INTRODUCTION
TO SOCIOLOGY

INTRODUCTION TO SOCIOLOGY

ANTHONY GIDDENS

Cambridge University
University of California, Santa Barbara

W · W · NORTON & COMPANY
New York · London

Printed in the United States of America.

The text of this book is composed in Bembo, with the display
set in Futura.
Composition by New England Typographic Service, Inc.
Manufacturing by R. R. Donnelley and Sons.
Book design by Guenet Abraham.
Page makeup by Roberta Flechner.
Cover painting: *Black Pouring over Color,* by Jackson Pollock,
© 1952. Reprinted by permission of Jason McCoy, Inc.

FIRST EDITION.

Library of Congress Cataloging-in-Publication Data

Giddens, Anthony.
Introduction to sociology / by Anthony Giddens.
    p. cm.
Includes bibliographical references and index.
ISBN 0-393-95753-5
1. Sociology. I. Title.
HM51.G444 1991
301—dc20   90-46670
                                                      CIP

ISBN 0-393-95753-5

W.W. Norton & Company, Inc., 500 Fifth Avenue,
New York, N.Y. 10110
W.W. Norton & Company, Ltd., 10 Coptic Street,
London WC1A 1PU

1 2 3 4 5 6 7 8 9 0

CONTENTS

PART ONE

CULTURE, THE INDIVIDUAL, AND SOCIAL INTERACTION

CHAPTER 4   SOCIAL INTERACTION AND EVERYDAY LIFE   109

CHAPTER 5   DEVIANCE   141

CHAPTER 6   GENDER AND SEXUALITY   189

P A R T   T W O

STRUCTURES OF POWER

■

CHAPTER 7   STRATIFICATION AND CLASS STRUCTURE 253

CHAPTER 8   ETHNICITY AND RACE   296

CHAPTER 9   GROUPS AND ORGANIZATIONS   342

P A R T   T H R E E

SOCIAL INSTITUTIONS

■

CHAPTER 12   KINSHIP, MARRIAGE, AND THE FAMILY   469

CHAPTER 13 EDUCATION, COMMUNICATION, AND MEDIA 509

CHAPTER 14   RELIGION · 548

CHAPTER 15   WORK AND ECONOMIC LIFE 593

P A R T F O U R

SOCIAL CHANGE IN THE MODERN WORLD

CHAPTER 17   MODERN URBANISM   673

CHAPTER 18   POPULATION, HEALTH, AND AGING   706

CHAPTER 19   REVOLUTIONS AND SOCIAL MOVEMENTS   740

CHAPTER 20 UNDERSTANDING SOCIAL CHANGE 776

P A R T   F I V E

METHODS AND THEORIES IN SOCIOLOGY

■

PREFACE

This book was written in the belief that sociology has a key role to play in modern intellectual culture and a central place within the social sciences. After teaching at all levels of sociology for many years, I became convinced of the need to filter some of the discipline's current advances and developments into an elementary introduction to the field.

My aim has been to write a work that combines some originality with an analysis of all the basic issues of interest to sociologists today. The book does not try to introduce overly sophisticated notions; nevertheless, ideas and findings drawn from the cutting edge of the discipline are incorporated throughout. I hope it is not a partisan treatment; I endeavored to cover the major perspectives in sociology in an even-handed, although not indiscriminate, way.

MAJOR THEMES

The book is constructed around a number of basic themes, each of which helps to give the work a distinctive character. One major theme is that of the *world in change.* Sociology was born of the transformations that wrenched the industrializing social order of the West away from the ways of life characteristic of preceding societies. The world that was created by these changes is the primary object of concern of sociological analysis. The pace of social change has continued to accelerate, and it is possible that we stand on the threshold of transitions as fundamental as those that occurred in the late eighteenth and nineteenth centuries. Sociology has prime responsibility for charting the transformations that have taken place in the past, and for grasping the major lines of development taking place today.

A second important theme of the book is the *globalizing of social life.* For far too long, sociology has been dominated by the view that societies can be studied as independent unities. But even in the past, societies have never really existed in isolation. In current times we can see a clear acceleration in processes of global integration. This is obvious, for example, in the expansion of international trade across the world. The emphasis on globalization in this book also connects closely with the weight given to the interdependence of First and Third Worlds today.

Third, the book takes a strongly *comparative* stance. The study of sociology cannot be taught solely by understanding the institutions of any one particular society. While I have of course slanted the discussion especially towards the United States, such discussion is always balanced by a rich variety of materials drawn from other societies or cultures. These include researches carried out in other Western countries, but I have also referred frequently to the Soviet Union and the East European societies, societies currently undergoing substantial changes. This book also includes much more material on Third World countries than has been usual hitherto in introductions of sociology. In addition, I strongly emphasize the relationship between sociology and anthropology, whose concerns overlap comprehensively. Given the close connections that now mesh societies across the world with one another, and the virtual disappearance of many forms of traditional social system, sociology and anthropology increasingly become indistinguishable.

A fourth theme is the necessity of taking an *historical orientation* to sociology. This involves far more than just filling in the "historical context" within which events occur. One of the most important developments in sociology over the past few years has been an increasing emphasis upon historical analysis. This should not be understood solely as applying a sociological outlook to the past, but as a way of contributing to our understanding of institutions in the present. Recent work in historical sociology is used widely in the book, and provides a framework for the interpretations offered within most of the separate chapters.

Fifth, particular attention is given throughout the text to *issues of gender.* The study of gender is ordinarily regarded as a specific field within sociology as a whole—and this volume contains a chapter devoted to thinking and research on the subject (Chapter 6). However, questions about gender relations are so fundamental to sociological analysis that they cannot simply be relegated to a subdivision of the discipline. Thus many of the chapters contain sections concerned with issues of gender.

A sixth theme is the relation between the *social* and the *personal.* sociological thinking is a vital help to self-understanding, which in turn can be focused back upon an improved understanding of the social world. Studying sociology should be a liberating experience: sociology enlarges our sympathies and imagination, opens up new perspectives on the sources of our own behavior, and creates an awareness of cultural settings different from our own. Insofar as sociological ideas challenge dogma, teach appreciation of cultural variety, and allow us insight into the working of social institutions, the practice of sociology enhances the possibilities of human freedom.

ORGANIZATION OF THE BOOK

There is no abstract discussion of basic sociological concepts at the beginning of this book. Instead, concepts are explained when they are introduced in the relevant chapters, and I have sought throughout to illustrate ideas, concepts, and theories by means of concrete examples. While these are usually taken from sociological research, I have quite often used material from other sources (such as newspaper reports) for illustrative purposes. I have tried to keep the writing style as simple and direct as possible, while endeavoring to make the book lively and "full of surprises."

The chapters follow a sequence designed to help achieve a progressive mastery of the different fields of sociology, but I have taken care to ensure that the book can be used flexibly and is easy to adapt to the needs of individual courses. Chapters can be deleted, or studied in a different order, without much loss. Each chapter has been written as a fairly autonomous unit, with cross-referencing to other chapters at relevant points.

The five parts of the book provide a comprehensive coverage of the major areas of sociology. Part 1 concentrates on culture, society, and the individual, analyzing the interplay between social influences and personal experience, with gender a major theme. The chapters included here cover culture, the development of different types of human society, socialization, everyday social interaction, and deviance. In Part 2, the themes of inequality, power, and ideology are explored. Several core areas of sociology are discussed here: stratification, ethnicity and race, groups and organizations, politics and the state, and war and the military. Part 3 deals with basic social institutions and analyzes their influence on key areas of human behavior. The chapters in this part are concerned with marriage and the family, education and the media, religion, and work and economic life. Part 4 groups together chapters in which the theme of *change* is developed with special emphasis, analyzing globalization, modern urbanism, population, health, and aging, and revolution and social movements. It concludes with a discussion of social change in general.

Finally, in Part 5, the major research methods and theoretical perspectives employed in sociology are discussed. Although this material has been placed at the end of the book, it can be read at any point. My reason for not including it earlier, as most texts do, is simply that in my experience students are better able to handle issues in methodology and theory once they are familiar with the basic subject matter and research findings of sociology. I have avoided the practice found in other texts whereby "functionalist," "conflict," and "symbolic interactionist" theories are continually played off one another. Rather than force theoretical debates into these boxes, I have integrated the work of leading theorists, past and present, with the subject matter in the various chapters. In addition, I have given a much fuller exposition of theoretical ideas and perspectives in Chapter 22 than is usual in other texts.

CHAPTER SUMMARIES AND GLOSSARIES

Each chapter has been carefully structured to make the learning process as entertaining, yet systematic, as possible. Every chapter is followed by a concise summary, plus a list of basic concepts and important terms that it introduced. All these concepts and terms are included in the glossaries at the end of the book, which provide a very extensive reference source. Whenever a new term is first mentioned in the text itself, it is printed in **boldface.**

FURTHER RESEARCH: READING AND LIBRARIES

Libraries contain abundant sources of information that can be used to follow up, or expand upon, issues discussed here. References are given throughout the text and listed fully in the Bibliography at the end. Also, I have included a short appendix that provides a guide to library resources and how to use them.

ACKNOWLEDGMENTS

During the writing of this book, many individuals offered comments and advice on particular chapters and, in some cases, large parts of the text. They helped me see many issues in a different light, clarified some difficult points, and allowed me to take advantage of their specialist knowledge in their respective fields. I am deeply indebted to them.

Deirdre Boden, Washington University, St. Louis

Richard J. Bord, Pennsylvania State University

Stephen E. Cornell, University of California, San Diego

Lynn Davidman, University of Pittsburgh

Judith F. Dunn, Pennsylvania State University

John V.A. Ehle, Jr., Northern Virginia Community College

Eliot Freidson, New York University

William Gibson, Southern Methodist University

Paul Kingston, University of Virginia

Janet Koenigsamen, West Virginia University

Cora B. Marrett, University of Wisconsin

Greg Matoesian, Fontbonne College

Katherine McClelland, Franklin and Marshall College

Allan Pred, University of California, Berkeley

Roland Robertson, University of Pittsburgh

Andrew Scull, University of California, San Diego

Joel C. Tate, Germanna Community College

Timothy P. Wickham-Crowley, Georgetown University

Paul Root Wolpe, University of Pennsylvania

Dennis H. Wrong, New York University

Irving M. Zeitlin, University of Toronto

In providing the comparative perspectives of the book, many European friends also provided invaluable help. I should like to thank in particular:

Teresa Brennan, University of Amsterdam

Abigail Buckle, University of Cambridge

Kevin Bonnett, Anglia Polytechnic

David Held, The Open University

Michelle Stanworth, Anglia Polytechnic

John Thompson, University of Cambridge

Andrew Webster, Anglia Polytechnic

I also have many others to acknowledge, including Sam Hollick, Michele Giddens, and Avril Symonds. I am especially grateful to Harriet Barry and to Margie Brassil at Norton, who each did a marvelous job of copyediting the book in its various versions. To them I owe numerous suggestions for alterations and improvements that have contributed in very important ways to the final form of the volume.

My greatest debt of all is to Don Fusting, at Norton. He has poured an enormous amount of work into the book, has made many innovations in the original chapters that I submitted to him, and has given the text much of whatever is worthwhile in it. It has been a pleasure working with him.

I would also like to express special thanks to Richard P. Appelbaum of the University of California, Santa Barbara, and Karen Shapiro. In addition to devoting a great amount of time to reading the entire manuscript and offering informed comments on nearly every page, they came up with numerous ideas and selections for illustrating the book.

INTRODUCTION
TO SOCIOLOGY

CHAPTER ONE

SOCIOLOGY: PROBLEMS AND PERSPECTIVES

WE LIVE TODAY—APPROACHING THE TWENTY-FIRST CEN-
tury—in a world that is intensely worrying, yet full of
the most extraordinary promise for the future. It is a
world awash with change, marked by the terrifying possibility of nuclear war and by the destructive onslaught of
modern technology on the natural environment. Yet we
have possibilities of controlling our destiny, and shaping
our lives for the better, that would have been quite unimaginable to earlier generations. How did this world
come about? Why are our conditions of life so different
from those of our forebears? What directions will change take in the
future? These questions are the prime concern of sociology, a discipline that consequently has a fundamental role to play in modern intellectual culture.

Examples are everywhere. Think, for instance, of the massive
changes that have taken place since 1989 in Eastern Europe—changes
that have affected not only the millions of people living there, but
have many consequences for the rest of the world. Will the world become a safer place to live in now the Berlin Wall has become a relic of
history? How will people's lives be reshaped in countries that have
broken away from Communist government? What can we learn

about our own social problems from the new paths of development being charted in Europe, or indeed from changes going on in other parts of the world? All these issues, and many more like them, can be illuminated through sociological study.

THE SCOPE OF SOCIOLOGY

SOCIOLOGY IS THE STUDY OF HUMAN SOCIAL LIFE, groups, and societies. It is a dazzling and compelling enterprise, having as its subject matter our own behavior as social beings. The scope of sociology is extremely wide, ranging from the analysis of passing encounters between individuals in the street up to the investigation of global social processes. A few examples will provide an initial taste of the nature and objectives of the subject.

LOVE AND MARRIAGE

Why do people fall in love and get married? The answer to such a question at first sight seems obvious. Love expresses a mutual physical and personal attachment two individuals feel for one another. These days, many of us might be sceptical of the idea that "love is forever." But "falling in love," we tend to think, derives from universal human sentiments and emotions. It seems entirely natural for a couple who fall in love to want to set up house together, and to seek personal and sexual fulfillment in their relationship.

Yet this view, which seems so self-evident, is in fact quite unusual. Falling in love is not an experience most human beings have and is rarely associated with marriage. The idea of romantic love did not become widespread until fairly recently in the West, and has never existed in most other cultures. It is only in modern times that love, marriage, and sexuality have been regarded as closely bound up with one another. In the Middle Ages, and for centuries afterwards, people married mainly in order to perpetuate the ownership of a title or property in the hands of family, or to raise children to work the family farm. Once married, they may have sometimes become close companions, but this happened after marriage rather than before. There were sexual liaisons outside marriage, but these involved few of the sentiments we connect with love. Love in the past was regarded "as at best a necessary weakness and at worst a kind of sickness" (Monter, 1977).

The scope of sociology takes us from an analysis of our society—a recent one in human history . . .

Romantic love first made its appearance in courtly circles as a characteristic of extramarital sexual adventures indulged in by members of the aristocracy. Until about two centuries ago, it was wholly confined to such circles, and kept specifically separated from marriage. Relations between husband and wife among aristocratic groups were often cool and distant—certainly compared to our expectations of marriage today. The wealthy lived in large houses, each spouse having his or her own bedroom and servants; they may rarely have seen each other in private. Sexual compatibility was a matter of hazard and was not considered relevant to marriages. Among both rich and poor, the decision of whom to marry was made by family and kin, not by the individuals concerned, who had little or no say in the matter.

This remains true in many non-Western countries today. In India, for example, the vast majority of marriages are arranged by parents or other relatives. The opinions of prospective marriage partners are quite often taken into account, but by no means always so. A study of marriage in Kerala, a state in India, showed that just over half the young people thought that meeting the prospective spouse before marriage was relevant to marital happiness. Among parents, only one percent were willing to let their children choose their own marriage partners. Romantic love is recognized to exist, but it is equated with temporary infatuation, or actually seen as a barrier to a happy marriage.

Neither romantic love, then, nor its association with marriage, can be understood as "given" features of human life. Both love and marriage are shaped by broad social influences. These are the influences that sociologists study—and which make themselves felt even in

. . . to other societies—more long lasting . . .

seemingly purely personal experiences. Most of us see the world in terms of familiar features of our own lives. Sociology demonstrates the need to take a much wider view of why we act as we do.

HEALTH AND ILLNESS

We normally think of health and illness as matters involving the physical condition of the body. A person feels aches and pains, or gets feverish. How could this have anything to do with wider social influences? In fact, social factors have a profound effect upon both the experience and the occurrence of illness, as well as upon how we react to being ill. Our very concept of "illness," as involving physical malfunctioning of the body, is not shared by people in all societies. In some other cultures, sickness and even death are thought to be produced by evil spells, not by treatable physical causes (Evans-Pritchard, 1950). In our society, Christian Scientists reject most orthodox medical thinking about illness, believing that we are really spiritual and perfect in the image of God, with sickness coming from a person's misunderstanding of God, or "letting error in."

How long one can expect to live, and the chances of contracting serious diseases such as heart troubles, cancer, or pneumonia, are all strongly influenced by social characteristics. The more affluent the background people are from, the less likely they are to suffer from a serious illness at any point in their life. In addition, there are strongly defined social rules concerning how we are expected to behave when we become ill. A person who is ill is excused from many or all of the

. . . to the ways by which we have related to one another in love . . .

normal duties of everyday life. But the sickness has to be acknowledged as "serious enough" to be able to claim these benefits without criticism or rebuke. Someone who is thought to be suffering only from a relatively mild form of infirmity, or whose illness has not been precisely identified, is likely to be seen as a faker or malingerer—as not really having the right to escape from the daily round of obligations (Segal, 1976; Cockerham, 1986).

A FURTHER EXAMPLE: CRIME AND PUNISHMENT

The following horrific description concerns the final hours of a man put to death in 1757, having been accused of plotting to assassinate the king of France. This unfortunate individual was condemned to have flesh torn from his chest, arms, and legs, and a mixture of boiling oil, wax, and sulphur spread over the wounds. His body was then to be drawn and quartered by four horses, and the dismembered parts subsequently burnt. An officer of the watch left this account:

> The executioner dipped an iron in the pot containing the boiling potion, which he poured liberally over each wound. Then the ropes that were to be harnessed to the horses were attached with cords to the condemned man's body; the horses were then harnessed and placed alongside the arms and legs, one at each limb. . . . The horses tugged hard, each pulling straight on a limb, each horse held by an executioner. After a quarter of an hour, the same ceremony was repeated and finally, after several attempts, the direction of the horses had to be changed, thus: those at the thighs towards the arms, which broke the arms at the joints. This was repeated several times without success.
>
> After two or three attempts, the executioner Samson and he who had used the pincers each drew out a knife from his pocket and cut the body at the thighs instead of severing the legs at the joints; the four horses gave a tug and carried off the two thighs after them, namely, that of the right side first, the other following; then the same was done to the arms, the shoulders, and the four limbs; the flesh had to be cut almost to the bone. The horses, pulling hard, carried off the right arm first and the other afterwards. (Foucault, 1979)

The victim was alive until the final severance of his limbs from his torso.

Prior to modern times, punishments like this were not uncommon. As John Lofland has written, describing traditional forms of execution:

> Early historic executions were calculated to maximize the condemned's period of dying and his consciousness during it. Pressing to death by a progressively heavy weight placed upon the chest, breaking upon the wheel, crucifixion, strangling, burning at the stake, cutting off strips of flesh, stabbing non-vital parts of the body, drawing and quartering, and other techniques all consumed rather prolonged periods of time. Even hanging was a slow-working technique for most of its history. When the cart was merely driven from beneath the condemned or the trapdoor merely opened, the condemned slowly strangled, writhing for many minutes before succumbing . . . to shorten this struggle, the executioner sometimes went beneath the scaffold to pull the condemned's legs. (Lofland, 1977)

Executions were often carried out in front of large crowds—a custom that persisted well into the eighteenth century in some countries. Those who were to be done to death would be drawn through the streets in an open cart, to meet their end as part of a well-publicized

. . . in adversity . . .

spectacle. The crowds would cheer or hiss according to their attitude towards the particular victim. Hangmen were public celebrities having something of the fame and following conferred upon film stars in modern times.

Today, we find such modes of punishment repellant. Few of us could imagine gaining enjoyment from watching someone being tortured or violently put to death, whatever crimes they might have committed! Our penal system is based upon imprisonment rather than the infliction of physical pain. In most Western countries (though not in the United States), the death penalty has been abolished altogether. Why did things change? Why did prison sentences replace the older, more violent forms of punishment?

. . . and in war.

It is tempting to suppose that in the past people were simply more brutal, while we have become humane. To a sociologist, such an explanation is unconvincing. The public use of violence as a means of punishment for many crimes, not just homicide, had been established in Europe for centuries. People did not suddenly change their attitudes towards such practices "out of the blue"; there were wider social influences at work, connected with major processes of change occurring in that period. The European societies in the late eighteenth century were becoming *industrialized* and *urbanized.* The old, rural order was being rapidly replaced by one in which more and more people were being employed in factories and workshops that were moving to the rapidly expanding city areas. Social control over large urban-based populations simply could not be maintained by older forms of punishment, which, relying on setting a fearful example, were only appropriate in small, tightly knit communities where the number of cases was small.

Prisons developed as part of a general trend towards the establishment of organizations in which individuals were kept "locked away" from the outside world as a means of controlling and disciplining their behavior. Those shut away at first included not only criminals of all kinds, but vagabonds, the sick, the unemployed, the feeble-minded, and the insane. Prisons only gradually became separated from asylums and hospitals for the physically ill. In prisons, criminals were supposed to be "rehabilitated" to become good citizens. Punishment for crime became oriented towards creating the obedient citizen, rather than publicly displaying to others the terrible consequences that follow from wrong-doing. What we now see as more humane attitudes towards punishment followed from these changes, rather than caused them in the first place. Changes in the treatment of criminals were part of processes that swept away traditional orders which people had accepted for centuries. These processes created the societies in which we live today.

THE NATURE OF SOCIOLOGY

At this point, we can take stock of the examples discussed so far. In each of the three cases—love, marriage, and sexuality, health and illness, and punishment for crime—we have seen that what might be understood to be "naturally given" human sentiments and feelings are in fact pervasively influenced by social factors. Understanding the subtle, yet complex and profound ways in which our lives reflect the contexts of our social experience is basic to the sociological outlook. Sociology focuses in particular upon social life in the *modern world*—the world brought into being by the sweeping changes in human societies that have occurred over the last two hundred years or so.

CHANGE IN THE MODERN WORLD

The changes in human ways of life in the last two hundred years have been far-reaching. We have become accustomed, for example, to the fact that most of the population do not work on the land, and live in towns and cities rather than in small rural communities. But this was *never* the case until the modern era. For virtually all of human history, the vast majority of people had to produce their own food and shelter and lived in tiny groups or in small village communities. Even at the height of the most developed traditional civilizations—like ancient Rome or traditional China—less than 10 percent of the population lived in urban areas; everyone else was engaged in food production in a rural setting. Today, in most of the industrialized societies, these proportions have become almost completely reversed. Quite often, more than 90 percent of the people live in urban areas, and only 2–3 percent of the population work in agricultural production.

It is not only the environment surrounding our lives that has changed; these transformations have radically altered, and continue to alter, the most personal and intimate side of our daily existence. To extend a previous example, the spread of ideals of romantic love was strongly conditioned by the transition from a rural to an urban, industrialized society. As people moved into urban areas and began to work in industrial production, marriage was no longer prompted mainly by economic motives—by the need to control the inheritance of land and to work the land as a family unit. "Arranged" marriages —fixed through the negotiations of parents and relatives—became less and less common. Individuals increasingly began to initiate marriage relationships on the basis of emotional attraction, and in order to seek personal fulfillment. The idea of "falling in love" as a basis for contracting a marriage tie was formed in this context. (For further discussion, see Chapter 12: Kinship, Marriage, and the Family.)

Similarly, before the rise of modern medicine, popular views of health and illness resembled those found today in many non-Western countries. Modern methods of diagnosis and treatment, together with an awareness of the importance of hygiene in preventing infectious disease, only date from the early nineteenth century. Our current views of health and sickness emerged as part of social changes that influenced many aspects of people's beliefs about biology and nature.

Sociology had its beginnings in the attempts of thinkers to understand the initial impact of these transformations that accompanied industrialization in the West. It remains the basic discipline concerned with analyzing their nature. Our world today is radically different from that of former ages; it is the task of sociology to help us understand this world and what future it is likely to hold for us.

SOCIOLOGY AND "COMMON SENSE"

The practice of sociology involves gaining knowledge about ourselves, the societies in which we live, and other societies distinct from ours in space and time. Sociological findings both *disturb* and *contribute* to our **common-sense beliefs** about ourselves and others. Consider the following list of statements:

1. Romantic love is a natural part of human experience and is therefore found in all societies in close connection with marriage.

2. How long people live depends on their biological makeup and cannot be strongly influenced by social differences.

3. In previous times, the family was a stable unit, but today there is a great increase in the proportion of "broken homes."

4. In all societies some people will be unhappy or depressed; therefore rates of suicide will tend to be the same throughout the world.

5. Most people everywhere value material wealth and will try to get ahead if there are opportunities to do so.

6. Wars have been fought throughout human history. If we face the threat of large-scale war today, this is due to the fact that human beings have aggressive instincts that will always find an outlet.

7. The spread of computers and automation in industrial production will greatly reduce the average workday of most of the population.

Sociology takes up social groups in worship . . .

These assertions seem to make sense, but each is wrong or questionable—as we already know of statements 1 and 2. Knowing why will help us understand the questions sociologists ask, and try to answer, in their work. (These points will be analyzed in greater detail in later chapters.)

1. The idea that marriage ties should be based on romantic love is a recent one, not found either in the earlier history of Western societies or in other cultures. Romantic love is actually unknown in most societies.

2. How long people live is very definitely affected by social influences. This is because ways of social life act as "filters" for biological factors that cause illness, infirmity, or death. The poor are less healthy on average than the rich, for example, because they usually have worse diets, live a more physically demanding existence, and have access to inferior medical facilities.

3. If we look back to the early 1800s, the proportion of children living in homes with only one natural parent was probably as high as at present, because many more people died young, particularly women in childbirth. Today the main causes of "broken homes"—separation and divorce—differ from earlier times, but the overall level has not changed much.

4. Suicide rates are certainly not the same in all societies. Even if we only look at Western countries, we find that suicide rates vary considerably. The suicide rate in the United States, for example, is four times as high as that of Spain, but only a third of that of Hungary. Suicide rates increased quite sharply during the main period of industrialization of the Western societies, in the nineteenth and early twentieth centuries.

5. The value that many people in modern societies place upon wealth and "getting ahead" is for the most part a recent development. It is associated with the rise of "individualism" in the West—the stress which we tend to place on individual achievement. In many other cultures, individuals are expected to put the good of the community above their own wishes and inclinations. Material wealth often is not highly regarded compared to other values, such as religious or family ones.

6. Far from having an aggressive instinct, human beings do not have instincts at all, if "instinct" means a fixed and inherited pattern of behavior. Moreover, throughout most of human history, when people lived in small tribal groups, warfare did not exist in the form it came to have subsequently. Although some such groups were warlike, many were not. There were no armies, and when skirmishes occurred, casualties would often be deliberately avoided or limited. The threat of large-scale war today is bound up with a process of the "industrialization of war" that is a major aspect of industrialization in general.

. . . in work . . .

. . . and in protest.

7. The assumption that computers and automation will mean more free time for everyone is rather different from the others, because it refers to the future. There is in fact good reason to be at least cautious about this idea. The automated industries are still fairly few and far between. Jobs eliminated by automation might be replaced by new ones created elsewhere or by the new automation itself. We cannot as yet be sure. One of the tasks of sociology is to take a hard look at the actual evidence available on issues such as this.

Obviously sociological findings do not always go against common-sense views. Common-sense ideas often provide sources of insight about social behavior. What needs emphasizing, however, is that the sociologist must be prepared to ask of any of our beliefs about ourselves—no matter how cherished—*is this really so?* By this means, sociology also helps to contribute to whatever "common sense" is at any time and place. Much of what most of us today would regard as common sense, "what everyone knows"—for example, that divorce rates have risen greatly over the period since World War II—is in fact due to the work of sociologists and other social scientists. A great deal of research, of a permanent kind, is necessary to produce material from year to year on patterns of marriage and divorce. The same is true of very many other areas of our common-sense knowledge.

SOCIOLOGICAL QUESTIONS

SOME OF THE QUESTIONS SOCIOLOGISTS ASK, AND TRY TO answer, are largely **factual.** As we are all members of a society, we already have a certain amount of factual knowledge about it. For example, everyone in the United States is aware that there are laws that they are supposed to observe, and that to go against these is to risk criminal punishment. But the knowledge the average individual has of the legal system, and of the nature and types of criminal activity, is likely to be sketchy and incomplete. Most aspects of crime and justice need direct and systematic sociological investigation. Thus the sociologist might ask: What forms of crime are most common? What proportion of people who engage in criminal behavior are caught by the police? How many of these are in the end found guilty and imprisoned? Factual questions are often much more complicated and difficult to answer than might be imagined. Official statistics on crime, for example, do not accurately reflect the real level of criminal activity. Many crimes never come to the attention of the police at all. For instance, only a relatively small number of women who are raped report the attack to the police because they do not want to face the personal examinations, interviews, court-room procedures, and possible humiliation they will have to undergo.

COMPARATIVE QUESTIONS

Factual information about one society, of course, will not always tell us whether we are dealing with an unusual case or a very general set of influences. Sociologists often want to ask **comparative questions,** relating one social context within a society to another, or contrasting examples drawn from different societies. There are significant differences, for example, between the social and legal systems of the United States and Canada. A typical comparative question might be: How much do patterns of criminal behavior and law enforcement vary between the two countries? (Some important differences are in fact found between them.)

DEVELOPMENTAL QUESTIONS

In sociology we need to look not only at existing societies in relation to one another, but also to compare their present and past. The questions sociologists ask here are **developmental.** To understand the nature of the modern world, we have to look at previous forms of society and also study the main direction that processes of change have taken. Thus we can investigate, for example, how the first prisons originated and what they are like today—an issue already touched upon earlier.

THEORETICAL QUESTIONS

Factual—or what sociologists usually prefer to call **empirical**—investigations, show *how* things occur. Yet sociology does not just consist of collecting facts, however important and interesting they may be. We also want to know *why* things happen, and in order to do so we have to learn to pose **theoretical questions.** For instance we know that industrialization has had a major influence upon the emergence of modern societies. But what are the origins and preconditions of industrialization? Why do we find differences between societies in their industrialization processes? Why is industrialization

TABLE 1.1	A SOCIOLOGIST'S LINE OF QUESTIONING	
FACTUAL QUESTION	What happened?	During the 1980s, there was an increase in the proportion of women in their thirties bearing children for the first time.
COMPARATIVE QUESTION	Did this happen everywhere?	Was this a global phenomenon, or did it occur just in the United States, or only in a certain region of the United States?
DEVELOPMENTAL QUESTION	Has this happened over time?	What have been the patterns of childbearing over time?
THEORETICAL QUESTION	What underlies this phenomenon?	Why are more women now waiting until their thirties to bear children? What factors would we look at to explain this change?

associated with changes in ways of criminal punishment, or in family and marriage systems? To respond to such questions, we have to develop theoretical thinking (Table 1.1).

Theories involve constructing abstract interpretations that can be used to explain a wide variety of empirical situations. A theory about industrialization, for example, would be concerned with identifying the main features that processes of industrial development share in common, and would try to show which of these are most important in explaining such development. Of course, factual and theoretical questions can never completely be separated. We can only develop valid theoretical approaches if we are able to test them out by means of empirical study. (See Chapter 21: "Working with Sociology: Methods of Research.")

We need theories to help us make sense of facts. Contrary to popular assertion, facts do not speak for themselves. Many sociologists work primarily on empirical questions, but unless they are guided in research by some knowledge of theory, their work is unlikely to be illuminating. This is true even of research carried out with strictly practical objectives.

"Practical people" tend to be suspicious of theorists, and may like to see themselves as too "down-to-earth" to need to pay attention to more abstract ideas, yet all practical decisions have some theoretical assumptions lying behind them. A manager of a business, for example, might have scant regard for "theory." Nonetheless, every approach to business activity involves theoretical assumptions, even if these often remain unstated. Thus the manager might assume that employees are motivated to work hard mainly by money—the level of wages they receive. This is not only a theoretical interpretation of human behavior, it is also a mistaken one, as research in industrial sociology tends to demonstrate.

INTENDED AND UNINTENDED CONSEQUENCES OF HUMAN ACTION

SOCIOLOGISTS DRAW AN IMPORTANT DISTINCTION BEtween the purposes of our behavior—what we intend to do—and the **unintended consequences** that our behavior brings about. The purposes for which we do things may be very different from the consequences we produce. We can understand a great deal about societies in this way. Schools are set up, for example, for the purpose of teaching skills of reading and writing, and to allow children to acquire new knowledge. Yet the existence of schools also has consequences that are not so plainly recognized or intended. Schools keep children out of the job market for extended periods of time, thereby lowering the number of people looking for work. Although modern school systems are designed to reduce social inequalities by giving everyone the same opportunities to succeed, they often in fact have the opposite effect. Schools frequently reinforce existing inequalities because students from poorer backgrounds find the school an alien environment, and hence may tend to perform poorly within it.

Many of the major changes in history were largely unintended. Prior to the 1917 Russian Revolution, there were various political groups at work trying to overthrow the existing regime. None of these, however—including the Bolshevik (Communist) party that eventually came to power—anticipated the process of revolution that in fact occurred. A series of minor tensions and clashes brought about a process of social transformation much more radical than anyone initially tried to accomplish (Skocpol, 1979).

Sometimes behavior initiated with a particular aim in view actually has consequences that *prevent* the achievement of that aim. Some years ago in New York City, laws were introduced compelling the owners of deteriorating buildings in low-income areas to bring their buildings up to a minimum standard for habitation. The intention

Sociology examines how we structure our life in urban settings . . .

was to improve the basic level of housing available to people in poorer sections of the community. The result was in fact the opposite. Rather than conform to the laws, owners of run-down buildings abandoned them altogether or put them to uses other than residential ones. The result was an even greater shortage of affordable housing than before (Sieber, 1981).

We can find a comparable example by returning to the case of prisons and asylums. Over the past few years, in the United States and some other Western countries, the process of shutting people away from the community has been partly reversed. In an effort to extend civil rights and create "community care" for offenders and for the mentally ill, some of the inmates of prisons and mental hospitals were released to live in the outside world. However, the results have substantially rebounded on the hopes of the liberal reformers who supported the innovation. For many erstwhile mental patients in particular, the consequences were disastrous; they found themselves living in acute poverty, unable to cope with their new environment.

Both continuity and change in social life have to be understood in terms of a mix of intended and unintended consequences in people's actions. Sociology has the task of examining the balance between two major processes: **social reproduction** and **social transformation.** Social reproduction refers to how societies "keep going" over time and social transformation to the changes they undergo. A society is not a mechanical device like a clock or an engine, which "keep going" because they have a momentum of forces built into them. Social reproduction occurs because there is continuity in what people do from day to day and year to year and in the social practices they follow. Changes occur partly because people intend them to occur, and partly—as the example of the Russian Revolution indicates—because of consequences that no one either foresees or intends.

WHAT CAN SOCIOLOGY SHOW US ABOUT OUR OWN ACTIONS?

AS INDIVIDUALS, ALL OF US KNOW A GREAT DEAL ABOUT ourselves and about the societies in which we live. We tend to think we have a good understanding of why we act as we do, without needing sociologists to tell us! And to some degree this is true. Many of the things we do in our day-to-day lives we do because we understand the social requirements involved. Yet there are definite boundaries to such self-knowledge, and it is one of the main tasks of sociology to show us what these are.

On the basis of the discussion so far, we can illuminate the nature of these boundaries quite easily. As we saw earlier, people make many common-sense judgements about themselves and others that turn out to be wrong, partial, or ill-informed. Sociological research helps to identify the limitations of our social judgements, and at the same time it "feeds back" into our knowledge of ourselves and the social environment. Another essential contribution of sociology lies in showing that, although most of us understand most of what we do and why, much of the time we have little knowledge of the consequences of our actions. The unintended and unforeseen consequences of actions affect all aspects and contexts of social life. Sociological analysis explores the delicate and subtle connections between intentional and unintentional features of the social world.

. . . and in rural areas.

SOCIAL STRUCTURE AND HUMAN ACTION

An important concept that helps us understand these connections is that of **social structure.** The social environments in which we exist do not consist of just random assortments of events or actions. There are underlying regularities, or patternings, in how people behave and in their relationships with one another. It is these regularities to which the concept of social structure refers. To some degree it is helpful to picture the structural characteristics of societies as resembling the structure of a building; its walls, floors, and roof together give it a particular shape or form. But the analogy can be a very misleading one if applied too strictly. Social structures are made up of human actions and relationships: what gives these their patterning is their *repetition* across periods of time and distances of space. Thus, the ideas of social reproduction and social structure are very closely related to one another in sociological analysis. We should understand human societies to be *like buildings that are at every moment being reconstructed by the very bricks that compose them.* The actions of all of us are influenced by the structural characteristics of the societies in which we are brought up and live; at the same time, we recreate (and also to some extent alter) those structural characteristics through our actions. The two-party political system, for example, is a structural part of American society—an enduring feature which has lasted over many lifetimes. Yet it only continues to exist insofar as people fill political positions, make policy decisions, participate in voting, and so forth.

DEVELOPING A SOCIOLOGICAL OUTLOOK

LEARNING TO THINK SOCIOLOGICALLY MEANS CULTIVATING powers of the imagination. Studying sociology *cannot* be just a routine process of acquiring knowledge. A sociologist is someone who is able to break free from the immediacy of personal circumstances. Sociological work depends upon what C. Wright Mills (1967), in a famous phrase, called the **sociological imagination.**

The sociological imagination necessitates, above all, being able to "think ourselves away" from the familiar routines of our daily lives in order to look at them anew. Consider the simple act of drinking a cup of coffee. What could we find to say, from a sociological point of view, about such an apparently uninteresting item of behavior? The answer is—an enormous amount.

We could point out that coffee is not just a drink that helps maintain the liquid intake of the individual. First, it has *symbolic value* as part of day-to-day social rituals. Often the ritual associated with coffee drinking is much more important than the act of consuming the drink itself. For example, two people who arrange "to have coffee" together are probably more interested in meeting and chatting than in what they drink. In all societies, drinking and eating are occasions for social interaction and the enactment of rituals—and these offer a rich subject matter for sociological study.

Second, coffee contains a drug, caffeine, which has a stimulating effect on the brain. Coffee addicts are not regarded by most people in Western cultures as "drug users." It is an interesting sociological question to consider why this should be so. Like alcohol, coffee is a "socially acceptable" drug, whereas marijuana for instance, is not. Yet there are cultures that tolerate the consumption of marijuana, but disfavor both coffee and alcohol. (For further discussion of these issues, see Chapter 5: "Conformity and Deviance.")

Third, an individual sipping a cup of coffee is caught up in an extremely complicated set of *social and economic relationships* stretching worldwide. The production, transportation, and distribution of coffee requires continuous transactions between many people thousands of miles away from the coffee-drinker. Studying such global transactions forms an important task of sociology, since many aspects of our lives are now affected by worldwide trading exchanges and communications.

FIGURE 1.1   **THE SOCIOLOGY OF COFFEE**

1. <u>Symbolic Value</u>. For most Americans, the morning cup of coffee is a personal ritual followed later in the day by coffee with others, a more social ritual.

Sociology tries to explain the many dimensions of a cup of coffee.

2. <u>Use as a drug</u>. Many drink coffee for that "extra lift." Some cultures prohibit its use.

3. Social and Economic Relationships. The growing, packaging, distributing, and marketing of coffee is a global enterprise affecting several cultures, social groups and organizations within those cultures, and thousands of individuals. Much of the coffee consumed in the United States is imported from South America.

4. <u>Past Social and Economic Development</u>. The "coffee" relationships currently set in motion were not always there. They developed gradually, and might well break down in the future due to change.

Finally, the act of sipping a cup of coffee presumes a whole process of *past social and economic development*. Along with many other now-familiar items of Western diets—like tea, bananas, potatoes, and white sugar—coffee only became widely consumed after the nineteenth century. Although coffee originated in the Middle East, virtually all of the coffee we drink in the Western countries today comes from areas (South America and Africa) that were colonized by the Europeans (Figure 1.1).

Developing the sociological imagination means using materials from **anthropology** (the study of nonmodern societies) and *history* as well as from sociology itself. The *anthropological* dimension of the sociological imagination is vital because it allows us to see what a kaleidoscope of different forms of human social life exist. In contrasting these with our own, we learn more about the distinctiveness of our specific patterns of behavior. The *historical* dimension of the sociological imagination is equally fundamental: we can only grasp the distinctive nature of our world today if we are able to compare it with the past. The past is a mirror which the sociologist must hold up to understand the present. Each of these dimensions involves "thinking ourselves away" from our own customs and habits in order to develop a more profound understanding of them.

There is yet another aspect of the sociological imagination—the one upon which, in fact, Mills laid most emphasis. This concerns *our possibilities for the future.* Sociology helps us not only to analyze existing patterns of social life, but to see some of the "possible futures" open to us. The imaginative pursuit of sociological work can show us not just what *is the case,* but what *could become the case* should we seek to make it so. Unless based upon an informed sociological understanding of current trends, our attempts to influence future developments will be ineffective or frustrated.

IS SOCIOLOGY A SCIENCE?

SOCIOLOGY OCCUPIES A PRIME POSITION AMONG A GROUP of disciplines (including anthropology, economics, and political science, among other subjects) that are usually termed "the social sciences." But can we really study human social life in a "scientific" way? To answer this question, we have first of all to understand the main characteristics of science as a form of intellectual endeavor. What is **science?**

Science is the use of systematic methods of investigation, theoretical thinking, and the logical assessment of arguments, to develop a body of knowledge about a particular subject matter. Scientific work depends upon a mixture of boldly innovative thought and the careful marshaling of evidence to support or disconfirm ideas and theories. Information and insights accumulated through scientific study and debate are always to some degree *tentative*—open to being revised, or even completely discarded, in the light of new evidence or arguments.

When we ask "Is sociology a science?" we mean two things: "Can the discipline be closely modeled upon the procedures of natural science?" and "Can sociology hope to achieve the same kind of precise, well-founded knowledge that natural scientists have developed with respect to the physical world?" These issues have always been to some degree controversial, but for a long period most sociologists answered them in the affirmative. That is to say, they held that sociology can, and should, resemble natural science both in its procedures and in the character of its findings.

This view today has generally come to be seen as naive. Like the other social sciences, sociology *is* a scientific discipline in one sense: it involves systematic methods of investigation, the analysis of data, and the assessment of theories in the light of evidence and logical argument. Studying human beings, however, is different from observing events in the physical world, and neither the logical framework nor the findings of sociology can adequately be understood simply by comparison with natural science. In investigating social life we deal with activities that are *meaningful* to the people who engage in them. Unlike objects in nature, humans are self-aware beings, who confer sense and purpose upon what they do. We cannot even describe social life accurately unless we first of all grasp the meanings that people apply to their behavior. For instance, to describe a death as a "suicide" necessitates learning something about what the person in question was intending when killed. "Suicide" can only occur when an individual actively intends self-destruction. A person who accidentally steps in front of a car and is killed cannot be said to have committed suicide; the death was not willed by that person.

The fact that we cannot study human beings in exactly the same way we study inanimate objects in nature is in some ways an advantage to sociology; in other respects it creates difficulties not encountered by natural scientists. Sociological researchers profit from being able to pose questions directly to the objects of their study—other human beings. On the other hand, people who know that their activities are being scrutinized will often not behave as they would normally. For example, when individuals answer questionnaires, they may consciously or unconsciously give a view of themselves that differs from their usual attitudes. They may even try to "assist" the researcher by giving responses they believe the investigator wants to find.

OBJECTIVITY

Sociologists strive to be detached in their research and theoretical thinking, trying to study the social world in an open-minded way. So far as possible, a good sociologist will seek to put aside prejudices that might prevent ideas or evidence from being assessed in a fair-minded manner. But nobody is completely open-minded on all topics, and the degree to which anyone can succeed in developing such attitudes towards contentious issues is bound to be limited. However, **objectivity** does not depend solely, or even primarily, upon the outlook of specific researchers. It also has to do with methods of observation and argument. Here the *public character* of the discipline is of major importance. Because findings are available for scrutiny—as published in articles, monographs, or books—others can check the conclusions reached. Claims made on the basis of research findings can be critically assessed and personal inclinations discounted by others.

Objectivity in sociology is thus achieved substantially through the effects of mutual *criticism* by members of the sociological community as a whole. Many of the subjects studied in sociology are controversial, because they directly affect disputes and struggles in society itself. Yet through public debate, the examination of evidence, and the logical structure of argument, controversial issues can be analyzed in a fruitful and effective fashion in the discipline as a whole (Habermas, 1979).

THE PRACTICAL SIGNIFICANCE OF SOCIOLOGY

SOCIOLOGY IS A SUBJECT THAT HAS MANY PRACTICAL IMPLIcations for our personal lives, and also for policymaking and social reform. Sociological thinking, and sociological research, can aid practical efforts towards social change in a variety of ways.

UNDERSTANDING SOCIAL SITUATIONS

First, sociology contributes to policymaking simply through providing *clearer or more adequate understanding* of given social situations than existed hitherto. This can be achieved either on the level of factual knowledge, or through gaining an improved grasp of *why* something is happening (in other words, by means of theoretical understanding). For instance, research may disclose that a far greater proportion of the population is living in poverty than was previously believed. Any attempt to foster improved living standards would obviously stand more chance of success if based upon accurate rather than faulty information. The more we understand about why poverty remains widespread, the more likely it is that successful policies can be implemented to counter it.

AWARENESS OF CULTURAL DIFFERENCES

A second way in which sociology aids in practical policymaking is through helping to foster greater *cultural awareness* on the part of different groups in society. Sociological research provides a means of seeing the social world from a diversity of cultural perspectives, thereby helping to dispel prejudices that groups hold towards one another. No one can be an enlightened policymaker who does not have a cultivated awareness of varying cultural values. Practical policies that are not based upon an informed awareness of the ways of life of those they affect have little chance of success. Thus a white social worker operating in a black neighborhood, like Watts in Los Angeles or Harlem in New York City, will not gain the confidence of its members without developing a sensitivity to the cultural differences that often separate whites and blacks in the United States.

ASSESSMENT OF THE EFFECTS OF POLICIES

Third, sociological research has practical implications in terms of *assessing the results of policy initiatives.* A program of practical reform may simply fail to achieve what its designers sought, or bring in its train a series of unintended consequences of an unpalatable kind. For instance, in the years following World War II, large public-housing blocks were built in city centers in many countries. These were planned to provide high standards of accommodation for low-income groups from slum areas, and offered shopping amenities and other civic services close at hand. However, subsequent research showed that many of those who moved from their previous dwellings to large apartment blocks felt isolated and unhappy in their new surroundings. High-rise buildings and shopping malls often rapidly became dilapidated, providing breeding grounds for muggings and other violent crimes.

THE INCREASE OF SELF-KNOWLEDGE

Fourth, and in some ways most important of all, sociology can provide **self-enlightenment**—increased self-understanding—to groups in society. The more people know about the conditions of their own actions and about the overall institutions of their society, the more they are likely to be in a position to influence the circumstances of their own lives. We must not picture the practical role of sociology only as assisting policymakers—that is, powerful groups—to make informed decisions. Those in power cannot be assumed always to have in mind the interests of the less powerful or underprivileged in the policies they pursue. Self-enlightened groups can respond in an effective way to policies pursued by government officials or other authorities, and can also form policy initiatives of their own. Self-help groups (like Alcoholics Anonymous) and social movements (like women's movements) are examples of social associations that directly seek to bring about practical reforms they see as necessary (see Chapter 9: "Groups and Organizations").

THE SOCIOLOGIST'S ROLE IN SOCIETY

Should sociologists themselves actively advocate, and agitate for, practical programs of reform or social change? Some argue that sociology can preserve its objectivity only if practitioners of the subject are studiously neutral in moral and political controversies. But there is no reason why we should suppose that scholars who remain aloof from issues of the day are necessarily more impartial in their assessment of sociological issues than others. There is bound to be a connection between studying sociology and the promptings of social conscience. No one who is sociologically sophisticated can be unaware of the inequalities that exist in the world today, the lack of social justice in many current social situations, or the deprivations suffered by millions of human beings. It would be strange if sociologists were not to take sides on practical issues and it would be illogical as well as impractical to try to ban them from drawing upon their sociological expertise in such involvements.

A LOOK FORWARD

IN THIS CHAPTER WE HAVE DESCRIBED SOCIOLOGY AS A DIScipline in which we set aside our personal view of the world to look more carefully at the influences that shape our lives and those of others. Sociology emerged as a distinct intellectual endeavor with the early development of modern industrialized societies, and the study of such societies remains its principal concern. But sociologists are also preoccupied with a broad range of issues concerning the nature of social interaction and human societies in general. In Chapter 2 we shall investigate the diversity of human culture, looking at the enormous contrasts between the customs and habits that different peoples follow. To do so, we need to embark upon a voyage of cultural exploration around the world. We have to retrace, on an intellectual level, the travels that Christopher Columbus, Captain Cook, and other adventurers undertook when they set off on their perilous journeys across the globe. But as sociologists, we cannot look at these only from the explorers' point of view—as voyages of discovery. For these expeditions initiated a process of Western expansion that had a dramatic impact upon other cultures and upon subsequent world social development.

SUMMARY

1. Sociology can be identified as the systematic study of human societies giving special emphasis to modern, industrialized systems. The subject came into being as an attempt to understand the far-reaching changes that have occurred in human societies over the past two to three centuries.

2. Major social changes have also occurred in the most intimate and personal characteristics of people's lives. The development of romantic love as a basis for marriage is an example of this.

3. Sociologists investigate social life by posing distinct questions and trying to find the answers to these by systematic research. These questions may be factual, comparative, developmental, or theoretical. In sociological research it is important to distinguish between intended and unintended results of human action.

4. The practice of sociology involves the ability to think imaginatively and to detach oneself as far as possible from preconceived ideas about social relationships.

5. Sociology has close ties with other social sciences. All the social sciences are concerned with human behavior, but tend to concentrate on different aspects of it. The connections between sociology, anthropology, and history are particularly important.

6. Sociology is a science in that it involves systematic methods of investigation and the evaluation of theories in the light of evidence and logical argument. But it cannot be modeled directly upon the natural sciences, because studying human behavior is in fundamental ways different from studying the world of nature.

7. Sociologists attempt to be objective in their studies of the social world, approaching their work in an open-minded way. Objectivity depends not only upon the attitudes of the researcher, but upon the critical evaluation of research and theory, which is an essential part of sociology as a scholarly discipline.

8. Sociology is a subject with important practical implications. Sociology can contribute to social criticism and practical social reform in several ways. First, the improved understanding of a given set of social circumstances often gives us a better chance of controlling them. Second, sociology provides the means of increasing our cultural sensitivities, allowing policies to be based upon an awareness of divergent cultural values. Third, we can investigate the consequences (intended and unintended) of the adoption of particular policy programs. Finally, and perhaps most important, sociology provides self-enlightenment, offering groups and individuals an increased opportunity to alter the conditions of their own lives.

BASIC CONCEPTS

SOCIOLOGY
SOCIAL STRUCTURE
SCIENCE
OBJECTIVITY

IMPORTANT TERMS

COMMON-SENSE BELIEFS
FACTUAL QUESTIONS
COMPARATIVE QUESTIONS
DEVELOPMENTAL QUESTIONS
EMPIRICAL INVESTIGATION
THEORETICAL QUESTIONS

UNINTENDED CONSEQUENCES
SOCIAL REPRODUCTION
SOCIAL TRANSFORMATION
THE SOCIOLOGICAL IMAGINATION
ANTHROPOLOGY
SELF-ENLIGHTENMENT

CULTURE, THE INDIVIDUAL AND SOCIAL INTERACTION

In this part of the book, we start our exploration of the diverse field of sociology by looking at the connections between individual development and culture and analyzing the major types of society within which human beings live today, or have lived in the past. Our personalities and outlooks are strongly influenced by the culture and society in which each of us happens to exist. At the same time, in our day-to-day behavior we actively recreate and reshape the cultural and social contexts in which our activities occur.

In the first chapter of this part (Chapter 2), we examine the unity and the diversity of human culture. We consider how far human beings resemble the animals and how far they differ from them; and we analyze the range of variations found between different human cultures. The extent of human cultural variability has only come to be studied as a result of changes that have in fact altered or destroyed many cultures in which people lived prior to modern times. These changes are outlined, and the main types of society that dominate the world today are contrasted to those that preceded them in history.

Next, Chapter 3 discusses socialization, concentrating upon the process by which the human infant develops into a social being. To some degree, socialization continues through the life span, so studying socialization thus also means analyzing the "cycle of the generations"—the relationships between young, middle-aged, and older people.

In Chapter 4, we discuss how people interact with each other in everyday life. We look at the delicate, yet profoundly important, mechanisms whereby individuals interpret what others say and do in their face-to-face encounters. The study of social interaction can in fact tell us a great deal about the larger social environments in which we live. Chapter 5 moves on to look at wider social processes, beginning with the study of deviance and crime. We can learn much about the way the majority of a population behaves by studying people whose behavior deviates from generally accepted patterns.

The last chapter in this part (Chapter 6) discusses problems of gender, analyzing how changing social conditions have affected the position of women in modern societies. This chapter also includes an examination of the nature of sexuality, looking at the main influences governing patterns of sexual behavior.

CULTURE AND SOCIETY

SOME HALF A CENTURY AGO, SOME ISLANDERS IN THE WEST-
ern Pacific began constructing elaborate, large wooden
models of airplanes. Hours of patient labor went into
their construction, although no one there had ever seen a
plane at close hand. The models were not designed to fly,
but were at the center of religious movements led by local
prophets. The religious leaders proclaimed that if certain
rites were performed, "cargo" would arrive from the
skies. Cargo consisted of the goods Westerners had been
seen to bring into the islands for themselves. The whites
would then disappear, and the ancestors of the native peoples would
return. The islanders believed that, as a result of faithful observation
of certain rites, a new era would arrive, in which they would enjoy
the material wealth of the white intruders, while otherwise continuing their traditional ways of life (Worsley, 1968).

Why did these "cargo cults" come into being? They originated in
the clash between the traditional customs of the islanders and ways of
life introduced through Western influence. The wealth and power of
the whites were plain to see. The islanders assumed that the mysterious flying objects that delivered the riches the interlopers enjoyed
were the very source of such wealth. From the islanders' point of

view, it was quite logical to attempt to bring the airplanes under their own control by religious and ritual means. At the same time, they were seeking to protect and preserve their own customs, threatened by the arrival of the newcomers.

The islanders' knowledge of Western patterns of behavior and technology was relatively slight; they interpreted the activities of the Europeans in terms of their own beliefs about, and outlook upon, the world. In this respect, their reactions to a foreign culture were similar to those of most societies prior to modern times. Even people in the great civilizations of previous ages had only a vague awareness of the ways of life of other peoples. When Western adventurers and merchants sailed off to remote parts of the globe in the sixteenth and seventeenth centuries, they regarded those with whom they came into contact as "barbarians" or "savages."

THE MEETING OF CULTURES

The Europeans who traveled to the Americas in the 1500s went looking for giants, amazons, and pygmies, the Fountain of Eternal Youth, women whose bodies never aged, and men who lived to be a hundred years or more. The familiar images of traditional European myths helped guide the voyages undertaken. The American Indians were initially regarded as wild creatures having more affinity with animals than with humans. Paracelsus, the sixteenth-century medical writer, pictured North America as a continent peopled with creatures that were half-man, half-beast. Nymphs, satyrs, pygmies, and wild men were held to be soulless beings created spontaneously from the earth. The bishop of Santa Marta in Colombia, South America, described the local Indians as "not men with rational souls but wild men of the woods, for which reason they could retain no Christian doctrine, no virtue nor any kind of learning" (Pagden, 1982).

Conversely, the Europeans who established contact with the Chinese Empire during the seventeenth and eighteenth centuries were treated with disdain by its rulers. In 1793, King George III of England sent a trade mission to China to foster commercial exchange. The "barbarian" visitors were allowed to set up some trading posts in China and to benefit from the luxuries the country could provide. The Chinese themselves, the visitors were told, were quite uninterested in anything the Europeans had to offer: "Our Celestial Empire possesses all things in prolific abundance and lacks no products within its borders. There is therefore no need to import the manufactures of outside barbarians in exchange for our own produce." A request for permission to send Western missionaries to China met with

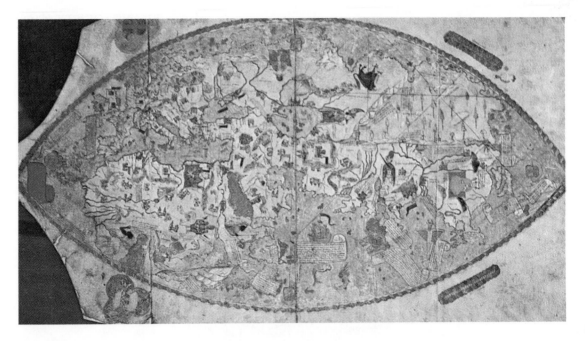

This fifteenth-century map of the world shows Europe on the left, China toward the right, and no western hemisphere.

the answer: "The distinction between Chinese and barbarians is most strict, and your Ambassador's request that barbarians shall be given full liberty to disseminate their religion is utterly unreasonable" (Worsley, 1973).

The gulf between East and West was so great that each held the most bizarre beliefs about the other. For example, even as late as the closing part of the nineteenth century it was widely believed in China that foreigners, particularly the English, would die of constipation if deprived of rhubarb. Until two centuries ago, no one had the "overall view" of the world that we now take for granted.

One of the most dramatic first contacts between Westerners and other cultures occurred as late as 1818. An English naval expedition looking for a passage to Russia between Baffin Island and Greenland, within the Arctic Circle, had a chance encounter with the polar Eskimos. Before that meeting, the Eskimos had thought they were the only people in the world! (Oswalt, 1972).

THE CONCEPT OF CULTURE

IN THIS CHAPTER, WE SHALL LOOK AT THE UNITY AND DI-versity of human life and culture. The concept of culture, together with that of society, is one of the most widely used notions in sociology. **Culture** consists of the **values** the members of a given group hold, the **norms** they follow, and the *material*

Chinese painting showing trading posts, which were confined to a certain area in Canton (c. 1800).

goods they create. Values are abstract ideals, while norms are definite principles or rules that people are expected to observe. Norms represent the "dos" and "don'ts" of social life. For instance, monogamy—being faithful to a single marriage partner—is a prominent value in most Western societies. In many other cultures, a person is permitted to have several wives or husbands simultaneously. Norms of behavior in marriage include, for example, how husbands and wives are supposed to behave towards their in-laws. In some societies, a husband or wife is expected to develop a close relationship with the parents-in-law; in others, by contrast, they are expected to keep a clear distance.

When we use the term in ordinary daily conversation, we often think of "culture" as equivalent to the "higher things of the mind," such as art, literature, music, and painting. As sociologists use it, the concept includes such activities, but also far more. Culture refers to the whole way of life of the members of a society. It includes how they dress, their marriage customs and family life, their patterns of work, religious ceremonies, and leisure pursuits. It covers also the goods they create and which become meaningful for them—bows and arrows, ploughs, factories and machines, computers, books, dwellings. Culture has been described by the anthropologist Clyde Kluckhohn (1985; orig. pub. 1949) as a "design for living," acquired—as we shall see later—through learning rather than by instinct.

How might we describe American culture? It involves, first, a particular range of values shared by many, if not all, Americans—such as the belief in the merits of individual achievement, or in equality of opportunity. Second, these values are connected to specific norms: for example, it is usually expected that people will work hard in order to achieve occupational success. Third, it involves the use of material artifacts created mostly through modern industrial technology, such as cars, mass-produced food, clothing, and so forth.

Culture can be conceptually distinguished from society, but there are very close connections between these notions. While culture concerns the *way of life* of the members of a given society, **society** refers to the *system of interrelationships* that connects together the individuals who share a common culture. Thus the United States, vast though it is, is a social system largely separate from the neighboring societies of Mexico and Canada. All three are distinct—and of course, physically separated by thousands of miles of ocean—from European societies, such as France, Sweden, or Britain, or those in Asia, such as India or China. There are many different societies in the world today, and we shall discuss their overall characteristics towards the end of the chapter. It is important to recognize from the outset, however, that no society is a closed entity—far from it. There are many social, economic, and political connections that crosscut the boundaries between societies; and these are of rapidly growing importance in the present day. For instance, many goods are now produced and traded worldwide. Your local supermarket may seem to be simply part of the local community, and therefore of American society as a whole, but the goods it sells are regularly imported from all over the world; the supermarket is an outpost in a global set of economic relationships.

Why should we distinguish the concepts of culture and society? We need the distinction because cultural characteristics can be transmitted from society to society, and different societies may share common cultural characteristics. For instance, some of the cultural characteristics of the United States have come from societies in Europe as a result of immigration and other processes.

However, no culture could exist without a society, and equally no society could exist without culture. If we lacked culture, in fact, we would not be human at all in the sense in which we usually understand that term. We would have no language in which to express ourselves, no sense of self-consciousness, and our ability to think and reason would be severely limited—as we shall show in this chapter and in Chapter 3 ("Socialization and the Life Cycle").

The chief theme of both the current chapter and the next, in fact, is the biological versus the cultural inheritance of humankind. The relevant questions are: What distinguishes human beings from the

One definition of culture: the ability of people not only to invent and use something, but also to teach others how to do so.

animals? Where do our distinctively human characteristics come from? What is the nature of human nature? These questions are crucial to sociology because they set the foundation for the whole field of study. To answer them, we shall analyze what human beings share in common and how cultures differ.

Cultural variations among human beings are linked to differing types of society, and we shall compare and contrast the main forms of society found in history. The point of doing this is to tie together closely the two aspects of human social existence—the different cultural values and products that human beings have developed, and the contrasting types of society in which such cultural development has occurred. Too often, culture is discussed separately from society as though the two were quite disconnected; whereas in fact, as has already been emphasized, they are closely meshed. Throughout the chapter, attention will be concentrated upon how social change has affected human cultural development—particularly since the time when Europeans began to spread their ways of life across the world.

THE HUMAN SPECIES

Charles Darwin (1809–1882)

In spite of the clashes and misunderstandings that occurred, the increasing intrusion of Westerners into other parts of the globe gradually made it possible to understand what human beings share in common as a species, as well as the variabilities of human culture (Hirst and Woolley, 1982). Charles Darwin, an ordained minister of the Church of England, published his book *On the Origin of Species* in 1859, following two journeys around the world on HMS *Beagle.* Painstakingly amassing observations of different animal species, Darwin set out a picture of the development of human beings quite different from those existing hitherto.

As we have seen, it was not uncommon for people in earlier centuries to believe in beings that were half-beast, half-human. But with Darwin's findings, such possibilities were completely swept away. Darwin claimed to have found a continuity of development from animals to human beings. Our characteristics as humans, according to him, have emerged from a process of biological change that can be traced back to the initial origins of life on earth, more than three billion years ago. Darwin's view of humans and animals was for many even harder to accept than that of half-beast, half-human creatures. He set in motion one of the most debated, yet persuasive, theories in modern science—the theory of **evolution.**

Evolution

According to Darwin, the development of the human species came about as a result of a *random process*. In many religions, including Christianity, animals and human beings are seen as created by divine intervention. Evolutionary theory, by contrast, regards the development of the animal and human species as devoid of purpose. Evolution is a result of what Darwin called *natural selection*. The idea of natural selection is simple. All organic beings need food and other resources, such as protection from climatic extremes, in order to survive. Not enough resources exist to support all types of animals that exist at any given point in time, because they produce far more offspring than the environment can provide food for. Those best adapted to their environment survive, while others, less able to cope with its demands, perish. Some animals are more intelligent, faster, or have superior eyesight than others. In the struggle for survival, they have advantages over those less endowed. They live longer and are able to breed, passing on their characteristics to subsequent generations. They are "selected" to survive and reproduce.

There is a continuous process of natural selection, because of the biological mechanism of **mutation.** A mutation is a random genetic

Great moments in evolution.

change, altering the biological characteristics of some individuals in a species. Most mutations are either harmful or useless in terms of survival value. But some give an animal a competitive advantage over others: individuals possessing the mutant genes will then tend to survive and reproduce while others will not. The phrase *survival of the fittest,* although coined by the sociologist Herbert Spencer rather than by Darwin, describes the phenomenon. The "fittest" are those best adapted to a particular environment. This random process explains both minor changes within species and major changes leading to the disappearance of entire species. For example, many millions of years ago, giant reptiles flourished in various regions of the world. Their size became a handicap as mutations occurring in other, smaller, species gave them superior adaptive capabilities. The early ancestors of humans were among these more adaptable species.

Although the theory of evolution has been refined since Darwin's day, the essentials of Darwin's account are widely accepted. Evolutionary theory allows us to piece together a clear understanding of the emergence of different species and their relation to one another.

Human Beings and the Apes

The evolution of life, it is now firmly established, began in the oceans. About four hundred million years ago, the first land-based creatures emerged. These gradually evolved into the large reptiles, which were in turn displaced by mammals. Mammals are warm-blooded creatures who reproduce through sexual intercourse. Although the mammals were much smaller in bodily size than the giant reptiles, they were more intelligent and maneuverable. Mammals have a greater capacity to learn from experience than other animals. This capacity has come to its highest development in the human species. Human beings are part of a group of higher mammals, the primates, that originated some seventy million years ago.

Our closest relatives among animal species are the chimpanzee, gorilla, and orangutan. On learning about Darwin's account of evolution, the wife of the bishop of Worcester is said to have remarked: "Descended from monkeys? My dear, let us hope that it is not true. But if it is true, let us hope that it does not become widely known." Like many others since, the lady mistook what evolution involves. Human beings are not descended from the apes. Humans and apes all trace their evolution from much more primitive groups of ancestor species living many millions of years ago.

The ancestors of human beings were primates who walked erect and were about the size of modern pygmies. Their bodies were probably fairly hairless, but in other respects they looked more like apes than humans. Various other types of hominid (beings belonging to the human family) existed between this period and the emergence of the human species as it exists today. Human beings recognizably identical in all respects to ourselves appeared about fifty thousand years ago. There is good evidence that cultural development preceded, and probably shaped, the evolution of the human species. The use of tools and the development of fairly elaborate forms of communication, together with the formation of social communities, almost certainly played a major part in the evolutionary process. They offered greater survival value for the ancestors of the human species than was available to animals lacking them. Groups that possessed them were able to master their environment much more effectively than those that did not. However, with the emergence of the human species proper, cultural development became intensified.

Because of their parallel lines of development, the human species shares a number of characteristics with other primates. The physical structure of the human body is similar in most respects to that of the apes. Like human beings, the apes tend to live in social groups, have large brains compared to their body size, and have a long period during which the young are dependent upon their elders.

In some ways, however, human beings differ appreciably from their nearest relatives. Human beings stand erect, while apes crouch. The human foot differs strikingly from the hand, while in most apes these are more similar. The human brain is distinctly larger in relation to body size, than the brain of even the most intelligent of the

Humans are not descendants of the apes though we do share a common ancestry. Hence, we share some characteristics, but differ in many ways.

apes. While the period of infant dependency among the higher animals is two years or less, among human beings it is some seven to eight years.

NATURE AND NURTURE

As human beings, we all have physical or biological characteristics that are part of our genetic makeup. We are all also members of a society and adopt some of its cultural characteristics. In other words, "nature" and "nurture" intermingle in our actions. But what is the relationship between these? Is our behavior directly influenced by our biological constitution (nature)? There is general agreement among sociologists and social scientists about some, but not all, aspects of the answers to these questions. The fundamental importance of culture (nurture) in human life is not denied by anyone. But disagreements exist about whether or not some forms of human activity are genetic rather than cultural in derivation. In the following sections we shall survey this issue, considering the origins of some of our main human characteristics and analyzing common features of human social life as well as human diversity.

Sociobiology

Although they recognized the evolutionary continuity between the animals and human beings, until recently most biologists tended to emphasize the distinctive qualities of the human species. This position has come under challenge from the work of *sociobiologists,* who see close parallels between human behavior and that of the animals. The term **sociobiology** derives from the writings of the American entomologist, Edward O. Wilson (1975, 1978). It refers to the application of biological principles to explain the social activities of all social animals, including human beings. According to Wilson, many aspects of human social life are grounded in our genetic makeup. For example, some species of animals have elaborate courtship rituals whereby sexual union and reproduction are achieved. Human courtship and sexual behavior, in the view of sociobiology, generally involve similar rituals, also based on inborn characteristics. In most animal species, to take a second example, males are larger and more aggressive than females, and tend to dominate the "weaker sex." According to these researchers, this perhaps explains why, in all human societies we know of, men tend to hold positions of greater authority than women. Similarly, sociobiologists even look at altruism, which has been considered a distinctively human quality. We often hear of stories in which an individual gives up his or her life to save another. What could be more human? But here as well, sociobiologists draw parallels with other nonhuman species, particularly some species of birds that will risk sacrificing their lives to save their young. According to Wilson and his followers, by demonstrating that many such aspects of human behavior are genetically programmed, sociobiology will increasingly be able to absorb sociology and anthropology into a single, biologically based, discipline.

The issues thus raised have been much debated over recent years, and they remain highly controversial (Montagu, 1980; Sahlins, 1976; Caplan, 1978; Wiegele, 1982; Kitcher, 1985). Scholars tend to fall into two camps, depending to some degree on their educational background. Authors sympathetic to the sociobiological viewpoint are mostly trained in biology, rather than the social sciences, while the large majority of sociologists and anthropologists tend to be skeptical of the claims of the sociobiologists. Probably they know rather little about the genetic foundations of human life; while those with a background in biological science have similarly limited knowledge of sociological or anthropological research. Each side finds it a little difficult to fully understand the force of the arguments advanced by the other.

Some of the passions generated early on by Wilson's work have now abated, and it is possible to produce a reasonably clear assessment of it. Sociobiology is important—but more for what it has shown about the life of the animals than for what it has demonstrated about human behavior. Combined with the studies of ethologists (biologists who carry out fieldwork among animal groups, rather than studying animals in artificial circumstances in zoos or laboratories), sociobiologists have been able to demonstrate that many animal species are more social than was previously thought. Animal groups have a considerable influence over the behavior of individual members of the species. On the other hand, little evidence has been found to demonstrate that genetic inheritance controls complex forms of human activity. The ideas of the sociobiologists about human social life are thus at best no more than speculative. Our behavior, of course, is genetically *influenced,* but our genetic endowment, as members of the human species, probably conditions only the potentialities and limits of our actions, not the actual content of what we do.

Instincts

Most biologists and sociologists agree that human beings do not have any "instincts." Such a statement runs contrary, not only to the hypotheses of sociobiology, but to what most ordinary people believe.

FIGURE 2.1
THE "MATING DANCE"
OF THE STICKLEBACK

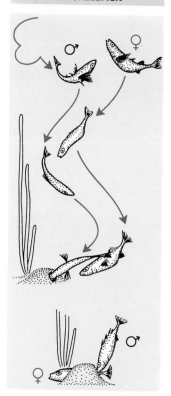

This figure shows the elaborate but pre-programmed, instinctual, movements brought about in the male by the appearance of the female stickleback.

Aren't there many things we do "instinctively?" For instance, if someone throws a punch, don't we instinctively blink or shy away? In fact, this is not an example of an instinct when the term is used precisely. As understood in biology and sociology, an **instinct** is a *complex pattern* of behavior that is genetically determined. The courtship rituals of many of the lower animals are instinctive in this sense. The stickleback (a small freshwater fish), for example, has an extremely complicated set of rituals that have to be followed by both male and female if mating is to occur (Tinbergen, 1974). Each fish produces an elaborate array of movements, to which the other responds, creating an elaborate "mating dance." This is genetically patterned for the whole species (Figure 2.1). A spontaneous blinking of the eye, or movement away of the head, in the face of an anticipated blow, is a *reflex act* rather than an instinct. It is a single, simple response, not an elaborate behavior pattern. To speak of this as instinctive in the technical sense is thus mistaken.

Human beings are born with a number of basic reflexes similar to the eye-blink reaction, most of which seem to have some evolutionary survival value. Very young human infants, for example, will suck when presented with a nipple, or a nipple-like object. A young child will throw up his arms to catch at support when suddenly losing his balance, and pull his hand back sharply if he touches a very hot surface. Each of these reactions are obviously useful in coping with the environment.

Human beings also have a number of biologically given *needs.* There is an organic basis to our needs for food, drink, sex, and the maintenance of certain levels of body temperature. But the ways in which these needs are satisfied or coped with vary widely between—and within—different cultures.

For example, all cultures tend to have some kind of standardized courtship behavior. This is obviously related to the universal nature of sexual needs, but their expression in different cultures—even including the sexual act itself—varies enormously. The normal position for the sexual act in Western culture involves the woman lying on her back, and the man on top of her. This position is seen as absurd by people in some other societies, who usually have intercourse lying side by side, with the man facing the woman's back, with the woman on top of the man, or in other positions. The ways in which people seek to satisfy their sexual needs thus seem to be culturally learned, not genetically implanted.

Moreover, humans can override their biological needs in ways that seem to have no parallel among the animals. Religious mystics may fast for very long periods. People sometimes go on a "hunger strike" as a means of political protest, and have on occasion starved themselves to death. All animals, including human beings, have a drive towards self-preservation. Unlike other animals, however, humans are able deliberately to go against that drive, risking their lives in hazardous pursuits, or actually committing suicide.

CULTURAL DIVERSITY

The study of cultural variation drives home the centrality of cultural learning to our existence as humans. The diversity of human culture is remarkable. Values and norms of behavior vary widely from culture to culture, often contrasting radically with what people from Western societies consider "normal."

In the West, we eat oysters, but we do not eat kittens or puppy dogs, both of which are regarded as delicacies in some parts of the world. Jews do not eat pork, while Hindus eat pork but avoid beef. Westerners regard kissing as a normal part of sexual behavior, but in many other cultures the practice is either unknown or regarded as disgusting. All these different traits of behavior are aspects of broad cultural differences that distinguish societies from one another.

Small societies (like the "hunting and gathering" societies, which will be discussed later in the chapter) tend to be culturally uniform, but industrialized societies are themselves culturally diverse, involving numerous different **subcultures.** In modern cities, for example, there are many subcultural communities living side by side. Gerald Suttles (1968) carried out a now classic fieldwork study of a slum area on Chicago's West Side. In just this one neighborhood, he found many different subcultural groupings: Puerto Ricans, blacks, Greeks, Jews, gypsies, Italians, Mexicans, and Southern whites. All of these groups had their own "territories" and ways of life.

CULTURAL IDENTITY AND ETHNOCENTRISM

Every culture contains its own unique patterns of behavior, which seem alien to people from other cultural backgrounds. As an example, we can take the Nacirema, a group described in a celebrated research investigation by Horace Miner (1956). Miner concentrated his attention upon the elaborate body rituals in which the Nacirema engage, rituals that have strange and exotic characteristics. His discussion is worth quoting at length:

> The fundamental belief underlying the whole system appears to be that the human body is ugly and that its natural

tendency is to debility and disease. Incarcerated in such a body, man's only hope is to avert these characteristics through the use of the powerful influences of ritual and ceremony. Every household has one or more shrines devoted to this purpose. . . . The focal point of the shrine is a box or chest which is built into the wall. In this chest are kept the many charms and magical potions without which no native believes he could live. These preparations are secured from a variety of specialized practitioners. The most powerful of these are the medicine men, whose assistance must be rewarded with substantial gifts. . . .

However, the medicine men do not provide the curative potions for their clients, but decide what the ingredients should be and then write them down in an ancient and secret language. This writing is understood only by the medicine men and by the herbalists who, for another gift, provide the required charm.

The Nacirema have an almost pathological horror of and fascination with the mouth, the condition of which is believed to have a supernatural influence on all social relationships. Were it not for the rituals of the mouth, they believe that their teeth would fall out, their gums bleed, their jaws shrink, their friends desert them, and their lovers reject them. They also believe that a strong relationship exists between oral and moral characteristics. For example, there is a ritual ablution of the mouth for children which is supposed to improve their moral fibre.

The daily body ritual performed by everyone includes a mouth-rite. Despite the fact that these people are so punctilious about care of the mouth, this rite involves a practice which strikes the uninitiated stranger as revolting. It was reported to me that the ritual consists of inserting a small bundle of hog hairs into the mouth, along with certain magical powders, and then moving the bundle in a highly formalized series of gestures. (Miner, 1956)

Who are the Nacirema, and in which part of the world do they live? You will be able to answer these questions for yourself, as well as identifying the nature of the body rituals described, simply by spelling "Nacirema" backwards. Almost any familiar activity will seem strange if described out of context, rather than being seen as part of the whole way of life of a people. Western cleanliness rituals are no more, or less, bizarre than the customs of some Pacific groups who knock out their front teeth to beautify themselves, or of certain South American tribal groups who place discs inside their lips to make them protrude, believing that this enhances their attractiveness.

We cannot understand these practices and beliefs separately from the wider cultures of which they are part. A culture has to be studied in terms of its own meanings and values—a key presupposition of sociology. Sociologists endeavor as far as possible to avoid **ethnocentrism,** which is judging other cultures by means of one's own. Since human cultures vary so widely, it is not surprising that people coming from one culture frequently find it difficult to sympathize with the ideas or behavior of those from a different culture. The cargo-cult example that opened this chapter illustrated one culture's difficulty in dealing with another.

This difficulty is not something that merely belongs to the past, nor is it a trivial matter, amusing though the example of the Nacirema might be. Consider the cultural differences that exist between nations in the modern world. Misunderstanding of these differences might involve distrust between them which, in times of crisis, could help fuel a war. How many people living in the United States have a good understanding of the cultural characteristics of Iranian society —or vice versa?

Different cultures value different characteristics: San woman in Botswana (left), film star in the United States (right).

In sociology, we have to ensure that we remove our own cultural blinders in order to see the ways of life of different peoples in an unbiased light. More than this, it is one of the primary tasks of sociology to work to remove these blinders. It is a task in which, as was stressed in the opening chapter of the book, the sociological imagination must be brought fully into play. To adequately understand cultures other than our own, we have to be able to actively project ourselves, in our imagination, out of our mundane lives and into cultural domains that might initially seem puzzling or even quite bizarre.

CULTURAL UNIVERSALS

Amid the diversity of human cultural behavior there are some common features. Where these are found in all, or virtually all, societies they are called **cultural universals** (Oswalt, 1972; Hiebert, 1983; Friedl, 1981). There is no known culture without a grammatically complex language. All cultures have some recognizable form of family system in which there are values and norms associated with the care of children. The institution of marriage is a cultural universal as are religious rituals and property rights. All cultures also have some form of incest prohibition—the banning of sexual relations between close relatives, such as father and daughter, mother and son, or brother and sister. A variety of other cultural universals have been identified by anthropologists—including the existence of art, dancing, bodily adornment, games, gift giving, joking, and rules of hygiene (Murdock, 1945).

Yet rather less is universal than would appear from this list, because there are so many variations within each category. Consider, for example, the prohibition against incest. What is defined as incest in different cultures varies considerably. Most often, incest is regarded as sexual relations between members of the immediate family, but among many peoples it includes cousins, even, in some instances, all people bearing the same family name. There also have been societies in which at least a small proportion of the population have been permitted to engage in incestuous practices. This was the case within, for instance, the ruling class of traditional Egypt.

Among the cultural characteristics shared by all societies, two stand out particularly. All cultures incorporate ways of expressing meaning and communication, and all depend on material means of production. In all cultures, *language* is the primary vehicle of meaning and communication. It is not the only such vehicle, however. Material culture itself carries meanings, as we shall show in what follows.

Language

The possession of language is one of the most distinctive of human cultural attributes. Animals can communicate with one another, yet there is no animal species that possesses a developed language. Some of the higher primates can be taught linguistic skills—but only in a highly rudimentary way. One of the most famous chimpanzees known to sociology, called Washoe, was taught a vocabulary of well over a hundred words using the American Sign Language for the Deaf (Gardner and Gardner, 1969, 1975). Washoe was also able to put together a few very rudimentary sentences. For example, she could communicate "Come hug-love sorry sorry," meaning that she wanted to apologize after behaving in a way she knew would be disapproved of.

The use of language, and the ability to pass it on from generation to generation, is a distinctly human attribute.

The experiments with Washoe were much more successful than similar ones done with other chimpanzees—hence Washoe's fame in the sociological literature. But Washoe was not able to master what is basic to human language—rules of grammar—nor could she teach other chimps what she knew. Even after she had been trained for several years, her linguistic capacity was far below that of the average human child of two. Every competent adult human language speaker has a vocabulary of thousands of words and is able to combine them according to rules so complex that linguists spend their entire careers trying to find out what they are (Linden, 1976).

Language is one of the best examples for demonstrating both the unity and diversity of human culture. For there are no cultures without language, yet there are thousands of different languages spoken in the world. Anyone who has visited a foreign country armed with only a dictionary knows how difficult it is to either understand anything or to be understood. Although languages that have similar origins have words in common with one another—as for example, German with English—most of the world's languages have no words in common at all. Even languages that are very close to each other in origin have many words and phrases that the other does not possess, that is, which cannot be directly translated. For instance, German has two words meaning "you," involving a distinction that does not exist in English. *Du* is used when a person knows another well, and when adults speak to children; *Sie* is employed in circumstances where two people are relative strangers, or to indicate respect or deference.

Language is involved in virtually all of our activities. In the form of ordinary talk or speech, it is the means whereby we organize most of what we do. We shall discuss the importance of talk and conversation in social life at some length in a subsequent chapter (Chapter 4:

One of the earliest (15,000–10,000 B.C.) forms of human expression. Cave drawings at Lascaux, France, by Cro-Magnons.

"Social Interaction in Everyday Life"). However, language is involved not just in mundane, everyday activities, but also in ceremony, religion, poetry, and many other spheres. One of the most distinctive features of human language is that it allows us to vastly extend the scope of our thought and experience. Using language, we can convey information about events remote in time or space, and can discuss things we have never seen. We can develop abstract concepts, tell stories, make jokes, and construct imaginative flights of fancy.

Speech and Writing

All societies use speech as a vehicle of language. However, there are other ways of "carrying" or expressing language—most notably, writing. The invention of writing marked a major transition in human history. Writing first began as the drawing up of lists. Marks would be made on wood, clay, or stone to keep records about significant events, objects, or people. For example, a mark, or sometimes a picture, might be drawn to represent each field possessed by a particular family or set of families (Gelb, 1952). Writing began as a means of storing information, and as such was closely linked to the administrative needs of the early civilizations (which will be discussed a little later in the chapter). A society that possesses writing can "locate itself" in time and space. Documents can be accumulated that record the past, and information can be gathered about present-day events and activities. (One of the most important traditions of thought that has analyzed these issues in sociology and anthropology is *structuralism*—which is discussed extensively in Chapter 22: "The Development of Sociological Theory.")

Writing is not just the transfer of speech to paper or some other durable material. It is a phenomenon of interest in its own right. Written documents or *texts* have qualities in some ways quite distinct from the spoken word. The impact of speech is always by definition limited to the particular contexts in which words are uttered. Ideas and experiences can be passed down through generations in cultures without writing, but only if they are regularly repeated and passed on by word of mouth. Texts, on the other hand, can endure for thousands of years, and through them those from past ages can in a certain sense "address" us directly. This is, of course, why documentary research is so important to historians. Through interpreting the texts that are left behind by dead generations, historians can reconstruct what their lives were like. The Biblical texts, for example, have formed an enduring part of the history of the West for the past two thousand years. We can still read, and admire, the plays of the great dramatists of ancient Greece.

An example of early writing and counting (c. 3200–3100 B.C.). The signs above represent fifty-four, and those below are for "cow" and "bull"; hence, "fifty-four cows and bulls."

Semiotics and Material Culture

The symbols expressed in speech and writing are the chief ways in which cultural meanings are formed and expressed. But they are not the only ways. Both material objects and aspects of behavior can be used to generate meanings. A *signifier* is any vehicle of meaning—any set of elements used to convey communication. The sounds made in speech are signifiers, as are the marks made on paper or other materials in writing. Other signifiers, however, include dress, pictures or visual signs, modes of eating, forms of building or architecture, and many other material features of culture (Hawkes, 1977). Styles of dress, for example, normally help signify differences between the sexes. In our culture, at least until relatively recently, women used to wear skirts and men pants. In other cultures, this is reversed: women wear pants and men skirts (Leach, 1976).

Semiotics—the analysis of nonverbal cultural meanings—opens up a fascinating field for both sociology and anthropology. Semiotic analysis can be very useful in comparing one culture with another. Given that cultural meanings are symbolic, it allows us to contrast the ways in which different cultures are structured. For example, the buildings in cities are not simply places in which people live and work. They often have a symbolic character. In traditional cities, the main temple or church was usually placed on high ground in or near the city center. It symbolized the all-powerful influence that religion was supposed to have over the lives of the people. In modern societies, by contrast, the skyscrapers of big business often occupy that symbolic position.

Of course, material culture is not simply symbolic, but is vital to catering for physical needs—in the shape of the tools or technology used to acquire food, make weaponry, construct dwellings, and so forth. We have to study both the practical and the symbolic aspects of material culture in order to understand it completely.

CULTURE AND SOCIAL DEVELOPMENT

Cultural traits are closely related to overall patterns in the development of society. The level of material culture reached in a given society influences, although by no means completely determines, other aspects of cultural development. This is easy to see, for example, on the level of technology. Much of the cultural paraphernalia characteristic of our lives today—cars, telephones, computers, running water, electric light—depend upon technological innovations that have been made only very recently in human history.

The same is true at earlier phases of social development. Prior to the invention of the smelting of metal, for example, goods had to be made of organic or naturally occurring materials like wood or stone —a basic limitation upon the artifacts that could be constructed. Variations in material culture provide the main means of distinguishing different forms of human society, but other factors are also influential. Writing is an example. As has been mentioned, not all human cultures have possessed writing—in fact, for most of human history, writing was unknown. The development of writing altered the scope of human cultural potentialities, making different forms of social organization possible than those that had previously existed.

We now turn to analyzing the main types of society that existed in the past and that are still found in the world today. In the present day, we are accustomed to societies that contain many millions of people, many of them living crowded together in urban areas. But for most of human history, the earth was much less-densely populated than it is now, and it is only over the past hundred years or so that any societies have existed in which the majority of the population were city dwellers. To understand the forms of society that existed prior to modern industrialism, we have to call upon the historical dimension of the sociological imagination.

TYPES OF PREMODERN SOCIETY

THE EXPLORERS, TRADERS, AND MISSIONARIES SENT OUT during Europe's great age of discovery met with many different peoples. As the anthropologist Marvin Harris has written in his work *Cannibals and Kings:*

> In some regions—Australia, the Arctic, the southern tips of South America and Africa—they found groups still living much like Europe's own long-forgotten stone age ancestors: bands of twenty or thirty people, sprinkled across vast territories, constantly on the move, living entirely by hunting animals and collecting wild plants. These hunter-collectors appeared to be members of a rare and endangered species. In other regions—the forests of eastern North America, the jungles of South America, and East Asia—they found denser populations, inhabiting more or less permanent villages, based on farming and consisting of perhaps one or two large

communal structures, but here too the weapons and tools were relics of prehistory. . . .

Elsewhere, of course, the explorers encountered fully developed states and empires, headed by despots and ruling classes, and defended by standing armies. It was these great empires, with their cities, monuments, palaces, temples and treasures, that had lured all the Marco Polos and Columbuses across the oceans and deserts in the first place. There was China—the greatest empire in the world, a vast, sophisticated realm whose leaders scorned the "red-faced barbarians," supplicants from puny kingdoms beyond the pale of the civilised world. And there was India—a land where cows were venerated and the unequal burdens of life were apportioned according to what each soul had merited in its previous incarnation. And then there were the native American states and empires, worlds unto themselves, each with its distinctive arts and religions: the Incas, with their great stone fortresses, suspension bridges, over-worked granaries, and state-controlled economy; and the Aztecs, with their bloodthirsty gods fed from human hearts and their incessant search for fresh sacrifices. (Harris, 1978)

This seemingly unlimited variety of premodern societies can actually be grouped into three main categories, each of which is referred to in Harris's description: hunters and gatherers (Harris's "hunters and collectors"); larger agrarian or pastoral societies (involving agriculture or the tending of domesticated animals); and nonindustrial civilizations or traditional states. We shall look at the main characteristics of these in turn.

HUNTERS AND GATHERERS

For all but a tiny part of our existence on this planet, human beings lived in small groups or tribes, which often numbered no more than thirty or forty people. The earliest type of human society consisted of **hunters and gatherers.** Rather than growing crops, or tending animals, these groups gained their livelihood from hunting, fishing, and gathering edible plants growing in the wild. Hunting and gathering cultures continue to exist today in some parts of the world, such as the jungles of Brazil and New Guinea, but most have been destroyed or absorbed by the global spread of Western culture, and those that remain are unlikely to stay intact for much longer (Wolf, 1983). Cur-

Hunters and gatherers in Botswana (Africa).

rently, less than a quarter of a million people in the world support themselves chiefly through hunting and gathering—only .003 percent of the total global population.

Research by anthropologists over the past fifty years has provided a great deal of information about hunting and gathering societies. Given the diversity of human culture, we have to be careful in generalizing about even one type of society. But there are some common characteristics of hunting and gathering communities that set them apart from other types (Bicchieri, 1972; Diamond, 1974; Schrire, 1984).

Compared to larger societies—particularly modern industrial systems—little inequality is found in hunting and gathering groups. Hunters and gatherers move about a good deal; since they are without animal or mechanical means of transport, they can take few goods or possessions with them. The material goods they need are limited to weapons for hunting, tools for digging and building, traps, and cooking utensils. Thus there is little difference in the level of material possessions between any members of the society. Differences of position or rank tend to be limited to age and sex. Males seem virtually everywhere to be the hunters, while women may gather wild crops and concern themselves with the upbringing of the children. The "elders"—the oldest and most experienced men in the community—usually have an important say in major decisions affecting the group. But just as there is little variation in wealth between members of a community, differences of power are much less than in larger types of society. Hunting and gathering societies are usually "participatory"—all adult (male) members tend to assemble together when important decisions are made or crises faced.

Hunters and gatherers do not just move about in a completely erratic way. Most have fixed territories, around which they migrate in a regular way from year to year. Many hunting and gathering communities do not have a stable membership. People often move between different camps, or groups split up and join others within the same overall territory.

The Mbuti Pygmies

Of the hundreds of descriptions of hunting and gathering societies that have been written, we shall pick just one to illustrate their way of life: the society of the Mbuti (pronounced "Mubooti") pygmies, who live in an area of Zaire, in central Africa (Turnbull, 1983; Mair, 1974). The Mbuti inhabit a heavily forested area, difficult for outsiders to penetrate. They themselves know the forest intimately, and move about in it as they please. There is plenty of water everywhere, edible wild plants, and animals to be hunted. The houses of the Mbuti are not permanent dwellings but are made of leaves on a framework of branches. They can be set up in a matter of hours, and abandoned when the Mbuti move on—as they do continuously, never staying more than a month at any one site.

The Mbuti live in small groups, made up of four or five families. The groups have a fairly permanent membership, but there is nothing to stop either an individual or a family from leaving one group and joining another. Nobody "runs" any group—there are no chiefs. Older men have a duty, however, to quiet "noise"—bickering or quarreling—which the pygmies believe displeases the spirits of the forest. If a conflict gets too severe, the members of a group split up and go to join others.

The Mbuti were first studied in the 1960s, when their traditional way of life remained intact. Since then, it has come under increasing strain. The outside world has encroached more and more on the forest, and the Mbuti are becoming drawn into the money economy of the villages around the forest's perimeters. We have presented the account of their way of life in the present tense, but it is now on the verge of extinction. Much the same is true of the examples of other types of traditional society that will be given later.

The "Original Affluent Societies"?

Unlike the case of the Mbuti, most hunting and gathering societies remaining in existence today are confined to inhospitable areas. Such groups may live close to starvation level, because the environment is too harsh to extract more than a minimal living. Hunters and gatherers have long since been driven out of the more fertile areas of the world. The fact that most now live in circumstances where survival is a perennial struggle has led many scholars to assume that all such peoples lived in conditions of material deprivation. This was probably not in fact the case in the past. A prominent anthropologist, Marshall Sahlins, has called hunter-gatherers the "original affluent societies"—because they had more than enough to provide for their wants (Sahlins, 1972). Hunters and gatherers living in the more hospitable regions of the world in the past did not have to spend long portions of the day engaged in production, since these areas were rich in resources. Many may have worked for a shorter average number of hours per day than the modern factory or office employee.

Hunters and gatherers have little interest in developing material wealth beyond what is needed to cater for their basic wants. Their main preoccupations are usually with the pursuit of religious values and with ceremonial and ritual activities. Many hunters and gatherers have elaborate ceremonials in which they regularly participate. They may spend a large amount of their time preparing the dress, masks, paintings, or other sacred objects used in such rituals.

Some authors, especially those influenced by sociobiology, have tried to link the prominence of hunting in these societies with universal human impulses towards war. According to them, hunting expresses aggressive impulses that naturally lead to hostility and warfare with surrounding peoples. This view has been strongly criticized, however, by anthropologists who specialize in the study of hunters and gatherers. Their research indicates, in fact, that hunting and gathering societies mostly seem to be unwarlike. The implements used for hunting are rarely employed as weapons against other human beings. Occasionally, clashes may occur between different groups, but these are usually very limited in nature with few or no casualties involved. Warfare in the modern sense is completely unknown among hunters and gatherers. In such communities, there are no specialist warriors, no armies or arms technology. In an important sense, hunting is a cooperative activity. Individuals may go off hunting alone, but almost always share the results of the hunt—say, the meat from a wild pig or boar—with the rest of the group.

Hunters and gatherers are not merely "primitive" peoples whose ways of life no longer hold any interest for us. Studying these cultures allows us to see more clearly that some of our institutions are far from being "natural" features of human life. We should not idealize the circumstances in which hunters and gatherers have lived, which few, if any of us, would want to cope with. Their way of life is dependent on preserving natural resources, which can become scarce if there is a bad winter or a drought through which food or water supplies diminish. Nonetheless, the absence of war, the lack of major inequalities of wealth and power, and the emphasis upon cooperation rather than competition, are all instructive reminders that the world created by modern industrial civilization is not necessarily to be equated with "progress."

PASTORAL AND AGRARIAN SOCIETIES

About twenty thousand years ago, some hunting and gathering groups turned to the raising of domesticated animals and the cultivation of fixed plots of land as their means of livelihood. **Pastoral societies** are those relying mainly on domesticated livestock, while **agrarian societies** are those that grow crops (practice agriculture). Many societies have had mixed pastoral and agrarian economies.

Pastoral Societies

Depending upon the environment in which they live, pastoralists rear and herd animals such as cattle, sheep, goats, camels, or horses. There are many pastoral societies still in existence in the modern world. They are concentrated especially in areas of Africa, the Middle East, and central Asia. These remaining societies are usually to be found in regions in which there are dense grasslands, deserts, or mountains. Such regions are not amenable to fruitful agriculture, but may support various kinds of livestock.

Pastoral societies usually migrate between different areas according to seasonal changes. Because they have means of animal transport, they move across much larger distances than the hunting and gathering peoples. Given their nomadic habits, people in pastoral societies do not normally accumulate many material possessions, although their way of life is more complex in material terms than that of hunters and gatherers. For example, in addition to raising animals, they may engage in extensive trading relations, exchanging their own products for precious metals, cloths, or spices. Since the domestication of animals permits a regular supply of food, these societies are usually much larger than hunting and gathering communities. Some pastoral societies number a quarter of a million people or more.

Ranging as they often do over large tracts of territory, pastoralists regularly come into contact with other groups. They frequently engage in trade—and also in warfare. Many pastoral cultures have been peaceful, wishing only to tend to their livestock and engage in community ritual and ceremonies. Others have been highly warlike, deriving their livelihood from conquest and pillage as well as from the herding of animals. Pastoral societies display greater inequalities of wealth and power than hunting and gathering communities. In particular, chiefs, tribal leaders, or warlords often wield considerable personal power.

A classic description of a pastoral society was given by the British author, E. E. Evans-Pritchard (1940) who studied the Nuer, a society in the southern Sudan, in Africa. The livelihood of the Nuer depended mainly on raising cattle, although they also grew some crops. The people lived in villages situated from five to twenty miles away from one another. In the 1930s, when Evans-Pritchard carried out his study, the Nuer numbered about two hundred thousand people. They spoke the same language and followed similar customs, but there was no central political authority or form of government. The Nuer were divided into tribes, which sometimes collaborated with one another but mostly lived separately.

Each tribe had its own area of land, the divisions mostly marked by watercourses. The Nuer attached no particular significance to land, however, except insofar as it provided a place to graze their cattle. Part of the year, during the dry season, the Nuer moved their villages to live in camps near water holes. Much of the life of the Nuer was bound up with their cattle, which were in many ways central to their culture. They had a profound contempt for neighboring societies that had few or no cattle. Every major phase of life—birth, entering adulthood, marriage, and death—was marked by rituals involving cattle. Men were often addressed by the names of their favorite oxen and women by their favorites among the cows they milked.

The Nuer tribes quite often waged war upon each other, and also sometimes formed an alliance to fight outsiders. Just as they lived for their cattle, so they fought wars for them—for instance, raiding the nearby Dinka, another pastoral society, to steal their herds. A Nuer saying went, "More people have died for the sake of a cow than for any other cause."

Agrarian Societies

Agrarian societies seem to have originated at about the same date as pastoral ones. At some point, hunting and gathering groups began to sow their own crops rather than simply collecting those growing in the wild. This practice first developed as what is usually called "horticulture," in which small gardens are cultivated by the use of simple hoes or digging instruments. There are still many societies in the world that rely primarily upon horticulture for their means of subsistence.

Chinese engraving of agrarian workers in rice paddies.

Like pastoralism, horticulture provides for a more assured supply of food than is possible by hunting and gathering, and therefore can support much larger communities. Since they are not on the move, peoples gaining a livelihood from horticulture can develop larger stocks of material possessions than can either pastoral or hunting and gathering communities. Once groups are settled in places of habitation, regular trading and political ties can be developed between separate villages. Warlike behavior is common in horticultural societies, although the level of violence tends to be less pronounced than among some pastoral groups. Those who grow crops are not ordinarily practiced in arts of combat; nomadic pastoral tribesmen, on the other hand, can mass together as marauding armies.

An example of this type of society was the Gururumba, a New Guinea tribe (Newman, 1965). The Gururumba numbered just over a thousand people and lived in six villages. In each village there were several gardens, fenced off from one another. Different families owned plots within these fenced areas. Everyone, adults and children, was involved in tending the plots, although men and women were responsible for separate types of fruits and vegetables. Each family had more than one plot and cultivated different plants at certain times of the year, thus providing a consistent annual food supply. Gururumba culture also had a complicated system of ceremonial gift exchanges that families carried on with one another, through which prestige in the community could be achieved. The people thus had plots in which they grew crops to cater for their day-to-day needs, and other plots in which they cultivated "prestige" crops to be used only as gifts. "Prestige" crops were given far more care than those relating to ordinary needs.

The Gururumba also raised pigs, which were not mainly kept for food but again as items of gift exchange designed to achieve status in the community. Every few years a massive pig feast was held in which hundreds of pigs were killed, cooked, and given as gifts. As in pastoral groups, among the Gururumba there was more inequality than in hunting and gathering cultures. Chiefs and tribal leaders played a prominent role, and there were substantial differences in the material wealth people possessed.

NONINDUSTRIAL CIVILIZATIONS OR TRADITIONAL STATES

From about 6000 B.C. onwards, we find evidence of larger societies than ever existed previously, contrasting in distinct ways with earlier types (Burns et al., 1986). These societies were based upon the development of cities, showed very pronounced inequalities of wealth and power, and were associated with the rule of kings or emperors. Because they involved the invention of writing, and a flourishing of science and art, they are often called *civilizations*. However, since they developed more coordinated governments than other forms of society, the term **traditional states** is also often used to refer to them.

Most traditional states were also *empires; they* achieved the size they did through the conquest and incorporation of other peoples (Eisenstadt, 1963; Claessen and Skalnik, 1976; Kautsky, 1982). This was true, for instance, of traditional China and Rome. At its height, in the first century A.D. the Roman Empire stretched from Britain in Northwest Europe to beyond the Middle East. The Chinese Empire, which lasted for more than two thousand years, up to the threshold of the present century, covered most of the massive region of eastern Asia now occupied by modern China. No traditional states continue to exist in the world today. Although some, like China or Japan, remained more or less intact up to the twentieth century, all have now been destroyed or dissolved into more modern systems.

FIGURE 2.2   TRADITIONAL SOCIETIES IN THE ANCIENT WORLD

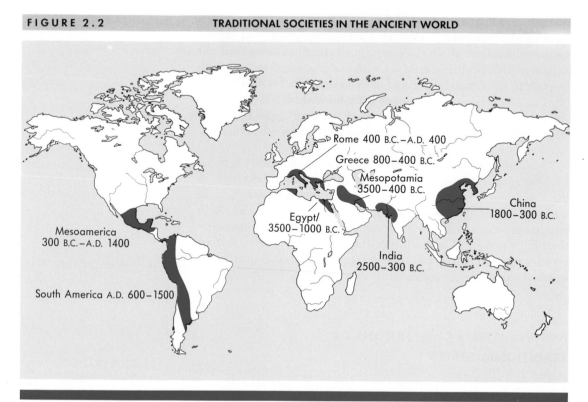

The color areas on the map show the locations and approximate dates of some of the major traditional civilizations of the past.

The earliest traditional states developed in the Middle East, usually in fertile river areas (Kramer, 1959). The Chinese Empire originated in about 2000 B.C., at which time powerful states were also found in what is now India and Pakistan. A number of large traditional states existed at a later date in Mexico and Latin America, such as the Aztecs of the Mexican peninsula and the Inca of Peru. The Aztec state had been established for about a century before the arrival of the Spanish adventurer, Cortés. Cortés landed in 1519 with only a small force of soldiers. Yet by building alliances with other native tribes hostile to the Aztecs, he was rapidly able to bring about the downfall of the Aztec state and claim the area for Spain. Thus was initiated the series of encounters between Western influences and traditional states that would eventually lead to their complete disappearance.

The Maya

As an example of a traditional state we shall take a third American civilization, that of the Maya, who lived in the Yucatán Peninsula, by the Mexican Gulf. One of the great epochs of Mayan civilization was from A.D. 300 to 800, when the Maya built elaborate religious centers, surrounded by their dwellings, all built in stone. The religious shrines took the form of large pyramids, at the top of which were temples. At Tikal, the biggest of the pyramids, the surrounding city held some forty thousand inhabitants. It was the main administrative center—effectively the capital city—of the Mayan state.

Mayan society was ruled by an aristocratic class of warrior-priests. They were both the highest religious dignitaries and its military leaders, and they fought continuous wars with surrounding groups. The majority of the population were peasant farmers. All of these were required to give up a proportion of their production to their aristocratic rulers, who lived in conditions of some luxury.

It is not known for certain why the original Mayan civilization collapsed, but it was probably conquered by neighboring tribes. Although reverting to smaller communities, the Mayans themselves survived, and aspects of their ancient culture are still preserved by their descendants living in the area today.

Features of the Traditional State

The traditional state was the only type of society in history, prior to the emergence of modern industrialism, in which a significant proportion of the population was engaged in occupations other than the

City of the Teotihuacán civilization (300 B.C.–A.D. 700) which overlapped with the Mayan civilization.

production of food. In hunting and gathering communities, and in pastoral and agrarian societies, there was a fairly simple **division of labor** (division between different occupations). The most important separation of tasks was between men and women. In traditional states, by contrast, a more complicated occupational system existed. A strict division of labor by sex was still found, the activities of women being mainly confined to the household and working in the fields. However, among men we see the emergence of specialized trades, such as those of merchant, courtier, government administrator, and soldier.

There was also a basic division of classes between aristocratic groups and the remainder of the population. The ruler was at the head of a "ruling class" that maintained the exclusive right to hold the higher social positions. The members of the ruling class usually lived in circumstances of considerable material comfort or luxury. The conditions of life of the mass of the population, on the other hand, were frequently quite abject. Slave-owning was also a common feature of these societies.

A few traditional states were built up mainly through trade and were ruled by merchants. But most were either established through military conquest or depended on a substantial buildup of armies and navies (McNeill, 1982; Mann, 1986). Traditional states saw the development of professional armies, anticipating modern types of military organization. The Roman army, for example, was a highly disciplined and intensively trained body of men and was the foundation upon which the expansion of the Roman Empire was built. We also find in traditional states the start of a process of the mechanization of war. The swords, spears, shields, and siege equipment carried by the Roman army were manufactured by specialized craftsmen. In the wars conducted between traditional states, and between these states and "barbarian" tribes, casualties were far higher than they had ever been previously.

SOCIETIES IN THE MODERN WORLD

TRADITIONAL STATES HAVE NOW COMPLETELY DISAPPEARED from the face of the world (Figure 2.3). Although hunting and gathering, agrarian, and pastoral societies continue to exist in some regions, they are only to be found in relatively isolated territories—and, in most cases, even these last surviving ex-

FIGURE 2.3   **GROWTH AND DECLINE OF DIFFERENT TYPES OF SOCIETIES**

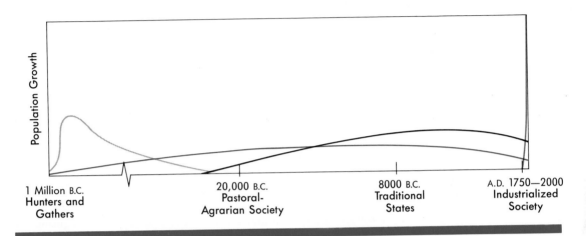

This chart shows the relationships in population over time among the various types of societies.

amples are disintegrating. What has happened to destroy the forms of society that dominated the whole of world history up to two centuries ago? The answer, in a word, is the impact of *industrialization*— the emergence of machine production based upon the use of inanimate power resources (like steam or electricity). The **industrialized societies** are utterly different in many respects from any previous type of social order, and their development has had consequences stretching far beyond their European origins.

THE INDUSTRIALIZED SOCIETIES

Modern industrialization first came into being in England as a result of the "Industrial Revolution" initiated in the late eighteenth century. This term is really a shorthand name for a complex set of technological changes affecting the means whereby people gain their livelihood. These changes involved the invention of new machines (like the spinning jenny for weaving yarn), the harnessing of power resources (especially water and steam) to production, and the use of science to improve production methods. Since discoveries and inventions in one field lead to those in others, the pace of technological innovation in the industrialized societies is extremely rapid compared to traditional forms of social system.

We shall not discuss the industrialized societies in any detail here and will simply describe their main characteristics—because most of the subsequent chapters of the book are focused upon them. The major industrialized sectors of the world today are found in Europe, the Soviet Union, Japan, North America, and Australasia.

A prime distinguishing feature of industrialized societies is that the large majority of the employed population works in factories or offices, rather than in agriculture. Even in the most advanced of traditional states, only a tiny proportion of the population was not engaged in working on the land. The relatively rudimentary level of technological development simply did not permit more than a small minority to be freed from the chores of agricultural production. In industrialized societies, by contrast, only some 2–5 percent of the population works in agriculture, and their produce provides food for the rest.

Industrialized societies are also much more highly urbanized than any type of traditional social system. In some industrialized countries, well over 90 percent of the people live in towns and cities, where most jobs are to be found and new job opportunities are continually created. The size of the largest cities is vastly greater than the urban settlements found in traditional civilizations. In these new urban areas, social life has become more impersonal and anonymous than before; many day-to-day encounters are between strangers rather than between individuals known to one another on a personal basis. Large-scale organizations, such as business corporations or government agencies, influence the lives of virtually everyone.

A further characteristic of industrialized societies concerns their political systems. These systems are much more developed and intensive than forms of government in traditional states. In traditional civilizations, the political authorities (monarchs and emperors) had little direct influence upon the customs and habits of most of their subjects, who lived in fairly self-contained local villages. With the coming of industrialization, transportation and communications became much more rapid, making for a more integrated "national" community. The industrialized societies were the first **nation-states** to come into existence. Nation-states are political communities having clearly delimited borders dividing them from each other, rather than the vague "frontier areas" that used to separate traditional states. In nation-states, governments have extensive powers over many aspects of the lives of the citizenry, framing laws that have universal application to those living within their borders. Today, all modern societies—like the United States—are nation-states.

Industrial technology has been by no means limited in its application to peaceful processes of economic development. From the earliest phases of industrialization, modern production processes have been put to military purposes, radically altering ways of waging war and creating weaponry and modes of military organization greatly in advance of those possessed by nonindustrial cultures. Superior economic strength, political cohesion, and military might underlie the seemingly irresistible spread of Western ways of life across the world over the past two centuries.

If traditional societies and cultures have now disappeared, this is not because their ways of life were "inferior." It is because they were unable to resist the impact of the combination of industrial and military *power* that the Western countries developed. The concept of **power**—and a closely associated notion, that of **ideology**—are of great importance in sociology. By power is meant the capability of individuals or groups to make their own concerns or interests count, even where others resist. Power sometimes involves the direct use of force, but is almost always also accompanied by the development of ideas (ideologies), which are used to *justify* the actions of the powerful. In the case of Western expansion, the Western intruders justified their activities by seeing themselves as "civilizing" the "heathen" peoples with whom they came into contact.

THE "THREE WORLDS"

From the seventeenth to the early twentieth centuries, the Western countries established colonies in many areas previously occupied by traditional societies, using their superior military strength to do so where necessary. Although virtually all of these colonies have now attained their independence, the process of **colonialism** reshaped the social and cultural map of the globe. In some regions, like North America, Australia, and New Zealand, which were only thinly populated by hunting and gathering communities, the Europeans became the majority population. In other areas, including much of Asia, Africa, and South America, the local populations remained in the majority. Societies of the first of these types, such as the United States, have become industrialized. Those in the second category are mostly at a much lower level of industrial development and are often referred to today as **Third World societies.**

Third World Societies

Third World societies include China, India, most of the African countries (such as Nigeria, Ghana, or Algeria) and those in South America (for example Brazil, Peru, or Venezuela).

In Third World countries there is only a low level of industrialization, and the large majority of the population is engaged in agricultural production. Since many of these societies are situated below the

TABLE 2.1	TYPES OF HUMAN SOCIETY	
Type	Period of Existence	Characteristics
HUNTING AND GATHERING SOCIETIES	50,000 B.C. to the present (now on the verge of complete disappearance)	Consist of small numbers of people, gaining their livelihood from hunting, fishing, and the gathering of edible plants Few inequalities Differences of rank limited by age and sex
AGRARIAN SOCIETIES	12,000 B.C. to the present Most are now part of larger political entities, and are losing their distinct identity	Societies based on small rural communities, without towns or cities Livelihood gained through agriculture, often supplemented by hunting and gathering Stronger inequalities than among hunters and gatherers Ruled by chiefs
PASTORAL SOCIETIES	12,000 B.C. to the present Today mostly part of larger states; their traditional ways of life are becoming undermined	Societies dependent on the tending of domesticated animals for their material subsistence Size ranges from a few hundred people to many thousands Marked by distinct inequalities Ruled by chiefs or warrior kings
TRADITIONAL STATES OR CIVILIZATIONS	6000 B.C. to the nineteenth century All traditional states have disappeared	Societies based largely on agriculture Some cities exist, in which trade and manufacture are concentrated Very large in size, some numbering millions of people (though small compared to larger industrialized societies) Distinct apparatus of government headed by a king or emperor Major inequalities exist among different classes

equator, they are sometimes referred to collectively as the "South," and contrasted to the wealthier, industrialized "North." While they may incorporate peoples living in traditional fashion, Third World countries are quite different from earlier forms of traditional culture. They have political systems derived from, or modeled upon, the systems first established in the Western societies—that is to say, they are nation-states. While most of the population still live in rural areas, many of these societies are now experiencing a very rapid process of

FIRST WORLD SOCIETIES	Eighteenth century to the present	Societies based on industrial production and generally free enterprise Majority of people live in towns and cities, few in rural agricultural pursuits Major class inequalities, though less pronounced than in traditional states Distinct political communities or nation-states
SECOND WORLD SOCIETIES	Early twentieth century (following the Russian Revolution of 1917) to the early 1990s	Societies with an industrial base, but where the economic system is centrally planned Small proportion of the population works in agriculture; most live in towns and cities Major class inequalities persist Distinct political communities or nation-states Until 1989, included the Soviet Union and Eastern Europe, but current social and political changes might transform them into free-enterprise economic systems making them First World Societies.
THIRD WORLD SOCIETIES	Eighteenth century (mostly as colonized areas) to the present	Societies where the majority of the population works in agriculture using traditional methods of production Some agricultural produce sold on world markets Some have free enterprise systems, others centrally planned Distinct political communities or nation-states

urbanization. Although agriculture remains the dominant form of economic activity, crops are often produced for sale on world markets instead of being used for local consumption. Third World countries are not merely societies that have "lagged behind" the more industrialized countries of the West. The conditions in which billions of people now live in the Third World have been in large part brought about by contact with the West, which undermined their earlier, more traditional, systems.

First and Second World Societies

The term **First World** refers to the industrialized countries of Europe, the United States, Australasia, and Japan. First World countries nearly all have multiparty, parliamentary systems of government. **Second World** societies are industrialized societies like the Soviet Union ruled by governments having an affiliation to communism. Before the democratic movements of 1989 and 1990, these included the East European societies such as Czechoslovakia, Poland, and Hungary.

There are significant differences between First and Second World societies on an economic as well as a political level. Whereas the economic systems of the First World countries are based on market principles—allowing a major role for free enterprise—those of Second World states are centrally planned. In other words, many economic decisions that are made by business leaders in a country like the United States—such as setting production targets for corporations—are made by government officials in the Soviet Union. As of 1990, this system looks set to undergo major change, almost certainly moving towards a more competitive, market-based economy. If this happens, the "Second World" will largely disappear.

The greatest contrasts are between the industrialized societies as a whole, on the one side, and Third World countries on the other. By comparison with the industrialized nations, the Third World societies are mostly very poor. Many of them have experienced massive rates of population growth, placing an extreme strain upon their capability to generate sufficient resources to provide even a minimally adequate standard of living for their citizenry.

In Chapter 1, it was pointed out that the chief focus of sociology is upon the study of the industrialized societies. As sociologists, can we thus safely ignore the Third World, leaving this as the domain of anthropology? We certainly cannot. The industrialized and the Third World societies have developed in *interconnection* with one another and are today more closely related than ever before. Those of us living in the industrialized societies depend upon many raw materials and manufactured products coming from Third World countries to sustain our lives. Conversely, the economies of most Third World states depend upon trading networks that bind them to the industrialized countries. We can only fully understand the industrialized order against the backdrop of the Third World societies—in which, in fact, by far the greater proportion of the world's population lives. (For further discussion, see Chapter 16: "The Globalizing of Social Life.")

Industrialized and Third World societies are radically different from the traditional types of social order that dominated world history for thousands of years up to some two centuries ago. The explorations that Western travelers undertook across the globe set off processes of change that have destroyed many premodern cultures. There remains enormous cultural diversity, however, both within and between societies. As human beings, we all share major traits in common—but we are also strongly influenced by the cultural values and habits of the societies in which we exist. In the following chapter, we shall look at some of the processes that affect our individual development from infancy through to the later phases of life.

SUMMARY

1. *Culture* consists of the *values* held by a given group, the *norms* they follow, and the *material goods* they create.

2. The human species emerged as a result of a long process of biological evolution. Human beings are part of a group of higher mammals, the primates. There seems to be strong evidence that cultural development preceded, and probably shaped, the evolution of the human species.

3. *Sociobiology* is important primarily for its insights concerning animal behavior. The ideas of the sociobiologists about human social life are highly speculative. Our behavior is genetically influenced, but our genetic endowment probably conditions only the potentialities of our behavior, not the actual content of our activities.

4. Human beings have no instincts in the sense of complex patterns of unlearned behavior. A certain set of simple reflexes, plus a range of organic needs, are innate characteristics of the human individual.

5. Forms of behavior found in all, or virtually all, cultures are called *cultural universals*. Language, the prohibition against incest, institutions of marriage, the family, religion, and property are the main types of cultural universals—but within these general categories there are many variations in values and modes of behavior between different societies.

6. Several types of premodern society can be distinguished. In *hunting and gathering* societies, people do not grow crops or keep livestock, but gain their livelihood from gathering plants and hunting animals. *Pastoral* societies are those that raise domesticated animals as their major source of subsistence. *Agrarian* societies depend upon the cultivation of fixed plots of land. Larger, more developed, urban societies form *traditional states* or *civilizations*.

7. The development and expansion of the West led to the conquest of many parts of the world, and the process of *colonialism* radically changed long-established social systems and cultures.

8. In industrialized societies, industrial production (whose techniques are also used in the production of food) is the main basis of the economy. *First World* industrialized countries include the nations of the West, plus Japan, Australia, and New Zealand. *Second World* countries are industrialized societies ruled by communist governments. *Third World* countries, in which most of the world's population live, are almost all formerly colonized areas. The majority of the population works in agricultural production, some of which is geared to world markets.

BASIC CONCEPTS

CULTURE   NORMS

SOCIETY   POWER

VALUES   IDEOLOGY

IMPORTANT TERMS

EVOLUTION   AGRARIAN SOCIETIES

MUTATION   TRADITIONAL STATES

SOCIOBIOLOGY   INDUSTRIALIZED SOCIETIES

INSTINCT   DIVISION OF LABOR

SUBCULTURE   NATION-STATE

ETHNOCENTRISM   COLONIALISM

CULTURAL UNIVERSALS   THIRD WORLD

SEMIOTICS   FIRST WORLD

HUNTING AND GATHERING SOCIETIES   SECOND WORLD

PASTORAL SOCIETIES

SOCIALIZATION AND THE LIFE CYCLE

ANIMALS LOW DOWN ON THE EVOLUTIONARY SCALE, SUCH as most species of insects, are capable of fending for themselves very soon after they are born, with little or no help from adults. There are no generations among the lower animals, because the behavior of the "young" is more or less identical to that of the "adults." As we go up the scale, however, these observations apply less and less; the higher animals have to *learn* appropriate ways of behavior. Among most of the more developed mammal species, the young are quite often completely helpless at birth and have to be cared for by their elders. The human infant is most dependent of all. A human child cannot survive unaided for at least the first four or five years of life.

Socialization is the process whereby the helpless infant gradually becomes a self-aware, knowledgeable person, skilled in the ways of the culture into which he or she is born. Socialization among the young allows for the more general phenomenon, social reproduction —the process whereby societies have structural continuity over time (a concept introduced in Chapter 1: "Sociology: Problems and Perspectives"). During the course of socialization, especially in the early years of life, children learn the ways of their elders, thereby perpetu-

ating their values, norms, and social practices. All societies have characteristics that endure over long stretches of time, even though their members change as individuals are born and die. American society, for example, has many distinctive social and cultural characteristics that have persisted for generations—such as the fact that English is the main language spoken.

Socialization connects the different generations to one another (Turnbull, 1983). The birth of a child alters the lives of those who are responsible for its upbringing—who themselves therefore undergo new learning experiences. Parenting usually ties the activities of adults to children for the remainder of their lives. Older people still remain parents when they become grandparents, of course, thus forging another set of relationships connecting the different generations with each other. Although the process of cultural learning is much more intense in infancy and early childhood than later, learning and adjustment go on through the whole life cycle.

In the sections to follow, we shall continue the theme of "nature versus nurture" introduced in the previous chapter. We shall first analyze the development of the human individual from infancy to early childhood, identifying the main stages of change involved. A number of theoretical interpretations have been put forward by different writers about how and why children develop as they do, and we will describe and compare these. Finally, we shall move on to discuss the main groups and social contexts that influence socialization during the various phases of individuals' lives.

"UNSOCIALIZED" CHILDREN

WHAT WOULD CHILDREN BE LIKE IF, IN SOME WAY OR ANother, they were raised without the influence of human adults? Obviously no humane person could bring up a child away from social influence. There are, however, a number of much-discussed cases of children who have spent their early years away from normal human contact. We shall begin the chapter by looking at two of these cases, then move on to study more orthodox patterns of child development.

THE "WILD BOY OF AVEYRON"

On January 9, 1800, a strange creature emerged from the woods near the village of Saint-Serin in southern France. In spite of walking erect, he looked more animal than human, although he was soon identified as a boy of about eleven or twelve. He spoke only in shrill, strange-sounding cries. The boy apparently had no sense of personal hygiene, and relieved himself where and when he chose. He was brought to the attention of the local police and taken to a nearby orphanage. In the beginning he tried constantly to escape, and was only recaptured with some difficulty. He refused to tolerate wearing clothes, tearing them off as soon as they were put on him. No parents ever came forward to claim him.

The child was subjected to a thorough medical examination, which turned up no major physical abnormalities. On being shown a mirror, he seemingly saw an image, but did not recognize himself. On one occasion, he tried to reach through the mirror to seize a potato he saw in it. (The potato in fact was being held behind his head.) After several attempts, without turning his head, he took the potato by reaching back over his shoulder. A priest who was observing the boy from day to day, and who described this incident, wrote: "All these little details, and many others we could add prove that this child is not totally without intelligence, reflection, and reasoning power. However, we are obliged to say that, in every case not concerned with his natural needs or satisfying his appetite, one can per-

The frontispiece for the book on the "wild boy of Aveyron."

ceive in him only animal behavior. If he has sensations, they give birth to no idea. He cannot even compare them with one another. One would think that there is no connection between his soul or mind and his body" (Shattuck, 1980; see also Lane, 1976).

Later the boy was moved to Paris and a systematic attempt was made to change him "from beast to human." The endeavor was only partly successful. He was toilet-trained, accepted wearing clothes, and learned to dress himself. Yet he was uninterested in toys or games, and was never able to master more than a few words. So far as anyone could tell, on the basis of detailed descriptions of his behavior and reactions, this was not because he was mentally retarded. He seemed either unwilling or unable to fully master human speech. He made little further progress, and died in 1828.

GENIE

It cannot be proved how long the wild boy of Aveyron lived on his own in the woods, or whether or not he suffered from some congenital defect that made it impossible for him to develop like a normal human being. However, there are more recent examples that reinforce some of the observations made about his behavior. One case is provided by the life of Genie, a Californian girl who was locked in a room from the age of about one-and-a-half until she was over thirteen (Curtiss, 1977). Genie's father kept his wife, who was going blind, more or less completely confined to the house. The main connection between the family and the outside world was through a teenage son, who attended school and did the shopping.

Genie had a hip defect from birth that prevented her from walking properly. Her father frequently beat her. When Genie was twenty months old, her father apparently decided she was retarded and put her away in a closed room with the curtains drawn and the door shut. She stayed there for the next eleven years, seeing the other members of the family only when they came to feed her. Genie had not been toilet-trained, and spent part of her time harnessed, naked, to an infant's potty seat. Sometimes at night she was removed, only to be put into another restraining garment, a sleeping bag within which her arms were imprisoned. Tied up in this way, she was also enclosed in an infant's crib with wire-mesh sides and a mesh cover overhead. Somehow, in these appalling circumstances she endured the hours, days, and years of her life. She had almost no opportunity to overhear any conversation between others in the house. If she attempted to make a noise, or to attract attention, her father would beat her. Her father never spoke to her, but instead made barking, animal-like sounds if she did anything to annoy him. She had no proper toys, or other objects with which to occupy her time.

In 1970 the mother escaped from the house, taking Genie with her. The condition of the girl came to the notice of a social worker, and she was placed in the rehabilitation ward of a children's hospital. When she was first admitted to the hospital, she could not stand erect, could not run, jump, or climb, and was only able to walk in a shuffling, clumsy fashion. She was described by a psychiatrist as "unsocialized, primitive, hardly human." Once in a rehabilitation ward, however, Genie made fairly rapid progress. She learned to eat quite normally, was toilet-trained, and tolerated being dressed like other children. Yet she was silent almost all of the time, except when she laughed, her laugh being high-pitched and unreal. She masturbated constantly in public situations, refusing to abandon the habit. Later she lived as a foster child in the home of one of the doctors from the hospital. She gradually came to develop a fairly wide vocabulary and could make a limited number of basic utterances. Yet her mastery of language never progressed beyond that of a three or four year old.

Genie's behavior was studied intensively and she was given a variety of tests over a period of some seven years. These seemed to indicate that she was neither feeble-minded nor suffered from any other congenital defects. What seems to have happened to Genie, as to the wild boy of Aveyron, is that by the time she came into close human contact, she had grown beyond the age at which the learning of language and other human skills is readily accomplished by children. There is probably a "critical period" for the learning of language and other complex accomplishments, after which it is too late to master them fully. The wild boy and Genie provide some sense of what an "unsocialized" child would be like. Each retained many "nonhuman" responses. Yet, in spite of the deprivations they suffered, neither displayed any lasting viciousness. They responded quickly to others who treated them sympathetically, and were able to acquire a certain minimum level of ordinary human capabilities.

Of course, we have to be cautious about interpreting cases of this sort. In each of these examples it is possible that there was a mental abnormality that remained undiagnosed. Alternatively, the experiences to which the children were subjected may have inflicted psychological damage that prevented them from gaining the skills most children acquire at a much earlier age. Yet there is sufficient similarity between these two case histories, and others that have been recorded, to suggest how limited our faculties would be in the absence of an extended period of early socialization.

EARLY INFANT AND CHILD DEVELOPMENT

The forming of attachment between infant and caretaker (usually the mother) marks a fundamental threshold in socialization.

LET US NOW TURN TO LOOKING DIRECTLY AT THE EARLY phases of child development. In so doing, we will be able to understand more comprehensively the processes whereby the infant becomes recognizably "human." All human infants are born with the capability to make certain perceptual distinctions and respond to them (Richards and Light, 1986). It was once thought that the newborn infant was swamped by a mass of sensation that it had no way of sorting through. In a famous observation, the psychologist and philosopher William James wrote: "The baby, assailed by eyes, ears, nose, skin and entrails all at once, feels it all as one great blooming, buzzing confusion" (James, 1981; orig. pub. 1890). This is no longer seen as an accurate portrayal by most students of infant behavior—even newborn infants react selectively to their environment.

PERCEPTUAL DEVELOPMENT

Infants of only a few days old can tell the smell of their own mothers' milk. In a research study, three-day-old infants were placed on their backs and breast pads from their nursing mothers put on one side of their heads. Breast pads from other nursing women were placed on the other side. The newborns virtually all the time turned their heads towards their own mothers' pads, no matter on which side the pads were placed (Stern, 1985).

From the age of one week, a patterned surface (stripes, concentric circles, or a face-like picture) is looked at more often than even a brightly colored plain surface. A baby is very shortsighted up to about age two months. Since most objects are outside this range, the infant may appear to the onlooker to be uninterested in the exterior world. But if objects are brought very close up, the child will often make excited reaching gestures. This behavior begins as early as two weeks of age. After four or five weeks, the baby will stop crying at the close-up sight of the mother's face, but not at others' (Rayner, 1986). By the age of about four months a baby will keep in sight a person moving about the room. Sensitivity to touch and pleasure in warmth are present from birth.

CRYING AND SMILING

Just as infants selectively respond to the environment, adults discrim-inate among the patterns of behavior of the baby and assume that these give clues to what the infant wants or needs. Crying is seen to indicate hunger or discomfort, smiling or certain other facial expres-sions to mean contentment. This very recognition treats these re-sponses as social actions on the part of the infant. Cultural assumptions are deeply involved in this process, however. Crying is a good example. In Western culture, the baby is physically separate from the mother for most of the day, in a cot, baby carriage or play area. Crying here tends to be a signal that the infant needs attention. In many other cultures, the newborn infant spends much of the day, for a period of many months, in direct contact with the mother's body, carried in a sling. Where this is the practice, a mother may pay attention only to extreme bouts of crying, which are treated as emer-gencies. Squirming movements of the infant are taken as the main signal that he needs food or some special treatment (Liederman, Tul-kin, and Rosenfeld, 1977).

Cultural differences have also been demonstrated in the interpreta-tion of smiling. All normal babies smile, in certain circumstances, after about a month or six weeks. An infant will smile if presented with a face-like shape containing only two dots in place of eyes. She will also smile at a human face if the mouth is hidden just as readily as when it is not. Smiling seems to be an inborn response, not learned, or even triggered, by seeing another smiling face. One reason why we can be sure of this is that children born blind begin smiling at the same age as sighted children, although they have had no chance to copy others doing so. The situations in which smiling is regarded as appropriate, however, vary between cultures, and this is related to the early reactions adults give to the smiling response of infants. Infants do not have to learn to smile, but they have to learn when and where it is thought proper to do so. The Chinese, for example, smile less often in public settings than Westerners do—say, when greeting a stranger.

INFANTS AND MOTHERS

An infant is able to distinguish his mother from other people by three or four months of age (Schaffer, 1976). The baby still does not recog-nize the mother as a "person," rather, he responds to certain charac-

teristics, probably the mother's eyes and voice, and the manner in which she holds him. The infant's recognition of the mother is shown in reactions such as stopping crying only when she (rather than anyone else) picks the infant up, smiling more at her than at other people, lifting his arms or clapping to mark the mother's appearance in the room, or, once the child is mobile, crawling to be close to her. Cultural differences influence which reactions tend regularly to appear. In a study of a Ugandan culture, Mary Ainsworth found that embracing, hugging, and kissing between mothers and infants was rare, but clapping hands to express pleasure, on the part of both mother and child, was much more common than in Western families (Ainsworth, 1977).

The infant's attachment to its mother only becomes firm after about the first seven months of life. Prior to this time, separation from the mother will not produce any specific protest and other care-taking agents will be accepted without any change in usual levels of responsiveness. At about the same age, children will start to smile only at some individuals rather than indiscriminately. It is also at this stage that an infant begins to get an understanding of the mother as a distinct person. The child recognizes that the mother exists even when she is absent from his or her immediate presence, and can hold some sort of image of her in mind. This also implies the beginning of the experience of time, because the baby has both a memory of the mother and anticipation of her return. Infants of eight or nine months are able to look for hidden objects, and begin to understand that objects have an independent existence, regardless of whether or not they are in view at any particular moment.

Selma Fraiberg illustrates this phase of the infant's behavior brilliantly in the course of a classic work designed to inform parents about children's growth:

> Have you a six- or seven-month-old baby who snatches the glasses off your nose? If you do, you hardly need this piece of advice. Remove the glasses when the baby reaches for them, slip them in a pocket or behind a sofa pillow (and don't forget where you hid them!). Don't trouble to be sneaky about it, let the baby see you hide them. He will not go in search of them. He will stare at the place he last saw them—on your nose—then lose interest in the problem. He does not search for the glasses because he cannot imagine that they have an existence when he does not see them.

> When the baby is around nine months old, don't rely on the old tricks. If he sees you remove your glasses and slip them

behind a sofa pillow he will move the pillow and pounce on your glasses. He has learned that an object can be hidden from sight, yet can still exist! He can follow its movements in your hand to the place of hiding and actively search for it there. This is a tremendous step in learning and one that is unlikely to be overlooked by the parents whose glasses, earrings, pipes, fountain pens, and keycases are now not only lifted from their persons, but defy safekeeping. Parents who have babies in this stage of development are little interested in the theoretical aspects of the problem as posed here, but a theory can always bring some practical benefits. We still have some tricks up our sleeve. Let's try this: Let the baby see you slip your glasses behind the pillow. Let him find them, persuade him to give them to you, then hide the glasses under a second pillow. Now he is confused. He will search for the glasses under the first pillow, in the first hiding place, but he will not search for them in the second hiding place. This means that the baby can conceive of the glasses having an existence when hidden, but only in one place, the first hiding place where his search had earlier been successful. When the baby does not find the glasses under the first pillow, he continues to search for them there, but it does not occur to him to search for them in the second hiding place or anywhere else. An object can still vanish. In a few weeks he will extend his search from the first hiding place to the second one and he is on his way to the discovery that an object can be moved from place to place and still have a permanent existence. (Fraiberg, 1984)

The early months of a child's life are also a period of learning for the mother. Mothers (and other caretaking agents, like fathers or older children) learn to grasp the communications conveyed by the infant's behavior and to respond to them appropriately. Some mothers are much more sensitive to these cues than others. Different cues tend to be emphasized, and reacted to, in varying cultural settings. The "readings" mothers make of their children's behavior strongly influence the pattern of interaction that develops between them. For instance, one mother might see a child's restlessness as indicating fatigue and put the infant to bed. Another might interpret the same behavior as meaning that the child wants to be entertained. Mothers often project their own characteristics onto their babies. A mother who finds it hard to maintain a stable caring relationship with her child might perceive the infant as aggressive and rejecting towards herself.

The forming of attachments to specific individuals marks a fundamental threshold in socialization. The primary relationship, virtually always between infant and mother, becomes one in which strong feelings are invested, and on the basis of which complex social learning processes start to occur.

THE DEVELOPMENT OF SOCIAL RESPONSES

The relationship between child, mother, and other caretakers alters around the first year of the baby's life. Not only do children of this age begin to speak, but they are able to stand, and most are able to walk alone at about age fourteen months. In their second and third years, children develop an increasing capacity to understand the interactions and emotions of other family members. Children of that age know how to comfort, as well as how to annoy, others. A child of two years old will show distress if one parent gets angry with the other, and may hug that person if he or she is visibly upset. A child of the same age is also able to tease a brother or sister, or a parent (Dunn, 1985).

From about one year onwards, play starts to occupy much of the child's life. At first, a child will mainly play alone, but increasingly demands someone else to play with. Through play, children further improve their bodily coordination and start to expand their knowledge of the adult world. They try out new skills, and they imitate the behavior of the grownups.

In an early study, Mildred Parten (1932) set out some categories of the development of play that are still generally accepted today. Young children first of all engage in *solitary independent play.* Even when in the company of other children, they play alone, making no reference to what the others are doing. This is followed by *parallel activity,* in which a child copies what the others are doing, but does not try to intervene in their activities. Subsequently (at age three or thereabouts) the children engage more and more in *associative play,* in which they relate their own behavior to that of others. Each child still acts as he wishes, but takes notice of and responds to what the others do. Later, at around age four, children take up *cooperative play* —activities that demand that each child collaborates with the other (as in playing at "mommies" and "daddies").

Over the period from age one to four or five, the child is also learning discipline and self-regulation. One thing this means is learning to control bodily needs and deal with them appropriately. Children become toilet-trained (a difficult and extended process), and learn how to eat their food politely. They also learn how to "behave themselves" in the various contexts of their activity, particularly when interacting with adults.

By about age five, children become fairly self-sufficient. They are no longer babies, but almost independent in the elementary routines of life at home—and ready to venture further into the outside world. For the first time, the developing individual is able to spend long hours away from parents without too much worry.

THE LEARNING OF LANGUAGE

The learning of language by infants—commonplace and virtually universal though it is—is one of the most extraordinary phenomena in the whole of human life. As adults, accustomed to speaking a language, and doing so more or less effortlessly, we tend not to realize how immensely complicated linguistic skills are. Every language has thousands of words that have to be remembered by the competent speaker. But this captures only one aspect of language-use, as was pointed out in the preceding chapter. To speak a language is to master a huge number of rules of language and meaning. If you have tried to learn a foreign language, even one quite close in vocabulary and grammar to the one you know already, you will have some sense of how difficult language-learning is. When a person who can already speak a language attempts to learn another, she seems to have a tremendous advantage over an infant. For the infant, having no knowledge of language at all, has to start from nothing. The accomplished language-speaker can use her knowledge of one language to learn another. Yet infants normally begin to speak even before the end of the first year of life, and by about age three can carry on a reasonably complex conversation with others. As we will see, this is achieved by a complex combination of innate ability and social interaction.

Stages of Language Acquisition

From the earliest days of life, children make vocal sounds. In the beginning, these do not have much variety, and consist mainly of crying or cooing. At around four months, an infant will usually start to babble. Babbling is meaningless to adults and, so far as we can tell, to the baby too. But it involves a rich variety of sound—so much so, that some students of child development have claimed that babbling contains all the sounds necessary to speak any language on earth (Brown, 1973). Babbling seems to be a "vocal repertoire" out of which the sound differences involved in a specific language are selected as the child learns that language.

Babbling becomes socially responsive before children utter their first distinguishable word. By the time they are about six months old, infants will babble more often when an adult talks to them than when they are alone. Moreover, this connection of vocalizing with social interaction is accompanied by other developing forms of social contact: the exchange of looks, touches, and caresses with the child's caretakers. It seems likely that the association of babble and gesture in early interaction prepares the way for some of the most distinctive characteristics of language-use later on. For instance, the child learns that talking and being talked to involves "taking turns," so that each person in a conversation responds to the other in sequence (see Chapter 4: "Social Interaction in Everyday Life").

The very first few words a baby learns happen in the context of such social interaction. Babies and their caretakers develop common frames of reference about objects as they look and point at them. The mutual gesturing carried on by baby and parent is accompanied by the naming of objects and talking about situations. This helps establish what is meant when a word is *used*—for a word like "cat" is not just a label. To know how to use "cat" means learning what cats look like, how they differ from people, from dogs, or from inanimate objects. Although babies do not make these discriminations early on—the infant might first of all say "cat" whenever a person or an animal is around—they learn to make such distinctions progressively and rapidly (Bruner, 1975).

Babies learn to understand a few words before actually talking themselves. For instance, an infant of about six months will glance at the highchair if her mother says "dinner." Infants often start to say one or two words at about nine or ten months of age, although some take several months longer to do so. The first words seem to be more than just references to objects. When a child says "cat," seeing the cat come into the room, he appears to be making a comment, or sometimes asking a question or making a command. We cannot actually be sure, of course, what is in the infant's mind. Is the infant, for example, asking in a foreshortened way, "Where did the cat come from?" While we do not know for certain, many students of language learning think that children often do in fact normally have compressed sentences in mind when using isolated words (Greenfield and Smith, 1976).

At about age two, a rapid period of language development occurs. The child's vocabulary rises to several hundred words, and then he starts to combine words into simple sentences. Vocabulary expands, and the use of sentence structure becomes more and more complex throughout the second year of life. Five-year-olds have a vocabulary of five thousand to ten thousand words. Given that at age one they can only speak about ten words, and perhaps none at all, they must learn on average some five to seven words each day, week in and week out—an amazing feat that an adult would find very difficult to match (Gleitman, 1986).

Origins of Language Development

How do children do it? What makes possible early language learning? What is it in humans that allows for language that isn't in chimps whose brains are similar? We can be certain that children do not learn language just through imitation and parental instruction. We know this because even children of less than two years old use phrases they have never heard before. Language-use is inherently *creative,* and this applies just as much to early language-learners as to mature speakers. We can show that children do not just imitate or follow instruction by some of the very mistakes they make. A child might say, "I dided that yesterday," instead of the grammatically correct "I did that yesterday." Somehow the child has learned the rule that in the past tense in English *-ed* is added to verbs. No one has taught this to the child as a grammatical principle, nor could anyone possibly have done so, because it would require a complicated linguistic explanation! Children somehow infer grammatical rules and apply them creatively to say words, phrases, and sentences they have never said before. In the case of "dided," the inference is wrong, but the example shows clearly that a general rule is being applied.

The mystery is exactly how such rules, and the complex ways in which they are applied in particular contexts, are learned. As the histories of the "wild boy" of Aveyron and of Genie indicated, there may be thresholds in the development of children. At a certain age, the young brain is open to rapid learning of language. Some have suggested that this early receptivity is to some degree genetically programmed. The child's brain is biologically "set up" to be able to pick out linguistic rules and principles, and apply them in contexts of action (Chomsky, 1976). After the age of five or six, however, this native aptitude is progressively lost. Hence young children who have a basic knowledge of one language can pick up another quickly if taken to a foreign country, but as they get older, this feat becomes more difficult.

While there must be an innate basis to the *capacity* to learn language, the nature of what is learned very clearly depends upon the social and cultural environment. Children learn the language spoken by their parents or by those who care for them and with whom they come into contact in their early years. A child brought up by Chinese speakers learns Chinese, an infant raised by German speakers learns

German. In fact, one experience which drives home the remarkable nature of infant language-learning is when an adult hears a very young child chattering away with ease in a language to which he or she has devoted many hours of study, and yet can still only speak imperfectly.

The early learning of language is crucial to the development of the child, but so also are emotional attachments. As was mentioned earlier, the relationship between child and mother is usually of overing importance during the early phases of a child's life. Research suggests that if this relationship is in any way impaired, serious consequences can occur.

ATTACHMENT AND LOSS

Some thirty years ago, the psychiatrist John Bowlby carried out research indicating that a young child who did not experience a close and loving relationship with its mother would suffer major personality disturbances in later life (Bowlby, 1951). Bowlby claimed, for example, that a child whose mother died shortly after birth would be affected by anxieties that would have a long-term impact upon her or his subsequent character. This theory came to be known as **maternal deprivation,** and has since given rise to a large number of investigations into child behavior. The results claimed by Bowlby also received support from studies done on some of the higher primates.

Isolated Monkeys

Harry Harlow carried out some celebrated experiments rearing Rhesus monkeys away from their mothers in order to explore the ideas put forward by Bowlby. Apart from being isolated from contact with others, the material needs of the monkeys were carefully provided for. The results were very striking. The monkeys brought up in isolation showed an extreme level of behavior disturbance. When introduced to other, normal, adult monkeys they were either fearful or hostile, refusing to interact with them. They would spend much of their time sitting huddled in the corner of the cage, resembling in their posture human beings suffering from schizophrenic withdrawal. They were unable to mate with other monkeys, and in most cases could not be taught to do so. Females who were artificially impregnated devoted little or no attention to their young.

In order to see whether it was absence of the mother that produced these abnormalities, Harlow brought up some young monkeys in the company of others of the same age. These animals showed no sign of disturbance in their later behavior. Harlow concluded that what matters for normal development is that the monkey has the opportunity to form attachments to another or others, regardless of whether these include the mother herself (Harlow and Zimmerman, 1959; Harlow and Harlow, 1962; Novak, 1979).

Deprivation in Human Infants

It cannot be assumed that what happens in the case of monkeys will occur in the same way among human infants (nor did Harlow suggest that his experiments demonstrated anything conclusively about human experience). Nevertheless, research on human children suggests parallels with the observations Harlow was able to make, although demonstrating long-term consequences of deprivation in infancy is obviously difficult. Studies of human infants tend to bear out the conclusion that what matters for the security of a child is the development of consistent patterns of early emotional attachment. These need not be with the mother herself and therefore the term "maternal deprivation" is somewhat misconceived. It is the opportunity to form stable, emotionally close relations with at least one other human being in infancy and early childhood that matters. The immediate effects of deprivation of such ties upon young children have been well documented. Research upon children admitted to hospitals has shown that emotional distress is most pronounced within the age group between six months to four years of age. Older children tend to suffer less severely and in a less prolonged way. The reactions of young children are not just due to the effects of being placed in a strange environment; the same consequences are not found if the mother or other caretakers are continuously present in the hospital.

Long-Term Influences

While the evidence about long-term influences is more ambiguous, in general it seems that deprivation of close early attachments often does produce lasting behavior disturbances. Only in cases such as that of the wild boy of Aveyron, or Genie, are human children more or less completely isolated from other people. So we would not expect to find a clear demonstration of the profound disturbances that affected Harlow's animals. However, there is considerable evidence indicating that children without stable attachments in infancy show linguistic and intellectual retardation, as well as experiencing difficulties later in forming close and lasting relationships with others. Reversal of these characteristics becomes progressively more difficult after the age of about six.

GENERAL THEORIES OF CHILD DEVELOPMENT

BOWLBY'S WORK CONCENTRATED UPON LIMITED ASPECTS of child development, above all the importance of emotional bonds between infants and those who care for them. How should we understand other features of children's growth, especially the emergence of a sense of self—the awareness that the individual has a distinct identity, separate from others? During the first months of life, infants possess little or no understanding of differences between human beings and material objects in their environment, and have no awareness of self. Children usually do not begin to use concepts like "I," "me," and "you" until the age of two or afterwards. Only gradually do they then come to understand that others have distinct identities, consciousness, and needs separate from their own.

The problem of the emergence of self is much debated and is viewed rather differently in contrasting theoretical perspectives. To some extent, this is because the most prominent theories about child development emphasize different aspects of socialization. The work of the founder of psychoanalysis, Sigmund Freud, concentrates above all upon how the infant controls anxieties, and upon the emotional aspects of child development. The American philosopher and sociologist George Herbert Mead gives attention mainly to how children learn to use the concepts of "I" and "me." The Swiss theorist of child behavior Jean Piaget worked on many aspects of child development, but his most well-known writings concern **cognition**—the ways in which children learn to *think* about themselves and their environment.

FREUD AND PSYCHOANALYSIS

Sigmund Freud (1856–1939), a Viennese physician, not only strongly influenced the formation of modern psychology, but he was also one of the major intellectual figures of the twentieth century. The impact of his ideas has been felt in art, literature, and philosophy, as well as in the social sciences. Freud theorized that much of what motivates adult behavior has its origins in unconscious conflicts that may or may not get resolved very early on in life. Freud laid out a series of early psychosexual stages, each with related anxieties and conflicts.

Most of these early childhood "conflicts" are lost to our conscious memory, but to Freud, they were the source of the neuroses of his patients. To bring these lost memories to the surface, Freud developed **psychoanalysis,** the technique of psychotherapy based upon "free association"—setting up a situation in which an individual speaks freely, following whatever direction his thought takes. Psychoanalysis has sometimes been called the "talking cure."

Personality Development

According to Freud, infants are demanding beings with sources of energy they cannot control because of their essential helplessness. They have to learn that their needs or desires cannot always be satisfied immediately—a painful process. In Freud's view, infants have needs not just for food and drink, but for erotic satisfaction. Freud did not mean that infants have sexual desires in the same way as older children or adults do. The "erotic" refers to a general need for close and pleasurable bodily contact with others. The idea is not so distant from what emerged from Harlow's experiments and the literature on child attachments. Infants do indeed have a need for close connections with others, including cuddling and caressing.

Sigmund Freud (1856–1939)

As Freud described it, human development is a psychosexual process involving important tensions. Infants learn progressively to control their drives, but these remain powerful motives in the unconscious. Of the several psychosexual stages, Freud placed particular emphasis on the phase at which most children are able to relinquish the company of their parents and enter a wider social world, at around age four to five. Freud called this phase the *Oedipal stage.* The early attachments that infants and young children form to their mothers and fathers have a defined erotic element, in the sense noted previously. If such attachments were allowed to continue and further develop, as children matured physically they would become sexually involved with the parent of the opposite sex. This does not happen because children learn to repress their erotic desires towards their parents.

Little boys learn that they cannot continue to be "tied to their mother's apron strings." According to Freud, the young boy experiences intense antagonism towards his father, because the father has sexual possession of the mother. This is the basis of the **Oedipus complex.** The Oedipus complex is overcome when the child represses both his erotic attachments to his mother, and his antagonism towards his father (most of this happens on the unconscious level). This marks a major stage in the development of an autonomous self, because the child has detached himself from his early dependence upon his parents, particularly his mother.

Freud's portrayal of female development was much less well worked out and more obscure. He believed that something of a reverse process occurs to that found in boys. The little girl represses her erotic desires for her father and overcomes her unconscious rejection of her mother by striving to become like her—to become "feminine." In Freud's view, how children cope with the Oedipus complex strongly influences later relationships, especially sexual ones, in their lives.

Criticism of Freudian Theory

Freud's theories have been widely criticized and have often met with very hostile responses. Some have rejected the idea that infants have erotic wishes, as well as the thesis that what happens in infancy and early childhood establishes unconscious modes of coping with anxiety that endure throughout life. Feminist critics have seen Freud's theory as directed too much towards male experience, giving too little attention to female psychology. Yet Freud's ideas continue to exert a powerful influence. Even if we do not accept Freud's ideas in their entirety, some of them are very probably valid. There almost certainly are unconscious aspects to human behavior resting upon modes of coping with anxiety established first of all in infancy.

THE THEORY OF G. H. MEAD

The background and intellectual career of G. H. Mead (1863–1931) was in most respects quite different from that of Freud. Mead was primarily a philosopher who spent most of his life teaching at the University of Chicago. He wrote rather little, and the publication for which he is best known, *Mind, Self, and Society* (1967; orig. pub. 1934), was in fact put together by his students on the basis of their lecture notes and other sources. Since Mead's ideas form the main basis of a general tradition of theoretical thinking, **symbolic interactionism,** they have had a very broad impact in sociology. Symbolic interactionism emphasizes that interaction between human beings takes place through symbols and the interpretation of meanings. (For an extended discussion, see Chapter 22: "The Development of Sociological Theory.") But in addition, Mead's work provides an account of the main phases of child development, giving particular attention to the emergence of a sense of self.

Development of Self

There are some interesting similarities between the views Mead developed and those of Freud, although Mead saw the human personality as less tensionful than Freud. According to Mead, infants and young children first of all develop as social beings by imitating the actions of those around them. Play is one way in which this takes place, and in their play small children often imitate what adults do. A small child will make mud pies, having seen an adult cooking, or dig with a spoon, having observed someone gardening. Children's play evolves from simple imitation to more complicated games in which a child of four or five years old will act out an adult role. Mead called this "taking the role of the other"—learning what it is like to be in the shoes of another person. It is only at this stage that children acquire a developed sense of self. Children achieve an understanding of themselves as separate agents—as a "me"—by seeing themselves through the eyes of others.

We achieve self-awareness, according to Mead, when we learn to distinguish the "me" from the "I." The "I" is the unsocialized infant, a bundle of spontaneous wants and desires. The "me," as Mead used the term, is the **social self.** Individuals develop **self-consciousness,** Mead argued, by coming to see themselves as others see them. Both Freud and Mead saw the child becoming an autonomous agent, capable of self-understanding and able to operate outside the context of the immediate family, at about age five. For Freud, this was the outcome of the unconscious conflicts of the Oedipal phase, while for Mead it was the result of developing self-awareness achieved through social experience.

The Generalized Other

A further stage of child development, according to Mead, occurs when the child is about eight or nine years old. This is the age at which children tend to take part in organized games, rather than unsystematic play. It is at this period that children begin to understand the overall *values* and *morality* according to which social life is conducted. To learn organized games, children must understand the rules of play, and notions of fairness and equal participation. Children at this stage learn to grasp what Mead termed the **generalized other**—the general values and moral rules involved in the culture in which they are developing. This was placed at a somewhat later age by Mead than by Freud, but once more there are clear similarities between their ideas on this point.

According to Mead, children develop a sense of themselves through play and imitation, in effect, "getting into the shoes of another."

Mead's views are less controversial than those of Freud because they do not contain so many startling ideas, nor is his theory of development based on unconscious conflicts. Mead's insights on development have been very influential, particularly upon researchers studying the formation of the child's self-consciousness and the acquisition of cultural values.

JEAN PIAGET AND COGNITIVE DEVELOPMENT

Jean Piaget (1896–1980)

The influence of the work of Jean Piaget has not been far short of that of Freud. Born in Switzerland in 1896, Piaget spent most of his life directing an institute of child development in Geneva. He published an extraordinary number of books and scientific papers, not just on child development, but on education, the history of thought, philosophy, and logic. He continued his prodigious output right up to his death in 1980.

Unlike Freud and Mead who never studied children directly, Piaget, by contrast, spent most of his life observing the behavior of infants, young children, and adolescents. He based most of his work on the detailed observation of limited numbers of individuals, rather than studying large samples. Nonetheless, he claimed his major findings to be valid for child development in all cultures.

The Stages of Cognitive Development

Piaget placed great emphasis upon the child's active capability to make sense of the world. Children do not passively soak up information, but select and interpret what they see, hear, and feel in the world around them. Piaget described several distinct stages of cognitive development during which children learn to think about themselves and their environment. Each stage involves the acquisition of new skills and depends upon the successful completion of the preceding one.

Piaget called the first stage, which lasts from birth up to about age two, **sensorimotor,** because infants learn mainly by touching objects, manipulating them, and physically exploring their environment. Until about age four months or so, infants cannot differentiate themselves from their environment. For example, a child will not realize that his own movements cause the sides of his crib to rattle. Objects are not differentiated from persons, and the infant is unaware that anything exists outside his range of vision. As the research we have already looked at shows, infants gradually learn to distinguish people from objects, coming to see that both have an existence independent of their immediate perceptions. The main accomplishment of this stage is that by its close children understand their environment to have distinct and stable properties.

The next phase, called **preoperational,** is the one to which Piaget devoted the bulk of his researches. This stage lasts from ages two to seven. During the course of it, children acquire a mastery of language and become able to use words to represent objects and images in a symbolic fashion. A four-year-old might use a sweeping hand, for example, to represent the concept "airplane." Piaget termed the stage "preoperational" because children are not yet able to use their developing mental capabilities systematically. Children in this stage are **egocentric.** As Piaget used it, this concept does not refer to selfishness, but to the tendency of the child to interpret the world exclusively in terms of his own position. A child during this period does not understand, for instance, that others see objects from a different perspective to his own. Holding a book upright, the child may ask about a picture in it, not realizing that the other person sitting opposite can only see the back of the book.

Children at the preoperational stage are not able to hold connected conversations with another. In egocentric speech, what each child says is more or less unrelated to what the other speaker said. Children talk together, but not *to* one another in the same sense as adults. During this phase of development, children have no general understanding of categories of thought that adults tend to take for granted: concepts such as causality, speed, weight, or number. Even if the child sees water poured from a tall, thin container into a shorter, wider one, she will not understand that the volume of water remains the same—and conclude rather that there is less water because the water level is lower.

A third period, the **concrete operational stage,** lasts from age seven to eleven. During this phase, children master abstract, logical notions. They are able to handle ideas such as causality without much difficulty. A child at this stage of development will recognize the false reasoning involved in the idea that the wide container holds less water than the thin, narrow one, even though the water levels are different. She becomes capable of carrying out the mathematical operations of multiplying, dividing, and subtracting. Children by this stage are much less egocentric. In the preoperational stage, if a girl is asked, "How many sisters have you?" she may correctly answer "one." But if asked, "How many sisters does your sister have?" she will probably answer "none," because she cannot see herself from the point of view of her sister. The concrete operational child is able to answer such a question with ease.

A child on the "frustrating verge" of a new Piagetian stage.

The years from eleven to fifteen cover what Piaget called the **formal operational stage.** During adolescence, the developing child becomes able to grasp highly abstract and hypothetical ideas. When faced with a problem, children at this stage are able to review all the possible ways of solving it and go through them theoretically in order to reach a solution. The young person at the formal operational stage is able to understand why some questions are trick ones. To the question, "What creatures are both poodles and dogs?" the individual might not be able to give the correct reply, but will understand why the answer "poodles" is right and appreciate the humor in it.

According to Piaget, the first three stages of development are universal; but not all adults reach the formal operational stage. The development of formal operational thought depends in part upon processes of schooling. Adults of limited educational attainment tend to continue to think in more concrete terms and retain large traces of egocentricism.

Criticism of Piagetian Stages

A number of psychologists have criticized Piaget's stage theory. The general thrust of this criticism is that children are able to do more tasks earlier than suggested by Piaget's stages. One critic, Margaret Donaldson (1979), has questioned Piaget's view that children are highly egocentric, compared to adults. The tasks that Piaget set the children he studied, according to her, were presented from an adult standpoint, rather than in contexts that were understandable to the children. Egocentricism is equally characteristic of adult behavior—in some situations. To make the point, she quotes a passage from the autobiography of the British poet Laurie Lee describing his first day at school as a small boy:

> I spent that first day picking holes in paper, then went home in a smouldering temper.
>
> "What's the matter, Love? Didn't he like it at school then?"
>
> "They never gave me a present."
>
> "Present? What present?"
>
> "They said they'd give me a present."
>
> "Well now, I'm sure they didn't."
>
> "They did! They said: 'You're Laurie Lee, aren't you? Well just you sit there for the present.' I sat there all day but I never got it. I ain't going back there again." (Lee, 1965)

As adults, we tend to think that the child has misunderstood, in a comic way, the instructions of the teacher. Yet on a deeper level, Donaldson points out, the adult has failed to understand the child and has not recognized the ambiguity in the phrase "sit there for the present." The adult is guilty of egocentrism, not the boy.

Piaget's work has also been much criticized on methodological grounds. How can we generalize about findings based upon observations of small samples of children living in Geneva? Yet for the most part, Piaget's ideas have stood up well in the light of the enormous amount of subsequent research they have helped to generate. The stages of development he identified are probably less clearcut than he claimed, but many of his ideas are now generally accepted.

CONNECTIONS AMONG THEORIES OF DEVELOPMENT

There are major differences among the perspectives of Freud, Mead, and Piaget; yet it is possible to suggest a picture of child development that draws upon them all.

All three authors accepted that, in the early months of infancy, babies have no distinct understanding of the nature of objects or persons in their environment, or of their own separate identity. Throughout the first two or so years of life, before the mastery of developed linguistic skills, most of children's learning is unconscious because they have as yet no awareness of self. Freud was probably right to claim that ways of coping with anxiety established during this early period—related, in particular, to interaction with mother and father—remain important in later personality development.

It is likely that children learn to become self-aware beings through the process suggested by Mead—the differentiating of an "I" and a "me." Children who have acquired a sense of self retain egocentric modes of thinking, however, as Piaget indicated. The development of the child's autonomy probably involves greater emotional difficulties than either Mead or Piaget seemed to recognize—which is where Freud's ideas are particularly relevant. Being able to cope with early anxieties may well influence whether a child is later able to move successfully through the stages of cognition distinguished by Piaget.

Taken together, these theories explain a great deal about how we become social beings, having an awareness of self and able to interact with others. However, they concentrate upon socialization in infancy and childhood, and none of the authors provides a full account of the social contexts in which socialization takes place—a task to which we now turn.

AGENCIES OF SOCIALIZATION

WE CAN REFER TO THE GROUPS OR SOCIAL CONTEXTS within which significant processes of socialization occur as **agencies of socialization.** In all cultures, the **family** is the main socializing agency of the child during infancy. But at later stages of an individual's life, many other socializing agencies come into play.

THE FAMILY

Since family systems vary widely, the range of contacts that the infant experiences is by no means standard across cultures. The mother everywhere is normally the most important individual in the child's early life but, as has been pointed out, the nature of the relationships established between mothers and their children is influenced by the form and regularity of their contact. This is, in turn, conditioned by the character of family institutions and their relation to other groups in society.

In modern societies, most early socialization occurs within a small-scale family context. The majority of American children spend their early years within a domestic unit containing mother, father, and perhaps one or two other children. In many other cultures, by contrast, aunts, uncles, and grandchildren are often part of a single household and serve as caretakers even for very young infants. Yet within American society there are many variations in the nature of family contexts. Some children are brought up in single-parent households; some are cared for by two mothering and fathering agents (divorced parents and step-parents). A high proportion of women with families are now employed outside the home and return to their paid work relatively soon after the births of their children. In spite of these variations, the family normally remains the major agency of socialization from infancy to adolescence and beyond—in a sequence of development connecting the generations.

Families have varying "locations" within the overall institutions of a society. In most traditional societies, the family into which a person was born largely determined the individual's social position for the rest of his or her life. In modern societies, social position is not inherited at birth in this way, yet the region and social class of the family into which an individual is born affects patterns of socialization quite distinctly. Children pick up ways of behavior characteristic of their parents or others in their neighborhood or community.

Varying patterns of child rearing and discipline, together with contrasting values and expectations, are found in different sectors of large-scale societies. It is easy to understand the influence of different types of family background if we think of what life is like, say, for a child growing up in a poor black family living in a run-down city neighborhood, compared to one born into an affluent white family living in an all-white suburb.

Of course, few if any children simply take over unquestioningly the outlook of their parents. This is especially true in the modern world, in which change is so pervasive. Moreover, the very existence of a range of socializing agencies in modern societies leads to many divergences between the outlooks of children, adolescents, and the parental generation.

PEER RELATIONSHIPS

Another socializing agency is the **peer group**—a friendship group of children of a similar age. In some cultures, peer groups are formalized as **age-grades.** Each generation has certain rights and responsibilities, which alter as its members grow older. (Age-grade systems are normally confined to males.) There are often specific ceremonials or rites that mark the transition of individuals from one age-grade to another. An example is puberty rites—when boys begin to develop physically, and their voices deepen, they have to participate in collective ceremonials, after which they are defined as "men." Those within a particular age-set generally maintain close and friendly connections throughout their lives. A typical set of age-grades is childhood, junior warriorhood, senior warriorhood, junior elderhood, and senior elderhood. Men do not move through these grades as individuals, but as whole groups.

Peer relationships often remain influential throughout one's life.

It is rather obvious how important the family is in socialization, since the experience of the infant and very young child is shaped more or less exclusively within it. It is less apparent, especially to those of us living in modern societies, how significant peer groups are. Yet, although there are no formal age-grades, children usually spend a great deal of time in the company of friends of the same age from four to five years old onwards. Given the high proportion of women now in the work force, whose young children are together in day-care centers, peer relations are even more important today than before, and schools of course are a major influence here. The theories of Mead and Piaget each rightly stressed the importance of peer relations. Piaget particularly emphasized the fact that peer relations are more "democratic" than the relations between a child and parents.

The word "peer" means "equal," and friendship relations established between young children do tend to be reasonably egalitarian. A forceful, or physically strong, child to some extent may try to dominate others. Yet since peer relations are founded upon mutual consent, rather than on the dependence inherent in the family situation, there has to be a large amount of give and take. Piaget pointed out that, because of their power, parents are able (in varying degrees) to enforce codes of conduct upon their children. In peer groups, by contrast, a child discovers a different context of interaction, within which rules of conduct can be tested out and explored.

Peer relationships often remain important throughout a person's life. Particularly in rural areas or city neighborhoods where there is not a great deal of mobility, individuals may be members of the same informal clique, or keep the same group of friends, for most or all of their lives. Even when they do not, peer relations are likely to have a significant impact beyond childhood and adolescence. Informal groups of people of similar ages at work, and in other contexts, are usually of enduring importance in shaping individuals' attitudes and behavior.

SCHOOLS

Schooling in modern societies is a formal process: there is a definite curriculum of subjects studied. Yet schools are agencies of socialization in more subtle respects too. Alongside the formal curriculum there is what some sociologists have called a **hidden curriculum** conditioning children's learning (see Chapter 13: "Education, Communication, and Media"). Children are expected to learn to be quiet in class, punctual at lessons, and observe rules of school discipline. They are called upon to accept and respond to the authority of the teaching staff. Reactions of teachers also affect the expectations children have of themselves. These, in turn, become linked to their job experience when they leave school since many jobs involve settings of authority and work-discipline quite similar to those made familiar by school experience.

THE MASS MEDIA

Newspapers, periodicals, and journals flourished in the West from the end of the eighteenth century onwards, but were confined to a fairly small readership. It was not until early in this century that such printed materials became part of the day-to-day experience of mil-

lions of people, influencing their attitudes and opinions. The spread
of **mass media**—newspapers and magazines with a mass circulation,
plus the "electronic media" of TV, radio, and videos—have become
fundamentally important to our lives. American children spend the
equivalent of almost a hundred school days per year watching television. Adults watch almost as often. And somewhere along the way,
TV has gained people's trust: a research study showed that, if a news
report on TV differs from a newspaper account, more than twice as
many people would believe the televised version as the newspaper
one (Roper Organization, 1977).

A vast amount of research work has been carried out trying to analyze the influence of particular TV programs, or types of programs,
on the attitudes of children and adults. Most of this research is not
conclusive in its implications. It is still not agreed, for example, to
what degree the portrayal of violence on TV promotes aggressive behavior among children. But it cannot be doubted that the media profoundly influence people's attitudes and outlooks. For one thing,
they convey a whole variety of information that individuals would
not otherwise acquire. Newspapers, books, radio, TV, movies, recorded music, comics, and popular magazines convey experiences of
which we would otherwise have little awareness.

There are few societies in current times, even among the more traditional cultures, that remain completely untouched by the mass

In the days before television

Research on the effects of television remains a controversial area of study.

media. Electronic communication is accessible even to those who are completely illiterate, and in the most isolated areas of Third World countries it is common to find people owning radios, or even TV sets.

OTHER SOCIALIZING AGENCIES

As many other socializing agencies exist, besides those mentioned, as there are groups, or social contexts, in which individuals spend large parts of their lives. *Work* is in all cultures an important setting within which socialization processes operate, although it is only in industrial societies that large numbers of people go "out to work"—that is, go each day to places of work separate from the home. In traditional communities many people farmed the land close to where they lived, or had workshops in their dwellings. "Work" in such communities was not so clearly distinct from other activities as it is for most members of the work force in the modern West. In the industrialized countries, going "out to work" for the first time ordinarily marks a much greater transition in an individual's life than entering work in traditional societies. The work environment often poses unfamiliar demands, perhaps calling for major adjustments in the person's outlook or behavior.

Although the local community usually influences socialization much less in modern societies than in other types of social order, it has not become wholly irrelevant. Even within large cities there are quite often strongly developed neighborhood groups and organizations—such as voluntary associations, clubs, or churches—which powerfully affect the ideas and activities of those who become involved in them.

RESOCIALIZATION

IN SOME CONDITIONS, ADULT INDIVIDUALS MAY EXPERIENCE **resocialization,** which is marked by the disruption of previously accepted values and patterns of behavior, followed by the adoption of radically different ones. One type of circumstance in which this may happen is when an individual enters a **carceral organization**—a mental hospital, prison, barracks, or other setting in which he or she is incarcerated (separated) from the outside world and subjected to rigorous new disciplines and demands. In situations of extreme stress, called **critical situations,** the changes in an individual's outlook and personality may be quite dramatic. From the study of such situations, in fact, we get considerable insight into more orthodox processes of socialization.

BEHAVIOR IN THE CONCENTRATION CAMP

The psychologist Bruno Bettelheim has provided a famous description of resocialization among people placed in concentration camps in Germany by the Nazis in the late 1930s and 1940s. The account was partly based on his own experiences when interned in two of the most notorious camps, Dachau and Buchenwald. The conditions of camp life were appalling. The prisoners faced physical torture, constant verbal abuse, severe scarcity of food and other elementary provisions for the sustenance of life. As a practicing psychotherapist, Bettelheim was used to seeing people alter their outlook and behavior, in fairly fundamental ways, as they responded to treatment. But the changes the prisoners experienced under the enormous strains of camp life were much more radical and rapid. In the camps, Bettelheim wrote, "I . . . saw fast changes taking place and not only in behavior but personality also; incredibly faster and often much more radical changes than any that were possible by psychoanalytic treatment" (Bettelheim, 1971).

According to Bettelheim, all the prisoners interned in the camps for more than a period of a year or so underwent changes in personal-

The concentration camp—"socialization" of a radical and distinct kind.

ity that followed a definite sequence. The very process of initial imprisonment was shocking, for people were ruthlessly torn away from family and friends, and often subjected to torture during their transportation to the camps. Most new prisoners tried to resist the impact of camp conditions and sought to maintain the modes of conduct associated with their previous lives. But this proved impossible to do for long. Fear, deprivation, and uncertainty caused the prisoners' personalities to crumble. Some prisoners became what the rest called *Muselmänner,* "walking corpses," apparently devoid of will, initiative, or any interest in their own fate. These men and women soon died. Others became childlike in their behavior, losing a sense of time and an ability to "think ahead," and having marked swings of mood in response to apparently trivial events.

Most of those who had been in the camps for more than a year or so —the "old prisoners"—behaved quite differently. The old prisoners had experienced a process of resocialization, by means of which they coped with the brutalities of camp life. They were often unable to recall names, places, and events in their previous lives. The reconstructed personalities of the old prisoners developed by imitation the outlook and behavior of the very individuals they had found so repugnant when they first came into the camps—the camp guards themselves. They aped the guards' behavior and even used tattered pieces of cloth to attempt to imitate their uniforms.

Bettelheim writes:

> Old prisoners felt great satisfaction if, during the twice daily counting of prisoners, they really had stood well at attention or given a snappy salute. They prided themselves on being as tough, or tougher, than the SS. In their identification they went so far as to copy SS leisure-time activities. One of the games played by the guards was to find out who could stand being hit the longest without uttering a complaint. This game was copied by old prisoners, as if they were not hit often enough without repeating the experience as a game." (Bettelheim, 1971)

BRAINWASHING AND BATTLE TRAUMA

We can see similar resocialization responses and changes in other critical situations—for example, in the behavior of individuals subjected to forced interrogation or "brainwashing," and of soldiers returning from the trauma (shock) of war.

In the initial stages of forced interrogation, the individual attempts to resist the pressures imposed. Following this, he or she seems to regress to a childlike stage. Resocialization takes place when new traits of behavior are developed, modeled upon the authority figure in the situation—the interrogator. As William Sargant, who has studied numerous types of critical situations, notes: "One of the more horrible consequences of these ruthless interrogations, as described by the victims, is that they suddenly begin to feel affection for the examiner who has been treating them harshly" (Sargant, 1959).

What seems to happen in critical situations is that the socialization process is "thrown into reverse." Socialized responses are stripped away, and the individual experiences anxieties similar to those of a young child removed from parental protection. The individual's personality then becomes effectively restructured. These radical changes in personality and behavior represent an extreme case of normal processes of socialization but in unusual settings. People's personality, values, and outlook are never simply "fixed," but alter in relation to their experiences throughout the life cycle—but in this case, they alter in an extreme way.

An illustration of this is the experience of the young men who fought in Vietnam in the 1960s and early 1970s. Under the extreme pressures of fighting in an unfamiliar jungle environment, against a determined and resourceful enemy, many soldiers underwent personality changes resembling those identified by Bettelheim and Sargant. They became resocialized in order to survive in a harsh and brutal situation. On their return to the United States after the war, the combat veterans, as well as many women who served as nurses, found that they faced a new process of resocialization—back into the peacetime world for which they were now ill-suited. The many individuals now suffering from what psychiatrists call "post-traumatic stress disorder" offer evidence of the difficulties of moving out of the psychological limbo between the Vietnam War and everyday life in the United States.

Victims of natural and humanly created catastrophes, here battle trauma, are often faced with relearning old patterns of behavior if they are to readjust to the "normal" world.

THE LIFE CYCLE ACROSS CULTURES

THE VARIOUS TRANSITIONS THROUGH WHICH INDIVIDUALS pass during their lives seem at first sight to be biologically fixed—from childhood to adulthood and eventually to death. Things are much more complicated than this, however. The stages of the human life cycle are social as well as biological in nature. They are influenced by cultural differences and also by the material circumstances in which people live in given types of society. For example, in the West death is usually thought of in relation to old age, because most people enjoy a life span of seventy years or more. In traditional societies, however, more people died at a younger age than survived to old age.

CHILDHOOD

Prior to the present century, children were expected to go to work at a very young age. This twelve-year-old worked in a Vermont cotton mill.

To those living in modern societies, "childhood" is a clear and distinct stage of life; "children" are distinct from "babies" or "toddlers." Childhood intervenes between infancy and the onset of adolescence. Yet the concept of childhood, like so many other aspects of our social life today, has only come into being over the past two or three centuries. In traditional societies, the young moved directly from a lengthy infancy into working roles within the community. The French historian, Philippe Ariès, has argued that "childhood," as a separate phase of development, did not exist in medieval times (Ariès, 1965). In the paintings of medieval Europe, children were portrayed as "little adults," having mature faces and the same style of dress as their elders. Children took part in the same work and play activities as adults and did not have the distinct toys or games that we now take for granted.

Right up to the start of the twentieth century, in most Western countries, children were put to work at what now seems a very early age. In many countries in the world today, in fact, young children are engaged in full-time work, often in physically degrading or dangerous circumstances (for example, working in coal mines) (UNICEF, 1983). The idea that children have distinct rights, coupled with the notion that the use of child labor is morally repugnant, are quite recent developments.

Some historians, developing the standpoint put forward by Ariès, have suggested that in medieval Europe most parents were indifferent, or even hostile, to their children. This view has been rejected by others, however, and is not borne out by what we know of traditional cultures still existing today. Most parents, particularly mothers, almost certainly formed the same kinds of attachments to their children as are usual in modern times. However, because of the long period of "childhood" that we recognize today, modern societies are in some respects more "child-centered" than traditional ones. Both parenting and childhood have become more clearly distinct from other activities than was true of traditional communities.

It seems possible that, as a result of changes currently occurring in modern societies, "childhood" is again becoming eroded as a distinct status. Some observers have suggested that children now "grow up so fast" that the separate character of childhood is diminishing once more (Suransky, 1982; Winn, 1983). Children often watch the same TV programs as adults, for example, and are familiar with many aspects of the adult world at a much earlier age than previous generations were.

ADOLESCENCE

The existence of "teenagers" is also specific to modern industrialized societies. The biological changes involved in puberty (the point at which a person becomes capable of adult sexual activity and reproduction) are universal. Yet in many cultures these do not produce the turmoil and uncertainty often found among young people in the modern West. When there is an age-grade system, for example, coupled with distinct rituals that signal the person's transition to adulthood, the process of psychosexual development generally seems easier to accomplish. Adolescents in traditional societies had less to "unlearn" than their counterparts in modern ones, since the pace of change was slower. There is a time at which children in modern societies are required to be children no longer and must put away their toys and break with childish pursuits. In traditional cultures, where children were already working alongside adults, this process of "unlearning" was normally much less severe.

The distinctiveness of being a teenager in Western societies is related both to the general extension of child rights and to the process of formal education. Teenagers often try to follow adult ways, but are treated in law as children. They may wish to work, but are constrained to stay in school. Teenagers are "in between" childhood and adulthood, growing up in a society subject to continuous change (Elkind, 1984).

ADULTHOOD

Most young adults today can look forward to a life stretching right through to old age. In premodern times, few could expect such a future with much confidence. Death through sickness, plague, or injury was much more frequent among all age groups than is true today. Women in particular were at great risk because of the high rate of mortality in childbirth.

On the other hand, some of the strains present in modern societies were less pronounced in previous times. People usually maintained a closer connection with their parents and other kin than in today's more mobile populations, and the routines of work they followed were the same as those of their parents and grandparents. In the modern world, people must make decisions about careers, marriage, family life, and other social contexts they enter, and major uncertainties are involved. We have to "make" our own lives more than people did in the past. The creation of sexual and marital ties, for instance, now depends upon individual initiative and selection, rather than being fixed by parents. This represents greater freedom for the individual, but also can impose strains and difficulties.

Keeping a "forward-looking" outlook in middle age has a particular importance in modern societies. Most people do not expect to be "doing the same thing all their lives"—as was usually the case for the majority of the population in traditional cultures. Men or women who have spent their lives in one career might find the level they have reached in middle age unsatisfying and that further opportunities are blocked. Women who spent their early adulthood raising a family, and whose children have left home, may feel themselves without useful social value. The phenomenon of a "mid-life crisis" is very real for many middle-aged people in the modern world. At this period a person may feel he or she has thrown away the opportunities that life had to offer, or will never attain goals cherished since childhood. Yet there is no reason why the transitions involved should lead to resignation or bleak despair; a release from childhood dreams can be liberating.

OLD AGE

In traditional societies, older people were normally accorded a great deal of respect. Among cultures having age-grades, the "elders" usually had a major, often the final, say over matters of importance to the community as a whole. Within families, the authority of both men and women often increased with age. In modern industrialized societies, by contrast, because they are no longer seen as "productive" members of society, older people tend to lack authority either within the family or in the wider social community. Having retired from the labor force, and living on fixed incomes from pensions or social security, they may exist in circumstances of greater economic hardship than earlier in their lives. At the same time, there has been a great increase in the proportion of the population aged sixty-five or more. Only one in thirty people in the United States in 1900 was over sixty-five; the proportion today is one in five. The same sort of change is found in all the industrially advanced countries.

Transition to the age-grade of elder in a traditional culture often marked the pinnacle of the status an individual—at least a male—could achieve. In modern societies, retirement tends to lead to the very opposite consequences. No longer living with their children, ejected from the economic sphere, it is not easy for older people to make the final period of their life a rewarding one. It used to be assumed that those who successfully coped with old age did so by turning to their inner resources, becoming less interested in the external rewards social life had to offer. While this may no doubt often be true, it seems likely that, in a society in which many are physically healthy in old age, an "outward-looking" view will come more and more to the fore. Those in retirement might find renewal in what has been called the "Third Age" (following childhood and adulthood), in which a new phase of education and learning may begin. (For further discussion of old age, see Chapter 18: "Population, Health, and Aging.")

DEATH AND THE SUCCESSION OF THE GENERATIONS

In medieval Europe, death was much more visible than it is today. The loved one passed away in the presence of family, often friends. No less a sad event than today, death in past times was an event that often occurred *in* the community. In the modern world most people die in the enclosed environments of hospitals, removed from day-to-day contact with their relatives or friends. Death is often seen as the end of an individual life, not as a process of the renewal of the generations. For most people today death tends to be a subject that goes undiscussed. It is taken for granted that people are frightened of dying, and thus doctors or relatives quite commonly hide from a mortally ill person that they will shortly die.

According to Elisabeth Kübler-Ross (1986), the process of adjusting to the imminence of death is a compressed form of socialization that involves several stages. The first is *denial*—the individual refuses to accept what is happening. The second stage is *anger,* particularly among those dying at a relatively young age. The person feels resentful at having been robbed of the full span of life others are able to enjoy. This is followed by a stage of *bargaining.* The individual makes a deal with fate, or with the deity, to die peacefully if allowed to live to see some particular event of significance, such as a family marriage or birthday. Subsequently, the person frequently lapses into *depression.* Finally, if this state can be overcome, she or he might move towards a phase of *acceptance,* in which an attitude of peace is achieved in the face of approaching death.

Kübler-Ross notes that when she asks her lecture audiences what they fear most about dying, the majority of people say they dread the unknown, pain, separation from loved ones, or unfinished projects. According to her, these things are really only the tip of the iceberg. Most of what we associate with death is unconscious, and this has to be brought to light if people are to be able to face dying. Unconsciously, people cannot conceive of their own death except as a malicious entity come to punish them—which is how they also unconsciously think of serious illness. If they can see that this association is an irrational one—that, for example, being terminally ill is not a punishment for wrongdoing—the process is eased (Kübler-Ross, 1981).

In traditional cultures, in which children, parents, and grandparents often lived in the same household, there was usually a clear awareness of the connection of death with the succession of the generations. Individuals felt themselves to be part of a family, and a community, which would endure indefinitely, regardless of the transience of personal existence. In such circumstances, death was perhaps looked upon with less anxiety than in the more rapidly changing, individualistic social circumstances found in the industrialized world.

At the same time as children are shaped by agencies of socialization, they develop a sense of self-identity and the capabilities to alter those agencies.

SOCIALIZATION AND INDIVIDUAL FREEDOM

SINCE THE CULTURAL SETTINGS IN WHICH WE ARE BORN and come to maturity so influence our behavior, it might appear that we are robbed of any individuality or free will. We might seem to be merely stamped into pre-set molds that society has prepared for us. Some sociologists do tend to write about socialization—and even about sociology more generally!—as though this were the case. But such a view is fundamentally mistaken. The fact that from birth to death we interact with others certainly conditions our personalities, the values we hold, and the behavior in which we engage, yet socialization is also at the origin of our very individuality and freedom. In the course of socialization each of us develops a sense of *self-identity,* and the capability for *independent thought* and *action,* all of which feed back into the social system and in effect change the process of socialization itself.

This point is easily illustrated by taking the example of learning language. None of us invented the language we learned as children; we learned it simply by being in the culture in which it was spoken.

At the same time, however, understanding a language is one of the basic factors that make possible our self-awareness and creativity. Without language, we would not be self-conscious beings, and we would live more or less wholly in the here-and-now. Mastery of language is necessary for the symbolic richness of human life, for awareness of our distinctive individual characteristics, and for our practical mastery of the environment.

SUMMARY

1. Socialization is the process whereby, through contact with other human beings, the helpless infant gradually becomes a self-aware, knowledgeable human being, skilled in the ways of the given culture and environment.

2. The work of Sigmund Freud suggests that the young child learns to become an autonomous being only as she or he learns to balance the demands of the environment with pressing desires coming from the unconscious. A child's capabilities of self-awareness are built, painfully, upon the repression of unconscious drives.

3. According to G. H. Mead, the child achieves an understanding of being a separate agent by seeing how others behave towards him or her in social contexts. At a later stage, entering into organized games, learning the rules of play, the child comes to understand "the generalized other"—general values and cultural rules.

4. Jean Piaget distinguishes several main stages in the development of the child's capability to make sense of the world. Each stage involves the acquisition of new cognitive skills and depends upon the successful completion of the preceding one. According to Piaget these stages of cognitive development are universal features of socialization.

5. Agencies of socialization are structured groups or contexts within which significant processes of socialization occur. In all cultures, the family is the principal socializing agency of the child during infancy. Other influences include peer groups, schools, and the mass media.

6. Formal schooling becomes an extended process in modern societies, and thus a key aspect of socialization. To educate means to deliberately teach skills or values. The school also educates in more subtle ways, instilling attitudes and norms via the "hidden curriculum."

7. The development of mass communications has enlarged the range of socializing agencies. The spread of mass printed media was later accompanied by the use of electronic communication. TV exerts a particularly powerful influence, reaching people of all ages at regular intervals every day.

8. In some circumstances involving a marked alteration in the social environment of an individual or a group, people may undergo processes of resocialization. Resocialization refers to a restructuring of personality and attitudes, consequent on situations of great turmoil or stress.

9. Socialization continues throughout the life cycle. At each distinct phase of life there are transitions to be made or crises to be overcome. This includes facing death as the termination of personal existence.

BASIC CONCEPTS

SOCIALIZATION
SELF-CONSCIOUSNESS

IMPORTANT TERMS

MATERNAL DEPRIVATION
COGNITION
PSYCHOANALYSIS
OEDIPUS COMPLEX
SYMBOLIC INTERACTIONISM
SOCIAL SELF
GENERALIZED OTHER
SENSORIMOTOR STAGE
PREOPERATIONAL STAGE
EGOCENTRICISM
CONCRETE OPERATIONAL STAGE

FORMAL OPERATIONAL STAGE
AGENCIES OF SOCIALIZATION
FAMILY
PEER GROUP
AGE-GRADES
HIDDEN CURRICULUM
MASS MEDIA
RESOCIALIZATION
CARCERAL ORGANIZATION
CRITICAL SITUATIONS

SOCIAL INTERACTION
AND EVERYDAY LIFE

TWO PEOPLE PASS ONE ANOTHER ON A CITY SIDEWALK. Both briefly exchange glances, rapidly scanning the other's face and style of dress. As they get close and pass by, each looks away, avoiding the other's eyes. What is happening here goes on millions of times a day in the towns and cities of the world.

When passersby quickly glance at one another, then look away again when they come near, they demonstrate what Erving Goffman (1967, 1972) calls the **civil inattention** we require of one another in many situations of social life. Civil inattention, he pointed out, is not at all the same as merely ignoring another person. Each individual indicates to the other recognition of that person's presence, but avoids any gesture that might be taken as too intrusive. According civil inattention to others is something we do more or less unconsciously, but it is of fundamental importance in our day-to-day lives. By their civil inattention, people imply to one another that they have no reason to suspect others' intentions, to be hostile to them, or in any other way to specifically avoid them (Goffman, 1963).

The best way to see the importance of this is by thinking of examples where it doesn't apply. On some occasions a person may stare fixedly at another, allowing her or his face to express openly a particular emotion. But this only happens in an exchange of looks between lovers, or when one individual is angry with another. Strangers or chance acquaintances, whether encountered on the street, at work, or at a party, virtually never hold the gaze of another in this way. To look fixedly at another person is often taken as an indication of hostile intent. It is only when two groups are strongly antagonistic to one another that strangers might indulge in such practices of which the "hate stare" is one type. Thus, sometimes a boxer at the start of a fight will give his opponent a "hate stare" to intimidate the other or to show that he is not afraid. Another example is the hostile look that members of some animal-rights groups might give a woman walking down the street wearing a fur coat.

Even friends in close conversation have to be careful about how they look at one another (Goodwin, 1981). Each individual demonstrates attention and involvement in the conversation by regularly looking at the eyes of the other, but not staring into them. To look too intently at someone might be taken to be a sign of mistrust about, or at least failure to understand, what the other is saying. Yet, if each party to the conversation does not engage the eyes of the other at all, he or she is likely to be thought evasive, shifty, or otherwise odd.

STUDYING DAY-TO-DAY SOCIAL LIFE

GOFFMAN WAS ONE OF THE FIRST SOCIOLOGISTS TO STUDY the subtleties of seemingly trivial forms of social interaction. But why should sociologists concern themselves with these aspects of social behavior? Passing someone on the street or exchanging a few words with a friend seem minor and uninteresting activities, things we do countless times a day without needing to give them any thought. In fact, the study of such apparently insignificant forms of social interaction is of major importance in sociology and, far from being uninteresting, is one of the most absorbing of all areas of sociological investigation.

There are two reasons why studying day-to-day social interaction is so important:

1. The routines of daily life, which involve us in more or less constant face-to-face interaction with others, make up the bulk of our social activities. Our lives are organized around

the repetition of similar patterns of behavior from day to day, week to week, month to month, and even year to year. Think of what you did yesterday, for example, and the day before that. If they were both weekdays, in all probability you got up at "about the same time as usual" (an important routine in itself). You may have gone off to class fairly early in the morning, involving a journey from home to campus that you make on virtually every weekday. You perhaps met some friends for lunch, returning to classes or private study in the afternoon. Later, you retraced your steps back home, possibly going out later in the evening with other friends. Of course, the routines we follow from day to day are not identical, and our patterns of activity on weekends are usually different than on weekdays. If a major change occurs in a person's life—like leaving college to take up a job—major alterations in daily routines usually have to be made. Normally, however, a new and fairly regular set of habits is established. Our day-to-day routines, then, and the interactions in which they involve us with others, give structure and form to what we do. We can learn a great deal about ourselves as social beings, and about social life itself, from studying such routines.

2. Studying social interaction in everyday life sheds light on larger social systems and institutions. All large-scale social systems, in fact, depend upon the patterns of social interaction we engage in during the course of our daily lives. This is easy to demonstrate. Consider again the case of two strangers passing on the street, the most transient type of social interaction one could imagine. When we take such an event on its own, it perhaps has little direct relevance to large-scale, more permanent, forms of social organization. But when we take into account many such interactions, this is no longer so. Extremely wide-ranging features of social life are sustained through civil inattention and other interactional devices whereby we relate to strangers. In modern societies, most people live in towns and cities, and constantly interact with others whom they do not know on a personal basis. Civil inattention is one among other mechanisms that gives city life, with its bustling crowds, and many fleeting, impersonal contacts, the character it has.

We will return to this point at the end of the chapter. Before this, we will provide a general account of the nature of social interaction in day-to-day life and discuss the nonverbal cues (facial expressions and bodily gestures) that all of us use when interacting with each other. We will then move on to analyze everyday speech or talk—how we use language to communicate to others the meanings we wish to get across. In the following section, we shall focus upon looking at how our lives are structured by daily routines, giving particular attention to how we coordinate what we do across space and time. Our over-riding concern in the chapter is to show how complicated, and intriguing, are the features of our everyday behavior that we usually take for granted—and how important these are for understanding human social institutions as a whole.

NONVERBAL COMMUNICATION

SOCIAL INTERACTION INVOLVES A NUMEROUS VARIETY OF **nonverbal communication**—the exchange of information and meaning through facial expressions, gestures, or movements of the body. Nonverbal communication is sometimes referred to as "body language." We characteristically use such non-verbal cues to amplify, or expand upon, what is said verbally.

THE FACE, GESTURES, AND EMOTIONS

One major aspect of nonverbal communication is the facial expression of emotion. Paul Ekman and his colleagues have developed what they call the Facial Action Coding System (FACS) for describing movements of the facial muscles giving rise to particular expressions (Ekman and Friesen, 1978). By this means they have tried to inject some precision into an area notoriously open to inconsistent or contradictory interpretations—for there is little agreement among scholars about how emotions are to be identified and classified. Charles Darwin, the originator of evolutionary theory, claimed that basic modes of emotional expression are the same among all human beings. Although some have disputed the claim, Ekman's researches among people from widely different cultural backgrounds seem to confirm this. Ekman and Friesen (1971) carried out a study of an isolated community in New Guinea, whose members had previously had virtually no contact with Westerners. Pictures of facial expressions of six emotions (happiness, sadness, anger, disgust, fear, surprise), shown in other studies to be recognized by many different peoples, were presented to the New Guinea group. They identified the same emotions from the pictures as the members of other cultures

do. According to Ekman, such results support the view that the facial expression of emotion, and its interpretation, are innate in human beings. However, he acknowledges that his evidence does not conclusively demonstrate this, and it may be that widely-shared cultural learning experiences are involved.

When New Guinea tribesmen were asked to show expressions of happiness, sadness, disgust, or anger, they displayed facial expressions similar to those of other cultures (viewed from left to right).

Ekman's conclusions have been supported by other types of research. I. Eibl-Eibesfeldt (1972) studied six children born deaf and blind to see whether their facial expressions were the same as those of normal individuals in particular emotional situations. He found that the children smiled when engaged in obviously pleasurable activities, raised their eyebrows in surprise when sniffing at an object with an unaccustomed smell, and frowned when repeatedly offered a disliked object. Since they could not have seen or heard others behaving in these ways, it seems that these responses must have been innate.

Using FACS, Ekman and Friesen identified a number of the discrete facial-muscle actions in newborn infants that are also found in the adult expression of emotion. Infants seem, for example, to produce facial expressions similar to the adult expression of disgust (pursing the lips and frowning) in response to sour tastes. But although the facial expression of emotion seems to have innate aspects, individual and cultural factors influence exactly what form facial movements take, and the contexts in which they are deemed appropriate. How people smile, for example, the precise movement of the lips and other facial muscles, and how fleeting the smile is, all vary widely between cultures (Birdwhistell, 1970).

There are no gestures or aspects of bodily posture that have been shown to characterize all, or even most, cultures. In some societies, for instance, people nod when they mean "no," the opposite to our practice. Gestures that we tend to use a great deal, such as pointing, seem not to exist among certain peoples (Bull, 1983). Other gestures employed frequently elsewhere are unknown in Anglo-American culture. A gesture called the "cheek-screw," where a straightened forefinger is placed in the center of the check and rotated, is used in parts of Italy as a gesture of praise. It appears to be unknown in other parts of Europe.

Without the benefit of learning from others, children blind from birth display the same facial expressions as sighted children.

Like facial expressions, gestures and bodily posture are continually used to fill out utterances, as well as to convey meanings when nothing is actually said. Few of us can completely control the nonverbal impressions that we "give off"—convey without consciously meaning to—which often indicate that what we say is not quite what we really mean. Blushing is perhaps the most obvious example, but there are innumerable more subtle indicators that can be picked up by others. Genuine facial expressions tend to evaporate after four or five seconds, and a smile or display of surprise that lasts longer could very well indicate deceit. Like any of the forms of talk and activity around which our day-to-day lives are built, facial expressions, gestures, or body postures can be used to joke or show irony or scepticism. A facial expression of surprise that lasts too long, for example, may deliberately be used as a parody—to show that the individual is not in fact surprised after all by a given event or happening, even though he or she might have reason to be.

"FACE" AND CULTURE

We can speak of "face" in a broader sense than we have done thus far, referring to the *esteem* in which an individual is held by others. In daily social life, we normally give a good deal of attention to protecting or "saving" each other's "face." Much of what we usually call "politeness" or "etiquette" in social gatherings consists of disregarding aspects of behavior that might otherwise lead to a "loss of face." Episodes in an individual's past, or personal characteristics that might produce embarrassment if mentioned, are not commented on. Jokes about baldness are avoided if it is realized that a person is wearing a hairpiece—unless those concerned are very well known to one another (Goffman, 1974). Tact is a sort of protective device that we employ in the expectation that, in return, our own fallibilities and weaknesses will not deliberately be exposed to general view. Our day-to-day lives, therefore, do not just "happen." Without realizing it most of the time, all of us skillfully maintain a close and continuous control over facial expressions, body postures, and gestures in the interaction we carry on with others.

Some people—for example, diplomats—are "specialists" in the control of facial expression and the tactful organizing of interaction with others. A good diplomat, while giving every appearance of ease and comfort, has to be able to interact with others whose views she or he might disagree with, or even find distasteful. The degree to which this is managed successfully can affect the fate of whole nations. Skillful diplomacy, for instance, might defuse tensions between nations and prevent an armed conflict.

SOCIAL RULES, CONVERSATIONS, AND TALK

ALTHOUGH THERE ARE MANY NONVERBAL CUES WE ROU-tinely use in our own behavior and in making sense of that of others, much of our interaction is carried out through **talk** or **conversation.** Sociologists have always considered language fundamental to social life. Recently, however, they have become specifically concerned with how people *use* language in the ordinary contexts of everyday life. Most language-use is in fact talk —casual verbal exchange—carried on in informal conversations with others. The study of conversations has been strongly influenced by Goffman's work, but the most important figure influencing this type of research is Harold Garfinkel, the founder of **ethnomethodology** (Garfinkel, 1985).

Ethnomethodology is the study of the "ethno-methods"—the folk or lay methods—people use to make sense of what others do, and particularly what they say. All of us apply methods of *making sense* in our interaction with others, which we normally employ without having to give any conscious attention to them. We can only make sense of what is said in conversation by knowing the social context that does not appear in the words themselves. Take the following conversation (Heritage, 1985):

A: "I have a fourteen year old son."
B: "Well, that's all right."
A: "I also have a dog."
B: "Oh, I'm sorry."

What do you think is happening here? What is the relation between the contributors to the conversation? Looked at "cold," there seems no relation between the sentences. Why should it be "all right" to have a fourteen-year-old son? Why is B "sorry" that A owns a dog? We can understand what was said, and why, quite easily, however, as soon as we guess or are told that it is a conversation between a prospective tenant and landlord. The conversation then becomes sensible and "obvious." Yet without knowing the social context, the responses of individual B seem to bear no relation to the statements of A. *Part* of the sense is in the words, and *part* is in the way in which the social context emerges from the talk.

SHARED UNDERSTANDINGS

The most inconsequential forms of daily talk presume complicated, shared knowledge "brought into play" by those involved. We take this for granted, but our small talk is so complex that it has thus far proved impossible to program even the most sophisticated computers to converse with human beings as we do among ourselves. The words used in ordinary talk do not have precise meanings and we "fix" what we want to say, or our understanding of what is said, through the unstated assumptions that back it up. If one person asks another "What did you do yesterday?" there is no obvious cue to the expected answer provided by the words themselves in the question. A day is a long time, and it would be logical for someone to answer "Well, at seven-sixteen, I woke up. At seven-eighteen I got out of bed and started to brush my teeth. At seven-nineteen I turned on the shower. . . ." We understand the type of response the question calls for by knowing who the individual is asking it, what sort of activities are normally carried on together, what the other person usually does on a particular day of the week, and many other things.

GARFINKEL'S EXPERIMENTS ON DAY-TO-DAY TALK

The "background expectancies" by means of which we organize ordinary conversations were highlighted by some experiments Garfinkel undertook with student volunteers. The students were asked to engage a friend or relative in conversation and insist on clarifying any commonplace remarks made. Casual remarks, or day-to-day comments, were to be actively pursued to make their meaning precise. If someone said, "Have a nice day," the students were to respond, "Nice in what sense, exactly?", "Which part of the day do you mean?", and so forth. One of the transcripts of the exchanges that resulted ran as follows:

> (S *waved his hand cheerily.*)
> S: "How are you?"
> E: "How am I in regard to what? My health, my finance, my school work, my peace of mind, my . . . "
> S: (*red in the face and suddenly out of control*) "Look! I was just trying to be polite. Frankly, I don't give a damn how you are."
> (Garfinkel, 1963)

Why do people get so upset when apparently minor conventions of talk are not followed? The answer is that the stability and meaningfulness of our daily social life depend upon the sharing of common—but unstated—cultural assumptions about what is said and why. If we were not able to take these for granted, meaningful communication would literally be impossible. Any question or contribution to a conversation would have to be followed by a massive "search procedure" of the sort Garfinkel's subjects were told to initiate in response to everyday remarks. Interaction would simply break down. What seem at first sight to be unimportant conventions of talk, therefore, turn out to be fundamental to the very fabric of social life, which is why their breach is so serious.

In everyday life people will on occasion deliberately feign ignorance of the unstated knowledge involved in interpreting a statement, remark, or question. This may be done to rebuff or poke fun at the other, cause embarrassment, or call attention to a double meaning in what was said. Consider, for example, this classic exchange between parent and teenager:

> P: "Where are you going?"
> T: "Out."
> P: "What are you going to do?"
> T: "Nothing."

The responses of the teenager are effectively the opposite of those of the volunteers in Garfinkel's experiments. Rather than pursuing enquiries where this is not normally done, the teenager declines to provide appropriate answers at all—effectively saying, "Mind your own business!" The initial question might get quite a different response from another person in another context, such as:

A: "Where are you going?"
B: "I'm going crazy trying to finish my term paper!"

B deliberately "misreads" A's question ironically to convey worry or frustration. Comedy, joking, and wit thrive upon such deliberate misunderstandings of the unstated assumptions involved in talk. There is nothing threatening about this so long as the parties concerned recognize the intent to provoke laughter.

FORMS OF TALK

It is a sobering experience to hear a tape recording or read a transcript of a conversation to which one has contributed. Conversations are much more fractured, hesitant, and ungrammatical than most people realize. When we take part in everyday talk, we tend to think that what is said has a polished character, because we unconsciously "fill in" the background to the actual words exchanged. Real conversations look quite different from fictional accounts of conversations in novels. Dialogue that characters speak in fictional literature is usually well formed and grammatical. Consider the following sequence of talk, which is entirely characteristic of most real-life conversation (Heritage, 1985):

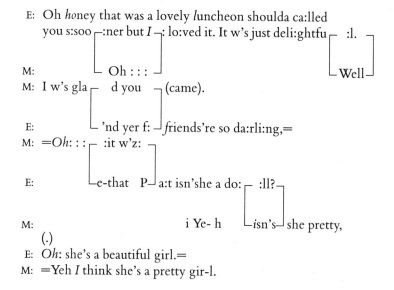

E: Oh: she's a beautiful girl.=
M: =Yeh *I* think she's a pretty gir-l.

Key:
[ ] One speaker is talking at the same time as the other.
ho Italic type represents a stress upon a particular utterance, word or phrase, such as a change in the pitch of the voice or in its degree of loudness.
= Indicates that speech carries on without a gap, even though one person takes over talking from another.
: Indicates very slight pause, with change of stress or intonation, within a word.
( ) Indicates slightly larger gap than usual between utterances.

Neither party to this conversation finishes a sentence. Each interrupts the other, talks across the other, or leaves words "hanging in the air."

As in the case of Goffman's work on civil inattention, it might easily be presumed that the analysis of ordinary conversations is at best rather marginal to the main concerns of sociology. Many sociologists have been severely critical of ethnomethodological research for just this reason. Yet some of the arguments given to show why Goffman's work is so important to sociology also apply to ethnomethodology. Studying everyday talk has shown how complicated is the mastery of language that ordinary people command. In addition, talk is an element of every realm of social life. The conversations recorded on the Watergate tapes of President Richard Nixon and his advisers, for instance, reveal various "dirty tricks" designed to adversely affect the 1972 Democratic campaign for the presidency, and were part of the exercise of political power at the highest levels (Molotch and Boden, 1985).

As a concrete example, however, we might take studies of gender differences in conversation. The ways in which women and men talk to one another in everyday conversations express—and help perpetuate—relations of inequality between the sexes. Don Zimmerman and Candace West (1975) recorded conversations in a number of informal settings, such as in drugstores, coffee shops, and cafés. They found that despite the popular belief that women talk all the time, men generally expect to "hold the floor." Men interrupt women far more than the reverse. Zimmerman and West also found that men interrupt women more than they do other men.

Zimmerman and West discovered similar imbalances in conversations between parents and children, with parents interrupting children much more often than the reverse. The person who interrupts, they concluded, is exercising power over the other, not only through the immediate act of assertion, but by channeling the conversation in a desired way.

RESPONSE CRIES

There are some kinds of utterances that are not talk, but consist of muttered exclamations, or what Goffman has called **response cries** (Goffman, 1981). As an example, consider when someone says "Oops!" after knocking over or dropping something. "Oops!" seems to be merely an uninteresting reflex response to a mishap, rather like blinking the eye when a person moves a hand sharply towards another's face. It is not, however, an involuntary response of this type at all, and lends itself to detailed analysis that illuminates general characteristics of our actions as human beings. That "Oops!" is not an involuntary reaction to misadventure is shown by the fact that people do not usually make the exclamation when alone. "Oops!" is normally directed towards *others* present on the scene—it is interactional rather than merely reactive. The exclamation demonstrates to those witnessing a mishap that the lapse is only minor and momentary, not something that should cast doubt upon the individual's command of his or her actions.

"Oops!" is only used in situations of minor failure, rather than in major accidents or calamities—which also demonstrates that the exclamation is part of our controlled management of the details of social life. Moreover, the exclamation may also be offered by someone observing the lapse, rather than the individual experiencing it. The "Oops!" may be used to sound a warning to another while at the same time conveying the assurance that the mishap is not being treated as indicating incompetence on the part of the person responsible for it. "Oops!" is normally a curt sound. But the "oo" in it may be prolonged in some situations. Thus someone might extend the sound to cover a part of a task in which a hazardous moment has to be overcome to be successful; or a parent may utter an extended "Oops!" or "Oopsadaisy!" when playfully tossing a child in the air. The sound covers the brief moment when the child may feel a loss of control, reassuring it, and probably at the same time developing its understanding of response cries.

This may all sound very contrived and exaggerated. Why bother to analyze such an inconsequential utterance in this detail? Surely we do not pay as much deliberate attention to all aspects of what we say, and how we act, as this example suggests? Of course we don't—on a conscious level. The crucial point, however, is that we *take for granted,* in ourselves and others, an immensely complicated, continuous control of our appearance and actions. Even in situations of unfocused interaction, we are never expected just to be "present" on the scene. Others expect, and we expect of others, the display of what Goffman calls "controlled alertness." A fundamental part of "being human" is continually demonstrating to others our competence and capability in the routines of daily life.

SLIPS OF THE TONGUE

"Oops" is a response to a minor bodily mishap. We all also make mistakes in speech and pronunciation in the courses of conversations, lectures, speeches, and other situations of talk. In his investigations into the "psychopathology of everyday life," Freud analyzed numerous examples of such lapses of the tongue (Freud, 1971). According to Freud, no mistakes in speaking, including mispronounced or misplaced words, momentary stammering or stuttering, are in fact accidental. All are symptoms of inner conflicts, associated with ways in which our unconscious influences what we consciously say and do. Slips of the tongue are unconsciously motivated—by motives or feelings that we feel on an unconscious level, but which are repressed from our conscious minds—or which we try consciously but unsuccessfully to suppress. These often, but by no means always, involve sexual associations. Thus a speaker may try to say "organism," but instead pronounces "orgasm." Or, in an example Freud gave, someone was asked, "What regiment is your son with?" She answered, "With the 42nd Murderers" (*Mörder* in German, rather than the word she intended to say, *Mörser,* "Mortars").

As in other cases of the misunderstanding of actions or talk, slips of the tongue are often humorous, and could pass as jokes. The difference lies simply in whether or not the speaker consciously intended the words to come out as they did. Slips of the tongue shade over into other types of "inappropriate" speech, which Freud also believed are often unconsciously motivated—as when a person fails to see that something he or she says has a clear double meaning. These again can be taken as jokes if deliberately intended—but are otherwise lapses in the controlled production of talk that we expect people to sustain.

One of the best ways of illustrating these points is to look at lapses in the talk of radio and TV announcers. Announcers' speech is not like ordinary day-to-day talk, because it is not spontaneous, but scripted. It is also expected to be more nearly "perfect" than ordinary talk—delivered with fewer hesitations and more clearly articulated. Hence, when announcers, such as newscasters, make "bloopers," they are much more visible and obvious than in casual conversations. Yet announcers do, of course, make slips of the tongue, and many are funny or have the "only too true" nature to which Freud called attention. Here are some examples of mispronunciations of this type (Goffman, 1981):

> In closing our TV Church of the Air, let me remind all of our listeners that time wounds all heals.

> This is the Dominion network of the Canadian Broad Corping Castration.

> Viceroys—if you want a good choke.

> Beat the egg yolk and then add the milk, then slowly blend in the sifted flour. As you do you can see how the mixture is sickening.

Other examples fall into the category of "inappropriate speech," where a double meaning unintentionally occurs:

> Ladies who care to drive by and drop off their clothes will receive prompt attention.

> Folks, try our comfortable beds. I personally stand behind every bed we sell.

> The loot and the car were listed as stolen by the Los Angeles Police Department.

> And here in Hollywood it is rumored that the former movie starlet is expecting her fifth child in a month.

We tend to laugh more at verbal mistakes when announcers (or professors in lectures) make them than in ordinary conversation. Broadcasters and professors are supposed to be specialists in the production of faultless talk. The humor does not only reside in what is said, or mis-said, but in the discomfiture that the person might show at delivering a less than perfect performance. We temporarily see behind the mask of cool professionalism to the "ordinary individual" behind.

FACE, BODY, AND SPEECH
IN INTERACTION

LET US SUMMARIZE AT THIS POINT WHERE WE HAVE GOTTEN to so far. Everyday interaction, we have emphasized, depends upon subtle relationships between what we convey with our faces and bodies and what we convey in words. We use the facial expressions and bodily gestures of others to expand upon what

Different modes of greeting have evolved across cultures. Americans are familiar with the handshake. More elaborate, though, is this highly stylized greeting of two Buddhist monks.

they communicate verbally, and to check how sincere they are in what they say. Mostly without realizing it, each of us keeps a tight and continuous control over facial expression, bodily posture and movement in the course of our daily interaction with others.

Sometimes, however, we make verbal slips which, as Freud's example of the "murderers" indicates, briefly reveal what—consciously or unconsciously—we wish to keep concealed. Lots of verbal slips have an "only too true" quality—like, "the mixture is sickening" in the example of the cake mix, which the announcer probably thinks is quite unappetizing. Verbal slips often inadvertently display our true feelings.

Face, bodily management, and speech, then, are used to convey certain meanings and to hide others. We also organize our activities in the *contexts* of social life to achieve the same ends—as we shall now go on to show.

ENCOUNTERS

In many situations of day-to-day social activity, we engage in what Goffman calls **unfocused interaction** with others. Unfocused interaction takes place whenever individuals in a given setting exhibit an overall mutual awareness of one another's presence. This is usually the case in any circumstance in which large numbers of people are assembled together, as on a busy street, in a theater crowd, or at a party. When individuals are in the presence of others, even if they do not directly talk to them, they continually engage in nonverbal communication. In their bodily appearance, movement, and position, facial and physical gestures, they convey certain impressions to others.

Focused interaction occurs when individuals directly attend to what each other says or does. Except when an individual is standing alone, say at a party, all interaction when individuals are co-present with one another involves both focused and unfocused exchanges. Goffman calls a unit of focused interaction an **encounter.** Much of our day-to-day life consists of continuous encounters with other individuals—family, friends, co-workers—frequently occurring against the background of unfocused interaction with others present on the scene. Small talk, formal discussion, games, and routine face-to-face contacts (with ticket clerks, waiters, sales people, and so forth) are all examples of encounters.

Encounters always need "openings," demonstrating the discarding of civil inattention. Where strangers meet and begin to talk—for example, at a party—the moment at which civil inattention shades over into focused interaction is always risky, since misunderstandings can easily occur about the nature of the encounter being established (Goffman, 1972). Hence, the joining of eye contact may first of all be ambiguous and tentative. A person can then act as though no direct move were intended if the overture is not accepted. In focused inter-

Inadvertently, Roy dooms the entire earth to annihilation when, in an attempt to be friendly, he seizes their leader by the head and shakes vigorously.

Cartoonist Gary Larson draws an extreme case of what often happens when a member of one culture fails to take account of the modes of interaction of another culture. With the globalization of business, international business consultants now offer courses on how to conduct oneself in another culture.

action, each individual communicates as much by facial expression and gesture as by the words actually exchanged. Goffman distinguishes in this context between the expressions individuals "give" and those they "give off." The first are the words and facial expressions by means of which people deliberately try to produce certain impressions upon others. The second concerns other, more subtle and unintentional cues that are in fact often used to check a person's sincerity or truthfulness. For instance, a restaurant owner listens with a polite smile to the statements by customers that they enjoyed the food they were served. At the same time, the owner would be noting how much enjoyment was displayed in the eating of the food, whether a lot was left over, as well as the tone of voice in which the customers expressed their satisfaction.

CONTEXTS AND LOCATIONS

Daily social life takes place as a series of encounters with others in varying contexts and locations. Most of us meet and talk to a variety of others in the course of the average day. A woman gets up, eats breakfast with her family, perhaps accompanies her children to school, stopping briefly to exchange pleasantries with a friend at the school gates. She drives to work, probably listening to the morning radio. During the course of the working day, she enters into many interchanges with colleagues and visitors, ranging from transitory conversations to more formal meetings. Each of these encounters is likely to be separated by "markers," or what Goffman calls *brackets,* which distinguish each episode of focused interaction from ones going before and from unfocused interaction going on in the background. The wave which the woman gives to her family when she drives off is one sort of marker; another is where she firmly shuts her office door to put an end to the persistent attempts of a colleague to waste her time chatting when she wants to get on with her work (Goffman, 1974).

Where others are close at hand in an open space, those holding a conversation will tend to position themselves and control their voice levels, so as to create a "huddle" separate from others. Their physical positioning marks them off from others present on the scene. They may stand facing one another, for example, effectively making it difficult for others to intrude until they decide to break up or "soften the edges" of their focused interaction by moving to different positions in the room. On more formal occasions, recognized cueing devices are often used as markers to signal the opening and ending of a particular encounter or phase of interaction. To signal the opening of a play, for instance, a bell rings, the lights go down and the curtain is raised. At the end of the act or performance the auditorium lights go on again as the curtain falls.

Markers are particularly important either when an encounter is especially divergent from the ordinary conventions of daily life or when there might be ambiguity about "what is going on." When models pose naked in front of art classes, they do not usually undress or dress in the presence of the group. Undressing and dressing in private mark the boundaries of the episode, and convey that it is devoid of the sexual meanings that otherwise might be involved.

In very confined spaces, such as in elevators, it is difficult or impossible to mark off a unit of focused interaction. Nor can others present easily display that they are "not listening" to—not a part of—whatever conversation is being carried on. It is also difficult for strangers to avoid being seen looking at others more directly than the norms of civil attention allow. Thus in elevators, people often adopt an exaggerated "not listening" and "not looking" pose, staring into space or at the elevator buttons—anywhere but at their fellow passengers! Conversation is usually suspended or kept confined to brief exchanges. Similarly, if several people are sitting talking to one another, and one is interrupted to take a phone call in the same room, the others cannot readily show complete inattention to what is being said, and may carry on a sort of hesitant, limp conversation (Goffman, 1963).

IMPRESSION MANAGEMENT

Goffman and other writers on social interaction often use notions from the theater in analyzing social interaction. The concept of **role,** widely used for this purpose (and also more generally in sociology), originated in a theatrical setting. Roles are socially defined expectations about behavior that a person in a given *status* or **social position** follows. A teacher's role, for example, consists of acting in specified ways towards students. In the theater-like or **dramaturgical model** that Goffman employs, social life is seen as though played out by actors on a stage—or on many stages, because how we act depends on the roles we are playing at a particular time. People are very sensitive to how they are seen by others and use many forms of *impression management* to ensure that others react to them in the ways they wish. This is sometimes done in a calculated fashion; an entire industry of political and media consultants now advises presidential candidates on how to dress, how to use "body language" and so on. For most though, impression management is among the many things we do without conscious attention. A person will dress and behave quite

During the early "cooling off" summit meetings, Soviet leader Mikhail Gorbachev and former president Ronald Reagan made every effort to portray appearances of ease and comfort despite a past history of U.S. and Soviet disagreement and distrust.

differently when attending a business meeting than when relaxing
with friends at a football game.

Front and Back Regions

Much of social life, Goffman suggests, can be divided up into **front
regions** and **back regions.** Front regions are social occasions or encounters in which individuals act out formal or stylized roles—these
are "on-stage performances." The back regions are where they assemble the props and prepare themselves for interaction in the more
formal setting. Back regions resemble the backstage of a theater, or
the off-camera activities of filming or TV productions. When they
are safely "behind the scenes," people relax and give vent to feelings
and styles of behavior they keep in check when "on front stage."
Thus a waitress may be the soul of quiet courtesy when serving a customer in the dining room of a restaurant, but may become loud and
aggressive once behind the swing-doors of the kitchen. There are
probably very few restaurants customers would like to eat in if they
were able to see all that goes on in the kitchens.

Back regions permit "profanity, open sexual remarks, elaborate
griping . . . rough informal dress, 'sloppy' sitting and standing posture, use of dialect or substandard speech, mumbling and shouting,
playful aggressivity and 'kidding,' inconsiderateness for the other in
minor but potentially symbolic acts, minor self-involvements such as
humming, whistling, chewing, nibbling, belching, and flatulence"
(Goffman, 1974).

Teamwork is often involved in creating and preserving front-
region performances. Thus, two prominent politicians in the same
political party might put on an elaborate show of unity and friendship before the television cameras, even though each detests the
other. A wife and husband may take care to conceal their quarrels
from the children, preserving a front of harmony, but fight bitterly
once the children are safely tucked away in bed.

Adopting Roles: Intimate Examinations

As an example of collaboration in "impression management," we
shall describe a particular study in some detail. James Henslin and
Mae Briggs (1971) studied a very specific, and highly delicate, type of
encounter—what happened when a woman visited a physician for a
gynecological examination. In the past, most pelvic examinations
were carried out by male doctors, and the experience was fraught
with potential ambiguities and embarrassment for both parties involved. Men and women in Western cultures are socialized to think
of the genitals as the most private part of the body. Seeing, and partic-

ularly feeling, the genitals of another person is ordinarily associated with intimate, sexual encounters. Many women are made so uneasy by pelvic examinations that they refuse to visit their doctors even when they suspect there are good reasons to do so.

Henslin and Briggs analyzed material from a large number of gynecological examinations, collected by Briggs who was a trained nurse. They interpreted what they found in terms of several phases that such encounters typically go through. Adopting the dramaturgical metaphor, they suggested that each phase can be treated as a distinct "scene," in which the parts the actors play alter as the episode unfolds. The "prologue" is when the woman enters the waiting room, preparing to assume the role of patient, temporarily discarding her outside identity. Called into the consulting office, she adopts the patient role and the first "scene" opens. The doctor takes up a businesslike, professional manner towards his patient, but treats her as a proper and competent person, maintaining eye contact and listening politely to what she has to say about her state of health. If he decides an examination is called for, he tells the patient so, and leaves the room; "scene one" is over.

As he leaves, the nurse comes in. She is an important "stagehand" in the "main scene" shortly to begin. She soothes any worries the patient might have, acting as both a confidant—as one who is familiar with the experience—and a collaborator in what is to follow. Crucially, the nurse helps alter the patient from a "person" to a "non-person" for the vital scene—a body to be scrutinized, rather than a complete human being. The nurse not only supervises the patient's undressing, but takes over aspects of behavior that normally the individual herself would control. Thus, she takes the patient's clothes and folds them. Most women wish their underwear to be out of sight when the doctor returns, and the nurse makes sure that this is so. She guides the patient to the examining table, and covers most of her body with a sheet before the physician comes back into the room.

The "central scene" now opens, with nurse as well as doctor present. The presence of the nurse helps ensure that the interaction between doctor and patient is free of sexual overtones, and also provides a legal witness should the physician be charged with unprofessional conduct. The examination proceeds as though the personality of the patient were absent—the sheet across her separates the genital area from the rest of the body, and her position does not allow her to see the procedures of the examination itself. Save for any specific medical queries, the doctor ignores her, sitting on a low stool, out of sight of her face. The patient collaborates in becoming a temporary "non-person," not initiating conversation and keeping any movements to a minimum.

In the "interval" between this and the "final scene," the nurse

again plays the role of stagehand, helping the patient to become a
"full person" once more. At this juncture, the two may again engage
in conversation, the patient expressing relief that the examination is
over. Having dressed and re-groomed herself, the patient is ready to
face the "concluding scene." The doctor re-enters, and in recounting
the results of the examination again treats the patient as a complete
and responsible person. Resuming his polite, professional manner, he
conveys that his reactions to her are in no way altered by the intimate
contact with her body that he has been permitted. The "epilogue" is
played out when she leaves the physician's office, taking up again her
identity in the outside world.

A medical examination such as this suspends some of the norms
that usually govern our interaction with one another. Ordinarily, we
preserve social distance through ensuring that the physical spacing of
encounters is carefully controlled. The maintenance of "personal
space" is an important aspect of how we interact on a face-to-face
level, and is to some extent culturally variable.

ENCOUNTERS AND PERSONAL SPACE

In Western culture, on most occasions, people maintain a personal
distance of at least three feet when engaged in focused interaction
with others. When standing side by side, even if not within the same
encounter, they may stand more closely together. There are cultural
differences in the definition of **personal space.** In the Middle East,
for example, people often stand closer to one another than is thought
acceptable in the West. Westerners visiting that part of the world are
likely to find themselves disconcerted by this unexpected physical
proximity.

Edward T. Hall, who has worked extensively on nonverbal communication, distinguishes four zones of private space. *Intimate distance,* of up to one-and-a-half feet, is reserved for very few social
contacts. Only those involved in relationships in which regular bodily touching is permitted—such as parents and children, or lovers—
operate within this zone of private space. *Personal distance* (from
one-and-a-half to four feet) is the normal spacing for encounters with
friends and reasonably close acquaintances. Some intimacy of contact
is permitted, but this tends to be strictly limited. *Social distance,* from
four feet to twelve feet, is the zone usually maintained in formal settings of interaction, as in interviews. The fourth zone is that of *public
distance,* of beyond twelve feet, preserved by those who are perform-
ing to a watching audience.

In day-to-day interaction, the most tensional zones are those of
intimate and personal distance. If these spaces are "invaded," people

Humans, as well as several species of animals, tend to maintain a certain distance to preserve some personal space.

try to recapture their space. A stare might convey to the other "move away!" or the individual might elbow the intruder aside. In cases where people are forced into proximity closer than they deem desirable, some kind of physical boundary might be established, as when a reader at a crowded library desk physically demarcates a private space by stacking books around its edges (Hall, 1973, 1969).

INTERACTION IN TIME AND SPACE

SEEING HOW ACTIVITIES ARE DISTRIBUTED IN SPACE—AND time as well—is fundamental to analyzing encounters, and also to understanding basic aspects of social life in general. All interaction, of course, is *situated*—it occurs in a particular place and has a specific duration in time. Our actions over the course of a day tend to be "zoned" in time as well as in space. Thus, for example, people who go out to work spend a "zone"—say, from 9 A.M. to 5 P.M.—of their daily time working. Their weekly time is also zoned: they are likely to work on weekdays and spend weekends at home, altering the pattern of their activities on the weekend days. Time spent at work normally means spatial movement as well; a person journeying between home and work may take a bus from one area of the city to another, for example, or perhaps commute in to the city from the suburbs. When we analyze the contexts in which social interaction goes on, therefore, it is often useful to analyze people's movements across *time-space*. As we move through the temporal zones of the day, we are also often moving across space as well.

Social geographers have introduced the notion of **time-space convergence** to analyze how social development and technological change affect patterns of social activity. Time-space convergence refers to the way in which, with improved transportation systems, distances "shrink." Thus the time taken to travel from the east to the west coast of the United States can be calculated in terms of advances in transportation methods. On foot, the journey takes more than two years; on horseback, eight months; by stagecoach, four months; by rail in 1910, four days; non-stop driving by car today, two-and-a-half days; by regular air services, five hours; by the fastest available jet transport, just over two hours; by space shuttle, a few minutes (Janelle, 1968; Carlstein, Parkes, and Thrift, 1978). Modes of social life become radically reorganized with increasing time-space convergence, affecting the lives of all of us. Many of the goods we use and much of the food we eat, for instance, are transported over large distances, even from the other side of the world. This has helped to produce much greater global economic interdependence—the need of people in each country to import goods from others—in present times than was ever the case before. (See Chapter 16: "The Globalizing of Social Life.")

We can understand how social activities are organized in time and space by means of the concept of **regionalization,** which refers to how social life is organized in time and space. Take the example of a private house. A modern house is regionalized into rooms, hallways, and floors if there is more than one story. These various spaces of the house are not just physically separate areas, but are distinct in time as well as space. The living room and kitchen are used most in the daylight hours, the bedrooms at night. The interaction that occurs in these various "regions" is bounded by both spatial and temporal divisions. Some areas of the house form back regions, with "performances" being put on in the others. The whole house, at a given period of the week, can become a back region, as can paths across time and space traced outside. Once again these matters are beautifully captured by Goffman:

Of a Sunday morning, a whole household can use the wall around its domestic establishment to conceal a relaxing slovenliness in dress and civil endeavor, extending to all rooms the informality that is usually restricted to kitchen and bedrooms. So, too, in American middle-class neighborhoods, on afternoons the line between children's playground and home may be defined as backstage by mothers, who pass along it wearing jeans, loafers, and a minimum of make-up. . . . And, of course, a region that is thoroughly established as a front region for the regular performance of a particular routine often functions as a back region before and after each performance, for at these times the permanent fixtures may undergo repairs, restoration, and rearrangement, or the performers may hold dress rehearsals. To see this we need only glance into a restaurant, or store, or home, a few minutes before these establishments are opened to us for the day. (Goffman, 1974)

CLOCK TIME

Monasteries were the first organizations to try to schedule the activities of their inmates in a precise manner across the day and week, a practice originating as early as the fourteenth century. Today there is virtually no group or organization that does not do so—the greater the number of people and resources involved, the more precise the scheduling has to be. Eviatar Zerubavel (1979) demonstrated this in his study of the temporal structure of a large modern hospital. A hospital has to operate on a twenty-four-hour basis, and coordinating the staff and resources is a highly complex matter. For instance, the majority of nurses work for set periods on different wards, moving around the different sectors of the hospital, and they are also called upon to alternate between day and night shift work. All these individuals, and the resources they need, have to be integrated together both in time and in space.

In modern societies, the zoning of our activities is very strongly influenced by the experience of clocks and **clock time.** Without clocks, and the precise timing of activities—and thereby their coordination across space—industrialized societies could not exist (Wright, 1968; Mumford, 1973). The measuring of time by clocks today is standardized across the globe, making possible the complex international transportation and communications systems upon which our lives now depend. But it was not always this way. World standard time was not introduced until 1884, at a conference of nations held in

Washington, D.C. The globe was partitioned into twenty-four time zones, each one hour apart, and an exact beginning of the universal day was fixed (Zerubavel, 1982). This was a landmark of sorts for the globalization of social and economic life.

TIME GEOGRAPHY

The Swedish social geographer Torsten Hägerstrand has analyzed activities across time and space by using an approach called **time geography** (Hägerstrand, 1973; Carlstein, Parkes, and Thrift, 1978). Dealing with movements in time-space, the time-geographic approach looks at the physical environment (streets, buildings, roads, neighborhoods) in which social activities are carried on and traces how this influences—and is influenced by—the daily and weekly movements of individuals and groups. We can map the daily paths that individuals trace—what people do, at which parts of the day, and where—in the course of a typical day or a typical week.

Two individuals, let us say A and B, live in different neighborhoods in a city. Their time-space paths across the course of the day bring them into contact with one another at point X for a certain duration—perhaps they meet in a coffee shop or restaurant and share a conversation—after which their paths diverge as each moves off to other activities in separate places. By recording the typical daily activities of individuals or groups, it is quite easy to construct a "time-space picture" of their lives. In this way, we can portray the mosaic of activities in time and space that compose the life of urban neighborhoods and communities.

TIME-SPACE CONSTRAINTS

We can understand some of the factors influencing the patterning of urban life by identifying simple, yet basic, characteristics of human activity that affect how time-space is organized. Three kinds of constraints set limits on how day-to-day activities unfold in terms of their location in time and space.

1. *Capability constraints* are limits set by the physical constitution of individuals. For instance, all human beings have needs for food and sleep, which have to be catered for in the time-space ordering of their activities. Those who work in one area have to be transported, or transport themselves, back to their homes in which they prepare their food and rest for the night.

2. *Coupling constraints* are limits set by the capabilities of people to come together in particular places to interact with one another. Where (as in cluttered traditional cities) there are few roadways providing easy access from one area to another, most forms of interaction are necessarily confined to distances that can easily be covered on foot. Moreover, all physical settings have what Hägerstrand calls a "packing capacity"—a limit to the numbers of persons who can occupy a particular space for the purposes of a given type of activity. The rush hour in a modern city is a graphic example of this. There are strict limits to the volume of traffic that streets can carry; at peak times, no one in fact gets anywhere in a "rush" but usually at a slow crawl.

3. *Authority constraints* concern limits set by the system of power in a community or broader society. How much power people have to live where they want, for example, is limited by their financial resources. Most people might want to live in neighborhoods having elegant and luxurious homes, but only relatively few have the resources to do so. Zoning regulations also often limit the types of dwellings that can be constructed in different areas.

APPLYING A TIME-SPACE APPROACH

As an illustration of how these concepts help inform actual research, we can take a study conducted from a time-geographic perspective in the city of Newcastle, in New South Wales, Australia. The research project investigated some of the problems involved in setting up a new community health-care center, located in a socially mixed area about fourteen miles from the middle of the city. When the center was first established, those running it did not realize that many people in the area to which it catered were on shift work. Far more clients than had been anticipated needed to come into the center either before 7 A.M. or after 5 P.M. At the same time, most of the clientele also assumed the center would be open, and its facilities available, during normal hours.

The center thus faced severe capacity and coupling problems. It was difficult to find staff who would work outside the usual hours; those who were willing to do so could not necessarily get transportation into the area at the required times from the neighborhoods where they lived. Acute crowding difficulties were faced in the scheduling of the center's services. Some periods of the day were quite slack, with little for the staff to do, while at other times—particularly towards the end of the day and right at the end of the week —the center would be too jammed with people to cope. By studying the time-space paths of a number of workers and clients at the center, the researchers could pinpoint the origins of these problems. They were also able to suggest positive steps that could be taken to alleviate them by means of the more systematic allocation of resources (Parkes and Thrift, 1980).

ZONING

The distribution of activities in time-space over the past century or so —particularly in quite recent times—has been influenced by what has been called the *colonization of time*. Processes of spatial migration to, and within, cities have been accompanied by a "migration" into the time zones of evening and night. As Murray Melbin observes:

> The last great frontier of human immigration is occurring in time: a spreading of wakeful activity throughout the twenty-four hours of the day. There is more multiple-shift factory work, more police coverage, more use of the telephone at all hours. There are more hospitals, pharmacies, airplane flights, hostels, always-open restaurants, car rental, and gasoline and auto repair stations, bowling alleys, and radio stations always active. There are more emergency services such as auto-touring, locksmiths, bail bondsmen, drug and poison and suicide and gambling "hot lines" available incessantly. Although different individuals participate in these events in shifts, the organizations involved are continually active. (Melbin, 1978)

Melbin (1987) estimates that after midnight in the United States there are some 30 million people active, excluding those getting ready to go to sleep. Even during the "depths of the night"—3 A.M. to 5 A.M.—well over 10 million people are up and about. On a global level, this migration into the night occurs in nations across the world, particularly among workers in one country (time zone) who monitor what is occurring in another. In order to keep a close watch on the world stock exchanges and money markets, stockbrokers and other financial managers are among the "migrators into the night."

These changes, of course, always have spatial implications and are affected by the various types of constraint influencing time-space zoning. The nighttime activities of one area demand corresponding processes in the daytime in other regions. For instance, a plane that travels overnight might arrive very early in the morning at the place of its destination, requiring the mobilizing of airport facilities and transport links. The organizations that cater to the increased level of activity in evening and nighttime hours face the sort of coupling constraints mentioned in the research on the Newcastle community health-care center.

EVERYDAY LIFE IN CULTURAL AND HISTORICAL PERSPECTIVE

SOME OF THE MECHANISMS OF SOCIAL INTERACTION ANAlyzed by Goffman, Garfinkel, and others seem to be universal; but many are not. "Markers" that signal the opening and closing of encounters, for example, are no doubt characteristic of human interaction everywhere. Various means used to organize encounters are also found in all gatherings of human beings—such as keeping the body turned away from others when forming a conversational "knot." Yet in many respects our day-to-day lives in modern societies are very different from those of people in other cultures. For instance, some aspects of civil inattention are irrelevant to the behavior of members of very small societies where there are no strangers and few, if any, settings in which more than a handful of people are present together at any one time. Much of Goffman's discussion of civil inattention, and other aspects of interaction, primarily concerns societies in which contact with strangers is commonplace.

Our day-to-day lives have been shaped in fundamental ways by the changes associated with industrialism, urbanism, and the development of modern states. An example will help to demonstrate some of the contrasts between social interaction in modern and traditional societies. One of the least technologically developed cultures remaining in the world is that of the !Kung* (also sometimes known as the Bushmen), who live in the Kalahari desert area of Botswana and Namibia, in southern Africa (Lee, 1968, 1969). Their way of life is changing now because of the impact of outside influences, but we shall concentrate upon their traditional patterns.

The !Kung live in groups of some thirty or forty people in temporary settlements near to waterholes. Food is a scarce resource in their environment, and they must walk far and wide to find it. Such roaming takes up most of the average day. Women and children often stay

---

* The exclamation mark refers to a click sound made before the name is pronounced.

The !Kung can construct their temporary huts in a matter of hours; when food supplies run out the !Kung move on to new settlements. Societies today have organized their "settlements" differently to deal with the time-space constraints of everyday life.

back in the camp, but equally often the whole group may spend the day walking. Members of the community will sometimes fan out over an area of up to 100 square miles in the course of a day, returning to the camp at night to eat and sleep. The men in particular may be alone, or in twos and threes, for much of the day. There is one period of the year, however, when the routines of their daily activities change. This is during the winter rainy season, when water is abundant and food much easier to come by. The everyday life of the !Kung during this period is centered around ritual and ceremonial activities, preparation for and enactment of which is very time-consuming.

The members of most !Kung groups never see anyone they do not know reasonably well. Until contacts with the outside became more common over recent years, they had no word for "stranger," making the idea of civil inattention irrelevant. While the !Kung, particularly the males, may spend long periods of the day out of contact with others, in the community itself there is little or no opportunity for privacy. Families sleep in flimsy, open dwellings, with virtually all activities open to public view. No one has studied the !Kung with Goffman's observations on everyday life in mind, but it is easy to see that some aspects of his work have limited application to !Kung social life. There are few opportunities, for example, to create front and back regions. The "closing off" of different gatherings and encounters by the walls of rooms, separate buildings of many kinds, and into the different neighborhoods of cities are aspects of daily life in modern societies that are remote from the everyday activities of the !Kung.

Tommy Carlstein (1982) has analyzed aspects of !Kung social life using the concepts of time-geography. Like all hunters and gatherers, he argues, the !Kung face a "time-space" conflict between food storage and social movement that affects the nature of their day-to-day lives. The more food they try to store, to protect against lean times, the more they are pinned down in one place. But if they should concentrate their activities in a fixed settlement, their sources of food supply would become limited, because they would not be able to travel far enough afield to collect the food they need in the first place. The !Kung cope with this dilemma in precisely the way that gives their mode of life the shape it has. They possess settlements, but only live in them irregularly, moving camp as a whole when necessary.

MICROSOCIOLOGY AND MACROSOCIOLOGY

THE STUDY OF EVERYDAY BEHAVIOR IN SITUATIONS OF face-to-face interaction is usually called **microsociology. Macrosociology** is the analysis of large-scale social systems, such as the political system or the economic order. Macrosociology also includes the analysis of long-term processes of change—such as the development of industrialism. At first sight it might seem as though micro and macro analysis are quite distinct from one another. In fact the two are closely connected (Knorr-Cetina and Cicourel, 1981; Giddens, 1985), as we have tried to demonstrate throughout this chapter.

Macro analysis is essential if we are to understand the institutional background of daily life. The ways in which people live their everyday lives are greatly affected by the broader institutional framework within which they exist, as is obvious when the daily cycle of activities of a culture like that of the !Kung is compared to life in an industrialized urban environment. In modern societies, as has been pointed out, we are constantly in contact with strangers. Indeed, the term "stranger" has lost the significance it once had. A stranger was literally a "strange person" who came from "outside." Individuals who live in an urban area today constantly meet others not known to them personally. In these circumstances, the boundaries between unfocused and focused interaction are crossed much more often. The city dweller constantly has to open and break off interaction with others he or she has not previously met.

Micro studies are in their turn necessary for illuminating broad institutional patterns. Face-to-face interaction is clearly the main basis of all forms of social organization, no matter how large scale. Suppose we are studying a business corporation. Many of the activities of the corporation could be discovered simply by looking at face-to-face behavior. We could analyze, for example, the interaction of directors in the boardroom, people working in the various offices, or the workers on the shop floor. We would not build up a picture of the whole corporation this way, since many of its activities do not place people in face-to-face contact. Through printed materials, letters, the telephone, and computers, many connections transcend the immediacies of personal interaction. Yet we could certainly contribute significantly to understanding how the organization works.

In later chapters, we will meet with many further examples of how interaction in micro contexts affects larger social processes, and how such processes in turn influence more confined settings of social life.

SUMMARY

1. Many apparently trivial aspects of our day-to-day behavior turn out on close examination to be both complex and important aspects of social interaction. An example is the gaze—looking at other people. In most interaction, eye contact is fairly fleeting. To stare at another person could be taken as a sign of hostility—or on some occasions, of love. The study of social interaction is a fundamental area in sociology, illuminating many aspects of social life.

2. Many different expressions are conveyed by the human face. It is widely held that basic aspects of the facial expressions of emotion are innate. Cross-cultural studies demonstrate quite close similarities between members of different cultures both in facial expression and in the interpretation of emotions registered on the human face.

3. "Face" can also be understood in a broader sense to refer to the esteem in which an individual is held by others. Generally, in our interaction with other people, we are concerned with "saving face"—protecting our self-esteem.

4. The study of ordinary *talk* and *conversation* has come to be called *ethnomethodology*, a term first coined by Harold Garfinkel. Ethnomethodology is the analysis of the ways in which we actively —although usually in a taken-for-granted way—make sense of what others mean by what they say and do.

5. We can learn a great deal about the nature of talk by studying "response cries" (exclamations) and slips of the tongue (what happens when people mispronounce or misapply words and phrases). Slips of the tongue are often humorous and are in fact closely connected psychologically to wit and joking.

6. *Unfocused interaction* is the mutual awareness individuals have of one another in large gatherings when not directly in conversation together. *Focused interaction,* which can be divided up into distinct *encounters* or episodes of interaction, is when two or more individuals are directly attending to what the other or others are saying and doing.

7. Social interaction can often be illuminatingly studied by applying the *dramaturgical model*—studying social interaction as if those involved were actors on a stage, having a set and props. As in the theater, in the various contexts of social life there tend to be clear distinctions between *front regions* (the stage itself) and *back regions,* where the actors prepare themselves for the performance and relax afterwards.

8. All social interaction is situated in time and space. We can analyze how our daily lives are "zoned" in time and space combined by looking at how activities occur during definite durations and at the same time involve spatial movement. *Time-geography* provides one means of documenting this.

9. The study of face-to-face interaction is usually called *microsociology*—as contrasted to *macrosociology,* which studies larger groups, institutions, and social systems. Micro and macro analysis are in fact very closely related and each complements the other.

BASIC CONCEPTS

ENCOUNTER
ROLE
SOCIAL POSITION

IMPORTANT TERMS

CIVIL INATTENTION	FRONT REGION
NONVERBAL COMMUNICATION	BACK REGION
TALK	PERSONAL SPACE
CONVERSATION	TIME-SPACE CONVERGENCE
ETHNOMETHODOLOGY	REGIONALIZATION
RESPONSE CRIES	CLOCK TIME
UNFOCUSED INTERACTION	TIME GEOGRAPHY
FOCUSED INTERACTION	MICROSOCIOLOGY
DRAMATURGICAL MODEL	MACROSOCIOLOGY

DEVIANCE

AS WE HAVE SEEN FROM PREVIOUS CHAPTERS, HUMAN SOCIAL
life is governed by norms or rules. Our activities would
collapse into chaos if we did not stick to rules that define
some kinds of behavior as appropriate in given contexts
and others as inappropriate. Orderly behavior on the
highway, for example, would be impossible if drivers did
not observe the rule of driving on the right side of the
road and other traffic conventions. The norms we follow
in our actions give the social world its orderly and predictable character. A great deal of sociology is concerned
with showing how social order is achieved. But there is another side
to the story. Not everyone conforms to social expectations all of the
time. Drivers sometimes disregard the rules of traffic behavior, even
if the lives of others are thereby endangered. When in a great hurry,
or under the influence of drink, a person might drive recklessly, perhaps even taking a short cut up a one-way street. People quite often
deviate from the rules they are expected to follow.

The study of deviant behavior is one of the most fascinating tasks
of sociology. It is a complex area of analysis because there are as many
types of rule-violation as there are social norms and rules. Since
norms vary between different cultures, and between differing subcul-

tures within the same society, what is normal in one cultural setting is deviant in another. Smoking marijuana is a deviant activity in American culture while drinking alcohol is not. Exactly the reverse is the case in some Middle Eastern societies.

WHAT IS DEVIANCE?

DEVIANT BEHAVIOR MAY BE DEFINED AS NONCONFORMITY to a given norm or set of norms that are accepted by a significant number of people in a community or society. No society can be simply divided between those who **deviate** from norms and those who **conform** to them. Most of us on some occasions transgress generally accepted rules of behavior. Many people have at some point committed minor acts of theft, like taking something from a store without paying for it, or appropriating small items from work—such as office stationery—and putting them to private use. Large numbers of individuals have smoked marijuana, purchased alcohol while under age, used illegal drugs, or taken part in prohibited sexual practices.

The scope of the concept of deviance is very wide. Some examples will help make this clear. The legendary billionaire Howard Hughes was a highly successful businessman who built up his massive fortune through a mixture of hard work, inventive ideas, and shrewd decisions. His drive to individual success and his activities in business conformed to some of the key values in American society—values emphasizing the desirability of material rewards and individual achievement. On the other hand, in some areas his behavior deviated psychologically from the norm:

> During at least the last half of his life, Hughes was apparently afflicted with a severe obsessive-compulsive disorder about infection. He lived as a recluse, but unlike most obsessives, he was rich enough to be able to hire a retinue of servants to carry out his rituals for him, rather than doing them himself. Hughes's fear of germs and contamination dominated his life. He wrote numerous memos in which he explained in detail what he wanted done to prevent the "back transmission" of germs to him. For example, in a three-page memo, he explained how he wanted a can of fruit opened to prevent "fallout" of germs. He required that special equipment be used to open the can, writing, "The equipment used in connection with this operation will consist of the follow-

ing items: 1 unopened newspaper, 1 sterile can opener; 1 large sterile plate; 1 sterile fork; 1 sterile spoon; 2 sterile brushes; 2 bars of soap; sterile paper towels." The ritual he devised for opening the can had nine steps: "preparing a table, procuring of fruit can, washing of can, drying the can, processing the hands, opening the can, removing fruit from can, fallout rules while around can, and conclusion of operation." (Barlett and Steele, 1981)

Hughes was both highly successful and highly deviant in his behavior. As a contrasting example, we might take the career of Ted Bundy, whose way of life, on the surface, conformed to the norms of behavior of a good citizen. Bundy not only led what seemed to be a normal life, but a most worthy one. He took part in various civic groups and community activities. For example, he played an active role in the Samaritans, an association that organizes a twenty-four-hour call-in service for people who are distressed or suicidal. Yet Bundy had another side to him that resulted in his being executed in the electric chair on January 24th, 1989, for a series of brutal murders of young women. Before sentencing him to death, the judge commented on Bundy's abilities (he had prepared much of his own defense), but finished by noting what a waste Bundy had made of his life. Bundy's career illustrates that a person can seem entirely normal, but secretly engage in extreme acts of criminal deviance.

Deviance does not just refer to the psychological or criminal behavior of individuals, but concerns the social activities of groups as well. An illustration is the Hare Krishna cult, a religious group whose beliefs and way of life are quite different from those of most people living in the United States. The cult was established in New York in 1965, when Sril Prabhupada came from India to spread the word of Krishna consciousness to the West. He aimed his message particularly at young people who were drug-users, proclaiming that one could "stay high all the time, discover eternal bliss," by following his teachings (Rockford, 1985). The Hare Krishnas became a familiar sight to many, dancing and chanting in the streets. They were regarded tolerantly by most of the population, even if their beliefs seemed eccentric.

The Hare Krishnas represent an example of a **deviant subculture.** Although their membership today has declined, they have been able to survive fairly easily within the wider society. The organization is a wealthy one, financed by donations given by members and sympathizers. Their position differs from that of another socially deviant subculture that might be mentioned here by way of contrast: the homeless. People who are down-and-out live on the streets by day, spending their time in parks or in public buildings. They may sleep

Billionaire Howard Hughes for many years was outwardly a normal successful American businessman.

People who find themselves homeless have to live on the margins of ordinary society.

outside as well, or find refuge in public shelters. Many of the homeless manage to eke out only a miserable existence on the fringes of the wider society.

NORMS AND SANCTIONS

WE MOST OFTEN FOLLOW SOCIAL RULES OR NORMS BEcause, as a result of socialization, it has become habitual for us to do so. Take, for example, the rules of usage involved in the language we speak. Using language means knowing a variety of rules of grammar and speech. Most of the time, we simply use these without having to give them any thought, since we learned them in early childhood. It is only when we try later to master a foreign language that we recognize how many rules have to be learned even to be able to speak simple sentences correctly. The norms governing interaction in social encounters, discussed by Goffman (see Chapter 4: "Social Interaction in Everyday Life") provide another illustration. Maintaining attitudes of civil inattention towards strangers, using tact in our conversations with friends, or following the procedures establishing "markers" between encounters—all these we usually do without even realizing that distinct rules of procedure are involved.

We follow other types of norms more in the belief that the behavior they entail is justified. This is true, for instance, of the norms of traffic behavior mentioned earlier. Drivers accept that they have to observe rules like driving on the right side of the road or stopping when the traffic light is red. Most of us are aware that if the majority of drivers did not abide by such rules most of the time, the roads would become vastly more dangerous than they are even at present.

There is less agreement regarding some other aspects of road behavior—like speed limits. No doubt the majority of drivers accept that speed limits of some type are necessary to protect each other, bicyclists, and pedestrians. But few motorists rigorously respect speed limits. They are likely to drive within those limits only if they know or suspect that there is a police car or helicopter in the vicinity. But once they are confident that there are no police to catch them, many drivers will speed up to well beyond the legal maximum.

This example directs our attention towards some very important aspects of conformity and deviance. All social norms involve **sanctions** that protect against **nonconformity.** A sanction is any reaction from others to the behavior of an individual or group, which has the aim of ensuring that a given norm is complied with. Sanctions may be positive (the offering of rewards for conformity) or negative (punishment for behavior that does not conform). They can also be formal or informal. Formal sanctions exist when there is a definite body of people or an agency whose task it is to ensure that a particular set of norms is followed. Informal sanctions are less organized, and more spontaneous, reactions to nonconformity.

The main types of formal sanction in modern societies are those used in the system of punishment administered by the courts and prisons. The police, of course, are the agency charged with bringing offenders to face trial and possible imprisonment. Most motoring offenses are punished with fines or loss of license, but these are sufficient to ensure that drivers who knowingly depart from the traffic regulations keep a watchful eye open for the police. Fines, imprisonment, or execution, are all cases of formal negative sanctions. There are not many formal positive sanctions to reward traffic behavior—although sometimes "road proficiency" or "good driving awards" are offered to stimulate observance of the rules of the road. Formal positive sanctions are found in many other areas of social life, however—for instance, the presentation of medals for bravery in combat, degrees or diplomas to mark academic success, or awards for performances in sports events.

Informal sanctions, positive and negative, are commonplace features of all contexts of social activity. Those of a positive type include saying "well done" to someone, or giving the person an appreciative smile or a pat on the back. Examples of negative informal sanctions are speaking insultingly to, scolding, or physically shunning a given individual. Although formal sanctions are usually more dramatic and visible than informal ones, informal sanctions are of fundamental importance in ensuring conformity to norms. Wanting to secure the approval of family, friends, and colleagues, or wishing to avoid being ridiculed, shamed, or rejected, often influences behavior more than formal rewards or punishments.

LAWS, CRIMES, AND PUNISHMENT

LAWS ARE NORMS DEFINED BY GOVERNMENTS AS PRINCIPLES that their citizens must follow, and formal sanctions are used by those authorities against people who do not conform to them. Where there are **laws,** there are also **crimes,** which can most simply be defined as any mode of behavior that breaks a law. What society regards as criminal behavior, the relative seriousness of different crimes, and the ways in which criminal activities are punished by government authorities has changed significantly over the past two or three centuries. As was mentioned in Chapter 1 ("Sociology: Problems and Perspectives"), the reasons for this can be traced to the replacement of traditional societies, based upon the local village community, by industrialized social systems, in which most people live in the more anonymous locations of towns and cities.

CRIMES IN PREMODERN TIMES

In preindustrial Europe, the most serious crimes, which received the highest penalties, were religious in nature, or were crimes against the property of the ruler or the aristocracy. These transgressions are either not treated as crimes at all today, or are thought of as minor offenses. Heresy (proclaiming religious doctrines other than those of Christianity), sacrilege (stealing or damaging church property), and even blasphemy (taking God's name in vain, or speaking negatively about religious matters) were for a long time punishable by death in many parts of Europe. Hunting or fishing, cutting down trees or bushes, or picking fruit on the lands of the king or aristocracy by the common people were also capital offenses (although the death penalty was not always actually enforced).

This sketch depicts a Church tribunal attempting to get a confession out of someone accused of heresy during the fifteenth century.

The murder of one commoner by another was not generally seen to be as serious as these other crimes. The culprit often could atone for the crime simply by paying a certain amount of money to the relatives of the victim. However, the victim's family would sometimes take justice into their own hands and put the murderer to death. One problem with this mode of punishment was that the family of the original killer might then respond in kind, leading to a pattern of multiple killings—often known as the *blood feud.* In a few areas, like southern Italy, the practice of the blood feud persisted into the twentieth century (and is still used as a mode of dispensing "justice" between rival "crime families" in the United States today).

CHANGES IN MODES OF PUNISHMENT

Before the early nineteenth century, imprisonment was rarely used to punish crime, either in Europe or the United States. Most towns of any size had a local jail, but these were normally very small, and were not capable of holding more than three or four prisoners at any one time. They were used to cool off drunks for the night, or occasionally as places where accused persons awaited trial. In the bigger European cities there were prisons of some size; most of the people interned in these were convicted criminals awaiting execution. These institutions were very different from the prisons that were built in great numbers after the turn of the nineteenth century. Prison discipline was lax or nonexistent. Sometimes those who were to be executed were plunged into dungeons and saw only the jailor before being taken to execution, but more often, the prison atmosphere was amazingly free and easy by modern standards.

Justin Atholl, a historian of crime, has described life in Newgate, one of the early London prisons. It was a bustling, lively place, full of visitors at most times of the day. In 1790, one of the condemned men held a ball at the prison, apparently not an uncommon event:

> Tea was served at 4 P.M. to the music of violins and flutes, after which the company danced until 8 P.M. when a cold supper was produced. The party broke up at 9 o'clock, the usual hour for closing the prison. (Atholl, 1954)

The main forms of punishment for crime until the nineteenth century were putting people in the stocks, whipping, branding with hot irons, or hanging. These were usually carried out publicly and were well attended. Some executions attracted thousands of people. Those about to be hanged would quite often make speeches, justifying their actions or proclaiming themselves innocent. The crowd would cheer, or boo and hiss, according to their assessment of the accused's claims.

Prisons and Asylums

Modern prisons have their origins, not in the jails and dungeons of former times, but in workhouses (also often referred to as "hospitals"). Workhouses date from the seventeenth century in most European countries, being established during the period when feudalism was breaking down and many peasant workers, who could no longer get work on the land, became vagrants. In the workhouses, they were provided with food, but were forced to spend most of their time in the institution, and had to undertake backbreaking hours of hard labor. The workhouses also, however, became places in which other groups were interned if no one was prepared to care for them outside: the sick, aged, feeble-minded, and mentally ill.

As late as 1785 it was written that the Bicêtre, one of the main Paris "hospitals,"

> "... shuts away poor people, who are admitted free, other poor paying for their board ... men and children who are epileptic, scrofulous, paralyzed, or insane, and men shut away by royal order. ... Children arrested by order of the police, or convicted for theft or an offense, children without

any vice or sickness who are admitted free; finally, men and women being treated for venereal disease." (Quoted in Castel, 1988)

The establishment was simultaneously a medical hospital, asylum, boarding house, and prison.

During the eighteenth century, prisons, asylums, and hospitals gradually became distinct from one another (Ignatieff, 1978; Doerner, 1984; McConville, 1981). Reformers objected to the physical hurt involved in traditional punishments, seeing deprivation of liberty as a more effective way of coping with criminal activities. As rights of individual freedom developed within the wider political system, murder became recognized as the most serious crime, for to kill another person was the ultimate attack upon that individual's rights. Since prisons were supposed to have the effect of training criminals in sober habits of discipline and conformity, the idea of punishing people in public progressively dropped away. Executions, for example, were hidden from public view, rather than put on public display.

The behavior of the mad increasingly came to be seen as evidence of a type of sickness; the concept of **mental illness** first made its appearance in the late eighteenth century (Scull, 1979), and was firmly established in the nineteenth century. Madness became *medicalized*— taken over by the medical profession. Since insanity was henceforth recognized as a disease (rather than a variant of feeble-mindedness or as possession of the mind by demons), it was regarded as something that only doctors were qualified to treat. People could still be placed in asylums against their will, but a doctor's certificate was needed to do so.

A typical cell in one of today's state prisons.

EXPLAINING DEVIANCE

THE NATURE AND CONTENT OF DEVIANT BEHAVIOR VARY widely both from the past to the present and from one society to another. This is something we must seek to explain. In the following sections, we shall discuss some of the leading theories of deviance, giving particular attention to biological, psychological, and sociological theories of crime. None of the theories provides a comprehensive explanation of crime as a whole, let alone all deviance. But they overlap in some ways and can be combined together in others to provide a reasonable understanding of major aspects of deviant behavior.

THE ARGUMENT FROM BIOLOGY

Some of the first attempts to explain crime and other forms of deviance were essentially biological in character. Paul Broca, an early French anthropologist, claimed to discern peculiarities in the skulls and brains of criminals that distinguished them from the law-abiding population. The Italian criminologist Cesare Lombroso, working in the 1870s, claimed that certain people were born with innate criminal tendencies, throw-backs to a more primitive type of human being (Lombroso, 1911). Criminal types, he believed, could be identified by the shape of the skull. He accepted that social learning could influence the development of criminal behavior, but regarded most criminals as biologically degenerate or defective.

These ideas became thoroughly discredited, but the thesis that criminality is influenced by biological makeup has repeatedly been suggested in various guises (Eysenck, 1977; Mednick and Moffitt, 1984). At one time, a popular method of trying to demonstrate the likely influence of heredity upon criminal tendencies was to study family trees. Richard Dugdale investigated the Dukes family in the United States, which included 140 criminals among its 1,200 members (Dugdale, 1877). He compared the Dukes with the descendants of Jonathan Edwards, a well-known clergyman in colonial America. The Edwards progeny included no criminals, but more than one president of the United States, as well as high-ranking justices, writers, and religious leaders. Comparison with the Dukes was supposed to show the difference in genetic inclinations to criminality (Estabrook, 1916). As a demonstration of its case, however, the research was less than convincing, because Jonathan Edwards's *forebears* included people who had been convicted of crimes! If criminality were indeed an inherited trait, some of his descendants therefore should have been criminals too. Studies of family histories demonstrate virtually nothing about the influence of heredity, because it is impossible to disentangle inherited and environmental influences. The conditions under which children in the Edwards family were raised contrasted with those of the Dukes, who grew up among thieves. No one can say from this type of evidence where the causal influences lie.

The idea of a connection between biological makeup and criminality was revived in the work of William A. Sheldon in the 1940s. Sheldon distinguished three main types of human physique, claiming one to be directly associated with delinquency. Muscular, active types (*mesomorphs*), he proposed, were more likely to become delinquent than those of thin physique (*ectomorphs*), or more fleshy people (*endomorphs*). Subsequent studies carried out by other researchers claimed rather similar findings (Sheldon et al., 1949; Glueck and Glueck, 1956). However, while views of this sort still have their advocates, such research has been widely criticized. Even if there were an overall relationship between bodily type and delinquency, this would show nothing about the influence of heredity. People of the muscular type of physique may be drawn towards gang activities because these offer opportunities for the physical display of athleticism. Moreover, nearly all studies in this field have been restricted to delinquents in reform schools. If there is any link with body build, it may be that the tougher, athletic-looking delinquents are more liable to be "put away" than fragile-looking, skinny ones.

More recently, some researchers have tried to link criminal tendencies to a particular set of chromosomes in genetic inheritance (Cowen, 1979). They claimed that criminals, particularly those guilty of violent crimes, include a disproportionately high number of men having an extra Y chromosome. Some studies of maximum-security prisons indicated that one in a hundred of the male inmates had the abnormality, compared to one in a thousand men in the population as a whole. Subsequent research along these lines, however, proved inconclusive and contradictory. Observers soon realized that the inconsistent findings resulted from the small size of the samples being investigated. Research with a large representative population indicated that XYY men are not more likely to be involved in violent crime than are XY men (Mednick, 1982).

Similarly, some have suggested that criminal tendencies might break down racially. Viewing statistics of violent crime among blacks in the United States has led some researchers to conclude incorrectly that blacks are biologically predisposed to crime. But violence in American society has absolutely nothing to do with the biological characteristics that separate blacks from whites. Studies demonstrate that homicide rates in communities in Africa are generally extremely low compared to rates for American blacks. Research by Marvin Wolfgang in Philadelphia showed blacks to have an annual rate of 246 homicides per one million between 1948 and 1952. African groups studied at the same period by Paul Bohannan had annual rates of homicide of less than 12 per one million—among the lowest in the world (Wolfgang, 1958; Bohannan, 1960).

CRIME AND THE PSYCHOPATHIC PERSONALITY: THE PSYCHOLOGICAL VIEW

Like biological interpretations, psychological theories of crime associate criminality with particular types of personality. Freud's ideas have had some influence upon psychological interpretations of crime even though he wrote little or nothing in the field of criminology. But drawing upon Freud's ideas, others suggest that, in a certain minority of individuals, an amoral or *psychopathic* personality develops. According to Freud, much of our sense of morality derives from the self-restraints we learned as young children during the Oedipal phase of development (see Chapter 3: "Socialization and the Life Cycle"). Because of the nature of their relationships with their parents, some children never develop these restraints, and therefore lack an underlying sense of morality. **Psychopaths** are said to be "emotionless" characters, who delight in violence for its own sake, and who crave excitement and adventure.

Individuals having psychopathic traits do sometimes commit violent crimes (Taylor, 1982), but there are major problems with the concept of psychopathy. It is not at all proven that these traits are inevitably criminal. Nearly all studies of individuals said to possess psychopathic characteristics have been of convicted prisoners, and these characteristics almost inevitably tend to be presented negatively. If we describe these traits positively, the personality type sounds quite different, and there seems no particular reason why people of this sort should be inherently criminal. Should we be looking for noninstitutionalized psychopathic individuals for a research study, we might place the following ad:

ARE YOU ADVENTUROUS?
Researcher wishes to contact adventurous, carefree people, who've led exciting, impulsive lives. If you're the kind of

person who'd do almost anything for a dare, call 337-xxxx any time.

(Widom and Newman, 1985)

Such people might be explorers, heroes, gamblers, or just those who get bored with the routines of day-to-day life. They might be prepared to contemplate criminal adventures, but would seem just as likely to look for challenges in socially respectable avenues.

Whether derived from Freud or from other perspectives in psychology, psychological theories of criminality can at best only explain aspects of crime. While a small minority of criminals may have personality characteristics distinct from the remainder of the population, it is highly unlikely that the majority do so. There are many different types of crime, and it is implausible to suppose that those who commit them share some specific psychological characteristics.

Even if we confine ourselves to one distinct category of crime, such as crimes of violence, many different circumstances are involved. Some such crimes are carried out by lone individuals, while others are committed by organized groups. It is not likely that the psychological makeup of those who are "loners" will have much in common with the members of a close-knit gang. If consistent differences could be linked to forms of criminality, we still could not be sure which way the line of causality would run. It might easily be that becoming involved with groups in which criminal activity is common influences the attitudes and outlooks of individuals, rather than these actually stimulating the criminal behavior in the first place.

SOCIETY AND CRIME: SOCIOLOGICAL THEORIES

A satisfactory account of the nature of crime must be sociological, for what "crime" is depends upon the social institutions of a society. Sociological thinking about crime emphasizes the interconnections between conformity and deviance in different social contexts. Modern societies contain many different subcultures, and behavior that conforms to the norms of a particular subcultural setting may be regarded as deviant outside it. For instance, within the subculture of a boys' gang, it may be a norm for a member to "prove himself" by stealing a car—an act that is deviant according to the norms of the larger society. Moreover, there are extreme differences of wealth and power in society that greatly influence opportunities open to different groups. Crimes like theft and burglary, not surprisingly, are carried out

Sociological theories emphasize the importance of a person's social surroundings in the development of criminal activities.

mainly by people from the poorer segments of the population. Other crimes like embezzling or tax evasion are, due to circumstances, limited to persons in positions of some affluence (Box, 1984).

Differential Association

Edwin H. Sutherland linked crime to what he called **differential association** (Sutherland, 1949). The idea of differential association is very simple: in a society that contains many different subcultures, some social environments tend to encourage illegal activities, whereas others do not. Individuals become delinquent or criminal by associating with others, particularly peers, who are the carriers of *criminal norms.* This theory differs from the psychological view in that Sutherland sees criminals as being psychologically normal. Criminal activities are learned in much the same way as law-abiding ones, and in general are directed towards the same needs and values. Thieves try to make money in much the same way as people in orthodox jobs, but they choose illegal methods of doing so.

Anomie as a Cause of Crime

Robert K. Merton's interpretation of crime, which links criminality to other types of deviant behavior, similarly emphasizes the normality of the criminal (Merton, 1957). Merton drew upon the concept of **anomie**—first introduced by Émile Durkheim (1858–1917), one of the founders of sociology—to develop a highly influential theory of deviance. According to Durkheim, anomie exists when there are no clear standards to guide behavior in a given area of social life. In modern societies, traditional norms and standards had become undermined, without being replaced by new ones; in these circumstances, Durkheim believed, people feel disoriented and anxious. In his famous study on suicide Durkheim saw anomie as one of the social factors influencing dispositions to suicide.

Merton modified the concept of anomie to refer to the strain placed upon people's behavior when accepted norms conflict with social reality. In American society—and to some degree in all modern Western societies—generally held values emphasize "getting ahead," "making money," and so on: material success. The means of achieving these are supposed to be self-discipline and hard work. According to these beliefs, people who really work hard can succeed, no matter what their starting point in life. But this is not the reality, because most of the disadvantaged have very limited opportunities for advancement. Yet those who do not "succeed" find themselves condemned for their apparent inability to make material progress. In this situation, there is great pressure to try to "get on" by any means, legitimate or illegitimate.

Merton identified five possible reactions to the tensions between socially endorsed values and the limited means of achieving them:

1. CONFORMISTS. These individuals accept both the generally held values and the conventional means of trying to realize them, whether or not they meet with success. The majority of the population falls into this category.

2. INNOVATORS. Merton called those who continue to accept socially approved values, but use illegitimate or illegal means to try to follow them, innovators. Criminals concerned with acquiring wealth through illegal activities exemplify this type of response.

3. RITUALISTS. These people conform to socially accepted standards, although they have lost sight of the values that originally prompted their activity. The rules are followed compulsively for their own sake, without a greater end in view. A ritualist would be someone who is dedicated to a boring job, even though it has no career prospects and provides few rewards.

4. RETREATISTS. These people have abandoned the competitive outlook altogether, thus rejecting both

the dominant values and the approved means of
achieving them. An example would be the members of
a self-supporting commune.

5.   REBELS. These individuals reject both the existing
values and the normative means, but wish actively to
substitute new ones and reconstruct the social system.
The members of radical political groups fall into this
category.

Anomie and Differential Association

Merton wrote rather little about criminal activity as such. He also
provided few suggestions as to why some reactions to anomie are
chosen over others. These gaps were filled in by later researchers,
who linked Sutherland's idea of differential association (the idea that
the group of people with whom we associate influences us for or
against crime) to Merton's definitions. An example is Richard A.
Cloward and Lloyd E. Ohlin's (1960) research on delinquent boys'
gangs. They argued that such gangs arise in subcultural communities
where the chances of legitimately achieving success are small—such
as communities of deprived ethnic minorities. The members of the
gangs accept some aspects of the desirability of material success, but
these values are filtered through local community subcultures. In
neighborhoods where established criminal networks exist, gang subcultures help lead individuals from petty acts of theft into an adult
life of crime. In areas where such networks are not found, gang delinquency tends to take the form of fighting and vandalism, as there is
little opportunity in such areas for gang members to become part of
criminal networks. Those who cannot cope either with the legitimate social order or the gang subcultures tend to withdraw into the
retreatism of drug addiction.

Cloward and Ohlin's work has close parallels with a somewhat
earlier study of delinquent subcultures by Albert Cohen (1955).
Cohen identified "delinquency neighborhoods" in the larger American cities, within which gang culture has become a way of life. According to Cohen, rather than being interested in material gain, gang
members tend to steal for much the same reasons as they might engage in fighting and vandalism. All these activities express a rejection
of "respectable" society. Recognizing their deprived position within
the social order, the gangs create oppositional values of their own.

The studies of Cloward and Ohlin, and Cohen, are important because they place normal individuals on a conformity/deviance continuum where the lack of opportunity for success in the dominant

society is the main factor determining who engages in criminal behavior and who doesn't. Yet there is in fact little evidence to support the thesis that people in poorer communities accept the same level of aspiration to "success" as those in more affluent circumstances. On the contrary, most people tend to adjust their aspirations to what they see as the reality of their situation. It is also mistaken to suppose that discrepancies between aspirations and opportunities are confined to the less-privileged. It might be suggested that there are pressures towards criminal activity—and perhaps some of the other types of deviance suggested by Merton—whenever there is a major gap between aspirations and opportunities. Such a gap may be relevant, for example, to the white-collar crimes of embezzlement, fraud, or tax evasion. Even very wealthy people might feel pressures to accumulate more money than would be possible through legal means.

Labeling Theory

One of the most important approaches to understanding criminality is called **labeling theory**—although this term itself is a label for a cluster of related ideas, rather than a unified approach. Labeling theorists interpret deviance not as a set of characteristics of individuals or groups, but as a *process* of interaction between deviants and nondeviants. In their view, we have to see why some people become tagged with a deviant label in order to understand the nature of deviance itself. Those who represent the forces of law and order, or are able to impose the boundaries of conventional morality and proper behavior upon others, provide the main sources of labeling. The labels applied to create categories of deviance thus express the power structure of society. By and large, the rules by which deviance is defined, and the contexts in which they are applied, are framed by the wealthy for the poor, by men for women, by older people for younger people, and by ethnic majorities for minority groups.

For example, many children engage in activities such as climbing into other people's gardens, breaking windows, stealing fruit, or playing truant. In an affluent neighborhood, these might be regarded by parents, teachers, and police alike as relatively innocent aspects of the process of growing up. In poor areas, on the other hand, such activities might be seen as evidence of tendencies towards juvenile delinquency.

Once a child is labeled as a delinquent, he or she is stigmatized as a criminal and is likely to be considered, and treated, as untrustworthy by teachers and prospective employers. The individual then relapses into further criminal behavior, widening the gulf with orthodox social conventions. Edwin Lemert (1972) calls the initial transgression

primary deviation. Secondary deviation occurs when the person comes to
accept the label that has been attached, seeing himself or herself as
deviant, and acts in a way that fulfills the expectations of the label.

Take, for example, a boy who smashes a store window while
spending a Saturday night out with his friends. The act may perhaps
be defined as the accidental result of over-boisterous behavior, an excusable characteristic of young men. The youth might escape with a
reprimand and a small fine. If he is from a "respectable" background,
this is a likely result. The smashing of the window stays at the level
of primary deviance if the youth is seen as someone of "good character" who on this occasion became too rowdy. If, on the other hand,
the police and courts have a more punitive reaction, perhaps handing
out a suspended sentence and making the boy report to a social
worker, the incident could become the first step in a process of secondary deviance. The process of "learning to be deviant" tends to be
accentuated by the very organizations supposedly set up to correct
deviant behavior—reform schools, prisons, and mental hospitals.

Labeling theory begins with the assumption that no act is intrinsically criminal. Definitions of criminality are established by the powerful, through the formulation of laws and their interpretation by
police, courts, and correctional institutions. Critics of labeling theory
have sometimes argued that there are in fact a number of acts consistently prohibited across all, or virtually all, cultures, such as murder,
rape, and robbery (Wellford, 1975). This view is surely incorrect:

even within our own culture, killing is not always regarded as murder. In times of war, killing the enemy is positively approved of, and until recently, some countries did not recognize sexual intercourse forced on a woman by her husband as rape.

But we can criticize labeling theory on two grounds. First, in emphasizing the interactive process of labeling, the processes that *lead* to acts defined as deviant tend to get lost (Fine, 1977). Labeling certain behaviors as deviant is clearly not arbitrary; what leads one to engage in such behaviors might result from differences in socialization, attitudes, and opportunities. Second, it is still not clear whether or not labeling actually does have the effect of increasing deviant conduct. Delinquent behavior tends to increase following conviction, but is this the result of the labeling itself? It is very difficult to judge, since many other factors, such as increased interaction with other delinquents, or learning of new criminal opportunities, may be involved (Farrington, Ohlin, and Wilson, 1986).

Rational Choice and "Situational" Analyses of Crime

None of the theories mentioned so far finds much place for understanding criminal behavior as a deliberate and calculated act. Each tends to see criminality as "reaction" to outside influences, rather than as conduct in which individuals actively engage in order to get definite benefits. But some writers suggest that people who engage in criminal acts, whether regularly or more sporadically, do so purposefully, and usually recognize the risks they are running. This approach to understanding criminal behavior is called *rational-choice analysis* (Cornish and Clarke, 1986).

Research indicates that many criminal actions, particularly more minor types of crime—like nonviolent theft or burglary—are "situational" decisions. An opportunity presents itself, and seems too good to pass up—as when someone sees that a house is empty, tries the backdoor, and finds that it is easy to get in. There are few "specialists" in crime; most people are "generalists," supplementing their other sources of income by sporadically taking part in acts of theft or burglary when opportunities to do so crop up (Walsh, 1986).

Floyd Feeney (1986) studied a sample of male Californian robbers, some convicted of crimes of robbery with violence. He found that over half said they had not planned in advance for the crime or crimes for which they were convicted. Another third reported only minor planning, such as finding a partner, thinking about where to leave a getaway car, or whether to use a weapon. Such planning usually took place the same day as the robbery, often within a few hours of it. Of the 15 percent who had used a carefully planned approach, 9 percent simply followed a pattern they had established before. Over 60 percent said that before the robbery they had not even thought of being caught. The belief was perhaps well founded: the sample included one person who had committed over 1,000 robberies by the age of twenty-six, but had only been convicted once.

The fact that many property crimes are "situational" emphasizes how similar much criminal activity is to day-to-day decisions of a nondeviant kind. Given that an individual is prepared to consider engaging in criminal activities (which some of the other theories might assist in explaining) many criminal acts involve quite ordinary decision-making processes. The decision to take something from a store when no one is looking is not so different from deciding to buy a particular product that catches the eye—in fact, a person might do both during the same shopping expedition.

MAKING USE OF THE THEORIES

What then, should we conclude from this survey of the many theories of crime that exist? We must first of all reiterate a point made earlier. Even though "crime" is only one subcategory of deviant behavior, it covers such a variety of forms of activity—from taking a bar of chocolate without paying for it to mass murder—that it is unlikely that any single theory could account for all forms of criminal conduct. Each of the above theories contributes to our understanding either of some aspects or of some types of crime. Biological and psychological approaches can serve to identify some of the personality characteristics which—given particular social contexts—predispose certain individuals to contemplate criminal acts. For example, individuals with traits usually termed "psychopathic" may be more heavily represented among some categories of violent criminals than among the general population. On the other hand, they are probably also over-represented among those recognized as having carried out acts of extreme heroism, or involving themselves in other risk-taking activities.

The general contributions of the sociological theories of crime are important because they correctly emphasize the continuities between criminal and "respectable" behavior. The situations in which particular types of activity are seen as "criminal," and punishable by law, vary widely. Each of the theories agrees that there is a strong *contextual* element in the occurrence of criminal activities. Whether people engage in criminal acts, or come to be regarded as "criminals," is fundamentally influenced by social learning, and by the social circumstances in which individuals find themselves.

In spite of its deficiencies, labeling theory is the most widely used approach. When integrated with a historical perspective, labeling theory sensitizes us to the conditions in which some types of activity come to be defined as punishable by law, the relations of power involved in the forming of such definitions, as well as the circumstances in which particular individuals "fall foul of the law." Also, situational interpretations of crime can be quite easily linked to the labeling approach, because they clarify one feature of criminality about which labeling theory is silent—why many people who are in no obvious way "abnormal" choose to engage in acts that they know could be followed by legal sanctions.

These theories of crime raise some very general issues that stretch over into other areas of sociology. Should we see crime primarily in terms of deviation from values and norms held by the law-abiding population? Or should we rather pose the question: *Whose* "law and order" do legal sanctions protect? Perhaps most types of "crime" are simply types of behavior that threaten the privileges of the affluent and the powerful (Chambliss and Seidman, 1982). These questions about deviance reflect broader concerns in sociology. Some sociologists tend to see societies as more consensual and integrated than do others, who focus more upon differential power, social divisions, and tensions. These are differences in overall theoretical perspective, which we shall come back to at various points in other chapters (see also Chapter 22: "The Development of Sociological Theory").

We now turn to an examination of the levels and character of criminal activities occurring in modern societies, giving particular attention to crime in the United States.

CRIME AND CRIMINAL STATISTICS

STATISTICS ON CRIME AND DELINQUENCY WERE COLLECTED, though haphazardly, in the United States during the early part of the nineteenth century, but no effective national system of crime reporting existed until the first publication of the *Uniform Crime Reports* by the FBI in 1930. Although they are usually discussed in the popular press as though they were accurate, statistics about crime and delinquency remain the least reliable of all social statistics. The official crime statistics are perhaps not entirely without value. They are a valuable guide to the deployment and behavior of police forces. Yet they are far from representing the real level of most forms of crime.

Their most basic limitation of these statistics is that they only include crimes actually recorded by the police. There is a long chain of
problematic decisions between a possible crime and its registration in
the police files. The majority of crimes, especially petty thefts, are
never reported to the police at all. People vary in their ability to recognize crimes, and their willingness to report them. Of the crimes
that do come to the notice of the police, a proportion are not recorded
in the statistics because the police are skeptical of their validity. Surveys estimate that at least half of all serious crimes, such as robbery or
aggravated assault (assault with the purpose of inflicting severe injury) are not reported. The Bureau of the Census since 1973 has been
interviewing people in random samples of sixty thousand households, to see how many were victims of particular crimes during the
preceding six months. This research, which is called the National
Crime Survey, has confirmed that many serious crimes go unreported. Reporting is highest for commercial robbery (86 percent) and
lowest for household thefts of under $50 (15 percent).

To find the true rates of crime we cannot simply add unreported
crimes to the official police rate, because practices of police departments in reporting crime vary. Some departments report fewer
crimes than others, either because of inefficiency or because their
ratio of arrests to number of crimes thereby looks better. Studies have
shown, for example, that rapid increases in crime shown officially in
some large cities in the 1960s were probably in a large degree the result of changes in reporting practices (*Task Force on Assessment,* 1967).
Citizens themselves may alter their reporting habits as attitudes or
values change. For instance, rapes are more likely to be reported
when women perceive a more sympathetic framework of response
developing from police and courts.

Between 1971 and 1980 in the United States, the number of officially reported serious crimes rose by 42 percent. Although this increase gave rise to much public alarm, the real trend was in all
probability much less pronounced than this. Serious crimes, as documented by the National Crime Survey, did not alter greatly over the
period, showing only a slight increase, although apparently a progressive one (Rutter and Giller, 1984). Murder and negligent manslaughter rates rose by 11 percent between 1977–1981 (subsequently
falling somewhat).

"Victim surveys," like the National Crime Survey, have difficulties of their own. People are more prone to report some crimes to interviewers than to the police, but the reverse may be the case with
other criminal activities. A woman may notify the police when as-
saulted by her husband, but when talking to an interviewer several
months afterwards she might not mention the incident, particularly

if the husband is present during the interview. One research study, carried out in San José, California, looked at cases of people who had reported assaults to the police, and who were later interviewed in the National Crime Survey. Only 48 percent admitted to the assaults in the later interview, the proportion being lowest among those who had reported to the police that the assailant was a relative (Turner, 1981).

HOMICIDE AND OTHER VIOLENT CRIME

Rates of homicide (murder) are probably the most accurate of crime statistics. Yet even here there are problems. For a death to be classified as a murder it has to be known to have occurred. This usually means a body has to be found; few deaths where a body remains undiscovered are categorized as homicides. Given that a body is located, murder will only be suspected given circumstances that indicate that the death was "non-natural"—such as gunshot wounds, severe bruising, or lacerations of the skull or body. Once a case is brought against someone, it may be decided that the accused was guilty of manslaughter (intent to harm, but not kill), rather than homicide.

Despite the inaccurate crime statistics, nobody disputes the exceptionally high level of homicide in the United States compared to other industrialized countries. There are more reported murders each year in Detroit, with a population of just over 1.5 million, than in the whole of the United Kingdom, which has a population of 55 million people. Viewed in comparative context, the United States is a culture in which crimes of violence flourish. Why should this be?

One answer given is the widespread availability of handguns and other firearms. This is surely relevant, but cannot on its own be the answer. Switzerland has very low rates of violent crime, yet firearms are easily accessible. There, all males are members of the citizen army and may keep weapons in their homes, including rifles, revolvers, and sometimes other automatic weapons, plus ammunition; nor are gun licenses difficult to obtain (Clinard, 1978). The most likely explanation for the high level of violent crime in the United States is a combination of the availability of firearms, the general influence of the "frontier tradition," and the existence of subcultures of violence in the large cities. Violence by frontiersmen and vigilantes is an honored part of American history. Some of the first, established immigrant areas in the cities developed their own informal modes of neighborhood social control, backed by violence or the threat of violence. Similarly, young people in black and Hispanic communities today have developed subcultures of manliness and honor associated

with rituals of violence, and some belong to gangs whose everyday life is one of drug-dealing, territory protection, and violence.

A notable feature of most crimes of violence is their mundane character. Most assaults and homicides bear little resemblance to the murderous, random acts of gunmen nor to the carefully planned homicides given most prominence in the media. Murders generally happen in the context of family and other interpersonal relationships. The victim usually knows his or her murderer. Alcohol consumption is often a factor, which is hardly surprising given the prevalence of alcohol consumption in the United States (Cook, 1982).

A substantial proportion of homicides are "victim precipitated," that is, the victim initiates the fatal outburst by making the first menacing gesture or striking the first blow. For example:

> A victim became incensed when his eventual slayer asked for money which the victim owed him. The victim grabbed a hatchet and started in the direction of his creditor, who pulled out a knife and stabbed him. (Wolfgang, 1958; see also Campbell and Gibbs, 1986)

PRISONS AND PUNISHMENT

For a long time now, prison sentencing has been aimed at correcting criminal behavior: rehabilitating criminals to become law-abiding citizens while protecting the citizenry from them. But do prisons actually have these effects upon those who are interned in them for specific periods of time? The evidence strongly suggests that they don't.

Prisoners are generally no longer physically maltreated as was once a common practice—although physical beatings are by no means unknown, even in women's prisons (as will be indicated below). However, prisoners suffer many other types of deprivation. Not only are they deprived of their freedom, but of a proper income, the company of their families and previous friends, heterosexual relationships, their own clothing, and other personal items. They frequently live in overcrowded conditions and have to accept strict disciplinary procedures and the regimentation of their daily lives (Table 5.1).

This might seem fine to those who believe that the purpose of criminal justice is to punish wrong-doers. But those who favor rehabilitation see this as a situation with unfortunate consequences.

Rather than adjusting their behavior to the norms of society, living in these conditions tends to drive a wedge between prison inmates

TABLE 5.1	WHO IS IN PRISON: STATE PRISON INMATES BY AGE AND RACE	
	1979	1986
AGE		
UNDER 18 YRS.	2,220	2,057
18–24	97,860	120,384
25–34	116,284	205,817
35–44	37,296	87,502
45–54	13,987	23,524
55–64	4,786	8,267
65 AND OVER	1,499	2,808
RACE		
WHITE	136,295	223,648
BLACK	131,329	221,021
OTHER	6,939	15,412

Source: U.S. Bureau of Justice Statistics, *Profile of State Prison Inmates*, 1986, January, 1988.

and the outside society. Prisoners have to come to terms with an environment quite distinct from "the outside," and the habits and attitudes they learn in prison are quite often exactly the opposite of those they are supposed to acquire. For instance, they may develop a grudge against the ordinary citizenry, learn to accept violence as normal, acquire contacts with seasoned criminals that they maintain when freed, and acquire new criminal skills. In effect, they are socialized more firmly into a deviant subculture, learning or refining its norms, beliefs, and attitudes. It is therefore not surprising that rates of *recidivism*—repeat offending by those who have been in reform schools or prison before—are disturbingly high. Over 60 percent of all men set free after serving prison sentences are rearrested within four years of their original crimes. The actual rate of recidivism is presumably higher than this, since some of those returning to criminal activities are not caught.

Although prisons do not seem to work in rehabilitating prisoners, it is possible that they do deter people from carrying out crimes. While those who are actually imprisoned are not deterred, the unpleasant qualities of prison life might very well deter others on the outside. But there is an almost intractable problem here for prison reformers. Making prisons thoroughly unpleasant places probably helps deter potential offenders; but it makes the rehabilitating goals of prisons extremely difficult to achieve. Yet the less harsh prison conditions are, the more imprisonment loses its deterrent effect.

Probation and Parole

At any one time, many more people who have been convicted of crimes are on probation or parole than in prison. Probation is widely used as a method for dealing with minor crimes. A person who is put on probation has to follow certain prescriptions like holding down a job and committing no further offense within a specified period. Following that period, the case is closed. Parole is a reduction in the length of a sentence, given to reward "good behavior" while an individual is in prison. When a prisoner comes before a parole board, after serving a certain period of the sentence, the board may grant the parole, refuse parole but set a future date for another hearing, or decide that the prisoner must serve the full sentence.

THE DEATH PENALTY

Ever since prison sentencing became the main form of criminal punishment, the death penalty has been increasingly controversial.

TABLE 5.2	PRISONERS EXECUTED IN THE UNITED STATES, 1930–1987		

| | CRIME | | |
	Murder	Rape	Total*
1930–1939	1,514	125	1,667
1940–1949	1,064	200	1,284
1950–1959	601	102	717
1960–1964	145	28	181
1965–1967	10	—	10
1968–1976**	—	—	—
1976–1980	3	—	3
1981	1	—	1
1982	2	—	2
1983	5	—	5
1984	21	—	21
1985	18	—	18
1986	18	—	18
1987	25	—	25

* Includes other offenses (armed robbery, kidnapping, burglary, espionage, aggravated assault).
** The U. S. Supreme Court abolished capital punishment, 1972–1976.
Source: U.S. Law Enforcement Assistance Administration through 1976; thereafter, U.S. Bureau of Justice Statistics, Correctional Projections in the U.S. annual.

Given that prisons are supposed to rehabilitate, executing people for crimes has seemed to most reformers illogical as well as barbaric; for to put someone to death is to recognize that altering their behavior is impossible.

As was mentioned in Chapter 1, the United States is almost the only Western country that still uses the death penalty. The death penalty was in fact abolished by the Supreme Court in 1972, but reinstated by a subsequent Court decision in 1976. Executions were resumed in some but far from all states in 1977. The number of people sentenced to death each year is growing, but so far appeals and other factors have limited the actual number of those executed (Table 5.2).

In other countries there is public pressure to bring back the death penalty, at least for certain types of crime (like terrorism or the murdering of a policeman). In Britain, for example, opinion polls consistently show that a majority of the population would like the death penalty reinstated. The public apparently believes that the threat of execution deters potential murderers. How valid is this view? Although the arguments continue, there is little or no evidence to support the idea that the death penalty is a deterrent. Countries that have abolished the death penalty do not have notably higher homicide rates than before. Although the United States retains the death penalty, American rates of homicide are the highest in the industrialized world. Here again, we return to the mundane, everyday aspect of homicide. Most homicides are not premeditated, that is, thoughtful, fully-planned-out acts. Rather, homicides arise out of ordinary, albeit often passionate, interactions during which the slayer has little time to reflect on the possibility of being executed for his or her crime.

Of course, the strength of public feeling on this issue may reflect attitudes towards punishment, rather than the idea that the death penalty is a deterrent. People may feel that someone who takes another person's life should be punished in kind. Another, contrary, view holds that it is morally wrong for a society to put its citizens to death, whatever their crime. Yet a further view suggests that the legal system can neither decide fairly who should and who should not be executed nor be absolutely sure of a person's guilt. These latter views, together with the lack of proof that it has a deterrent effect, are what have swayed most legislators against the death penalty.

GENDER AND CRIME

As in other areas of sociology, criminological studies have traditionally ignored half the population, women (Morris, 1987). Most theories of deviance similarly disregard women almost completely. An example is Merton's account of social structure and anomie. The "pressure to succeed" is supposed to touch virtually everyone in modern societies. Logically, one could argue that women should figure more prominently than men in the various categories of deviance identified by Merton, including crime, as there are fewer opportunities open for women "to get on" than for men. Yet rates of criminality of women are—or seem to be—exceptionally low. Even if women are for some reason less prone to participate in deviant activities than men, this is hardly any reason to omit them from consideration.

Male and Female Crime Rates

The statistics on gender* and crime are startling. For example, there is an enormous imbalance in the ratio of men and women in prison, not only in the United States (Table 5.3) but in all the industrialized countries. Women only make up some 4 percent of the American prison population. There are also contrasts between the types of crime men and women commit, at least as indicated in the official statistics. The offenses of women rarely involve violence, and are almost all small-scale. Petty thefts, like shoplifting, and public-order offenses, such as public drunkenness and prostitution, are typical female crimes (Gillen, 1978; Flowers, 1987).

Of course, it may be that the real gender difference in crime rates is less than the official statistics show. Police and other officials might regard female offenders as less dangerous than men, for example, letting pass activities for which men would be arrested. Victimization surveys provide a means of checking upon such a possibility. In one study in the United States, the National Crime Survey materials of 1976 were compared with FBI statistics to see whether there was any divergence in proportions of women involved in criminal activities (Hindelang, 1979). Little variation was found in respect to serious crimes committed by women, the FBI statistics actually showing somewhat higher proportions than the survey reported. Some observers argue that the proportion of women involved in "male" crimes, such as armed robbery, is likely to increase; however there is no clear-cut evidence of such a trend (Dobash, Dobarth, and Gutteridge, 1986).

"Lost-letters" experiments have provided one source of information about gender, opportunity, and crime (Farrington and Kidd, 1980). In these experiments, money enclosed in letters was dropped in public places. Various conditions were altered in different versions —the amount of money involved, whether it was in cash or another form (like a money order), and the apparent loser (an old lady or an affluent man). The characteristics of the individuals who picked up the letters were observed, and the researchers could tell from a particular code number whether a letter was posted or kept.

Stealing the money was most common when the apparent victim

**TABLE 5.3
STATE PRISON INMATES
BY SEX**

	1979	1986
MALE	263,484	430,604
FEMALE	11,080	19,812

Source: U.S. Bureau of Justice Statistics, *Profile of State Prison Inmates, 1986,* January 1988.

---

* In comparing the behavior of men and women, sociologists often prefer to use the term "gender" rather than "sex." "Sex" refers to the biological/anatomical differences between women and men, "gender" to the psychological/social/cultural differences between them—differences between masculinity and femininity (see Chapter 6: "Gender and Sexuality").

was an affluent man and cash was involved, and females were as likely to steal as males—except when larger sums of money were concerned. About half of the men observed stole in this situation, compared to less than a quarter of the women. Perhaps pocketing a small amount of cash is not seen as "stealing," while taking a large amount is—and men are more prepared to profit in this way.

The only crime where the female rate of conviction approximates that of men is shoplifting. Some have argued that this fact indicates that women will engage in criminal activities when they find themselves in a "public" context—out shopping—rather than in a domestic situation. In other words, when the opportunity to commit crime is more or less equal between men and women, they are equally likely to commit offenses. There have been few investigations comparing female and male rates of shoplifting. A recent study, however, found that men are proportionately twice as likely to shoplift as women (Buckle and Farrington, 1984).

The Girls in the Gang

There has been little work on female members of youth gangs, or on female gangs where these exist. Numerous accounts have been written of male street-corner groups and male gangs, but in these studies women appear only fleetingly. Anne Campbell (1984), however, has studied women in New York street gangs. She selected three gangs for intensive study: one was ethnically mixed, one Puerto Rican, the other black. The age of the members ranged from fifteen to thirty. Campbell spent six months living with each gang, focusing especially upon the gang leaders.

Connie was the leader of the Sandman Ladies, a female group associated with the Sandman bikers, a gang headed by her husband. She was thirty at the time of the research (1979), and led a mixed Hispanic and black gang in Harlem. The major source of income of the Sandman bikers was drug dealing. The group was involved in a longstanding feud with the Chosen Ones, another Harlem gang. Those who joined the Sandman Ladies had to prove their fighting capabilities; entry was decided by Connie, who made an initial judgement about whether a girl could "hang around" for a trial period, and whether she later got her "patches" (insignia). Connie always carried a flick knife and also possessed a gun; she said that when she fought, it was to kill. Fighting involving physical brawls was just as constant a preoccupation of the female as of the male group.

Weeza and the Sex Girls were a Hispanic gang, having a male and female section. Weeza could not read or write, and was unsure of her true age—which was probably twenty-six. At the gang's height, there were more than fifty female members. The women cultivated a reputation for physical toughness, fighting and beatings-up were commonplace. The male members of the gang admired this, while still encouraging traditional roles in other respects, such as caring for children, cooking, and sewing.

The third group studied was The Five Percent Nation, which was a black religious organization. According to the beliefs of the group, the United States is a society dominated by exploitation: 10 percent of the population exploit 85 percent of the remainder. The other 5 percent are enlightened believers of Islam who have the duty of educating blacks. The police regarded the Five Percent Nation as a street gang. The individual upon whom Campbell concentrated her attention, Sun-Africa, had rejected what she called her "government name." As with the other groups, she and other female members frequently engaged in fighting. Group members had been arrested for robbery, possession of dangerous weapons, burglary, and auto theft.

In another study, Campbell interviewed working-class schoolgirls about fighting, finding that they engaged in this activity more often than is commonly believed (Campbell, 1986). Almost all those she contacted admitted to having been involved in a fight; a quarter had been in more than six fights. The majority rejected the statement, "I think fighting is only for boys."

Prison Violence Among Women

Autobiographical accounts of female prisoners contain numerous episodes of violence, which is portrayed as a constant feature of female prison life. One inmate described how the "heavy mob" of female guards specialized in violent retribution towards prisoners they saw as ill-behaved. Beatings by the "heavy mob" and by other prisoners were common:

> "One particular officer always steamed in and started poking you in the chest because she wanted you to hit her—that's what she got off on, the struggling and the fighting. They carry you by the "necklace," the key chains, and you can have three chains round your neck at any one time. You get purple bruises round your neck, a necklace of purple . . . you begin to black out and you think, 'This is it, I'm going to die now' . . . I could have died. But I didn't and I was lucky. I was a survivor." (Quoted in Carlen et al., 1985)

Such studies of female gangs and prisons clearly show that violence is not exclusively the province of men. Statistically women are much less likely than men to participate in violent crime, but in certain situations they will do so.

Differences in Crime and Gender Roles

Why are female rates of criminality so much lower than those of men? The reasons are almost certainly the same as those that explain gender differences in other spheres. There are, of course, certain specifically "female crimes"—most notably, prostitution—for which women are convicted while their male clients are not. "Male crimes" remain "male" because of differences in socialization and the fact that male activities and involvements are still more nondomestic than those of most women. The gender difference in crime used to be explained by the supposedly innate biological or psychological differences of women—in terms of differential strength, passivity, or preoccupation with reproduction (Smart, 1978). Nowadays "womanly" qualities are seen as largely socially generated, in common with the traits of "masculinity." Many women are socialized to value different qualities in social life from those of men (caring for others and the fostering of personal relationships). Even though a high proportion of women are now in the labor force, most spend much more of their lives in domestic settings than men do. In the domestic sphere the opportunities and motivation for most forms of criminal activity are less than in the public settings in which men more often move.

At the moment, it is difficult to say with any certainty whether female rates and patterns of crime will increasingly resemble those of men as gender divisions become more blurred than they once were. Ever since the late nineteenth century, criminologists have predicted that increasing gender equality would reduce or eliminate the differences in criminality between men and women, but as yet these differences remain pronounced. We take this up further in Chapter 6: "Gender and Sexuality."

CRIMES OF THE AFFLUENT AND POWERFUL

Although the poor make up the bulk of the prison population, engaging in criminal activities is by no means confined to them. Many wealthy and powerful people carry out crimes whose consequences are often much more far-reaching than the often petty crimes of the poor. In the following sections, we shall study some of these forms of crime.

White-Collar Crime

The term "white-collar crime" was first introduced by Edwin Sutherland (1949). It refers to crime carried out by those in the more affluent sectors of society, and it covers many types of criminal activity including tax frauds, antitrust violations, illegal sales practices, securities and land frauds, embezzlement, the manufacture or sale of dangerous products, and illegal environmental pollution, as well as straightforward theft. The distribution of white-collar crimes is even harder to measure than that of other types of crime; most forms of such crime do not appear in the official statistics at all. We can distinguish between **white-collar crime** and **crimes of the powerful.** White-collar crime mainly involves the use of a middle-class or professional position to engage in illegal activities. Crimes of the powerful are those in which a person in a position of power uses that power in criminal ways—as when an official accepts a bribe to favor a particular public policy.

Efforts made to detect white-collar crime are ordinarily quite limited, and it is only on rare occasions that those who are caught go to jail. One researcher offers a vivid example of differences in judicial attitudes to white-collar and "orthodox" crime (Napes 1970). A

"Kickbacks, embezzlement, price fixing, bribery . . . this is an extremely high-crime area."

partner in a New York firm of brokers was found guilty of illegal trading in Swiss banks involving a sum of $20 million. He received a suspended sentence plus $30 thousand fine. On the day that this case was tried, the same judge handed down a decision upon an unemployed black shipping clerk who stole a television set worth $100. He was sentenced to a year in jail (Table 5.4).

Although the authorities regard white-collar crime in a much more tolerant light than crimes of the less-privileged, the cost of white-collar crime is enormous. It has been calculated that the amount of money involved in white-collar crime in the United States is forty times as great as that in ordinary crimes against property such as robberies, burglaries, larceny, forgeries, and car thefts (President's Commission on Organized Crime, 1986). Some forms of white-collar crime, moreover, affect much larger numbers of people than lower-class criminality. An embezzler might rob thousands—or today, via computer fraud, millions—of people, and tainted foods or drugs sold illegally can affect the health of many, and might lead to fatalities.

Violent aspects of white-collar crime are less visible than in the cases of homicide or assault, but are just as real—and may on occasion be much more serious in their consequences. For example, violating regulations concerning the preparation of new drugs, safety in the workplace, or pollution, may cause physical harm or death to large numbers of people (Hopkins, 1980; Geiss and Stotland, 1980). Deaths from hazards at work far outnumber murders, although precise statistics about job accidents are difficult to obtain (Box, 1983). Of course, we cannot assume that all, or even the majority, of these deaths and injuries are the result of employer negligence about safety factors for which they are legally liable. Nevertheless, there is some

TABLE 5.4	CONVICTIONS IN FEDERAL COURT FOR WHITE-COLLAR CRIMES			
	1981	1983	1985	Median length of sentence, 1985
OFFENSES INCLUDE TAX FRAUD, CREDIT FRAUD, EMBEZZLEMENT, FORGERY, ETC.	31,819	37,295	40,649	1.5 years

Source: U.S. Bureau of Justice Statistics, *White Collar Crime*, September 1987, and unpublished data.

basis for supposing that many are due to neglect of legally binding safety regulations by employers or managers.

About 40 percent of job injuries in the United States each year are the direct result of illegal working conditions, while a further 24 percent derive from legal but unsafe conditions. No more than a third are due to unsafe acts on the part of workers themselves (Hagan, 1988). There are many documented examples of employers knowingly introducing or maintaining hazardous practices even when these are contrary to the law. For instance, some large companies continued to use asbestos in production processes, or tolerate its existence in the work environment, long after it was known to be a substance having cancer-inducing properties. Ermann and Lundman (1982) argue that deaths resulting from these circumstances should be called corporate homicides, because they effectively involve the illegal (and avoidable) taking of life on the part of business corporations.

Governmental Crimes

Can government authorities ever be said to engage in crime? If "crime" is defined more broadly than it was at the beginning of the chapter (see p. 146), to refer to moral wrongs having harmful consequences, the answer is resoundingly clear. Nations have perpetrated many of the most dreadful crimes in history, including wiping out whole peoples, indiscriminate mass bombings, the Nazi holocaust, and Stalin's concentration camps. However, even if we define crime in terms of the breaking of codified laws, governments frequently act criminally. That is to say, they ignore or transgress the very laws their authority is supposed to defend. In the history of the United States, this was the case, for example, when legal guarantees offered to native Americans promising protection of their land and way of life were repeatedly disregarded. Government officials in the past have openly or tacitly permitted vigilantes and other groups to harass blacks and other minority groups. During the Reagan Administration, the members of the executive branch provided funds and equipment to the *contras* in Nicaragua, despite congressional bans on such activities.

The police, the government agency established to control crime, are sometimes themselves involved in criminal activities. This involvement does not just consist of isolated acts, but is a widespread feature of police work. Criminal activities of police officers include intimidating, beating up or killing suspects, accepting bribes, helping organize criminal networks, fabricating or withholding evidence, and keeping some or all of the proceeds when money, drugs, or stolen goods are recovered (Binder and Scharf, 1982).

ORGANIZED CRIME

Organized crime refers to forms of activity having many of the characteristics of orthodox business, but where the activities engaged in are illegal. Organized crime in America is a massive business, rivaling any of the major orthodox sectors of economic enterprise, such as the car industry. National and local criminal organizations exist providing illegal goods and services to a huge clientele, and some **criminal networks** also extend internationally.

Precise information about the nature of organized crime is obviously difficult to obtain. In romantic portrayals of gangsters, organized crime in the United States is depicted as being controlled by a secret society of national dimensions, "the Mafia." The Mafia as such —like the cowboy—is in some degree a creation of American folklore. There is almost certainly no group of mysterious mobsters of Sicilian origin who sit at the top of a coherent nationwide organization. Yet it does seem that established criminal organizations exist in nearly all major American cities, and some have connections with one another (Bequai, 1980). Rather than being part of one "Mafia," organized crime goes by various names in different parts of the country, at least to those directly involved in it. In Chicago the usual terms are "the Syndicate" or "the Outfit." It is called "the People" in many Western states and in upstate New York "the Arm." Police agencies often use the name "the Confederation," or simply "the Mob."

The most detailed study carried out into organized crime dealt mainly with an Italian-American crime "family" in New York City (Ianni and Reuss-Ianni, 1973). The Iannis assert that there had never been a single unified Mafia organization in Sicily, let alone in the United States. What were exported to America were social values involving the primacy of kin attachments, and stressing personal honor as being more important than law. The Lupullos, the group studied, maintained contacts nationally and internationally, but operated largely independently of any other criminal organizations.

Organized crime in the United States is much more firmly established, pervasive, and tenacious than in other industrialized societies. In France, for example, there are documented networks of organized crime, but they are largely limited in their influence to two major cities, Paris and Marseille. In southern Italy, the region of origin of the stereotypical Sicilian gangster, criminal networks are very powerful, but they are linked to traditional patterns of family organization and community control, within largely poor, rural areas.

Organized crime has probably become so significant in American society because of an early association with—and in part was modeled on—the activities of the industrial "robber barons" of the late nineteenth century. Many of the early industrialists made fortunes by exploiting immigrant labor, largely ignoring legal regulations on working conditions and often using a mixture of corruption and violence to build their industrial empires. Organized crime flourished in the deprived ethnic ghettos where people were ignorant of their legal and political rights, using similar methods to curtail competition and build networks of corruption. The power of the Chicago mob boss, Al Capone, for example, was built as much upon the network of contacts he established with local business leaders, government and police officials, as upon the gun-battles in which he was involved with rival criminal groups.

Illicit gambling on horse races, lotteries, and sporting events, together with drug trading and prostitution, represent the greatest sources of income generated by organized crime. A President's Commission on Organized Crime was established in 1983, charged with acquiring detailed information on the extent of organized crime in the United States. The transcripts of interviews with individuals involved with criminal networks have been published, together with basic statistics. According to the commission, in 1983 the total amount of money taken in illegal gambling per year was about $30 billion (President's Commission on Organized Crime, 1985 and 1986). Many Western countries, among them the United States, have legal off-track betting; in the United Kingdom there are licensed public betting shops. While these do not escape all criminal influence, gambling is not controlled by illegal organizations to anything like the same extent as in the United States.

VICTIMLESS CRIME

So-called **victimless crimes** are activities in which individuals more or less freely engage without directly harming others, but which are defined by the state as illegal (taking narcotics, various forms of gambling, or prostitution) (Schur, 1965; Geis, 1972). The term "victimless" crime is not entirely accurate, because those, for example, who become drug addicts, gamblers, or prostitutes in a sense fall victim to organized crime. However, many argue that since whatever harm befalls such individuals is mainly of their own doing, it is not the role of the government to intervene in such activities—and these habits should be "decriminalized."

Some authors propose that no activities in which people indulge of their own free will should be illegal (so long as they do not impinge upon others' freedom or cause them harm). Opponents claim that the state must have a role as moral guardian of the population subject to

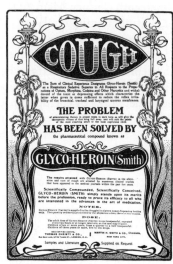

The drug problem in the United States presents law-enforcement officials with one of their greatest challenges, as the cartoon illustrates. At one time, though, the victimless crime of taking heroin was not a crime at all, as this early twentieth-century advertisement shows.

its administration, and that therefore it is justified to define at least some of these types of activity as criminal. Curiously, this argument is most often advocated by conservatives, who in other respects lay an emphasis upon freedom of the individual from interference by the state. Of course, the issue is very complicated. Is someone doing harm to others by hurting themselves, such as a heroin addict hurting her or his family? After all, alcohol is also a drug, and alcoholism damages many families; but alcohol consumption is not a crime.

DEVIANCE AND MENTAL ILLNESS

LET US AT THIS POINT TURN TO A DISCUSSION OF THE SEC-
ond major area of deviant behavior, which involves individuals, the state, and the sciences of medicine and
psychology—mental illness. The idea that the insane are mentally "ill," as has been mentioned, dates from only two centuries ago. Before that time, people we would now regard as mentally disordered were considered "possessed," "unmanageable," or "melancholic," rather than sick. Accordingly, society has dealt with the mentally ill in different ways over time, from banishing them from the walls of the city or tossing them in workhouses or prisons along with crimi-

nals, the poor, and the aged, to establishing separate asylums for voluntary or involuntary commitment. Today, there is an enormous psychiatric and psychological industry in collaboration with the state attempting to cope with mental illness.

FROM PSYCHOSIS AND NEUROSIS TO *THE DIAGNOSTIC AND STATISTICAL MANUAL* (DSM-III-R)

Psychiatrists traditionally divided mental disorders into two main categories, psychoses and neuroses. The **psychoses** were the most serious type; the afflicted had such a severely disturbed sense of reality that they could not deal with everyday life. **Schizophrenia** was the most commonly recognized form of psychosis, and diagnosed schizophrenics made up a substantial proportion of the inmates of mental hospitals. Symptoms characterizing schizophrenia included talking in seemingly illogical or disconnected ways, hearing or seeing hallucinations, having illusions of grandeur or persecution, and being unresponsive to surrounding circumstances or events.

The other main category, the **neuroses,** were less-severe disorders that caused the afflicted much anxiety, but such individuals retained a sense of reality and could carry on their ordinary day-to-day lives. The main feature of behavior classified in this category was a pervasive and at times debilitating worry about matters that other people would see as trivial. A person might experience extreme anxiety, for instance, when meeting strangers for the first time; another might

This painting depicts the eighteenth-century French reformer Philippe Pinel ordering the removal of chains from mental patients, who, until that time, had been mainly locked up and left untreated.

have such an exaggerated fear (*phobia*) of leaving the house, or getting into an elevator. Some individuals are *obsessive compulsives* who will perform the same activity over and over again. For instance, someone might make and remake a bed thirty or forty times each morning before being satisfied enough to go on to another domestic chore (Prins, 1980).

All of these disorders—schizophrenia, phobia, obsessive-compulsion—still exist along with numerous others, depression being among the most prevalent. But the way by which they are categorized has changed. Instead of using the psychoses-neuroses distinction, the American Psychiatric Association now uses, as an all-encompassing categorization, *The Diagnostic and Statistical Manual,* Third Edition, Revised (DSM-III-R). For each disorder, DSM-III-R is a formidable document, but it is still the subject of much controversy particularly regarding diagnosis and treatment.

DIAGNOSING MENTAL ILLNESS

To many, the diagnostic categories employed in psychiatry are quite unreliable. One of the most telling indications of this is to be found in David Rosenhan's pseudo-patient study of mental-hospital admissions (Rosenhan, 1973). In this research, eight sane people presented themselves to the admissions units of different mental hospitals located on the east and west coasts of the United States. They had falsified their employment records and disguised the fact that all had received professional psychological training; they did not change their personal biographies in any other way. The pseudo-patients claimed to hear voices.

All were diagnosed as schizophrenic and admitted. Once in the hospitals, they returned to their normal behavior. None were detected by hospital staff as "fakes," although the real mental patients correctly saw them as imposters. All the collaborators in the study regularly and openly took notes on their experiences. Rather than discussing this writing with the pseudo-patients, the staff simply saw the writing as one aspect of their pathological behavior. The length of hospitalization of these people ranged from seven to fifty-two days, and each was eventually discharged with a diagnosis of schizophrenia "in remission." As Rosenhan points out, the phrase "in remission" did not mean that the normality of the pseudo-patients had been discerned, rather it clearly indicated how easily and unreliably a person could be diagnosed schizophrenic.

Rosenhan's research caused a great deal of controversy; critics point out that its results were not quite as dramatic as was claimed.

The nursing reports on the collaborators indicated that they "exhibited no abnormal indications" (Rosenhan, 1973). Length of hospitalization perhaps indicates very little, since the study was conducted at a time when it was difficult, if not impossible, to be discharged from mental hospitals in the United States on short notice.

The characteristics used by psychiatrists to diagnose schizophrenia clearly do exist. A minority of people, for example, persistently hear voices when no one is present, experience hallucinations, or display behavior seemingly quite disjointed and illogical. On the other hand, Rosenhan's experiment indicates the vague character of some forms of psychiatric diagnosis and the influence of labeling (described earlier in this chapter). If the pseudo-patients had not been collaborators in a research investigation, but had for some other reason found themselves in mental hospitals, there is little doubt that they would have been thereafter stuck for the rest of their lives with the diagnostic label of "schizophrenic in remission."

In 1987, an American city launched a program whereby teams of social workers and medical technicians went into various city areas to offer assistance to those living on the street. Controversy arose when one woman was taken to a mental health facility for psychiatric diagnosis. This woman (left) was diagnosed as schizophrenic by one team of psychiatrists but not so by another team. The same woman is pictured (right) sometime after the diagnoses, without having been involuntarily hospitalized or treated. This case illustrates the problems society has in determining who is and who is not mentally ill.

TREATING MENTAL DISORDERS

Today there are innumerable treatments, from psychodynamic, behavioral, and cognitive therapies to a group of physical treatments, for the multitude of disorders in the DSM-III-R. Yet, there remains among mental health professionals much disagreement on which treatment to use with which disorder. The history of physical treatment illustrates this.

Physical Treatments

Many different physical treatments for mental illness have been proposed in the past century. Claims have repeatedly been made that a physiological basis of the major mental disorders (particularly schizophrenia) has been discovered. Yet the physical treatment of mental illness, and the thesis that it has an identifiable biological basis, have proved problematic. Physical methods employed to treat schizophrenia have included insulin shock therapy, electroconvulsive therapy (E.C.T.), and prefrontal lobotomy (the surgical severing of neural connections in the frontal lobes of the brain). In shock treatments, the patient suffers a short but intense convulsion, followed by memory loss that can sometimes last for weeks or months. At the end of this, in theory, there is a return to normality. This procedure has been largely abandoned for schizophrenia, but is still used in extreme cases of depression. Many have seen it as little more than a barbaric form of punishment. Today, after having used E.C.T. so often, psychiatrists still do not know why it did not work with schizophrenia nor why it seems to help lift severe depression.

Lobotomy was introduced by a Portuguese neurologist, Antonio Egas Moniz, in 1935, and for a period was extensively used in many countries. Broad claims were made for its effectiveness in improving the behavior patterns in psychotic patients, but it became apparent that many patients showed a conspicuous deterioration in their intellectual capabilities, and developed apathetic personalities. By the 1950s the technique had become largely discarded—although partly because of the discovery of new tranquilizing drugs. Drug therapy is now widely used for disorders from anxiety to schizophrenia. There is no doubt that the drugs "work" to some degree—even if no one knows exactly why they do so—in that they subdue some of the symptoms that make it difficult for patients to live effectively in the wider society. How effective they are even in this limited respect, however, remains disputed (Scull, 1984).

THE NATURE OF MADNESS: RESIDUAL RULE-BREAKING

Such examples have made many sociologists skeptical about the tendency to try to explain, and cure, mental illness primarily in physical terms. In reaction, they have drawn upon labeling theory to interpret the nature of mental illness. Thomas Scheff (1966) has suggested that mental disorders, especially schizophrenia, can be understood by the concept of **residual rule-breaking.** *Residual norms* are the basic rules of action and conversation structuring day-to-day life. They concern the conventions studied by Erving Goffman and ethnomethodologists (see Chapter 4: "Social Interaction and Everyday Life")—for example, looking at the person who is talking to you, grasping the meaning of what other people say and do, and controlling body posture and gestures. Violating these norms, Scheff suggests, is essentially what schizophrenia is.

Many or all of us are residual rule-breakers in some circumstances. A person who is deeply upset about the death of a loved one, for example, might behave quite "unnaturally" in interaction with others. In such a situation, behavior of this kind is tolerated and even expected. Were an individual to act in such a way without any apparent reason, however, the reaction of others would be quite different and it is possible the person would be regarded as mentally ill. Once such a label has been applied, the person's subsequent experiences are likely to reinforce secondary deviance, that is, to lead them to behave in the expected way (Smith, 1978).

Scheff's theory does not explain *why* some individuals become residual rule-breakers. There may possibly be genetic factors involved. Sociological studies and theories of mental illness do not refute the possibility, or even probability, that there is a biological input to some of the main types of mental disorder (Roth and Kroll, 1986), but they do lay out a much wider context for understanding mental disorders.

POLITICS, SOCIAL PRESSURE, AND PSYCHIATRY

Even if it were true that the major recognized forms of mental illness have a biological foundation, it would not necessarily follow that it is desirable to keep mental patients separated from the wider community, particularly when people are placed in mental hospitals against their will. An extreme case of involuntary commitment existed, according to some, up until quite recently in the Soviet Union, where dissidents, with no distinguishable signs of mental disorder save for their opposition to the Soviet system, were declared mentally ill and lodged in mental hospitals. Such a use of psychiatry allows for the removal of critics of the system from public view, without the need of a trial. Active political opposition is equated with lunacy, while a "cure" is represented by retraction of whatever accusations were made against the state. The practice was widely condemned by psychiatrists and human-rights groups outside the Soviet Union. It was by any token an illegitimate use of state power to seek to control opposition.

Some have argued however that such control through the use of psychiatry exists to a certain extent in the West as well. A psychiatrist, Thomas Szasz (1970), proposed that the concept of mental illness is a myth, justifying persecution in the name of mental health. Involuntary detainment in a mental hospital is essentially a form of imprisonment for deviants who have not committed any crimes in law. According to Szasz, what are seen as mental illnesses today should more properly be regarded as "problems in living" that some individuals experience in an acute way. People currently called "mentally ill" should be incarcerated only if they transgress laws, like any "sane" member of the population. The homeless old woman singing to herself on a street corner, for instance, who does not want to be in a hospital or shelter because she is afraid "they" will hurt her, should be allowed to live as she has chosen because she is not committing a crime in doing so. Everyone should be free to express whatever views or feelings they might have, and to live as they so wish. Those who feel they need help should be able to seek psychotherapy on a voluntary basis, like any other service.

DECARCERATION

Over the past twenty-five years in most Western countries, there have been major changes affecting inmates of carceral organizations (Cohen, 1985). The mentally ill and the physically and mentally handicapped have been released in large numbers, with the object of replacing institutional confinement with community care. These reforms have been prompted largely by humanitarian motives, combined to some extent with cost-saving endeavors, since the expense to the state of maintaining custodial organizations is very considerable.

Decarceration has radically affected mental-health treatment. Many liberal reformers had been concerned about the effects of incarceration upon mental patients, since people kept away from the outside world became "institutionalized" and were only able to function within the very organizations that were supposed to care for or rehabilitate them. In addition to pressure from reformers to "do away with the asylum walls," two other factors in the 1950s and 1960s enabled this change in the treatment of the mentally ill. One, first introduced in Britain, was the development of methods of psychiatric therapy emphasizing the need of individuals to relate to groups and communities. The second, and more influential, factor was the marketing of new drugs that seemingly provided a breakthrough in the treatment and management of mental illness, as well as forms of mental retardation and mental disorders of old age. Between 1955 and 1974, the mental-hospital population in the United States was reduced by over 60 percent (Rose, 1979), although many of those released were old people. In some states the decline was particularly steep and dramatic. For instance, in California, the numbers of the elderly in state and county hospitals dropped by nearly 95 percent in only two years between 1975 and 1977.

What have been the consequences of decarceration? Many mental patients in fact seem worse off than they were before. Those discharged often find themselves living in circumstances in which others are unwilling or unable to care for them (Wallace, 1987). In many areas there is a serious lack of funds for providing community-care systems. Governmental agencies saving money on the upkeep of mental hospitals are usually not prepared to devote large-scale expenditures to the creation of community services. It is not clear to what extent people with serious and persisting mental disabilities can be treated in existing community medical-health centers. Many of those released from mental hospitals make up a part of the homeless population. They lack adequate means of support, and have drifted to decaying inner-city areas. There they live in poverty and isolation, on the streets or as trapped in city shelters as they ever were in asylums.

Michael Dear and Jennifer Wolch refer to the environments in which many ex-mental patients live as "landscapes of despair" (Dear and Wolch, 1987). It would surely be a retrograde step to suggest that those living in such circumstances be returned to the asylums. Dear and Wolch call for the creation of a "landscape of caring" that would begin to realize the promise of community care. This would require the provision of adequate shelter and services, backing these up with employment opportunities offered to those released from custodial care. In such a context, we could begin to speak of genuine progress in the community treatment and understanding of people suffering from mental anguish and disability.

DEVIANCE AND SOCIAL ORDER

IT WOULD BE A SERIOUS MISTAKE TO REGARD DEVIANCE wholly in a negative light. Any society that recognizes that human beings have diverse values and concerns must find space for individuals or groups whose activities do not conform to the norms followed by the majority. People who develop new ideas, in politics, science, art, or other fields are often regarded with suspicion or hostility by those who follow orthodox ways of doing things. The political ideals developed in the American Revolution, for example—freedom of the individual and equality of opportunity —were fiercely resisted by many people at the time, yet they have now become accepted across the world. To deviate from the dominant norms of a society takes courage and resolution, but is often crucial in securing processes of change that later are seen to be in the general interest.

Is "harmful deviance" the price a society has to pay where considerable leeway is allowed for people to engage in nonconformist pursuits? For example, are high rates of criminal violence and homicide a cost that is exacted in American society in exchange for the wide range of individual liberties its citizens enjoy? Some have certainly suggested as much, arguing that crimes of violence are inevitable in a society in which rigid definitions of conformity do not apply. But this view does not hold much water when examined closely. In some societies in which a wide range of individual freedoms are recognized, and deviant activities tolerated (such as in Holland) rates of violent crime are low. Conversely, countries in which the scope of individual freedom is restricted (like South Africa) may show high levels of violence.

A society that tolerates deviant behavior need not suffer social disruption. This outcome can probably only be achieved, however, where individual liberties are joined to social justice—in a social order where inequalities are not glaringly large, and in which the population as a whole has the chance to lead a full and satisfying life. If freedom is not balanced with equality, and if many people find their lives largely devoid of self-fulfillment, deviant behavior is often likely to be channeled towards socially destructive ends.

SUMMARY

1. Deviant behavior refers to action that transgress commonly held norms. What is regarded as deviant can shift from time to time and place to place; "normal" behavior in one cultural setting may be labeled "deviant" in another.

2. *Sanctions,* formal or informal, are applied by society to reinforce social norms. *Laws* are norms defined and enforced by governments; *crimes* are acts that are not permitted by those laws.

3. Biological and psychological theories have been developed claiming that crime and other forms of deviance are genetically determined, but these have been largely discredited. Sociologists argue that conformity and deviance intertwine in different social contexts. Divergencies of wealth and power in society strongly influence opportunities open to different groups of individuals and determine what kinds of activities are regarded as criminal. Criminal activities are learned in

much the same way as are law-abiding ones, and in general are directed towards the same needs and values.

4. Labeling theory (which assumes that labeling someone as deviant will reinforce their deviant behavior) is important because it begins from the assumption that no act is intrinsically criminal (or normal). However, this theory needs to be supplemented with the enquiry: what caused the behavior (which has come to be labeled "deviant") in the first place?

5. The extent of crime in any society is difficult to assess, as not all crimes are reported. But some societies seem to experience much higher levels of crime than others—as is indicated by the high rates of homicide in the United States as compared to other Western countries.

6. As "crime" has varied between different periods and cultures, so have forms of punishment. Prisons have developed partly to protect society and partly with the intention of reforming the criminal. In this they seem to be mostly ineffective. The death penalty has been abolished in most countries partly because it is regarded by many people as immoral in itself, and partly because it seems to have no discernible effect on deterring crime.

7. Rates of criminality are much lower for women than for men, probably because of general socialization differences between men and women, plus the greater involvement of men in nondomestic spheres.

8. *White-collar crime* and *crimes of the powerful* refer to crimes carried out by those in the more affluent sectors of society. *Organized crime* refers to institutionalized forms of criminal activity, in which many of the characteristics of orthodox organizations appear, but where the activities engaged in are systematically illegal.

9. Sociological studies of mental illness have raised questions about the precision of the diagnostic categories used by psychiatrists, and have indicated that some people "learn" to become mentally ill by the very process supposed to treat them. Labeling probably plays an important part in producing this outcome.

10. Decarceration is the process whereby inmates of custodial organizations are returned to the community. The unintended consequences of decarceration have often been unfortunate, as many former inmates of mental hospitals struggle to survive in the unfamiliar circumstances in which they find themselves "on the outside."

BASIC CONCEPTS

DEVIANCE
CONFORMITY
CRIME
MENTAL ILLNESS

IMPORTANT TERMS

DEVIANT SUBCULTURE
SANCTION
NONCONFORMITY
LAWS
PSYCHOPATH
DIFFERENTIAL ASSOCIATION
ANOMIE
GANG
LABELING THEORY
WHITE-COLLAR CRIME

CRIMES OF THE POWERFUL
ORGANIZED CRIME
CRIMINAL NETWORK
VICTIMLESS CRIME
PSYCHOSES
SCHIZOPHRENIA
NEUROSES
RESIDUAL RULE-BREAKING
DECARCERATION

GENDER AND SEXUALITY

TWO NEWLY BORN INFANTS LIE IN THE NURSERY OF A HOSPI-
tal maternity ward. One, a male baby, is wrapped in a blue
blanket, the other, a female, is in a pink blanket. Both
babies are only a few hours old and are being seen by their
grandparents for the first time. The conversation between
one pair of grandparents runs along these lines:

GRANDMA A: There he is—our first grandchild, and a
boy.

GRANDPA A: Hey, isn't he a hefty little fellow? Look at
that fist he's making. He's going to be a
regular little fighter, that guy is. *(Grandpa
A smiles and throws out a boxing jab to his
grandson.)* At-a-boy!

GRANDMA A: I think he looks like you. He has your
strong chin. Oh, look, he's starting to cry.

GRANDPA A: Yeah—just listen to that set of lungs. He's
going to be some boy.

GRANDMA A: Poor thing—he's still crying.

GRANDPA A: It's okay. It's good for him. He's exercising
and it will develop his lungs.

GRANDMA A: Let's go and congratulate the parents. I know they're thrilled about little Fred. They wanted a boy first.

GRANDPA A: Yeah, and they were sure it would be a boy too, what with all that kicking and thumping going on even before he got here.

When they depart to congratulate the parents, the grandparents of the other child arrive. The dialogue between them goes like this:

GRANDMA B: There she is . . . the only one with a pink bow taped to her head. Isn't she darling.

GRANDPA B: Yeah—isn't she little. Look at how tiny her fingers are. Oh, look—she's trying to make a fist.

GRANDMA B: Isn't she sweet . . . you know, I think she looks a little like me.

GRANDPA B: Yeah, she sorta does. She has your chin.

GRANDMA B: Oh, look, she's starting to cry.

GRANDPA B: Maybe we better call the nurse to pick her up or change her or something.

GRANDMA B: Yes, let's. Poor little girl. *(To the baby)* There, there, we'll try to help you.

GRANDPA B: Let's find the nurse. I don't like to see her cry. . .

GRANDMA B: Hmm. I wonder when they will have their next one. I know Fred would like a son, but little Fredericka is well and healthy. After all, that's what really matters.

GRANDPA B: They're young yet. They have time for more kids. I'm thankful too that she's healthy.

GRANDMA B: I don't think they were surprised when it was a girl anyway . . . she was carrying so low. (Walum, 1977)

The contrast between the two sets of conversations sounds so exaggerated that it is tempting to think they were made up. In fact, they are composed of transcripts of actual dialogue recorded in a maternity ward. The very first question usually asked of a parent—in Western culture at least—is, "Is it a boy or a girl?" Our images of others are fundamentally structured around sexual identity, as seen in the experiences of people who have lived for part of their lives as men and then undergone surgery in order to become women (Morris, 1977). Family, friends, and colleagues find it enormously difficult to call someone they have known as a "him," a "her." The alterations in behavior and attitudes that this implies are immense.

Astronaut Sally K. Ride

In the discussion that follows, we study the nature of sex differences, analyzing the complex character of what it means to be a "man" or a "woman." We shall first of all look at the historical differences between the sexes, then at the aspects of socialization that influence **femininity** and **masculinity.** Subsequently we shall discuss the social and economic position of women in modern societies, before moving on to an analysis of sexuality. In the present chapter, we weight our discussion mainly towards the analysis of the position and experience of women in different types of society. For many aspects of sociology are implicitly concerned primarily with the experience of men, who dominate the "public" spheres of social life—for instance, in politics or the military and even, as we saw in the preceding chapter, in crime. In spite of changes that have occurred over recent years in the industrialized societies, inequalities between the sexes remain very marked—as will be shown in some detail below.

SEX, GENDER, AND BIOLOGY

JAMES MORRIS, A NOTED BRITISH JOURNALIST AND A MEMBER of Sir Edmund Hillary's expedition to climb Mount Everest, underwent a sex-change operation after he was well into his adulthood. Some time after living as a woman, now known as Jan Morris, she described how different her life had become:

We are told that the social gap between the sexes is narrowing, but I can only report that having, in the second half of the twentieth century, experienced life in both roles [male and female], there seems to me no aspect of existence, no moment of the day, no contact, no arrangement, no response, which is not different for men and for women. The very tone of voice in which I was now addressed, the very posture of the person next in [line], the very feel in the air when I entered a room or sat at a restaurant table, constantly emphasized my change of status.

And if others' responses shifted, so did my own. The more I was treated as a woman, the more woman I became. I adapted willy-nilly. If I was assumed to be incompetent at reversing cars, or opening bottles, oddly incompetent I found myself becoming. If a case was thought too heavy for me, inexplicably I found it so myself. . . .

It amuses me to consider, for instance, when I am taken out to lunch by one of my more urbane men friends, that not so many years ago that fulsome waiter would have treated *me* as he is now treating *him*. Then he would have greeted me with respectful seriousness. Now he unfolds my napkin with a playful flourish, as if to humor me. Then he would have taken my order with grave concern, now he expects me to say something frivolous (and I do). (Morris, 1974)

Sexual differences, the quotation shows, are far more comprehensive, and subtle, than just the more obvious characteristics of physical appearance and dress. Treated from early infancy as either "girls" or "boys," most of us take for granted experiences that for Morris, changing from one sex to another, came as a shock. "She" lived effectively in an entirely different world from the one that "he"—her former self—had inhabited.

The word "sex," as used in ordinary language, is ambiguous, referring both to a category of person and to acts in which people engage —that is, as in "having sex." For the sake of clarity, we must separate these two senses. We can distinguish **sex**—meaning *biological or anatomical differences* between women and men—from **sexual activity**. We need also to make a further important distinction, between sex and gender. While sex refers to physical differences of the body, **gender** concerns the *psychological, social,* and *cultural* differences between males and females. The distinction between sex and gender is fundamental, since many variations between males and females are not biological in origin.

THE ORIGINS OF SEX DIFFERENCES

A first place to start in any discussion of sex is with human genetics. Our sex, and much of our biological makeup, is a result of genes contributed by our father's sperm cell and our mother's egg cell at conception, that is, at the formation of a new cell. All of this genetic material is contained in twenty-three pairs of chromosomes that reside in that new cell. The sperm and egg each contribute genetic information to one member of each pair.

We are concerned with the twenty-third pair of chromosomes, the sex chromosomes. This pair is notated XX for female or XY for male. It is the logic of genetics that an egg (female cell) can contribute only an X to the twenty-third chromosome pair, since it has the XX pair. But since the sperm (male cell) contains the XY pair, it can contribute either an X, resulting in an XX pair (female child) or a Y, resulting in an XY pair (male child).

After conception, the new cell divides and forms new identical cells (with identical chromosomes), which then divide, and before long, the human embryo takes shape. At an early stage, the embryo contains the biological apparatus, the gonads, from which either male testes or female ovaries can develop. We speak of the gonads as being at that point undifferentiated. If a Y chromosome is present, the gonads develop into testes. If the Y chromosome is absent, they develop into ovaries. Once this determination is made, sex differentiation moves from genetic to hormonal control. The testes secrete two hormones. One causes the genital tissues to form external male genitals. Should this hormone not be forthcoming at this stage, the tissues develop into female genitals. The second hormone stops the undeveloped ducts from forming a uterus and fallopian tubes, as happens in the course of female development (Figure 6.1). In other words, the existence or absence of a Y chromosome acts like a switch, early in the development of the embryo, moving the physical development of the organism along one or other of two tracks (Lewontin, 1984).

Mechanisms of further sexual development—involving for example, the growth of pubic hair, the onset of menstruation for females, and the growth of facial hair for males—are also under hormonal control and are triggered in both sexes at puberty. The average age of the onset of puberty has been declining in the industrial societies. A hundred years ago, the average age of first menstruation for girls was fourteen-and-a-half years; today it is twelve. Boys reach puberty somewhat later than girls. Physical differences in strength are at a maximum at puberty; adult men on average possess 10 percent more muscle than women, and a higher proportion of the muscle fiber associated with physical power. Whether this is "in-built" is not easy

FIGURE 6.1   **SEXUAL DIFFERENTIATION IN THE HUMAN FETUS**

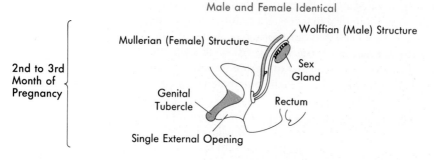

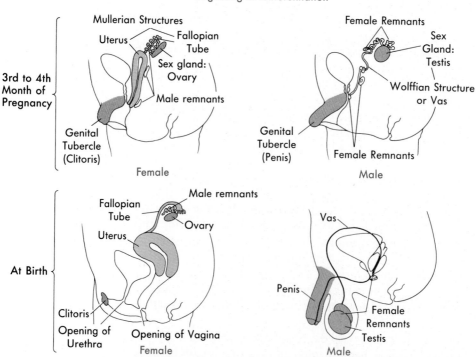

The male and female genitalia develop from common embryonic structures. It is the presence or absence of the Y chromosome and certain hormones that determines sexual differentiation (Money and Ehrhardt, 1972).

to assess with precision, however, because it is affected by training and exercise. Mechanical efficiency (how much force the body can produce per minute for a given unit of fuel consumption) is the same for men and women.

ORIGINS OF GENDER DIFFERENCES: NATURE-NURTURE REVISITED

When we move from the physical differences—sex differences—between women and men to differences in attitudes and behavior—gender differences—we enter a much more disputed area. There is general agreement about what the main physical differences between males and females are, and how those develop (see Figure 6.2 on p. 194). Opinions are radically divided, however, about what general differences in the behavior of men and women are found in all cultures and, given that these do exist, how they should be explained. Many authors hold that there are biologically built-in differences of behavior between women and men that appear, in some guise or another, in every society. Some believe that the findings of sociobiology point strongly in this direction. (For a discussion of sociobiology, see Chapter 2: "Culture and Society.") They are likely to draw attention to the fact, for example, that in all known early cultures, men rather than women took part in hunting. Surely, they argue, this demonstrates that men have biologically-based tendencies towards aggression that women lack. Others are unimpressed by this argument. The level of aggressiveness of males, they say, varies widely between different cultures; women are expected to be more "passive" or "gentle" in some cultures than in others (Elshtain, 1987). Moreover, they add, because a trait is more or less universal, it does not follow that it is biological in origin. There may be cultural factors of a very general kind that produce such traits. For instance, in all cultures most women spend much of their lives caring for children and could not readily take part in hunting. According to this standpoint, differences in the behavior of men and women develop mainly through the social learning of female and male identities. (See Chapter 11: "War and the Military," where the question of "male aggressiveness" and war is further analyzed.)

Studies of Animals: The Development of Aggression

What does the evidence on the issue of male aggression show? One possible source of relevant information concerns differences in hormonal makeup between the sexes. Some have claimed that the male sex hormone, testosterone, which is secreted by the testes, is associated with the male propensity to aggression (Rutter and Giller, 1984). Research has indicated, for instance, that male monkeys cas-

FIGURE 6.2   SEXUAL DIFFERENTIATION AND GENDER IDENTITY

This schematic connects the biological process of sexual differentiation to social influences, which results in the development of a gender identity (Williams, 1987).

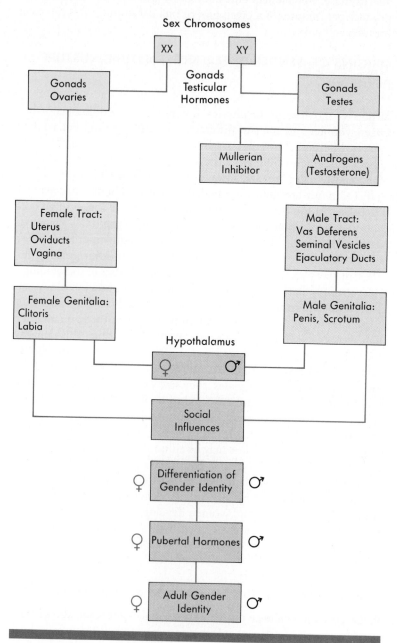

trated at birth are less aggressive than normal males; and female monkeys given testosterone are more aggressive than normal females. However, it has also been found that providing male monkeys with opportunities to dominate actually increases their testosterone level. In other words, aggressive behavior may affect the production of the hormone, rather than the hormone causing increased aggression.

Other evidence derives from direct observations of animal behavior. Those who connect male aggression to biological origins often lay much emphasis on male aggressive behavior among nonhuman primates. If we look at the behavior of the primates, they say, male animals are invariably more aggressive than females. Yet there are in fact large differences between types of primates in this respect. Among gibbons, for instance, there are few noticeable differences in aggression between the sexes, whereas these are marked in baboons. Moreover, many female primates are highly aggressive in some contexts—such as when their young are threatened. Material derived from studies of animals is thus inconclusive even on its own terms, and does not allow us to draw any clear inferences about human behavior in respect to aggressiveness (Epstein, 1988).

Studies of Humans

Studies of two types of congenital abnormality found among a small number of human individuals provide some of the most illuminating evidence we possess concerning the debate over the dominance of biological or social influences. One is called **testicular feminization syndrome,** the other **androgenital syndrome.** In the first of these conditions, individuals are born with the normal male chromosome (XY) makeup, testes, and distribution of hormones. Were such people given a sex examination based upon chromosome tests, such as those administered to women Olympic athletes, they would be designated as "male." But because their genital tissue does not react to testosterone during the development of the embryo, they appear externally to have female genitals. These children are almost always raised as girls, since their condition is not diagnosed until they fail to menstruate at the time of puberty.

Androgenital syndrome is the reverse situation. Individuals with normal female chromosomal (XX) characteristics secrete extra male androgen hormones prior to birth, then develop male external genitals. Some of these infants have genitalia of both sexes, which can be altered by surgery to be female in form. But many such children are brought up as males, their abnormality only being noted at a later stage in their development.

On balance, research into each of these types of abnormality points to the importance of socialization, as opposed to biological influences, in the development of differences between the behavior of boys and girls. In the case of testicular feminization syndrome, infants designated as "female" at birth, though chromosomally "male," tend to develop female gender identity in behavior and attitudes. Babies treated as male since birth, as in androgenital syndrome, acquire male gender characteristics (Money and Ehrhardt, 1973).

A case concerning identical twins is relevant here. Identical twins derive from a single egg and have exactly the same genetic makeup. If it were the case that biological influences were the prime determinants of gender behavior, identical twins would have similar behavior patterns. In this case, one of a pair of identical male twins was seriously injured while being circumcised and a decision was made to reconstruct the genitalia as female. The individual was thereafter raised as a girl. Observations of the behavior of these twins at six years old demonstrated typical male and female traits as found in Western culture. The little girl enjoyed playing with other girls, helped with the housework, and when she grew up wanted to "get married." The boy preferred the company of other boys, his favorite toys were cars and trucks, and he wanted to become a fireman or policeman when he grew up.

For some time, this case was treated as a conclusive demonstration of the overriding influence of social learning upon gender differences. But the girl, as a teenager, was subsequently interviewed during a television program. The interview revealed her to have considerable unease about her gender identity; she felt that perhaps she was "really" a boy after all. However, by then she had learned of her unusual background, so it is not really surprising that she should come to feel uncertain about her "real" identity at that point (Ryan, 1985).

Thus the study does not wholly refute the possibility that there are biological determinants of observed behavior differences between men and women. If these do exist, however, their physiological origins have not yet been identified. Many observers would probably agree with the conclusions drawn by Richard Lewontin, one of the world's leading geneticists:

> The primary self-identification of a person as a man or a woman, with the multitude of attitudes, ideas, and desires that accompany that identification, depends on what label was attached to him or her as a child. In the normal course of events, these labels correspond to a consistent biological difference in chromosomes, hormones and morphology. Thus biological differences become a signal for, rather than a cause of differentiation in social roles. (Lewontin, 1982)

How might we sum up the implications of this section as regards the questions raised earlier concerning male aggressiveness? Like many of the attitudes that are supposed to distinguish between the behavior of men and women in general, "aggressiveness" is a vague notion. There are some areas of conduct falling under this category, however, where there seem to be clear differences between females and males. Thus the use of force or violence for sexual purposes is overwhelmingly a male action (see the discussion of rape later in the chapter). There is no adequate evidence to show that sexual assaults are directly related to biologically given differences between men and women however, although the possibility cannot be discounted. Rather, tendencies towards sexual violence probably have their origins in socialization, which associates masculinity with an active, dominating orientation towards the world. Consider again the attitudes expressed by the two grandparents looking at the newborn babies. Talk of a "regular little fighter," "having a strong chin," "kicking and thumping," and so forth all suggest a view of how boys are "supposed to be," which is likely to influence early socialization. It is not difficult to imagine how these attitudes might later contribute to the use of physical strength in connection with sexual ends.

GENDER SOCIALIZATION

SO FAR, WE HAVE LOOKED AT BIOLOGICAL EVIDENCE CONtributing to our understanding of the origins of gender differences. Here, we take another route toward unravelling these origins by studying **gender socialization.** Many studies have been carried out on whether or not gender differences are the result of social factors. Most forms of gender discrimination are more subtle than the responses of the grandparents that opened the chapter, but they are still powerful and pervasive.

REACTIONS OF PARENTS AND ADULTS

Studies of mother-infant interaction show differences in treatment of boys and girls even when parents believe their reactions to both are the same. Adults asked to assess the personality of a baby give different answers according to whether or not they believe the child to be a girl or a boy. In one experiment, five young mothers were observed in interaction with a six-month-old called Beth. They tended to

| FIGURE 6.3 | GENDER-BASED LANGUAGE |

Sturdy?   Dainty?

Handsome?   Sweet?

Tough?   Charming?

Offer a truck?   Offer a doll?

What words would you use to describe this child named Francis? Or Frances? (The child's sex is revealed on p. 202.)

smile at her often and offer her dolls to play with. She was seen as "sweet" and having a "soft cry." The reaction of a second group of mothers to a child the same age, named Adam, was noticeably different. The baby was likely to be offered a train or other "male toy" to play with. Beth and Adam were actually the same child, dressed in different clothes (Will, Self, and Datan, 1976).

It is not only parents and grandparents whose perceptions of infants differ in this way (Figure 6.3). One study analyzed the words used about newborn babies by the medical personnel attending births. Newborn male infants were most often described as "sturdy," "handsome," or "tough"; female infants were more often talked of as "dainty," "sweet," or "charming." There were no overall size or weight differences between the infants in question (Hansen quoted in Scanzoni and Fox, 1980).

GENDER LEARNING

Early aspects of gender learning by infants are almost certainly unconscious. They precede the stage at which children can accurately label themselves as either "a boy" or "a girl." A range of preverbal clues are involved in the initial development of gender awareness. Male and female adults usually handle infants differently. The cosmetics many women use contain different scents from those the baby learns to associate with men. Systematic differences in dress, hair style, etc., provide visual clues for the infant in the learning process. By age two, children have a partial understanding of what gender is. They know which label is attached to themselves and can usually categorize others accurately. Not until age five or six, however, does a child know that a person's sex does not change or that differences between girls and boys are anatomically based.

The toys, picture books, and TV programs with which young children come into contact all tend to emphasize differences between male and female attributes. Toy stores and mail-order catalogs usually categorize their products by gender. Even some toys that seem "gender neutral" are not so in practice. For example, toy kittens or rabbits are recommended for girls, while lions and tigers are seen as more appropriate for boys.

Vanda Lucia Zammuner (1986) studied the toy preferences of children in two different national contexts—Italy and Holland. Children's views of, and attitudes towards, a variety of toys were analyzed; stereotypically "masculine" and "feminine" toys, as well as toys presumed not to be sex-typed, were included. The children were mostly aged between seven and ten. Both the children and their parents were asked to assess which toys were "boys' " toys and which were suitable for girls. There was close agreement between the adults and children. On average, the Italian children chose sex-differentiated toys to play with more often than the Dutch children—a finding which conformed to expectations, since Italian culture tends to have a more "traditional" view of gender divisions than Dutch society. As in other studies, girls from both societies chose "gender neutral" or "boys' " toys to play with far more than boys wanted to play with "girls' " toys. The implication that could be drawn from this is that male orientations tend to be the dominant ones. Girls are prepared to play with "non-feminine" toys, but boys choose to scorn "feminine" ones.

Books and Television

Lenore Weitzman and her colleagues carried out an analysis of gender roles in some of the most widely used preschool children's books, and found several clear differences in gender roles portrayed (Weitzman et al., 1972). Boys played a much larger part in the stories and pictures than girls, outnumbering them by a ratio of 11 to 1. If animals with gender identities were included, the ratio was 95 to 1. The activities of boys and girls also differed. The boys engaged in adventurous pursuits and outdoor activities demanding independence and strength. Where girls did appear in the stories, they were shown as passive and confined themselves mostly to indoor activities. Girls cooked and cleaned for the males, or awaited their return (Figure 6.4).

Much the same was true of the adult men and women represented in the storybooks. Women who were not wives and mothers were imaginary creatures like witches or fairy godmothers. Not one woman in all the books analyzed had an occupation outside the home. By contrast, the men were depicted in a large range of roles, as

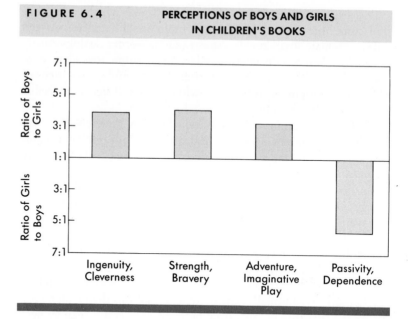

FIGURE 6.4   **PERCEPTIONS OF BOYS AND GIRLS IN CHILDREN'S BOOKS**

In a study of children's books, boys were more likely to be depicted as clever, strong, and adventurous; girls, as passive and dependent (Women on Words and Images, 1972).

fighters, policemen, judges, kings, and so forth. Later studies show some change in these ratios. An analysis of eight separate studies of American children's literature disclosed similar findings in all of them. Some studies only counted the main characters in the stories, while others counted every character, but the percentages were about the same in each case. Some 75 percent of the characters were boys or men, 25 percent girls or women (Butler and Paisley, 1980; Friedman, 1977).

Picture books and storybooks written from a nonsexist perspective have still made little impact in the overall market for children's literature. Fairy tales, for example, embody very traditional attitudes towards gender, and towards the sorts of aims and ambitions girls and boys are expected to have. "Some day my prince will come"—in versions of fairy tales several centuries ago, this usually implied that a girl from a poor family might dream of wealth and fortune. Today, its meaning has become more closely tied to the ideals of romantic love. Feminists have tried to rewrite some of the most celebrated fairy tales, reversing their usual emphases:

The child pictured on p. 200 is female.

I really didn't notice that he had a funny nose.
And he certainly looked better all dressed up in fancy
    clothes.
He's not nearly as attractive as he seemed the other night.
So I think I'll just pretend that this glass slipper feels too
    tight. (Viorst, 1986)

As in this version of "Cinderella," however, these "rewrites" are mainly in books directed to adult audiences and have scarcely at all affected the tales represented in innumerable children's books.

Although there are some notable exceptions, analyses of TV programs designed for children conform to the findings on children's books. Studies of the most frequently watched cartoons show that virtually all the leading figures are male, and that males dominate the active pursuits depicted. Similar images are found in the commercials that appear at regular intervals through the programs.

Schools

By the time they start school, children have clear ideas about gender differences, and such ideas are difficult to alter. Schools might provide an opportunity for change, and in theory, are not supposed to encourage gender differentiation. In practice, though, an array of factors affect girls and boys differently. In many Western countries, although not in the United States, there are still differences in the curriculum girls and boys follow—home economics or "domestic service" are studied by the former, for example, woodwork or metalwork by the latter. Boys and girls are often encouraged to play different sports. The attitudes of teachers may subtly or more openly vary towards their female pupils as compared to their male pupils, reinforcing the expectation that the boys are expected to be the "performers," or tolerating greater rowdiness among the boys than the girls (see Chapter 13: "Education, Communication, and Media"). Peer-group socialization tends to play a major part in reinforcing and further shaping gender identity throughout a child's school career. Children's friendship circles, in and out of school, are normally either all-boy or all-girl groups. In effect, schooling still tends to reinforce the separate gender identities and roles that children learn as toddlers.

Nonsexist Child Rearing

June Statham (1986) studied the experiences of a group of parents committed to nonsexist child rearing. Thirty adults in eighteen families of children aged from six months to twelve years were involved in the research. The parents were of middle-class background, mostly involved in academic work as teachers or professors. Statham found that most of the parents did not simply try to reverse traditional gender roles—seeking to make girls more like boys—but wanted to foster new combinations of the "feminine" and "masculine." They wished boys to be more sensitive to others' feelings and capable of expressing warmth. Girls were encouraged to be more assertive in seeking opportunities for learning and self-advancement.

Even with this focus, all the parents found existing patterns of gender learning difficult to combat, as their children were exposed to these with friends and at school. The parents were reasonably successful at persuading the children to play with nongender-typed toys, but this proved more difficult than many of them had at first imagined. One mother commented to the researcher:

> "If you walk into a toyshop, it's full of war toys for boys and domestic toys for girls, and it sums up society the way it is. This is the way children are being socialized: it's all right for boys to be taught to kill and hurt, and I think it's terrible, it makes me feel sick. I try not to go into toy shops, I feel so angry."

Practically all the children, in fact, possessed and played with gender-typed toys, given to them by relatives. Most had a preference for these toys over those that were "gender neutral."

Statham found that the parents knew of storybooks with strong, independent girls as the main characters, but had discovered few showing boys in nontraditional roles. A mother of a five-year-old boy told of how she tried to reverse the sex of the characters in a story she read to him:

> "In fact he was a bit upset when I went through a book which has a boy and a girl in very traditional roles, and changed all the 'he's' to 'she's' and the 'she's' to 'he's.' When I first started doing that, he was inclined to say 'you don't like boys, you only like girls.' I had to explain that that wasn't true at all, it's just that there's not enough written about girls." (Quoted in Statham, 1986)

GENDER IDENTITY AND SEXUALITY: THREE THEORIES

HOW DOES ONE'S GENDER IDENTITY EMERGE? WHAT FACtors are important? Over the years, various theorists have contributed to our understanding of how gender differences emerge. We look here at the work of three such theorists, Sigmund Freud, Nancy Chodorow, and Carol Gilligan.

FREUD'S THEORY OF GENDER DEVELOPMENT

Perhaps the most influential—and controversial—theory of the development of gender identity is Freud's. According to Freud, the learning of gender differences in infants and young children is centered on possession or absence of the penis. "I have a penis" is equivalent to "I am a boy," while "I am a girl" is defined by "I lack a penis." Freud was careful to say that it is not just the anatomical distinctions that matter here; possession or absence of the penis is symbolic of masculinity and femininity (Freud, 1982; orig. pub. 1905).

In the Oedipal phase, at around age four to five, a boy feels threatened by the discipline that his father tends to impose on him at that age, and fantasizes that his father wishes to remove his penis, that is, castrate him. Partly consciously, but mostly on an unconscious level, the boy recognizes his father as a rival for possession of the affections of his mother. In repressing the erotic feelings towards his mother, and accepting the father as a superior being, the boy identifies with the father and becomes aware of his male identity. The boy gives up his love for his mother out of an unconscious fear of castration by his father. A girl, on the other hand, supposedly suffers from "penis envy" because she does not possess the visible organ that distinguishes boys. The mother becomes devalued in the little girl's eyes, because she is also seen to lack a penis and be unable to provide one. When the girl identifies with the mother, she takes over the submissive attitude involved in recognition of being "second best" (see Chapter 3: "Socialization and the Life Cycle").

Once the Oedipal phase has been gone through, children have learned to repress their erotic feelings. The period from about five

As part of the Oedipal phase, according to Freud, the boy develops a strong identity with his father.

FIGURE 6.5   **FREUD'S THEORY OF GENDER IDENTITY**

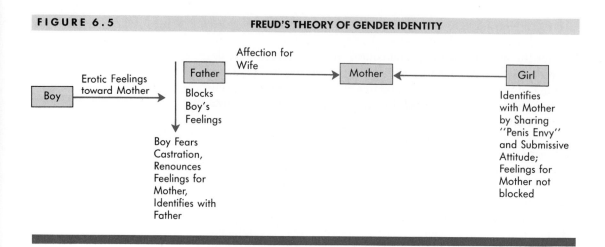

years old to puberty, according to Freud, is one of latency—sexual activities tend to be suspended until the biological changes involved in puberty reactivate erotic desires in a direct way. The latency period, covering the early and middle years of school, is the time at which same-sex peer groups become very important in a child's life. By then, according to Freud, children have already internalized male or female identities and, along with those, a sense of superiority or inferiority (Figure 6.5).

Major objections have been raised against Freud's views, particularly by some feminists, but also by others. First, he seems to identify gender identity too closely with genital awareness; many other, more subtle, factors are surely involved also—cultural factors, for instance, like style of dress or modes of expected behavior for boys compared to girls. Second, the theory seems to depend upon a notion that the penis is "naturally" superior to the vagina, which is thought of as just a "lack" of the male organ. Yet why shouldn't the female genitals be thought of as superior to those of the male? Third, Freud treated the father as the primary disciplining agent, whereas in many cultures the mother plays a more significant role in imposing discipline. Fourth, Freud believed that gender learning is concentrated in the Oedipal phase, at about age four or five. Later authors have emphasized the importance of much earlier learning, beginning in infancy.

CHODOROW'S THEORY OF GENDER DEVELOPMENT

In spite of all these criticisms, Freud's writings have remained central to the work of many subsequent authors concerned with the psychology of gender differences. For although it needs modification, Freud's theory probably casts more light upon the origins of male and female identity than that of any other author. An example of an approach influenced by Freud is the work of Nancy Chodorow (1978, 1988). Chodorow argues that learning to feel male or female is a very early experience, deriving from the infant's attachments to its parents. In addition, she places much more emphasis than Freud does on the importance of the mother as compared to the father. Children tend to become emotionally involved with the mother, since the mother is easily the most dominant influence in the early life of the infant. This attachment has to be broken at some point in order to achieve a separate sense of self—the child is required to become less closely dependent upon the mother.

Chodorow argues that the breaking process—described by Freud as the Oedipal transition—occurs in a different way for boys and girls. Unlike boys, girls remain closer to the mother—able, for example, to go on hugging and kissing her, and imitating what she does. The little girl stays attached to her mother for longer than the boy. Because there is no sharp break from the mother, the girl, and later the adult woman, has a sense of self which is more continuous with others. Her identity is more likely to be merged with and/or dependent on another's: first her mother, later a man. In Chodorow's view, this tends to produce—and to reproduce across the generations—characteristics of sensitivity and emotional compassion in women.

Boys gain a sense of self via a more radical rejection of their original closeness to the mother, forging their understanding of masculinity from what is *not* feminine. They have to learn not to be "sissies" or "mommy's boys." As a result, boys become less skilled in relating closely to others; they develop more analytical ways of looking at the world. They take a more active view of their lives, emphasizing "achievement"; but they have repressed their capabilities to understand their own feelings and those of others (Figure 6.6).

FIGURE 6.6   CHODOROW'S THEORY OF GENDER IDENTITY

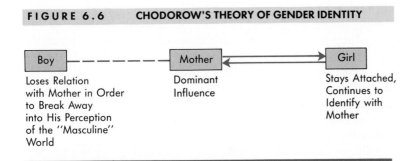

Boy — Loses Relation with Mother in Order to Break Away into His Perception of the "Masculine" World

Mother — Dominant Influence

Girl — Stays Attached, Continues to Identify with Mother

To some extent Chodorow here reverses the Freudian emphasis. Masculinity rather than femininity is defined by a "loss," the forfeiting of continuing close attachment to the mother. Male identity is formed through separation; thus men unconsciously later in life feel their identity is endangered if they become involved in too close an emotional relationship with others. Women, on the other hand, feel the opposite; absence of a close relationship to another person threatens their self-esteem. These patterns are passed on from generation to generation because of the primary role women play in the early socialization of children. Women express and define themselves mainly in terms of relationships. Men have repressed these needs and take a more manipulative attitude towards the world.

Chodorow's work has met with certain criticisms. Janet Sayers (1986), for example, has suggested that Chodorow does not explain the struggle of women—particularly in current times—to become autonomous, independent beings. Women (and men), she points out, are more mixed or contradictory in their psychological makeup than Chodorow's theory suggests. "Femininity" may conceal feelings of aggressiveness or assertiveness, which are revealed only obliquely or in certain contexts (Brennan, 1988). In spite of their limitations, Chodorow's ideas are important. They help us to understand the origins of what psychologists have called **male inexpressiveness**—the difficulty men have in revealing their feelings to others (Balswick, 1983). They explain a great deal about the nature of femininity, and are directly relevant to understanding the universal nature of male dominance over women—a phenomenon that we shall move on to document in following sections of this chapter.

GENDER, SELF, AND MORALITY

Carol Gilligan (1982) has further developed Chodorow's analysis. Her work concentrates on the images adult women and men have of themselves and their attainments. Women, she agrees with Chodorow, define themselves in terms of personal relationships, and judge their achievements by reference to the ability to care for others. Women's place in the lives of men is traditionally that of caretaker and helpmate. But the qualities developed in these tasks are frequently devalued by men, who see their own emphasis upon individual achievement as the only form of "success." Concern with relationships on the part of women appears to them as a weakness rather than as the strength that in fact it is.

Gilligan carried out intensive interviews with about two hundred American women and men of varying ages and social backgrounds.

She asked all of the interviewees a range of questions concerning their moral outlook and conceptions of self. Consistent differences emerged between the views of the women and the men. For instance, the interviewees were asked: "What does it mean to say something is morally right or wrong?" Whereas the men tended to respond to this question by mentioning abstract ideals of duty, justice, and individual freedom, the women persistently raised the theme of helping others. Thus a female college student answered the question in the following way:

> "It [morality] has to do with responsibilities and obligations and values, mainly values. . . . In my life situation I relate morality with interpersonal relationships that have to do with respect for the other person and myself." The interviewer then asked: "Why respect other people?" receiving the answer, "Because they have a consciousness or feelings that can be hurt, an awareness that can be hurt." (Gilligan, 1982)

The women were more tentative in their moral judgments than the men, seeing possible contradictions between following a strict moral code and avoiding harming others. Gilligan suggests that this outlook reflects the traditional situation of women, anchored in caring relationships, rather than in the "outward-looking" attitudes of men. Women have in the past deferred to the judgments of men, while being aware that they have qualities that most men lack. Their views of themselves are based upon successfully fulfilling the needs of others, rather than pride in individual achievement.

PATRIARCHY AND PRODUCTION

ALTHOUGH THERE ARE CONSIDERABLE VARIATIONS IN THE respective roles of women and men in different cultures, there is no known instance of a society in which women are more powerful than men. Women are everywhere primarily concerned with child rearing and the maintenance of the home, while political and military activities tend to be resoundingly male. Nowhere in the world do men have primary responsibility for the rearing of children. Conversely, there are few if any cultures in which women are charged with the main responsibility for the herding of large animals, the hunting of large game, deep-sea fishing, or plough agriculture (Brown, 1977). In modern societies, the division of labor between the sexes has become less clear-cut than it was in premodern cultures; but men still outnumber women in all spheres of power and influence.

Male dominance in a society is usually referred to as **patriarchy.** Why should it be that patriarchy is—in one form or another—universal? Many answers have been suggested, but the most likely explanation is relatively simple. Women give birth to and care for children. The helplessness of the human infant demands that such care be intensive and prolonged—hence the centrality of "mothering" to women's experience, as emphasized by Chodorow. Because of their role as mothers, women are absorbed primarily in domestic activities. Women become what the French novelist and social critic Simone de Beauvoir (1974; orig. pub. 1949) called "the second sex," because of their exclusion from the more "public" activities in which men are free to engage. Men are not dominant over women as a result of superior physical strength, or any special intellectual powers, but because, prior to the development of birth control, women were at the mercy of their biological constitution. Constant childbirth, and continuous caring for infants, made them dependent on males for material provision (Firestone, 1971; Mitchell, 1975).

WOMEN AND THE WORKPLACE

For the vast majority of the population in premodern societies (and for many people in Third World societies today), productive activities and the activities of the household were closely connected. Production was either carried on in the home or nearby. All members of the family in medieval Europe participated in work on the land or in handicrafts. In the towns, workshops were normally in the home, and family members contributed to various aspects of the production process. In the weaving trade, for instance, children did carding and combing, older daughters and wives spun, and the fathers wove. Wives and children similarly worked directly with men in tailoring, shoemaking, and baking. Women often had considerable influence within the household as a result of their importance in the economic process, even if they were excluded from the male realms of politics and warfare. Wives of craftsmen often kept business accounts, as did those of farmers, and widows quite commonly owned and managed businesses.

In the early part of the nineteenth century, in Britain and many other European countries, employers often hired family units. If the father was hired to work in the factory, for example, the wife and children would be taken on as domestic servants or farm hands to supplement his income. Much of this was changed by the separation of the workplace from the home, brought about with the expansion of modern industry. The movement of production into mechanized factories was probably the largest single factor. Work was performed at the machine's pace by individuals hired specifically for the task. Employers wished to contract workers as individuals, not as families, to work in factories, not at home. The old way of treating families as one unit began to fade.

As this practice declined, a widening division became established between home and workplace. Women came to be associated with "domestic" values, although the idea that "a woman's place is in the home" had different implications for women at various levels in society. Affluent women enjoyed the services of maids, nurses, and domestic servants. The burdens were harshest for poorer women, who had to cope with most of their own household chores as well as those of the more affluent families for whom they worked. In some cases, too, they were employed in the emerging factories.

Rates of employment of women outside the home, for all classes, were quite low until well into the twentieth century. Even as late as 1910 in the United States, more than a third of gainfully employed women were maids or house servants. The female labor force consisted mainly of young, single women. Where they worked in factories or offices, employers often sent their wages straight home to their parents. When they married, they withdrew from the labor force.

Since then, women's participation in the paid labor force has risen more or less continuously. One major influence was the labor shortage experienced during the First World War. During the war years, women carried out many jobs previously regarded as the exclusive province of men. On returning from the war, men again took over most of those jobs, but the established pattern had been broken. Today over 50 percent of women aged sixteen to sixty, in the United States, and nearly as many in most other industrialized countries, hold paid jobs outside the home (Figure 6.7). The most significant rise has been among married women. Some 55 percent of married women with children aged three or younger are now in the work force (Mallier and Rosser, 1986; U.S. Bureau of Labor Statistics, 1988). The proportion of employed women, nevertheless, is still well below that of men. Nearly 80 percent of the male population between twenty-five and sixty years old is employed. The proportion of employed men over the past century has not altered much. Expanding levels of employment for women are not a result of them displac-

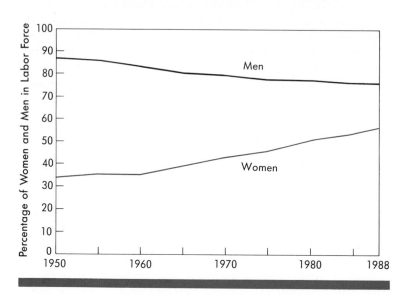

FIGURE 6.7   WOMEN AND MEN (AGE 16 AND OVER) IN THE U.S. LABOR FORCE

ing men from the jobs, but have come about through a general increase in the overall number of jobs available (Table 6.1).

INEQUALITIES AT WORK

Women workers today are overwhelmingly concentrated in routine, poorly paid occupations. The fate of the occupation of "clerk" provides a good illustration of some of the processes involved. In 1850 in the United States, less than 1 percent of clerks were women. Clerks held responsible positions, requiring accountancy skills and carrying managerial responsibilities. The twentieth century has seen a general mechanization of office work (starting with the introduction of the typewriter in the late nineteenth century). Office mechanization has been accompanied by a marked downgrading of the status of "clerk"—together with another related occupation, that of "secretary"—into a routine, low-paid occupation. Women filled these occupations as the pay and prestige of such jobs declined. Today, most secretaries and clerks are women.

Studies of particular types of occupations have shown how gender-

| TABLE 6.1 | LABOR FORCE AND EMPLOYMENT EXPERIENCE OF WOMEN WITH YOUNG CHILDREN (in percentages) |

| | Married, Husband Present | | |
Labor Force Status	1960	1985	1988
Women with children age 3 and younger			
In the labor force	15.3	50.9	54.5
Employed full-time	9.5	30.7	33.7
Employed part-time	4.5	16.3	17.1

Source: U.S. Bureau of Labor Statistics (BLS), April 1961, Tables G and I; and unpublished BLS data.

typing occurs in the workplace. Expanding areas of work of a lower-level kind, such as secretarial positions, or retail sales, draw in a substantial proportion of women. These jobs are relatively poorly paid and have few career prospects. Most men who have good educational qualifications aspire to something higher, while others choose blue-collar work. Once an occupation has become gender-typed—seen as mainly "a woman's job"—inertia sets in. Job hierarchies are

> built around the assumption that men will occupy superior positions, while a stream of women will flow through subordinate jobs. Employers are guided in future hiring decisions by gender labels. And the very conditions of most female jobs lead to adaptive responses on the part of women —low job commitment, few career ambitions, high turnover, seeking alternative rewards in social relations—which fortify the image of women as suitable for only lower-level jobs. (Lowe, 1987)

These social conditions often tend to reinforce outlooks produced by early gender socialization. Women may grow up believing that they should put their husband's career before their own. (Men also are frequently brought up to believe the same thing.)

Women have recently made some inroads into occupations once defined as "men's jobs," but so far only to a limited degree (Table 6.2). Making up over 50 percent of the paid labor force in the United States in 1984, women occupied only 17 percent of higher managerial positions. Women own no more than 5 percent of all businesses, and these produce under 1 percent of all business wealth.

TABLE 6.2	WOMEN AS A PERCENTAGE OF ALL WORKERS IN "MALE" OCCUPATIONS	
Occupation	1975	1988
Airplane pilot, navigator	—	3.1
Architect	4.3	14 .6
Bartender	35.2	49.6
Bus driver	37.7	48.5
Carpenter	0.6	1.5
Dentist	1.8	9.3
Economist	13.1	35.3
Firefighter	—	2.1
Lawyer, judge	7.1	19.5
Mail carrier	8.7	22.0
Physician	13.0	20. 0
Police officer	2.7	13.4
Telephone installer, repairer	4.8	12.1
Welder	4.4	4.9

Source: U.S. Bureau of Labor Statistics. January 1976, Table 2 and January 1989, Table 22.

The Problems of Success

Women who are successful economically have to fit into a world to which they feel they do not fully belong. In their book, *The Managerial Woman,* Margaret Hennig and Anne Jardin compare the experiences of women executives to someone going to a foreign country for an extended stay. It is essential to take good guides and maps, and to observe the rules of the local inhabitants. A good deal of "culture shock" is involved, and even the foreigner who stays on permanently is never accepted. In the long run, however, Hennig and Jardin anticipate that women may exert a modifying effect on the masculine value system, bringing family responsibilities into line with work imperatives (Hennig and Jardin, 1977; Kanter, 1977).

One of the major factors affecting women's careers is the male perception that work comes second to having children for female employees. One study carried out in Britain investigated the views of managers interviewing female applicants for positions as technical staff in the health services. The researchers found that the interviewers always asked the women about whether or not they had, or intended to have, children. They virtually never followed this practice with male applicants. When asked why, two themes ran through their answers: (a) women with children may require extra time off for school holidays or if a child falls sick, and (b) responsibility for child care is seen as a mother's problem rather than as a parental one.

Some managers saw their questions on this issue as indicating an attitude of "caring" towards female employees. But most saw such a line of questioning as part of their task to assess how far a female applicant would prove a reliable colleague. Thus one manager remarked:

> "It's a bit of a personal question, I appreciate that, but I think it's something that has to be considered. It's something that can't happen to a man really, but I suppose in a sense it's un-fair—it's not equal opportunity because the man could never find himself having a family as such." (Homans, 1987)

While men cannot biologically "have a family" in the sense of bear-ing children, they could be fully involved in and responsible for childcare. Such a possibility was not taken into account by any of the managers studied. The same attitudes were held about the promotion of women. Women were seen as likely to interrupt their careers to care for young children, no matter how senior a position they might have reached. A top male manager commented:

> "Males tend to dominate the higher levels because simply the women drop out to have babies and that sort of thing. . . . I don't think that is necessarily selective promo-tion but just the facts of life that women tend to go off and get married and have their families and therefore they have a fragmented career. They come back and have a gap in expe-rience or training and when you come down to it and you are selecting candidates, it is not the sex of the candidate but what they can contribute to their job. You've got the candi-date who is perhaps a woman who has been three years out of a job for family reasons and a man who has been on the job. It is fairly evident, given that the rest is equal between the candidates, that he is likely to get the job." (Homans, 1987)

The few women who were in senior management positions were all without children, and several of those who planned to have children in the future said they intended leaving their jobs, and would perhaps retrain for other positions subsequently.

How should we interpret these findings? Are women's job oppor-tunities hampered mainly by male prejudices? Some managers ex-pressed the view that women with children should not work, but should occupy themselves with childcare and the home. Most, however, accepted the principle that women should have the same career opportunities as men. The bias in their attitudes had less to do with the workplace itself than with the domestic responsibilities of parenting. So long as most of the population take it for granted that parenting cannot be shared on an equal basis by both women and men, the problems facing women employees will persist. It will remain a "fact of life," as one of the managers put it, that women are severely disadvantaged, compared to men, in their career opportunities.

In addition, the average wage of employed women is well below that of men, although the difference has narrowed somewhat over the past twenty years. Women are over-represented in the more poorly paid job sectors, but even within the same occupational categories as men, women on average have lower salaries. For instance, female clerical workers are paid 60 percent of the earnings of their male counterparts; women salesclerks earn 57 percent of male earnings in the same occupation.

Are things different in other countries? As a basis for comparison, we shall consider Sweden and the Soviet Union. Each of these nations has introduced a greater range of measures concerned with improving the economic status of women than has been the case in the United States.

THE CASE OF SWEDEN

Sweden leads the Western world in legislation designed to promote the equality of the sexes (Scriven, 1984). A high proportion of women in Sweden are in paid employment—in 1986, 80 percent of those between ages sixteen and sixty-four did some form of paid work (Allmän/månad statistik, 1987). State benefits, providing for 90 percent of normal earnings, are available to anyone having a child to cover the period of one month before birth until six months afterwards. These six months can be divided between parents depending on who takes time from work to care for the child. A further 180 days' benefit are available, which may be taken by either mother or father at a subsequent period. Many childcare centers exist in Sweden, designed to provide after-school and vacation facilities for children up to the age of twelve.

These measures seem to have been partially successful in providing opportunities for women to achieve positions of influence. For example, women hold a quarter of the seats in the Swedish Parliament, one of the highest percentages internationally. Yet few women are found at the highest levels of business firms, and in most occupations women are not much more significantly represented than in other Western societies. In 1985 45 percent of Swedish women worked in part-time occupations, which have poorer career opportunities, social benefits, and pension rights than full-time jobs. Only 5 percent of men aged sixteen to sixty-four were in part-time work in Sweden. Many women do not wish to leave their children at the day-care centers for the long periods necessary for them to take full-time employment and women continue to be primarily responsible for the home and for childcare. Paradoxically, because of the existence of the day-care centers, men may think they have less need to participate in childcare than they would otherwise (Wistrand, 1981).

WOMEN IN THE SOVIET UNION AND EASTERN EUROPE

The Soviet Union has been said to be "the first country in the world to declare the equality of men and women and to commit itself to policies to ensure this equality" (Attwood and McAndrew, 1984). Following the Russian Revolution of 1917, the new Soviet government publicly declared that it would establish equal occupational opportunities for women, coupled with state provision of childcare facilities.

A women's section of the Central Committee of the Bolshevik Party, known as *Zhenotdel,* was set up in September 1919. It was supposed to bring women into a central role in political as well as economic life. *Zhenotdel* has been compared to modern women's centers—putting on exhibitions, meetings, consciousness-raising sessions, and organizing campaigns. However, it was regarded with suspicion by the male-dominated Communist Party committees. In some parts of the Soviet Union the women's sections were abolished almost immediately after they were first set up. In other regions of the country the women's committees were very active, but met with great resistance from most of the male-dominated organizations. Eventually all were dissolved, becoming incorporated within the orthodox committees of the Party—and instructed to concentrate upon increasing productivity rather than upon women's issues as such.

The Communist Party continued nonetheless to encourage extensive female involvement in the paid-labor force. There is today a markedly higher proportion of women in paid employment in the Soviet Union, and in other Eastern European societies, than in most Western countries. Compared to the West, rates of participation in the work force are especially high for mothers with small children. In the United States, as mentioned, some 55 percent of women with children under three years of age are in the labor force. In Czechoslovakia, by comparison, the figure is over 80 percent (Heitlinger, 1979). Women are spread far more equally across the range of available jobs than in the West. Soviet women perform "physical" work thought in most countries to be the province of men; for example, they work in mining, steel production, and the engineering industry. Women compose about half the blue-collar industrial labor force. They are also well-represented in most professional jobs. Over 75 percent of doctors and dentists in the Soviet Union, and more than 50 percent of medical administrators, are women. By comparison, women make up only a small proportion of doctors and dentists in the United States.

But gender equality in the Eastern European countries is much less developed than might appear from such figures. As in the West, occupations in which there is a high percentage of women have lower average wages and less prestige than comparable occupations in which men dominate. For example, being a physician in the Soviet Union is much less prestigious than in the United States. It follows that doctors receive lower average wages than Soviet engineers, a profession in which women are still out-numbered by men. Average earnings for women in the Soviet Union are about 75 percent of those of men. Women are poorly represented in higher positions in the national government.

Most important of all, in spite of their high rates of labor-force participation, women in the Soviet Union and Eastern Europe retain primary responsibility for care of the home. The amount of effort involved in domestic work in the Soviet Union is much greater than in most Western countries. Shopping is time-consuming, as it is often necessary to wait in long lines to purchase even basic items of food, housing space is limited, and domestic technology is less advanced. Washing machines and refrigerators are expensive relative to wages, while dishwashers and clothes driers are virtually nonexistent. Soviet men mostly have disparaging attitudes towards housework. Although a much higher proportion of women in the Soviet Union work full time outside the home than in the United States, the average contribution of husbands to housework and childcare is smaller.

HOUSEWORK

Regardless of the percentage of women in the paid work force, women everywhere still perform those tasks that make up **housework**. In its current form housework came into existence with the industrial revolution. As we will see in a later chapter on work (Chapter 15), industrialization brought about the separation of the home and workplace (Oakley, 1975). The home became a place of consumption rather than production of goods. Domestic work became "invisible," as "real work" was defined more and more as that which received a direct wage. The period of the development of a separate "home" also saw other changes. Before the inventions and facilities provided by industrialization influenced the domestic sphere, work in the household was hard and exacting. The weekly wash, for example, was a heavy and demanding task. The Maytag Washing Machine Company carried out research reconstructing what washing involved in the nineteenth century, concluding that "the old washday was as exhausting as swimming five miles of energetic breast stroke, arm movements and general dampness supplying an almost exact parallel" (quoted in Hardyment, 1987).

Copyright 1985 G. B. Trudeau. Reprinted with permission of Universal Press Syndicate. All rights reserved.

The introduction of hot and cold running water, at around the turn of the present century, eliminated many time-consuming tasks. Previously, water had to be carried to the home and heated there whenever hot water was required. The wiring of electricity and piping of gas made coal and wood stoves obsolete. Chores such as chopping wood, carrying coal, and continuous cleaning of the stove were thereby largely eliminated. Labor-saving inventions like the vacuum cleaner and washing machine reduced hard work. Declining family size meant fewer children to care for.

Yet, surprisingly, the average amount of time spent on domestic work by women did not decline very markedly. The amount of time American women not in the work force spend on housework has remained quite constant over the past half century. Household appliances eliminated some of the heavier chores, but new tasks were created in their place. Time spent on childcare, stocking the home with purchases, and caring for and improving it, all increased.

The women's movement has had some effect upon men's attitudes towards work inside and outside the home, yet "liberated" men still retain conventional masculine standards. Mirra Komarovsky studied sixty-two male seniors at Columbia University, in New York City, to investigate changing views of masculinity. Many of these individuals clearly shared some feminist objectives, yet they still retained the idea of men as strong-willed and assertive. They expressed desire for intellectual companionship, but were cautious about becoming involved with intelligent, self-confident women. Although they did not have a high opinion of women who became full-time housewives, most still believed that a husband's career should come first. Judgments recognized to be valid in the abstract were disclaimed for the individual. One man commented, for example, "It is only fair to let a woman do her own thing, if she wants a career. Personally, though, I would want my wife at home" (Komarovsky, 1976).

The trend towards an increasing number of women entering the labor force has had a discernible impact on housework activities (Vanek, 1974). Married women employed outside the home do less domestic work than others, although they almost always shoulder the main responsibility for care of the home. The pattern of their activities is of course rather different. They do more housework in the early evenings and for longer hours at weekends than those who are full-time housewives.

Unpaid domestic work is of enormous significance to the economy. It has been estimated that housework accounts for between 25 and 40 percent of the wealth created in the industrialized countries. Domestic work props up the rest of the economy by providing "free" services on which many of the working population depend.

FEMINIST MOVEMENTS

FEMINIST AUTHORS HAVE BEEN LARGELY RESPONSIBLE FOR pointing out and analyzing the importance of housework. For many years, sociologists were guilty of defining "work" as "paid work outside the home." Feminists have shown how misleading such a view was, and have prompted studies of women's activities and attitudes in many areas of social life where they were previously largely ignored. Although this particular influence has been a recent one, **feminism**—the struggle to defend and expand the rights of women—in fact has a lengthy history, going back to the late eighteenth century.

One of the earliest works to advance feminist ideas was the English writer Mary Wollstonecraft's book, *A Vindication of the Rights of Women,* first published in 1792. "Women," she declared, "have acquired all the follies and vices of civilization, and miss the useful fruit" (Wollstonecraft, 1982). Sixteen years previously, as the United States was forming its new government, Abigail Adams made a plea for improving the situation of women when writing to her husband John Adams, who would later become the second president, "I desire you would Remember the Ladies, and be more favorable and generous to them than your ancestors. . . . Remember all Men would be tyrants if they could" (Rossi and Calderwood, 1973).

The first groups actively organized to promote women's rights date from the period immediately following the French Revolution in 1789 (Evans, 1977). In the 1790s, inspired by the ideals of freedom and equality for which the revolution had been fought, several women's clubs were formed in Paris and major provincial cities. The clubs provided meeting places for women, but also developed political programs petitioning for equal rights in education, employment, and government. Marie Gouze, a leader of one of the clubs, drew up a statement entitled *Declaration of the Rights of Women,* based upon the *Declaration of the Rights of Man and Citizen,* the main constitutional document of the revolution. Rights of free and equal citizenship, she argued, could not be limited to men; how can true equality be achieved when half the population were excluded from the privileges that men share?

The response from the male revolutionary leaders was less than sympathetic—Marie Gouze was executed in 1793, charged with "having forgotten the virtues which belong to her sex." The women's clubs were subsequently dissolved by government decree. Feminist groups and women's movements have been formed and reformed repeatedly in Western countries since that date, almost always encountering hostility, and sometimes provoking violence, from the established authorities. Marie Gouze was by no means the only feminist to give her life to the cause of achieving equal rights for her sex.

In the nineteenth century, feminism became more advanced in the United States than elsewhere, and most leaders of women's movements in other countries looked to the struggles of American women as a model. In the 1840s and 1850s, American feminists were closely involved with groups devoted to the abolition of slavery. Antislavery petitions usually carried a high proportion of female signatures. Yet, having no formal political rights (the Constitution did not give women the right to vote), women were excluded from the political lobbying through which reformers could pursue their objectives. No women were allowed to participate in a world antislavery convention held in London in 1840. This very fact led the women's groups to turn more directly to considering gender inequalities. In 1848, just as their French counterparts had done a half century before, women leaders in the United States met to approve a *Declaration of Sentiments* modeled upon the *Declaration of Independence.* "We hold these truths to be self-evident," it opened, "that all men and women are created equal." The declaration set out a long list of the injustices to which women were subject (Hartman and Banner, 1974). However, few real gains in improving the social or political position of women were made during this period. When slavery ended, Congress ruled that only freed *male* slaves should be given the vote.

Sojourner Truth.

Black women played a part in the early development of the women's movement in the United States, although they often had to contend with hostility from their white sisters. Sojourner Truth was a black woman who spoke out against both slavery and the exclusion of women from the vote, linking the two issues closely. When she forcefully and passionately addressed an antislavery rally in Indiana in the 1850s, a white man yelled at her: "I don't believe you really are a woman." She publicly bared her breasts to demonstrate her femininity. In 1852, when she lectured at a women's rights convention in Akron, Ohio, white women in the audience heckled her to prevent her speaking. She overcame this resistance to play a prominent part in women's struggles of the period (Hooks, 1981). But other black women who tried to participate became disillusioned with the prejudice they encountered from their white sisters. Black feminists as a result were very few in number.

One of the most important events in the early development of feminist movements in Europe was the presentation of a petition, signed by 1,500 women, to the British Parliament in 1866. It demanded that the electoral reforms then being discussed include full

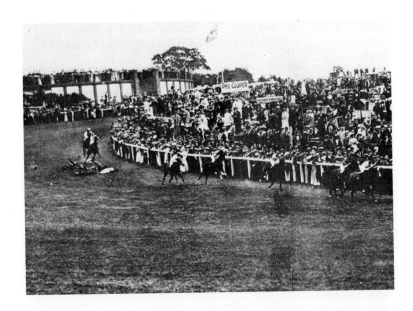

To call attention to the suffragist cause, Emily Davison died after throwing herself in front of the king's racehorse at the Epsom Derby, England, 1913.

voting rights for women. The petition was ignored; in response, its organizers set up the National Society for Women's Suffrage the following year. The members of the society became known as **suffragists,** and throughout the remainder of the nineteenth century they petitioned Parliament to extend voting rights to women. By the early twentieth century, the world influence of British feminism rivaled that of feminists in the United States. In the early 1900s, frequent marches and street demonstrations were organized in both countries. An open-air meeting held in London in June 1908 attracted a crowd numbering half a million people. During this period, women's movements mushroomed in all the major European countries, together with Australia and New Zealand.

Emmeline Pankhurst, a leading figure among the suffragists, went on several speaking tours of the United States, recounting the British struggles to large audiences. Two Americans who had become involved in the campaigns in Britain, Alice Paine and Harriet Stanton Blatch, organized a series of massive marches and parades through New York and other major Eastern cities from 1910 onwards.

By 1920, women had attained the right to vote in many Western countries (Table 6.3). After achieving that right, though, most feminist movements in the United States and elsewhere fell into decline, although numerous small groups remained politically active. Radical women tended to be absorbed into other movements, such as those combating fascism, a political doctrine of the extreme right wing gaining ground in Germany, Italy, and elsewhere in the 1930s. While

TABLE 6.3   THE YEAR IN WHICH WOMEN ACHIEVED THE RIGHT TO VOTE ON AN EQUAL BASIS WITH MEN BY COUNTRY

Year	Country	Year	Country
1893	New Zealand	1945	France, Hungary, Italy, Japan, Vietnam, Yugoslavia, Bolivia
1902	Australia		
1906	Finland		
1913	Norway	1946	Albania, Rumania, Panama
1915	Denmark, Iceland		
1917	Soviet Union	1947	Argentina, Venezuela
1918	Canada	1948	Israel, Korea
1919	Austria, Germany, the Netherlands, Poland, Sweden, Luxembourg, Czechoslovakia	1949	China, Chile
		1950	El Salvador, Ghana, India
		1951	Nepal
		1952	Greece
1920	United States	1953	Mexico
1922	Ireland	1954	Colombia
1928	Britain	1955	Nicaragua
1929	Ecuador	1956	Egypt, Pakistan, Senegal
1930	South Africa	1957	Lebanon
1931	Spain, Sri Lanka, Portugal	1959	Morocco
1932	Thailand	1962	Algeria
1934	Brazil, Cuba	1963	Iran, Kenya, Libya
1936	Costa Rica	1964	Sudan, Zambia
1937	Philippines	1965	Afghanistan, Guatemala
1941	Indonesia	1977	Nigeria
1942	Dominican Republic, Uruguay	1979	Peru, Zimbabwe

Source: Lisa Tuttle, *Encyclopedia of Feminism* (NY: Facts on File, 1986).

many pursued feminist aims in these contexts, little was left of feminism as a distinct movement combating male-dominated institutions. The achievement of equal political rights did little to extend equality to other spheres of women's lives.

THE RESURGENCE OF FEMINISM

In the late 1960s, women's movements again burst back to prominence (Chafe, 1974, 1977). Over the quarter of a century since then, feminism has become a major influence in countries throughout the world, including many Third World societies. The resurgence of feminism began in the United States, influenced by the civil rights movement and by the student activism of the period. Many women were active in these causes, but found themselves often treated by male activists in a traditionally subordinate role. Civil rights leaders were resistant to women's rights being included in the manifestos of equality for which they fought. Women's groups began to establish their own independent organizations concerned primarily with feminist issues.

The women's movement today in fact involves a variety of differing interest groups and organizations. Among the most prominent is the National Organization for Women (NOW), which has a membership of about 160,000 (men may belong as well as women, although the large majority of members are female). Another group is the National Women's Political Caucus (NWPC), which has about half the level of membership of NOW. Some other organizations are "single-issue" groups, concerned with particular issues such as abortion, education, or pension rights. Yet other groups consist of more long-established associations of women in various occupations or professions—like the American Association of University Women (Palley, 1987).

Women's movements today have addressed a much wider range of issues than their predecessors. They have pressed for economic equality, the availability of abortion, and alterations in laws concerning divorce—among other concerns. In addition to significant practical achievements, feminists today have made an intellectual impact far beyond anything previously achieved. Throughout the social sciences, and in many other fields, feminist authors have forced a rethinking of established notions and theories. A great deal of the research carried out in recent years into historical and cultural factors affecting the position of women, and into gender relations more generally, has been prompted by the influence of modern feminism.

DOMESTIC VIOLENCE, SEXUAL HARASSMENT, AND RAPE

WE SHALL NOW TURN TO CONSIDER SOME BASIC PROBLEMS that very many women face, directly or indirectly. They are all to do with ways in which males use their superior social or physical power against women: domestic violence, sexual harassment, and rape. While the first two of these are sometimes practiced by women against men, in the vast majority of cases men are the culprits and women the victims.

The home is often idealized as a haven of security and happiness, but **domestic violence** is part of the experience of many women. This is not a new social ill. Violence towards women was a common aspect of marriage in medieval times and in the early days of industrialization. Until the late nineteenth century, there were no laws in the United States prohibiting a man from physically abusing his wife, short of serious injury or murder. Women now have more legal protection, yet such violence remains widespread. Violence against women in the home is sometimes thought to be mostly minor, but evidence from refuge houses for battered women suggests otherwise. One study notes: "Some women are appallingly injured; they suffer broken bones, knife wounds and severe bruising; some are hit over the head with furniture, some are thrown downstairs and one had a nail hammered into her foot" (Pahl, 1978).

In spite of an improving legal position, recourse to the law for women subjected to domestic violence is difficult. The attitude of the police is sometimes unhelpful. The police normally have a policy of nonintervention in "domestic disputes." When called out in such circumstances, they tend to restrict their intervention to calming down the disputants, rather than pressing charges. Women in relationships involving violence often find it difficult to leave the household. Local government-housing departments are sometimes wary of women who come to them with complaints of physical abuse, suspecting these to be exaggerated for the purposes of securing housing rapidly.

SEXUAL HARASSMENT

In the work setting, the rights of women are more easily enforceable and levels of actual violence against women are low. **Sexual harassment,** nevertheless, is extremely common. Sexual harassment in the workplace may be defined as the use of occupational authority or power to try to enforce sexual demands. This may take blatant forms, as when it is suggested to a female employee that she consent to a sexual encounter or be dismissed. Most kinds of sexual harassment are somewhat more subtle. They involve hints, for example, that the granting of sexual favors would bring other rewards; or that if such favors are not offered some kind of punishment, such as a blocked promotion, will ensue.

Choice about where, and with whom, we have sexual relationships is a basic part of exercising control over our lives. Sexual harassment denies this choice. Although the men involved may see the milder forms of sexual harassment as harmless, women often experience them as humiliating. Women are expected to tolerate unwanted sexual talk, gestures, or physical approaches, and to "play along." To do so demands not only tolerance, but great skill. A cocktail waitress, whose tips are a major part of her income, and who consequently has to please customers, observes that a woman in her job "must learn to be sexually inviting at the same time as she is unavailable. This of course means that men will take out their lust through lewd and insinuating words, subtle propositions, gestures. She must manage to turn him off gently without insulting him, without appearing insulted. Indeed she must appear charmed by it, find a way to say no which also flatters him " (Quoted in Mackinnon, 1979).

It is obviously not easy to draw a line between harassment and what might be regarded as a legitimate approach from a man to a woman. On the basis of self-reporting, however, it has been estimated that seven out of ten women are directly affected by sexual harassment during the course of their working lives. Sexual harassment may be a single occurrence or a consistent pattern of behavior. Where the second of these is involved, women frequently experience difficulty in maintaining their usual work rate, may take sick leave, or quit the job altogether.

RAPE

The rate of occurrence of **rape** is very difficult to assess with any accuracy. Only a small proportion of rapes actually come to the attention of the police and are recorded in the statistics (Table 6.4). The real figure might be as much as five times as high as the official statistics show—although estimates vary widely. A study of 1,236 women in London, England, revealed that one in six had been raped, one in five of the remainder had fought off an attempted rape, and that half of the assaults had taken place either in the woman's own house or in that of her assailant (Hall, 1985). The majority of women who are raped either wish to put the incident out of their minds, or are unwilling to participate in what can be a humiliating process of medical examination, police interrogation, and courtroom cross-examination. The legal process often takes a long time; it might be as much as eighteen months after the incident before a court verdict is reached.

The trial itself can be intimidating. Courtroom procedure is public and the victim must come face-to-face with the accused. Men are not usually convicted on the basis of the testimony of the victim alone. Confirming evidence has to be obtained from others. Proof of penetration, the identity of the rapist, and that the act occurred without the woman's consent, all have to be forthcoming. Corroborative evi-

TABLE 6.4 FORCIBLE RAPES REPORTED IN THE UNITED STATES	
1970	37,990
1975	56,090
1980	82,990
1985	87,670
1987	91,110

Source: U.S. Federal Bureau of Investigation, *Crime in the United States Annual.*

dence of the identity of an assailant is likely to be hard to obtain if the crime occurred in a dark street or alley. A woman who walks alone at night is liable to be portrayed by a defense attorney as encouraging the attentions of men. Wherever the rape occurs, the woman may be interrogated about the history of her previous sexual relationships (although some states have dropped this practice). The defendant's sexual history is not deemed relevant in the same way. In fact, prior convictions for rape or assault on the part of the accused cannot be mentioned in rape cases.

According to a 1736 English ruling, a husband "cannot be guilty of rape committed by himself upon his lawful wife, for by their mutual matrimonial consent and contract the wife hath given up herself in this kind unto her husband which she cannot retract" (quoted in Hall, James, and Kertesz, 1984). This formulation remains the law in England and Wales. Unless a non-molestation injunction, personal-protection order, or legal separation, has been obtained, even women separated from their husbands have no legal defense against rape by them. Rape within marriage is illegal only in a minority of Western countries, such as Denmark, Sweden, Norway, and Canada—although most countries in Eastern Europe and the Soviet Union have passed legislation abolishing the husband's immunity from prosecution.

In the United States, the first case of prosecution for rape in marriage was won against James K. Chretien in 1979. Prior to the Chretien case, rape within marriage was illegal in only five states. Since then, many others have brought in legislation or introduced test cases establishing the crime.

Conventional attitudes as to what is and what is not rape can be very strong. Researchers studying forcible sex within established relationships reported the following case. A man who was drunk started to attempt anal intercourse with his girlfriend. She refused and screamed, at which point he became violent, held her down so that she could not move, and forced her to submit. Yet when asked by the researchers whether she had ever been forced to have sex against her will, she said "no" (Finkelhor and Yllo, 1982).

Research has shown that many common beliefs about rape are false. It is not true, for example, that rape cannot happen if the victim resists; that only young, "attractive" women are likely to be raped; that some women enjoy the experience of being raped; or that most rapists are in some way psychologically disturbed (Hall, 1985). Most rapes are not spontaneous, but at least partly planned in advance (Amir, 1971; Clark and Lewis, 1977). Rape is clearly related to the association of masculinity with power, dominance, and toughness. It is not for the most part the result of overwhelming sexual desire, but of the ties between sexuality and rituals of power and superiority. There seems to be little connection between lust and rape. A substantial proportion of rapists in fact are only able to become sexually aroused once they have terrorized and degraded the victim. The sexual act itself is less significant than the debasement of the woman (Estrich, 1987).

Over the last few years, women's groups have fought to alter both legal and public thinking about rape. They have stressed that rape should not be seen as a sexual offense, but as a type of violent crime. It is not just a physical attack but an assault upon an individual's integrity and dignity. As one writer put it, rape is "an act of aggression in which the victim is denied her self-determination. It is an act of violence which, if not actually followed by beatings or murder, nevertheless carries with it the threat of death" (Griffin, 1980). The campaign has had some real results in respect to changing legislation. Rape is today recognized in law to be a specific type of criminal violence.

Rape and Female Anxiety: Brownmiller's Thesis

There is a sense in which all women are victims of rape. Women who have never been raped often experience similar anxieties to those who have. They may be afraid to go out alone at night, even on crowded streets—and may be almost equally fearful of being on their own in a house or apartment. Emphasizing the close connection between rape and male sexuality as a whole, Susan Brownmiller (1986) has argued that rape is part of a system of male intimidation that keeps all women in fear. Those who are not raped are affected by the anxieties thus provoked, and by the need to be much more cautious in everyday aspects of life than men have to be.

Brownmiller's view may sound extreme, but a moment's thought shows how careful a woman has to be if she wishes to minimize the chance of being raped. The following is a list of "dos" and "don'ts" for women to avoid a rape confrontation, published by a women's organization in the United States. This list supplies compelling support for the view that rape is a crime that affects the behavior of all women (Katz and Mazur, 1979.)

1. Make your home as safe as possible; locks, windows, and doors should be in good working condition. If you move to a new apartment or home, change the locks. The Crime Prevention Unit of the local police can give advice on making the residence burglar-proof—and thus rape-proof.

2. If you live alone:

- leave lights on to give the impression of more than one occupant;

- pretend that there is a male in the house when you answer the door (call out loudly, "I'll get the door, Bob!");

- do not list your first name on the doorbell or in the telephone book; instead, use initials.

3. In general, be aloof to strangers and never open the door to a stranger. Always ask for identification from a delivery or service man (their I.D. card can be slipped beneath the door). If children live in the house, be sure that they do not open the door to a stranger.

4. If you live in an apartment house, do not enter or remain alone in a deserted basement, garage, or laundry room.

5. If you receive an obscene telephone call, say nothing but hang up immediately and report the call to the police.

6. Avoid being alone on the streets or on a university campus late at night. However, if necessary, carry in your hand a "practical" weapon, such as a lighted cigarette, a hat pin, a plastic lemon, an umbrella, a pen, a kitchen fork, a key chain, a hair brush or comb (to slash his face), or a police whistle (not tied around the neck, but on a key chain).

7. Do not hitchhike. (Everyone agrees that this is primary!) If absolutely necessary, go in groups and only in heavy traffic.

8. If you drive a car:

- be sure your gas tank is never below one-quarter full;

- always lock your car when you leave;

- check back seat and floor before getting into a car;

- if you have car trouble, do not accept help from a man or group of men; instead, lift the hood, and wait inside the locked car for the police to come.

9. Be wary of picking up strange men in bars, particularly if you have been drinking heavily or using drugs.

10. Do not ride the elevators alone with a man. Either get off immediately or stand by the control panel.

11. On a date, communicate your limits of sexual activity early so that no misunderstandings occur later.

12. Babysitters should check on the family's reputation before taking the job. Parents should be very careful in the selection of a babysitter.

13. If you are attacked, do *not* cry "rape," cry "fire!"

The study of rape shows how complex are human sexual attitudes and behavior. Rape, as has been pointed out, is rarely if ever the spontaneous expression of sexual desire. It is conditioned by gendered learning, and is a symbolic as well as a physical assertion of male dominance.

HUMAN SEXUAL BEHAVIOR

IN THE FOLLOWING SECTIONS, WE SHALL LOOK IN A MORE general way at the nature of human sexual behavior. We shall first of all consider "normal" human sexuality —that is, heterosexual behavior. In thinking of what is "normal" sexual conduct, we have to bear in mind all that was said in the preceding chapter about the complicated nature of normality and deviance. Homosexual conduct is considered to be a deviant form of activity in Western culture, although widely practiced. In some other societies, however, it is generally approved of, or encouraged, among certain categories of people—as we shall see below. What is regarded as conventional heterosexual behavior differs considerably from culture to culture; and if we consider even just the fairly recent history of Western culture, we find that major changes have occurred in public attitudes towards sexuality.

CROSS-CULTURAL DIFFERENCES IN HETEROSEXUAL BEHAVIOR

Many people suppose that human sexual behavior is mainly governed by biological influences, since sexual intercourse is obviously a necessity for the reproduction of the species. In fact, unlike most of the an-

Auguste Rodin's Eternal Springtime.

imals, our sexual responses are not genetically given, but are almost all learned—and human sexual behavior includes many other kinds of activities besides **heterosexual intercourse** (intercourse between a man and a woman). **Homosexual behavior** (sexual relations between persons of the same sex), for example, is common in many cultures. We shall discuss homosexuality in the following section, concentrating for the time being upon heterosexual activities and involvements.

Accepted types of heterosexual behavior vary widely between different cultures—which is one way in which we know that most sexual responses are learned rather than innate. The most extensive survey of sexual practices across different cultures was carried out several decades ago by Clellan Ford and Frank Beach (1951). They surveyed anthropological evidence from more than two hundred societies and found striking variations in what is regarded as "natural" sexual behavior, and in norms of sexual attractiveness. For example, in some cultures, extended foreplay, perhaps lasting some hours, is thought desirable and even necessary prior to intercourse. In others, foreplay is virtually nonexistent. Kissing is an accepted sexual practice in some societies, but either not indulged in, or thought disgusting, among many peoples.

The position adopted by partners in the sexual act also varies widely. Some cultures accept that a diversity of positions may be adopted in lovemaking, while in others only one is regarded as "normal." Variation was rare in Western culture until recently, the usual position being for the woman to lie underneath the man, with the couple face to face. In many other societies this position is hardly ever used, the most common one being where the man enters the woman from the rear, both partners taking a squatting position. In some cultures, it is believed that overly frequent intercourse leads to physical debilitation or illness. Advice on the desirability of spacing out love-making among the Seniang of the South Pacific is given by the elders of the village—who also believe that a person with white hair may legitimately copulate every night!

In most cultures, norms of sexual attractiveness (held by both females and males) focus more on physical looks for women than for men—a situation which seems to be gradually changing in the West today, as other gender differentials begin to diminish. The traits seen as most important in female beauty, however, are quite different across cultures. In some cultures, for example, a slim, small body build is admired, while in others a much more generous shape is regarded as most attractive. Sometimes the breasts are not seen as a source of sexual stimulus, whereas in others great erotic significance is attached to them. Some societies place great store upon the shape of the face, while others emphasize the shape and color of the eyes, or the size and form of the nose and lips.

SEXUALITY IN WESTERN CULTURE

Western attitudes towards sexual behavior were for nearly two thousand years molded primarily by Christianity. Although different Christian sects and denominations have held widely divergent views about the proper place of sexuality in life, the dominant Christian view was that all sexual behavior is suspect, and to be kept to the minimum needed to secure the production of children. At some periods, and in some places, this view produced an extreme prudishness in society at large. But at other times, many people ignored or reacted against Christianity's teachings, commonly engaging in various practices (such as adultery), which the religious authorities forbade. As was mentioned in Chapter 1 ("Sociology: Problems and Perspectives"), the idea that sexual fulfillment can and should be sought through marriage was rare.

In the nineteenth century, religious presumptions about sexuality became partly replaced by medical ones. Most of the early writings by doctors about sexual behavior, however, were as stern as church views. Some argued that any type of sexual activity unconnected with reproduction brings serious physical harm to those indulging in it. Masturbation was said to bring on blindness, insanity, heart disease, and many other ailments, while oral sex was claimed to cause cancer (Feldman and MacCulloch, 1980). In Victorian times, sexual hypocrisy abounded. Virtuous women were believed to be indifferent to sexuality, accepting the attentions of their husbands only as a duty. Yet in the expanding towns and cities, prostitution was rife, and often more or less openly tolerated, "loose" women being placed in an entirely different category from their respectable sisters.

Many men who were considered to be sober, well-behaved citizens and devoted to their wives, regularly frequented prostitutes or kept mistresses. Such behavior on the part of men was treated leniently, whereas women who took lovers were regarded as scandalous, and shunned in "polite society" if such behavior came to light. The differing attitude towards the sexual activities of men and women formed a *double standard* that has long existed, and whose residues still linger on today.

In current times, traditional attitudes of this type exist alongside much more liberal attitudes towards sexuality, which had developed strongly in the 1960s. Many people, particularly those influenced by Christian teachings, believe that premarital sexual experience is wrong, and generally frown upon all forms of sexual behavior save for heterosexual activity within the confines of marriage—although it is now much more widely accepted that sexual pleasure is a desirable and important feature of the marital relationship. Others, by contrast, condone or actively approve of premarital sexual activity, and a wide range of sexual practices. Sexual attitudes have undoubtedly become more permissive over the past thirty or so years in most Western countries. In the cinema and theater, scenes are shown that previously would have been completely unacceptable, while pornographic material is readily available to most adults who wish to obtain it.

SEXUAL BEHAVIOR

We can speak much more confidently about public values concerning sexuality in the past than we can about private practices, for by their nature such practices have mostly gone undocumented. When Alfred Kinsey began his researches in the United States in the 1940s and 1950s, it was the first time a major investigation of actual sexual behavior had been undertaken. Kinsey and his co-researchers faced condemnation from many religious organizations, and his work was denounced as immoral in the newspapers and in Congress. But he persisted, and eventually obtained sexual life-histories of eighteen thousand people, a reasonably representative sample of the white American population (Kinsey et al., 1948, 1953).

Kinsey's results were surprising to most, and shocking to many, because they revealed a great difference between the norms of sexual behavior prevailing at that time and actual sexual conduct. He found that almost 70 percent of men had visited a prostitute, and 84 percent had had premarital sexual experience. Yet, following the double standard, 40 percent expected their wives to be virgins at the time of marriage. More than 90 percent had engaged in masturbation, and nearly 60 percent in some form of oral sexual activity. Among women, about 50 percent had had premarital sexual experience, although mostly with their prospective husbands. Some 60 percent had masturbated, and the same percentage had engaged in oral-genital contacts (Table 6.5).

Kinsey's findings demonstrated the gap that can exist between publicly accepted attitudes and actual behavior in sexual matters. But the discrepancy was probably especially great at that particular period, just after the Second World War. A phase of sexual liberalization had begun rather earlier in the 1920s, when many young people felt freed from the strict moral codes that had governed earlier generations. Sexual behavior probably changed a good deal at this time, but issues concerning sexuality were not openly discussed in the way that has become familiar now. People participating in sexual activities that were still strongly disapproved of publicly concealed them, not realizing the full extent to which others were engaging in similar practices. The more permissive era of the 1960s brought openly declared attitudes more into line with the realities of sexual behavior (Reiss, 1960, 1972).

Other factors were also involved in the sexual liberalism of the 1960s. The social movements which challenged the existing order of things—like those associated with the "New Left," or more generally with countercultural or "hippy" lifestyles—also broke with existing sexual norms. Many such groups preached sexual freedom, and the invention of the contraceptive pill for women allowed sexual pleasure to be clearly separated from reproduction. Women's groups also started pressing for greater independence from male sexual values, the rejection of the double standard, and the need for women to achieve greater sexual satisfaction in their relationships.

No survey of comparable scope to that carried out by the Kinsey researchers has since been attempted in any country. Because of the fragmentary nature of subsequent research, we cannot be entirely sure how far sexual behavior today differs from that of the immediate postwar period. But some trends seem fairly clear. There has been a progressive increase in the level of premarital sexual experience, par-

**TABLE 6.5
FREQUENCY OF MARITAL
INTERCOURSE**

Age	Weekly
16–25	2.5
25–35	2.0
36–45	1.5
46–55	0.9
56–60	0.5

Source: Adapted from Kinsey, 1948, 1953.

ticularly among women, in the United States and most European countries (Kantner and Zelnik, 1972). It seems that most Western societies will sooner or later reach the point already reached by Sweden in the early 1970s, when about 95 percent of both women and men had experienced sexual intercourse prior to marriage. Women generally have much higher aspirations towards sexual fulfillment than two decades ago, demanding sexual competence in their lovers and husbands. Extramarital sexual activity has increased for both sexes, but particularly for women.

Two opposing influences now seem to be at work. Many previously hidden sexual practices have been made public. "Swinging," spouse-swapping, transvestism (dressing in the clothes of the opposite sex, mainly on the part of males), sadomasochism (inflicting pain to bring sexual pleasure), and other sexual activities and inclinations are now openly discussed. Yet at the same time there is a strong current of "sexual Puritanism," linked to some degree with Rightist thinking in politics. Such people are highly critical of sexual permissiveness, and preach a return to more rigid standards of behavior. The spread of AIDS (see p. 240) is a further important factor creating pressure towards the sustaining of monogamous relationships—whether inside or outside marriage.

HOMOSEXUALITY

Homosexuality has existed in all cultures. Yet the idea of a "homosexual person"—someone clearly marked off in terms of his or her sexual tastes from the majority of the population—is only a relatively recent one. Before the eighteenth century the notion seems barely to have existed. The act of sodomy (anal intercourse) was denounced by church authorities and by the law; in England and several other countries it was punishable by death. However, sodomy was not defined specifically as a homosexual offense. It applied to relations between men and women, men and animals, as well as men amongst themselves. The term "homosexuality" was coined in the 1860s, and from then onwards homosexuals were increasingly regarded as being a separate type of people having a particular sexual aberration (Weeks, 1986). Use of the term **lesbian** applied to women dates from a slightly later time.

The death penalty for "unnatural acts" (such as anal and oral sex) was abolished in the United States following independence, and in Europe in the late eighteenth and early nineteenth centuries (Katz, 1976; Hyde, 1970; Greenberg and Bystryn, 1984). Until relatively few decades ago, however, homosexuality remained a criminal activity in the United States in common with virtually all Western countries.

Homosexuality in Non-Western Cultures

There are many non-Western cultures in which homosexual relations are tolerated or even encouraged, although normally only among certain groups within the population. The Batak people of northern Sumatra, for example, permit male homosexual relationships prior to marriage. At puberty, a boy leaves his parents' house and sleeps in a dwelling with a dozen to fifteen males of his age or older. Sexual partnerships are formed between couples in the group and the younger boys are initiated into homosexual practices. This situation continues until young men marry. Once married most, but not all, men abandon their homosexual activities (Money and Ehrhardt, 1973).

Among the people of East Bay, a village in Melanesia, in the Southwest Pacific, homosexuality is similarly tolerated—although again only in males. Prior to marriage, while living in the men's house, young men engage in mutual masturbation and anal intercourse. Homosexual relationships also exist, however, between older men and younger boys, often involving boys too young to be living in the men's house. Each type of homosexual relationship is completely acceptable and discussed openly. Many married men are bisexual, having relations with younger boys while still continuing an active sexual life with their spouses. Homosexuality without an interest in heterosexual relationships seems to be unknown in this culture—a very common finding (Davenport, 1965; Shepherd, 1987).

Homosexuality in Western Culture

Kenneth Plummer has distinguished four types of homosexuality within modern culture. *Casual homosexuality* is a passing homosexual encounter that does not substantially structure the overall sexual life of the individual. Schoolboy crushes, or mutual masturbation, are examples. Homosexuality as a *situated activity* refers to circumstances in which homosexual activities are regularly carried on, but where these do not become an individual's overriding preference. In many enclosed settings, such as prisons or military camps, homosexual behavior of this kind is common. It is regarded as a substitute for heterosexual behavior rather than as preferable to it.

Personalized homosexuality refers to cases of individuals who have a preference for homosexual activities, but who are isolated from group supports. Homosexuality here is a furtive activity, hidden away from friends and colleagues. Homosexuality as a *way of life* refers to individuals who have "come out," and have made association with others of similar sexual tastes a key part of their lives. Such people usually belong to gay subcultures, in which homosexual activities are integrated into a definite type of lifestyle (Plummer, 1975).

The proportion of the male and female population who have had homosexual experiences, or experienced strong inclinations towards homosexuality, is much larger than those who follow an openly gay lifestyle. The probable extent of homosexuality in Western cultures first became known with the publication of the Kinsey researches into sexuality. According to Kinsey's findings, no more than half of American men are "completely heterosexual"—that is, restrict themselves entirely to heterosexual experiences—judged by their sexual activities and inclinations following puberty. Eight percent of Kinsey's sample had been involved in exclusively homosexual relationships for periods of three years or more. A further 10 percent had mixed homosexual and heterosexual activities in more or less equal quantities. Kinsey's most striking finding was that 37 percent of men had at least one homosexual experience to the level of orgasm. An additional 13 percent had felt homosexual desires but had not acted upon them.

Rates of homosexuality among women indicated by the Kinsey researchers were lower. About 2 percent of women were exclusively homosexual. Thirteen percent reported homosexual experiences, while a further 15 percent admitted homosexual desires without acting on them. Kinsey and his colleagues were startled by the level of homosexuality disclosed among the population. The results were rechecked using various different methods, but the conclusions remained the same.

Attitudes Towards Homosexuality

Attitudes of intolerance towards homosexuality have been so pronounced in the past that it is only over recent years that some of the myths surrounding the subject have been dispelled. Homosexuality is not a sickness and is not distinctively associated with any forms of psychiatric disturbance. Homosexual males are not limited to any particular sector of occupations, like hairdressing, interior decorating, or the arts, although some popular stereotypes suggest this is so. There is little direct connection between homosexuality and transvestism; the majority of transvestites are heterosexual men (Spada, 1979; Fisher, 1972).

Gay Subcultures

It is difficult to analyze changes in homosexual activities because there was almost no research prior to the period at which distinct gay subcommunities developed. Gay subcultures in large cities today tend to have exclusively homosexual meeting places, such as clubs and gay bars. Although transient relationships are common, the majority of homosexuals who have "come out" have long-lasting relationships. Outside the women's movement, lesbian communities tend to be less highly organized than male subcultures, and have a lower proportion of casual relationships.

San Francisco and New York are two major centers where the gay community has become a significant political force. Gay rights organizations have campaigned particularly actively since the Stonewall Inn confrontation of June 27, 1969. On that day, the police raided the Stonewall Inn, a gay bar in the Greenwich Village section of New York, expelling customers into the street. Rather than leaving, the angry patrons of the inn locked the police inside the bar, from where it took them some while to escape. Lesbians and gay males took part in several marches over the next three days, protesting against police discrimination against the gay community. Following these events, gay liberation groups sprang up in numerous cities throughout the United States.

There are some four thousand gay organizations, male and female, today in the United States. Many previously isolated homosexuals have spoken of the impact that has been thereby made on their own lives. Allen Young, a prominent activist, has commented, "Before gay liberation, I was lost in a morass of isolation and self hatred . . . for myself and many thousands of others—not only 'activists' but ordinary gay people . . . around the world—the movement launched at Stone Wall has meant an incredible opportunity for . . . rebirth and growth" (Young, 1972). While meeting bitter opposition, the movement has helped stimulate major policy changes. The Civil Service Reform Act of 1978 forbade most federal agencies from discriminating against gays in respect to employment or promotion. Several states, and more than thirty-five cities, have followed suit. Yet there have also been counteractions from hostile groups. A gay rights ordinance in Dade County, Florida, was repealed following protests led by the singer Anita Bryant.

Lesbianism

Male homosexuality tends to receive more attention than lesbianism, and lesbian activist groups are often treated as if they were identical

A lesbian couple.

with male groups. While there is sometimes close cooperation between male gays and lesbians, and they share many similar experiences, there are also differences (Cruikshank, 1982). For example, many lesbians have been closely involved with women's rights organizations—and have campaigned against sexist attitudes held by gay as well as by heterosexual men.

Lesbian couples often have children, some through a relationship with a man, others through artificial insemination. Child custody has not been easy for lesbians to win. In the United States and Britain, courts decide whether a mother's lesbianism makes her an "unfit" parent before allocating custody in divorce suits. Several cases were fought through the U.S. courts in the late 1970s and early 1980s establishing that lesbianism is not relevant to deciding whether or not a woman should be given custody of her child; but this has only been accepted as a principle in some states (Rights of Women Lesbian Custody Group, 1986).

AIDS

More recently, male homosexuality has been associated with the social impact of the disease **AIDS** (Acquired Immune Deficiency Syndrome). In medical terms, AIDS is a moving target, new and elusive. Medical knowledge about the illness dates very quickly. AIDS is a condition that causes the body's immune system to collapse. The immune system is the body's natural defense against infection. When invaded by germs or bacteria, it calls out antibodies to ward off infection. AIDS victims lose this defense. AIDS itself does not cause death, but the sufferer becomes prey to a range of illnesses, including cancers, which are fatal. Much of the evidence thus far seems to link AIDS to a virus (HIV), or possibly to several related viruses (Table 6.6).

Media discussion of the illness only dates from late 1981, although within gay circles the illness was familiar earlier. AIDS came into public consciousness just at the time at which it seemed that many of the established prejudices against homosexuality were collapsing. AIDS seemed to those who were repelled by homosexuality, especially some religious groups, to provide concrete evidence for their accusations. The idea that AIDS is a plague sent by a divine hand to punish perversion even found expression in some respectable medical quarters. An editorial in a medical journal asked: "Might we be witnessing, in fact, in the form of a modern communicable disorder, a fulfilment of St. Paul's pronouncement: 'The due penalty of their error?' " (quoted in Altman, 1986). The idea is absurd in more than

TABLE 6.6	AIDS CASES REPORTED BY AGE AND SEX			
	1981–82	1984	1986	1988
Age				
UNDER 13 YRS.	13	50	186	414
13–29	202	962	2825	4844
30–39	399	2118	6122	10,868
40–49	178	923	2689	4916
50–59	61	313	969	1665
60 AND OVER	5	82	378	789
Sex				
MALE	799	4155	12,177	21,019
FEMALE	59	293	1052	2476

Source: U.S. Centers for Disease Control (unpublished data).

one way—for female homosexuals are one of the lowest-risk groups for the disease.

AIDS seemed at first to be limited almost exclusively to large American cities with significant gay populations. The rapid spread of AIDS among the gay community was undoubtedly due in some degree to the increased opportunities for homosexual encounters offered by male gay subcultures in North America and elsewhere. Headlines in the press set the early tone: "Gay plague baffling medical detectives," claimed the *Philadelphia Daily News* of August 9, 1982. "Being gay is a health hazard," announced the *Saturday Evening Post,* of October 1982, while the *Toronto Star* carried the banner "Gay plague has arrived in Canada." The magazine *US* reported: "Male homosexuals aren't so gay any more." At that time it was already known that probably a third of those having AIDS in the United States were not homosexual, but in the initial publicity this was virtually ignored. When Rock Hudson, the movie star, died of AIDS in 1985, what shocked much of the world's press was not so much the nature of his illness, but the fact that this symbol of male virility had been a homosexual.

Rather than looking for the source of the disease in a particular virus, medical researchers first of all tried to discover its origins in specific aspects of gay practices. The discovery that AIDS can be transmitted through heterosexual contact forced a reappraisal. Most of the initial evidence came from central Africa, where AIDS was widespread but had no particular relation to male homosexuality. The "gay plague" soon became redefined by the press as a "heterosexual nightmare."

Volunteers stitching the memorial quilt made up of panels bearing two thousand names and images of people who have died of AIDS. The quilt was stretched out on Washington's Capitol Mall in 1987.

The impact of AIDS is likely to influence many forms of sexual behavior. In the homosexual community, marked changes are already noticeable, with the level of casual sexual encounters becoming radically reduced. Some of the most widely condemned homosexual practices, paradoxically, turn out to be the safest. For example, sadomasochistic activities, involving the infliction of discomfort or pain upon a partner, are often entirely safe, because no direct genital contact is involved. The dilemma facing male gay communities is how to foster procedures of "safe sex," while warding off the renewed attacks to which the gay community is subject.

AIDS and the Heterosexual Population

There are radical discrepancies in estimates of the prevalence of AIDS. The numbers of carriers of the AIDS virus in the United States as of 1988 have been variously estimated between 160,000 and 3 million! (Langone, 1987; Masters, Johnson, and Kolodny, 1987). AIDS is believed to be solely transmitted either by direct blood-to-blood contact (as when drug users share needles), or through sexually emitted fluids (semen or vaginal secretion). Homosexual men still account for over 70 percent of all AIDS cases in the United States, and a higher proportion in most European countries (Vass, 1986). In Central Africa, by contrast, where the disease is widespread, the majority of carriers are heterosexuals.

There is some evidence that high risk heterosexual groups are altering their behavior. A study of London prostitutes found that 70 percent had changed their behavior since they had heard of AIDS, and required all clients to wear condoms for penetrative sex. However, 10 percent of the group studied said they would continue to work as prostitutes even if they knew they were infected with the virus (Barton et al., 1985).

In most countries today, legal controversies are developing about whether there should be some form of compulsory screening for AIDS, and whether or not discrimination against AIDS sufferers should be legalized. Civil rights groups argue that the introduction of any type of compulsory screening would mark a deterioration in individual freedom. Opponents claim that this price is worth paying if the spread of what is becoming an illness of major proportions can be halted. Some countries are introducing legal penalties for individuals who knowingly infect others—this carries a prison sentence of eight years in Norway, for example. In the United States, a case is awaiting trial of an AIDS patient who spat in the face of two police officers; the individual was charged with intent to murder. Under the Texas Communicable Disease and Prevention Act 1982, the city of San Antonio, Texas, has introduced penalties of up to ten years' imprisonment for AIDS sufferers who have sexual intercourse with healthy people.

PROSTITUTION

PROSTITUTION CAN BE DEFINED AS THE INDISCRIMINATE granting of sexual favors for monetary gain. There is no clear-cut distinction between the paid mistress, whose main reason for granting sexual access to her patron is the money he provides, and street prostitution as such, except that the prostitute sells sexual access to numerous buyers. The word "prostitute" began to come into common usage in the late eighteenth century. Prior to that time, most purveyors of sex for economic reward were courtesans and concubines (kept mistresses), or slaves. Courtesans and concubines often had a high position in traditional societies.

A key aspect of modern prostitution is that women and their clients are generally unknown to one another. Although men may become "regular customers," the relationship is not initially established upon the basis of personal acquaintance. This was not true of most forms of prostitution in previous times. Modern prostitution is directly connected to the breakup of small-scale communities, the development of large, impersonal urban areas and the commercializing of social relations. In small-scale, traditional communities, sexual relations were controlled by their very visibility. In the newly developed urban areas, more anonymous social connections have become established.

PROSTITUTION TODAY

Prostitutes in the United States today still come mainly from poorer social backgrounds, as they did in the past, yet they have been joined by larger numbers of middle-class women than previously. The increasing divorce rate has drawn newly impoverished women into prostitution. In addition, some women unable to find jobs after graduation work in massage parlors or in call-girl networks while looking for other employment opportunities (Rosen, 1982).

Paul J. Goldstein has classified types of prostitution in terms of *occupational commitment* and *occupational context*. *Commitment* refers to the frequency with which a woman is involved in prostitution. Many women are only involved temporarily, engaging in a few episodes, then abandoning prostitution for a long while. "Occasional prostitutes" are those who quite often take part in the activity, but in a sporadic fashion, to supplement income from other sources. Others are continually involved in prostitution, deriving their main source of income from it. *Occupational context* means the type of work environment and interaction process in which a woman is involved. A "streetwalker" is someone who solicits business on the street. A "call girl" solicits clients over the phone, men either coming to her house or apartment, or the woman visiting them. A "house prostitute" is a woman who works in a private club or brothel. A "massage-parlor prostitute" provides sexual services in an establishment supposedly offering only legitimate massage and health facilities. Many women also engage in barter (payment in goods or other services rather than money) for sexual services. Most of the call girls Goldstein studied regularly engaged in sexual bartering—in exchange for TV sets, repairs of autos and electrical goods, clothes, legal and dental services (Goldstein, 1979).

A United Nations Resolution passed in 1951 condemns those who organize prostitution, or profit from the activities of prostitutes, but does not ban prostitution as such. A total of fifty-three member states, excluding the United States, have formally accepted the resolution, although their legislation about prostitution varies widely. In some countries, prostitution itself is illegal. Others prohibit only certain types, such as street soliciting, or child prostitution. Some national or local governments license officially recognized brothels or sex parlors—such as the "Eros Centers" in West Germany or the sex houses in Amsterdam. Only a few countries license male prostitutes.

Legislation against prostitution is virtually everywhere confined to one side of the transaction between prostitutes and clients. Those who purchase sexual services are not arrested or prosecuted, and in court procedures their identities may be kept hidden. There are far fewer studies of clients than of prostitutes, and it is rare for anyone to suggest—as is often stated or implied about prostitutes—that they are psychologically disturbed. The imbalance in research surely expresses an uncritical acceptance of orthodox stereotypes of sexuality, according to which it is "normal" for men to actively seek a variety of sexual outlets, while the women who cater to these needs are condemned.

PROSTITUTES AND THEIR CLIENTS

Bernard Cohen (1980) studied streetwalkers in New York City. He found that they carried on their trade as part of what he called "deviant street networks"—in networks of people engaged in a mixture of illegal or morally dubious behavior, such as drug taking or gambling. The pimp or "manager" played a key role in these networks, and quite often engaged in various other deviant activities (like drug trafficking) as well as "looking after" his woman or women. A pimp may be a husband, lover, friend, or merely an acquaintance of the prostitute, who shares the proceeds from her work and provides services for her. He gives on-the-spot protection and supervision, and serves as a look-out for the police. Pimps who have several girls working for them employ other men to carry out these supervisory activities. The pimp usually controls the business details; he pays the rent and gives the woman an allowance.

According to Jennifer James, author of a well-known study on prostitution, women can leave their pimps more easily than is often assumed. She compares the prostitute-pimp relationship to a marriage: the relation is very often a sexual one, there is a joint income, money to be earned and apportioned, and rent paid for. Pressures from women to have autonomy and influence in the social world at large have influenced prostitutes, who now demand better treatment than previously, opt to "go it alone" or, in some cases, form alliances with other prostitutes for mutual help and protection. Nonetheless, pimps still have considerable power over "their" women, and normally tell them when to work and how much money they must try to earn (Miller, 1978).

Other studies in the late 1980s question the idea that the pimp-prostitute relationship is one based mainly on mutual benefit, and place the emphasis instead on its exploitative nature. The allowance provided by the pimp is often meager, and pimps frequently maintain their power over the women in their "employ" by regular beatings or by the continual threat of violence (Davidson and Loken, 1987).

Who are the men who patronize prostitutes? It is part of the double-standard in sexual behavior that we have far fewer studies of male clients than of female prostitutes. What research has been carried out in the United States shows that most of the regular patrons of prostitutes are "white, middle-aged, middle-class, and married" (James et al., 1975). Many such men use prostitutes only when they are away from home, probably because the risk of being observed by family members or friends is much less. It has been suggested by some authors that the average age of clients has risen over the past few decades or so. When there were stricter controls over courtship, young men quite often turned to prostitutes to gain sexual experience difficult to attain elsewhere. With rather freer sexual standards today, this pattern has become less common. Given the relative frequency of violence by men towards women in the larger social world, it is not surprising that prostitutes are particularly at risk. Pimps cannot supply complete protection, because by the nature of the case women are usually alone with their clients. Many prostitutes carry tear-gas pistols, knives, and other weapons (Winick and Kinsie, 1971).

CHILD PROSTITUTION

Prostitution frequently involves children—boys as well as girls. Some 40 percent of street prostitutes in the United States are under 18 years old. David Campagna (1985) has analyzed the extent of child prostitution in the United States, basing his study on a large-scale research project that collected information from 596 police departments and 125 social-service agencies throughout the country. According to figures calculated by Campagna, the annual revenue from child prostitution may amount to as much as $2 billion. In spite of the massive sums of money involved, child prostitution for the most part does not seem to be controlled by networks of organized crime. A study of child prostitutes in the United States, Britain, and West Germany indicated that the majority are involved in "small-scale" operations in which, for example, children who have run away from home and have no income turn to prostitution to gain a livelihood. Most clients do not seem specifically attracted to children, looking rather for youthfulness in those whose sexual services they buy.

The fact that many runaway children turn to prostitution is in part an unintended consequence of laws that protect children against underage employment. By no means all child prostitutes consist of those who have run away from home. Janus and Heid Bracey (1980) distinguish three broad categories of child prostitute:

1. *Runaways,* who either leave home and are not traced by their parents, or who persistently leave each time they are found and brought back.

2. *Walkaways,* who are basically living at home, but spend periods away, for example staying out periodically for several nights.

3. *Throwaways,* whose parents are indifferent to what they do, or actively reject them—the most distressing category of all.

All categories involve male as well as female child prostitutes.

Child prostitution is part of the "sex tourism" industry in several areas of the world—in, for instance, Thailand and the Philippines. Package tours, oriented towards prostitution, draw men to these areas from Europe, the United States, and Japan. Members of Asian women's groups have organized public protests against these tours, which nonetheless still continue. Sex tourism in the Far East has its origins in the sources of prostitution that provided sexual services to

American troops during the Korean and Vietnam wars. "Rest and Recreation" centers had been built in Thailand, the Philippines, Vietnam, Korea, and Taiwan. Some still remain, particularly in the Philippines, catering to regular shipments of tourists as well as to the military stationed in the region.

PROSTITUTION AND GENDER INEQUALITY

Why does prostitution exist? Certainly it is an enduring phenomenon, which resists the attempts of governments to eliminate it. It is also usually a matter of women selling sexual favors to men, rather than the reverse—although there are some instances, as in Hamburg, West Germany, where "houses of pleasure" exist to provide male sexual services for women. Also, of course, boys or men prostitute themselves for other men.

Thinking about the origins of heterosexual prostitution actually serves to focus the main issues with which this chapter has been concerned. It involves behavior that is gender divided (paying for sexual favors) and it is marked by distinct inequalities, at least in many situations (for example, prostitutes are regarded with disapproval, and may be subject to legal penalties, while their clients more often than not escape social sanctions).

No single factor can explain prostitution. It might seem that men simply have stronger, or more persistent, sexual needs than women, and therefore require the outlets that prostitution provides. But this explanation is unpersuasive. Most women seem capable of developing their sexuality in a more intense fashion than men of comparable age (Hyde, 1986). If prostitution existed simply to serve sexual needs, there would surely be many male prostitutes catering to women.

The most apt general conclusion to be drawn is that prostitution expresses, and to some extent helps perpetuate, the tendency of men to treat women as sex objects who can be "used" for sexual purposes. Prostitution is an aspect of patriarchal relations, representing in a particular context the inequalities of power between men and women. Of course, many other elements are also involved. Prostitution offers a means of obtaining sexual satisfaction for people who, because of their physical shortcomings, or the experience of restrictive moral codes, cannot find other sexual partners. Prostitutes cater to men who are away from home, desire sexual encounters without commitment, or have unusual sexual tastes that other women will not accept. But these factors are relevant to the extent of the occurrence of prostitution rather than to its overall nature.

SOCIOLOGY AND GENDER RELATIONS

FEW AREAS OF SOCIOLOGY HAVE DEVELOPED AS SIGNIFI-
cantly over recent years, or have emerged as so central to
the discipline as a whole, as the study of gender relations.
In some large part, this reflects changes in social life itself. Established differences between male and female identities, outlooks, and
typical modes of behavior, are coming to be seen in a new light today.
These changes affect numerous other social institutions besides sexual behavior and family life. We shall trace out their influence further in many of the chapters that follow. Yet, as the present chapter
has demonstrated, there are many aspects of male/female relations
that are deeply persistent and seem unlikely to alter substantially in
the near future. Differences in gender identity, and political and economic inequalities between women and men, remain ingrained features of our society, as they have been for centuries past.

The study of gender poses difficult problems for contemporary sociology—all the more so because it has not traditionally been seen as
one of the central concerns of the discipline. What concepts are best
used to understand the importance of gender in society? Why *is*
gender so universally linked to inequalities? Could one imagine a society in which gender differences disappear, so that we are all andro-
gynous (have the same gender characteristics)? These questions form
part of one of the main "theoretical dilemmas"—problems of theoretical explanation and analysis—which sociology faces today (see
Chapter 22: "The Development of Sociological Theory").

SUMMARY

1. The term "sex" is ambiguous. As commonly used, it denotes
   physical and cultural differences between males and females as
   well as the activity of engaging in sexual behavior. It is useful to
   distinguish between *sex,* in the physiological sense, and *gender,*
   which is a cultural construct (a set of learned behavior patterns).
   These in turn should be conceptually separated from "having
   sex"—that is, engaging in sexual activity.

2. Gender socialization begins virtually as soon as an infant is born.
   Even parents who believe they treat children equally tend to
   produce different responses to boys than girls. These differences
   are reinforced by many other cultural influences.

3. Patriarchy refers to male dominance over women. There are no known societies that are not patriarchal, although the degree and character of inequalities between the sexes varies considerably cross-culturally.

4. Gender identity and modes of expressing sexuality develop together. It has been argued that masculinity depends upon denial of intimate emotional attachment to the mother, thus producing "male inexpressiveness."

5. In all the industrialized countries, women are under-represented in positions of power and influence. The average wage of women is well below that of men; many more women than men in paid employment are in part-time jobs.

6. Sexual harassment directly affects a high proportion of women. Domestic violence and rape are also much more common than the official statistics reveal. There is a sense in which all women are victims of rape, since they have to take special precautions for their protection.

7. Homosexuality seems to have existed in all cultures, yet the concept of "a homosexual" is a relatively recent idea. Only over the past century or so has homosexual activity been considered as a category of abnormality and deviance constructed in opposition to the category of the "normal" heterosexual.

BASIC CONCEPTS

GENDER
PATRIARCHY
FEMINISM
GENDER SOCIALIZATION

IMPORTANT TERMS

FEMININITY
MASCULINITY
SEX
SEXUAL ACTIVITY
TESTICULAR FEMINIZATION SYNDROME
ANDROGENITAL SYNDROME
MALE INEXPRESSIVENESS
HOUSEWORK (DOMESTIC LABOR)
SUFFRAGIST

DOMESTIC VIOLENCE
SEXUAL HARASSMENT
RAPE
HETEROSEXUALITY
HOMOSEXUALITY
LESBIANISM
AIDS
PROSTITUTION

PART TWO

STRUCTURES OF POWER

Power is an ever-present phenomenon in social life. In all human groups, some individuals have more authority or influence than others, while groups themselves vary in terms of the level of their power. Power and inequality tend to be closely linked. The powerful are able to accumulate valued resources, such as property or wealth; while possession of such resources is in turn a means of generating power itself.

In this part, we discuss some of the main systems of power and inequality. The first chapter looks at stratification and class structure—the ways in which inequalities are distributed within societies. This chapter is followed by a discussion of race and ethnicity, which examines the tensions and hostilities often found between people who are physically or culturally different from one another.

In Chapter 9 we move on to connect power and inequality with various types of groups and organizations. Attention is given in particular to the study of the large organizations—like government agencies, industrial firms, hospitals, or colleges—that dominate so much of modern social life. The final two chapters analyze two types of organization whose impact is particularly far reaching—the state, in Chapter 10, and the military, in Chapter 11. Governments are "specialists" in power; they are the source of the directives that influence many aspects of our daily activities. On the other hand, they are also the focus of resistance and rebellion.

From their earliest origins, states have been associated with the development of military power. Military rivalries and wars have shaped human social development in far-reaching ways in the past, and continue to do so in the twentieth century. We look at the nature of the military in the modern world, the relation between the military and politics, and the global trade in armaments.

C H A P T E R   S E V E N

STRATIFICATION AND CLASS STRUCTURE

WHY ARE SOME GROUPS IN SOCIETY MORE WEALTHY AND
powerful than others? How unequal are modern societies? How much chance does someone from a lowly background have of reaching the top of the economic ladder?
What are the reasons for the persistence of poverty in affluent countries today? These are some of the questions
we shall try to answer in this chapter. The study of social
inequalities is one of the most important areas of sociology, because the material resources that people have access to determine a great deal about their lives. To
describe inequalities, sociologists speak of **social stratification.**
Stratification can be defined as the system of structured inequalities
among different groups of people.

Stratification is not just an abstract notion, but concerns fundamental aspects of people's lives—what they strive for, the satisfactions
and rewards they are able to gain, and the deprivations they suffer.
The following passage comes from Ellen Israel Rosen's study of married working women in "Milltown," an industrial city in New England. The women were mostly factory workers who essentially held
down two jobs, because they also shouldered a heavy burden of man-

aging their homes. Some were born in America, others were immi-grants—Celia Triano, for instance, is of Portuguese background:

> When we spoke with her, Celia Triano was sixty years old. She was currently employed full-time as an assembler in a small firm that made electrical wires and cables. Her hus-band, Bud, was a metal worker in a local plant that manufac-tured machine tools. As our interviewer walked through the door, she was welcomed, offered a seat, and almost instantly regaled with photographs of the Trianos' two grown sons. Both had graduated from college and Celia proudly showed the pictures of her sons' graduations—and then the photo-graphs of their weddings.
>
> Celia began working in 1939 when she was eighteen in a rubber factory where, for thirteen years, she made golf balls. Unlike most of her contemporaries, she married late, at the age of thirty-two, the year Eisenhower was first elected pres-ident. She stopped working for a full eighteen years while she bore and reared her two sons. In 1970, at the age of fifty, Celia went back to work to put her two sons through college.
>
> Celia's children are somewhat unusual. Most of her friends at work have grown sons who are blue-collar workers and daughters who are secretaries. Yet there is a sizable minority of women who have children who are currently enrolled at the state university. Others have sons and daughters who have already become nurses, engineers, and accountants. One woman on our study, a stitcher in a garment shop, has a son who is a student at Yale. Clearly he is somewhat atypical. Yet, Tina Bologna, his mother, expressed the feelings and aspirations many women have for their children when she told us, "I would stitch any time to send him to school."
>
> When Celia decided to go back to work ten years ago the only job she could find was as a part-time file clerk in a real estate office in her town. She worked there for about nine months and quit when the production job she now holds be-came available. Working in the cable plant paid more money —money she felt she needed at that point. She has worked there, full-time, for the past nine years.
>
> Celia admits that her husband does not believe that women should work. Yet, he apparently acknowledges that they

couldn't have sent their two boys to school without her salary. He would like her to quit now that their children are out of school and on their own, but Celia continues to work. She says she likes having the extra money. She doesn't have anything special to do now that her children are gone and enjoys being with her friends at work. She says she would like to retire at sixty-two when she becomes eligible for a small pension. (Rosen, 1987)

Rosen's research illustrates some of the forms of inequality with which we shall be preoccupied in this chapter. The circumstances under which Celia Triano has lived out her life are very different from those of some other Americans. She has had to struggle constantly to make ends meet—and has never known the ease and comfort that a high income can bring. Her work in the factory and real estate office has always been seen as of secondary importance to that of her husband, although the couple could not have pursued their aspirations—such as providing adequately for their children—without it.

Although her own life has been hard, Celia Triano hopes for better things for her children and, together with her husband, has worked relentlessly to make these dreams come true. These endeavors have met with some success since her sons have graduated from college and are likely to find better-paying jobs than either of their parents held. In sociological terms, the children are *socially mobile,* having the ability to move up the social scale, as compared to their parents. In a sense, all the members of the Triano family are lucky. They are white and do not face the same barriers to social advancement that confront blacks (see Chapter 8: "Ethnicity and Race"). Yet even for whites, American society is much less "open" than many of its citizens believe it to be, and major inequalities between groups persist.

SYSTEMS OF SOCIAL STRATIFICATION

AMERICAN SOCIETY INVOLVES A SYSTEM OF STRATIFICATION, because the chances for material success that individuals have are strongly influenced by the social background from which they come. We shall study stratification in the United States in some detail later in the chapter, but first of all we have to analyze the different types of stratification that exist, and have existed

in the past. Modern stratification systems differ considerably from those characteristic of previous periods of history, and from those found in nonindustrial parts of the world in the present-day. Four basic systems of stratification can be distinguished: slavery, caste, estates, and class.

SLAVERY

Slavery is an extreme form of inequality, by which certain people are owned as property by others. The legal conditions of slave ownership have varied considerably among different societies. Sometimes slaves were deprived of almost all rights in law—as was the case on southern plantations in the United States—while in other societies, their position was more akin to that of servant. For example, in the ancient Greek city-state of Athens, some slaves occupied positions of great responsibility. They were excluded from political positions and from the military, but they held most other types of occupation. Some were literate and worked as government administrators; many were trained in craft skills. Even so, not all slaves could count on such good fate. For many, their days began and ended in hard labor in the mines (Finley, 1968, 1980).

Those subjected to slavery quite often fought back against their subjection, and many slave rebellions have occurred through history. Because of the phenomenon of resistance, systems of forced slave labor have tended to be economically unstable. High productivity could only be achieved through constant supervision and brutal punishment. Slave-labor systems eventually broke down, partly because of the struggles they provoked, and partly because economic or other incentives motivate people to produce more effectively than direct compulsion. Slavery is simply not economically efficient.

From about the eighteenth century on, many people in Europe and America came to see slavery as morally wrong. Since the freeing of slaves in North and South America, something over a century ago, slavery as a formal institution has almost completely disappeared from the world.

CASTE

Caste is associated above all with the cultures of the Indian subcontinent. The term "caste" itself is not an Indian one, but comes from the Portuguese *casta,* meaning "race" or "pure stock" (Littlejohn, 1972). The Indian caste system is extremely elaborate, and varies in its structure from area to area—so much so that it does not really constitute one "system" at all, but is a loosely connected diversity of varying beliefs and practices. However, there are certain principles that are widely shared. Caste membership is hereditary; no individual may move between castes. Those in the highest caste, the Brahmins, represent the most elevated condition of purity; the untouchables the lowest. The Brahmins must avoid certain types of contact with the untouchables, and only the untouchables are allowed physical contact with animals or substances regarded as unclean.

The caste system is closely bound up with the Hindu belief in reincarnation. Individuals who fail to abide by the rituals and duties of their caste, it is believed, will be reborn in an inferior position in their next incarnation. The Indian caste system is rigid compared to other forms of stratification, but has never been completely static. Although individuals are debarred from moving between castes, whole groups can change, and frequently have changed, their position within the caste hierarchy.

ESTATES

Estates were prominent in European feudalism, but also existed in many other traditional civilizations, tending to develop wherever there was a ruling group based on noble birth. The feudal estates consisted of different levels of social position with their own obligations and legal rights.

In Europe, the highest estate was composed of the aristocracy and gentry, whose wealth and power emanated from large-scale land holdings. The clergy formed another estate, having lower status but possessing various distinctive privileges and often enormous power. The Church itself owned much land and exerted considerable influence over the power of the aristocrats. Those in what came to be called the "third estate" were the commoners—serfs, free peasants, merchants, and artisans. A certain degree of intermarriage and individual mobility was tolerated between estates. Commoners might be knighted, for example, for having performed special services for the monarch; wealthy merchants could sometimes purchase titles and become aristocrats. A remnant of the system persists in Britain today where hereditary titles are still recognized, though the power to rule based on these inherited titles no longer exists. Business leaders, civil servants, and others may be knighted or receive peerages in recognition of their services.

CLASS

The concept of **class** is most important for analyzing stratification in industrialized societies like the United States. Everyone has heard of the notion of class, but most people in everyday talk use it in a vague way. As employed in sociology, the term has some precision. It can easily be understood in comparison with the other forms of stratification. Class systems differ from slavery, castes, or estates in four respects:

1. CLASS SYSTEMS ARE FLUID. Unlike the other types of strata, classes are not established by legal or religious provisions. Class systems are typically more fluid than the other types of stratification and the

boundaries between classes are never clear-cut. There are no formal restrictions upon intermarriage between people from different classes.

2. CLASS POSITIONS ARE IN SOME PART ACHIEVED. An individual's class is at least in some degree *achieved*, not simply "given" at birth as is common in the other types of stratification systems. Social mobility—movement upwards and downwards in the class structure—is more common than in the other types.

3. CLASS IS ECONOMICALLY BASED. Classes depend upon *economic* differences between groups of individuals—inequalities in possession and control of material resources. In the other types of stratification systems, noneconomic factors (such as the influence of religion in the Indian caste system) are generally most important.

4. CLASS SYSTEMS ARE LARGE-SCALE AND IMPERSONAL. In the other types of stratification systems, inequalities are expressed primarily in personal relationships of duty or obligation—between serf and lord, slave and master, or lower and higher caste individuals. Class systems, by contrast, operate mainly through large-scale, impersonal associations. For instance, one major basis of class differences is to be found in inequalities of pay and working conditions; these affect all the people in specific occupational categories, as a result of very general economic circumstances pertaining to the economy as a whole.

TABLE 7.1		SYSTEMS OF STRATIFICATION
System	Basis	Mobility
Slavery	Legal (by force)	None
Caste	Religious	Some (by the movement of whole caste groups, but not by individuals)
Estates	Legal	Some (through intermarriage, purchase of titles, or knighthood)
Class	Economic	Much

In the light of these criteria, then, what is a class? We can define a class as a large group of people who share common economic resources, which strongly influence the opportunities they have to lead certain kinds of lives. Ownership of *wealth,* together with *occupation,* are the chief bases of class differences. For example, someone who comes from a rich background has opportunities closed to a person born into a poor, inner-city area.

The major classes that exist in Western societies are the **upper class** (the wealthy, employers, and industrialists, plus top executives—those who own or directly control productive resources); the **middle class** (which includes most white-collar workers and professionals); and the **working** or **lower class** (those in blue-collar or routine service jobs). Celia Triano and her husband are working-class people, but their sons are likely to enter middle-class occupations. In some of the industrialized countries, such as France and Japan, a fourth class —**peasants** (people engaged in traditional types of agricultural production)—has also until recently been important. Celia Triano actually came from a peasant background in her country of origin, Portugal. In Third World countries, peasants remain the largest class.

CLASSES IN WESTERN SOCIETIES TODAY

HISTORIANS GENERALLY AGREE THAT A CENTURY AND A half ago, in the early period of the development of industrial capitalism, there were major class differences. The economic gap between the laboring poor and the wealthy industrialists who were their employers was enormous. Since then, some claim, material inequalities have lessened greatly in industrialized countries. Incomes as a whole have risen, the rich are now heavily taxed, and the welfare system benefits those who cannot easily earn a living for themselves. Because of these changes, these observers say, class today has become relatively unimportant.

In reality, this is far from the case. Some kinds of inequalities have been alleviated, but many remain. As we shall see below, there are still major differences in wealth, income, and power between those at the top and those at the bottom of the social scale. Most people are considerably better off materially than in the nineteenth century, but a sizable minority still live in conditions of poverty.

Even physical differences are correlated with class membership. People at the bottom levels of the class system have lower birth

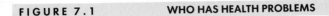

FIGURE 7.1 **WHO HAS HEALTH PROBLEMS**

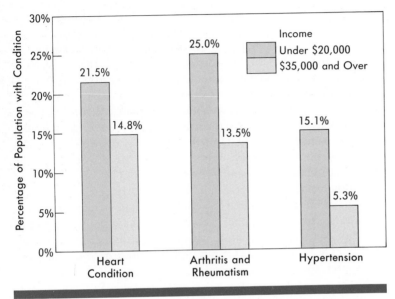

This graph shows the percentage of people with various chronic conditions by income level (1985).

Source: U.S. National Center for Health Statistics. 1985. *Vital and Health Statistics*, ser. 10.

weights, higher rates of infant mortality, are on average smaller at maturity, less healthy, and die at a younger age, than those in higher class categories. Major types of mental disorder and physical illnesses, including heart disease, cancer, diabetes, pneumonia, and bronchitis, are all more common at lower levels of the class structure than towards the top (Figure 7.1) (Zola and Kosa, 1975; Luft, 1978; Waitzkin, 1986).

DIFFERENCES OF WEALTH AND INCOME

Let us begin our exploration of class differences by looking at basic divisions of wealth and income within the population as a whole.

Wealth refers to all assets individuals own: cash, savings and checking accounts, investments in stocks, bonds, and estate properties, and so on. **Income** refers to wages and salaries coming from paid occupations, plus "unearned" money deriving from investments. While most people get what money they have from their work, the wealthy often derive the bulk of their income from investments, some of them inherited.

Wealth

Reliable information about the distribution of wealth is difficult to obtain. Some countries keep more accurate statistics than others, but there is always a considerable amount of guesswork involved. The affluent tend not to publicize the full range of their assets; we know far more about the poor than we do about the wealthy. What is certain is that wealth is concentrated in the hands of a very few. One percent of the adult population in the United States today owns more than 20 percent of the total wealth of the country. More specifically, the wealthiest 10 percent of families own 90 percent of corporate stocks and business assets and 95 percent of bonds. The richest 0.5 percent of the population (four hundred thousand households) owns 40 percent of corporate stocks and bonds. Lower down the scale, 80 percent of the adult American population owns no more than 25 percent of all wealth (U.S. Bureau of the Census, 1989; Institute of Social Research Newsletter, 1986–87).

Income

One of the most significant changes occurring in Western countries over the past century has been the rising real income of the majority of the working population. (*Real income* is income with rises due to inflation excluded, to provide a fixed standard of comparison from year to year.) Blue-collar workers in Western societies now earn between three to four times as much in real income as their counterparts at the turn of the century. Gains for white-collar, managerial, and professional workers have been slightly higher still. In terms of earnings per person (per capita) and the range of goods and services that can be purchased, the majority of the population today are vastly more affluent than any peoples have previously been in human history. One of the most important reasons for this growth is the increasing *productivity*—output per worker—that has been secured through technological development in industry. The volume of goods and services produced per worker has risen more or less continually , in many industries at least, since the 1900s.

Nevertheless, just as in the case of wealth, income distribution is very unequal. The top 5 percent of earners in the United States receive 16 percent of total income; the highest 20 percent obtain 42 percent of the total. The bottom 20 percent of earners receive only 5 percent of overall income. In 1987, 13.5 percent of the population lived below the federal government's poverty line. In a country in which many are affluent by any standards, and some enormously wealthy, more than thirty million live in conditions in which, according to the official definition, they are unable to afford basic necessities of food, clothing, and adequate housing.

In most Western countries, wealth and income have become more equally distributed than was the case half a century or more ago. But this trend has been less pronounced in the United States than elsewhere. Since the fortunes possessed by the richest Americans are so very large, the disparity between the wealthy and the poor is considerably greater than in most other industrialized countries (Figure 7.2).

CLASS DIVISIONS

Ownership of wealth is a basic dimension by which we categorize groups in a class system. Let us at this point proceed to analyze the main class divisions in the United States. We offer a general portrayal even though there are more complexities and subcategories within the classes than we have space to mention here. Moreover, the identification of classes and class boundaries is a debated issue among sociologists, and no such portrayal would command universal agreement.

FIGURE 7.2   **WHO IS MAKING THE MONEY, 1987**

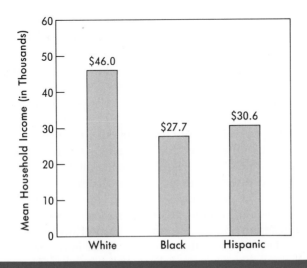

This graph compares the average (mean) household income of those in the prime of their working life (age 45–54) by race and Hispanic origin.

Source: U.S. Bureau of the Census. 1987. *Current Population Reports,* ser. P–60, no. 161.

The Upper Class

The upper class in American society consists of a small number of individuals and families who own considerable amounts of property—thinking of them as the top 1 percent of the wealthy provides an approximate statistical guide. The upper class includes a core of the "super-rich." There are about 150 families in the United States worth at least $100 million. To them, it has been said, "a fortune of a million is only respectable poverty" (Jaher, 1980).

The extravagant and sometimes bizarre habits of the super-rich have horrified liberal observers and titillated generations of the less fortunate. Some have lived a frugal and self-denying life while administering their vast assets. Others have made a cult of ostentation, particularly in the 1920s and 1930s. Many of the very wealthy at this period lived in extravagant homes, quite often modeled upon European palaces or chateaux. The estate of newspaper publisher William Randolph Hearst, at San Simeon, California, had grounds one-third the size of Rhode Island containing his own private zoo. The estate of John D. Rockefeller in Tarrytown, New York, needed 350 employees to run it; its annual upkeep cost $400,000 in the 1930s—equivalent to several million dollars today. Much money was spent ostentatiously on costume balls and "coming out" events—several hundred thousand dollars were spent upon entertainment each season by those who lived in the most opulent style. Some of the very wealthy devoted themselves to art collecting, building up fabulous accumulations of treasures. The richest man in the United States in the 1920s, Andrew Mellon, spent $31 million buying paintings—whose value when he died had grown to even larger proportions. On the other hand, some devoted a proportion of their fortunes to charitable ends. John D. Rockefeller and Andrew Carnegie were particularly prominent in establishing charity foundations. Carnegie gave away 90 percent of his wealth of $350 million before he died, and left most of the remainder to colleges, libraries, and scientific institutes. Andrew Mellon and Henry Ford also gave large sums of money to set up charitable foundations.

The gaudy expressions of wealth subsided in the postwar period. Even the Texas oil magnates, who amassed some of the largest fortunes during those years, spent less ostentatiously than their predecessors of the 1920s and 1930s. The collection of art and antiques remains a favorite preoccupation however. The oilman J. Paul Getty spent well over $50 million accumulating such treasures.

Forbes magazine publishes each year a list of the richest people in America. The list currently includes sixty-six billionaires—individuals who own more than one billion dollars in assets. The wealthiest of them all is the media magnate and financier, John Kluge, whose fortune amounts to $5 billion. The owner of the magazine, Malcolm Forbes, was himself extremely wealthy, and went in for the sort of flamboyant spending that has in recent years become relatively uncommon. In 1989, for example, he celebrated his seventieth birthday with a lavish party held in Morocco, attended by the rich and famous invited from all over the world.

The newer entrants among the small group of the very rich tend to have made their wealth from finance rather than industry. An example is Michael Milken, who invented "junk bonds"—share issues giving high interest rates in the short term, designed to help companies finance takeovers. At the peak of his earnings, Milken had an income of nearly half a billion dollars a year. Fate changed for Milken in 1989 as he was indicted by federal prosecutors on ninety-six counts. In April, 1990, Milken pleaded guilty to six felony counts and was fined $600 million.

Such wealth confers power. The influence of the wealthy stems in part from direct control of industrial and financial capital, and in part from their access to leading positions in the political, educational, and cultural spheres.

The Middle Class

The phrase "the middle class" covers people working in many different occupations. According to many observers, the majority of the population of the United States today falls into this class category, because the proportion of white-collar jobs has risen markedly relative to blue-collar ones (see Chapter 15: "Work and Economic Life").

There are three fairly distinct sectors within the middle class. The *old middle class* consists of the owners of small businesses, the proprietors of local shops, and small farmers. The numbers of people in this category have declined steadily over the past century, but they still compose a significant proportion of the overall working population (6 percent of the work force in the United States in 1985). Small businesses are much more unstable than larger ones. Most small enterprises fail within two years of being set up; only some 20 percent of those established in any one year in the United States are still in business five years later. Small firms and shops are often unable to compete effectively with the large companies, supermarkets, and restaurant chains. If the old middle class has not shrunk as much as some once thought would be the case, it is because there is a large reservoir of people wanting to try their hand at starting a business of their own. Most of those who go out of business are thus replaced by others.

The *upper-middle class* is made up mainly of those holding managerial or professional occupations. The category includes large numbers of individuals and families, and generalizing about their attitudes and outlooks is risky. Most have experienced some form of higher education, and the proportion holding liberal views on social and political issues, especially among professional groups, is fairly high. In the United States, those from White Anglo-Saxon Protestant (WASP) and Jewish backgrounds are disproportionately represented, although there is now also a small "black bourgeoisie."

The *lower-middle class,* an even more heterogeneous category, includes people working as office staff, sales representatives, teachers, nurses, and others. People in this class group tend to have similar social and political attitudes to most blue-collar workers, although there are many variations of outlook.

The diverse character of the middle class as a whole is a reflection of the "contradictory" situations in which middle-class people find themselves. They are often caught between conflicting pressures and influences. Many lower-middle-class people, for example, identify with the same values of those in more remunerative positions, but may find themselves living on incomes below those of the better-paid manual workers who do not have a middle-class position.

The Working Class

The working class consists of those working in blue-collar, manual occupations. As with the middle class, there tend to be marked divisions within the working class as a whole. One important source of such divisions is skill level. The *upper-working class,* consisting of skilled workers, has frequently been an "aristocracy of labor"; its members have had superior incomes, better working conditions, and more job security than those in other blue-collar occupations (Mackenzie, 1973). Some skills, though, have been undermined by technological developments, resulting in a weakening of the position of the workers, or even the extinction of certain occupations. For example, the skilled Linotype operators who used to set the type for newspapers, books, and other printed materials have now nearly all disappeared. The Linotype machine has been supplanted by new print technology based on a computerized photo-electronic process that requires less skilled workers.

The *lower-working class* is made up of those in unskilled or semi-skilled jobs, which need little training. Most of these jobs have lower incomes than, and inferior job security to, skilled occupations.

Working-class occupations also differ depending on whether they are full time or part time, and how much job security workers have. Distinguishing between *central* and *peripheral* areas of the economy helps illuminate this. Central sectors are those in which workers are in full-time jobs, obtaining high earnings, and enjoying long-term job security. Peripheral sectors are those in which jobs are insecure, having low earnings, with a high proportion of part-time workers. Skilled workers, and a proportion of semi- and unskilled employees, (mostly white males) predominate in the central sectors. This group also makes up a large proportion of labor-union membership. Others find themselves in the peripheral sector, where the level of unionization is low (Form, 1985).

Another line of demarcation at the lower levels of the class structure is between the white working class and underprivileged minorities—who compose an **underclass.** Members of the underclass have markedly inferior conditions of work and living standards to the majority of the population. Many are among the long-term unemployed, or drift in and out of jobs. In the United States, blacks are disproportionately represented in the underclass—and have been ever since slavery ended.

STUDYING CLASS CONSCIOUSNESS: DIFFERENT APPROACHES

In studying class, it is not enough only to analyze social and economic differences alone. We must also consider how people think about class—not just about what class they believe they belong to, but their attitudes towards others differently situated from themselves. In other words, we have to study not only class but also **class consciousness**—that is, how people think about class and class divisions.

Studies of class consciousness have used various approaches among them, the *reputational* and *subjective methods,* as well as a rather different one, concerned with class imagery.

The Reputational Method

In the reputational method, respondents are asked in which classes they would place other people. One of the best-known studies of this type was carried out by W. Lloyd Warner and Paul Lunt in Newburyport, a small town in Massachusetts (Warner and Lunt, 1941; Warner et al., 1949). Lengthy interviews were conducted with many of the residents of the community in order to build up a picture of their views of the class divisions within it. Class categories like "the folks with the money," "poor folk but decent," and "nobodies" were consistently referred to by respondents. Six social classes were identified on the basis of these responses: an upper, middle, and lower class, each having a subdivision.

This reputational approach has been used often since the original studies by Warner and his associates, but can only be effectively applied in small communities in which people tend to know each other. Moreover, the method mixes up two phenomena that should be kept separate—class and class consciousness. Class differences exist regardless of whether people are conscious of them.

The Subjective Method

The subjective method simply involves asking people to which class they believe themselves to belong. An early study of this type was carried out by Richard Centers, who obtained responses from a national random sample (Centers, 1949). Centers undertook his research in reaction to a poll organized by the business magazine *Fortune,* which claimed that 80 percent of Americans identified themselves as middle class. Centers observed that the poll had offered respondents only three choices: upper class, middle class, and lower class. He found that if a fourth choice, "working class," were added, about half of those in his sample placed themselves in this category. People were prepared to see themselves as "working class," but were unhappy about placing themselves in the "lower class." Since responses vary according to the questions asked in this way, it is not very clear what value can be placed upon the results of studies of this type.

However, Jackman and Jackman (1983) have recently tried to build upon Centers's approach to class. They used data from a national survey of attitudes towards and awareness of class in the United States, conducted by the Survey Research Center of the University of Michigan. People were asked to say which of the following classes they considered they belonged to: the poor, the working class, the middle class, the upper-middle class, or the upper class. All but 3 percent of the respondents identified themselves with one of the five class categories. About 8 percent saw themselves as poor, 37 percent as working class, 43 percent as middle class, 8 percent as upper-middle class, and 1 percent as upper class. There was a high level of agreement over which occupations were associated with these classes. For instance, business executives, doctors, and lawyers almost invariably were in the upper-middle or upper-class categories. There were no significant differences between blacks and whites in these assessments.

Images of the Class Structure

A third approach to studying class consciousness involves investigating *images of the class structure.* Research of this sort tends to be more informative than either of the other two approaches, because it looks more directly at *how* people think about the nature and sources of social inequality. For example, there are attitudes and outlooks that do not employ the word "class" itself, but nonetheless express important aspects of class consciousness. Thus upper-class or upper-middle-class people may sometimes deny that classes exist at all. We may see this sociologically, however, as *itself* an expression of class consciousness. Such people tend to interpret the social world as a hierarchy of positions in which opportunities for advancement are fairly equal for everyone. Their image of stratification corresponds to the contexts of their own experience, but is generalized to the whole society.

Those at lower levels of the class structure, on the other hand, tend more often to see stratification in terms of an opposition between "us" and "them." "They" are people who are in authority—officials, bosses, or managers. "We" are those who are subject to that authority in similar conditions of work or are in a situation of relative powerlessness. An illustration of this can be taken from a study of an automated chemical plant in New Jersey (Halle, 1984; Levison, 1974). The blue-collar workers in the plant made a clear distinction between "working men" or "working women" (which refers to their own experience) and people who hold office jobs or are in positions of authority—plus the "people above them," "the rich." Being a working man or woman involves a cluster of related attitudes. Interviewees repeatedly commented "it's working with your hands," "we get our hands dirty," "we do the same thing over and over again," and "we're told what to do." Those in managerial or professional jobs "do not really work," they "just sit on their butts all day."

A typical portion of an interview between the researcher and a worker at the plant went as follows:

RESEARCHER: "What do you mean when you talk about the working man?"

WORKER: "The working man really refers to laboring work, hard physical work."

RESEARCHER: "Are big businessmen working men?"

WORKER: [derisively] "Of course not. They don't do nothing all day."

RESEARCHER: "Am I [a professor] a working man?"

WORKER: "Well, you have a job, but you're not really a working man. It really refers to physical work. Everyone here in the plant is a working man."

Women in lower-level, or "pink-collar," jobs in the plant also felt themselves to be separate from those above them. Here is another extract from an interview:

RESEARCHER: "Are you a working woman?"

SECRETARY: "Oh yes, I have a job."

RESEARCHER: "Are managers working women?"

SECRETARY: "Well, they're not really like us. Like, I do a lot of my boss's job. I screen visitors, I know who he'll want to see and who he won't. And I do a lot of his writing for him, I write a lot of his memos. He doesn't tell anyone else, but he says I write better than he does, so he often tells me what he wants and I write it out." (Halle, 1984)

GENDER AND STRATIFICATION

THE DESCRIPTION OF THE LIFE OF CELIA TRIANO, GIVEN AT the beginning of the chapter, indicates that women's work—in the workplace and the home—plays a central part in the stratification system. Yet studies of stratification were for many years "gender blind"—they were written as though women did not exist, or as though, for purposes of analyzing divisions of power, wealth, and prestige, women were unimportant and uninteresting. Gender in fact is one of the most profound dimensions of stratification. There are no societies in which men do not have more wealth, status, and influence than women.

One of the main problems posed by the study of gender and stratification in modern societies sounds simple, but turns out to be difficult to resolve. This is the question of whether we can understand gender inequalities in modern times mainly in terms of class divisions. Inequalities of gender are more deep-rooted historically than class systems. Men had superior standing to women even in hunting and gathering societies, where there were no classes. Yet class divisions are so marked in modern societies that there is no doubt that they "overlap" substantially with gender inequalities. The economic position of many women tends to reflect that of their husbands, since males are usually the main breadwinners; hence it can be argued that we have to explain gender inequalities mainly in class terms.

Frank Parkin has expressed this point of view very well:

Female status certainly carries with it many disadvantages compared with that of males in various areas of social life including employment opportunities, property ownership, in-

come, and so on. However, these inequalities associated
with sex differences are not usefully thought of as components of stratification. This is because for the great majority
of women the allocation of social and economic rewards is
determined primarily by the position of their families and, in
particular, that of the male head. Although women today
share certain status attributes in common, simply by virtue of
their sex, their claims over resources are not primarily determined by their own occupation but, more commonly, by
that of their fathers or husbands. And if the wives and
daughters of unskilled laborers have something in common
with the wives and daughters of wealthy landowners, there
can be no doubt that the *differences* in their overall situation
are far more striking and significant. Only if the disabilities
attaching to female status were felt to be so great as to override differences of a class kind would it be realistic to regard
sex as an important dimension of stratification. (Parkin,
1971)

Women, it can be claimed, tend to be confined to a "private" domain
—the domestic world of the family, children, and the household.
Men, on the other hand, live in more of a "public" domain, from
which variations in wealth and power primarily derive. Their world
is that of paid work, industry, and politics (Elshtain, 1981). Even if
there are now many women in the labor force, the managerial sphere
is still dominated by men.

The view that class inequalities govern gender stratification has
become the subject of some debate. John Goldthorpe has defended
what he calls the "conventional position" in class analysis—that the
paid work of women is relatively insignificant compared to that of
men, and that therefore women can be regarded as being in the same
class as their husbands (Goldthorpe, 1983). This is not, Goldthorpe
emphasizes, a view based upon an ideology of sexism. On the contrary, it recognizes the subordinate position in which most women
find themselves in the labor force. Women have part-time jobs more
often than men, and tend to have more intermittent experience of
paid employment, since many withdraw from the work force for
lengthy periods to bear and care for children. Since the majority of
women are in a position of economic dependence upon their husbands, Goldthorpe agrees with Parkin that their class position is most
often governed by the husbands' class situation.

Goldthorpe's argument can be criticized in several ways. First, in a
substantial proportion of households the income of women is essential to maintaining the family's economic position and way of life. In

these circumstances women's paid employment in some part actually determines the class position of households. Second, a wife's employment may strongly influence that of her husband, not simply the other way around. Although women rarely earn more than their husbands, the working situation of a wife might still be the "lead" factor in influencing the class of her husband. This could be the case, for instance, if the husband is an unskilled or semi-skilled blue-collar worker and the wife is the manager of a store. The wife's occupation in such a case would then determine the family's class position.

Third, many "cross class" households exist, in which the work of the husband is in a higher class category than that of the wife, or (less commonly) the other way around. Since few studies have been carried out looking at the consequences of this, we cannot be confident that it is always appropriate to take the occupation of the male as the determining influence. There may be some purposes for which it is more realistic to treat men and women, even within the same households, as being in different class positions.

Fourth, there is an increasing proportion of families in which women are the sole breadwinners. Unless the woman has an income derived from alimony which puts her on the same economic level as her ex-husband, she is by definition the determining influence upon her own class position (Stanworth, 1984; Walby, 1986).

Recent research has supported the conclusion that the economic position of women cannot simply be deduced from that of their husband. A study carried out in Sweden showed cross-class families to be common (Leiuffsrud and Woodward, 1987). In most such cases, the husband had the superior occupation, although in a minority of instances the reverse was the case. The research showed that individuals in such families tended to "import" aspects of their differing class position into the family. Decisions, for instance, about who stays home to care for a sick child were related to the interaction of class and gender in the family. Where the wife's job was superior to that of the husband, he would usually have this responsibility.

WOMEN AND MEN IN STRATIFICATION RESEARCH

Women have only rarely been directly included in research into occupations and work situations (Stromberg and Harkness, 1977; Barker and Allen, 1976). Even where women do appear in research studies, less attention is paid to their activities and attitudes than to those of men. Roslyn Feldberg and Evelyn Glenn (1984) have distinguished two conceptual models used in the study of class and gender differences. One, the *job model,* has been applied mainly to men; the other, the *gender model,* has been used primarily in relation to women. The job model assumes that basic social relationships are determined by work; that families are headed by men; and that employment and financial earnings are the main influence over an individual's life activities. The gender model accepts that the family is male-headed, but sees the family as determining basic social relationships, rather than work, and treats domestic roles as the main focus of a person's life.

Looking at some studies of occupations, Feldberg and Glenn show that the use of these models actively distorts the conclusions reached. One piece of research they examined, for example, is Robert Blauner's work, *Alienation and Freedom* (Blauner, 1964). Blauner's research included a comparison of men and women working within the textile industry. The jobs studied were mostly routine and uninteresting. Those of the women were more demanding than the men's jobs, because the women's work was more closely paced by machines requiring a consistently fast rhythm of work. Even though the women had worse working conditions than the men, they did not express greater dissatisfaction with their jobs. Blauner comments that this is because work did not have a central importance in their lives, their most important roles were those of wife and mother. In other words, he invokes the gender model. He provides no evidence to support this interpretation, however, although detailed information was gathered about why men held the attitudes they did. The reader of Blauner's book is not told what proportion of the women were mothers and housewives, or what their domestic responsibilities were. Women were presumed to be little affected by the nature of the paid work they did, while considerable research effort was expended to document the ways in which the men related to their jobs.

Feldberg and Glenn concluded:

> When several alternative explanations could plausibly be invoked, the one that is most consistent with job or gender models is favored without adequate discussion . . . the search for alternative interpretations is short-circuited. The models offer a ready-made explanation and the researcher follows the path of least resistance. These distortions are serious enough. An even more serious consequence of the models is that they bias the entire direction of research. As is the case of basic paradigms in science, the job-gender paradigm determines *what* is studied. (Feldberg and Glenn, 1984)

Problems in Studying Gender and Stratification

At the present moment, there does not exist an adequate framework within which problems of gender and stratification can effectively be analyzed. Theoretical and conceptual innovations are needed as well as a reorientation of empirical research. The two models identified by Feldberg and Glenn express long-established shortcomings in analyses of class and the domestic sphere. Those interested in stratification have concentrated upon men, with their households presumed to be "pulled along" with them. Where the situation and outlook of women has been studied at all in sociology, it has been almost always in the domestic setting. Not nearly enough is known of the connections between these two environments.

SOCIAL MOBILITY

IN STUDYING STRATIFICATION, WE HAVE TO CONSIDER NOT only the differences between economic positions or occupations, but what happens to the individuals who occupy them. **Social mobility** refers to the movement of individuals and groups between different socioeconomic positions. **Vertical mobility** means movement up or down the socioeconomic scale. Those who gain in property, income, or status are said to be *upwardly mobile,* while those who move in the opposite direction are *downwardly mobile.* In modern societies there is also a great deal of **lateral mobility,** which refers to geographical movement between neighborhoods, towns, or regions. Vertical and lateral mobility are often combined. For instance, an individual working in a company in one city might be promoted to a higher position in a branch of the firm located in another town, or even in a different country.

There are two ways of studying social mobility. First, we can look at individuals' own careers—how far they move up or down the socioeconomic scale in the course of their working lives. This is called **intragenerational mobility.** Alternatively, we can analyze where children are on the scale compared to their parents or grandparents. Mobility across the generations is called **intergenerational mobility.**

MOBILITY STUDIES

The amount of vertical mobility in a society is a major indication of its "openness." Do individuals born into the lower strata have opportunities to move up the socioeconomic ladder? How "open" are the industrialized countries? Is there more equality of opportunity in the United States than elsewhere? Pitrim Sorokin carried out the earliest studies of comparative social mobility (Sorokin, 1927). Sorokin included a vast array of different societies, ranging from traditional Rome and China to the United States. He concluded that opportunities for rapid ascent in the United States were much more confined than American folklore suggested. The techniques Sorokin used to gather his data, however, were relatively primitive.

Research carried out by Peter Blau and Otis Dudley Duncan (1967), forty years later, was far more sophisticated and comprehensive. Surveying a national sample of twenty thousand males, Blau and Duncan concluded that there was a great deal of vertical mobility in the United States, but nearly all of this was between occupational positions quite close to one another. "Long range" mobility, that is, from working class to upper-middle class, was rare. Although downward movement occurred both within the careers of individuals and intergenerationally, it was much less common than upward mobility. The reason for this latter finding was that white-collar and professional jobs had grown much more rapidly than blue-collar ones. This shift created the openings for some sons of blue-collar workers to move into white-collar positions.

Perhaps the most celebrated international study of social mobility was that carried out by Seymour Martin Lipset and Reinhard Bendix (1959). They analyzed data from nine industrialized societies—Britain, France, West Germany, Sweden, Switzerland, Japan, Denmark, Italy, and the United States. The research concentrated upon mobility of men from blue-collar to white-collar work. Contrary to the researchers' expectations, they discovered no evidence that the United States was more open than the European societies. Total vertical mobility across the blue-collar–white-collar line was 30 percent in the United States, with the other societies varying between 27–31 percent. Lipset and Bendix concluded that all the industrialized countries were experiencing similar changes in respect to the expansion of white-collar jobs. This led to an "upward surge of mobility" of comparable dimensions in each of them.

Other researchers since have questioned these findings. They have argued that there are significant differences between countries if more attention is given to downward mobility, and if long-range mobility is also brought into consideration. There seems to be more long-range mobility in the United States, for instance, than in most other Western societies. But on the whole, the similarities in patterns of mobility are more striking than the differences (Miller, 1960, 1971; Heath, 1981; Tyree, Semyonov, and Hodge, 1979; Grusky and Hauser, 1984).

Robert Erikson and John Goldthorpe (1986) carried out a substantial study of cross-national similarities and variations in mobility, including in their work both Western and Eastern European societies. They studied nine countries, including England and Wales, France, Sweden, Hungary, and Poland among others. The results again showed a general similarity between mobility rates and patterns. However, they also found some significant variations as well. Sweden, for example, was found to be considerably more "open" than the other Western countries. Poland also showed high rates of mobility, substantially greater than those of Hungary.

DOWNWARD MOBILITY

Although downward mobility is less common than upward mobility, it is still widespread. Over 20 percent of men in the United States are downwardly mobile intergenerationally, although most of this movement is short range. Downward intragenerational mobility is also a common occurrence. Mobility of this latter type is often associated with psychological problems and anxieties. Some individuals are simply unable to sustain the life style into which they were born. Another source of downward mobility among individuals arises through no fault of their own. Corporate America is flooded with instances in which middle-aged men lose their jobs because of mergers or company take-overs. These executives either find it hard to gain new employment at all, or can only obtain work at a lower level of income than before. Other employers are reluctant to invest in them because of their age.

Many of the downwardly mobile intragenerationally are women. It is still common for women to abandon promising careers on the birth of a child. After spending some years bringing up a family, such women later return to the paid work force, often at a level lower than they left—for instance, in poorly paid, part-time work. This situation is changing, although not as fast as many might hope.

One finding emerges fairly clearly from the literature: Levels of mobility are low compared to ideals of equality of opportunity. In the United States, as elsewhere, most people remain close to the same level as the family from which they came. While many do experience vertical mobility, this is most often the result of changes in the occupational structure, not because there is a high level of equality of opportunity built into the social system.

OPPORTUNITIES FOR MOBILITY

Many people in modern societies believe it is possible for anyone to reach the top through hard work and persistence. Why should it be difficult to do so? In one respect, the answer is very simple. Even in a "perfectly fluid" society, in which everyone had an exactly equal chance of reaching the highest positions, only a small minority would do so. The socioeconomic order is shaped like a pyramid, with relatively few positions of power, status, and wealth at the top. No more than two or three thousand people, out of a total population of 200 million in the United States, could become directors of the two hundred largest corporations.

In addition, those who already hold positions of wealth and power have many chances available to them to perpetuate their advantages, and to pass them on to their offspring. They can make sure their children have the best available education, and this will often lead them into the best jobs. Despite estate taxes, the rich still find ways to pass on much of their property to their descendants. Most of those who reach the top had a head start; they came from professional or affluent backgrounds. Studies of people who have become wealthy show that hardly anyone begins with nothing. The large majority of people who have "made money" did so on the basis of inheriting or being given at least a modest account initially—which they then used to make more (Jaher, 1973; Rubinstein, 1986).

PROBLEMS IN STUDYING SOCIAL MOBILITY

The study of social mobility presents various problems: for example, it is not clear whether mobility from blue-collar to white-collar work is always "upward" (Hopper, 1981). Skilled blue-collar workers may be in a superior economic position to many people in more routine white-collar jobs. The nature of jobs alters over time, and it is not always obvious that what are regarded as the "same" occupations are in fact still such. Clerical occupations, for instance, have changed greatly over the past several decades as a result of the mechanization of office work.

Another problem is that, in studies of intergenerational mobility, it is difficult to decide at what point of the respective careers to make comparisons. A parent may still be at mid-career when a child begins his or her work life; parents and their offspring may simultaneously be mobile, perhaps in the same direction or (less often) in different directions. Should we compare them at the beginning or at the end of their careers?

All of these difficulties can be dealt with to some extent. Care can be taken to alter occupational categories when it is clear that the nature of jobs has shifted radically over the period covered by a particular study. For example, we might decide to group higher blue-collar and routine white-collar jobs together and examine mobility into and out of these jobs as a whole. The problem about where in individuals' careers to make comparisons in studying intergenerational mobility can be resolved—where the data permit—by comparing parents and children both at the beginning and at the end of their respective careers. But these strategies are not entirely satisfactory. What may appear to be precise figures offered in mobility studies have to be approached with caution. We can only draw general conclusions from mobility research, particularly where international comparisons are involved.

YOUR OWN MOBILITY CHANCES

What implications might be drawn from mobility studies about the career opportunities that you are faced with, as someone searching for a good job in the 1990s? Like previous generations, you are likely to enjoy upward mobility. It seems probable that the proportion of managerial and professional jobs will continue to expand relative to lower-level positions (for more information about changes in the occupational structure, see Chapter 15: "Work and Economic Life"). Those who have done well in the educational system are most likely to fill these openings (Figure 7.3).

FIGURE 7.3 INCOME AND EDUCATIONAL ACCOMPLISHMENT, 1987

This graph shows the correlation between the level of education achieved and the average (mean) income.

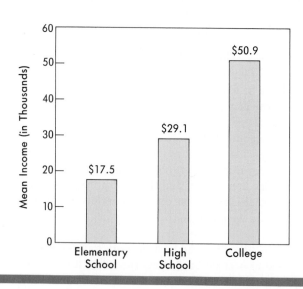

Source: U.S. Bureau of the Census. 1987. *Current Population Reports,* ser. P–60, no. 161.

Yet there are not nearly enough higher-status positions open for all who wish to enter them, and some of you are bound to find that your careers do not match your expectations. Although a higher proportion of jobs are being created at managerial and professional levels than existed before, the overall number of jobs available in the economy may not, in the future, keep pace with the number of people actively seeking work. One reason for this is the growing numbers of women entering the labor force. Another (whose consequences are difficult to sort out fully as yet) is the increasing use of information technology in production processes. Because computerized machinery can now handle tasks—even of a highly complicated kind—that once upon a time only human beings could do, it is possible, and perhaps even likely, that many jobs will be eliminated in future years.

If you are a woman, although your chances of entering a good career are improving, you face two major obstacles to your progress. Male managers and employers still discriminate against female applicants, compared to males seeking the same positions. They do so at least partly because of their beliefs that "women are not really interested in careers," and that they are likely to leave the work force to begin families. This latter factor substantially affects opportunities for women. This is less because they are uninterested in a career than

FIGURE 7.4   **WHO GETS PAID BETTER**

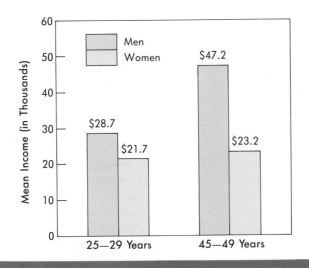

This graph shows the average (mean) income at various ages for men and women (1986) who have graduated from college.

Source: U.S. Bureau of the Census. 1986. *Current Population Reports,* ser. P–60, no. 159.

because they are often forced to choose between a career and having children. Men are rarely willing to share equal responsibility for domestic work and childcare. Although many more women than before are following nontraditional paths—determinedly organizing their domestic lives in order to pursue a career—there are still major barriers in their way.

POVERTY AND INEQUALITY

RIGHT AT THE BOTTOM OF THE CLASS SYSTEM ARE THE MIL-lions of people in the United States who exist in conditions of poverty. Many do not have a proper diet and live in miserable conditions; their average life expectancy is lower than the majority of the population. In addition, the number of individuals and families who have become homeless has greatly increased over the past decade (Table 7.2).

Many affluent people pay little attention to the existence of poverty, so some have made it their goal to bring the phenomenon to public consciousness. In 1889, Charles Booth published a work showing that a third of Londoners were living in dire poverty (Booth, 1904). The result was a public outcry. How could it happen that, in a country which at that time was probably the wealthiest on earth, at the center of a massive empire, poverty should be so widespread? Booth's work was taken up by his namesake, General William Booth of the Salvation Army. His book *In Darkest England and the Way Out* (1984; orig. pub. 1890) opened with figures derived from Charles Booth's calculations, showing there to be 387,000 "very poor" people in London, 220,000 "near to starving," and 300,000 "starving." Almost a quarter of a million copies of William Booth's book were sold within a year, so dramatically did he capture the public imagination. Poverty, he proposed, could be drastically reduced by the means of practical programs of reform and welfare.

Seventy years later, a somewhat parallel situation occurred in the United States. In his book *The Other America*, Michael Harrington shocked the American public with the finding that many millions of people in the country were without the basic requisites for meeting minimum standards of life (Harrington, 1963). Harrington's book also became a bestseller. In May 1964, President Lyndon B. Johnson declared an "unconditional War on Poverty," whose object would be "to eliminate the paradox of poverty in the midst of plenty." The United States had long since supplanted Britain as the world's richest nation, a country vastly more wealthy than Britain had been at the

TABLE 7.2	PROFILE OF THE HOMELESS*
Average income	$181.90 per month
Receiving public assistance	45%
Average age	36
Race:	
Black	63%
White	25%
Hispanic and other	12%
Sex	63% male
Average years of education	11
Currently Married	6%
Single women with children	21%
Jail experience	53%
Prison experience	11%
Symptoms of alcoholism	19%
Hospitalized for mental illness	20%
Those exhibiting symptoms of mental illness needing treatment	45%
First-time homeless	50%
Reasons for homelessness:	
Eviction	50%
Arguments	21%
Building destroyed	17%
Received court order for eviction	14%

* Based on interviews at soup kitchens with 535 meal recipients who are homeless.
Source: "Homeless in Chicago": 1988 study by the School of Social Service Administration of the University of Chicago.

time of the work of the two Booths. Yet large numbers of the population continued to live in circumstances that denied them the bare essentials of social health and housing. The War on Poverty was designed finally to achieve the objectives that William Booth had planned some three generations earlier.

THE WAR ON POVERTY

After his inauguration into office, President Lyndon B. Johnson pushed his "Great Society" legislation through Congress. Not only would there be large-scale increases in spending on existing social welfare programs, but numerous new programs would be established to deal with an affluent America's impoverished. Welfare spending went up by 400 percent, from $77.2 billion in 1965 to $286.5 billion

TABLE 7.3
FAMILIES BELOW THE
POVERTY LEVEL

	In Millions	Percentage
1970	9.78	15%
1975	9.63	13%
1980	10.87	12%
1983	12.70	14%
1986	12.27	13%

Source: Congressional Budget
Office, *Trends in Family Income:*
1970–1986. February 1988.

ten years later. The increase in spending on welfare did have discernible effects in reducing the level of poverty, although these fell far short of anticipations. In 1972, as measured by official statistics, the numbers of the poor fell to their lowest mark in the postwar period. Those living below the officially defined poverty line fell from just under 40 million to about 23 million. Since then, however, the numbers of the poor have again climbed, although the actual proportion to the general population of individuals and families living in poverty has remained fairly stable (Table 7.3).

The War on Poverty programs fell victim to various economic and political forces, which reduced their level of success. For example, the Job Corps was designed to teach young people the skills needed to enter the job market. But the U.S. economy was such that the job openings were simply not there for them. In the early seventies, a new period of recession set in, reducing job opportunities still further. The Head Start program, which offered preschool education to the poor, made some real gains over time, but it became unpopular among some sections of the white working class, who did not see immediate results for the large price the program cost. Politically, the United States was deepening its commitment to the Vietnam War at the same time, which competed with the antipoverty programs for funding. The War on Poverty frequently lost out.

WHAT IS POVERTY?

How should "poverty" be defined? A distinction is usually made between *subsistence* or **absolute poverty** and **relative poverty.** Charles Booth was one of the first to try to establish a consistent standard of subsistence poverty, which refers to lack of basic necessities needed to sustain a physically healthy existence—sufficient food and shelter to make possible the physically efficient functioning of the body. Booth assumed that these requirements would be more or less the same for people of equivalent age and physique living in any country.

This is essentially the definition that is used most frequently in the analysis of poverty in the United States. The official poverty line is fixed by calculating the average cost of food providing adequate nutrition, this figure is then trebled to cover clothing, housing, medical care, and other necessities. Weightings are introduced for size of family and area of residence. The official poverty line for a family of four living in an urban area in 1985 was $10,989. Using this figure, in 1985, 14 percent of the population of the United States, about 33 million people, were living below the poverty line. This figure hides major differences between people of various ethnic background; whereas 11 percent of whites live in poverty, 29 percent of people of Hispanic origins do so, and 31 percent of blacks (U.S. Bureau of the Census, 1987).

Subsistence definitions of poverty have definite shortcomings. Defining what the "basic necessities" of life are is more problematic than it sounds, because it is hard to separate the notion from the living standards of the majority of the population. The majority of the world's population lives in dwellings that do not contain a bath or shower; but it would be hard not to see piped water as a necessity in an economically developed society. It makes sense to see poverty in relative rather than absolute terms. As the economist John Kenneth Galbraith has written in a classic work:

> People are poverty-stricken when their incomes, even if adequate for survival, fall markedly below those of the community. Then they cannot have what the larger community regards as the necessary minimum for decency. . . . They are degraded for, in the literal sense, they live outside the grades or categories which the community regards as acceptable. (Galbraith, 1985)

In some ways it is more accurate to speak of "poverties" rather than "poverty" when we survey a society like the United States (Figure 7.5). In the very poorest parts of the South, particularly between Vir-

FIGURE 7.5   PERSONS BELOW THE POVERTY LEVEL BY RACE AND HISPANIC ORIGIN

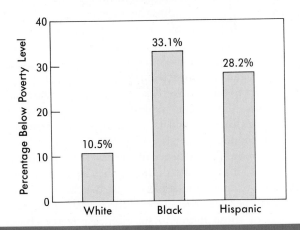

Source: U.S. Bureau of the Census. 1987. *Current Population Reports,* ser. P–60, no. 161.

ginia and Louisiana, people (the majority of whom are black) live in conditions close to those found in an impoverished Third World country. According to the National Association of the Southern Poor, "People in the area . . . live in houses insulated by cardboard with tin roofs, in converted stables or chicken coups. Many have no toilets, indoors or out. Often they must transport water from long distances. Most babies are born without the assistance of any medical advice. The sleep of residents is sometimes disturbed by children crying from hunger; and our organization has witnessed hunger pacified by sugar and water for entire households, including babies, for periods of up to 10 days" (Harrington, 1984). Their level of poverty is considerably greater than that of most blacks living in even the most deprived neighborhoods in Northern cities.

The poorest groups of all in the United States are those whose land it once was, the Native Americans. Their rate of unemployment is the highest of any minority; their life expectancy is well below that of blacks, and their rate of infant mortality very high. Yet some of Native Americans still retain enough of their traditional culture to provide a meaningful focus for their lives.

Why Are the Poor Still Poor?

Well-developed and systematically administered welfare programs, in conjunction with government policies that actively assist in keeping down unemployment, reduce poverty levels. There exist societies —such as Sweden—in which subsistence poverty has been almost completely eliminated. An economic and political price has to be paid for this. First, such societies require high levels of taxation. Second, the integration of a full welfare system into an already bureaucratic government inevitably gives those agencies a great deal of power.

Where the distribution of wealth and income in a country is mainly left to mechanisms of the market—as in the case in the United States—greater material inequalities tend to be found. For example, the Reagan administration (1981–1988) pursued a market strategy in order to take the burden of providing welfare off the federal government. The theory underlying "Reaganomics" was that cutting tax rates for individuals and corporations would generate high levels of economic growth, the fruits of which would "trickle down" to the poor. The evidence of the past few years does not support this thesis. This type of economic policy may or may not generate acceleration of economic development, but the result is to expand the differentials between the poor and the wealthy, actually swelling the numbers of those living in subsistence poverty (Block et al., 1987).

Most Americans, of all social classes, have more negative attitudes

TABLE 7.4	COMPARATIVE PUBLIC OPINION ON WELFARE	
	Strongly agree/agree that the government should . . .	
	provide everyone with a guaranteed basic income	spend more on benefits for the poor
Hungary	78%	72%
Italy	67%	83%
West Germany	51%	80%
Britain	59%	82%
Netherlands	48%	55%
Australia	36%	59%
United States	20%	58%

Source: Smith, Tom W. (1989).

towards welfare provisions and benefits than is the case in other Western countries (Table 7.4). Surveys repeatedly show that the majority of Americans regard the poor as being responsible for their own poverty, and they are antagonistic to those who live on "government handouts." Most believe that people on welfare could find work if they were determined to do so (Waxman, 1977). These views are completely out of line with the realities of poverty. About a quarter of those officially living in poverty are actually working. They are, however, in a difficult situation because they earn too little to bring them over the poverty threshold and too much to allow them to be candidates to receive any welfare. Of the remainder, over 60 percent consist of children under fourteen years of age, those aged sixty-five and over, the ill or disabled. Only a minute proportion (about 2 percent) of able-bodied men are on welfare.

Other myths about the poor abound. Families on welfare are not, as is often thought, large; the average number of children is the same as for the rest of the population. In spite of popular views about the high level of welfare cheating, fewer than 1 percent of welfare applications involve fraudulent claims—much lower than in the case of income-tax fraud, where it is estimated that more than 10 percent of tax is lost through misreporting or evasion.

What accounts for the marked disparities between beliefs about poverty and welfare spending, and the actual facts? One reason is the sheer strength of the beliefs in economic individualism that are so dominant in the United States. Even if overall rates of social mobility are no higher in the United States than elsewhere, successive genera-

"WELL, AT LEAST THESE STUDIES, ARTICLES, PROPOSALS, SPEECHES ABOUT US MAKE A GREAT PILLOW..."

tions of immigrants have risen from conditions of initial poverty to positions of some affluence. The persistence of discrimination against blacks and Native Americans dovetails with views that they make up the majority of welfare recipients and are disinclined to seek work where it is available.

Yet the strength of public reaction to the periodic disclosure of the level of poverty suggests that a contributing factor is also the lack of "visibility" of the poor. Most of those in the more privileged sections of society rarely visit the urban or rural areas in which poverty is concentrated. Some issues connected with poverty, such as high rates of crime, regularly command public attention, but the widespread existence of poverty tends otherwise to be put out of mind. Poverty has periodically been "rediscovered" from the time of Charles Booth on. For a while the plight of the poor stirs the conscience of the more favored, but public concern soon fades away.

THEORIES OF STRATIFICATION
IN MODERN SOCIETIES

SO FAR, WE HAVE DEFINED STRATIFICATION, EXAMINING closely types of class division, the influence of gender, social mobility, and poverty. In this section we step back and examine some broad theories by which thinkers have attempted to *understand* stratification. The most influential theoretical approaches are those developed by Karl Marx (1818–1883) and Max Weber (1864–1920). Most subsequent theories of stratification are heavily indebted to their ideas. We shall also analyze two later theories put forward by Erik Olin Wright and by Frank Parkin. The ideas of Marx and Weber have made a deep impact upon the development of sociology, and have influenced many other areas of the discipline besides the study of stratification. Other aspects of their writings will show up in subsequent chapters. (For an overall survey of their work, see Chapter 22: "The Development of Sociological Theory.")

KARL MARX: MEANS OF PRODUCTION AND THE ANALYSIS OF CLASS

Marx was born in Germany but spent much of his life in Britain. Although his ideas have always been controversial, Marx's writings have been influential worldwide. Many authors (including Max Weber) who reject Marx's political views have drawn widely upon his writings.

Most of Marx's work was concerned with stratification and, above all, with social class, yet surprisingly he failed to provide a systematic analysis of the concept of class. The manuscripts Marx was working on at the time of his death (subsequently published as part of Marx's major work, *Das Kapital*) break off just at the juncture where he posed the question, "What constitutes a class?" Marx's concept of class thus has to be reconstructed from the body of his writings as a whole. Since the various passages in which Marx discusses class are not always consistent, there have been many disputes between scholars about "what Marx really meant." The main outlines of his views, however, are fairly clear.

The Nature of Class

For Marx a class refers to people who stand in a common relationship to the **means of production**—the means by which they gain a livelihood. Prior to the rise of modern industry, the means of production consisted primarily of land and the instruments used to tend to crops or pastoral animals. In preindustrial societies, therefore, the two main classes were those who owned the land (aristocrats, gentry, or slaveholders) and those actively engaged in producing from it (serfs, free peasantry, and slaves). In modern societies, factories, offices, machinery, and the wealth or capital needed to buy them become more important. The two main classes are those who own these new means of production—industrialists or **capitalists**—and those who earn their living by selling their labor to them—the working class or, in the now somewhat archaic term Marx sometimes favored, the "proletariat."

The relationship between classes, according to Marx, is an exploitative one. In feudal societies, exploitation often took the form of the direct transfer of produce from the peasantry to the aristocracy. Serfs were compelled to give a certain proportion of their production to their aristocratic masters, or had to work for a number of days each month in the lord's fields to produce crops consumed by the lord and his retinue. In modern capitalist societies, the source of exploitation is less obvious, and Marx devoted much attention to trying to clarify its nature. In the course of the working day, Marx reasoned, workers produce more than is actually needed by employers to repay the cost of hiring them. This **surplus value** is the source of profit, which capitalists are able to put to their own use. A group of workers in a clothing factory, say, might be able to produce a hundred suits a day. Selling half the suits provides enough income for the manufacturer to pay the workers' wages. Income from the sale of the remainder of the garments is taken as profit.

The Complexity of Class Systems

Although in Marx's theory there are two main classes in society, those who own the means of production and those who do not, he recognized that actual class systems are much more complex than this model suggests. In addition to the two basic classes, there exist what Marx sometimes called **transitional classes.** These are class groups left over from an earlier type of production system, which persist long after that system has disappeared. In some modern societies, for example (like France, Italy, or Spain for much of the current century), substantial numbers of people remain peasants, working in much the same way as their predecessors did—although, of course, they no longer stand in a feudal relation to aristocratic landowners.

Marx also drew attention to splits that tend to occur within classes:

1. Among the upper classes, for instance, there are often conflicts between financial capitalists (like bankers) and industrial manufacturers.

2. There are divisions of interest between small business people and those who own or manage the large corporations. Both belong to the capitalist class; but policies that favor large businesses are not always in the interests of small ones.

3. Within the working class, those who are more or less permanently unemployed have worse conditions of life than

the majority of workers. These groups often consist largely of ethnic minorities.

Marx believed that the maturing of industrial capitalism would bring about an increasing gap between the wealth of the minority and the poverty of the mass of the population. According to him, the wages of the working class could never rise far above subsistence level, while wealth would pile up in the hands of those owning capital. In addition, laborers would daily face work that is physically wearing and mentally tedious, as is the situation in many factories. At the lowest levels of society, particularly among those frequently or permanently unemployed, there would develop an "accumulation of misery, agony of labor, slavery, ignorance, brutality, moral degradation. . ." (Marx, 1977; orig. pub. 1864). Marx was right about the persistence of poverty within the industrialized countries, and in anticipating that large-scale inequalities of wealth and income would continue. He was wrong in supposing that the income of most of the population would remain extremely low, as well as in claiming that a minority would become more and more wealthy relative to the majority. Most people in Western countries today are much better off materially than were comparable groups in Marx's day.

MAX WEBER: CLASS AND STATUS

Like Marx, Max Weber was also German. Although illness prevented him from following an orthodox academic career, he had a private income and was able to devote much of his life to scholarly study. He is regarded as one of the founders of sociology; his writings range more widely than the study of stratification, spanning many fields of history, legal theory, economics, and comparative religion.

Weber's approach to stratification is built upon the analysis developed by Marx, but modifies and elaborates it. There are two main differences between Weber's theory and that of Marx.

First, although Weber accepted Marx's view that class is founded upon objectively given economic conditions, he saw a greater variety of economic factors as important in class formation than was recognized by Marx. According to Weber, class divisions derive not only from control or lack of control of the means of production, but from economic differences that have nothing directly to do with property. Such resources include especially the *skills* and *credentials,* or qualifications, that affect the types of jobs people are able to obtain. Those in managerial or professional occupations earn more, and have more favorable conditions of work, for example, than people in blue-collar jobs. The qualifications they possess, such as degrees, diplomas, and the skills they have acquired, make them more "marketable" than others without such qualifications. At a lower level, among blue-collar workers, skilled craftsmen are able to secure higher wages than the semiskilled or unskilled.

Second, Weber distinguished another aspect of stratification besides class, which he called **status.** He in fact adapted the notion of status groups from the example of medieval estates—the German word he used *(Stand)* means both "status" and "estate." Status refers to differences between social groups in the social honor or prestige they are accorded by others. Status distinctions often vary independently of class divisions. Social honor may be either positive or negative. Positively privileged status groups include any groups of people who have high **prestige** in a given social order—for instance, doctors and lawyers have high prestige in American society. **Pariah groups** are negatively privileged status groups, subject to discrimination that prevents them from taking advantage of opportunities open to most others. The Jews were a pariah group in medieval Europe, banned from participating in certain occupations, and from holding official positions.

Possession of wealth normally tends to confer high status, but there are many exceptions to this principle. The term "genteel poverty" refers to one example. In Britain, for instance, individuals from aristocratic families continue to enjoy considerable social esteem even after their fortunes have been lost. Conversely, "new money" is often looked upon with some scorn by the well-established wealthy.

Whereas class is objectively given, status depends upon people's subjective evaluations of social differences. Classes derive from the economic factors associated with property and earnings; status is governed by the varying *styles of life* groups follow.

Weber's writings on stratification are important because they show that other dimensions of stratification besides class strongly influence people's lives. Most sociologists hold that Weber's scheme offers a more flexible and sophisticated basis for analyzing stratification than that provided by Marx.

RECENT THEORIES OF CLASS

The ideas developed by Marx and Weber are still used extensively in sociology today, although rarely without modification. Those who have worked in the Marxian tradition have further elaborated Marx's original ideas, and followers of Weber have built upon his formulations. Yet, since the views of Marx and Weber were complementary, many subsequent authors have drawn upon both. We can find examples in the work of Erik Olin Wright and Frank Parkin.

Erik Olin Wright and Contradictory Class Locations

The American sociologist Erik Olin Wright has developed a theoretical position that owes much to Marx, but also incorporates ideas from Weber (Wright, 1978, 1985). According to Wright, there are three means of control over economic resources in modern capitalist production, and these allow us to identify the major classes that exist. These three modes of control are:

1. control over investments or money capital;

2. control over the physical means of production (land or factories and offices);

3. control over labor power.

Those who belong to the capitalist class have control over each of these elements within the production system. Members of the working class have control over none of them. In between these two main classes, however, there are groups whose position is more ambiguous. These people are in what Wright calls **contradictory class locations,** because they are able to influence some aspects of production, but are denied control over others. Many white-collar and professional employees, for example, have to contract their labor power to employers in order to obtain a living, in the same way as manual workers do. Yet at the same time, they have a greater degree of control over their work setting than those in blue-collar jobs. For instance, lawyers who work for large corporations might be in a contradictory class location. While they do not own the means of production, they still have a considerable amount of control over their work situation. Wright terms the class position of such workers "contradictory," because it incorporates the characteristics of the classes both above and below them. Workers in contradictory class locations are neither capitalists nor manual workers, yet share certain common features with each.

Frank Parkin and Social Closure

Frank Parkin (1971, 1979), a British author, has proposed an approach drawing more heavily from Weber than from Marx. Parkin agrees with Marx, as Weber did, that ownership of property—the means of production—is the basic foundation of class structure. Property, however, according to Parkin, is only one form of **social closure** that can be monopolized by one group and used as a basis of power over others. We can define social closure as any process whereby groups try to maintain exclusive control over resources, limiting access to them. Besides property or wealth, most of the characteristics Weber associated with status differences, such as ethnic origin, language, or religion, may be used to create social closure.

Two types of processes are involved in social closure. The first type, *exclusion,* refers to strategies that groups adopt to separate outsiders from themselves, preventing them from having access to valued resources. Thus white unions in the United States have in the past excluded blacks from membership, as a means of maintaining power and privilege.

An emphasis on credentials is another major way by which groups exclude others in order to hold on to their power and privilege. In some U.S. school systems, for example, only those who have earned a secondary-school teaching certification in their subject, awarded by a school of education, are allowed to teach in the public schools. The second type, *usurpation,* refers to attempts by the less privileged to acquire resources previously monopolized by others—as where blacks struggle to achieve rights of union membership.

The strategies of exclusion and usurpation may be used simultaneously in some circumstances. Labor unions, for instance, might engage in usurpatory activities against employers (going on strike to obtain a greater share of the resources or a position on the board of directors of a firm) but at the same time exclude ethnic minorities from membership. Parkin calls this *dual closure.* Here there is clearly a point of similarity between Wright and Parkin. Dual closure concerns much the same processes as those discussed by Wright under contradictory class locations. Both notions indicate that those in the middle of the stratification system in some part cast their eyes towards the top, yet are also concerned with distinguishing themselves from others lower down.

STRATIFICATION, STRUCTURE, AND ACTION

STUDYING STRATIFICATION RAISES ACUTELY ONE OF THE perennial theoretical problems of sociology. We are all deeply influenced by the social circumstances in which, as children, we are raised, and the position in society in which we find ourselves as adults. Those who are born and brought up in an impoverished ghetto area of a city do not choose their circumstances of life. Those circumstances affect individuals' lives in an objective fashion, molding their views of themselves and their general attitudes towards society at large. These views and attitudes, in other words, result from structural characteristics of the societies of which people are members. As Emile Durkheim (1982, orig. pub. 1895) expressed this, social structure is *external* to individuals and *constrains* their behavior.

On the other hand, no one is completely a prisoner of their social environment. People from disadvantaged backgrounds sometimes attain high positions. We all actively make choices, seek to achieve ambitions of various sorts, and to some extent can overcome barriers that society places in our way. A society is plainly not external to our actions in the same fashion as a building is—for societies only *consist* of human actions and relationships. We create society in the diversity of social activities we carry on day in and day out.

It has not proved easy for sociologists to show how these two aspects of society can be reconciled. The main theoretical traditions of sociology tend to divide up according to where they place their main emphasis. Some—like traditions of thought indebted to Durkheim—concentrate attention upon how our actions are conditioned by the social world. Others (like symbolic interactionism) stress much more the active, creative character of social conduct. Each view has some truth in it. The problem is to analyze how these views mix. You should reflect on this as you read through subsequent chapters, because there are few areas of sociology in which the issue does not emerge in one way or another. The issue is discussed in some detail, along with other major theoretical dilemmas in sociology, in Chapter 22 ("The Development of Sociological Theory").

SUMMARY

1. Social stratification refers to the division of people socioeconomically into layers or strata. When we talk of social stratification, we draw attention to the unequal positions occupied by individuals in society. In the larger traditional societies and in industrialized countries today there is stratification in terms of wealth, property, and access to material goods and cultural products.

2. Four major types of stratification systems can be distinguished: slavery, caste, estates, and class. Whereas the first three of these depend upon legal or religiously sanctioned inequalities, class divisions are not "officially" recognized, but stem from economic factors affecting the material circumstances of people's lives.

3. Classes derive from inequalities in possession and control of material resources. An individual's class position is at least in some

part achieved, for it is not simply "given" from birth. Social mobility, both upwards and downwards in the class structure, is a fairly common feature.

4. Class is of major importance in industrialized societies, although there are many complexities in the class system within such societies. The main class divisions are between people in the *upper, middle,* and *working* classes, and the *underclass.*

5. Most people in modern societies are more affluent today than was the case several generations ago. Yet the distribution of wealth and income remains highly unequal. The wealthy have various means open to them of transmitting their property from one generation to the next.

6. Analyses of stratification have traditionally been written from a male-oriented point of view. This is partly because of the assumption that gender inequalities simply reflect class differences; but this assumption is highly questionable. Gender influences stratification in modern societies in some part independently of class.

7. In the study of social mobility, a distinction is made between *intragenerational* and *intergenerational* mobility. The first of these refers to movement up or down the social scale within an individual's working life. Intergenerational mobility is movement across the generations, as when the daughter or son from a blue-collar background becomes a professional. Social mobility is mostly of limited range. Most people remain close to the level of the family from which they came, though the expansion of white-collar jobs in the last few decades has provided the opportunity for considerable short-range upward mobility.

8. Poverty remains widespread in the United States. Two methods of assessing poverty exist. One involves the notion of *subsistence poverty,* which is a lack of the basic resources needed to maintain a healthy existence. *Relative poverty* involves assessing the gaps between the living conditions of some groups and those enjoyed by the majority of the population.

9. The most prominent and influential theories of stratification are those developed by Marx and Weber. Marx placed the primary emphasis on *class,* which he saw as an objectively given characteristic of the economic structure of society. He saw a fundamental split between the owners of capital and the workers who do not own capital. Weber accepted a similar view, but distinguished another aspect of stratification, *status.* Status refers to the esteem or "social honor" given to individuals or groups.

BASIC CONCEPTS

SOCIAL STRATIFICATION

CLASS

SOCIAL MOBILITY

STATUS

IMPORTANT TERMS

SLAVERY

CASTE

ESTATE

UPPER CLASS

MIDDLE CLASS

WORKING OR LOWER CLASS

PEASANTS

WEALTH

INCOME

UNDERCLASS

CLASS CONSCIOUSNESS

VERTICAL MOBILITY

LATERAL MOBILITY

INTRAGENERATIONAL MOBILITY

INTERGENERATIONAL MOBILITY

ABSOLUTE POVERTY

RELATIVE POVERTY

MEANS OF PRODUCTION

CAPITALISTS

SURPLUS VALUE

TRANSITIONAL CLASSES

PRESTIGE

PARIAH GROUPS

CONTRADICTORY CLASS LOCATIONS

SOCIAL CLOSURE

ETHNICITY AND RACE

IN JAPAN, THERE EXISTS A GROUP OF PEOPLE WHO ARE PHYSI-
cally indistinguishable from other Japanese, who have
lived in the country for hundreds of years, and who share
the same religion. Yet they are regarded with hostility or
disdain by the majority of the Japanese population. The
origins of this prejudice can be traced back to the eighteenth century. As a result of the wars that reigned
between local rulers, some groups of people were dispossessed from their land and became outcasts and vagrants.
They were called *eta* (a term that means "very dirty"),
and later on *burakumin* (derived from the isolated communities, or
buraku, in which they came to live). Both names have survived up to
today, *eta* being the most offensive (Dore and Aoyagi, 1965).

The outcasts were forced to take menial jobs that other people de-
spised. In local religious beliefs, many of these occupations were regarded as unclean, a trait that was subsequently extended to the
people who worked in them. Consequently, they were systematically
discriminated against by the majority. They lived in special settlements, were forbidden to change occupations, and compelled to
marry only amongst themselves. With the modernization of Japan,
beginning in the second half of the nineteenth century, the *buraku-*

min were made formally equal to everyone else. A decree by the Japanese emperor stated that they should become full citizens and allowed to follow any occupation they desired. The term *eta* disappeared from official pronouncements in much the same way as "nigger" has done in the United States. It continued to be used as an epithet, however, and the actual practices of discrimination changed little.

Today the *burakumin* still form an oppressed minority within a country that has risen to become one of the largest economic powers in the world. Many *burakumin* live in the same areas as their ancestors did, these being overcrowded slums. Even people from other depressed neighborhoods nearby look down upon them. Rates of intermarriage with the rest of the population continue to be low. A family will often exhaustively check the background of a prospective wife or husband to ensure that there is no *buraku* connection. Various kinds of organizations seeking to advance the position of the *burakumin* within Japanese society have sprung up, but prejudice and discrimination remain strong. The *burakumin* are still widely thought to be "mentally inferior, incapable of high moral behavior, aggressive, impulsive and lacking any notion of sanitation or manners" (Neary, 1986).

ETHNIC GROUPS, MINORITIES, AND RACE IN PLURAL SOCIETIES

THE CASE OF THE *BURAKUMIN* DEMONSTRATES HOW ENgrained and enduring the prejudices towards a minority group can be, even when they are not physically different from the remainder of the population. Long-standing persecution of minorities, unfortunately, has been all too common in human history. The Jews have been repeatedly subjected to discrimination and persecution in the Christian West for nearly two thousand years. The most horrific instance of brutal destructiveness against a minority group was the massacre of millions of Jews in the German concentration camps during World War II. Nazi ideology claimed Jews to be an inferior race to the "Aryan" people of Germany and northern Europe (Weinstein, 1980). The term "Aryan" originally referred to a group of languages spoken by people of differing physical stock. It was appropriated by the Nazis, and their so-called "race scientists," to refer to characteristics that have little or no basis in reality.

The Jews in Germany, like the *burakumin* in Japan, were a group having distinct *ethnic* characteristics. Ethnic groups are based upon cultural differences. **Ethnicity** refers to cultural practices and outlooks of a given community of people that set them apart from others. Members of ethnic groups see themselves as culturally distinct from other groups in a society, and are seen by those others to be so in return. Many different characteristics may serve to distinguish ethnic groups from one another, but the most usual are language, history or ancestry—real or imagined—religion, and styles of dress or adornment. Ethnic differences are *wholly learned,* a point that seems self-evident until we remember how often some such groups have been regarded as "born to rule" or, alternatively, have been seen as "shiftless," "unintelligent," and so forth.

Most modern societies include numerous different ethnic groups. The United States and Soviet Union, for instance, are both ethnically very diverse (Figure 8.1). The United States incorporates communities deriving from all corners of the world. Irish- and Italian-Americans, Chicanos, Puerto Ricans, blacks, and numerous other distinct ethnic groups are to be found in American society. Although Russian is the official language of the Soviet Union, Russia is only one part of the country; other regions have their own languages and customs. There are more than one hundred different ethnic groups in the Soviet Union, twenty-three of which have populations of a million or more. The Russians made up 52 percent of the total population in 1979, when the last census was taken (Kesselman et al., 1987).

MINORITIES

Ethnic groups whose members are particularly disadvantaged in a given society—like blacks in the United States—are often referred to as **minority groups.** As used in sociology, this is more than a merely numerical distinction. There are many minorities in a statistical sense, such as people having red hair or weighing more than 250 lbs, but these are not minorities according to the sociological concept. As understood in sociology, a minority group has a number of distinctive features. Its members are *disadvantaged,* as compared to the majority population, and have some sense of *group solidarity,* of "belonging together." Experience of being the subject of prejudice and discrimination usually heightens feelings of common loyalty and interests. Members of minority groups often tend to see themselves as "a people apart" from the majority. Minority groups are usually to some degree physically and socially isolated from the larger community. They tend to be concentrated in certain neighborhoods, cities, or re-

FIGURE 8.1   **WHERE AMERICANS CAME FROM**

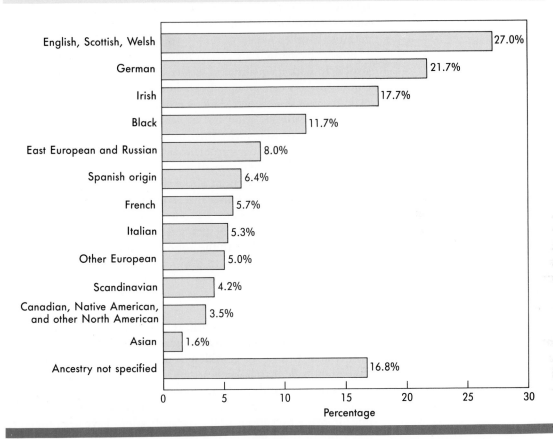

Source: U.S. Bureau of the Census. 1980 Census of the Population. *Ancestry of the Population by State, 1980,* April 1983 (in Ladd, 1989).

The graph shows the ancestry of Americans in percentages. (The percentages add up to over 100 because many Americans have multiple ancestral roots.)

gions of a country. There is little intermarriage between those in the majority and members of the minority group, or between minority groups. Those within the minority sometimes actively promote endogamy (marriage within the group) in order to keep alive their cultural distinctiveness.

Minority groups are always to some degree ethnically distinct from the majority population, but how far this is so varies. The *burakumin* are a minority group in Japanese society, although the degree of ethnic difference between them and the majority population is low. They look and act like other Japanese. Many minorities, however, are both ethnically and physically distinct from the rest of the population of the societies in which they live. This is the case with blacks, Native Americans, Chinese, and certain other groups in the United States. Physical differences, in skin color or other characteristics, are commonly called *racial.*

Ethnic distinctions are rarely "neutral," but are characteristically associated with inequalities of wealth and power, as well as with antagonisms between groups. Explaining why this is so will be the main focus of this chapter. Among ethnic-group tensions, racial divisions and hostilities stand out as being particularly prevalent. We shall have to consider why this is so, and examine the concept of "race" as such—for it is a problematic one. From there we move on to discuss theoretical interpretations of ethnic prejudice and discrimination. In subsequent sections of the chapter we will analyze race relations in a comparative framework, contrasting South Africa, Brazil, and the United States. Since the ethnic composition of the United States is so complex, we shall survey American ethnic groups in some detail. We begin, then, with the notion of **race.**

RACE AND BIOLOGY

Many people today believe—mistakenly—that humans can be readily separated into biologically different races. It is perhaps not surprising that this belief is widespread, because numerous attempts have been made by scholars to establish racial categorizations of the peoples of the world. Some authors have distinguished four or five major races, while others have recognized as many as three dozen. But too many exceptions to these classifications have been found to make any of them workable. A commonly used type, for example, that of "negroid," is supposed to be composed of people with dark skin, tightly curled, black hair, and certain other physical characteristics. Yet the original inhabitants of Australia, the Aboriginals, have dark skin but wavy, and sometimes blonde, hair. Many other examples can be found that defy any clear classification. There are no clear-cut "races," only a range of physical variations between human beings.

Differences in physical type between groups of human beings derive from population inbreeding, which varies according to the degree of contact between different social or cultural units. Human population groups are a continuum. The genetic diversity *within* populations that share certain visible physical traits is as great as the diversity between groups. In virtue of these facts, many biologists, anthropologists, and sociologists believe the concept of race should be dropped altogether.

There are clear physical differences between human beings and some of these differences are inherited. But the question of why some physical differences, and not others, become matters for social discrimination and prejudice has nothing to do with biology. Racial differences, therefore, should be understood as *physical variations singled out by the members of a community or society as socially significant.* Differences in skin color, for example, are often treated as significant in this way, whereas differences in color of hair are not (Rex, 1986). **Racism** is prejudice based on socially significant physical distinctions. A racist is someone who believes that some individuals are superior, or inferior, to others as a result of these racial differences.

ETHNIC ANTAGONISM, PREJUDICE, AND DISCRIMINATION

THE CONCEPT OF "RACE" IS MODERN, BUT PREJUDICE AND discrimination have been widespread in human history and we must first clearly distinguish between them. **Prejudice** refers to *opinions* or *attitudes* held by members of one group about another, whereas **discrimination** refers to *actual behavior* towards the other group. Prejudice means holding preconceived views about an individual or group, often based upon hearsay rather than on direct evidence, views that are resistant to change even in the face of new information. People may have favorable prejudices about groups with which they identify and negative prejudices against others. Someone who is prejudiced against a particular group will refuse to give them "a fair hearing."

Discrimination refers to activities that disqualify the members of one group from opportunities open to others—as when a black person is refused a job made available to a white. Although prejudice is very often the basis of discrimination, the two may exist separately. People may have prejudiced attitudes that they do not act upon. Equally important, discrimination does not necessarily derive directly from prejudice. For example, white house buyers might steer away from purchasing properties in certain predominantly black neighborhoods of a city, not because of attitudes of hostility they might feel towards blacks, but because of worries about declining property values. Prejudiced attitudes here influence discrimination, but in a partly indirect fashion.

PSYCHOLOGICAL INTERPRETATIONS

To explain why ethnic differences become the focus of inequalities, and of conflicts, we need to make use of both psychological and sociological concepts. Psychological theories help explain why ethnic differences become so emotionally charged, and clarify aspects of the nature of prejudiced attitudes. Sociological interpretation is necessary to show *how* and *why* ethnic divisions become institutionalized as forms of discrimination "built into" a given society.

Two types of psychological approach to understanding ethnic hostilities are important. One puts forward a number of general psychological mechanisms relevant to analyzing prejudice in general. The other concentrates upon the idea that there is a particular type of person who is most prone to hold prejudiced attitudes against minority groups.

Stereotypes and Scapegoats

Prejudice operates mainly through the use of **stereotypical thinking,** which means thinking in terms of fixed and inflexible categories. All thought involves categories by means of which we classify our experience. Sometimes, however, these categories are both ill-

The socialization of prejudice and discrimination at a Ku Klux Klan meeting.

informed and rigid. A person may have a view of blacks or Jews, for example, that is based upon a few firmly held ideas through which information about, or encounters with them, are interpreted.

Stereotypical thinking may be harmless if it is "neutral" in terms of emotional content and distant from the interests of the individuals concerned. Americans might have stereotypical views of what the British are like, for example—such as that they all talk with clipped accents, or wear striped pants—but these may be of little consequence for most people of either nationality. Where stereotypes are associated with anxiety or fear, the situation is likely to be quite different. Stereotypes in such circumstances are commonly infused with attitudes of hostility or hatred towards the group in question. A white person may believe, for example, that all blacks are lazy and worthless and use this belief to justify attitudes of contempt towards them.

Stereotyping is often closely linked to the psychological mechanism of **displacement.** In displacement, feelings of hostility or anger become directed against objects that are not the real origin of those anxieties. People vent their antagonism against scapegoats, who are blamed for whatever is the source of their troubles. The term "scapegoat" originated with the ancient Hebrews, who each year ritually loaded all their sins onto a goat, which was then chased out into the wilderness. A scapegoat is a person or group forced to shoulder the blame for happenings that are not their fault. **Scapegoating** is common in circumstances in which two deprived ethnic groups come into competition with one another for economic rewards. Those involved in racial attacks directed against blacks, for example, are often in a similar economic position to them. They blame the blacks for grievances whose real causes lie elsewhere.

Scapegoating is normally directed against groups that are clearly distinctive and relatively powerless, because they form a fairly easy target. Minority groups show both these characteristics. Protestants, Catholics, Jews, Italians, racial minorities, and very many others have played the unwilling role of scapegoats at various times throughout Western history.

Scapegoating frequently involves **projection,** the unconscious attribution to others of one's own desires or characteristics. In circumstances in which people experience considerable frustration, or must carefully control their own desires, they may be unable to recognize their own inner feelings and project them instead upon others. The bizarre ideas held by white men in the old American South about the lustful nature of black men, for instance, probably originated in their own frustrations, since sexual access to white women was limited by the formal nature of courtship. Research has consistently demonstrated that where the members of a dominant group have practiced violence against a minority, and exploited it sexually, they are likely to believe that the minority group itself displays these traits of sexual violence. Similarly, in South Africa, the belief that black males are exceptionally potent sexually and that black women are voluptuous is widespread among whites. Black males are thought to be highly dangerous sexually, in terms of the threat they pose to white women—while in fact virtually all sexual contact is initiated by white men against black women (Simpson and Yinger, 1986).

The Authoritarian Personality

It is possible that some types of people, as a result of early socialization, are particularly prone to stereotypical thinking and projection on the basis of repressed anxieties. A famous piece of research carried out by Theodor Adorno and his associates in the 1940s, diagnosed a character type they termed the **authoritarian personality** (Adorno et al., 1950). The researchers developed several measurement scales, each for a particular area of social attitudes, for assessing levels of prejudice. On one scale, for instance, people were asked to agree or disagree with a series of statements expressing rigid, particularly anti-Semitic, views. Those who were diagnosed as prejudiced on one scale also tended to be so on the others; prejudice against Jews went along with the expression of negative attitudes towards other minorities. People having an authoritarian personality, the investigators concluded, tend to be rigidly conformist, submissive to those seen as their superiors, and dismissive towards inferiors. Such people are also highly intolerant in their religious and sexual attitudes.

The characteristics of an authoritarian personality, it was suggested by the researchers, derive from a pattern of upbringing in which parents are unable to express direct love for their children, and are aloof and disciplinarian. In these circumstances, the adult individual suffers from anxieties that can be controlled only by the adoption of a rigid outlook. Such individuals have an inability to cope with ambiguous situations, and ignore inconsistencies, tending to think in a strongly stereotypical way. The researchers included some contradictory statements in the anti-Semitism scale. For example, each of the following items was included:

> Jews tend to remain a foreign element in American society, trying to preserve their old social standards and resist the American way of life.

> Jews go too far in hiding their Jewishness, especially such extremes as changing their names, straightening their noses, and imitating Christian manners and customs.

The majority of people who agreed with the first item also agreed with the second. In much the same way, those who agreed with statements that Jews are too oriented towards the acquisition of money, and control big business, also agreed with the view that Jews are subversive and critical of business enterprise.

The research and conclusions drawn from it have been subjected to a barrage of criticism. Some have doubted the value of the measurement scales used. Others have argued that authoritarianism is not a characteristic of personality, but reflects the values and norms of particular subcultures within the wider society. The investigation may be more valuable as a contribution to understanding authoritarian patterns of thought in general, rather than distinguishing a particular personality type (Wellman, 1977). Yet there are clear similarities between these findings and other research on prejudice. For example, a classic study by Eugene Hartley investigated attitudes towards thirty-five ethnic minorities, also finding that those prejudiced against one ethnic group were also likely to express negative feelings against others. Jews and blacks were disliked just as much as Wallonians, Pireneans, and Danireans (Hartley, 1946). The three latter groups in fact are nonexistent! The names were coined by Hartley in order to see whether people would be prejudiced against groups they could not have even heard of.

SOCIOLOGICAL INTERPRETATIONS

The psychological mechanisms mentioned above—stereotypical thinking, displacement, and projection—are universal in nature. They are found among the members of all societies, and are relevant to explaining why ethnic antagonism is such a common element in cultures of many different types. However, they explain little about the social processes involved in discrimination. To study such processes, we must bring into play three sociological ideas.

Ethnocentrism, Group Closure, and Resource Allocation

Sociological concepts relevant to ethnic conflicts on a general level are those of *ethnocentrism, ethnic-group closure,* and *resource allocation.* Ethnocentrism—a suspicion of outsiders combined with a tendency to evaluate the culture of others in terms of one's own culture—is a concept we have encountered previously (see Chapter 2: "Culture and Society"). Virtually all cultures have been ethnocentric in greater or lesser degree, and it is easy to see how ethnocentrism combines with stereotypical thought. "Outsiders" are thought of as aliens, barbarians, or as morally and mentally inferior. This was how most civilizations viewed the members of smaller cultures, for example, and it has helped to fuel innumerable ethnic clashes in history.

Ethnocentrism and group closure frequently go together. "Closure" means the process whereby groups maintain boundaries separating themselves from others—we have already encountered it in discussing the boundaries between classes in the previous chapter (Chapter 7: "Stratification and Class Structure"). The anthropologist Frederick Barth (1969) has tried to show how ethnic-group boundaries are organized, and how they contribute to conflicts. These boundaries are developed and sustained, he argues, by means of "exclusion devices," which sharpen the divisions between one ethnic group and another. Such devices include, for instance, limiting or prohibiting intermarriage between the groups, restrictions on social contact or economic relationships like trading, and the physical separation of groups from one another (as in the case of ethnic ghettos). American blacks have experienced all three exclusion devices at one time or another: Racial intermarriage has been illegal in some states, economic and social segregation was enforced by law in the South, and segregated black ghettos still exist in most major U.S. cities.

Sometimes groups of equal power may mutually enforce principles of closure: Their members keep separate from each other, but neither group dominates the other. More commonly, however, the members of one group are in a position of power over another ethnic group or groups. In these circumstances, ethnic-group closure coincides with the *allocation of resources:* in other words, with inequalities in the distribution of wealth and material goods. There are many contexts in which this may happen—for example, through the military conquest of one group by another or the emergence of an ethnic group as economically dominant over others. Ethnic-group closure provides a means of defending the economic position of the dominant group. For instance, in South Africa (discussed further below), laws were established forcing blacks to live separately from whites and forbidding sexual relations across racial lines. By these means, the white minority population tried to ensure that they would retain their economically privileged situation as compared to nonwhites.

Some of the fiercest conflicts between ethnic or racial groups center upon the lines of closure between them, precisely because these lines usually signal inequalities in the distribution of wealth, power, or social standing. The concept of ethnic-group closure helps us understand both the dramatic and the more insidious differences that separate communities or categories of people from one another —not just why the members of some groups get shot, lynched, beaten up, or harrassed, but also why they don't get good jobs, good education, or a desirable place to live. Wealth, power, and social

| TABLE 8.1 | SOCIOLOGICAL CONCEPTS RELEVANT TO ETHNIC CONFLICTS |

ETHNOCENTRISM

>   suspicion of outsiders
>   evaluation of other cultures in terms of one's own

ETHNIC-GROUP CLOSURE

>   maintenance of boundaries against others
>   prohibition against intermarriage between groups
>   restrictions on social contact with other groups

RESOURCE ALLOCATION

>   limited resources resulting in inequalities in distribution of wealth and
>   goods

status are scarce resources—some groups have more of them than others. To hold onto their distinctive positions or possessions, privileged groups are sometimes prepared to undertake extreme acts of violence against others. The members of underprivileged groups may also turn to violence as a means of trying to improve their own situation. The combination of group closure with ethnic prejudice and racism is frequently explosive.

A HISTORICAL PERSPECTIVE

These various concepts, psychological and sociological, help us to understand factors underlying many forms of ethnic conflicts both today and in previous ages. But to more fully analyze ethnic relations in current times we must take a more historical perspective. It is impossible to comprehend ethnic divisions in the present era without giving prime place to the impact of the expansion of Western colonialism upon the rest of the world. We have sketched out this history in Chapter 2 ("Culture and Society"), and the account given there provides the necessary background for the remainder of this chapter.

From the fifteenth century onwards, the Europeans began to venture into previously unchartered seas and unexplored landmasses, pursuing the aims of exploration and trade, but also conquering and subduing native peoples in many areas. They poured out by the millions from Europe to settle in these areas. In the shape of the slave trade, they also brought about a large-scale movement of population from Africa to the Americas. The following are the major shifts in population that have occurred over the past three hundred and fifty years or so (Berry and Tischler, 1978).

1. **EUROPE TO NORTH AMERICA.** From the seventeenth century to the present, some 45 million people have emigrated from Europe to what is now the United States and Canada. Many went back to Europe again, but most remained, and about 150 million people in North America today can trace their ancestry to this migration.

2. **EUROPE TO CENTRAL AND SOUTH AMERICA.** About 20 million people from Europe, mostly coming from Spain, Portugal, and Italy, migrated to Central and South America. Some 50 million people in these areas today are of European ancestry.

3. **EUROPE TO AFRICA AND AUSTRALASIA.** Approximately 17 million people in these continents are of European ancestry. In Africa, the majority emigrated to the state of South Africa, which was colonized mainly by the British and the Dutch.

4. **AFRICA TO THE AMERICAS.** Starting in the sixteenth century, about 15 million blacks were unwillingly transported to the North and South American continents. Under a million came in the sixteenth century; some 1.3 million in the seventeenth century; in the eighteenth century, about 6 million; and roughly 2 million in the nineteenth century. Black Africans were brought to the Americas in chains to serve as slaves; families and whole communities were brutally destroyed in the process.

These population flows, therefore, were the main basis of the current ethnic composition of the United States, Canada, the countries of Central and South America, South Africa, Australia, and New Zealand. In all of these societies, the indigenous populations were subjected to European rule—becoming relatively small ethnic minorities in North America and Australasia. Since the Europeans were from ethnically diverse backgrounds, they implanted numerous ethnic divisions in their new homelands. At the height of the colonial era, in the nineteenth and early twentieth centuries, Europeans also ruled

FIGURE 8.2 **COLONIZATION AND ETHNICITY**

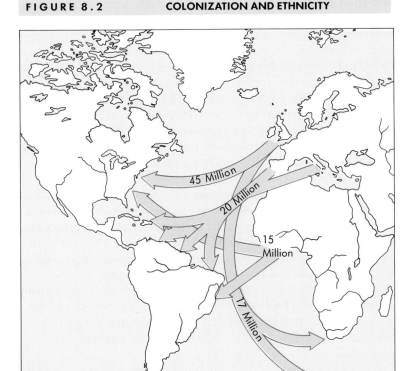

This map shows the massive movement of peoples from Europe who colonized the Americas, South Africa, Australia, and New Zealand, resulting in the ethnic composition of people there today. People from Africa were brought to the Americas to be slaves.

over native populations in many other regions: in parts of the Middle East, and in India, Burma, and Malaya.

For most of the period of European expansion, ethnocentric attitudes were rife among the colonists, who believed themselves to be on a civilizing mission to the rest of the world. Even the more liberal European colonists thought themselves superior to the indigenous peoples they encountered. The fact that many of those peoples thought precisely the same about the colonists is not so relevant, since the Europeans possessed the power to make their outlook count.

The early period of colonialism coincided with the rise of racism, and ever since then racial divisions and conflicts have tended to have a prime place in ethnic conflicts as a whole. In particular, racist views separating "whites" from "blacks" became central to European attitudes.

THE RISE OF RACISM

Why did this happen? There were several reasons. One is that an opposition between white and black, as cultural symbols, was deeply rooted in European culture. White had long been associated with purity, black with evil (there is nothing "natural" about this symbolism; in some other cultures it is reversed). The symbol "blackness" held the following meanings *before* the West came into extensive contact with black peoples: "Deeply stained with dirt; soiled, foul . . . having dark or deadly purposes, malignant; pertaining to or involving death, deadly; baneful, disastrous, sinister . . . indicating disgrace, censure, liability to punishment" (Kovel, 1970).

These symbolic meanings tended to infuse the Europeans' reactions to blacks when they were first encountered on African shores. They helped reinforce a sense that there was a radical difference between black and white peoples which, combined with the "heathenism" of the Africans, led many Europeans to regard blacks with a mixture of disdain and fear. As a seventeenth-century observer expressed it, blacks "in colour as in condition are little other than Devils incarnate" (Jordan, 1968). Although the more extreme expressions of such attitudes have disappeared today, it is difficult not to believe that elements of this black/white cultural symbolism remain widespread.

A second important factor influencing modern racism was simply the coining and diffusion of the concept of "race" itself. Racist attitudes have existed in many cultures and at very early periods of history. In China of A.D. 300, for example, we find recorded descriptions of barbarian peoples "who greatly resemble monkeys from whom they are descended" (Gossett, 1963). But the notion of "race," as referring to a cluster of inherited characteristics, comes from European thought of the eighteenth and nineteenth centuries. Count Joseph Arthur de Gobineau (1816–1882), who is sometimes called "the father of modern racism," proposed ideas that became influential in many circles. According to de Gobineau, three races exist: the white, black, and yellow. The white race possesses superior intelligence, morality, and willpower to the others, and these inherited qualities underlie the spread of Western influence across the world. The blacks are the least capable of the three races, marked by an animal nature, a lack of morality, and emotional instability.

These ideas of de Gobineau and others who proposed similar views were pronounced as supposedly scientific theories. They later influenced Adolf Hitler, who, as mentioned earlier, used them as part of the ideology of the Nazi party. The notion of "the superiority of the white race," although completely without value factually, remains today a key element of white racism. It is an explicit part, for example, of the ideology of the Ku Klux Klan in the United States, and it is the basis of *apartheid* (separate racial development) in South Africa, a phenomenon that will be described in more detail a little later.

A third reason for the rise of modern racism lies in the exploitative relations that the Europeans established with nonwhite peoples. The slave trade could not have been carried on were it not widely believed by Europeans that blacks belonged to an inferior, perhaps even sub-human, race. Racism helped justify colonial rule over nonwhite peoples and denied them the rights of political participation that were being won by whites in their European homelands. Using the concept mentioned previously, we can say that racism played an important part in the group closure whereby Europeans were the rulers and nonwhites the ruled.

The relations between whites and nonwhites varied according to different patterns of colonial settlement—and were influenced as well by cultural differences between the Europeans themselves. To demonstrate these points, we now turn to look at race relations in Brazil and South Africa before analyzing racial and ethnic divisions in the United States at greater length.

ETHNIC RELATIONS IN HISTORICAL PERSPECTIVE: SOME EXAMPLES

BRAZIL IS SOMETIMES QUOTED AS AN EXAMPLE OF A SOCIETY free from ethnic prejudice between black and white, although as we shall see this is not wholly accurate. South Africa, by contrast, is a country in which prejudice and discrimination have developed in an extreme form, and segregation of black and white is institutionalized and backed by the law.

ETHNIC RELATIONS IN BRAZIL

Nearly four million Africans were transported to Brazil before the cessation of the slave trade in the middle of the nineteenth century. In the southern United States, blacks coming from different African cultures were usually dispersed, but in Brazil, those shipped from similar culture areas were normally kept together. Hence they were able to retain more of their original culture than was possible in North America. Slaves in Brazil were allowed to marry even if their masters disapproved, as long as they continued serving them as before. A married couple could not be thereafter sold as individual slaves. Sexual contact between white men and slave women was frequent, and the children of such unions were often freed. They were sometimes fully accepted as part of the white family. Slavery was finally abolished in 1888, but well before then whites had become well used to the existence of free blacks (Swartz, 1985).

Following the ending of slavery, many black Brazilians moved into the towns and cities. There most of them lived (and live today) in considerable poverty. Yet they were not debarred from membership in labor unions, and a proportion have risen to positions of wealth and power. There is a much-quoted Brazilian saying that "A rich black man is a white and a poor white man is a black." The phrase neatly catches both the relatively relaxed views of racial differences, as well as the fact that "whiteness" is still clearly identified with superiority. Whites continue to dominate the higher positions in all sectors of the society.

Brazilians had long interpreted their own system of race relations in a charitable light, comparing it positively to the more segregated patterns of the United States. In the 1960s and 1970s, as moves to secure greater civil rights for American blacks gathered strength, such comparisons became somewhat less favorable to Brazil. In the early 1960s, the Brazilian Congress had to pass a law forbidding discrimination in public places after a touring American black, Katherine Dunham, complained of being refused accommodation in a São Paulo hotel. The law was largely a symbolic gesture, however, as the government made no effort to investigate the extent of possible discrimination.

Most observers agree that such discrimination has been fairly rare in Brazil, but there have been few government programs designed to improve the social and economic opportunities of nonwhites. The Brazilian belief in "whitening" stands in some contrast to the continued concentration of blacks in the poorest sections of the society. Brazil has nonetheless avoided the recurrent lynchings and race riots that have punctuated the history of the United States, and has escaped most of the more extreme forms of anti-black prejudice (Skidmore, 1974).

We can understand patterns of race relations in Brazil in terms of factors that acted against complete closure on the part of white and black ethnic groups. First, as was mentioned, sexual contact between whites and blacks was from the beginning quite commonplace.

White males also quite often took Indian women as mates or even wives. Second, the Portuguese came from an area of Europe where the Moors—North Africans—had held considerable power, hence they did not associate dark skin with the same degree of racial inferiority as most northern Europeans. The level of racial prejudice, in other words, was from the outset less than in either South Africa or North America.

THE SOCIAL DEVELOPMENT OF SOUTH AFRICA

In South Africa, the first white settlers were Dutch. Finding the local population resistant to working in European enterprises, they began the practice of importing large numbers of slaves from elsewhere in Africa and from the Dutch East Indies. The British later established a dominant position in South Africa, putting an end to slavery in the 1830s. Divisions between whites and indigenous Africans were not at first as absolute as they later became. When slavery was abolished, new taxes were introduced for blacks, which forced many of them to contract themselves to European employers. Young African men had to look for employment away from home in order to pay the tax. There developed a system of "migrant labor," which set the pattern for the subsequent evolution of the South African economy. Many Africans went to work in gold or diamond mines, living in special camps well away from the neighborhoods where Europeans lived. Gradually a segregated system grew up that was later formalized in law (Western, 1981; Smith, 1982; Lapping, 1987).

Apartheid

Under the **apartheid** system, legalized following the Second World War, the population of South Africa is classified into four "registration groups"—the 4.5 million white descendants of European immigrants; the 2.5 million so-called "colored people," whose descent is traced from members of more than one "race"; the 1 million people of Asian descent; and the 23 million black Africans. The system is designed to secure "racial purity," with each "race" developing separately.

It is not just the enormous disparities of wealth and opportunity between whites and blacks that distinguish South Africa from other industrialized countries, because these exist elsewhere. It is the sharp and pervasive contrasts that divide white and nonwhite. As one author has described this,

Exclusive boutiques and luxuriant shopping malls, hushed
tree-lined streets, enclosed and well-manicured gardens, and
so forth, shape the environment of the affluent white residential areas . . . In contrast, it is difficult to imagine the monotony and abject sparseness of the black townships and
ghettos. Pockets of relative affluence do exist, but these are
the exception rather than the rule. It is the persistent repetition of identical images—cheerless dusty streets, bare-footed
and shabbily dressed children, endless [lines] of tired travelers, ribbons of exhausted workers trudging home, the sul-
len stares and probing glances—that creates an unforgettable
collage of deprivation. In the townships, daily life is an endless grind, a seemingly ceaseless struggle for existence and
survival. (Murray, 1987)

Pierre van den Berghe (1970) has distinguished three levels of segregation in South African society:

1. **Microsegregation**—The segregation of public places
   (which was also the case in the American South).
   Washrooms, waiting rooms, railway carriages, and other
   public areas have separate facilities for whites and
   nonwhites.

2. **Mezzosegregation**—the segregation of whites and nonwhites by neighborhoods in urban areas; blacks are compelled to live in specially designated zones.

3. **Macrosegregation**—the segregation of whole peoples in
   distinct territories set up as "native reserves."

The existence of separate facilities in public places has a strong symbolic value in reinforcing apartheid. However, it provides little or no
direct support to the political and economic power that the white minority maintains over the black population. Such microsegregation
has been relaxed in recent years, as successive South African governments have responded to international pressures to reduce discriminatory practices. The other types of segregation, however, are more
significant for the maintenance of white control (Saul and Gelb,
1986).

It has long been impossible for the South African economy to carry
on without the labor-power of the millions of nonwhites living in or
near the cities (Lipton, 1986). At one time there used to be various
ethnically mixed neighborhoods in the major urban areas. But more

and more of the blacks have been placed in "model townships" situated a number of miles away from the white neighborhoods. Millions of people have also been herded into so-called "homelands" well removed from the cities. These regions have been organized into partially autonomous states subject to the overall control of the white central government.

The homelands are separate territories where the black majority would supposedly be able to exercise political rights denied them in white South Africa. Under the provisions of the 1970 Homelands Citizenship Act, those in a homeland were automatically deprived of their South African citizenship on the day it became "independent." So-called "frontier commuters" live with their families in the homelands and travel daily across the "national borders" into white South Africa. It has been estimated that 80 percent of the inhabitants of the homelands live below the officially designated poverty line (Giliomee and Schlemmer, 1985).

In South Africa, the principle of ethnic-group closure has been carried to an extreme. Apartheid is a formal, legal means of establishing clear racial boundaries, and of consolidating the privileges of the whites. It remains a distinct method of keeping power in the hands of the few.

ETHNIC RELATIONS IN THE UNITED STATES

LIKE BRAZIL AND SOUTH AFRICA, THE UNITED STATES ORIGI-
nated as a colonial society. However, in contrast to these
countries, in the United States the native population was
swamped by the settlers, who became the overwhelming majority. As a result of massive migrations from Europe and other parts of the world, the United States became one of the most ethnically diverse societies in the world. In the sections that follow, we shall provide a broad portrayal of the ethnic development of the United States. We will give particular prominence to the divisions that have separated whites and nonwhite minority groups, such as blacks, Native Americans, Hispanic-Americans, and others. We shall place the emphasis on *struggle*. The members of these groups have repeatedly made efforts to defend the integrity of their cultures, and advance their social position, in the face of persistent prejudice and discrimination in the wider social environment.

EARLY COLONIZATION

The first European colonists in what was to become the United States were actually of quite homogenous background. At the time of the Declaration of Independence, the majority of the colonial population was of British descent and almost everyone was Protestant. Settlers from outside the British Isles were at first admitted only with some reluctance, but the desire for economic expansion meant having to attract immigrants from other areas. Most came from countries in northwest Europe, such as Holland, Germany, or Sweden. Large-scale migration into North America dates from about 1820 (Hutchinson, 1981). In the century following, about 33 million immigrants entered the United States. No migrant movement of population on such a scale has ever been seen before or since.

The early waves of immigrants came mostly from the same countries of origin as the groups already established in the United States. They left Europe to escape economic hardship, religious and political oppression, and because of the opportunities offered for acquiring land as the drive westwards gained momentum. As a result of successive potato famines that had produced widespread starvation, 1.5 million people left Ireland to come to the United States. The Irish for the most part settled in the coastal areas, in contrast to most other immigrants coming from rural backgrounds. Seeing farm work as a way of life marked by hardship and despair, most of the Irish immigrants opted for city life and, where they could get it, industrial work. A major new influx of immigrants arrived in the 1880s and 1890s, coming this time mainly from southern and eastern Europe—the Austro-Hungarian Empire, Russia, and Italy.

Each successive group of immigrants was subject to considerable discrimination on the part of those previously established in the country. When the Irish first arrived they were a target of prejudice. Negative views of the Irish emphasized their low level of intelligence and drunken behavior. Job vacancies often specifically stated "No Irish need apply." Being concentrated within the cities on the other hand, the Irish-Americans began to organize to protect their interests and gained a strong influence over political life (Wittke, 1956). The Italians and Polish, when they arrived were in turn discriminated against by the Irish.

Asian immigrants first came to the United States in large numbers in the late nineteenth century, encouraged by employers who needed cheap labor in the developing industries of the West. Some two hundred thousand Chinese emigrated at this period (Lee, 1960). Most were men, who came with the idea of saving money to send back to their families in China, anticipating that they would also later return

FIGURE 8.3   **IMMIGRATION TO AMERICA**

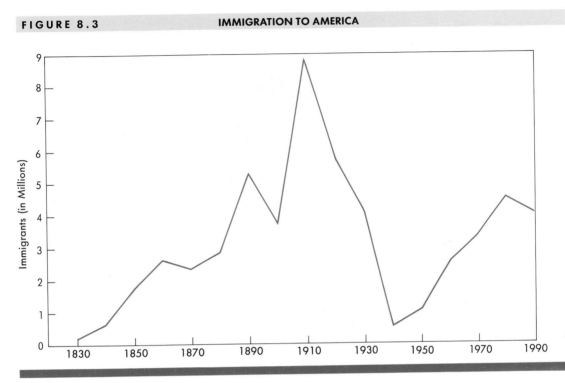

Source: U.S. Immigration Service. 1989. *Statistical Yearbook.*

This graph shows the number of immigrants arriving in America since 1820.

there. Bitter conflicts broke out between white workers and the Chinese when employment opportunities diminished. The Chinese Exclusion Act, passed in 1882, cut down further immigration to a trickle until after World War II (McKee, 1977). Japanese immigrants began to arrive not long after the cessation of Chinese immigration. They were soon subject to great hostility from whites, although less so than the Chinese. Opposition to Japanese immigration intensified in the early part of the century, leading to strict limits being placed on the numbers coming to the United States.

Most immigrant groups arriving in the early twentieth century found themselves in urban areas, engaged in the developing industrial economy. They also tended to cluster in ethnic neighborhoods of their own. Chinatowns, Little Italies, and other clearly defined areas became features of most large cities. The very size of the influx provoked various sorts of backlash on the part of the Anglo-Saxon sections of the population. During the 1920s, new immigration quotas were set up, discriminating against those coming from southern and eastern Europe.

Immigrants after landing at Ellis Island, New York, as they appeared in a 1905 issue of National Geographic *magazine.*

Many immigrants found their conditions of life in their new land little better, and sometimes worse, than the areas from which they originated. Ewa Morawska, the author of a recent historical study of immigrants coming from east central Europe to Johnstown, Pennsylvania, observes:

> The ambivalence and heart-rending uncertainty that accompanied the immigrants when they made their decision to cross the ocean to try their luck in America became further sharpened in this country by feelings of bewilderment and nostalgia, and by disillusionment with the reality of the "Promised Land" as compared with the dreams they had harbored in Europe. To a number of East Central Europeans, the arrival in Johnstown was bitterly disappointing. The town was soiled and the air filled with soot and fumes from the furnace chimneys. "My disappointment was unspeakable," recalls an eighty-four-year-old Galician, "when after a twelve-day journey I saw the city of Johnstown: squalid and ugly, with those congested shabby houses, blackened with soot from the factory chimneys—this was the America I saw." (Morawska, 1986)

The immigrants may have gained greater religious and political freedom in their new land, but they met with prejudice and discrimination if their ways of life differed from those of the dominant Anglo-Saxon community. The large flow of immigration, and competition for jobs, allowed employers to compel workers to accept very long working days, low levels of pay, and unhealthy working conditions. Since new immigrants were quite commonly used as strikebreakers, conflicts between them and established groups were frequent. In spite of all this, the economy was rapidly growing and a substantial proportion of immigrant workers in the end managed to improve their standards of living.

BLACKS IN THE UNITED STATES

Millions of blacks were brought from Africa to the United States during the period of the slave trade. Liverpool in Britain was the leading slave-trading port, importing from the American South the raw cotton upon which the cotton industry of Lancashire was founded. The slave plantations of the southern United States were for a period in some part economically dependent on Lancashire. The most powerful and economically advanced country in the world at that time, Britain, helped develop one of the most oppressive and backward institutions—the system of plantation slavery.

By 1780, there were nearly 4 million slaves in the American South. Given that there was little incentive for them to work, physical punishment often had to be used. Slaves who ran away were hunted with dogs and on their capture were manacled, sometimes branded with their master's mark, and occasionally even castrated. Slaves had virtually no rights in law whatsoever.

The position of black women slaves was frequently worse than that of the men. On plantations with a considerable proportion of female slaves, women carried out the same tasks as men, plowing and planting and harvesting crops. They also worked in the white households as nurses, cooks, and washerwomen. Although sometimes black women were reasonably well treated by the white families, they were also often beaten; many also lived in fear of rape (Davis, 1971). The famous black orator, Frederick Douglass, speaking at an abolitionist rally in 1859, said that "every slaveholder is the legalized keeper of a house of ill-fame." Rape of black women had no status as a crime in law.

The other side of the absolute power of the slave owner was the almost complete dependence of the slave. Masters and slaves, particularly domestic slaves, sometimes developed affectionate relationships. More common, however, were brutal forms of punishment inflicted upon slaves to keep them docile and obedient.

The slaves did not simply passively accept the conditions which their masters imposed upon them. The struggles of slaves against their oppressive conditions of life sometimes took the form of direct opposition or disobedience to orders, and occasionally outright rebel-

A newspaper advertisement offering a reward for the capture of runaway slaves.

$200 Reward.

RANAWAY from the subscriber, on the night of Thursday, the 30th of Sepember,

FIVE NEGRO SLAVES,

To-wit : one Negro man, his wife, and three children.

The man is a black negro, full height, very erect, his face a little thin. He is about forty years of age, and calls himself *Washington Reed,* and is known by the name of Washington. He is probably well dressed, possibly takes with him an ivory headed cane, and is of good address. Several of his teeth are

lion (although collective slave revolts were more common in the Caribbean than in the United States). On a more subtle level, their response took the form of a cultural creativity—a mixing of aspects of African cultures, Christian ideals, and cultural threads woven from their new environments. Some of the art forms they evolved, such as in music, were genuinely new (Bastide, 1978; Cone, 1984).

The work of historians has shown that feelings of hostility towards blacks were in some respects more strongly developed in states where slavery had never been known than in the South itself. The celebrated French political observer, Alexis de Tocqueville, noted in 1835 that, "The prejudice of race appears to be stronger in the states that have abolished slavery than in those where it still exists; and nowhere is it so intolerant as in those states where servitude has never been known" (Tocqueville, 1969). Moral rejection of slavery seems to have been confined to a few more educated groups.

The main factors underlying the Civil War between South and North were political and economic; most Northern leaders were more interested in sustaining the Union than in abolishing slavery, although this was the eventual outcome of the conflict. The formal abolition of slavery changed the real conditions of life for blacks in the South relatively little. The "black codes" placed restrictions upon the behavior of the former slaves, and punished their transgressions in much the same way as under slavery. A number of methods, including the open use of violence, were used to restrict access to civil and political rights. In some respects, these efforts were redoubled with the passing of time. Thus, in Louisiana, in 1896, there were 130,334 registered black voters, but only 1,342 by 1904. Acts were also passed legalizing segregation of blacks from whites in public places, such as trains and restaurants. In other words, one form of group closure (slavery) was replaced by another (based upon social, political, and economic discrimination).

A badge, issued in South Carolina, to be worn by blacks who had gained their freedom.

INTERNAL MIGRATION OF BLACKS

Industrial development in the North, combined with the mechanization of agriculture in the South, produced a progressive movement of
blacks northwards from the turn of the century onwards. In 1900,
more than 90 percent of black Americans lived in the South, mostly
in rural areas. Today, less than half of the black population remains in
the South; three-quarters of blacks now live in Northern urban areas.
Blacks used to be farm laborers and domestic servants, but over a period of little more than two generations, they have become mainly
urban, industrial, and service-economy workers.

The migration of black Americans to the North began during
World War I, when the interruption of immigration from Europe
caused employers to look for additional sources of labor-power.
Hundreds of thousands of Southern blacks moved North during this
early period; job opportunities continued to expand as the laws restricting immigration were passed during the 1920s. Northern employers actively began to seek black workers, who provided cheaper
labor than that available from established and unionized sources. Like
the more recent immigrants, black workers were sometimes used as
strikebreakers, producing extreme tensions between white and black
ethnic groups—although the blacks mainly suffered as innocent
scapegoats. In East St. Louis in 1917, and in Chicago in 1919, violent
race riots broke out. Migrant blacks also met with numerous forms of
discrimination in work, housing, and politics.

During the Second World War, the demand for labor grew still
further and more than a million blacks moved North during this period. Migration continued in the postwar years, as Southern agriculture became more mechanized and large-scale black unemployment
ensued. Blacks heading North in the period after World War II found
job opportunities harder to come by. Greater sophistication in manufacturing production had decreased the need for unskilled labor.
Unionized workers maintained a control over many craft occupations, and a high proportion excluded blacks from membership.

Blacks have not become assimilated into the wider society in the
way in which the successive groups of white immigrants were. They
have for the most part been unable to break free from the conditions
of neighborhood segregation and poverty that other immigrants first
faced when they arrived. Together with those of Anglo-Saxon origin, blacks have lived in the United States far longer than most other
immigrant groups. What was a transitional experience for most of
the later, white immigrants, has become a seemingly more or less
permanent experience for blacks. In the majority of cities, both South
and North, blacks and whites live in separate neighborhoods and are

educated in different schools. It has been estimated that 80 percent of either blacks or whites would have to move in order to desegregate housing fully in the average American city (Vanveley et al., 1977; Farley and Allen, 1987). We shall look at the reasons why blacks have not experienced greater social and economic integration later in this chapter.

THE RISE OF THE CIVIL RIGHTS MOVEMENT

Struggles by minority groups to achieve equal rights and opportunities have for a long while been a part of American history. Most minorities have been successful in achieving access to political influence and economic rewards, and in pressing claims to equal status with the majority. Blacks were largely excluded from such processes of self-advancement, however, until the early 1940s. The National Association for the Advancement of Colored People (NAACP) and the National Urban League were founded in 1909 and 1910 respectively. Both fought for black civil rights, but the struggle only began to have some real effect during and after World War II.

Before the United States entered the war, the leaders of the NAACP and the Urban League met with President Franklin D. Roosevelt, petitioning for the desegregation of the armed forces. Not only was this refused, but the administration made a public statement to the effect that the civil rights leaders had agreed at the meeting to the continuation of segregation. Angry at this apparent deception, a black union leader who had attended the meeting with the president, A. Philip Randolph, called for a march of a hundred thousand blacks to protest in Washington. A few days before the march was due to take place, Roosevelt signed an executive order forbidding discrimination in the defense industries based on ethnic differences, and he pledged action on the question of segregation in the armed forces (Finch, 1981; Zangrando, 1980). Two years later, the newly established Congress of Racial Equality (CORE) began challenging segregation in restaurants, swimming pools, and other public areas in Chicago. Although not a great deal was gained, and a fierce reaction was provoked from whites, this marked the beginning of militant action on behalf of black civil rights—which fifteen years later became a mass movement (Meier and Rudwick, 1973).

Shortly after the Second World War, the NAACP instituted a campaign against segregated public education, which came to a head when the organization sued five school boards, challenging the concept of separate but equal schooling which then held sway. In 1954, in *Brown v. Board of Education of Topeka, Kansas,* the Supreme Court unanimously decided that "separate educational facilities are inher-

ently unequal." This decision became the platform for struggles for
civil rights from the 1950s to the 1970s. When the Supreme Court
decision was first reached, several state and local governments made
efforts to limit its effects. Public-school integration proceeding under
Federal orders was violently resisted by the Ku Klux Klan, the organization of White Citizens Councils, and local vigilante groups. Even
by 1960 well under 1 percent of Southern black students attended de-
segregated schools (Issel, 1985; Sitkoff, 1981).

The very strength of the resistance from many whites persuaded
black leaders that mass militancy was necessary to give civil rights
any real substance. In 1955 a black woman, Rosa Parks, was arrested
in Montgomery, Alabama, for declining to give up her seat on a bus
to a white man. As a result, almost the complete black population of
the city, led by a Baptist minister, Martin Luther King, Jr., boycotted
the transportation system for 381 days. Eventually the city was forced
to abolish segregation in public transportation. Further boycotts and
sit-ins followed, with the object of desegregating other public facilities. The marches and demonstrations began to achieve a mass following from blacks and white sympathizers. King planned
campaigns of active but nonviolent resistance to discrimination. Responses to the movement were far from nonviolent. In 1957 Gover-
nor Orval Faubus of Arkansas called out the national guard to
forcibly stop black students from entering the Central High School
in Little Rock. In Birmingham, Alabama, in April 1963, Police Commissioner "Bull" Connor ordered the police to disperse protesters
with fire hoses, clubs, and police dogs.

*Even after being freed, blacks faced
much hostility and overt
discrimination.*

Following the episode in Birmingham, several hundred demonstrations took place in many American cities over a period of some
ten weeks and more than fifteen thousand protesters were arrested. In
1963, a quarter of a million civil rights supporters staged a March on
Washington, hearing King announce "We will not be satisfied until
justice rolls down like the waters and righteousness like a mighty
stream." In 1964, a Civil Rights Bill was passed by Congress comprehensively banning discrimination in public facilities, education, employment, and in any agency receiving government funds. Further
bills in following years were aimed at ensuring that blacks became
fully registered voters, and outlawed discrimination in housing.

The civil rights movement provided a sense of cultural freedom
and affirmation for black activists, going well beyond the formal objectives for which they were fighting. The Student Nonviolent Coordinating Committee (SNCC), which had organized the sit-in
movement, also had its "Freedom Singers," who translated their beliefs in civil disobedience as a mechanism of change into music and
song. Vincent Harding has described the energy and sense of a fresh
beginning which blacks in particular felt:

A number of civil rights workers died in their struggle. Among them was Reverend Martin Luther King, Jr. (second from right) shown here on the balcony of the motel where he was later slain. With him are Hosea Williams (far left), Reverend Jesse Jackson, and Reverend Ralph D. Abernathy (far right).

There was an indescribable hope, idealism, courage and determination in those early months of organizing, marching, singing, and going to jail. . . . They were believers. When they sang in jail, in mass meetings, in front of policemen and state troopers, "We shall overcome," they meant it . . . overcoming meant "freedom" and "rights" and "dignity" and "justice" and black and white together and many other things that people in a movement feel more than they define. (Harding, 1980)

Attempts to implement the new civil rights legislation continued to meet with ferocious resistance from opponents. Civil rights marchers were insulted, beaten up, and some lost their lives. Between 1965 and 1968, major riots broke out in black ghetto areas in cities from Los Angeles to Newark, where civil rights legislation had made little or no impact on black urban poverty. By 1966, a more aggressive black militancy, under the title of "Black Power," developed as a response to white prejudice (Carmichael and Hamilton, 1967). Moderates dissociated themselves from this development, continuing to press for legal and political reforms.

Stokely Carmichael, one of the most militant black leaders, described the position of blacks in the United States as an extension of colonialism. Most other Western nations colonized countries outside themselves, but in the United States, beginning with Southern slavery, the colonialism was within. Carmichael remarked:

> It is more than a figure of speech to say that black communities in America are the victims of white imperialism and colonial exploitation. This is in practical economic and political terms true.
>
> There are over thirty million of us in the United States. For the most part we live in sharply defined areas in the black belt and shanty towns of the South, and more and more in the slums of the Northern and Western industrial cities. . . . In these cities we do not control our resources. We do not control the land, the houses or the stores. They are owned by whites who live outside the community. These are very real colonies, as their capital and cheap labor are exploited by those who live outside the cities. White power makes the laws and enforces those laws with guns and nightsticks in the hands of white racist policemen and black mercenaries!

In spite of the barriers that hampered the full realization of its provisions, the Civil Rights Bill proved to be fundamentally important. Its principles applied not just to blacks, but to anyone subject to discrimination, including other ethnic groups and women. It served as the starting point for a range of movements concerned with developing the rights of oppressed groups.

During the course of the struggles of the 1960s, the goals of the black civil rights movement in some part altered. The ambition of most civil rights leaders had always been the full integration of blacks into the wider American culture. The rise of militant black power groups helped shift these ideals towards a stress upon the dignity of being black and the intrinsic value of black culture. Blacks then began to demand an independent position in the community, looking towards the development of a genuinely plural society rather than assimilation within the white social order. This changing outlook was also prompted by the general feeling that equality before the law is of little use if discrimination persists in practice. The black power groups advocating violence to achieve their ends, like the Black Panthers, were either crushed by the authorities or broke up into disputing factions. By the 1970s, many black activists turned to the ballot box as a means of generating political power for blacks.

Affirmative Action

Although there was such violent early resistance to desegregating schools in the South, in the long term desegregation in the North posed even greater problems. Schools in the North were not segregated by law, but the pronounced segregation of black and white was caused by the patterns of neighborhood residence. Since blacks and whites lived in largely separate neighborhoods, their children attended different schools. The busing of children between school districts in order to achieve greater integration began as a result of a Supreme Court decision, which came into force in 1971. Busing is an example of **affirmative action,** which is the development of programs that take positive steps to redress the balance where minority groups are disfavored (Bullock, 1984). Other examples of affirmative action tried out in the 1970s and 1980s included allocating a certain proportion of college places to members of minorities and ensuring that at least a certain percentage of those hired for jobs in public agencies come from disadvantaged groups.

Most forms of affirmative action have proved highly controversial. The debates over busing came to a climax in Boston in 1976, when whites stormed buses carrying black students to previously all-white schools. Busing has for the most part progressed peacefully, but probably has had the unintended consequence of adding to the movement of whites away from central areas of cities. (However, whites were leaving the central cities in large numbers before busing started.)

The Supreme Court lent partial support to the principle of affirmative action in the case of *Bakke v. The University of California* (1977). Bakke was a student who had applied to the medical school of the University of California at Davis. Since his grades and test scores were higher than a number of applicants from minority groups, who were accepted while he was rejected, he claimed he had suffered "reverse discrimination." The Supreme Court ruled that he should be admitted to the university. The Court decided, however, that universities have the right to use ethnic background as a relevant criterion in deciding student entry. Fixed quotas, on the other hand, were declared illegal.

Current Developments

In August 1983, some three hundred thousand civil rights supporters commemorated the anniversary of the Washington March held twenty years earlier. What progress has in fact been made since then? The trends of development are not entirely clear-cut, and sociologists disagree about how they should be interpreted. There has been increased equality in some areas of social life, but certainly less than was hoped for by the civil rights leaders of the 1960s. Differences between blacks and whites in levels of educational attainment have lessened, but these seem more the result of long-established trends rather than the direct outcome of the struggles of the 1960s. In 1984,

77 percent of whites aged eighteen and nineteen were in college, compared to 48 percent of blacks. Blacks now hold a slightly higher proportion of managerial and professional jobs than in 1960. Yet these positions are still very heavily dominated by white males. The proportion of black males who are blue-collar workers is about twice as high as that of white males (Farley, 1985).

Disparities between the earnings of black and white men are gradually becoming less, while those between black and white women are decreasing rapidly. In 1959, white males earned an average wage of $8.03 per hour, black males $4.93. As expressed in standard terms (that is, discounting the effects of inflation), the figures in 1984 were $9.88 per hour and $7.30 respectively; the differential lessened considerably. As measured in terms of average hourly income, black males now earn 74 percent of the level of pay of whites. In 1959, the proportion was only 49 percent. The gap in earnings between women has more or less completely disappeared. Black and white women have become equal in their inequality, both earning about 55 percent of the wages of white men.

However, the economic position of black women is still worse on average than that of white women (Malveaux, 1985). Although the incomes of white and black women in paid work have converged, there are far more black than white women who are heads of households—and therefore dependent solely upon their own income (see Chapter 12: "Kinship, Marriage, and the Family"). Moreover, the rate of unemployment of black women is twice that of white women (12.6 percent for black women as against 5.4 percent for white women in 1985).

The unemployment rate of black men outstrips that of whites by the same degree today as was the case in the early 1960s. Twice as many black as white men are registered as unemployed. Employment opportunities for black men have worsened, which this statistic does not reveal. Unemployment rates only measure those known to be looking for work. A higher proportion of blacks than whites have simply opted out of the occupational system, neither working nor looking for work. They have become disillusioned by the frustration of searching for employment which is not there.

Neighborhood segregation seems to have declined little over the past quarter century. Studies show that discriminatory practices between black and white clients in the housing market continue (Lake, 1981). Black and white children now attend the same schools in most rural areas of the South, and in many of the smaller and medium-size cities throughout the country. Most black college students now also go to the same colleges and universities as whites, instead of the traditional all-black institutions (Bullock, 1984). Yet in the larger cities a

TABLE 8.2	BLACK MEMBERS OF THE U.S. CONGRESS	
	Representatives (435 total)	Senators (100 total)
94th Congress, 1975	15	1
95th Congress, 1977	16	1
96th Congress, 1979	16	0
97th Congress, 1981	17	0
98th Congress, 1983	21	0
99th Congress, 1985	20	0
100th Congress, 1987	23	0
101st Congress, 1989	24	0

Source: Congressional Quarterly Weekly Report, vol. 46, No. 46, Nov. 12, 1988.

high level of educational segregation persists as a result of the continuing movement of whites to suburbs or rural environs.

Blacks have made some gains in holding local elective offices; the number of black public officials has increased from 103 in 1964 to over 5,000 today. The numbers of black mayors and judges have increased appreciably. Yet these changes are still relatively small scale. Black officials still make up only just over 1 percent of the half million elective offices in the United States. Most of these are in relatively minor local positions. In 1986, only five public officials elected on a statewide basis were black; there were only eight black judges on state supreme courts, and less than one hundred black state senators. Blacks make up over 20 percent of the electorate in Alabama, Louisiana, North Carolina, and South Carolina, but not a single black has been elected to Congress in these states since the Reconstruction period nearly a century ago (Davis et al., 1987). The Reverend Jesse Jackson did infuse some hope in the political sphere by running a strong and widely publicized campaign during the 1988 Democratic presidential primaries.

THE BLACK MIDDLE CLASS

It seems probable that a division has opened up between the minority of blacks who have obtained white-collar, managerial, or professional jobs—who form a small black middle class—and the majority whose living conditions have not improved. In 1960, most of the nonmanual-labor jobs open to blacks were those serving the black community—a small proportion of blacks could work as teachers, social workers, or less often, lawyers or doctors. No more than some 13 percent of blacks held white-collar jobs, contrasted to 44 percent of whites. Since that date, however, there have been significant changes. Between 1960 and 1970, the percentage of blacks in white-collar occupations doubled—although this level of growth slowed markedly in the 1980s. This increase was greater than that for the half century previous to 1960.

Bart Landry carried out a systematic study of the growing black middle class (1988). He surveyed white-collar blacks and whites in twenty-one metropolitan areas across the country, and also analyzed government statistics from the early 1980s. Landry found that middle-class blacks were much better off, and much more numerous, than their predecessors twenty years before. Opportunities have opened up partly through changes in legislation brought into being as a result of the civil rights movement. However, the population of blacks in middle-class jobs remains well below that of whites, and their average incomes are less.

William Julius Wilson (1980; see also Wilson et al., 1987) has argued that race is of diminishing importance in explaining inequalities between whites and blacks. In his view, these inequalities are now based upon class rather than skin color. The old racist barriers are crumbling. What remain are inequalities similar to those affecting all lower-class groups.

Wilson's work has proved controversial. His book was awarded a prize by the American Sociological Association, but the Association of Black Sociologists passed a resolution stating that the book "omits significant data regarding the continuing discrimination against blacks at all class levels." "It is the consensus of this organization," the resolution continues, "that this book denies the overwhelming evidence regarding the significance of race and the literature that speaks to the contrary." The resolution criticized the view that the circumstances of blacks have substantially improved, or even that racism has declined significantly. Most of the changes, it was argued, have been relatively minor, and racism has only become less vocal since the 1964 Civil Rights Act, rather than diminishing in any substantial sense (Pinkney, 1984).

Yet Wilson had made it clear in his book that the living conditions of poor blacks were deteriorating. In Wilson's view, his critics have almost completely ignored this aspect of his work. He has since extended his analysis of the most deprived sectors of the black population. Middle-class blacks today tend no longer to live in ghetto neighborhoods. Their exodus has led to an even higher concentration of the disadvantaged in these areas than previously was the case. Wilson recognizes that racism plays a part in this situation of disadvantaged, but points out that other class-related and economic factors are at least equally important—in particular, the very high rate of unemployment and welfare dependency characteristic of the poorest neighborhoods. Wilson's argument is not so much that racism as such has declined, but that it has declined in its *significance* for blacks. Other mechanisms of discrimination based more upon economic disadvantages are as important.

Are racial inequalities to be explained primarily in terms of class? For racial divisions provide a means of social closure, whereby economic resources can be monopolized by privileged class groups. The thesis that ethnic subordination should be explained primarily in terms of class domination, however, has never been a satisfactory one. Ethnic discrimination, particularly of a racial kind, is partly independent of class differences: the one cannot be reduced to the other. This still seems to remain true in the United States today. We shall return to this point subsequently, when summing up why the relative experience of different ethnic groups has been so variable.

WHITE ATTITUDES AND INSTITUTIONAL RACISM

Attitude surveys show a general decline in hostile attitudes towards blacks over the past twenty years among white Americans (Schuman, Steel, and Bobo, 1985). The overall level of prejudice seems to be diminishing fairly markedly. David Wellman has argued that the concept of prejudice only captures the more open and pronounced forms of hostile attitudes towards ethnic minorities. Racism can also be expressed in more subtle ways—in terms of beliefs which, regardless of the intentions involved, defend the position of privileged groups. Many sociologists, according to Wellman, have underestimated the true incidence of racism, because they have looked only at its more obvious manifestations. Most studies have investigated prejudice using surveys; but these do not get at the less obvious, complex aspects of people's views about such emotive topics as ethnicity and race.

Wellman sought to illuminate these complex aspects of racism by means of in-depth interviews with 105 white Americans of varying backgrounds. Most of those he interviewed said that they believed that everyone is equal, and that they held no hostility towards blacks. Their beliefs and attitudes did not show the rigidities characteristic of prejudice and stereotypical thinking. Yet their views about contexts of social life (such as education, housing, or jobs) in which black rights threatened their own position were effectively anti-black. Their opposition to change was expressed in ways that did not directly express racial antagonism. People would say, for instance, "I'm not opposed to blacks; but if they come into the neighborhood house prices will be affected"—or, as one individual put it, "I favor anything that doesn't affect me personally" (Wellman, 1987).

These attitudes can still underlie quite rigid patterns of discrimination. Ethnic inequalities are structured into existing social institutions and modes of behavior having no immediate connection to ethnicity can serve to reinforce them. Rights and opportunities are not the same thing. Even if it were true that every member of the population accepted that members of all ethnic groups have the same civil rights, major inequalities would persist. There are many examples that demonstrate this. A black person who wishes to obtain a bank loan in order to be able to make home improvements finds it hard to borrow money. The bank might use purely "objective" measures in reaching such decisions, based on the likelihood of the loan repayments being successfully made. Nevertheless, the effect is the perpetuation of ethnic discrimination. This is usually referred to as **institutional racism,** to distinguish it from racism involving directly prejudiced attitudes.

OTHER AMERICAN ETHNIC GROUPS

DIVISIONS BETWEEN "WHITE" AND "BLACK," OF COURSE, only capture one aspect of ethnicity in the United States today, albeit a persistent and troubling one. There are many other ethnic groups in the United States. Here we shall concentrate attention upon four prominent examples, Indians or Native Americans, Hispanic-Americans, and Asian-Americans. The fortunes of some of these communities have diverged substantially from others, and we shall ask why this is so.

NATIVE AMERICANS

American Indians have now been aliens in their own land for more than two centuries. During the course of the nineteenth century they were herded onto areas of land, officially called reservations, where agriculture was difficult or impossible, hunting was forbidden, and where they had few opportunities to obtain industrial work. Indians thus lived for many years as forgotten members of American society.

Native Americans, 1902—aliens in their own land.

In the present century the Native American population has grown from a low ebb of 250,000 in the early 1900s, to more than 1.5 million. Half the population continues to live either on reservations or in rural areas, mostly west of the Mississippi River. The Native Americans are the poorest ethnic minority in the country. Their average length of schooling is only eight years, their school drop-out rate being double the national average; their rate of alcoholism is more than five times that of the rest of the population. Ninety percent of their housing is below officially defined minimum standards. The rate of Indian unemployment is about 45 percent, reaching nearly 80 percent in some areas. They have much higher levels of infectious disease, and sickness due to vitamin deficiency, than the rest of the American population. Some 30 percent of Native Americans live below the poverty line.

The majority of Native Americans lived in rural areas until the 1950s and 1960s, when there was a large migration into industrial cities, particularly in the West. Urban Indians have not, however, necessarily abandoned their original cultures any more than their rural counterparts. Research on urban Indians in Kansas, for example, showed a strong persistence of cultural identity. Local Indian groups had their own clubs, associations, and centers (Steele, 1975). The Navajo, who have the largest and most heavily populated reserve in the United States, have maintained their cultural distinctiveness in spite of the fact that many have spent time working in large cities.

Recent years have seen the growth of Native American activism, inspired in some part by black civil rights struggles. Some tribes have pursued legal suits to try to either recover ancient privileges or to prevent any further violation of their territorial rights. The American Indian Movement (A.I.M.) has tried to band together Indians from different tribes to pursue common objectives. Those supporting the movement for "red power" stress the need to preserve authentic Indian cultures, while seeking the self-determination that Indians have for so long effectively been denied. Some significant successes have been achieved, but Native Americans are now only a tiny proportion of the overall population of the country, and the capability of the Indian rights movement to make substantial headway is likely to be limited.

HISPANIC-AMERICANS

The wars of conquest that created the modern United States were not only directed against the Indian population. Much of the Southwest —along with a quarter of a million Mexicans—was annexed by the United States in 1848 as a result of the American military success in the war with Mexico. The term "Hispanic" includes the descendants of these people, together with subsequent immigrants from Mexico and, more recently, other Spanish-speaking areas.

The three main groups of Hispanics in the United States are Mexican-Americans (around nine million); Puerto Ricans (some two million); and Cubans (just under one million). There are also a further three million Spanish-speaking residents of the United States from areas in Central and South America. The Hispanic population of the United States is increasing at an extraordinary rate. In some degree this is due to their tendency to have large families, but it is mainly due to the large-scale flow of new immigrants since the 1960s, particularly those coming across the Mexican border. If current trends continue, the Hispanic residents of the country will outstrip the black population within the next decade or two.

The Mexican-American population continues to be found mainly in the Southwestern states, although there are substantial groups in some Northern cities. The majority have come over, legally and illegally, to work at menial jobs. In periods of labor shortage, illegal Mexican immigration has been encouraged by employers, only to be followed by extensive deportations in times of economic slump. In the post–World War II period up to the early 1960s, Mexican workers were admitted without much restriction. This was succeeded by a phase in which numbers were again limited and efforts

TABLE 8.3 IMMIGRANTS TODAY: WHERE DID THEY COME FROM?	
	(in thousands)
Mexico	72.4
Philippines	50.1
Korea	35.8
Central America	29.3
Cuba	28.9
India	27.8
China	25.8
Dominican Republic	24.9
Vietnam	24.2
Jamaica	23.1

Source: U.S. Immigration and Naturalization Service, *Statistical Yearbook.* 1987; and releases.

TABLE 8.4 IMMIGRANTS TODAY: IN WHICH U.S. CITY DID THEY SETTLE?	
	(in thousands)
New York	97.5
Los Angeles	64.5
Miami-Hialeah	37.9
Chicago	20.3
Washington, D.C.	17.9
San Francisco	16.2
Anaheim-Santa Anna	13.0
San Diego	12.7
Houston	11.4
San Jose	11.1

Source: U.S. Naturalization Service, *Statistical Yearbook.* 1987.

United Farmworkers leader Cesar Chavez with supporters in California.

made to deport those who had entered illegally. Illegal immigrants today continue to flood across the border. Large numbers are intercepted and sent back each year by immigration officials, but most simply try again, and it is estimated that four times as many as are caught elude the officials. Since Mexico is a Third World country, existing alongside the much more wealthy United States, it seems unlikely that this flow of people northwards will diminish in the near future. Illegal immigrants can be employed more cheaply than indigenous workers, and are prepared to do jobs that most of the rest of the population would not accept. Legislation was passed by Congress in 1986 making it possible for illegal immigrants who had lived in the United States for at least five years to claim legal residence.

The majority of Mexican-Americans used to be farm laborers. During the 1960s, Cesar Chavez, the leader of the United Farm Workers, achieved notable success against the large landowners in his fight to improve the wages and working conditions of agricultural workers in California and the Southwest, the majority of whom were of Mexican origin. Now most Mexican-Americans live in urban areas, concentrated especially in the *barrios,* the Spanish-speaking neighborhoods. Twenty percent live below the poverty line and since many speak English only inadequately, the level of job opportunities for young people is low. Many Mexican-Americans have long resisted assimilation into the dominant English-speaking culture, and in common with other ethnic groups, have begun to lay increasing stress upon building pride in their own cultural identity within the United States.

Puerto Ricans and Cubans

Puerto Rico is another territory acquired by the United States through war, and Puerto Ricans have been American citizens since 1917. Puerto Rico is poor, and many of its inhabitants have migrated to the mainland United States to improve their conditions of life (Fitzpatrick, 1971). Large numbers of Puerto Ricans settled in New York City, but there and elsewhere have continued to live in considerable poverty. Nearly 40 percent of Puerto Ricans on the mainland exist below the poverty line. A "reverse migration" of Puerto Ricans began in the 1970s—more have left than arrived in the United States since that date. One of the most important issues facing Puerto Rican activists is the political destiny of their homeland. Puerto Rico is at present a commonwealth, not a full state within the United States. For many years Puerto Ricans have been divided about whether the island should retain its present status, opt for independence, or attempt to become the fifty-first state of the Union.

A third Hispanic group in the United States, the Cubans, differs from each of the others in some key respects. Half a million Cubans left their country following the rise of Fidel Castro to power in 1959, and the majority settled in Florida. Unlike other Hispanic immigrants, these were mainly people from white-collar and professional backgrounds. They have managed to thrive within the host society, many finding positions comparable to those they had abandoned in Cuba. A further wave of Cuban immigrants, from less affluent origins, came over in 1980. Lacking the qualifications held by many of the first wave of immigrants, they tend to live in circumstances closer to those of most of the rest of the Hispanic communities in the United States. Both sets of Cuban immigrants are mainly political refugees rather than economic migrants. The later immigrants to a large extent have become the "working class" for the earlier. They are paid low wages, but Cuban employers tend to take them on in preference to other ethnic groups. In Miami, nearly one-third of all businesses are owned by Cubans and 75 percent of the labor force in construction is Cuban (Bach, 1980).

Over the past few years, an influx of migrants from Nicaragua, Guatemala, El Salvador, and other Central American states has occurred. Many of these groups have settled in Florida or in California and New Mexico. A considerable proportion are illegal immigrants, and most are living in conditions of some poverty.

ASIAN-AMERICANS

About two percent of the population of the United States is of Asian origin—some five million people. Chinese, Japanese, and Filipinos (immigrants from the Philippines) form the largest groups. However, there are also significant numbers of Asian-Indians, Pakistanis, Koreans, and Vietnamese now living in America. As a result of the war in Vietnam, some 350,000 refugees from that country have entered the United States since the early 1970s.

As was mentioned earlier in the chapter, Chinese and Japanese workers were imported into the United States by employers in the late nineteenth and early twentieth centuries. Most of the Chinese settled in California, where they were employed mainly in heavy industries, such as mining and railroad construction. They were faced with intense prejudice and discrimination, especially from lower-class whites, who saw them as a source of threat to their jobs. The retreat of the Chinese into distinct "Chinatowns" was not primarily their choice, but was enforced by the hostility they faced. Since Chinese immigration was ended by law in 1882, the Chinese remained largely isolated from the wider society—at least until fairly recently.

Most of the early Japanese immigrants also settled in California and the other Pacific states. During World War II, following the attack on Pearl Harbor by Japan, all Japanese-Americans in the United States were made to report to "relocation centers"—which were effectively concentration camps, surrounded by barbed wire and gun turrets. In spite of the fact that most of these Japanese were American citizens, they were compelled to live in the hastily established camps for the duration of the war. Paradoxically, this eventually led to their greater integration within the wider society since, following the war, Japanese-Americans did not return to the separate neighborhoods in which they had previously lived. They have become extremely successful in terms of their levels of educational attainment and income, marginally outstripping whites. The rate of intermarriage of Japanese-Americans with whites is now nearly 50 percent.

Following the passing of a new Immigration Act in 1965, large-scale immigration of Asians into the United States again took place. Foreign-born Chinese-Americans today outnumber those brought up in the United States. The newly arrived Chinese have avoided the "Chinatowns" in which the long-established Chinese have tended to stay, mostly moving into other neighborhoods. Many Chinese, including the vast majority of those recently arrived, work in menial occupations. But a higher proportion of Chinese-Americans as a whole are in professional and managerial jobs than is the case for the white population. On average, native-born Chinese-Americans earn 30 percent more than the recent immigrants.

DIVERGENT FORTUNES

Surveying the development and current position of the various major ethnic groups in America, one conclusion that emerges clearly is the differences in their fortunes. Whereas successive waves of European immigrants managed to overcome most of the prejudice and discrimination they originally faced, and became assimilated into the wider society, other groups have not. These include two of the minorities that have been in North America for centuries: the Native Americans and the blacks. The others are the Mexicans, Puerto Ricans, and to some extent the Chinese.

What distinguishes the first four groups is not just that they are nonwhite, but that they were originally present in America as colonized peoples rather than as willing immigrants. Robert Blauner (1972) has suggested that a fairly sharp distinction should be drawn between groups who came voluntarily to settle in the new lands, and those who were incorporated into the society through force or violence. The Native Americans are part of American society because they were subjected militarily; the blacks were brought over in the slave trade; Puerto Rico was colonized as a result of war; and, originally at least, the Mexicans were incorporated as a result of the conquest of the Southwest by the United States in the nineteenth century. These groups have consistently been the target of racism, which both reflects and perpetuates their separation from other ethnic communities.

The situation of the Chinese and Japanese has been rather different. Some of them came voluntarily, others were "shanghaied" or pressed into service by their countrymen more or less against their will. Although they first of all faced severe discrimination, they were later able to gain greater acceptance than other nonwhites. The Chinese and Japanese had more choice and self-direction than the other groups, and historically, Asiatic people have not been regarded by Europeans with the same degree of antipathy as that held towards those with dark skins.

Although both open and institutional racism seem to be declining in the United States, the differences between white and nonwhite ethnic groups are long enduring (Ringer, 1985). Moreover, the relative success of white ethnics has been to some degree purchased at the expense of nonwhites. A combination of continued white immigration and white racism, up to at least the World War II period, served to keep nonwhites out of the better-paid occupations, forcing them into the least-skilled, most marginal sectors of the economy. With the slowing down of white immigration, this situation is changing, although some newly-arrived groups, like the Cubans in Miami, seem to be repeating the process.

LIKELY FUTURE
DEVELOPMENTS

THREE MODELS HAVE BEEN SUGGESTED TO INTERPRET THE likely future development of ethnic relations in the United States (Gordon, 1964, 1978). One is **Anglo-conformity,** or **assimilation,** meaning that immigrants abandon their original customs and practices, molding their behavior instead to the values and norms of the English-speaking majority. Generations of immigrants faced pressures towards being "assimilated" in this way, and many of their children became more or less completely "American" as a result. Indeed, it is only as a consequence of such a process that the "Anglo" majority is a majority at all, since the proportion of the population of English descent is considerably outweighed by that of people from other backgrounds.

A second model is that of the **melting pot**—rather than the traditions of the immigrants becoming adapted to those of the preexisting population, all are blended to form new, evolving cultural patterns. Many have argued that this should be actively striven for as the most desirable outcome of ethnic diversity in the United States. To a limited degree, this model is an accurate expression of some aspects of American cultural development. Although the "Anglo" culture has remained preeminent, it has been influenced by the many different groups that now comprise the American population.

The third model is that of **pluralism.** In this view, the most appropriate course of development for the United States is to foster the development of a genuinely plural society, in which the equal validity of numerous different subcultures is recognized. This has become the dominant view of many leaders of minority-group organizations, who want to secure an independent but equal position for their different ethnic communities. It does seem at least possible to create a society in which ethnic groups are separate but equal, as is shown by the case of Switzerland, where French, German, and Italian groups coexist in the same nation. But this situation is unusual, and it seems unlikely that the United States could even approximate it in the near future.

As in the past, the most likely path for the foreseeable future is a mixture of these three types, with a stronger emphasis upon pluralism than before. It would be a mistake, however, to see ethnic pluralism only as a result of different cultural values and norms "brought in" from the outside to American society. Cultural diversity has also been *created* by the experience of ethnic groups as they adapt to the wider social environment in which they find themselves.

The situation of blacks, and other nonwhites, continues to be different from that of white immigrant groups. Blacks have persistently been excluded from the process of ethnic "succession," whereby each new wave of immigrants first of all lives in circumstances of some deprivation, but eventually successfully finds a secure and prosperous position within the social order. While prejudice and discrimination may be diminishing, it is doubtful that a fundamental alteration in the varying fortunes of whites and blacks in America is occurring.

SUMMARY

1. *Ethnic groups* have common cultural characteristics that separate them from others within a given population. Ethnic differences are wholly learned, although they are sometimes depicted as "natural."

2. A *minority group* is one whose members are discriminated against by the majority population in a society. Members of minority groups often have a strong sense of group solidarity, deriving in part from the collective experience of exclusion.

3. *Race* refers to physical characteristics, such as skin color, that are treated by members of a community or society as socially significant—as signaling distinct cultural characteristics. Many popular beliefs about race are mythical. There are no distinct characteristics by means of which human beings can be allocated to different races.

4. *Racism* is prejudice based on socially significant physical distinctions. A *racist* is someone who believes that some individuals are superior, or inferior, to others as a result of racial differences.

5. *Displacement* and *scapegoating* are psychological mechanisms associated with *prejudice* and *discrimination.* In displacement, feelings of hostility become directed against objects that are not the real origin of these anxieties. People project their anxieties and insecurities onto scapegoats. Prejudice involves holding preconceived views about an individual or group; discrimination refers to actual behavior that deprives members of a group of opportunities open to others. Prejudice usually involves *stereotypes*—fixed and inflexible categories of thought.

6. *Group closure* and *differential allocation of resources* are important parts of many situations of ethnic antagonism. However, some of the fundamental aspects of modern ethnic conflicts, espe-

cially racist attitudes held by whites against blacks, have to be understood in terms of the expansion of the West and of colonialism.

7. Historical examples illustrate various ways in which societies have dealt with ethnic diversity, ranging from slavery and apartheid to cultural integration.

8. The civil rights movement of the 1950s and 1960s, which involved numerous episodes of violence, had a significant effect upon ethic relations in the United States. New forms of legislation ended open segregation and discrimination, although the long-term impact of these in producing greater equality between whites and blacks has been much less than many of the leading activists had hoped for.

9. *Affirmative action* refers to programs of change that take positive steps to reduce the disadvantages suffered by minority groups. Some recent types of affirmative action, which have been most widely introduced in the United States, such as busing, have led to major conflicts.

10. A remarkable diversity of ethnic minorities is found in the United States today, each group having its own distinctive cultural characteristics. Some of the most important minority communities numerically, after blacks, are the Native Americans, Mexican-Americans, Puerto Ricans, Cubans, Chinese, and Japanese.

11. Three models of possible future developments in race and ethnic relations can be distinguished—the first stressing Anglo-conformity, or *assimilation,* the second the *melting pot,* and the third *pluralism.* In recent years there has been a tendency to emphasize the third of these avenues, whereby different ethnic identities are accepted as equally valid within the context of the overall national culture.

BASIC CONCEPTS

ETHNICITY

RACISM

PREJUDICE

DISCRIMINATION

IMPORTANT TERMS

MINORITY GROUP
  (OR ETHNIC MINORITY)
RACE
STEREOTYPICAL THINKING
DISPLACEMENT
SCAPEGOATING
PROJECTION
AUTHORITARIAN PERSONALITY
APARTHEID

MICROSEGREGATION
MEZZOSEGREGATION
MACROSEGREGATION
AFFIRMATIVE ACTION
INSTITUTIONAL RACISM
ANGLO-CONFORMITY
ASSIMILATION
MELTING POT
PLURALISM

GROUPS AND ORGANIZATIONS

THE FRENCH PHILOSOPHER AND DRAMATIST JEAN-PAUL Sartre once wrote that "hell is other people." There are indeed many situations, intimate and more impersonal, where our relations with others can be oppressive. One way to make people uncomfortable, and even despairing, is to place them in close and continuous relationships with others—as is often the case, for example, in prisons. Yet a far more severe punishment is to deprive someone of human contact altogether. Being held in solitary confinement, even if in a reasonable degree of comfort in other respects, is something most people find unendurable. Living and interacting with others in groups, associations, and organizations is a pervasive aspect of the lives of virtually everyone.

Most of us belong to numerous groups including, for example, the families into which we are born, but also a variety of other organizations, such as schools, colleges, or business firms. Groups and organizations dominate much of our lives, and the systems of authority they involve consistently influence and constrain our behavior. In this chapter we shall discuss some of the main characteristics of groups, putting particular emphasis upon the authority systems of large-scale organizations.

FORMS OF ASSOCIATION

THE CONCEPT OF SOCIAL GROUP SHOULD BE DISTINGUISHED
from two other related notions, aggregates and social categories. A **social group** is simply a number of people
who interact with each other on a regular basis. Such regularity of interaction tends to weld participants together as a distinct unit with an
overall social identity. Members of a group expect certain forms of
behavior from one another that are not demanded of nonmembers.
Groups differ in size, ranging from intimate associations, like a married couple, up to large organizations, such as a government bureaucracy. **Aggregates** are collections of people who are in the same place
at the same time but share no definite connections with one another.
Passengers waiting at an airport, a cinema audience, or students waiting in the lines for class registration, are examples of aggregates. To
use Erving Goffman's phrase, aggregates are gatherings of people in
unfocused interaction with one another (see Chapter 4: "Social Interaction and Everyday Life"). Of course, within aggregates various
kinds of group relationships are usually found.

A **social category** is a statistical grouping—people classified together on the basis of a particular characteristic they share, such as
having the same level of income or being in the same occupation. A
social category isn't based on whether people within it interact with

each other or gather together in one place; nor do the people in the same category necessarily attach any particular importance to the common characteristic they share. Social categories are quite often referred to in sociological research. For instance, if we were interested in economic inequalities in the United States, we might want to analyze the difference in average earnings between people in varying occupations.

PRIMARY AND SECONDARY GROUPS

The groups to which we belong are not all of equal importance to us. Some groups tend to influence many aspects of our lives and bring us into personal and familiar association with others. The early sociologist Charles Horton Cooley (1864–1929) used the term **primary group** to refer to a small association of people connected by ties of an emotionally involving nature. The family is an example, as are friendship groups, sororities, and fraternities. Cooley tended to idealize primary groups, but this emphasis should be questioned. Life in families, for example, is not by any means always intrinsically satisfying and enjoyable; families are often the source of great tensions and hostilities. You may find life in a sorority or fraternity group worthwhile and emotionally rewarding; but to some it can be threatening and uncomfortable.

A **secondary group** is made up of people who meet regularly, but whose relationships are mainly impersonal. Individuals in secondary groups do not have intimate ties with one another, and normally come together for specific practical purposes. A committee, a sports club, or an intramural swim team are examples of secondary groups. In actual social situations, the distinction between primary and sec-

An Amish family working together in Pennsylvania's Lancaster County would be an example of a primary group tied together not only by family, but also by religion and work.

ondary groups is not defined. People who regularly attend committee meetings together, for example, might become very friendly and spend time with one another informally.

FORMAL ORGANIZATIONS

An **organization** is a large association of people run on impersonal lines, set up to achieve specific objectives. Most social systems in the traditional world developed over lengthy periods as a result of custom and habit. Organizations, on the other hand, are mostly *designed* —established with definite aims in view and housed in buildings or physical settings specifically constructed to help realize those aims. The edifices in which hospitals, colleges, or business firms carry on their activities are mostly "custom-built."

In traditional societies, most people lived in small group settings. In a society like traditional China, it was rare for members of a local village community ever to meet a government official. Government edicts barely affected their lives. Compare our situation today. What we do is constantly conditioned by the decisions of officials. Every major life event—birth, marriage, or death—has to be registered. Government organizations provide, or at least are partly responsible for, some of the most basic resources affecting our activities, such as education, sanitation, road systems, public utilities, control of the environment, the national monetary system—the list is almost endless.

Many of us are born in large hospitals, and are tagged so that we can be identified among several dozen other newborn babies. Virtually all of us attend schools, and some go on to colleges. We may spend much of our adult lives working within an industrial organization, financial company, bank or government agency. Throughout our lives we also depend upon organizations to be able to communicate with others by means of the mail or the telephone; to provide light and heat for our homes; to give us information, or entertainment, should we wish to read a newspaper, listen to the radio, or watch television.

It is easy to see why organizations are so important to us today. In the premodern world, families, close relatives, and neighbors provided for most needs—food, the instruction of children, work, and leisure-time activities. In modern times, the mass of the population is much more *interdependent* than was ever the case before. Many of our requirements are catered for by people we never meet, and who indeed might live many thousands of miles away. A tremendous amount of coordination of activities and resources—which organizations provide—is needed in such circumstances.

One of the best ways to begin to think about the nature of organizations is to consider the university or college to which you belong. These institutions vary in size, but even the smallest are very large compared with virtually any groups in premodern societies. "Small" colleges may have two or three thousand members, while the biggest universities number seventy thousand or more. Running a college involves a permanent administrative apparatus, together with rules or procedures that students and professors are expected to follow—governing, for example, the teaching and grading of courses. Besides the student body, there are numerous different types of people involved in a college, when it is looked at as an organization. Professors, administrators, service personnel, campus officers of various sorts, police, and many others form part of the system. For the college to keep going from day to day, the activities of these groups have to be coordinated with one another, and resources have to be fed in from the outside (for example, finances to pay salaries, maintain buildings and services).

A college is not just a collection of people but has a definite physical setting. The campus (or sometimes a number of linked campuses in a big university) helps give "shape" to the college as an organization. In general, the architectural and the social characteristics of an organization are closely connected with one another. This is easily seen if we compare an "open" organization like a university—where people enter and leave the site freely—with a "closed" organization like a high-security prison. A prison is normally surrounded by high walls and has a forbidding exterior, while internally its architecture is geared to the control of inmates whose membership of the organization is involuntary.

What are the distinctive characteristics that modern organizations tend to have in common? What features of organizations make possible the functions that they are established to undertake? How do the social and physical settings of organizations interrelate? These are the questions with which we shall be concerned in the following sections. We shall start by looking at the most important classic account of the nature of organizations, provided by Max Weber. Weber saw organizations as strongly hierarchical, and we shall examine whether or not he was right in this emphasis. If he was indeed right, it matters a great deal to all of us. For Weber diagnosed a clash—as well as a connection—between modern organizations and democracy that he believed had far-reaching consequences for social life.

In assessing Weber's views, we shall consider some types of organization that have been deliberately set up in a nonhierarchical way. We shall also compare Western organizations with those from other cultural contexts, looking especially at the nature of Japanese business corporations. Although Japanese firms are very hierarchical in some ways, in others they seem to diverge from the Weberian model —and it would be difficult to deny that they are efficient! Weber neglected the influence of the physical settings of organizations, and we will need to look at this aspect in some detail. Finally, we shall analyze the importance of self-help groups, which provide a further contrast with more hierarchical forms of organization. The overriding themes of this chapter thus focus upon the connections, and the tensions, between *hierarchy, administrative effectiveness,* and bureaucracy or *participation* in organizations.

BUREAUCRACY

MOST MODERN ORGANIZATIONS ARE TO A LARGE DEGREE bureaucratic in nature. The word **bureaucracy** was invented by a Monsieur de Gournay in 1745. He added to the word "bureau," meaning in French both an office and a writing table, a term derived from the Greek verb "to rule." "Bureaucracy" is the rule of officials. It was first used only to apply to government officials, but gradually became extended to refer to large organizations in general. The concept was from the beginning used disparagingly, by its inventor and by others. De Gournay spoke of the developing power of officials as "an illness called bureaumania" (Albrow, 1970). The French novelist Balzac spoke of bureaucracy as "the giant power wielded by pigmies." This sort of view has persisted into current times. Bureaucracy is frequently associated with red tape, inefficiency, and wastefulness.

The satirist C. Northcote Parkinson (1957) produced a celebrated discussion of bureaucracy based upon the idea that officials informally expand the scope of what they do to take care of any free time they find on their hands. "Parkinson's Law" states that work expands to fill the time available for its completion. Bureaucracies tend to grow, not because the officials have taken on new duties that they did not have before, but because they have to be constantly seen to be busy. They create tasks where none really exist, and then have to supervise their subordinates, who in turn must spend a great deal of time writing reports and memoranda for them. And so the process continues—most of the form-filling, memo-writing, and file-keeping actually being quite unnecessary to carry out the tasks the bureaucracy was initially set up to achieve.

Many other writers, however, have seen bureaucracy in a different light—as a model of carefulness, precision, and effective administration. Bureaucracy, they argue, is in fact the most efficient form of organization human beings have devised, because all tasks are regulated by strict rules of procedure. The most influential account of bureaucracy, given by Max Weber, steers a way between these two extremes. According to Weber, the expansion of bureaucracy is inevitable in modern societies. The development of bureaucratic authority is the only way of coping with the administrative requirements of large-scale social systems. However, Weber also believed bureaucracy to have a number of major failings, which have important implications for the nature of modern social life.

WEBER'S VIEW OF BUREAUCRACY

A few types of bureaucratic organizations, Weber pointed out, already existed in the larger traditional societies. For example, there was a bureaucratic officialdom in Imperial China responsible for the overall affairs of government. The other main type of bureaucracy in the traditional world was the military. But it is only in modern times that bureaucracies have become fully developed, and are found in most areas of social life. In order to look at the origins and nature of the expansion of bureaucratic organizations, Weber constructed an **ideal type** of bureaucracy. "Ideal" here does not refer to what is most desirable, but to a "pure form" of bureaucratic organization. An ideal type is an abstract description constructed by accentuating certain features of real cases so as to pinpoint their most essential characteristics. Weber noted several of these characteristics (Weber, 1979):

An automobile assembly line—one level of a much larger bureaucracy.

1. **HIERARCHY.** There is a definite *hierarchy of authority,* such that tasks in the organization are distributed as "official duties." A bureaucracy looks like a pyramid, with the positions of highest authority at the top. A "chain of command," formed by the **officials** located at each level, stretches from top to bottom, making coordinated decision making possible. Each higher office controls and supervises the one below it in the hierarchy. Take as an example the administrative personnel in a college. From the president down to the clerks there is a hierarchy of administrative posts; the higher up the system a person is, the greater the authority he or she has in making decisions.

2. **WRITTEN RULES.** A clear set of rules governs the conduct of officials at all levels of the organization.

This does not mean that bureaucratic duties are just a matter of routine. The higher the office, the more the rules involved tend to encompass a wide variety of cases and demand flexibility in their interpretation. All colleges, for example, have statutes or codes of procedure that set out "how things are done"—what the duties of college officers are, the principles of college government, the criteria for grading and assessment, and so forth.

3. FULL-TIME AND SALARIED OFFICIALS. Each job in the hierarchy has a definite and fixed salary attached to it. The individual is expected to make a career within the organization. Promotion is possible on the basis of capability, seniority, or a mixture of the two. Unlike the student body, the administrative officials in a college—the bureaucrats—receive a salary from it, and many spend most of their lives working in the organization.

4. SEPARATION OF WORK AND HOME LIFE. There is a separation between the tasks of the official within the organization and life outside. The "home life" of the official is distinct from her or his activities in the workplace, and is also physically separated from it. The official duties of college administrators, to pursue the same illustration we have been using, are quite separate from their domestic lives. (This was not true of most work settings in premodern societies. For example, on peasant farms, the place of work was also the family dwelling, and domestic tasks and work tasks were closely bound up with one another.)

5. OWNERSHIP NOT IN THE WORKERS' HANDS. No member or members of the organization own the material resources with which they operate. The development of bureaucracy, according to Weber, separates the workers from control of their means of production. In traditional communities, farmers and craft workers usually had close control over their processes of production, and owned the tools they used. In bureaucracies, officials do not own the offices in which they work, the desks at which they sit, or the office machinery they utilize. Thus college adminis-

trators are not the owners of the buildings where they carry out their work or of the resources they utilize to keep the college running from day to day.

THE EFFECTIVENESS OF BUREAUCRACY

Modern bureaucracy, Weber argued, is a highly effective mode of organizing large numbers of people. There are several reasons for this:

1. Bureaucratic procedures might in some ways limit initiative, but they also ensure that decisions are made according to general criteria rather than individual whim or caprice.

2. Training officials to be experts in the area to which their duties apply cuts out the "talented amateur," but ensures a general level of overall competence.

3. Making official positions salaried and full time reduces, although it does not eliminate, possibilities of corruption. Traditional systems of authority were actually based in large part on what we would today regard as corrupt practices. Officeholders used their position, for instance, to tax those they governed, taking most of the money for their own use.

4. The fact that performance is judged by examinations or other formal credentials reduces—although it does not entirely put a stop to—the obtaining of positions through personal favor or kinship connections.

Weber believed that the more an organization approaches the ideal type of bureaucracy, the more effective it will be in pursuing the objectives for which it was established. He often compared bureaucracies to sophisticated machines. Yet he recognized that bureaucracy could cause red-tape problems, and accepted that many bureaucratic jobs are dull, offering little opportunity for the exercise of creative capabilities. Bureaucratic routine, and the authority of officialdom over our lives, are prices we pay for the technical effectiveness of bureaucratic organizations.

FORMAL AND INFORMAL RELATIONS

Weber's analysis of bureaucracy gives prime place to **formal relations** within organizations. The more bureaucratized an organiza-

Business leaders often develop informal groups and "meet" during their pursuit of more leisurely goals. Women have often been excluded from such informal networks (and thus from advancement) because of the male-only nature of some of the "meeting" places (see Chapter 15: "Work and Economic Life").

tion is, in Weber's terms, the more that tasks are fixed and detailed. He had little to say about the informal connections and small group relations that exist in all organizations. In bureaucracies, informal ways of doing things are often the chief means by which a measure of flexibility is achieved.

In an influential study, Peter Blau studied **informal relations** in a government agency (Blau, 1963). The tasks of the officials in the agency involved investigating possible income-tax violations. Agents who came across problems that they were unsure how to handle were supposed to discuss them with their immediate supervisor. The rules of procedure stated that they should not consult colleagues working at the same level as themselves. Most officials were wary of approaching their supervisors, however, because they felt this might suggest a lack of competence on their part, and reduce their chances for promotion. Hence they usually consulted each other, violating the official rules. This not only helped to provide concrete advice, it reduced the anxieties involved in working alone. A cohesive set of loyalties, of a primary-group kind, developed among those working at the same level. The problems these workers faced, Blau concludes, were probably coped with much more effectively as a result. The group was able to evolve informal procedures allowing for more initiative and responsibility than provided for by the formal rules of the organization.

Informal networks tend to develop at all levels of organizations. At the very top, personal ties and connections may be more important in the real structure of power than the formal situations in which decisions are supposed to be made. For example, meetings of boards of directors and shareholders supposedly determine the policies affecting the activities of business corporations. In practice, a few members of the board usually run the corporation, making their decisions informally and expecting the board to approve them. Informal networks of this sort also stretch across different corporations. Business leaders from different firms frequently consult one another informally, and belong to the same clubs and leisure-time associations.

John Meyer and Brian Rowan (1977) argue that formal rules and procedures in organizations are usually quite distant from the practices actually adopted by the organizations' members. Formal rules, in their view, are often "myths" that people profess to follow but which have little substance in reality. They serve to legitimate—to justify—ways in which tasks are carried out, even while these ways may diverge greatly from how things are "supposed to be done."

Formal procedures, Meyer and Rowan point out, often have a ceremonial or ritual character. People will make a show of conforming to them in order to get on with their real work using other, more informal procedures. For example, rules governing ward procedure in a hospital help justify how nurses act towards patients in caring for them. Thus a nurse will faithfully fill in a patient's chart that hangs at the end of the bed, but will check the patient's progress by means of other, informal criteria—"how well the person is looking," and whether he or she seems alert and lively. Rigorously keeping up the charts impresses the patients and keeps the doctors happy, but is not always essential to the nurse's assessments.

Deciding to what degree informal procedures generally help or hinder the effectiveness of organizations is not a simple matter. Systems that resemble Weber's ideal type tend to give rise to a multitude of unofficial ways of doing things. This is partly because the flexibility that is lacking can be achieved by unofficial tinkering with formal rules. For those in dull jobs, informal ways of doing things often help also to create a more satisfying work environment. Informal connections between officials in higher positions may be effective in some ways that aid the organization as a whole. On the other hand, those involved may be more concerned to advance or protect their own interests rather than those of the overall organization.

BUREAUCRACY AND OLIGARCHY

It follows from Weber's model of bureaucracy that power tends to be concentrated at the top. A large organization is pyramid shaped, with the majority being in relatively powerless positions near the bottom. A student and colleague of Weber's, Robert Michels, (1967, orig. pub. 1911), made use of this observation to set out what he termed the *iron law of oligarchy*. **Oligarchy** means rule by the few. According to Michels, the larger and more bureaucratized an organization becomes, the greater the degree to which power is concentrated in the hands of a small number of people in high positions. Michels based his thesis upon the development of the Social Democratic Party in Germany, which was explicitly committed to ideals of mass participation in political decision making. The party was developing into a major force in German politics at that period (the first decade of this century). Its very success brought about increasing internal bureaucracy as the party grew in size.

Real power, Michels tried to show, was increasingly becoming monopolized by those running the party bureaucracy at the top—a few high party officials. Ironically, the Social Democratic Party had become dominated by a small clique in just the same way as the conservative parties it opposed had. Every large-scale organization, according to Michels, shows the same tendencies. Rule by the few is simply an inevitable aspect of the bureaucratic nature of large organizations. If Michels's argument is valid, the consequences are serious for anyone who values democratic participation. Michels himself progressively abandoned the socialist ideals he once supported.

In common with Weber, Michels identified a genuine source of tension in modern societies between trends towards bureaucracy, on the one hand, and the development of **democracy** on the other. Mass democracy can only exist if there are regular voting procedures and well-developed party organizations, but these procedures bring about the advance of bureaucracy, because there have to be full-time officials whose job is to supervise or run them. Democracy is supposed to involve mass participation in the political system; yet the very furtherance of democratic parties leads to the development of large, bureaucratized party machines, dominated by cliques of leaders. (For further discussion of mass democracy, see Chapter 10: "Politics, Government, and the State.")

Was Michels right? It surely is correct to say that large-scale organizations involve the centralizing of power. Yet there is good reason to suppose that the "iron law of oligarchy" is not quite as hard and fast as Michels claimed. The connections between oligarchy and bureaucratic centralization are more ambiguous than he supposed.

We should recognize first of all that unequal power is not just a function of size. In modest-sized groups there can be very marked differences of power. In a small business, for instance, where the activities of employees are directly visible to the directors, much tighter control might be exerted than in offices in larger organizations. As organizations expand in size, power relationships often in fact become looser. Those at the middle and lower levels may have little influence over general policies forged at the top. On the other hand, because of the specialization and expertise involved in bureaucracy, people at the top also lose control of many administrative decisions, which become handled by those lower down (Crozier, 1967). Individuals in subordinate authority positions always have some control over their superiors. For example, a civil-service official is often able to present the background of a case to a superior in such a way that only one decision appears plausible.

Power is also quite often openly delegated downwards from superiors to subordinates within organizations. Ray Pahl and Jack Winkler (1974) studied business directors in corporations of differing sizes. They found that open transfer of power downwards was more common in the larger than in the smaller firms. In the larger companies, directors were so busy coordinating different departments, coping with crises, and analyzing budget and forecast figures, that they had little time for original thinking. They handed over consideration of policy issues to others below them, whose task was to develop proposals about them. Many directors frankly admitted that for the most part they simply accepted the conclusions given to them.

NONHIERARCHICAL
ORGANIZATIONS

SINCE THE TIME AT WHICH MICHELS WROTE, THERE HAVE been many attempts to set up organizations in such a way as to counter tendencies towards the centralization of power. Two examples are the Israeli kibbutz and the system of workers' self-management in Yugoslavian industry. The **kibbutzim** were set up in Israel specifically to create an egalitarian system of production, in which there would be few differences of income or power. Save for certain small possessions, property is owned collectively, and work-groups are headed by elected supervisors. (For further information about the kibbutzim, see Chapter 12: "Kinship, Marriage, and the Family.") The Yugoslavian enterprises have a formal system of industrial democracy, with workers voting to elect directors of firms.

Tannenbaum and his colleagues (1974; Rosner and Tannenbaum, 1987) carried out a comparative study of firms in five countries, including the kibbutzim and the industrial plants in Yugoslavia. Business organizations were also studied in Austria, Italy, and the United States. Small and large firms were included in the research in each of the countries. The researchers explicitly addressed their work to Michels's views on organization and oligarchy.

The results showed substantial differences between organizations in the various societies. Size of organization did not prove to be the main correlate of centralization and hierarchy. Both within and across different countries some small firms were more hierarchical than larger ones. In the kibbutz and the Yugoslavian enterprises, whether small or large, there was less hierarchy than in the industrial plants in the other countries. The kibbutz, for example, showed few graduations of authority, and no large differences in income between those at the various levels; individuals rotated between different tasks frequently (Bartolle et al., 1980). The researchers also found, however, variations in the degree to which informal participation alleviated hierarchy. In Yugoslavia, participation in decision making is formally part of the organizational structure. Informal practices tended to produce *more,* rather than less, hierarchy in such a setting. In the case of American firms, on the other hand, the reverse was more often true. In Yugoslavia, informal connections were used to get round procedures of industrial democracy, while in the United States they served to alleviate hierarchical inequalities.

The international comparisons involved here are all from a Western context. In assessing the questions with which this chapter is concerned it is worthwhile spreading the cultural net more widely than this. To do so, we now turn to look at organizations in a very different cultural environment—that of Japan.

JAPANESE CORPORATIONS

Japan is the only non-Western country to have become fully industrialized. The economic progress of the country is remarkable for more than one reason. At the midpoint of the nineteenth century, just before industrialization got fully under way, Japan was still essentially a feudal society—far more traditional and rural than most Western countries at that period—yet it experienced a very rapid process of industrial development in the late 1800s and early twentieth century. At a later period, following its defeat in World War II, the Japanese economy was shattered. Yet—aided initially by financial resources provided by the American victors—Japan has since that time shot to near the top of leading economic powers. In terms of volume of wealth produced, Japan is today the third largest economy in the world. The rates of economic growth of the two biggest economic systems, the United States and the Soviet Union, are currently well behind that of Japan. If present trends are maintained, Japan will be the wealthiest country in the world shortly after the year 2000 (Pascale and Athos, 1982).

The economic success of Japan is frequently said to be due mainly to the distinctive characteristics of the large Japanese corporations—which differ substantially from most business firms in the West (Vogel, 1979). Japanese companies diverge from the characteristics that Weber associated with bureaucracy in several ways:

1. BOTTOM-UP DECISION MAKING. The big Japanese corporations do not form a pyramid of authority as Weber portrayed it, with each level being responsible only to the one above. In Japanese firms, workers low down in the organization are consulted about policies being considered by management, and even the very top executives regularly meet with them. The Japanese speak of "bottom-up" decision making to refer to this system.

2. LESS SPECIALIZATION. In Japanese organizations, employees specialize much less than their counterparts in the West. Take as an example the case of Sugao, as described by William Ouchi (1982). Sugao is a university graduate who has just joined the Mitsubeni Bank, in Tokyo. He will enter the firm in a management-training position, spending his first year learning generally how the various departments of the bank operate. He will then work in a local branch for a while, working directly with the tellers, and will subsequently be brought back to the bank's headquarters to learn commercial banking. Then he will move out to yet another branch dealing with loans, learning about that side of the business. From there he is likely to come back again to headquarters, working in the personnel department. Ten years will have elapsed by this time, and Sugao will have reached the position of section chief. But the process of job rotation will not stop. He will move on to a further branch of the bank,

Japanese training to be managers.

perhaps dealing this time with the financing of small businesses, and then return to yet a different job at the headquarters.

By the time Sugao reaches the peak of his career, some thirty years after having begun as a trainee, he will have mastered all the important tasks in which the bank is involved. Sugao's likely career contrasts dramatically with that stretching ahead of a typical American bank-management trainee of the same age. American trainees will almost certainly specialize in one area of banking early on, and stay in that specialty for the remainder of their working life.

3. JOB SECURITY. The large corporations in Japan are committed to the lifetime employment of those they hire—the employee is guaranteed a job. Pay and responsibility are geared to seniority—how many years a manager has been with the firm—rather than to a competitive struggle for promotion.

4. GROUP ORIENTED. At all levels of the corporation people are involved in small "teams" or work groups. The groups, rather than individual members, are evaluated in terms of their performance. Unlike their Western counterparts, the "organization charts" of Japanese companies—maps of the authority system—show only groups, not individual positions.

5. MERGING OF WORK AND PRIVATE LIVES. In Weber's depiction of bureaucracy, there is a clear division between the work of people within the organization, and their activities outside. This is in fact true of most Western corporations, in which the relation between firm and employee is largely an economic one. Japanese corporations, by contrast, provide for many aspects of their employees' needs, expecting in return a high level of loyalty to the firm. Japanese employees, from workers on the shop floor right through to top executives, often wear company uniforms. They may assemble to sing the "company song" each morning, and regularly take part in leisure activities organized by the corporation at weekends. (A few Western corporations, like IBM and Apple, now also have com-

pany songs.) Workers receive many material benefits
from the company over and above their salaries. The
electrical firm Hitachi, for example, studied by Ronald
Dore (1980), provided housing for all unmarried
workers and nearly half of its married male employees.
Company loans were provided for the education of
children, and to help with the cost of weddings and
funerals.

THE IMPLICATIONS OF THE JAPANESE SYSTEM FOR ORGANIZATION THEORY

Many observers have argued that firms in the United States and Europe should copy the Japanese corporations if the Western economies
are to match the rate of development of Japan. This is an important
issue, not only on an economic level, but as regards our understanding of the nature of organizations and bureaucracy in general. For the
Japanese companies are definitely in some ways more "democratic"
than Western corporations—there is far more effort to secure consultation at all levels and to encourage a developed sense of corporate
loyalty. In respect to their authority system, emphasis upon work
teams, promotion by seniority rather than competition, and overall
provision for employees' needs, the Japanese firms deviate quite substantially from Weber's model of bureaucracy. If they are efficient *because* of these deviations from bureaucratic hierarchy, considerable
doubt would be thrown upon conclusions usually drawn from the
study of organizations in a Western context. For, in spite of the criticisms to which it has been subject, Weber's interpretation of bureaucracy is still taken by most observers to be correct in its broad outlines.
That is to say, it is generally agreed that Weber's "ideal type" of bureaucratic organization does promote productive efficiency.

Are there factors other than their "nonbureaucratic" nature that
might explain the effectiveness of Japanese corporations? It is actually not difficult to point to other potential influences. Consultation
at all levels is perhaps only possible because of the marked attitudes of
deference that subordinates in Japan show towards their superiors,
which means that the final decisions of supervisors and managers are
accepted even when subordinates disagree with them. In Japan, it is
common to see junior managers carrying the briefcases of their seniors as a matter of course. Lifetime employment is only guaranteed in
large firms (and not in all of these). The Japanese economy contains a
high percentage of small firms, in which pay and employment conditions are often very poor.

Japan's superior economic performance may come mainly from the sheer intensity of work and the long hours involved as much as anything else. Satoshi Kamata, a freelance journalist, worked for a period at Toyota, the Japanese car manufacturer, and described his experiences there in vivid detail in a book published not long afterwards (Kamata, 1982). The company housing in which he lived was regulated like an army camp would be in the West. Health standards in the living quarters and in the workplace were bad, and the working conditions oppressive. Kamata wrote:

> Workers are urged on to production, day and night. So tightly are their lives bound to the conveyor belts in the plants that they cannot even take days off when they want to. The thoroughgoing enforcement of rationalization has eliminated all relief workers. Not only team leaders, the lowest management people, but also unit leaders have been required to work on conveyor lines. Even foremen, normally part of higher management, may sometimes put on working gloves and lend a hand. Then these men have to take home their paper work such as the writing of daily reports and the calculation of day-to-day work units. Through it all the conveyor belts are kept running, with the absolute minimum number of men necessary. . . . Workers are forced to work on Sundays and holidays. The reinforcement work and Sunday-holiday work are a lubricant without which the conveyors could not run. . . . Whenever I come to this city and talk with the workers, I feel as though I have strayed into some foreign land. But this is a nightmare that I have lived, and the anger will not go away.

One test of whether Japanese managerial methods depend upon an especially compliant, deferential, and hard-working labor force is provided by the experience of Japanese-run firms recently set up in Western countries. The number of studies of these carried out thus far are few, and the evidence patchy. But it does seem in fact that Japanese management practices can be detached from the cultural environment of Japan and operate effectively. It appears that they can be applied with some success among a more individualistic labor force used to reasonable working conditions.

Studies of Japanese-run plants in the United States and Britain indicate that "bottom-up" decision making does work outside the Japanese cultural context. Workers seem to respond positively to the greater level of involvement these plants provide, as compared to the Western-style firms in which they were previously employed (White and Trevor, 1983). It seems reasonable to conclude, therefore, that the "Japanese model" does carry some lessons relevant to assessing the Weberian conception of bureaucracy. Organizations that closely resemble Weber's "ideal type" are probably much less effective than they appear "on paper," because they do not permit lower-level employees to develop a sense of autonomy over, and involvement in, their work tasks and the way work is organized.

Drawing upon the example of Japanese corporations, Ouchi (1979, 1982) has argued that bureaucratic hierarchy, as emphasized by Weber, has clear limits to its effectiveness. Overtly bureaucratized organizations lead to "internal failures" of functioning because of their rigid, inflexible, and uninvolving nature. What Ouchi terms *clan forms* of authority contrast with bureaucratic systems and, in many settings of modern societies, are more efficient than bureaucratic types of organization. "Clans" are groups having close ties and personal connections with one another. The work groups in Japanese firms are one example, but clan-type systems also often develop informally within Western organizations.

ORGANIZATIONS, PROFESSIONALS, AND NEW TECHNOLOGY

LET US NOW TURN BACK TO THE WESTERN CONTEXT. IN pursuing the themes introduced at the beginning of the chapter—hierarchy, effectiveness, and participation in organizations—there are some further questions that need to be raised. One concerns the role of professionals—such as accountants, lawyers, doctors, or professors—in organizations. Such groups, for reasons that will be outlined, do not fit readily into hierarchical authority systems. A second question is raised by the changes occurring in organizations today, particularly as a result of the increasing use of information technology. Some have suggested that the spread of such technology might lead both to greater flexibility in organizations and to their decentralization. How valid is this idea?

PROFESSIONALS

Many positions in modern organizations depend upon detailed knowledge and expertise in the understanding and transmitting of

information. Often, managers have to go outside the ranks of management personnel and hire professionals to fill such positions. **Professionals** are those who specialize in the development or application of technical knowledge. Because a long period in higher education is presumed, and because professionals belong to national and even international bodies that define the nature of their tasks, professional expertise cannot easily be reduced to bureaucratic duties. When professionals are employed within large organizations, they do not "fit" neatly within the hierarchy of authority. Professionals usually have more autonomy in their work than others in middle and lower levels of an organization. Companies like IBM, which in so many ways epitomizes the modern corporation from organization to dress code, has under its wing research units staffed by professionals (scientists) whose work habits, hours, dress, and so on differ from those of people in other divisions.

How much control professionals within organizations enjoy over their work tasks varies according to several factors: the size and level of bureaucratization of the organization, the nature of the profession in question, and the strength of the professional association to which the individual worker belongs (Freidson, 1986). As contrasting examples, we might take nursing and law. Nurses are usually recognized as professionals, but the amount of control most have over their conditions of work is relatively limited. The larger hospitals are usually strongly bureaucratized organizations, in which nurses are subordinate to nursing supervisors as well as to other medical staff. Nursing associations set out guidelines for the employment of nurses, but do not have much power over how far these are followed within particular organizations.

For lawyers, the situation is different. Even when working in corporations rather than law firms, lawyers normally have more control over their work tasks than nurses do. The professional associations in law are very strong, and are able to define the codes of conduct which lawyers follow. Lawyers accept some administrative constraints, but their work can only be fully assessed or supervised by other members of the legal profession. Suppose a lawyer working in a given company has to prepare a legal case defending the firm against a suit that a disgruntled customer has brought against it. The company can instruct the lawyer to take charge of the case, but would not ordinarily insist on how the case would be argued in court. This is almost always assumed to be within the sphere of the lawyer's professional autonomy, and not subject to interference on the part of the employer.

Part of the power of professionals in organizations derives from their role as *gatekeepers* for the wider publics that these organizations cater to. A gatekeeper is someone who controls access to desired goods—in this case, to qualifications. For example, professional surveyors or engineers control the licenses needed before building construction can be undertaken; professors determine grades and who shall get degrees and diplomas; caseworkers assess who is eligible for various types of welfare benefit. How much autonomy professionals have in these matters is again influenced by the factors noted in the previous paragraph.

A general increase is taking place in the proportion of people working in professional occupations in modern societies. As organizations come increasingly to rely upon their services, hierarchical bureaucratic systems are liable to come under strain. A growing tendency exists for professionals to work outside large organizations, founding smaller firms of their own, and hiring out their services as they are needed. Organizations that have a high proportion of professional workers tend to have a flexible administrative character, as compared to traditional types of organization.

INFORMATION TECHNOLOGY

The development of **information technology**—computers and electronic communication devices—is another factor currently influencing organizational structures. Automatic data-processing systems have been widely introduced in a range of settings. Anyone who draws money out of a bank, or buys an airline ticket, depends upon a computer-based communications system. Since data can be processed instantaneously in any part of the world linked to such a system, there is no need for physical proximity between those involved (Winch, 1983; Sommerville, 1983; Gill, 1985; Davies, 1986).

A fully integrated "electronic office," in which the bulk of the work done is carried out by machines rather than humans, is still a long while off, and there are many problems facing its realization. Nevertheless, there is a strong trend towards the transfer of office activities to electronic machinery. For example, banks have automated many aspects of processing bank accounts. A study carried out in a branch of Citicorp, in New York, showed that, prior to automating coded operations, fourteen people were involved in processing a letter of credit, a process that took three days to accomplish. Following the introduction of electronic equipment, one person using a mini computer, which stores records electronically, could carry out the same job in a matter of minutes (Meteis, 1979). The bank in question reduced its clerical staff from ten thousand to six thousand during the 1970s.

One view of the "electronic office."

One of the most recent developments in office technology is the introduction of computer work stations that allow access to a large data base, automated filing, data-analysis capabilities, the presentation of reports, computer mail, and telecommunications with other similar work stations. It has been predicted that, by 1995, 85 percent of top managers in the largest two hundred corporations will have executive work stations. They will not necessarily spend much of their time looking at monitor screens: by this date, the keyboard may be superseded by the human voice as the means of inputting materials to the computer. In other words, the executive will be able to dictate instructions directly to the machine.

In 1982, a particular company found the sales of some of its products falling, and was faced with the need to reduce costs. The traditional route in such circumstances would be to lay off staff. But instead, the firm set up those who might have been laid off as independent consultants, and established a computerized support network called Xanadu to provide basic office services to each of them working out of their homes. The company then "bought back" a substantial proportion of their working time for a number of years, but also left them free to use other time to work for different clients. The idea was that the new system would provide the corporation with access to the skills possessed by their former employees, but at a cheaper rate since it no longer needed to provide office space or company benefits (pension, life insurance, etc.). The former employees, in their turn, had the opportunity to build up their own businesses. Thus far, at least, the scheme seems to have worked well for both parties (Handy, 1984). In such a scheme, though, the burden is placed on the former employees since they have to match the loss of company benefits with their ability to attract new business clients.

It might appear from such evidence that large organizations will become leaner as the more routine tasks disappear, reinforcing the tendency towards smaller, more flexible types of enterprises. Yet we should be cautious about reaching such conclusions. Some trends along these lines are appearing, but their impact is as yet fairly limited.

In principle, organizations could become much more decentralized than the case at present. A good deal of office work, for instance, could be carried out at home through computer terminals linked through a telecommunications system. Several large firms in the United States and elsewhere have set up computer networks connecting employees who work from home on consulting contracts. However, these schemes have not yet become nearly as widespread as many anticipated for at least two reasons. First, the employees lose the human side of work; computer terminals are not an attractive substitute for face-to-face interaction with colleagues and friends at work. Second, management cannot easily monitor the activities of employees not under direct supervision.

"Could you fellas tell me if there's anyplace around here where I could find a fax machine?" Drawing by Koren; © 1989 The New Yorker Magazine, Inc.

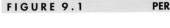

FIGURE 9.1   **PERSONAL COMPUTERS IN USE**

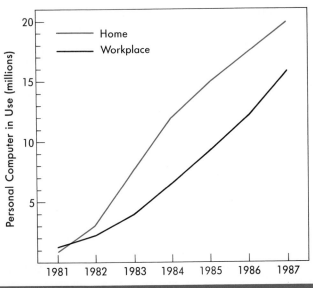

The curves in this graph show the growth of computers in use in the workplace and at home. Some suggest that more and more of these home computers will be hooked up to computers in the workplace, but so far, this work-at-home movement is not that widespread.

Source: Future Computing/Datapro, Inc. Dallas, TX, unpublished data.

Both of these situations demand physical proximity. This observation leads us to give attention to the physical environments within which organizations operate, because these are a key element of their social form. In what follows, we shall consider how the architecture of organizations expresses and influences what goes on in them. We shall also shift the emphasis away from business firms towards other organizations, especially "closed" organizations in which inmates are kept separate from the outside world for lengthy periods.

THE PHYSICAL SETTINGS OF ORGANIZATIONS

AS WAS MENTIONED EARLIER, MODERN ORGANIZATIONS mostly exist in specially designed physical settings. The buildings in which organizations are housed have specific features relevant to their activities, but also share important architectural characteristics with other organizations. The architecture of a hospital, for instance, differs in some respects from that of a business firm or a university building. In the hospital, there are separate wards, consulting rooms, operating rooms, and offices, which give the overall building a definite layout, while a university building has classrooms, laboratories, and a sports hall. Yet there is a general resemblance between hospital buildings and those of universities. Both are likely to be constructions having a large number of hallways with doors leading off, and to have standard decoration and furnishings throughout. Apart from the different dress of the people moving through the corridors, the buildings in which modern organizations are housed have a definite "sameness" to them. They often look quite similar from the outside as well as in their interiors.

For many years, sociologists discussed organizations as though they floated in some kind of ethereal void. It is still common to find large tomes written on organizations that make no mention at all of the fact that they operate in definite physical settings. Yet, as Michel Foucault and others have shown, the architecture of organizations is very directly linked to their social makeup and system of authority (Foucault, 1973, 1979; Gregory and Urry, 1985). By analyzing the physical characteristics of organizations, Foucault demonstrates, we can shed new light upon the problems Weber had analyzed. The "offices" that Weber discussed abstractly are also *architectural settings*— rooms, separated by corridors—within organizations. The buildings of large business firms are sometimes actually constructed physically as a hierarchy. The more elevated one's position in the hierarchy of authority, the nearer the top of a skyscraper one's office is—the phrase "the top floor" is sometimes used to mean "those who hold ultimate power" in the organization.

In many other ways, the geography of an organization will affect its functioning, especially in cases where systems rely heavily on informal relationships. Physical proximity enables the formation of primary groups, while physical distance can enhance the polarization of groups—a "them" and "us" attitude between departments, for example.

SURVEILLANCE AND DISCIPLINE IN ORGANIZATIONS

The arrangement of rooms, hallways, and open spaces in an organization's buildings provides basic clues to how its system of authority operates. (Of course, many organizations exist in buildings *not* specifically designed for them, and this can affect the activities of the staff in significant ways.) In some kinds of organizations, open settings are provided, in which numbers of people work collectively. Because of

The forms of surveillance have altered over time with technological advances. Here, managers oversee workers in a textile manufacturing company. Today, surveillance can be carried out through modern computer systems.

the dull, repetitive nature of certain kinds of industrial work—like assembly-line production—regular supervision is needed to ensure that the pace of labor is sustained. The same is often true of routine work carried out by typists, who sit together in the "typing pool," where their activities are visible to their superiors. Foucault lays great emphasis upon how "visibility," or lack of it, in the architectural settings of modern organizations influences and expresses patterns of authority. The degree to which the activities of subordinates is visible to those of higher grades affects whether they can easily be subject to what Foucault calls surveillance.

Surveillance

Surveillance takes two forms: one, the direct supervision of work tasks of subordinates by superiors; and second, the maintenance of personal records on subordinates. In modern organizations everyone, even in relatively high positions of authority, is subject to surveillance. But the more lowly an individual is, the more his or her behavior tends to be closely scrutinized. Consider the example of a school classroom. Pupils sit at tables or desks, usually arranged in a circle or in rows, putting them all in view of the teacher. The teacher often sits or stands on a raised platform, allowing a clear sight of the pupils' activities. Children are usually supposed to look alert more or less continually, or otherwise to be absorbed in their work. Of course, whether this actually happens in practice depends upon the capabilities of the teacher and the inclinations of the children to conform to what is expected of them.

The second type, more subtle, but equally important, consists of keeping files, records, and case-histories of employees in the organization. Weber saw the importance of written records (nowadays often computerized) in modern organizations, but did not fully consider how they are used to regulate behavior.

Employee records usually provide complete work histories, register personal details, and often give character assessments. Such records are used to monitor employees' behavior and for recommendations for promotion. In many business firms, individuals at each grade in the organization prepare annual reports on the performance of those in the grades just below them. School records and college grade transcripts are other examples of case-history records used to monitor individuals' performance as they make their way through the organization. A further illustration is given by the references that are kept on file about academic personnel.

Of course, people do not always passively accept the surveillance to which they are subject. They find all sorts of ways to create "free space" and "free time" for themselves, out of sight of supervisors. People may get to look at their records even though they are not supposed to do so, and discover means of encouraging or pressuring their superiors to write good reports about them. The creation of "back regions," away from supervisory control, is one main method used to combat over-strict supervision (see Chapter 4: "Social Interaction and Everyday Life"). Middle-level supervisors often connive in this, because they want to keep the trust of the workers, but have to be seen to be "doing a good job" when they themselves are inspected by superiors. Thus an early sociological study of a shipyard reported:

> It was amusing to watch the sudden transformation whenever word got round that the foreman was on the hull or in the shop or that a front-office superintendent was coming by. Quartermen and leadermen would rush to their groups of workers and stir them to obvious activity. "Don't let him catch you sitting down," was the universal admonition, and where no work existed a pipe was busily bent and threaded, or a bolt which was already in place was subjected to further and unnecessary tightening. This was the formal tribute invariably attending a visitation by the boss, and its conventions were as familiar to both sides as those surrounding a five-star general's inspection. (Archibald, 1947)

Discipline

Surveillance is important in modern organizations because of their strong connection with *discipline*—the coordinated regulation of people's behavior. Organizations cannot operate effectively if what goes on in them is haphazard. In business firms, for example, as Weber pointed out, people are expected to work regular daily hours. We have come to take this more or less for granted, but in the early days of industrialization it was a long while before people could be persuaded to work for the same number of hours each day, every week. Rural work in traditional communities was irregular and seasonal. People were used to working only as long as they needed to work in order to meet their needs. The setting up of factories and separate workplaces, which made constant supervision possible, was a means of achieving the necessary labor discipline (Thompson, 1967).

Discipline is promoted both by the physical settings of organizations and by the precise scheduling provided by detailed timetables. Timetables regularize activities across time and space—in Foucault's words, they "efficiently distribute bodies" around the organization. Timetables are the condition of organizational discipline, because they "slot" the activities of large numbers of people together. If a university did not have a lecture timetable that was fairly strictly observed, for example, students wouldn't know where and when to find lecturers and several lecturers might attempt to use the same lecture hall—in short, there would be chaos. A timetable makes possible the intensive use of time and space: each can be "packed" with many people and many on-going activities.

CARCERAL ORGANIZATIONS

IN COMMON WITH ERVING GOFFMAN, FOUCAULT HAS GIVEN a great deal of attention to studying organizations in which individuals are physically separated for long periods from the outside world. In such organizations, people are *incarcerated*—kept hidden away—from the external social environment. According to Goffman, prisons, asylums, and other carceral systems differ radically from other organizations because of their "totally closed" nature (Goffman, 1961). Foucault agrees with this, but also tries to show that the study of **carceral organizations**—settings in which people are separated from the outside world and subjected to strict disciplines—can illuminate how other organizations are run.

Surveillance and discipline were pioneered in carceral settings before becoming widely applied in other types of organizations. Prisons, asylums, and barracks show up in clear detail the nature of surveillance and discipline precisely because they seek to maximize control over their inmates' behavior (Foucault, 1979).

THE DEVELOPMENT OF CARCERAL ORGANIZATIONS

Carceral organizations were rare in premodern times. Jails and dungeons sometimes existed, but they were few and far between, and were not places in which convicted criminals served fixed sentences. People were thrown in them either as a means of stifling political opposition, to be tortured in order to extract information, or to await trial. The mentally ill either lived within the community, or were forced to roam the countryside. There were no asylums or mental hospitals for the population.

Carceral institutions can be traced back to the early 1700s, although prisons and asylums only became common more than a century afterwards (Ignatieff, 1978). Both grew out of the earlier foundations of what were called "general hospitals." As the word was used at the period, "hospital" did not mean primarily a place where the sick were cared for. Rather, it signified a place of "confinement," mostly filled with vagrants, the feeble-minded, and the mentally ill. The "hospitals" were supposed to help reform their inmates, and to this end they were often places where forced labor, for very low wages, was carried on.

Mental asylums began to be built in the late eighteenth century in Europe and somewhat afterwards in the United States. Prisons in their modern form were set up at about the same period. It took some while, however, for these to become more or less completely disentangled from the older "hospitals." The prison reformer, John Howard, wrote of his visit in 1781 to a Berlin "hospital," that it was full of "idlers," "rogues and libertines," "infirm and criminals," and "destitute old women and children," all mixed together.

According to Foucault, the Panopticon—designed by Jeremy Bentham in the early nineteenth century—expressed in purest form the differences between the old "hospitals" and the new prisons. The Panopticon was the name Bentham gave to an ideal prison he designed, which he tried on various occasions to sell to the British government. The design was never fully implemented, but some of its main principles were taken up in prisons built in the nineteenth century in the United States, Britain, and several countries of continental Europe. The Panopticon was circular in shape, with the cells built around the outside edge. In the center was an inspection tower. Two windows were placed in every cell, one facing the inspection tower and the other facing the outside. The aim of the design was to make prisoners visible at all times. The windows in the tower itself were to be covered by venetian blinds, so that while the prison staff could continually keep the prisoners under observation, they themselves would be invisible.

Among other influences, the plan of the Panopticon helped spread the principle of separate cells for individuals or small numbers of prisoners. In the old houses of internment, people were much more together in very large rooms, in which they both worked and slept. The architectural design of prisons directly influenced the design of other types of organization. Some of the early factories, for example, were planned by prison architects.

Carceral organizations, of course, remain in a minority among modern organizations in general. People either spend only part of the day or week "on the site" in most organizations or they are "inmates" continuously for only short periods. Being in school or being at work occupies only a proportion of the individual's time. Many of those who go into hospital do so only for short stays. Yet there are evident similarities between carceral and noncarceral organizations, and Foucault is right to point out that the study of the former can help illuminate the latter, as well as vice versa.

To round off our discussion in this chapter, we shall switch right to the other end of the spectrum, moving from carceral institutions to organizations that are much more open in nature than any type of bureaucratic system. These are organizations formed by mutual collaboration between people, in which few of the characteristics noted in Weber's depiction of bureaucracy apply. Such examples provide one final way of considering the relations between hierarchy (or lack of it), effectiveness, and participation in organizations.

NONBUREAUCRATIC ORGANIZATIONS: SELF-HELP GROUPS

SOCIOLOGISTS SOMETIMES SEEM TO WRITE AS IF THE ONLY collectivities of any importance in modern societies are primary groups and bureaucratic organizations. This is far from the case. There have long been a variety of voluntary associations, charities, and self-help organizations existing alongside the other two types. In the early period of industrialism, for example, many forms of workers' groups of this sort were established, such as working men's clubs or workers' educational associations. (See also the discussion of another very important type of nonbureaucratic organization, *social movements,* in Chapter 19: "Revolutions and Social Movements.")

In our discussion here, we shall concentrate upon self-help organizations, which contrast most markedly with bureaucratic systems. The number and variety of self-help groups as a whole has risen substantially over the past century. Medical clinics, legal cooperatives, alcoholics anonymous, drug rehabilitation groups, the Samaritans, and hundreds of other self-help associations have come into existence (Robinson, 1979; Hatch and Kickbusch, 1983). A few have a continuous history lasting back over a hundred years or more, while others come and go with some rapidity. Some self-help groups themselves have become large, bureaucratic organizations. The original workers' self-help groups, for instance, sometimes later grew into labor unions.

The right to form self-help groups has by no means always been accepted in law. In many countries the early workers' associations met with hostile reactions from the authorities, and were sometimes actively prohibited. The right to form groups according to freely chosen interests and objectives was one that had to be fought for in most societies.

Self-help groups are made up of people who are in a similar situa-

An Alcoholics Anonymous (AA) meeting—an example of a non-bureaucratic self-help organization.

tion, and who come together to assist one another to pursue shared interests or cope with common problems. Self-help groups tend to be nonhierarchical and lack the fixed positions associated with bureaucracies. They often have a fluctuating membership. Individuals may come for one or a few meetings, then leave the group. Self-help groups are normally dependent upon money collected by members, or upon donations, rather than having fixed forms of income. If paid staff exist, they usually have low salaries compared to their counterparts in orthodox organizations. Usually some kind of moral ideal binds the members of the group to one another.

FEATURES OF SELF-HELP GROUPS

The two main characteristics of self-help groups can be designated as *sharing* and *project work* (Robinson, 1980). Sharing means the pooling of information and similar experiences. This might be either in face-to-face meetings or via other contacts. For example, in a self-help group for parents of mentally handicapped children, people contact one another through correspondence magazines. Parents participate in exchanges of letters; magazines circulate around the group continuously, so that every member receives up to a dozen letters every few weeks, although they only write one each themselves.

Self-help groups ordinarily seek to influence both their members and the attitudes of others outside. One of the aims of the group just mentioned is to educate the general population about the problems of the mentally handicapped. "Project work" usually consists of cooperative activities organized to achieve these and other goals. For example, much of the program of Alcoholics Anonymous is made up of a series of projects designed to help fellow alcoholics. When a person recounts his or her past experiences and current problems, the information is used to develop discussion and policies in the group as a whole.

Self-help groups have frequently been set up in opposition to established bureaucratic organizations. For example, some medical self-help groups have been started to permit patients to care for themselves directly, on the basis of the belief that orthodox medical settings fail to give them sufficient responsibility for their own well-being. Self-help groups *are* in some ways clearly a counter to bureaucracy. They provide spheres outside bureaucratic organizations where individuals can meet in circumstances of cooperation and equality. Yet they are always likely to exist alongside formal organizations, rather than replacing them. Self-help groups that become permanent, and grow in size, probably tend to become like other organizations. They develop specialized authority positions, have to ensure a regular income, and generally take on more of the trappings of a bureaucracy.

It seems that there are important shifts towards more flexible types of organizations in modern societies. We are not (as Weber and many others have feared) all about to become tiny cogs in a vast administrative machine that runs our lives. Bureaucratic systems are more internally fluid than Weber believed, and their dominance is constantly challenged by less hierarchical types of groups and associations. Yet it is wishful thinking to suppose, as some have, that large impersonal organizations will progressively disappear and be replaced by more decentralized, loosely structured agencies (Toffler, 1984). Rather, there is likely to be a continuing "push and pull" between tendencies towards large size, impersonality, and hierarchy in organizations on the one hand and opposing influences on the other.

SUMMARY

1. A *social group* is a number of people who regularly interact with each other. This regularity encourages familiarity, solidarity, and shared habits. *Aggregates* are collections of people, such as at a bus stop, without a common sense of identity. A *social category* is a statistical grouping—people classified together on the basis of a particular characteristic they share.

2. All modern organizations are in some degree bureaucratic in nature. *Bureaucracy* is characterized by a clearly defined hierarchy of authority; written rules governing the conduct of *officials* (who work full time for a salary); and a separation between the tasks of the official within the organization and life outside it. Members of the organization do not own the material resources with which they operate. Max Weber argued that modern bureaucracy is a highly effective means of organizing large numbers of people, ensuring that decisions are made according to general criteria.

3. Informal networks tend to develop at all levels both within and between organizations. The study of these informal ties is as important as the more formal characteristics upon which Weber concentrated his attention.

4. The work of Weber and Michels identifies a tension between bureaucracy and democracy. On the one hand, there are long-term processes of the centralization of decision making associated with the development of modern societies. On the other hand, one of the main features of the past two centuries has been expanding pressures towards democracy. The trends conflict, with neither one in a position of dominance.

5. Japanese corporations differ significantly from most Western companies in terms of their characteristics as organizations. There is more consultation of lower-level workers by managerial executives, pay and responsibility are linked to seniority, and groups, rather than individuals, are evaluated for their performance. Some Western firms have adopted aspects of Japanese management systems in recent years, although it is by no means proven that these explain why Japan's economic performance has outstripped that of most Western countries.

6. All modern organizations depend upon the specialization of knowledge and the transmitting of information. *Professionalization,* together with the increasing use of *information technology,* may be leading to a general increase in the flexibility of organizations. The impact of these changes—thus far, at any rate, has often been exaggerated.

7. The physical settings of organizations strongly influence their social features. The architecture of modern organizations is closely connected to surveillance as a means of securing obedience to those in authority. *Surveillance* refers to the supervision of people's activities, as well as to the keeping of files and records about them.

8. Carceral organizations are those in which individuals spend virtually the whole of their time, separated from the outside world. The main types of carceral organization are prisons and mental hospitals. Carceral organizations maximize discipline and supervision, but these are to some degree characteristic of all organizations.

9. Self-help groups (and voluntary associations of various types) contrast with bureaucratic organizations, tending to be non-hierarchical and participatory. Large numbers of self-help groups are found in most modern societies. They exist alongside, and sometimes in a tense relationship with, larger, more bureaucratic systems. Some grow to become bureaucratic.

BASIC CONCEPTS

SOCIAL GROUP
ORGANIZATION
FORMAL RELATIONS
INFORMAL RELATIONS

IMPORTANT TERMS

AGGREGATE   OLIGARCHY
SOCIAL CATEGORY   DEMOCRACY
PRIMARY GROUP   KIBBUTZIM
SECONDARY GROUP   PROFESSIONALS
BUREAUCRACY   INFORMATION TECHNOLOGY
IDEAL TYPE   SURVEILLANCE
OFFICIALS   CARCERAL ORGANIZATION

POLITICS, GOVERNMENT, AND THE STATE

◼

AS WAS POINTED OUT IN THE PREVIOUS CHAPTER, THE STATE impinges on many aspects of our lives today. Yet for the greater part of human history, distinct political institutions did not exist at all. In hunting and gathering communities, and in small agrarian cultures, there were no separate political authorities. But such **stateless societies** did not lapse into chaos, for there were informal ways by which decisions affecting the community were channelled and disputes managed. Decisions were made within the family group; should several groups of kin living within one band fundamentally disagree, they split off into separate units, subsequently perhaps recombining with others (see Chapter 2: "Culture and Society").

Other small cultures had an element of political centralization, without becoming fully-fledged states. In these societies, there was a chief to whom the rest of the population owed allegiance. Chiefs were themselves either warriors or priests, or both, and sometimes had the right to call upon armed retainers to back up whatever decisions they made. The chief usually ruled with the assistance of a council or court. In **state societies** (traditional civilizations), these rulers became kings or emperors, had elaborate courts and households, and controlled armed forces used to ensure obedience and extend the scope of their dominion. They had full-time officials who dealt with regular issues of administration, together with specialized courts within which trials were organized and criminals punished.

In trying to understand political systems, traditional and modern, we have to make full use of the sociological imagination (see Chapter 1: "Sociology: Problems and Perspectives"). Why do modern states —like the United States, Soviet Union, Britain, or France—differ so much from the types of political order found in traditional civilizations? What accounts for the fact that virtually all countries in the world today regard themselves as democratic? What are the conditions and limits of democratic participation in government? We can only answer such questions by looking at a broad sweep of comparative evidence, and by being aware of the variety of political systems under which people had lived previously and which exist today.

In this chapter, we shall concentrate upon identifying the distinctive characteristics of modern states, placing particular emphasis upon exploring the nature of democracy. All states in the world today, without exception, are "nation-states"—a concept that we shall explain in some detail. Nation-states are as specific to the modern era as any of the other social phenomena that have become central to our lives over the past two centuries—such as industrialization and urbanism. Having looked at the connections between the nation-state and democracy—connections which make clear the basic importance of citizenship—we shall analyze different forms of party systems, voting processes, and movements of political opposition. From there we move on to consider which groups hold most political power in modern societies, contrasting the political systems of the United States and the Soviet Union.

Let us first of all make clear the concept of "the state," and other important notions connected with it.

THE CONCEPT OF THE STATE

ALL STATES,[*] TRADITIONAL AND MODERN, SHARE SOME GENeral characteristics. A **state** exists where there is a **political apparatus** (governmental institutions like a court, parliament, or congress, plus civil-service officials), ruling over a given *territory,* whose authority is backed by a *legal system* and by the

---

[*] As used in this chapter, "state" refers to the national political community—the nation-state. The "states" within the Union should be seen as forms of regional government within the "U.S. state" as a whole.

The range of political activity is great. From a legislative meeting of the House of Chiefs in Nigeria to a television network's coverage of a U.S. presidential election or two individual protesters getting ready to lobby politicians, politics takes many shapes.

capability to use *force* to implement its policies. To get a clear understanding of the nature of the state, consider each of these characteristics.

THE POLITICAL APPARATUS

Government refers to the regular enactment of policies and decisions on the part of the officials within a political apparatus. These officials include kings or emperors and their courts, presidents and prime ministers, elected representatives, and members of the civil service. We can speak of "government" as a process, or "the government" to refer to the apparatus responsible for the administrative process. **Politics** concerns the means whereby power is used to affect the scope and content of governmental activities. It includes, therefore, voting in local and national elections, the actions of political leaders, the influence of newspapers and TV, and much more besides. The sphere of the "political" may therefore range well beyond that of state institutions themselves, for there may be many ways in which those who are not part of the governmental apparatus seek to influence it. In modern societies, for instance, social movements operating outside accepted political channels may try to exert pressure upon a government or, in extreme circumstances, even overthrow it. The civil rights movement was such a force challenging American politics in the 1960s and 1970s by calling for reform (see Chapter 8: "Ethnicity and Race").

TERRITORY

Hunting and gathering societies had no fixed territories, but moved around over large areas of land pursuing their livelihood. Small agrarian communities were more fixed in one spot, but usually they had no boundaries separating them from other groups. But with the rise of states came the establishment of specific territories over which political authorities claimed rule. In contrast to preceding types of society, states have consistently been expansionist. Where rulers have seen an opportunity to acquire more territory—and thus expand the scope of their dominion—they normally have taken advantage of it. From the empires of ancient Assyria and Rome to the massive colonization of the Americas, Africa, and the Far East by England, France, Spain, and Portugal many centuries later, rulers have looked well beyond their own shores. At present, however, the boundaries between states are fixed by international agreement, and the aggressive acquisition of new territories is much less an option than it once was.

LAW AND THE USE OF FORCE

A legal system exists where there are codes of law and individuals who specialize in the administration of justice. In smaller societies, conflicts were resolved by a meeting of the whole community, or by the actions of kinship units. There was no group that held prime responsibility for using **force**—physical compulsion, violence, or the threat of violence to achieve an aim—to back up communal decisions. Sometimes a family or kinship group would take matters into its own hands, initiating a "blood feud." With the development of states, however, there emerged a specialized judicial system—codified laws and law courts—backed by the capability to enforce them. In traditional states there were usually no clear distinctions between the army and internal police forces; the military were used to back up juridical decision making.

MODERN STATES

ALL MODERN STATES, LIKE THE UNITED STATES FOR INstance, are nation-states. **Nation-states** incorporate each of the characteristics mentioned above along with a few more that distinguishes them from traditional states.

1. SOVEREIGNTY. The territories ruled by traditional states were always rather ill-defined in character, the level of control wielded by the central government being quite weak. The notion of **sovereignty**—that a government has authority over clearly defined borders, within which it is the supreme power—had little relevance to traditional states. All nation-states, by contrast, are sovereign states. Thus the United States has distinct boundaries that separate it from Canada and Mexico and, in the case of Alaska, from Canada and the Soviet Union.

2. CITIZENSHIP. In traditional states, most of the population ruled by the king or emperor had little awareness of, or interest in, who governed them. Normally only the dominant classes, or more affluent, cosmopolitan groups felt a sense of belonging to an overall national community. In nation-states, by contrast, most of those living within the borders of the political system are **citizens,** having common rights and duties, and knowing themselves to be part of a nation. While there are some people who are political refugees and "stateless," almost everyone in the modern world today is identified as a member of a definite national political order. The United States is an immigrant society, and all immigrants are keenly aware of the importance of achieving full American citizenship when they have foregone, or been denied, it elsewhere.

3. NATIONALISM. Nation-states are associated with the rise of **nationalism** (Smith, 1979; Breuilly, 1982; Gellner, 1983). Nationalism can be defined as the sense of being part of a single political community, often expressed through the use of symbols and ideology. Thus, individuals feel a sense of pride and belonging in being American, Canadian, or Japanese. Probably people have always felt some kind of identity with social groups of one form or another—for example, their family, clan, or religious community. Nationalism, however, only made its appearance with the development of the modern state.

Nationalistic loyalties do not necessarily always fit the borders demarcating the territories of states in the world today. Virtually all nation-states were built from communities of diverse backgrounds. "Local nationalisms" have frequently arisen in opposition to the dominant nationality of a state. In Canada, nationalist feelings among the French-speaking minority population in Quebec remain strong. Nationalist sentiments have also recently emerged in several parts of the Soviet Union, such as Lithuania, Latvia, and Georgia.

In the light of these considerations, we can now offer a comprehensive definition of the concept of nation-state. A nation-state refers to a political apparatus, recognized to have sovereign rights within the borders of a demarcated territorial area, able to back its claims to sovereignty by control of military power, many of whose citizens have positive feelings of commitment towards its national identity.

CITIZENSHIP RIGHTS

Most nation-states became centralized and effective political systems through the activities of monarchs who successfully concentrated more and more power in their own hands. Citizenship did not originally carry rights of political participation in these states. These rights were achieved largely through struggles that limited the power of monarchs, as in Britain, or actively overthrew them—sometimes by a process of revolution, as in the case of the United States in 1776 and France in 1789.

Three types of rights are associated with the growth of citizenship (Marshall, 1973). **Civil rights** refer to the rights of the individual in law. These include prerogatives many of us take for granted today, but which took a long while to achieve, and which are by no means fully recognized in all countries even now. Civil rights include the freedom of individuals to live where they choose; the freedoms of speech and religion; the right to own property; and the right to equal justice before the law. These rights were not fully established in most European countries until the early nineteenth century, and even where they were achieved, some groups were omitted. Although the U.S. Constitution granted such rights to Americans well before most of the European nations, women and blacks were excluded. Even after the Civil War, when blacks were formally given these rights, they were not able to make them effective in reality.

The second type of citizenship rights is **political rights,** especially the right to participate in elections and to run for public office. Again, these were not won easily or quickly. Universal voting rights are relatively recent in most countries, and had to be struggled for against reluctant governments. In most European countries, the vote was at first limited to male citizens owning a certain amount of property—effectively limiting voting rights to an affluent minority. Not only women, but the majority of the male population was therefore without the vote. Property ownership qualifications were eliminated and most men had obtained the vote by the early years of the present century. Women had to wait longer (until after the Second World War in some countries). In most Western societies, women achieved the right to vote partly as a result of the struggles of women's movements in the nineteenth and early twentieth century, and partly as a consequence of the mobilization of women into the economy during the First World War (see Chapter 6: "Gender and Sexuality").

While citizens in Europe were winning civil and political rights in the eighteenth and nineteenth centuries, colonized peoples were excluded from full citizenship of the parent states of the colonial regimes (and normally within the colonial states themselves). Those who were not enslaved were regarded by white administrators as too "primitive" to be allowed to participate in government and in very few if any areas were they treated as equal to the white settler communities. The majority of the populations in colonial states only acquired legal and political rights with the disappearance of colonialism in the twentieth century.

The third type of citizenship rights is **social rights,** the prerogative of every individual to enjoy a certain minimum standard of living and economic security. These include such rights as health-care benefits, social security in case of unemployment, and a minimum wage. Social rights, in other words, involve *welfare provisions.* Although in some countries, such as nineteenth-century Germany, var-

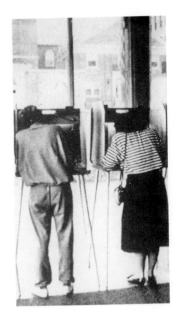

Voting—one expression of political rights.

ious kinds of welfare benefits were introduced before legal and political rights were fully established, in most societies social rights have been the last to develop. This is because the achievement of civil, and particularly political, rights have usually been the basis upon which social rights have been fought for.

The Welfare State

The broadening of social rights is the basis for what has come to be called the **welfare state,** which has become firmly established in the Western societies only since World War II, although its origins go back much earlier. A welfare state exists where government organizations provide material benefits for those who are unable to support themselves adequately through paid employment—the unemployed, sick, disabled, and the elderly. Elements of a welfare state in the United States date back to the 1930s, when President Franklin D. Roosevelt established federal programs known as the New Deal (Ashford, 1988). All Western countries today have extensive welfare provisions, although the United States has less extensive programs than most. On the other hand, in many of the poorer countries of the world these benefits are virtually nonexistent.

There are several major differences between U.S. welfare policy and that of most European countries. First, in many of the European countries, programs of health, housing provision, and child or family allowances are highly coordinated and relatively well-funded. These systems in the United States are much more of a patchwork and are poorly integrated with one another. Second, many more welfare provisions in Europe are universal—they are open to everyone, rather than being available only to the very poor. Third, European governments quite often intervene more directly in the economy, so as to influence the distribution of benefits. For instance, in Sweden, public resources have been used to keep the unemployment rate low (Rodgers, 1986).

DEMOCRACY

CITIZENSHIP AND DEMOCRACY ARE INTRINSICALLY CONnected for political citizenship rights are the very essence of modern democracy. A society where there are no civil and political rights is the opposite of democracy—a tyranny. Without the political participation of citizens, democracy is, by definition,

Democracy in the United States takes the form of a representative multiparty system. Shown here is the seat of much of this representative activity—the U.S. Capitol with the 100-member Senate chamber on the left and the 435-member House of Representatives on the right.

impossible. In all democratic systems today, moreover, there is at least some recognition of the necessity of according social rights to the population.

The word "democracy" has its roots in the Greek term *dēmokratia,* the parts of which are *dēmos* (people) and *kratos* (to rule). The basic meaning of democracy is therefore a political system in which the people, not monarchs (kings or queens), or aristocracies (people of noble birth, like dukes, lords, or counts), rule. This sounds simple and straightforward, but as David Held (1987) has pointed out, questions can be raised about each part of the phrase: "Rule," "rule by," and "the people." If we start with "the people":

1. Who are "the people"?

2. What kind of participation is envisaged for them?

3. What conditions are assumed to be conducive to participation?

As regards "rule":

1. How broadly or narrowly should the scope of rule be?

2. Should rule be confined, for example, to the sphere of government, or can there be democracy in other spheres—such as popular control over factories and workplaces (industrial democracy)?

3. Can rule cover the daily administrative decisions that governments must make, or should it refer only to major policy decisions?

In the case of "rule by":

1. Must the rule of "the people" be obeyed? What is the place of dissent?

2. Are there circumstances in which some of "the people" should act outside the law, if they believe existing laws to be unjust?

3. Under what conditions, if any, should democratic governments use coercion against those who happen to disagree with their policies?

Answers to these questions have taken contrasting forms, both at varying periods and in different nation-states. For example, "the people" has been variously understood to be owners of property, white men, educated men, men, and all adults. In some societies, the officially accepted version of democracy is limited to the political sphere, whereas in others it is held to extend to other areas of social life. Let us therefore look at the main types of democratic systems.

TYPES OF DEMOCRACY

The three main types of democracy are representative multiparty democracy, representative one-party democracy, and participatory democracy (this third type is sometimes called *direct democracy*). Representative democracy means that decisions affecting a community are made by people elected for this purpose, not by its members as a whole. Versions of representative democracy exist in many organizations. For instance, a sports club may be run by a council elected from among the club's members. In the area of government, representative democracy takes the form of elections to congresses, parliaments, or similar national bodies. Representative democracy also exists at other levels where collective decisions are made. Provinces or states within an overall national community, cities, counties, boroughs, and other regions, all often have their own councils.

Representative Multiparty Systems

Representative multiparty democracy is found at any or all of these levels of government when voters have at least two parties to choose from in the political process. Systems of multiparty representative democracy, in which the mass of the adult population has the right to vote at all the various levels, are usually called **liberal democracies.** The United States, the European countries, Japan, Australia, and New Zealand all fall into this category. A certain number of Third World countries, such as India, also have liberal democratic systems.

Representative One-Party Systems

When people living in the West use the term "democracy" without qualification, they are usually referring to liberal democratic systems. Yet states in which there is effectively only one party (such as China, Cuba, and until very recently, the Soviet Union and most of the states in Eastern Europe) also regard themselves as democracies. In these countries, while voters do not have a choice between different parties, there are elections to select representatives at the various local and national levels. Sometimes the only "choice" voters have is whether or not to cast their vote for a sole candidate nominated by the ruling party. In other one-party states, there may be two or more candidates for a given position, but the voter is choosing between individual representatives of the same party, rather than between candidates from separate parties as in the West.

The usual principle underlying such **representative one-party democracies** is that the single party expresses the overall will of the community. According to Marxist thinkers, the parties in liberal democracies represent divisive class interests. In socialist societies, which have supposedly eliminated antagonistic classes, there is presumed to be a need only for one party. Voters choose, therefore, not between parties, but between different candidates, proposing different policy programs. Most one-party democracies are organized in terms of **democratic centralism**—a pyramid structure in which each level elects representatives to a council, which, in turn, elects representatives to the body above it, and so forth. In the system that existed in the Soviet Union until 1990 there was a pyramid of councils, or "soviets," descending from the Supreme Soviet to those at the local village and neighborhood grass roots. At each level there were executive committees, all members of which were elected. There was a separate, but somewhat similar, system that operated at the various levels of the Communist Party. There were also complex connections between the Party and levels of union representation in industry, which were supposed to render the economic sphere democratic (Hill, 1985).

How far one-party systems are genuinely democratic, that is, offer real opportunities for political influence for members of the population is, of course, debatable. We shall discuss this question further below, in relation to a wider assessment of the nature and possibilities of democratic systems.

Participatory Democracy

In **participatory democracy** (or direct democracy), decisions are made communally by those affected by them. This was the "original" type of democracy found in the cities of ancient Greece. Those who were citizens, a small minority, regularly assembled together to consider policies and make major decisions. Direct democracy is of limited importance in modern societies where the majority of the population have political rights. It would be impossible for everyone in a large-scale society to actively participate in making all the decisions that affect them. It is inconceivable that the voters in the United States could directly run the federal government in Washington. Yet there are dimensions of direct democracy that do have relevance to modern societies; and there are many organizations within such societies in which direct democracy is practiced. Many U.S. cities, counties, and states hold referenda on specific issues, which allow voters directly to enact legislation or even constitutional amendments.

THE UNIVERSAL APPEAL OF DEMOCRACY AND THE DECLINE OF MONARCHIES

While some modern states (such as Britain or Belgium) still have monarchs, these are now rare. There are a tiny number of countries, such as Saudi Arabia and Jordan, where monarchs continue to hold some degree of control over the reins of government. But in most cases where monarchies continue to exist, they are symbols of national identity rather than having any direct control over political life. The queen of England, the king of Sweden, and even the emperor of Japan, are all **constitutional monarchs**—the amount of real power they have is severely restricted by a constitution, which vests authority in the elected representatives of the people. In almost every modern state, including constitutional monarchies, there is a professed adherence to democracy.

Even in countries subject to military rule, elections may be held and a certain façade of democratic politics adhered to. Most military rulers profess allegiance to democratic principles and claim that their rule is a means of achieving stability until there can be a return to

The universal appeal of democracy became even more evident in 1989 and 1990. Here, thousands of pro-democracy demonstrators march through Moscow streets.

some form of representational democracy (see Chapter 11: "War and the Military").

Why has democracy become a near-universal feature of modern states? The answer is no doubt partly to be found in the intrinsic attractiveness of democratic ideals, which promise an escape from subjection to arbitrary power. But a fundamental factor is the integrated character of nation-states compared to traditional civilizations (discussed in Chapter 2: "Culture and Society"). Those who rule in modern states cannot do so unless they secure the active compliance of the majority of the population. Democratic ideals represent a way of expressing, as well as securing, that compliance. Thus although individual dictators may sometimes achieve power through the use of force, they cannot rule effectively unless they enjoy widespread personal popularity. Like military rule, this form of government tends to be unstable and even reverts to a more representative system.

Professed democratic ideals, as was mentioned earlier, do not necessarily correspond to reality. The fact that appeals to democracy are so consistently made by ruling authorities today shows little about how democratic they are in practice. Few would accept, for example, that the former one-party systems of Eastern Europe offered much in the way of real political choice to the population. On the other hand, it is not easy to assess how much influence voters have in multiparty systems. Theorists of democracy disagree, in fact, about the potentialities and limitations of possible forms of democratic involvement in modern societies. We will now go on to examine some of the main theories of democracy: democratic elitism and pluralist theories.

DEMOCRATIC ELITISM

One of the most influential views of the nature and limits of modern democracy was set out by Max Weber and, in rather modified form, by the economist Joseph Schumpeter (1983; orig. pub. 1942). The ideas they developed are sometimes referred to as the theory of **democratic elitism.**

Max Weber's View

Weber began from the assumption that direct democracy is impossible as a means of regular government in large-scale societies. This is not only for the obvious logistical reason that millions of people cannot meet to make political decisions, but because running a complex society demands *expertise.* Participatory democracy can only work, Weber believed, in small organizations in which the work to be carried out is fairly simple and straightforward. Where more complicated decisions have to be made, or policies worked out, even in modest-sized groups—like a small business firm—specialized knowledge and skills are necessary. Experts have to carry out their jobs on a continuous basis; positions that require expertise cannot be subject to the regular election of people who may only have a vague knowledge of the necessary skills and information. While higher officials, responsible for overall policy decisions, are elected, there must be a large substratum of full-time bureaucratic officials who play a large part in running a country (Weber, 1979).

In Weber's view, the development of mass citizenship, which is so closely connected with the idea of general democratic participation, greatly expands the need for bureaucratic officialdom. For example, provision for welfare, health, and education demands permanent large-scale administrative systems. As Weber expresses this, "It is obvious that technically the large modern state is absolutely dependent upon a bureaucratic basis. The larger the state, and the more it is a great power, the more unconditionally this is the case . . ." (Weber, 1979).

Representative multiparty democracy, according to Weber, helps defend against both arbitrary decision making on the part of political leaders, because they are subject to popular elections, and against power being completely usurped by bureaucrats, because elected official set overall policy. But under these circumstances the contribution of democratic institutions is less than many advocates of a more pure democracy would hope. "Rule by the people" is possible in only a very limited sense. In order to achieve power, political parties themselves must become organized in a systematic way. In short, they, too, must become bureaucratized. "Party machines" develop, which threaten the autonomy of parliaments or congresses as places in which policies are discussed and formulated. If a party with a majority representation is able to dictate policy, and if that party is itself mainly run by officials who are permanently in control, the level of democracy that has been achieved is slim indeed.

In order for democratic systems to have some degree of effectiveness, Weber argues, two conditions have to be met. First, there must be parties that represent different interests and have different outlooks. If the policies of competing parties are more or less the same, voters are denied any effective choice. Weber rejects the idea that one-party systems can be democratic in any meaningful way. Second, there must be political leaders who have the imagination and courage necessary to escape the inertia of bureaucracy. Weber places a great deal of emphasis upon the importance of *leadership* in democracy— which is why his view is referred to as "democratic elitism." He argues that rule by elites is inevitable; the best we can hope for is that those elites effectively represent our interests and that they do so in an innovative and insightful fashion. Parliaments and congresses provide a breeding ground for capable political leaders able to counter the influence of bureaucracy and to command mass support. Weber valued multiparty democracy more for the quality of leadership it generates than for the mass participation in politics it makes possible.

Joseph Schumpeter—Democratic Elitism Modified

Joseph Schumpeter fully agreed with Weber about the limits of mass political participation. For Schumpeter, as for Weber, democracy is more important as a method of generating effective and responsible government than as a means of providing significant power for the majority. Democracy cannot offer more than the possibility of replacing a given political leader or party by another. Democracy, Schumpeter stated, is the rule of *the politician,* not *the people*. Politicians are "dealers in votes" much as brokers are dealers in shares on the stock exchange. To achieve voting support, however, politicians must be at least minimally responsive to the demands and interests of the electorate. Only if there is some degree of competition to secure votes can arbitrary rule effectively be avoided.

PLURALIST THEORIES

The ideas of Weber and Schumpeter influenced some of the **pluralist theorists** of modern democracy, although the pluralists developed their ideas somewhat differently. Pluralists accept that individual citizens can have little or no *direct* influence on political decision making. But they argue that tendencies towards the centralization of

A more cynical view of interest-group politics.

power in the hands of government officials are limited by the presence of **interest groups.** Competing interest groups or factions are vital to democracy because they divide up power, reducing the exclusive influence of any one group or class (Truman, 1981).

According to the pluralist view, government policies in a democracy are influenced by continual processes of bargaining among numerous groups representing different interests—business organizations, trade unions, ethnic groups, environmental organizations, religious groups, and so forth. A democratic political order is one in which there is a balance among competing interests, all having some impact on policy but none dominating the actual mechanisms of government. Elections are influenced by this situation also, for to achieve a broad enough base of support to lay claim to government, parties must be responsive to numerous diverse interest groups. The United States, it is held, is the most pluralistic of industrialized societies and, therefore, the most democratic. Competition between diverse interest groups occurs not only at the national level but within the states and in the politics of local communities.

EVALUATION OF THE THEORIES

Democratic elitism and pluralist theories alike have met with considerable criticism (Held, 1987). Several different criticisms have been made against the democratic elitist view. First, critics have pointed out, the mass of the electorate is portrayed as passive and unenlightened, without evidence being given to show that this is so. Second, the only choice seen by Weber and Schumpeter is between creatively led elites and unresponsive bureaucratic rule, yet there are wide variations between types of bureaucracy, some being more open and responsive to public interests and needs than others. Moreover, requirements of expertise can often be fulfilled by professionals, rather than bureaucratic officials. Third, there might be possibilities for introducing cooperative enterprises and "open" forms of association in both the political and economic spheres, which would reduce bureaucratic tendencies. Fourth, if the pluralist view is right, a significant measure of political involvement is made possible by interest groups, which represent the concerns of broad segments of the population.

Yet pluralist theories have also been strongly criticized. The interest groups referred to by pluralists, critics point out, are not equal in their power. Business organizations particularly often have far greater sway over government policies than other interest groups. It is misleading in any case, they continue, to see the influence of business as being expressed through specific interest groups, because it is business enterprise that supplies the overall *framework* in which political processes occur and decisions are made (Lindblom, 1977; Mintz and Schwartz, 1985). In other words, it is taken for granted by almost everyone that business activity must be generally fostered and kept profitable, because it generates the wealth upon which government revenues depend.

These criticisms all have some validity; but it is impossible to deny the validity of some of the arguments developed both by democratic elitism and pluralism. Elements of the two can be combined to give a fuller picture of democratic institutions. In modern societies, groups with many different interests cannot get recognition unless they can organize to make their views known. Competition among such groups can in principle serve to produce something of a "balance": the strongest do not simply impose their views on others, while minorities can get their interests represented (Bobbio, 1987).

Moreover, Weber and Schumpeter were right to raise the question of expertise. The mass of the electorate lack the time and training to master the intricacies of the decisions that governments constantly have to make. Civil-service officials and elected members of representative bodies have the time to acquire specialist knowledge of issues. While experts need to be constrained by the views of those affected by policies they formulate, they can make decisions on an informed basis. Where their activities are overseen by elected representatives, these decisions can be made responsive to broad social interests and pressures.

We cannot analyze such issues solely on an abstract level, of course; we have to look at the operation of actual political systems. This is the task to which we now turn, beginning with the nature of political parties.

POLITICAL PARTIES AND VOTING IN WESTERN COUNTRIES

A POLITICAL PARTY IS AN ORGANIZATION OF INDIVIDUALS, with broadly similar political aims, oriented towards achieving legitimate control of government through an electoral process. In some situations, there may be political organizations that seek to achieve power but are denied the legal status or economic means to do so. Such organizations are best regarded as political sects or movements, until they achieve legal recognition. In the early 1980s in Poland, for example, the Solidarity Party, a strong labor-oriented, non-communist movement, was outlawed by the communist leadership. They were an organized political force, operating outside orthodox channels. But by August, 1989, they not only had achieved recognition as a party, they had actually also gained a dominant position in the government.

PARTY SYSTEMS

There are many types of party systems within the overall category of multiparty democracies. Whether a two-party system, or one involving more parties, flourishes depends in large part upon the nature of electoral procedures in a given country. Two parties tend to dominate the political system where elections are based on the principle of winner-take-all, as in the United States. The candidate who gains the most votes wins the election, no matter what proportion of the overall vote he or she gains (Duverger, 1954). Where elections are based on different principles, such as proportional representation (in which seats in a representative assembly are allocated according to the proportions of the vote attained), five or six different parties, or even more, may be represented in the assembly. To form a government, where they lack an overall majority, some of the parties have to form a coalition—an alliance with one another.

In the United States, the system has become effectively a two-party one between the Republicans and Democrats, although no formal restriction is placed upon the number of parties. The nation's founders made no mention of parties in the Constitution because they thought that party conflict might threaten the unity of the new republic. The same is true of constitutional arrangements in many European countries; parties have therefore developed as a means of representing interests alongside formal political frameworks.

In the Western European countries there are many types of party organization not found in American politics. Some parties are based upon religious denominations (like the Social Christian Party or the Catholic People's Party in Belgium); some are ethnic parties, representing specific nationalist or linguistic groups (such as the Scottish National Party in Britain or the Swedish People's Party in Finland); others are rural parties, representing agrarian interests (for example, the Center Party in Sweden or the People's Party in Switzerland); yet others are environmental parties, concerned with ecological objectives (such as the "Greens" in West Germany, who have achieved representation in parliament). There are also numerous parties representing different shades of political opinion (Kesselman et al., 1987).

The largest parties are those associated with general political interests—socialist, communist, liberal, or conservative parties. Socialist or labor parties have formed governments at some time in most West European societies, mainly since the Second World War. There are officially recognized communist parties in virtually all Western countries, some of which are fairly large (such as those in Italy, France, and Spain). There are many conservative parties (like the Parti Republican in France or the Conservative and Unionist Party in Britain), and "centrist" parties that occupy the middle ground between Left and Right (such as the Social and Liberal Democrats in Britain). (The term *Left* is used to refer to radical or progressive political groups who lean towards socialism; *Right* refers to more conservative groups.)

In some countries, the leader of the majority party in the representative body—for example, Great Britain's House of Commons—or of one of the parties in a coalition, automatically becomes prime minister, the highest public official in the land. In other cases (like the United States) a president is elected separately from the party elections to the main representative bodies. (In 1988, Americans voted in a Republican president, George Bush, but a Democratic House and Senate.) Hardly any of the electoral systems in Western countries are exactly the same as one another, and most are more complicated than that of the United States.

Two-party systems, like that of the United States, Britain, or Australia on the national level tend to lead to a concentration upon the "middle ground," where most votes are to be found, excluding more radical views. The parties in these countries often cultivate a moderate image, and sometimes come to resemble one another so closely that the choice they offer is relatively slight. A plurality of interests may supposedly be represented by each party, but can become blended into a bland program with few distinctive policies. Multiparty systems allow divergent interests and points of view to be expressed more directly, and provide scope for the representation of radical alternatives. Green Party representatives or representatives of Far Right parties, found in some European parliaments, are cases in point. On the other hand, no one party is likely to achieve an overall majority, and the government by coalition that results can lead to indecision and stalemate, if compromises can't be worked out, or to a rapid succession of elections and new governments, none able to stay in power for long.

Some writers have studied the connection between voting patterns and class differences: liberal and leftist parties tend to gain most of their votes from those in lower-class groups, while conservative or rightist parties are more strongly supported by affluent groups. The party system in the United States is quite distinct from that of virtually all other Western societies, since there is no large leftist party. Class-based voting is less pronounced than in other Western democracies. While the Democratic Party has tended to appeal more to lower-class groups, and the Republicans have drawn support from the more affluent sectors of the population, the connections are far from absolute. Each party has a conservative and a liberal wing; it is relatively common for conservative and liberal members of one party to align themselves with those holding parallel opinions in the other party on particular issues.

POLITICS AND VOTING IN THE UNITED STATES

The founders of the American governmental system did not foresee a role for parties in the political order. George Washington recognized that interest groups would develop, but spoke out forcefully against "the harmful effects of the spirit of party." Thomas Jefferson echoed these sentiments, but in fact became the leader of one of the earliest party organizations, the Republicans—who were subsequently called the Democratic-Republicans, and in 1831, the Democrats. Policy disputes arose between Jefferson and Alexander Hamilton during Washington's administration. Each had a group of followers: Hamilton's faction was called the Federalists. Jefferson's Republicans were the first to endorse candidates for Congress, leading the Federalists to do likewise. The national division of parties later spread to the state legislatures, and the parties soon developed into state organizations representing specific interests and points of view. A two-party system was well established by the 1830s, and although the parties themselves underwent subsequent changes, the fundamental nature of that system has not altered greatly to this day.

Building mass support for a party in the United States is difficult, because the country is so large and includes so many different regional, cultural, and ethnic groups. The parties have each tried to develop their electoral strength by forging broad regional bases of support and by campaigning for very general political ideals. The Republican Party became a major force at the time of the Civil War, and until the 1890s had roughly equal strength to the Democrats. There followed a period in which the Republicans had the edge in voting support. From the early 1930s to the 1960s, however, the Democrats achieved majority-party status, on the basis of President Franklin Roosevelt's New Deal coalition, which brought together southerners, northern industrial workers, ethnic minorities, and big-city poor. During the 1970s and 1980s, support has again swung towards the Republicans, particularly in the presidential elections. The Republicans have been victorious in five of the last six presidential elections, covering the period from 1972 to 1989—and most of these wins have been landslides. One clear swing in political support has occurred over this period: white southerners have moved increasingly toward the Republican party.

DECLINING PARTY SUPPORT

As measured by their levels of membership, party identification, and voting support, each of the major American parties is in decline (McKay, 1985). A study carried out covering the years 1952 to 1980 showed that the numbers declaring themselves to be "independent" of either party grew from 22 percent in 1952 to over 30 percent in 1980 (Lipset, 1981). Only some 2 percent of the adult population are active members of party organizations, nearly all of which are locally based. Most activists over the past few years have become increasingly concerned with supporting particular candidates and mobilizing support over specific issues, which has weakened party organizations even further.

Some of the changes that broke up earlier coalitions within the parties can be traced to the election of 1964. Barry Goldwater's candidacy brought about a presidential election based more clearly upon ideological differences than was usually the case. While some conservative Democratic states of the South deserted the Democrats for the conservative Republican Goldwater, many more traditional Republican voters, more liberal in outlook, turned out to support Texas Democrat Lyndon Johnson, who won by a handsome margin. The Southern states have continued to drift away from the Democrats, while Republican defectors in the 1964 election returned to the party. Since that time patterns of party support and presidential voting have been more unstable than previously.

TABLE 10.1   PARTY IDENTIFICATION IN 1988, BY SOCIOECONOMIC POSITION (IN PERCENTAGES)

	Democrat	Republican	Independent
EDUCATION			
Less than high school	50%	20%	30%
High school graduate	37	29	34
Some college	35	32	33
College graduate	30	35	34
INCOME			
Less than $15,000	48	22	31
$15,000–24,999	37	33	31
$25,000–34,999	35	30	35
$35,000–49,999	35	29	36
$50,000–74,999	31	36	33
$75,000 and up	24	43	34

Source: Combined surveys taken for the Americans Talk Security project, February–June 1988.

For instance, nearly 40 percent of votes for Richard Nixon in 1968 came from people who had voted for Johnson four years previously (Dolbeare and Edlelman, 1974). In *The Changing American Voter,* Norman Nye and his colleagues found that political issues such as inflation and world peace were more significant than professed party affiliation in determining how people voted (Nie, Verba, and Petrocik, 1976). Some observers saw Ronald Reagan's victory in 1980 as signalling the beginning of a period in which the Republicans would become a majority party. This does not in fact seem to have become the case; although Reagan was reelected in 1984, the overall level of Republican support has not increased. In the 1986 Senate elections, the voting turnout was the lowest in more than forty years—only 37.7 percent of the electorate voted—but the outcome was to return control of the Senate to the Democrats.

Rather than a realignment in favor of the Republicans, we may be seeing a process of party de-alignment—where voters choose between presidential candidates more for their stands on particular issues, and for their personalities, than in terms of fixed party loyalties. This interpretation gains support from the results of opinion polls, which show that only about 20 percent of voters regard the party a presidential candidate belongs to as an important factor in their choice (Ladd, 1989).

VOTING BEHAVIOR

Since the early 1960s the proportion of the population that turns out to vote in the United States has steadily decreased. Only just over half the electorate votes in presidential elections; the turnout for congressional elections is lower still. Levels of voting are typically much lower than in the other Western societies, even with the declining patterns of voting in other countries in recent years. The average voter turnout in Britain, West Germany, and France since the Second World War has been over 75 percent in each country. In American presidential elections over the same period, by contrast, the average turnout was 59 percent (Ladd, 1989).

The differences in voter participation between the United States and Western Europe are real, but less pronounced than they appear, for two reasons. First, voter turnout in the United States is computed rather differently from elsewhere. In most other countries, the percentage of people voting in an election is calculated on the basis of the population of *registered* voters. The American statistics are expressed as a percentage of the entire *voting-age population.* Since in the European countries some people, for one reason or another, are not on the voting register at any one time, the proportion of actual voters to those eligible to vote appears higher than in the U.S. system of calculation.

Second, there is a much more extensive range of elections in the United States than in other Western societies. There is no other country in which such a variety of offices at all levels—including sheriffs, judges, city treasurers, and many other posts—are open to election. Americans are entitled to do about three or four times as much electing as elsewhere. Low rates of voter turnout thus have to be balanced against the wider extent of voter choice.

INTEREST GROUPS

Interest groups and lobbying play a distinctive part in American politics. An interest group is any organization that attempts to influence elected officials to consider their aims when deciding on legislation. The American Medical Association, the National Organization of Women, and the National Rifle Association are but three examples. Interest groups vary in size; some are national; others, statewide. Some are permanently organized, while others are short-lived. Lobbying is the act of contacting influential officials to present arguments to convince them to vote in favor of a cause or otherwise lend support to the aims of an interest group. The word *lobby* originated in the British parliamentary system. In days past, members of Parliament did not have offices so their business was conducted in the lobby of the Parliament buildings.

Professional lobbyists are a highly paid group. In 1987 there were eleven thousand registered lobbyists in the United States. Many are not officially registered, so the real number is probably much larger. Interest groups provide a great deal of money in donations to the election campaigns at all levels of political office. To run as a presidential candidate is enormously expensive. Even to run for the House or Senate costs hundreds of thousands, often millions, of dollars. About a quarter of this funding in congressional or senatorial elections comes from Political Action Committees (PACs), which were set up by interest groups to raise and distribute campaign funds (Green and Newfield, 1980).

Interest Group Politics: A Case Study

Interest groups affect virtually every area of American politics, and the aims they pursue are highly variable. They may work to get a law changed, a new law instituted, alter regulations, provide funding for a program, develop new policy goals, and many more political objectives. As an example, however, let us take the struggles of interest groups to get new environmental legislation introduced (Ladd, 1989). Following the Santa Barbara oil spill of 1969, a groundswell of public opinion developed, expressing concern about environmental pollution. Environmental groups such as the Sierra Club and the National Wildlife Federation started to press very actively for new legislation on the issue. Business firms, however, objected to their proposals on the grounds that their activities would be adversely affected, which would in turn harm the U.S. economy as a whole. The battle came to a head over an important item of legislation, the Clean Air Act.

The Clean Air Act was passed by Congress in 1970, following much lobbying by both sides. Its aim was to ensure that set safety levels for air pollutants were not exceeded. This was necessary, proponents of the act argued, to protect health and to prevent pollution damage to crops and buildings near industrial areas. By the early 1980s, some of the industrial producers most directly affected by the legislation, particularly in auto, oil, and chemical production, had come to feel strongly that the act unreasonably hampered their operations. They began to lobby intensively to weaken the act's main clauses; environmental groups were determined to resist them.

In the ensuing struggle, corporations and trade associations lobbied actively on an individual level, but they also got together to form coalitions. Some of the corporations in the business coalition, like Exxon, the giant oil company, were directly affected by the Clean Air Act, but they also made great efforts to gain support from firms whose interests were not as immediately involved—like IBM. To oppose them, the environmental groups used similar tactics, bringing to their support labor unions and associations such as the League of Women Voters.

Who came out on top in this interest-group power struggle? The two political parties were each internally divided on the issues involved, although the Reagan administration strongly backed the position of the business corporations. A stalemate developed, and the House Energy and Commerce Committee was deadlocked. The result was not a decisive victory for either side. Modifications were made to the act, but they were not as sweeping as the business lobby had sought, and on the whole the environmentalists were the victors.

The debate over the Clean Air Act was in some ways typical of interest-group conflicts over major policy matters. It was a clash between two sets of coalitions, drawing in many specific groups. It served to check initiatives towards change, rather than promote new changes—a common phenomenon of interest-group politics. What was perhaps atypical was that the corporate interests were unable to get their way.

Interest groups are not officially part of the electoral process, and this has made many people critical of them. While they ensure that a diversity of interests are represented at the higher levels of politics, it is not clear that the average voter has much influence on them; not being subject to elections, lobbyists and the more powerful interest groups are not accountable to the majority of the electorate. Also, many of their activities are carried on in secret. Thus it is possible that they contribute to the sense of powerlessness many people feel toward the state, particularly at the national level.

PARTY POLITICS IN THE LATE TWENTIETH CENTURY

THE PAST TWENTY YEARS, AS THE PRECEDING SECTIONS have suggested, have seen some significant changes in patterns of traditional party politics. This period is also one in which, in several Western countries, the welfare state has come under attack. Rights and benefits, fought for over long periods, have been contested and cut back. Rightist parties, such as those led by Margaret Thatcher in Britain and Helmut Kohl in West Germany, together with the former Reagan administration, have attempted to reduce levels of welfare expenditure in their countries (Krieger, 1986). Even in states led by socialist governments, like France under President François Mitterrand, commitment to government provision of public resources has been restricted (Ross, Hoffmann, and Malzacher, 1987). One reason for this governmental retrenchment is the declining revenues available to governments as a result of the general world recession beginning in the early 1970s. Yet there also seems to have developed an increasing skepticism, shared not only by some governments but by many of their citizens, about the effectiveness of relying on the state for the provision of many essential goods and services.

STATE OVERLOAD AND LEGITIMATION CRISIS

Two theories have been put forward by different authors to account for this changing political situation. One is the theory of **state overload** (Brittan, 1975; Nordhaus, 1975). According to this view, governments in the twentieth century have acquired more responsibilities than they can capably fund and manage, from establishing public ownership of industries, utilities, and transportation, to creating extensive welfare programs. One reason for this situation is that political parties have tried to woo voters by promising to provide too many benefits and services. Governments are unable to deliver on these promises because the level of state expenditure has risen beyond the resources provided by tax revenues: state responsibilities are overloaded (Etzioni-Halevy, 1985).

Consequently, it is argued, voters have become skeptical about claims made by governments and political parties. The Democratic party in the United States and leftist parties elsewhere have lost some of their traditional support from lower-class groups, as it became apparent that states could no longer deliver the promised benefits. The rise of New Right politics is explained as an attempt to cope with this situation by trimming back the state and encouraging private enterprise.

The rival theory is that of **legitimation crisis,** as developed by the German social thinker, Jürgen Habermas and others (Habermas, 1975; Offe, 1984, 1985). According to this theory, modern governments now lack the legitimacy they need to carry out tasks they are required to undertake. These theorists assume that state intervention in economic life, and in the provision of welfare resources, is necessary for keeping the economy on a stable course, because a society that depends extensively upon goods and services generated by private capitalist production produces great economic fluctuations and instability. Governments must also provide many services that private companies are unwilling to fund because they are insufficiently profitable—such as highways, public housing, and health-care systems. However, since private individuals and businesses resist being taxed, the state does not have the revenue necessary to accomplish all of these tasks. Governments cannot cope with the contradictory demand of less taxes and more responsibilities, leading to a partial withdrawal of public support and general disillusionment with the capabilities of politicians: in sum, a "legitimation crisis." New forms of Rightist politics have arisen on the basis of resistance to high levels of taxation by those in higher income groups.

ASSESSING THE THEORIES

The two theories have common elements. Each holds that government authority and established patterns of party support have become undermined in the face of growing responsibilities and functions that are required. Both suggest that governments find it difficult to control the many aspects of social and economic life, which they are charged to oversee. The practical remedies that flow from the two theories, however, are quite different.

Overload theory suggests that attempts to roll back levels of state spending can be fruitful. But legitimation crisis theory implies that such retrenchment will rebound, probably causing worsening social conflicts because there will be inadequate funding to cope with major problems of health, welfare provision, deteriorating inner cities, and so on. Overload theory is probably the less illuminating of the two. There seems to be a "push and pull" in the provision of resources between governments and private bodies that Habermas successfully analyzes. Those who feel they pay most to the cost of services—the more affluent—are likely to believe they gain least from them. For instance, in many countries there are persistent public debates about whether health services should be funded from taxation, and provided by the state, or whether they should be directly paid for by those who receive them. Health care is sometimes "pulled" into state control, but then may later be partly "pushed" out again into private insurance systems, under pressure from high tax-paying groups. According to Habermas, legitimation crises can only be overcome if the electorate can be persuaded to accept high taxation by seeing the necessity for supporting a wide range of fundamental government services.

THE POLITICAL PARTICIPATION
OF WOMEN

VOTING HAS A SPECIAL MEANING FOR WOMEN AGAINST THE background of their long struggle to obtain universal suffrage. The members of the early women's movements saw the vote both as the symbol of political freedom and as the means of achieving greater economic and social equality. In the United States, where the attempts by women to gain voting rights were more active, and provoked more violence, than elsewhere, women's leaders underwent considerable hardships to reach this end. Even today, in many countries, women do not have the same voting rights as men, although Saudi Arabia is the only state where women cannot vote at the national level (Randall, 1984).

The short answer is no. In most Western countries, when they first achieved voting rights, women voted in far fewer numbers than men. In the first national election for which they were eligible in the United States, in 1920, only about one-third of women voted, as compared to two-thirds of men. The proportions were roughly the same in Britain, and a similar pattern is found in other states in the early period after the instituting of universal voting rights (Baxter and Lansing, 1983; Flanz, 1983). Women still do not vote with the same frequency as men in many nations, although in some cases the discrepancy has almost completely disappeared. Voter turnout by women in the last three American presidential elections has only been slightly less than that of men. In parliamentary elections in Britain since 1970 (including the election of that year), the differential has been roughly the same. Gender differences in voting have completely disappeared in Sweden, West Germany, and Canada, while in Italy, Finland, and Japan women vote at slightly higher rates than men.

How far do the political attitudes of women differ from those of men? Many suffragists, early supporters of women's right to vote, believed that the entry of women into politics would radically transform political life, bringing in a new sense of altruism and morality. Those who were against extending the vote to women similarly argued that the political participation of women would have momentous consequences—but of a disastrous kind. A prominent male opponent of female franchise in Britain warned that "a revolution of such boundless significance cannot be attempted without the greatest peril to England" (quoted in Currell, 1974). Women's involvement in politics, it was widely held, would trivialize political life and would at the same time undermine the stability of the family.

Women's right to abortion has increasingly become a major political issue: here, pro-choice political activists.

Neither of these extreme consequences has come to pass. Women obtaining the vote has not greatly altered the nature of politics. Women's voting patterns, like those of men, are shaped by party preferences, policy options, and the choice of available candidates. Worldwide, there are only a few consistent differences between female and male voting. Women voters on the whole tend to be more conservative in their inclinations than men as judged by level of voting for Rightist parties. This is true, for example, in France, West Germany, and Italy. The relationship is more ambiguous in Britain and the United States. In Britain young women vote in higher numbers for the Labor Party than young men, but older women disproportionately vote Conservative. The two tendencies more or less balance one another. In the United States a conservative orientation cannot be easily associated with either of the two main parties, since the difference between the Republicans and Democrats is not a straightforward opposition between political Right and Left. In recent elections, women have voted Democrat in slightly higher proportions than men, with younger women being particularly inclined to favor the Democrats.

The influence of women upon politics cannot be assessed solely through voting patterns, however. Feminist groups have made an impact upon political life independently of the franchise, particularly in recent decades. Since the early 1960s, the National Organization of Women (NOW) and other women's groups in the United States have played a significant role in the passing of equal opportunity acts, and have pressed for a range of issues directly affecting women to be placed on the political agenda. Such issues include equal rights at work, the availability of abortion, changes in family and divorce laws, and lesbian rights. In 1973, women achieved a legal victory when the Supreme Court ruled in *Roe v. Wade* that women had a legal right to abortion. The 1989 Court ruling in *Webster v. Reproductive Health Services,* which placed restrictions on that right, resulted in a resurgence of involvement in the women's movement.

In most of the European countries, comparable national women's organizations have been lacking, but the "second wave" of feminism, characteristic of the 1960s and since, has brought the same issues to the center of the political stage (see Chapter 6: "Gender and Sexuality"). While many of these matters—like the question of whether abortion should be freely available—have proved highly controversial among women as well as men, it seems clear that many problems and concerns that particularly affect women, which previously had seemed to be "outside politics," are now central to political debates.

WOMEN IN POLITICAL ORGANIZATIONS

Women have never been complete strangers to political power. From Cleopatra onwards individual women have on occasion wielded vast influence as heads of state. Where they have not been formally installed as rulers, women have sometimes held great power informally, as the wives or mistresses of monarchs, presidents, and prime ministers. One of the most famous of such examples is that of Madame de Pompadour in the seventeenth century; as the mistress of Louis XIV of France, she was effectively able to make most of the important decisions of state. In the twentieth century, women have occasionally been heads of government—examples include Golda Meir in Israel, Indira Gandhi in India, Margaret Thatcher in the United Kingdom, Benazir Bhutto in Pakistan, and Corazon Aquino in the Philippines.

Yet in general, as in so many other sectors of social life, women are poorly represented among political elites. Following the 1980 national elections in the United States, there were nineteen female members in the House of Representatives, making up just over 4 percent of the total membership (Randall, 1984). This number has remained more or less stable since the early 1970s. In 1981 there were only two women in the Senate, representing 2 percent of those sitting in the upper chamber. There were no women at all in the preceding session, and in its entire history there have only been a total of thirteen women senators.

In Britain, after the 1981 election, there were nineteen female members of Parliament, making up 3 percent of the membership of the House of Commons. In the preceding period there were twenty-seven female members representing 4.5 percent of the total. Women have fared somewhat better in the legislatures of some other countries. In West Germany in 1981, women made up 8.5 percent of the parliament, the Bundestag. Women formed 28 percent of the legislators in Sweden and 26 percent in Finland.

The representation of women in local governments is generally greater than in national assemblies. In 1983, 9.8 percent of the members of state assemblies in the United States were women. Women composed some 16 percent of local councillors in the United Kingdom in 1981. In most other European countries, women are more strongly represented in local than in national assemblies, with the exception of the Scandinavian countries, where the local and national percentages are more similar. The overall pattern of women's representation in government parallels that of most other spheres of society. While at the middle levels of power there may be a fairly substantial proportion of women—although nothing approaching equal numbers with men—the higher up the system, the fewer women are to be found.

Exactly the same pattern is found within political party organizations. Women make up about a third of the delegates to the Democratic and Republican National Conventions in the United States. In Britain, 11 percent of Labor Party Annual Conference delegates in 1980 were women, with the comparable figure for the Conservative party being 38 percent. At the top of the party hierarchies, however, the proportion of women shrinks dramatically. In the Carter administration, there were two women in a cabinet of eleven people. The cabinet formed by President Reagan after the 1980 election contained no women at all, while the Bush cabinet also had only two. The Scandinavian countries are virtually the only ones in which women have figured prominently. The cabinets in Sweden, Finland, and Norway have long included women, although still in a clear minority. In 1980, for example, five out of twenty cabinet members in Sweden were women.

What is surprising about the figures on women's involvement at the higher levels of political organizations is not this lack of representation itself, but the slowness with which things seem to be changing. In the business sector, men still monopolize the top positions, but women are now making more inroads into the strongholds of male privilege than previously. As yet at least, this does not seem to be happening in the political sphere—in spite of the fact that nearly all political parties today are nominally committed to securing equal opportunities for women and men.

The factors that present difficulties for women's advancement in the economy also exist in the realm of politics. To rise within a political organization requires a great deal of expenditure of effort and time, which women who have major domestic burdens can rarely generate. But there may be an additional influence in political life. A high level of power is concentrated in the political area: perhaps men are especially reluctant to abandon their dominance in such a sphere.

From considering the position of women in politics, we now broaden our scope to look at some of the basic mechanisms of political power. First, we analyze the nature of political legitimacy, and from there we move on to consider how and why groups contest the legitimate political order—the study of political protest. Finally, we take up the issue of who actually holds the reins of power, drawing on comparative materials to help illuminate the discussion.

POLITICAL LEGITIMACY AND IMPRESSION MANAGEMENT

THE MAINTENANCE OF LEGITIMACY (ACCEPTANCE BY MOST of the population of the right of a set of rulers or a government to hold power) is one of the most important elements in modern political systems. Study of the means whereby leaders actively try to sustain their legitimacy provides one area in which we can readily connect political institutions with characteristics of social interaction on the "micro" level (discussed in Chapter 4: "Social Interaction and Everyday Life"). Peter M. Hall's study of the American presidency provides a good example of this (Hall, 1979).

In everyday interaction, Hall points out, people are much preoccupied with what Erving Goffman calls "impression management"— the cultivation of the "right image" of themselves in the eyes of others. In trying to manage the impressions which others have of them, people "give off" what they want to convey in how they act, what they look like, and through their facial expressions—as well as in what they say. In political life, impression management, aimed at sustaining the legitimacy of leaders and their policies, tends to be more explicitly designed and controlled than in ordinary day-to-day activity, but the basic mechanisms are the same. Hall analyzes the presidency of John F. Kennedy to demonstrate political impression management in operation. According to Hall, Kennedy

> believed in the power of facts, the need to be tough, cool, and objective, and was interested in results and action. He disdained abstractions, theories, emotion, and ideology. He basically accepted American society as given and had few so-

cial change goals, and saw his role as an educator or mobilizer. He did, however, want to be a hero, and this could be done by acting tough and courageous in crises which could best be found in the international realm. Because of his view of history, which saw monolithic Communistic expansion, Kennedy could find his heroic role in standing opposed to the ubiquitous challenge of the Russians. Every international conflict was a crisis, a test of will and nerve. Any wavering or retreat would only encourage our enemies. (Hall, 1979)

One might contest some aspects of this portrayal—surely Kennedy was more oriented to changing American society than Hall claims—but it accurately describes the image of the strong and forceful leader that Kennedy and his aides were concerned to get across to the public. Hall analyzes the Cuban missile crisis of October 1962 to show how Kennedy made use of the situation to demonstrate his toughness and determination. The crisis began when U.S. reconnaissance missions identified the presence of Soviet offensive missiles in Cuba, which is only ninety miles off the U.S. mainland. Five possible interpretations of the situation were made by Kennedy and his advisers:

1. It was part of Cold War politics, and the Soviet Union was testing U.S. resolve by planting the missiles, anticipating little response, and presuming the United States would look impotent to the rest of the world.

2. Placing missiles in Cuba was a diversionary tactic: the Soviets were really concerned with taking over West Berlin and were trying to focus U.S. attention elsewhere.

3. The Soviets were determined to defend Cuba at any cost from the threat of U.S. invasion.

4. It was a bargaining ploy: the Soviets wanted to use the missiles in Cuba as bargaining chips to get a reduction of U.S. missile strength in Europe.

5. The Soviets were simply building up their military strength, and placing missiles in Cuba was the simplest and cheapest means to do so.

John F. Kennedy, only two years into his presidency before being felled by an assassin's bullet, fostered an image of dynamism as well as that of a family man.

Kennedy saw little evidence for the last four of these possibilities, and approached the crisis by focusing on the first interpretation (Sorenson, 1966). The confrontation with the Soviets, in other words, was taken as a test of U.S.—and especially of Kennedy's own—credibility and willpower in world affairs.

While the reconnaissance missions reported the existence of missiles, there was less evidence that actual nuclear warheads were in Cuba. These were said to be on Soviet vessels approaching the island. Kennedy's response was to blockade Cuba and threaten to order the Navy to fire on the Soviet vessels if they attempted to run the blockade. After some very tense days during which the outbreak of nuclear war seemed a real possibility, the crisis ended; the Russian ships turned back. By not backing down, Kennedy sought to give public demonstration of his resolve and his nerve. Political credibility (not just in the Cuban missile crisis, but as a more general feature of Kennedy's government) was seen to depend upon fostering the impression that the United States not only possessed great power but was prepared to use it.

The way by which leaders handle the media plays a key role in impression management, both in terms of the information they reveal and the ways that this information is conveyed. Much of the information upon which Kennedy based his reactions to the missiles in Cuba was not made available publicly. Press releases were written in such a way as to reflect a definite "style" of leadership that Kennedy wished to embody. Whereas Kennedy was able to carry through this form of impression management very successfully, later presidents Jimmy Carter and Gerald Ford were unable to present themselves effectively as decisive leaders, nor were they able to manage the media effectively. Both, in fact, tried to move away from the tough or heroic imagery, but as a consequence were widely seen as weak and irresolute.

Impression management depends partly upon real qualities of the individual, and partly upon how impressions are conveyed to others. In the presidency of Ronald Reagan, we again saw the attempt to foster an image of determination and resolve. When Reagan ordered a military strike against Libya in 1986, he did so in order to give public demonstration of U.S. determination to resist terrorism, which the Libyans were held to be centrally involved in organizing. Reagan's age, and his "folksy" approach, however, precluded creating the imagery of the bold and dashing hero in the Kennedy mold. Reagan had to struggle against the public impression that his mastery of the political scene was less than complete, that he was indifferent to detail and prone to errors of judgement. He was able to counter these negative images by successful management of the media, particularly television, and to some extent actually drew upon these weaknesses to reassure the people of his "ordinariness."

The importance of impression management in political leadership and legitimacy drives home the lesson that apparently minor aspects of personal activity (personal style, the impressions people have of others) can have fundamental implications for institutions as well. "How one is seen" is of key importance for political leaders—all the more so now that they *are* seen constantly on television.

This also relates back directly to issues mentioned near the beginning of the chapter. The United States is a nation-state in a world of other nation-states; its closest rival for global influence is the Soviet Union. Each state is autonomous within its own territories but, in seeking to maintain its influence outside, uses a mixture of diplomacy, threat, and active military engagement. Fostering impressions of determination and will is a major aspect of the relations between the two superpowers and between other nations. Impression management is central even to the nuclear arms race itself, because nuclear weapons can only work as a deterrent if both sides believe that the other, if pushed, has the resolve to use them. (For a discussion of some of the paradoxes of nuclear deterrence, see Chapter 11: "War and the Military.")

NONINSTITUTIONALIZED POLITICAL ACTION: PROTEST MOVEMENTS

POLITICAL LIFE IS BY NO MEANS CARRIED ON ONLY WITHIN the orthodox framework of political parties, voting, and representation in government bodies. It often happens that groups find that their objectives or ideals cannot be achieved within, or are actively blocked by, this framework. The most dramatic and far-reaching example of nonorthodox political action is *revolution*—the overthrow of an existing political order by a mass movement using violence to achieve this result. We take up revolutions in Chapter 19: "Revolution and Social Movements"; here we shall focus on how governments respond to protest movements.

Protest movements normally, but not always, arise amongst the poorer and more underprivileged groups in society. In Western countries today, it is legal to form political associations of more or less any sort, and to stage street demonstrations or marches. But this was not always the case. These rights had to be won from the political authorities. During the nineteenth century, for example, European legislatures introduced "combination acts" banning the assembling of large groups in public places for political purposes. These attempts at government regulation were mostly abandoned when it became clear that they could not be realistically enforced. Ironically, people turned out *en masse* to demonstrate against these acts. Such laws apparently stimulated the very activities they were supposed to prevent.

Many protest movements tend to operate within the margins of what is defined as legally permissible by governments. A police license, for example, normally has to be obtained before a mass demonstration is staged. Where such a license is denied, the organizers may decide to go ahead anyway, bringing them into confrontation with the authorities. Protesters who feel strongly about a cause are often prepared to transgress the law in order to make their actions more effective. People involved in peace movements over the past few years, for instance, have blockaded army camps in an endeavor to stop weapons from being moved in and out, climbed over the wire fences to stage sit-ins, and entered missile silos.

GOVERNMENT RESPONSE TO PROTEST MOVEMENTS

Government leaders have three main options when confronted by political protest movements. First, they might simply ignore them. Groups that can muster no real popular support are likely to draw little response from government circles. In such circumstances, a particularly determined group or movement may turn to violence, since this inevitably calls forth a reaction, even if only a punitive one. Small political sects, for example, which have few followers among the population at large, have turned to terrorism as a means of dramatizing their causes (see Chapter 11: "War and the Military").

A second response on the part of government authorities might be to clamp down immediately upon those involved, or believed to be involved, in the activities in question. Repressive measures have very frequently been used by the political authorities to quell what are seen as "disturbances to public order." Sometimes such responses have been savage; riot police or troops have been used against unarmed marchers, for example, occasionally producing extensive loss of life. This was the case in China during the democracy movement in the summer of 1989.

The third possible reaction is to blunt the edge of the protest by agreeing to at least some of the protesters' demands. These three responses might very well follow from one another. In the first stage of the development of a protest movement, the authorities may either pay little attention to it, or believe that it will fade away of its own accord. If the movement gathers strength, especially if it is directly hostile to government policies, the response might be to control its impact by force. If this fails, or produces a public outcry, the political authorities might at that point give way on some issues, and perhaps incorporate them within their own political program.

Protests quite often produce major revisions in official policies in this way (Piven and Cloward, 1977). Such was the case, for example, with the civil rights movement. Involving a mixture of poor Southern blacks, middle-class black leaders, and white liberals recruited mostly from the North, the civil rights movement brought about far-reaching political changes. Reactions to the movement by governmental authorities broadly followed the sequence mentioned above. At first, neither central nor local government agencies were particularly interested, and treated the early marches and disturbances as phenomena that would evaporate of their own accord (although some local vigilante groups reacted violently from the beginning). When it became clear that this was not to be the case, some local authorities began to harass the movement's leaders, using force to try to prevent marches and demonstrations from occurring. Later on, however, once the federal government became involved, local governments were compelled to introduce legislative changes promoting greater equality between blacks and whites, such as desegregating schools. (For a further discussion of the civil rights movement, see Chapter 8: "Ethnicity and Race.")

Students have often been involved in political protests. These French students protested the educational system in 1968. In the early 1970s, American students protested against the Vietnam War, and in June 1989, Chinese students rallied for democracy in Tiananmen Square.

WHO RULES?

POLITICAL PROTEST MOVEMENTS ARE DIRECTED AGAINST those who hold power, attempting to influence their decisions, or to actively overthrow them, by nonorthodox means. But who are the power-holders in modern societies, and from what types of social background do they come? In answering this question, we shall contrast the political systems of the United States and the Soviet Union. The Soviet Union is often thought of in the West as a society of extreme political inequality, having little fluidity or "openness"; but this is in some ways a misconception, as we shall see.

We saw earlier that pluralist theory emphasizes the competitive nature of group interests in the United States. Such competition supposedly prevents power from falling too much into the hands of any one group or class. Like the advocates of the theory of democratic elitism, the pluralists agree that "the people" do not, and cannot, rule, yet they see the United States, and other Western societies, as essentially democratic.

THE POWER ELITE

The view suggested by C. Wright Mills in his celebrated work, *The Power Elite,* is quite different from pluralist theories (Mills, 1956). According to Mills, in earlier periods of its history, American society did show flexibility and diversity at all levels; however, this has since changed.

Mills argues that during the course of the twentieth century a process of institutional centralization occurred in the political order, the economy, and the sphere of the military. On the political side, individual state governments used to be very powerful and were only loosely coordinated by the federal government. Political power today, Mills argues, has become tightly coordinated at the federal level. Similarly, the economy was once made up of many small units, businesses, banks, and farms across the country, but has now become dominated by a cluster of very large corporations. Finally, since World War II, the military, once kept restricted in size, has grown to a giant establishment at the heart of the country's institutions.

Not only has each of these spheres become more centralized, according to Mills, but they have become increasingly merged with one another to form a unified system of power. Those who are in the highest positions in all three institutional areas come from similar social backgrounds, have parallel interests, and often know one another on a personal basis. They have become a single **power elite** that runs the country—and, given the international position of the United States, also influences a great deal of the rest of the world.

The power elite, in Mills portrayal, is composed mainly of white Anglo-Saxon Protestants (WASPs). Many are from wealthy families, have been to the same prestigious universities, belong to the same clubs, and sit on government committees with one another. They have closely connected concerns. Business and political leaders work together, and both have close relationships with the military through weapons contracting and the supply of goods for the armed forces. There is a great deal of movement back and forth between top positions in the three spheres. Politicians have business interests; business leaders often run for public office; higher military personnel sit on the boards of the large companies.

In opposition to pluralist interpretations, Mills argues that there are three distinct levels of power in the United States. The power elite occupies the highest level, formally and informally making the most important policy decisions affecting both the domestic arena and foreign policy. Interest groups, upon which the pluralists concentrate their attention, operate at the middle levels of power, together with local government agencies. Their influence over major policy decisions is limited. At the bottom is the large mass of the population, who have virtually no influence upon the decisions at all, since these are made within the closed settings in which the members of the power elite come together. The power elite spans the top of both party organizations, each party being run by individuals with similar overall interests and outlooks. Thus the choices open to voters in presidential and congressional elections are so small as to be of little consequence.

Since Mills published his study, there have been numerous other research investigations analyzing the social background and interconnections of leading figures in the various spheres of American society (Dye, 1986). All studies agree upon the finding that the social backgrounds of those in leading positions are highly unrepresentative of the population as a whole (Domhoff, 1971, 1979, and 1983).

Mills's Thesis: An Assessment

How should we assess Mills's thesis in the light of discussion and empirical research over the last thirty years? It seems reasonable to conclude that in the United States, as in other Western countries, there is a distinguishable upper class, holding a disproportionate share of the wealth of the country; its members have much higher chances of achieving top positions in a variety of areas than others from less privileged backgrounds. There is a strong meshing of business and governmental interests, often facilitated by direct personal contacts. Many major decisions are made in contexts outside the public arena—in boardrooms, meetings of the president and a few colleagues, and in the more informal settings in which some of these individuals come into regular contact with each other.

On the other hand, it is dubious whether, either in the United States or elsewhere, there exist groups as coordinated and cohesive as Mills's power elite. There tend to be major divisions of opinion and interest between powerful groups, who may collaborate in some circumstances but are more diverse and fragmented than in Mills's portrayal. The true picture seems some way between that given by the pluralists and the analysis offered by Mills.

In concluding this chapter, we shall switch from the United States to the Soviet Union—studying two such different political systems helps us gain a fuller perspective upon power and privilege.

ELITES IN THE SOVIET UNION

Information about elites in the Soviet Union is much more difficult to obtain than in Western societies, where there is greater access to governmental and corporate documents. The Soviet Union differs from the United States in that both its political and economic systems are dominated by a single party, the Communist Party of the Soviet Union (CPSU). But, in spite of the preeminent position of the Party, the official view is that there are no favored elites in the Soviet Union, let alone a distinct upper class. The Party regards itself as the "tried and tested militant vanguard of the Soviet people," the "leading and guiding force of Soviet society" (quoted in Hill and Frank, 1986). As the representative of the industrial workers, the Party claims to express the collective interests of the majority of the population.

Membership in the CPSU is in principle open to any citizen of the Soviet Union. In practice though, entry tends to be controlled by members of local Party organizations, and applications for membership may be rejected by the local Party branches. Party members are expected regularly to attend meetings and take part in discussions; membership is more than just a process of formal registration. Party membership is not formally a prerequisite for entry into the majority of high positions in the country, but greatly facilitates chances of reaching the top in most spheres. Full-time officials make up only a small proportion of the overall Party membership, but include within their ranks some of the most powerful individuals in the Soviet Union.

About 18.5 million people belonged to the CPSU in 1986—about 6 percent of the total population. Forty-two percent of the membership is composed of blue-collar workers, 14 percent are agricultural workers, and the remainder are in white collar and professional jobs (Hill and Frank, 1986). The Politburo, Central Secretariat, and Central Committee stand at the apex of the Party organization. The Central Committee is in fact a large body consisting of over four hundred members. Top leadership is concentrated in the Politburo and Central Secretariat; the former consists of about twenty men (only one woman has ever been a member), the latter about a dozen, with some people being members of both.

Recruitment, Prestige, and Privilege

How elitist is the political system in the Soviet Union as compared to the United States? The answer has to be a mixed one. Although political leaders are drawn from a wide range of the population, their power and privilege is more concentrated than in Western countries. In terms of social background, however, recruitment to top Party positions is much more open than in the case of political leadership in most Western nations. Thus, *all* the members of the Politburo in 1957 came from working-class or peasant backgrounds. Of the members of the Central Committee in 1961, more than 85 percent originated from such backgrounds. Much the same was true of those in leading positions in industry, the military, education, and the arts (Matthews, 1972). This situation has since altered, with a trend towards a higher proportion of the leadership being drawn from white-collar backgrounds; yet the Party elite continues to include a far higher proportion of people drawn from lower-class backgrounds than is typical in the West. Among members of the Politburo and secretaries of the Central Committee in 1985, only one came from a background of some privilege—the son of a senior official in a government ministry (Walker, 1987).

In spite of the egalitarian ideology of the Soviet Union, top leadership in the CPSU carries privileges denied to most of the rest of the population. Party officials are able to travel internationally outside the Soviet bloc and have access to special shops containing superior goods; they can skip food lines, obtain the best living accommodation, and may possess second homes in the countryside. Yet, because there is no private ownership of industrial enterprise, opportunities for the accumulation of large fortunes are lacking. There is no proportied upper class in the Soviet Union that, by means of its wealth, can transmit material advantages across the generations. Although those in the leading positions in the Party have sometimes been regarded as a "new class," it is more appropriate to see them as a distinctively privileged—and very powerful—elite (Djilas, 1967; Gouldner, 1982).

Those in top Party positions generally wield far more power than their counterparts in Western countries. While there are often divisions of interest and outlook within the Party, and between Party officials and the leaders of other organizations, power is more highly concentrated. This is because of the lack of effective political opposition, the control over the media which the Party maintains, and the coordination of political and economic power in the same hands. In the West, political and business leadership are substantially separate, while in the Soviet Union they are combined (Hill, 1985).

TOTALITARIANISM

The Soviet Union and the East European societies, prior to 1989, together with other Communist systems such as China, have often been labelled **totalitarian.** The term has also been used to characterize fascist regimes, such as those of Germany and Italy during the Second World War. (Fascism is an extreme Rightist form of government, marked by an authoritarian outlook.) The word totalitarian

Totalitarian Adolf Hitler's Nazi soldiers.

was in fact coined by a philosopher whose ideas became important in Italian fascism, Giovanni Gentile, and was used by the Italian dictator Mussolini to favorably describe his own regime. Thereafter, the term acquired a pejorative meaning (Schapiro, 1972). It has been commonly applied not only to Communist countries but to traditional states, and even to fictional societies like Plato's Republic.

Carl Friedrich's definition of totalitarianism has probably been most influential. According to Friedrich (1954), totalitarianism contains four elements:

1. *A totalist ideology*—a comprehensive or all-embracing set of political doctrines to which everyone is expected to adhere (for example, the commitment to the "fatherland" stressed by the Nazis).

2. *A single party* committed to this ideology and usually led by one individual, a dictator.

3. *A secret police* seeking out and punishing those said to be enemies of the regime.

4. *Monopoly control* of economic organizations, the mass media, and the military.

Is totalitarianism, thus defined, a useful way of referring to the Communist societies? Most scholars today agree that it is not (Hill and Frank, 1986; Holmes, 1987; Walker, 1987). The Soviet Union and other Communist countries are more internally diverse than such a conception presumes. For example, the Soviet Union has a federal system, which includes many different cultural, ethnic, and regional groups. Moreover, their governments command at least a considerable measure of popular support. Finally, they are not ruled over by dictators, but by Party bureaucrats.

Totalitarianism should rather be regarded as a form of political regime that is more transitional, in which a dictator rises to power, promoting totalist ideologies with the use of mass terror. The periods of rule by Stalin in the Soviet Union, Hitler in Germany, or Pol Pot in Cambodia, may be regarded as examples of totalitarian governments. In these circumstances, Friedrich's four characteristics can be clearly identified. Each of these governments concentrated extreme power in the hands of one individual and were supported by an ideology to which no exceptions were permitted. In addition, all were marked by great savagery and killing directly instigated by the actions of the state authorities. As Frederick Barghoorn writes,

> Totalitarianism describes not so much a type of political system as a historical situation in which a dictator integrates and mobilizes a society beset by a crisis that threatens disintegration, barring emergency measures. If we identify totalitarianism with practices and perspectives implicit perhaps in Leninism but fully developed only by Stalin, then the Russia of today still has not fully recovered from the trauma of totalitarian rule. However, its dynamism and rigor have in large measure been supplanted by business-as-usual routines and rituals. (Barghoorn, 1972)

DIFFERENCES BETWEEN EAST AND WEST

What conclusions can we draw about the similarities and differences between the political systems of the United States and the Soviet Union? In both countries—as in all industrialized societies—there is a considerable concentration of power at the top. By any reckoning, this concentration is more pronounced in the Soviet Union than in the United States as a result of the dominance of the Communist Party. On the other hand, the Soviet political system, even prior to 1989, was more pluralistic than many Western observers allowed. There are interest groups in the Soviet Union, although their scope for independent action is less than in Western countries; and there are divisions of interest between different sections of the elite. Elite recruitment is notably more open in the Soviet Union than in the United States, and there is a sense in which the level of political participation is higher, because of mass involvement in Party activities.

At the present time, important changes are being introduced into the Soviet political system, although it is too soon to know what their full impact will be. In June 1988, the Soviet leader, Mikhail Gorbachev, proposed that the government should no longer be headed by the Politburo, but by a president appointed by and answerable to a supreme National Congress. The members of the Congress —some two thousand in number—elect from among themselves about four hundred deputies who make up a permanent Soviet Parliament. The electoral system involved is a complicated one, with several levels of elected bodies below the Congress and Parliament.

The push for reform (*perestroika*) within the Soviet political order comes at least partly from a genuine desire for a more pluralistic system on the part of Gorbachev, as well as many others in the Soviet Union. However, these changes are also motivated by economic concerns. The performance of the Soviet economy over recent years has been poor, in the sphere of manufacturing industry and particularly in the area of agriculture. A shakeup of the political system is to be combined with economic innovations aimed at introducing greater flexibility into the production system and expanding workplace democracy. As of 1990, how far the Soviet Union will move toward a free-market system and other, radical, political changes that will in effect overthrow the existing order is unknown.

SUMMARY

1. A *state* exists where there is a political apparatus, ruling over a given territory, whose authority is backed by a legal system and by the capability to use force to implement its policies.

2. *Government* refers to the regular enactment of policies, decisions, and matters of state on the part of officials within a political apparatus. *Politics* concerns the means whereby power is used to affect the scope and content of governmental activities. The sphere of the political may range well beyond that of state institutions themselves.

3. Modern states are *nation-states,* usually having some form of congressional or parliamentary system. The notion of *sovereignty* (the authority of a government over a clearly defined territory) suggests both the acknowledged legitimacy of the

nation-state and the recognition of the state's borders by others. Each community acquires a distinct character through its association with *nationalism.*

4. Citizenship is associated with certain rights: civil, political, and social; where these have been established in some form, a nation can be said to be democratic.

5. There are several major types of democratic system. In a representative multiparty democracy, the adult population has the right to vote with a choice between parties. In a *representative one-party democracy,* the adult population has the right to vote with no choice of party. In a *participatory democracy,* communal decisions are discussed and made by the people directly.

6. According to Weber and Schumpeter, the level of democratic participation which can be achieved in a modern, large-scale society is limited. The rule of elites is inevitable, but multiparty systems provide the possibility of choosing *who* exercises power. The pluralist theorists add the claim that the competition of interest groups limits the degree to which ruling elites are able to concentrate power in few hands.

7. A political party is an organization oriented towards achieving legitimate control of government through an electoral process. In most Western states, the largest parties are those associated with general political interests—socialism, communism, liberalism, or conservatism. There is usually some connection between voting patterns and class differences. In many Western countries there has recently been a decline in allegiance to traditional parties and a growing disenchantment with the party system in general.

8. Women achieved the right to vote much later than men in all countries, and continue to be poorly represented among political elites. They have been influential on social and civil rights issues, and most Western countries have passed equal rights legislation over recent years.

9. Political activity is not confined to political parties. *Protest movements* and *interest groups* can be very influential.

10. In Western societies there is a distinguishable upper class, holding a disproportionate share of the country's wealth, whose members have better chances of achieving and retaining top positions in a variety of areas than others from less-privileged backgrounds.

11. The Soviet Union and East European societies have in the past been more "open" than Western countries in terms of the social backgrounds of top leaders. Yet Communist Party elites had many distinctive privileges compared to the rest of the population.

12. *Totalitarianism* involves a totalist ideology, a single party led by a dictator, a secret police, and monopoly control of major institutions. It is not a term that usefully describes a distinct type of society, but refers rather to exceptional circumstances in which a dictator wields immense power.

BASIC CONCEPTS

STATE
GOVERNMENT
POLITICS
NATION–STATE

IMPORTANT TERMS

STATELESS SOCIETY
STATE SOCIETIES
POLITICAL APPARATUS
FORCE
SOVEREIGNTY
CITIZEN
NATIONALISM
CIVIL RIGHTS
POLITICAL RIGHTS
SOCIAL RIGHTS
WELFARE STATE
DEMOCRACY
LIBERAL DEMOCRACY

REPRESENTATIVE MULTIPARTY DEMOCRACY
REPRESENTATIVE ONE-PARTY DEMOCRACY
DEMOCRATIC CENTRALISM
PARTICIPATORY DEMOCRACY
CONSTITUTIONAL MONARCH
DEMOCRATIC ELITISM
PLURALIST THEORIES OF DEMOCRACY
INTEREST GROUPS
POLITICAL PARTY
STATE OVERLOAD
LEGITIMATION CRISIS
POWER ELITE
TOTALITARIANISM

WAR AND THE MILITARY

ON JULY 1, 1916, THE BRITISH AND FRENCH ARMIES launched an attack against German forces occupying an area close to the Somme River in Northeastern France. By that date, the First World War had been in progress for some two years. Each side had prepared a complex array of trenches and fortifications, and neither had made much progress in pushing back the other. The Allied plan at the Battle of the Somme was to launch an all-out offensive that would drive the Germans back decisively from the lines they occupied. The British army bore the brunt of the responsibility for the attack. Following a massive artillery bombardment of the German encampments, thousands of men swept out of their trenches across "no man's land" towards the Germans.

Although many German soldiers perished in the artillery bombardment, most of their defensive fortifications remained intact. As the Allies advanced, they were met by a pitiless stream of rifle and machine-gun fire. The larger German guns behind the lines also sent over a hail of high explosive shells, whose jagged pieces sprayed across the battlefield. Small groups of British forces did manage to penetrate the German front line, and a few even pressed beyond. But behind them the enemy fire continued to dominate no man's land,

and only meager numbers of other troops got through to reinforce them. By the end of the first day's fighting, the British had advanced only a mile further than their own trenches. Fifty-seven thousand British troops lost their lives to achieve that gain, while eight thousand German soldiers died.

The offensive was resumed on July 3, and the attacks continued for over four months thereafter. Some got further through the German lines than before, but at the cost of appalling casualties. By mid-November, when the campaign ended, the German front remained largely intact. Well over half a million Allied soldiers, and an equivalent number of Germans, were killed at the Battle of the Somme. No military encounter previously in human history had ever seen so many hundreds of thousands of soldiers in action on a battlefield; and none had generated casualties even remotely approaching those suffered by both sides (Wilson, 1986).

Since the First World War, developments in the destructive strength of weaponry have continued apace. In the Second World War, and subsequent military engagements all over the world, armed forces and civilians alike have suffered horrific levels of casualties. The acceleration in the scale and intensity of war is as distinctive an aspect of modern societies as any other institutional change that has occurred since the emergence of industrialism. How and why has modern war come to develop to such a pitch? What impact has war and the military had on modern social development? How should we analyze war and military power in sociological terms? These are the problems we shall tackle in this chapter.

WARFARE IN THE PAST

IN HUNTING AND GATHERING SOCIETIES, AND SMALLER agrarian cultures, there were few if any specialized warriors. Since everyone was routinely engaged in the day-to-day production of food, which usually could not be stored for long, there were simply no bands of men free to engage in chronic fighting. If skirmishes with rival groups did occur, some or all of the adult men who were not too old would be called upon to fight, but it is misleading to speak of "war" among such peoples, as long battles were rarely if ever fought. Conflicts occurring between smaller cultures were fundamentally different from those between large-scale societies. There were no armies, little technology of war (for exam-

ple, no metal shields, swords, or pikes), and few tendencies towards the conquest or subjugation of other cultures (Brock and Galtung, 1966; Otterbein, 1985).

Much of World War I was fought in and out of trenches—a network of mud, stone, and timber stretching across Europe—and, to a certain extent, in the skies in the form of "dog fights."

TRADITIONAL STATES

The fighting of wars that are often protracted and very bloody is one of the most obvious features of the first development of states. The larger traditional states, such as ancient Rome, were empires, usually built by the military conquest and subordination of less-powerful groups and cultures. Military technology, in this case the development of methods of working metal to produce armor and weapons, was pioneered within these early civilizations. In traditional states there were **standing armies,** that is to say, bodies of men who were full-time professional soldiers. In those societies whose position depended upon the use of sea power, there were also specialized navies. Standing armies and navies were usually small and often primarily formed a means whereby the sovereign or emperor protected his court and household. Larger armies were raised by conscripting peasants and by forming alliances with other military leaders.

Prior to the sixteenth and seventeenth centuries, the Chinese and the Mongols were the most powerful military civilizations. Again,

one reason for this was technology. In weaponry, as in the arts and literary culture, the Chinese were far more developed than the societies of the West. Evidence relating to two Chinese government arsenals in the late eleventh century shows that they were producing thirty-two thousand suits of armor every year, indicating a very extensive scale of military development (Needham, 1975). The Chinese pioneered the use of gunpowder, in about the ninth century, and invented the first guns. Their ships also ranged far and wide. An edict of the Chinese emperor in 1371, prohibiting foreign trade and military adventures abroad, put a stop to these voyages and the Chinese withdrew to their own territories. If the emperor had not decided upon this prohibition, the subsequent history of the world might have been completely different. For only slightly later the Europeans began their voyages of discovery that provided the basis for the expansion of European power.

WARFARE IN EUROPE AND ITS COLONIES

The increasing economic development of Europe from the fifteenth century onwards, coupled with changes in military organization and technology, propelled Western states into what eventually became a commanding global position. Wars and battles have played a primary role in shaping the map of the world as it exists today. Within Europe itself, military strength determined which states survived and which did not. In 1500 there were some five hundred or more states in Europe; by 1900 this had shrunk to twenty-five (Tilly, 1975). Wars have also shaped the borders between societies in Europe in the present century. For example, the divisions between Poland, Czechoslovakia, Hungary, and Austria were an outcome of the First World War.

The Europeans' explorations into the wider world also depended substantially upon their superior military organization and weaponry. Cultures like those native to the Americas were only intermittently able to hold up the advance of white colonists into their territories. Warfare between the Europeans themselves largely determined the distribution of social and political units in North and South America. While the Spanish and Portuguese divided up South and Central America between them, the shape of North American society was resolved by military encounters first between the English and the French, and then between the English and the American colonists. The victory of the English over the French settled the boundaries and ethnic character of Canada, with a French-Canadian culture surviving only in Quebec. The military triumph of the American colonial settlers over their parent English government in the Revolutionary War resulted in the creation of the United States.

FROM LIMITED TO TOTAL WAR

PRIOR TO THE TWENTIETH CENTURY, EVEN WHEN LARGE battles were fought, they were limited to only small segments of the population—soldiers directly involved with the fighting (normally a small percentage of the adult males of a society), or civilians living in the immediate regions where the wars were fought. These can be characterized as **limited wars.** But World War I, epitomized by battles involving enormous bodies of soldiery, such as those involved in the Battle of the Somme, was clearly not limited. **Total war** involves several antagonistic nations, high proportions of their male populations, the mobilization of their overall economies, and fighting throughout the world. The First World War, or the "Great War," was in many ways a watershed in military development in the twentieth century. It fully justified its name; in terms of the number of countries involved—most of the European nations, together with Russia, Japan, and the United States—there were no historical parallels. The numbers of combatants and noncombatants killed were much higher than in any previous episode of armed conflict. As the social historian Maurice Pearton observes, "War had changed from being the concern of the army as an elite to being the business of society as a whole, and from the limited and rational application of force to unrestricted violence" (Pearton, 1984). At least

Artist William Draper's depiction of a World War II battle scene for National Geographic Magazine, *1942.*

two major developments promoted this transition from limited to total war: **the industrialization of war** and the rise of the mass-military organization. We shall look at these in some detail in the following sections. The industrialization of war refers to the application of modern industrial methods to the production and further development of weaponry. Modern mass-military systems have significantly changed the nature of organizing and fighting wars.

TECHNOLOGY AND THE INDUSTRIALIZATION OF WAR

The development of modern military potential was closely intertwined with the emergence of industrialism. From the early eighteenth century onwards, the armed forces possessed by the leading states became vastly larger than had ever been the case before—in some part a reflection, of course, of the fact that the size of their populations was expanding in general. But the main reason was that weapons could then be produced on a massive scale. By 1860, the Woolwich Arsenal in London was able to produce a quarter of a million bullets a day and nearly as many completed cartridges (Ropp, 1959). While governments sponsored their own arsenals devoted to

The industrialization of war, as depicted by artist Thornton Oakley for National Geographic Magazine, *1942.*

TABLE 11.1		NINETEENTH-CENTURY WARS	
Location	Date	Identification of conflict	Deaths
NORTH AMERICA			
United States	1861–65	Civil War, Confederacy vs. Union govt	650,000
LATIN AMERICA			
Brazil	1864–70	Peru vs. Brazil and Argentina	1,000,000
Colombia	1899–1903	Liberals vs. Conservative govt	150,000
Cuba	1868–78	Cuba vs. Spain	200,000
	1898	U.S. vs. Spain over Cuba and Philippines	200,000
EUROPE			
Germany	1870–71	France vs. Germany/Prussia	250,000
Greece	1821–28	Greek revolt against Turkey	120,000
Turkey	1828–29	Russia vs. Turkey	130,000
	1877–78	Russia vs. Turkey	285,000
Russia	1853–56	Turkey vs. Russia; Britain, France, Italy invading	267,000
FAR EAST			
China	1860–64	Taiping rebellion; Britain intervening	2,000,000
	1860–72	Moslem rebellions vs. China	150,000
Indonesia	1873–78	Achinese vs. Netherlands	200,000
Philippines	1899–1902	Philippine revolt against U.S.	215,000
		Total	5,817,000

Source: Ruth Leger Sivard, *World Military and Social Expenditures* (Washington, D.C.: World Priorities, 1983), p. 26.

military production, industrialists also started producing weaponry, which they sold both nationally and internationally. The arms trade in its modern sense came into being during the second half of the nineteenth century. Large corporations, devoted either wholly or partly to the manufacture of armaments and placing stress upon technical innovation, have ever since played a leading part in military development and war.

During World War I, processes of scientific discovery were applied in a concerted way to develop new forms of weaponry. A good example was the development of the tank (first introduced in the Battle of the Somme). Tanks were originally the equivalents of armor-plated ships brought ashore and made maneuverable on land. Tanks were first commonly known as "land cruisers"—or, more popularly, as "motor-monsters," "touring forts," or "giant toads." While the part

TABLE 11.2		TWENTIETH-CENTURY WARS	
Location	Date	Identification of conflict	Deaths
LATIN AMERICA			
Bolivia	1932–35	Paraguay vs. Bolivia	200,000
Colombia	1949–62	'La Violencia': civil war, Liberal vs. Conservative govt	300,000
Mexico	1910–20	Liberals and Radicals vs. govt	250,000
EUROPE			
Greece	1945–49	Civil war; Britain intervening	160,000
Poland	1919–20	USSR vs. Poland	100,000
Spain	1936–39	Civil war; Italy, Portugal and Germany intervening	1,200,000
Turkey	1915	Armenians deported	1,000,000
Russia	1904–05	Japan vs. Russia	130,000
	1918–20	Civil war; Allied intervention	1,300,000
EUROPE AND OTHER			
	1914–18	First World War	38,351,000
	1939–45	Second World War	19,617,000
MIDDLE EAST			
Iraq	1961–70	Civil war, Kurds vs. govt; massacre of Christians	105,000
	1982–88	Iran attack following Iraq invasion	600,000
Lebanon	1975–76	Civil war, Moslems vs. Christians; Syria intervening	100,000
Yemen	1962–69	Coup; civil war; Egypt intervening	101,000
SOUTH ASIA			
Afghanistan	1978–86	Civil war, Moslems vs. govt; USSR intervening	500,000
Bangladesh	1971	Bengalis vs. Pakistan; India invading; famine and massacres	1,500,000
India	1946–48	Moslems vs. Hindus; Britain intervening; massacres	800,000

they played in the First World War was limited, they have subsequently become basic to war on land. Similarly, the development of the airplane was greatly advanced as a result of its role as a weapon first in World War I, but even more so during World War II.

Three technological developments that now dominate military power were pioneered during the Second World War: the creation of nuclear weapons, the invention of rocket-propelled missiles, and the use of radar tracking to organize offensive and defensive strategies. In

TABLE 11.2		TWENTIETH-CENTURY WARS	
Location	Date	Identification of conflict	Deaths

FAR EAST

Location	Date	Identification of conflict	Deaths
Cambodia	1970–75	Civil war, Khmer Rouge vs. govt; N. Vietnam, U.S. intervening	156,000
	1975–78	Pol Pot govt vs. people; famine and massacres	2,000,000
China	1928	Moslem rebellion vs. govt	200,000
	1930–35	Civil war, Communists vs. govt	500,000
	1937–41	Japan vs. China	1,800,000
	1946–50	Civil war, Communists vs. Kuomintang govt	1,000,000
	1950–51	Govt executes landlords	1,000,000
	1956–59	Tibetan revolt	100,000
Indonesia	1965–66	Abortive coup; massacres	500,000
	1975–80	Annexation of East Timor; famine and massacres	100,000
Korea	1950–53	Korean war; UN intervening	2,889,000
Vietnam	1945–54	War of independence from France	600,000
	1960–65	Civil war, Vietcong vs. govt; U.S. intervening	300,000
	1965–75	Peak of Indochina War; U.S. bombing	2,058,000

AFRICA

Location	Date	Identification of conflict	Deaths
Algeria	1954–62	Civil war, Moslems vs. govt; France intervening	320,000
Burundi	1972	Hutu vs. govt; massacres	100,000
Ethiopia	1974–86	Eritrean revolt and famine	545,000
Mozambique	1981–86	Famine worsened by civil war	100,000
Nigeria	1967–70	Civil war, Biafrans vs. govt; famine and massacres	2,000,000
Rwanda	1956–65	Tutsis vs. govt; massacres	108,000
Sudan	1963–72	Christians vs. Arab govt; massacres	300,000
Tanzania	1905–07	Revolt against Germany; massacres	150,000
Uganda	1971–78	Civil war, Idi Amin coup; massacres	300,000
	1981–85	Army vs. people; massacres	102,100
Zaire	1960–65	Katanga secession; UN, Belgium intervening	100,000
		Total	83,642,000

Source: Ruth Leger Sivard, *World Military and Social Expenditures* (Washington, D.C.: World Priorities, 1983), p. 26.

the post–Second World War period, all three have become connected with one another: missiles can be furnished with nuclear warheads and guided by means of electronic tracking equipment. Some of the most important technological innovations influencing civilian life over the past half century had their origins in the Second World War or in weapons-related developments shortly afterwards. These include advances in jet travel, telecommunications, and information technology (Milward, 1984).

THE RISE OF MODERN
MILITARY ORGANIZATION

THE WORD "DISCIPLINE" ORIGINALLY MEANT A PROCESS OF learning. It is sometimes still used in this way, as when we speak of sociology or other academic subjects as "disciplines." During the seventeenth century, however, as part of the rise of the development of modern military organizations, it came to refer to military training and the controlled behavior it produces. First of all in the Dutch armies, and then rapidly spreading throughout Europe, standardized forms of military organizations were developed. Maurice, the Prince of Orange (1567–1625), set up the first military academy in Europe; his doctrines later became standard practice throughout the continent.

The modern sense of "uniform" as well as "discipline" can be traced to Maurice's teachings. "Uniform" was originally used as an adjective, but became a noun as standardized clothing became the norm in armies. Prior to this time, troops had often dressed more or less as they pleased. During the course of the seventeenth century, the wearing of uniforms became firmly established among all ranks of soldiery. Maurice also developed regularized marching, keeping men in step. He set up chains of command extending from generals to the enlisted men. From this period onwards, the armed forces became bureaucratic organizations, in which professional careers could be made.

By the twentieth century all the major European countries, as well as the United States and Russia, had set up military training schools using bureaucratic methods of recruitment and advancement. The soldiery came to consist of men recruited for periods of time in regular service. They were augmented in times of war or potential war by conscripts. Governments started to introduce large-scale conscription as the scale of war increased. The practice had its origins in France; in 1813 Napoleon was able to call up an army of 1.3 million Frenchmen (Challener, 1965; Finer, 1975). **Universal conscription**—the drafting of all able-bodied men within a certain age-range—was a significant development in the nature of modern war. It was an explicit recognition that all male citizens should be involved in wars waged for national objectives.

Modern armies are bureaucracies, staffed on the officer level by full-time officials. The terms "officer" and "official" in fact have a common origin, both referring to the office or position that an individual occupies in a hierarchy. In armies, some kinds of bureaucratic elements tend to be especially prominent. For example, divisions of rank are often the same throughout all branches of the military organization, no matter how large it is or how far flung its personnel. In other respects, the armed forces are quite distinctive as compared to most other modern organizations. Where national service exists, entry into the military is not voluntary. Anyone who seeks to leave before their period of service is ended—whether they are national-service conscripts or soldiers recruited on longer contracts—is subject to military trial and imprisonment. The army is also a carceral organization in which most members spend all their waking and sleeping hours. Even those military personnel who do not live in barracks tend to reside in housing specially set aside for them, physically separate from the civilian population (see Chapter 9: "Groups and Organizations").

CHARACTERISTICS OF THE MODERN MILITARY

Samuel Huntington, one of the most astute analysts of war, has argued that the modern military has four basic characteristics that distinguish it from earlier forms of military organization (Huntington, 1981):

1. EXPERTISE IN THE MANAGEMENT OF VIOLENCE. Military technology today is highly complex, with immense destructive capabilities. The military specializes in the control and use of this weaponry. In premodern armies, the difference between weaponry used in the military and that available to the civilian population was not great. Swords, bows, and guns were owned by many who were not themselves professional soldiers. Today, the armaments possessed by the military are vastly more powerful than those available to ordinary civilian populations—especially, of course, where nuclear armaments are involved.

2. CLIENTSHIP. With the exception of guerrilla and revolutionary movements, the armed forces in modern times are responsible to their major "client," the government of the state of which they are part. In premodern cultures, a military leader could secede from a political organization to which he and his armies were connected. He could move off elsewhere, subjugate the indigenous population, and set up a new adminis-

trative regime. This is no longer possible in the modern world because the military depends upon finances provided by the state through taxation and upon arms manufactured in industrial production.

3. CORPORATENESS. The armed forces, especially on the officer levels, tend to have a strong sense of corporate identity, separating them from civilians. The military often have their own schools, associations, publications, and customs. Those who make their careers within the armed forces have to start at the lowest officer grades and, unlike in the case of business firms, there are no opportunities for moving into higher management or obtaining directorships by changing organizations. Since members of the armed forces tend to live and work separately from the rest of society, their professional contacts and informal friendships tend to be within the military sphere.

4. THE IDEOLOGY OF THE MILITARY MIND. Premodern warfare tended to emphasize warrior values that glorified battle for its own sake, and placed an emphasis upon the valor of the individual warrior. Paradoxically, the modern military is usually not keen to engage in war, and these values have become largely irrelevant, or at least greatly reduced in their influence, in the military today. The modern "military mind" emphasizes attitudes of cooperation, the subordination of individual motives to group demands, and the primacy of order and discipline.

Overall, the outlook of the modern military tends to be based upon a desire to maintain its organizational strength and level of technological advancement. As Huntington puts it,

> The military man rarely favors war. He will always argue that the danger of war requires increased armaments; he will seldom argue that increased armaments make war practical or desirable. He always favors preparedness, but he never feels prepared. Accordingly, the professional military man contributes a cautious, conservative, restraining voice to the formulation of state policy. This has been his typical role in most modern states including fascist Germany, Communist Russia and Democratic America. (Huntington, 1981)

A painting of brutal hand-to-hand combat in the U.S. Civil War during which 650,000 soldiers lost their lives.

THE MILITARY IN THE UNITED STATES

The development of a professionalized, bureaucratic military came about later in the United States than in almost any other Western country. A few years after the Revolutionary War, in 1784, the Continental Congress ordered the disbanding of the only standing army in the United States, the last remaining units of the force that had been mobilized to fight the English. Congress proposed that standing armies in peacetime were inconsistent with the principles of republicanism and constituted a danger to individual liberties. The regular army was replaced with a militia whose sole role was to guard the western frontier.

The geopolitical situation of the United States was quite different from that of the European countries, which were in constant conflict with one another both on the European continent itself and in the areas of their colonial influence. Most immigrants to the United States in the nineteenth century wished to leave such conflicts behind them, and governing circles were largely indifferent to international affairs. The military was seen as the ally of monarchy and aristocracy. Prior to the present century, with the exception of the Civil War, large-scale military power was rarely deployed in the United States, and never gave rise to military organizations as powerful as those in the leading European countries.

The American Civil War has in fact been regarded by some historians as the forerunner of modern total war, since the numbers of soldiery involved on both sides were so considerable and both North and South mobilized their economies to provide full-scale support for the conflict. There was a large body of armed forces in the United States in 1865 when the war ended, even if the level of discipline and training were to European eyes very low. Yet, rather than trying to consolidate its military strength, the federal government set about dismantling the military establishment that had been created. Only a small army and navy remained; the army mainly deployed against the Indians along the frontier. Numbers were progressively pared down and funds cut back during the last half of the century.

Nevertheless, during this period a number of schools devoted to military education were established, and the Army War College was set up in 1901. In some respects, the very lack of public support for military organizations led to an extreme glorification of military values by those still in the service. With the increasing industrial strength of the United States in the late nineteenth and early twentieth centuries came spreading commercial contacts overseas. The military used this as a basis for arguing that far more military resources were needed, specifically for the protection of these commercial interests abroad. In addition, Leonard Wood, Chief of Staff from 1910 to 1914, pressed for the introduction of regular national service. When the United States entered the First World War, not long before its end, its industries could not supply the military hardware the armed forces claimed to need. Two million American soldiers were sent over to Europe, but much of their heavy equipment was provided by the French.

In spite of the widespread revulsion felt in the United States against the horrors of World War I, the armed forces from that time onwards became progressively more established and powerful. Several of the enterprises that had been turned to military production during the war years continued in the armaments business. During World War II, in which American troops were involved on several fronts in Europe and in the Pacific, the U.S. armed forces became the most powerful in the world. Since then, military preparedness in the face of possible conflict with the Soviet Union has dominated the concerns of the American armed forces. During this "Cold War" and since, the military establishment began to have more influence within the country than was ever the case outside the conditions of actual war. International military commands were set up, integrating the United States "defense community" across the world. Closer links were developed between military and business leaders than formerly was the case. Armaments manufacturers continued producing weaponry with increasing technological sophistication and in greater volume than before.

SOVIET MILITARY POWER

The Russian Revolution of 1917 occurred in the context of war. Devastating loss of life among the soldiery, together with incompetent battlefield command, led to desertions and mutinies. Before they came to power, the Bolsheviks, led by Vladimir I. Lenin and Leon Trotsky, were hostile to standing armies for reasons similar to those characteristic of early American political thought. They associated standing armies with aggression abroad and oppression at home. Soon after they assumed the reins of government, however, the Bolshevik government was forced to raise an army in order to fight off hostile Western powers which invaded the country during their civil war. The Red Army was organized by Trotsky, who recruited more than fifty thousand former Tsarist officers, stressing centralized control and strict military discipline. It was originally intended that the Red Army would be disbanded, and replaced by militia, following the civil war. Although the issue was publicly debated, and government reports heard, the army was not dissolved. It was instead systematically reorganized and placed under the control of military commissars—political officials connecting the army with the Communist Party, whose aim was to guarantee the subservience of the army to the Party (Erickson, 1974).

In the 1920s and 1930s, the Soviet Union was ringed with countries hostile to its political system. The need to develop the armed forces in conjunction with the industrialization of the country became a major emphasis. Under Joseph Stalin's leadership, a rapid process of expansion of industrial production was initiated, driven in part by military considerations. High priority was given to the development of the armaments industry. By the opening of the Second World War, the Soviet Union was militarily very strong. Since its level of economic advancement was well behind that of the leading Western countries, however, its approach to military organization was different from theirs. Rather than stressing relatively small, highly mechanized forces, the policy was to develop strength in numbers, creating a mass basis for the army. Stalin built up heavy industry as a means of providing both for economic growth in general and for developing military strength. The Soviet Union thus created a "war economy" prior to the Second World War and such a system has remained in place subsequently.

The Soviet Union entered the Second World War when it was invaded by Germany in June 1941, and became allied to the United States, Britain, and France. While many men and women from these other countries were killed during the course of the war, the loss of life suffered by the Soviet population was far more devastating. Over

20 million of the Soviet population were killed, and thousands of towns and villages were wiped out. The continuing development of the Soviet military today is partly due to a determination that such events should never be repeated. Since the Second World War, the Soviet Union has built up its own network of security alliances rivaling those of the United States.

In the Soviet Union there is no privately owned armaments industry; the armed forces also stand in a different relation to the government, as compared to Western countries. There are many direct connections between Party and military leaders, with members of each sitting on the ruling councils of the other. A commissariat of the defense industry is responsible for the overall coordination of weapons production, with subministries involved with particular branches, such as the nuclear weapons program (Holloway, 1984). The weapons industry tends to be clearly separated from other economic sectors in the Soviet Union, being given highest priority, and having superior rates of pay to comparable areas of production elsewhere. It is technologically more advanced than any other industry in the country. While the bulk of Soviet military production is used by its own armed forces, weapons and military equipment are sold extensively to other countries.

GLOBAL MILITARY EXPENDITURE

THE TWENTIETH CENTURY HAS BEEN UNQUESTIONABLY THE most war-ridden and destructive in human history. Thus far, more than 100 million human beings have been killed in war, an average of 3,500 a day. Most were killed in the two world wars. Military budgets grow larger and larger; military weaponry gets increasingly sophisticated and more readily available to those throughout the world who can pay for it.

In 1977, world military expenditures passed $1 billion a day, representing a rate of spending of $50 million each hour. Since then, the overall rate of spending has almost doubled again, amounting to a yearly total of $820 billion in 1989 (Stockholm International Peace Research Institute, 1990). By far the greater proportion of this is spent by First World countries, their share amounting to $600 billion in that year. World military expenditure is greater than the overall gross product of the whole of the African continent, South Africa included. It is more than that of all of Asia, if Japan is left out.

The ratio of military spending to total government expenditure within particular countries varies. West Germany allocates 3.3 percent of its overall production for military purposes, Britain 5.4 percent, and the United States 6.6 percent (Stockholm International Peace Research Institute, 1988). The Soviet Union does not provide figures, which makes any comparison difficult, but its rate of military expenditure is certainly much higher than that of the United States; it has been estimated at no less than 20 percent. This crippling burden on the Soviet economy was one of the main factors leading to the economic problems that the Soviet Union experienced in the 1980s, and which helped provoke the reforms initiated under Gorbachev.

THE NUCLEAR STOCKPILE

Although there are nonproliferation treaties, which are supposed to limit the spread of nuclear weapons, the world's stockpile of nuclear armaments until very recently continued to increase. As of early 1990, there are still some fifty thousand nuclear warheads in the hands of the countries possessing nuclear capability—the vast majority of these are held by the United States and the Soviet Union. The nuclear arsenals of other countries are much smaller, but even the possession of a few nuclear weapons yields immense destructive capacity. Countries having nuclear weaponry include Britain, France, India, and China—and in all probability, Israel, Pakistan, and South Africa.

In addition there are also major links between nuclear power and the capacity to manufacture nuclear weapons. If dependence upon nuclear power as a source of energy becomes increasingly widespread throughout the world, it will offer more and more countries the potential to develop their own nuclear weapons. In 1981, the Israeli Air Force bombed Iraq's nuclear reactor just outside Baghdad. The Israelis alleged that what was claimed to be a power station was in fact being devoted to the production of nuclear weapons. Israel was condemned by many other states for its action, but it is generally agreed that the Iraqi technology program was being put to military purposes (Durie and Edwards, 1982). There are virtually insoluble problems in detaching the spread of nuclear power, which some Western countries are keen to encourage, from the proliferation of nuclear weaponry.

THE ARMS RACE

The enormous nuclear stockpile is a result of what came to be called the **arms race** between the United States and the Soviet Union.

Why have governments been concerned with building up their military strength? There are several reasons. A country that is militarily strong can hope to *deter* others from using force against it. Conversely, military strength can be used to acquire new territories or pursue national interests through active conflict or war. The traditional states, ancient Greece, Persia, and Rome, built up their militaries to expand their empires. According to the celebrated nineteenth-century military thinker, Karl von Clausewitz, war is a means of achieving national ends where peaceful or diplomatic measures fail (von Clausewitz, 1982; orig. pub. 1873). In times of peace, military power can be used as a means of *coercion,* because the threat of its use might be sufficient to achieve a desired objective. In the nuclear age, this can be a frightening prospect. During the Cuban missile crisis in 1962, President John F. Kennedy and Soviet Premier Nikita Khrushchev threatened the world with nuclear war over the issue of Russian land-based nuclear weapon sites in Cuba. Finally, military power provides a basis for *defense* if one country is attacked by another. "Defense" has come to be used as a synonym for military needs, because no government wishes to advertise itself as a likely aggressor against others.

The arms race is characterized by what has been called **action-reaction**—the government of one country looks to innovations going on in another in order to adjust its own program of weapons development. The military in each society also presses its claims on the basis of what it believes military planners on the other side are planning. Costly research goes on continuously to fill each nation's perceived gaps or to get a step ahead of the other nation (Figure 11.1).

FIGURE 11.1   **THE ARMS RACE: MILITARY EXPENDITURES**

This figure shows the action-reaction increase (prior to 1989) in military expenditures by nations aligned with the Soviet Union, in the Warsaw Pact, and with the United States, in the North Atlantic Treaty Organization (NATO).

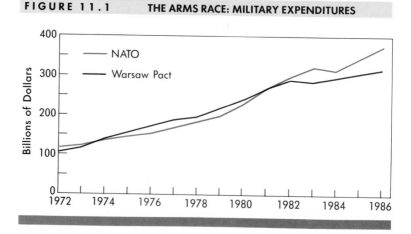

Source: U.S. Arms Control and Disarmament Agency, *World Military Expenditures and Arms Transfers* (Washington, D.C.: Government Printing Office, 1988).

This latter was the case, for example, with the development of the first atomic bomb toward the end of World War II. Warned that Nazi Germany was working on such a weapon, the Roosevelt administration assembled the Manhattan Project, one of the largest scientific research teams ever brought together, to "get there first." The project, which took five years and cost some $2 billion, resulted in the two bombs dropped on Japan that ended the war and began the nuclear age.

Today, weapons development has become an on-going "project." Corporations regularly approach the armed forces with new weapons ideas which the military then finds a reason for needing. Thus when it was discovered that several warheads, having multiple targets, could be put on one intercontinental missile, the armed forces enthusiastically adopted the new technology. Their rationale as to why new weapons systems are necessary changes whenever the technology alters further (Sheehan, 1983).

THE DETERRENCE DEBATE

The arms race became decisively influenced by the advent of nuclear armaments, particularly since long-range missiles have existed to deliver them. There exists no mode of defense that is effective against nuclear missiles. Deterrence was once only one among other reasons why states kept themselves armed. In the case of the massively destructive nuclear weapons that now exist, it is the *only* possible reason. As the effect of using them would be catastrophic to all, nuclear weapons are supposedly kept only to deter the other side from using them.

Deterrence is essentially a psychological concept, since what is important is that each side believes both that the other would retaliate if attacked and that the outcome would be so devastating that no military aggression can be risked. The deterrent strategy of the United States from the 1950s up to the early 1970s was based upon the concept of "Mutual Assured Destruction" (MAD). Since the United States and the Soviet Union possessed such large nuclear arsenals, neither could immobilize the other by suddenly mounting an attack. It would not be rational for either country to precipitate a nuclear war, because each knew that its own population and resources would be largely wiped out by any retaliation. This outlook was criticized from a number of standpoints. Activists in peace movements argued that in fact this doctrine produced a paradoxical situation of extreme danger. For MAD to work, each side must believe that the other would be willing to destroy it by unleashing its missiles, if attacked. Yet each side must simultaneously believe that the other had no intention of using its nuclear weapons. Each must be frightened into holding back from using its weaponry, and must believe the other to be so deterred; yet each must accept that the other *would* use that weaponry if called upon to do so. Jonathan Schell remarks:

> We cannot both threaten ourselves with something and hope to avoid that same thing by making the threat—both intend to do something and intend not to do it. The head-on contradiction between these aims has set up a cross current of tension within the policies of each superpower. Safety may be emphasized at one moment, and at the next moment it is the "terror" that comes to the fore. And since the deterrence doctrine pairs the safety and the terror, and makes the former depend on the latter, the world is never quite sure from day to day which one is in the ascendent—if, indeed, the distinction can be maintained in the first place. (Schell, 1982)

People throughout much of the world have demonstrated against the arms race.

Arms Limitation Discussions

Strategic Arms Limitations Talks (SALT) were held on several occasions in the 1960s and 1970s and lead to two sets of agreements, one signed in 1972 and the other in 1979. These did not, however, prevent a resurgence of military spending by the superpowers in the late 1970s and early 1980s. Such spending was also prompted by President Ronald Reagan's "Star Wars" program—officially known as the Strategic Defense Initiative (SDI). This program proposed to develop a system of defense against missiles using space weapons and lasers. It seems probable that the Soviet Union was independently working upon similar possibilities, although not on the same scale of investment that the United States devoted to it (Bulkeley and Spinardi, 1986).

Given the irrationalities of MAD, MAS (Mutually Assured Security) would obviously be vastly preferable if it worked (if defensive weapons could be effectively deployed on both sides). However, critics argue that SDI can never work, because to do so it must be virtually perfect. A system could be 99.9 percent effective, yet with current missile deployments still allow eight warheads through, capable of killing 60 million people in the United States. Supporters claim that SDI will increase stability by turning the emphasis from destructive to protective systems. SDI would offer far greater possibilities for world peace in the relatively near future than the current reliance upon offensive weapons.

The United States and the Soviet Union reached an agreement in 1988 to scrap medium-range nuclear missiles stationed in Europe. This initiative was originally proposed by Western leaders, but made a realistic option by a concrete agenda put forward by Mikhail Gorbachev, the Soviet premier. The agreement marked the first effective reversal in the arms race. In 1989, Gorbachev put forward more far-reaching proposals still: Soviet armed strength would be substantially cut, particularly the troops stationed in or near Europe. Gorbachev promised further cuts if they were matched by the Western side. The United States responded positively to these ideas, and at meetings between Gorbachev and President George Bush in December 1989 and May 1990, both sides agreed to pursue substantial arms reductions in Europe. A new agreement is due to be signed between the United States and the Soviet Union late in 1990 that will radically reduce the nuclear arsenals held by both sides. These proposals might also mean the abolition of most or all weapons with multiple nuclear warheads.

THE ARMS TRADE

While the arms race between the United States and the Soviet Union might be slowing down substantially, the same cannot be said of the **arms trade,** which, like so much in the military sphere today, is dominated by the same two countries. Each of the superpowers transfers arms within its global system of alliance. Since the Second World War, the United States has provided some $80 billion, in the form of loans or grants, for assistance for military projects in countries covered by its various alliances. It has also made available many kinds of on-location training personnel. Soviet military assistance has been lent to its allies in similar ways, but on a less extensive basis. The Soviet Union has concentrated attention upon its Warsaw Pact nations in Eastern Europe and on a few strategically important clients, particularly in the Middle East, to whom it has provided very large stocks of armaments.

The United States is by a large margin the leading exporter of armaments, with the Soviets lagging some way behind in second place. About two-thirds of the arms trade concerns weaponry passing between the industrialized and the Third World countries. A high proportion of this consists of major weapons systems, rather than just small arms and support equipment (Kaldor, 1982). In the first twenty years after World War II, much of the weaponry exported to developing countries was of kinds being phased out by the armed forces of the United States and other industrialized nations. Today, however, even the most sophisticated weapons systems, with the exception of

those having nuclear capability, are sold to anyone with the money to buy. Thus, some Third World countries possess equipment almost as advanced as that of the American or Soviet military. Several leading Western industrial powers besides the United States are also major arms exporters, including especially France and Britain.

Since the early 1980s, the overall volume of the world arms trade has remained at a fairly stable level. Many Third World countries, suffering from the global economic recession and growing foreign debts, can no longer afford to import new armaments at the same level. On the other hand, an increasing number of developing countries now have their own arms industries. Not only are they less reliant on Western or Soviet sources, they are actively starting to compete with them in offering their own military goods for sale on world markets.

Effects of Arms Trading on the Economy

The arms trade has important effects on the economies of many countries. The leading Western exporting countries and the Soviet Union gain financially from the world trade in weapons. Governments and businesses that produce military hardware invest a great deal in research and development, pioneering new weapons technologies. The costs of such investment can be significantly lessened by selling the weapons to customers outside their own countries. This wide marketing of weapons can rebound in times of war; a country could find itself attacked by weapons it or one of its allies produced.

For example, in 1986 an American ship in the Middle East was partially destroyed and sailors' lives lost by a sophisticated French-made Exocet missile fired (by mistake) by the Iraq military.

Third World countries that purchase armaments from the industrialized nations quite often do so at the price of placing great strain on their economies—which are mostly much weaker than those of the industrialized world. For them, the arms trade has unfortunate consequences. Where the military are particularly powerful, or actually governing, it is able to push for the constant importing of new equipment. This in turn further strengthens their position, while draining away economic resources that might be desperately needed for other projects—such as buying agricultural machinery, power plants, or manufacturing technology—that would help the impoverished population.

Among the most heinous weapons being stockpiled are chemical weapons. They were responsible for many deaths during the 1980s Iran-Iraq war.

THE MILITARY, POLITICS, AND SOCIETY

THERE ARE MANY COUNTRIES THROUGHOUT THE WORLD where the armed forces are the rulers or that have experienced periods of military government. In the present century, most South American countries, and many states in Africa, the Middle East, and Europe have experienced military takeovers. In one guise or another, military rule is "normal" in some parts of the world and, over the past fifty years, has become more rather than less common. As compared to Third World countries, the industrialized, liberal-democratic societies of the West and the East European societies, including the Soviet Union, have been relatively immune from direct military rule. Why should this be so? Why aren't *all* societies, in fact, ruled by the military, given that they are far more tightly organized than any civilian groups and have a monopoly over the most powerful weaponry?

There are several reasons. First, the higher the level of a society's industrialization, the more complicated its administrative system tends to be. Depending as they do upon their own internal codes of discipline and duty, the armed forces are not equipped to undertake the task of administering a complex social order. Specialist civilian administrators are necessary to govern such systems, as can be seen from the experiences of the Allied military governments of occupation in Germany and Italy following World War II. Although faced with defeated and compliant populations, rather than rebellious ones, the occupying powers still found it necessary to reinforce their military personnel with large numbers of specialized civilian officials.

Second, the military lacks the **legitimacy**—the morally accepted right—to rule. Government by force can only be transitory. To sustain continuing political power, a group must be widely recognized by the people they govern as having the right to govern. In societies with established traditions of civilian rule, this is very difficult for the military to achieve.

Third, in societies without histories of military government, there is normally a clear separation between the military and police forces. During the period of the development of modern police forces, in the early to middle nineteenth century, the military was often called in to quell civil disturbances. The more civil order is maintained by the police, however, the more the role of the armed forces is defined as being concerned with *external* threat. The police may be armed and have their own paramilitary antiriot squads, but the firepower available to them is vastly less than that of the armed forces, and the police could not stage a *coup d'état* (seizure of government) as the military could (Finer, 1962). Where civil order is maintained by a clearly defined police force, with the armed forces concerned only with defense of borders, the chances of a military takeover of government are minimized.

POLITICAL INFLUENCE AND ECONOMIC EFFECTS OF THE MILITARY

Even in societies in which they do not rule, the military does influence political and economic life. This is virtually guaranteed by the fact that the modern armed forces depend upon tax revenue raised by the government. The sway of the military over political decisions varies considerably within modern societies. Military leaders can use various routes to try to affect, or control, political and economic policies. At one end of the spectrum, the military might confine themselves to employing "usual" channels in influencing politicians and business leaders. That is to say, they may form a lobby or pressure group like any other, not straying outside conventional processes of political bargaining. At the other end of the spectrum, they may blackmail or intimidate civilian authorities by the threat or actual use of violence. In Japan, in the 1930s, the army was implicated in the murders of prominent politicians and trade-union leaders and carried on a campaign of threats against others. The French armed forces in Algeria blackmailed the French government by refusing to cooperate with any of its policies unless General De Gaulle was brought to power (Williams et al., 1979). More recently, the military in Latin American countries such as El Salvador or Guatemala has been involved in organizing death squads that murder civilians whose views or policies disagree with the government's.

The Military-Industrial Complex

In those states in which the direct role of the military in politics is confined, the close meshing of military and industrial interests may still strongly influence government decision making. President Dwight D. Eisenhower coined the phrase **military-industrial complex,** in the late 1950s, to describe the close integration of military and economic development in American society. Eisenhower originally used the phrase to refer in a positive way to the application of science and technology to military production. Later, however, he came to see the development of such connections as threatening. The military-industrial complex had achieved such power that major decisions affecting the social and economic life of the country were being made outside the political domain. Many subsequent observers argued that, as a result of the Cold War, the military-industrial complex became prominent both in the United States and in the Soviet Union.

How valid is this view? Unfortunately, the idea of the military-industrial complex has often been used vaguely, and the extent of its power over political decision making hinted at rather than directly specified. If such a system is said to *dominate* a modern political economy, however, two conditions are implied: (1) that large areas of economic activity are dependent upon military production for their prosperity; (2) that in consequence of this, those in government positions find themselves compelled to acquiesce in the production needs demanded by military leaders and armaments manufacturers.

In some Western countries defense contractors are giant corporations. About three-quarters of the firms having the biggest military contracts with the government in the United States are also among the largest five hundred American corporations (Kennedy, 1983). There are many documented ties between military leaders and the top executives within these corporations. In the Soviet Union, arms-related industries outstrip all others in technological advancement. Industries concerned with military needs account for a higher proportion of Soviet economic activity as a whole than in most Western countries.

Yet it does not follow that in either economy the main productive organizations are primarily dependent upon military-related activi-

"On the other hand, gentlemen, what if we gave a war and EVERYBODY came?"

ties for their prosperity. Few of the largest American corporations are engaged in military production. Those whose scale of business does depend upon military contracts tend to move in and out of this production area according to shifts in the political and economic climate (Lieberson, 1972).

During the Vietnam War, the largest twenty-five military contractors in the United States derived some 40 percent of their business from defense production. Five years after the end of the war, this had slumped to under 10 percent (Gansler, 1980). The level of involvement in military production, in other words, tends to respond to political needs and pressures, rather than the other way around. Much the same is true in the Soviet Union. It is the Communist Party leaders who retain the final say in questions of military expenditure.

We can conclude that there is not a military-industrial complex directly controlling or manipulating civilian policies in either of these societies. Nonetheless, production of military-related goods and services is a major part of the economy of both, and expenditure on these is a matter of prime political concern. Hence, military leaders and manufacturers, sometimes acting as combined pressure groups, are often able to wield considerable direct and indirect influence over political policies. The same can be said for the other industrialized countries, although there are some (such as Switzerland and Canada) where the influence of the military is particularly weak.

ARMED FORCE IN THE THIRD WORLD

Why should there be so many *coups d'état,* and military governments, in developing countries? To reach an answer, we have to understand the distinctive nature of these societies. Many have only a low degree of administrative unity. They are the legacy of colonial regimes or are "new nations" established where there was previously little or no centralized government. Colonial regimes did not encourage ideals of democratic participation, and when they ended there were often few established bases of legitimate political power. In countries in which there are multiple ethnic, tribal, and regional loyalties, and where most of the population may have little knowledge or interest in the mechanisms of central government, political-party systems are highly unstable. In these circumstances, as an internally coherent group with its own interests, the military organization frequently steps directly into the political void. In many such countries the distinction between the military and the police is ambiguous, the two often being connected through military intelligence units used to maintain compliance among the civilian population (Janowitz, 1977). A separate system of internal policing, similar to those of the industrialized countries, has not been effectively developed.

In most Third World countries in which the armed forces are a major presence, **military rule** is strategically indirect. The military places puppet politicians in power, whose activities are controlled behind the scenes by the military leaders. Should the politicians deviate from policies the armed forces consider desirable, a *coup d'état* will be staged. The military temporarily assumes power, before handing the government over to another puppet regime.

TERRORISM AND GUERRILLA MOVEMENTS

As compared to traditional social orders, and in contrast to some Third World countries, the industrialized societies are mostly highly *pacified*—internally peaceful. Of course, a great deal of criminal, domestic, and other types of violence exist. Yet save for cases in which strong revolutionary movements arise, there are no agencies internal to the society capable of challenging the armed forces. This was very rarely the case in traditional societies, where the power of the ruling authority was often threatened by warlords, pirates, brigands, and others.

The remains of a jet cockpit rests in Lockerbie, Scotland, after a terrorist bomb destroyed a U.S.-bound flight from Germany, killing over two hundred civilians.

Terrorism

We can only understand what has come to be called **terrorism** against the background of the internal pacification of modern states. Terrorism can be defined as *the threat or use of violence, for political ends, on the part of individuals or groups who otherwise have no formal political power.* Understood in this way, terrorism acquires a particular significance within modern states, precisely because governments claim a monopoly over the right to deploy violence for political motives—as a threat against other nations or in war. Terrorism draws upon the same symbols of legitimacy as the government to which it is opposed. Terrorists tend to assert that their actions are "legal," and often call themselves soldiers, adopting military terms for their organizations —such as the Irish Republican Army (IRA), the Red Brigade in Italy and so forth. They talk of "political rights" and announce "trials," "sentences," and "executions" (Wardlaw, 1983; Wilkinson, 1986).

If the majority of the population do not accept the claim that the activities of a terrorist group are legitimate military ones, they are likely to see the group as engaging in wanton violence. One of the characters in Sean O'Casey's play *The Shadow of a Gunman* expresses this attitude when talking of armed resistance to the British presence in Ireland:

> "Its the civilians that suffer; when there's an ambush they don't know where to run. Shot in the back to save the Brit-

TABLE 11.3	SOME OF THE PRINCIPAL TERRORIST GROUPS ACTIVE DURING THE 1980s		
Name	Aim/type of group	Target	Area of operation
Action Directe	Revolutionary anticapitalism	Military, business, United States, and defense	France
Black September	Palestinian state	Israel and Israeli support	Western Europe
El Fatah	Palestinian state	Israel and Israeli support	Western Europe, Middle East
Euzkadi ta Askata-suna (ETA)	Basque nationalism	Spanish police and administration	Spain (sometimes France)
Front de la Libération Nationale Corse (FLNC)	Corsican nationalism	French state and property, especially businesses	France
Irish Republican Army (IRA)	Irish nationalism	Security forces	United Kingdom
Palestine Liberation Organization (PLO)	Palestinian state	Israel and Israeli support	Western Europe, Middle East
Red Army Faction (RAF)	Revolutionary socialism	Military and business	West Germany (suspected of Italian link)
Red Brigades	Revolutionary socialism	Military and business	Italy

Many other groups, particularly nationalists and regionalists, operate in Europe; these include Armenians, Jugoslavs, South Tyroleans and Jurassians.
Source: Social Studies Review, March 1987, p. 5.

ish Empire, an' shot in the breast to save the soul of Ireland. I'm a Nationalist meself, right enough. . . . I believe in the freedom of Ireland, an' that England has no right to be here, but I draw the line when I hear the gunmen about dyin' for the people, when it's the people that are dyin' for the gunmen!" (O'Casey, quoted in Wilkinson, 1974)

The word "terrorism" has its origins in the French Revolution of 1789. During the Reign of Terror thousands of people—originally just the aristocrats, but later many ordinary citizens—were hunted down by the new political authorities and put to the guillotine. "Terror," meaning the use of violence to intimidate, has been used by governments on a wide scale since that time. The practices of the Nazis and of the secret police under Stalin are particularly horrific examples. States have been responsible for far more outrages against human dignity and life over the past two centuries than have insurrection groups. But for our purposes here, the term "terrorist" means those who set out to *challenge* the authority of a state.

Guerrilla Movements

Terrorism in the twentieth century has been closely connected with **guerrilla movements,** and the two really have to be considered together. The only real difference between them is that guerrillas are usually thought of as operating against military targets, and terrorists against civilian ones—but this distinction is blurred in practice. Guerrillas are irregular fighters, lacking the organized military power and personnel commanded by regular armed forces. They use sporadic acts of violence as a means of dramatizing their case, because they cannot hope to win in open battle. There are many examples of guerrilla movements and wars in the twentieth century, involving groups of a variety of different political persuasions. Sometimes such movements have remained weak, or have been wiped out by superior military force; on other occasions they have been successful enough to bring about wholesale political change, a revolution.

The movements that resisted the Germans during the Nazi occupation in France, Holland, Belgium, Scandinavia, the occupied parts of Russia, and elsewhere, were guerrilla organizations. So too were the movements led by Mao Tse-Tung in China and by Fidel Castro in Cuba, prior to their successful takeover of governmental power. Guerrilla movements include the Algerian insurrectionists who forced the French to put an end to their colonial government in that country in the 1960s; the Mau Mau revolts in Kenya of roughly the same period; the Tupamaros in Uruguay and Monteneros in Argentina in the 1960s and 1970s; the groups who operated in South Vietnam fighting the Americans during the Vietnam war; and the Islamic groups opposed to the Russian presence in Afghanistan in the 1980s.

Guerrilla organizations have sprung up in many different circumstances, among them, situations in which there is either acute political oppression or in which there is a very unequal distribution of wealth. Walter Laqueur (1976) provides a summary of some of the main characteristics of twentieth-century guerrilla warfare, while cautioning that guerrilla movements "are an awkward topic for generalization":

1. Guerrilla movements develop in relatively inaccessible parts of a country, in which the regular military cannot easily use their superior numbers and firepower. Guerrillas normally operate out of inhospitable mountain areas, forests, jungles, or swamps. They usually change their bases periodically, seeking to escape offering a clear target for enemy attack.

2. Guerrilla wars often occur in areas where numerous wars

and battles have occurred before. This is obviously in some part because these regions tend to be fiercely contested in terms of political affiliations and loyalties. The same factors that give rise to military rule also facilitate the emergence of guerrilla movements, opposed to the military leaders.

3. Guerrilla warfare is most commonly found in less-developed countries, where traditional social structures have been broken down by the impact of political or economic ties with the industrialized world. Peasants whose livelihood has suffered, or who wish to escape the influence of large landowners, are often recruited by guerrilla movements.

4. There have been three main types of guerrilla war in the present century. One consists of hostilities waged against foreign invaders; a second is warfare conducted by separatist movements in conflict with the central government (such as the IRA); the third consists of guerrilla activities conducted against governments thought to be corrupt or exploitative (as in the case of the Tupamaros and Monteneros in South America).

5. Guerrilla war has developed in conjunction with the modernization of warfare generally. Guerrilla movements cannot deploy the range of sophisticated weaponry available to orthodox armies. On the other hand, particularly given appropriate terrain, they can and do develop means of countering or frustrating it. The Vietcong guerrillas in Vietnam, for instance, had very little weaponry compared to the Americans, yet they were still able to invent tactics that frustrated the sophisticated military technology deployed against them —such as the elaborate system of underground tunnels that they disappeared into after carrying out raids.

6. Most guerrilla movements do not operate autonomously; they are funded or supported by countries outside the particular region in which they operate. Funding and support received from one of the two major military alliances (centered on the United States and the Soviet Union) means that guerrilla struggles today are frequently extensions of the global competition between the major powers. Both the United States and the Soviet Union have provided resources for guerrilla movements in several parts of Africa, Latin America, and Southeast Asia.

Victims of urban guerrilla warfare in Lebanon.

Urban Guerrillas and Terrorists

Over the past twenty years, tactics originally used mainly by rural guerrilla movements have been widely adopted by groups operating within urban settings, especially in Europe and Japan. The hijacking of airplanes, kidnapping and murder of prominent individuals, and bombings have become familiar events in many countries. Those involved hold political views ranging from extreme Left to extreme Right, and include a variety of separatist and nationalist groups. In the late 1960s and early 1970s, bombings, kidnappings, and assassinations were carried out by the Rengo Sekigun in Japan, the Red Army Faction in West Germany, and the Red Brigades in Italy. In the United States, the Weathermen and Black Panthers advocated strategies of urban violence. In the mid-1980s, a further wave of urban guerrilla activity occurred in Milan, Paris, Berlin, and other European cities. Most terrorist groups have proved to be transient, either meeting with widespread condemnation and so failing to recruit members or obtain money, or being broken up by the authorities. Others have more sustained sources of funding and represent causes having some measure of popular support, particularly where they are connected with separatist movements. Such groups include the Irish Republican Army (IRA) and the Basque separatist movement in Spain (Lodge, 1981).

Most of even the more permanently organized groups remain small. Violence is used to dramatize particular causes, to create anxieties that might reflect upon the competence of the existing government, and to achieve a following among those impressed by the fact that such movements do not merely "talk" but "mean business." As such groups become more persecuted by the state, and forced to operate more and more in a secretive, closed fashion, their use of violence sometimes becomes more ruthless (Mommsen, 1982).

In the popular press, terrorists are often represented as driven by bloodlust and as having incomprehensible motives for their actions (Schmid and DeGraaf, 1982; Crenshaw, 1983). This characterization is usually far from the truth. Most groups prepared to use violence to further their ends have a coherent philosophy about why they act as they do. Controversial though their ideas may be, these groups are not normally composed of people who claim to value violence for its own sake. Political authorities and the general public often have ambivalent, or even hypocritical, attitudes towards terrorism. They may feel outrage at the brutality of activities carried out within their own borders, but at the same time support and encourage guerrilla movements using identical tactics in other regions of the world.

Guerrilla movements have sometimes included women who have taken an active fighting role. Women have also participated in terrorist actions, such as hijacking planes or planting bombs. But these instances are relatively uncommon, and if we look back over the history of the military, we find that war has everywhere been preeminently a male activity. Why should this be so? The question is very important, because if it should be the case that war is somehow linked to a biologically determined male aggressiveness, war would perhaps be an inescapable part of the human condition—a terrifying prospect in an era of nuclear weapons.

WOMEN AND WAR

MEN HAVE EVERYWHERE STAFFED THE FIGHTING FORCES OF armies, and have been the commanders and generals; warrior values, emphasizing adventure, daring, and *esprit de corps* (the sense of involvement with others in the pursuit of shared ends) have always been mainly associated with men rather than women. The enthusiasm of men for war, and the absence of women from the ranks of the warriors, has led some to speculate that genetic factors must be responsible. In other words, men may be biologically disposed to engage in aggressive behavior—fighting against others—while women are not. Some who have held such a view include writers influenced by sociobiology (See Chapter 2: "Culture and Society"), as well as some early feminists. Elizabeth Cady Stanton expressed this idea forcefully when she wrote in 1868,

> The male element is a destructive force, stern, selfish, aggrandizing, loving war, conquest, acquisition, breeding in the material and moral world alike discord, disorder, disease, and death. See what a record of blood and cruelty the pages of history reveal! . . . The male element has held high carnival thus far, it has fairly run riot from the beginning, overpowering the feminine element everywhere, crushing out the diviner qualities in human nature. (Stanton, Anthony, and Gage, 1969; orig. pub. 1889)

Perhaps we might hope in the future, Stanton went on to add, that the female values of gentleness, caring, and sympathy will be brought more to the fore in society, balancing the aggressive impulses of men. The female values are held by one-half of humankind, but because of the dominance of men in public activities, they have never had much influence.

How valid is the view that men are constitutionally predisposed towards war, whereas women are not? On the whole, the evidence is

A female drill instructor—U.S. Army.

against this thesis. Warfare (in the sense of violent and bloody battles, in which many are killed) barely existed before the emergence of traditional states. States fight wars in order to acquire territory for their use, to gain new resources, to advance religious causes, and for other reasons not directly connected with aggressiveness as such.

Moreover, women have sometimes been combatants in times of war, and as noncombatants have very often lent support to war aims. Although the vast majority of commanders have been men, there are historical cases of women military leaders who have actively led soldiery on the battlefield. Two of the best-known examples are Boadicea, the Saxon warrior monarch, and Joan of Arc, who led the French against the English in the fifteenth century. Female monarchs (like Queen Elizabeth I of England) have assumed overall control over their country's fighting forces, and have not hesitated to proclaim militaristic values (Elshtain, 1987).

Women's regiments have been formed in most modern armies, although the majority of these do not participate in actual combat. However, Israeli women soldiers have formed part of fighting units, and during the Second World War, Soviet women regularly engaged in combat. Some 8 percent of militarily active Soviet personnel in 1943, the time of peak strength of the Soviet armed forces during the war, were women. They served as machine gunners and snipers, and in the artillery and tank corps (Cottam, 1980). A Soviet woman bomber pilot, Nadya Popova, wrote of her wartime experiences in a way that closely parallels countless male observations of war:

> "They were destroying us and we were destroying them. . . .
> I killed many men, but I stayed alive. . . . War requires the
> ability to kill, among other skills. But I don't think you
> should equate killing with cruelty. I think the risks we took
> and the sacrifices we made for each other made us kinder
> rather than cruel." (Quoted in Saywell, 1985)

Women today form a larger percentage of the armed forces in most Western countries than ever before. The United States has the highest proportion of women military personnel (10 percent). These soldiers, although not in combat units, are not kept away from zones in which fighting occurs. For example, female soldiers formed part of the U.S. force that invaded Panama in 1989. Among some, there is strong pressure to lift the regulations that prevent women from being in combat units. The majority of women in the U.S. armed forces, surveys show, are strongly in favor of such a move.

TABLE 11.4	WHERE WOMEN SERVE IN THE U.S. ARMED FORCES*				
Category	Army	Navy	Marines	Air Force	Total
Medical and dental specialists	26.1%	19.2%	**	28.5%	24.7%
Functional support and administration	25.8	21.6	14.5	24.5	23.5
Communications, intelligence specialists	10.6	13.7	7.2	16.0	12.1
Service and supply handlers	11.7	7.8	5.9	12.1	10.3
Other technical and allied specialists	9.5	18.8	6.4	9.4	10.1
Electronic equipment repairers	6.6	4.0	3.5	6.4	5.3
Crafts workers	3.3	5.5	4.8	5.1	4.9
Electrical, mechanical equipment repairers	5.0	3.3	2.6	4.6	4.1
Infantry, gun crews, seamanship	0.3	3.2	0.0	2.6	0.8

* Women as a percentage of active enlisted personnel in occupational categories in the fiscal year 1987.
** The Navy provides the Marine Corps with medical support
Source: Defense Manpower Data Center

Noncombatant women have not infrequently protested against the barbarism of war, but just as commonly they have supported and praised military values. Women have cared for the wounded and dying, "kept the home fires burning," and staged celebrations when the soldiers went off to war and when they returned. During the two world wars, women contributed to the war effort of most countries in a crucial way by entering the paid labor force in large numbers. In the world wars, particularly in World War I, women played a major role in pacifist organizations; but the majority of organizations in which women were prominently involved were dedicated to the goal of victory. Emmeline Pankhurst in Britain, one of the leaders of the women's movement in the early 1900s, declared her support for the Allied war aims near the beginning of the war. The magazine she headed, *The Suffragette,* was in fact redirected to war propaganda and renamed *Britannia* in 1915 (Wiltsher, 1985). In the United States, the National American Woman Suffrage Association proclaimed women's loyalty to the war effort, and promised its dedication to the virtues of patriotism and duty.

If warfare—or at least active participation in combat—has been an overwhelmingly male activity in the past, then this probably has little to do with any biologically given differences that make one sex more gentle than the other. Men have monopolized war as they have the other institutions in which power is concentrated. Participation in war has always involved long periods of military training and discipline, and has usually demanded that the soldier be able to go wherever military duties require. Wars have been mostly fought by young men, at the age that has represented the prime childbearing years for women. Women's confinement to the domestic sphere, in most previous periods of history, has separated them decisively from the role of warrior.

WOMEN'S CAMPAIGNS AGAINST WAR

Although these differences are not genetically given, women in fact have often held opposing attitudes towards war from those of most men. Ancient Greek dramas contain episodes in which women try to dissuade husbands and sons from going off to fight, or in which they protest against the futility of warfare. From the early origins of modern feminism in the late eighteenth century, sections of the women's movement have consistently promoted **pacifism.** As in the case of male attitudes to war, women's pacifist groups have normally represented the views of only a minority of their sex; but such groups have had a significant part in the struggles that women's associations have carried on against a male-dominated society.

Women's pacifist organizations were particularly active during the First World War. Prior to the war, women had played a substantial part in the international peace movements that had gained momentum in the early years of the twentieth century. While many women later followed Emmeline Pankhurst and other feminist leaders in changing their views to support the war effort, others vigorously defended an antiwar stance. In the United States, which remained outside the war until 1917, women opposing the war were not subjected to harassment by the government authorities, as was the case in Europe. In August 1914, fifteen thousand women participated in a peace parade in New York, rejecting offers of cooperation from males holding similar views (Steinson, 1980). A Women's Peace Party (WPP), formed in the same year, drew widespread support. Without female participation, there would have been very little agitation in favor of peace in the United States during World War I.

Feminist pacifist organizations were less prominent (as were their male counterparts) during the Second World War—there was general agreement that Nazism was such a menace that military violence was necessary to stop it. But in the postwar period, particularly since nuclear weapons have become widespread, women's groups have again become prominent in peace movements. Female pacifist groups have developed in most Western countries—such as Women's Action for Nuclear Disarmament in the United States and Women for Peace in West Germany and the Netherlands.

WAR AND AGGRESSION

WHAT IS THE GENERAL RELATION BETWEEN WAR AND AG-
gressiveness? Perhaps all human beings, men and women,
in some circumstances tend to be aggressive, and this aggressiveness finds an outlet in the destructiveness of war? Such a view
does not in fact stand up to examination. War has little to do with the
expression of aggressive impulses, although the battlefield might
permit certain individuals the chance to give vent to murderous feelings they would otherwise have kept concealed. Aggression is a feature of many aspects of human activity, but it leads very few of us to
murder anyone. The vast majority of those who have killed others
have done so in times of war. Some of us no doubt know, or have met,
people who have killed others in war—perhaps many others, using
machine guns, grenades, or bombs. But we do not usually fear them,
because we recognize that their actions in war are quite different
from the personal aggression that individuals might feel in ordinary
life.

All armies use drill training and the learning of discipline to develop physical fitness and the group solidarity important for success
in battle. But such training also helps alter people's usual attitudes towards indiscriminately shedding the blood of others. Gwynne Dyer
(1985), who has made a systematic study of war and aggressiveness,
comments as follows:

> The business of armies, at the end, is killing, and so a crucial
> part of training people to be soldiers is teaching them to ig-
> nore the limits they normally place on the actual use of vio-
> lence, so that in the right circumstances against the
> "enemy," they will go all the way and actually kill him. For
> the vast majority of people, killing has to be taught—
> though there are exceptions. There is such a thing as a "nat-
> ural soldier": the kind of man who derives his greatest
> satisfaction from male companionship, from excitement,
> and from the conquering of physical and psychological ob-
> stacles. He doesn't necessarily want to kill people as such,
> but he will have no objections if it occurs within a moral
> framework which gives him a justification—like war—and
> if it is the price of gaining admission to the kind of environ-
> ment he craves. . . . But armies are not full of such men.
> They are so rare that they form only a modest fraction even
> of small professional armies, mostly congregating in the

The Wreckage of War, *by Francis Goya.*

commando-type paid forces. In large conscript armies they virtually disappear beneath the weight of numbers of more ordinary men. And it is those ordinary men, who do not like combat at all, that the armies must persuade to kill.

United States Army Colonel S. L. A. Marshall carried out a large number of interviews with men in some four hundred infantry companies during the Second World War, to investigate their reactions to battle. The results greatly surprised him. He found that on average only 15 percent of troops fired their guns at all in battle, even when their positions were directly under attack and their lives in danger. The findings were as startling to the infantrymen as to their officers, because each had believed himself to be alone in defecting from his duty. They fired their weapons when others were present, especially officers, but not when they were more isolated. Their unwillingness to fire had nothing to do with fear, but reflected a disinclination to kill when there was "no need" (Marshall, 1947).

The fighting of war, then, does not derive directly from human aggressiveness. The origins of war, and the frequency with which wars have been fought, can be traced to other factors. The most important influence was the rise of state-based societies—from traditional states to the nation-states of today. As was mentioned earlier, among hunting and gathering peoples, war did not exist in any recognizable sense. The armed conflicts they fought were exciting and dangerous rituals, more like sport than war, in which bloodshed was minimized rather than deliberately sought after. With the development of larger societies having centralized forms of government, things changed. Armies were established and military discipline introduced. From that time onwards, hundreds or thousands of men operating in tight formations met on the fields of battle.

War, simply, is an ever-present possibility in a world in which states possess the means of wielding military violence through the deployment of their armed forces. Although the events precipitating an outbreak of war are varied, warfare is what happens when states clash, and when their disagreements cannot be handled successfully through negotiation, treaty, or diplomacy. A government may go to war because of a desire to acquire some or all of the territory of another, because of a struggle over resources (such as control of a major sea route), or as a result of ideological or religious clashes. There is no single "cause" or war. War is the ultimate test of power in the international arena.

A WORLD WITHOUT WAR?

IN TODAY'S WORLD, HOWEVER, THIS ULTIMATE TEST OF power could result in nuclear annihilation. In the event of a full-scale nuclear exchange, the global effects would be so horrendous that probably only small numbers of people in remote regions would survive. No one can be entirely confident just how complete the destruction would be; it is possible that, because of atmospheric and ecological effects, after a short period the human race —along with most other life on the planet—would disappear altogether. The result might be "a republic of insects and grass"— with all the higher animals eliminated (Schell, 1982).

The development of weaponry capable of destroying the whole of human society is the outcome of the industrialization of war, a process initiated some two hundred years ago. Unless all states agree to outlaw nuclear weapons, everyone must live for the indefinite future in the shadow of a possible nuclear holocaust. Chancellor Helmut Kohl of West Germany expressed a view held by many political leaders when he said, in May 1990, that to seek a world free from nuclear weapons was a "utopian demand." Those who might wish to create such a world he labelled "the great simplists." Even if all nu-

Vietnam War Memorial, Washington, D.C.

clear weapons were completely scrapped, which looks unlikely, the knowledge that produced them cannot be unlearned. Moreover, it seems improbable that the continuing application of science and technology to weapons development will diminish. Nuclear weapons may not necessarily be the most horrific or destructive armaments that human beings are capable of inventing and constructing.

Yet some of the chief ambitions that led to war in the past, particularly the acquisition of new territories, have become less relevant in the contemporary world. Modern societies are today much more interdependent on a global level than ever was the case before, and for the most part their boundaries are fixed (Rosecrance, 1986). Full-scale war fought with nuclear weapons already has no rational purpose: nuclear war is so cataclysmic in its consequences that it cannot be used to achieve any realistic political or economic objectives.

Recognition of this situation might perhaps create a growing understanding that nonviolent means of resolving global social conflicts must be found. The recent agreements to reduce levels of military expenditures by the United States and the Soviet Union, and the end of the cold war, are positive steps in this direction. Although humanity still has a long and dangerous road to tread, it is not wholly unrealistic in the long-term future to envisage a world free from major war.

SUMMARY

1. The fighting of wars is one of the most obvious features of the first development of states. Wars and battles played a primary role in shaping the map of the world as it exists today. The development of the modern military was closely intertwined with the emergence of industrialization. Large corporations, devoted either wholly or partly to the manufacture of armaments and stressing technical innovation, have ever since played a leading part in military development and war.

2. Modern armies are bureaucracies, staffed on the officer level by full-time officials. Armies are highly organized, specialized, and hierarchical. Although the sheer complexity of most modern states works against the possibility of military dominance, the army still often has a key voice in the policy-making process.

3. The arms trade is carried on by governments as well as by industrial firms. The competitive development of conventional weapons and nuclear arms by the United States and the Soviet Union has been characterized as the "arms race."

4. Some countries are directly ruled by the military, although most military governments are unstable. While most have been concentrated in the Third World, several industrialized countries have experienced periods of military rule in the twentieth century.

5. An important characteristic of modern societies is the degree to which the military and police are able successfully to acquire more or less exclusive control over the use of force. Terrorist groups and guerrilla movements draw upon the same symbols of legitimacy as established armies and governments.

6. As guerrilla groups become more persecuted by the state, and forced to operate more and more in a clandestine fashion, their use of violence sometimes becomes more ruthless. Although governments oppose the activities of terrorists within their own borders, they nonetheless often encourage guerrilla movements using identical tactics in other regions of the world.

7. War has always been preeminently a male activity, although women have tended to support wars, and today some armed forces include women in combat roles. Women have also played a prominent part in campaigning for peace. There is unlikely any biologically innate reason why women are less involved in wars than are men.

8. Wars are not the result of innate aggressive instincts. People usually have to be *trained* to kill. Wars are usually fought to acquire territory or resources or because of ideological or religious clashes.

9. We are the first generation, in the history of the human race, to live with the threat of global extinction. The industrialization of war has produced this outcome. Yet states are now so interdependent, and the consequences of nuclear war are known to be so cataclysmic, that there is a realistic hope that a world without war might be created.

BASIC CONCEPTS

THE INDUSTRIALIZATION OF WAR
MILITARY RULE

IMPORTANT TERMS

STANDING ARMY
LIMITED WAR
TOTAL WAR
UNIVERSAL CONSCRIPTION
MANAGEMENT OF VIOLENCE
CLIENTSHIP
CORPORATENESS
MILITARY MIND
ARMS RACE

ACTION-REACTION
DETERRENCE
ARMS TRADE
LEGITIMACY
MILITARY-INDUSTRIAL COMPLEX
TERRORISM
GUERRILLA MOVEMENT
PACIFISM

PART THREE

SOCIAL
INSTITUTIONS

Social institutions are the "cement" of social life. They concern the basic living arrangements that human beings work out in their interaction with one another and by means of which continuity is achieved across the generations.

We open by discussing the institutions of kinship, marriage, and the family. Although the social obligations associated with kinship vary widely between different types of society, the family is everywhere the context within which the young are provided with care and protection. Marriage is in turn more or less universally connected to the family, since it is a means of establishing new kin connections, and of forming a household in which children are brought up. In traditional cultures, much of the direct learning or formal instruction a child receives occurs within the family context. In modern societies, however, children spend many years of their lives in special places of instruction outside the family—that is, in schools and colleges. Chapter 13 looks at the ways in which formal education is organized, concentrating particularly upon how the educational system relates to wider processes of learning and communication.

In Chapter 14 we discuss religion. Although religious beliefs and practices are found in all cultures, the changes affecting religion in modern societies have been particularly acute. We analyze the nature of these changes, considering in what ways traditional types of religion still maintain their influence. Finally, in Chapter 15, we study work and economic life. Economic institutions affect many aspects of social activity. Although the nature of work varies widely both within and between different societies, it is one of the most pervasively important of all human pursuits.

KINSHIP, MARRIAGE, AND THE FAMILY

THE STUDY OF THE FAMILY AND MARRIAGE IS ONE OF THE most important areas of sociology. Virtually everyone, in all societies, is brought up in a family context; and in every society the vast majority of adults are, or at some point have been, married. Yet, as with other aspects of social life, there is great variation in family and marriage patterns across different cultures. What counts as a "family," its connections with other kin, whom one is permitted to marry, how spouses are selected, the connections between marriage and sexuality—all these differ widely. In this chapter we shall study some of these variations, showing how they help illuminate distinctive aspects of family life and patterns of marriage and divorce in the modern West. The Western family has altered markedly over the centuries, and we shall compare family life and marriage relationships in the modern period with those of earlier times. Fundamental changes in the nature of the family and marriage are occurring today also, and in the concluding sections of the chapter these will be analyzed in some detail.

You can probably trace out some of these changes in your own experience. A generation ago, only a few parents were divorced or living in separate households from one another. Today, marriage breakup is very common, with about half of American marriages expected to end in divorce. If you think of yourself and your friends, it is very unlikely that no one has divorced parents. Divorce has become so frequent, in fact, that you may know more people of your own age with divorced parents than with parents who have remained together.

While the incidence of divorce has increased dramatically over the past few decades, marriage has remained popular. Most people who have been divorced remarry and, in some cases, divorce and marry again on several occasions. The prevalence of remarriage means that many children are brought up in step-families. This is a new experience in recent history (although it was common in the premodern era, when death rates were much higher than they are now, and marriages were often broken by the death of a spouse at a relatively young age). Step-families introduce new relationships and issues into family life. People with step-parents have "double" sets of kinship relations—for example, two "fathers" or two "mothers."

Not all divorced people remarry; moreover, at any one time there are considerable numbers of people "between marriages," having left one partner but not yet entered into a long-term relationship with another. Thus the proportion of adults living alone or in single-parent households has risen quite sharply. Since an increasing number of unmarried couples today are living together, this means that many alternatives to traditional marriage exist. Where is all this leading us? Is family life disintegrating? What new patterns are emerging? These are the main questions we shall focus upon in this chapter.

BASIC CONCEPTS

WE NEED FIRST OF ALL TO DEFINE THE BASIC CONCEPTS OF family, kinship, and marriage. A **family** is a group of persons directly linked by kin connections, the adult members of which assume responsibility for caring for children. **Kinship** ties are connections between individuals, established either through marriage or through the lines of descent that connect blood relatives (mothers, fathers, other offspring, grandparents, etc.). **Marriage** can be defined as a socially acknowledged and approved sexual union between two adult individuals. When two people marry, they become kin to one another; the marriage bond also, however, connects together a wider range of kinspeople. Parents, brothers, sisters, and other blood relatives become relatives of the partner through marriage.

KINSHIP

In most Western societies, kinship connections are for all practical purposes confined to a limited number of close relatives. Most people, for example, have only a vague awareness of relatives more distant than first or second cousins. In many other cultures, however, especially small-scale ones, kinship relations are of overriding importance in most spheres of life. In most traditional societies there are large kinship groupings that go well beyond immediate family relationships. An example is the **clan.** A clan is a group from which all members believe themselves to be descended, either through the men or through the women, tracing their origin to a common ancestor several generations back. They see themselves, and are seen by others, as a collectivity with a distinct identity. The clans in Scotland were groups of such a kind; and there are many African and Pacific societies where such corporate groups remain significant. The *tsu,* a clan group in traditional China, sometimes included thousands of people.

Sometimes kinship categories recognized in clan groups completely cut across those we in the West would take to be "natural." For example, a father's sister may be called "father," with the addition of the qualification "female"; a mother's brother might be called "mother," with the added qualification "male." In these groups, it is not unusual to hear a man refer to another man, who may be much younger than himself, as his "mother." Strange as this sounds to us, it is entirely logical within a society organized in terms of clans. The individual is aware of who his real mother is. When he uses the word, he identifies the person referred to as coming from the same descent group as his mother, and therefore having strong ties to himself.

FAMILY RELATIONSHIPS

FAMILY RELATIONSHIPS ARE ALWAYS RECOGNIZED WITHIN wider kinship groups. In virtually all societies we can identify what sociologists and anthropologists have come to call the **nuclear family,** which consists of two adults living together in a household with their own or adopted children. In most traditional societies, even when there are no clans, the nuclear family is embedded in larger kinship networks of some type. Where kin other than a married couple and children live either in the same household, or in close and continuous relationship with one another, we speak of the **extended family.** An extended family can be de-

Nuclear families.

fined as a group of close relatives living either within the same dwelling or very close at hand. It may include grandparents, brothers and their wives, sisters and their husbands, aunts, or nephews.

Whether nuclear or extended, so far as the experience of each individual is concerned, families can be divided into **families of orientation** and **families of procreation.** The first is the family into which a person is born; the second is the family into which an individual enters as an adult and within which a new generation of children is brought up. A further important distinction concerns place of residence. In the United States when a couple marries they are usually expected to set up a separate household. This can be in the same area in which the bride's parents or the groom's parents live, but may very well be in some different town or city altogether. In many societies, however, everyone who marries is expected to live close to, or within the same dwelling as, the parents of the bride or groom. Where the couple moves to live near or with the bride's parents, the arrangement is called **matrilocal.** In a **patrilocal** pattern, the couple goes to live near to or with the parents of the groom.

MONOGAMY AND POLYGAMY

In Western societies, marriage, and therefore the family, is associated with **monogamy.** It is illegal for a man or woman to be married to more than one individual at any one time. Monogamy is not the most common type of marriage in the world as a whole. In a comparison of several hundred present-day societies, George Murdock found that polygamy was permitted in over 80 percent (Murdock, 1949). **Polygamy** refers to any type of marriage that allows a husband or wife to have more than one spouse. There are two types of polygamy: **polygyny,** in which a man may be married to more than one woman at the same time, and **polyandry,** which is much less common, in which a woman may have two or more husbands simultaneously.

Polyandry

Murdock found that only four societies out of the 565 he analyzed practiced polyandry—under 1 percent. Polyandry creates a situation, absent in polygyny, in which the biological father of a child is usually not known. Among the Todas of southern India, a polyandrous culture, husbands seem uninterested in establishing biological paternity. Who is deemed the father of a child is established by means of a ceremony in which one of the husbands presents the pregnant wife with a toy bow and arrow. If other husbands subsequently wish to become fathers, the ritual is reenacted during further pregnancies. Polyandry seems to exist only in societies living at an extreme level of poverty, in which female infanticide (the killing of female infants) is practiced. In such societies, men may substantially outnumber women; and thus the women are "shared around."

Polygyny

Most men in polygynous societies in fact have only one wife. The right to have several wives is often limited to individuals of high social status; where there are no such restrictions, the sex ratio and economic factors keep polygyny in check. There are no societies in which women so far outnumber men that the majority of males could have more than one wife.

In polygynous families, co-wives sometimes live in the same dwelling as one another but often are in different households. Where separate households exist, each having the children of one wife, there are effectively two or more family units. The husband usually has one home as his primary dwelling, but may spend a certain number of nights per week or month with each wife in rotation. Co-wives are frequently cooperative and friendly; but their situation is obviously one that can lead to rivalry and tensions, since they may see themselves as competitors for the husband's favors. Among the Ruanda of East Africa, the word for "co-wife" is the same as that for "jealousy" (Maquet, 1961). The discord provoked by polygyny is sometimes eased by a system of hierarchical grading among wives. The senior wife or wives have more authority over family decisions than juniors.

Western missionaries have always been extremely hostile to polygyny and from the days of colonialism onwards sought to combat its influence. Polygyny still exists in many parts of the world, but where Western influence is strong, attitudes may have become mixed. The anthropologist John Beattie quotes a case of a young schoolteacher whom he got to know while working in Bunyoro in western Uganda. This individual had one wife, whom he married in the Christian church, and with whom he cohabited when he lived at the school. He had another wife and two children in his home village. This wife he had married in the traditional way of his people. He hid the existence of the second wife from his superiors at the school, and asked Beattie to keep the matter completely secret (Beattie, 1968).

These comparisons illustrate the variability of family and marriage patterns across cultures. What of the historical picture? In order to appreciate what is happening to the family and marriage today, we have to have an understanding of how these institutions have developed in past history.

THE FAMILY AND MARRIAGE IN HISTORY

PRIOR TO THE DEVELOPMENT OF MODERN INDUSTRY IN THE eighteenth century, most families were also domestic enterprises, working the land or engaged in craft production. Even people who did not establish their own families of procreation tended to live and work in the family settings of others. Selection of marriage partners was not usually determined by love or affection, but by social and economic interests involved in the continuation of the family enterprise and care of dependents. Landlords often directly influenced choice of marriage partners, because they were concerned with ensuring the effective working of their properties (Mitterauer and Sider, 1984). In most parts of central Europe, a person wishing to be married had to obtain the landlord's permission. The landless poor, who had little hope of obtaining a cottage or farm, were sometimes prohibited from marrying altogether.

Sexual relationships before and outside marriage were common in many areas of premodern Europe, among both poor and wealthier strata. In some regions, it was permissible for a man to test the childbearing capacity of his future wife by trying to impregnate her prior to marriage. If she became pregnant, the marriage would go ahead, but if not, she would stay unmarried. Rates of illegitimacy in many parts of Europe (particularly central Europe) were extraordinarily high by modern standards. Little shame was attached to illegitimacy, and children of extramarital activities were frequently taken into the family and raised alongside legitimate offspring. As was mentioned in Chapter 1 ("Sociology: Problems and Perspectives"), sexual passion within marriage seems to have been rare in all sectors of the population. Within the aristocracy and gentry, erotic liaisons were recognized, but were almost always extramarital.

Many sociologists once thought that, prior to the modern period, the predominant form of family in western Europe was of the extended type. Research has shown this view to be mistaken. The nuclear family seems long to have been preeminent. Premodern household size was larger than present day, but the difference is not especially great. In the United States, for example, throughout the seventeenth, eighteenth, and nineteenth centuries, the average household size was 4.75 persons. The current average is 3.04. Since the earlier figure includes domestic servants, the difference in family size in the domestic unit is small. Extended family groups were more important in eastern Europe and Russia.

Children in preindustrial Europe were often "out at work"—helping their parents on the farm—from about seven or eight years old. Those who did not remain in the family enterprise frequently left the parental household at an early age and were sent off to do domestic work in the houses of others or to follow apprenticeships. Children who went away to work in other households would rarely, or perhaps never, see their parents again.

Other factors made family groups even more impermanent than they are now—in spite of the high rates of divorce in current times. Rates of mortality (numbers of deaths per thousand of the population in any one year) for people of all ages were much higher than those of today. A quarter or more of all infants in premodern Europe did not survive beyond the first year of life (in contrast to well under 1 percent today), and women frequently died in childbirth. The death of children, or of one or both spouses, frequently dislocated or shattered family relationships, and, as mentioned previously, remarriages, with their attendant step-relationships, were frequently found.

THE DEVELOPMENT OF FAMILY LIFE

The historian Lawrence Stone has charted some of the changes leading from premodern to modern forms of family life in Europe (Stone, 1980). Stone distinguishes three dominant phases in the development of the family over a period of three hundred years from the 1500s to the 1800s. In the early part of this period, the main family form was a type of nuclear family, that lived in fairly small households, but had deeply embedded relationships within the community, including with other kin. This family structure was not clearly separated from the community. According to Stone (although other historians have challenged this), the family at that time was not a major focus of emotional attachment or dependence for its members. People did not experience, or look for, the emotional intimacies we associate with family life today. Sex within marriage was not regarded as a source of pleasure but as a necessity to propagate children.

Individual freedom of choice, in contracting marriage and in other aspects of family life, was subordinated to the interests of others, such as parents, other kin, or the community. Outside aristocratic circles, where it was sometimes actively encouraged, erotic or romantic love was regarded by moralists and theologians as a sickness. As Stone puts it, the family during this period "was open to support, advice, investigation and interference from the outside, from neighbors and from kin, and internal privacy was non-existent. The family, therefore, was an open-ended, low-keyed, unemotional, authoritarian institution. . . . It was also very short-lived, being frequently dissolved by the death of the husband or wife or the death or very early departure from the home of the children" (Stone, 1980).

This type of family was succeeded by a transitional family form that lasted from the early sixteenth century to the opening of the eighteenth century, but was largely confined to the upper reaches of society. It was nevertheless very important, because from it spread attitudes that have since become almost universal. The nuclear family became a more separate entity, distinct from ties to other kin and to the local community. It was a phase of family development associated with a growing stress upon the importance of marital and parental love, although there was also an increase in the authoritarian power of fathers.

Gradually the type of family system we are most familiar with in the West today evolved. This is a group tied by close emotional bonds, having a high degree of domestic privacy, and preoccupied with the rearing of children. It is marked by the rise of **affective individualism,** the formation of marriage ties on the basis of personal selection, guided by norms of affection or romantic love. Sexual aspects of love began to be glorified within marriage instead of in extramarital relationships. The family became a unit geared to consumption rather than production, as a result of the increasing spread of workplaces separate from the home.

Originating among more affluent groups, this family type gradually became more or less universal in Western countries with the spread of industrialization. The choice of a mate became based upon the desire for a relationship offering affection or love.

CHANGES IN FAMILY PATTERNS WORLDWIDE

There remains a diversity of family forms in different societies across the world. In some areas, such as more remote regions in Asia, Africa, or the Pacific, traditional family systems are little altered. In most Third World countries, however, widespread changes are occurring in preestablished family patterns. The origins of these changes are complex, but several factors can be picked out as especially important. One is the spread of Western culture. Changes in the family and marriage in the West have had an extensive impact elsewhere. Ideals of romantic love, for example, have spread to societies in which it was previously unknown. Another factor is the development of forms of centralized government in areas previously composed of largely autonomous smaller societies. People's lives become influenced by their involvement in a national political system; moreover, governments often make active attempts to alter traditional ways of behavior. Particularly because of the problem of rapidly expanding population growth, states frequently try to intervene in family life, introducing programs advocating smaller families, the use of contraception, and so forth.

A further influence is the mushrooming of towns and cities. Large-scale processes of migration from rural to urban areas have occurred in many Third World countries. Often men go to work in towns or cities, leaving wife, children, and other family members in the home village. Alternatively, a nuclear-family group will move as a unit from the rural area to the city. In both cases, traditional family forms and kinship systems may become weakened. Finally, and perhaps most important, employment opportunities away from the land lead people to be involved in organizations outside family influence. Employment in government bureaucracies, mines, plantations, and—where they exist—industrial firms, tends to have disruptive consequences for family systems previously centered upon landed production in the local community.

In general, these changes are creating a worldwide movement towards the predominance of the nuclear family, breaking down extended-family systems and other types of kinship group. This was first documented by William J. Goode in his book *World Revolution in Family Patterns* (1963). Goode probably over-simplified some of the directions of change, but his claim that a general shift is occurring towards the increased prominence of the nuclear family has been borne out by subsequent research.

Directions of Change

The most important changes occurring worldwide are the following:

1. Clans and other corporate-kin groups are declining in their influence. The postwar history of China offers an example. When the Communist government came to power in 1949, it set out to try to dissolve the influence of the *tsu* over family life and economic affairs. *Tsu* landholdings were broken up and redistributed among the peasants. Communes largely replaced the traditional *tsu* organization. Since then, other changes in social and economic life have further undermined its influence.

2. There is a general trend towards the free choice of spouse. Extended-family systems tend to be associated with arranged marriages. Obligations to the family group are of overriding importance in establishing marriage ties. Partly because of the influence of Western ideas emphasizing romantic love, and partly because of the other factors weakening extended-family systems, marriage by arrangement is coming under strain. Members of the younger generation—particularly where they are involved in living and working in urban areas—are often claiming the right to choose their own marriage partners.

3. The rights of women are becoming more strongly recognized, in respect to both the initiation of marriage and decision making within the family. Higher levels of employment for women outside the home, coupled with the liberalizing of divorce, are bound up with these changes. In some societies, husbands traditionally had almost complete discretion in divorcing their wives—for example, having only to tell the wife in front of witnesses that she was no longer wanted. Women's organizations are now widely pressing for equal rights of divorce—although there are many societies where little progress has been made in this respect.

4. Most marriages in traditional cultures were "kin marriages." People were expected, or obliged, to marry a partner chosen

With more and more women in the workforce, some women take their children into the workplace. Here, actor Sheila Ellis deals with conflicting demands of career and motherhood by bringing her son to the theater.

from a specific range of people, defined by means of kinship relations. For example, where strong clan groups existed, individuals were usually not allowed to marry anyone who was a member of the same clan, however distant the kin connection. This practice is called **exogamy. Endogamy** is the reverse, where individuals are obligated to be married to others within a kin group. In both instances, kin membership is the organizing principle for the formation of marriage relationships. This practice is generally becoming less and less common.

5. Higher levels of sexual freedom are developing in those societies that were very restrictive. Sometimes this process has not proceeded very far, and there have been changes in the opposite direction, as happened following the Islamic revolution in Iran in the late 1970s when the Iranian authorities sought to reanimate laws and customs limiting sexual freedom. However, such examples are exceptional. It should be pointed out that many traditional societies were more liberal sexually than has ever been the case in the West, up to and including the present day.

6. There is a general trend towards the extension of children's rights. In many countries, children are still subject to extreme deprivation, or are sexually exploited and abused. Most governments have established legal frameworks protecting children's rights, although there is a long way to go before these are universal.

It would be a mistake to exaggerate these trends, or to suppose that the nuclear family has everywhere become the dominant form. In most societies in the world today, extended families are still the norm and traditional-family practices continue. Moreover, family systems are diverse, and begin from varied starting points in this process of change. There are differences in the speed at which change is occurring, and there are many reversals and counter trends. In a study in the Philippines, for example, a higher proportion of extended families was found in urban areas than in surrounding rural regions. These had not just developed from traditional extended-family households, but represented something new. Leaving the rural areas, cousins, nephews, and nieces went to live with their relatives in the cities to try to take advantage of the employment opportunities available there. Parallel examples have also been noted elsewhere in the world (Stinner, 1979). Similar processes have been observed in some industrialized nations. In certain regions of Poland, for instance, a rejuvenation of the extended family has been documented. Many industrial workers in Poland have farms that they tend part time. Grandparents move in with their children's family, run the household, and bring up the grandchildren, while the younger generation is engaged in outside employment (Turowski, 1977).

Having analyzed some of these global processes of changes in the family, we now turn to look in some detail at the development of family and marriage patterns in the United States. We shall first of all analyze what the major trends of change have been, and sketch out the main characteristics of the institutions of the family and marriage today. Given the ethnically diverse character of the United States, there are considerable variations in family and marriage within the country. Some of the most striking of such variations cover differences between white and black family patterns, and we need to consider why this is so. We will then move on to examine divorce, remarriage, and step-parenting in relation to contemporary patterns of family life.

FAMILY AND MARRIAGE IN THE UNITED STATES

AS IN EUROPE, EXTENDED FAMILIES WERE RELATIVELY RARE in the early development of the United States. Households were larger than today, but—again as in Europe—mainly because of the existence of servants and a higher proportion of children. A study carried out in Rhode Island, covering the period from 1887 to 1960, showed that, at the earlier date, 82 percent of the families were of the nuclear type compared to 85 percent in 1960. The percentage remained almost exactly the same.

Some aspects of family life, of course, have been radically transformed over the past century, expressing broader patterns of social change. At the time of the first national census in 1790, the population was 95 percent rural; today it is 90 percent urban, with the vast majority of people working in non-farming occupations. Moreover, the fact that later immigrants came from many points of origin meant that a variety of different family systems have coexisted in this country. There remain today many subcultural variations in the family organization throughout the society; a characterization of "family and marriage in America" can thus only be given in very broad outlines.

The main characteristics of the American family are as follows:

A sign of the times—father at work.

1. The American family is monogamous, monogamy being established in law. Until near the end of the nineteenth century, the Mormons practiced polygamy. However, in 1896, they embraced monogamy as one of the conditions made for the admission of Utah to the Union. Given the high rate of divorce that now exists in the United States, however, some observers have suggested that the American marriage pattern should be called **serial monogamy.** That is to say, individuals are permitted in law to have a number of spouses in sequence, although nobody may have more than one wife or husband at any time. It is misleading, though, to confuse monogamy with actual sexual practice. It is obvious that a high proportion of Americans are not in fact monogamous. That is to say, they engage in transitory or more regular sexual relations with individuals other than their spouses.

2. American marriage is based upon the idea of romantic love. Affective individualism has become the major element influencing the formation of marital ties in the United States as in Europe. Couples are expected to develop mutual affection, based upon personal attraction and compatibility, as a basis for contracting marriage relationships. Romantic love has become naturalized in contemporary America; it seems to be a normal part of human existence, rather than peculiar to modern culture (Cancian, 1987). The connection between love and marriage has proved in some part paradoxi-

cal. Given the emphasis upon personal satisfaction through the marriage relationship, there is often more of a burden placed on partners than one or both thinks it reasonable to bear—one factor involved in increasing rates of divorce.

3. The American family is patrilineal and neolocal. **Patrilineal inheritance** means that children take the surname of the father, and property usually passes down through the male line. (Many societies in the world are **matrilineal**—surnames, and often property, pass down through the female line.) A **neolocal residence** pattern means that married couples move into a dwelling away from both of their families of orientation. Neolocalism, however, is not an absolutely fixed trait of the American family. Many families, particularly in lower-class neighborhoods, have a definite tendency to be matrilocal—the newlyweds settle in an area close to where the bride's parents live.

4. The American family is of the nuclear type, consisting of one or two parents living in a household with their children. However, nuclear-family units are by no means completely isolated from other kin ties. A survey carried out in 1980 by the National Opinion Research Center, for instance, showed that more than half the American population see relatives socially several times a month, while a third visit, or are visited by, relatives on a daily basis (N.O.R.C., 1981). Such relatives—especially parents, brothers, and sisters—provide material support, help with childcare and babysitting, assist during sickness, sometimes buy gifts such as major household appliances, and may offer financial benefits (such as help with the down payment on a house). Studies of blue-collar families have demonstrated similar results, and comparable findings have also been reported for other industrialized countries.

CURRENT TRENDS

The United States has long been characterized by high marriage rates. Nearly every American adult eventually marries; almost 95 percent of adults in their early fifties today are, or have previously been, married (Cherlin, 1981). The age at which first marriages are contracted has risen, however, over the past twenty years (it was also high at the turn of the century, declining in the 1922–1950 period).

"Bob and Ruth! Come on in . . . . Have you met Russell and Bill, our 1.5 children?" *The Far Side* © 1988; Universal Press Syndicate. Reprinted with permission.

This is partly because of an increase in the numbers of people living together without being married, and partly a result of factors such as the growing proportion of the population attending college—most of whom tend to defer marriage until some while after completing their education.

In 1960, the average age of first marriages was 22.5 years for men and 20 for women. The comparable ages today are 24 for men and 21.5 for women. Another way of measuring the relations between age and first marriage is to look at the numbers of people who remain unmarried prior to a certain age. Thus in 1960 just under 30 percent of women aged less than 24 years had never married. Today, that proportion is 45 percent. The U.S. census now incorporates a category of "unmarried couples sharing the same household." As this practice is new, it is not easy to make direct comparisons with preceding years. Nonetheless, we cannot doubt that the number of couples among younger age groups who live together without being married has risen steeply.

An extraordinary increase in the proportion of people living alone in the United States has taken place over recent years—a phenomenon that partly reflects the high levels of marital separation and divorce now characteristic of society. One in every five households now consists of one person, a rise of 44 percent since 1960. There has been a particularly sharp rise in the proportion of individuals living alone in the 24–44 age bracket.

Many people suppose that the "average American family" is made up of a husband who works in paid employment and a wife who looks after the home, living together with their two children. This is very different from the real situation. Only some 7 percent of households in the United States fit this picture! One factor is the impact of the rising rates of divorce: a substantial proportion of the population lives either in single-parent households or in stepfamilies, or both. Another is the high proportion of women who now go to work. Dual-career marriages are now the norm. The majority of married women working outside the home have a child or children of less than eighteen years old. Most working women do not have careers outside the home in the sense in which males in the better-paid occupations do. That is to say, women are concentrated in jobs having poor or non-existent promotion prospects. Yet the standard of living of many American couples is dependent upon the income contributed by the wife—as well as upon the unpaid work she undertakes in the home.

BLACK FAMILIES

The trends in family patterns among the overall American population conceal important differences between classes, ethnic, or racial groups. This is especially true of differences between white and black family patterns—although within each of these there are also a variety of differing systems and customs. Numbering over twenty-four million, black people comprise easily the largest minority in the United States. Some 30 percent of the black population lives below the officially defined poverty line (compared to 9 percent of the white population). Although there are affluent black families, the large majority of black people are concentrated in lower-income groups.

One of the most striking differences between white and black families as a whole is that far fewer black women aged 25–44 are married and living with a husband than white women in the same age group. This fact has given rise to heated disputes about the nature of black families in the United States. It was said by Daniel Moynihan, for example, that black families are "disorganized" and caught up in a "tangle of pathology" (Moynihan, 1965). Moynihan, among others, traced these circumstances to the long-term history of the black family.

The early development of black family patterns was, of course, largely governed by the conditions imposed by slavery. The circumstances under which slaves were brought over from Africa prevented blacks from maintaining the cultural customs of their societies of origin. Members of similar tribal groups were deliberately dispersed to different plantations. Some owners treated their slaves considerately, fostering the development of family life. Many others, however, regarded their slaves as little better than livestock, seeing them as inherently promiscuous and therefore believing marriage formalities to be unnecessary. Plantation overseers were mainly interested in securing high levels of production and usually kept the men separate from the women and children. Many owners provided a separate cabin for the women and children to live in, issuing direct rations of food to them.

It seems possible that these dislocations of family life have persisted through to the present day: perhaps a "mother-centered family," developed under conditions of slavery, formed an enduring pattern? There is reason to have some doubt about this. Recent work by historians has indicated that family and kinship relationships among blacks in the antebellum period were rather stronger than was once believed. Herbert Gutman studied plantation records and other documents covering the period 1750–1925. The evidence indicates that most slaves lived in stable family groups until one died or was sold to another owner. Larger kin connections were also well developed. He found much the same to be true among blacks who were living in New York City in 1925 (Gutman, 1976; see also Engerman, 1977). Patterns of family life established under slavery probably had a long-term impact, but it is unlikely that this was the decisive factor affecting patterns today.

Some have argued that the main influence on current black family patterns was the disruptive effect of the migration of blacks to the North in the current century. People from a rural background were plunged into an unfamiliar urban-industrial environment in the North, where many found themselves unemployed. The disorientation this brought about may have eroded family patterns already relatively weak from the influence of slavery (Frazier, 1939). But recent historical research tends to run counter to this view also. A study of Philadelphia in 1880, for instance, showed that blacks born in the South, most of whom were originally slaves or the children of slaves, were more likely to be living in a family with husband and wife both present than blacks born in the North (Furstenberg, Jr., Hershberg, and Modell, 1975).

Trends Since 1960

The divergence between black and white family patterns has become much greater since the early 1960s, and it seems probable that we have to look mainly to present-day influences to explain them (Wilson, 1987). In 1960, 21 percent of black families were headed by females; among white families, the proportion was 8 percent. By 1984, the proportion of black families maintained by a woman had risen to 46 percent, while that for white families was under a third of this figure, at 12 percent. Female-headed families are more prominently represented among poorer blacks. Blacks in central-city neighborhoods have experienced little rise in living conditions over the past two decades: the majority are confined to low-wage jobs, or are more or less permanently unemployed. In these circumstances—given the absence of a "traditional" family outlook, characteristic of most other ethnic groups—there is little to foster continuity in marital relationships.

However, we should not see the situation of black families purely in a negative light. The director of the National Urban League, a black organization, coined the phrase "the strengths of black families" as the title of a research report produced in the 1970s. Black families, the report claimed, have several characteristics promoting stability, including strong and adaptable kin ties. Extended kinship networks are important among poor blacks—much more significant, relative to marital ties, than is the case in most white communities. A mother heading a one-parent family is likely to have a close and supportive network of relatives to depend upon. This contradicts the idea that black single parents and their children form unstable families (Stack, 1974). A far higher proportion of female-headed families among blacks have other relatives living with them, compared to white families headed by females.

In her book *Lifelines* (1983), Joyce Aschenbrenner provides a comprehensive portrayal of extended kin relationships in black families. She gained a new perspective upon both white and black family types in the United States as a result of fieldwork she had earlier carried out in Pakistan. From the point of view of the Pakistanis, the white family in the United States is weak or nonexistent. They could not understand how a couple, let alone a single parent, could bring up children. They viewed with abhorrence the practice of hiring a stranger to babysit while the parents went out. Where were the uncles and grandparents? Why aren't a woman's brothers on hand to lend assistance if she is left on her own to bring up her children? The way they thought of "the family" was closer to the situation of many black families rather than to the usual family structure among whites. Seen from their standpoint, the *white* family seems weak and "disorganized."

Discussions of the black family, Aschenbrenner suggests, have focused too strongly on the marriage relationship. This emphasis is in line with the overriding importance of marriage in American society, but it is this which is unusual, rather than the structure of the black family. In most societies having extended families, relationships such as mother-daughter, father-son, or brother-sister, may be more socially significant than that between husband and wife (Aschenbrenner, 1983).

DIVORCE AND SEPARATION

THE PAST THIRTY YEARS HAVE SEEN MAJOR INCREASES IN rates of divorce, together with a relaxation of the attitudes of disapproval previously held towards it. For many centuries in the West, marriage was regarded as virtually indissoluble. Divorces were granted only in very limited situations, such as nonconsummation of marriage. Some countries, such as Spain, still do not recognize divorce. In a recent referendum in Ireland, the majority voted against the introduction of laws permitting couples to divorce. Yet these are now isolated examples. Most countries have moved rapidly towards making divorce more easily available. The so-called "adversary system" used to be characteristic of virtually all industrialized countries. Under this system, for a divorce to be granted, one spouse had to bring charges (for example, cruelty, desertion, or adultery) against the other. The first "no-fault" divorce laws in the United States were introduced in California in 1970. Over the ten years following, every state save South Dakota and Illinois adopted no-fault legislation of some form. Illinois introduced new laws in 1984, leaving South Dakota as the only state operating with the traditional type of divorce provisions.

Divorce rates are calculated by looking at the number of divorces per thousand married men or women per year. Rates of divorce in the United States have fluctuated in different periods. They rose, for example, following World War II, then dropped off before climbing to much higher levels. The divorce rate increased steeply from the 1960s to the late 1970s, reaching a peak in 1981 (thereafter declining somewhat). The likelihood of a married individual of thirty years old in 1985 either to have been divorced, or to be divorced in the future, was about one in three. Over the 1970s the proportion of separated or divorced mothers heading families including children under eighteen increased by 86 percent (Cherlin, 1981). One of the most important changes that has occurred is that separated or divorced individuals continue to maintain their own households, rather than going to live with relatives. It used to be common for divorced women to move back to their parents' homes after separation; today, most set up their own households.

TABLE 12.1	WHERE CHILDREN LIVE (in percentages)			
Children Living With	1980		1988	
	White	Black	White	Black
Two parents	82.7%	42.2%	78.9%	38.6%
Mother only	13.5	43.9	16.0	51.1
Father only	1.6	1.9	2.9	3.0

Source: U.S. Bureau of the Census, January 1989a, Table A-4.

Divorce makes an increasing impact upon the lives of children. Since 1970, more than one million American children per year have been affected by divorce. It has been calculated that nearly 40 percent of children born in 1970 will at some stage in their lives be members of a one-parent family. Since 75 percent of women and 83 percent of men who are divorced remarry within three years, they will nonetheless grow up in a family environment. Only just over 2 percent of children under fourteen in the United States today are not living with either parent.

Lenore Weitzman (1985) has argued that no-fault divorce laws have helped positively to recast the psychological context of divorce (reducing some of the hostility it once generated), but have had strong negative consequences for the economic position of women. Laws that were designed to be "gender-neutral" have had the unintended consequence of depriving divorced women of the financial protections that the old laws provided. Women are expected to be as capable as men of supporting themselves after divorce. Yet because most women's careers are still secondary to their work as homemakers, they lack the qualifications and earning power of men. Weitzman's research showed that the living standards of divorced women and their children on average fell by 73 percent in the first year following the divorce settlement. The average standard of living of divorced men, by contrast, rose by 42 percent. Most court judgments left the former husband with a high proportion of his income intact; therefore he had more to spend on his own needs than while he was married.

MARRIAGE, DIVORCE, AND SELF-FULFILLMENT

Divorce rates are obviously not a direct index of marital unhappiness. For one thing, they do not include people who are separated but have

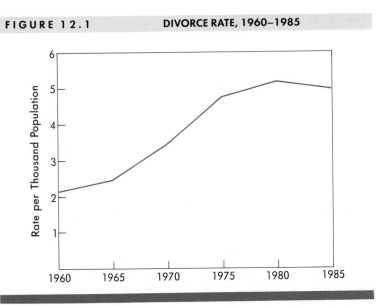

FIGURE 12.1 **DIVORCE RATE, 1960–1985**

Source: U.S. National Center for Health Statistics, *Vital Statistics of the United States,* annual.

not been legally divorced. Moreover, people who are unhappily married may choose to stay together—because they believe in the sanctity of marriage, or are wary about the consequences they will suffer in the case of a breakup, or wish to remain with one another for the sake of the children.

Why has divorce become much more common over recent years? Several factors are involved, having to do with the wider changes going on in modern societies. Except for a very small proportion of wealthy people, marriage today no longer has much connection with the desire to perpetuate property and status from generation to generation. As women become more economically independent, marriage is less of a necessary economic partnership than it used to be. Greater overall prosperity means that it is easier to establish a separate household, in case of marital disaffection, than formerly was the case. The fact that little stigma now attaches to divorce is in some part the result of these developments, but adds momentum to them also. A further important factor is the growing tendency to evaluate marriage in terms of the levels of personal satisfaction it offers. Rising rates of divorce do not seem to indicate a deep dissatisfaction with marriage as such, but an increased determination to make it a rewarding and satisfying relationship.

THE EXPERIENCE OF DIVORCE

It is extremely difficult to draw up a "balance sheet" of the social advantages and costs of high levels of divorce. More tolerant attitudes towards divorce mean that couples can terminate an unrewarding relationship without incurring social ostracism. On the other hand, marriage breakup is almost always emotionally stressful and may create financial hardship, especially for women.

Uncoupling

In her study *Uncoupling,* Diane Vaughan (1986) analyzed relationships between partners during the course of separation or divorce. She carried out a series of interviews with 103 recently separated or divorced people (mainly from middle-class backgrounds) to chart the process of transition from living together to living apart. The notion of "uncoupling" refers to how people make the transition out of intimate relationships to living alone. She found that, in many cases, prior to the actual physical parting there was a "social separation"— at least one of the partners developed a new life pattern, becoming interested in new pursuits and making new friends, in contexts in which the other was not present. This usually meant keeping secrets from the other—especially, of course, when a relationship with a lover was involved.

"Darling, let's get divorced."
Drawing by Koren; © 1975,
The New Yorker Magazine, Inc.

According to Vaughan's research, uncoupling is often unintentional in its beginnings. One individual—whom she calls the "initiator"—becomes more dissatisfied with the relationship than the other. The initiator creates a "territory" independent of the activities in which the couple engages together. For some while previously, the initiator may have been trying unsuccessfully to change the partner, to get him or her to behave in more acceptable ways, foster shared interests, and so forth. At some point, the initiator feels that this attempt has been a failure, and that the relationship is fundamentally flawed. From then onwards, he or she becomes preoccupied with the ways in which the relationship or the partner is defective. Vaughan suggested that this is the opposite of the process of "falling in love" at the beginning of a relationship, when an individual focuses on the attractive features of the other, ignoring those that may be more dubious.

Initiators seriously considering a break normally discuss their relationship extensively with others, "comparing notes." In so doing, they weigh the costs and benefits as applied to their own position. Can they survive on their own? How will friends and parents react? Will the children suffer? Will they be financially solvent? Having thought about these and other problems, some decide to try again to make the relationship work. For those who proceed with a separation, these discussions and inquiries help make the break less intimidating, building confidence that they are doing the right thing. Most initiators tend to become convinced that a responsibility for their own self-development takes priority over commitment to the other. Of course, uncoupling is not always wholly led by one individual. The other partner by this time may have also decided that the relationship cannot be changed. In some situations, an abrupt reversal of roles occurs. The person who previously wanted to save the relationship becomes determined that it should end, while the erstwhile initiator wishes to salvage it.

Transitions in Divorce

Should a couple decide to divorce, a number of major transitions of lifestyle and outlook have to be made. Paul Bohannan (1970) distinguishes six overlapping "stations of divorce" that a couple who part have to face. All may create difficulties and tensions, affecting the two people themselves, their children, relatives, and friends:

1. *The emotional divorce,* expressing the deteriorating marriage itself—increasing tensions between partners, leading usually to separation.

2. *The legal divorce,* involving the grounds upon which the marriage is ended.

3. *The economic divorce,* concerned with the division of wealth and property.

4. *The co-parental divorce,* representing issues of child custody and visiting rights.

5. *The community divorce,* concerning the alterations in friendships and other social relations that a divorced person undergoes.

6. *The psychic divorce,* whereby the individual has finally to sever ties of emotional dependence and face the demands of living alone.

A series of interviews that Robert Weiss (1976) carried out with divorced men and women in the United States showed a definite "trajectory" of adjustment. Women suffer from divorce on an economic level far more than men, but the process of psychological and social adjustment seems quite similar for both sexes. In the majority of instances Weiss studied, the respect and liking a couple may have felt for one another disappears some time before they separate. Hostility and mistrust take their place. At the same time, a sense of being bound emotionally to the other person persists. Thus, even though a couple may argue bitterly just prior to parting, they tend to experience profound feelings of what Weiss calls "separation distress." The sudden lack of availability of the other spouse creates feelings of anxiety or panic. A minority of individuals have an opposite experience— a feeling of euphoria in response to being free and able to deal with their lives on their own. Feelings of depression and euphoria might also alternate with one another.

After a certain period, distress and euphoria both give way to sensations of loneliness. People feel separated from the secure family worlds in which others, for all their problems, seem to live. Friendship relations in fact do almost always alter. Although friends might attempt to maintain contact with both ex-partners, gradually they tend to see much more of one than the other.

Divorce and Children

The effects of divorce upon children are difficult to gauge. How conflictual the relationship is between the parents prior to separation, the age of the children at the time, whether or not there are brothers or sisters, the availability of grandparents and other relatives, their relationships to their individual parents, how frequently they continue to see both parents—all these and other influences can affect the process of adjustment. Since children whose parents are unhappy with one another but stay together may be affected by the resulting tensions, assessing the consequences for children is doubly problematic.

Research indicates that children do often suffer a period of marked emotional anxiety following the separation of their parents. Judith Wallerstein and Joan Kelly studied the children of sixty families in Marin County, California, following the separation of the parents. They contacted the children at the time of the divorce in court, a year-and-a-half afterwards, and five years later. According to the authors, almost all the 131 children involved experienced intense emotional disturbance at the time of the divorce. Preschool-age children were confused and frightened, tending to blame themselves for the separation. Older children were better able to understand their parents' motives for divorce, but frequently worried deeply about its effects upon their future and often expressed sharp feelings of anger. At the end of the five-year period, however, the researchers found that two-thirds of the children were coping at least reasonably well with their home lives and their commitments outside. A third remained dissatisfied with their lives, were subject to depression, and expressed feelings of loneliness, even in some cases where the parent with whom they were living had remarried (Wallerstein and Kelly, 1980).

We cannot say, of course, how the children might have fared if their parents had stayed together. The sample of parents and children studied all came from an affluent white area, and might or might not be representative of the wider population. Moreover, the families were self-selected: they had approached counselors seeking help. Those who actively seek counseling might be less (or more) able to cope with separation than those who do not. One finding that does seem to emerge from this and other research is that children fare better when they have a continuing relationship with both parents following separation than when they only see one parent regularly.

REMARRIAGE AND STEPPARENTING

REMARRIAGE INVOLVES VARIOUS DIFFERENT SCENARIOS. Some remarried couples are in their early twenties, neither bringing a child to the new relationship. People who remarry in their late twenties, thirties, or early forties might each bring one or more children from the former marriage or marriages to live in the same dwelling with their new partner. Those who remarry at later ages might have adult children who never live in the new homes the parents establish. There may also be children of the new marriage itself. Either one of the new couple may previously have been single, divorced, or widowed, adding up to eight possible combinations. Generalizations about remarriage therefore have to be made with considerable caution. However, some general trends can be reliably identified.

Prior to 1900, about nine-tenths of all marriages in the United States were first marriages. Most remarriages involved at least one widowed person. With the progressive rise in the divorce rate, the level of remarriage also began to climb, and an increasing proportion of remarriages began to involve divorced people. In the 1960s, the remarriage rate increased rapidly, trailing off during the 1970s and early 1980s.

Today, twenty-eight out of every one hundred marriages involve at least one previously married person. Up to age thirty-five, the majority of remarriages are between divorced people. After that age, the proportion of remarriages involving widows or widowers rises. By age fifty-five, the proportion of such remarriages is larger than those following divorce.

Odd though it might seem, the best way to maximize the chances of marriage, for both sexes, is to have been married previously. People who have been married and divorced are more likely to marry again than single people in similar age groups are to marry for the first time. At all age levels, divorced men are more likely to remarry than divorced women. Three in every four divorced women remarry, but five in every six divorced men eventually marry again. In statistical terms, at least, remarriages are less successful than first marriages. Rates of divorce of people from second marriages are higher than those from first marriages.

This does not show that second marriages are doomed to "fail." People who have once been divorced may have higher expectations of marriage than those that remain married to their first spouses. Hence they may be more ready to dissolve new marriages than those only married once. The second marriages that endure might be more satisfying, on average, than first marriages (Glenn and Weaver, 1956).

A **stepfamily** may be defined as a family in which at least one of the adults is a stepparent (Vischer and Vischer, 1979). Many who remarry become stepparents of children who regularly "visit," rather than live in the same household as themselves. Using such a definition, the number of stepfamilies is much greater than shown in available official statistics, since these usually refer only to families with whom stepchildren live.

The existence of stepfamilies brings into being kin ties that resemble those of some traditional societies. Children may now have two "mothers" and two "fathers"—their natural parents and their stepparents. Some stepfamilies regard all the children and close relatives from previous marriages as "part of the family." If we consider that at least some of the grandparents may be closely involved, the result is a situation of some complexity.

There is in addition the factor of adoption. Brenda Maddox has estimated that more than one-third of all adoptions in the United States are of stepchildren (Maddox, 1975). Adoption is a way in which the non-biological parent makes public his or her connection to the child. Adoptive parents have legal rights and obligations towards their children. Other stepparents lack these, and in most cases their relationship with their stepchildren endures only as long as the marriage lasts. According to the law in most countries, if the biological parent in a stepfamily dies or is divorced from the stepparent, the stepparent has no legal rights of custody over the children. Even if a child has lived with a stepparent for many years, if the natural parent dies the stepparent has little recourse in law if the other natural parent wishes to have custody.

Certain particular difficulties and problems tend to arise in stepfamilies. In the first place, there usually exists a biological parent living elsewhere whose influence over the child or children is likely to remain powerful. Cooperative relations between divorced individuals often become strained when one or both remarries. Take as an illustration the case of a woman with two children who marries a man also having two children, all six living together. If the "outside" parents demand the same times of visitation as previously, the tensions involved in welding such a newly established family together are likely to be intense. For example, it may prove impossible ever to have the new family all together at weekends.

Stepfamilies merge children from different backgrounds, who may have varying expectations in the family milieu. Since most stepchildren "belong" to two households, the possibilities of clashes of habits and outlooks are considerable. Finally, there are few established norms defining the relationship between stepparent and stepchild. Should a child call a new stepparent by name, or is "Dad" or "Mom" more appropriate? Should the stepparent play the same part in disciplining the children as the natural parent? How should a stepparent treat the new spouse of his or her previous partner when the children are picked up? This letter and response appeared in "Dear Abby," a "problem column" syndicated in many United States newspapers:

Dear Abby:

A year ago I married Ted. His wife (Maxine) died and left him with two children, ages six and eight. This is my first marriage. I say that after Maxine died, Ted is no longer related to Maxine's relatives. Ted says Maxine's parents will always be his in-laws. Well, I have parents, too, so where does that leave them? A person can only have one set of in-laws at a time, and my parents should be regarded as grandparents, too, and they aren't. The titles of "grandma" and "grandpa" go to Maxine's parents. My parents are called "papa Pete" and "mama Mary." Do you think this is fair? . . . and what can I do about it?

In-Law Trouble

Dear In-Law Trouble:

Even though technically Ted is no longer the son-in-law of Maxine's parents, I advise you not to be so technical. There is a strong bond between Ted's former in-laws and their grandchildren, so if you're wise you won't tamper with these bonds because they were established before you came into the picture. Grandparents are grandparents for ever.

(Quoted in Vischer and Vischer, 1979)

Stepfamilies are developing types of kinship connection that are new in modern Western societies. Members of these families are developing their own ways of adjusting to the relatively uncharted circumstances in which they find themselves. Perhaps the most appropriate conclusion to be drawn is that while marriages are broken up by divorce, families on the whole are not. Especially where children are involved, many ties persist despite the reconstructed family connections brought into being through remarriage.

THE DARK SIDE OF
THE FAMILY

SINCE FAMILY OR KIN RELATIONS FORM PART OF EVERYONE'S experience, family life encompasses virtually the whole range of emotional experience. Family relationships—between wife and husband, parents and children, brothers and sisters, or between more distant relatives—can be warm and fulfilling. But they can equally well be full of the most extreme tension, driving people to despair, or imbuing them with a deep sense of anxiety and guilt. The "dark side" of family life is very extensive, and belies the rosy images of family harmony with which we are relentlessly bombarded in TV commercials and elsewhere in the popular media. There are many aspects to the unattractive side of the family, including the conflicts and hostilities that lead to separation or divorce that have just been analyzed. Among the most devastating in their consequences, however, are the incestuous abuse of children and domestic violence.

SEXUAL ABUSE

The sexual abuse of children is a widespread phenomenon, but of course is not confined to the sphere of the family. **Sexual abuse** can most easily be defined as the carrying out of sexual acts by adults with children below the age of consent (usually placed at sixteen years old). *Incest* refers to sexual relations between close kin. Not all incest is sexual abuse. For example, sexual intercourse between brother and sister is incestuous, but does not fit the definition of abuse, unless one is considerably older than the other. In sexual abuse, an adult is essentially exploiting an infant or child for sexual purposes (Ennew, 1986). It is impossible to get precise figures on the occurrence of incest, because of its forbidden and generally furtive character. But there is no doubt that the most common form of incest is one that is also sexual abuse—incestuous relations between fathers and young daughters.

Incest, and child sexual abuse more generally, are phenomena that have been "discovered" only over the past ten to twenty years. Of course, it has long been known that such sexual acts occasionally occurred, but it was assumed by most researchers that the strong moral taboos that exist against such behavior meant that it was not widespread. Such unfortunately is not the case. Child sexual abuse is proving to be disturbingly commonplace and exists at all levels of the social hierarchy. Statistics reported to the nationwide data collection system in the United States charted an increase of 600 percent in reported cases of sexual abuse between the years 1976–1982 (Finkelhor, 1984). It is virtually certain that this increase results from more direct attention being paid to the problem by welfare agencies and the police. It is equally certain that such statistics represent no more than the tip of the iceberg. In some surveys carried out in the 1980s, more than a third of women were found to have been victims of sexual abuse in childhood, meaning that they had experienced some degree of unwanted sexual touching. The figure for males is about 10 percent (Russell, 1984).

Children are highly vulnerable to exploitation and abuse within the family unit.

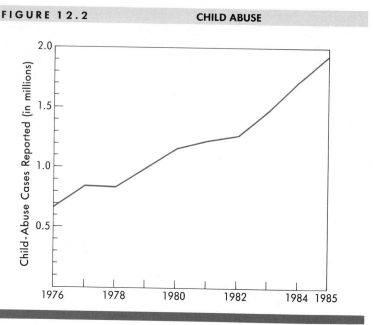

FIGURE 12.2   **CHILD ABUSE**

This graph shows the increase of child-abuse cases reported. Such cases range from physical injury and emotional maltreatment to deprivation of necessities and sexual abuse, the last category comprising 3.2 percent of child-abuse cases in 1976, rising to 11.7 percent in 1985.

Source: American Humane Association, Denver, CO, *National Study on Neglect and Abuse Reporting,* annual.

Why have incest and child sexual abuse been so hidden from public view until quite recently? Part of the answer seems to be that the taboos against such activity led welfare workers and social researchers to be wary of asking questions about possible abuse to parents or children. The women's movement played an important role in initially drawing public attention to sexual abuse, as one element in wider campaigns against sexual harassment and exploitation. Once researchers began to probe into suspected cases of child sexual abuse, many more came to light. The "discovery" of child sexual abuse, which began in the United States, has become an international phenomenon. Studies in Britain, for example, show parallel findings to those in the United States (CIBA Foundation, 1985).

We do not know exactly what proportion of child sexual abuse is incestuous, but probably most does in fact occur in a family context. Both the nature of the incestual relation and the sexual acts committed vary quite widely. Most studies indicate that 70–80 percent of incest cases are father-daughter or stepfather-daughter relationships. However, uncle-niece, brother-sister, father-son, mother-daughter, and even grandparent-grandchild relationships also occur. Some incestual contacts are short-lived and involve no more than a fondling of the child's sexual organs by the adult, or the child being encouraged to touch the adult's genitals. Others are much more extensive and may be repeated over several years. The children are usually over two years old, but there are many reported instances of sexual acts with infants. In one case, for example, a baby died from suffocation induced by fellatio (oral sex) (Goodwin, 1982).

Sometimes multiple incestuous relationships exist within the same family group. A British study, for instance, reports a case in which the father had had sexual intercourse with his daughter, aged fourteen, and had also committed sodomy (anal intercourse) with his thirteen-year-old son, who in turn had had sexual intercourse with his sister, as had another brother. The mother knew of these activities, but was too frightened of her husband to report any of them to the authorities. The full extent of the abuse within the family only came to light when the father was arrested for physically beating his daughter (CIBA Foundation, 1985).

Force or the threat of violence is involved in many cases of incest. It is quite rare for children to be willing participants. Children are sexual beings, of course, and quite often engage in mild sexual play or exploration with one another. But the large majority of children subject to sexual contact from adult family members find the experience repugnant, shameful, or disturbing. There is now considerable material indicating that child sexual abuse might have long-term consequences for its sufferers. Studies of prostitutes, juvenile offenders, adolescent runaways, and drug-users show that a high proportion have a history of child sexual abuse (De Young, 1982). Of course, correlation is not causation (see Chapter 21: "Working with Sociology: Methods of Research"). Demonstrating that people in these categories have been sexually abused as children does not show that such abuse was a causal influence over their later behavior. Probably a range of additional factors is involved, such as family conflicts, parental neglect, physical abuse, and so on.

Understanding Sexual Abuse

To explain why incest and, more broadly, child sexual abuse occur, we have to account for two things. First, why adults should be attracted to sexual activities involving children and second, why men should make up the vast majority of abusers. Each of these raises complex issues, given the variable nature of the acts and the relationships concerned. We can say with some certainty that only a minority of the perpetrators of child sexual abuse are mentally ill. In other words, we cannot explain what attracts adults to sexual involvement with children mainly in terms of some mental disorder.

Most child abusers do not seem to have a *preference* for sexual relationships with children over adults. Rather, it is a matter of availability, coupled to power. Children within the family are dependent beings and highly vulnerable to parental demands or pressures. Adults who commit incest with their children seem often to be timid, awkward, and inadequate in their dealings with other adults. Many appear not just to be satisfying sexual impulses, but searching for affection they cannot attain elsewhere. We can make a connection here with the fact that the large majority of abusers are men. In an earlier chapter (Chapter 6: "Gender and Sexuality"), we discussed "male inexpressiveness"—the difficulty many men have in expressing feelings, a phenomenon that probably has deep psychological origins. Men come to associate the expression of feeling directly with sexuality, whereas women focus more on whole relationships. Males also associate sexuality with the assertion of power and with submissiveness in their partners. Therefore, there is less of a distance for men between adult sexuality and sexual attention to children than for women.

As one of the leading students of child abuse, David Finkelhor has argued that this interpretation, if correct, suggests what changes might be needed in our society to help reduce the sexual exploitation of children:

> First, we might benefit from the opportunity to practice affection and dependency in relationships that did not involve sex, such as male-to-male friendships and nurturant interaction with children. Second, the accomplishment of heterosexual sex might be de-emphasized as the ultimate criterion of male adequacy. Third, men might learn to enjoy sexual relationships based on equality. Men who are comfortable relating to women at the same level of maturity and competence will be less likely to exploit children sexually. As men's relationships with women change, so will their relations with children. (Finkelhor, 1984)

VIOLENCE WITHIN THE FAMILY

Violence within family settings (as elsewhere in society) is also primarily a male domain, but less decisively so than in the case of child sexual abuse. We may define domestic violence as physical abuse directed by one member of a family against another or others. Studies show that the prime targets of physical abuse are again children, especially little children under the age of six. Violence by husbands against wives is the second most common type, a phenomenon we have also previously referred to in Chapter 6, which dealt with gender and sexuality. Women, however, are also quite often perpetrators of physical violence in the household, against young children and against husbands. The home is in fact the most dangerous place in modern society. In statistical terms, a person of any age or either sex is far more likely to be subject to physical attack in the home than on the street at night. One in four murders in the United States are committed by one family member against another.

It is occasionally claimed that women are almost as violent as men in the home, and some surveys indicate that wives hit husbands nearly as often as the reverse (Strauss, Gelles, and Steinmetz, 1980). However, violence by women is more restrained than that by men, and much less likely to cause enduring physical harm. "Wife-battering"—the regular physical brutalizing of wives by husbands—has no real equivalent the other way around. Men who physically abuse children are also much more likely to do so consistently, so as to cause long-standing injuries, than are women.

Why is domestic violence so commonplace? Several sets of factors can explain this. One is the combination of emotional intensity and personal intimacy characteristic of family life. Family ties are normally charged with strong emotions, often mixing love and hate. Quarrels that break out in the domestic setting can unleash antagonisms that would not be felt in the same way in other social contexts. What seems only a minor incident can precipitate full-scale hostilities between spouses, or between parents and children. A man who tolerates eccentricities in the behavior of other women may become furious if his wife talks too much at a dinner party, or confides intimacies he wishes to keep secret.

A second influence is the fact that a good deal of violence within the family is culturally tolerated and even approved of. Although socially sanctioned family violence is relatively confined in nature, it can quite easily spill over into more severe forms of assault. There are few children in modern America who have not at some time been slapped or spanked by one or both of their parents. Such actions quite often meet with general approval and are probably not even thought of as "violence." If a stranger slapped a child in a shop because he disapproved of something the child said or did, it would be a different matter. Yet there is no difference in the physical assault involved.

There is also some social approval of violence between spouses. Murray Straus has argued that parenthood provides a "license for hitting," and that "the marriage license is a hitting license" (Straus, 1978). The cultural acceptability of this form of domestic violence is expressed in an old ditty:

Domestic violence has increased the need for services that enable abused women, and sometimes their children, to get help.

A woman, a horse, and a hickory tree
The more you beat 'em the better they be.

In the workplace and other public settings, it is a general rule that no one can hit anyone else, no matter how objectionable or irritating he or she may be. This is not the case within the family. Many research studies have shown that a substantial proportion of couples believe that in some circumstances it is legitimate for a spouse to strike the other. But, while about one in four Americans of both sexes take the view that there can be a good reason for a husband to strike his wife, a somewhat lower proportion believe that the reverse also holds (Greenblat, 1983).

However, violence within the family does also reflect broader patterns of violent behavior. Many husbands who physically abuse their wives and children have records of violence in other contexts. A study by Jeffrey Fagan and his coresearchers (1983) of a national sample of battered wives showed that more than half their husbands were violent with others as well as with their partners. More than 80 percent of these men had in fact been arrested at least once for episodes of nondomestic violence.

ALTERNATIVES TO MARRIAGE AND THE FAMILY

THE FAMILY HAS LONG HAD ITS CRITICS. IN THE NINETEENTH century, numerous thinkers proposed that family life should be replaced by more communal forms of living arrangements, and some of their ideas gave rise to actual communities. One of the most well-known examples was the Oneida Community of New England, set up in the second part of the nineteenth century. Based upon the religious beliefs of John Humphrey Noyes, it involved the principle that every man in the community was married to every woman. All were supposed to be parents to the community's children. After various initial difficulties, the group expanded to include about three hundred people and endured for about thirty years before breaking up. Many other communes have been founded since then, in the United States as well as many other Western countries. A large variety of communal groups were established in the 1960s, often based on free sexual relations within the group and collective responsibility for the raising of children. A small number of these are still in existence.

The most important current example of communal domestic life is that of the **kibbutzim** in Israel. A kibbutz is a community of families and individuals that cooperates in the raising of children. Originally most of the kibbutzim were collective-farming enterprises, but today many have also moved into industrial production. There are more than 240 kibbutzim in Israel, having nearly one hundred thousand members in all. Some are small, with no more than fifty members, while others include as many as two thousand people. Each kibbutz operates as though it were a single household, treating childcare as the responsibility of the whole community rather than of the family. In some, children live in special "children's houses" rather than with their parents, although they usually spend weekends with their families.

The kibbutzim were originally established with a radical intent. Communal ownership of property, together with the group rearing of children, was supposed to allow kibbutzim members to escape the individualistic, competitive nature of life in modern societies. These ideals have by no means been abandoned. Yet over the years the majority of kibbutzim have opted for more conventional living arrangements than those favored in the early stages. It is more common now for children to sleep in their parents' quarters, for instance, than used to be the case.

COHABITATION

Cohabitation—where a couple lives together in a sexual relationship without being married—has become increasingly widespread in most Western societies. In Sweden, Denmark, and some other countries, it has become the norm for couples to live together prior to marriage. Since it is only recently that a high proportion of people have been cohabiting in this way, it is difficult as yet to say whether it primarily signals a postponement of marriage or a permanent living situation. In a Swedish survey of unmarried parents living together to whom children were born in 1971, the majority were shown still to be living together in 1975, by the time the offspring had reached aged four. Only 43 percent of these couples had since actually gotten married (Agell, 1980).

In the United States, until very recently, cohabitation was generally regarded as somewhat scandalous. During the 1970s, however, the number of unmarried men and women sharing a household went up by nearly 300 percent. Cohabitation has become widespread among college and university students. Surveys indicate that about one in four college students lives with a partner with whom they have a sexual relationship at some point during the course of their college careers (Macklin, 1978). In a national survey of cohabitation in the United States, a sample of 2,510 men aged twenty to thirty were contacted. While only 5 percent were living with a woman at the date of the interview, 18 percent had cohabited for at least six months at previous dates in their lives (Clayton and Voss, 1977).

Cohabitation in the United States today seems to be, for the most part, an "experimental" stage prior to marriage. In the case of young people living together, this is usually the result of a gradual drift rather than of calculated planning. A couple already having sexual relations gradually spend more and more time together, and eventually one or the other gives up their original place of residence. Young people living together almost always anticipate getting married at some date, but not necessarily to their current partners. Only a minority of such couples pool their finances.

Living with a member of the opposite sex remains a rather furtive activity for some people in their late teens. Some women still attempt to conceal the true nature of their living arrangements from parents —although men are less troubled by this. It does not seem at the moment that trends toward extensive cohabitation in the United States will proceed as far as in Sweden and some other European countries in the near future. Living together is not yet established as a significant alternative to marriage, although it is possible that it will become so. In some countries, including some places in the United States, the law now recognizes that people living together have rights similar to married couples. Should the relationship break up, individuals can sue for a property settlement and for maintenance. One highly publicized case concerned the relationship between the actor Lee Marvin and his companion Michelle Triola Marvin. When their relationship ended, Michelle Marvin claimed financial support, some of which was ultimately granted by a California court.

GAY-PARENT FAMILIES

A lesbian couple with their child.

Many homosexual men and women live in stable relationships as couples. Some gay couples have been formally married even if these ceremonies have no standing in law. Relaxation of previously intolerant attitudes towards homosexuality has been accompanied by a growing inclination on the part of courts to allocate custody of children to a mother living in a gay relationship. The availability of techniques of artificial insemination means that gay women may start a family without any heterosexual contacts. While virtually every gay family with children in the United States involves two women, for a period social-welfare agencies in several cities placed homeless gay teenage boys in the custody of gay male couples. The practice was discontinued largely because of adverse public reaction.

STAYING SINGLE

Several factors combine to increase the numbers of people living alone in modern societies. One is the trend towards later marriages; another, the rising rates of divorce. Yet another is the growing numbers of old people in the population whose partners have died. "Being single" means different things at different periods of the life cycle. A larger proportion of people in their twenties are unmarried than used to be the case. By the mid-thirties, however, only a small minority of men and women have never been married. The majority of single people aged thirty to fifty are divorced and "in between" marriages. Most single people over fifty are widowed.

Peter Stein (1980) interviewed sixty single individuals in the age range of twenty-five to forty-five. Most felt ambivalent about single-hood. They recognized that being single often helped their career opportunities, made available a wider variety of sexual experiences,

FIGURE 12.3   **WHO IS SINGLE?**

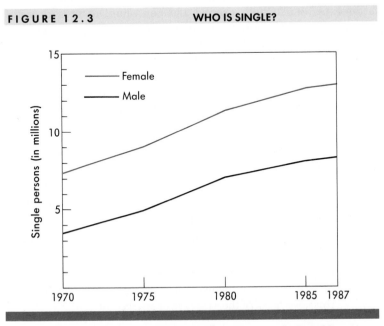

Source: U.S. Bureau of the Census, *Current Population Reports,* series P-20, No. 423.

and promoted overall freedom and autonomy. On the other hand, they acknowledged the difficulty of being single in a world in which most people their age were married, and suffered from isolation or loneliness. On the whole, most found the pressures to marry greater than the incentives to stay single.

THE DECLINE OF THE FAMILY?

In 1859, a contributor to the *Boston Quarterly Review* wrote that "the family, in its old sense, is disappearing from our land, and not only our free institutions are threatened but the very existence of our society is endangered" (quoted in Lantz, Schulz, and O'Hara, 1977). This sort of judgment has echoed down the years in most Western countries, expressed anxiously by those who feel that the family is threatened with disintegration. Critics of the family, on the other hand, have looked forward with approval to the decline, and even the disappearance, of family institutions.

Since it has so often been said—with little real justification—that the family is disappearing, we should be skeptical of sweeping judgments. Yet it would be difficult to deny that major shifts in the nature of both marriage and the family are taking place today. We are witnessing some basic alterations in the nature of marriage and family relationships, which both express and contribute to broader social changes. It seems almost certain that alternative forms of social and sexual relationships to those of the past will flourish still further. It seems equally clear that the family is not on the verge of crumbling or falling into terminal decay.

SUMMARY

1. *Kinship, family,* and *marriage* are closely related terms of key significance for sociology and anthropology. Kinship comprises either genetic ties or ties initiated by marriage. A family is a group of kin having responsibility for the upbringing of children. Marriage is a union of two persons living together in a socially approved sexual relationship.

2. A *nuclear family* refers to a household in which a married couple or single parent live with their own or adopted children. Where kin other than a married couple and children live in the same household, or are involved in close and continuous relationships, we speak of the existence of an *extended family.*

3. In Western societies, marriage, and therefore the family, is associated with *monogamy* (a culturally approved sexual relationship

between one man and one woman). Many other cultures tolerate or encourage *polygamy,* where an individual may be married to two or more spouses at the same time. *Polygyny,* in which a man may marry more than one wife, is far more common than *polyandry,* in which a woman may have more than one husband.

4. In Europe and the United States, nuclear-family patterns were strongly implanted well before the development of industrialization, although they were profoundly influenced by it. Elsewhere in the world there remains a diversity of family forms. Changes in family patterns are generated by such factors as the development of a centralized government, the expansion of towns and cities, and employment within organizations outside family influence. These changes are tending to produce a worldwide movement towards nuclear-family systems, eroding extended-family forms and other types of kinship group.

5. There have been major changes in patterns of family life in the United States during the postwar period: a high percentage of women are in the paid labor force, there are rising rates of divorce, and substantial proportions of the population are either in single-parent households or are living with stepfamilies. *Cohabitation* (where a couple lives together in a sexual relationship outside of marriage) has become increasingly common in many industrial countries.

6. Family life is by no means always a picture of harmony and happiness. The "dark side" of the family is found in the patterns of *sexual abuse* and domestic violence that often occur within it. Most sexual abuse of children is carried out by males and seems to connect with other types of violent behavior in which some men are involved.

7. Cohabitation, people choosing to live alone, and homosexuality have become more common in recent years. It seems certain that alternative forms of social and sexual relationships to those prevalent in the past will flourish still further. Yet marriage and the family remain firmly established institutions.

BASIC CONCEPTS

SOCIAL INSTITUTION

FAMILY

KINSHIP

MARRIAGE

IMPORTANT TERMS

CLAN

NUCLEAR FAMILY

EXTENDED FAMILY

FAMILY OF ORIENTATION

FAMILY OF PROCREATION

MATRILOCAL FAMILY

PATRILOCAL FAMILY

MONOGAMY

POLYGAMY

POLYGYNY

POLYANDRY

AFFECTIVE INDIVIDUALISM

EXOGAMY

ENDOGAMY

SERIAL MONOGAMY

PATRILINEAL INHERITANCE

MATRILINEAL INHERITANCE

NEOLOCAL RESIDENCE

STEPFAMILY

SEXUAL ABUSE

KIBBUTZIM

COHABITATION

CHAPTER THIRTEEN

EDUCATION, COMMUNICATION, AND MEDIA

IMAGINE BEING IN THE SHOES—OR THE WOODEN CLOGS—of Jean-Paul Didion, a peasant boy growing up in a French farming community two centuries ago. In 1750 Jean-Paul is fourteen years old. He cannot read or write, but this is not uncommon; only a few of the adults in his village have the ability to decipher more than the odd word or two of written texts. There are some schools in nearby districts run by monks and nuns, but these are completely removed from Jean-Paul's experience. He has never known anyone well who attended school, save for the local priest. For eight or nine years, Jean-Paul has been spending most of his days helping with domestic tasks and working in the fields. The older he gets, the longer each day he is expected to share in the backbreaking chores demanded by the intensive tilling of his father's plot of land.

Jean-Paul is likely never to leave the area in which he was born, and may spend virtually the whole of his life within the confines of the village and surrounding fields, only occasionally traveling to other local villages and towns. He may have to wait until he is in his late fifties before inheriting his father's plot of land, sharing control

Education takes many forms. Here, Navajo culture is passed from one generation to another.

of it with his younger brothers. Jean-Paul is aware that he is "French," that his country is ruled over by Louis XV, and that there is a wider world beyond even France itself. But he only has a vague awareness even of "France" as a distinct political entity. There is no such thing as "news," nor any regular means by which information about events elsewhere reaches him. What he knows of the wider world comes from stories and tales he has heard told by adults and by visiting travelers. Like others in his community, he only learns about major events—like the death of the king—days, weeks, or sometimes months, after they have occurred.

Although in modern terms Jean-Paul is "uneducated," he is far from "ignorant." He has a sensitive and developed understanding of the family and children, having had to care for those younger than himself since he was very young. He is already highly knowledgeable about the land, methods of crop production, and ways of preserving and storing food. His mastery of local customs and traditions is profound, and he can turn his hand to many different tasks over and above agricultural cultivation, such as weaving or basket making.

Jean-Paul is an invented figure, but the above description portrays the typical experience of a boy growing up in preindustrial Europe. Compare this with our situation today. In the industrialized countries, virtually everyone can read and write—that is, people are *literate.* We have all gone through a process of formal schooling. We are all aware of the common characteristics we share with other members of the same society, and have at least some sort of knowledge of its geographical and political position in the world, and of its past history. Our lives are influenced at all ages beyond infancy by information we pick up through books, newspapers, magazines, radio, and television, in short, the various *media.* We live in a media-saturated world. The printed word and electronic communication, combined with the formal teaching provided by schools and colleges, have become fundamental to our way of life. This being so, schooling and the media extend the process of socialization, which we took up earlier in Chapter 3 ("Socialization and the Life Cycle"). There, we focused on early influences, especially mother-infant interaction, but we only touched briefly upon schooling and the media.

In this chapter, two themes dominate: education and media as socializing processes, and education and media as sources of power. First, we shall show how present-day education developed and analyze its socializing influence, which at times complements, and at others competes with, the family. We will also look at education in relation to social inequality, and consider how far the educational system serves to encourage or to reduce such inequality. We then move to studying the nature of modern systems of communication.

THE EARLY DEVELOPMENT OF LITERACY AND SCHOOLING

THE TERM "SCHOOL" HAS ITS ORIGINS IN A GREEK WORD meaning "leisure" or "recreation." In premodern societies, schooling existed for the few who had the time and resources available to pursue the cultivation of the arts and philosophy. For some, their engagement with schooling meant much the same as when we take up a hobby. For others, like religious leaders or priests, schooling was a way of gaining skills and thus increasing their knowledge to interpret sacred texts. But for the vast majority of people, growing up meant learning by example the same social habits and work skills as their elders. Socialization was a family affair. Children often began assisting in domestic duties and farming work at a very young age, rapidly becoming full-fledged members of the community, much the way we saw with Jean-Paul Didion—fully socialized, but illiterate.

One reason why so few were able to read and write in former times was that all texts had to be laboriously copied by hand, so texts or books simply were not available except to a few. The invention of printing altered that situation. The first printing press in the West was constructed by the German Johann Gutenberg, who produced his first book in 1454. Printing made texts and documents more widely available. These included books and pamphlets, but also many kinds of routine materials that we take for granted but are essential to the running of a complex society. Codes of law, for instance, became written down and widely diffused. Records, reports, and the collection of routine data increasingly became part of government, economic enterprise, and organizations in general. Printing spread across Europe and arrived in America before the pilgrims did. Juan Pablo set up a press in Mexico City in 1539, producing religious books (De Fleur and Dennis, 1985).

The spread and increasing use of printed materials in different spheres of life eventually led to the development of higher levels of **literacy**—the ability to read and write at a basic level—than had ever been the case previously. **Education** in its modern form, involving the instruction of pupils within specially constructed school premises, gradually began to emerge in the first few decades of the nineteenth century, when systems of primary schools began to be constructed in Europe and the United States. One main reason for the rise of large educational systems was the process of industrialization with its ensuing expansion of cities. Great numbers of people now

A page from a Chinese book written in 688, and printed in 1124, three centuries before the European printing of the Gutenberg Bible.

worked in many different occupations, and work skills could no longer only be passed on from parents to children, or even from master craftsman to apprentices. The acquisition of knowledge based on abstract learning (of subjects like math, science, or history) became increasingly important. With the development of modern society, people had to be furnished with the basic skills of reading, writing, and calculating; and it became important that they be able to master new, sometimes very technical, forms of information.

SCHOOLING IN THE UNITED STATES

SCHOOLING ON A SMALL SCALE PREDATED THE INDUSTRIAL revolution, and evolved from other perceived needs. Schooling in the United States has its origins in the disciplining of children. The states of Massachusetts and Connecticut instituted compulsory schooling in 1647. The basis of this early development was the Puritan belief that all children should obey their parents without question, a belief which these colonies had in fact made part of their legal statutes. A legal provision of 1642 promised severe sanctions against the "great neglect of many parents and masters in training up their children in learning and labour" (Bailyn, 1960). Because this measure was ineffectual, however, the Puritan authorities commanded every town to provide schooling, and by doing so took on some of the socializing roles of parents especially, in this case, discipline.

It was almost two centuries later, however, before schooling became a common experience for the by then much-expanded American population. All states provided free elementary schooling by the 1850s, although at first attendance was not compulsory and large numbers of the population still went without formal education. Compulsory education was introduced in most states towards the end of the nineteenth century. This was a period of extremely rapid expansion in the building of schools and colleges. There were only 160 public high schools in the country in 1870, but by 1900 there were in excess of six thousand.

The diverse cultural makeup of America at the turn of the century presented a particular challenge to the public-school system. By that time large groups of immigrants from Europe and elsewhere, each with a different native language and all with great hopes for the future, had settled in the United States. School then became a major

American classroom, 1937.

transmission point in linguistically, and to some extent culturally, anglicizing the immigrants. In addition, the schools propagated American ideals of equality of opportunity, thus encouraging the immigrants to set about making a new life. The notion that everyone is "born equal" caused mass public education to develop in the United States well before comparable systems were set up in other countries. Education was seen as an avenue of mobility in a society in which the "aristocratic ideal"—that some people are born with superior rights to others—had never held sway. And along with the idea of equality, other American values and beliefs were, and continue to be, taught more or less explicitly.

The system of higher education, colleges and universities, did not expand as early as the elementary and high school systems. In 1940, only 15 percent of the 18–21 age group were enrolled in college. In the period after World War II, however, there was a rapid expansion that carried on until the early 1970s. In 1950, the proportion of the college-age group enrolled in college had risen to 30 percent, and a decade later had reached nearly 40 percent. It has gone up to 48 percent today. The numbers of students carrying on through graduate school has also risen progressively over the postwar period.

In spite of the importance of public education in America, it is only since World War II that schooling has come to be seen as more or less essential to career advancement. For a long while, the Horatio Alger view of the self-made and self-educated individual held sway alongside the belief in the value of education. But this idea has moved more to the sidelines as educational qualifications have become more and more valued by employers. For this reason, the day that colleges and universities notify those who have been accepted or rejected has become a day of reckoning for many high school students.

There are wide differences between countries in ways of organizing educational systems. Some systems of education are highly centralized. In France, for example, all students follow nationally determined curricula, sitting for uniform national examinations. In contrast, the American system is much more fragmentary. Individual states provide substantial funding for schools, contributing about 40 percent of the necessary finance, with the federal government being responsible only for some 10 percent. The rest comes from taxation revenue in local school districts. As a result, schools are administered by local school boards elected by community vote; the boards have a wide range of powers including the hiring of teachers and other school officials, and the selection (and occasional banning) of texts and other reading or viewing materials.

Such community control of schooling has mixed consequences. It has clear benefits in that schools are kept responsive to the needs and interests of the areas they serve. On the other hand, the system also leads to very wide differences in school funding, depending upon how wealthy a given community is. Class size, available facilities, and the capability to attract well-qualified teachers, all vary enormously between different school districts. As we shall see later in this chapter, these variations are important factors in perpetuating social inequalities between more affluent groups and the less privileged.

HIGHER EDUCATION

There are also large differences among societies in the organization of **higher education** (education after high school, usually at university or college). In some countries, all universities and colleges are public agencies, and receive their funding directly from government sources. Higher education in France, for instance, is organized nationally, with centralized control being almost as marked as in primary and secondary education. All course structures have to be validated by a national regulatory body responsible to the minister of higher education. Two types of degree can be gained, one awarded by the individual university, the other by the state. National degrees are generally regarded as more prestigious and valuable than those of specific universities, since they are supposed to conform to guaranteed uniform standards. Some occupations in government are only open to the holders of national degrees, which are also favored by most industrial employers. Virtually all teachers in schools, colleges, and universities in France are state employees. Rates of pay and the broad framework of teaching duties are fixed centrally.

The United States has a much higher proportion of private colleges and universities than most other industrialized countries—over half of American institutions of higher education are privately funded. The difference between "public" and "private" in American higher education, however, is not as clear-cut as it is in other countries. Students at private universities are eligible for public grants and loans, and such universities receive public research funding. Public universities often possess substantial private endowments, or are given donations by private firms. They also often obtain research grants from private industrial sources.

Certainly one clear difference between public and private colleges in the United States is their tuition and board. The cost of studying at a private college is three to four times that of attending a public one (Table 13.1). Private colleges generally have smaller enrollments than public ones and can therefore provide more intensive teaching. Hence, although private colleges are in the majority, only about 20 percent of all students are educated in them (Lerner, 1982).

The educational sociologist Martin Trow predicted in 1960 that educational development in the United States would eventually lead to a situation in which almost everyone receives some form of higher education (Trow, 1961). The expansion of American higher education has in fact since then largely come to a stop. Yet a very high proportion of the American population, compared to elsewhere, has experience of higher education. There is also a general trend towards a greater proportion of students staying in high school, moving on to college, and carrying on through graduate school.

TABLE 13.1	WHAT IT COSTS TO ATTEND COLLEGE	
	Public	Private
1970	$1,362	$2,920
1988	$4,760	$13,330

Figures represent average cost of tuition, fees, room, and board, some of which get as high as $20,000 for some private universities.
Source: U.S. Department of Education, National Center for Education Statistics, *Digest of Education Statistics,* annual.

EDUCATION, POWER, AND SOCIETY

THUS FAR, WE HAVE TOUCHED ON THE DEVELOPMENT OF literacy and education and the nature of the educational system in the United States. In the next few sections, we continue to depict education as a socializing influence, while at the same time examining issues of power and individual development: education and inequality, intelligence and inequality, gender and education, and education in the Third World.

EDUCATION AND INEQUALITY

The expansion of education has always been closely linked to the ideals of democracy. Reformers value education, of course, for its own sake—for the opportunity it provides for individuals to develop their capabilities and aptitudes. Yet education has also consistently been seen as a means of equalization. Access to universal education, it has been argued, could help reduce disparities of wealth and power. Has education, in fact, proved to be a "great equalizer" in this way? A great deal of sociological research has been devoted to answering this question.

Coleman's Study of Inequalities in American Education

One of the classic investigations of educational inequality was undertaken by James Coleman in the United States in the 1960s. As a result of the Civil Rights Act of 1964, the United States commissioner of education was required to prepare a report on educational inequalities resulting from differences of ethnic background, religion, and national origin. James Coleman, a sociologist, was appointed director of the research program. The outcome was a study, published in 1966, based on one of the most extensive research projects ever carried out in sociology.

Information was collected on more than half a million pupils, who were also given a range of achievement tests assessing verbal and nonverbal abilities, reading levels, and mathematical skills. Sixty thousand teachers also completed forms providing data for about four thousand schools. The results provided a general survey of schooling across the country, but Coleman's research also came up with some surprising results.

The report found that a large majority of children were in schools that effectively segregated black from white. Almost 80 percent of schools attended by white students contained only 10 percent or less black students. White and Asian-American students scored higher achievement-test results than blacks and other ethnic minority students. Coleman had supposed his results would also show mainly black schools to have worse facilities, larger classes, and inferior buildings than schools that were predominantly white. But surprisingly, the results showed far fewer differences of this type than had been anticipated.

Coleman therefore concluded that the material resources provided in schools made little difference to educational performance; the decisive influence was the children's backgrounds. In Coleman's words, "Inequalities imposed on children by their home, neighborhood, and peer environment are carried along to become the inequalities with which they confront adult life at the end of school" (Coleman et al., 1966). There was, however, some evidence that students from deprived backgrounds having close friendships with those from more favorable circumstances were likely to be more successful educationally.

Not long after Coleman's study, Christopher Jencks produced an equally celebrated work that reviewed empirical evidence accumulated on education and inequality up to the end of the 1960s (Jencks et al., 1972). Jencks reaffirmed the conclusions (1) that educational and occupational attainment are governed mainly by family background and nonschool factors, and (2) that, on their own, educational reforms can have only minor effects on existing inequalities. Jencks' work has been criticized on methodological grounds, but the overall conclusions he drew remain persuasive (Oakes, 1985).

Later Research

While subsequent research, like Jencks's study, has confirmed some of Coleman's findings, aspects of his work have also been challenged. Since Coleman's research covered students at a single point in time, it was not really well set up to analyze change. Subsequent investigations with a more extended time perspective suggest that the school environment is more relevant to academic performance than Coleman argued. A study by Michael Rutter, carried out in London, looked at the educational development of groups of boys over a period of several years. The children studied were first contacted in 1970, when they were on the point of finishing their primary schooling. Information was collected on social background and academic performance. The survey was repeated in 1974, when the boys had been in secondary school for three years. A number of schools were selected for intensive study: pupils and teachers were interviewed and classroom activities observed.

The findings indicated that schools do in fact have an influence upon the academic development of children. The factors Rutter found to be important were left largely unanalyzed in Coleman's investigation. They included, for example, the quality of teacher-pupil interaction, an atmosphere of cooperation and caring between teachers and students, and well-organized course preparation. Schools that provided superior learning environments were not always the best equipped in terms of material resources or buildings (Rutter et al., 1979).

Rutter's results do not go against the finding that influences prior to, and outside of, school are most decisive in perpetuating social inequalities. Since the factors to which Rutter pointed are often maximized in schools catering to well-motivated students, and which provide good support for their teachers, they help explain just why schooling tends to maintain inequalities more often than to diminish them. There is a self-repeating cycle in which students from relatively privileged homes, where education is often highly valued, attend a particular school, and perpetuate its good qualities; good teachers are attracted and motivation is maintained. A school mainly attended by deprived children will have to work far harder to achieve a similar result.

Yet Rutter's conclusions do suggest that differences in school organization and atmosphere can in some degree affect academic attainment. The improvement of teaching quality, the social climate of the school, and patterns of school work can have a positive effect on the academic performance of those from disadvantaged backgrounds (Hurn, 1985). In subsequent research, Coleman has in fact reached similar conclusions (Coleman, Hoffer, and Kilgore, 1981).

Tracking and Inequality

The practice of tracking—dividing students into groups that receive different instruction on the basis of assumed similarities in ability or attainment—is common in American schools. In some schools students are tracked just for certain subjects, in others for all. Tracking partly explains why schooling seems to have little effect on existing social inequalities. For being in a particular track labels a student as either "able" or otherwise. As we have seen in the case of labeling and deviance (Chapter 5: "Deviance"), once attached, such labels are hard to break away from. Children from more privileged backgrounds, where academic work is encouraged, are likely to find themselves in the higher tracks early on—and by and large stay there.

The tracking of students early in their schooling can greatly influence their chances in higher education.

Jeannie Oakes (1985) studied tracking in twenty-five junior and senior high schools. Some were large, others small; she included schools in both urban and rural areas in her sample. But she concentrated upon differences *within* schools rather than between them. She found that many schools claimed they did not track students. But virtually all of them had mechanisms for sorting students into groups that seemed to be alike in ability and achievement, to make teaching easier. In other words, they had tracking but did not choose to use the term itself. Even where tracking only existed in this informal fashion, she found strong labels developing—high ability, low achieving, slow, average, and so on. Individual students in these groups came to be defined both by teachers, other students, and themselves, in terms of such labels. A student in a "high-achieving" group was seen as a high-achieving *person*—bright, smart, and quick. One in a "low-achieving" group came to be seen as slow, below average, and when people are more forthright in their vocabulary, dummies, sweathogs, or yahoos.

The usual reason given for tracking is that bright children learn more quickly and effectively in a group of others who are equally able, and that clever students are held back if placed in mixed groups. Surveying the evidence, Oakes was able to show that these assumptions are not valid. The result of different research investigations are not wholly consistent, but the majority have found that the brightest students do not learn more, or more quickly, when taught in equal-ability groups. The learning of average and slow students, however, *is* reduced by tracking.

THEORIES OF SCHOOLING

From these and other studies, various theories of schooling and inequality have developed. Some focus on children's language and cognitive abilities; others attempt to understand educational institutions in the context of wider social and economic influences. At least one prominent educational theorist, taking a more radical approach to education, has proposed a full-scale "deschooling" of society.

Language Codes

The British sociologist Basil Bernstein (1977) has argued that children from varying backgrounds develop different "codes," or forms of speech, during the early years of life, which affect their subsequent school experience. He is not concerned with differences in vocabulary or in grammatical correctness; his interest is in systematic differences in ways of using language, in particular those that contrast children from poorer environments with children from more affluent backgrounds.

The speech of lower-class children, Bernstein argues, represents a **restricted code,** a type of speech that is tied to the cultural setting of a lower-class community or district. Many lower-class people live in a strong familial or neighborhood culture, in which certain values and norms are taken for granted and not put into explicit language. Lower-class parents tend to socialize their children in a concrete rather than an abstract way, by the use of rewards or reprimands to correct their child's behavior. For example, a lower-class parent is likely to scold a child for a transgression without explaining why it might be injurious to him or to others. Language in a restricted code is more likely to be used to communicate practical experiences than to teach abstract ideas, processes, or relationships. Speech is oriented to the norms of the group, without anyone easily being able to explain *why* they follow the patterns of behavior they do.

By contrast, the language development of children from higher class backgrounds, according to Bernstein, involves the acquisition of an **elaborated code**—a style of speaking in which the meanings of words can be individualized to suit the demands of particular situations. These children also use restricted codes—in their talk with one another on the playground, for example—in addition to mastering an elaborated code. They can "switch over" from one to the other when they wish. The ways in which children from higher class backgrounds learn to use language are less bound to particular contexts; the child is more easily able to generalize and express abstract ideas. Their mothers, when controlling their children, explain the reasons and principles that underlie their reactions to a child's behavior. A lower-class mother might admonish her child for wanting to eat too much candy by simply saying, "No more candy for you!" A mother from a higher class background is more likely to explain that eating too much candy is bad for the child's health and the state of her teeth. Whether or not the child eats the candy, she at least comes away from this situation with further knowledge.

Children who have acquired elaborated codes of speech, Bernstein proposes, are better able to deal with the demands of formal academic education than children confined to restricted codes. The reason for this is that formal schooling involves learning abstract concepts, as opposed to more concrete cultural, or even neighborhood-bound, topics. Such symbolic knowledge requires a flexibility of language for which lower-class children are at a disadvantage. This does not imply that lower-class children have an "inferior" type of speech, or that their codes of language are "deprived." Rather, the way in which they use speech clashes with the academic culture of the school. Those who have mastered elaborated codes and the flexible use of language fit much more easily within the school environment.

There is some evidence to back up Bernstein's theory, although it remains controversial. Joan Tough has studied the language of working- and middle-class children, finding systematic differences. She backs up Bernstein's thesis that lower-class children rarely have their questions answered, nor are they offered explanations about the reasoning of others (Tough, 1983; Tizard and Hughes, 1985).

Bernstein's ideas might help explain why those from low socioeconomic backgrounds tend to be underachievers at school. The following traits are probably associated with restricted-code speech, all of which inhibit the lower-class child's educational chances:

1. LACK OF CURIOSITY. The child probably receives limited responses to questions asked at home, and therefore is likely to be both less informed and less curious about the wider world than those mastering elaborated codes.

2. PROBLEM WITH ABSTRACT CONCEPTS. The child will find it difficult to respond to the unemotional and abstract language used in teaching, as well as to appeals to general principles of school discipline. The child will experience little difficulty with rote or "drill" learning but will have major difficulties in grasping conceptual distinctions involving generalization and abstraction.

3. DIFFERENT LANGUAGE USAGE. Much of what the teacher says is likely to be incomprehensible, as he or she might use different linguistic forms than those the child is accustomed to. The child may attempt to cope by "translating" the teacher's language into something familiar—but then could fail to grasp the very principles the teacher intends to convey.

Recent research seems to show that the difference in the speech of lower-class black groups (black English vernacular) directly affects performance in mathematical school tests. This is not "bad English," or "bad grammar," but a complex English dialect. Those who speak black English are not culturally deprived, but speak a form of English that conflicts with the "standard English" by means of which teachers approach school tasks that appear to be purely nonverbal. For example, black English tends to merge "as . . . as" statements with "more than" statements. A student who hears the sentence "John has twice as many books as Harry" will interpret it to mean "John has two times more books than Harry." In other words, rather than picking up the *multiplication* sense of "twice as many as," it is interpreted in an *additive* way. In the case of standard English, if Harry has four books, John will be seen as having eight; in the case of black English vernacular, twelve (four plus "twice more"). Something which sounds ungrammatical to standard English speakers—"twice as large than"—is how a black English speaker may express the idea (Orr, 1987).

The ways of thinking encouraged by black English may be superior to standard English for handling some kinds of tasks and situations. Thus, additive interpretation is a way of grasping connections quickly, aiding the sort of "thinking on one's feet" that is part of being "streetwise." But linguistic structures of this sort cut across some of the requirements of mathematical calculation in the school curriculum. For instance, a student might find it hard to see that 2.5×2.5 is not 5, since $2.5 + 2.5 = 5$. The problem here is not that students speaking black English cannot master multiplication tasks, but that teachers must have greater sensitivity to the linguistic differences involved if such mastery is to be achieved. If this does not happen, Eleanor Orr writes,

> Students will not understand why their teachers tell them their answers are wrong, since to the students these answers make sense; and teachers will not understand why students arrive at the answers they give. Wrong answers will therefore persist despite what may seem the most appropriate ex-

planation; teachers will think that these students, who seem not to understand the most basic explanation, must be limited in some way. (Orr, 1987)

Schools and Industrial Capitalism

The material discussed above suggests that the use of language strongly influences inequalities of educational achievement. In their studies of education and inequality, Samuel Bowles and Herbert Gintis take a different approach to the question of how schools maintain social inequality—one that is concerned mainly with the institutional development of the modern school system (Bowles and Gintis, 1976). They base their theory on schools in the United States, but consider that their interpretation applies to other Western societies also. Modern education, they propose, is a response to the economic needs of industrial capitalism. Schools help to provide the technical and social skills required by industrial enterprise; and they instill discipline and respect for authority into the labor force.

Authority relations in school, which are hierarchical and place strong emphasis upon obedience, directly parallel those dominating the workplace. The rewards and punishments held out in school also replicate those found in the world of work. Schools help to motivate some individuals towards "achievement" and "success," while discouraging others, who find their way into low-paid jobs.

Bowles and Gintis accept that the development of mass education has had many beneficial consequences. Illiteracy rates are low, compared with premodern times, and schooling provides access to learning experiences that are intrinsically self-fulfilling. Yet because education has expanded mainly as a response to economic needs, the school system falls far short of what enlightened reformers had hoped from it. That is, schooling has not become the "great equalizer," rather, schools merely produce for many the feelings of powerlessness that continue throughout their experience in industrial settings. The ideals of personal development central to education can only be achieved if people have the capability to control the conditions of their own life, and develop their talents and abilities of self-expression. Under the current system, schools "are destined to legitimate inequality, limit personal development to forms compatible with submission to arbitrary authority, and aid in the process whereby youth are resigned to their fate" (Bowles and Gintis, 1976). If there were greater democracy in the workplace, and more equality in society at large, Bowles and Gintis argue, a system of education could be developed that would provide for greater individual fulfillment.

Deschooling Society

One of the most controversial writers on educational theory in recent years is Ivan Illich. Illich is noted for his criticisms of modern economic development. His central thesis is that education is part of a process whereby previously self-subsistent peoples are dispossessed of their own skills and made to rely on a series of "experts"—that is, doctors for their health, teachers for their schooling, television for their entertainment, and employers for their subsistence. Illich argues that the very notion of compulsory schooling—now accepted throughout the world—should be placed in question. Like Bowles and Gintis, he stresses the connection between the development of education and economic requirements for discipline and hierarchy. According to Illich, schools have developed to cope with four basic tasks: the provision of custodial care, the distribution of people among occupational roles, the learning of dominant values, and the acquisition of socially approved skills and knowledge. The school has become a "custodial" organization because attendance is obligatory and children are "kept off the street" for the period of time between early childhood and their entry into work.

Illich places a good deal of stress upon the **hidden curriculum** of schools. Much of what is learned in school has nothing directly to do with the formal content of lessons. Schools, by the nature of the discipline and regimentation they entail, tend to teach students values of what Illich calls "passive consumption"—an uncritical acceptance of the existing social order. These "lessons" are not consciously taught; they are implicit in school procedures and organization. The hidden curriculum teaches children that their role in life is "to know their place and to sit still in it" (Illich, 1983).

Illich advocates *deschooling* society. Compulsory schooling is a relatively recent invention, he points out; there is no reason why it should be accepted as somehow inevitable. Since schools do not promote equalization or the development of individual creative capabilities, why not do away with them in their current form? Illich does not mean by this that all forms of educational organization should be abolished. Education, he argues, should provide everyone who wants to learn with access to available resources—at any time in their lives, not just in their childhood or adolescent years. Such a system should make it possible for knowledge to be widely diffused and shared, not confined to "specialists." Learners would not have to submit to a standardized curriculum, but they would have a personal choice about which areas or issues they study.

What all this means in practical terms is not wholly clear. In place of schools, however, Illich proposes a completely different distribution of educational resources. Several types of "educational framework" would exist: material resources for formal learning would be stored in libraries, rental agencies, laboratories, and information storage banks, available to any student. "Communications networks" would be set up, providing data about the skills possessed by different individuals and stating if they would be willing to offer training to others, or engage in mutual learning activities. Students would be provided with educational vouchers allowing them to use these various services as and when they wished.

Are these proposals utopian? Many would say so. Yet if paid work becomes substantially reduced or restructured in the future, as looks possible, they appear less unrealistic (see Chapter 15: "Work and Economic Life"). Should paid work become less central to social life, people might instead engage in a wider variety of pursuits than they typically do today. Against this backdrop, some of Illich's ideas make good sense. Education would not just be a form of early training, confined to special institutions, but would become available to whoever wished to take advantage of it. On the other hand, there are obvious criticisms that might be made against Illich's standpoint. How would access to educational resources be controlled, and by whom? If the criteria for employment remain based on education levels, social inequalities might become much more marked than today if a process of deschooling occured. Children from more affluent backgrounds, encouraged by their parents and motivated to succeed, might be in an even better position than now to monopolize access to the best-paid jobs.

EDUCATION AND SOCIAL REPRODUCTION

At this point, we should take stock and see if there is a way to connect some of the themes of these three theoretical perspectives. One such way is through the idea of **social reproduction,** already mentioned quite often in previous chapters. In the context of education, social reproduction refers to the ways in which schools, in conjunction with other social institutions, help perpetuate social and economic inequalities across the generations. The concept directs our attention to the means whereby, via the "hidden curriculum," schools influence the learning of values, attitudes, and habits. Schools reinforce variations in cultural values and outlooks picked up early in life; when children leave school, these have the effect of limiting the opportunities of some, while facilitating those of others. The French sociologist Pierre Bourdieu calls this process the transmission of *cultural capital* (Bourdieu, 1984, 1988). Those who own economic capital—wealth, or stocks and shares—often manage to pass much of it on to their sons and daughters (see Chapter 7: "Stratification and Class Structure"). The same is true, Bourdieu argues, of the cultural advantages that coming from "a good home" confers. These advantages are "capital," which succeeding generations "inherit" from one another, thus perpetuating inequalities.

The modes of language-use identified by Bernstein no doubt connect to the broad cultural differences that underlie variations in interests and tastes. Children from lower-class backgrounds, particularly those from minority groups, develop ways of talking and acting that conflict with the environment of the school. As Bowles and Gintis emphasize, schools impose rules of discipline upon pupils, and the authority of teachers is devoted to a process of academic learning alien to children from poorer backgrounds, who find themselves, in effect, in a foreign cultural environment. Not only are they less likely to be motivated towards high academic performance; their habitual manner of speech and action do not "mesh" with those of the teachers, even if they are trying their best to communicate with each other.

Children spend long hours in school. As Illich stresses, they learn a great deal more in the school context than is contained in the lessons they are actually taught. Children get an early taste of what the world of work will be like, learning that they are expected to be punctual and apply themselves diligently to the tasks which those in authority set for them.

Social Reproduction: A Case Study

An example of social reproduction is provided in a fieldwork study that Paul Willis carried out in a school in Birmingham, England (Willis, 1981). The question Willis set out to investigate was how social reproduction occurs—or, as he put it, "how working-class kids get working-class jobs." It is often thought that, during the process of schooling, children from lower-class or minority backgrounds simply come to see that they "are not clever enough" to get highly paid or high-status jobs in their future work lives. In other words, the experience of academic failure teaches them to accept what they think are their intellectual limitations; having accepted their "inferiority," they move into occupations with limited career prospects.

As Willis points out, this interpretation does not conform at all to the reality of people's lives and experiences. The "street wisdom" of those from poor neighborhoods may be of little or no relevance to the academic setting, but it involves as subtle, skillful, and complex a set of abilities as any of the intellectual capabilities taught in school.

Few if any children leave school thinking, "I'm so stupid that it's fair and proper for me to be stacking boxes in a factory all day." If children from less-privileged backgrounds accept menial jobs, without feeling themselves throughout life to be failures, there must be other factors involved.

Willis concentrated his work upon a particular boys' group in the school he studied, spending a great deal of time with them. The members of the gang, who called themselves "the lads," were white; the school itself contained considerable numbers of black and Asian children. Willis showed how the lads had an acute and perceptive understanding of the school's authority system—but used this to fight that system rather than to pursue the academic values of the organization. The lads saw the school as an alien environment, but one that they could manipulate to their own ends. They derived positive pleasure from the running battles—confined mostly to minor skirmishes—they carried on with teachers. They were adept at seeing the weak points of the teachers' claims to authority, as well as the ways in which they were vulnerable as individuals.

In class, for instance, the children were expected to sit still, be quiet, and get on with their work. But the lads were all movement, save when the teacher's stare might freeze one of them momentarily; they would gossip surreptitiously or pass open remarks that were on the verge of direct insubordination, but could be explained away if challenged.

Willis describes all this beautifully:

> "The lads" specialize in a caged resentment which always stops just short of outright confrontation. Settled in class, as near a group as they can manage, there is a continuous scraping of chairs, a bad-tempered "tut-tutting" at the simplest request, and a continuous fidgeting about which explores every permutation of sitting or lying on a chair. During private study, some openly show disdain by apparently trying to go to sleep with their heads sideways down on the desk, some have their backs to the desk gazing out of the window, or even vacantly at the wall. . . . A continuous hum of talk flows around injunctions not to, like the inevitable tide over barely dried sand and everywhere there are rolled-back eyeballs and exaggerated mutterings of conspiratorial secrets. . . . In the corridors there is a foot-dragging walk, an over-friendly "hello" or sudden silence as the deputy [senior teacher] passes. Derisive or insane laughter erupts which might or might not be about someone who has just passed. It is as demeaning to stop as it is to carry on. . . . Opposition to the school is principally manifested in the struggle to win

symbolic and physical space from the institution and its rules and to defeat its main perceived purpose: to make you "work." (Willis, 1981).

The lads referred to conformist children as "the ear-'oles" (earholes). The ear-'oles were those who actually listened to the teachers, behaving as they were instructed. The ear-'oles would go on to be more "successful," in terms of getting well-paid, comfortable jobs on leaving school, than the lads. Yet their awareness of the complexities of the school environment, according to Willis, was in many respects less profound than that of the lads. For, unlike the lads, the ear-'oles found it relatively easy to adapt to the modes of life of the school and accepted them unquestioningly. Most pupils in the school were somewhere between the lads on the one side and the ear-'oles on the other—less openly confrontational than the first group, and less consistently conformist than the second.

The lads recognized that work would be much like school, but they actively looked forward to it. They expected to gain no direct satisfaction from the work environment, but were impatient for the wages work would bring. Far from taking the jobs they did—in tire fitting, carpet laying, plumbing, painting, and decorating—from feelings of inferiority, they held an attitude of dismissive superiority towards work, as they had towards school. They enjoyed the adult status that came from working, but were uninterested in "making a career" for themselves. As Willis points out, work in blue-collar settings often involves quite similar cultural features to those the lads had developed in their counter-school culture—banter, quick wit, and the skill to subvert the demands of authority figures where necessary.

Willis's work demonstrates how working-class children often tend to end up in working-class jobs by a process of the perpetuation of inequalities, but one that works in a subtle way. The lads felt uneasy in the school environment, and rebelled against it. The result of their rebellious attitudes was an orientation towards work that led them to be prepared to accept dull, poorly paid jobs—like the ones their parents had. Although they actively chose this type of work, the overall result was still the reproduction of inequality, because they had no interest in trying to obtain better-paid jobs with career prospects.

INTELLIGENCE AND INEQUALITY

The discussion so far neglects the possible importance of inherited differences in ability. Suppose it were the case that differences in educational attainment, and in subsequent occupational positions and incomes, directly reflected differential intelligence? In such circumstances, it might be argued, there is in fact equality of opportunity in the school system, for people find a level equivalent to their innate potential.

What Is Intelligence?

For many years psychologists, geneticists, statisticians, and others have debated whether there exists a single human capability that can be called **intelligence** and, if so, whether it rests upon innately determined differences. Intelligence is difficult to define because, as the term is usually employed, it covers many qualities that may be unrelated to one another. We might suppose, for example, that the "purest" form of intelligence is the capability to solve abstract mathematical puzzles. However, people who are very good at such puzzles sometimes seem to have low capabilities in other areas, such as history or art. Since the concept has proved so resistant to accepted definition, some psychologists have proposed (and many educators have by default accepted) that intelligence should simply be regarded as "what **IQ** (intelligence quotient) tests measure." Most IQ tests consist of a mixture of conceptual and computational problems that the testee is required to answer. Points are given for each correct response. The tests are constructed so that the average score is 100 points: anyone scoring below is thus labeled "under-average intelligence," and anyone scoring above is "above-average intelligence." In spite of the fundamental difficulty in measuring intelligence, IQ tests are widely used in research studies, as well as in more practical contexts in schools and businesses.

IQ and Genetic Factors: The Jensen Controversy

Scores on such tests do in fact correlate highly with academic performance (which is not surprising, since IQ tests were originally developed to predict success at school). They therefore also correlate closely with social, economic, and ethnic differences, since these are closely associated with variations in levels of educational attainment. White students score better, on average, than blacks or members of other disadvantaged minorities. On this basis, some have suggested that the IQ differences between blacks and whites are partly the result of hereditary factors. An article published by Arthur Jensen in 1969 caused a furor by attributing IQ differences between blacks and whites in part to genetic variations (Jensen, 1967, 1979).

Jensen's views have been extensively criticized, and most psychologists reject them. Jensen drew widely upon the work of the British psychologist Cyril Burt (1977), who was later shown to have falsified evidence relating IQ to heredity. We do not really know whether IQ tests measure stable abilities, let alone whether such abilities are inherited. Critics of Jensen deny that the IQ difference between blacks and whites—usually amounting to an average of about 15 IQ points —is genetic in origin. IQ tests relate to a range of linguistic, symbolic, and mathematical skills. Arguments advanced by Bernstein and others suggest that these skills may be strongly influenced by early learning processes. The tests leave out other intellectual aptitudes not usually thought significant in school curricula. These may include, for instance, the sorts of capabilities that the "streetwise" person may perhaps possess in abundance.

IQ tests are probably always to some degree culture bound. They pose questions—to do with abstract reasoning, for example—more likely to be part of the experience of more affluent white students rather than of blacks and ethnic minorities. Scores on IQ tests may also be influenced by factors that have nothing to do with the abilities supposedly being measured—such as whether the testing is experienced as stressful. Research has demonstrated that blacks score some 6 points lower on IQ tests when the tester is white than when the tester is black (Kamin, 1974).

The average difference in IQ scores between blacks and whites in the United States is remarkably similar to that of deprived ethnic minorities in other countries around the world—such as the "untouchables" in India (who are at the very bottom of the caste system), the *maoris* in New Zealand, or the *burakumin* of Japan. Children in these groups score an average of 10 to 15 IQ points below those belonging to the ethnic majority. The *burakumin* (discussed in Chapter 8: "Ethnicity and Race") are a particularly interesting example. They are not in any way physically distinct from other Japanese, although they have suffered from prejudice and discrimination for centuries. In this case, the difference in average IQ results cannot derive from genetic variations since there are no genetic differences between them and the majority population; yet the IQ difference is as thoroughly fixed as that between blacks and whites. *Burakumin* children in America, where they are treated like any other Japanese, do as well on IQ tests as other Japanese.

Such observations strongly suggest that the IQ variations between blacks and whites in the United States result from social and cultural differences. This conclusion receives further support from a recent comparative study of fourteen nations. The study shows that, in all the countries studied (including the United States), average IQ scores have risen substantially over the past half century for the population as a whole (Coleman, 1987). IQ tests are regularly updated. Where old and new versions of the tests are given to the same group of people, they get significantly higher scores on the old tests. It was found that present-day children taking IQ tests from the 1930s outscored 1930s groups by an average of 15 points—just the kind of average difference that currently separates blacks and whites. Children today are not innately superior in intelligence to their parents or grandparents; the shift presumably derives from increasing prosperity and social advantages over the period. The average social and economic gap between whites and blacks is at least as great as that between the different generations, and is sufficient to explain the variation in IQ scores. While there may be genetic variations between individuals that influence scores on IQ tests, these have no overall connection to racial differences. The average degree of difference in IQ between blacks and whites is much smaller than variations found within each of these groups.

Disentangling Genetics and IQ: Identical Twins

We do not actually know to what degree genetic factors may influence IQ scores. There is no way of disentangling, for any particular individual, the relative influence of heredity and environment on development. The only means whereby an approximate assessment can be attempted is through comparison of identical twins, who by definition have exactly the same genetic characteristics, in situations in which they were separated at birth and raised in different environments. There are a few such studies (including the now partly discredited research work of Cyril Burt), but these do not permit any absolute conclusions. Even within this small sample of cases it is not always possible to say with certainty that the twins were in fact identical ("fraternal" twins are born from separate eggs and therefore have different genetic characteristics; twins may look physically alike even when they are in fact fraternal).

After reworking the evidence provided by studies of identical twins, Leon Kamin concluded that they had almost no value. The material is too unreliable, and the number of cases too few, to supply any authoritative conclusions about the influence of heredity on IQ. In Kamin's words, "There are no data sufficient for us to reject the hypothesis that differences in the way in which people answer the questions asked by the testers are determined by their palpably different life experiences" (Kamin, 1974).

The IQ and nature-nurture controversy has by no means fully abated. It connects directly to other aspects of education and inequality. One of the most important is the relationship between education and gender, to which we now turn.

GENDER AND SCHOOLING

In the 1960s, a school in California initiated an experiment called a Program for Educational and Occupational Needs, based on a study of the aptitudes and interests of several generations of previous graduates of the school. Two groups, white and black students, took part in the program. Research had made clear that white students had a definite aptitude for, and interest in, professional and managerial occupations, while blacks tended more to turn to manual labor, or preferred to remain unemployed. The white students hence were taught using more academic methods, while the black classes put heavy emphasis on physical exercise, in order to increase strength and agility. Since blacks do not usually aspire to positions of leadership, the games they were taught to play emphasized submissiveness and docility. The teaching staff were enthusiastic about the program, believing it to be ideally tailored to the needs of the two groups.

This example is imaginary, of course. Even those who believe that there are genetic differences in intelligence and other aptitudes between ethnic groups would not propose such a blatantly discriminatory program. It would be quite shocking to even consider such an idea in the context of ethnic divisions. Yet, such an approach was for many years applied to the educational curricula of the sexes. Consider, for example, an article that appeared in 1966 in a widely read educational journal, the *National Elementary Principal.* The article outlined a new teaching program in Wakefield Elementary School, Fairfax County, Virginia, and suggested that this program be widely adopted elsewhere. The program proposed that boys and girls be taught in separate classes. The emphasis for boys should be upon developing initiative and self-reliance and for the girls, the fostering of cheerfulness and adaptability. In the boys' classes, emphasis was placed on science materials, building, and practical activities; the girls' classes stressed tasks such as sewing and housekeeping. Different reading stories were used for boys as compared to girls (Frazier and Sadker, 1973).

The program at the Wakefield Elementary School made explicit what has for a long time been part of the hidden curriculum in schools—the fostering of gender differences in outlook and behavior. Although this has become less common today, regulations that compelled girls to wear dresses or skirts in school formed one of the most obvious ways in which gender typing occurred. The consequences went beyond mere appearance. As a result of the clothes they had to wear, girls lacked the freedom to sit casually, to join in rough-and-tumble games, or sometimes to run as fast as they were able. While the strict enforcement of styles of school dress has become quite rare, differences in informal styles of dress still persist, influencing gender behavior in school. School reading texts also help to perpetuate gender images. Although this again is changing, storybooks in elementary school often portray boys showing initiative and independence, while girls, if they appear at all, are more passive and watch their brothers. Stories written especially for girls often have an element of adventure in them, but this usually takes the form of intrigues or mysteries in a domestic or school setting. Boys' adventure stories are more wide-ranging, having heroes who travel off to distant places or who in other ways are sturdily independent (Statham, 1986).

Studies of how gender differences affect interaction between pupils and teachers in the classroom are few. The research that exists indicates that girls are rewarded for silence, neatness, and conformity, whereas somewhat more rebellious behavior is tolerated in boys (Frazier and Sadker, 1973; Delamont, 1983; Walker and Barton, 1983). It has been suggested that one reason why the academic performance of boys is worse in primary school than in secondary school may be that they are confronted with an unfamiliar "feminine" environment. The atmosphere in the primary-school classroom, which has a high proportion of female teachers, may run contrary to the assertive and independent attitudes that parents usually try to encourage in their sons. In secondary schools, on the other hand, where the majority of teachers are male, these attitudes are looked upon favorably (Sharpe, 1976).

Female children from ethnic minorities are in some respects doubly disadvantaged. Beverley Bryan and her colleagues have described what it was like to be a black female pupil in a school in the same area of Britain where Willis studied his white boys' group. Unlike the lads, the black girls were initially enthusiastic about school but altered their attitudes because of the difficulties encountered there. Even when they were quite small, aged seven or eight, teachers would disperse the black girls if they were standing chatting in a group on the playground—in contrast to their treatment of the white children, whose similar behavior was tolerated. In other ways too, the black girls came to feel that they were regarded with suspicion and hostility by their teachers and by the white pupils. Once treated as "troublemakers," they rapidly became so (Bryan, Dadzie, and Scafe, 1987).

Women in Higher Education

Women's organizations in the United States and elsewhere have made a series of attempts to attack sex discrimination in higher edu-

TABLE 13.2	WHO RECEIVES DOCTORATES	
	1979	1989
Men	71.4%	63.5%
Women	28.6%	36.5%

Source: National Research Council

cation. Women are still heavily underrepresented among the teaching faculty in colleges and universities. A survey of 454 colleges and universities in the United States, published in 1970, showed that no more than 8 percent of those in top-level administrative positions were women (Oltman, 1970). No comparable study has been published bringing these statistics up to date, but it is doubtful whether this situation has changed very substantially in the last twenty years. Women also hold only a small proportion of teaching positions in higher education. No more than 10 percent of full professorships and 25 percent of associate professorships are held by women in U.S. universities today. A comparative investigation of women academics in Britain and the United States disclosed that in both countries, women on average have higher teaching loads than male colleagues, and are less often involved in postgraduate teaching. Heavy teaching loads are likely to cut into time available for research and publication; level of publication plus involvement in postgraduate teaching are important criteria for promotion (Blackstone and Fulton, 1975).

EDUCATION AND LITERACY IN THE THIRD WORLD

LIVING IN THE WEST, WE HAVE BECOME USED TO CIRCUM-stances in which the vast majority of the population can read and write and attends school for many years. But universal education is far from being the norm throughout the world (Webster, 1984). Over the past quarter of a century, the educational systems of most Third World countries have expanded rapidly; yet there are still several societies (such as Senegal, Africa), where well under half of the children in the relevant age groups receive no formal schooling whatsoever. Literacy is the "baseline" of education.

Without it, schooling cannot proceed. We take it for granted in the West that the majority of people are literate, but as has been mentioned, this is only a recent development in Western history, and in previous times, no more than a tiny proportion of the population had any skills of literacy.

Today some 30 percent of the population of Third World countries are still illiterate. The Indian government has estimated the number of illiterate in that country alone to be over 250 million people, a number that exceeds the total population in the United States. Even if the provision of primary education increased to match the level of population growth, illiteracy would not become markedly reduced for many years, because a high proportion of those who cannot read or write are adults. The absolute number of illiterate people is actually rising (Coombs, 1985). According to UNESCO estimates, the total grew from 569 million in 1970 to 625 million in 1980, and is likely to be 900 million by 2000.

Classroom in Nigeria.

Many countries have instituted literacy programs, but they have made only a small contribution to a problem of large-scale dimensions. Television, radio, and the other electronic media can be used, where these are available, to "skip" the stage of learning literacy skills, conveying educational programs directly to adults. But educational programs are usually far less popular than commercialized entertainment.

During the period of colonialism, the colonial governments regarded education with some trepidation. Until the twentieth century, most believed indigenous populations to be too primitive to be worthy of educating. Later, education was seen as a way of making local elites responsive to European interests and ways of life; at the same time, it was recognized that educating colonized peoples could serve to foment discontent and rebellion. To some extent this was what happened, since the majority of those who led anti-colonial and nationalist movements were from educated elites who had attended schools or colleges in Europe. They were able to compare first-hand the democratic institutions of the European countries with the absence of democracy in their lands of origin.

The education that the colonizers introduced usually pertained to Europe, not the colonial areas themselves. Africans, for instance, had to learn the language of their European masters and about European history and culture. Educated Africans in the British colonies knew about the kings and queens of England, read Shakespeare, Milton, and the English poets, but knew next to nothing about their own history or past cultural achievements. Policies of educational reform since the end of colonialism have not completely altered the situation even today.

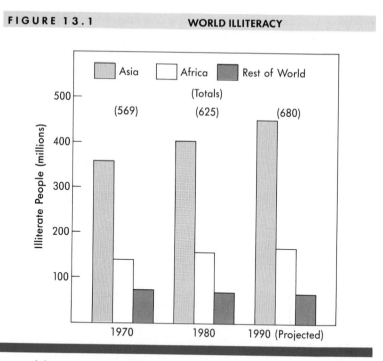

FIGURE 13.1   **WORLD ILLITERACY**

Source: Philip H. Coombs, *The World Crisis in Education: The View from the Eighties* (New York: Oxford University Press, Inc., 1985), p. 268.

Partly as a result of the legacy of colonial education, which was not directed towards the majority of the population, the educational system in many Third World countries is "top-heavy." Higher education is disproportionately developed, relative to primary and secondary education. The result is a correspondingly "overqualified" group who, having attended colleges and universities, cannot find white-collar or professional jobs. Given the low level of industrial development, most of the better-paid positions are in government; and there are not enough of those to go around.

Many Third World countries have tried in recent years to redirect their educational programs towards the rural poor, recognizing the shortcomings of the curricula inherited from colonialism. These have had limited success, because usually there is insufficient funding to pay for the scale of the innovations that would be necessary. Recognizing this, some countries, including India, have begun programs of self-help education. Communities draw upon existing resources without creating demands for high levels of finance. Those who can read and write, and perhaps possess job skills, are encouraged to take others on as "apprentices," whom they coach in their spare time. Some of these schemes bear a close similarity to ideas suggested by Illich in his critique of orthodox education. This is not surprising, because Illich developed his approach in Third World contexts where, apart from basic teaching of literacy, formal school systems often do not correspond closely to the real needs of the population.

COMMUNICATION AND MEDIA

THE MODERN WORLD DEPENDS UPON THE CONTINUOUS **communication** or interaction between people widely separated from one another. If we were not so dependent upon "communication across distance," schooling would be less necessary. In traditional cultures—as that of Jean-Paul Didion in France, the example with which we opened the chapter—most knowledge was what the anthropologist Clifford Geertz has called **local knowledge** (Geertz, 1983). Traditions were passed on through the local community, and although general cultural ideas gradually spread across large areas, processes of cultural diffusion were long, drawn out, slow and inconsistent. Today, we live in "the whole world" in a way which would have been quite inconceivable to Jean-Paul Didion, or anyone else living in cultures of the past.

We learn a great deal about the world from formal schooling. But we also learn much from the various communication media, which operates outside the context of schools. All of us are aware of situations and events that happen thousands of miles away—electronic communication makes such awareness almost instantaneous. Changes in the spread of information, and in information technologies, are as much a part of the development of modern societies as any aspect of industrial production (Kern, 1983). In the twentieth century, rapid transportation and electronic communication have greatly intensified the global diffusion of information.

The **mass media**—newspapers, magazines, cinema, and TV—are often associated with entertainment, and therefore seen as rather marginal to most people's lives. Such a view is quite misleading. Mass communications enter in at many different points of our social activities. For instance, a bank account is no longer a pile of bank notes kept in a safe, but a series of digits printed on an account sheet and stored in computers, and monetary transactions are now mainly performed through the exchange of information between computers.

Anyone who uses a credit card is connected with a very complex system of electronically stored and transmitted information that has now become the very basis of modern financial accounting.

Even "recreational" media like newspapers or TV have a wide-ranging influence over our experience. This is not just because they affect our attitudes in specific ways, but because they are the *means of access* to the knowledge upon which many social activities depend. Voting in national elections, for example, would be quite different if information about current political events, candidates, and parties were not generally available. Even those who are largely uninterested in politics, and have little knowledge of the personalities involved, have some awareness of national and international events. Only a complete hermit would be entirely detached from the "news events" that impinge to some degree upon the consciousness of all of us—and we could suspect that a modern hermit might very well own a transistor radio!

THE DEVELOPMENT OF NEWSPAPERS

Newspapers in their modern form derive from pamphlets and information sheets printed and circulated in the 1700s. The newspaper was a basic invention in the history of modern media because it packaged many different types of information—on current affairs, entertainment, and advertising—within a limited, and easily reproducible, format. News and advertising developed together. Distinctions shift between news, advertising, and entertainment and are difficult to make. For example, the announcement that a ship is leaving or arriving may in one context be news; in another, an advertisement; or, if it concerns particular passengers, written as part of a gossip column, it becomes entertainment (Smith, 1980a).

The cheap daily press was pioneered in the United States. The one-cent daily paper was originally established in New York in 1833, then copied in other major eastern cities. The invention of low-priced newsprint (the paper used) was the key to the mass diffusion of newspapers from the late nineteenth century onwards when circulation of the dailies reached thousands and millions. By the early 1900s there were city or regional newspapers covering most of the American states, although in contrast to the countries of Europe, no national newspapers were set up. During the period of mass immigration, there were many foreign newspapers written and published in the United States. For example, in 1892, ninety-seven German language daily newspapers were being published in cities in the midwest and northeast (Tunstall, 1977).

The two most prestigious newspapers at the turn of the century were the *New York Times* and, in Europe, *The Times* of London. Most of the influential newspapers in other countries took these newspapers as their models. Newspapers at the "top end" of the market became a major political force and have remained so to the present day. The European press, however, for a long time concentrated more upon political news than any American newspaper.

For a period of a half a century or more, newspapers were the chief basis upon which information was conveyed quickly and comprehensively to a mass public. The influence of newspapers waned with the rise of radio, cinema, and—much more important—TV. As recently as 1960, more than one newspaper was sold per day for each household in the country: an average of 112 newspapers for every 100 households. This figure has progressively declined since then. Today there are less than 90 papers sold for each 100 households (Smith, 1980a). Sales of newspapers have fallen especially among young adults (Bogart, 1975).

NEWSPAPER PUBLISHING

Newspapers have long been associated with the image of the powerful tycoon, the head of a publishing empire. This picture is not in fact so far from the truth. In virtually all Western countries, newspaper ownership is highly concentrated in the hands of a few large corporations, and these are often dominated by particular individuals or families. Many of these firms today also have extensive holdings in TV and entertainment industries. In Britain, companies run by the press baron, the Lords Northcliffe, Beaverbrook, and Kemsley, developed on the basis of their control of mass-circulation newspapers in the 1920s and 1930s. France has seen the development of the Hersant information empire. The German Springer and Grüner organizations are vast concerns. In the United States, the number of cities in which there are competing newspaper firms has steadily declined, from more than five hundred at the turn of the century to just over thirty in 1984. Only 3 percent of cities in the country have competing papers—newspaper publishing in most cities has become a monopoly enterprise.

With the exception of the United States, all Western countries boast a number of national newspapers. A situation of oligopoly rather than monopoly exists: there is choice between nationally available papers, often geared to different political standpoints. Although newspapers in the United States are local, they are by no means all locally owned. More than 70 percent are controlled by publishing chains. In some of these, as in the case of many mass-circulation papers in Europe, the owners set editorial policies that those who produce the newspaper are expected to follow. In the Hearst chain of newspapers, several editorials are sent out each day to the eight major editors, some of which have to be used, while others are left to each editor's judgment. The editors do not write their own copy.

The fact that newspaper ownership is so concentrated has worried most Western governments (Jenkins, 1986). In many countries anti-trust actions have been brought against the large chains to prevent the takeover of the smaller newspapers, although these have mostly not met with much success. In some societies, policies have been instituted to try to achieve a political balance in the press. In Norway, for example, a scheme was set up to equalize investments between newspapers representing different sides of the political spectrum. Most local Norwegian communities have two or more well-produced and comprehensive papers providing different points of view on national and international news.

It is possible that the development of computer-based technologies will lead to a greater proliferation of newspapers than in the recent past. Newspapers have become much cheaper to print and produce than used to be the case. On the other hand, electronic modes of communication organized through computers might in fact bite further into newspaper circulations. For instance, teletext systems provide news information that is constantly updated during the course of the day and available on the TV screen.

TELEVISION AND THE CULTURE INDUSTRY

The increasing influence of TV is probably the single most important development in media of the past thirty or so years (Barnouw, 1975). If current trends in TV watching continue, by age eighteen, the average child born today will have spent more time watching TV than in any other activity save for sleep. Virtually every household now possesses a TV set. In the United States, the average set is switched on between five and six hours a day. Much the same is true in the European countries (Goodhardt, Ehrenberg, and Collins, 1987). The number of hours individuals actually watch TV is lower than this, of course, since the set is in use by different members of the household at various times of the day. The average period of TV watching for adults each day in the United States is three hours.

The advent of television has strongly influenced patterns of day-to-day life, since many people schedule what they do around planned periods of viewing. In one study covering eleven countries, the investigators sought to analyze the influence of television watching on

Country	Telephones per 100 population	Televisions per 1,000 population	Radios per 1,000 population
United States	76.0	813	2,126
Brazil	8.8	188	365
Canada	76.9	546	877
China	0.7	10	140
Czechoslovakia	23.9	281	577
Egypt	2.8	83	313
France	60.8	402	896
Israel	41.6	261	463
Japan	55.5	585	824
Mexico	9.6	117	197
Nigeria	0.3	6	162
Poland	11.8	259	415
Soviet Union	11.3	321	660
United Kingdom	52.4	534	1,157
West Germany	64.0	379	955

TABLE 13.3 ELECTRONIC COMMUNICATIONS—A CROSS-NATIONAL LOOK

Data as of 1986; 1984 for U.S.; 1985 for France, Nigeria, Soviet Union.
Source: Statistical Office of the United Nations, New York, NY, *Statistical Yearbook.*

daily life, comparing the characteristic activities of owners and non-owners of television sets. The countries covered included the United States, a range of West and East European countries, and Peru. Respondents were asked to list all their activities over the course of a full twenty-four-hour day. Those possessing a TV spent less time than the nonowners on other leisure activities, meeting friends, conversation, household duties, and sleeping.

The researchers concluded that television has had a larger impact on daily life than any other technical innovation outside the sphere of paid employment. Those who own automobiles, for instance, spend on average only 6 percent more time in transit than nonowners. Domestic appliances like refrigerators, washing machines, and dryers do not tend to alter time spent on housework (Rubenstein et al., 1972a, 1972b).

TV Companies

Like mass newspapers, TV today is big business. In most countries, the state directly administers television broadcasts. In Britain, for example, the British Broadcasting Corporation (BBC), which initiated the first television programs ever produced, is a public organization (although in 1990 its status was being exhaustively reexamined by the government). It is funded by a license fee which has to be paid by every household that possesses a set. For some years, the BBC was the only organization permitted to broadcast either radio or television programs in Britain. Today, alongside the two BBC TV channels, BBC1 and 2 there exist two commercial TV channels (ITV channels 3 and 4), put together from programs produced by regional companies whose number is kept strictly limited. The frequency of advertising is controlled by law, with a maximum of six minutes per hour (Pragnall, 1985).

In the United States, the three leading TV organizations are all commercial networks—the American Broadcasting Company (ABC), Columbia Broadcasting System (CBS), and the National Broadcasting Company (NBC). These networks are limited by law to owning five licensed stations, which they have located in the biggest cities. The "big three," therefore, reach over a quarter of all households in the country via their own stations. Some two hundred affiliated stations are also attached to each network, comprising 90 percent of the seven hundred or so TV stations that exist in the country. The networks depend on revenue derived from selling advertising time for their income. The National Association of Broadcasters lays down guidelines about the proportion of viewing time per hour that may be devoted to advertising. These specify 9.5 minutes per hour during "prime time" and 16 minutes per hour at other times. TV companies use regularly collected ratings, showing how many people watch specific programs, upon which advertising costs are based. The ratings also, of course, strongly influence whether or not a program becomes a long-running one.

Each of the networks spends about $1.5 billion per year for prime-time programming. A one-hour pilot program may cost well over a million dollars to produce, but if audience response, as measured by the ratings, is deemed insufficient, it will not be further developed. Children's programs are not usually piloted because of the dominance of cartoon animation. A network purchasing a children's series from a producer usually guarantees that each episode will be shown at least four times. Unlike adult shows, children's programs can be shown again and again to the same age group, since its composition changes as the children grow up. An important fact about children's viewing is that most spend at least part of their time watching programs produced for adults.

The development of cable TV has led to a proliferation of channels in most large cities in the United States over recent years. Some of the cable companies have become quite large, and the market shares of

ABC, CBS, and NBC have generally tended to decline. It is possible that the whole nature of the TV industry will change in the future. At the moment, the large networks still dominate, but it is not clear that they can retain their preeminence much longer. In 1984, over 50 percent of U.S. households during a typical evening's viewing were tuned to one of the "big three." By 1989, this proportion had fallen to 41 percent. More than half of all homes in the United States are now wired for cable TV, and 60 percent have VCRs—each introducing more diversity into viewing patterns.

The Effects of Television on Behavior

Vast amounts of research have been carried out to try to assess the effects of television programs upon the audiences they reach. Most of this research has concerned children—understandably enough, given the sheer volume of their viewing and the possible implications for socialization. The three most commonly researched topics are the impact of television upon propensities to crime and violence, the effects of news broadcasting, and the role of television in political life. We shall concentrate here on the first of these topics.

The incidence of violence in television programs is well documented. The most extensive studies are those carried out by Gerbner and his collaborators, who have analyzed samples of prime-time and weekend daytime TV for all the major American networks each year since 1967. The number and frequency of violent acts and episodes is charted for a range of various types of TV program. Violence is defined in the research as the threat or use of physical force, directed against the self or others, in which physical harm or death occurs. Television drama emerges as highly violent in character. On average 80 percent of such programs contain violence, with a rate of 7.5 violent episodes per hour. Children's programs show even higher levels of violence, although killing is less commonly portrayed. Cartoons contain the highest number of violent acts and episodes of any type of television program (Gerbner et al., 1979; Gerbner et al., 1980; Gunter, 1985).

In what ways, if at all, does the depiction of violence influence the watching audience? F. S. Anderson collected the findings of sixty-seven studies, conducted over the twenty years from 1956 to 1976, investigating the influence of TV violence upon propensities to aggression among children. About three-quarters of the studies claimed to find some such association. In 20 percent of cases there were no clear-cut results, while in 3 percent of the studies the investigators concluded that watching TV violence actually decreases aggression (Anderson, 1977; Liebert, Sprafkin, and Davidson, 1985).

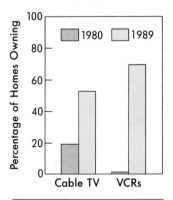

**FIGURE 13.2
U.S. HOUSEHOLDS WITH CABLE TV AND VCRS**

Source: Nielsen Media Research, *Nielsen Report on Television and VCR Trends, 1988.*

The studies Anderson surveyed, however, differ widely in the methods used, the strength of the association supposedly revealed, and the definition of "aggressive behavior." In crime dramas featuring violence (and in many children's cartoons) there are underlying themes of justice and retribution. A far higher proportion of miscreants are brought to justice in crime dramas than happens with police investigations in real life. In cartoons, harmful or threatening characters usually tend to end up getting their "just desserts." It does not necessarily follow that the high levels of violence portrayed create directly imitative patterns among those watching, who may perhaps be more influenced by the underlying moral themes.

In general, research on the "effects" of television upon audiences has tended to treat viewers—children and adults—as passive and undiscriminating in their reactions to what they see. Robert Hodge and David Tripp (1986) emphasized that children's responses to TV involve interpreting or "reading" what they see, not just registering the content of programs. They suggested that most research has not taken account of the complexity of children's mental processes. TV watching, even of trivial programs, is not an inherently low-level intellectual activity; children "read" programs by relating them to other systems of meaning in their everyday lives. For example, even very young children recognize that media violence is "not real." According to Hodge and Tripp it is not the violence alone that has effects upon behavior, but rather the general framework of attitudes within which it is both presented and "read."

Yet it is difficult to believe that the continuing depiction of violence on television has no impact at all on children's attitudes or behavior. A U.S. government investigation into the influence of television on violent behavior among children and young people, initiated by the Surgeon General, included a large number of different studies. It produced an ambiguous and inconclusive final report, which masked differences of opinion among the various researchers concerned (Surgeon General, 1972). The report did, however, fuel efforts to use television in a constructive and positive way in children's development—particularly through public-service television. Although they only have about 5 percent of the revenue obtained by commercial broadcasters, public-television stations put on numerous educational programs. "Sesame Street" is an example of a program specifically designed to entertain yet also foster the intellectual and cultural development of children (Cook et al., 1975).

Television as Purveyor of Social Attitudes

The influence of television as a cultural medium cannot properly be assessed by the content of programs alone. Television helps to provide the "frames of experience," the overall cultural outlooks, within which individuals in modern societies interpret and organize information. Television is as important as books, magazines, and newspapers in the expansion of indirect forms of communication characteristic of modern societies. It frames the ways in which individuals *interpret* and *respond* to the social world by helping to *order our experience* of it. Assumptions built into the overall character of TV production and distribution may perhaps be more significant than whatever particular programs are shown.

For instance, television has served in some degree to change the nature of modern elections, because of its importance in providing a platform for presentation of issues and candidates. To take another example: the symbols and semiotic codes involved in advertising might have a more profound influence upon social behavior than the stated "messages" the advertisers wish to get across. Thus, gender divisions are often symbolized in what goes on in the setting or the background of a commercial rather than what it is explicitly selling. In many ads, men appear mentally and physically alert, while women are shown dreamily gazing into the distance (Goffman, 1979).

As in the case of schooling, TV and the "culture industry" raise questions about the balance between power, responsibility, and freedom. Schools provide for many learning experiences—inside and outside the formal curriculum—which are inherently fulfilling and contribute towards individual development. The teaching of reading and writing is the most obvious example of this. If we did not have access to such skills, our existence would be radically impoverished. On the other hand, the school system helps perpetuate social and economic inequalities, expressing aspects of broader patterns of differential privilege.

The modern media of communication are similarly central to our lives today, providing many necessary informational services as well as offering innumerable possibilities for self-enlightenment and entertainment. Yet the media on the whole tend to reflect the outlook of dominant groups in society. This is not because of direct political censorship, in the United States at least, but results from the fact that ownership of television, newspapers, data banks, and so forth, are concentrated in relatively few hands. Who should control the media? How can the less privileged make their voices heard? These are complex and difficult problems. They now have an international dimension, given the domination of world communications by a limited number of countries. This phenomenon is further discussed in Chapter 16 ("The Globalizing of Social Life").

SUMMARY

1. Education in its modern form, involving the instruction of pupils within specially designated school premises, began to emerge with the spread of printed materials, records, and higher levels of *literacy.* Knowledge could be retained, reproduced, and consumed by more people in many different places. With the advent of industrialism, work became specialized, and knowledge was increasingly acquired in more abstract rather than practical ways—the skills of reading, writing, and calculating.

2. The expansion of education in the twentieth century has resulted from the need for a literate and disciplined work force. Although reformers have seen education for all as a means of reducing inequalities, its impact in this respect has been fairly limited. Education tends to express and reaffirm existing inequalities more than acting to change them.

3. According to Bernstein's theory, children who have acquired *elaborated codes* of speech are better able to deal with the demands of formal academic education than those confined to *restricted codes.* "Intelligence tests," such as IQs, rely on a standardized conception of "useful" abilities and skills. Critics argue that they are culture-bound and thus misleading.

4. The formal school curriculum is only one part of a more general process of *social reproduction* influenced by many informal aspects of learning, education, and school settings. The *hidden curriculum* plays a significant role in such reproduction.

5. The ways schools are organized and how classes are taught have tended to sustain gender inequalities. Rules specifying distinct dress for girls and boys encourages sex typing, as do the texts

containing established gender images. There is evidence that teachers treat girls and boys differently, and there is a long history of specialized subjects for separate sexes. In higher education, women are still underrepresented among administrators and teachers.

6. Primary education is far from being established throughout the world; there are still some Third World countries in which most children receive no formal education whatsoever. The absolute number of people in the world who are illiterate is rising rather than declining at present.

7. Schooling has to be understood as one element in the systems of mass communication that have emerged with industrialism and the modern state. Modern political systems depend upon an informed citizenry: through mechanical printing and the electronic media of telegraph, telephone, radio, TV, and computer-transmitted information, the "global" and the "local" have moved nearer to each other.

8. In spite of many studies of television and violence, it is still not clear how far, and in what ways, the portrayal of violence on TV encourages aggressive behavior in real life. Most of the research has underestimated how much viewers selectively interpret what they see, and the complex ways in which the "fictional" and the "real" interrelate.

9. The influence of TV, and other mass media, upon our lives is profound. The media do not just provide entertainment, but provide and shape much of the information that we utilize in our daily lives. Questions about who owns the media, and how far the media allow for the expression of diverse viewpoints, are of great importance in analyzing questions of power and inequality in modern societies.

BASIC CONCEPTS

EDUCATION   COMMUNICATION

SOCIAL REPRODUCTION

IMPORTANT TERMS

LITERACY   INTELLIGENCE

HIGHER EDUCATION   IQ

RESTRICTED CODE   LOCAL KNOWLEDGE

ELABORATED CODE   MASS MEDIA

HIDDEN CURRICULUM

RELIGION

BY THE LIGHT OF DAY, AND BY THE FALL OF NIGHT, YOUR
Lord has not forsaken you, nor does He abhor you. The
life to come holds a richer prize for you than this present
life.
You shall be gratified with what your Lord will give you.
Did He not find you an orphan and give you shelter? Did
He not find you in error and guide you? Did He not find
you poor and enrich you? Therefore do not wrong the or-
phan, nor chide away the beggar.
But proclaim the goodness of your Lord.

This scriptural passage gives a good insight into the hold that religion has had over the lives of human beings for thousands of years.
God cares for each of us, the scripture asserts, providing us with care
and comfort, food and shelter. In worshipping God, and believing in
his goodness, we shall reap benefits in the life to come.

Not all religions, as we shall see a little later in this chapter, share
the same beliefs as these, but in one form or another, religion is found
in all known human societies. The earliest societies on record, of
which we have evidence only through their archaeological remains,
show clear traces of religious symbols and ceremonials. Throughout

subsequent history, **religion** has continued to be a central part of human experience, influencing how we perceive and react to the environments in which we live.

The scripture just quoted presents religion as a source of personal solace and support. Yet religion has often been the origin of intense social struggles and conflicts. Consider the advice and sentiments contained in the following scriptural statement:

> Let love for our brotherhood breed warmth of mutual affection. Give pride of place to one another in esteem.
> With unflagging energy, in ardor of spirit, serve the Lord.
> Let hope keep you joyful; in trouble stand firm; persist in prayer.
> Contribute to the needs of God's people, and practice hospitality.
> Call down blessings on your persecutors—blessings, not curses. . .
> If possible, so far as it lies with you, live at peace with all men.

Like the first text, these words convey a sense of universal love and of God's goodness. It is difficult to suppose that believers who followed the teaching of the first of these scriptures would be out of sympathy with the sentiments of the second. Yet for many centuries these two groups of believers have frequently come into bloody conflict. The first quotation is in fact from the Koran, the holy book of Islam. The second comes from the New Testament of the Christian Bible. Islam and Christianity have overlapping origins and recognize many of the same prophets. Each, however, rejects the God of the other and regards those who follow the alternative religion—or any other religion at all—as outsiders.

Between the eleventh and thirteenth centuries, European armies invaded parts of the Near East with the object of capturing the Holy Land from the Moslems for Christianity. These wars, which the Christians called "Crusades," were some of the bloodiest ever fought, but were carried out both in the name of God and of Allah. Thousands were slaughtered and atrocities were committed by Christian and Islamic armies alike over the course of two hundred years. The Europeans captured large tracts of land and important cities, including Jerusalem, in the First Crusade, but by the end of the Ninth, in 1272, the Moslems had recaptured all of the Holy Land.

St. Bernard, abbot of a large monastery at Clairvaux, France, was one of the most fervent advocates of the crusades. "How blessed are the martyrs who die in the battle!" he wrote. "Rejoice, stout champion, if you live and conquer in the Lord, but exalt and glory even more if you die and join the Lord" (Koenisberger, 1987).

How can religion have such a purchase upon individuals' lives that they would be prepared to sacrifice themselves for its ideals? Why has religion been such a pervasive aspect of human societies? Under what conditions does religion unite communities, and under what conditions does it divide them? These are the questions that we shall try to answer in this chapter. In order to do so, we shall have to ask what religion actually is, and look at some of the different forms that religious beliefs and practices take. We shall also consider the main sociological theories of religion and analyze the various types of religious organization that can be distinguished. Finally, we will consider the fate of religion in the modern world; for it has seemed to many observers that, with the rise of science and modern industry, religion today has become a less central force in social life than it ever was prior to the modern age.

The study of religion is a challenging enterprise, which places quite special demands upon the sociological imagination. In analyzing religious practices, we have to make sense of the many different beliefs and rituals found in the various human cultures. We must be sensitive to ideals that inspire profound conviction in believers, yet at the same time take a balanced view of them. We have to confront ideas that seek the eternal, while recognizing that religious groups also promote quite mundane goals—such as acquiring finance or soliciting for followers. We need to recognize the diversity of religious beliefs and modes of conduct, but also probe into the nature of religion as a general phenomenon.

DEFINING RELIGION (AND MAGIC)

THE VARIETY OF RELIGIOUS BELIEFS AND ORGANIZATIONS IS so immense that scholars have found great difficulty in reaching a generally accepted definition of religion. In the West, most people identify religion with Christianity—a belief in Jesus Christ as the Son of God, who commands them to behave in a moral fashion on this earth and promises an afterlife to come. Yet we certainly cannot define religion as a whole in these terms. These beliefs, and many other aspects of Christianity, are absent from most of the world's religions.

Ancestor worship in China.

WHAT RELIGION IS NOT

In order to overcome the pitfalls of culturally biased thinking about religion, it is probably best to begin by saying what religion *is not* (Wilson, 1972). First, religion should not be identified with **monotheism** (belief in one God). Most religions do not involve a single deity, but many. Even in some versions of Christianity, there are several figures having sacred qualities: God, Jesus, Mary, the Holy Ghost, and the Angels. In certain religions, like Confucianism, there are no gods at all.

Second, religion should not be identified with *moral prescriptions* controlling the behavior of believers—like the Ten Commandments Moses carried down from the Mount. The idea that the gods are consumingly interested in how we behave on this earth is alien to many religions. To the Ancient Greeks, for example, the gods were largely indifferent to how human beings chose to conduct themselves, and considering the gods' behavior, were they to prescribe moral rules of conduct, it would clearly be a case of their not practicing what they preached.

Third, religion is not necessarily concerned with *explaining how the world came to be as it is*. In Christianity, the creation myth of Adam and

Eve explains the origins of human existence. Many religions have "myths of origin" of this sort. But many do not.

Fourth, religion cannot be identified with the *supernatural* that implies a universe "beyond the realm of the senses." There are some religions where such ideas are not found. Confucianism, for example, is concerned with accepting the "natural harmony" of the world, not with finding truths that "lie beyond" it.

WHAT RELIGION IS

Having dismantled our ethnocentric notions of religion, let's look at some characteristics that all religions seem to share. Religions involve a set of *symbols,* invoking feelings of *reverence* or *awe,* and are linked to **rituals** practiced by a community of *believers.* Each of these elements needs some elaboration. Whether or not the beliefs in a religion involve gods, there are virtually always symbolic beings or objects inspiring attitudes of awe or wonder. In some religions, for example, people believe in a "divine force," rather than personalized gods, towards which such attitudes are held. In other religions, there are figures who are not gods, but who are thought of with reverence —such as Buddha or Confucius.

The rituals associated with religion are many. Ritual acts may include praying, chanting, singing, eating certain kinds of foods—or refraining from doing so—fasting on certain days, and so on. Since ritual acts are oriented towards religious symbols they are usually seen as quite distinct from the habits and procedures of ordinary day-to-day life. Lighting a candle to honor or placate a god has quite a different significance from doing so to provide illumination in the dark. Religious rituals are often carried on by individuals in isolation, but all religions also include ceremonials practiced collectively by believers. Such ceremonials normally take place within special places—churches, temples, or ceremonial grounds. Many religions also involve rituals practiced in the home, but even there, a separate place —such as a small shrine or special room—is sometimes set aside for them.

Sociologists usually regard the existence of collective ceremonial as one of the main factors distinguishing religion from magic, although the boundary lines between the two are by no means always distinct. **Magic** is the use of potions, chantings, or ritual practices to influence natural events. It is generally practiced by individuals or small groups, rather than by a community of believers. People often have resorted to magic in situations of misfortune or danger. Thus Bronislaw Malinowski's classical study of the Trobriand Islanders of the Pacific described a variety of magical rites performed before any hazardous voyage by canoe was undertaken (Malinowski, 1982). The islanders omit these rites when they are simply going fishing on the safe and placid waters of a local lagoon.

Although magical practices have become less common in modern societies, comparable superstitions are still found. Many who work in occupations that are either dangerous or depend on chance factors that can affect performance—such as miners, deep-sea fishermen, or athletes—indulge in small superstitious rituals or carry a charm in times of stress. An example might be a tennis-player who insists on wearing a particular ring during big matches. Astrological predictions, which have been inherited from magical beliefs in medieval Europe, still command a following.

We now proceed to analyze some of the main types of religion, placing the emphasis primarily upon the more "developed" forms of religious belief and practice—those that have come to be most prominent in the contemporary world. From there we move to a consideration of theoretical interpretations of religion.

VARIETIES OF RELIGION

IN TRADITIONAL SOCIETIES, RELIGION USUALLY PLAYS A comprehensive part in social life. Religious symbols and rituals are often integrated with the material and artistic culture of the society—music, painting or carving, dance, storytelling, and literature. In small hunting and gathering cultures there is no professional priesthood, but there are always certain individuals who specialize in knowledge of religious (and often magical) practices. Although there are various sorts of such specialists, one common type is the **shaman.** A shaman is an individual believed to be able to direct the activities of spirits or nonnatural forces through ritual means. Shamans are sometimes essentially magicians rather than religious leaders, however, and are often consulted by people dissatisfied with what is offered in the orthodox religious rituals of the community.

TOTEMISM AND ANIMISM

Two forms of religion found frequently in smaller cultures are **totemism** and **animism.** The word "totem" originated among Native

American tribes, but has become widely used to refer to any species of animals or plants believed to have supernatural powers. Usually each kinship group or clan within the society has its own particular totem, with which various ritual activities are associated. Totemic beliefs might at first seem quite alien to modern thinking. Yet in certain contexts, symbols similar to those of totemism are familiar—as when a sports team has an animal or plant for its emblem. Mascots are totems.

Animism is a belief in spirits or ghosts, which are believed to populate the same world as human beings. Such spirits may be seen as either benign or malevolent, and may influence human behavior in numerous respects. In some cultures, for example, spirits are believed to cause illness or madness. Spirits may also "possess" or take over individuals in such a way as to control their behavior. Animistic beliefs are not confined to small cultures, but are found to some degree in many other religious settings. In medieval Europe, those believed to be possessed by evil spirits were frequently persecuted as sorcerers or witches.

Totemism and animism are mostly found among small, seemingly "simple" premodern societies, but some small societies have far more complex religions. The Nuer of southern Sudan, for instance, have an elaborate set of theological ideas centered upon the "high god" or "sky spirit" (Evans-Pritchard, 1956). Monotheistic religions, however, are found rather infrequently among smaller traditional cultures. Most are **polytheistic**—there is a belief in many gods.

JUDAISM, CHRISTIANITY, AND ISLAM

The three most influential monotheistic religions in world history are *Judaism, Christianity,* and *Islam.* All originated in the Near East and each has influenced the others.

Judaism

Judaism is the oldest of the three religions, dating from about 1000 B.C. The early Hebrews were nomads living in lands adjacent to and in ancient Egypt. The Hebrew **prophets** ("inspired" leaders or teachers) drew their ideas from religious beliefs existing in the region, but were also often critical of them. Their commitment to a single, almighty God distinguished their beliefs from those of surrounding religions, most of which were polytheistic. They emphasized that obedience to God meant the following of strict moral codes. The Hebrew prophets also strongly insisted on their claim to a monopoly of truth, seeing their beliefs as the only true religion (Zeitlin, 1985, 1988).

The holy book of Judaism is the Tenakh—the "Old Testament" of the Christian Bible. The Tenakh is divided into three sections, the Torah, Nevi'im, and Ketubim. The Torah, also often referred to as the Five Books of Moses, is the most important of the three and begins with the creation of the world by the word of God, who said, "Let there be light, and there was light." Much of the Torah describes God's communications to Moses and through him to the Hebrew people, instructing them how to live and how to worship. Devotion to a single God, the "jealous God" of Judaism, is expressed in the Sheina, a passage in the Scripture that contains the first religious words a Jewish child should learn, and the last a Jew should utter when leaving this world:

Jews reading the Torah during Sabbath service.

> Hear O Israel, the Lord God is one.
> And you shall love the Lord thy God with all thy heart.
> And with all thy soul and all thy might.

The Torah plays a key role in worship. When not in use, it is kept in the Ark, a cupboard placed in the wall of the synagogue, the Jewish place of worship, facing in the direction of Jerusalem. In the course of a service, the text of the Torah, which is inscribed on a scroll, is taken out and carried in procession to a lectern from which a reading is made. The scroll is usually capped with a silver crown, and the Torah is also known as the "crown of life." The other two parts of the Tenakh do not have the same status as the Torah, because they are regarded as the expression of religious traditions rather than the words of God.

Christianity

Christianity began as a sect of Judaism and incorporated many Judaic views. It is not certain that Jesus, who himself was an orthodox Jew, had wished to found a religion distinct from Judaism, but his disciples came to think of him as the promised "Messiah"—a Hebrew word meaning "the anointed," for which "Christ" was the Greek word. St. Paul, a Greek-speaking Roman citizen and contemporary of Jesus, was a major initiator of the spread of Christianity. He preached extensively in the Near East and Greece, though not always to receptive ears. From the crucifixion of Christ and some of his disciples to the tearing apart of believers by lions in The Roman Colosseum, Christians were savagely persecuted. The Emperor Constantine eventually adopted Christianity as the official religion

A sixth-century artist's depiction of Jesus Christ.

of the Roman Empire, but not until the fourth century. Since then, Christianity spread to become a dominant force in Western culture.

The New Testament of the Bible is a collection of books of Christian authorship. It interprets the Tenakh from a Christian standpoint as well as setting out a range of distinctive teachings. The first writings of Christianity were letters sent by St. Paul to churches that he had founded. The gospels were not written until some while later and are thought to be the work of many hands. Although the gospels of Matthew and John have been connected with the disciples of those names, these individuals almost certainly did not write them, while Mark and Luke were not among the twelve original disciples of Jesus. The main purpose of the gospels is to justify the belief that Jesus was indeed the true Messiah and was God in human form. John's gospel refers to Jesus as expressing the word of God in his person: "And the Word became flesh and dwelt among us, full of grace and truth; we have beheld his glory, glory of the only Son from the Father."

Christianity today commands the greatest number of adherents, and is more generally spread across the world, than any other religion. Over a billion individuals regard themselves as Christians, but there are many divisions, each with their own theology and church organization. Besides its main branches—Roman Catholicism, Protestantism, and Eastern Orthodoxy—there are many small subdivisions.

Islam

The origins of Islam, the second largest religion in the present-day world, overlap with those of Christianity. Islam derives from the teachings of the prophet Mohammed, in the seventh century. The single God of Islam, Allah, is believed to hold sway over all human and natural life. The Pillars of Islam are the five essential religious duties of the Moslem (as the believer is called in Islam). The first is the compulsory recitation of the Islamic creed, "There is no god but Allah, and Mohammed is the apostle of Allah." The second is the saying of formal prayers five times each day, each preceded by ceremonial washing. The worshipper at these prayers must always face towards the holy city of Mecca in Saudi Arabia, no matter how far away that is.

The third pillar is the observance of Ramadan, a month of fasting during which no food or drink may be taken during the daylight hours. The fourth is the giving of alms (money to the poor), set out in Islamic law, which often has been used as a source of taxation by the state. Finally, there is the expectation that every believer will make the attempt, at least once in life, to undertake a pilgrimage to

Mecca. Moslems believe that Allah spoke through earlier prophets—including Moses and Jesus—before Mohammed, but his teachings most directly express Allah's will.

The Islamic scriptures, which are known collectively as the Koran, are a collection of the messages that Mohammed received from God. Mohammed could not read or write, so he memorized God's words, passing them on to those who became his followers. After Mohammed's death, some of the followers decided to write down his sayings in an authoritative form. "Koran" comes from an Arabic term meaning to "recite," and simply means "the recitation"—the words of God as revealed to the Prophet. The Koran sets out the Pillars of Islamic faith and also provides teachings on the conduct of business affairs, law, and personal behavior. In Islamic services, the opening passage of the Koran is always recited before further prayer:

Islamic worshippers.

> In the name of God, the merciful and the benign;
> All praise is due to God, Lord of the worlds, the merciful,
> the mercy-giving,
> Master of the day of judgment.
> Thee alone do we worship and from thee alone do we ask
> help.
> Guide us on the straight path,
> the path of those upon whom is thy favor,
> not the path of those who have sought thine anger or who
> have gone astray. Amen.

Islam has come to be very widespread, having some 600 million adherents throughout the world. The majority of Moslems are concentrated in North and East Africa, the Middle East, and Pakistan.

THE RELIGIONS OF THE FAR EAST

Hinduism

The oldest of all the great religions still prominent in the world today is *Hinduism,* the core beliefs of which date back some six thousand years. Hinduism is a polytheistic religion containing an array of beliefs and rituals. It is so internally diverse, in fact, that some scholars have suggested that it should be regarded as a cluster of related religions rather than a single religious orientation.

Most Hindus accept the doctrine of the cycle of *reincarnation*—the belief that all living beings are part of an eternal process of birth, death, and rebirth. A second key feature of Hinduism is the caste system, according to which individuals are born into their positions in the social and ritual hierarchy, their level in that hierarchy being determined by their activities in previous incarnations. There is a different set of duties and ritual prescriptions for each caste, and one's fate in the next life is governed mainly by how well these duties are performed.

Hindus recognize female as well as male gods, but hold that ultimately the divine force is beyond such categories, since it is found in all living beings. A passage from the Upanishads, one of a group of ancient writings regarded as sacred in Hinduism, expresses this belief in speaking of the atman, or soul, present in all creatures:

> You are woman, and you are man,
> You are the youth and the maiden too,
> You are the old man tottering on his staff.
> You are born again facing all directions.
> You are the blue fly and the red-eyed parrot,
> the cloud pregnant with lightening.
> You are the seasons and the seas,
> The Beginningness, the Abiding Lord
> from whom the spheres are born.

Hinduism accepts the possibility of numerous different religious standpoints, and does not draw a clear line between believers and nonbelievers. There are as many Hindus as Moslems—about 600 million—however, they are virtually all situated in India. Hinduism, unlike Christianity and Islam, is not a form of religious outlook that seeks to convert others into "true believers."

Buddhism, Confucianism, and Taoism

The **ethical religions** of the East encompass *Buddhism, Confucianism,* and *Taoism.* These religions have no gods, at least not in a sense akin to the Christian God or Allah. Rather, they emphasize ethical ideals that relate the believer to the natural cohesion and unity of the universe. Buddhism derives from the teachings of Siddhārtha Gautama, the Buddha (Enlightened One) who was a Hindu prince in a small kingdom in south Nepal in the sixth century B.C. According to the Buddha, human beings can escape the reincarnation cycle by the renunciation of desire. The path of salvation lies in a life of self-discipline and meditation, separated from the tasks of the mundane world. The overall objective of Buddhism is the attainment of Nirvana, complete spiritual fulfillment. The Buddha rejected Hindu ritual and the authority of the castes. Like Hinduism, however, Buddhism tolerates many local variations, including belief in local deities, and does not insist upon an "exclusivist" view. Buddhism today is a major influence in several states in the Far East, including Thailand, Burma, Sri Lanka, China, Japan, and Korea.

Confucianism was the basis of the culture of the ruling groups in traditional China. "Confucius" is the latinized form of K'ung Fu-tzu, who lived in the sixth century B.C., the same period as Buddha. Confucius, like Lao-tzu, the founder of Taoism, was a teacher, not a religious prophet in the manner of Judaism or Islam. Confucius is not seen by his followers as a god, but as "the wisest of wise men." Confucianism seeks to adjust human life to the inner harmony of nature and lays emphasis upon the veneration of ancestors. Taoism shares similar principles, stressing meditation and nonviolence as means to the higher life. Although some principles survive in the practices of many Chinese, Confucianism and Taoism have lost much of their influence in China as a result of determined opposition from the current Communist government.

Buddha, the Enlightened One.

Any sociological theory of religion with claims to generality must allow us to analyze all the religious systems just outlined, from totemism and animism right through to the sophisticated religions of the Near and Far East. In practice, as we shall see, the main contributors to theoretical thinking about religion in sociology have tended to focus only on certain aspects of it, or have concentrated their attention more on some types of religion than others.

THEORIES OF RELIGION

SOCIOLOGICAL APPROACHES TO RELIGION ARE STILL strongly influenced by the ideas of the three "classical" sociological theorists: Marx, Durkheim, and Weber. None of the three was religious themselves, and all believed that religion would become less and less significant in modern times. Each accepted that religion was fundamentally an illusion: the very diversity of religions, and their obvious connection to different types of society and regions of the world made the claims by their advocates inherently implausible. An individual born into an Australian society of hunters and gatherers would plainly have different religious beliefs than someone born into the caste system of India or the Catholic Church of medieval Europe.

MARX AND RELIGION

In spite of the influence of his views on the subject, Karl Marx never studied religion in any detail. Marx's views on religion were mostly derived from the writings of a number of theological and philosophical authors of the early nineteenth century. One of these was Ludwig Feuerbach, who wrote a famous work called *The Essence of Christianity* (Feuerbach, 1957; orig. pub. 1841). Through a process Feuerbach called **alienation,** human beings tend to attribute their own culturally created values and norms to "alien" or separate beings (i.e., divine forces or gods), because they do not understand their own history. Thus the story of the Ten Commandments given to Moses by God is a mythical version of the origins of the moral precepts which govern the lives of Jewish and Christian believers.

So long as we do not understand the nature of the religious symbols we ourselves created, Feuerbach argued, we are condemned to be prisoners of forces of history we cannot control. While the effects of alienation have in the past been negative, the understanding of religion as alienation, according to Feuerbach, promised great hope for the future. Once human beings realized that the values projected onto religion were really their own, those values would become capable of realization on this earth, rather than deferred to an afterlife. For instance, Christians believe that while God is all-powerful and all-loving, human beings themselves are imperfect and flawed. But the powers believed to be possessed by God in Christianity could be appropriated by human beings themselves. Feuerbach held that the potentiality for love and goodness, and the power to control our own lives, were present in human social institutions and could be brought to fruition once we understand their true nature.

Marx accepted the view that religion represents human self-alienation. In his famous phrase, Marx declared that religion was the "opium of the people." Religion defers happiness and rewards to the afterlife, teaching the resigned acceptance of existing conditions in the earthly life. Attention is thus diverted away from inequalities and injustices in this world by the promise of what is to come in the next. Religion has a strong ideological element: religious belief and values often provide justifications for the inequalities of wealth and power. For example, the teaching that "the meek shall inherit the earth" suggests attitudes of humility and nonresistance to oppression.

While it is often believed that Marx held a completely dismissive attitude towards religion, this was far from the case. Religion, Marx wrote, was the "heart of a heartless world"—a haven from the harshness of day-to-day reality. In Marx's view, religion would, and should, disappear in its traditional form. Yet, as with Feuerbach, this was because the positive values embodied in religion could be made guiding ideals for the improvement of the lot of humanity on this earth, *not* because the ideals and values were themselves mistaken. We should not fear the gods we ourselves created, and we should cease endowing them with values we ourselves could realize.

DURKHEIM: RELIGION AND FUNCTIONALISM

In contrast to Marx, Émile Durkheim spent a good part of his intellectual career studying religion, concentrating particularly upon religion in small, traditional societies. Durkheim's work, *The Elementary Forms of the Religious Life,* first published in 1912, is perhaps the most influential single study in the sociology of religion (Durkheim, 1965). Durkheim did not connect religion primarily with social inequalities or power, but with the overall nature of the institutions of a society. He based his work upon a study of totemism as practiced by Australian aboriginal societies. Durkheim's argument was that totemism represented religion in its most "elementary" or simple form —hence the title of his book.

A totem, as has been mentioned, is an animal or plant believed to have particular symbolic significance for a group. The totem, Durkheim argued, is a *sacred* object, regarded with an attitude of veneration and surrounded by various ritual activities. Durkheim defined religion in terms of a distinction between the **sacred** and the **profane.** Sacred objects and symbols, he held, are treated as "apart" from

One function of religion is to foster a sense of community among worshippers, as in this funeral procession in Tibet (left), or in this Catholic mass in Poland (above).

the routine, utilitarian aspects of day-to-day existence—the realm of the profane. It is usually forbidden to eat the totemic animal or plant, except on special ceremonial occasions. As a sacred object, the totem is believed to have divine properties which separate it completely from other animals that might be hunted, or crops gathered and consumed.

Why is the totem sacred? According to Durkheim, it is because it is the emblem of the group itself. The totem stands for the values central to the group or community. The attitudes of reverence that people feel for the totem actually derive from the respect they hold for their central social values. In religion, the object of worship is actually society itself.

Durkheim strongly emphasized that religions are never just a matter of belief. All religion involves regular ceremonial and ritual activities, in which the group of believers meets together. In collective ceremonials, a sense of group solidarity is affirmed and heightened. Ceremonials take individuals away from the concerns of profane social life, into an elevated sphere, in which they feel in contact with higher forces. These higher forces, attributed to totems, divine influences, or gods, are really the expression of the influence of the collectivity over the individual.

Ceremony and ritual, in Durkheim's view, are essential to binding the members of groups together. This is why they are found not only in regular situations of worship, but at the various "crises of life" in which major social transitions are experienced. Groups tend to gather together, for example, to celebrate birth and marriage, and in circumstances of mourning at funerals. In virtually all societies, ritual and ceremonial procedures are observed at such gatherings. Durkheim reasons that collective ceremonials reaffirm group solidarity at a time when people are forced to adjust to major changes in their lives. Funeral rituals demonstrate that the values of the group outlive the passing of particular individuals, and at the same time provide a means for bereaved persons to adjust to their altered circumstances. Mourning is not simply the expression of grief—or, at least, it is only so for those personally affected by the death—it is also a duty imposed by the group.

Durkheim's theory of religion is a good example of the *functionalist* tradition of thought in sociology—to which his writings make a prime contribution. To analyze the function of an item of social behavior or social institution—like religion—is to study the contribution it makes to the continuation of a group, community, or society. According to Durkheim's view, religion has the function of cohering a society by ensuring that people meet regularly to affirm common beliefs and values. (For further discussion of functionalism, see Chapter 22: "The Development of Sociological Theory.")

In small, traditional cultures, Durkheim argued, almost all aspects of life are permeated by religion. Religious ceremonials are the origin of new ideas and categories of thought at the same time as they reaffirm existing values. Religion is not just a series of sentiments and activities, it actually conditions the *modes of thinking* of individuals in traditional cultures. Even the most basic categories of thought, including how time and space are thought of, were first framed in religious terms.

Durkheim's Expectations of Religious Change

The influence of religion would wane, Durkheim believed, with the development of modern societies. Scientific thinking increasingly would replace religious categories, and ceremonial and ritual activities would come to occupy only a small part of people's lives. Durkheim agreed with Marx that traditional religion—that is, religion involving divine forces or gods—was on the verge of disappearing. "The old gods," Durkheim wrote "are dead." Yet there is a sense in which religion, in altered form, is likely to continue. Even modern societies depend for their cohesion upon rituals that reaffirm their values; new ceremonial activities can thus be expected to emerge to replace the old. Durkheim provided only vague allusions as to what these might be. It seems, however, that he had in mind the celebration of humanist and political values such as those of freedom, equality, and social cooperation.

It could be argued that most modern states have in fact fostered **civil religions.** In the United States, symbols such as the flag, songs like "America the Beautiful," and rituals like the July 4 celebrations, all act to endorse the "American way of life" (Bellah, 1970). The government of the Soviet Union was until very recently openly hostile to traditional forms of religion, on the basis of Marx's ideas. Yet, Marx, Engels, and Lenin themselves became symbols within a state-sponsored "civil religion." The May Day celebrations held annually in Red Square in Moscow, and other less grand rituals, reinforced a commitment to the ideals of the Russian Revolution.

Whether it is accurate to speak of "religion" in these contexts is debatable; these symbols and practices coexist with traditional religions. Yet it is difficult to deny that civic symbols and rituals draw on similar social mechanisms to those found in traditional forms of religion.

WEBER, THE WORLD RELIGIONS, AND SOCIAL CHANGE

Durkheim based his arguments upon a very restricted range of examples, even though he claimed his ideas applied to religion in general.

Max Weber, by contrast, embarked on a massive study of religions worldwide. No scholar before or since has undertaken a task of the scope Weber attempted. Most of his attention was concentrated upon what he called the "world religions"—those religions that have attracted large numbers of believers and have decisively affected the course of global history. He produced detailed studies of Hinduism, Buddhism, Taoism, and Ancient Judaism (Weber, 1958, 1951, 1952, 1963). In his book *The Protestant Ethic and the Spirit of Capitalism* (1977; orig. pub. 1904–5), and in other works, he also wrote extensively about the impact of Christianity upon the history of the West. He did not, however, complete his projected study of Islam.

Weber's writings on religion differ from those of Durkheim because they concentrate upon the connection between religion and social change, something to which Durkheim gave little direct attention. They contrast with those of Marx, because Weber argued that religion was not necessarily a conservative force; on the contrary religiously inspired movements have often produced dramatic social transformations. Thus Protestantism, particularly Puritanism, according to Weber, was the source of the capitalistic outlook found in the modern West. The early entrepreneurs were mostly Calvinists. Their "drive to succeed," which helped initiate Western economic development in modern times, was originally prompted by a desire to serve God. Material success was for them a sign of divine favor. (For a fuller exposition of Weber's account of Puritanism and capitalism, see Chapter 22: "The Development of Sociological Theory.")

Weber conceived of his research on the world religions as a single project. His discussion of the impact of Protestantism upon the development of the West was connected to a comprehensive attempt to understand the influence of religion on social and economic life in various cultures. Analyzing the Eastern religions, Weber concluded that they provided insuperable barriers to the development of industrial capitalism, such as took place in the West. This was not because the non-Western civilizations were "backward"; they were simply oriented towards different values than those that came to predominate in Europe.

In traditional China and India, Weber pointed out, there was at certain periods a significant development of commerce, manufacture, and urbanism. But these did not generate the radical patterns of social change involved in the rise of industrial capitalism in the West. Religion was a major influence inhibiting such change. Consider, for example, Hinduism. Hinduism is what Weber called an "other-worldly" religion. That is to say, its highest values stress escape from the toils of the material world to a higher plane of spiritual existence. The religious feelings and motivations produced by

Hinduism do not focus upon controlling or shaping the material world. On the contrary, Hinduism sees material reality as a veil hiding the true spiritual concerns to which humankind should be oriented. Confucianism also acts to direct activity away from economic "progress," as this came to be understood in the West. Confucianism emphasizes harmony with the world, rather than promoting an active mastery of it. Although China was for a long while the most powerful and culturally most developed civilization in the world, its dominant religious values acted as a brake upon a stronger commitment to economic development.

Weber regarded Christianity as a *salvation religion*. According to such religions, human beings can be "saved" if they are converted to the beliefs of the religion and follow its moral tenets. The notions of "sin," and of being rescued from sinfulness by God's grace, are important here. They generate a tension and an emotional dynamism essentially absent from the Eastern religions. Salvation religions have a "revolutionary" aspect. While the religions of the East cultivate an attitude of passivity or acceptance within the believer, Christianity demands a constant struggle against sin, and so can stimulate revolt against the existing order. Religious leaders—like Luther or Calvin —have arisen, who reinterpret existing doctrines in such a way as to challenge the existing power structure.

THE INFLUENCE OF RELIGION

Marx, Durkheim, and Weber each identified some important general characteristics of religion, and in some ways their views complement one another. Marx was right to claim that religion often has ideological implications, serving to justify the interests of ruling groups at the expense of others. There are innumerable instances of this in history. Take as an example the influence of Christianity upon the endeavors of the European colonialists to subject other cultures to their rule. The missionaries who sought to convert "heathen" peoples to Christian beliefs were no doubt sincere in their efforts. Yet the effect of their teachings was in large part to reinforce the destruction of traditional cultures and the imposition of white domination. The various Christian denominations almost all tolerated, or endorsed, slavery in the United States and other parts of the world up to the nineteenth century. Doctrines were developed proclaiming slavery to be based upon divine law, disobedient slaves being guilty of an offense against God as well as their masters (Stampp, 1956).

Yet Weber was certainly correct to emphasize the unsettling, and often revolutionary, impact of religious ideals upon the established social order. In spite of the churches' support for slavery in the United States early on, many church leaders later played a key role in fighting to abolish the institution. Religious beliefs have prompted many social movements seeking to overthrow unjust systems of authority. In modern times, for instance, religious sentiments played a prominent part in the civil rights movements of the 1960s. Religion has also generated social change through the armed clashes and wars fought for religious motives.

These divisive influences of religion, so prominent in history, find little mention in Durkheim's work. Durkheim emphasized above all the role of religion in promoting social cohesion. Yet it is not difficult to redirect his ideas towards explaining religious division, conflict, and change as well as solidarity. After all, much of the strength of feeling which may be generated *against* other religious groups derives from the commitment to religious values generated *within* each community of believers.

Among the most valuable aspects of Durkheim's writings is his stress upon ritual and ceremonial. All religions comprise regular assemblies of believers, at which ritual prescriptions are observed. As Durkheim rightly points out, ritual activities also mark the major transitions of life—birth, entry to adulthood (rituals associated with puberty are found in many cultures), marriage, and death (Van Gennep, 1977).

TYPES OF RELIGIOUS ORGANIZATION

ALL RELIGIONS INVOLVE COMMUNITIES OF BELIEVERS. YET there are various ways in which such communities are organized as practicing religious groups. One of the most important ways of classifying religious organizations was first put forward by Max Weber and his colleague, the religious historian Ernst Troeltsch (Troeltsch, 1981). Weber and Troeltsch distinguished between churches and sects. Other authors have further developed the church-sect typology. Howard Becker (1950) has added two further types: the denomination and the cult.

CHURCHES AND SECTS

Churches are large, established religious bodies—like the Catholic Church or the Church of England. Churches normally have a formal, bureaucratic structure, with a hierarchy of religious officials. Churches often (although by no means always) represent the conservative face of religion, since they are integrated within the existing institutional order. Most of their adherents are born into and grow up with the church.

Sects are smaller, less highly organized groups of committed believers, usually set up in protest against a church—as Calvinists or Methodists did initially. Sects aim at discovering and following "the true way," and either try to change the surrounding society or tend to withdraw from it into communities of their own. The members of sects regard established churches as corrupt. Many sects have few or no officials and all members are regarded as equal participants. For the most part, people are not born into sects, but actively join them in order to further commitments in which they believe.

DENOMINATIONS AND CULTS

A **denomination** is a sect which has "cooled down" and become an institutionalized body rather than an activist protest group. Sects that survive over any period of time inevitably become denominations. Thus Calvinism and Methodism were sects in their early period of formation, when they generated great fervor among their members; but over the years they have become more established. Denominations are recognized as legitimate by churches and exist alongside them, quite often cooperating harmoniously with them.

Cults resemble sects, but have different emphases. Cults are the most loosely-knit and transient of all religious organizations. They are composed of individuals who reject what they see as the values of the outside society. Their focus is upon individual experience, bringing like-minded individuals together. People do not formally "join" a cult but rather follow particular theories or prescribed ways of behavior. Those who are members are usually allowed to maintain other religious connections. Like sects, cults quite often form around the influence of an inspirational leader. Instances of cults in modern societies would include groups of believers in spiritualism, astrology, or transcendental meditation.

RELIGIOUS MOVEMENTS

Religious movements represent a subtype of social movement in general (which are discussed extensively in Chapter 19: "Revolutions and Social Movements"). A religious movement is an association of people who join together to seek to spread a new religion or to promote a new interpretation of an existing religion. Religious movements are larger than sects, and less exclusivist in their membership—although like the distinction between church and sect, movements and sects (or cults) are not always clearly separable from one another. Examples of religious movements include the groups that originally founded and spread Christianity in the first century, the Lutheran movement that split Christianity in Europe about fifteen hundred years afterwards, and the groups involved in the more recent Islamic Revolution (which is discussed in more detail later in the chapter).

Religious movements tend to go through certain definite phases of development (Nottingham, 1971) In the first phase, the movement frequently derives its life and cohesion from a powerful leader. Max Weber classified such leaders as *charismatic,* that is, having inspirational qualities capable of capturing the imagination and devotion of a mass of followers. (Charismatic leaders in Weber's formulation include political as well as religious figures—revolutionary China's Mao Tse-tung or President John F. Kennedy would be examples in the political world; Jesus or Mohammed in the religious.) The leaders of religious movements are usually critical of the religious establishment, and seek to proclaim a new message. In their early years, religious movements are fluid—they do not have an established authority system. Their members are normally in direct contact with the charismatic leader, and together they spread the new teachings.

The second phase of development occurs following the death of the leader. Rarely does a new charismatic leader arise from the masses so this phase is crucial. The movement is now faced with what Weber termed the "routinization of charisma." To survive, it has to create formalized rules and procedures, since it can no longer depend upon the central role of the leader in organizing the followers. Many movements fade away when their leaders die or for some other reason lose their influence. A movement that survives, and takes on a permanent character, becomes a church. In other words, it becomes a formal organization of believers having an established authority system and established symbols and rituals. The church might at some later point itself be the origin of other movements, which question its teachings and either set themselves up in opposition to it or break away completely.

One type of religious movement that appears periodically is the **millenarian movement.** Millenarian movements have been an important feature of the development of Christianity both in European history and in other cultural contexts. A millenarian movement is one that anticipates immediate, collective salvation for a group of believers, either because of some cataclysmic change in the present, or through a recovery of a golden age that was supposed to have existed in the past. (The term "millenarian" actually derives from the thousand-year reign of Christ, the "millennium" prophesied in the Bible.) Millenarian movements are deeply entwined with the history of Christianity. In medieval Europe, millenarian movements were frequently the last, desperate resort of those who found themselves suddenly impoverished. Peasants in times of famine, for example, were drawn to follow prophets who offered a vision of a "world turned upside down," in which the poor would finally inherit the earth. Such movements have arisen in two major contexts—among the poor in the past development of the West, and among colonized people in other parts of the world (Lantenari, 1968; Worsley, 1970).

A number of common elements which most or all millenarian movements share can be identified. Virtually all seem to involve the activities of prophets, who draw upon established religious ideas and proclaim the need to revitalize them. Such prophets successfully develop a following if they manage to put into words what others only vaguely feel, and if they tap emotions that stir people to action. Prophecy has always been strongly associated with salvation religions, especially Christianity, and most of those who have led millenarian movements in colonized areas have been familiar with Christian practices and beliefs. Many have in fact been mission teachers, who have turned their adopted religion against those who schooled them in it.

Millenarian movements among colonized peoples tend to develop when a traditional culture is being destroyed by the impact of Western colonizers, as was the case with the Ghost Dance cult that arose among the Plains Indians of North America in the late nineteenth century. Prophets preached that a general catastrophe would occur, heralding the millennium. Storms, earthquakes, whirlwinds, and floods would destroy all the white intruders. The Indians would survive to see again the prairies covered with herds of buffalo and other game. After the catastrophe all ethnic divisions would be dissolved, and any further whites who come to the land would live amicably with the Indians. The Ghost Dance ritual spread from community to community in the plains areas, just as cargo cults have spread more recently from village to village in New Guinea (Burridge, 1969). The rituals of the Ghost Dance, which included singing, chanting, and the attainment of trancelike states, were based partly upon ideas derived from contacts with Christianity, and partly upon the traditional Sun Dance which the Indians used to perform previous to the white man's arrival. The Ghost Dance disappeared after the massacre at Wounded Knee, at which 370 Indian men, women, and children were slaughtered by white soldiers.

APPLYING THE CATEGORIES

The five categories just discussed are useful in analyzing aspects of religious organization, but we have to apply them with caution because they partly reflect specifically Christian traditions, and are not necessarily representative of non-Western religious cultures. For example, a heterogeneous religion such as Hinduism does not have a bureaucratic hierarchy, one of the characteristics of a "church." Nor would it make sense to call its various subdivisions "denominations"; yet Hinduism is every bit as established a religion as the Christian churches.

While these concepts may be culture-bound, they do help us analyze the tension between institutionalization and revivalism present in all religions. Established religious organizations tend to become bureaucratic and inflexible. Yet their religious symbols have extraordinary emotive power for believers and resist becoming reduced to the level of the routine. We can find a use here for Durkheim's distinction between the sacred and the profane. The more religious activities become standardized, a matter for habitual re-enactment, the more the element of "sacredness" is lost, and religious ritual and belief become mundane aspects of the everyday world. Churches that are sensitive to this tension might revitalize a sense of the distinct qualities of religious experience through ceremonies. But when bureaucratic inflexibility dominates over inspirational experiences, certain subgroups or sects might diverge from established orthodoxy. They might break away from the main community, mobilize protest or separatist movements, or otherwise differ from patterns of established ritual and belief.

RELIGION AND THE STATE

MANY COUNTRIES THROUGHOUT THE WORLD RECOGNIZE A particular church as having a special relationship to the state—as in the case of Anglicanism in Britain, Catholicism in Italy, or Shinto in prewar Japan. The United States is the exception here, since its constitution prohibits any state-sponsored religion.

Where state and church are closely linked, religion is often a conservative force, used to supplement governmental power. British kings often called upon and received the support of Anglican Church leaders. After all, it was King Henry the Eighth who established the Church in a break with the pope. But this supporting role is by no means always accepted. Both in the traditional world and in more modern times political and religious authorities have often been in sharp conflict with one another. For example, when the dictator Juan Perón came to power in Argentina in the 1940s, he sponsored legislation giving special privileges to the Catholic Church as the state religion. He did so to build popular support for his policies, since the population of the country was overwhelmingly Catholic. At that time, the leading figures in the Argentinian Catholic hierarchy were strongly in favor of Perón, and for a while, things went well. But later, bitter dissent arose as Perón's government developed policies of which Church leaders disapproved. Perón himself became a bitter antagonist of the Church, which came to condemn him as a tyrant.

Just as political authorities have frequently sought to enlist religious support for their policies so also have state-backed religious organizations often enlisted governmental power to maintain or further their own interests. For several hundred years, up to about the end of the eighteenth century, successive English governments intermittently hounded Catholics (called "papists" then because they followed the pope) denying them the right to practice their religion openly. Seeing this, the Catholic Church in other countries enlisted their governments to retaliate. In France, for example, Protestants were subjected to a series of attacks by the political authorities, at the instigation of the Catholic Church, forcing many of them to leave the country. The early Puritan settlers in the United States, of course, and many later groups of other religious backgrounds, migrated partly to escape persecution at home. In most countries today, the separation of church and state is more pronounced than it used to be, and state-sponsored religious persecution is relatively uncommon. But there remain many instances where an alliance of political and religious authorities keeps a firm grip upon religious dissent, and where religious minorities are subjected to harassment—as, for instance, in the case of non-Islamic groups in Pakistan.

THE ISLAMIC REVOLUTION

One view that Marx, Durkheim, and Weber all shared was that traditional religion would become more and more marginal to the modern world. Of the three, probably only Weber would have suspected that a traditional religious system like Islam could undergo a major revival, and become the basis of important political developments in the late twentieth century. Yet this is exactly what occurred in the 1980s in Iran. In recent years, Islamic fundamentalism has also had a significant impact upon other Middle Eastern countries, including Egypt, Syria, and Lebanon among others.

The image of the Ayatollah Khomeini provides the background for these Iranian worshippers.

To understand the phenomenon, we have to look at Islam as a traditional religion and at the secular changes affecting modern states. Islam, like Christianity, is a religion that has continually stimulated activism. The Koran is full of instructions to believers to "struggle in the way of God." This struggle is both against unbelievers and those within the Moslem community who introduce corruption. For centuries there have been successive generations of Moslem reformers, and Islam has become as internally divided as Christianity.

The Islamic Revolution was fuelled initially by internal opposition to the shah (the king) Mohammad Reza Pahlavi (1941–1979). The shah had accepted and tried to promote forms of modernization modeled on the West—for example, land reform, extending the vote to women, and developing secular education. He also brutally repressed those who opposed his regime, by means of the army and secret police. The movement that overthrew the shah brought together people of diverse interests, all of whom were by no means attached to Islamic fundamentalism. A dominant figure, however, was the Ayatollah Ruhollah Khomeini, a religious leader exiled in France during the shah's reign, who provided a radical re-interpretation of Shi'ite ideas.

Khomeini established a government in strict accordance with traditional Islamic law, calling that government the "Representative of Alī." The Islamic Revolution fused religion and the state. It made Islam, as specified in the Koran, the direct basis of all political and economic life in Iran. Under the revived Islamic law, men and women are kept rigorously segregated, women are obliged to cover their heads and faces in public, homosexuals face the possibility of being sent to the firing squad, and adulterers are stoned to death. The strict code is accompanied by a pronounced nationalistic outlook, strongly rejecting Western influences.

Islamic revivalism plainly cannot be understood wholly in religious terms; it represents in part a reaction against the impact of the West, and is a movement of national and cultural assertion. It is doubtful whether, even in its most fundamentalist forms, it should be seen only as a renewal of traditionally held ideas. What has occurred is something more complex. Traditional practices and modes of life have been revived, but are combined with concerns that relate specifically to modern times.

CHURCH AND STATE IN THE SOVIET UNION AND EASTERN EUROPE

In contrast to government-sponsored religions like Islam in Iran, the state in the Soviet Union and East European societies, while under

Communist influence, was mostly hostile to religion, and attempted to promote an official creed of atheism (denial of religion and the existence of God). Communist governments took this position on the basis of Marx's supposition that, in a socialist society, there is no longer any need for religion. Following the Russian Revolution of 1917, church property was confiscated by the government. A seven-day work week was established, mainly to get the economy going, but also partly to discourage religious services on Sundays. Communist Party members were prohibited from being members of any religious organization; a body sponsored by the Party, the League of Militant Godless, devoted itself to eradicating the influence of religion.

However, these efforts to combat religion were fairly short-lived. They were not effective in weaning many of the population away from their strong religious beliefs, and the government came to see that it stood more to gain by placating religious leaders than by being hostile towards them. The seven-day work week was abandoned and restrictions on religion relaxed by the 1930s. During the Second World War, the leader of the Russian Orthodox Church, the Patriarch of Moscow, came out in firm public support of the Communist government.

In the postwar period this attitude of mutual accommodation between the Communist Party and the major religious organizations was maintained, although there was also much tension between them. Nikita Khrushchev, for example, the Soviet political leader in the 1950s, conducted an extensive campaign against the churches on the basis that they were a focus for dissent. Thousands of church buildings were forcibly closed by the authorities at that time (Hill, 1985). Under Mikhail Gorbachev today, policies towards religion have become more favorable. Among other radical changes in the USSR, Gorbachev has accepted the right of Soviet citizens to practice their religions without restriction.

In several Eastern European countries in the 1970s and 1980s, the churches were often centers of dissent and resistance to Communist rule. A notable example was the association of Catholic Church leaders with the Solidarity movement in Poland. Solidarity was one of the first movements to effectively challenge the Communist Party's monopoly of power. In 1989, it formed the first non-Communist government in Eastern Europe, which helped stimulate major changes in the other East European societies.

Some religious leaders and socialist intellectuals, however, have seen Marxism and Christianity as compatible rather than as inevitably in conflict with one another. This has particularly been true of Catholic political activists in Europe, Central, and South America. Rather than picking up on Marx's negative statements about religion, they are inspired by the idea that "religion is the heart of a heartless world." Religious belief and social reform, they argue, can go hand in hand. Their outlook is sometimes referred to as *liberation theology*—the use of religious thought to promote human social betterment and freedom. Liberation theologians have been widely condemned by orthodox Catholic organizations, especially in Central and South America, but their writings and activities have been widely influential among political dissidents in several parts of that continent.

GENDER AND RELIGION

CHURCHES AND DENOMINATIONS RESEMBLE OTHER INSTITUtions in social life in that women have been mostly excluded from power. This is clear in Christianity, but is also characteristic of virtually all the major religions. In the following sections, we shall examine some of the interrelations of religion and gender. The issue is an important one, because this is an area in which significant changes are taking place.

RELIGIOUS IMAGES

The Judeo-Christian tradition, as well as the Islamic religion, is a resolutely male affair in its symbolism as well as in its hierarchy of authority. While Mary, the mother of Jesus, may sometimes be treated as if she had divine qualities, God is "the Father," a male figure, and Jesus took the human shape of a man. Genesis, the first book of the Bible, reveals that woman was created from a rib taken from man. Yet other biblical texts portray women as capable of acts of charity and bravery. The Book of Judith, for instance—contained in the Apocrypha—tells the story of a young Israelite woman's courage against the Assyrian army. Before a critical battle between the out-numbered Israelites and the Assyrians, Judith entered the enemy's camp under the pretext of betraying the Israelites. After being entertained at a great banquet, the Assyrian general Holofernes fell into a drunken stupor. Judith cut off his head, put it into a basket, and took it back to the Israelites' camp, where they hung it from their wall. When the Assyrians discovered their general's headless corpse, they scattered in fear, and the Israelites plundered their camp. Yet, such stories are few and the prime roles in the Bible are reserved for men. There is no female equivalent to Moses, for example, and in the New Testament, all the apostles are men.

These facts have not gone unnoticed by those involved in women's movements. Nearly a hundred years ago Elizabeth Cady Stanton published a series of commentaries on the scriptures, entitled *The Woman's Bible*. In her view, the deity had created women and men as beings of equal value, and the Bible should fully reflect this fact. Its "masculinist" character, she believed, reflected not the authentic word of God, but the fact that the Bible was written by men. In 1870, the Church of England established a Revising Committee to continue what had been done many times before—revise and update the biblical texts. As she pointed out, the committee contained not a single woman. She asserted that there was no reason to suppose that God is a man, since it was clear in the scriptures that all human beings were fashioned in the image of God. When a colleague opened a women's rights conference with a prayer to "God, our Mother," there was a virulent reaction from the church authorities. Yet Stanton pressed ahead organizing a Women's Revising Committee, composed of twenty-three women, to advise her in preparing *The Woman's Bible*, which was published in 1895. In her introduction she summed up her position:

> The canon and civil law; church and state; priests and legislators; all political parties and religious denominations have alike taught that woman was made after man, of man, and for man, an inferior being, subject to man. The fashions, forms, ceremonies and customs of society, church ordinances and discipline all grow out of this idea.. . . . Those who have the divine insight to translate, transpose and transfigure this mournful object of pity into an exalted, dignified personage, worthy of our worship as the mother of the race, are to be congratulated as having a share of the occult mystical power of the eastern Mahatmas. (Stanton, 1972; see also Gage, 1972; orig. pub. 1893)

Female deities are quite often found in religions across the world. They are sometimes thought of as "womanly," gentle and loving; in other instances, goddesses appear as feared destroyers. Warrior goddesses, for example, are found fairly often, even though in actual social life few women have been military leaders.

In Buddhism, females appear as important figures in the teachings of some Buddhist orders. In one branch of the religion especially, Mahayana Buddhism, women are represented in a particularly favorable light. But on the whole, Buddhism, like Christianity, is "an overwhelmingly male-created institution dominated by a patriarchal power structure," in which the feminine is mostly "associated with the secular, powerless, profane, and imperfect" (Paul, 1985). The contrasting pictures of women that appear in the Buddhist texts mirror no doubt the ambiguous attitudes of men towards women in the secular world: women are portrayed as wise, maternal, and gentle yet also as mysterious, polluting and destructive, threatening evil.

In sum, there are few, if any, religions in which females are the dominant figures, either symbolically or as religious authorities. When they appear, female gods are usually fairly minor figures compared with male deities (Bynum, Harrell, and Richman, 1986). This, of course, is not surprising if one accepts Feuerbach's view that religion expresses the deeply held values of society.

THE ROLE OF WOMEN IN RELIGIOUS ORGANIZATIONS

In Buddhism, and later on in Christianity, women were allowed to express strong religious convictions by choosing to become nuns. Western monastic life derives from the practices of first century Christian men who lived a life of extreme poverty given over to meditation. These individuals, many of whom were hermits, lived, worked, and prayed together, but had few connections with the established church. By the early Middle Ages, the church controlled most of the monastic orders, subjecting them to its authority system.

The first orders for women were probably established in the fourteenth century. Their membership remained small, however, until the 1800s (Southern, 1970). Many women at that time became nuns in order to become teachers and nurses, since these occupations were largely controlled by the religious orders. All along, however, female religious orders remained subject to a male hierarchy, and this subjugation was reinforced by some elaborate rituals. For example, all nuns were regarded as "brides of Christ." Until changes were made in some of the orders in 1950s and 1960s, "marriage" ceremonies were carried out, during the course of which the novice would cut her hair, receive her religious name, and sometimes be given a wedding ring. After several years, a novice takes a vow of perpetual profession, after which she must receive dispensation if she chooses to leave.

Women's orders today show a considerable diversity in their beliefs and modes of life (Campbell-Jones, 1979). In some convents, sisters still dress in full traditional habit and live together in communities removed from the secular world. In other convents, by contrast, the nuns wear ordinary dress and may live in apartments or houses. There are now few restrictions on talking to others at certain periods of the day, together with rules about the position of the body, such as walking with the hands folded and hidden under the habit.

These changes were made possible by edicts from the Vatican Council in the 1960s.

Over the past two decades or so women have succeeded in forging a significant role for themselves in the major religious organizations in some countries. Women's groups have pressed to achieve equal status in religious orders. Increasingly, the Catholic and Episcopalian Churches are under strong pressure to allow women an equal voice in their hierarchies (Franklin, 1986; Dowell and Hurcombe, 1987). Yet in 1977, the Sacred Congregation for the Doctrine of the Faith, in Rome, declared formally that women were inadmissible to the Catholic priesthood. The reason given was that Jesus had not called a woman to be one of his disciples (Noel, 1980). The year 1987 was officially designated as the "Year of the Madonna" in which women were advised to recall their traditional role as wife and mother. The barriers to Catholic women in the hierarchy of the Church remain formidable.

Since 1981 the Anglican church has permitted women to be deacons, but that role is ambiguous. They are officially part of the laity and are not allowed to conduct basic religious rituals, like pronouncing blessings or solemnizing marriages. On the other hand, at the direction of an Anglican priest, a deacon may administer certain sacraments and conduct baptisms, among other duties. A report was issued by the standing committee of the General Synod in 1986 examining the legislation that would be needed were women to be admitted to the priesthood. The group was composed of ten men and two women. Their task was to consider the "safeguards" necessary to meet the objections of "those within the Church of England who are unable to accept, for one reason or another, the ordination of women as priests" (Quoted in Aldridge, 1987). The feelings and aspirations of women themselves found little mention.

The Christian church was born out of what was essentially a revolutionary movement. But in respect to attitudes towards women, it has become one of the most conservative of organizations in modern societies. The churches are the last major institutions to persist in formally supporting inequalities of gender. The Anglican bishop of London, Graham Leonard was asked on a radio program in August 1987 if he thought the Christian notion of God would be affected by seeing a women regularly up at the altar. He replied: "I think it would. My instinct when faced with her would be to take her in my arms. . . ." The possibility of sexual attraction between a woman priest and the congregation, he stated, was a reason why women should not be admitted as full members of the priesthood. In religion as elsewhere, he stated, "it is the male who takes the initiative and the female who receives" (Jenkins, 1987).

The first female Episcopal bishop, Barbara Harris.

The Anglican Church in the United States (the Episcopal Church) has been more open and has allowed women into its priesthood since 1976. When it overthrew tradition and appointed its first female bishop, Barbara Harris, Dr. Leonard's comment was that he did not feel himself to be in communion with Bishop Harris, and he did not accept her consecration.

So far in this chapter we have looked at religion on a comparative basis, and analyzed aspects of religious organization. In the remaining sections, we focus our attention upon religion in the United States more specifically, analyzing patterns of membership of religious organizations and other aspects of religious beliefs and practices. To conclude the chapter, we will consider to what extent religion retains the same central importance it once had in social life.

RELIGION IN THE UNITED STATES

FREEDOM OF RELIGIOUS EXPRESSION WAS MADE AN ARTICLE of the American Constitution long before tolerance of varied religious beliefs and practices was widespread in any other Western society. The early settlers were refugees from religious oppression by political authorities, and were suspicious of the close association between state and church that existed in their lands of origin. State and church remain more separate in the United States today than in most other industrialized countries.

The United States also contains a far greater diversity of religious groups than any other industrialized country. In most Western societies the majority of the population are formally affiliated with a single church, such as the Italians with the Catholic Church. Some 90 percent of the American population are Christian, but belong to a diversity of churches and denominations. While many groups might number only hundreds, more than ninety religious organizations claim memberships of more than fifty thousand, twenty-two of these reporting memberships of over a million. The largest body by far in the United States is the Catholic Church, which numbers some fifty million members. However, it makes up only about 28 percent of total membership of religious organizations. About 60 percent of the population are Protestant, but they are divided among numerous denominations and their relative share is declining (Roof and McKinney, 1988). The Southern Baptist Convention is largest, with over thirteen million members, followed by the United Methodist

Church, the National Baptist Convention, and the Lutheran and Episcopal Churches. Among non-Christian groups, the largest are the Jewish congregations, numbering about six million members.

SOCIAL CORRELATES OF RELIGION

Membership of religious organizations correlates quite closely with socioeconomic differences. The majority of Baptists are comparatively poor, whereas Presbyterians and Jews are disproportionately represented among those in higher income positions. Catholics have a higher average income than any major Protestant denomination. These general comparisons are important, but they have to be interpreted with care. Many of the poorest groups in the United States are Catholics—including especially people of Hispanic background. There are large differences in income within all the major Protestant denominations.

Religion is also related to political preferences and attitudes towards social issues. Catholics and Jews show higher levels of support for the Democratic Party than Protestants. Attitude surveys indicate that Jews have a more liberal outlook than Catholics, who in turn are more liberal in their views than Protestants. A National Opinion Research Center survey of 1978 investigated what proportion of various religious groups would oppose a hypothetical atheistic book being removed from a public library. The results showed that 87 percent of Jews would be so opposed, as compared to 65 percent of Catholics, and 56 percent of Protestants (NORC, 1978).

These figures conceal important subvariations. For example, over three-quarters of black Protestants are Democrats, a higher proportion than Jews or Catholics as a whole. Reasons for party support also vary. Black support for the Democratic Party is largely because of its favorable attitude to social welfare and civil rights issues. Catholic patterns of Democratic voting originated during the period when immigrants were first absorbed into big-city politics, gaining favors from the Democratic "party machines." Protestant views on social issues are weighted in a conservative direction by the influence of fundamentalist groups. Some denominations are much more liberal than others. None of these correlations, moreover, demonstrate to what degree religion is the determining factor in the observed differences. Religious affiliation is associated with many other social characteristics—such as ethnicity. Finally, the figures on church membership are less than completely reliable. Some denominations include as members anyone who was ever baptized by them, while others include only those who are active churchgoers.

RELIGION AND RACE

The divisions between whites and blacks in American society are perhaps more clearly seen in religion than in any other area of social life. The saying that "eleven o'clock on a Sunday morning is the most segregated hour of the week" is as valid in 1990 as any time in the past. The racial separation of religious organizations is more rigid than in most other areas of American social life.

Before the Civil War it was fairly common for whites and blacks to attend church together as members of the same congregations. Religious segregation derived in large part from subsequent attempts on the part of whites to ensure that blacks were excluded from mixing with them culturally or socially. An additional factor, however, was the wish of leaders of some of the black denominations to secure their free and independent development. Black Baptist groups were among the first to break away, in the late 1860s. Most other denominations had followed suit by the turn of the century, at which point the independent black churches claimed nearly three million members in a total black population of just over eight million. It has been said that black religion "was the one institution over which blacks maintained control. The price of autonomy and self-control was a separate and segregated church, one effectively cut off socially and religiously from white America" (Roof and McKinney, 1988).

Many different black religious organizations have been formed or have splintered off from more established groups during the course of the present century. The largest black denomination today is the National Baptist Convention, with over five million members, followed by the National Baptist Convention of America, which has just over half that number. About 85 percent of all black Protestant members of religious organizations are in the black denominations (this compares with an estimate of 88 percent made by H. Richard Niebuhr in the 1920s [Niebuhr, 1929]).

The majority of white denominations have only 2–3 percent black members; the two groups with the largest proportions are the American Baptists and the Seventh-Day Adventists. Even in these denominations, however, blacks mainly belong to all-black congregations, so it would scarcely be meaningful to speak of a significant degree of integration here. Some steps have been taken in recent years to promote wider racial inclusiveness. The United Methodists, Episcopalians, and the United Church of Christ, have been particularly prominent in giving leadership positions to blacks. Yet the general picture is one of persistent and entrenched separation between whites and blacks in the religious sphere.

RELIGIOUS BEHAVIOR

Some 40 percent of the American population on average attend a church or synagogue service each week. This is much higher than comparable rates for most other industrialized countries. The upper socioeconomic groups attend church more regularly than those in the poorer sections of society—a finding that holds in the other industrialized societies also. The same is true within each church or denomination: Catholics on average attend church more regularly than Protestants, but more affluent Catholics show higher rates of attendance than their poorer counterparts (Chalfant, Beckley, and Palmer, 1986).

Almost 70 percent of Americans belong to churches, synagogues, or other religious organizations. The majority of these claim to be active within their congregations. When questioned about their personal attitudes, virtually all Americans—some 95 percent—say they hold religious beliefs of one kind or another. Most express beliefs in God, life after death, and accept that the Bible was divinely inspired (Stark and Bainbridge, 1985). A survey carried out in sixty countries showed the United States to have a higher level of stated religious commitment than any other country save India. Over 70 percent of Americans, for example, say they believe in life after death, compared to 46 percent in Italy or 35 percent in Scandinavia (Gallup Opinion Index, 1976).

RELIGIOUS CHANGE IN THE UNITED STATES

Catholicism

Church attendance by Catholics has shown a sharp decline over the past few decades, beginning in the 1960s and leveling off in the mid-1970s. One of the main reasons for the falloff in rates of Catholic churchgoing seems to have been the papal encyclical of 1968, which restated the ban on the use of contraceptives among Catholics. This upset a great many American Catholics who were hoping for some kind of change. But the encyclical offered no leeway for those whose conscience allowed for the use of contraceptives. They were faced with disobeying the Church and many Catholics did just that. Over three-quarters of Catholic women of childbearing age use contraceptive devices, and more than 80 percent of all Catholics are in favor of the use of contraception (Greeley, 1977). In addition, almost half of all American Catholics reject the notion that the pope infallibly rep-

Catholics demonstrating against Pope John Paul II during his 1987 visit to San Francisco.

resents the voice of God. A large proportion of Catholics have therefore come to doubt or defy the Church's authority over various areas of their lives.

When Pope John Paul II visited San Francisco, in September 1987, he received a muted reception from Catholics in the city, mixed with vociferous protests from gay and pro-abortion groups. In a public speech, the pope discussed homosexuality in a sympathetic way, but reiterated his strong stance against "pleasure-seeking" and "immorality." In an earlier meeting with senior bishops in Los Angeles he had condemned the waywardness of U.S. Catholics. Only fifty thousand people, instead of the anticipated eight hundred thousand, turned out to see the papal procession through San Francisco. At Saint Mary's Cathedral in the city, Donna Hanson, a prominent member of the Catholic laity, was greeted with applause from the congregation when she told the pope,

> I know the church is not a democracy, ruled by popular vote, but I expect to be treated as a mature, educated, responsible adult.

She went on to criticize the Church for its sexism, its stance against contraception, and its refusal to allow the laity a greater part in administering Church affairs (Brummer, 1987). For Catholics in the United States these issues have also contributed to their declining attendance in Church services.

Protestantism

Church attendance by Protestants has remained fairly stable over the period from 1950 to the present, but other significant changes are occurring within Protestantism today. One such change is the dividing of Protestant denominations into modernists and fundamentalists (Marty, 1970). Modernists are politically liberal, do not interpret the Bible literally, and have an "intellectual" commitment to their beliefs. The fundamentalists are conservative in their politics, view the Bible literally as the word of God, and are committed emotionally to their religious values and practices. Both types are found in many churches and denominations, the more established churches being primarily modernist.

The more liberal Protestant denominations include the Methodists, Episcopalians, and Lutherans. Their membership has remained stable or declined in recent years. The fundamentalist organizations, on the other hand, have been attracting a growing following. We shall come back to them a little later in the chapter, since they warrant special consideration.

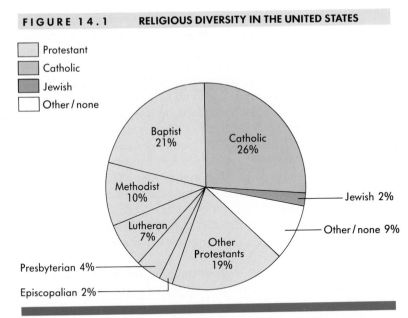

FIGURE 14.1   RELIGIOUS DIVERSITY IN THE UNITED STATES

☐ Protestant
▨ Catholic
▦ Jewish
☐ Other / none

Baptist 21%
Catholic 26%
Jewish 2%
Methodist 10%
Other / none 9%
Lutheran 7%
Other Protestants 19%
Presbyterian 4%
Episcopalian 2%

Source: General Social Surveys, 1985, 1986, 1987; National Opinion Research Center, University of Chicago; in Ladd, 1989.

Judaism

Jews in the United States are both a religious denomination and an ethnic minority. There are more Americans who see themselves as Jewish, and are regarded by others as Jewish, than who subscribe to any of the core religious beliefs of Judaism or participate in Jewish religious activities. Attendance at temple or synagogue services has always been lower than for Christian denominations. Well under 20 percent of American Jews attend services more than once a month, although there is little indication that this proportion is declining.

Judaism is not a faith that actively seeks converts. Consequently, one change likely to affect American Jews is the rising rate of intermarriage with non-Jewish partners. Twenty-five years ago, no more than 5 percent of Jews married outside their religion; today more than a third do so. Given that many of the children of these marriages may be raised outside the Jewish faith, this trend seriously threatens the continuity of Judaism within the United States.

NEW RELIGIONS AND CULTS

Since World War II, more religious movements have been founded in the United States than at any previous time in its history (Robbins,

1988). Over this period there has occurred an unprecedented series of mergers and divisions between denominations. Most have proved short-lived, but a few have achieved notable followings. An example is the Unification Church, founded by the Korean Sun Myung Moon. This cult was introduced into the United States at the beginning of the 1960s, and it appealed to many who at the time were rejecting traditional religion and looking for insight in Eastern religious teachings. The Unification Church mixed Eastern ideas with aspects of fundamentalist Christianity and had a strong bent towards anticommunism. Moon's followers accepted his prediction that the world would come to an end in 1967. Though this event seems not to have taken place, the mis-prediction did not spell the end of the cult. As many previous leaders of such movements have done, Moon readjusted his ideas in the light of his failed prediction, and his new doctrines in fact gained even more adherents than before.

The sect claims to have a membership of forty thousand in the United States today. Its members are expected to fraternize only with one another, to donate their property to the cult, and to obey Moon's commands. Moon's doctrine of "heavenly deception" permits members to mislead the public when asking for money—for instance, by posing as a charity. Large funds were accumulated in this way, and in fact Moon was imprisoned for a year and a half in 1984 on charges of tax evasion.

Since this cult lives separately from the outside world, and its members undergo strict religious training, there is the suspicion that it tries to "brainwash" its members. This may be true, yet there are many established religious organizations, that also demand the complete absorption of the believer within a rigidly structured framework of values and practices. The beliefs involved in the new cults might seem bizarre mixtures of traditional and modern religious ideas, but in fact all long-established religions mix elements taken from diverse cultural sources.

Sectarian diversity for a long time has been characteristic of the United States. The main growth period for the new cults was the 1970s and early 1980s. Since then, their dynamic fervor seems to have been on the wane. Many of the cults have achieved some degree of stable membership, but "without essentially changing the map of American religion." By the mid-1980s, "most of these religions had begun to fit quietly into the larger landscape . . . as only slightly less conventional denominations among the denominations, study accents among other Great Book interests, or, most of all, as merely self-preservative groups constantly fighting for legal rights and privilege" (Marty, 1985).

RELIGIOUS FUNDAMENTALISM

The growth of fundamentalist religious organizations in the United States is one of the most notable features of the past twenty or so years. **Fundamentalism** is a loose label for a variety of viewpoints that emphasize a return to literal interpretations of the scriptural texts. Fundamentalism is both a trend within existing religious organizations and an outlook stimulating the development of new sects.

A prominent fundamentalist group for a while was the Jesus People movement, which had its origins in the Haight-Ashbury area in San Francisco, the center of countercultural movements in the 1960s. The Jesus People rejected conventional religions as well as many existing social institutions. They saw their mission as that of redeeming the world from the state of inequity into which it had supposedly fallen. The cult derived its followers almost completely from young whites of affluent background. Before undergoing their religious conversion, many were involved in illegal drug use—over 90 percent (Harder et al., 1972; Richardson, Stewart, and Simmonds, 1979). The Jesus Movement has today largely disintegrated. Many ex-Jesus people gravitated towards more conventional fundamentalist churches, while others became members of groups such as the Children of God or the Alamo Foundation.

More influential fundamentalist groups are the Southern Baptist Convention, the Assemblies of God, and the Seventh-Day Adventists. Fundamentalism is a reaction against liberal theology and against attendance at church by people who do not really take much active interest in religion. The fundamentalist groups are mostly affiliated with the conservative political Right, and many have been active in the political sphere. One expression of this political activism is the Moral Majority, founded by the Reverend Jerry Falwell in 1980. The Moral Majority is nominally a political body, but gains its membership and financial resources from its association with fundamentalist religious organizations. The secular influence of the Moral Majority is considerable. Falwell claims to have recruited seventy-two thousand ministers and four million lay citizens to his cause, raising millions of dollars to intervene in political campaigns.

The political influence of the Moral Majority, and more generally of the fundamentalist "Religious Right," has probably often been exaggerated. These groups supported Ronald Reagan's 1980 and 1984 presidential campaigns, but Reagan's success really came from larger, nonreligious groups (such as alliances of business interests) pursuing broadly similar political ends, which were undoubtedly much more influential. In 1988, George Bush handily defeated fundamentalist preacher Pat Robertson in the Republican primaries before going on to win the presidency. Studies of these campaigns suggest that the Religious Right rode upon a wave of conservatism caused by other sources and events, rather than creating it. Religion was only one of several priorities among voters holding Rightist views (Demerath and Williams, 1989).

The "Electronic Church"

The electronic media (television and radio) have been centrally involved in changes affecting religion in the United States since the 1960s. The Reverend Billy Graham was the first to preach regularly to the nation across the airwaves, and through effective use of the media, he amassed a large following. Increasingly, over the last twenty years, we have seen even more sophisticated and systematic use of the media for spreading religious messages and raising money for ministries. The "electronic church"—religious organizations that operate primarily through the media, rather than depending upon local congregation meetings—has come into being. Through satellite communications, religious programs can now be beamed across the world into Third World countries (for example, to nations in Africa and Latin America) as well as to other industrialized societies.

Fundamentalist groups, and others seeking to convert nonbelievers, have been the main pioneers of the electronic church, particularly in the United States. While the reasons for this are complex, one factor is the "star system" which has long been a feature of such groups. Religious revivalism has frequently been led by inspirational preachers, who have drawn followers to themselves on the basis of their personal appeal. Some such preachers are ideally suited to the electronic media, by means of which these qualities can be projected to an audience of many thousands, or even millions, of people. Besides Billy Graham, other "electronic preachers" have made the media their main preoccupation, relying almost wholly on broadcasting to gain a following. Among them are Oral Roberts, Jerry Falwell, Jimmy Swaggart, Pat Robertson, and the married couple, Jim and Tammy Bakker.

While their individual preaching styles differ, as do the formats of their programs, they all concentrate upon providing a colorful and dramatic presentation of religious ideas. An example of their mode of religious broadcasting was Jim and Tammy Bakker's PTL (Praise the Lord) Club, a weekday program. The PTL Club was like a talk show, in which Jim and Tammy presided over a running discussion of their faith and their lives, interspersed with contributions from invited guests. Music was a major element of the program, provided by the gospel music of the "PTL Singers," visiting musicians, and the singing of Tammy Bakker herself. The program was strongly geared to fundraising efforts—so much so that some of its critics sarcastically accused it of being the "Pass the Loot Club." On the basis of the revenue they generated, the Bakkers built a huge vacation and entertainment complex geared to religious themes, including a miniature Holy Land. Jimmy and Tammy Bakker were forced to resign from PTL in 1987, following a series of sexual and financial scandals in which they were involved.

Other leading religious broadcasters, such as Jimmy Swaggart, have also been caught up in scandals that have seriously damaged their reputations. Because the standing of such individuals has suffered, some have suggested that the peak of the influence of the electronic church has passed. This may possibly be true for the dominant position achieved by revivalist and fundamentalist groups, but the broader connections between religious organizations and the electronic media are unlikely to come to an end. As we saw in the previous chapter, TV, radio, and other forms of electronic communication have a prime influence in the modern world, and this is bound to continue to stimulate religious programming.

SECULARIZATION

The vast majority of Americans hold religious beliefs of some sort, and in the United States, hundreds of sects and cults thrive alongside the established churches. In Iran and other areas of the Middle East, Africa, and India, a vital and dynamic Islamic fundamentalism challenges Westernization. In Northern Ireland, Protestants and Catholics keep alive a set of divided religious loyalties established for centuries, while the more activist members of each denomination engage in open warfare against one another. The pope tours South America, and millions of Catholics there enthusiastically follow his progress. In the face of all this, it might appear strange to suggest that the influence of religion in the modern world is declining.

However, sociologists generally agree that such a decline has taken place, considered as a long-term trend. Until the modern period, the churches rivalled, and frequently surpassed, monarchs and governments in the political power they wielded and the wealth they managed to accumulate. The priesthood maintained a monopoly control over the skills of literacy, scholarship, and learning. Even when education became more widespread, the churches continued for a long while to have the leading role in its organization. As in so many other

While there is a greater worldwide trend toward secularization, Pope John Paul II has been met by great crowds on his trips. Here, he celebrates Mass in South Korea in 1989.

areas of social life, much of this changed as industrialization took hold. Churches and religious organizations in Western countries lost most of the secular power they formerly had. Governments took over most of the tasks that the churches had previously controlled, including education.

Scientific thought and technology increasingly challenged religion and magic as ways of understanding and coping with the world. In medieval times, many people in Europe believed not only in Christian ideas, but in ghosts, spirits, witches, and demons (Camporesi, 1988). The more science provided physical explanations, the less the world was seen to be governed by spiritual beings or ghostly entities. In the Middle Ages, mystical experiences had been commonplace among the general population. Joan of Arc was not unusual, for example, in claiming to have heard the voices of angels instructing her to save France from the marauding English. Three centuries later, not only was it rare for anyone to claim to experience mystical states, but these very same experiences came to be regarded as symptoms of mental disorder if anyone admitted to them.

Towards the end of the nineteenth century, the German philosopher Friedrich Nietzsche announced, "God is dead!" Religions, he argued, used to be a point of reference for our sense of purpose and meaning. Henceforth, we would have to live without this security, Nietzsche asserted, and indeed without any fixed moral reference points at all. Living in a world without God would mean creating our own values and getting used to what Nietzsche called "the loneliness of being"—understanding that our lives were without purpose and that no superior entities watched over our fate.

Secularization is the process whereby religion loses its influence over the various spheres of social life. It is a complex phenomenon, with a number of dimensions. One concerns the *level of membership* of religious organizations—how many people belong to a church or other religious body and are active in attending services or other ceremonials. Using this index, the United States, and Western European countries, including Catholic countries such as France and Italy, have all experienced considerable secularization over the past century. More Italians than French attend church regularly and participate in the major rituals (such as Easter communion), but the overall pattern of declining religious observance is similar in both cases (Acquaviva, 1979).

A second dimension of secularization concerns how far churches and other religious organizations *maintain their social influence, wealth, and prestige.* In earlier times, as we saw, religious organizations usually wielded considerable influence over governments and social agencies, and commanded high respect in the community. To what extent is this still the case? The answer to the question is clear. Even if we only confine ourselves to the present century, religious organizations have progressively lost much of the social and political influence they previously had. The trend is worldwide. With some notable exceptions (such as in Iran), church leaders can no longer automatically expect to influence the powerful. Although some established churches remain very wealthy by any standards, and new religious movements may rapidly build up fortunes, the material circumstances of many established religious organizations are insecure. Churches and temples have to be sold off or are in a state of disrepair.

The third dimension of secularization concerns beliefs and values. We can call this the dimension of *religiosity*. Levels of churchgoing and the degree of social influence of churches are obviously not necessarily a direct expression of the beliefs or ideals that people hold. Many who have religious beliefs do not regularly attend services or take part in public ceremonials. On the other hand, regularity of such attendance or participation does not always mean that people hold strong religious views—people may attend services or ceremonies out of habit or because it is expected of them in their community.

As with the other dimensions of secularization, we must have an accurate understanding of the past to see how far religiosity has declined today. In many traditional societies, including medieval Europe, commitment to a religious belief was less strong, and less important in day-to-day life, than might be supposed. Research into English history, for example, shows that a lukewarm commitment to

TABLE 14.1
WHO ATTENDS RELIGIOUS SERVICES REGULARLY, 1987 (in percentages)

United States	54
Italy	45
Austria	39
W. Germany	29
Netherlands	28
Australia	25
Britain	20
Hungary*	7

* Hungary data, 1986
Source: Davis and Jowell, 1989.

The appeal of religion stretches far back in human history. Here, Egyptian papyrus records the god Osiris sitting in judgment on a princess over four thousand years ago.

religious beliefs was common among the ordinary people (Thomas, 1986). Religious skeptics could be found in most cultures, particularly in the larger traditional societies (Ginzburg, 1982).

Yet there can be little doubt that the hold of religious beliefs today is less than was generally the case in the traditional world—particularly if we include under the term "religion" the whole range of supernatural phenomena in which people believed. Most of us do not any longer experience our environment as permeated by spirits and demons. Some of the major tensions in the world today—like those that afflict Israel and neighboring Arab states—derive primarily, or in some part, from religious differences, but the majority of conflicts and wars are now mainly secular in nature—concerned with divergent political creeds or economic interests.

The influence of religion has diminished along each of the three dimensions of secularization. Should we conclude that the nineteenth-century authors were correct after all? Perhaps the death pangs of religion have merely been more long-drawn-out than they anticipated? Such a conclusion would certainly be misleading. The appeal of religion, in its traditional forms, as well as in novel forms of religious expression, is likely to be long enduring. Modern rationalist thought and a religious outlook exist in an uneasy state of tension. A rationalist perspective has conquered large aspects of our existence, and its hold in all probability will not become weakened in the fore-seeable future. Yet there are bound to be reactions against rationalism, leading to periods of religious revivalism. There are probably few individuals on the face of the earth who have not been touched by religious sentiments at some time in their lives. Science and rationalist thought remain silent on questions of the meaning and purpose of life, matters that have always been at the core of religion.

SUMMARY

1. There are no known societies that do not have some form of religion, although religious beliefs and practices vary from culture to culture. All religions involve a set of *symbols,* invoking feelings of reverence, linked to *rituals* practiced by a community of believers.

2. *Totemism* and *animism* are common types of religion in smaller cultures. In totemism, a species of animal or plant is perceived as possessing supernatural powers. Animism means a belief in spirits or ghosts, populating the same world as human beings, sometimes "possessing" them.

3. The three most influential *monotheistic* religions (religions in which there is one God) in world history are Judaism, Christianity, and Islam. *Polytheism* (belief in several or many gods) is common in other religions. In some religions, like Buddhism and Confucianism, there are no gods or supernatural beings.

4. Sociological approaches to religion have been most influenced by the ideas of the three "classical" thinkers: Marx, Durkheim, and Weber. All believed that religion is fundamentally an illusion. They held that the "other" world which religion creates is *our* world, distorted through the lens of religious symbolism.

5. Several different types of religious organization can be distinguished. A *church* is a large, established religious body, having a bureaucratic structure. *Sects* are small, and aim at restoring the original purity of doctrines that have become "corrupted" in the hands of official churches. A *denomination* is a sect that has become institutionalized, having a permanent form. A *cult* is a loosely-knit group of people who follow the same leader or pursue similar religious ideals.

6. *Religious movements* have played a central part in the development of religion in general, as well as influencing other aspects

of social life. *Millenarian movements,* which anticipate the coming of the "millenium," or "golden age," have been an important feature of the history of Christianity.

7. Religious organizations are generally dominated by men. In most religions, particularly Christianity, the images and symbols are mostly masculine; female imagery stresses gentleness and passivity.

8. Secularization refers to the declining influence of religion. Measuring the level of secularization is complicated, because several dimensions of change are involved. Although the influence of religion has definitely declined, religion is certainly not on the verge of disappearing, and continues to show great diversity in the modern world. Religion can act as both a conservative and revolutionary force in society.

BASIC CONCEPTS

RELIGION

RITUAL

MAGIC

SECULARIZATION

IMPORTANT TERMS

MONOTHEISM   PROFANE

SHAMAN   CIVIL RELIGION

TOTEMISM   CHURCH

ANIMISM   SECT

POLYTHEISM   DENOMINATION

PROPHETS   CULT

ETHICAL RELIGIONS   RELIGIOUS MOVEMENT

ALIENATION   MILLENARIAN MOVEMENTS

SACRED   FUNDAMENTALISM

WORK AND ECONOMIC LIFE

ALL HUMAN BEINGS DEPEND UPON SYSTEMS OF PRODUCTION for their existence. We could not survive were it not for the provision of regular sources of food, drink, and shelter. Even in societies where no food is cultivated—the hunting and gathering cultures—there are systematic arrangements for the regular supply and distribution of necessary material resources. For most people in all societies, productive activity, or work, occupies a larger part of their lives than any other single type of behavior. In modern societies, we are used to people working in a large variety of occupations, but this has only come about with industrial development. The majority of the population in traditional cultures were engaged in one main pursuit—food-gathering or food production. Various crafts, such as carpentry, stonemasonry, or shipbuilding, were practiced in the larger traditional societies, but only a small minority of the population engaged in them as a full-time endeavor.

Work may be defined as the carrying out of tasks, which involves the expenditure of mental and physical effort, and has as its objective the production of goods and services that cater to human needs. An **occupation** or *job* is work that is done in exchange for a regular wage or salary. In all cultures work is the basis of the *economic system* or

Detroit Industry, *by Diego Rivera*

economy. The economic system consists of those institutions that provide for the production and distribution of goods and services.

The study of economic institutions is of major importance in sociology, because the economy influences all segments of society and therefore social reproduction in general. Hunting and gathering, pastoralism, agriculture, industrialism—these different ways of gaining a livelihood have a fundamental influence upon the lives people lead. The distribution of goods, and variations in the economic position of those who produce them, also strongly influence social inequalities of all kinds. Wealth and power do not inevitably go together, but in general the privileged in terms of wealth are also among the more powerful groups in a society.

In this chapter, we shall analyze the nature of work in modern societies, and discuss the major changes affecting the economic order today. We shall investigate the origins of industrial conflict, the ownership structure of the large business corporations and the importance of informal economic relationships. We will also take up some of the most significant issues affecting work in current times: the problem of unemployment and the possibility that work may be becoming less central to social life than was the case in the past.

To tackle these problems, we have to relate work to the broad contours of the economic system and to industrial organization as a whole. We quite often associate the notion of "work" with drudgery —with a set of tasks that we want to minimize and, if possible, escape from altogether. You may have this very thought in mind as you set out to read this chapter! Do most people have such an attitude towards their work and, if so, why? This is a question we shall try to answer in the following pages. Work has more going for it than the above view suggests or people would not feel so "lost" and disoriented—as many do—when they become unemployed. Yet work has had its critics, and many have felt that a general reduction in work tasks is the key to satisfying human existence.

A major focus of this chapter will be on the relation between paid employment and other forms of work. Neither work nor the economy can be adequately understood as concerning only the area of paid employment. While most members of the population engage in paid work at some point in their lives, paid employment is by no means the only way in which people gain the resources necessary for their lives. Children, many married women, retired people in their sixties or older (now a very large slice of the population, see Chapter 18: "Population, Health, and Aging"), and the unemployed, are outside the paid-labor force. Yet much of what they do certainly counts as work and contributes substantially to the overall economic system. Children work in school developing skills and acquiring knowledge that will be crucial to the economic order in the future. Married women who are not in paid employment work as housewives—as do the vast majority, in fact, of those women who also hold down paid jobs. Retired older people work at housework or the maintenance of the home, in charity organizations, local clubs, and other spheres. Many people who are unemployed are so only on a temporary basis, and many also spend much of their time when out of a job doing unpaid work about the home. While we will not study all these groups in this chapter, we shall give considerable space to showing how paid employment and other forms of work interrelate.

First, however, we look at the formal economic system—the world of paid employment—taking up broader questions of the nature of work later. We start by considering some of the factors influencing the character of the work tasks involved in modern industrial production.

THE DIVISION OF LABOR AND ECONOMIC DEPENDENCE

ONE OF THE MOST DISTINCTIVE CHARACTERISTICS OF THE economic system of modern societies is the development of a highly complex **division of labor:** work has become divided into an enormous number of different occupations in which people specialize. In traditional societies, nonagricultural work entailed the mastery of a craft. Craft skills were learned through a lengthy period of apprenticeship, and the worker normally carried out all aspects of the production process from beginning to end. For example, a metalworker making a plough would forge the iron, shape it, and assemble the implement itself. With the rise of modern industrial production, most traditional crafts have disappeared altogether. They have been replaced by skills that form part of more large-scale production processes. An electrician working in an industrial setting today, for instance, may inspect and repair only a few parts of one type of machine; different people will deal with the other jobs and other machines.

The contrast in the division of labor between traditional and modern societies is truly extraordinary. Even in the largest traditional societies, there usually existed no more than twenty or thirty major craft trades, together with a few other specialized pursuits, such as those of merchant, soldier, or priest. In a modern industrial system, there are literally many thousands of distinct occupations. The U.S. Census Bureau lists some twenty thousand distinct jobs in the American economy. In traditional communities, most of the population worked in farming and were economically self-sufficient. They produced their food, clothes, and other necessities of life for themselves. One of the main features of modern societies, by contrast, is an enormous expansion of **economic interdependence.** All of us are dependent upon an immense number of other workers for the products and services involved in sustaining our lives. With few exceptions, the vast majority of people in modern societies do not produce the food they eat, the dwellings in which they live, or the material goods they consume.

Industrialization radically changed the nature of work and material production. Compare the Medieval weaver with the large 1848 German textile-manufacturing facility.

PRIMARY, SECONDARY, AND TERTIARY SECTORS

To make comparisons and examine contrasts between societies in different stages of industrial development, it is useful to divide occupations into three sectors. The proportion of the labor force within each of these sectors tends to vary at different stages of industrialization. The primary industries are those involving the collection or extraction of natural resources. Thus the **primary sector** of an economy includes agriculture, mining, forestry, and fishing, among other industries. Most workers in a society in the first phases of industrial development are to be found in the primary sector. With the increasing use of machinery and the construction of factories, a larger proportion of workers are drawn into the **secondary sector:** industries that convert raw materials into manufactured goods. The **tertiary sector** refers to **service industries**—occupations that offer services to others instead of directly producing goods. Medicine, teaching, managerial, and clerical jobs are examples of types of work usually included as service occupations.

Although it is a crude indicator, the distinction between primary, secondary, and tertiary sectors allows us to draw illuminating contrasts between different types of society. In most Third World countries, some three-quarters of the workforce is engaged in agriculture, with the remainder distributed about equally between manufacture and services. In the industrialized countries, on the other hand, only a tiny proportion of the population is engaged in agricultural production. Less than 2 percent of the American labor force now works in agriculture—as compared to almost 70 percent in 1840. A major trend within the industrialized societies is the expansion of the service sector. In 1840, 15 percent of the labor force in the United States worked in the secondary sector and 16 percent in the tertiary sector. By 1950, the tertiary sector had grown to equal the size of the other two sectors combined. Today, just over two-thirds of the labor force works in the tertiary sector.

INDUSTRIAL DIVISION OF LABOR: TAYLORISM AND FORDISM

Writing in the late 1700s, Adam Smith, one of the founders of modern economics, identified various advantages that the division of labor provides in terms of increasing productivity. His most famous work, *The Wealth of Nations,* opens with a description of the division of labor in a pin factory. A person working alone could perhaps make 20 pins per day. By breaking down that worker's task into a number of simple operations, however, ten workers carrying out specialized jobs in collaboration with one another could collectively produce 48,000 pins per day. The rate of production per worker, in other words, is increased from 20 to 4,800 pins, each specialist operator producing 240 times more than when working alone (Smith, 1982).

Charles Babbage (who also invented an early form of computer) subsequently extended Smith's analysis further (Babbage, 1986; orig. pub. 1835). According to the "Babbage Principle," technological progress can be measured by the degree to which the tasks of each worker are simplified and integrated with those of other workers. This process reduces the price employers have to pay for hiring workers, and the time needed to learn each job, as well as weakening the workers' bargaining power, thus keeping wage costs down.

Sixty years later, these ideas reached their most developed expression in the writings of Frederick Winslow Taylor, an American management consultant (Braverman, 1974). Taylor's approach to what he called *scientific management* involved the detailed study of industrial processes in order to break them down into simple operations that could be precisely timed and organized. **Taylorism,** as scientific management came to be called, was not merely an academic study. It was a system of production designed to maximize industrial output. Taylorism had a widespread impact upon the organization of industrial production and technology in many countries, although its influence varied. Japan in particular was resistant, and Japanese industrialization took a substantially different path from that of most Western societies, emphasizing the use of work teams, lacking precise job divisions, and offering considerable job flexibility.

Taylor was concerned with improving industrial efficiency, but gave little consideration to the results of that efficiency. Mass production demands mass markets, and the industrialist Henry Ford was among the first to see this link. **Fordism** is the name used to designate the system of mass production tied to the cultivation of mass markets (Hounshell, 1984). It extended Taylor's principles of scientific management to mass production. Ford designed his first plant at Highland Park, Michigan, in 1908, to manufacture only one product —the Model T Ford—thereby allowing the introduction of specialized tools and machinery designed for speed, precision, and simplicity of operation (Sabel, 1982). One of Ford's most significant innovations was the construction of a moving assembly line—said to have been inspired by Chicago slaughterhouses, in which animals were "disassembled" section by section on a moving line. Each worker on Ford's assembly line had a specialized task, such as fitting the leftside door handles, as the car bodies moved along the line. By 1929, when production of the Model T ceased, over fifteen million cars had been made.

A 1913 Ford Motor Company assembly line. Compare with 1990s robotic assembly line on p. 603.

Work on the Assembly Line

Having seemingly maximized productive efficiency, Ford began to discover problems with assembly-line production. Rates of absenteeism and labor turnover soon became extremely high. According to the head of Ford's personnel department, it cost only $38 to train a new worker in 1913, so simple and routine were the tasks required on the assembly line. Yet, because the annual turnover was more than fifty thousand workers, the total cost of training amounted to $2 million per year (Meyr, 1981). Ford sought to develop worker discipline by extending his influence outside the factory gates. His "five dollar day" offered workers wage incentives for changing their personal as well as their work habits. Bonuses, and possibilities of obtaining company loans, depended upon employees leading exemplary private lives, with alcohol and tobacco consumption being frowned upon. The company even set up its own "Sociological Department" to investigate and report upon workers' private lives.

Fordism—manufacture carried on in large plants, producing for mass markets using assembly-line processes—became central to the automobile industry worldwide and was adopted in other industrial settings. The Ford Motor Company and its main competitor, General Motors, set up subsidiary companies in Britain, Germany, Japan, and other countries. Citroen, in France, set up assembly-line production as early as 1919 and hired American engineers to act as advisers. It was followed in France by Renault, by Fiat in Italy and later by Austin-Morris in England.

A vivid picture of work on the assembly line is provided by an employee in a Citroen factory in the 1970s:

> " . . . each man has a well-defined area for the operations he has to make, although the boundaries are invisible: as soon as a car enters a man's territory, he takes down his blowtorch, grabs his soldering iron, takes his hammer or his file, and gets to work. A few knocks, a few sparks, then the soldering is done and the car's already on its way out of the 3 or 4 yards of this position. And the next car's already coming into the work area. And the worker starts again. Sometimes, if he's been working fast, he has a few seconds respite before a new car arrives: either he takes advantage of it to breathe for a moment, or else he intensifies his effort and 'goes up the line' so that he can gain a little time . . . if, on the other hand, the worker's too slow, he 'slips back,' that is he finds himself progressively beyond his position, going on with his work when the next laborer has already begun his. Then he has to push on fast, trying to catch up. And the slow gliding of the cars, which seems to me so near to not moving at all, looks as relentless as a rushing torrent which you can't manage to dam up . . . sometimes it's as ghastly as drowning." (Quoted in Linhart, 1981)

The Limitations of Fordism and Taylorism

At one time it looked as though Fordism represented the likely future of industrial production as a whole. This proved not to be the case. Fordism became prominent only in a few industrial sectors—most notably, the car industry itself (Sabel, 1982). The system can only be applied in industries producing standardized products for large markets; to set up mechanized production lines is enormously expensive. Once a Fordist system is established, it is quite rigid—to alter a product, for example, substantial reinvestment would be needed. Fordist production is easy to copy, if sufficient funding is available to set up the plant. Firms in countries in which labor power is expensive find it difficult to compete with those where wages are cheaper. This was one of the factors originally leading to the rise of the Japanese car industry (although Japanese wage levels today are no longer low) and, more recently, that of South Korea.

Taylorist techniques of management, as compared to Fordism, do not necessarily involve expensive capital investment. The limitations of Taylorism are due more to the fact that human beings are not like machines, and resent being treated as though they were. Where jobs are subdivided into monotonous tasks, they offer little scope for the creative involvement of the worker (Salaman, 1986). In such circumstances, it is difficult to motivate workers to do more than the bare minimum necessary to get by, and levels of job dissatisfaction are high (Wood, 1984). In its extreme form as promoted by Taylor, "scientific management" did not have a wide influence. But some of the features of modern industry to which Taylor drew attention—especially the need to break down jobs into simple, routine activities—have become very widespread. To some degree Taylorism simply tried to accentuate characteristics of the division of labor that the mechanization of production widely developed.

WORK AND ALIENATION

KARL MARX WAS ONE OF THE FIRST WRITERS TO GRASP THAT the development of modern industry would reduce many people's work to dull, uninteresting tasks. According to Marx, the division of labor *alienates* human beings from their work. In traditional societies, he pointed out, work was often exhausting—peasant farmers sometimes had to toil from dawn to dusk, caring for their fields. Yet peasants held a real measure of control over their work, which involved many forms of knowledge and skill. Many industrial workers, by contrast, have little control over the nature of the job task, only contribute a fraction to the creation of the overall product, and have no influence over how or to whom it is eventually sold. Work thus appears as something *alien,* a task that the worker must carry out in order to obtain an income, but which is intrinsically unsatisfying.

Marx saw a major paradox at the heart of modern societies. On the one hand, the development of industry had generated enormous wealth, far greater than was found in any preceding type of society. But large numbers of those whose labor was the very source of this wealth were denied any effective control over the work they did. Marx described this phenomenon in graphic terms:

> What constitutes the alienation of labor? First, that work is *external* to the worker, that it is not part of his nature; and that, consequently, he does not fulfill himself in his work

but denies himself, has a feeling of misery rather than well-being, does not develop freely his mental and physical energies but is physically exhausted and mentally debased. The worker, therefore, feels himself at home only during his leisure time, whereas at work he feels homeless. His work is not voluntary but imposed, *forced labor.* It is not the satisfaction of a need, but only a *means* for satisfying other needs. Its alien character is clearly shown by the fact that as soon as there is no physical or other compulsion it is avoided like the plague. . . . We arrive at the result that man (the worker) feels himself to be freely active only in his animal functions —eating, drinking and procreating, or at most also in his dwelling and personal adornment—while in his human functions he is reduced to an animal. The animal becomes human and the human becomes animal! (Marx, 1963)

For Marx, **alienation** refers not only to feelings of indifference or hostility to work, but to the overall framework of industrial production within a capitalist setting. In Marx's view, alienation expresses the material lack of control workers have over the settings of their labor. Many studies have documented how common such a situation is in the modern workplace. An example is a report produced by the United States Department of Health, Education and Welfare, entitled *Work in America* (1973). Unlike most official reports, this study attracted major public attention and became a bestseller. The investigation found that many work settings involved "dull, repetitive, seemingly meaningless tasks, offering little challenge or autonomy," thereby "causing discontent among workers at all occupational levels."

Blue-collar workers in particular, the report concluded, feel they have little control over their working conditions and are denied the possibility of influencing decisions about their jobs. Their work schedules tend to be fixed and they are subject to close and continuous supervision. Only 24 percent of blue-collar workers studied said they would choose the same kind of job if they could have their lives over again. Almost twice as many white-collar workers said they would do so. However, levels of dissatisfaction with work were high among those in white-collar jobs also. People in lower-level office work found their jobs routine and boring and provided little scope for initiative. Many working in middle management similarly expressed dissatisfaction with their work, feeling that they were required to put policies into practice that they had had no say in. Those in higher positions were more likely to be satisfied with their work, considering themselves to have a measure of independence, challenge, and variety.

LOW-TRUST SYSTEMS AND HIGH-TRUST SYSTEMS

Fordism and Taylorism—systems of production that maximize worker alienation—are what some industrial sociologists call **low-trust systems** (Fox, 1974). Jobs are set by management and are geared to machines. Those who carry out the work tasks are closely supervised and are allowed little autonomy of action. A **high-trust system** is one in which workers are permitted to control the pace, and even the content, of their work, within overall guidelines. Such systems are usually concentrated at the higher levels of industrial organizations. Where there are many low-trust positions, the level of worker alienation is high, industrial conflict common, and rates of absenteeism often acute.

From the early 1970s onwards, firms in various industries in Western Europe, the United States, and Japan have experimented with alternatives to low-trust organizations. These include, among other programs, the automation of assembly lines, eliminating some of the more routine work previously done by human operators; and the introduction of group production, in which the work group has a recognized role in influencing the nature of the work task. Although they have rarely found favor among employers, there have also been some notable attempts to establish systems of industrial democracy (Kelly, 1982). We shall look at these various strategies in turn.

AUTOMATION

Automation has thus far affected relatively few industries, but with advances in the design of industrial robots, its impact is certain to become greater (P. Marsh, 1982; Large, 1984). A robot is an automatic device that can perform functions ordinarily done by human workers.

The term "robot" came from the Czech word *robota,* or serf, popularized about fifty years ago by the playwright Karel Capek. The concept of programmable machinery goes back much further. Christopher Spencer, an American, invented the Automat, a programmable lathe that made screws, nuts, and gears, in the mid-1800s. Robots were first introduced into industry in some numbers in 1946, when a device was invented to automatically regulate machinery in some simple areas of production technology in the engineering industry.

Robots of greater complexity, however, date only from the development of microprocessors—basically since the 1970s. The first robot controlled by a mini-computer was developed in 1974 by

Robotic-based Chrysler Corporation assembly line for producing the K–car.

Cincinnati Milason. Robots today can execute numerous tasks like welding, spray-painting, lifting and carrying parts, and have microprocessors for their "brains." Some robots can distinguish parts by "feel" or touch, while others can "see" by distinguishing a certain range of objects visually.

As Robert Ayres and Steven Miller have pointed out,

> There can be no more dedicated and untiring factory worker than a robot. Robots can repeat tasks such as spot-welding and spray-painting flawlessly on a variety of workpieces, and they can quickly be reprogrammed to perform entirely new tasks. . . . In the next few years, we can expect to see many industrial robots installed in medium-batch manufacturing plants. Robots will feed workpieces to clusters of automatic machines in "workcells," which may be serialized to form a "closed loop" manufacturing system controlled by micro-processors. (Ayres and Miller, 1985)

These manufacturing systems may form the factories of the future. Precursors of such systems have already been built in the United States and Japan. The main stage on the way to the completely auto-mated factory is the Flexible Manufacturing System (FMS). This system consists of a computer-controlled machining center which sculpts metal parts at high speed, robots that handle these parts, and remotely guided carts that transport materials to and from the site of production. FMSs can be instantly reprogrammed to make new parts or entire products. They are able to manufacture goods cheaply in small volumes and different products can be made on the same line. The implications are far-reaching. In Fordist production, a massive schedule is necessary for efficient production. But flexible manufacturing systems can turn out a small batch of goods as efficiently as an assembly line designed to turn out a million identical items.

FMSs are at the moment most advanced in Japan. In the Japanese plants, skeleton crews work with the machines during the day, while at night the robots and machines work alone. In the factory of Fanuc Inc., near Mount Fuji, automatic machining centers and robots toil through the night, the unmanned delivery carts rolling quietly through the semi-darkness, which is relieved only by the subdued flashing of blue warning lights. At night a single controller super-vises the whole operation, watching the machinery on closed-circuit television. If anything goes wrong, the supervisor can close down part of the operation and reroute production around it. A new factory is planned by Yamazaki, which will be operated by remote control from the firm's headquarters twenty miles away. The work done in the factory (making machine tools) will be fully programmed from the headquarters. The plant will have 200 workers, producing as many goods as 2,500 would be able to do in a conventional factory (Ayres and Miller, 1983).

The majority of the robots used in industry worldwide are to be found in automobile manufacture. In spite of the imminent arrival of automated factories, the usefulness of robots in production thus far is relatively limited, because their capacity to recognize different objects and manipulate awkward shapes is still at a fairly rudimentary level. Yet it is virtually certain that automated production will spread rapidly in forthcoming years. The sophistication of robots is fast increasing, while their costs decrease.

GROUP PRODUCTION

Group production—abandoning the assembly line and establishing collaborative work groups—has sometimes been used in conjunction with automation as a way of reorganizing work. The underlying idea is to increase worker motivation by letting groups of workers collaborate in production processes rather than each worker spending the whole day doing a single repetitive task—such as putting the screws in the door-handle of a car. An example is the experiment set up by Volkswagen in one of its engine plants in West Germany in 1975. Car engines are usually built on an assembly line, and each worker has about one or two minutes to complete a standard task. Volkswagen instead set up four groups of seven workers, whose tasks were separated from the machine-based line. Within each group, four worked on assembly, two worked on testing, while one individual was placed in charge of supplying materials. The group had to meet a quota of making seven engines per day. The members of each group were trained so that they could carry out all of the team jobs, and were allowed to rotate job assignments as they wanted. Although the groups met their quotas, levels of production were not high enough to satisfy the Volkswagen management and in 1978 they ended the experiment.

A comparable innovation is that of so-called *quality circles* (QCs). These are groups of between five to twenty workers, which meet regularly to study and resolve production problems. Workers who belong to QCs receive extra training enabling them to contribute technical assistance to the discussion of production issues. QCs were initiated in the United States, taken up by a number of Japanese companies, then re-popularized in the West in the late 1970s.

The system of quality circles represents a break from the assumptions underlying Taylorism, since it recognizes that workers have the expertise to contribute towards the definition and method of the tasks they carry out. In 1980, the Ford Corporation, under the stimulus of Japanese competition, decided to set up the system in all of its twenty-five manufacturing and assembly plants in Western Europe. The object of the program was to improve the quality and reliability of its products, together with encouraging worker involvement.

INDUSTRIAL DEMOCRACY

The idea of **industrial democracy** is more long established than these recent schemes. Marx pointed out in the nineteenth century that the rights of political participation enjoyed by the citizenry stopped short at the gates of the workplace. Political democracy, he suggested, should be complemented by the introduction of democratic rights within industry. These claims have been taken seriously by the national governments of some countries and by the founders of cooperative firms in certain sectors of industry. Workers' self-management is built into Yugoslavian industry, with workers having the right to elect directors and have a say in personnel policies. According to Swedish law, workers must be represented on the boards of directors of companies having more than a hundred employees. Worker directors also exist in West Germany and Norway.

Good evidence exists to show that organizations where workers have some influence over decisionmaking have high morale and a good productivity record. In an early analysis of seventeen experiments with systems of industrial democracy, Paul Blumberg concluded that:

> There is hardly a study in the entire literature which fails to demonstrate that satisfaction in work is enhanced or that other generally acknowledged beneficial consequences accrue from a genuine increase in workers' decision-making power. Such consistency of findings, I submit, is rare in social research. (Blumberg, 1968)

Blumberg's findings have been criticized because the cases he discussed were mostly short-lived, lasting only some two or three years. But subsequent research supports Blumberg's conclusions. A study of plywood cooperatives in the Pacific Northwest of the United States showed that firms having a cooperative system were 30–50 percent more efficient than orthodox companies of similar size in the same industry (Berman, 1982).

Cooperative organizations, in which workers have a range of powers usually held by management, are to be found in several Western European countries as well as in the United States. For example, the Mondragon cooperatives, in the Basque country of northern Spain, have achieved a high degree of economic success in the manufacture of various consumer goods. Yet there is often resistance to the extension of industrial democracy by both management and unions. Managers are loath to give decision-making powers within their own command to workers, while unions sometimes see industrial democracy as eroding their rights of collective bargaining (Thornley, 1981).

The development of industrial democracy has been seen as a means of overcoming the tensions or conflicts to which industry is frequently subject. Although many conflicts are local and fragmentary, involving for instance, a brief stoppage of work by employees who have a minor grievance, others are much more major. A strike that receives union backing may bring a whole sector of industry to a stop. In some cases, a "national strike" may be called, designed to cause complete economic disruption in a country.

In the next sections, we discuss the development of labor unions and their current position, following with an analysis of the nature of strikes, which concern mainly lower-level workers. We then move on to consider those at the top in the economic system: the owners and managers of business firms.

LABOR UNIONS AND INDUSTRIAL CONFLICT

THERE HAVE LONG BEEN CONFLICTS BETWEEN WORKERS and those in economic and political authority over them. Riots against conscription and high taxes, and food riots at periods of harvest failure, were common in urban areas of Europe in the eighteenth century. These "premodern" forms of labor conflict continued up to not much more than a century ago in some countries. For example, there were food riots in several large Italian towns in 1868 (Geary, 1981). Such traditional forms of confrontation were not just sporadic, irrational outbursts of violence: the threat or use of violence had the effect of limiting the price of grain and other essential foodstuffs (Rudé, 1964; Thompson, 1971; Booth, 1977).

THE DEVELOPMENT OF UNIONS

Industrial conflict between workers and employers first of all tended to follow these older patterns. In situations of confrontation, workers would quite often leave their places of employment and form crowds in the streets; they would make their grievances known through their unruly behavior or by engaging in acts of violence against the authorities. Workers in some parts of France in the late nineteenth century would threaten disliked employers with hanging (Holton, 1978).

Use of the *strike* as a weapon, today commonly associated with organized bargaining between workers and management, developed only slowly and sporadically.

Most early strikes were spontaneous, in the sense that they were not called by any specific organizations of workers. A report by the U.S. Commissioner of Labor in 1907 showed that somewhere near half of all strikes at the time were not initiated by unions (Ross, 1954). This situation changed by the end of the First World War, and since then, the proportion of strikes occurring among non-unionized workers has become small.

One of the most important early labor organizations in the United States was the Knights of Labor (founded 1869), a body with a chequered career. Initially involved in organizing local strike actions, its membership by 1886 had grown to seven hundred thousand. Later, its leaders turned against the strike as a medium of industrial conflict, and its membership dwindled away. Unions wishing to lead the labor movement without the use of the strike have not survived —although, of course, some unions have been much more reluctant than others to call workers out on strike.

Unions tended to develop first among skilled or craft workers. The American Federation of Labor (AFL) was established in 1886 as an alliance of craft unions. The AFL became the central organization of the American labor movement, but its coordinating role was challenged on a number of occasions. For instance, in the early 1900s it was in conflict with the Industrial Workers of the World (IWW), a far more militant organization that had strong revolutionary leanings. However, the IWW largely disintegrated some twenty years later, and the moderate AFL retained its prime position. A body known as the Committee (later, Congress) for Industrial Organization (CIO) split away from the AFL in the 1930s, subsequently acquiring about as many members as the original association. After some years of division, the two organizations reunited in 1955, as the AFL-CIO. This body, however, does not represent all unions in the United States; the two largest unions in the country, the International Brotherhood of Teamsters and the United Automobile Workers, are not members.

Like the United States, unions in England are more long established than in other European societies. The British trade-union movement was coordinated by a central body that was founded in 1868, the Trades Union Congress (TUC), which has since developed strong links with the Labor Party. In contrast, the German unions were largely destroyed by the Nazis in the 1930s and had to be reestablished following the Second World War. The main development of the French union movement did not occur until the 1930s, when the freedom to organize unions and negotiate collective labor contracts was formally recognized by the government.

Levels of union membership differ considerably among Western societies. Today, only 20 percent of the labor force in the United States are union members, compared to just below 50 percent in Britain. Other European countries are below the British figure, but Belgium and Denmark have rates of union membership of around 65 percent, while in Sweden it is as high as 90 percent. Sweden is an example of a country in which the labor movement plays a major and direct part in influencing governmental policies. In that country, there is continuous consultation between union representatives, employers, and the government on a national basis.

WHY DO LABOR UNIONS EXIST?

Although their levels of membership, and the extent of their power, vary widely, union organizations exist in all Western countries, which also all legally recognize the right of workers to strike in pursuit of economic objectives. Why have unions become a basic feature of Western societies? Why does union-management conflict seem to be a more or less ever-present possibility in industrial settings?

Some have proposed that unions are effectively a modern version of medieval guilds—associations of people working in the same trade—reassembled in the context of modern industry. Thus, Frank Tannenbaum has suggested that unions are associations built upon the shared outlook and experience of those working in similar jobs (Tannenbaum, 1964). This interpretation might help us understand why unions often emerged first among craft workers, but does not explain why they have been so consistently associated with wage bargaining and industrial conflict. A more satisfactory explanation must look to the fact that unions developed to protect the material interests of workers in industrial settings in which they hold very little formal power.

TABLE 15.1	LABOR UNION MEMBERSHIP, 1988			
	Austria	West Germany	U.K.	USA
		(percentages)		
All	52	32	47	17
Men	58	39	51	21
Women	40	20	41	12
In manual occupations	61	44	53	28
In non-manual occupations	45	27	42	12

Hungarian data are for 1986.
Source: Blanchflower and Oswald, 1989.

In the early development of modern industry, workers in most countries were both without political rights and had little influence over the conditions of work in which they found themselves. Unions developed as a means of redressing the imbalance of power between workers and employers. Whereas workers had virtually no power as individuals, through collective organization their influence was considerably increased. An employer can do without the labor of any particular worker, but not without that of all or most of the workers in a factory or plant. Unions originally were mainly "defensive" organizations, providing the means whereby workers could counter the overwhelming power that employers wielded over their lives.

Workers today have voting rights in the political sphere, and there are established forms of negotiation with employers, by means of which economic benefits can be pressed for and grievances expressed. However, union influence, both at the level of the local plant and nationally, still remains primarily *veto power.* In other words, using the resources at their disposal, including the right to strike, unions can only *block* policies or initiatives of employers, not help formulate them in the first place. There are exceptions to this, as in instances where unions and employers negotiate periodic contracts covering conditions of work. An increasing tendency is for these negotiations to include "no-strike" agreements for the duration of the contract. Nationally—especially in the Scandinavian countries—union officials may have a significant role in formulating a country's economic policies.

Yet unions in many countries have had to face a constant battering from hostile employers and governments. The bargaining rights that industrial workers hold have been won against bitter opposition, and once achieved have frequently been subjected to further attacks. Employers in some industries have consistently refused to employ union members or allow company union branches to be established. The employers' resistance to the unions has been especially pronounced in the United States—one factor in the low union membership in the country. For instance, in the 1920s and 1930s, under the slogan of the "American Plan," the National Association of Manufacturers fought against some of the key bargaining rights claimed by unions. "Yellow-dog" contracts (under which employees agree not to join a union) were promoted, together with more positive schemes like profit sharing, designed to show workers that rewards could be achieved without unions. The early history of the labor movement in the United States was plagued by violence. Some employers ruthlessly suppressed union organizations in their plants, using every means to achieve their ends, including murder. Many bloody battles fought outside the gates of factories and mines pitted the workers against strike-breakers and police.

RECENT DEVELOPMENTS

Unions themselves, of course, have altered over the years. Some have grown very large and have become bureaucratized. These are staffed by full-time officials, who may themselves have little direct experience of the conditions under which their members work. The activities and views of union leaders can thus become quite distant from those of the members they represent. Shop-floor groups sometimes find themselves in conflict with the strategies of their own unions. Most unions have not been successful in recruiting a high level of women workers. Although some have initiated campaigns to increase their female membership, many have in the past actively discouraged women from joining.

In current times, unions in Western countries are facing a threat from three related changes—the recession in world economic activity, associated with high levels of unemployment, which weakens the unions' bargaining position; the decline of the older manufacturing industries, in which the union presence has traditionally been strong; and the increasing intensity of international competition, particularly from Far Eastern countries, where wages are often lower than in the West. In the United States and several European countries, including Britain, France, Germany, and Denmark, Rightist governments came to power in the 1970s or 1980s, mostly determined to limit what they saw as excessive, and negative, union influence in industry.

In the United States, the unions face a crisis of greater dimensions than their counterparts in most European countries. Union-protected working conditions and wages have eroded in several major industries over the past decade. In recent years, the teamsters, steelworkers, and autoworkers have all accepted reduced economic conditions from those previously negotiated. The unions have come out second best in several major strikes, perhaps the most notable example being the crushing of the air traffic controllers' union (PATCO) by the Reagan administration in the early 1980s. Union membership as a whole has dipped considerably. From a peak of over 30 percent of the labor force in the mid-1950s, the level of union membership has declined to its level of 20 percent today (Edwards and Podgursky, 1986, Goldfield, 1987).

STRIKES

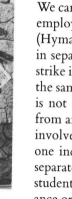

We can define a **strike** as a temporary stoppage of work by a group of employees in order to express a grievance or enforce a demand (Hyman, 1984). All the components of this definition are important in separating strikes from other forms of opposition and conflict. A strike is *temporary,* since workers intend to return to the same job with the same employer; where workers quit altogether, the term "strike" is not appropriate. As a *stoppage of work,* a strike is distinguishable from an overtime ban or "slow down." A *group* of workers has to be involved, because a strike is a collective action, not the response of one individual worker. That those involved are *employees* serves to separate strikes from protests such as may be conducted by tenants or students. Finally, a strike involves seeking to make known a grievance or press a demand; workers who miss work to go to a ball game could not be said to be on strike.

Strikes represent only one aspect or type of conflict in which workers and management may become involved. Other closely related expressions of organized conflict are lockouts (where the employers rather than the workers bring about a stoppage of work), output restrictions, and clashes in contract negotiations. Less-organized expressions of conflict may include high labor turnover, absenteeism, and interference with production machinery.

Workers choose to go out on strike for many specific reasons. They may be seeking to gain higher wages, forestall a proposed reduction in their earnings, protest against technological changes that make their work duller or lead to redundancies, or obtain greater security of employment. However, in all these circumstances the strike is essentially a mechanism of power: a weapon of people who are relatively powerless in the workplace, and whose working lives are affected by managerial decisions over which they have little or no control. It is usually a weapon of "last resort," to be used when other negotiations have failed, because workers on strike either receive no income, or depend upon union funds, which might be limited.

We cannot explain a high-strike rate in a given country simply in terms of the strength of its union movement. Sweden, for instance, which has very strong labor unions, has a low-strike rate. But the nature of the overall *organization* of the labor movement is important. Countries in which the labor unions are highly centralized (like Sweden) tend to have lower strike rates than those where they are more fragmentary (like the United States or Italy). Where the unions are centralized and cover much of the workforce, they usually have more negotiating power than where they are more disaggregated: they can achieve their ends without resorting to strikes.

So far in this chapter, we have been looking at industry mostly from the perspective of occupations and employees. We have studied how patterns of work have changed and the factors influencing the development of labor unions. But we have also to concern ourselves with the nature of the business firms in which the workforce is employed. (It should be recognized that many people today are employees of government organizations, although we shall not consider these here.) What is happening to business corporations today, and how are they run?

CORPORATIONS AND CORPORATE POWER

SINCE THE TURN OF THE TWENTIETH CENTURY, MODERN economies have been more and more influenced by the rise of large business **corporations.** The share of total manufacturing assets held by the two hundred largest manufacturing firms in the United States has increased by 0.5 percent each year from 1900 to the present day. These two hundred corporations now control over half of all manufacturing assets. The two hundred biggest financial organizations—banks, building societies, and insurance companies—account for more than half of all financial activity. There are many connections between large firms. For example, financial institutions hold well over 30 percent of the shares of the largest two hundred firms.

Of course, there still exist many thousands of smaller firms and enterprises within the American economy. In these companies, the image of the **entrepreneur**—the boss who owns and runs the firm—is by no means obsolete. The large corporations are a different matter. Ever since Adolf Berle and Gardiner Means published their celebrated study, *The Modern Corporation and Private Property,* more than half a century ago, it has been accepted that most of the largest firms are not run by those who own them (Berle and Means, 1967; orig. pub. 1932). In theory, the large corporations are the property of their shareholders, who have the right to make all important decisions affecting them. Since share ownership is so dispersed, however, Berle and Means argued that actual control over decisions of large corporations has passed into the hands of the managers who run firms on a day-to-day basis. *Ownership* of the corporations is thus separated from their *control.*

On the basis of the findings of Berle and Means, and subsequent research pointing in the same direction, some authors have diagnosed major shifts in the nature and outlook of the large corporations. The managers who now control the giant companies, they claim, do not share the same interests as shareholders. While shareholders want to maximize the returns they get on their investment, managers are more concerned with the growth of the corporation and its image in the outside world. Some suggest that, as a consequence, the large corporations have become more "socially responsible" than in the past, looking as much to their public role as to cultivating their profits.

However, this view is of dubious validity. Many managers in fact own considerable stocks in their own companies and presumably wish to gain a high return on these. The salaries of executives tend to be linked to the financial success of the firms, and success is usually measured by the profit they generate. When asked where their priorities lie, managers place the emphasis upon profitability. A study of about 190 senior executives and directors of a number of large corporations in Great Britain, for example, showed that precedence was given to "maximizing growth of total profits" and "maximizing rate of return on capital." Objectives such as "provision of service to the community at large" were well down the list (Francis, 1980).

Just how many of the large corporations are manager-controlled is difficult to gauge. An individual (or family) who owns even as little as 15–20 percent of the total shares may effectively control the company, if the remainder of the shareholding is widely fragmented between different individuals. Moreover, a good deal of the shareholding in large companies is now in the hands of *other* corporations—usually banks, insurance firms, and other financial organizations. Where these corporations are still dominated by shareowning interests themselves, a whole network of firms may be in the control of shareholders rather than managers. Nevertheless, there is general agreement that the majority of very large corporations are under management control (Scott, 1980).

Whether run by owners or managers, the power of the major corporations is very extensive. Where one, or a handful, of firms dominate in a given industry, they often cooperate in setting prices rather than freely competing with one another. Thus the giant oil companies normally follow one another's lead in the price charged for gasoline. Where one firm has a commanding position in a given industry, it is said to be in a **monopoly** position. More common is a situation of **oligopoly,** in which a small group of giant corporations predominate. In situations of oligopoly, firms are able more or less to dictate the terms on which they buy in goods and services from smaller firms who are their suppliers.

TYPES OF CORPORATE CAPITALISM

There are three general stages in the development of the business corporations—although each overlaps with the others, and all continue to coexist today. The first phase, characteristic of the nineteenth and early twentieth centuries, was dominated by **family capitalism.** Large firms were run either by individual entrepreneurs or by a handful of members of the same family—and then passed on to their descendants. The famous corporate "dynasties"—such as the Rockefellers or Fords—belong in this category. These individuals and families owned not just a single large corporation, but held a diversity of economic interests, standing at the apex of economic empires.

Most of the big firms founded by entrepreneurial families have since become public companies—that is, shares of their stock are traded on the open market—and have passed into managerial control. But important elements of family capitalism remain, even within some of the very largest corporations—like the Ford Motor Company, where Henry Ford IV has a leading managerial role. Among small firms, such as local shops run by their owners, small plumbing and housepainting businesses, and so forth, family capitalism of course continues to be the primary type of enterprise. Some of these firms are also "dynasties" on a minor scale, as where a shop remains in the hands of the same family for two or more generations. However, the small business sector is a highly unstable one, in which economic failure is very common; the proportion of firms that are owned by members of the same family across extended periods of time is minuscule.

TABLE 15.2   **THE WORLD'S FIFTEEN LARGEST INDUSTRIAL COMPANIES (1987)**

Company	Headquarters	Industry	Sales (billion dollars)
General Motors	Detroit	Motor vehicles and parts	102.8
Exxon	New York	Petroleum refining	69.9
Royal Dutch/Shell Group	The Hague/London	Petroleum refining	64.8
Ford Motor	Dearborn, MI	Motor vehicles and parts	62.7
International Business Machines (IBM)	Armonk, NY	Computers	51.3
Mobil	New York	Petroleum refining	44.9
British Petroleum	London	Petroleum refining	39.9
General Electric	Fairfield, CT	Electronics	35.2
American Tel. & Tel.	New York	Electronics	34.1
Texaco	White Plains, NY	Petroleum refining	31.6
IRI	Rome	Metals	31.6
Toyota Motor	Toyota City (Japan)	Motor vehicles and parts	31.6
Daimler-Benz	Stuttgart	Motor vehicles and parts	30.2
E.I. du Pont de Nemours	Wilmington, DE	Chemicals	27.1
Matsushita Electric Industrial	Osaka	Electronics	26.5

Source: Fortune Magazine, 3 August 1987, p. 18.

In the large corporate sector, family capitalism was increasingly succeeded by **managerial capitalism.** As managers came to have more and more influence, through the growth of very large firms, the entrepreneurial families were displaced. The result has been described as "the replacement of family role of the company by the supremacy of the company itself" (Useem, 1984). The corporation emerged as a more defined economic entity. In studying the two hundred large industrial corporations, Michael Allen found that, in cases where profit showed a decline, family-controlled enterprises were unlikely to replace their chief executive, but manager-controlled firms did so rapidly (Allen, 1981).

Managerial capitalism has today partly ceded place to a third form of corporate system: **institutional capitalism.** This term refers to the emergence of a consolidated network of business leadership, concerned not only with decisionmaking within single firms, but with the development of corporate power beyond them. Institutional capitalism is based upon the spread of shareholding of corporations by other firms. This to some degree reverses the process of increasing managerial control since the managers' shareholdings are dwarfed by the large blocks of shares owned by other corporations. In effect, a situation arises by which interlocking boards of directors exercise control over much of the corporate landscape. Shareholding of this type often takes effective power away from managers within the firms in question. One of the main reasons for the spread of institutional capitalism is a shift in patterns of investment that has occurred over the past thirty years of so. Rather than investing directly by buying shares in a business, individuals now invest in money markets, trusts, insurance and pension funds that are controlled by large financial organizations, which in turn invest these grouped savings in industrial corporations (Scott, 1980; Stollman, Ziegler, and Scott, 1985).

UNEMPLOYMENT

PEOPLE WHO OWN SUFFICIENT STOCKS AND SHARES CAN LIVE without working as the income from these generates the resources needed for their lives. Such people are "unemployed," but of course only a minority at the top of the class system are able to live off investments in this way, and they deliberately choose not to hold a paid job. The vast majority of those who we term unemployed are in a very different situation. They wish to find paid work, but cannot do so. For them, being without work means they also lack the resources to lead a satisfying life, and it often brings psychological as well as material hardship. Unemployment is one of the most important and pervasive aspects of the economic order in Western societies, and we need to analyze its extent and consequences at some length.

Unemployment.

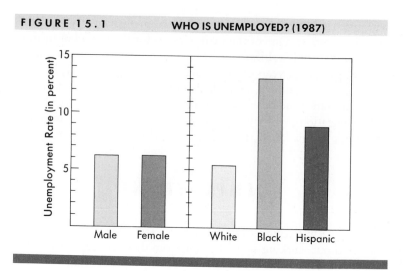

FIGURE 15.1   **WHO IS UNEMPLOYED? (1987)**

Source: U.S. Bureau of Labor Statistics, *Employment and Earnings,* monthly and unpublished data.

UNEMPLOYMENT RATES

Rates of unemployment have fluctuated considerably during this century. In Western countries, unemployment reached a peak during the Great Depression in the early 1930s, with a quarter of the labor force being out of work in the United States in 1933. Not until the ideas of the British economist John Maynard Keynes were put into practice did unemployment in the United States and Europe recede. Keynes believed that unemployment resulted from the lack of sufficient purchasing power to buy goods; governments can intervene to increase the level of demand in an economy, leading to the creation of new jobs. State management of economic life, many came to believe, meant that high rates of unemployment belonged to the past. Commitment to "full employment" became part of government policy in virtually all Western countries. Until the 1970s, these policies seemed successful, and economic growth was more or less continuous.

Over the past fifteen years or so, however, unemployment rates have risen in many countries, and Keynesianism has been largely abandoned as a means of trying to control economic activity. The rate of unemployment in the United States in 1969 was 3.4 percent. By 1975 it had reached 9 percent, and in 1983 stood at 10.8 percent, with eleven million workers out of a job. Since that date it has dropped back considerably, but in many other Western countries it has remained high. In Canada, it stood at 12 percent in 1985, in Great Britain it was 12 percent, while in Holland the rate reached 17 percent (Fineman et al., 1987). Japan, so far largely exempt from these trends, might perhaps succumb to them, as the country faces increasing competition from other Far Eastern countries like Taiwan or Hong Kong. The official rate of unemployment in Japan in 1988 was only 4 percent.

Unemployment is not equally distributed within countries. It varies by race or ethnic background, by age, and by industry and geographic region. These irregular patterns are hidden by a single national unemployment figure, but they are no less real. Ethnic minorities living in central cities in the United States have much higher rates of long-term unemployment than the rest of the population. A substantial proportion of young people are among the long-term unemployed, again especially among minority groups. More than half of male teenage unemployment is among those out of work for six months or more.

BEING IN AND OUT OF WORK

The experience of unemployment can be very disturbing to those accustomed to having secure jobs. Obviously, the most immediate consequence is a loss of income, but the effects of this vary between countries, because of differences in the level of unemployment benefits. In the United States and some other Western countries, unemployment benefits are short term, and the economic strain upon those without work is correspondingly greater than in countries where a welfare system is more fully developed. For example, in Britain, long-term welfare benefits are provided for the unemployed. Unemployment may produce acute financial difficulties but, unlike in the case of the United States, does not affect access to health care and other welfare benefits.

In modern societies, having a job is important for maintaining self-esteem. Even where work conditions are relatively unpleasant and the tasks involved dull, work tends to be a structuring element in a person's psychological makeup and in the cycle of daily activities. The experience of unemployment can therefore only be properly understood in terms of what holding a job provides. Six main characteristics of paid work are relevant in this respect:

1. MONEY. A wage or salary is the main resource most people depend upon to meet their needs. Without such an income, anxieties about coping with day-to-day life tend to multiply.

2. ACTIVITY LEVEL. Employment often provides a basis for the acquisition and exercise of skills and competencies. Even where work is routine, it offers a structured environment in which a person's energies may be absorbed. Lacking employment, the opportunity to exercise such skills and capacities might be reduced.

3. VARIETY. Employment provides access to contexts that contrast with domestic surroundings. In the working environment, even when the tasks are relatively dull, individuals may enjoy doing something different from home chores. Unemployment reduces this source of contrast with the domestic milieu.

4. TEMPORAL STRUCTURE. For people in regular employment, the day is usually organized around the rhythm of work. While this rhythm may sometimes be oppressive, it provides a sense of direction in daily activities. Those who are out of work frequently find boredom a major problem and develop a sense of apathy in relation to the passing of the days. As one unemployed man remarked, "Time doesn't matter now as much as it used to. . . . There's so much of it" (Fryer and McKenna, 1987).

5. SOCIAL CONTACTS. The work environment often provides friendships and opportunities to participate in shared activities with others. Separated from the work setting, a person's circle of possible friends and acquaintances is likely to dwindle.

6. PERSONAL IDENTITY. Employment is usually valued for the sense of stable social identity it offers. A person's self-esteem is often bound up with the economic contribution made to the maintenance of the household.

Against the backdrop of this formidable list, it is not difficult to see why unemployment may undermine individuals' confidence in their social value. Thus an unemployed teacher remarked:

It's difficult when you strip away all the things that supposedly hold you together in terms of an identity. Your work, your money, whatever is power to you, whatever is responsi-

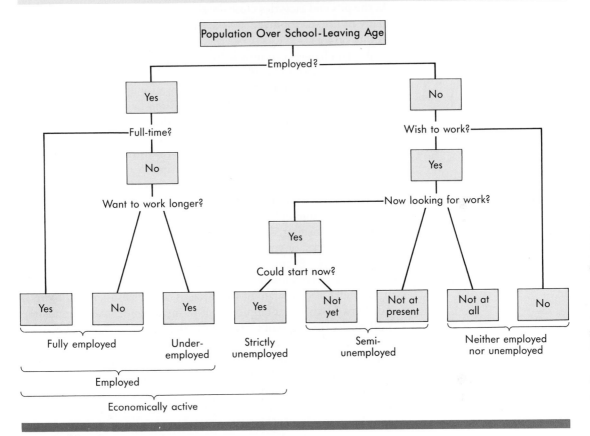

FIGURE 15.2 **A TAXONOMY OF POSSIBLE EMPLOYMENT, UNEMPLOYMENT, AND NON-EMPLOYMENT STATES**

Source: Sinclair, 1987.

bility, whatever means freedom and choice. I have to ask myself, "Who am I now? What will I do now?" (Holt, 1979)

In some part, recent rises in unemployment in Western countries are the result of the decline of the older, manufacturing industries. This means that unemployment varies substantially between the different regions of a country. In areas where heavy industry has traditionally been concentrated, 20 percent or more of the work force may be unemployed. In some industrial neighborhoods or towns, the outcome is a partial disintegration of long-standing social communities. Mining and steel towns, for example, from the environs of Detroit and Pittsburgh to South Wales and the Ruhr, now quite often lie in decay. As the pits and factories close down, property values plummet; while many of the unemployed are moving away, others can no longer afford to do so.

Similar changes can now be seen in Japan, the last fully developed industrial society to be affected by them. In the past, many Japanese workers enjoyed much greater security of employment than their Western counterparts, the large corporations having pursued a policy of "lifetime employment"—taking on their employees for life (see Chapter 9: "Groups and Organizations"). For such workers, the experience of unemployment is even more disturbing than for most employees in the West. A recent description of unemployment in Japan quoted the case of forty-seven-year-old Atsuhiko Tateuchi, who was fired from his job as a section chief in a middle-sized company. Seeing unemployment as utterly demeaning, he left home at 7:30 every morning, dressed in a suit and tie. He spent the day in coffee shops, parks, or cinemas, and did not inform his family about the loss of his job. Eventually his wife and children became suspicious, because he arrived home at 6:30 P.M. rather than at midnight!

Consider also the fate of the citizens of Kamaishi, a steel town in northern Japan. Most employment in the town depends upon a steel mill run by the Nippon Corporation, the largest steel producer in the world. The mill was the first in Japan, having opened in 1886. It was shut down completely in 1990 and the 2,300 employees lost their jobs; several thousands of others in the town, running services dependent upon the mill, have also become unemployed. The mayor of Kamaishi says the town will return to what it was a hundred years ago, "just a village" (McGill, 1987), but the dislocation in people's lives and in the local economy is profound.

WHY HAVE RATES OF UNEMPLOYMENT RISEN?

A combination of factors probably explains the increase in unemployment levels in Western countries in recent years. One important element is the rise of international competition in industries upon which Western prosperity used to be founded. In 1947, 60 percent of steel production in the world was carried out in the United States. Today the figure is only about 15 percent, while steel production has risen by 300 percent in Japan and the Third World countries (principally Singapore, Taiwan, and Hong Kong—which are now undercutting Japanese prices). A second factor is the worldwide economic recession, which was either caused or triggered by the Oil Crisis of 1973—a recession that has still not fully abated. A third influence is the increasing use of microelectronics in industry, the net effect of which has been to reduce the need for labor power. A further factor is that more women are seeking paid employment, meaning that more people are chasing the limited number of available jobs.

It is not certain whether the current high rates of unemployment will continue—or perhaps become even more pronounced—in the immediate future. Some countries seem to be better placed to combat large-scale unemployment than others. Rates of unemployment have been reduced more successfully in the United States than in some of the major European nations. This is perhaps because the sheer economic strength of the country gives it more power in world markets than smaller, more fragile economies. Alternatively, it may be that the exceptionally large service sector in the United States provides a greater source of new jobs than in countries where more of the population has traditionally been employed in manufacturing.

It is much less easy to define unemployment than may appear at first sight. The official unemployment statistics, for example, only count as unemployed those who are registered as actively looking for paid employment. But many people who are not in this category might like to obtain paid work if they thought this were possible, or would do so if they could get a job at a reasonably high level of income. These include many older people, married women, and members of minority groups who have become discouraged in actively looking for a regular job.

Moreover, as has been emphasized earlier, being unemployed is by no means the same as being "out of work," since "work" has a much broader meaning than "paid employment." In the concluding sections of the chapter, we will consider the implications of this fact, beginning with an analysis of women's work and following with a discussion of the "informal economy" which stands alongside the formal production system.

WOMEN AND WORK

IN MUCH OF THE SOCIOLOGICAL LITERATURE ABOUT WORK, at least until very recently, unwaged work—labor carried on without direct payment—was never considered. Marx's discussion of alienated labor concentrates wholly upon the worker in the enterprise, and most discussions in industrial sociology since that time have followed suit. Unpaid work, particularly that of women in the domestic sphere, was largely ignored. Yet such work is just as necessary to the economy as paid employment. It has been estimated that housework is equivalent in value to about a third of the total production per year in a modern economy.

HOUSEWORK

The notion of **housework**—work concentrated upon maintaining the home and raising children—had little meaning when the home was a production unit, prior to industrialization. Most women carried out a variety of tasks, in addition to caring for children and chores in the home. For example, women would cultivate gardens in which the vegetables consumed in the home were grown, tend sheep, goats, cows, and other animals, make their own bread and preserve food for storage. Save for the homes of the wealthy, the tasks associated with housework today—cleaning, tidying, dusting, shopping, and so forth—were not the major chores. Rooms in premodern houses did not have individual uses and were sparsely furnished. Cooking, eating, and working at the spinning wheel or loom were all done in the same space (Tilly and Scott, 1978). Women's tasks were often closely coordinated with those of men, and the household formed an integrated productive unit.

A proportion of married women, and virtually all unmarried women, were engaged in paid work from the beginning of industrialization. But many women became confined to the domestic sphere ("not working") as paid employment for men in separate workplaces became the norm (Oakley, 1976, 1981). This coincided almost exactly with the period in which the numbers of household servants declined sharply. As J. K. Galbraith has remarked, paid servants became employed only by a small minority, while "the servant-wife is available, domestically, to almost the entire present male population" (Galbraith, 1974). Many men were enabled by their wives' work at home to do far more in their paid jobs than would have been possible had they been looking after themselves.

With the development of workplaces separate from the home, production also became separated from consumption. Men, the "producers," "went out to work"; the home, the domain of women, became a place in which goods were consumed in the process of family life. The housewife became a "consumer," someone "who does not work," her productive activity concealed from view. Yet housework patently *is* work, as exhausting and demanding as most types of industrial labor. In Oakley's (1975) study of housework, women frequently drew attention to its "unending" character—it is work that is more or less continuous, which is "never done." Housewives value the fact that they have a considerable amount of control over what they do, and when they do it. Like industrial workers, however, they dislike most of the tasks that are purely routine—like ironing or dusting.

WOMEN'S WORK OUTSIDE THE HOME

During the period between the two world wars, the numbers of women who were solely housewives reached a peak. Although it was common for unmarried women to be in paid employment, the large majority of married women at that time were not in paid work. During both wars, women were encouraged to enter employment in place of men who joined the armed forces; after the First World War they were displaced, but after World War II the expulsion was not so thorough. The growth in women's employment since then (see Chapter 6: "Gender and Sexuality") has been closely connected with the trend towards the expansion of service jobs. Women are disproportionately concentrated in the service sector, although not in managerial or professional positions. Women's jobs are concentrated in secondary labor markets. The **primary labor market** is made up of

TABLE 15.3	OCCUPATIONAL DISTRIBUTION, 1988	
Occupation	Women	Men
	(percent)	
Executive, administrative, managerial	10.8	13.6
Professional specialty	14.4	11.9
Technicians and related support	3.3	2.9
Sales occupations	13.0	11.1
Administrative support (including clerical)	28.3	5.7
Private household	1.7	0.1
Service (except private household)	16.2	9.5
Precision, production, craft, and repair	2.3	19.7
Machine operators, assemblers, and inspectors	6.4	7.6
Transportation and material moving occupations	0.8	6.9
Handlers, equipment cleaners, helpers, and laborers	1.6	6.4
Farming, forestry, and fishing	1.1	4.5

Source: U.S. Bureau of Labor Statistics, January 1984, Table 1, and January 1989, Table 21; Women's Research and Education Institute, 1990.

work in large corporations, unionized industries, or government agencies. In these, workers receive relatively high wages, enjoy good job security and promotion possibilities. **Secondary labor markets** comprise forms of employment that are unstable, where job security and wages are low, there are few opportunities for promotion, and working conditions are frequently poor. Waitressing, sales work, cleaning, and many other service jobs mostly carried out by women fall into this category.

Women are also much more heavily concentrated than men in part-time paid work. Women make up 80 percent of part-time workers in the United States; about 38 percent of the working women are in part-time paid employment. Many women move to part-time work following the birth of a first child, if they do not leave the work force altogether. Older women who return to paid work once their children are grown up often take part-time jobs—either from choice or because few full-time positions are available to them.

HARD CHOICES: WOMEN AND WORK TODAY

In her book, *Hard Choices,* Kathleen Gerson (1985) has investigated how women make choices today about work, careers, and motherhood (see also Rowbotham, 1974; Ehrenreich, 1983; Anyon, 1987). Gerson distinguishes four paths that different women follow in their home and work lives. Some still follow a traditional path. They settle down to full-time mothering and only work outside the home for short periods, if at all. For them, motherhood is a career, with which they are reasonably satisfied. A second group of women found themselves caught between the traditional outlook and an awareness of the rewards a good job outside the home can offer. They experience *rising work aspirations* and *ambivalence toward motherhood.* These women may have married while in their late teens or early twenties, but either became disillusioned with their married state, or found themselves divorced and in the job market a few years later.

A third group follows a *nontraditional path.* Women in this category know early on that they want a career in paid work, and try to ensure that their domestic circumstances permit this. Prior to the 1960s, most might have succumbed to pressures to forsake career ambitions in favor of the family and motherhood. But today there are sufficient social supports to allow for a more resolute outlook, even though having a successful career and a family remains far harder for women than for men. A fourth pattern is represented by women who experience *falling work aspirations,* and come to see *the home as a haven.* They

enter the world of work with high hopes, but for one reason or another find their ambitions thwarted, and turn to the home as a retreat from the disappointments of work. A complexity of different attitudes, feelings, and life experiences influence in which direction a woman chooses to try to channel her activities.

THE INFORMAL ECONOMY

SOCIOLOGISTS AND ECONOMISTS OFTEN THINK IN TERMS OF people being either employed or unemployed, as though these were exhaustive categories; but this is an over-simplified view of work. Not only housework but other kinds of non-paid labor (such as repairing one's own car) are important aspects of many people's lives in modern societies. Many types of work do not conform to orthodox categories of paid employment. Much of the work done in the informal economy is not recorded in any direct fashion in the official statistics of employment. The **informal economy** refers to transactions outside the sphere of regular employment, sometimes involving the exchange of cash for services provided, but also the direct exchange of goods or services (Henry, 1978; Feige, 1981; Gaertner and Wenig, 1985; Pahl, 1987).

Someone who comes to fix the plumbing, for example, may be paid in cash, without any receipt being given, or details of the job recorded. People sometimes exchange pilfered or stolen goods with friends or associates in return for other favors. The informal economy includes not only "hidden" cash transactions, but many forms of self-provisioning that people carry on inside and outside the home. The use of domestic machinery (like washing machines or dryers) and household tools, for instance, provide goods and services that would otherwise have to be purchased (Gershuny and Miles, 1983).

To illustrate this, Ray Pahl (1984) gives the example of fixing a leaking roof. The roof might be mended in several ways:

1. The owner of the home might do the work with the help of other members of the household. The materials needed could be bought from a store, or could be acquired from a friend or neighbor who had saved them from surplus materials. In such a case, it is possible that no money changes hands at all. The members of the household may choose to fix their own roof because they cannot afford the cost of paying for the work to be done by a contractor, or perhaps because they take pride in their capability to maintain the dwelling without outside assistance.

2. The roof might be mended by a friend or neighbor in exchange either for cash or benefits provided in return. The work relations here are based on informal ties, quite different to those between employer and employee. If the work is done by a relative, payment may not be made for months or even years later.

3. A contractor could be hired to do the work. In this case, the transaction might be a "normal" one in which a full fee is paid for the service and receipted in the accounts of the contractor. Alternatively, the contractor might charge a lower rate, be paid in cash, and not record the transaction in order to avoid declaring income which might be taxed.

The informal economy is particularly significant among poorer groups and in areas having high rates of unemployment. Many goods or services that could not otherwise be paid for are provided in this way. Self-provision, of course, is not just a matter of economic necessity; it may bring satisfactions that cannot be derived from the environment in which paid work is done.

The household is usually where the connections between the informal and formal economies are handled. Members of a household collectively decide what constitutes an overall level of income that will meet their needs, and to some degree—where circumstances allow—distribute paid and unpaid labor tasks accordingly. For example, a husband or wife might work overtime in their paid employment to cover various domestic costs (like paying a carpenter to put in new cupboards). Alternatively, they might reject overtime work and undertake the tasks in the home themselves. One or more of the family members might turn to illegal activities to supplement their income, or as full-time pursuits. The "illegal economy" is very large, both on the level of organized crime and as regards more sporadic, or petty, criminal activities (see Chapter 5: "Deviance").

SOME SPECULATIONS ON THE FUTURE OF WORK

WHAT COUNTS AS "WORK," THEN, IS A COMPLEX MATTER involving many types of activities in addition to orthodox employment. "Everyone has the right to work" declared the Universal Declaration of Human Rights, signed at the United Nations following World War II. At that time, this meant the right to a paid job. If, however, the trend towards large-scale unemployment proves to be long term, the manifesto may prove to be unrealizable. Perhaps we should rethink the nature of paid work, and in particular the dominant position it often has in people's lives?

Unemployment tends to be seen by employers and workers alike as a negative phenomenon, but this outlook might be becoming archaic. After all, the identification of "work" with "paid employment" is peculiarly limiting. If someone spends enormous effort on an activity such as cultivating a beautiful garden, for interest rather than for any material reward it might bring, why should this be regarded as clearly separate from "work"? The word "unemployment" only came into the language in the late nineteenth century. Perhaps it might disappear in the twenty-first if not having a job ceases to be regarded as equivalent to being "out of work." Why not, some observers suggest, classify all the unemployed as self-employed, giving subsidies to those who need them to follow their chosen pursuits? (Handy, 1984; Jones, 1985; Merritt, 1982).

In all the industrialized countries the average length of the working week has become reduced. Many workers still undertake long stretches of overtime, but some governments are beginning to introduce new limits on permissible working hours. In France, for example, annual overtime is restricted to a maximum of 130 hours a year. In most countries, men retire at sixty-five and women at sixty, but there seems a general tendency towards further shortening the average working career (Blyton, 1986). More people would probably quit the labor force at sixty, or earlier, if they could afford to do so.

If the amount of time given over to paid employment continues to shrink, and the need to "have a job" becomes less central, the nature of working careers might become substantially reorganized. Job sharing or flexible working hours, for example, might become increasingly common. Some work analysts have suggested that sabbaticals, such as exist in universities, should be extended to workers in other spheres. People would be entitled to take a year off in order to study or pursue some form of self-improvement. Perhaps more and more individuals will engage in "life planning," in which they arrange to work in different ways (paid, unpaid, full, or part time, etc.) at different stages in their lives. Thus some people might choose to enter the labor force in their late thirties, having followed a period of formal education in their early twenties with time devoted to pursuits like travel. Many people might opt to work part time throughout their lives, rather than being forced to because of a lack of full-time employment opportunities.

Some recent surveys of work indicate that, even under existing conditions, part-time workers register higher levels of job satisfaction than those in full-time employment. This may be because most part-time workers are women, who have lower expectations of their career prospects than men, or who are particularly relieved to escape from domestic monotony. Yet many people seem to find reward precisely in the fact that they are able to balance paid work with other activities to produce a more variegated life (Humphries, 1983).

Other individuals may choose to "peak" their lives, giving full commitment to paid work from their youthful to their middle years, then perhaps changing to a second career that would open up new interests. Studies of those choosing deliberately to retire early provide a possible indication of how many people might organize their activities. A study by Ann McGoldrick (1973) of men who had retired early showed much diversity in the lifestyles followed. In the sample of 1,800 people studied, 75 percent described themselves as "more at ease" and "under less stress and strain" than they had been in their jobs. The minority who were disappointed with their new lives, however, included some individuals living in financial hardship or suffering from some form of debility or illness.

The French sociologist and social critic André Gorz has used findings like these to criticize traditional ideas about the course of development of modern societies, and to provide an alternative mapping of their likely future organization. Gorz bases his views upon a critical assessment of Marx's work. Marx believed that the working class—to which he thought more and more people would belong—would lead a revolution that would bring about a more humane type of society, in which work would be central to the satisfactions life has to offer. However, rather than the working class becoming the largest group in society, it has actually shrunk. Blue-collar workers have now become a minority—and a declining minority—of the labor force.

In Gorz's view it no longer makes much sense to suppose that workers can gain much control over the conditions of their labor. Nor is there any real hope of transforming the nature of paid work, because it is organized according to technical considerations that are unavoidable if an economy is to be efficient. "The point now," Gorz writes, "is to free oneself *from* work . . ." (Gorz, 1982). This is particularly necessary where work is organized in a Taylorist way, or is otherwise oppressive or dull.

Rising rates of unemployment together with the spread of part-time work, Gorz argues, have already created what he calls a "non-class of non-workers," alongside those in paid full-time employment. Most people, in fact, are in this "non-class," because the proportion of the population in stable paid jobs at any one time is relatively small—if we exclude the young, the retired, and housewives, together with people who are in part-time work or unemployed. The spread of microtechnology, Gorz believes, will further reduce the numbers of available full-time jobs. The result is likely to be a swing towards a rejection of the "productivist" outlook of Western society, with its emphasis upon wealth, economic growth, and material goods. A diversity of lifestyles followed outside the sphere of permanent, paid work, will be pursued by the majority of the population in coming years. According to Gorz, we are moving towards a "dual society." In one sector, production and political administration will be organized to maximize efficiency. The other sector will be a sphere in which individuals occupy themselves with a variety of nonwork pursuits offering enjoyment or personal fulfillment.

How valid is this viewpoint? That there *are* major changes going on in the nature and organization of work in the industrialized countries is beyond dispute. It does seem possible that more and more people will become disenchanted with "productivism"—with the stress upon constant economic growth and the accumulation of material possessions. It is surely valuable, as Gorz has suggested, not to see unemployment entirely in a negative light, but as offering opportunities for individuals to pursue their interests and develop their talents. Yet, thus far at least, progress in this direction has been slight. We seem at the moment to be far away from the situation Gorz envisages. Now that women are pressing for greater job opportunities, there has been a rise, not a fall, in the numbers of people actively interested in securing paid employment. Paid work remains for many the key basis of generating the material resources necessary for economic survival, or for sustaining a varied life.

SUMMARY

1. *Work* is the carrying out of tasks, which involves the expenditure of mental and physical effort, and has as its objective the production of goods and services catering to human needs. An *occupation* is work that is done in exchange for a regular wage. In all cultures work is the basis of the *economic system.*

2. A distinctive characteristic of the economic system of modern societies is the development of a highly complex and diverse division of labor. The economy of the industrialized countries is comprised of three sectors: the *primary sector* (involving the collection or extraction of natural resources), the *secondary sector* (converting raw materials into commodities), and the *tertiary sector* (providing services).

3. Union organizations, together with recognition of the right to *strike,* are characteristic features of economic life in all Western countries. Unions emerged as "defensive" organizations, providing a measure of control for workers over their conditions of labor. Today, union leaders quite often play an important role in formulating national economic policies—although this is less true in the United States than elsewhere.

4. The modern economy is dominated by the large corporations. When one firm has a commanding influence in a given industry, it is in a *monopoly* position. When a cluster of firms wields such influence, a situation of *oligopoly* exists. Through their influence upon government policy, and upon the consumption of goods, the giant corporations have a profound effect on people's lives.

5. A *primary labor market* consists of workers in large corporations, in unionized industries, and in government agencies, and offers opportunities for promotion and advancement. A *secondary labor market* consists of unstable forms of employment, where job opportunities are restricted and insecure, and working conditions are poor.

6. Unemployment has been a recurrent problem in the industrialized countries in the twentieth century. As work is a structuring element in a person's psychological makeup, the experience of unemployment is often disorientating. The impact of new technology seems likely to further increase unemployment rates.

7. Work should not be understood as applying only to paid employment. Domestic work and the *informal economy* are major spheres of unpaid work, but their contribution to the production of wealth as a whole is very considerable. The informal economy refers to transactions involving the exchange of cash, goods, or services. Aside from being a matter of economic necessity, self-provisioning may provide satisfactions unavailable in the work environment.

8. The nature of women's work has been greatly affected by the separation of the workplace from the home. Many married women become "housewives" and are regarded as "not working," even though the hours of labor they put into domestic tasks may be far more than the working hours of their husbands. Far more women are now in paid employment than was the case some decades ago; but women are disproportionately concentrated in low-paid jobs.

9. Major changes are currently occurring in the nature and organization of work. It seems certain that these will become even more important in the future. Nonetheless, work remains for many people the key basis of generating resources necessary to sustain a varied life.

BASIC CONCEPTS

WORK
ECONOMY
DIVISION OF LABOR
ALIENATION

IMPORTANT TERMS

OCCUPATION
ECONOMIC INTERDEPENDENCE
PRIMARY SECTOR
SECONDARY SECTOR
TERTIARY SECTOR
SERVICE INDUSTRIES
TAYLORISM
FORDISM
LOW-TRUST SYSTEMS
HIGH-TRUST SYSTEMS
AUTOMATION
GROUP PRODUCTION
INDUSTRIAL DEMOCRACY

STRIKE
CORPORATIONS
ENTREPRENEUR
MONOPOLY
OLIGOPOLY
FAMILY CAPITALISM
MANAGERIAL CAPITALISM
INSTITUTIONAL CAPITALISM
HOUSEWORK
PRIMARY LABOR MARKET
SECONDARY LABOR MARKET
INFORMAL ECONOMY

PART FOUR

SOCIAL CHANGE IN THE MODERN WORLD

All the chapters in this book emphasize the sweeping nature of the social changes that have taken place in the modern era. For virtually the whole of human history, the pace of social change was relatively slow compared to the period in which we now live. Most people followed more or less the same ways of life as their forebears. By contrast, we live today in a world subject to dramatic and continuous transformation. In the chapters in this part of the book, we look at some of the major areas in which change is concentrated.

The first chapter analyzes a particular direction of change that affects us all: the increasing interdependence of different societies within global systems. The globalizing of social life both influences, and is influenced by, changing patterns of urbanization. Urbanism—the factors swelling the numbers of people living in cities worldwide—is the subject of Chapter 17. We then discuss in Chapter 18 one of the most far-reaching changes occurring in modern times, the tremendous growth in world population. Population growth has been greatly influenced by the spread of Western techniques of hygiene and medicine, and in this chapter we study the social contexts of health and disease. One effect of people living longer has been to change the age distribution (proportions of the population in different age groups) of modern populations, and in this respect there are major contrasts between the industrialized and the less-developed nations.

The concluding two chapters look directly at processes of change. One of the main characteristics of the modern era is the deliberate attempt to secure social and political change through collective action. In Chapter 19, we study some of the major processes of revolutionary change from the eighteenth century to the present day, and also analyze some general mechanisms of protest and collective violence. In the final chapter of this part, we consider general interpretations of the nature of social change. We discuss what social change actually is and why change has become so profound and constant today. We then take a look into the future, considering where present-day patterns of change are likely to lead us as we prepare to move into the twenty-first century.

CHAPTER SIXTEEN

THE GLOBALIZING OF SOCIAL LIFE

TAKE A CLOSE LOOK AT THE ARRAY OF PRODUCTS FOR SALE the next time you walk into the local store or supermarket. The diversity of goods which we in the West have come to take for granted as available, for anyone with the money to buy them, depends upon amazingly complex economic connections stretching across the world. The products on display have been made in, or use ingredients or parts from, a hundred different countries. All of these have to be regularly transported to and fro across the globe; constant flows of information are necessary to coordinate the millions of daily transactions involved.

"Until our day," wrote the anthropologist Peter Worsley (1973), "human society has never existed," meaning that it has been only in quite recent times that we could speak of the development of forms of social association that span the earth as a whole. In important respects, the world has become a single social system as a result of growing ties of interdependence that now affect virtually everyone.

Global social relations are not just an "environment" within which particular societies—like the United States—develop and change. The social, political, and economic connections that cut across borders between countries decisively condition the fate of those living within them. The general term for the increasing world interdependence is **globalization.** It would be a mistake to think of globalization simply as a process of the growth of world unity. The globalizing of social relations is primarily a reordering of time and distance in our lives. Our lives, in other words, are more and more influenced by activities and events happening well away from the social contexts in which we carry on our day-to-day activities. Although developing rapidly today, globalization is by no means completely new; it dates from the time when Western influence started to expand across the world some two or three centuries ago. (We have already discussed aspects of this phenomenon in Chapter 2: "Culture and Society.")

Our main concern in this chapter will be to analyze the *uneven,* or *fragmented,* nature of the processes that have drawn different parts of the globe into interrelation with one another. The globalizing of social relations has not proceeded even-handedly: from its beginnings it has been associated with inequalities between different regions in the world. Especially important are the processes that created the *Third World* societies. Large disparities of wealth and living standards separate the industrialized (First and Second World) countries from those in the Third World—in which most of the planet's population live. We shall begin this chapter by looking at the development of Third World societies and their relationships to the industrialized nations today. We shall then analyze international organizations and the global influence of the mass media, before discussing some of the most important theories of world development and inequality.

THIRD WORLD SOCIETIES

THE TERM "THIRD WORLD" (ORIGINALLY COINED BY THE French demographer, Alfred Sauvy) has become a conventional way of referring to the less-developed countries, but in some respects it is not very satisfactory. The label makes it sound as though these societies are quite separate from the industrialized countries—a world apart from ours. But this is not true at all. The Third World countries were shaped by the impact of Western colonization, and by the trading links that the Western states forged with them. In turn, the connections that the West established with these countries have strongly affected its own development. For example, the fact that there is a large black population in the United States, and in Brazil, is a result of the "trade in people"—the slave trade–that the West engaged in until less than two centuries ago.

As a result of accelerating processes of globalization, the ties between the industrialized societies and Third World countries are now becoming ever more complex. Many raw materials used in Western manufacture are imported from Third World societies. Large numbers of food products (cash crops) come regularly from the Third World to the industrialized nations. Finally, to an increasing degree, goods are now manufactured in Third World countries, where many Western companies have established plants.

THE FORMATION OF NATIONS

The large majority of Third World societies in Asia, Africa, and South and Central America were once under Western colonial rule. One or two are still colonies (Hong Kong, for example, is a British colony, although control is due to pass to China in 1997). A few colonized areas gained independence early, like Haiti, which became the first autonomous black republic in January 1804, and Brazil, which broke away from Portuguese rule in 1822. In most early examples of independent states, European settlers were instrumental in separating themselves from the original colonizing country (Haiti was an exception). This was the case, of course, with the founding of the United States.

Some countries were strongly influenced by colonial relationships, but did not fall completely under European mastery. The most notable example was China, which was never completely conquered by the Europeans, but by force of arms was compelled to enter into trading agreements with European powers. The Europeans were allocated certain areas within which they governed, which included a number of major seaports. Hong Kong is the last remnant of these.

Most Third World nations have only become independent states in the Second World War period—often following bloody anticolonial struggles. Examples include India, which very shortly after achieving its right to self-rule split into India and Pakistan; a range of other Asian countries, like Burma, Malaysia, and Singapore; and many states in Africa, including Kenya, Nigeria, Zaire, Tanzania, and Algeria.

Many Third World countries were not distinct "societies" prior to the arrival of the Europeans, but were created as such by European rule. The colonists usually forced together many different cultures under a single governmental administration, or split cultures where territorial boundaries between two European powers were established. Although substantial colonial expansion began in the sixteenth century, most of the regions that have now become Third World states were only colonized in the nineteenth century. India did

FIGURE 16.1   **EUROPEAN COLONIZATION OF AFRICA**

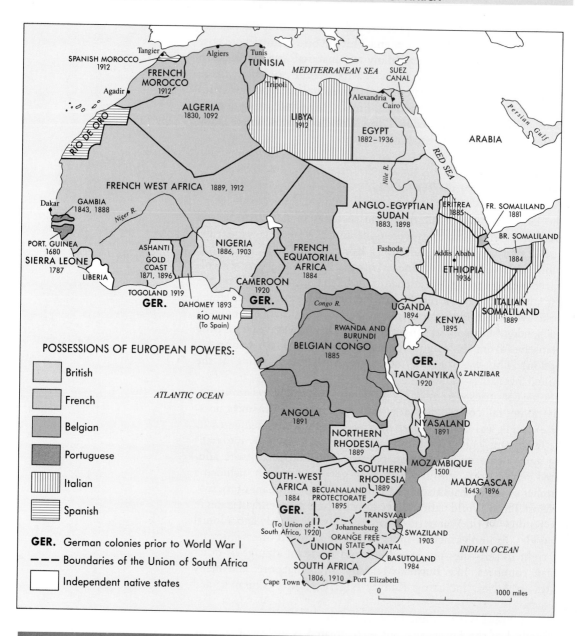

This pre–World War II map shows the dominance of European powers in Africa from the eighteenth through the twentieth century. Colonization had also taken place earlier in the Americas.

Source: Burns et al., *World Civilizations,* Eighth Edition, Vol. 2, (New York: Norton, 1991).

not come fully under British rule until the 1860s, about the same time as Malaya, Singapore, and Burma.

Africa was the "dark continent" to Europeans, largely unexplored until the mid-nineteenth century. In the 1870s and 1880s, the leading European countries competed with one another to acquire possessions in different parts of Africa. Not until some while later were effective systems of colonial government established there. The period of colonial rule was thus in some instances not long enough to integrate a diversity of indigenous groups under an effective administration. This explains why many Third World states today are internally so diverse and fragmented. At the time of Kenyan independence in 1963, for instance, the memory of some Kenyans extended back to before the establishing of white rule (Goldthorpe, 1984).

THE ECONOMIC CONSEQUENCES OF COLONIALISM

The European powers acquired colonies for a number of reasons. Colonial possessions added to the political influence of the parent country and provided military bases. Most Westerners also saw colonialism as a civilizing enterprise, helping to upgrade native peoples from their "primitive" conditions of life. Missionaries wished to bring the Christian message to the "heathen." A further important motive was economic. From the early years of Western expansion, food, raw materials, and other goods were taken from the colonized areas to fuel Western economic development. Where colonies were not acquired primarily for economic gain, the colonizing country nevertheless almost always strove to achieve sufficient economic return to cover the costs of its administration of the area.

In some regions, the existing economic activities of the local peoples generated a sufficient basis for trade. However, in the majority of instances, particularly in tropical areas, the Europeans encouraged the development of **cash-crop production**—crops produced for sale on international markets. The colonizers often set up plantations, farms, or mines, for which they were the overseers, drawing their labor-power from the native populations. In most of these cases, large tracts of land were taken over to become the property of European settlers. A significant economic invention set up by the colonial countries was the **concession company**—a company licensed by the colonizing state with a monopoly over the production of certain goods or crops within a particular area (Weatherby et al., 1987). A few of these companies, including both state-controlled enterprises and private firms, became very large, having a leading influence over the regions to which they were assigned. The descendants of some of the concession companies are very prominent in world trade today.

Many, although not all, of the Third World countries are impoverished compared to the industrialized nations, due to their lack of an industrial base. Most of their populations are engaged in agriculture, using traditional methods of production. In some cases, these countries were drained of resources by the colonizing countries, who kept them in a state of subjection. In addition, most of the Third World societies have experienced high rates of population growth over the course of the present century (see Chapter 18: "Population, Health, and Aging"). This situation has made it very difficult for them to achieve any sustained economic development, because increases in production are taken up by the extra mouths that have to be fed.

In the poorer Third World countries, many people exist in conditions that are almost inconceivable to those who live in the West. Agostino Neto, the first president of Angola, wrote a poem that graphically describes the life of a poor quarry worker. With deliberate irony, it is entitled "Western Civilization":

> Sheets of tin nailed to posts
> driven in the ground
> make up the house.
>
> Some rags complete
> the intimate landscape.
>
> The sun slanting through cracks
> welcomes the owner.
>
> After twelve hours of slave
> labor.
>
> breaking rock
> shifting rock
> breaking rock
> shifting rock
> fair weather
> wet weather
> breaking rock
> shifting rock
>
> Old age comes early
>
> a mat on dark nights
> is enough when he dies
> gratefully
> of hunger.
>
> (Quoted in Bennett and George, 1987)

The inequalities that separate the poorest Third World countries from the wealthy societies of the First World are massive. We can chart these out, in a general way at least, by drawing some direct comparisons between different nations.

THE DIVERGENCE BETWEEN RICH AND POOR COUNTRIES

About twenty countries in the world (the Western countries, Japan, Australia, and New Zealand) are markedly wealthier than any others. The United States, Canada, Sweden, and Switzerland are at the top of this group and have the highest **gross national product (GNP).** There is another group whose GNP per capita (per head of population)* approaches that of the industrialized countries: the "oil rich" states in the Middle East. Their position fluctuates as the price of oil changes, however, and their domestic economies have not developed non-oil-based industries to the same extent as those of the West and Japan. The Soviet Union and Eastern Europe have lower per capita GNPs than the Japanese and Western societies, although there is a good deal of variation within this category, East Germany being the most prosperous. The poorest countries in the world are concentrated in Asia and Africa.

If we take the wealthiest forty countries, and the forty poorest (each making up about a quarter of humankind), we find that the second group produces only about 5 percent of the GNP of the first. In other words, the population of the richest forty countries has a "cake" twenty times larger than the one shared between the equivalent number of poorest nations. This gap is widening rather than narrowing at the present time. It has been estimated that at current rates of development, the gap between the wealthiest and poorest countries will have widened by a further 300 percent by the year 2000 (Kubalkova and Cruickshank, 1981).

The position of Third World countries within the world economy is made especially precarious by their dependence upon cash-crop production. There are many countries in which one or two crops form the basis of the economic system. These are often crops strongly affected by climatic fluctuations from year to year (like coffee or

TABLE 16.1
GNP PER CAPITA—
A GLOBAL LOOK

	(U.S. Dollars)
United States	16,240
Switzerland	15,320
Canada	13,220
Sweden	11,380
Japan	10,920
Britain	7,882
Soviet Union	7,635
Nigeria	749
China	342
Kenya	291
Zaire	150

Data for 1985.
Source: U.S. Arms Control and Disarmament Agency, *World Military Expenditures and Arms Transfers,* annual. Data from International Bank for Reconstruction and Development and U.S. Central Intelligence Agency.

---

* The GNP of a society is the value of all the goods and services produced in that country per year. GNP per head of population is the normal measure used for comparing differences in wealth between nations, although it has many drawbacks. For example, since it is an average figure, it conceals variations between rich and poor *within* countries.

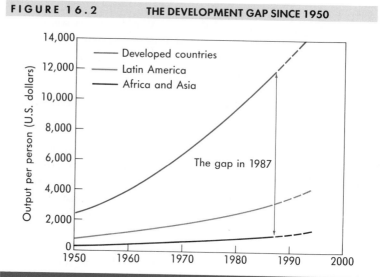

The economic dominance of developed nations, like the United States, Japan, and Western European countries, has greatly increased over the last forty years. Projections are that the gap in growth between the developed nations and the less-developed countries will continue to widen through the 1990s.

FIGURE 16.2   **THE DEVELOPMENT GAP SINCE 1950**

Source: Reed, 1987.

cocoa). Prices of such products on world markets vary far more than those for manufactured goods. Since in some countries the whole economy is more dependent on foreign trade than in the case of the wealthier nations, the problems for Third World countries are severe (Goldthorpe, 1984; Stavrianos, 1981).

Conditions in the poorer Third World countries have deteriorated as a result of the world recession that has existed for the past fifteen years or so. The recession has also significantly affected the First World countries, as high rates of inflation, coupled with increasing unemployment, were for a period found in most industrialized countries—Japan being an exception. While inflation has since gone down, unemployment, as pointed out in Chapter 15, has remained high in many Western societies. Yet the difficulties faced by the industrialized countries have been slight compared to those that have confronted the Third World. The economic adjustments the wealthier countries have made have produced serious consequences for poor Third World countries. Because of the recession, the richer countries cut down on imports coming from the poorer ones, which depressed prices. Prices for some of the cash-crop goods, such as tea and rubber, are today at their lowest in thirty years. The level of aid (as opposed to loans) going from richer to poorer countries has actually declined during this period. Given high rates of population growth, the outlook for the poorest Third World countries is bleak indeed.

THE NEWLY INDUSTRIALIZING COUNTRIES

While the majority of Third World countries lag well behind the Western societies and those of Eastern Europe, some have now successfully embarked upon a process of industrialization (Saunders, 1981). These countries are sometimes referred to as the **newly industrializing countries (NIC).** The NICs include Brazil and Mexico in South America, and Hong Kong, South Korea, Singapore, and Taiwan in East Asia.

The rates of economic growth of the most successful NICs, such as Taiwan, are several times those of most of the mature industrial economies (Harris, 1987). No developing economy figured among the top thirty exporters of manufactured products in the world in 1965. Twenty years later, Hong Kong and South Korea were in the top fifteen, with export shares similar to those of Sweden and Switzerland. Brazil is easily the largest of the NICs. The country increased its GNP by an average of 6.5 percent annually from 1932 to the mid-1980s. In the late 1960s and 1970s in particular, growth rates were spectacular compared to most of the industrialized world. Mexico's growth rate paralleled this, averaging just below 8 percent annually for these two decades. On the other hand, both countries are very heavily indebted to Western banks, with little chance of being able to repay their loans even in the moderate-term future. Much of the newly-created wealth is monopolized by the privileged and doesn't filter down to the urban and rural poor.

FOOD PRODUCTION AND WORLD HUNGER

The distribution of the world's food supply reflects the general inequalities between rich and poor countires. World food requirements are normally analyzed by reference to what experts regard as a minimum adequate daily diet necessary to keep a person in a good state of health. The usual measure is that a diet should contain 2,354 calories a day, which must include 90 grams of protein. This is only an average calculation. The range of minimum nutritional requirements runs from 820 calories for a female child aged less than one year to 3,500 for a sixteen-year-old boy.

Using the figure of 2,354 calories, the World Health Organization estimates that ten million children under five in the world are living close to starvation levels. Many more than ten million children die in infancy or early childhood each year as a result of vulnerability to illness brought about by their own or their mother's malnutrition. There are probably about 700 million adults who are seriously undernourished (Bennett and George, 1987; Lappe and Collins, 1979).

Yet world food supplies have been steadily increasing, and have not, as many feared some years ago, so far been outstripped by population growth. The average world yield of grain over the past few years has been about 1.3 billion tons, which is sufficient to feed the five billion people who are alive today (Marstrand and Rush, 1978).

Virtually all surplus food, however, is produced within the industrialized societies. North America is the largest source of exportable food supplies. Before World War II, it shared this position with South America, Argentina being especially prominent as a source of grains and livestock. Since then, population growth in South America, combined with lack of agricultural reform and modernization, has eliminated the surplus coming from that continent. Today, most South American countries do not produce sufficient food to meet their own needs and must import. In the United States, Canada, and Europe, by contrast, there is a large excess capacity in agricultural production, and governments regularly pay farmers to keep some of their acreage idle, storing very large amounts of food which cannot find buyers on world markets.

Under Public Law 480, passed in 1954, the policy of the United States has been to use its "abundant productivity to combat hunger and malnutrition and to encourage economic development in the developing countries," through providing direct food aid and sales at low prices to the needy. Levels of aid supplied under the program, however, have varied and have never involved more than a slight proportion of the available surplus. Moreover, political considerations have strongly influenced where food has been exported. In the mid-1970s, during the Vietnam War, about half of all American food aid went to two countries alone: South Vietnam and Cambodia. During the same period, the United States rejected a request from Chile, at that time governed by the socialist administration of Salvador Allende, to buy wheat on credit. The action probably contributed to bringing about the downfall of Allende's government, which the United States government had also been trying to achieve by other means.

The Soviet Union is not in a position to contribute to world food supplies, since its own agriculture is inefficient compared to that of most Western countries. The Soviet Union, in fact, is periodically dependent upon securing grain exports from the United States. At one time, the Soviet Union managed surreptitiously to buy up a large share of the exportable wheat crop of the United States, purchasing some 28 million tons of grain through various Third World agencies. The Soviet government was thus able to purchase the food at a much lower price than normal, taking advantage of United States government subsidies. Available food exports to the rest of the world were severely reduced, while the Soviet Union got its grain at bargain prices.

Famine

If extreme hunger in Third World countries is largely ignored by the richer states, it is partly because the nature of famine has changed. Famine is commonly seen as a temporary condition affecting a particular area as a result of specific, and transitory, circumstances. Thus, for instance, there was famine in Ireland at certain periods during the nineteenth century when the potato crop failed. Famines of this sort still do occur—such as happened in Uganda in 1985 and 1986—but in general, severe shortages of food have become a permanent condition among the poor of the world, rather than limited to particular times and places.

The most widespread conditions of malnutrition and famine today are found in Africa. Most African countries are net importers of food, but the proportion of their national income which can be devoted to this purpose is shrinking. A spiral of deteriorating conditions has set

Famine in Mali (northwest Africa).

in, as populations increase while lack of foreign currency makes it impossible to buy the fertilizers, pesticides, and agricultural machinery that could increase levels of food production. Wars, political upheavals, and unusual periods of drought have made matters even worse. Countries in which two-thirds or more of the labor force are engaged in agriculture now have to import nearly 10 percent of all their food (Canon, 1987).

Even if the richer countries were more generous than they are in providing food aid, fundamental problems would still remain. The provision of aid does not in and of itself help improve the capacity of poor countries to develop their agriculture more effectively, and may even have unfortunate, unintended consequences. In some parts of Africa, for example, imports of wheat and rice have changed local diets, and also tastes. These products are extremely expensive to grow, so money is spent to import them which may previously have been devoted to developing local agriculture. Because of such paradoxical consequences, some have argued that food aid should actually be confined to emergency situations. What is really needed is a large-scale transfer of production resources (such as agricultural machinery and the means to run and repair it), which would create more effective methods of indigenous agriculture (Brandt Commission, 1983).

Agribusiness

Despite the fact that many among their own populations go hungry, Third World countries are important food suppliers to the West as a result of the influence of the Western food-producing companies—the **agribusiness** enterprises. The term "agribusiness" was coined by Ray Goldberg, of the Harvard Business School, to refer to the industrialization of food production by machinery and organized through systematic processing, transport, and storage. Many millions of people in the world (mostly in the industrialized countries) no longer produce their own food. The food products they consume include large numbers of crops, minerals, and other goods imported from the Third World. These are mainly not "basic" foods (like grain or meat), but include many that are a common part of Western diets (such as coffee, tea, and cane sugar).

Many of the large agribusiness firms operating in Third World countries originated in the concessionary companies established there by colonial governments. For instance, one of the first plantations owned by a foreign company in Africa was set up by William Hesketh Lever in the nineteenth century. Lever was the prime mover behind the development of Lever Brothers, which has since become

Unilever, which was until recently the largest food business in the world. Its activities in Africa were first based upon controlling palm oil supplies used in the company's soap factories in Port Sunlight, in the northwest of England.

Other examples are the Firestone Rubber Company and the Brooke Bond Tea Company. The Firestone Rubber Company bought a million acres from the government of Liberia in 1926 to establish an extremely large rubber plantation. While the resources fed permanently into the Liberian economy were few, the country nonetheless became so dependent on the company that it was often called the "Firestone Republic" (Dinham and Hines, 1983). Brooke Bond set up the first tea plantation in Africa in the 1920s and also established such plantations in India, Pakistan, and Ceylon (now Sri Lanka).

Several sectors of world-exportable crop production are controlled today by a small number of large agribusiness companies. Four corporations (Gill and Duffus, Cadbury-Schweppes, Nestlé, and Rowntree) handle 60–80 percent of world cocoa sales. Five European and three United States companies control 90 percent of the tea marketed in Western Europe and North America. A third of the world trade in margarine and table oil is in the hands of one firm (Unilever). Prices paid for crops are primarily governed by activities on the New York and London stock exchanges, far removed from the circumstances of local producers.

Taxation of agribusiness enterprises provides a source of foreign currency for Third World governments. The corporations often provide sources of employment, at rates of pay higher than those available in competing local industries. Yet the overall effects usually are largely negative for the host countries. While agribusiness enterprises are usually highly efficient, the bulk of their production is devoted to the needs of the industrialized regions of the world. More traditional modes of agricultural production tend to be undermined, as workers are drawn into agribusiness employment. Once this has happened, local populations are at the mercy of foreign corporations should they decide to switch their investment elsewhere. Local elites generally become richer through their connections with the agribusiness enterprises, while divisions between them and the peasantry grow larger.

Agribusiness firms are one type of large corporation that has played an important part in the shaping of global patterns of development. But world development has been shaped fundamentally by other forms of business corporation also. In the following sections we move on to look more generally at these large corporations, concentrating on their impact upon global interdependence.

TRANSNATIONAL CORPORATIONS AND GLOBAL INTERDEPENDENCE

LARGE COMPANIES OPERATING ON A WORLD SCALE ARE usually referred to as **transnational** or *multinational* companies. The term "transnational" is preferable, indicating that these companies operate *across* different national boundaries rather than being simply situated *within* several or many nations. A transnational corporation is a company that has plants or offices in two or more countries.

The largest transnationals are gigantic companies, their wealth outstripping that of many countries. Half of the one hundred largest economic units in the world today are nations; the other half are transnational corporations (Benson and Lloyd, 1983). The scope of the operations of the large transnational companies is staggering. Combining industrial and service corporations, the sales of the top two hundred companies in 1986 were equivalent to one third of the world's total GNP. Revenues of the largest two hundred companies rose tenfold from the mid-1970s to the mid-1980s. Over the past twenty years, the big transnational companies have become increasingly global in the scope of their involvements. Only three of the world's 315 largest companies in 1950 had manufacturing subsidiaries in more than twenty countries; there are some fifty today which do so. These are still, of course, a small minority among companies operating transnationally. The majority of companies have subsidiaries in between two to five countries.

Of the top two hundred transnational corporations in the world today, eighty-nine are based in the United States and contribute just over half of the total sales of those corporations. The share of American companies has, however, fallen significantly since 1960, while Japanese companies have grown dramatically. Only five were in the top two hundred in 1960, as compared to twenty-five in 1983. Contrary to what is often believed, most of the investment of transnational companies is within the industrialized world: three-quarters of all foreign direct investment is between the industrialized countries. Nevertheless, the involvement of transnationals in Third World countries is very extensive; the highest levels of foreign investment being in Brazil, Mexico, and India. Since 1970 the most rapid rate of increase in corporate investment has been in the Asian NICs of Singapore, Hong Kong, South Korea, and Malaysia (Dicken, 1986).

TYPES OF TRANSNATIONAL CORPORATION

The transnationals have assumed an increasingly important place in the world economy over the course of this century. Just as national economies have become increasingly *concentrated*—dominated by a limited number of very large companies—so has the world economy. In the case of the United States and several of the other leading industrialized countries, the firms that dominate nationally also have a very wide-ranging international presence. In many sectors of world production (as in agribusiness) the largest companies are oligopolies —three or four corporations control production and dominate the market. Over the past two or three decades international oligopolies have developed in automobile production, microprocessors, the electronics industry, and other goods marketed worldwide. A particularly important recent trend is the growth of **conglomerates**—companies straddling many different types of production and service. An example is R. J. Reynolds, which recently merged with Nabisco to form R.J.R. Nabisco, the largest food conglomerate in the world. Nabisco now owns, among other companies, Del Monte (fruit), Heublein (alcohol), Sealand Services (shipping), Kentucky Fried Chicken (food retailing), and Aminoil (oil and petroleum) (Transnationals Information Exchange, 1985).

Howard Perlmutter (1972) divides transnational corporations into three types.

1. ETHNOCENTRIC TRANSNATIONALS. These corporations set company policy, and as much as possible put it into practice, from the headquarters in the country of origin. Companies and plants that the parent corporation owns around the world are cultural extensions of the originating company—its practices are standardized across the globe.

2. POLYCENTRIC TRANSNATIONALS. In this second type, overseas subsidiaries are managed by local firms in the countries in which they are situated. The headquarters in the country or countries of origin of the main company establish broad guidelines within which local companies manage their own affairs.

3. GEOCENTRIC TRANSNATIONALS. These are international in their management structure. Managerial systems are integrated on a global basis and higher managers are very mobile, moving from country to country as needs dictate.

FIGURE 16.3   **TYPES OF TRANSNATIONAL CORPORATIONS**

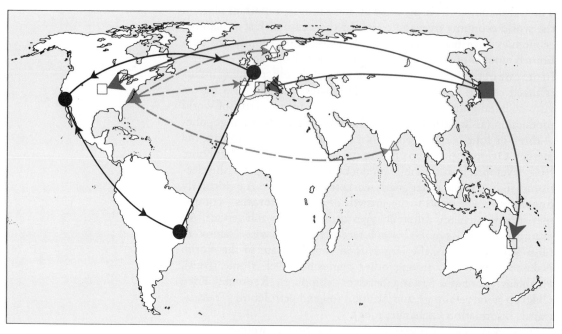

■ Ethnocentric Transnational
(strong central home office
manages far-flung offices☐)

▲ Polycentric Transnationals
(home office establishes
broad guideline for subsidiaries
△ run by locals)

● Geocentric Transitionals
(globally integrated
management structure with
higher managers moving from
country to country)

According to Perlmutter, while a few companies are ethnocentric, the large majority of transnationals at the moment are of the polycentric type. But there is a strong movement towards the geocentric type: many companies are becoming more and more truly international in character.

Of all transnationals, the Japanese companies tend to be most strongly ethnocentric in Perlmutter's terms. Their worldwide operations are usually controlled tightly from the parent corporation, sometimes with the close involvement of the Japanese government. The Japanese Ministry of International Trade and Industry (MITI) plays a more direct part in overseeing Japanese-based foreign enterprises than Western governments do. MITI produced a series of development plans coordinating the overseas spread of Japanese firms over the past two decades. One distinctive Japanese type of transnational consists of the giant trading companies or *sogo shosha*. These are colossal conglomerates whose main concern is with the financing and support of trade. They provide financial, organizational and information services to other companies. About half of Japanese exports and imports are routed through the ten largest *sogo shosha*. Some, like Mitsubishi, also have large manufacturing interests of their own.

THE GROWTH OF THE TRANSNATIONALS

What accounts for the growth of the transnational companies? First, the corporations are an expression of the tendency of modern economic enterprise to become internationalized. Firms that buy and sell goods at a profit—the very rationale for their existence—would be foolish to confine the scope of their operations to one country. The more they seek to expand, the more it makes sense to look for sources of profitable investment wherever they can be found. Second, by expanding overseas, a firm can take advantage of sources of cheap labor power and, often, the absence of unions. Third, having subsidiaries in several countries may permit access to a diversity of natural resources. Fourth, transnational companies with subsidiaries in numerous countries can sometimes gain tax advantages by spreading their profits between them. Finally, the transnational corporations are able to internalize numerous transactions that otherwise are sources of uncertainty for a company. By integrating plants and services in several countries, they can avoid having to depend upon other companies for raw materials and services they need. The parent firm can set its own prices for goods and services transferred between its various subsidiaries (Buckley and Casson, 1976).

The growth of the transnationals over the past thirty years would not have been possible without the advances that have taken place in transport and communications. Jet travel allows people to move from point to point around the world at a speed that would have seemed inconceivable even half a century ago. The development of extremely large ocean-going vessels ("super freighters"), together with containers that can be shifted directly from one type of transport to another, make possible the easy transportation of bulk materials. Telecommunications technologies permit almost instantaneous communication from one part of the world to another. Satellites have been used for commercial telecommunications since 1965. The first satellite could carry 240 telephone conversations at once; current satellites can carry twelve thousand simultaneous conversations. The larger transnationals now have their own satellite-based communications systems. The Mitsubishi corporation, for instance, can transmit five million words across its communications network to and from its headquarters in Tokyo each day (Naksase, 1981).

INTERNATIONAL ECONOMIC INTEGRATION

The transnational companies have helped create a new **international division of labor**—economic interdependence between societies—which now profoundly affects all countries in the world (Frobel et al., 1980; Nyilas, 1982). Although it is true that the Third World countries are much more dependent upon—vulnerable to—movements in some global markets than the industrialized societies are, there is a sense in which *all* societies have become more dependent upon one another. For even the most highly industrialized countries cannot control their own economic development to the degree that they could formerly (Kahn, 1986).

The transnationals have contributed to growing global economic interdependence by the sheer scale of their activities, but also by the way in which the largest companies have integrated their administrative and production systems worldwide. One of the most noteworthy examples of this is provided by the automobile industry.

An Example: The Automobile Industry

The manufacture of cars, together with the goods and services associated with them—the production and refining of oil, the building of gas stations, motels, and hotels, and highway construction—have been at the heart of Western development in the postwar period. The automobile industry directly employs about one in ten of all manufacturing workers in France and Japan, and one in twenty in the United States and Britain. Many millions more are employed in the ancillary industries and services parasitic upon the automobile.

The car industry is controlled by a small number of huge corporations, all of which are transnationals. In the early 1980s, twenty-two firms accounted for some 90 percent of global production in the industry (UNCTNC, 1983; Tolliday and Zeitlin, 1987). The United States used to be the leading producer of cars in the world; in 1980 it was surpassed by Japan. Its share is now only 18 percent, compared to the 25 percent produced by Japanese manufacturers. Well over 50 percent of the automobiles manufactured by the Japanese companies are exported.

The automobile producers have pioneered the **vertical integration** of their companies and their subsidiaries, welding together a diversity of plants and companies, operating in different areas of the

FIGURE 16.4   **AUTOMOBILE PRODUCTION BY CORPORATE VERTICAL INTEGRATION**

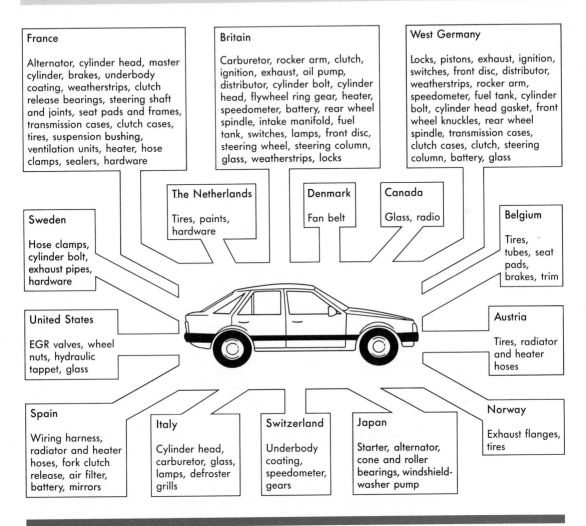

France

Alternator, cylinder head, master cylinder, brakes, underbody coating, weatherstrips, clutch release bearings, steering shaft and joints, seat pads and frames, transmission cases, clutch cases, tires, suspension bushing, ventilation units, heater, hose clamps, sealers, hardware

Britain

Carburetor, rocker arm, clutch, ignition, exhaust, oil pump, distributor, cylinder bolt, cylinder head, flywheel ring gear, heater, speedometer, battery, rear wheel spindle, intake manifold, fuel tank, switches, lamps, front disc, steering wheel, steering column, glass, weatherstrips, locks

West Germany

Locks, pistons, exhaust, ignition, switches, front disc, distributor, weatherstrips, rocker arm, speedometer, fuel tank, cylinder bolt, cylinder head gasket, front wheel knuckles, rear wheel spindle, transmission cases, clutch cases, clutch, steering column, battery, glass

The Netherlands

Tires, paints, hardware

Denmark

Fan belt

Canada

Glass, radio

Sweden

Hose clamps, cylinder bolt, exhaust pipes, hardware

Belgium

Tires, tubes, seat pads, brakes, trim

United States

EGR valves, wheel nuts, hydraulic tappet, glass

Austria

Tires, radiator and heater hoses

Spain

Wiring harness, radiator and heater hoses, fork clutch release, air filter, battery, mirrors

Italy

Cylinder head, carburetor, glass, lamps, defroster grills

Switzerland

Underbody coating, speedometer, gears

Japan

Starter, alternator, cone and roller bearings, windshield-washer pump

Norway

Exhaust flanges, tires

This schematic shows how automobile parts are produced in several countries, and then sent to a central plant for final production of the car.

world within a single administrative framework. Ford has the most extensive range of subsidiaries collaborating in car manufacture. The Ford Escort was designed as a "world car." It is produced from parts assembled in numerous countries and is supposed to be suitable for motoring on all continents. In Europe, the car is built of parts manufactured by Ford's subsidiaries in twelve European countries, Canada, the United States, and Japan. Final assembly is carried out in Germany, Britain, and Spain (Figure 16.4). It is not yet truly a "world car," however, because the degree of integration between European and North American production is fairly low. The Escort in the United States and Canada is assembled primarily from parts made in those countries.

Like the Western companies, the Japanese car firms have integrated production systems stretching across different countries, centered mainly in the East. However, in the 1970s and 1980s they set up manufacturing plants in the United States and Europe, largely because many countries place limits upon the numbers of Japanese autos that can be imported each year. Honda set up a plant in Ohio in 1982, followed by Nissan in Tennessee. Toyota, Mazda, and Mitsubishi have subsequently opened plants in the United States. Toyota and Nissan have also set up assembly plants in Australia and Europe. Cars are now also produced in South Korea by the Hyundai Group, which is a large conglomerate that first began to build cars under license from Ford. It has since developed its own models and has captured a significant portion of the North American import market.

CURRENT CHANGES IN GLOBAL INTERDEPENDENCE

Changes taking place in the automobile industry are part of the global process of the spatial reorganization of industry that is gaining pace, and which will have profound consequences for the Western countries (Morgan and Sayer, 1988). The overall proportion of manufacturing jobs in the world economy has gone up at the same time as high rates of unemployment have developed in many countries in the West. The creation of jobs in manufacture, in other words, is proceeding in areas outside the West—especially in the newly industrializing countries, where either the transnationals have set up production, or the local government has successfully promoted economic development, or a combination of the two.

Given the staggering economic success of Japan, the increasing prosperity of other, smaller Asian countries, and the possibility that rapid economic advancement might potentially be achieved by China, is the center of global power shifting back to where it lay before the rise of Europe? Will Asia and the Pacific become the new "core" of global social and economic relationships, with the United States and Europe becoming more marginal? This is almost certainly too simple a view. Major changes in global production are undoubtedly taking place, however, these are not all located in the Far East. It is possible that some South American countries, notably Brazil, will rise to world prominence. Moreover, what happens over the next few decades will not depend only on economic changes, but on political and military considerations also. The military and political strength of the United States and the Soviet Union is likely to set limits on the degree to which a fundamental eastward shift of world power will occur.

It is not only in terms of the international division of labor that the world is becoming more interdependent. Since early in this century —but again, particularly following World War II—there has been a continuing enlargement in the number of noncommercial, international organizations. Together with the transnational corporations, these are often referred to as **nonstate actors,** because their activities are not bound to the policies of particular states or governments.

NONSTATE ACTORS IN GLOBAL INTERDEPENDENCE

THERE ARE SEVERAL MAJOR TYPES OF NONSTATE ACTORS BEsides the transnational companies. First, there are organizations representing the international community of states, including especially the United Nations and its affiliated organizations (like UNESCO, the UN Educational, Scientific, and Cultural Organization). Second, there exists a large number of organizations concerned with processes that demand international collaboration or communication, such as postal services, telecommunications, navigational regulations for shipping, and so forth. Third, there are organizations linking states or other economic enterprises having mutual international interests. The largest of such organizations is the EEC (European Economic Community). We shall look briefly at each of these types in turn.

THE UNITED NATIONS

Following the First World War, there was widespread revulsion against the tremendous loss of life that it produced. Political leaders were united in the view that war on such a scale must never be repeated—although, of course, their hopes turned out to be vain. In order to provide an organization that might stand above the squabbles of nations, the League of Nations was set up shortly after the war. President Woodrow Wilson was especially influential in its planning and organization. Wilson conceived of the League of Nations as an organization that would help secure the future peace of

The United Nations building in New York a few years ago, during its fortieth anniversary celebration.

the world and generally enhance international cooperation. In Wilson's words, "We [i.e., nations] are all participants, whether we would or not, in the life of the world. The interests of all nations are our own also. We are partners with the rest . . . citizens of the world" (Scott, 1918).

Wilson's vision was not realized. Some of the other participants saw the League as a means of pursuing their own national interests rather than as a force transcending them. In addition, the League did not include members from countries in the world as a whole, being made up mainly of those who had fought the war. A decision was made, for instance, to exclude the Soviet Union. In the end, the United States did not join either because the Senate couldn't agree on the level of U.S. participation and therefore never ratified the Treaty of Versailles, which contained provisions for the League. While the League was only a partially representative organization, and was able to do nothing to prevent the occurrence of another world war, it did become the focus of numerous new forms of international agency, which still exist today. For example, it established its own health organization concerned with documenting and checking the spread of infectious diseases throughout the world. This was later renamed the World Health Organization (WHO) when the League of Nations was replaced by the United Nations following the Second World War.

The United Nations today includes representatives from all states in the world, but this achievement was not without its difficulties. The American government early on tried to use the organization to advance its own political views. For this and other reasons, in 1950 the Soviet Union withdrew to develop a rival body, the Partisans of Peace. During the Russian absence, however, the Americans gained the support of the United Nations for their military intervention in South Korea, which had been invaded from the Communist north. The Russians then decided to resume their participation in order to prevent the UN being used to generate support for Western interests.

Like the League of Nations before it, the United Nations has little chance of independently protecting or enhancing world peace. The only military forces it possesses are small and composed of soldiery drawn from the member states. Yet it has had a profound influence upon the world system, because discussions carried on under its auspices led to the recognition of a large number of new Third World nations. In the mid-1950s, there was a mass admission to the United Nations of postcolonial Asian and African countries. Without the United Nations, the map of the world would not look as it now does, because it completed the process of dividing the world into self-governing states.

Even if it is not in any sense a form of "world government," with a membership of over 150 countries, the United Nations expresses the increasing integration of the world system. Of course, it also reflects the material and ideological conflicts that divide the global social order.

OTHER INTERNATIONAL ORGANIZATIONS

Many of the organizations that are concerned with international collaboration are linked to the United Nations in one way or another. For instance, the Universal Postal and International Telecommunications Union existed before the foundation of the United Nations, but has since become connected to it. This organization establishes standard measures of payment for letters or packages sent across the world, or messages passed through airborne communications systems, such as telephone calls beamed off satellites.

We tend to take many of the organizations that maintain international order for granted, because the activities of such bodies are not very visible. Yet the standardization of many forms of global relationship are relatively recent in origin. For example, in 1850 there were some 1,200 different postal rates operating in the various parts of Europe. Standardization of European postal charges was not fully accomplished until the turn of the present century, and the coordination of worldwide postal charges and procedures took much longer (Luard, 1977). There are many similar international organizations now in existence, concerned with diverse aspects of the coordination of global relationships and concerns. *The Year Book of International Organizations* listed 1,000 agencies in 1958. By 1972 this had grown to 2,190. The number today is over 4,000.

TRADING NETWORKS

The European Economic Community (EEC), also called the Common Market, was set up shortly after the Second World War, and consisted originally of six European countries. Membership has now expanded to twelve. The EEC originated as a first step towards the development of a European Federation, which the founders believed would eventually become a strong political union. While there is a European Parliament, its powers are as yet relatively restricted. The EEC remains fundamentally an economic network, offering favorable conditions for trading and economic exchange between its member countries. In 1992, however, many existing barriers to trade and mobility within the EEC are due to come down—something that is likely to produce greater political as well as economic integration.

Many similar **trading networks,** although smaller in size, have been formed in other areas of the world. The Soviet Union, for instance, set up the Council for Mutual Economic Assistance (COME-CON), to facilitate trading relationships among the Eastern European societies. One of the most important international economic networks established was the Organization of Petroleum Exporting Countries (OPEC). The control that OPEC exerted over world oil supplies allowed its members to quadruple the price of oil in the early 1970s, causing shock waves throughout most of the world economy, but with the declining demand for oil since the early 1980s, its influence has declined. Various attempts have been made, however, to set up similar organizations among producers of goods in short supply. While organizations of this type are not worldwide, they still express—and are at the same time a response to—the acceleration of globalizing influences.

We now turn to a fundamental influence upon globalization, which partly underlies those discussed so far: the communications media, particularly electronic media like radio, television, and modern information systems. Information can be transmitted almost instantaneously to all parts of the globe, transcending distance in ways that were impossible until some thirty years or so ago, with the initiating of satellite communication systems.

THE GLOBALIZING OF MEDIA

IF TODAY WE ALL LIVE IN "ONE WORLD," IT IS IN LARGE part a result of the international scope of the communications media. Anyone who switches on the TV set and watches "the world news" ordinarily gets what the description suggests: a presentation of events that occurred that day or shortly before in many different parts of the world. Television programs are sold to large international markets and hundreds of millions of people watch them. The development of a **world information order**—an international system for the production, distribution, and consumption of information—like other aspects of the global society, has been uneven and reflects the divisions between the developed societies and Third World countries.

NEWS

Flows of news are dominated by a small number of news agencies, which supply up-to-the-minute information to newspapers, as well as to radio and TV stations throughout the world. Reuters, a British agency, was one of the first in the field. In 1870, Reuters, together with Agence Havas, a French company, divided up the globe into exclusive news territories. Reuters dealt with Britain, Holland, and their imperial dependencies, which at that time stretched across large segments of Africa and Asia. Havas took France, Italy, Spain, Portugal, and part of the Middle East. In 1876, Reuters agreed that Havas could have exclusive claim to South America, while Reuters was given the whole of the Far East, except for what was then Indo-China, but including Australia and New Zealand. Both agencies exchanged news with the most prominent American agency, the Associated Press (AP).

AP at that time was largely dependent upon the two European agencies for international news used by newspapers in the United States. Following World War I, the leading American agencies began to compete with their European rivals in many parts of the world. The two largest agencies, AP and UPI (United Press International), still gain much of their revenue from newspapers, radio, and televi-

Media agencies travel far and wide to report the news. Here, a TV crew tapes a Palestinian demonstration in the Israeli-occupied West Bank.

sion in the United States, but have become very influential in providing news material used internationally.

Together with Agence France-Presse, (which replaced Havas), Reuters, AP, and UPI are responsible for most of the international news transmitted throughout the world, partly excluding the Soviet Union. Information assembled by these agencies, once sent by Morse code, or telephone line, is now transmitted via computer and satellite links. Between them the four agencies send out thirty-four million words each day and claim to provide nine-tenths of the total news output of the world's press, radio, and television (Smith, 1980b).

Another news agency of world importance is TASS (the Telegraphic Agency of the Union of Soviet Socialist Republics). TASS provides virtually all the international news that reaches provincial newspapers and broadcasting stations in the Soviet Union. The major national newspapers and television also rely heavily upon its services, although a few have their own offices overseas which supply them with material directly. When TASS was first set up, in 1925, it was given sole authority to distribute information about the Soviet government inside the country and abroad. TASS maintains offices in many parts of the world, although it is particularly well-established in Eastern Europe (Hopkins, 1970). It is essentially an arm of the Soviet government, explicitly dedicated not only to reporting international news but to portraying the Soviet Union in a favorable light to the rest of the world. Information supplied by TASS reaches foreign clients without charge, leading many Third World countries to make use of the agency. TASS has an extensive network, reporting from about three-quarters of the countries of the world.

Partly to counter the dominance of TASS, the Union of Journalists and Writers in the USSR established NOVOSTI in 1961. This agency has no direct links with either the Soviet Government or the Communist Party, although like all organizations in the Soviet Union it is subject to their general supervision. NOVOSTI has grown rapidly over the period since it was first set up, publishing foreign-language magazines and newspapers as well as maintaining a large chain of foreign bureaus. These are linked through communication technologies as sophisticated as that possessed by the leading Western media organizations. Outside the Soviet Union, TASS and NOVOSTI have nothing like the global influence of the Western agencies. Western media use TASS and NOVOSTI as sources for official Soviet pronouncements, or for news events in the Soviet Union that Western agencies for one reason or another are unable to cover. However, the press and TV in Eastern Europe—especially in countries other than the Soviet Union itself—make extensive use of the Western agencies for international reporting.

The influence of the U.S. film industry is seen in this Japanese use of Hollywood movie images and in Taiwan's use of film star Mickey Mouse.

CINEMA, TELEVISION, ADVERTISING, AND ELECTRONIC COMMUNICATION

American companies are dominant in the production and distribution of television programs, movies, advertisements, and other forms of electronic communication.

In the 1920s, when "feature films" first began, Hollywood made four-fifths of all films screened in the world. The United States continues today to be easily the largest influence in the cinema industry. The governments of many countries provide subsidies to aid their own film industries, but no other country rivals the United States as an exporter of feature films. In Britain, for instance, American films account for 40 percent of all films shown annually (Smith, 1981). Most of the other countries which have a film export industry, such as Italy, Japan, and West Germany, are themselves large importers of American products. Many Third World countries import substantial quantities of American films. In most South American countries, for example, over 50 percent of all films shown each year come from the United States. The same ratio also applies to many societies in Asia, Africa, and the Middle East. In Thailand, as many as 90 percent of all films shown per year are American.

In the field of television programs, the British are an important global presence alongside American corporations. If feature films on television are excluded, earnings for British television exports are about the same as those for the United States. However, a substantial proportion of British programs are actually sold to a single market—the United States itself—so the worldwide influence of American television programs sales is in fact more considerable.

Nine of the largest ten advertising firms in the world are North American. Half the major agencies in Canada, West Germany,

France, Britain, and Australia are American; in many states in Asia, Africa, and South America the largest agencies are either American or owned by U.S. companies. The top ten advertising agencies are transnationals, some with a host of subsidiaries in other countries. The big advertising agencies, like Saatchi and Saatchi, are regularly employed by the giant transnational corporations to coordinate programs of advertising put out simultaneously in many countries.

American influence is also strong over the electronic channels used to communicate much of the information upon which modern states, and large corporations depend. Telecommunication links now essential to banking, world monetary transactions, and some kinds of TV and radio broadcasting, are mostly in American hands. International Business Machines (IBM), based in the United States, is one of the largest of all transnational corporations. It has enormous influence over international information flow and control, particularly in respect of the supply of computer resources. It has been estimated that nine-tenths of all records held in databases throughout the world are accessible to the American government or other organizations in the United States.

MEDIA IMPERIALISM

The paramount position of the industrialized countries, above all the United States, in the production and diffusion of media has led many observers to speak of *media imperialism*. A cultural empire, it is argued, has been established, and Third World countries are especially vulnerable, because they lack the resources with which to maintain their own cultural independence. Control of the world's news by the major Western agencies inevitably means the predominance of a "First World" outlook in the information conveyed throughout the world. Attention is given to the Third World in news broadcasts in the developed countries mainly in times of disaster, crisis, or military confrontation. The daily files of other types of news, which are kept on the industrialized world, are not maintained on the Third World (Tatarian, 1978).

The quantity of television and movie exports coming from the United States, as a proportion of the world's total, has declined since its peak in the late 1960s. Elihu Katz and his colleagues studied the development of radio and television networks in ten Third World countries and proposed that there were "phases of institutionalization" in the introduction of radio and television in the less-developed societies. In the first phase, a model of broadcasting is adopted from elsewhere, usually from the United States, Britain, or France, and serves as the basis for the fledgling system. During this period, the media are saturated by imported products. In the second phase, local production facilities become more developed, and the system becomes more oriented towards the local society. In the third phase, governments tend to intervene to promote conditions in which the onslaught of Western influence can to some degree be resisted (Katz et al., 1978).

It would be impossible to deny the prime role which Western media in general, and English-speaking countries and organizations in particular, play in the global production and diffusion of media. Some Third World leaders have advocated the creation of controls upon information production and flow in order to create more equality in international communications media. At a conference of nations not affiliated by treaty either to the United States or the Soviet Union, a "non-aligned news pool" was set up in the early 1970s. The eighty-five countries involved agreed to share information from their national agencies, in order to try to foster more-informed news releases than those coming from the Western and Soviet agencies. Its influence thus far, however, has been limited. Many of the national agencies involved are hardly known for scrupulous or unbiased reporting of events in their homelands. It has seemed to critics of such endeavors that some Third World governments try to exert rigorous internal control over their own media, ensuring that the "official" way of seeing things is maintained—while denouncing "bias" from abroad (McPhail, 1987).

Some observers believe that world inequalities in telecommunications technology are likely to become more pronounced in the future than is the case thus far. In the words of a prominent media researcher, Anthony Smith:

> The threat to independence in the late twentieth century from the new electronics could be greater than was colonialism itself. We are beginning to learn that de-colonization and the growth of supra-nationalism were not the termination of imperial relationships but merely the extending of a geo-political web which has been spinning since the Renaissance. The news media have the power to penetrate more deeply into a "receiving" culture than any previous manifestation of Western technology. The results could be immense havoc, an intensification of the social contradictions within developing societies today. In the West we have come to think of the 2,500 communications satellites which presently circle the earth as distributors of information. For many societies they may become pipettes through which the data which confers sovereignty upon a society is extracted for processing in some remote place. (Smith, 1980b)

UNDERSTANDING GLOBAL
INEQUALITY

WHAT ACCOUNTS FOR THE HUGE DIFFERENCES IN WEALTH and power between the industrialized countries and the Third World societies? Several theories have been proposed to try to explain why such marked global inequalities have developed. We now move on to look at these theoretical approaches. Each of them takes a broad historical perspective and is oriented towards explaining the legacy of colonialism for subsequent relationships between rich and poor countries.

IMPERIALISM

An early theoretical view, first advanced by the English historian J. A. Hobson and later by the Soviet leader Vladimir I. Lenin, placed a particular emphasis on the importance of **imperialism** in explaining world inequalities. Hobson's work was published in the early 1900s, at the time of the "scramble for Africa" among Western nations. In Hobson's view, colonialism derived from the attempt to find new markets for investment as capacity for production expanded beyond what could profitably be sold in the home markets. According to Hobson, the majority of the population are only able to afford to buy a relatively small proportion of the goods that can be produced. There is a constant striving both for new markets in which to sell and for ways of cheapening production by gaining access to sources of inexpensive raw materials and labor power in other parts of the world. Imperialism—the drive to conquer and subjugate other peoples, of which colonialism was one expression—results from these pressures towards external expansion (Hobson, 1965).

This process both assisted the economic development of the Western countries and impoverished much of the rest of the world, because resources were drained off from the nonindustrialized regions. Thus was set in motion an increasing divergence between the wealth that the West was able to accumulate and the poverty of the Third World. Lenin argued that large business corporations played a leading role in this development, although they were supported by their national governments. The corporations led the drive to exploit the nonindustrialized parts of the world, establishing trading relations with poorer countries on terms highly favorable to themselves.

NEO-IMPERIALISM

More recent authors have borrowed from the ideas of Hobson and Lenin to develop theories of **neo-imperialism.** The advocates of these theories are more concerned with the present-day world than with the period which Hobson and Lenin analyzed. The old colonial empires, like the British Empire, have more or less completely disappeared, and virtually all the old colonial areas have become self-governing countries. Yet, so these theorists argue, while the industrialized states have withdrawn from direct administration of colonized territories, they still maintain their control through their leading economic position in world trade, and through the influence of the large transnational corporations. The Western countries are able to perpetuate their privileged position by ensuring that they control the terms upon which world trade is carried on (Warren, 1981).

DEPENDENCY THEORY

An approach linked to theories of neo-imperialism is **dependency theory.** This approach was developed originally in a South American context (Cardoso, 1972; Furtado, 1984). According to the dependency theorists, global society has developed *unevenly,* such that the main core of the industrialized world (United States, Europe, and Japan) has a dominant role, with the Third World countries being dependent upon it. The origins and nature of dependence vary according to how far a specific country was colonized and by whom. Dependence usually means the reliance of Third World countries upon selling case crops to the developed world.

For instance, Brazil became—and remains today—the major producer of coffee for export to the industrialized countries. Other cash crops include sugar, rubber, and bananas—hence the name "banana republics," scornfully applied to the unstable political regimes of South America by those surveying them from the more prosperous North (Munck, 1984). The strong presence of traditional forms of agriculture in such countries, combined with cash-crop production for export, limited the development of modern manufacturing production. Once the South American countries had fallen too far behind the industrialized countries of Europe and the United States, and had become dependent upon them for manufactured goods, stagnation set in.

The economist André Gunder Frank coined the phrase "the development of underdevelopment" to describe the evolution of the Third

Third World countries have always provided the cash crops for the expansion of Western-dominated agribusiness. Here, a coffee picker in Colombia at work.

World countries. These societies became impoverished, he held, as a direct result of their subordinate position to the industrialized countries. The industrialized countries became rich *at the expense* of the Third World, which they created through colonialism and neo-imperialism. In Frank's words, "development and underdevelopment are two sides of the same coin" (Frank, 1969). The rich countries form a "metropolitan center," around which "satellite" (Third World) countries are grouped, their economies being dependent upon those of the more advanced countries, while they themselves become largely impoverished.

WORLD SYSTEM THEORY

World system theory, pioneered by Immanuel Wallerstein (1974, 1979), is the most sophisticated approach to patterns of global inequality. According to Wallerstein, from the sixteenth century onwards there developed a **world system**—a series of economic and political connections stretching across the globe—based on the expansion of a *capitalist world economy.* The capitalist world economy is made up of the core countries (which correspond roughly to Frank's metropolitan center), the semi-periphery, the periphery, and the external arena. The **core countries** are those in which modern economic enterprises first emerged and which subsequently underwent processes of industrialization. The core first consisted of England, Holland, and France. Other societies located in northwest Europe, such as Germany, came to form part of the core at a later date. The core areas contained a range of emerging manufacturing industries and relatively advanced forms of agricultural production. The core states also developed centralized forms of government.

Societies situated in the south of Europe, around the Mediterranean (such as Spain), became a **semi-periphery** of the core countries. In other words, they were linked in various kinds of dependent trading relationships with the northern states, but remained economically fairly stagnant. Until two centuries ago, the **periphery**—the outer edge—of the world economy was situated mainly in the eastern fringes of Europe. In these areas, such as what is now Poland, cash crops were sold directly to the core countries.

Much of Asia and Africa were at this date part of the **external arena**—that is to say, they remained outside the commercial connections established by the core countries. As a result of colonialism, and subsequently the activities of the large corporations, these regions have been drawn into the world economy. Today, the Third World nations form the periphery of what is by now a very comprehensive world system, in which the United States and Japan have come to join, and now dominate, the core. The Soviet Union and the East European societies (the Second World societies), whose economies were centrally planned, were until recently the only large group of countries that remained to some degree outside the global economy. Now that they are turning more to systems of competitive enterprise, they will become drawn more and more into the global economic order.

Since the core countries dominate the world system, Wallerstein argued, they are able to organize world trade to favor their interests. Much as the dependency theorists say, the First World countries have established a position in which they are able to exploit the resources of the Third World societies for their own ends.

CRITICAL ASSESSMENT OF THE THEORIES

How valid are these theories? They all agree that the imbalance in wealth and resources between First and Third Worlds has its origins in colonialism. In this they are surely correct, and without doubt it is also right to claim that the dependency relationships established during the colonial period have been maintained, and even accentuated, since then. Most Third World countries find themselves enmeshed in economic relations with the core states that hamper their economic development, but from which it is very difficult for them to break free. The result is that the industrialized areas of the world become increasingly more prosperous, while many Third World countries stagnate. Wallerstein's theory is especially important, because it is not just concerned with global inequalities but with analyzing the world as a single social system. The industrialized societies and the Third World countries emerged as different parts of an overall set of processes of development. This perspective is vital, even if the details of Wallerstein's account can be criticized (Brenner, 1977; Skocpol, 1977; Stinchcombe, 1982).

But it is false to argue, as Frank does in particular, that the prosperity of the industrialized societies has been achieved *as a result* of their exploitation of the poorer countries. The resources they derived from these countries were of minor importance compared to the processes of industrial growth generated within the industrialized societies themselves (Blomstrom and Hettne, 1984).

None of these theories helps much to understand the rapid acceleration of global interdependencies in the post–World War II period. There has been a clear "speed-up" in globalization over the past few decades. As we have seen, one factor in this is largely technological— the development of systems of transportation and communication that allow people, goods, and information to be carried at great speed from place to place.

U.S. corporate influence in Hong Kong.

A further weakness of each of these theories is that they concentrate almost exclusively upon economic factors in the development of the world system. Economic influences are very important but so are others. The impact of war has been profound (see Chapter II: "War and the Military"). Political considerations and cultural factors have also had a major impact upon the forging of increasing global interdependence.

A GLOBAL PERSPECTIVE

WHAT WILL BE THE END-RESULT OF THE GLOBAL PROCESSES described in this chapter? Is the whole globe likely at some future point to become a single political system supervised by some form of world government? Certainly processes of globalization are among the most important social changes occurring at the current time. Sociological analysis that confines itself to the study of single societies is becoming increasingly archaic. As human beings, we more and more share a common fate. Many of the fundamental problems that beset human life today, such as ecological issues or avoiding large-scale military confrontations, are necessarily global in scope.

Yet in spite of growing economic and cultural interdependence, the world global system is riven with inequalities, and divided up into a patchwork of states having divergent as well as common concerns. There is no real indication of a political convergence which will overcome the conflicting interests of states in the near future. A world government may eventually come into being, but if this does happen it will be a result of a long-term process of development. One of the most worrying features of world society today is that increasing globalization is not matched either by political integration or by the reduction of international inequalities of wealth and power.

The study of global development and inequality brings into focus one of the chief "theoretical dilemmas"—perplexing questions of theoretical interpretation—which confronts us in sociology today. It is a long-standing dilemma that can be traced back to differences between the views of Max Weber and Karl Marx. Is the expansion of capitalism the main force producing tendencies towards globalization? Or is globalization happening mainly as a result of other influences, such as what Weber called the *rationalization* of modern social life—the development of ever-more systematic connections between previously separate groups and communities?

Most of the theories we have looked at in this chapter have been indebted to Marx, and thus incline towards the first view. But we probably need to combine elements from each perspective to develop a more adequate understanding of global changes than we currently possess. We shall take up these issues again in the following chapters. (See Chapter 20: "Understanding Social Change" and Chapter 22: "The Development of Sociological Theory.")

SUMMARY

1. World society has become increasingly interdependent—a process known as *globalization.* The development of world social relations involves large-scale inequalities between the industrialized and Third World societies. The largest disparities of wealth and living standards are those separating the rich industrialized countries from the poorer Third World states.

2. Most Third World societies are in areas of the world that underwent Western colonial rule. Many have only become independent states since the Second World War. Although most Third World societies are impoverished compared to the industrialized nations, a minority (the NICs, or newly industrialized countries) have experienced rapid economic development.

3. Millions of people in the world each year die of hunger or of diseases associated with malnutrition. Yet sufficient food is produced today to feed everyone in the world, even with rapid population growth. Large amounts of food are destroyed, or stored indefinitely, by the Western countries even though people in other parts of the world are starving. The level of regular food aid provided by the rich to the poor countries is low.

4. The distribution of the world's food supplies is strongly influenced by the impact of agribusiness—the industrial production, processing, and storage of food. Agribusiness firms operating in Third World countries are geared to export for Western markets rather than to stimulating local agriculture.

5. A significant feature of the process of world development is the growth of *transnationals*—companies operating in two or more countries, thus operating across different national boundaries. Countries in the world economy have become interdependent largely as a result of the activities of the transnationals.

6. The invention of telecommunications technologies permits more or less instantaneous communication from one part of the world to the other. Advances made in transportation have also

facilitated a frequent and rapid exchange of goods from country to country. *Nonstate actors*—organizations concerned with processes demanding international collaboration or communication —have emerged to help cope with these trends.

7. The sense today of inhabiting *one world* is in large part a result of the international scope of the communications media. TV news programs provide a mosaic of international images offering a "window on the world." A world information order—an international system for the production, distribution, and consumption of informational goods—has come into being. Given the paramount position of the industrial countries in the world information order, many believe that the Third World countries are subjected to a form of *media imperialism*.

8. Three types of theoretical thinking have contributed to our understanding of the developments leading to global inequalities. Theories of *imperialism* and *neo-imperialism* see the dynamics of such developments in economic pressures towards external expansion of industrial enterprise. *Dependency theories* place emphasis on the capability of the industrialized countries to dominate the terms of their relationships with Third World states. *World system theory* describes a centralized world economy linking *core countries,* the *semi-periphery,* the *periphery,* and the *external arena*.

BASIC CONCEPTS

GLOBALIZATION	WORLD SYSTEM THEORY
IMPERIALISM	WORLD SYSTEM

IMPORTANT TERMS

THIRD WORLD	INTERNATIONAL DIVISION OF
CASH-CROP PRODUCTION	LABOR
CONCESSION COMPANY	VERTICAL INTEGRATION
GROSS NATIONAL PRODUCT (GNP)	NONSTATE ACTORS
NEWLY INDUSTRIALIZING	TRADING NETWORKS
COUNTRIES (NIC)	WORLD INFORMATION ORDER
AGRIBUSINESS	NEO-IMPERIALISM
TRANSNATIONAL COMPANIES	DEPENDENCY THEORY
CONGLOMERATES	CORE COUNTRIES
ETHNOCENTRIC TRANSNATIONALS	SEMI-PERIPHERY
POLYCENTRIC TRANSNATIONALS	PERIPHERY
GEOCENTRIC TRANSNATIONALS	EXTERNAL ARENA

CHAPTER SEVENTEEN

MODERN URBANISM

THE CITY PROVIDES SOCIOLOGISTS WITH A LABORATORY FOR studying the diversity of social life and conflict. Cities are the capitals of civilization: they are culturally lively, commercially dynamic, and alluring. They are efficient in providing for so much of the population in so little space. However, they can be dirty, polluted, crime-ridden, and expensive; an entire literature has been devoted to the grimness of city life.

There are tensions within all city areas. Speculative developers are at odds with urban dwellers and local businesses. Gentrification—the restoring and rebuilding of old downtown city centers—benefits some groups, but dispossesses others of their homes. Between city dwellers and their cousin suburbanites there are competing interests. Beyond the city lines there are also tensions. Each city, itself, is now engaged in a game of survival among cities of the world within the new and competitive global economy.

In studying modern cities, and examining these tensions, we shall analyze some of the most basic changes that separate our world from the traditional one. For in all industrialized countries, in contrast to the premodern era, most of the population live in urban areas. Moreover, modern urban life affects everyone, not only those who live in

City life: Street musicians in San Francisco . . .

the cities themselves. We shall first of all study the origins of cities and the vast growth in the numbers of city dwellers that has occurred over the past century. The discussion then moves on to consider patterns of urban development in North America, which we compare to cities in Eastern Europe and the Third World. Finally, we will take up the main theories that have been advanced to help understand the distinctive characteristics of urban life.

CITIES IN TRADITIONAL SOCIETIES

CITIES IN TRADITIONAL SOCIETIES WERE VERY SMALL BY modern standards. Babylon, for example, one of the largest ancient Near Eastern cities, only extended over an area of 3.2 square miles—and at its height around 2000 B.C. probably had a population of no more than 15,000–20,000 people. The world's first cities appeared about 3500 B.C., in the river valleys of the Nile in Egypt, the Tigris and Euphrates in what is now Iraq, and the Indus in what is today Pakistan. Rome under Emperor Augustus in the first century B.C. was easily the largest premodern city outside of China, having some 300,000 inhabitants, the population of Birmingham, Alabama, or Tucson, Arizona, today.

Most cities of the ancient world shared certain common features despite the variety of the civilizations in which they were established. They were usually surrounded by walls that served as military defense, and emphasized the separation of the urban community from the countryside. The central area of the city was almost always occupied by a religious temple, a royal palace, government and commercial buildings, and a public square. This ceremonial, commercial, and political center was sometimes enclosed within a second, inner wall, and was usually too small to hold more than a minority of the citizens. Although it usually contained a market, the center was quite different from the business districts found at the core of modern cities because the main buildings were nearly always religious and political (Sjoberg, 1960, 1963; Fox, 1964; Wheatley, 1971).

The dwellings of the ruling class or elite tended to be concentrated in or near the center. The less-privileged groups lived towards the perimeter of the city or outside the walls, moving within them if the city came under attack. Different ethnic and religious communities were often allocated to separate neighborhoods, where their members both lived and worked. Sometimes these neighborhoods were also surrounded by walls. Communication among city dwellers was erratic. Lacking any form of printing press, public officials had to shout at the tops of their voices to deliver pronouncements. There were few streets as we know them. "Streets" were usually strips of land on which no one had yet built.

In a few traditional states there were sophisticated road systems linking various cities. But these existed mainly for military purposes, and transportation for the most part was slow and limited. Merchants and soldiers were the only people who regularly traveled over extensive distances.

While cities were the main centers for science, the arts, and cosmopolitan culture in traditional states, their level of influence over the rest of the country was always relatively low. No more than a tiny proportion of the population lived in the cities, and the division between cities and countryside was pronounced. By far the majority of eople lived in small rural communities, and rarely if ever came into contact with more than the occasional state official or merchant from the towns.

. . . a drug arrest in New York . . .

INDUSTRIALIZATION AND URBANIZATION

THE CONTRAST IN SIZE BETWEEN THE LARGEST MODERN cities and those of premodern civilizations is extraordinary. The most populous cities in the industrialized countries have 20 million or more inhabitants. A **conurbation**—a cluster of cities and towns forming a continuous network—may include much larger numbers of people than this. The peak of urban life today is represented by what is called the **megalopolis,** the "city of cities." The term was originally coined in ancient Greece to refer to a city-state that was planned to be the envy of all civilizations. In its current usage though, it has little relation to that utopia. It was first applied in modern times to refer to the Northeast corridor of the United States, a conurbation covering some 450 miles from north of Boston to below Washington, D.C. In this region, about 40 million people live at a density of over 700 persons per square mile. An urban population almost as large and dense is concentrated in the lower Great Lakes region (Gottman, 1961).

. . . night life in Tokyo.

Britain was the first society to undergo industrialization, beginning in the mid-eighteenth century. The process of industrialization generated increasing **urbanization**—the movement of the population into towns and cities, away from the life on the land. In 1800, well under 20 percent of the British population lived in towns or cities having more than 10,000 inhabitants. By 1900, this proportion had become 74 percent. The capital city, London, held about 1.1 million people in 1800; it increased in size to a population of over 7 million by the beginning of the twentieth century. London was at that date by far the largest city ever seen in the world; it was a vast manufacturing, commercial, and financial center at the heart of a still-expanding British Empire.

The urbanization of most other European countries, and the United States, took place somewhat later, but in some cases, once under way, accelerated even faster. In 1800, the United States was more of a rural society than were the leading European countries at the same date. Less than 10 percent of the population lived in communities with populations of more than 2,500 people. Today, well over three-quarters of Americans are city dwellers. Between 1800 and 1900, as industrialization grew in the United States, the population of New York leapt from 60,000 people to 4.8 million.

Urbanization in the twentieth century is a global process, into which the Third World is increasingly being drawn. From 1900 to 1950, world urbanization increased by 239 percent, compared with a global population growth of 49 percent. The past forty years or so have seen an increased acceleration in the proportion of the world's population living in cities. From 1950 to 1986, urban growth worldwide was 320 percent, while the population grew by 54 percent. Most of this growth has occurred in cities in Third World societies. In 1975, 39 percent of the world's population lived in urban localities; the figure is predicted to be 50 percent in 2000 and 63 percent in 2025. Eastern and southern Asia will contain about a half of the world's population in 2025. By that date the urban populations of the Third World countries will each exceed those of Europe or the United States.

Along with this worldwide urbanization comes the effects of globalization. For example, the rise of urban-industrial areas in Third World countries has brought intensified economic competition to industries in U.S. cities. South Korea's shoe industry has led to the impoverishment of areas in Massachusetts cities that formerly relied on that industry for their prosperity. Similarly, Baltimore had to adjust to losing much of the market for its steel industry to Japan. We shall examine later in the chapter how the global economy has influenced forms of city life in recent years.

INTERPRETATIONS OF CITY LIFE

The development of modern cities has had an enormous impact not only on habits and modes of behavior, but on patterns of thought and feeling (Lees, 1985). From the beginning of large urban agglomerations in the eighteenth century, views about the effects of cities upon social life have been polarized—and remain so today. Some saw cities as representing "civilized virtue," centers of dynamism and cultural creativity (Schorske, 1963). For these authors, cities maximized opportunities for economic and cultural development, and provided the means of living a comfortable and satisfying existence. James Boswell constantly praised the virtues of London, which he compared to a "museum, a garden, to endless musical combinations" (Quoted in Byrd, 1978). Others branded the city a smoking inferno thronged with aggressive and mutually distrustful crowds, and riddled with crime, violence, and corruption.

During the nineteenth and early twentieth centuries, as cities mushroomed in size, these contrasting views found new voices. Critics found easy targets for their attacks, as the living conditions of the poor in the most rapidly developing urban areas were frequently appalling. George Gissing, an English novelist and social analyst, personally experienced extreme poverty both in London and in Chicago in the 1870s. His descriptions of the East End of London, one of the poorest sections in the city, conveyed a grim picture. Gissing portrayed the area as "a region of malodorous market streets, of factories, timber-yards, grimy warehouses, of alleys swarming with small

A soup kitchen in Manchester, England, 1862, and homeless in Washington, D.C., 1990.

trades and crafts, of filthy courts and passages leading into pestilential gloom; everywhere toil in its most degrading forms; the thorough-fares thundering with high-laden wagons, the pavements trodden by working folk of the coarsest type, the corners and lurking-holes showing destitution at its ugliest" (Gissing, 1983; orig. pub. 1892).

At this period, poverty in American cities received less attention than in Europe. Towards the end of the century, however, reformers began increasingly to condemn the squalor of large parts of New York, Boston, Chicago, and other major cities. The extent of urban poverty, and the vast differences among city neighborhoods, were among the main factors prompting early sociological analyses of urban life. A Danish immigrant, Jacob Riis, a reporter for the *New York Tribune,* traveled extensively across the United States, docu-menting conditions of poverty and lecturing about needed reforms. Riis's book, *How the Other Half Lives,* which appeared in 1890, reached a wide audience (Riis, 1957; Lane, 1974). Others added their voices to what became a chorus of description of grim urban life. As one anonymous poet put it, speaking of the Boston poor:

> In a great, Christian city, died friendless, of hunger!
> Starved to death, where there's many a bright banquet hall!
> In a city of hospitals, died in a prison!
> Homeless, died in a land that boasts free homes for all!
> In a city of millionaires, died without money!
> (Quoted in Lees, 1985)

URBANISM IN THE UNITED STATES

NEW YORK CITY OFFERS THE MOST READY EXAMPLE OF THE contrasts of urban life. It is common to capture in one pic-ture frame a homeless person rummaging through a trash can and a business executive getting out of a limousine. In other cities, like San Francisco, Los Angeles, or Dallas, the well-to-do and the disadvantaged are more likely to be found in different sections of the city. Canadian cities, like Toronto, Montreal, and Vancouver, as well as most cities in Europe, contrast with the large U.S. urban areas. Rates of urban crime are generally well below those of cities in the United States, and most have not experienced the same level of urban decay. What are the main trends that have affected city development in the United States over the past several decades? How can we explain the decay of central-city areas? These are questions we shall take up in the following sections. One of the major changes that has affected urban patterns in the period since World War II is the movement of large parts of city populations to newly constructed suburbs. Although it has not been wholly a one-way process, this movement outwards has been a particularly pronounced feature of U.S. urbanism and is certainly related directly to central-city decay. We therefore begin with a discussion of suburbia before moving on to look at the inner city. We shall then place the discussion in a broader global context by studying city development in two quite different situations from the United States: in the Third World and in Eastern Europe and the Soviet Union.

SUBURBANIZATION

A measure of the high density of urbanization in the United States today is the fact that three-quarters of the population lives in 1.5 percent of the land area of the country. To measure urban density, the Bureau of the Census uses the concept of the Standard Metropolitan Statistical Area (SMSA), defined as any region that contains an urban area with a population of at least 50,000. There are 320 SMSAs in the United States, most of them in the Northeast and Great Lakes areas, with rapid expansion occurring in the South and West, especially in California. The Census Bureau also reports that more people now live in the suburbs of metropolitan areas than in the downtown areas.

The word "suburb" has its origins in the Latin term *sub urbe*, meaning "under city control," an appropriate meaning throughout most of the history of urbanism. Suburbs were small pockets of dwellings dependent upon urban centers for their amenities and livelihood. Today, "suburb" refers to any residential or commercial area adjoining a city, regardless of whether or not it is subject to central-city control. Many suburbs are effectively autonomous areas, over which city administrations have little direct influence.

In the United States, **suburbanization,** the massive development and inhabiting of towns surrounding a city, reached its peak during the 1950s and 1960s, a time of great economic growth. World War II had previously absorbed most industrial resources, and any development outside the war effort was restricted. But by the 1950s, war rationing had ended, automobiles instead of tanks were being mass produced, and people were encouraged to pursue at least one part of "the American Dream"—owning a house and a piece of land. During that decade, the population in the cities increased by 10 percent, while in the suburban areas it grew by no less than 48 percent.

The prevailing economic scene also made it easy to move out of the city. The Federal Housing Administration (FHA) provided assistance in obtaining mortgage loans, making it possible in the early postwar period for families to buy housing in the suburbs for less than they would have paid for rent in the cities (K. Jackson, 1981, 1985). FHA policy did not provide financial assistance to improve older homes, or to build new homes in the central areas of ethnically-mixed cities. Instead, the FHA offered large-scale aid only to the builders and buyers of suburban housing. The FHA, together with the Veterans Administration, funded almost half of all suburban housing built during the 1950s and 1960s.

A significant role was played by housing and highway lobbies in Congress. Early in the 1950s, groups promoting highway construction launched "Project Adequate Roads," aimed at inducing the federal government to support the building of highways. President Dwight D. Eisenhower responded with a giant construction program for interstate roadways. In 1956, the Highway Act was passed authorizing $32 billion to be used for building such highways. Coinciding with a period of expansion in the automobile industry, such that many families came to own more than one car, the result was that previously out-of-the-way suburban areas, with lower property taxes, became accessible to places of work. At the same time, the highway program led to the establishment of industries and services in suburban areas themselves. Many suburban towns became themselves es-

Suburbia.

"And now, Randy, by use of song, the male sparrow will stake out his territory . . . an instinct common in the lower animals."

sentially separate cities, connected by rapid highways to the other suburbs around them. From the 1960s on, the proportion of people commuting between suburbs increased more steadily than those commuting to cities.

In 1954, the Supreme Court, in *Brown v. Board of Education of Topeka, Kansas,* effectively outlawed segregated public schools. Cities could no longer systematically place black and white children in separate schools. One unintended consequence of school-integration policies was the flight of whites from the cities to the suburbs. In addition to the house and the lawn, the new suburbanites wanted well-financed white-only schools, and this they got. Blacks found it far more difficult to move to the suburbs. They were not in as good a position as whites to benefit from government programs offered by the FHA and the Veterans Administration, which helped encourage white migration from the cities (Issel, 1985). Those blacks who might have had the financial resources to move to the suburbs were confronted with another barrier, housing discrimination. In many parts of the country, it was a common practice for a new white home buyer to pledge that when the time came, he would sell his house only to another white family. In the 1970s fair-housing laws were passed barring such practices, but the results of earlier discrimination were still strongly felt.

Suburbia remains today heavily white-dominated. Prior to 1960, only about 3 percent of suburban residents were black. Over the years since then, black representation in suburbia has risen to about 8 percent. (This represents, however, over 20 percent of the total black population in the United States.) Three out of every five blacks continue to live in the central cities, compared to only one in every four whites. Most of the black suburban residents in fact live in towns bordering central-city neighborhoods (Lake, 1981; Muller, 1981).

CENTRAL CITIES

Inner-city decay—the Harlem section of New York.

City populations are far more varied ethnically and culturally than those of the suburbs. Herbert Gans distinguished five types of residents in central cities. The *cosmopolitans*—writers, artists, students, and some professionals—are urban dwellers because cities are cultural centers important to their way of life. Cities offer everything from art museums, the theater, and bookstores to the latest movies and ethnic cuisines. The *unmarried and childless* remain in, or move into, the city because of the job opportunities and lively entertainments. Such individuals usually live in rental apartments and frequently move out to the suburbs once they marry or begin to raise children.

The *ethnic villagers* are another group. They continue traditional ways of life within close-knit neighborhoods. These groups include long-established residents who maintain a firm sense of community identity, and who prefer to remain in contact with friends and kin rather than move away to the suburbs.

The *deprived* consist of those who are too poor to live anywhere save in low-rent neighborhoods, often in run-down housing. At the same time, they have strong feelings of community identity and may prefer city life. The *trapped* are individuals who would like to leave the central city, but cannot do so because they lack sufficient economic resources. Included here are people living on low fixed incomes, such as the elderly with small pensions, together with others who have become unemployed or who have suffered a decline in earnings. They feel that their neighborhoods are being "taken over" by other ethnic groups, but are compelled by economic circumstances to stay (Gans, 1962, 1968).

Inner-city decay is a partial consequence of the growth of the suburbs. The movement of high-income groups away from the city resulted in a loss of tax revenues. Since those that remained, or replaced them, include many living in poverty, the possibilities of generating increased tax revenues are limited. When taxes are raised in the central city, wealthier groups and businesses tend to move further out to take advantage of lower tax rates. This situation is worsened by the fact that the buildings in central cities are more run down than in the suburbs, crime rates have become higher, and there is a larger proportion of unemployed. The city must spend more on welfare services, schools, the upkeep of buildings, police, and fire services. A cycle of deterioration thus develops, in which the more suburbia expands, the greater become the problems faced by those living in the central cities. In many American urban areas, the outcome has been quite devastating—particularly in the older cities, such as New York, Philadelphia, or Washington, D.C. In some neighborhoods in these cities, the deterioration of property is probably worse than in large urban areas anywhere else in the industrialized world. Decaying tenement blocks, boarded-up and burnt-out buildings alternate with empty areas of land covered in rubble.

Lack of adequate systems of mass transportation has aggravated the problems of central cities. About 60 million people still live in central cities, while many more commute in to work. Yet federal and local governments still tend to give more assistance to highway programs than to public transport. Once the city has been geared to the automobile, it is usually difficult to reintroduce public transport effectively. The San Francisco Bay Area Rapid Transit System (BART), which opened in 1972, was the first newly constructed urban rail system in the United States for half a century. City planners saw this new train network as the prototype of public rapid-transit systems that might be introduced in other cities. So far, however, it has proved less than wholly successful. Running costs are higher and rates of passenger use lower than was anticipated, and it has not appreciably reduced automobile use in the Bay area.

In addition to financial crises, city managers and dwellers also have to contend with increasing environmental problems—here, smog in Los Angeles.

FINANCIAL CRISES

City governments today operate against a background of almost continual financial crisis. In the 1970s and early 1980s, several cities in the United States came close to bankruptcy and virtually all were compelled to cut back many of their services. The city of Cleveland defaulted in 1979, being unable to pay off debts equivalent to about a fifth of its annual budget. Chicago and San Francisco also faced deficits of many millions of dollars that they were unable to pay. But the most well-known urban financial crisis affected New York City.

In common with most other older industrial cities, New York had suffered a major decline in manufacturing jobs after World War II. Expansion in the areas of finance and insurance were not sufficient to compensate for this, and the net result was a steadily declining fund of resources for the city's revenue. From the 1950s on, New York also attracted large numbers of blacks, Puerto Ricans, and other low-income groups.

By 1974, the city had accumulated debts of $1.2 billion. During the years 1974 and 1975, there was a general economic downturn throughout the United States and banks refused to extend their loans to the city, while Congress and the state legislature reduced their assistance. New York City avoided bankruptcy only when the city government made major cutbacks in expenditures. Some fifty thousand public jobs were eliminated and the municipal payroll cut by nearly 20 percent. Schools, sanitation services, and police and fire departments were all drastically affected. Some social welfare programs were abandoned more or less completely. On the other hand, new tax benefits were given to businesses. The policies pursued since 1975 have been called a "tale of two cities" by critics. Manhattan has experienced a boom in office and hotel construction, attracting new capital investment. The majority of the urban population, on the other hand, is made up of low-income residents whose needs are largely disregarded by policy makers (Tabb, 1982).

New York today has a huge homeless population and, on a minor scale, is starting to look a little like a Third World city, such as will be discussed below. The homeless are visible to even a casual traveler through the city; they not only occupy park benches for the night, but make their homes in bus stations, train stations, and even airports. City-run shelters have been opened in various parts of the city, but many of the homeless reject these shelters, believing them to be unsafe. A 1987 decision in the New York State Supreme Court ruled that the thousands of single homeless people in the city were entitled to medical care and welfare grants—which had previously been denied to them. This assistance provides for some basic needs that most of the homeless cannot meet, but creates pressure upon the resources available to fund other welfare services (Bingham, Green, and White, 1987).

URBAN RENEWAL AND GENTRIFICATION

Urban decay is not a one-way process, but stimulates various countertrends, particularly those towards **urban renewal** or **gentrification.** Delapidated areas or, on a smaller scale, buildings, may become renovated as more affluent groups move back into them. Such a renewal process is called "gentrification," because those areas or buildings become upgraded and return to the control of the urban "gentry"—high-income dwellers—rather than remaining in the hands of the poor.

An example is the gentrification of the Society Hill area in Philadelphia. Some forty years ago, Society Hill, located in downtown Philadelphia, was "submerged in slums . . . [having] streets which were the dirtiest in the country" (Lowe, 1967). Most of the better-off groups had fled to the suburbs, leaving the inner city impoverished. Today, Society Hill is revitalized, many existing buildings have been renovated and new ones constructed. This has come about because of several influences. One was a feeling among civic leaders that the neighborhood had become a blight on the city as a whole. Members of a City Policy Committee, composed mainly of local business leaders, began a movement for the improvement of the area. This group was convinced that only comprehensive city planning could help transform the downtown district.

When the renewal program began in 1956, priority was given to the creation of high-quality residential streets, interspersed with green spaces, pedestrian malls, and secluded parks. Care was taken to preserve historical buildings as well as more ordinary dwellings and storefronts. Where buildings were demolished and replaced with others, the new constructions were designed to blend in style and scale with those that remained. Enormous financial resources were necessary to finance the redevelopment. Edmund Bacon, who was the executive director of the city commission overseeing the project, recalls that, in the beginning, "Everyone thought the idea was screwy" (quoted in Cybriwsky et al., 1986). Who could be persuaded to support the necessary program of investment? Wouldn't whatever buildings were renovated or constructed simply be isolated amid a downtown wasteland? Many businesses and construction companies did in fact invest in the redevelopment, while a number of leading citizens led the way in moving into the area and refurbishing homes there. As the trend towards private renovation caught on, more developers were persuaded to invest, generating further impetus to the process.

Society Hill became widely regarded as a model whose success could be repeated in other cities blighted by central-city decay. The Philadelphia program was both skilfully managed and received much popular support. These conditions are not easy to generate, and the high level of civic pride felt by many Philadelphians is not always shared by those living in cities with less-illustrious pasts. Moreover, a higher level of urban planning is necessary to achieve such results than many city governments are prepared to accept and pay for. Similar schemes, however, have been successful in cities like Boston, Baltimore, and Charleston. One lesson learned is that any urban renewal program requires comprehensive planning. Where urban renewal has been attempted by means of individual projects, its success has been limited. One such project, the Renaissance Center in Detroit, illustrates a fear that Philadelphians had: it has remained an isolated development amid an urban wasteland.

The Other Side of Gentrification

The trend towards central-city gentrification still does not match the continuing movement out of the cities by affluent groups. Poor immigrants moving into the cities outnumber the higher income groups returning to city life. Moreover, the renovation of an area rarely improves the living standards of its existing poor, who are usually simply displaced to other impoverished neighborhoods. So, while some areas are renovated, others as a direct result may be subject to further deterioration and decay. Gentrification can also contribute to homelessness, as the low-rent housing is never replaced, adding to the shortage of affordable housing and forcing more people onto the street.

URBANISM AND
INTERNATIONAL INFLUENCES

IN URBAN ANALYSIS TODAY—AS IN MANY AREAS OF SOCIOLogy—we must often be prepared to link global and local issues. Changes happening well beyond the borders of the United States affect the cities within them. For example, the problems suffered by Detroit and Pittsburgh originated in the decline of their major industries—cars and steel—in the face of international competition.

The global economic scene has forced sociologists to reconsider how they categorize cities. John Logan and Harvey Molotch (1987) have distinguished five city types that have recently emerged. One is the **headquarters city.** Cities of this type are those in which large, transnational corporations house their key activities, including those oriented to global concerns. New York, for example, has become one of the world's leading headquarters cities—the center of financial and industrial transactions, and of networks of communication and transportation, which stretch worldwide. Hong Kong, Tokyo, Toronto, and London would also be included here.

A second type of city is the **innovation center.** This is an urban area in which research and development industries become concentrated, developing technical and scientific processes used in goods produced elsewhere. The most influential world center is Silicon Valley in northern California. Innovation centers, at least in the United States, are often directly connected to military production needs. The research and development budget of the Defense Department makes up about a third of all research and development expenditure in the United States; where these contracts are placed strongly affects the level of prosperity of innovation centers.

The third type of city is the **module production place.** In the complex international division of labor that now exists, goods are made and assembled in regions spatially distant from one another across the world. Some urban areas become the sites for production processes in which parts of products are made, and final assembly is carried out in other regions or countries.

Detroit has become a city of this type, as a result of its position within the international organization of automobile production. It is not a "headquarters" city, even though the large automobile companies have traditionally been based there. These firms developed in the Detroit area, and concentrated many of their activities there, because of the expensive production facilities that had been constructed in the giant factories. But the more the car industry has become internationalized, the more the auto firms are becoming oriented to the major headquarter cities elsewhere—like New York and Los Angeles —and to the innovation centers where technical advance is fastest.

The fourth form of city, the **Third World entrepôt,** is a border center having substantial new immigrant populations drawn from Third World countries. Examples are cities like Miami with its large Cuban population, and Los Angeles with its growing Mexican areas.

Finally, there are cities developing as **retirement centers.** Retired people now move in considerable numbers to places with good climates. In the United States, this is mainly internal migration; people move from the North and Midwest to urban centers in the South and West. In Europe, however, retirement areas have a strongly international flavor. For example, British people who have holiday houses in Spain may move to them when they retire.

THIRD WORLD URBANIZATION

THE TOKYO-YOKAHAMA REGION IN JAPAN IS CURRENTLY the world's largest urban area, having a population of about 20 million. Seven of the ten biggest urban areas in the world, however, are now in Third World countries, including, for example, Mexico City, São Paolo, and Buenos Aires. If current trends continue, in about ten years time Mexico City will become the world's largest single urban area, having perhaps some 28 million people. The urban population in Third World countries by 2000 will be double that of the industrialized societies.

FIGURE 17.1   **THE WORLD'S FIFTEEN MOST HIGHLY POPULATED URBAN AREAS**

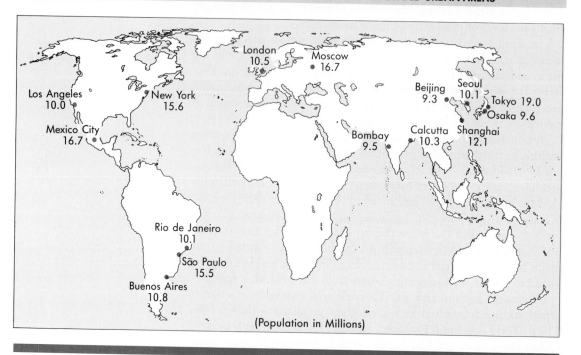

(Population in Millions)

Data for 1985.
Source: United Nations, Department for International Economic and Social Affairs,
New York, NY, *The Prospects of World Urbanization: Revised as of 1984–1985,*
forthcoming.

The urban areas now developing rapidly in Third World countries
differ dramatically from most cities in the industrialized countries.
People are drawn to cities in the Third World either because their traditional systems of rural production have disintegrated, or because
the urban areas offer better job opportunities. They may intend to
migrate to the city only for a relatively short while, aiming to return
to their villages once they have earned enough money. Some actually
do return, but in the end most find themselves forced to stay, having
lost their positions in their former communities.

When they do arrive, migrants crowd into squatters' zones mushrooming around the edges of Third World cities. This pattern differs
from Western urban areas, where newcomers are most likely to settle
in neighborhoods close to the center of the city. Third World city
dwellers live in conditions that are almost unbelievable to someone
accustomed to Western conditions of life, even in slum neighbor-

hoods. So appalling are these conditions that these areas have come to be known as the "septic fringe" of the city.

TWO CASE STUDIES OF THIRD WORLD URBANIZATION

As illustrations of Third World cities we shall consider Delhi in India and Mexico City in Latin America. India is a society in which there is still enormous population growth. Since the increasing numbers cannot find jobs in the traditional agricultural economy in the rural areas, the rate of migration to cities, even by Third World standards, is exceptionally high. Delhi, the capital, has been the fastest growing of all, but Calcutta, Bombay, and Madras all have populations numbering several million inhabitants.

These cities are massively congested. In many areas, large numbers of individuals wander the streets during the day because they have nowhere else to go. Many sleep on the streets at night and have no permanent dwelling at all. Others exist in shanty dwellings made of spare tin, sheet metal, or cardboard, set up around the edges of the city wherever there is a little space. Even if some of the immigrants do find jobs, the rate of urban immigration is much too high for the provision of permanent housing. The shanty dwellers in Indian cities have virtually no personal possessions. On the other hand, there are often strongly developed forms of community and self-help organizations within these neighborhoods.

The example of Delhi shows how different patterns of neighborhood organization are from Western cities. The Delhi urban area incorporates an ancient "old city" and New Delhi, a section built much later in which government buildings are concentrated. As in the case of other large Indian cities, some areas have an extremely high population density in relatively small neighborhoods, with quite low-density population in other areas. The old city is a convoluted maze of small streets, while some adjoining neighborhoods have broad avenues. Most of the population move across the city on foot or by bicycle, rather than by car or bus.

There is no distinct downtown business district on the model of Western cities; banks and offices are mostly out of the center. In the old city, there are innumerable small businesses. Many of the shops are no more than a few feet wide. It is common to find the manufacture and sale of articles combined in these establishments. There are large numbers of sidewalk sellers and hawkers. The New Delhi sections of the city are relatively open and quiet. Those who work in them tend to live in comparatively affluent suburbs situated several miles away towards the edge of the urban area. Makeshift squatter

City squatters.

housing surrounds the outer edges of the city, however, and is found along many access routes. Squatter housing tends to spring up in any cleared or undeveloped area, including public parks, and occasionally in formerly affluent neighborhoods. Squatter dwellings are sometimes found in small clumps, or more often in clusters of many thousands. The city authorities periodically clear some of the squatter areas, only to see the makeshift huts reappear elsewhere.

Writing of Delhi, a contributor to *India Today*, the leading Indian news magazine, says that the city, in common with other large cities in the country, is:

> ". . . heading for a total breakdown. The endless stream of migrants pour in, turning metropolises into giant slums. A third of the urban population lives in ramshackle huts with gunny sacks as doors and pavements for toilets. Another half of the populace is squeezed into one-room tenements or lives in monotonous rows of multi-storeyed flats.
>
> Civic services are going bust. Overcrowded buses, chaotic roads, lengthening water [lines], clogged drain-pipes that spew out filth and uncleared garbage piles are ominous portents of a still more apocalyptic future. And the giant melting pot of cultures that cities are, is coming to a boil. The naked display of wealth by a few in the midst of appalling misery is heightening tension. Riots break out at the slightest provocation, crime graphs spiral and youth take to drugs." (Quoted in Singh, 1988)

Mexico City consists of an old cultural center, an international business district, an entertainment zone, and affluent housing areas, which are all most tourists see of the city. The poor and destitute live in extensive shanty neighborhoods on the perimeter of the city. These inhabitants include recent migrants from rural areas and families who were displaced from other sections of the city because of urban renewal or highway construction. Over a third of Mexico City's population lives in dwellings without running water; many of these buildings also lack sewerage.

While there is a large amount of state-subsidized housing, only a minority of the city's population has the level of income required to obtain it. Only about 10 percent of the city's inhabitants are able to buy or rent on the private housing market. The majority of the city's population, therefore, are excluded from access to available housing (Castells, 1983).

Three types of "popular housing" areas are found in Mexico City. The *colonias proletarias* are composed of shanty dwellings, mainly put up illegally by the inhabitants themselves, on the edges of the city.

Over half the population of the metropolitan area of Mexico City lives in such housing. Most of these areas were not spontaneously colonized by the squatters, but were organized with the connivance of local authorities and illegal private developers. The developers have their local network of organizers to whom regular money payments have to be made by those living in the shanties. Most of the land occupied by the *colonias* was in fact originally public or communal, supposedly protected by the Mexican Constitution from being sold or transferred.

A second type of housing is the *vecindadas* (slums). These are mostly located in the older sections of the city, and are characterized by the multifamily occupation of dilapidated rental units. Two million people live in such slums, in conditions that are at least as deprived as those in the squatters' areas.

The third type is the *ciudades perdidas,* or shanty towns. These are similar to the *colonias proletarias,* but are put up in the middle of the city rather than on the periphery. They are also illegal settlements, but because of their centrality, their inhabitants try to take advantage of existing urban services, such as cheap transportation facilities. Some of these settlements have been demolished by the city authorities in recent years and their inhabitants moved out to the *colonias.*

Ninety-four percent of Mexico City consists of built-up areas, with only 6 percent allocated to open spaces. The amount of "green spaces"—parks and open stretches of green land—is far below that found in even the most densely populated U.S. or European cities (Ward, 1981). Pollution is a major problem in Mexico City, coming mostly from the cars, buses, and trucks that pack the inadequate roads of the city. The rest comes from industrial pollutants (Fox, 1972). The smog is much worse than notorious areas in the United States, such as the Los Angeles basin. It has been estimated that living in Mexico City is equivalent to smoking forty cigarettes a day.

CITIES IN EASTERN EUROPE
AND THE SOVIET UNION

IF CITIES IN THE THIRD WORLD CONTRAST WITH THOSE IN the West, so do those of Eastern Europe—although in a different way. In most Western countries, private land and industrial development, and private housing markets, determine patterns of urban growth. Planning and financial control by national and local governments have often taken second place. This is reversed in Eastern Europe and the Soviet Union, where government-directed city planning has been much more common, and the design of urban environments has been integrated with the overall planning of the economy.

There was a time, up to 1917, when major Soviet cities resembled their counterparts in the United States. Moscow and St. Petersburg (now Leningrad) had central business districts, and the patterning of poor- and high-income group areas was clearly demonstrated. Pre-revolutionary Russian cities, however, were much more crowded, and housing was in far shorter supply than in large Western cities of the same period. Post–World War II construction of government-sponsored housing altered this situation. Most of the dwellings built are large apartment blocks—although these are still over-crowded by Western standards. The apartments have only two or three rooms in which whole families live. Many families in older buildings still live in one-room apartments, sharing communal kitchens and bathrooms.

Soviet urban planners believe that urban areas should not grow too large, that the length of daily commuting between home and work-place should be kept to a minimum, and that public transport should be the main source of mobility (Bater, 1977). The organization of urban space is determined by social-welfare considerations (as deter-mined by government authorities), rather than by market values, as in Western cities (French, 1979). Rents, for example, are not directly related to the quality of dwellings, but are largely determined by other considerations. They are fixed by the government so as to make up only a small percentage of household expenditure—much less than in Western countries, where rent or mortgage costs can run as high as 30 percent of gross income. Families (not individuals) have a right to housing independently of their capability to pay particular rents.

The result of this government city planning, with its standardized apartment houses and controlled growth, is that population density tends to remain the same in all neighborhoods. Rather than more space being provided for individual family homes in the outer sub-urbs, as in Western cities, Soviet suburbs usually have the largest number of high-rise, high-density buildings, because these were the most recently built. Soviet urban areas do not gradually fade into rural areas but end suddenly, with highly built-up areas of apartments facing open forest and farmland.

Ivan Szelenyi (1983) has documented some further differences be-tween urbanization in the West and East. In Eastern Europe, dwell-ings built by private contractors, and bought and sold on the market, form a small proportion of the total housing. Privately-owned hous-ing is largely in the hands of people in lower-income groups, in di-rect contrast to most Western cities where wealthier people tend to own private housing. Eastern Europeans of higher status, such as government officials or professionals, live in apartments owned and maintained by the state. These are greatly superior to dwellings in which the majority of the population live.

Eastern European city zoning is strongly influenced by the government. There are deteriorating areas, but these do not cluster around the city centers as is usually the case in the West. Most central-city land is owned by the government, and has the best housing. The poorer zones lie further out, towards the edges of the city. Typical government housing tends to be more homogeneous in both character of ownership and architectural style than in Western cities (Szelenyi, 1983). Also, industry and commerce are much more scattered over different areas of the city than in the West, where residential and industrial areas are usually quite distinct. For example, Moscow is divided for planning purposes into sixty-five zones; the aim is to distribute industry evenly across these, to reduce daily commuting time.

Rates of urban growth in Eastern Europe since World War II have for the most part not been as high as those in most other regions of the world. Until the 1950s, Moscow and Leningrad were the only cities in the Soviet Union having over a million inhabitants—which was already the case prior to the Russian Revolution of 1917. Today there are twenty cities with more than a million inhabitants. Since Soviet citizens need residents' permits to live where they want, however, population migration has been much more strictly controlled than in the West.

Will these distinctive features of East European urbanism survive the social and economic changes introduced following the revolutions of 1989? The introduction of competitive markets will certainly affect city life directly. Much state-owned housing will pass into private hands, and migration between city areas and different parts of the country will no longer be determined by the government. These changes are bound to substantially alter city environments and will probably cause urban areas in Eastern Europe to shift towards Western models. But great differences will still remain.

THEORIES OF URBANISM

WE HAVE EXAMINED VARIOUS TRENDS AND THEIR EFFECTS on urbanism since industrialization; we have described the rise of suburbs, the problems of central cities, urban renewal, and the survival of cities in the global economy. How do we make sense of all of this? What general theories help us to understand fundamental characteristics of modern urban life?

THE CHICAGO SCHOOL

A number of writers associated with the University of Chicago in the 1920s and 1930s, especially Robert Park, Ernest Burgess, and Louis Wirth, developed ideas that were for many years the chief basis of theory and research in urban sociology. We will examine two conceptions developed by the Chicago School: one, the **ecological approach** to urban analysis; the other, the characterization of **urbanism** as a "way of life," developed by Wirth (Park, 1952; Wirth, 1938; McKenzie, 1933).

Urban Ecology

Ecology is a biological term that has to do with the adaptation of plant and animal organisms to their environment. In the natural world, organisms tend to be distributed over the terrain such that a balance or equilibrium among different species is achieved. The **urban ecology** approach advanced by the Chicago School maintained that the location of major urban settlements, and the distribution of different types of neighborhoods within them, can be understood in similar terms. Cities did not grow up at random, but in relation to advantageous features of the environment—along the shores of rivers, in fertile plains, or at the intersection of trading routes or railways.

"Once set up," Park wrote, "a city is, it seems, a great sorting mechanism which . . . infallibly selects out of the population as a whole the individuals best suited to live in a particular region or a particular milieu" (Park, 1952). Cities become ordered into "natural areas," through processes of **competition, invasion,** and **succession**—all of which occur in biological ecology. If we look at the ecology of a lake in the natural environment, we find that competition among various species of fish, insects, plants, and other organisms operates to reach a fairly stable distribution among them. This balance is disturbed if new species "invade"—try to make the lake their home. Some of the organisms that proliferated in the central depths of the lake are driven out to follow a more precarious existence around its fringes. The invading species become their successors, and a new balance is forged.

Similar processes occur in cities, according to the ecological theorists, as the inhabitants of different neighborhoods struggle to make their livelihoods. For instance, in the early stages in the development

of modern cities, industry tends to cluster at sites where there are good communications and supplies of raw materials, and working-class neighborhoods develop around these areas. As a city becomes more well-established and wealthy, land values rise and areas near the center become attractive for establishing large-scale business enterprises and entertainments (cinemas, theaters, new shops). The newcomers "invade" these areas and replace the older industries, thus driving out the established inhabitants because their jobs are gone. Gradually, a new equilibrium comes about between the various different groups in the city. But this may become disturbed again by new processes of invasion and succession, introducing a further cycle of readjustment between neighborhoods. The competitive struggle for urban space is never-ending.

In the initial stages of urban growth, industries often develop near supply lines such as rivers—for example, Richmond, VA, on the James (left)—or on major trade routes—as in Hong Kong (right).

Cities can be seen as formed in concentric rings, broken up into segments. In the center are the **inner-city** areas, a mixture of big-business prosperity and decaying private houses. Beyond these are older neighborhoods, housing stably employed, lower-class workers. Further out still are the suburbs in which higher-income groups tend to live. Processes of invasion and succession occur within the segments of the concentric rings. Thus as property decays in a central or near-central area, ethnic-minority groups might start to move into it. As they do so, more of the original population start to leave, precipitating a whole-scale "flight" to neighborhoods elsewhere in the city, or out to the suburbs.

Although for a period, the urban ecology approach fell into disrepute, it was later revived and elaborated in the writings of a number of authors, particularly those of Amos Hawley (Hawley, 1950, 1968). Rather than concentrating upon the competition for scarce resources, as his predecessors did, Hawley emphasized the *interdependence* of different city areas. Human beings adapt to their environment through "differentiation"—the specialization of groups and occupational roles. Groups upon which many others depend will have a dominant position, often reflected in their spatial centrality. Business groups, for example, like banks or insurance companies, provide key services for many in a community, and hence are found in the center of a city or town. The zones that develop in urban areas, Hawley pointed out, concern not just space but time. Business dominance, for example, is expressed not only in patterns of land use, but in the rhythm of activities in daily life—an illustration is the rush hour.

Many studies of cities as a whole, and of particular neighborhoods within cities, have been prompted by the ecological approach—concerned, for example, with the processes of "invasion" and "succession" just mentioned. However, various criticisms can justifiably be made of the ecological standpoint. The ecological perspective tends to under-emphasize the importance of conscious design and planning. The models of spatial organization developed by Park, Burgess, and their colleagues were drawn from American experience, and only fit some types of cities in the United States, let alone most cities in Europe, Japan, Eastern Europe, or the Third World.

Urbanism as a Way of Life

Louis Wirth's approach to urbanism as a "way of life" is concerned less with the internal differentiation of cities than with what urbanism *is* as a form of social existence. Wirth observed:

> "The degree to which the contemporary world may be said to be 'urban' is not fully or accurately measured by the proportion of the total population living in cities. The influences which cities exert upon the social life of man are greater than the ratio of the urban population would indicate; for the city is not only increasingly the dwelling-place and the workshop of modern man, but it is the initiating and controlling center of economic, political and cultural life that has drawn the most remote communities of the world into its orbit and woven diverse areas, peoples and activities into a cosmos." (Wirth, 1938)

Comparing cities with small traditional villages, Wirth pointed out that large numbers of people live in close proximity without really knowing each other. Most contacts between city dwellers are fleeting and partial, and are means to other ends rather than satisfying relationships in themselves. Interactions with salesclerks, bank tellers, or other commuters are passing encounters, entered into not for their own sake but as means to complete some daily task.

Since many who live in urban areas tend to move a great deal, there are relatively weak bonds between them. People are involved in numerous different activities and situations each day: the "pace of life" is faster than in rural areas. Competition prevails over cooperation. Wirth accepted, however, that the density of social life in cities also leads to the formation of neighborhoods with distinct characteristics, some of which may preserve characteristics of small communities. In immigrant areas, for example, traditional connections between families are found, and most people know each other on a personal basis. The more such areas are absorbed into wider patterns of city life, however, the more these characteristics disappear.

Wirth's ideas have deservedly enjoyed wide currency. There are any number of examples of the impersonality of cities and the lack of involvement of their residents with one another. One is the infamous case of the murder of Katherine Genovese on March 13, 1964, in New York City. Genovese was attacked three times on her way home to her apartment late at night in an affluent, tree-lined section of Queens, an area quite close to Manhattan. The third assault, which happened in the hallway of her building, proved fatal. What linked this to the impersonality of city life was the apparent apathy on the part of the onlookers. A total of thirty-eight, respectable citizens witnessed the attacks, but not a single person either went to Genovese's help or even called the police. A phrase that appeared in a newspaper editorial after this event was "The city has robbed Katherine Genovese of friends" (Latane and Darley, 1970). She certainly had friends. Where were her friends when she needed them? Given the far-flung nature of big-city life, they were probably in their homes elsewhere —in Manhattan, Long Island, or Brooklyn—and ignorant of her plight.

The impersonality of many day-to-day contacts in modern cities is undeniable—and to some degree this is true of social life in general in modern societies. Wirth's theory is important because he saw that urbanism is not just part of a society, but expresses and influences the nature of the wider social system. Aspects of the urban "way of life" are characteristic of social life in modern societies as a whole, not just the activities of those who happen to live in big cities. Yet Wirth's ideas also have marked limitations. Like the ecological perspective, with which it shares a good deal in common, Wirth's theory was based mainly on observations of American cities, yet generalized to urbanism everywhere. Urbanism is not the same at all times and places. As has been mentioned, for example, premodern cities were in many respects quite different from those found in modern societies. Life for most people in the premodern city was often no more anonymous or impersonal than for those living in village communities.

Wirth also exaggerated the impersonality of modern cities. Communities involving close friendship or kinship links are more persistent within modern urban communities than Wirth allowed. Everett Hughes, a colleague of Wirth's at the University of Chicago, wrote of his associate: "Louis used to say all those things about how the city is impersonal—while living with a whole clan of kin and friends on a very personal basis" (Quoted in Kasarda and Janowitz, 1974). Groups such as those Herbert Gans called "the urban villagers" are common in modern cities (Gans, 1982). Gans's urban villagers were Italian-Americans living in an inner-city Boston neighborhood. Such white-ethnic areas are probably becoming less significant in American cities than once was the case, but they are being replaced by inner-city communities of newer immigrants—for instance, Asian-Americans and Hispanic-Americans. More important, neighborhoods having close kinship and personal ties often seem to be actively *created* by city life; they are not just remnants of a preexisting way of life that had survived for a period within the city.

Claude Fischer has proposed that urbanism actually tends to promote diverse subcultures, rather than swamping everyone within an anonymous mass. Those who live in cities, he pointed out, are able to collaborate with others of like background or interests to develop local connections and interests; and they can join distinctive religious, ethnic, political, and other subcultural groups. A small town or village does not allow the development of such subcultural diversity (Fischer, 1975, 1984). Those who form ethnic communities within cities, for instance, might have had little or no knowledge of one another in their land of origin. When they arrive, they gravitate to areas in which others from a similar linguistic and cultural background are living, and new subcommunity structures are formed. Individuals drawn to artistic pursuits might find few others in a village or small town with whom to associate. In a large city, on the other hand, they might become part of a significant artistic and intellectual subculture.

Other studies show that characteristics which Wirth regarded as urban are frequently found in life in small towns or villages in the countryside. Peter Mann compared a small rural community in Sussex, in the south of Britain, with Huddersfield, a large industrial town in the north. The village is on a fast train and road route to London, and many of its inhabitants are commuters. They are more sophisticated and cosmopolitan than most of the inhabitants of the northern city, which is situated in a more provincial region of the country. There are more personal and kinship ties between those liv-

ing in various areas of the larger Huddersfield than is the case among
the residents of the Sussex village (Mann, 1970). Much the same
could be said of the "bedroom" communities that surround cities like
New York or Toronto. These villages used to be more tight-knit, but
with the influx of commuters, they serve mainly as "bedrooms" during the few hours that their inhabitants are there.

A large city is a "world of strangers," yet supports and creates personal relationships. This is not paradoxical. We have to separate
urban experience into the public sphere of encounters with strangers,
and the more private world of family, friends, and work colleagues. It
may be difficult to "meet people" when one first moves to a large
city, but anyone moving to a small, established rural community may
find the "friendliness" of the inhabitants to be largely a matter of
public politeness—it may take years to become "accepted." This is
not the case in the city. As Edward Krupat has commented:

> The urban egg . . . has a harder shell to crack. Lacking the
> occasion and circumstances for making an entrée, many per-
> sons who see each other day after day at a bus or railroad sta-
> tion, in a cafeteria or passing in the hallways at work, never
> become anything more than "familiar strangers." Also,
> some people may remain totally on the outside because they
> lack social skills or initiative. Yet the overwhelming evi-
> dence is that because of the diversity of strangers—each one
> is a *potential friend*—and the wide range of lifestyles and in-
> terests in the city, people do move from the outside in. And
> once they are on the inside of one group or network, the
> possibilities for expanding their connections multiply
> greatly. As a result, the evidence indicates that the positive
> opportunities in the city often seem to outweigh the con-
> straining forces, allowing people to develop and maintain
> satisfying relationships. (Krupat, 1985)

While Wirth's ideas retain some validity, in the light of these subsequent contributions it is clear that they were over-generalized. Modern cities are frequently marked by impersonal, anonymous, social
relationships, but they are also sources of diversity—and, sometimes,
intimacy.

URBANISM AND THE CREATED ENVIRONMENT

Theories of urbanism put forth in the 1970s and 1980s have stressed
that we should not look only at the city itself when studying urban-

ism. Instead, the focus should be on the city in relation to major patterns of political and economic change. The two leading writers in urban analysis today, David Harvey and Manuel Castells, were both strongly influenced by Marx, and link modes of urban organization to broader characteristics of industrial capitalism (Harvey, 1973, 1984, 1985; Castells, 1977).

Harvey: The Restructuring of Space

David Harvey emphasized that urbanism is one aspect of the **created environment** brought about by the spread of industrial capitalism. In premodern societies, the social and economic life of city and countryside were clearly differentiated. The walls surrounding traditional cities were evidence of more than just defense—they separated the urban environment from rural life. In the modern world, industry blurs the division between city and countryside. Agriculture has become mechanized and brought under the sway of economic supply and demand, price and profit, just like industry, and this process has lessened the social differences between urban and rural people.

In modern urbanism, Harvey pointed out, space is continually "restructured." The nature of an urban area is determined by where large firms choose to place their industries, research and development centers, and so forth; government control of both land and industrial production; and the activities of private investors, buying and selling houses and land. Business firms, for example, are constantly weighing the relative advantages of new locations against existing ones. As production becomes cheaper in one area than another, or as the firm moves from one product to another, offices and factories will be closed down in one place and opened up elsewhere. Thus at one time, when there are considerable profits to be made, there might be a spate of office-building construction in the downtown areas of large cities. Once the offices have been built, and the central area "redeveloped," investors look for sources of further speculative building elsewhere. Often what is profitable in one period will not be so in another, when the financial climate changes.

The activities of private home buyers are strongly influenced by how much, and where, business interests buy up land, as well as by rates of loans and taxes fixed by local and federal governments. Following World War II, for instance, there was vast expansion of suburban development in major cities in the United States. This was partly due to ethnic discrimination and the tendency of whites to try to escape from inner-city areas. However, it was only made possible, Harvey argued, because of government decisions to provide tax concessions to home buyers and construction firms, and by financial organizations that set up special credit arrangements. These provided the basis for the building and buying of new homes on the outer periphery of cities, and at the same time promoted demand for industrial products such as the automobile.

In effect, according to Harvey, the city is not an urban environment where many "species" contend for resources and eventually form a balanced ecology. Rather, the underlying influences generating city growth are those associated with competitive capitalism and resistances against it.

Castells: Urbanism and Social Movements

Like Harvey, Castells stressed that the spatial form of a society is closely linked to the overall mechanisms of its development. To understand cities, we have to grasp the processes whereby spatial structures are created and transformed. The layouts and architectural features of cities and neighborhoods express struggles and conflicts between different groups in society. Urban environments represent symbolic and spatial manifestations of broader social forces. The building of skyscrapers, for example, may be encouraged by the possibility of profitable investment, but the giant buildings also symbolize the power of big business and are "the cathedrals of the period of rising corporate capitalism" (Castells, 1983).

Castells saw the city not only as a distinct location—the urban area —but as an inherent aspect of wider processes of **collective consumption** (the public consumption of goods and services) which in turn are an integral part of industrial capitalism. Homes, schools, transport services, and leisure amenities are ways in which people "consume" the products of modern industry. The taxation system influences who is able to buy or rent where, and who builds where. Large corporations, banks, and insurance companies, which provide capital for building projects, have a great deal of power over these processes. But government agencies also directly affect many aspects of city life, by building roads and public housing, planning green spaces, and so forth (Lowe, 1986). The physical shape of cities is thus a product of both market forces and the power of government.

But the nature of the created environment is not just the result of policies initiated by the wealthy and powerful. Castells also emphasized the importance of the struggles of underprivileged groups to alter the conditions of their existence. Urban problems stimulate a range of social movements concerned with improving housing, protesting against air pollution, defending parks and green belts, and combatting building development that changes the nature of an area. For example, Castells studied the gay movement in San Francisco, which succeeded in reorganizing neighborhoods around its own cultural values—allowing many gay organizations, clubs, and bars to flourish—and gained a prominent position in local politics.

Harvey and Castells both stressed that cities are almost wholly artificial environments, constructed by the people living in them. Even most rural areas do not escape the influence of human intervention and modern technology. Human activity has reshaped and reordered the world of nature. Food is not produced for local inhabitants, but for national and international markets. In mechanized farming, land is rigorously subdivided and specialized in its use, ordered into physical patterns that have little relationship to natural features of the environment. Those who live on farms and in isolated rural areas are economically, politically, and culturally tied to the larger society, however different some of their modes of behavior may be from those of city dwellers.

INTEGRATING THE THEORIES

The views of Harvey and Castells have been important, though controversial, in redirecting problems of urban analysis (Pahl, 1977; Pickvance, 1985; Saunders, 1987). According to these authors, land and the created environment reflect social and economic systems of power—a significant shift away from the approach of Wirth and the urban ecologists, who were more concerned with "natural" spatial processes. Yet the ideas of Harvey and Castells are often stated abstractly and have not generated a similar volume of empirical research to that stimulated by the Chicago School.

In some ways, however, the views set out by Harvey and Castells and those of the Chicago School usefully complement each other and can be combined to give a comprehensive picture of urban processes. The differences between city areas described in urban ecology do exist, as does the impersonality of city life. But these are more varied than the members of the Chicago School believed, and are primarily governed by the social and economic influences analyzed by Harvey and Castells (Micklin and Choldin, 1984). John Logan and Harvey Molotch (1987), referred to earlier, have suggested an approach that connects the perspectives of authors like Harvey and Castells with some features of the ecological standpoint. They agree with Harvey and Castells that broad features of economic development, stretching nationally and internationally, directly affect urban life. But these wide-ranging economic factors, they argue, are focused through local organizations, including neighborhood businesses, banks, government agencies, together with the activities of individual home buyers.

Land and buildings are bought and sold, Molotch and Logan say, just like other goods in modern societies. But the markets that generate city environments are influenced by how different local groups want to *use* the property they buy and sell. Many tensions and conflicts arise as a result of this process—and these are the key factors structuring city neighborhoods. For instance, an apartment development is seen as a home by its residents, but as a source of rent by its landlord. Financial and business firms are most interested in buying, selling, or developing property in an area either to locate their production sites, or to make profits in land speculation. Their interests and concerns are quite different from residents, for whom the neighborhood is a place to live. Further tension arises since companies are rarely concerned with the social and physical effects of their activities upon a given neighborhood—whether or not, for example, attractive older residences are destroyed to make room for large new office buildings. Local businesses or residents may come together in neighborhood groups in order to defend their interests. Such local associations can influence planning and zoning boards and thereby restrict development, push for green areas and parkland, or press for more favorable rent regulations. In brief, Logan and Molotch see urban change as not dominated by an overall industrial capitalist machine, but rather as the result of a conflict between that machine and the interests and concerns of urban dwellers and local businesses.

New York fog.

What does the future hold out for cities and city dwellers? The patterns analyzed in this chapter form a complicated mosaic, and no single overall trend emerges from them. In the industrialized countries, it is likely that tendencies towards the "spreading" of urban life will continue. Improved systems of transportation and communication technology will allow people to live further from the places of work than before. At the same time, their places of work are coming to them, as new industries move away from city centers and into new suburban neighborhoods. Some older cities, particularly those based on manufacturing industries, will continue to decline in population, as people are drawn away to other areas. These same circumstances will stimulate further gentrification. The more dilapidated central cities become, in fact, the more opportunities there are for gentrification. Yet gentrification does little or nothing to help the urban poor, and often makes their plight worse than it was before.

While cities in the industrialized countries are likely to remain stable, or diminish, in population, those in Third World societies will continue to expand. Conditions of life in Third World cities seem likely to decline even further than today, at least for the poor. The problems of First and Second World cities, important as they are, pale almost into insignificance when compared to those faced in the Third World.

SUMMARY

1. Traditional cities differed in many ways from modern urban areas. They were mostly very small by modern standards, were surrounded by walls, and their centers were dominated by religious buildings and palaces.

2. In traditional societies, only a small minority of the population lived in urban areas. In the industrialized countries today, between 60 percent and 90 percent do so. Urbanism is also developing very rapidly in Third World societies.

3. The expansion of *suburbs* has contributed to inner-city decay. Wealthier groups and businesses tend to move out of the central city in order to take advantage of lower tax rates. This begins a cycle of deterioration, in which the more suburbia expands, the greater the problems faced by those living in the central cities. *Urban renewal* (also called gentrification)—the refurbishing of old buildings to put them to new uses—has become common in many large cities.

4. Urban analysis today must be prepared to link global and local issues. Factors that influence urban development locally are sometimes part of much more international processes. The structure of local neighborhoods, and their patterns of growth and decline, often reflect changes in industrial production internationally.

5. Massive urban development is occurring in Third World countries. Cities in these societies differ in major respects from those characteristic of the West. The majority of the population live in illegal makeshift housing, in conditions of extreme poverty.

6. Urbanism in the East European countries and the Soviet Union, in contrast to the West, is part of the overall planned economy. Cities are planned in conjunction with the overall development of industry and the realization of egalitarian ideals. The urban-growth rate in Eastern Europe since World War II has been comparatively low. Patterns established there are likely to change as a result of the recent upheavals in the East European countries.

7. Early approaches to urban sociology were dominated by the work of the Chicago School. The members of this school saw urban processes in terms of ecological models derived from biology. Louis Wirth developed the conception of urbanism as a "way of life." These approaches have more recently been challenged, without being discarded altogether.

8. Later approaches to urban theory, associated with David Harvey and Manuel Castells, have placed more emphasis on the influence of broader socio-economic factors—particularly those deriving from industrial capitalism—on city life.

BASIC CONCEPTS

URBAN ECOLOGY
INNER CITY
CREATED ENVIRONMENT

IMPORTANT TERMS

CONURBATION

THIRD WORLD ENTREPÔT

MEGALOPOLIS

RETIREMENT CENTER

URBANIZATION

ECOLOGICAL APPROACH

SUBURBANIZATION

URBANISM

URBAN RENEWAL

COMPETITION

GENTRIFICATION

INVASION

HEADQUARTERS CITY

SUCCESSION

INNOVATION CENTER

COLLECTIVE CONSUMPTION

MODULE PRODUCTION PLACE

CHAPTER EIGHTEEN

POPULATION, HEALTH, AND AGING

■

I have understood the population explosion intellectually
for a long time. I came to understand it emotionally one
stinking hot night in Delhi a few years ago. My wife and
daughter and I were returning to our hotel in an ancient
taxi. The seats were hopping with fleas. The only functional gear was third. As we crawled through the city, we
entered a crowded slum area. The temperature was well
over a 100° Fahrenheit; the air was a haze of dust and
smoke. The streets seemed alive with people. People eating, people washing, people sleeping. People visiting, arguing, and screaming. People thrusting their hands
through the taxi window, begging. People defecating and
urinating. People clinging to buses. People herding animals. People, people, people, people. As we moved
slowly, through the mob, hand-horn squawking, the
dust, noise, heat, and cooking fires gave the scene a hel-
lish aspect. Would we ever get to our hotel? All three of
us were, frankly, frightened. It seemed that anything
could happen—but, of course, nothing did. Old India

hands will laugh at our reaction. We were just some over-privileged tourists, unaccustomed to the sights and sounds of India. Perhaps since that night I've known the *feel* of over-population. (Ehrlich, 1976)

With the exception of the spread of nuclear weaponry and threats of ecological disaster (although these are problems enough!) population growth is the most pressing and urgent issue currently faced by humanity. The affluent countries have more food than they need for themselves, and in most of them, levels of population growth are low or declining. In much of the remainder of the world, population expansion is staggering and the pressure placed on available resources immense.

Those of us who live in the industrialized countries might feel Third World population growth is not "our" problem, and that those societies should deal with their swelling populations as best they can. There are two reasons why such a view cannot be justified, quite apart from the immorality of taking a disinterested stand on the fate of three-quarters of the world's human beings.

One reason is that the plight of the Third World is in some part the result of Western influences. Population growth in the Third World is largely due to factors deriving from Western contacts. Some of these are intrinsically beneficial, particularly improvements in hygiene and health care. But these positive influences have spread in conjunction with other processes—such as dependence upon international trade—that have broken down traditional ways of life. Second, if it continues at the present rate, world population growth carries the risk of global catastrophe. The pressure placed upon the world's resources may lead to global conflict, which could end in major wars. At this point, the three great issues with which humanity must deal over the next few decades—the possibility of nuclear conflict, ecological dangers, and population growth—merge with one another. (See Chapter 20: "Understanding Social Change.")

Why has the world population increased so dramatically? What are the main consequences of this increase? In this chapter, we shall try to answer these questions, connecting our analysis with two related sets of issues: the study of health and illness, and the consequences of the "aging" of populations in the industrialized countries.

We will begin the discussion on world population with a look at some basic demographic concepts and the dynamics of population change. Then we turn to the Third World and its population problems, especially as they relate to economic growth. Finally, we will examine U.S. population growth, focusing on the enormous baby-boom generation.

WORLD POPULATION GROWTH

THERE ARE CURRENTLY OVER 5 BILLION PEOPLE IN THE world. It was estimated that "baby number 5 billion" was born on July 11, 1987, although of course no one can know when and where this event happened. Paul Ehrlich calculated in the 1960s that, if the rate of population growth at that time continued, nine hundred years from now (not a long period in world history as a whole) there would be 60,000,000,000,000,000 (60 quadrillion) people on the face of the earth. There would be one hundred people for every square yard of the earth's surface, including both land and water. The physicist, J. H. Fremlin, worked out that housing such a population would need a continuous two thousand-story building covering the complete planet. Even in such a stupendous structure there would only be three or four yards of floor space per person (Fremlin, 1964).

Such a picture, of course, is nothing more than nightmarish fiction designed to drive home how cataclysmic the consequences of continued population growth would be. The real issue is what will happen over the next thirty or forty years, by which time, if current trends are not reversed, the world's population will already have grown to intolerable levels. Partly because governments and other agencies heeded the warnings of Ehrlich and others twenty years ago, by introducing population control programs, there are grounds for supposing that world population growth is beginning to trail off. Estimates calculated in the 1960s of the likely world population by the year 2000 have recently been lowered. The World Bank now estimates the probable world population by 2000 at 6.5 billion, compared to some earlier estimates of over 8 billion. Nevertheless, considering that a century ago there were only 1.5 billion people in the world, this still represents growth of staggering proportions. Moreover, the factors underlying population growth are by no means completely predictable and all estimates have to be interpreted with caution.

POPULATION ANALYSIS: DEMOGRAPHY

The study of population is referred to as **demography.** The term was invented about a century and a half ago, at a time when nations were beginning to keep official statistics on the nature and distribution of their populations. Demography is concerned with measuring the size of populations and explaining their rise or decline. Population patterns are governed by three factors: births, deaths, and migra-

tions. Demography is customarily treated as a branch of sociology, because the factors that influence the level of births and deaths in a given group or society, as well as migrations of population, are largely social and cultural.

Much demographical work tends to be statistical. All the industrialized countries today gather and analyze basic statistics on their populations by carrying out censuses (systematic surveys designed to find out about the whole population of a given country). Rigorous as the modes of data collection now are, even in these nations demographic statistics are not wholly accurate. In the United States there is a comprehensive population census every ten years, and sample studies are regularly conducted. Yet for various reasons many people are not registered in the official population statistics. According to the Bureau of the Census, there were probably some 7 million people omitted from the 1980 census, including illegal immigrants, homeless people, vagrants, and others who for one reason or another avoided registration.

In many Third World countries, particularly those with recent high rates of population growth, demographic statistics are much more unreliable. For instance, some demographers have estimated that registered births and deaths in India may represent only about three-quarters of the actual totals (Cox, 1976). The accuracy of official statistics is even lower in parts of central Africa.

Governments find it difficult to acquire an accurate picture of their citizenry in such countries; and many of the inhabitants lack essential information about themselves that virtually everyone in the industrialized world possesses. All of us know our dates of birth, and hence our ages. This was not the case in premodern societies; and in Third World countries today many people do not know how old they are. "Age" is usually measured in traditional communities by reference to life experiences. A person is a "young adult," or "married with young children," or a "grandparent"—rather than twenty-one, thirty, or sixty years of age.

BASIC DEMOGRAPHIC CONCEPTS

Among the basic concepts used by demographers, the most important are crude birth rates, fertility, fecundity, and crude death rates. **Crude birth rates** are expressed as the number of live births per year per thousand of the population. They are called "crude" rates because of their very general character. Crude birth rates, for example, do not tell us what proportions of a population are male or female, or what the age distribution of a population is (the relative proportions of young and old people in the population). Where statistics are collected that relate birth or death rates to such categories, demographers speak of *specific* rather than crude rates. For instance, an age-specific birth rate might specify the number of births per thousand women in different age groups.

If we wish to understand population patterns in any detail, the information provided by specific birth rates is normally necessary.

FIGURE 18.1   **POPULATION GROWTH RATE, 1980–1987 (ANNUAL PERCENTAGE INCREASE)**

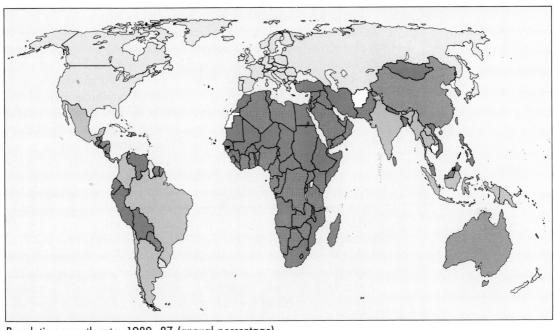

Population growth rate, 1980–87 (annual percentage)

■ 3.0 or more   ■ 2.2–3.0   ■ 1.5–2.1   ■ 1.0–1.4   □ Less than 1.0   □ No data

Source: The World Bank Atlas, 1988.

Crude birth rates, however, are useful for making overall comparisons between different groups, societies, and regions. Thus the crude birth rate in the United States is 16 per thousand. Other industrialized countries range from a low of 10 per thousand (West Germany and Denmark) to a high of 20 per thousand (U.S.S.R., Poland, and Ireland). In many other parts of the world, crude birth rates are much higher still. In India, for instance, the crude birth rate is 33 per thousand (1985); in Kenya it is 54 per thousand (World Bank, 1987).

Birth rates are an expression of the fertility of women. **Fertility** refers to how many live-born children the average woman has. A fertility rate is usually calculated as the average number of births per thousand women of childbearing age. The fertility rate in the United States in 1985 was 1.8, which is fairly typical of the industrialized countries. Using the previously mentioned countries as a basis of comparison, in India the rate was 4.5 and in Kenya 7.8. Since these are average figures, many families in these societies are considerably larger (although not every live-born child survives).

Fertility is distinguished from **fecundity,** which means the potential number of children women are biologically capable of bearing. It is physically possible for a normal woman to bear a child every year during the period when she is capable of conception. There are variations in fecundity according to age at puberty and menopause, both of which differ between countries as well as among individuals. While there may be families in which a woman bears 20 or more children, fertility rates in practice are always much lower than fecundity rates, because social and cultural factors limit breeding.

Crude death rates (also called *mortality rates*) are calculated in the same way as birth rates—the number of deaths per thousand of population per year. Again there are major variations among countries, but death rates in many Third World societies are becoming reduced to levels comparable to those of the West. The death rate in the United States in 1985 was 9 per thousand. In India it was 12 per thousand; in Kenya it was 13 per thousand. A few countries have much higher death rates. In Sierra Leone, for example, the death rate is 25 per thousand. Like crude birth rates, crude death rates only provide a very general index of **mortality** (the number of deaths in a population). Specific death rates give more precise information. A particularly important specific death rate is the **infant mortality rate:** the number of babies per thousand births in any year who die before reaching age one. One of the key factors underlying the population explosion has been reductions in infant-mortality rates.

Declining rates of infant mortality are the most important influence on increasing **life expectancy**—that is, the number of years the average person can expect to live. In 1900, life expectancy at birth in the United States was about forty years. Today it has increased to nearly seventy-four years (seventy-one for men and seventy-eight for women in 1985). This does not mean, however, that most people at the turn of the century died when they were about forty years of age. When there is a high infant-mortality rate, the average life expectancy—which is a statistical average—is brought down. Taking the life expectancy of people surviving the first year of life, in 1900 the average person could expect to live to age fifty-eight. Illness, nutrition, and the influence of natural disasters are the other factors influencing life expectancy. Life expectancy has to be distinguished from **life span,** which is the maximum number of years that an individual could live. While life expectancy has increased in most societies in the world, life span has remained unaltered. Only a small proportion of people live to be one hundred or more.

DYNAMICS OF POPULATION CHANGE

Rates of population growth or decline are measured by subtracting the number of deaths per thousand over a given period from the number of births per thousand—this is usually also calculated annually. Some European countries have negative growth rates—in other words, their populations are declining. Virtually all of the industrialized countries have growth rates of less than 0.7 percent. Rates of population growth were high in the eighteenth and nineteenth centuries in Europe and the United States, but have since leveled off. Many Third world countries today have rates of between 2–3 percent. These may not seem very different from the rates of the industrialized countries, but in fact, the difference is enormous.

The reason is that growth in population is **exponential.** There is an ancient Persian myth that helps to illustrate this. A courtier asked a ruler to reward him for his services by giving him twice as many grains of rice for each service than he had the time before, starting with a single grain on the first square of a chess board. Believing himself to be on to a good thing, the king commanded grain to be brought up from his storehouse. By the twenty-first square, the storehouse was empty; the fortieth square required ten billion rice grains (Meadows et al., 1972). In other words, starting with one item and doubling it, doubling the result, and so on, rapidly leads to huge figures: 1:2:4:8:16:32:64:128, etc. In seven operations the figure has risen by 128 percent. Exactly the same principle applies to population growth. We can measure this effect by means of the **doubling time,** the period of time it takes for the population to double. A population growth of 1 percent will produce a doubling of numbers in seventy years. At 2 percent growth, a population will double in thirty-five years, while at 3 percent it will double in twenty-three years.

MALTHUSIANISM

In premodern societies, birth rates were very high by the standards of the industrialized world today. Nonetheless, population growth remained low until the eighteenth century because there was a rough overall balance between births and deaths. The general trend of numbers was upwards, and there were sometimes periods of more marked population increase, but these were followed by increases in death rates. In medieval Europe, for example, when harvests were bad, marriages tended to be postponed and the number of conceptions fell, while deaths increased. These complementary trends reduced the number of mouths to be fed. No preindustrial society was able to escape from this self-regulating rhythm (Wrigley, 1968).

During the period of the rise of industrialism, many looked forward to a new age in which scarcity would be a phenomenon of the past. The development of modern industry, it was widely supposed, would create a new era of abundance. In his celebrated work *Essay on the Principle of Population* (1976; orig. pub. 1798), Thomas Malthus criticized these ideas and initiated a debate about the connection between population and food resources that continues to this day. At the time Malthus wrote, the population in Europe was growing rapidly. Malthus pointed out that, while population increase is exponential, food supply depends on fixed resources that can be expanded only by developing new land for cultivation. Population growth therefore tends to outstrip the means of support available. The inevitable outcome is famine, which, combined with the influence of war and plagues, acts as a natural limit to population increase. Malthus predicted that human beings would always live in circumstances of misery and starvation, unless they practiced what he called "moral restraint." His cure for excessive population growth was for people to strictly limit their frequency of sexual intercourse. (The use of contraception he proclaimed to be a "vice".)

For a while, **Malthusianism** was ignored, since the population development of the Western countries followed a quite different pattern from that which he had anticipated—as we shall see below. Rates of population growth trailed off in the nineteenth and twentieth centuries. Indeed, in the 1930s there were major worries about population decline in many industrialized countries, including the United States. The upsurge in world population growth in the twentieth century has again lent some credence to Malthus's views, although few support them in their original version. Population expansion in Third World countries seems to be outstripping the resources that those countries can generate to feed their citizenry.

POPULATION GROWTH IN THE THIRD WORLD

Virtually all the industrialized countries today have low birth and death rates compared with their past history and with Third World nations. In the majority of Third World countries, death rates have fallen but birth rates remain high. Because of the relatively sudden introduction of modern medicine and methods of hygiene, demographic changes that took more than two hundred years in the West have occurred within less than half a century in the Third World.

Population growth in Asia, Africa, and South America severely

TABLE 18.1 POPULATION AND GNP PER CAPITA GROWTH RATES, 1980–1987 (IN ANNUAL PERCENTAGES)

	Population growth rate	GNP per capita growth rate
DEVELOPING SOCIETIES		
Africa		
Ghana	3.4%	−2.0%
Sudan	2.8	−4.0
Zaire	3.1	−2.8
Zambia	3.5	−4.4
South America		
Equador	2.9	−1.9
Peru	2.6	−1.1
Asia		
Bangladesh	2.6	1.0
Philippines	2.4	−1.1
INDUSTRIALIZED SOCIETIES		
United States	1.0	2.0
Japan	0.6	3.1
Sweden	0.1	1.8

Source: The World Bank Atlas, 1988.

limits possibilities of economic development in these regions. In a population with zero growth, between 3–5 percent of national income has to be invested to produce a 1 percent increase in income per head. Where a population grows by 3 percent per year, up to 20 percent of national income has to be invested in order to create a similar increase in living standards. As the regions in which population is growing rapidly include most of the poorest countries in the world, such a level of investment cannot possibly be met; these countries fall further and further behind the industrialized sectors of the globe (see Chapter 16: "The Globalizing of Social Life").

The rapid drop in mortality, with little or no decline in fertility, has produced a completely different age structure in Third World countries compared to the industrialized ones. In Mexico, for example, 45 percent of the population is less than fifteen years old. In the industrialized countries, on the other hand, only about a quarter of the population is in this age group. The imbalanced age distribution in the nonindustrialized countries adds to their social and economic difficulties. A youthful population needs support and education, during which period its members would not be economically productive. But many Third World countries lack the resources to provide universal education, and as a result, large numbers of children must either work full time or scratch a living as "street children," begging for whatever they can. When the "street children," mature, most become unemployed, homeless, or both (Davis, 1976; Ennew, 1986).

A population that has disproportionate numbers of young people will continue to grow even if the birth rate should suddenly fall. If fertility declined to "replacement level"—one birth for every death in a population—it would still take seventy-five years before that population stopped increasing. In other words, until the population as a whole aged, there would be a disproportionate number of young people; the large numbers of young women would mean a large number of babies being born, keeping the population level above zero growth (Duncan, 1971).

THE DEMOGRAPHIC TRANSITION

Demographers often refer to the changes in the ratio of births to deaths in the industrialized countries from the nineteenth century onwards as the **demographic transition.** The notion was first worked out by Warren S. Thompson, who described a three-stage process in which one type of population stability would be eventually replaced by another as a society reached an advanced level of economic development (Thompson, 1929).

Stage one refers to the conditions characteristic of most traditional societies, in which both birth and death rates are high, and the infant-mortality rate is especially large. Population grows little if at all, as the high number of births is more or less balanced by the level of deaths. Stage two, which began in Europe and the United States in the early part of the nineteenth century—with wide regional variations—occurs when death rates fall while fertility remains high. This is therefore a phase of marked population growth. It is subsequently replaced by stage three, in which, with industrial development, birth rates drop to a level such that population is again fairly stable.

Demographers do not fully agree about how this sequence of change should be interpreted, or how long lasting stage three is likely to be. Fertility in the Western countries has not been completely stable over the past century or so; there remain considerable differences in fertility between the industrialized nations, as well as between classes or regions within them. Nevertheless, it is generally accepted that this sequence accurately describes a major transformation in the demographic character of modern societies.

The theory of demographic transition directly opposes the ideas of Malthus. Whereas for Malthus, increasing prosperity would automatically bring about population increase, the thesis of demographic transition emphasizes that economic development, generated by industrialism, would actually lead to a new equilibrium of population stability.

LIKELY PROSPECTS FOR THE THIRD WORLD

Will the demographic transition be repeated in the Third World? The answer to this question is as yet unclear. Fertility remains high in many Third World societies because traditional attitudes to family size have been maintained. Having large numbers of children is often still regarded as desirable, providing a source of labor on family-run farms. Some religions are influential in areas where population growth is high and are either opposed to birth control or affirm the desirability of having many children. Contraception is opposed by Islamic leaders in several countries and by the Catholic Church, whose influence is especially marked in South and Central America. The motivation to reduce fertility has not always been forthcoming even from political authorities. In 1974, contraceptives were banned in Argentina as part of a program to double the population of the country as fast as possible; this was seen as a means of developing its economic and military strength.

Yet it does seem that the phenomenal rate of world population increase of the past few decades may at last be slowing. A decline in fertility levels has occurred in some large Third World countries. An example is China, which currently has a population of over a billion people—almost a quarter of the world's population as a whole. The Chinese government established one of the most extensive programs of population control that any country has undertaken, with the object of stabilizing the country's numbers at close to their current level. The government instituted a range of incentives to promote single-child families (such as better housing, free health care and education), while families who have more than one child face special hardships (wages are cut for those who have a third child).

There is evidence that China's antinatal policies have had a substantial impact on its population (Mirsky, 1982). Yet there is also much resistance within the country to the measures. People are reluctant to regard parents with one child as a proper "family." In addition, the program demands a degree of centralized government control that is either unacceptable, or unavailable, in most other developing countries. In India, for instance, many schemes for promoting family planning and the use of contraceptives have been tried, but with only relatively small success. India in 1988 had a population of 789 million. Its average annual growth of population from 1975 to 1985 was 2.3 percent; this is projected to decline to 1.8 percent over the twenty years from 1980 to 2000. But by the latter year, however, the population of the country will be a billion people. Even if its population-growth rate does diminish, as the projection presumes, the increase in population will remain extremely large.

Technological advances in agriculture and industry are unpredictable, so no one can be sure how large a population the world might eventually be able to support. Yet even at current population levels, global resources may already be well below those required to create living standards in the Third World comparable to those of the industrialized countries. The consumption of energy, raw materials, and other goods is vastly higher in the Western countries than in other areas of the world. These consumption levels partly depend, moreover, upon resources transferred from Third World regions to the industrially developed nations (Ehrlich and Ehrlich, 1979). Each person in the United States consumes 32 times as much energy as an average individual in countries like China or India. Unless there are major changes in patterns of world energy consumption—such as expanding the use of solar energy and wind power—there seems little possibility of extending this level of energy consumption to everyone in the world. There are probably not enough known energy resources to go around (McHale et al., 1979; Gupte, 1984).

Let us now look at population distribution and change in the United States, before moving on to problems of health and illness.

POPULATION IN THE UNITED STATES

There are today about 240 million people living in the United States, with about 103 women to every 100 men. The most important change since the 1900s has been an overall decline in fertility. There have been fluctuations over this period, but for the most part, U.S. population growth is in the third stage of the demographic transition.

A marked but temporary rise in fertility occurred after World War II—the "baby boom." The birth rate rose from a low of 17 per thousand during the early 1930s to 25 per thousand in the late 1950s. The baby boom was not a consequence of a rise in larger families; in fact, there was little increase in the proportion of families with three or more children. Rather, there was a marked *decline* in the proportion of childless or one-child families.

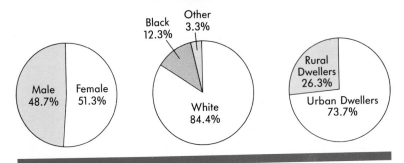

FIGURE 18.2 POPULATION IN THE UNITED STATES BY SEX, RACE, AND AREA OF RESIDENCE*

Sex and Race for 1988; residence for 1980.
Source: U.S. Bureau of the Census, *Current Population Reports,* series P-25, No. 1045.

One factor in the baby boom was the large number of soldiers returning home following the end of World War II, but other influences were also important. Increasing prosperity provided a sound economic basis for initiating families (and also provided the motivation for keeping them small). This was, moreover, the period during which the identification of women with the domestic role of "housewife and mother" was most pronounced. Many young women who had worked during the war years were now ready to have a family.

Demographers did not anticipate the baby boom, nor did they foresee the return to the lower levels of fertility in the early 1970s. In 1972, the fertility rate of the United States dropped below replacement level. In spite of this, the overall population of the country continues to increase. The baby boom, to change metaphors, has produced a "bulge" in the age distribution of the population. Those of the baby-boom generation born between 1946 and 1964 are now adults, having children of their own. Since the proportion of people of childbearing age will remain high for the next twenty years or so, the number of people born each year will still be greater than those who die.

But as the baby-boom generation gets still older, if the present low-fertility rate is maintained, the result will be a situation of zero population growth. In such a circumstance, those who are born each year, plus those who immigrate (come into the country), would be equal in numbers to those who die or emigrate (leave the country). Many demographers believed that zero population growth would be characteristic of some forty countries in the world by the end of the 1980s. If zero population growth should be characteristic of the

This graph shows the size of the
baby boom projected for 1990
relative to generations preceding
and following.

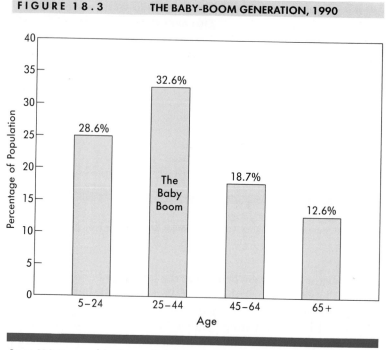

FIGURE 18.3   **THE BABY-BOOM GENERATION, 1990**

Source: U.S. Bureau of the Census, *Current Population Reports*, series P-25, No. 1018.

next few decades, there will be an even larger proportion of older
people in the population than at present. However, since demographers have not been particularly accurate in predicting trends in the
past, especially in the short-term, it cannot be assumed that such a
pattern of development will inevitably occur.

The impact of fluctuations in fertility on social institutions is well
evidenced by the consequences of the baby boom. In their early years,
this generation created the need to expand child-based medical services, the production of child-care goods, and welfare provisions. As
the baby boomers moved into the school system, strains were placed
upon existing personnel and resources. Now that they have entered
the labor market, the members of this generation have helped add to
the pressures upon employment opportunities. When they reach retirement age, a particular burden will be placed upon welfare and
medical services oriented to the elderly. Since the baby boom was followed by the "birth dearth" of the 1970s, the succeeding generation
is considerably smaller in size (Light, 1988). This has already brought
about a need for restructuring school resources, with a much lower
demand for elementary school teachers, and will create similar imbalances of resources as this generation itself ages.

A National Commission on Population Growth and the American Future, reporting in 1972, concluded that zero population growth would provide the most secure policy option for the United States. If the population were to increase much further, the commission suggested, the nation's social problems would become magnified. But just as important as national consequences are the global implications of American population patterns. Since the United States consumes an extremely high proportion of the world's material resources, each new American child places a special pressure upon global supplies of goods and services.

HEALTH AND ILLNESS

POPULATION ISSUES ARE INTIMATELY CONNECTED TO PROBlems of health and illness. How many children are born, the proportion who live beyond infancy, the ages to which people survive, and the major causes of death, are all bound up with health patterns. Health and illness, in turn, are strongly influenced by aspects of social structure. Social factors affect not simply life expectancy, but the chances individuals have of contracting major types of disease and the nature of the health care they receive.

TREATING ILLNESS IN THE PAST

All cultures have concepts of physical health and illness, but most of what we now recognize as "medicine" is a consequence of developments in Western society over the past two or three centuries. In premodern cultures, the family, or kinship unit, was the main institution coping with sickness or affliction. There have always been individuals who specialized as "healers," using a mixture of physical and magical remedies, and many of these traditional systems of medical treatment survive today in non-Western cultures throughout the world. Ayurvedic medicine (traditional healing) has been practiced in India, for instance, for nearly two thousand years. It is founded upon a theory of the equilibrium of psychological and physical aspects of the personality, imbalances of which are treated by nutritional means and herbal remedies. Chinese folk medicine is similarly based on a conception of the overall harmony of the personality, involving the use of herbs and other remedies, together with acupuncture, a technique whereby a patient is treated by strategic placement of needles.

It was common in traditional cultures for illness to be seen as one aspect of the overall psychological and social well-being of the individual. Similar views survived in Europe until the eighteenth century. Most schools of European medicine originated in Greek systems of treatment, which sought to explain illness in terms of the general mental and physical disposition of the individual (Patrick and Scambler, 1982; Porter, 1986). Physicians did not belong to a defined "profession," but were usually employed as healers by aristocrats or gentry. As was mentioned in Chapter 5 ("Deviance"), hospitals in the modern sense have only come into being in large numbers since the early nineteenth century. Up to that time, and in some areas even later, treatment of illness depended almost wholly on a mixture of folk remedies, prayer, and magic.

THE DEVELOPMENT OF MODERN MEDICINE

Modern medicine introduced a view of illness that sees its origins and treatment as physical and explicable in scientific terms. The application of science to medical diagnosis and cure was one major feature in the development of modern health-care systems. Other closely related features were the acceptance of the hospital as the setting within which serious illnesses were to be coped with or cured; and the development of the medical profession as a body having recognized codes of ethics and significant social power. The scientific view of disease was linked to the requirement that medical training be systematic and long-term; self-taught healers were excluded. Although professional medical practice is not limited to hospitals, the hospital provided an environment in which doctors for the first time were able to treat and study large numbers of patients, in circumstances permitting the concentration of medical technology.

In medieval times the major illnesses were infectious diseases such as tuberculosis, cholera, malaria, and plague. In the Black Death in the fourteenth century, the plague (which is spread by fleas carried by rats) killed a quarter of the population of England, and devastated large areas of Europe. Infectious diseases have now become a relatively minor cause of death in the industrialized countries, and several have also been substantially eradicated from other parts of the world. In the industrialized countries, the most common causes of death today are noninfectious illnesses, such as cancer and heart disease. Whereas in premodern societies the highest rates of mortality were among infants and young children, today mortality rates rise with increasing age.

In spite of the prestige that modern medicine has acquired, improvements in medical care accounted for only a relatively minor part of the decline in rates of mortality prior to the present century. Effective sanitation, better nutrition, control of sewage, and improved hygiene generally were more consequential, particularly in reducing the infant mortality rates and deaths of young children. Drugs, advances in surgery, and antibiotics did not significantly decrease mortality rates until well into the twentieth century. Antibiotics used to treat bacterial infections first became available in the 1930s and 1940s, while immunizations (against diseases such as polio) were developed still later.

THE THIRD WORLD: COLONIALISM AND THE SPREAD OF DISEASE

There is good evidence that the hunting and gathering communities of the Americas, prior to the arrival of the Europeans, were not as subject to infectious disease as the European societies of the period. Many infectious organisms only thrive when human populations are living above the density characteristic of hunting and gathering life. Permanently settled communities, particularly large cities, risk contamination of water supplies by waste products. Hunters and gatherers were less vulnerable in this respect because they moved continuously across the countryside.

The expansion of the West in the colonial era transmitted certain diseases into other parts of the world where they had not existed previously. Smallpox, measles, and typhus, among other major maladies, were unknown to the indigenous populations of Central and South America prior to the Spanish conquest in the early sixteenth century. The English and French colonists brought the same diseases to North America (Dubos, 1959). Some of these illnesses produced epidemics so severe that they ravaged or completely wiped out native populations, which had little or no resistance to them.

In Africa and subtropical parts of Asia, infectious diseases have almost certainly been rife for a long period of time. Tropical and subtropical conditions are especially conducive to diseases such as malaria, carried by mosquitoes, and sleeping sickness, carried by the tsetse fly. Yet it seems probable that, prior to contact with the Europeans, levels of risk from infectious diseases were lower. There was always the threat of epidemics, drought, or natural disaster, but colonialism led to major changes in the relation between populations and their environments, producing harmful effects upon health patterns. The Europeans introduced new farming methods, upsetting the ecol-

**TABLE 18.2
PERCENTAGE OF
POPULATION WITH ACCESS
TO CLEAN DRINKING WATER**

Third World	
Ethiopia	16%
India	42%
Tanzania	46%
Mexico	57%
Chile	85%
Soviet Union	76%
United States	99%

Sources: United Nations Children's Fund, 1983; Sivard, 1983; Pan American Health Organization, 1982.

ogy of whole regions. For example, wide tracts of East Africa today are completely devoid of cattle as a result of the uncontrolled spread of the tsetse fly, which multiplied as a result of the changes the intruders introduced. Before the arrival of the Europeans, Africans successfully maintained large herds in these same areas (Kjekshus, 1977).

The most significant consequence of the colonial system was its effect upon nutrition, and therefore on levels of resistance to illness, as a result of the changed economic conditions involved in producing for world markets. In many parts of Africa in particular, the nutritional quality of native diets became substantially depressed as cash-crop production supplanted the production of native foods.

This was not simply a one-way process, however, as the early development of colonialism also radically changed Western diets, having a paradoxical impact so far as health is concerned. On the one side, Western diets were improved by the addition of a range of new foods either previously unknown or very rare, like bananas, pineapples, and grapefruit. On the other hand, the importation of tobacco and coffee, together with raw sugar, which began increasingly to be used in all manner of foods, has had harmful consequences. Smoking tobacco, especially, has been linked to the prevalence of cancer and heart disease.

The Infectious Diseases Today

Although major strides have been made in reducing, and in some cases virtually eliminating, infectious diseases in the Third World, they remain far more common there than in the West. The most important example of a disease that has almost completely disappeared from the world is smallpox, which, even as recently as the 1960s, was a scourge of Europe as well as many other parts of the world. Campaigns against malaria have been much less successful. When the insecticide DDT was first produced, it was hoped that the mosquito, the prime carrier of malaria, could be eradicated. At first, considerable progress was made, but this has slowed down because some strains of mosquito have become resistant to DDT. Basic medical resources are still lacking in the vast majority of Third World countries. The hospitals that do exist, together with trained doctors, tend to be heavily concentrated in urban areas, where their services are mostly monopolized by the affluent minority. Most Third World countries have introduced some form of National Health Service, organized by the central government, but the medical services available are usually very limited. The small section of the wealthy utilize private health care, sometimes traveling to the West when sophisticated

FIGURE 18.4   LIFE EXPECTANCY AT BIRTH—A GLOBAL LOOK, 1987

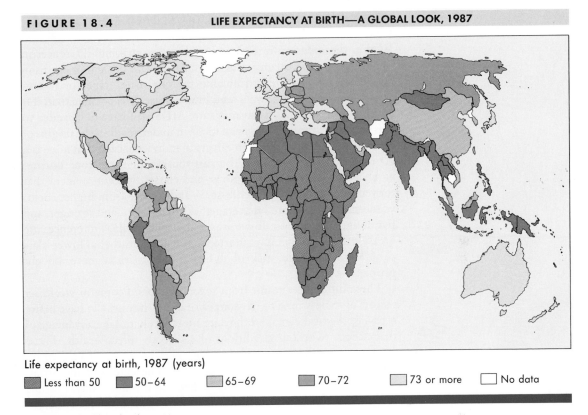

Life expectancy at birth, 1987 (years)

▨ Less than 50   ▨ 50–64   ▨ 65–69   ▨ 70–72   ▨ 73 or more   ☐ No data

Source: The World Bank Atlas, 1988.

medical treatment is needed. Conditions in many Third World cities, particularly in the shanty towns, make the control of infectious diseases very difficult: many shanty areas almost completely lack basic services such as water, sewage, and garbage disposal.

Studies carried out by the World Health Organization suggest that more than two-thirds of people living in urban areas in Third World countries draw their water from sources that fail to meet minimal health needs. It has been estimated that seventeen out of the twenty-five common water-related diseases in Third World nations could either be cut by half, or eradicated altogether, simply by the provision of ready supplies of safe water (Doyal and Pennell, 1981). Only about a quarter of the city residents in Third World countries have water-borne sewage facilities; some 30 percent have no sanitation at all. These conditions provide breeding grounds for diseases such as cholera (*The Lancet,* 1974; Dwyer, 1975).

HEALTH AND ILLNESS IN THE DEVELOPED COUNTRIES

Within the industrialized societies, there are striking differences in the distribution of the major diseases. Around 70 percent of deaths in Western countries are attributable to four major types of illness: cancer, heart disease, strokes, and lung disease. It is possible that, if it continues to spread at its current rate, AIDS will have to be added to this list. Some progress has been made in understanding the origins of these, and in controlling their effects in individual cases, but none can be effectively cured. Since the distribution of these four diseases varies between countries, regions, and classes, it seems evident that they are related to diet and life-style. Individuals from higher socio-economic positions are on average healthier, taller, and stronger, and live longer, than those lower down the social scale. Differences are greatest in respect to infant mortality and child death, but lower-class people are at greater risk of dying at *all ages* than more affluent people.

These differences result from several factors. People in wealthier sectors of society tend to have superior diets, they usually have better access to medical care, and they are more likely to take advantage of that access. Working conditions also directly affect health. Those who work in offices, or in domestic settings, are at less of a risk of injury or exposure to hazardous materials. The extent of industrial-based disease is difficult to calculate, because it is not always possible to determine whether an illness is picked up from working conditions or from other sources. However, some work-related diseases are well documented: lung disease is widespread in mining, due to dust inhalation; work in environments using asbestos has been shown to produce certain types of cancer.

It is generally accepted that the propensity to heart ailments is influenced by a diet rich in animal fats, a lack of exercise, and habitual smoking. Most of the evidence about this is indirect, inferred from correlational studies linking the rate of heart disease with different dietary habits and the amount of exercise. Twenty years ago, the United States had the highest rate of death from heart disease in the world. Over the past two decades, however, the level has dropped. This seems to be the result of changes in diet, a higher proportion of the population than before engaging in regular exercise, together with improved means of providing quick response to those suffering heart attacks.

Campaigns against smoking have also had an important effect. When the first reports were issued documenting a close correlation between cigarette smoking and cancer, in the early 1960s, over 50 percent of the male population were habitual smokers. That proportion has now declined to well under 30 percent. Yet there has been little change in the proportion of young people who smoke, while the proportion of women smoking on a regular basis has actually increased. Smoking is an even more widespread habit in many other Western countries than it is in the United States. It has been estimated that 20 percent of deaths from cancer worldwide could be prevented if cigarette smoking ceased completely.

In all modern societies vast amounts of money are spent regularly by governments and individual citizens upon health care of one sort or another, and each new health-related problem readjusts a nation's health-care system. We now move to analyzing such health-care systems in the United States and in other countries where, unlike the United States, there are national systems of socialized medicine.

HEALTH CARE IN THE UNITED STATES

An enormous sum of money is spent each year on health care in the United States. In fact, a higher proportion of total output is spent here than in any other nation. American medical services are supported primarily by private insurance programs or supplemented by government programs—Medicare for the elderly and Medicaid for the poor. The **health-care system** is much more fragmented and diverse than in most other countries where comprehensive government-run national health programs exist. For example, U.S. hospitals are owned by federal or state governments, city or county authorities, private organizations, religious orders, voluntary nonprofit groups, or some combination of these. In some other countries, like Britain, the vast majority of hospitals are owned and funded by the government.

Medicare is a program financed by the federal government for those aged sixty-five or more. One part covers all hospital costs, while other medical expenses must be paid in part by the individual. The federal Medicaid program finances health services for those who are "categorically needy" and "medically needy." The "categorically needy" covers people who are disabled, blind, or are children in special need. Those who are "medically needy" are only covered under Medicaid if the state in which they live has chosen to accept the program; a state may choose instead to provide its own coverage.

The American health-care system has changed markedly over the past twenty years because of the emergence of health-care organizations run primarily to make a profit. (Starr, 1982; Light, 1986, 1987). In 1968, Thomas F. Frist, a Nashville doctor, and Jack C. Massey, a businessman who was responsible for turning Kentucky Fried

Chicken into a national chain, began the first hospital chain set up explicitly for profit. Frist's hospital, Park View, was provided with capital for expansion by the Hospital Corporation of America (HCA), which the two had founded. Subsequently, HCA began acquiring other hospitals, and today has become the largest hospital chain of its type in the country. Prior to this, most privately-owned medical facilities were nonprofit organizations. Since then, clinics, consultancies, and specialized medical centers have also been set up to be profit making.

Medicine has traditionally been associated with an imagery of care, service, and charity. Has the development of for-profit organizations served to extend or to damage these ideals? Can medicine be run in a way similar to fast-food chains? Several studies have been undertaken to look at these questions, including a major investigation by the Institute of Medicine of the National Academy of Science (Krause, 1977; Fein, 1986). These researches do not support the claim of the for-profit chains that their hospitals are more efficient, and provide better value, than the nonprofit organizations. On average, charges are significantly higher in the for-profit hospitals.

Comparing quality of medical care is more difficult. The facilities of for-profit organizations seem to match those of others in terms of services available to people with good incomes. However, the for-profit hospitals have few patients who are uninsured, or who are only covered by welfare benefits. The for-profit organizations therefore shift much of the burden of health care onto other sectors of the system. Their overall impact seems to be to produce a pressure towards "cost cutting," which can lead to economizing on essential services (Waitzkin, 1986; Califano, 1986).

In spite of the country's high level of wealth, and the vast sums spent on health-care industries, the United States does not fare well in respect to some basic indices of health. The United States ranks quite low, for example, in respect to the two most common measures of the physical well-being of a population: average life expectancy and the rate of infant mortality. Life expectancy, even when differences in infant mortality are taken into account, is higher in some European countries than in the United States. In addition, virtually all the countries of Western Europe have lower rates of infant mortality than the United States. One reason for this is that there are an estimated 20 million people in the United States who do not possess private health insurance and who have virtually no access to public health care.

The logic of the health-care system in the United States is based upon the idea that competition produces the cheapest services, since it allows consumers to pick and choose. The weaknesses in this position are well known. Consumers cannot readily shop around when they are sick, and are usually unable to judge technically the services they are offered. Those with inadequate resources have very limited access to medical services. Affluent members of the population are quite often able to buy far superior medical provision than those who are less well off. People who are fully covered by medical insurance have little incentive to seek less-expensive care. The general result is a health-care system that is very expensive to run in proportion to the health levels achieved, and in which there are serious gaps in overall provision for the population.

NATIONAL HEALTH-CARE SYSTEMS

Because many Americans are not receiving adequate medical attention, some, including politicians, have pushed for establishing a national health-care system. Such a system, also known as *socialized medicine,* would put the federal government in charge of the now fragmented health-care system. The idea has been resisted in the United States by one of the more powerful institutions and government lobbyists, the American Medical Association, but such systems are common elsewhere in the world.

In the Soviet Union and the East European societies, for instance, there are very extensive systems of national health care. Most medical services are free, although the available facilities are often too few, and long waiting lists exist for many types of medical treatment. Virtually all other industrialized countries, Britain and Canada among them, have comprehensive systems of publicly provided medical services. The National Health Services (NHS) in Britain, for example, has been in existence since 1948. The stated principle underlying the founding of the NHS was that access to health care should depend upon medical need rather than on ability to pay (Eckstein, 1958).

The NHS is funded from national government revenues, collected as part of income tax. Access to general practitioners and hospital treatment is free to all users. Prescription drugs were originally supplied without charge, but legislation by recent governments has introduced a system of partial payments. When the NHS was first established, pressure from the medical profession, among others, ensured that a private market would remain in health care, operating alongside the publicly provided facilities. While the majority of general practitioners work exclusively for the NHS, there is a high proportion who maintain private practices. Some purely private hospitals and health-care facilities exist, together with medical personnel who work exclusively in the private sector. Only a small

TABLE 18.3 THE PROPORTION OF DOCTORS TO POPULATION	
Doctors per 100,000 people	
Soviet Union	357
Italy	294
Israel	270
Hungary	250
West Germany	222
Sweden	204
United States	192
Canada	182
Australia	179
France	172
Britain	154
Japan	128
Saudi Arabia	61
Brazil	59
China	52
India	27
Kenya	9

Source: Watkins and Worcester, 1986.

minority of the population, however, are members of private health-insurance programs.

Among the criticisms often made of the NHS is that patients are placed on long waiting lists to see specialists recommended by a general practitioner. A survey carried out by a royal commission, appointed to study the health service, however, found that on the whole this was not the case: 26 percent of patients were seen in seven days or less, while 60 percent waited less than three weeks (Royal Commission on the National Health Service, 1979). But since that study was carried out, the average waiting time has risen considerably. Average waiting time needed to see specialists is certainly greater than among fully insured patients in the United States. Another problem is that patients cannot shop around, but have to be registered with a particular general practitioner, who then contacts specialists on their behalf. The range of open "consumer choice" is quite limited when compared to the U.S. system (Richman, 1987). Such complaints are brought up whenever someone proposes that the United States adopt a national health-care system. However, those in favor of such a system point to the benefits which it might have for the poor, and to the fact that such a system could serve to place a stronger emphasis on preventative medicine than is now the case.

MEDICAL TECHNOLOGY AND ETHICS

Medical care does not just respond to illness and disability. The close involvement of modern medicine with science, mentioned earlier, has led to technological innovations that now venture into areas previously unknown to medicine. Along with these new technologies come ethical and legal problems.

Medical science is now well equipped to keep a person alive with machines for an extended period of time when that person's own body, because of illness or injury, cannot do so. At the same time, the technology does not exist for repairing the body so that it can take over in the case of some illnesses or injuries. What does a society do with such a person who now and in the future can exist only on a medical life-support system? Can the individual request the medical team to "pull out the plug"? If the individual is in a coma from which recovery is unlikely, what should be done? Many believe that the family, in consultation with the medical team and perhaps an outside adviser or member of the clergy, should decide whether the person is to be taken off the life-support system. Others disagree, stating that life under any circumstances is worth prolonging.

Reproductive technologies have had a tremendous impact on conception and childbearing and have raised another set of legal and ethical questions. Let's consider five areas in which medical intervention has affected different aspects of human reproduction (Stanworth, 1988).

Measuring and Screening Fetal Development

In the past, new parents had to wait until the day of birth to learn the sex of their newborn and whether it would be "healthy." Today, prenatal tests such as the sonogram (an image of the fetus produced using ultrasonic waves) and amniocentesis (which draws off some of the amniotic fluid from around the fetus for testing) can be used to discover any structural or chromosomal abnormalities prior to birth. Such new technology presents couples and society with ethical and legal decisions. Where a serious disorder is detected, the couple is faced with the decision of whether or not to have the baby knowing it may be seriously handicapped.

Labor and Childbirth

Medical science has not always been involved with all life events from birth to death. The "medicalization" of pregnancy and childbirth developed slowly, as local physicians and midwives were displaced by pediatric specialists. Today in the industrialized societies, most births occur in a hospital with the help of a specialized medical team. One consequence of this, and the development of other reproductive technologies, is the fact that women must rely on gynecologists and obstetricians, who are mostly male, for care and treatment before or during pregnancy.

Contraception

Various types of birth control were available in traditional societies although most were relatively haphazard or unsafe. Today, advances in contraceptive technology have enabled most women and men to control when and whether they choose to have children. The birth control pill is perhaps the single most important new form of contraception to appear over the last half century. So far, chemical control of contraception is limited to women, but various trials are proceeding with a "male pill," which will place more responsibility on men for birth control.

Abortion

Abortion technology has elicited a particularly heated debate, especially in the United States. A 1989 Supreme Court decision, *Webster v.*

Reproductive Health Services, threw the right to abortion into jeopardy. While not prohibiting abortion, the decision upheld part of a Missouri state law restricting abortion. One of the provisions of the Missouri law prohibited public employees and facilities from being used to perform abortions not necessary to save a woman's life. This ruling did not reverse a prior decision, *Roe v. Wade,* which in 1973 gave women the right to abortion, but *Webster* did open up to state legislatures the possibility to make laws restricting abortion. The debate over the issue continues as pro-life groups, who believe that abortion is the deliberate killing of an individual, battle pro-choice groups, who see abortion as a basic freedom of women's control of their own bodies. Making this question all the more complicated is the most recent advance in reproductive technology: RU486, a pill developed by medical researchers in France, which, when taken some hours after sexual intercourse, will cause the fertilized egg to detach from the uterus thus prohibiting any further development. This would give a woman even greater control over possible conception. But because of the drug's timing, anti-abortion groups will probably resist its marketing in the United States.

Influencing Conception Itself

New techniques have been developed for overcoming infertility. These began with the introduction of artificial insemination in the 1930s, followed some thirty years later by the discovery of "fertility drugs." Such drugs made it possible for some women to have children who had previously been unable to conceive. However, such drugs also frequently gave rise to multiple births.

There have also been major advances in techniques of *in vitro* fertilization (artificial fertilization of the woman's egg, outside the body). Various procedures are now available, including egg or embryo donation (from one woman to another), and low-temperature storage of gametes and embryo. Like fertility drugs, these procedures have given hope to couples who could not have children through natural processes. At the same time, they pose complicated ethical and legal problems. For example, a couple in Tennessee turned to *in vitro* fertilization because the wife was unable to conceive naturally. The woman's eggs were extracted and fertilized with the husband's sperm; nine embryos were produced in the laboratory. Two were reimplanted into the womb of the woman unsuccessfully. In the meantime, the couple had become estranged and planned to divorce. A court battle arose over the fate of the remaining seven frozen embryos. The wife wanted custody because she still wished to attempt a successful implantation of the embryos; the husband wanted custody because he did not want to become a father against his will. In September of 1989, the judge ruled that the wife should take temporary custody of the remaining embryos.

Similar court cases have arisen out of another reproductive method, **surrogate parenthood,** in which a woman contracts to be artificially inseminated with the sperm of a male from another couple, to whom custody of the child is to be transferred when born. One major issue here concerns the definition of parenthood. Who is the "parent" when a couple has paid a surrogate mother to bear the husband's child, and the surrogate mother decides she wishes to keep it? This was the situation in the "Baby M" case in which the New Jersey Supreme Court ruled in favor of the biological father but granted visitation rights to the surrogate mother as the natural mother. The courts in numerous countries are still debating this issue, and commercial surrogacy has been made illegal in several countries. As technological change continues, societies will have to face even more tangled dilemmas.

AGE AND AGING IN THE WEST

WE NOW TURN FROM THE YOUNG TO THE OLD. POPULAtion trends discussed earlier in the chapter have brought about a very large increase in the proportion of older people in Western societies (Jorgensen, 1980; Parnes, 1985; Zopf, 1986). At the same time, the social position of older people has become much more insecure than was the case in many earlier cultures. In traditional societies, old age brought prestige, wealth, and power. In the past, and to some extent in the many areas of the nonindustrialized world today, the needs of older people were often met within extended-family networks. Not only did they usually have a secure position in the community, they retained important duties within the family. Much of this has now disappeared in modern societies (Riley, 1987).

In the United States in 1850, the proportion of people over sixty-five years old was around 4 or 5 percent. The figure today is over 16 percent, and will grow over the next few decades. The average age of Americans has been rising for more than a century and a half. In 1800, the average age of the population was probably as low as sixteen. At the turn of the present century, it had risen to twenty-three. By 1970, it was twenty-eight, and today has reached over thirty. The average age of the population will go on rising for some time to come, given that no major changes in current demographic trends occur. It is likely to be thirty-five by 2000, and may climb to thirty-seven by 2030. By then, there may be as many as 50 million people over sixty-five in the population, a proportion of one in five. There has also been an expansion in the numbers of the very old. According to some estimates, the number of those over eighty-five years of age will be 60 percent above present levels by the year 2000, composing over 1.5 percent of the whole population (Acheson et al., 1981).

There are two main reasons for what has often been described as the "graying of America." One, as explained earlier, is that people on average live longer than they used to. Average life expectancy after the first year of life has increased by twelve years for men and fourteen years for women since 1900. The other is the future effect of the baby boom, as that enlarged generation "works its way through" the age structure.

RETIREMENT

The onset of old age is ordinarily associated with retirement. Old age today has a legal definition, in the sense that it refers to the time at which people can claim certain kinds of social security, welfare benefits, and pensions. Retirement can create social, economic, and psychological problems for individuals and, quite often, for households; it signals a major transition even for those able to treat their newfound free time as a means of acquiring fresh freedoms and opportunities (Parnes, 1985).

Retirement virtually always means a reduction of income. The average income for families in which at least one member is sixty-five or older is only just above half the average for the United States as a whole. There are wide variations of income among the over-sixty-five age group, since this now includes such a large segment of the population. However, many older people (15 percent of those aged sixty-five or over) live below the poverty line. Nearly 30 percent of those living alone, or with non-relatives, are below the poverty line. Older women living alone are on average poorest of all.

The social and psychological consequences of retirement vary according to previous job experience and standards of living. In a society geared to the value of work, retirement frequently means a loss of status. The absence of routines that may have structured an individual's life for as much as half a century may create a void difficult to fill. Knowledge and skills acquired over a lifetime do not any longer command the respect of the young, as used to be the case in most traditional cultures. Youth is prized more greatly than maturity, and the pace of social and technological change means that those in younger age groups often find the attitudes and outlook of their seniors largely irrelevant to their own aspirations.

For housewives, of course, there is no such thing as retirement, and the presence of a husband in the house during the day may make extra work; it certainly needs adjusting to.

SOCIAL PROBLEMS IN OLD AGE

Old age is often a time of loss in terms of relationships. Retirement spells the loss not only of a job itself but also of relationships with others at work. Children have normally moved to homes of their own. Contacts with relatives and friends are lost through death—or distance, since older people travel less frequently than when they were young (Matthews, 1979). The proportion of women aged sixty-five or more living alone is considerably larger than in the age group of forty-five to sixty-five (32 percent as compared to 15 percent in 1985). The proportion of men of sixty-five years or more who live alone, however, is actually slightly lower, at 8 percent, than those aged from forty-five to sixty-four (9 percent). Fear of violence is a strong influence on the elderly, which may restrict their activities, especially in city areas.

The aging process can affect individuals in different ways.

The social situation of older women is usually more problematic than that of men. It is easier for a man, if widowed or divorced, to find a new female companion or wife than for a woman to find a male companion, because far more women than men live to an old age; in addition, it is not socially disapproved of for men to go out with, or marry, much younger women. Older women, too, are generally less used to seeking companionship outside the home and family relationships. Most women respond to the death of their husbands with shock, depression, and guilt, quite often becoming physically ill themselves (Riley and Waring, 1976). On the other hand, a minority consider that their lives have improved following their husband's death. They may have been confined to the home as a result of the husband's illness, or perhaps restricted by having to fit in with his wishes (Lopata. 1977).

THE PHYSICAL EFFECTS OF AGING

Old age cannot as such be identified with ill health or disability, but advancing age of course brings increased health problems. Only during the past twenty years or so have biologists made a systematic attempt to distinguish the physical effects of aging from traits associated with diseases. Precisely to what extent the body inevitably "wears out" with advancing age is a debated issue. The effects of social and economic losses are also difficult to disentangle from the effects of physical deterioration as such. Loss of relatives and friends, separation from children who live elsewhere, and loss of employment may all take a physical toll.

In general, research findings demonstrate that poor health and advancing age are by no means completely synonymous. There are many people over sixty-five who claim to have almost perfect health. Nevertheless, a high proportion of people in this group reported "poor health" and "not enough medical care" as their most serious problems (Kart, 1985).

REDEFINING OLD AGE

In a society that places high value on youth, vitality, and physical attractiveness, older people tend to receive short shrift. Recent years, however, have seen the beginnings of altered attitudes towards old age on the part of older people themselves and of younger generations. Those in older age groups are unlikely to recover the full authority and prestige once held by "elders" of the community in

ancient societies. But as they become a more and more sizable proportion of the population, older people acquire more political influence than they previously possessed; they are already a powerful
political lobby. Under pressure from groups representing older people, the mandatory age of retirement was raised to seventy by Congress in 1978. In 1986, it was dissolved altogether, save for those in
some occupations, such as airline pilots or fire fighters.

Activist groups have also started to fight against "ageism," seeking
to foster a positive view of the capabilities of older people. **Ageism**
—discrimination against people on the basis of their age—is an ideology just as sexism and racism are. There are as many false stereotypes
of older people as in other areas of prejudice. For instance, it is often
believed that most people over sixty-five are confined to hospitals or
old-age homes; that a high proportion are senile; that older workers
are less competent than younger ones. All those beliefs are erroneous.
About 95 percent of people over sixty-five live in private dwellings;
only about 7 percent of those under the age of eighty show pronounced symptoms of senile decay; and the productivity and attendance records of older workers are superior to those of younger age
groups (Atchley, 1985).

A redefinition of the value and contributions of older people
would increase the general level of social tolerance in society. Benefits at the moment monopolized by the young and the middle-aged
might perhaps become more evenly distributed in future years. At the
moment, people in these age groups have a monopoly over education, work, power, and material rewards. A more even distribution of
these goods, from which older people can draw just as much profit as
younger individuals, would be in the interests of social justice.

SUMMARY

1. Population growth is one of the most significant global problems currently faced by humanity. About a quarter of the
   world's population suffers from malnutrition, and over 10 million people die of starvation each year. This misery is concentrated in the Third World countries.

2. The study of population growth is called *demography*. Much
   demographic work is statistical, but demographers are also concerned with trying to explain why population patterns take the
   form they do. The most important concepts in population analysis are *birth rates, death rates, fertility,* and *fecundity.*

3. The changes in population patterns that have occurred in the
   industrialized societies are usually analyzed in terms of a process

of *demographic transition*. Prior to industrialization, both birth and death rates were high. During the beginning of industrialization, there was population growth, because death rates were reduced while birth rates took longer to decline. Finally a new equilibrium was reached with low birth rates balancing low death rates.

4. World resources are finite, even if the limits of what can be produced are continually revised due to technological developments. Energy consumption and the consumption of raw materials and other goods are vastly higher in the Western countries than in other areas of the world. These consumption levels depend, moreover, upon resources transferred from Third World regions to the industrially developed nations. If resources were shared out equally, there would be a significant drop in Western living standards.

5. Population issues are intimately connected to problems of health and illness. All cultures have concepts of physical health and illness, but most of what we now recognize as "medicine" —such as the existence of hospitals and the application of science and technology to modes of medical treatment—is relatively recent in origin.

6. Susceptibility to the major illnesses in modern societies is strongly influenced by socioeconomic status. People from more affluent backgrounds tend to be healthier, taller, stronger, and to live longer, than those from poorer backgrounds.

7. *Reproductive technologies*—affecting fertilization, the growth of the embryo, and the nature of birth—pose difficult and controversial issues. Many debates continue to center on their use.

8. Retirement creates social, economic, and psychological problems for individuals (and often for households). For most people, retirement is a major transition. It usually means a reduction in income, and often a change in status. It can also be disorienting and lonely, since people must restructure much of their daily routine, and may lose contact with friends and colleagues.

9. In recent years, older people, who now make up a large proportion of the population of the industrialized countries have started to press for more recognition of their distinctive interests and needs. The struggle against ageism (discrimination against people on grounds of their age) is an important aspect of this development.

BASIC CONCEPTS

CRUDE BIRTH RATE
FERTILITY
CRUDE DEATH RATE
DEMOGRAPHIC TRANSITION

IMPORTANT TERMS

DEMOGRAPHY
FECUNDITY
MORTALITY
INFANT MORTALITY RATE
LIFE EXPECTANCY
LIFE SPAN
EXPONENTIAL GROWTH

DOUBLING TIME
MALTHUSIANISM
HEALTH-CARE SYSTEM
REPRODUCTIVE TECHNOLOGIES
SURROGATE PARENTHOOD
AGEISM

CHAPTER NINETEEN

REVOLUTIONS AND SOCIAL MOVEMENTS

REVOLUTIONS HAVE BROUGHT ABOUT SOME OF THE MOST momentous social changes in world history over the past two centuries. The American and French Revolutions, of 1776 and 1789 respectively, were the most important eighteenth-century revolutions. The ideals of those who led these revolutions—liberty, universal citizenship, and equality—have now become fundamental modern political values. But to have proclaimed them at all only two hundred years ago—and to suppose that they could be realized through mass action—represented a profound historical innovation. In previous eras, only idealistic dreamers had ventured to suggest that human beings could establish a social order in which political participation would be open to everyone.

The term **revolution** came to be employed in its modern sense at about the same time as that of **democracy.** It was not widely used until the success of the American and French struggles made clear that some new political process was afoot in the world. The European writer with more insight than anyone else about the United States and France at that period, Alexis de Tocqueville, observed: "What, to start with, had seemed to European monarchs and statesmen a mere passing phase, a not unusual symptom of a nation's growing pains, was now discovered to be something absolutely new, quite unlike any previous movement, and so widespread, extraordinary, and incalculable as to baffle human understanding" (Tocqueville, 1955).

At that time, "revolution" still carried a strong remnant of its original meaning, to "move in a circle" (the sense in which we still speak of the revolution of a wheel when a vehicle is in motion). The American and French revolutionary leaders, in fact, believed that they were "turning back" to a natural order of things. Human beings were born free and equal, but had been oppressed by the rule of kings and other self-appointed authorities; revolution was the means of restoring that happy, natural condition. In some respects, therefore, the innovative nature of the American and French revolutions was not apparent even to those who had played the greatest part in bringing them about.

As it became more and more obvious that at least some of the resulting changes were permanent, and as the influence of the ideals for which the revolutionaries had fought spread, "revolution" came increasingly to refer to mass action taken with the objective of bringing about fundamental social reconstruction (Abrams, 1982). Although some revolutions since then have been prompted by a concern with restoring a preexisting form of society (such as the Islamic revolution in contemporary Iran), the idea of revolution has been overwhelmingly associated with progress—representing a break with the past in order to establish a new order for the future (Arendt, 1977).

What is a revolution? What are the social conditions that lead to a process of revolutionary change? How should we best analyze movements of protest or rebellion? These are the main questions we shall concentrate upon in this chapter. We cannot understand revolution without knowing about the conditions under which revolutionary change occurs. Hence we shall look at several revolutions in some detail before discussing theories about radical political change and the impact of social movements.

The underlying theme of the whole chapter concerns *the roots of social protest*. Revolution is a particularly important example of mass protest operating outside orthodox political channels. But there are many other, more limited, situations in which uprisings or outbreaks of social violence occur—in the actions of street crowds, for example, or mass demonstrations. We shall also ask what prompts such activity and discuss how the behavior of individuals in crowds differs from their ordinary, everyday conduct.

Social movements—loose associations of people working collectively to achieve shared ends—play a key role in revolution. Indeed, as we shall see in the next section, the existence of such movements,

The democracy movement of 1989–1990 spread throughout Eastern Europe and forced Communist-led governments to relinquish their power. Here, part of the Berlin Wall that had divided this German city for almost thirty years is destroyed.

which receive mass support, is a defining characteristic of revolutions. However, as with mass action, social movements come into being in many other situations besides those of a revolutionary character. Besides political movements, we find religious movements, nationalist movements, women's movements, peace movements, ethnic movements, and very many others. All social movements are in some way oriented to change, although this might be a move backward (as in the case, for instance, of fundamentalist religious movements), rather than progressive. Classifying the different types of social movement, and explaining why social movements arise, are tasks we undertake in the closing parts of the chapter.

DEFINING REVOLUTION

AS A FIRST STEP, WE NEED TO DEFINE REVOLUTION SINCE everyday uses of the term vary widely. A ***coup d'état,*** which replaces one group of leaders by another without any changes in the existing political structure, for example, would not be an example of revolution in sociological terminology. For a set of events to be regarded as a revolution, they have to have several characteristics.

1. A revolution is a *mass social movement.* This serves to exclude instances in which either a party comes to power through electoral processes, or a small group, such as army leaders, seize power.

2. A revolution leads to *major processes of reform or change* (Skocpol, 1979). This means that those who seize state power must genuinely be more capable of governing the society over which they assume control than those they have overthrown (Dunn, 1972). The leadership must be capable of achieving at least some of its targets. A society in which a movement succeeds in gaining the formal trappings of power, but then is unable effectively to rule, cannot be said to have experienced a revolution; it is likely rather to be a society in chaos, or threatened with disintegration.

3. A revolution includes the *threat or use of violence* by those participating in the mass movement. Revolutions are political changes brought about in the face of opposition by existing

authorities, who cannot be persuaded to relinquish their power without the threatened or actual use of violence.

Assembling the three criteria together, we can define a **revolution** as *the seizure of state power through violent means by the leaders of a mass movement, where that power is subsequently used to initiate major processes of social reform.*

Revolutions differ from armed **rebellions,** which involve the threat or use of violence, but do not lead to substantial change. Until around three hundred years ago, the majority of uprisings were rebellions rather than revolutions. In medieval Europe, for example, serfs or peasants sometimes rose up in protest against the policies of the aristocracy (Scott, 1986; Zagorin, 1982). However, their objectives almost invariably were to secure more favorable treatment, or to replace a particularly tyrannical individual by someone less harsh. The idea of action taken to alter radically the existing political structure of society, that is, revolution, was virtually unthought of.

REVOLUTIONS IN THE TWENTIETH CENTURY

ALMOST ALL TWENTIETH-CENTURY REVOLUTIONS HAVE happened in developing societies, such as Mexico, Turkey, Egypt, Vietnam, Cuba, and Nicaragua, not in the industrial nations (Moore, 1965). The revolutions that have had the most profound consequences for the world in this century were the Russian Revolution of 1917 and the Chinese Revolution of 1949. Both took place in heavily rural, peasant societies, although Russia was beginning to industrialize. We shall begin our analysis of revolution by looking at these two cases and then at the revolution in Cuba.

THE RUSSIAN REVOLUTION

Prior to 1917, Russia was an economically backward society autocratically ruled by the tsars (emperors). The society was not completely stagnant, however. It had large armies, a well-organized civil service, and some large cities in which trade and manufacture were firmly established. Nonetheless, most of the population lived in rural poverty and the tsarist regime was for the most part dictatorial, making extensive use of a secret police and informers to suppress dissidents.

Serfdom (a system in which peasants were legally bound to a lord and his land) was not abolished in Russia until after 1860. The decision of the government to free the serfs was part of an attempt to modernize a society no longer able to compete militarily with the leading European powers. Russia had been the loser in the Crimean War of 1854–1855, and again lost in a war with the Japanese, fought in 1905. Largely in response to these defeats, programs of investment in industrial development were instituted, including the building of many new roads and railways. The Russian economy had some success but the tsarist government was too autocratic to permit the thorough social reforms that were taking place in the European countries.

Russia by 1905 was already a society under considerable tension. The beginnings of rapid industrialization had produced a developing class of industrial workers whose conditions of life were sometimes as miserable as those of most of the peasantry. Prevented from organizing effective unions, and completely excluded from political influence, the industrial workers became increasingly hostile to the government. For a far longer period, there had been growing hostility to the tsars among some sectors of the peasantry. During the Russo-Japanese war of 1905, there was a series of uprisings led by workers and some members of the armed forces disillusioned with the progress of the war. But that unrest was quelled when the government rapidly signed a peace treaty with the Japanese, disciplined

Vladimir Lenin (1870–1924), here speaking to crowds in Moscow, led the Russian Revolution.

the dissident troops, and brought them back to crush the rebels. Tsar Nicholas II introduced a few reforms, including the establishment of a representative parliament, but retracted them once he felt his power was again secure.

Between 1905 and 1917 discontent among industrial workers and peasants again became pronounced, with many strikes occurring. Some of these were led by the Bolsheviks, the most openly revolutionary party among a number of others that professed allegiance to socialism or Marxism. The influence of such parties increased during the early years of the First World War (1914–1918), a conflict in which Russia again fared badly—with much more serious consequences than before. Russia had 15 million men in its armies but, because of its lack of economic resources, was unable to equip them well enough to counter the Germans. Several million men were either killed, wounded, or taken prisoner, and a high proportion of officers were killed.

Food and fuel shortages became extreme among the civilian population as the war effort drained the country's resources. The wealthy as well as the poor started to turn decisively against the government. The tsar, continuing to exercise his privileges as absolute ruler, and guided by his adviser Rasputin, became more and more isolated from other groups in the country. In March 1917, workers and soldiers in the capital of Petrograd initiated a series of strikes and riots that rapidly spread through the western part of the country. Nicholas II was forced to abdicate and a new provisional government was set up.

The army, meanwhile, had more or less disintegrated, most of the soldiers returning to their home villages, towns, and cities. Peasants began to forcibly take over land from the larger landowners, and the provisional government was unable to contain continuing unrest and violence among workers and demobilized soldiers. Lenin, the leader of the Bolsheviks, determined to seize power, using as his slogan "Peace and Bread, Peace and Land"—an appeal to both the urban workers and the peasantry. In October 1917, the Bolsheviks forcibly dismissed the provisional government. Reorganizing and remobilizing the armed forces as the new Red Army, and successfully emerging from a period of bitter civil war, the new Soviet government set about implementing fundamental social changes, laying the basis for what has since become the second most powerful industrial and military power in the world (Carr, 1970).

The Russian Revolution was unusual in certain ways. The uprisings that initially undermined the tsarist regime were more spontaneous, and occurred on a larger scale, than in most other revolutions this century. At the beginning of 1917, not even the Bolsheviks anticipated that a successful revolution would be brought about within such as a short period of time. Yet the Russian Revolution teaches us a good deal about modern revolutions in general. Many revolutions have taken place against the background of war. A prolonged war places strain on the political and social institutions and, if conducted ineptly, is likely to result in a sharply declining level of support for the government. Disaffection within the armed forces removes the major instrument that a regime uses to subdue those who oppose it. Another important element was the role of the peasantry. Before the Russian Revolution, many (including Lenin) believed peasants to be an almost completely conservative force, wedded to traditional ways of life, and unlikely to join any movement for radical social change. This assumption was shown to be false: in this and subsequent twentieth-century revolutions, peasants have been directly involved.

REVOLUTION IN CHINA

Although much of what is now the Soviet Union is in Asia, Russia was always culturally oriented towards Europe. This was not true of China, which was culturally and geographically remote from the West until the nineteenth century. The development of steel-built passenger and cargo ships enabling extensive long-distance trade, combined with the colonizing of parts of the country by Western powers, broke down this separation between West and East. However, the continuity of the Chinese imperial state, stretching back at least two thousand years, remained unbroken until after the turn of the present century. Indeed, although some processes of modernization had been promoted within the government, much of Chinese society on the eve of the 1949 Communist revolution still followed long-established, traditional ways of life.

While China was too large for any Western power to attempt to colonize it completely, the impact of the extensive trading relations with the European states in the nineteenth century undermined the established economy. Largely because of the unfavorable conditions of trade imposed upon China, the imperial government in the late nineteenth century found itself increasingly impoverished. Unable to repay debts to European creditors, the government increased its taxation of the peasantry, which resulted in frequent riots and rebellions among peasants. In many parts of the enormous country, particularly where central political control had always been weak, warlords and bandits ruled unchecked. Although the Chinese believed deeply in the superiority of their civilization to all others, they were regularly humiliated by both the European states and the Japanese. China lost various territories in central and southeast Asia. The country was also

Mao Tse-tung (1893–1976) led the Chinese Revolution and established the Marxist-based People's Republic of China in 1949.

defeated in successive military encounters with the British, French, and Japanese.

In 1911 a major uprising forced the emperor to abdicate. Although sometimes spoken of as a "revolution," the events of 1911 and 1912 did not establish a government capable of unifying the country and promoting effective reforms. A Chinese Republic was set up, but local military leaders also established their own kingdoms, and some of the provinces declared their independence. The next few years brought a prolonged civil war among the various warlords, as well as a developing Communist party.

Stability was to some extent regained when one war leader, Chiang Kai-shek, won control over much of the country. To further solidify his rule, he hunted down and massacred members of the Communist party. As a result, the Communists, who had previously established themselves in the cities, moved out to remote peasant areas. Mao Tse-tung, at the head of the surviving elements of the Communist movement, attempted to adapt Marx's ideas to the Chinese context, giving particular importance to the peasantry as a revolutionary force. The movement Mao led also had strong nationalist overtones, emphasizing the need to rebuild Chinese society in the face of the inroads made by both Western and Japanese influences.

The Communists became the main group resisting the Japanese invasion that occurred during the Second World War, primarily by using guerrilla tactics. The Japanese occupation during this period

The quote behind these Chinese students reads: "We are not only able to destroy the old world, we are able to build a new world instead" —*Mao Tse-tung.*

threw the country back again into a state of almost complete disintegration. Following the war, the battles between the Communists and Chiang Kai-shek's followers resumed, ending in victory in 1949 for Mao's Red Army. The remnants of Chiang Kai-shek's forces moved with the aid of the American fleet to Formosa (now Taiwan).

When the new government came to power in 1949, China was on the verge of falling apart. If the Communists had not been as successful as they were in reforging national unity, China as it is today might not exist. The country could well have broken up into several states, as indeed happened to most traditional empires. There are several states now in North Africa and in the Middle East, for example, where the Ottoman Empire used to be (Dunn, 1972). The Communist government under Mao was able to build up a broad base of support by combining appeals to nationalism with very extensive rural reconstruction. Three years after the revolution, 45 percent of the cultivated land had been removed from the control of traditional landlords and distributed among 300 million peasants (Carrier, 1976).

Later, agricultural reforms were further expanded and, with the backing from the peasantry which these secured, the Communist government allowed other changes to take place. Trading, industrial, and financial organizations were nationalized (placed under the direct control of the government). Peasants were organized into "collectives": agricultural production was no longer carried on by individual families, but by groups of workers responsible to the Communist party. Although in very recent times other important reforms have been instituted in China, involving the encouragement of individual initiative and profit making, the basic system established soon after the revolution is still in place.

THE CUBAN EXPERIENCE

As a contrasting example to the cases of Russia and China it is illuminating to look at the Cuban revolution. Cuba is a small island with a population of only some eight million people. Unlike most other less-developed countries, prior to the revolution over half of Cuba's population lived in urban areas, the majority in Havana. The country was originally a colony of Spain, and the Spanish settlers treated the native population of the island brutally. These oppressive practices, together with the ravages of epidemics brought by the Europeans, virtually wiped them out. Slaves were therefore brought over from Africa to make up a labor force working the sugar, coffee, and tobacco fields.

A young Fidel Castro leads his followers in the early stages of the Cuban Revolution (left). An older Castro looks on during a 1989 press conference with Soviet leader Mikhail Gorbachev.

As a result of the Spanish-American War of 1898 (from which the United States also gained control of the Philippines, Puerto Rico, and Guam), Spain relinquished its control over Cuba, and the island was occupied by the U.S. army. After Spain's withdrawal, a treaty was signed with the new government giving the United States extensive rights to intervene in Cuba's internal affairs and in fact the marines were sent into Cuba on several occasions.

Before long, U.S. business firms dominated the Cuban economy. Americans owned 75 percent of the cultivated land, 63 percent of the sugar industry, and all of the railroads. Sugar made up over three-quarters of Cuba's exports, most of it shipped to the United States (Boorstein, 1967). Cuba was thus extremely dependent economically on the United States, which kept the price of sugar artificially low. It has been said that "even though a Cuban flag flew over the island, the real power sign was the American dollar" (Carrier, 1976).

Over the years, Cuba had a history of unrest and unstable governments. In the early 1930s, there were a series of uprisings across the island directed at the corrupt and ineffective government. Eventually, Cuban army officers led by Fulgencio Batista took control of the government and banned elections. Batista pursued policies favorable to United States business interests, while accumulating a vast fortune for himself. But eventually elections were reintroduced, and Batista lost power in 1944. He moved then for a while to Florida, enjoying the fruits of his personal fortune, but in 1952, he returned to power by means of a military *coup d'état.*

Batista was in turn overthrown by a band of revolutionaries led by Fidel Castro—although initially it was doubtful whether Castro would become a successful military leader. Castro formed his group in Mexico and originally landed in Cuba in July 1953. The attack failed, and Castro spent a period of time in jail. After his release, he returned with another revolutionary group in December 1956. This force consisted of only eighty-two soldiers, and was spotted by Batista's air force and attacked by the army. By the end of the battle, only twenty-two revolutionaries had survived, ten of whom were captured. The other twelve, including Castro, managed to reach the Sierra Maestra in Oriente, where they started building a new guerrilla group, joined by several hundred peasants.

Although Batista sent twelve thousand soldiers into the area to crush the guerrillas, they were not successful; the guerrilla movement drew more support than before, attracting a following from the urban areas in addition to the countryside. Castro's campaigning was largely inspired by patriotic sentiments, the promise of democracy, and the need for land reform. He was not at that time closely asso-

ciated with Marxism and initially the Communist-led Popular Socialist Party in Cuba did not give active encouragement. But the party
did add its support as it became apparent that the movement was
gaining more and more popular approval.

Even with this support, the guerrilla forces never exceeded more
than two thousand in number, deployed against an army of over forty
thousand plus an air force. The revolution was successful because of
the crumbling political support for the Batista government among
the population at large, and defections in the armed forces themselves. Castro was able to enter Havana without a shot being fired.
After Batista left the island in January 1959, the army surrendered to
the guerrillas.

The proximity of Cuba to the American mainland, combined with
the past history of intervention by the United States on the island,
made the new revolutionary state potentially vulnerable to invasion.
The dependence of the island upon sugar exports to the United States
was a further brake upon the capability of the new government to
consolidate its power. Castro managed to maintain control, however,
with support from the Soviet Union, which was only too willing to
acquire a political, and potentially a military, presence so near the
American mainland. When Cuba made an agreement to sell sugar to
the USSR in exchange for oil, the United States government reacted
by cancelling orders for the balance of Cuba's sugar imports in 1960.
The Cubans responded by nationalizing all American-owned sugar
fields, together with some other industries, utilities, and railroads.
Cuba in some part exchanged one form of dependence for another;
trade and material support from the Soviet Union became as essential
to the economy as sugar exports to the United States had been. Yet
the very rivalry between the United States and the Soviet Union over
the fate of the island allowed Castro space enough for the creation of
an effective and strong government.

Looking at the origins and nature of the Cuban revolution, we can
see that caution is needed in generalizing too readily from the examples of Russia and China. The Cuban revolution did not take place
against a background of war, as in the other two cases. The ideas that
originally prompted the guerrilla movement that Castro led were not
primarily derived from Marxism. Yet the Cuban example also allows
us to identify some factors probably characteristic of most revolutions, certainly twentieth-century ones. These include the influence
of nationalism; the role of intellectuals as leaders (Castro was originally a lawyer); the important part played by the peasantry; and the
fact that, at some point, the existing regime loses effective control of
at least a large part of the military.

THEORIES OF REVOLUTION

SINCE REVOLUTIONS HAVE BEEN FUNDAMENTAL TO SOCIAL development over the past two centuries, it is not surprising that a diversity of theories exists to try to account for them. The most influential was that of Karl Marx (1818–1883). Unlike other theorists, whose intentions were just to analyze revolutionary change, Marx also proposed his ideas as a means of furthering such change. Whatever the intrinsic validity of Marx's views, their practical importance for twentieth-century social change has been immense.

Other influential theories date from a much later time and have tried to explain both the "original" revolutions (such as the American and French) and subsequent ones. Some have cast the net even more widely, trying to analyze revolutionary activity in conjunction with other forms of rebellion or protest. We shall look at four frameworks for studying revolution: that of Marx; the theory of political violence suggested by Chalmers Johnson; the account of revolution and rising economic expectations put forward by James Davies; and the interpretation of collective protest proposed by the historical sociologist, Charles Tilly.

MARX'S THEORY

Marx's view of revolution was based on his more general interpretation of human history. According to Marx, the development of societies is marked by periodic class conflicts which, when they become acute, tend to terminate in a process of revolutionary change. Class struggles derive from the **contradictions**—unresolvable tensions—within societies. Marx traced the main source of contradiction to economic changes—changes in the "forces of production." In a stable society, there is a balance between the economic structure, social relationships, and the political system. But as the forces of production alter, contradiction is intensified, leading to open clashes between classes—which then ultimately provokes revolution. (For a lengthier discussion of Marx's ideas, see Chapter 22: "The Development of Sociological Theory.")

Marx applied this model both to feudalism of the past and to industrial capitalism of his time. The traditional, feudal societies of Europe were based on production by serfs who were ruled over by a class of landed aristocrats and gentry. Economic changes going on within these societies gave rise to towns and cities, in which trade and manufacture developed. This new economic system, created within feudal society, threatened its very basis. Rather than being founded upon the traditional lord-serf relationship, the emerging economic order encouraged industrialists to produce goods for sale on open markets. The contradictions between the old feudal economy and the newly emerging capitalistic one eventually became acute, taking the form of violent conflicts between the rising capitalist class and the feudal landowners. The outcome of this process was revolution, the most important example being the French Revolution of 1789. As a result of the French Revolution, and revolutionary changes that occurred in other European societies, Marx argued, the capitalist class managed to achieve dominance.

The evolution of capitalism, however, according to Marx, presented new contradictions, which would also eventually lead to revolution. Industrial capitalism is an economic order based upon the private pursuit of profit and upon competition between firms to produce and sell their products. This system creates a gulf between a rich minority, who own and control the industrial resources, and an impoverished majority of workers. Marx believed that workers and capitalists would come into more and more intense conflict with each other. Labor movements and political parties, representing the mass of the working population, would eventually mount a challenge to the rule of the capitalist class, and overthrow the existing political system. Where the position of a dominant class was particularly entrenched, Marx believed, violence was needed to bring about the required transition into socialism or communism. In other circumstances, this process might happen peacefully, using parliamentary mechanisms—a revolution (in the sense in which the term was defined earlier) would not be necessary.

Marx expected revolutions to occur in some Western countries during his lifetime. Towards the end of his life, when it became apparent that this was not to be, he turned his attention elsewhere. Interestingly, he looked particularly towards Russia. Russia, he argued, was an economically retarded society within which new forms of commerce and manufacture, borrowed from Western Europe, were being adopted. Marx thought that this was likely to create contradictions more severe than those developing within the European countries. For the introduction of novel types of production and technology into a backward society would lead to a highly explosive mixture of the old and the new. In his correspondence with Russian radicals, Marx claimed that these conditions might lead to a revolution in their country. But he added that the revolution would only be a successful one if it spread to other Western states. In these circumstances, a post-revolutionary government in Russia could take advantage of the more developed economic circumstances of the rest of Europe to push forward a rapid process of modernization.

Evaluation

Contrary to Marx's expectations, revolutions failed to occur in the advanced, industrialized societies of the West. In most Western countries (the United States being a notable exception) there are socialist or communist political parties, many of which claim to be following Marx's ideas. Where they have come to power, however, they have tended to become less rather than more radical. It is possible, of course, that Marx simply got the timetable wrong and that the revolutions he anticipated will one day take place in Europe, the United States, and elsewhere. But it is more plausible that Marx's predictions were at fault. The development of industrial capitalism does not lead, as Marx supposed, to more and more intense clashes between workers and capitalists.

At the same time, it does not follow from this that Marx's theory is irrelevant to the contemporary world. There is an important sense in which it *cannot* be, because it has become part of the ideals and values held both by revolutionary movements and established governments. Moreover, some of Marx's views can be adapted to make sense of Third World revolutions. The thesis he applied to Russia seems relevant to events in many peasant countries affected by the spread of industrial capitalism. Tensions are set up at the points of contact between the expansion of modern industry and traditional systems. As the traditional modes of life dissolve, those affected become a source of potentially revolutionary opposition to governments which try to preserve the old order of things.

CHALMERS JOHNSON: REVOLUTION AS "DISEQUILIBRIUM"

Marx had few cases of revolution upon which to base his analyses. Those trying to understand revolution today have more numerous historical examples to study. They can also see what impact Marx's ideas themselves have had in helping generate the momentum of revolutionary change.

The work of Chalmers Johnson is based upon ideas drawn from Talcott Parsons (Johnson, 1964, 1966). According to Parsons, societies are "self-regulating systems" that adjust to change by reordering their institutions so as to maintain a balance between them. This reordering keeps the system working effectively. The best way to understand this idea is by an analogy with the physiology of the body. When the bodily system is in working order, it is able to respond successfully to changes in its environment. If external temperature rises, for example, the body mobilizes certain mechanisms, such as the sweat glands, to keep its own temperature stable. It may happen, however, that conditions change in such a marked fashion that the whole system is thrown into disarray. If, say, the outside temperature rises too high, the mechanisms of the body would not be able to cope, and the result would be a major disturbance in the functioning of the physiological system. The bodily system at this point is in disequilibrium.

In Johnson's theory, the **disequilibrium** of societies is a necessary condition for the occurrence of revolution. The main source of disequilibrium, according to Johnson, is dislocation between the major cultural values of the society and the system of economic production. This can happen as a result of either internal or major external changes, but usually involves both. In nineteenth- and early twentieth-century China, for example, the traditional values of Chinese culture were placed more and more under strain by the impact of changes in the economic system brought about by Western trade and commerce. The old system of production, involving landlords and bonded peasants, began to disintegrate. The "reordering of institutions" was not enough to balance the system. Rather, the system was thrown into disequilibrium.

Once such disequilibrium has occurred, according to Johnson, many people become disoriented and look to new leaders who promise social transformation. This results in a loss of support for existing authorities. But revolution does not happen automatically at this point. If the political authorities react effectively to the situation, initiating policies that will restore equilibrium, they can avoid being overthrown. A stubborn ruling elite, however, might dig in its heels and deploy whatever armed force it has at its command to crush sources of protest, and if successful, a coercive regime or "police state" might come into being. Military force might be used in a ruthless fashion to stamp out sources of opposition, moving the whole society back in a conservative direction.

No society can be governed for long purely by the use of force. If the regime cannot persuade most of the population to readopt their traditional habits and attitudes, it will only be able to retain power for a short while. Once it becomes clear that the society is in fundamental disarray, the armed forces themselves become less loyal to the rulers. Several factors may hasten this process, the most important of which is defeat in war, as occurred in Russia before the 1917 Revolution, or in China during World War II. Such defeat has a demoralizing effect upon the military, as well as inherently weakening them. Without the full support of the military, the leadership collapses into chaos. Civil war or a revolution then occurs. A new government comes to power, putting into practice reforms that bring the society back into a new form of equilibrium.

Evaluation

Johnson's theory has the merits of being clear and comprehensive. What Johnson referred to as "disequilibrium" is similar to what Marx called "contradiction." Johnson's notion may or may not be superior to Marx's, but the idea that social change sets up dislocations that cannot be handled by existing institutions, without their radical restructuring, does seem to make sense of conditions likely to lead to revolutionary transitions.

A limitation of Johnson's view is the idea that societies normally exist in some kind of natural condition of harmony or equilibrium. This is surely not so. Most societies, particularly in the modern world, have many sources of tension or dislocation built into them, without becoming prone to revolution. Moreover, Johnson paid little attention to the actual *content* of the ideas which revolutionaries pursue. People do not become revolutionaries merely because a social system is undergoing strain. We cannot understand modern revolutions without seeing the distinctive impact that calls for freedom, democracy, and equality have made in promoting impulses to create new forms of social order (Smith, 1973). Finally, Johnson's theory cannot easily account for why revolution has become so common in the modern era, but was virtually unknown previously.

JAMES DAVIES: RISING EXPECTATIONS AND REVOLUTIONS

One clue as to why revolution has become common in the modern world is to be found in the work of James Davies. Davies pointed out that during innumerable periods of history people lived in dire poverty, or were subject to extreme oppression, but did not rise up in protest. Constant poverty or deprivation does not make people into revolutionaries; rather, they tend to endure such conditions with either resignation or mute despair. Revolutions are more likely to occur when there is a *rise* in people's living conditions. Once standards of living have started consistently to go up, people's levels of expectation also rise. If improvement in actual conditions subsequently slows down, propensities to revolt are created because gains are less than expectations.

Thus, social protest, and ultimately revolution, tends to occur in circumstances in which there is some improvement in people's conditions of life. It is not absolute deprivation that leads to protest, but **relative deprivation**—what matters is that there is a discrepancy between the lives people are forced to lead and what they think could realistically be achieved.

Assessment

This thesis offers an understanding of the connections between revolution and modern social and economic development. The influence of ideals of progress, together with expectations of economic growth, tend to induce rising expectations, which, if then frustrated, spark protest. Such protest gains further strength from the spread of ideas of equality and democratic political participation (Davies, 1962; Brinton, 1965). An example is to be found in the very recent history of China. In the late 1970s and 1980s, reforms were introduced by the Chinese Communist party designed to induce faster economic growth. The reforms later led to demands for greater democracy, producing violent clashes between pro-democracy groups and government forces in 1989.

As Charles Tilly has pointed out, however, Davies's theory does not discuss how and why different groups *mobilize* to seek revolutionary change. Protest might well often occur against a backdrop of ris-

Part of the aftermath of the suppression of the democracy movement by Chinese troops in June 1989.

ing expectations, but to understand how protest is transformed into the potential for revolution, we need to identify how groups become collectively organized to make effective political challenges.

CHARLES TILLY'S REVOLUTION THROUGH COLLECTIVE ACTION

In his book *From Mobilization to Revolution,* Charles Tilly attempted to analyze processes of revolutionary change in the context of an interpretation of broader forms of protest and violence. He distinguished four main components of **collective action**—action taken to contest or try to overthrow an existing social order (Tilly, 1978).

1. ORGANIZATION. There are many ways in which protest movements are organized, varying from spontaneous assemblies of crowds to tightly disciplined revolutionary groups. Castro's revolutionary movement in Cuba, for example, began as a small guerrilla band formed in exile in Mexico.

2. MOBILIZATION. This refers to the processes by which a group acquires control over the resources making collective action possible. Such resources may include supplies of material goods, political support, or weaponry. Castro was able to acquire material and moral support from a sympathetic peasantry and from many in the cities.

3. COMMON INTERESTS. Those engaging in collective action share what they see as the gains and losses resulting from policies or tactics they adopt. Some sort of common interests always underlie mobilization to collective action. Castro managed to weld together a broad coalition of support because many people had, or thought they had, a common interest in removing the existing government.

4. OPPORTUNITY. Many forms of collective action, including revolution, are greatly influenced by incidental happenings that provide opportunities for action which might not otherwise exist. Thus there was no inevitability to Castro's success, which depended upon a number of contingent factors—in the early stages,

Castro's "invasion" was almost a complete fiasco. If he had been one of the seventy captured or killed, would there have been a revolution?

Collective action, according to Tilly, can simply be defined as people acting together in pursuit of interests they share—for example, people gathering together to demonstrate in support of a cause. There may be various levels of activism among those who engage in such behavior, some being very intensively involved, others lending more passive or irregular support. To summarize, then, effective, collective action that culminates in revolution usually moves from (1) organization, to (2) mobilization, to (3) the perceiving of shared interests, and finally to (4) the occurrence of concrete opportunities to act effectively (Tilly, 1978).

Social movements, in Tilly's view, tend to develop as a means of mobilizing group resources either when people have no institutionalized means of making their voices heard, or where their needs are directly repressed by the state authorities. How far groups can secure active and effective representation within an existing political system is of key importance in determining whether their members turn to violence to achieve their ends. Collective action at some point involves open confrontation with the political authorities—"taking to the streets." However, only where such activity is backed by groups having systematic organization is it likely to have much impact upon established patterns of power.

Typical modes of collective action and protests vary with historical and cultural circumstances. In the United States today, for example, most people know how groups get together to represent their demands, and are familiar with forms of demonstration like mass marches, large assemblies, and street riots. For example, Martin Luther King, Jr., carried out a historic mass demonstration with his non-violent "March to Washington" for civil rights in 1963. There are many other types of collective protest, however, which have either become less common or have disappeared altogether in most modern societies (such as fights between villages, machine breaking, or lynching). Those who form protest movements can also build on examples taken from elsewhere, modifying their own practice. For instance, guerrilla movements proliferated in various parts of the world once disaffected groups learned how successful guerrilla actions can be against regular armies.

When and why does collective action become violent? After studying a large number of incidents occurring in Western Europe since 1800, Tilly concluded that most collective violence arises from nonviolent collective action. The occurrence of violence depends not so much on the nature of the action, as upon other forces—in particular, how the authorities respond. A good instance is the street demonstration. The vast majority of such demonstrations occur without personal or property damage. A minority lead to violence, and are then labeled in a different way—as "riots." Sometimes, of course, the authorities step in when violence has already come about; more often, as the historical record shows, the authorities are the originators of violent action. Moreover, where violent confrontations do occur, the agents of authority are responsible for the largest share of deaths and injuries. This is not particularly surprising given the special access they have to arms and military discipline. The groups they are attempting to control, conversely, cause more property damage (Tilly, 1978).

Revolutionary movements, according to Tilly, are a type of collective action that occurs in circumstances of what he calls **multiple sovereignty.** This is a condition in which a government, for one reason or another, lacks full control over the areas it is supposed to administer. Situations of multiple sovereignty can arise as a result of external war, internal political clashes, or the two combined. Whether a revolutionary take-over of power is accomplished depends upon whether the ruling authorities maintain control over the armed forces, the existence of conflict within the ruling group, and the level of organization of the protest movement seeking to seize power.

Assessment

Tilly's work represents one of the most sophisticated attempts to analyze collective violence and revolutionary struggles. His ideas seem to have wide application, and his use of them is sensitive to the variabilities of historical time and place. Questions of the nature of the organization and social movements, the resources they are able to mobilize, and the relation between groups contending for power, are all important circumstances of revolutionary transformation.

Tilly said little, however, about the circumstances that lead to multiple sovereignty. This is so fundamental to explaining revolution that it represents a serious omission. According to Theda Skocpol, Tilly assumed that revolutionary movements are guided by the conscious and deliberate pursuit of interests; successful processes of revolutionary change occur when people manage to realize these. Skocpol, by contrast, sees revolutionary movements as more ambiguous and indecisive in their objectives. Revolutions, she emphasizes, largely emerge as unintended consequences of more partial aims toward which groups and movement strive. She writes:

The purposive image is just as misleading about the process and outcome of historical revolutions as it is about their causes. For the image strongly suggests that revolutionary processes and outcomes can be understood in terms of the activity and intentions or interests of the key group(s) who launch the revolution in the first place . . . such notions are much too simple. In fact, in historical revolutions, differently situated and motivated groups have become participants in complex unfoldings of multiple conflicts. These conflicts have been powerfully shaped and limited by existing social, economic and international conditions. And they have proceeded in different ways depending upon how each revolutionary situation emerged in the first place. (Skocpol, 1979; see also Dunn, 1985)

This judgment is just as appropriate when we think of the revolutionary changes that occurred in the East European societies in 1989, compared with earlier revolutionary episodes. The changes of 1989 are too recent for us yet to form a full understanding of them; but very few people prior to these events anticipated that they would turn out the way that they did.

THE CONSEQUENCES OF REVOLUTION

DISCUSSING THE OUTCOME OF REVOLUTIONS IS EVERY BIT AS complex as analyzing their origins. What ensues after a revolution is partly influenced by the very events that led up to it. Following a period of revolutionary battles, a country may be economically impoverished and bitterly divided. Remnants of the defeated regime, or other groups contending for power, may regroup their forces and reinvade. If the attitude of surrounding states is hostile to the new government (as was the case following the 1917 Russian Revolution, for example), its success in producing desired social reconstruction may be much more limited than where they are sympathetic and prepared to lend active support. Also, there are major differences between the objectives of revolutionary governments themselves—some wish to pursue much more radical policies than others. Finally, although revolutions may have long-term consequences for the societies in which they occur, it is extremely difficult to disentangle these from other factors that affect that society's subsequent development.

SHORT-TERM CONSEQUENCES

Many revolutions are followed by a period of civil war, during which the incoming regime must bring about the military defeat of those who contest its position and claims. Revolutions tend to occur in circumstances in which the authority of a government has been radically undermined, and several movements may be competing to replace it. Some of these might be militarily strong enough to continue the fight against the new government, or receive funding from other nations supporting their cause. This was the case in the Russian, Chinese, and Cuban revolutions, although the degree of opposition they faced varied—Russia was actually invaded by Western forces to assist those loyal to the old regime.

Revolutions are made in the name of freedom, but they are often succeeded by a period in which there is severe social repression. This was not true of the American Revolution and there are other exceptions too. More commonly, however, revolutions have been succeeded by periods of widespread arbitrary imprisonment, executions,

The Reign of Terror during the French Revolution included the execution of King Louis XVI in January 1793.

and rigid censorship. The use of the term **revolutionary terror** to mean the systematic application of violence in order to induce obedience to the new authorities was first developed to describe the aftermath of the French Revolution of 1789 (see Chapter 10: "Politics, Government, and the State"). Large numbers of people deemed to be supporters of the old regime, or enemies of the revolution, were hunted down and publicly executed by guillotine.

Where they occur, such episodes tend to happen some years after the assumption of power by the new regime, rather than immediately. The reason is that there is usually a period of "settling down" before a revolutionary government tries to implement the radical new program it might be proposing. At this point, resistance either from supporters of the preceding regime, or other dissident groups, is likely to combine with opposition generated by the new policies which the authorities put into practice. In the Soviet Union, for example, Stalin pursued a vigorous policy of setting up collective farms, in the face of widespread resistance from the peasants. In this process, and in the purges of dissident groups, many people lost their lives or were transported to labor camps. It has been estimated that 5 percent of the Soviet population was arrested at this period (Kesselman et al., 1987). These events happened, however, more than a decade after the revolution itself.

LONG-TERM CONSEQUENCES

We can attempt to assess the long-term impact of revolution by contrasting societies that resemble one another save for the fact that some have experienced revolutions while others have not. For example, we can compare the development of China over the past forty years with that of India. Each country freed itself from direct Western influence at about the same time, but where China experienced a revolution, India did not. India had been under British colonial rule, but a strong protest movement, led by the nonviolent Mahatma Gandhi, caused much disruption and brought about British withdrawal without a revolution.

But since China's revolution and India's independence, the two societies have developed quite differently. In China, the Communist party established a strong, centralized government, imposing strict censorship upon the press and other media. India, by contrast, has a representative parliament based on the Western model, with multiparty elections. The level of political freedom in China is well below that of India. This is measured by the diversity of views which can be publicly expressed, and by types of political organization that can be

Through nonviolent civil disobedience, Mahatma Gandhi (right), along with Jawaharlal Nehru, led the independence movement that freed colonial India from British rule in 1947.

legally formed. On the other hand, China has made far more progress in reducing extreme poverty, eliminating official corruption, and in providing health and welfare facilities. The level of literacy is much higher in China than in India. Estimates of Chinese economic development vary widely, but it is generally agreed that the growth rate in China in the fifteen years following the revolution was higher than that of India and well ahead of population expansion—also unlike India. Agrarian reform was also much more successful in China than in India, the Chinese having broken the power of the rich landlords and distributing the land to the peasantry (Bergmann, 1977).

Neither India nor China has experienced a particularly stable process of development. In India, the central government has struggled to maintain control in a country where regional divisions remain pronounced. Between 1966 and 1968 the "Cultural Revolution" threw China into turmoil. During this period, millions of mostly young people sought to reimpose "proletarian values" upon professional, managerial workers and party officials whom they believed were ignoring the teachings of the revolution. Today, this process has been replaced by one which is in some ways its opposite: the Chinese government is currently emphasizing the need for "capitalist" mechanisms of personal incentive and profit in an effort to improve the efficiency of agricultural and industrial production. It is not entirely clear as yet how successful these new policies have been on the economic level. As mentioned earlier, in the political sphere they helped unleash major conflicts and tensions.

At this point, we turn from the study of revolutions, and their consequences, to other forms of uprising and protest. We shall separate out, and look at the nature of, two aspects of revolutionary activity: the organizing of individuals into crowds or mobs on the one hand, and the formation of social movements on the other. While these often appear together in other situations as well as in revolutions—as, for instance during the Civil Rights Movement (see Chapter 8: "Ethnicity and Race") in the 1960s and early 1970s—they also may be quite separate. Some kinds of crowd activity, such as the actions of lynch mobs in the southern United States in past years, are not closely bound up with a social movement.

CROWDS, RIOTS, AND OTHER FORMS OF COLLECTIVE ACTION

ALL REVOLUTIONS INVOLVE COLLECTIVE ACTION. BUT, AS Tilly's theory indicates, such action is found in many other circumstances besides those of revolutionary change. Collective action can occur wherever there is the chance of large numbers of people gathering together. The development of modern cities, where many people live in close proximity, offers ample opportunities to take protests "to the streets." The protest actions of urban groups are one example of **crowd activities.** A crowd is any relatively sizable collection of people who act in concert with one another in a public place. Crowds are an everyday part of urban life in one sense. We speak of a "crowded" shopping mall, or a "crowded" theater or amusement park, for instance, meaning that many people are jostling together in a physically confined space. These are individuals in circumstances of unfocused interaction (see Chapter 4: "Social Interaction and Everyday Life"). They are physically present in the same setting, and aware of one anothers' presence, but are broken up into many small knots of people going their own separate ways. However, in some situations—in a demonstration, riot, or panic—everyone's actions become bound up with those of all the others. The situation suddenly becomes one of focused interaction, because, however temporarily, the crowd starts acting as a single unit. Crowd action in this sense has stimulated the interests of sociologists and historians for many years—in fact, ever since the French Revolution of 1789.

LE BON'S THEORY OF CROWD ACTION

One of the most influential early studies of crowd action was Gustave Le Bon's book *The Crowd,* first published in 1895. Le Bon's work was stimulated by his studies of the revolutionary mobs during the French Revolution. In Le Bon's view, people act differently when caught up in the collective emotion of a crowd situation than they do in isolation. Under the influence of a **focused crowd,** individuals are capable of acts of barbarism, and of heroism, which they would not contemplate alone. The French revolutionary mobs that stormed the Bastille, for example, did so apparently regardless of the casualties they suffered. On the other hand, street crowds in 1789 also carried out numerous savageries.

What happens to produce this effect in crowd situations? According to Le Bon, when involved in the collective excitement generated by crowds, people temporarily lose some of the critical, reasoning faculties they are able to display in everyday life. They become highly suggestible and easily swayed by the exhortations of mob leaders or demagogues. Under the influence of the crowd, individuals regress to more "primitive" types of reaction than they would ordinarily produce. As Le Bon wrote, "Isolated, a person may be a cultivated individual; in a crowd, he is a barbarian—that is, a creature acting by instinct. He possesses the spontaneity, the violence, the ferocity, and also the enthusiasm and heroism of primitive beings" (Le Bon, 1960; orig. pub. 1895).

Although many subsequent authors have drawn upon Le Bon's ideas, we should treat them in historical context. Le Bon wrote as a conservative critic of democracy. He saw the French Revolution as signaling the opening of an era in which "crowds" (i.e., the mass of the ordinary population) would dominate their rightful rulers. Large groups, including parliamentary assemblies in Le Bon's eyes, cannot make rational decisions. They are liable to be as swayed by mass emotion, fashion, or whim, as street crowds are. Le Bon felt that democratic institutions would bring out the more primitive reactions of human beings, swamping the higher, more "civilized" faculties.

Some of Le Bon's ideas, however, at least regarding street crowds, do seem valid. The massing of large numbers of people together, in some circumstances, can generate an irrational, collective emotionality and produce unusual types of activity. Audiences have sometimes "gone wild" at pop concerts or rioted at sports events. When gripped by panic, people sometimes rush madly for safety, trampling others to death. Mobs have on occasion rampaged through the streets, beating up or killing those they see as their enemies—as happened, for example, in attacks upon the Jews in Nazi Germany.

RATIONAL ASPECTS OF CROWD ACTION

Yet most forms of crowd behavior are more discriminating and "rational" than in Le Bon's portrayal. Those engaging in collective action are often more clearly aware of their aims than Le Bon supposed. Nor do crowds always consist mainly of people already prone to behave irresponsibly—the crimminal riffraff—as Le Bon suggested. inal riffraff—as Le Bon suggested. George Rudé's studies of the French Revolution show that most of the 660 people killed in the mob that stormed the Bastille were "respectable" individuals who held orthodox occupations, not criminals or vagabonds (Rudé, 1959). Research into the urban riots of the 1960s in black neighborhoods in the United States showed that most rioters were not drawn from criminal elements, or even from people on social welfare. The average rioter was a man with a blue-collar job, more likely to be well informed about social and political issues, and to be involved in civil-rights activities, than other urban blacks. Moreover, although the rioting appeared haphazard, virtually all of the property attacked or looted was white-owned (U.S. Riot Commission, 1968).

Some authors have suggested that most crowd activities become intelligible when a quite opposite interpretation is put upon them to that given by Le Bon. Thus Richard Berk (1974) has argued that the activities of individuals in crowds are best understood as logical responses to specific situations. The gathering of crowds often offers opportunities to achieve aims at little personal cost. In crowd situations, individuals are relatively anonymous and can escape detection for acts that would otherwise result in their imprisonment—for instance, looting a store. When acting as a crowd, individuals temporarily have far more power than they have as isolated citizens (Turner and Killian, 1972).

Could this interpretation be applied to situations in which extreme violence towards innocent people is involved—say, to actions by lynch mobs in the South? The lynching of blacks was at one time a frequent occurrence. Following the Civil War, "nigger hunts" were regularly undertaken, in which freed slaves were sought out and put to death. Between 1889 and 1899, over 1,800 lynchings were reported—since some no doubt went unrecorded, the actual number was probably considerably higher (Cantril, 1963). The burning of blacks' homes, torture, and mutilation, were also carried out by mobs. It might seem as though only the view offered by Le Bon could make sense of such actions, and no doubt some of the features of mob violence that he identified are relevant. But there were some "rational" aspects to the lynchings. Those involved were usually semi-organized vigilante groups who saw themselves as having a righteous

In scenes such as the one on the left, people at a sports event act "irrationally" (Le Bon's idea), crushing others to escape a collapsed grandstand behind them (not in photo). These should be distinguished from others, in which crowds, often socially or politically motivated, act "rationally" (Berk's thesis), like in the French student uprising in May 1968 (right).

cause. Taking action as a mob reduced their individual responsibility for the events, while publicly proclaiming their fury at the freeing of the slaves. The violence also served as a means of social control upon blacks, emphasizing to the black population as a whole that the passing of a law in the North did not change the reality of white power in the South. It could be argued that, when in focused crowds, to some extent people are able to overcome the usual forms of social control; the power and anonymity of the crowd allows them to act as they might normally wish to, but feel unable to.

Mob action and rioting—as Tilly emphasizes—characteristically express the frustrations of people who cannot gain access to orthodox channels to express grievances or press for reforms. Ruling authorities of all types have always feared mob activity, not just because of the direct threat it poses, but because it gives a public and tangible form to felt social injustices. Even though some riots may on the surface seem abortive, giving rise to wanton destruction and loss of life, they may stimulate change and produce at least some desired benefits. For an example of this, one need only examine the spate of riots in black areas of cities, like Watts in Los Angeles, in the 1960s. These riots forced the white communities to pay attention to the deprivations blacks suffered and led to the creation of a number of new reform programs.

SOCIAL MOVEMENTS

BESIDES THOSE ENGAGED IN REVOLUTIONARY ACTIVITY, A wide variety of other social movements, some long-enduring, some which melt away almost overnight, have existed in modern societies. Social movements are as evident a feature of the contemporary world as are the formal, bureaucratic organizations they often oppose.

DEFINING SOCIAL MOVEMENTS

A **social movement** may be defined as *a collective attempt to further a common interest, or secure a common goal, through collective action outside the sphere of established institutions.* The definition has to be a broad one because of the variations between different types of movements. Many social movements are very small, numbering perhaps no more than a few dozen members; others might include thousands, or even millions, within their membership. Some movements carry on their activities within the laws of the society or societies in which they exist, while others operate as illegal or underground groups. Often, of course, laws are altered partly or wholly as a result of the action of social movements. For example, workers who organized strikes a century ago were engaging in illegal activity, punished with varying degrees of severity in different countries. Eventually, however, the laws were amended making strikes a permissible tactic of industrial conflict. Other modes of economic protest, by contrast, still remain outside the law in most countries—such as sit-ins in factories or workplaces.

The dividing lines between social movements and formal organizations are sometimes blurred, because movements that become well established usually take on bureaucratic characteristics. Social movements may thus in the course of time become formal organizations, while—less frequently—organizations may dissolve into social movements. The Salvation Army (a religious group concerned with humanitarian social causes), for example, began as a social movement, but has now taken on most of the characteristics of a more permanent organization. An example of the opposite process would be the case of a political party which is banned by a nation's leadership and forced to go underground, perhaps to become a guerrilla movement working outside the established political institutions.

Similarly, it is not always easy to separate social movements from **interest groups.** Interest groups are associations set up to influence government policymakers in ways that will favor their members. An example of an interest group would be the National Rifle Association, which lobbies to defend the interests of gun owners. But is the antinuclear coalition, which regularly lobbies against nuclear power, an interest group or part of a more wide-ranging mass movement? No clear-cut answer can be given in such a case; social movements often actively lobby for their causes through official channels while also engaging in more unorthodox and sometimes illegal forms of activity.

CLASSIFYING SOCIAL MOVEMENTS

Many different categories of social movements have been proposed. Perhaps the most comprehensive classification is that developed by David Aberle some quarter of a century ago (1966). Aberle distinguishes four types of movement. The first two, transformative and reformative movements, are concerned primarily with securing changes in society. The other two types, redemptive and alterative, are aimed at changing the habits or outlook of individuals.

Transformative movements aim at thorough-going change in the society or societies of which they are a part. The changes their members anticipate are cataclysmic, all-embracing, and often violent. Examples are revolutionary movements or some radical religious movements. Many millenarian movements (movements that anticipate the arrival of an era of religious salvation), for instance, have foreseen a more or less complete restructuring of society when the time of deliverance is at hand.

Reformative movements have more limited objectives, aspiring to alter only partial aspects of the existing social order. They concern themselves with specific kinds of inequality or injustice. Cases in point are movements against racism or anti-abortionist groups.

Redemptive movements seek to rescue individuals from ways of life seen as corrupting. Many religious movements belong in this category, in so far as they concentrate upon personal salvation. Examples are the Pentecostal sects, which propose that individuals' spiritual capacities and development are the true test of their worth (Schwartz, 1970).

Finally, there are the somewhat clumsily titled **alterative movements,** which aim at securing partial change in individuals. They do not aim at achieving a complete alteration in people's habits, but are concerned with changing certain specific traits. An illustration is Alcoholics Anonymous.

THEORIES OF SOCIAL MOVEMENTS

Theories of revolution inevitably tend to overlap with those of social movements. Charles Tilly's emphasis upon "resource mobilization," for example, has been applied to social movements, as has James Davies' interpretation of rising expectations and protest. Two additional theoretical perspectives on social movements, however, have been particularly important. These are the approaches of Neil Smelser and Alain Touraine.

Neil Smelser: Six Conditions for Social Movements

Neil Smelser (1963) distinguished six conditions underlying the origins of collective action in general, and social movements in particular. *Structural conduciveness* refers to the general social conditions promoting or inhibiting the formation of social movements of different types. For example, in Smelser's view, the sociopolitical system of the United States leaves open certain avenues of mobilization for protest because of the relative absence of state regulation in those areas. Thus there is no official state-sponsored religion. People are free to exercise their religious beliefs. This makes for a conducive environment in which religious movements might compete for individuals, so long as they do not transgress criminal or civil law.

Just because the conditions are conducive to the development of a social movement does not mean those conditions will bring them into being. There must be *structural strain*—tensions (or, in Marx's terminology, contradictions) that produce conflicting interests within societies. Uncertainties, anxieties, ambiguities, or direct clashes of goals, are expressions of such strains. Sources of strain may be quite general, or specific to particular situations. Thus sustained inequalities between ethnic groups give rise to overall tensions; these may become focused in the shape of specific conflicts when, say, blacks begin to move into a previously all-white area.

The third condition Smelser outlined is the spread of *generalized beliefs*. Social movements do not develop simply as responses to vaguely felt anxieties or hostilities. They are shaped by the influence of definite ideologies, which crystallize grievances and suggest courses of action that might be pursued to remedy them. Revolutionary movements, for instance, are based on ideas about why injustice occurs and how it can be alleviated by political struggle.

Precipitating factors are events or incidents that actually trigger direct action by those who become involved in the movement. In 1955, when a black woman named Rosa Parks refused to give up her seat to a white man on a bus in Montgomery, Alabama, her action helped spark the Civil Rights Movement (see Chapter 8: "Ethnicity and Race").

The first four conditions combined, Smelser argued, might occasionally lead to street disturbances or outbreaks of violence. But such incidents do not lead to the development of social movements unless there is a coordinated group that becomes mobilized for action. *Leadership* and some means of *regular communication* among participants, together with funding and material resources, are necessary for a social movement to exist.

Finally, the manner in which a social movement develops is strongly influenced by the *operation of social control.* The governing authorities may respond to initial protests by intervening in the conditions of conduciveness and strain that stimulated the emergence of the movement. For instance, in a situation of ethnic tension, steps might be taken to reduce ethnic inequality that generated resentment and conflict. Other important aspects of social control concerns the responses of the police or armed forces. A harsh reaction might encourage further protest and help solidify the movement. Also, doubt and divisions within the police and military can be crucial in deciding the outcome of confrontations with revolutionary movements.

Smelser's model is useful for analyzing the sequences in the development of social movements, and collective action in general. According to Smelser, each stage in the sequence "adds value" to the overall outcome; also, each stage is a condition for the occurrence of the next one. But there are some critical comments that can be made about Smelser's theory. Some social movements become strong without any particular precipitating incidents. Conversely, a series of incidents might bring home the need to establish a movement to change the circumstances that gave rise to them. Also, a movement itself might create strains, rather than develop in response to them. For example, the women's movement has actively sought to identify and combat gender inequalities where previously these had gone unquestioned. Smelser's theory treats social movements as *responses* to situations, rather than allowing that their members might spontaneously organize to achieve desired social changes. In this respect his ideas contrast with the approach developed by Alain Touraine.

Alain Touraine: From Historicity to Fields of Action

Alain Touraine (1977, 1981) developed his analysis of social movements on the basis of four main ideas. The first, which he called

historicity, explains why there are so many more movements in the modern world than there were in earlier times. In modern societies individuals and groups know that social activism can be used to achieve social goals and reshape society.

Second, Touraine focused on the *rational objectives* of social movements. Such movements do not just come about as irrational responses to social divisions or injustices; rather, they develop from specific views and rational strategies as to how injustices can be overcome.

Third, Touraine saw a process of *interaction* in the shaping of social movements. Movements do not develop in isolation; instead, they develop in deliberate antagonism with established organizations, and sometimes with other rival social movements. All social movements have interests or aims that they are *for;* all have views and ideas they are *against.* In Touraine's view, other theories of social movements (including that of Smelser) have given insufficient consideration as to how the objectives of a social movement are shaped by encounters with others holding divergent positions, as well as by the ways in which they themselves influence the outlooks and action of their opponents. For instance, the objectives and outlook of the women's movement have been shaped in opposition to the male-dominated institutions that it seeks to alter. The goals and outlook of the movement have shifted in relation to its successes and failures, and have also influenced the perspectives of men. These changed perspectives in turn stimulated a reorientation in women's movements, and so the process of shaping and reshaping continues.

Fourth, social movements and change occur in the context of what Touraine called **fields of action.** A field of action refers to the connections between a social movement and the forces or influences against it. The process of mutual negotiation among antagonists in a field of action may lead to the social changes sought by the movement as well as to changes in the social movement itself and in its antagonists. In either circumstance the movement may evaporate—or become institutionalized as a permanent organization. For example the labor-union movements became formal organizations when they achieved the right to strike and types of bargaining acceptable to both workers and employers. These changes in both the movement and the original worker-owner relationship were forged out of earlier processes involving widespread violent confrontation on both sides. Where there are continuing sources of conflict (as in the case of the relation between unions and employers) new movements still tend to reemerge.

Touraine's analysis can also be applied to movements concerned primarily with individual change—Aberle's redemptive and alterative categories—even though Touraine himself has said little about them. For instance, Alcoholics Anonymous is a movement based upon medical findings about the harmful effects of alcohol upon people's health and social activities. The movement itself has been shaped by its own opposition to advertising designed to encourage alcoholic drinking, and by its attempt to confront the outside pressures faced by alcoholics in a society in which drinking is easily tolerated.

Touraine's analysis helps us see that social movements have a double interest for the sociologist. They provide a subject matter for study but, more than this, they help shift the ways in which sociologists *look at* the areas of behavior they try to analyze. The women's movement, for instance, is not just relevant to sociology because it provides material for research investigation. It has identified weaknesses in established frameworks of sociological thought, and has used concepts (such as patriarchy) that help clarify issues of gender and power. There is a continuing dialogue not only between social movements and the organizations they confront, but between social movements and sociology itself.

SUMMARY

1. Revolutions have occurred in many areas of the world over the past two centuries. The American Revolution of 1776, and the French Revolution of 1789, introduced ideals and aspirations that have come to be widespread in political life. In the twentieth century, most revolutions have been inspired by socialist or Marxist aspirations, particularly in developing countries.

2. *Revolution* is a slippery concept to define. To count as a revolution a process of political change must involve the influence of a mass social movement that is prepared to use violence to achieve its ends and able to seize power and subsequently initiate reform.

3. Of the various theories of revolution, Marx's interpretation is particularly significant, not just because of its intellectual contribution—which can be questioned in various ways—but because it has served in some part to shape actual processes of revolution in the current century.

4. Since revolution is such a complex phenomenon, generalizing about the conditions leading to revolutionary change is diffi-

cult. Most revolutions occur in circumstances where governmental power has become fragmented (for instance, as a result of war), and an oppressed group has been able to create and sustain a mass movement. Revolutions are usually unintended consequences of more partial aims towards which movements initially strive.

5. Post-revolutionary regimes are often authoritarian, imposing censorship and other social controls. Revolutions normally have long-term consequences for the societies in which they occur, although it is difficult to disentangle these from other factors that affect the subsequent development of those societies.

6. Crowd activities occur not only in revolutions, but in many other circumstances of less dramatic social change—as in urban riots. The actions of rioting mobs might seem wholly destructive and haphazard, but often serve definite purposes for those involved.

7. Many types of social movement are found in modern societies. Social movements are a collective attempt to further common interests through collaborative action outside the sphere of established institutions. Sociology not only studies such movements but also responds to the issues they raise.

BASIC CONCEPTS

REVOLUTION
REBELLION
COLLECTIVE ACTION
SOCIAL MOVEMENT

IMPORTANT TERMS

DEMOCRACY
COUP D'ÉTAT
CONTRADICTION
DISEQUILIBRIUM
RELATIVE DEPRIVATION
MOBILIZATION
MULTIPLE SOVEREIGNTY
REVOLUTIONARY TERROR
CROWD ACTIVITY

FOCUSED CROWD
INTEREST GROUP
TRANSFORMATIVE MOVEMENT
REFORMATIVE MOVEMENT
REDEMPTIVE MOVEMENT
ALTERATIVE MOVEMENT
HISTORICITY
FIELD OF ACTION

UNDERSTANDING SOCIAL CHANGE

HUMAN BEINGS HAVE EXISTED ON EARTH FOR A HALF MIL-
lion years. Agriculture, the necessary basis of fixed settlements, is only about twelve thousand years old.
Civilizations date back no more than some six thousand
years or so. If we were to think of the entire span of
human existence as a day, agriculture would have been invented at 11:54 P.M., and civilizations would have come
into being at 11:57 P.M. The development of modern societies would get under way only at 11:59:30! Yet perhaps as
much change has gone on in the last thirty seconds of this
"human day" than in the whole of the time leading up to it. The pace
of change in the modern era is easily demonstrated by reference to
rates of technological development. As the economic historian David
Landes has observed:

> Modern technology produces not only more, faster; it turns
> out objects that could not have been produced under any
> circumstances by the craft methods of yesterday. The best
> Indian hand-spinner could not turn out yarn so fine
> and regular as that of the mule; all the forges in eighteen-
> century Christendom could not have produced steel sheets

so large, smooth and homogeneous as those of a modern strip mill. Most important, modern technology has created things that could scarcely have been conceived in the preindustrial era: the camera, the motor car, the airplane, the whole array of electronic devices from the radio to the high-speed computer, the nuclear power plant, and so on almost *ad infinitum*. . . . The result has been an enormous increase in the output and variety of goods and services, and this alone has changed man's way of life more than anything since the discovery of fire: the Englishman [and, we might add, the Englishwoman] of 1750 was closer in material things to Caesar's legionnaires than to his own great-grandchildren! (Landes, 1969)

Even greater are the differences between the American of 1750 and his or her descendants today.

The ways of life and the social institutions characteristic of the modern world are radically different from those of even the relatively recent past. During a period of only some two to three centuries—a minute sliver of time in the context of human history as a whole—human social life has become wrenched away from ways of life that people had followed for thousands of years. On a grand level, four major revolutions in America, France, Russia, and China have radically transformed the political, social, and individual ways of life in these countries, as well as influencing the rest of the world. On a more mundane and personal level, Landes, writing the above passage today rather than twenty years ago, would probably be sitting in front of a PC monitor tapping away.

In this chapter, we inquire into the nature and origins of social change, giving special attention to change in modern times. This inquiry will allow us to tie together some of the main threads of the book as a whole. In preceding chapters we looked at the transition from premodern to modern societies, emphasizing the contrasts between them. We now need to look at some of the interpretations that different social thinkers have offered to account for this transition—so fateful in its consequences for all of us today. We shall also consider some very general attempts to explain historical change, as well as posing the question: where are current processes of change likely to lead us in the future?

How should we define **social change?** There is a sense in which everything changes, all of the time. Every day is a new day; every moment is a new instant in time. The sixth-century B.C. Greek philosopher Heraclitus pointed out that a person cannot step into the same river twice. On the second occasion, the river is different, since water has flowed along it, and the person too has changed in subtle ways. While this observation is in a sense correct, we *do* of course normally want to say that it is the same river and the same person stepping into it on two occasions. There is sufficient continuity in the shape or form of the river, and in the physique and personality of the person with wet feet, to say that each remains "the same" through the changes that occur.

Identifying significant change means showing the alterations in the *underlying structure* of an object or situation over a period of time. In the case of human societies, to decide how much, and in what ways, a system is in a process of change, we have to show to what degree there is any modification of *basic institutions* during a specific period. All accounts of change also involve showing what remains *stable,* as a baseline against which to measure change. Even in the rapidly moving world of today there are continuities from the long-distant past. Major religious systems, for example, like Christianity or Islam, retain their ties with ideas and practices initiated some two thousand years ago. Yet most institutions in modern societies clearly change much more rapidly than was ever true in the traditional world.

THEORIES OF SOCIAL CHANGE

TWO GENERAL APPROACHES HAVE PROBABLY BEEN MORE INfluential than any others in the attempt to understand the general mechanisms of change over the course of human history. Both grew out of nineteenth-century thought. One is the approach suggested by **social evolutionism,** a viewpoint that tries to relate biological and social change. The second standpoint is that associated with **historical materialism**—originally worked out by Karl Marx, but elaborated upon subsequently by a diversity of writers.

EVOLUTIONARY THEORIES

Evolutionary approaches to social change start from a rather obvious fact. If we compare different types of human society in history, it seems rather evident that there is a development towards increasing *complexity.* Hunting and gathering societies, found at the earliest stages of human development (although some continue in existence today), seem to be relatively simple in structure compared with the

Today's world can produce something as technologically sophisticated as the radar-evading Stealth Bomber at a cost of billions of dollars, yet cannot solve major problems, such as world hunger and poverty.

agricultural societies that emerged at a later period in history. For instance, in hunting and gathering societies there were no separate ruling groups or political authorities, as in agrarian societies. Traditional civilizations, in China or Rome, for example, were larger and more complicated. In these societies, there were clearly distinct classes, plus separate political, legal, and cultural institutions. Finally, industrialized societies are far more complex than any preceding types: they are comprised of many separate institutions and organizations and, as we have seen, involve a global interdependency.

Social evolutionary thinkers have examined the development of increasing complexity by means of the concept of **differentiation.** As societies become more complex, areas of social life that once were mingled together become clearly differentiated—that is to say, distinct and separate from one another. Evolutionary thinkers argue that increasing differentiation and complexity in human society can be compared to processes involved in the biological development of species. The trend of biological evolution is also from simple to more complex. Organisms right at the bottom of the evolutionary scale, like the single-celled amoeba, are very simple in structure compared to more recently evolved animals.

In biological evolution, the development from simple to more complex organisms is explained by their adaptation to the environment, that is, how well animals and plants adjust to their material milieu (see Chapter 2: "Culture and Social Development"). More complex animals have a greater capacity to adapt to, and survive in, their environments than simpler organisms. According to social evolutionary theorists, therefore, there are direct parallels between biological development and the succession of human societies in history. The more complex a society is, the greater its "survival value" as compared with simpler types.

Social Darwinism

Early theories of social evolution in the nineteenth century frequently associated evolutionary change with *progress* in social, political, and cultural spheres. They saw more developed societies as morally superior to simpler, more traditional ones. One version of this view, which became very popular just prior to the twentieth century, was **social Darwinism.** As its name suggests, social Darwinism drew its inspiration (though not a seal of approval) from the evolutionary writings of Charles Darwin. Loosely applying the notion of "survival of the fittest," these theorists argued that human societies struggle among one another for survival in the environment just as biological organisms do. The modern societies of the West came out on top in this struggle—and thus the social Darwinists considered these to represent the highest stage of social progress yet achieved. Some such authors used these ideas to justify the supremacy of whites over blacks, working out supposedly "scientific" justifications for racism. This was particularly the case during Europe's colonizing of Africa, the so-called "scramble for Africa."

Social Darwinism was always to some extent an ideology justifying the dominant position of the West in relation to peoples who were considered inferior because they lacked a complex, differentiated society. The doctrine prospered before the rise of modern fieldwork anthropology, which helped document the diversity of human cultures and served to redress the Eurocentric outlook of social Darwinist thought. By the late 1920s, social Darwinism was thoroughly discredited, and the popularity of social evolutionism as a whole declined.

Unilinear and Multilinear Evolution

Nineteenth-century theories of social evolution often tended to be **unilinear** in character, asserting that there is a single line of development in human society, from simple to more complex. To ascend the evolutionary path, each society must pass through the same stages of development. Over the past few decades, social evolutionary theory has undergone something of a revival, but the emphasis is on **multilinear** rather than unilinear evolution (Sahlins and Service, 1960;

Lenski, 1966; Lenski and Lenski, 1982). Multilinear theories recognize that there may be various lines of development leading from one type of society to another. According to this view, different types of society can be categorized by their level of complexity and differentiation, but there is no single path of change they all follow.

Multilinear evolutionists still see the main mechanism of change as increasing adaptation to the environment. Each succeeding type of society is more effective in adapting to its environment than the previous, more simple types. Thus, for example, agrarian societies are more effective in generating consistent sources of food supply than hunting and gathering cultures. Contemporary evolutionists, however, are careful not to identify such increases in adaptive capacity as moral "progress."

Talcott Parsons's Theory of Evolution

Among the most influential evolutionary theories today is that put forward by Talcott Parsons. According to Parsons, social evolution is an extension of biological evolution, although the actual mechanisms of development are different. Both types of evolution can be understood by what Parsons called *evolutionary universals,* which are types of development that crop up on more than one occasion in different conditions and have great survival value. Vision is an example of an evolutionary universal in the animal world. Vision emerged not just in one part of the animal kingdom, but developed independently in several types of species. The ability to see allows for a much wider range of coordinated responses to the environment than is possible for unsighted organisms, and hence has great adaptive value. Vision is necessary to all animals at the higher stages of biological evolution.

Communication, as Parsons pointed out, is fundamental in all human culture, and language in turn is the basis of communication. Language is thus the first and most significant social evolutionary universal; there is no known human society that does not possess a language. Three other social evolutionary universals found even in the earliest forms of society are religion, kinship, and technology. These four universals constitute such essential aspects of any human society that no subsequent process of social evolution could get under way without them.

According to Parsons, social evolution is a process of continuous differentiation of social institutions, as societies move from the simple to the more complex. The earliest forms of society show only a very low level of differentiation, and are characterized by what Parsons called *constitutive symbolism*—the existence of a set of symbols, largely religious in character, that permeate virtually all aspects of so-

"And now there go the Wilsons! . . . Seems like everyone's evolving except us!"

cial life. As an example of a culture at the lowest stage of social evolution, Parsons took the case (as Durkheim did) of the aboriginal societies of Australia. These societies are structured almost wholly by kinship relations, which in turn express religious beliefs, and are integrated with economic activities. There is very little property; no distinct forms of chiefdom; and no productive economy, since hunting and gathering is the means of subsistence.

The next level of evolution is *advanced primitive society.* In this type, a stratification system has replaced the more egalitarian character of the simpler cultures. Advanced primitive societies often have ethnic as well as class divisions. They develop a distinct system of production through agriculture or pasturing of animals. They also have settled places of residence. Religion remains important, but it becomes separated to a certain degree from other aspects of social life. Religion is more organized and put under the guidance of a distinct priesthood.

Further up the scale are what Parsons called *intermediate societies.* Intermediate societies are civilizations or traditional states, such as ancient Egypt, Rome, or China. Here, writing and literacy emerge. Religion is further elaborated through systematic theologies and develops into an institution clearly distinct from the political, economic, and familial spheres. Political leadership develops in the shape of government administrations headed by aristocratic rulers. Several new social evolutionary universals come into being at this stage, including specialized forms of political legitimacy, bureaucratic organization, monetary exchange, and a codified system of law. Each of these, Parsons claimed, greatly increases the capability of a society to integrate large numbers of people within an overall community.

Industrialized societies stand at the highest point in Parsons's evolutionary scheme. They are far more internally differentiated than societies of the intermediate type. In industrialized societies, the economic and political systems become clearly separated from one another, and both are distinct from the legal system, as well as from religion. The development of mass democracy provides a means of involving the whole population within the political order. Industrialized societies have a much higher level of territorial unity than earlier societies, being distinguished by well-defined borders. The superior survival value generated by the institutions of industrialized societies is well demonstrated by the spread of industrialism worldwide, leading to the more or less complete disappearance of the earlier types of society.

Assessing Social Evolutionary Theories

Even in their more recent and sophisticated forms, social evolutionary theories are questionable (Gellner, 1964; Giddens, 1985). It is dubious whether the development of human societies at all closely resembles evolution in the natural world, and the concept of adaptation is probably of little value in sociology. In biology, **adaptation** has a fairly precise meaning, referring to the way in which the randomly generated characteristics of some organisms selectively promote their survival, thereby influencing the genes transmitted from one generation to another (Alland, 1967, 1970). No such clearly designated meaning exists in the case of social evolutionism.

It is not even certain that we can usefully classify societies, as we can biological organisms, in ascending levels of complexity. Hunting and gathering societies, for example, in some respects are *more* complex than industrialized ones, even if they are much smaller. Most hunting and gathering communities, for instance, have considerably more complicated kinship systems than those characteristic of industrialized societies.

More recent evolutionary theories, like Parsons's theory, are clearly superior to those developed in the nineteenth century. Yet although it makes sense to say that there is an overall "direction" of human social development, from smaller societies to larger ones, it is dubious whether this can be explained by adaptation and survival value. The theories provide plausible descriptions of social development, but they do not attach these descriptions firmly to any underlying mechanism of social change. The nature of social and cultural change seems altogether more complicated than evolutionary theories suggest.

KARL MARX AND HISTORICAL MATERIALISM

Marx's interpretation of social change shares something in common with social evolutionary theory. Both regarded the major patterns of change as being brought about by interaction with the material environment (i.e., the physical world of nature). According to Marx, every society rests upon an economic base or "infrastructure," changes in which tend to govern alterations in the "superstructure," the political, legal, and cultural institutions. Marx did not use the concept of adaptation in relation to social change. In Marx's view, human beings actively relate to nature, seeking to master and subordinate it to their purposes; they do not merely "adapt to" or "fit into" their environment, as the social evolutionists suggested.

Social change, Marx argued, can be understood through the ways in which, in developing more sophisticated systems of production, human beings progressively come to transform the material world. Marx referred to this process as the expansion of the **forces of production,** a term that refers to the level of economic advancement a society has reached. Social change does not occur only as a process of slow development but in the shape of revolutionary transformations. Periods of gradual development of the forces of production and other social institutions alternate with phases of more dramatic revolutionary change. This theory has come to be known more broadly as **historical materialism.**

The most significant processes of change, according to Marx's view, come about through tensions, clashes, and struggles—the most important of which are between class groups. Changes in the forces of production (i.e., economic advances) set up tensions in other institutions in the superstructure; the more acute these tensions become, the more there is a pressure towards the overall transformation of society. Struggles between classes become more and more acute, and ultimately produce either the disintegration of existing institutions or the transition to a new type of social order through a process of political revolution.

As an illustration of Marx's theory, we might take the changes involved in the replacement of feudalism by industrial capitalism in Eu-

Just five years before the publication of The Communist Manifesto *by Karl Marx and Friedrich Engels,* Punch *magazine ran this cartoon depicting the comforts of the capitalist class and the cruel hardships of the working class.*

rope. The economic system of feudalism was based on agricultural production; the two principal social classes were the aristocracy, who owned the land, and the peasantry, who worked for them. According to Marx, the growth of trade and advances in technology led to the emergence of a new set of economic relations centered on manufacture and industry in the towns and cities. A series of tensions thus developed between the old agricultural economic order of feudalism and the newly emerging, capitalistic manufacturing system. The more acute these tensions became, the greater the strains on other social and political institutions. Conflict between the aristocrats and the developing capitalist class ultimately led to a process of revolution, signaling the consolidation of a new type of society. In other words, industrial capitalism had come to replace feudalism.

Criticisms

Marx's ideas certainly help make sense of some major transitions in history. Many historians and sociologists who would not see themselves as "Marxists" have accepted much of Marx's interpretation of the decline of feudalism and the origins of modern capitalism. Yet as a general framework for analyzing social change, Marx's views have notable limitations. It is questionable whether other historical transitions fit into Marx's scheme. For instance, some archaeologists have drawn upon aspects of Marx's theory to try to explain the early development of civilizations (Childe, 1983, 1979). Civilizations emerged, it has been argued, when the forces of production had developed sufficiently to permit a class-based society to emerge. But at best this is an oversimplified view. Traditional states were more commonly formed as a result of military expansion and conquest rather than by changes in the economic infrastructure. Political and military power was often the *means* by which traditional states accumulated wealth, rather than by developing new forces of production. Moreover, Marx's theory has never been able to deal satisfactorily with the development of the large Eastern civilizations of India, China, and Japan.

WEBER'S INTERPRETATION OF CHANGE

Max Weber criticized both the evolutionary theories and Marx's historical materialism (Weber, 1979). Attempts to interpret historical change as a whole in terms of adaptation to the material world or by economic factors, he argued, are doomed to failure. Although there are many circumstances in which such influences are important, there is no sense in which they ultimately control overall processes of development. No single-factor theory of social change has a chance of accounting for the diversity of human social development from hunting and gathering and pastoral societies to traditional civilizations and the highly complex social systems of today. Other factors besides economic forces—including military power, types of government, and ideologies—are often equally or more important at one time or another.

If Weber's view is correct, as most would agree it is, there can be no single grand theory that explains the nature of social change. In analyzing social change, we can at most accomplish two tasks. First, we can identify some of the factors that have had a consistent and general influence upon social change in many contexts. Second, we can develop theories that account for certain phases or "episodes" of change —for instance, the early emergence of traditional states. Evolutionist and Marxist thinkers were not wrong to emphasize the importance of environmental and economic factors upon patterns of social change —they simply gave undue weight to these as compared to other influences.

Following Webster's lead, we can list the main influences upon social change in past history under three headings: the physical environment, political organization, and cultural factors.

The Physical Environment

As social evolutionists emphasized, the *physical environment* often had an effect upon the development of human social organization. This is clearest in more extreme environmental conditions. People in polar regions necessarily developed a different way of life from those who lived in the subtropical regions of the world. Less extreme physical conditions also often affected a society. For example, the native population of Australia always remained hunters and gatherers, since the continent contained hardly any indigenous plants suitable for regular cultivation, or animals that could be domesticated to develop pastoral production. In contrast, the world's early civilizations for the most part originated in river deltas where there was rich agricultural land. Other factors such as ease of travel across land, or the availability of sea routes, also influenced past social development. A society cut off from others by mountain ranges, impassable jungles, or deserts often remained relatively unchanged over long periods of time.

Yet the direct influence of the environment upon social change should not be overemphasized. Even peoples having quite simple technology were sometimes able to develop considerable productive wealth in relatively inhospitable areas. Conversely, hunting and gathering cultures frequently lived in highly fertile regions without shifting to pastoral or agricultural production. There is little direct or constant relation between the environment and the types of productive system that developed. The evolutionists' emphasis upon adaptation to the environment is thus less illuminating than Marx's stress upon the importance of productive relations in influencing social development. There is no doubt that the types of production systems strongly influenced the level and nature of change that went on in a society, although they did not have the overriding impact Marx attributed to them.

Political Organization

A second factor that strongly influenced social change was the type of *political organization*. In hunting and gathering societies, this influence was minimal, since there were no separate political authorities capable of mobilizing the community. In all other types of society, however, the existence of distinct political agencies—chiefs, lords, kings, and governments—strongly affected the course of development a society took.

Political systems were not, as Marx argued, expressions of underlying economic organization; different types of political order existed in societies having similar production systems. For instance, forms of production in small, nonstate pastoral societies were not very different from those of large, state-based civilizations. Rulers may have initiated processes of territorial expansion that greatly increased the wealth of the societies over which they exercised their sway. However, a monarch who embarked upon such adventures without success may have brought a society into economic disruption or ruin. Military strength has been an important aspect of political influences over social change. As was pointed out earlier, military power played a fundamental part in establishing most traditional states, as well as in influencing their subsequent survival or expansion.

Cultural Factors

A third set of influences consisted of *cultural factors,* which included the effects of religion, styles of thought, and consciousness. As we have previously seen (Chapter 14: "Religion"), religion may be either a conservative or an innovative force in social life. Many forms of religious belief and practice acted as a brake upon change, emphasizing above all the need to adhere to traditional values and rituals. Yet, as Weber emphasized, religious convictions also frequently played a mobilizing role in generating pressures for social change.

A particularly important cultural influence affecting the character and rapidity of change was the nature of communication systems. The invention of writing, for instance, influenced social change in more than one way. Writing allowed for record-keeping, which made possible the increased control of material resources, and thus the development of large-scale organizations. In addition, however, writing altered people's perception of the relationship between past, present, and future. Societies that possessed writing had a record of past events, knowing themselves to have a "history." Understanding history serves to develop a sense of the overall "movement" or "line of development" a society follows.

Under the general heading of cultural factors, we should also refer to the influence of *leadership.* Individual leaders have had an enormous influence upon some phases and aspects of world history—one only has to think of such figures as the great religious prophets (like Jesus), individual political and military leaders (like Julius Caesar), or innovators in science and philosophy (like Newton) to see that this is the case. A leader capable of pursuing dynamic policies, and able to generate a mass following, or someone who can radically alter existing modes of thought, can overturn a previously established social order of things.

However, individuals can only reach positions of leadership, and become effective in what they do, if favorable social conditions exist. Adolf Hitler was able to seize power in Germany in the 1930s, for instance, as a result of the tensions and crises that beset the country at that time. If those circumstances had not existed, he would no doubt have remained an obscure figure within a minor political faction.

Analyzing Episodes of Change

The impact of the factors just listed varies according to time and place. We cannot single out one as the determining influence over the whole of human social development, just as we cannot use one theory to explain social change. But we can develop theories about specific phases or **episodes of change** in history. As an illustration of this, we shall look at Robert Carneiro's interpretation of the initial development of traditional states or civilizations (Carneiro, 1970).

Carneiro accepted that warfare played a major part in the origin of traditional states, but pointed out that warfare was commonplace among societies that had reached a certain level of development, and therefore could not itself account for state formation. War led to the emergence of states when the peoples involved were penned into physically limited areas of agricultural land—which was the case in ancient Egypt (the Nile delta), the Valley of Mexico, or the coastal valleys of Peru, among other examples. In such circumstances, according to Carneiro, war tended to set up a pressure upon scarce resources. Migration out of the area was difficult, because of its physically confined character. Established ways of life therefore came under strain, which induced some groups to seek military ascendancy over others and encouraged attempts to centralize control over production. An entire valley eventually became unified under a single chiefdom, which was then able to concentrate administrative resources to become a governing apparatus or state.

The theory is an interesting and important one, and helps illuminate a substantial number of cases of state development. Yet not all early states developed in the physically circumscribed areas Carneiro identified (Claessen and Skalnik, 1976). Moreover, later forms of traditional state often developed in quite different circumstances. Once states actually existed, they stimulated further developments elsewhere; other peoples were able to mold their own political development upon them. The fact that Carneiro's theory only helps explain a limited number of instances of the formation of traditional states is no reason to condemn or reject it. It has sufficient generality to be a good and useful theory; and it is implausible to suppose that theories can be developed that will explain much broader phases of social transformation than this one covers.

CHANGE IN THE MODERN PERIOD

WHAT EXPLAINS WHY THE LAST TWO HUNDRED YEARS, THE period of modernity, has seen such a tremendous acceleration in the speed of social change? This is of course a very complex issue, but it is not difficult to indicate some of the factors involved. Not surprisingly, these can be categorized along lines similar to those involved in influencing social change throughout history. In analyzing them, we shall subsume the impact of the physical environment within the overall importance of economic factors.

ECONOMIC INFLUENCES

Of economic influences, the most far-reaching is the impact of *industrial capitalism*. Capitalism differs fundamentally from previous production systems because it involves the constant expansion of production and ever-increasing accumulation of wealth. In traditional production systems, levels of production were fairly static and were geared to habitual, customary needs. Capitalist development promotes the constant revision of the technology of production, a process into which science has increasingly been drawn. The rate of technological innovation fostered in modern industry is vastly greater than in any previous type of economic order.

Take as an example the automobile industry today. Almost every year, the major manufacturers bring out new models and constantly seek to improve and modify their existing ones. Or consider the current development of information technology: just over the past twenty years, the power of computers has increased by ten thousand times. The large computers of the 1960s required tens of thousands of handmade connectors; a computer today with the same power and memory is not only much smaller, but needs only ten elements in an integrated circuit. Other technological innovations affect virtually all aspects of our lives today.

In traditional societies, most production was local. Merchants may have journeyed far and wide, developing various kinds of long-distance trade, but most such trade was confined to luxury goods, consumed by the few. The development of modern industry did away with the localized character of traditional production and integrated producers and consumers in a division of labor that today has become global in scope. Marx described this process accurately. Modern capitalism, he pointed out,

A microchip, capable of handling millions of operations per second, is so small that a dozen could rest on a thumbnail.

has given a cosmopolitan character to production and consumption in every country. . . . It has drawn from under the feet of industry the national ground on which it stood. All old-fashioned national industries have been destroyed or are daily being destroyed. They are dislodged by new industries, whose introduction becomes a life and death question for all civilized nations, by industries that no longer only work upon indigenous raw materials, but raw materials drawn from the remotest zones; industries whose products are consumed, not only at home, but in every quarter of the globe. (Marx and Engels, 1965)

The development of industrial capitalism fundamentally altered people's basic ways of life. Most people in modern societies now live in cities rather than in rural communities, and work in factories and offices rather than in agricultural production. We tend to take these conditions of life for granted today, not realizing how unique our type of society is in human history. Ours is the first society in which the large majority of the population do not either live in small rural communities or gain their livelihood from the land. The changes associated with urbanism and the development of new work environments have affected—as well as been affected by—most other institutions.

POLITICAL INFLUENCES

The second major influence underlying change in the modern period is represented by political developments. The struggle between nations to expand their power, develop their wealth, and triumph militarily over their competitors, has been an energizing source of change over the past two or three centuries. Political change in traditional civilizations normally affected only the elite members. One aristocratic family would replace another and assume power, while for the majority of the population life would continue on relatively unchanged. This is no longer true in modern political systems, in which the activities of political leaders and government officials continually affect the lives of the mass of the population. Nationally and internationally, political decision making promotes and directs social change far more than in previous times.

Political development in the modern era has certainly influenced economic change as much as the reverse. Governments now play a major role in stimulating (and sometimes retarding) rates of economic growth. In all modern societies there is a high level of state in-

In World War II, two of Japan's major cities were virtually destroyed by atomic bombs; since, it has again become a major world economic power. Here, Hiroshima one month after the dropping of the bomb, August 6, 1945, and (at right) an electronics factory in Ibaragi today.

tervention in industrial production, with the government being far and away the largest employer.

Military power and war have also been of far-reaching importance in the modern period (Aron, 1981; Marwick, 1974; Howard, 1976; Giddens, 1985). The military strength wielded by the Western nations from the seventeenth century onwards allowed them to make their presence felt in all quarters of the world—and provided an essential backing to the global spread of Western styles of life. In the twentieth century, the effects of the two world wars have been profound: the devastation of many countries led to a rebuilding that brought about major institutional changes—such as happened in Germany and Japan. Even those states which were the victors—like the United States—experienced major internal changes as a result of the unsettling effects of the war economy.

CULTURAL INFLUENCES

Cultural factors have also greatly affected processes of social change in modern times. The development of science, and the secularization of thought, have been primary influences, each contributing to the *critical* and *innovative* character of the modern outlook. We no longer assume that customs or habits are acceptable merely because they have the age-old authority of tradition. On the contrary, in modern societies our ways of life are increasingly required to have a "rational" basis. That is to say, they have to be defended, and if necessary

changed, according to whether or not they can be justified based on persuasive arguments and evidence. For instance, a design for building a hospital would not be based mainly on traditional tastes, but would consider its capability for serving the purposes to which a hospital is put—effectively caring for the sick.

It is not just alterations in *how* we think that have influenced processes of change in the modern world; the *content* of ideas has also changed. Ideals of self-betterment, freedom, equality, and democratic participation are largely creations of the past two or three centuries. Such ideals have served to mobilize processes of social and political change, including revolutions. These are not ideas that can be tied to tradition, but rather suggest the constant revision of ways of life in the pursuit of human betterment. Although they initially were developed in the West, such ideals have become genuinely universal in their application, promoting change in most regions of the world.

CURRENT CHANGE AND FUTURE PROSPECTS

WHERE IS SOCIAL CHANGE LEADING US TODAY? WHAT ARE the main trends of development likely to affect our lives as the twenty-first century opens? Sociologists do not agree on the answers to these questions, which obviously involve a large element of speculation. We shall look at three different perspectives on the issues involved: the "convergence theory" of Clark Kerr; the notion that a "postindustrial society" is coming into being, connected particularly with the writings of Daniel Bell; and the idea, prominent in some traditions of social thought, that industrial capitalism will in the future cede place to socialism.

CONVERGENCE THEORY

One view about current processes of development has been offered by Clark Kerr and his colleagues, whose standpoint has come to be known as **convergence theory.** According to Kerr, "the world is entering a new age—the age of total industrialization. Some countries are far along the road; many are just beginning the journey. But everywhere, at a faster or slower pace, the peoples of the world are on the march towards industrialism" (Kerr et al., 1960). In Kerr's view, there is a "logic of industrialism," which ensures that social development produces a definite set of changes in social institutions. All industrialized societies tend to become alike; moreover, the rest of the world faces an industrial future because only through industrialization can Third World societies break free from their situation of poverty.

Kerr cites several social and economic processes that are fostered by industrialization. All societies in the future, whether or not they are currently industrialized, will tend to develop these characteristics, but the industrialized countries are already far along the road.

1. TECHNOLOGY AND PROFESSIONALISM. Modern large-scale production systems demand a wide range of technical skills and professional competence, producing a highly complex division of labor. Work in factories and offices, the predominant work settings in an industrialized society, follows regular and disciplined patterns—quite different than the more irregular types of labor characteristic of premodern economies. People accept that they have to work according to a set schedule each week, for example.

2. OPEN SOCIETIES. Industrialized societies are more open than premodern ones, with a high degree of lateral and vertical social mobility. There are strong tendencies toward equality of opportunity in the educational and occupational systems. Unlike tradi-

tional societies, work roles are not generally allocated on the basis of inheritance or kinship position.

3. HIGHER EDUCATION. A large educational sector develops to transmit the skills and knowledge required to do the many different tasks involved in an industrial economy. Not only is there a high level of literacy and basic educational achievement among the population at large, but specialized education for technical, managerial, and professional tasks becomes more and more important.

4. WIDESPREAD URBANISM. Industrialized societies necessarily become highly urbanized, with the majority of the population living in cities. Developed communications systems are also required—road, rail, and air systems, together with media of printed and electronic communication.

5. CULTURAL HOMOGENEITY. General agreement over cultural values emerges, influenced by the secularization of belief, the acceptance of the usefulness of science and technology, the opposition to tradition, and an acceptance of a work ethic.

6. DIMINISHING RISKS OF WAR. As industrialized societies become increasingly alike, and develop extensive networks of economic interdependence, the risks of war diminish. Wars derive from cultural clashes or from divisions of economic interest; as societies become more and more locked into an industrialized world, a common outlook and shared interests outweigh divisive influences.

Kerr's views were first set out in the 1960s, and he has subsequently elaborated on them. He later came to see convergence as less of a "blanket" process than he had originally. The industrialized societies, he now argues, tend to converge more closely in some aspects than in others. Convergence is most marked in the *means and methods of production*—in the use of similar technologies—and in terms of *the daily lives led by the mass of the population*. Forms of economic organization, political systems, and patterns of belief and ideology remain much more variable. For instance, although automobile production, and the lives of those working in that industry, are much the same in the United States and in the Soviet Union, the political systems and ideologies of the two societies remain different. "The process of convergence," in Kerr's words, "that has taken place thus far in history may be compared to a series of lines that approach one another at different but also at generally slower and slower rates, and that may at some point stop approaching one another at all" (Kerr, 1983).

Kerr's analysis stops short of endorsing convergence as a way to help humanity resolve some of its besetting problems. Others who have adopted a rather similar standpoint have not been so reluctant. Andrei Sakharov, who was a prominent Soviet dissident and Nobel Peace Prize recipient, accepted that convergence is occurring, and proposed that it should be actively encouraged. The greater the similarities that develop between the United States and the Soviet Union, Sakharov argued, the greater effect they will have on reducing global tensions. The Soviet Union has to become more liberalized (as has happened under Mikhail Gorbachev), as a prerequisite for more flexible and rapid economic development. The country lags behind the West as a result of the bureaucratic, repressive style of government and economic management that has controlled it for most of this century. On the other hand, the greater affluence of the Western countries has produced pronounced inequalities between the wealthy and the poor. These countries should spread their wealth more equally by means of greater government efforts towards redistribution. According to Sakharov, both systems "are capable of long-term development, borrowing positive elements from each other" (Sakharov, 1974; see also Galbraith, 1971).

Assessment of Convergence Theory

No one can dispute that industrialization has been a major force shaping social development worldwide over the past two centuries. Industrialization brings about major changes in the social institutions of any society, and without doubt, there are basic similarities between societies that have achieved a high level of industrial organization (Brzezinski and Huntington, 1964).

However, the convergence hypothesis has marked limitations that can be summarized as follows (Meyer, 1970; Goldthorpe, 1971; Ellman, 1980):

1. Pervasive as its influence is, industrialization is only one among other major sets of factors—such as political and cultural influences—shaping the development of modern societies.

2. Similarities between the industrialized countries do not necessarily stem directly from industrialization itself. They may derive, for example, from the competition of states to secure higher levels of economic development, or from the "borrowing" by one society of aspects of the institutions of another.

3. Industrialization is a complicated phenomenon, having a less unified character than Kerr seems to believe—at least in his original formulation of his ideas. For instance, there are major variations between industrialized countries in terms of the type of manufacturing industries that exist, the relation between manufacture and services, and the relative proportion of large corporations and smaller firms.

4. Even if it were the case, as it certainly seems today, that the United States and the Soviet Union were converging, it would not follow that military conflicts would necessarily diminish. Thus far, at least, the intensity of military conflict in the present century has grown rather than decreased. If the threat of major military confrontation recedes, it will not be because of increasing similarities between the United States and the Soviet Union, but rather because the factors that previously drove states to warfare are less important in an interdependent world (Rosenthau, 1980; Cooper, 1986).

TOWARDS A POSTINDUSTRIAL SOCIETY?

Many observers have suggested that what is occurring today is a transition to a new society no longer primarily based upon industrialism at all. We are entering, they claim, a new phase of development *beyond the industrial era altogether.* Alvin Toffler has argued that "what is occurring now is, in all likelihood, bigger, deeper, and more important than the Industrial Revolution. . . . The present moment represents nothing less than the second great divide in human history" (Toffler, 1970).

A variety of names have been coined to describe the new social order supposedly coming into being, such as the *information society, service society,* or *knowledge society.* They all refer to the idea that we are moving beyond the forms of industrial development characteristic of the modern era thus far. Therefore many authors have invented terms containing the prefix *post-* (meaning "after") to refer to such changes. They have spoken of *postmodern,* or *postscarcity* society, for example. The term that has come into most common usage, however —apparently first employed independently by Daniel Bell, writing in the United States, and Alain Touraine, working in France—is **postindustrial society** (Bell, 1976; Touraine, 1974).

The diversity of names that have been invented to refer to the changes now under way indicates the great diversity of ideas that have been put forward to interpret current social changes. But one theme which consistently appears is the significance of the use of *information* or *knowledge* in the society of the future. Our way of life, based upon the manufacture of material goods, centered upon the power machine and the factory, is being displaced by one in which information is becoming the main basis of the productive system.

In his work *The Coming of the Post-Industrial Society* (1973), Daniel Bell argued that the postindustrial society is distinguished by a growth of service occupations at the expense of those producing material goods. The blue-collar worker employed in a factory or workshop is no longer the most typical employee. White-collar workers increasingly outnumber those in blue-collar jobs, with professional and technical occupations growing fastest of all.

People working in white-collar occupations at higher levels specialize in the production of information and knowledge. The production and control of what Bell called *codified knowledge*— systematic, coordinated information—is the main strategic resource upon which the social order increasingly comes to depend. Those who are concerned with its creation and distribution—scientists, computer specialists, economists, engineers, and professionals of all kinds—become the leading social groups, replacing the industrialists and entrepreneurs of the old system. On the level of culture, there is a shift away from the "work ethic" towards an emphasis upon a freer and more pleasure-seeking lifestyle. The work-discipline characteristic of industrialism is relaxed in the postindustrial order; people are freer to be innovative in both their work and their domestic lives.

Reconsidering Postindustrialism

How valid is the idea that the old industrial order is being superseded by a postindustrial society? While the thesis has been widely accepted, there are good reasons to be cautious about its claims (Kumar, 1978; Williams, 1984). The empirical assertions upon which the notion depends are suspect in several ways.

1. The idea that information is becoming the main basis of the economic system is based upon a questionable interpretation of the shift towards service occupations. The trend towards the expansion of services at the expense of other production sectors dates back almost to the beginning of industrialism itself; it is not simply a recent phenomenon. From the early 1800s onwards, manufacture and services *both* expanded at the expense of agriculture, with the service sector consistently showing a faster rate of increase than manufacture. The blue-collar worker never really was the most common type of employee. A higher proportion of paid employees has *always* worked in agriculture and services, with the service sector increasing proportionally as the numbers in agriculture dwindled. Easily the most important change has not been from industrial to service work, but from farm employment to all other types of occupation.

2. The service sector is very heterogeneous. "Service occupations" cannot be simply treated as identical to "white-collar jobs"; many service jobs (such as that of gas-station attendant) are blue collar in the sense that they are manual. Most white-collar positions utilize very little specialized knowledge—and have become substantially mechanized. This is true of most low-level office work, such as secretarial or clerical occupations.

3. Many service jobs contribute to a process that in the end produces material goods—and therefore should be counted as part of manufacture. Thus a computer programmer working for an industrial firm, designing and monitoring the operation of machine tools, is directly involved in a process of making material goods. In analyzing service occupations, Jonathan Gershuny concludes that more than half are concerned with manufacturing production in such a way (Gershuny, 1978).

4. Daniel Bell proposes that the United States has advanced more than any other country towards becoming a postindustrial society; it is the furthest along a course of development that others will increasingly follow. Yet the American economy has long been different from that of other industrialized countries. Throughout this century, a relatively higher proportion of workers have been in service occupations in

the United States than in any other industrialized society. There remain today wide variations in the ratio between service and manufacturing occupations in different countries. It is not certain that other countries will become as "service-based" as the United States. What are seen as general trends might really be specific characteristics of American society.

5. No one can be sure what the long-term impact of the growing use of microprocessing and electronic communications systems will be. At the moment, these are integrated *within* manufacturing production, rather than *displacing* it. It seems certain that such technologies will continue to show very high rates of innovation, and will permeate more areas of social life. But any assessment of their impact still has to be speculative. To what extent we yet live in a society in which "codified knowledge" is the main resource is dubious (Gill, 1985; Lyon, 1989).

6. Like convergence theory, the postindustrial-society thesis tends to exaggerate the importance of economic factors in producing social change. The postindustrial society is described as the outcome of developments in the economy that then subsequently produce changes in other institutions. Most of those advancing the postindustrial hypothesis have been little influenced by or are directly critical of Marx; but their position is a quasi-Marxist one in the sense that they believe economic factors dominate social change.

Some of the developments pointed to by advocates of the theory of the postindustrial society are important features of the present era, but it is not obvious that the concept of postindustrial society is the best way to come to terms with them. Moreover, the origins of the changes going on today are political and cultural as well as economic.

CAPITALISM AND SOCIALISM

NEITHER CONVERGENCE THEORY NOR THE POSTINDUS-trial-society hypothesis cast much light upon political differences among societies. Up until 1989, the clearest differences among the industrialized societies today were between the liberal democratic states of the West and the communist societies of Eastern Europe. The ideological battles between these two "blocs" have been a major source of antagonism in international relations for well over forty years, and came to be known as the "Cold War." What does the future hold for the political and ideological clashes of capitalism and socialism? Political organizations and parties calling themselves "socialist" believe that a new type of society, which will overcome many of the shortcomings of those currently existing both West and East, can be created. How realistic are these aspirations? Will socialist ideals continue to mobilize social movements in the future? Socialism, as usually understood, is a much broader concept than "communism," which refers to movements and ideas associated with Marx and Lenin, such as became established in the Soviet Union. As of today, communism seems in radical decline, given the changes that have happened very recently in Eastern Europe and the USSR. But many socialist parties still exist, and are very powerful in the societies of both Western and Eastern Europe.

Socialism is held by its advocates to be a stage "beyond" the liberal democratic political systems and capitalist economies of modern societies. According to socialist thought, such societies cannot realize the goals of equality and democracy that they proclaim, because of their capitalistic framework. Rights of political participation are supposed to be open to all the citizenry, but in practice most of the population have little or no influence over the decisions that affect their lives. The economic system is supposedly based upon "free enterprise," but socialists argue that this is almost meaningless for the majority of the labor force. Workers have no choice but to contract themselves to employers if they are to obtain a living. Given the lack of industrial democracy, which would give workers formal avenues of expression, they have very little control over their work settings that dominate much of their waking hours.

The system of capitalist production may generate considerable wealth, socialists claim, but this is distributed very unequally; extensive poverty continues to exist in the midst of affluence. Moreover, in a market economy there are continual fluctuations of economic life, with periods of boom being succeeded by long phases of recession. At such times, there is sizable unemployment and many productive resources lie idle.

In a socialist society, it is held, these problems can be overcome, creating a more just and participatory social order. Although models of socialism differ very considerably, most hold that a socialist society presumes a combination of industrial democracy and central direction of economic enterprise. Government control of economic life is needed to control economic fluctuation and redistribute wealth. More extensive democracy, covering industry as well as the political

Below the statue of Lenin, Soviet President Mikhail Gorbachev lays the groundwork for change in the USSR.

sphere, is necessary to make sure that governmental power is not used to suppress individual liberties.

SOCIALISM: THE TWENTIETH-CENTURY RECORD

Until well into the twentieth century, socialism was just a concept—a dream, or a nightmare, according to different points of view—rather than a reality. There were no parties in power anywhere claiming to be implementing socialist ideals. Over the past half-century or so, this situation has changed greatly. Governments adhering to socialist ideals have come to power in most regions throughout the world. These include communist parties, which once dominated in Eastern Europe, but also many others, such as the democratic socialist parties of Western European countries. Self-professed socialist governments have also perpetrated some of the most barbaric events of twentieth-century history, for instance the mass killings and deportations during the period of Stalinism in the Soviet Union. In the light of this half-century of experience, we can be clearer both about the promise and the limitations of socialist thought.

Industrialized countries that have experienced centralized political and economic control—in particular the societies of Eastern Europe —do not show up well either in their level of economic development or in the degree of liberalism of their political systems. The attempt to supersede free-market mechanisms by strongly defined state planning has in most respects not been successful. It seems impossible to effectively organize a complex modern economy centrally. Market mechanisms appear to play a key role in efficiently allocating goods and resources. Moreover, the evidence is that strongly centralized economic planning tends to be associated with a high degree of authoritarianism in the political system. The movement towards greater democracy in Eastern Europe has been accompanied by the reintroduction of market mechanisms in all the countries involved.

Some Third World socialist countries have been more effective in promoting the social and economic welfare of their citizenry than their nonsocialist counterparts. Cuba, for example, has higher standards of literacy, general education, medical care, and other welfare provisions than comparable nonsocialist countries in South America. But although many Western socialists at one point saw Cuba as pioneering new modes of socialist organization, few would hold today that Cuban socialism represents a model that industrialized countries might profitably follow. Cuba remains at a low level of economic development, depends on extensive subsidies from the Soviet Union, and freedom of political expression is limited.

Democratic socialist parties in Western countries have usually found their more radical aspirations frustrated, either by electorates unwilling to endorse their views or by the opposition of business interests, but their impact has still been considerable. Such parties have played a leading part in establishing welfare institutions and in limiting the inequalities that unchecked market forces tend to bring about. In some societies, where socialist or labor parties have achieved power for lengthy periods, the results have been notable. Sweden is a good example, having by some measures a higher average income per head of the population than the United States, and having virtually eradicated poverty. Nonetheless, Sweden remains a "capitalist" society in its basic economic institutions. It is not clear how such a society might become more "fully socialist" without being authoritarian and overly centralized in the way the East European countries were when under communist domination (Himmelstrand et al., 1981). Sweden's combination of economic prosperity, liberalism, and social justice seems to derive from an effective compromise between socialist ideals and capitalistic mechanisms.

ISSUES FOR THE TWENTY-FIRST CENTURY

Socialist thought has been seriously compromised by the failures of central planning, and in recent years there has been a major challenge from Rightist political thought. Authors on this side of the political spectrum have not only attacked socialist doctrines as denying individual liberties, but have increasingly sought to develop positive alternatives of their own. According to such writers, expanding the realm of free-market operations is the key to a just and free social and political order—the very reverse of traditional socialist arguments. In the light of the dilemmas posed for socialism, together with the sorts of changes pointed to by the theorists of postindustrial society, many now argue that socialist ideas have become largely irrelevant to the fundamental problems of our age. Those making such arguments include Leftist as well as Rightist authors.

What are we to make of such arguments? Certainly socialist parties and movements are unlikely to disappear, or even diminish in importance, in forthcoming years. Socialism is a fundamental part of the Western political heritage. The number of countries in the world ruled by governments proclaiming themselves to be socialist (rather than communist) will probably grow rather than decline in the future. But it also seems certain that socialist ideas will become increasingly challenged in future years. The challenge will come not only from traditional opponents on the political Right, but from others associated with liberal views. New groups and movements are likely to have a larger place in political debates and struggles, and the issues and questions they are raising do not readily fit into the traditional debates about the relative merits of socialism and free-market capitalism.

One such set of issues concerns **environmental ecology.** Those on both the political Left and Right used to hold that economic growth could go on more or less indefinitely, even if they disagreed about the best means of achieving it. It has become increasingly apparent, however, that the earth's resources are finite; what may amount to irreparable damage to the environment has already been brought about by the spread of industrial production. Ecological questions do not only concern how we can best cope with and contain environmental damage, but are bound up with the very ways of life fostered within the industrialized societies. If the goal of continuous economic growth has to be abandoned, new social institutions will probably have to be pioneered. Technological progress is unpredictable, and it is possible that the earth might yet yield the resources to make possible the global process of industrialization envisaged by thinkers like Kerr. At the moment, however, this does not seem possible. If the Third World countries are to achieve living standards even moderately comparable to those currently enjoyed in the West, global readjustments will be necessary.

Protecting the environment has become a major challenge in the 1990s. Here, a clean-up crew attempts to restore an Alaskan beach back to its original beauty after the oil spill from the Exxon Valdez.

Other fundamental questions concern *gender divisions* and *violence.* Inequalities between men and women are deeply ingrained in all cultures, and establishing greater equality between the sexes is likely to demand major changes in our existing social institutions. While there are many debates about this issue, the established aspirations of socialism often ignore problems of gender. Much the same is true of attempts to meet the threat posed by the development of industrialized weaponry and military power. The problem of how to limit—and hopefully radically reduce—the risks of nuclear confrontation is by any token a most urgent task facing humanity in the 1990s and beyond. This issue goes beyond customary distinctions between "capitalism" and "socialism."

Stopping violence against world citizenry—another challenge for the modern world. Pablo Picasso's antiwar painting Guernica *is a protest against the bombing of an undefended city during the Spanish Civil War (1936–1939).*

SOCIAL CHANGE: LOOKING INTO THE FUTURE

WHETHER OR NOT WE ARE MOVING INTO A POSTINDUSTRIAL order, we do seem to be living through a period of social change that is dramatic even by the standards of the past two centuries. We know what the major dimensions of such change are, even if their interpretation remains problematic. They include the influences mentioned by the postindustrial-society theorists and others as well: exceptionally rapid rates of technological innovation coupled with the impact of information technology and microelectronics; an erosion of the established manufacturing industries of Western economies as a result of the transfer of basic industrial production to the Far East; the increasing global connections between industrialized societies; the occurrence of major changes in the domestic sphere—the home—associated with alterations in gender relations; the persistence of marked divisions of wealth and power between the industrialized and the poorer Third World countries; and, in the background to everything, a delicate balance between the possibility of long-lasting global peace and a nuclear conflict that could wipe out most of the population of the earth.

As we peer over the edge of our century into the next, we cannot foresee whether the coming hundred years will be marked by peaceful social and economic development, or by a multiplication of global problems—perhaps beyond the capacity of humankind to resolve. Unlike the early sociologists two hundred years ago, we see very clearly that modern industry, technology, and science are by no means wholly beneficial in their consequences. Our world is wealthier and more populous than ever before, and we have the potential to control our destiny and shape our lives for the better, unimaginable to previous generations. Yet the world hovers close to nuclear and ecological disaster. To say this is not in any way to counsel an attitude of resigned despair. If there is one thing that sociology offers us, it is a profound consciousness of the human authorship of social institutions. As human beings, aware of our achievements and limitations, we make our own history. Our understanding of the dark side of modern social change need not prevent us from sustaining a realistic and hopeful outlook towards the future.

SUMMARY

1. The modern period—from about the eighteenth century to the present day—has seen an extraordinary acceleration in processes of social change. Probably more profound changes have occurred in this period, which is only a tiny segment of time in human history, than in the whole existence of humankind previously.

2. Two of the most prominent interpretations of social change are *social evolutionism* and *historical materialism*. Both see change as deriving mainly from the ways in which human beings relate to the material environment. Major criticisms can be made against each of these approaches.

3. No "single-factor" theory can explain social change as a whole. A number of major influences upon social change can be distin-

guished, of which adaptation to the physical environment is one. Others are political, military, and cultural influences.

4. It is possible to develop theories of more restricted patterns or processes of change. An example is Robert Carneiro's theory of the development of traditional states.

5. Among the important factors relevant to social change in the modern era are the expansion of industrial capitalism, the development of centralized nation-states, the industrialization of war, and the emergence of science and "rational," or critical, ways of thought.

6. According to *convergence theory,* industrialization is the main force shaping the modern world; as they industrialize, societies tend to become more alike in certain basic respects. Although convergence theory helps us understand some features of change today, it has marked limitations centered on the prime causative role it gives to industrialization.

7. Another view of the directions of change going on today is associated with the idea of the *postindustrial society.* The old industrial order, it is believed by many, is being left behind in favor of the development of a new social order based on knowledge and information. These ideas underestimate the extent to which service work is embedded within manufacture, and also probably give too much emphasis to economic factors.

8. Traditional debates between the advocates of *free-market capitalism* and *socialism* may be becoming outdated. New issues are coming to the fore that cannot easily be grasped or responded to within the framework of established positions in political theory.

BASIC CONCEPTS

SOCIAL CHANGE
SOCIAL EVOLUTIONISM
POSTINDUSTRIAL SOCIETY

IMPORTANT TERMS

HISTORICAL MATERIALISM	ADAPTATION
DIFFERENTIATION	FORCES OF PRODUCTION
SOCIAL DARWINISM	EPISODES OF CHANGE
UNILINEAR EVOLUTION	CONVERGENCE THEORY
MULTILINEAR EVOLUTION	ENVIRONMENTAL ECOLOGY

METHODS AND THEORIES IN SOCIOLOGY

The first chapter in this part of the book discusses how sociologists set about doing research. A number of basic methods of investigation are available to help us find out what is going on in the social world. We have to make sure that the information upon which sociological reasoning is based is as reliable and accurate as possible. The chapter examines the problems that this raises, indicating how they are best dealt with.

In the final chapter of the book, we analyze some of the main theoretical approaches in sociology. Sociology is not a subject with a body of theories whose validity is agreed upon by everyone. In this chapter, differing theoretical traditions are compared and contrasted.

CHAPTER TWENTY-ONE

WORKING WITH SOCIOLOGY: METHODS OF RESEARCH

THE ISSUES WITH WHICH SOCIOLOGISTS ARE CONCERNED, both in their theorizing and their research, are often similar to those which worry many other people. How can mass starvation exist in a world that is far wealthier than it has ever been before? What effects will the increasing use of information technology have upon our lives? Is the family beginning to disintegrate as an institution? Do movies and TV encourage violent crime?

Sociologists try to provide answers to these and many other problems that worry or puzzle us. The answers reached are by no means necessarily conclusive. Yet it is always the aim of sociological theorizing and research to break away from the speculative or ill-informed manner in which the ordinary individual often responds to such questions. Good sociological work tries to make the questions asked as precise as possible, and seeks to assess factual evidence before coming to conclusions. To meet these objectives, we must utilize sound research procedures and be able accurately to analyze the material gathered. We have to know the most useful **research methods** to apply in a given study and how we should best analyze the results.

There are several aspects of sociological research. Research procedure or *strategy* refers to how research is planned and carried out.
Research *methodology* is the study of the logic underlying the interpreting of results and the analyzing of findings. Research *methods* are
the actual *techniques* of investigation used to study the social world
(Bulmer, 1984). Research methods include the use of questionnaires,
interviews, "participant observation," or fieldwork, together with
the interpretation of official statistics and historical documents—plus
other techniques not as widely used as these.

In this chapter, we shall begin by outlining the stages involved in
undertaking sociological research, together with the main principles
used in interpreting research findings. We shall then compare the
most widely used research methods, emphasizing actual projects and
investigations. There are often large differences between how research should ideally be carried out and real-life studies!

RESEARCH STRATEGY

ALL RESEARCH STARTS FROM A *RESEARCH PROBLEM.* THIS MAY
sometimes be mainly an area of factual ignorance: we may
simply wish to improve our knowledge of certain institutions, social processes, or cultures. The researcher might set out to
answer questions like "What proportion of the population holds
strong religious beliefs?" "Are people today really disaffected with
'big government'?" "How far does the economic position of women
lag behind that of men?" But the answers to these questions would be
mainly *descriptive.* The best sociological research, however, starts
from problems that are also *puzzles.* A puzzle is not just a lack of information, but a *gap in our understanding.* A large part of the skill of
producing worthwhile sociological research consists in correctly
identifying puzzles. Descriptive research simply answers the question "What is going on here?" Puzzle-solving research tries to contribute to our understanding of *why* events happen as they do, rather
than simply accepting them at their face value. Thus we might ask,
"Why are patterns of religious belief changing?" "What accounts
for the rise of the 'New Right' in politics in recent years?" "Why are
women so poorly represented in high-status jobs?"

No piece of research stands alone. Research problems come about
as part of on-going work. One research project may easily lead to another because it raises issues that the researcher had not previously
considered. Puzzles may also be suggested by reading the work of

The research methods used by sociologists will help in our attempts to understand the dismantling of communism in 1989–1990 in Eastern Europe in the years ahead.

other researchers in books and professional journals, or by an awareness of specific trends in society. For example, as mentioned in Chapter 5 ("Deviance"), over recent years there have been an increasing number of programs that seek to treat the mentally ill within the community setting, rather than confining them in asylums. Sociologists might be prompted to ask "What has given rise to this shift in attitude towards the mentally ill?" "What are the likely consequences both for the patients themselves and for the rest of the community?"

The first step taken in the research process is usually that of *reviewing the available evidence in the field.* It might be that previous research has already satisfactorily clarified the problem, so the would-be researcher must read other sociological work in this area. If the problem has not been clarified, the researcher will need to sift through relevant research to see how useful it is for the purpose at hand. Have previous researchers spotted the same puzzle? How have they tried to resolve it? What aspects of the problem has their research left unanalyzed? Drawing upon the ideas of others helps the researcher to clarify the issues that might be raised in a possible project, and the methods that might be used in the research.

The second stage involves working out a *clear formulation of the research problem.* Given that there is relevant research literature already in existence, the researcher might return from the library with a good notion of how the research problem should be approached. Hunches about the nature of the problem at this time perhaps can be turned into definite **hypotheses.** A hypothesis is a guess about the relationship between the phenomena in which the researcher is interested. If the research is to be effective, a hypothesis must be set out in such a way that the factual material gathered provides the opportunity to assess it.

The third stage is to work out a *research design.* In other words, the researcher must decide just how to collect the material involved in the research. There exists a range of different research methods, and which is chosen depends upon the overall objectives of the study, as well as the aspects of behavior to be analyzed. For some purposes, a survey (in which questionnaires are normally used) might be suitable. In other circumstances interviews or an observational study might be appropriate. None of these methods, of course, can be employed to study problems in historical sociology. For that purpose, documents relating to the period under study must be used.

The fourth stage is that of *carrying out the research itself.* At this point, unforeseen practical difficulties can easily crop up. It might prove impossible to contact some of those to whom questionnaires are due to be sent, or whom the researcher wishes to interview. A business firm or government agency, for example, might be unwilling to let the researcher carry out the work planned. Documentary materials might prove much harder to trace than was originally envisaged.

The fifth stage is *interpreting the results.* The material gathered has to be analyzed and applied to the problem that prompted the study. The troubles of the researcher are not over—it could even be said that they are just beginning! Working out the implications of the data collected, and relating these back to the research problem, is rarely easy, and applying the results to the original research formulation may pose difficulties of interpretation. While it may be possible to reach a clear answer to the questions with which the research was concerned, many investigations are in the end less than fully definitive.

The final stage is that of *reporting the research findings.* The research report, usually published as a journal article or book, provides an account of the nature of the research, and justifies whatever conclusions are drawn. This is a "final stage" only in terms of the individual research project. Most reports indicate the questions that remain unanswered and what sorts of research might profitably be done in the future. All individual research investigations are part of the continuing process of research by the whole sociological community.

THE OVERALL PROCESS

The preceding sequence of steps is a simplified version of what happens in actual research projects. In real sociological research, these stages rarely if ever succeed each other so neatly, and there may be a certain amount of sheer "muddling through" (Bell and Newby, 1977). The difference is a bit like that between the procedures outlined in a recipe book and the actual process of cooking a meal. People who are experienced cooks might not work from recipe books at all. Their work is often much more creative than those who do. Following fixed schemes can be unduly restricting; much of the most outstanding sociological research could not readily be fitted into the sequence just mentioned (Orenstein and Phillips, 1984).

GENERAL METHODOLOGY: UNDERSTANDING CAUSE

ONE OF THE MAIN PROBLEMS TO BE TACKLED IN RESEARCH *methodology* is the analysis of cause and effect. A **causal relationship** between two events or situations is an association in which one event or situation produces another. If the handbrake is released in an automobile pointing down a hill, it will roll down the incline, gathering speed progressively as it does so. Taking the brake off *caused* this to happen; the reasons for this can readily be understood by reference to the physical principles involved. Like natural science, sociology depends upon the assumption that all events have causes. Social life is not a random array of occurrences, happening without rhyme or reason. One of the main tasks of sociological research—in combination with theoretical thinking—is to identify causes and effects.

CAUSATION AND CORRELATION

Causation cannot be directly inferred from **correlation.** Correlation means the existence of a regular relationship between two sets of occurrences or **variables.** A variable is any dimension along which individuals or groups vary. Age, differences in income, crime rates, and social-class differences are some among the many variables sociologists study. It might seem as though when two variables are found to be closely correlated, one must be the cause of another; such is often not the case. There are many correlations without any causal relationship between the variables. For example, over the period since the Second World War, a strong correlation can be found between a decline in pipe-smoking and a decrease in numbers of people who regularly go to the movies. Clearly one change does not cause the other, and we would find it difficult to discover even a remote causal connection between them.

There are many instances, however, in which it is not so obvious that an observed correlation does not imply a causal relationship. Such correlations are traps for the unwary and easily lead to questionable or false conclusions. In his classical work *Suicide,* Emile Durkheim (1966) found a correlation between rates of suicide and the seasons of the year. In the societies Durkheim studied, levels of suicide increased progressively from January up to around June or July. From that time onwards they declined towards the end of the year. It might be supposed that this demonstrates that temperature or climatic change is causally related to the propensity of individuals to kill themselves. Perhaps as temperatures increase, people become more impulsive and hot-headed? However, the causal relation here has nothing directly to do with temperature or climate at all. In spring and summer most people engage in a more intensive social life than they do in winter. Individuals who are isolated or unhappy tend to experience an intensification of these feelings as the activity level of other people rises. Hence they are likely to experience acute suicidal tendencies more in spring and summer than in autumn and winter, when the pace of social activity slackens. We always have to be on our guard both in assessing whether correlation involves causation, and in deciding in which direction causal relations run.

Causal Mechanism

Working out causal connections involved in correlations is often a difficult process. There is a strong correlation, for instance, between level of educational achievement and occupational success in modern societies. The better the marks an individual gets in school, the better paying the job he or she is likely to obtain. What explains this correlation? Research tends to show that it is not mainly school experience itself; levels of school attainment are influenced much more by the type of home from which the person comes. Children from better-off homes, whose parents take a strong interest in their learning skills and where books are abundant, are more likely to do well than those coming from homes where these qualities are lacking. The causal mechanisms here are the attitudes of parents towards their children, together with the facilities for learning that a home provides. (For further discussion of the home and the school, see Chapter 13: "Education, Communication, and Media.")

Causal connections in sociology should not be understood in too mechanical a way. The attitudes people have, and their subjective reasons for acting as they do, are causal factors in relationships between variables in social life.

Controls

In assessing the cause or causes that explain a correlation, we need to distinguish **independent variables** from **dependent variables.** An independent variable is one that produces an effect upon another variable. The variable affected is the dependent one. In the example just mentioned, academic achievement is the independent variable and occupational income the dependent variable. The distinction refers to the direction of the causal relation we are investigating. The same factor may be an independent variable in one study, and a dependent variable in another. It all depends what causal processes are being analyzed. If we were looking at the effects of differences in occupational income upon lifestyles, occupational income would then be the independent variable rather than the dependent one.

To find out whether a correlation between variables is a causal connection we use **controls,** which means we hold some variables constant in order to look at the effects of others. By doing this, we are able to judge between explanations of observed correlations, separating causal from noncausal relationships. For example, researchers studying child development have claimed that there is a causal connection between maternal deprivation in infancy and serious personality problems in adulthood. ("Maternal deprivation" means that an infant is separated from its mother for a long period—several months or more—during the early years of its life.) How might we test whether there really is a causal relationship between maternal deprivation and later personality disorders? We would do so by trying to control, or "screen out," other possible influences that might explain the correlation.

One source of maternal deprivation is the admission of a child to a hospital for a lengthy period, during which it is separated from its parents. Is it attachment to the mother, however, that really matters? Perhaps if a child receives love and attention from *other* people during infancy, he or she might subsequently be a stable person? To investigate these possible causal connections, we would have to compare cases where children were deprived of regular care from anyone, with other instances in which children were separated from their mothers, but received love and care from someone else. If the first group developed severe personality difficulties, but the second group did not, we would suspect that regular care from *someone* in infancy is what matters, regardless of whether or not it is the mother. (In fact, children do seem to prosper normally as long as they have a loving,

The possible causal relationship between pornography and child molestation, which gave rise to this protest, is one of many current social concerns studied by sociologists (and others).

stable relationship with someone looking after them—this does not have to be the mother herself.)

Identifying Causes

There are a large number of possible causes that could be invoked to explain any given correlation. How can we ever be sure that we have covered them all? The answer is that we cannot be sure. We would never be able to carry out, and interpret the results of, a piece of sociological research satisfactorily if we were compelled to test for the possible influence of every causal factor we could imagine as potentially relevant. Identifying causal relationships is normally guided by previous research into the area in question. If we do not have some reasonable idea beforehand of the causal mechanisms involved in a correlation we would probably find it very difficult to discover what the real causal connections are. We would not know what to test *for*.

A good example of how difficult it is to be sure of the causal relations involved in a correlation is given by the long history of studies of smoking and lung cancer. Research has consistently demonstrated a strong correlation between the two. Smokers are more likely to contract lung cancer than nonsmokers, and very heavy smokers are more likely to do so than light smokers. The correlation can also be expressed the other way around. A high proportion of those who have lung cancer are smokers, or have smoked for long periods in their past. There have been so many studies confirming these correlations that it is generally accepted that a causal link is involved; but the exact causal mechanisms are thus far largely unknown.

However much correlational work is done on any issue, there always remains some doubt about possible causal relationships. Other interpretations of the correlation are possible. It has been proposed, for instance, that people who are predisposed to get lung cancer are also predisposed to smoke. In this view it is not smoking which causes lung cancer, but rather, some built-in biological disposition to smoking and cancer.

RESEARCH METHODS

AS WAS MENTIONED EARLIER, MANY DIFFERENT METHODS OF research are used in sociology, depending on the problems investigated. In this section, we will take a close look at several of these methods, including fieldwork, surveys, documentary research, experiments, and triangulation.

FIELDWORK

Various methods of research are used in sociology. In **participant observation** or **fieldwork** (the two terms can be used interchangeably), the investigator lives with a group or community being studied, and perhaps takes a direct part in their activities. An example of fieldwork research is Erving Goffman's celebrated study of behavior in an asylum (Goffman, 1961). Goffman spent several months in a mental hospital, working as an assistant athletic director. One or two of the staff knew him to be a sociological researcher, but the inmates were not told of his true identity. Hence Goffman was able to mix in an easy and informal fashion with the inmates of the asylum. He made contact even with the most severely ill patients in the "back wards." In this way he was able to build up a detailed picture of the life of the organization, together with the attitudes and views of those living and working in it. His research materials were the descriptions he wrote about daily life on the wards, together with accounts of conversations and contacts with the patients and staff.

He found, for example, that on the back wards, where many of the patients were resistant to ordinary social communication, the ward orderlies had one or two "working patients" from other wards, who helped them with their tasks. The working patients usually received a steady flow of favors as rewards for their cooperation, and mixed socially with the staff. This practice was not officially approved of by the hospital authorities, but was in fact essential for the smooth operation of the organization. An example comes from the field notes that Goffman kept, recording each day's activities:

> Am eating with a patient-friend in one of the large patient cafeterias. He says, "The food is good here but I don't like canned salmon." He then excuses himself, dumps his plateful of food into the waste-bucket, and goes to the dietary section of the steamtray line, coming back with a plate of eggs. He smiles in a mocking conspiratorial way and says: "I play pool with the attendant who looks after that." (Goffman, 1961)

Goffman managed to see the asylum from the point of view of the patients rather than in terms of the medical categories applied to them by the psychiatrists. "It is my belief," he wrote, "that any group of persons, primitives, pilots or patients, develop a life of their own that becomes meaningful, reasonable, and normal once you get close to it" (Goffman, 1961). Goffman's work indicates that what looks "insane" to an outside observer is not quite so irrational when seen in the context of the hospital. Asylums involve forms of discipline,

Fieldwork among Peruvian Indians.

dress, and behavior that make it almost impossible for inmates to behave like people in the outside world. When they were admitted to the hospital, patients' personal possessions were mostly taken away from them, they were undressed, bathed, and disinfected and issued with institutional clothing. From then on, virtually all their behavior occurred under the gaze of staff. There was very little privacy and staff often treated patients as though they were children. As a consequence, they developed patterns of behavior that seem bizarre to the outsider, but were in some part attempts to cope with the unusual demands of their environment.

The Demands of Fieldwork

A fieldworker cannot just "be present" in a community, but must explain and justify her or his presence to its members. The confidence and cooperation of the community or group must be obtained, and sustained over a period of time, if any worthwhile results are to be achieved. The conditions under which fieldworkers might have to live, especially when studying cultures very different from their own, may be difficult to adjust to. For a long while it was traditional for research based on participant observation to exclude any account of the hazards or problems that had to be overcome. More recently, the published reminiscences and diaries of fieldworkers have been more open about these. There are frequently feelings of loneliness to be coped with—it is not easy to "fit in" a community to which a person does not really belong. The researcher may be constantly frustrated because the members of the group or community refuse to talk frankly about themselves: direct queries may be welcomed in some cultural contexts but meet with a chilly silence in others. Some types of fieldwork may even be physically dangerous—for instance, a researcher studying a delinquent gang might be seen as a police informer, or might become unwittingly embroiled in conflicts with rival groups.

Like most types of social research, fieldwork is normally a one-sided endeavor, so far as those whose behavior is studied are concerned. The selection of a group for study is usually decided solely by the researcher; its members are rarely consulted in advance or involved in the design of the project (Georges and Jones, 1980). It is not surprising that fieldworkers are sometimes met with suspicion, or that attempts at field research quite frequently have to be abandoned as soon as they are initiated.

One of the very first anthropological fieldworkers, Frank Hamilton Cushing, who studied the Zuñi Indians of New Mexico, wrote an account of the problems he experienced (as well as the rewards he obtained) (Cushing, 1967; orig. pub. 1882–83). When he first arrived among the Zuñi, Cushing took numerous small gifts, and made various attempts to ingratiate himself with the members of the community. The Zuñi were reasonably friendly to him, but strenuously refused to let him study their religious ceremonials. Their leader tried to compel him to leave, but Cushing was eventually permitted to remain, if he agreed to adopt some of the Indian ways—to show that he did not regard their beliefs and practices as foolish. He was obliged to wear Zuñi clothing, which he found ill-fitting and uncomfortable; he had to eat Zuñi food; his hammock was torn down, and he was made to sleep on sheepskins on the floor, like the Zuñi themselves. One of his most difficult moments came when he was told that he was expected to take a wife, and a woman was sent to live with him. He tried to ignore her attentions, but without success. He was forced eventually to send her away, although this brought dishonor upon her in the eyes of the Zuñi.

Since then, the Zuñi—like many other American Indian groups—have become used to the visits of researchers, but their relationship with them has frequently been tense. The archaeologist F. W. Hodge aroused their enmity in the 1920s by starting excavations in one of their ancient religious shrines (Pandey, 1972). He was made to leave, and the cameras of his expedition's photographer were smashed. The celebrated anthropologist Ruth Benedict was better received among the Zuñi when she arrived to carry out fieldwork in the community not long afterwards. A Zuñi interpreter afterwards said that she was polite and distributed money generously; but the interpreter also felt Benedict's published descriptions of Zuñi life were not well founded, as she did not take an active part (as Cushing had done) in many aspects of Zuñi life. On various occasions since then other field-workers have been expelled from the Zuñi community. One man asked a researcher visiting more recently, "Are we still so primitive that you anthropologists have to come to study us every summer?" (Pandey, 1975).

The Advantages and Limitations of Fieldwork

Fieldwork—where it is successful—provides much richer informa-tion about social life than most other types of research method. Once we understand how things look "from the inside" of a given group, we are likely to have a much better understanding than before of why those involved act as they do. Fieldwork is virtually the only method available when the researcher is studying a group whose culture is largely unknown to outsiders, and has to be "learned" before their activities become fully comprehensible. For this reason, it is the main research method used in anthropology, which is concerned with doc-umenting and understanding non-Western cultures. However, it is used very widely in sociology as well. Fieldwork gives the investiga-tor more flexibility than other methods (such as questionnaires). The researcher in the field is able to adjust to novel or unexpected circum-stances and follow up leads that develop in the process of the research itself. Fieldwork is probably more likely to turn up unexpected re-sults than most other methods of investigation. The researcher may discover with a jolt that his or her preconceived ideas about the group or community in question were completely wrong. Fieldwork also has its limitations: only fairly small groups or communities can be studied in this way; and much depends upon the skill of the re-searcher in gaining the confidence of the individuals involved. Fail-ing this, the research is unlikely to get off the ground at all.

SURVEYS

There are usually problems of generalization involved in interpreting field studies. How can we be sure that what is found in one context will apply in other situations? This is usually less of a problem in **sur-vey** research, although such work has shortcomings of its own. In a survey, questionnaires are either mailed, or given directly in inter-views, to a selected group of people—sometimes as many as several thousand. Fieldwork is best suited for in-depth studies of social life. Survey research tends to produce information that is less detailed, but which we can be fairly confident applies over a broad area.

"Anthropologists!
Anthropologists!"

Standardized and Open-Ended Questionnaires

There are two sorts of questionnaires used in surveys. Some questionnaires have a *standardized* set of questions, to which only a fixed range of responses is possible. Either the respondents or the researcher mark certain categories of reply to the questions asked—for instance, "Yes/No/Don't know," or "Very likely/Likely/Unlikely/Very unlikely." Fixed-choice surveys have the advantage that responses are easy to compare and tabulate, since only a small number of categories are involved. On the other hand, because they do not allow for subtleties of opinion or verbal expression, the information they yield is likely to be restricted in scope. Other types of questionnaire are *open-ended,* giving opportunity for respondents to express their views in their own words: they are not limited to ticking fixed-choice responses. Open-ended questionnaires are more flexible and provide richer information than standardized ones. The researcher can follow up answers to probe more deeply into what the respondent thinks about any particular issues. On the other hand, because they are not so strictly standardized, responses may be more difficult to compare than where the choice of answers is fixed.

Survey questions have to be carefully constructed if the results are to be of value. A question like "What do you think of the government?" is worthless because it is much too vague. If they were able to answer it at all, respondents would interpret what the researcher meant in quite different ways. Survey researchers also have to pay particular attention to avoiding *leading* questions. A leading question is one expressed in such a way as to encourage a definite type of response. A question that begins "Do you agree that . . . ?" is leading, since it invites agreement from the respondent. A more neutral question would be one that begins "What is your opinion of . . . ?" There are many other sources of possible distortion or ambiguity in framing questions. For instance, a question may state a double choice: "Is your health better or worse now than it was a year ago?" The double choice is between "better-worse" and "now-then." A clearer formulation would be "Is your health better now than it was a year ago?" (Smith, 1975). Respondents might well answer "yes" or "no" to both questions; in the former case, the researcher could not interpret this. Questions should be as simple as possible so as to avoid ambiguous responses.

Questionnaire items are normally ordered so that a team of interviewers can ask the questions in the same predetermined order, recording responses in a fixed way. All the items have to be readily understandable to interviewer and interviewees alike for a major survey to be administered. In the large national surveys undertaken regularly by government agencies and research organizations, interviews are carried out more or less simultaneously across the whole country. Those who conduct the interviews and analyze the results could not do their work effectively if they constantly had to contact each other to check ambiguities in the questions or answers (Madge, 1985).

Questionnaires have to be carefully designed with a view to the characteristics of respondents. Will they see the point that the researcher has in mind by asking a particular question? Have they enough information to answer usefully? *Will* they answer? The terms with which the researcher may be working might be unfamiliar to the respondents. For instance, the question "What is your marital status?" might not be understood. It would be more appropriate to ask, "Are you single, married, or divorced?" Most surveys are preceded by *pilot studies* in order to pick up difficulties not anticipated by the investigator. A pilot study is a "trial run" in which a questionnaire is given to just a few people. Any difficulties found can be ironed out before the main survey is done.

Sampling

Often sociologists are interested in the characteristics of large numbers of individuals (for example, the political attitudes of the American electorate). It would be impossible to study all these individuals directly. In such situations, the research concentrates upon a proportion of the overall number of individuals—a sample of the total. It is usually possible to be fairly confident that results derived from a survey of a population sample can be generalized to the whole of that population. Studies of only some two to three thousand American voters, for instance, can give a very accurate indication of the attitudes and voting intentions of the whole population. But to achieve such accuracy, a sample must be *representative*. Representative **sampling** means ensuring that the section of individuals studied is typical of the population as a whole. Sampling is more complex than it might seem, and statisticians have developed various rules for working out the correct size and nature of samples.

A particularly important procedure is *random sampling,* in which a sample is chosen so that every member of the population concerned has the same probability of being included. The most sophisticated way of obtaining a random sample is to give each member of the population a number, and then use a computer to generate random numbers from which the sample is derived—for instance by picking every tenth number in a random series.

Example: *The People's Choice*

One of the most famous early examples of survey research was *The People's Choice,* a study carried out by Paul Lazarsfeld and a number of colleagues nearly half a century ago (Lazarsfeld, Berelson, and Gaudet, 1948). The study pioneered several of the main techniques of survey research in use to this day. At the same time, however, its shortcomings show rather clearly the limitations of the survey-research method. *The People's Choice* was based upon an investigation into the voting intentions of residents of Erie County, Ohio, during the 1940 campaign for the U.S. presidency. The study influenced the design of many subsequent political polls, not just those conducted by academic researchers (Clemens, 1983). In order to probe a little more deeply than a single questionnaire would do, the investigators interviewed each member of a sample of voters on seven separate occasions. The aim was to trace, and understand the reasons for, alterations in voting intentions.

The research was set up with a number of definite hypotheses in view. One was that relationships and events close to voters in a community influence voting intentions more than distant world affairs. The findings on the whole confirmed this hypothesis. The researchers developed sophisticated measurement techniques for analyzing political attitudes; yet their work was also strongly influenced by theoretical ideas and made significant contributions to theoretical thinking. Among the concepts the researchers helped to introduce were those of *opinion leaders* and the *two-step flow of communication.*

Some individuals—opinion leaders—tend to shape the political opinions of those around them. They take the lead in influencing responses to political events, by interpreting them to those with whom they associate. People's views on the political system are not just formed in a direct fashion, but in a "two-step" process: the views expressed by opinion leaders, filtered through personal relationships, influence the responses other individuals take towards political issues of the day.

The study was admired by many, but has also been widely criticized. Lazarsfeld and his colleagues claimed they were "interested in all the conditions which determine the political behavior of people." As critics pointed out, their research in fact only illuminated certain aspects of political behavior. The study contained little discussion of the actual institutions of the political system and how they work, concentrating instead upon political attitudes. The use of repeat interviewing—or what has come to be called a *panel study*—meant the findings were less superficial than many forms of survey research. But by their very nature, surveys normally only get at what people *say* about themselves—which may not correspond to what they really think or do.

Assessment

Surveys continue to be very widely used in sociological research. The reasons for the popularity of surveys are several (C. Marsh, 1982; Miller, 1983). Questionnaire responses can more easily be quantified and analyzed than material generated by most other research methods; large numbers of people can be studied; and, given sufficient funds, researchers can employ a research agency specializing in survey work to collect the material they need.

Many sociologists are critical, however, of what they see as overreliance on the survey method in sociological research. The results of surveys can often be easily quantified, and analyzed statistically; but critics argue that such quantification gives an appearance of precision to findings whose accuracy may be dubious, given the relatively shallow nature of most survey responses. There are other drawbacks too. Levels of non-response are sometimes high, especially where questionnaires are sent and returned through the mail. It is not uncommon for studies to be published based upon the results derived from little over half of those in a sample—although normally an effort is made to recontact non-respondents, or to substitute others for them. Little is known about those who choose not to respond to surveys, or refuse to be interviewed when the researcher turns up at the door. Survey research is often experienced as obtrusive and time-consuming by those approached (Converse and Schuman, 1974; Fitzgerald and Fuller, 1982; Goyder, 1988).

The conditions under which surveys are administered, and the language usually employed to describe the results, often distance survey research from the complexities of the flesh-and-blood individuals who react to the questions posed. Where mailed questionnaires are used, the investigator is so far removed from those concerned in the research that it may be difficult to remember that living people read and return the material that arrives through their mailboxes. Telephone surveys—used with increasing frequency in polling where "immediate" analysis is needed of opinions on a topical issue—are almost as anonymous. The language in which survey results are discussed, involving "subjects," "respondents," or "interviewees," expresses an abstracted and impersonal conception of the human individual. Treating human beings as essentially passive and reactive in this way is probably not just a convenient means of analyzing survey answers—it often expresses a limited and limiting view of human-reasoning processes.

Two people may hold an apparently similar attitude as measured by a questionnaire item, for example, but have quite different reasons for holding that view. Thus both might respond to a question on foreign policy by saying they believe "very strongly" that the United States should decrease the range of its military commitments abroad—and each would be counted as having the "same" view. But their real orientations might be utterly different from each other. One person might believe in a "fortress America"—in reducing overseas commitments because of an isolationist view that other countries should be left to deal with their own problems. The other might have a strong commitment to global disarmament, holding that the United States should use the influence it has in the world in other ways than by means of the deployment of force.

When interviewers have some flexibility in pursuing answers in some depth, they can sometimes cope with such problems. In general, the more intensive and direct the encounter between researcher and those involved in a study, the more informative and well-founded the conclusions that can be drawn from it. Survey-research findings need wherever possible to be complemented by in-depth material of the sort that field research provides.

DOCUMENTARY RESEARCH

Most discussions of research in sociology put their main emphasis upon fieldwork, survey research, or a combination of the two. **Documentary research**—the systematic use of printed or written materials for research investigation—is often regarded as less important. Yet there are very few pieces of fieldwork or survey research which do *not* involve some scrutiny of documentary materials. For example, in *The People's Choice,* newspapers and other materials were used extensively both in preparing and writing up the research. Documentary research, in one guise or another, is in fact one of the most widely used of all methods of gathering sociological data.

Some documents consulted most often in sociological research are public and private records, for example, government documents, church records, letters, or judicial records. These are usually termed *archival* sources, an archive being simply a place in which written records are deposited. The documents used in research virtually always also include information and findings produced by previous writers in the field in question. Many investigations are as much concerned with collecting together and analyzing materials from the work of others as with generating wholly new data.

An example of the use of historical documents is Anthony Ashworth's study of the sociology of trench warfare during the First World War (Ashworth, 1980). Ashworth was interested in analyzing what life was like for the men who had to endure being under constant fire, crammed together in close proximity with one another for weeks on end. To study the social relations they developed he drew upon a diversity of documentary sources. He used official histories of the war, including those written on different divisions and battalions. But he relied also upon archival materials, the notes and records kept informally by individual soldiers, personal accounts of war experiences, and other memoirs.

Although these materials were obviously in some respects very different from each other, by drawing upon such a diversity of sources Ashworth was able to develop a rich and detailed portrayal of life in the trenches. He discovered, for example, that soldiers developed their own norms about how often they would engage in combat with the enemy, often effectively ignoring the commands of the officers. For example, on Christmas Day the soldiers on both sides, the Germans and the Allies, suspended hostilities, and in one place even staged an impromptu soccer match with one another.

A major subtype of documentary research consists in the reanalysis of "data sets"—recorded research findings—generated by other investigators. Governments and other organizations regularly publish "official statistics" on a multitude of social phenomena: population, crime, marriage and divorce, suicide, rates of unemployment, and so forth. From the early development of sociology these have been used as a basis for sociological research. Researchers can utilize or reanalyze data derived from such statistics, applying that material to help resolve a given research problem. The data produced by governments is extremely extensive, and includes several major types of resource material. Population censuses, for example, are taken at regular inter-

Table 21.1	FOUR OF THE MAIN METHODS USED IN SOCIOLOGICAL RESEARCH	
Research Method	Strengths	Limitations
Fieldwork	Usually generates richer and more "in-depth" information than other methods.	Can only be used to study relatively small groups or communities.
	Provides flexibility for the researcher to alter strategies and follow up new leads that arise.	Findings might only apply to the groups or communities studied; it is not easy to generalize on the basis of a single fieldwork study.
Surveys	Make possible the efficient collection of data on large numbers of individuals.	The material gathered may be superficial; where a questionnaire is highly standardized, important differences between respondents' viewpoints may be glossed over.
	Allows for precise comparisons to be made between the answers of respondents.	Responses may be what people profess to believe rather than what they actually believe.
Documentary Research	Can provide sources of "in-depth" materials as well as data on large numbers—according to the type of documents studied.	The researcher is dependent on the sources that exist, which may be partial.
	Is often essential when a study is either wholly historical, or has a defined historical dimension.	The sources may be difficult to interpret in terms of how far they represent real tendencies—as in the case of some kinds of official statistics.
Experiments	The influence of specific variables can be controlled by the investigator.	Many aspects of social life cannot be brought into the laboratory.
	Experiments are usually easier for subsequent researchers to repeat.	The responses of those studied may be affected by their experimental situation.

vals, and provide data on many social and economic issues. Since response is obligatory, the material available from censuses is unusually comprehensive. Governments also carry out other surveys to provide more continuous information than that generated by the periodic censuses (Carley, 1981; Hakim, 1982).

Pitfalls in Documentary Research

Of course, documentary sources vary widely in terms of their accuracy, and a researcher making use of them has to evaluate their authenticity. Newspaper reports, for example, are notoriously casual in their standards of accuracy, particularly the more "popular" papers and magazines. Some years ago a letter was published in a prominent British newspaper, *The Guardian*. The letter writer, who called herself or himself "Student of the Press," had collected eight different newspaper accounts of the much-publicized wedding in Venice, Italy, of a young socialite, Ira von Furstenberg. The letter-writer reported that the press "has shown its enterprise and sturdy individuality. It refuses to conform to any agreed standard even when simple facts are in question." The bride was reported as being anywhere from thirty to seventy minutes late for the ceremony. Someone fell in the Grand Canal, but there were four different versions of who that was. The number of photographers said to be present varied from 50 to 250, and the guests from 250 to 600 (Mann, 1985).

Officially published statistics are of course more reliable. However, even such statistics must always be *interpreted* by the researcher, who has to be aware of the many limitations they can have. For example, all countries keep official statistics of different types of crime rates. Yet these reveal rather little about the real distribution of criminal behavior. The crimes registered are only those reported to the police. In the case of crimes like theft, these include only a small proportion of offenses that actually occur. Many simply never come to the notice of police. Large stores, for instance, report to the police only a fraction of the cases of shoplifting that occur each week— usually only when the store detective actually catches someone in the act. (For further discussion of crime statistics, see Chapter 5: "Deviance.")

EXPERIMENTS

In one respect, experiments offer major advantages over other research procedures. In an experimental situation, the researcher directly controls the relevant variables. An **experiment** can in fact be defined as an attempt, within artificial conditions established by an investigator, to test the influence of one or more variables upon others. Experiments are widely used in the natural sciences, but the scope for experimentation in sociology is restricted (Silverman, 1982). We can only bring small groups of individuals into a laboratory setting, and in a laboratory experiment, people know they are being studied and may behave differently from how they would in the outside world.

Nonetheless, experimental methods can sometimes usefully be applied in an illuminating way in sociology. An example is the ingenious experiment carried out by Philip Zimbardo (1972). Zimbardo set up a make-believe jail, allocating student volunteers to the roles of guards and prisoners. His aim was to see how playing these different roles led to changes in attitude and behavior. The results shocked the investigators, even though they were to some degree prepared for them. Those who played the guards quickly assumed an authoritarian manner, displaying real hostility towards the "prisoners." They started to order the "prisoners" around, verbally abuse and bully them. The others, by contrast, showed a mixture of apathy and rebelliousness often noted among inmates in real prison situations. These effects were so marked, and the level of tension so high, that the experiment had to be called off at an early stage. The researcher concluded that behavior in prisons is more influenced by the nature of the prison situation than by the individual characteristics of those involved.

OTHER RESEARCH METHODS

Interviews

There is no clear distinction between the survey method and interviews, since where questionnaires are directly administered, the researcher effectively interviews the respondents. Interviewing with a questionnaire is sometimes called "formal" or "controlled," to distinguish it from less-structured interviews, in which the interviewee is allowed to discuss freely various aspects of a topic. Some interview studies do not utilize a questionnaire at all. People may sometimes be interviewed at considerable length; where the objective is to develop in-depth information only a few respondents may be involved. Extended interviews provide richer material than is usually available from surveys. The disadvantages are that the influence of the interviewer may be greater, possibly affecting the results; and it is more difficult to compare responses in a rigorous way (Brenner, 1978).

Life Histories

Life histories consist of biographical material assembled about particular individuals—usually as recounted by themselves. No other method of research can give us as much detail about the development of people's beliefs and attitudes over time. Life histories are particularly valuable when research is concerned with connections between psychological development and social processes. However, such studies rarely rely wholly upon the memories of the persons involved. Normally documentary sources—such as letters, contemporary reports, or newspaper descriptions—are used to expand upon and check the validity of information provided by those concerned. There are different views about the value that can be placed upon life-history material. Some feel the method is too unreliable to provide useful research information. Others believe that life histories offer sources of insight that few other sociological research methods can match.

Life histories have been successfully employed in studies of major importance and are widely used in anthropology as well as sociology (Bertaux, 1981). A celebrated early study that used life history materials extensively was *The Polish Peasant in Europe and America,* by W. I. Thomas and Florian Znaniecki, the five volumes of which were first published between 1918 and 1920 (Thomas and Znaniecki, 1966). Thomas and Znaniecki were able to provide a much more sensitive and subtle account of the experience of migration than would have been possible without the life-history materials they collected. A more recent work, which became a bestseller, was Studs Terkel's book, *Working* (1977). The subtitle of Terkel's book was "people talk about what they do all day and how they feel about what they do." It provided a rich and moving account of the views of Americans about their daily work routines.

Life histories do not necessarily cover the whole span of an individual's life, or all of its main aspects. For instance, Edwin H. Sutherland published a well-known work based upon the life history of Chic Conwell, a professional thief; the material presented was largely limited to Conwell's criminal activities (Sutherland and Conwell, 1937). Life histories shade over into *oral history* more generally —verbal accounts of the past supplied by those who lived through the events.

Diaries

Diaries are sometimes used when sociologists want to keep track of the day-to-day activities of individuals in a given social environment. Fieldwork and surveys may not give us enough information about the regular round of people's lives. If we want to build up a picture of what they do at various parts of the day, and at different times of the day or month, it is often helpful to get them to keep their own records. Once again, there are very few studies that rely upon such information alone; it is nearly always used together with material gleaned by other methods.

Conversation Analysis

Tape recorders and videos are increasingly employed as means of generating sociological research materials. Both are frequently used in

conversation analysis, the study of how conversations are carried on in real-life settings. Using a tape recorder, all the audible characteristics of a conversation between two or more individuals can be put on record. Since we use facial expressions and gestures to convey meaning when we talk to one another, video recordings provide an even more complete register of the unfolding of a conversational exchange. Although much of the richness of the original context is lost, by the use of appropriate notation, recorded conversations can be transcribed onto the printed page. (For an illustration, see Chapter 4: "Social Interaction and Everyday Life.")

Many studies involving conversational analysis have been published over the past few years, offering a variety of insights into the nature of human interaction. An example is William B. Sanders's study of a very special type of conversation: police interrogations. Interrogation involves conversation, but not "just any talk"—as is indicated in one of the favorite phrases of police melodramas, "I'll ask the questions!" Sandero was able to analyze the distinctive character of interrogation so as to disclose features of the exchange that might otherwise escape notice. For instance, interrogators often do not actually say very much at all, stimulating the victim to talk by grunts and deliberately prolonged pauses (Sanders, 1974).

Conversation analysis can only be utilized in small-group settings, and frequently covers what might seem to be purely trivial aspects of day-to-day life. Its importance in sociology is much greater than would appear, however. Conversation and talk, after all, are universal features of social activity in both informal and more structured settings of interaction (see Chapter 4: "Social Interaction and Everyday Life").

TRIANGULATION

All research methods have their advantages and their limitations. Hence it is common to combine several methods in a single piece of research, using each to supplement and check upon the others, in a process known as **triangulation.** We can see the value of combining methods—and, more particularly, the problems and pitfalls of real sociological research—by looking at a specific research study.

An Example: Wallis and Scientology

Roy Wallis set out to investigate the movement known as Scientology. The founder of Scientology, L. Ron Hubbard, developed various religious doctrines that came to form the basis of a church. According to Scientology, we are all spiritual beings—Thetans—but we have neglected our spiritual nature. We can recover forgotten supernatural powers though training processes, which make us aware of our real spiritual capacities. Wallis admitted that he was first drawn to the research because of the "exotic" nature of Scientology. How could people believe in such apparently bizarre ideas? Scientology was very controversial, but had drawn a large following. Why had this particular movement, one of many new religious groups, become so prominent?

Initiating the research presented problems. Wallis knew that the leaders of the movement were likely to resist cooperating in sociological research because they had already been investigated by various government agencies. Reading about the movement's history, Wallis came across a book by one of its former members. He contacted that individual, and was eventually put in touch with a number of others who had also mostly severed their ties with Scientology. Many of these people agreed to be interviewed and some possessed a range of contacts with believers. These early interviewees also made available a range of papers and literature concerning their involvement with the movement. One such document was a mailing list of a Scientology organization. Wallis drew up and sent off a questionnaire to a sample of the names on the list. It proved to be so far out of date, however, that many of those to whom the questionnaires were sent were no longer living at the same address. Others had got on the list merely as a result of buying a single book on Scientology and had no real connections with the movement.

The survey thus turned out to be of limited value as a sample of Scientologists in general, although certain conclusions could be drawn from it. But it provided Wallis with a few further contacts. Among the completed questionnaires returned, some respondents indicated they would be willing to be interviewed. Wallis therefore travelled around the United States and Britain conducting interviews and collecting more documentary information at the same time. He began with a fixed schedule of questions, but soon found it more profitable to adopt a looser and more flexible style, allowing respondents to talk at length on matters they regarded as important. Some respondents were willing to be tape-recorded, others were not. Believing he needed more understanding of the doctrines of Scientology, Wallis applied to follow an introductory communications course put on by a Scientology group. He thus began participant observation, without revealing his identity as a researcher.

Staying at the Scientology lodging house during the course, Wallis found the role of covert participant observer difficult to sustain. Conversation with other members and progress in the course required a display of commitment to ideas that he did not share. Expressing disagreement with these views led to such difficulties that it became clear he could not continue without publicly assenting to some of the main principles of Scientology. Hence, he slipped away quietly without finishing the course. Later he wrote to the leaders of the movement, saying he was a sociologist engaged in research into Scientology. Pointing out that the movement had been under much attack, he suggested that his own research would provide a more balanced view. Subsequently he visited the headquarters of the sect in Britain, speaking to one of the officials there. This person was concerned about his having dropped out of the communications course, and knew about the questionnaires sent to the list of Scientologists. The official nonetheless gave Wallis permission to interview some staff members and students, supplying addresses to be contacted in the United States. Eventually Wallis felt he had enough material to publish a book on the Scientologists (Wallis, 1977).

Wallis faced particular difficulties because his research was about an organization jealous of its secrecy. In other respects, the problems he encountered, together with the need to use a combination of research methods, are typical of much sociological research. All of the material he gathered was partial, but combined together, the various methods he used produced an important and influential study.

ETHICAL PROBLEMS OF RESEARCH: THE RESPONDENTS ANSWER BACK

ALL RESEARCH CONCERNED WITH HUMAN BEINGS, NOT only in sociology, can pose ethical dilemmas (Barnes, 1979). Medical experiments are routinely carried out on human subjects, sometimes upon the sick and the dying. It is not easy to say to what degree such experiments are ethically justifiable. In order to be effective, experiments in medicine may involve misleading patients. In testing a new drug, one group of patients might actually be given the drug in question; others are told they are receiving the drug, but are not in fact doing so. Believing that one is being given a healing drug might itself lead to positive effects on health; this is controlled by only giving the real drug to half the patients involved in the experimental trials. But is this ethical? It surely approaches the limits of what can be justified, if there is a possibility that the real drug can have beneficial results, or save lives. On the other hand, if such procedures are not followed, it may be difficult or impossible to find out how effective the drug actually is.

Similar problems arise in sociological research wherever any deception is practiced upon those involved. An example is the celebrated, and highly controversial, series of experiments carried out by Stanley Milgram (1973). Milgram wished to see to what degree people would hurt others if they received commands from an authoritative source to do so. An electric shock machine was rigged up, by means of which the volunteers in the experiment were required to administer shocks to individuals who failed to respond correctly in a memory test. The experiments involved systematically deceiving those who volunteered to participate. They were not told the true purpose of the study, believing it to be an investigation into memory. Although they imagined they were delivering real shocks to other experimental subjects, in fact these were accomplices of the researcher feigning their reactions because the "shock machine" was in fact a fake.

Was such deception ethical, particularly since the people studied found the experience extremely unsettling? The general consensus of critics is that this investigation went "too far" since the deception involved was potentially psychologically harmful to those who volunteered to take part. But it is not at all clear where a line can be drawn in research between "excusable" and "inexcusable" deception. Milgram's research has become very well known, not just because of the deception involved, but because of the striking nature of the results he obtained. For the research indicated that many people will act brutally towards others if they are "under orders" to do so.

Wallis was less than truthful to those whose behavior he studied, because he did not disclose his identity as a sociologist when registering for the Scientology course. Moreover, he apparently gave his written agreement to conditions he did not intend to observe—for he proposed to publish his work as a sociological study. He tried to avoid any direct lies, but he did not disclose the real reason for his participation. Was this unethical? The answer is not obvious (Dingwall, 1980). The research might not have got as far as it did if Wallis had been completely frank from the beginning. It could be argued that it is in the interest of society at large to know what goes on inside organizations of a secretive kind, so we might consider his strategy justified.

Ethical issues are also often posed in sociology, however, by the potential consequences of the publication or utilization of research findings. Those who are the subjects of a particular study might find its results offensive, either because they are portrayed in a light they find unappealing, or because attitudes and behavior they would prefer to keep private are brought out into the open. In most settings of social life people engage in practices that they do not want to become public knowledge. For instance, some people working in factories and offices regularly "pilfer" materials; nurses sometimes wrap terminal patients in morgue sheets before their death, and give them little care; prison guards might accept bribes from inmates, and recognize certain prisoners as "trusties," having them do tasks the guards should take care of themselves.

In most circumstances, notwithstanding possible hostile reactions from those concerned, or from others, it is the obligation of the sociologist to make their findings public. Indeed, this is one of the main contributions sociological research can make to the fostering of a free and open society. "A good study," it has been said, "will make somebody angry" (Becker, 1976). There seems no reason for the sociological researcher to fear this, if the research work was done in a competent fashion and the conclusions drawn are justified by good arguments. But sociological investigators do have to consider carefully the possible consequences of the publication of findings and the form in which these should be announced. Often the researcher will wish to discuss these issues directly with those affected before deciding on a final form for publication.

PROBLEMS IN PUBLICATION: WALLIS'S EXPERIENCE

Prior to its publication, Wallis sent the manuscript of his book to the Scientology headquarters. As a result of the hostile responses of the Scientology officials, he altered the manuscript. Later they sent more detailed comments. Although he made further changes, the Scientologists then took the step of sending the manuscript to a lawyer experienced in libel cases. On his advice, there were further deletions. A commentary on the book, highly critical of Wallis's research methods and conclusions, was prepared by a sociologist who was also a practicing Scientologist. This was eventually incorporated into the published work as an appendix. The Scientologists also published an article analyzing the research in one of their own periodicals. In their discussion they quoted the Panel on Privacy and Behavioral Research set up by the U.S. President's Office of Science and Technology, which stressed that "informed consent" should be obtained by researchers engaged in work on human subjects. Informed consent, they emphasized, had not been secured. Wallis's published work, they went on to add, was based on information gained from a small circle of people, mostly hostile to the Church of Scientology.

At a later date, Wallis became involved in further entanglements arising from his research. In 1984, he was named as a potential witness in an extended legal battle between the Scientology church and another author of a book on Scientology. Wallis had contacted that author while carrying out his own work, and she had provided him with documents and information about the Scientologists and her own contacts with them. As a result of a Californian court order, he was obliged to release some of this material—which he had in fact received in confidence. Fortunately, the information in question was of no great significance to any of the parties concerned. But if it had been more damaging, Wallis would have had a difficult decision to make—to break a confidence, or resist the legal authorities (Wallis, 1987).

Wallis was dealing with a powerful and articulate group who were able to persuade him to modify earlier versions of his research reports. Many individuals or groups studied by sociologists and other social scientists do not have similar influence. If they did, the difficulties in which Wallis found himself might be much more common than they actually are.

It surely should be usual procedure for researchers to secure informed consent in all but a minority of research studies. There are bound to be some circumstances in which this principle is not fully followed. If we wish to study police brutality, there would probably be little chance of doing so effectively if we openly approached police agencies with this stated purpose. The aim of the research would have to be to some degree disguised to achieve any degree of cooperation. In such an instance, this might be justified given the potential importance of the results to the wider community. The overriding obligation of the sociologist, and every other social scientist, however, is to promote free and open discussion of social issues. Occasionally deception—paradoxically—can be the means of achieving this, by bringing to general awareness issues that otherwise would remain hidden from the general public.

THE INFLUENCE OF SOCIOLOGICAL RESEARCH

SOCIOLOGICAL RESEARCH IS RARELY OF INTEREST ONLY TO the intellectual community of sociologists. Its results are often either read by, or come to the knowledge of, many others in society. This is something that has far-reaching implications. Sociology is not just *about* the study of modern societies, it has become a major element in the continuing life of those societies themselves.

Take the example mentioned in Chapter 1 ("Sociology: Problems and Perspectives"): the changes going on in marriage, divorce, and the family. Very few people living in a modern society do not have some knowledge of the changing patterns of marriage and divorce as a result of the research into these matters. Our thinking and behavior are affected by sociological knowledge in complex and often subtle ways, thus reshaping the very field of sociological investigation. A way of putting this is to say that sociology stands in a *reflexive* relation to the human beings whose behavior is studied. "Reflexive" describes the interchange between sociological research and human behavior as people get to know about such research and think about its implications for their own actions. We should not be surprised that, while they might sometimes contradict our common-sense beliefs, sociological findings and common sense run quite closely together. The reason is not that sociology comes up with findings that we know already. It is rather that sociological research continually helps influence what our common-sense knowledge of society actually *is*.

SUMMARY

1. All research begins from a *research problem,* which interests or puzzles the investigator. Research problems may be suggested by gaps in the existing literature, theoretical debates, or practical issues in the social world. There are a number of clear steps in the development of research strategies—although these are rarely followed exactly in actual research.

2. Sound sociological research involves the selection of a reliable approach for analyzing a particular social phenomenon. Three aspects of sociological inquiry can be distinguished. *Research strategy* concerns the planning of any particular piece of research. *Research methodology* deals with the overall logic and principles of research. *Research methods* are how research is actually carried out, (e.g., by fieldwork or surveys).

3. In fieldwork, or *participant observation,* the researcher spends lengthy periods of time with a group or community being studied. A second method, *survey research,* involves sending or administering questionnaires to samples of a larger population. Documentary research uses printed materials, from archives or other resources, as a source for information. Other research methods include *experiments, in-depth interviews,* the use of *life histories* and *diaries,* and *conversation analysis.*

4. Each of these various methods of research has its limitations. For this reason, researchers will often combine two or more methods in their work, each being used to check or supplement the material obtained from the others. This process is called *triangulation*.

5. Sociological research often poses ethical dilemmas. These may arise either where deception is practiced against those who are the subjects of the research, or where the publication of research findings might adversely affect the feelings or lives of those studied. There is no entirely satisfactory way to deal with these issues, but all researchers have to be sensitive to the dilemmas they pose.

6. Sociological research stands in a complex relation to its subject matter—human social behavior. Research findings are routinely and constantly reincorporated back into social life, thus becoming part of "common-sense knowledge." This process represents a *reflexive* connection between sociology and social activity.

BASIC CONCEPTS

RESEARCH METHODS
CAUSATION
CORRELATION

IMPORTANT TERMS

HYPOTHESIS	DOCUMENTARY RESEARCH
CAUSAL RELATIONSHIP	EXPERIMENT
VARIABLE	LIFE HISTORIES
INDEPENDENT VARIABLE	CONVERSATION ANALYSIS
DEPENDENT VARIABLE	TRIANGULATION
CONTROLS	MEAN (APP. I)
PARTICIPANT OBSERVATION	MODE (APP. I)
(FIELDWORK)	MEDIAN (APP. I)
SURVEY	STANDARD DEVIATION (APP. I)
SAMPLING	CORRELATION COEFFICIENTS (APP. I)

APPENDIX: I. STATISTICAL TERMS

Research in sociology quite often makes use of statistical techniques in the analysis of findings. Some of these techniques are highly sophisticated and complex, but those used most commonly are easy to understand. The most widely employed are *measures of central tendency* (ways of calculating averages) and *correlation coefficients* (measures of the degree to which one variable relates consistently to another).

There are three methods of calculating averages, each of which has certain advantages and certain shortcomings. Take as a working example the amount of personal wealth owned by thirteen individuals. Suppose the thirteen own amounts as follows:

$ 000 (zero)	$ 80,000
$ 5,000	$ 100,000
$10,000	$ 150,000
$20,000	$ 200,000
$40,000	$ 400,000
$40,000	$10,000,000
$40,000	

The **mean** corresponds to the "average" as it is most often understood in ordinary usage. It is arrived at by adding together the wealth of all thirteen people, then dividing the result by that number (i.e., thirteen). The total is $11,085,000; dividing this by thirteen, we reach a mean of $852,692. The mean is often a useful calculation because it is based on the whole range of data provided. However, it can be misleading where one, or a small number, of cases are very different from the majority. In the above example, the mean is not in fact a very appropriate measure of central tendency, because the presence of one very large figure, $10,000,000, skews all the rest. One might get the impression from it that most of the people earn far more than they actually do.

In such instances, one of two other measures may be used. The **mode** is the figure that occurs most frequently in a given range of data. In the example given here, it is $40,000. The problem with the mode is that it does not take into account the overall distribution of the data, (i.e., the range of figures covered). The most frequently occurring case in a particular set of figures is not necessarily representative of their distribution as a whole, and may not be a very useful "average." Thus $40,000 does not give a very accurate idea of central tendency, because it is too close to the lower end of the figures.

The third measure is the **median,** which is the figure in the *middle* of any set of figures. In the example given here, this would be the seventh figure, $80,000. If there had been an even set of number figures in our example—for instance, twelve instead of thirteen—the median would be calculated by taking the mean of the two middle cases, figures six and seven. Like the mode, the median gives no idea of the actual *range* of the data measured. Sometimes a researcher will use more than one measure of central tendency, in order not to provide a deceptive picture of an average. More often, the **standard deviation** for the data in question would be calculated. A standard deviation is a way of calculating the *degree of dispersal,* or the range of a set of figures—which in this case ranges from zero to $10,000,000.

Correlation coefficients offer a useful way of expressing how closely connected two (or more) variables are with one another. Where two variables correlate completely, we can speak of a perfect *positive* correlation—expressed as a coefficient of 1.0. Where no relation is found between two variables—two variables that simply have no consistent connection at all—the coefficient is zero. A perfect *negative* correlation, expressed as −1.0, exists when two variables are in a completely *inverse* relation to one another. Perfect correlations are virtually never found in the social sciences. Correlations of the other of 0.6 or more, whether positive or negative, are usually regarded as indicating a strong degree of connection between the variables being analyzed. Positive correlations of this level might be found between, say, social class background and voting behavior. The higher a person is on the socioeconomic scale, the more likely he or she is to vote Republican rather than Democrat.

APPENDIX: 2. READING A TABLE

You will often come across tables in reading sociological literature. Tables sometimes look complex, but are in fact nearly always easy to decipher if a few basic principles are followed; with practice, these will become automatic. Do not succumb to the temptation always to skip over tables; they contain information in concentrated form, which can be "read off" more quickly than would be necessary if the same material were expressed in words. By becoming skilled in the interpretation of tables you will also be able to check how far the conclusions a writer draws from the material in question actually seem justified. Using the accompanying table as an example, the steps to follow in grasping the content of a table are these:

1. Read the title in full. Tables frequently have longish titles, which represent the attempt of the researcher or statistician to state accurately the nature of the information conveyed. The title of the table given here gives first, the *subject* of the material covered; second, the fact that it provides material for *comparison;* and third, the fact that material is offered only for a limited number of countries.

2. See if there are explanatory comments or notes about the data. A note at the foot of the table given here, linked to the subhead,

CAR OWNERSHIP: INTERNATIONAL COMPARISONS OF SEVERAL SELECTED COUNTRIES		
Number of cars* per thousand of the adult population		
1971	1981	1984
BRAZIL 12	78	84
CHILE 19	45	56
FRANCE 261	348	360
GREECE 30	94	116
IRELAND 141	202	226
ITALY 210	322	359
JAPAN 100	209	227
SWEDEN 291	348	445
BRITAIN 224	317	343
UNITED STATES 448	536	540
WEST GERMANY 247	385	412
YUGOSLAVIA 43	114	125

* Includes all licensed cars

Source: United Nations Annual Bulletin of Transport Statistics; World Road Statistics, International Road Federation, reported in *Social Trends,* (London: HMSO, 1987), p. 68.

points out that the data only cover licensed cars. This fact is important because in some countries the proportion of vehicles properly licensed may be less than in others. Notes may say how the material was collected, or why it is displayed in a particular way. If the data in the table have not been gathered by the researcher, but are based on findings originally reported elsewhere, a *source* will be given. The source usually gives some insight into how reliable the information is likely to be, as well as showing where you would have to look to find the original data on which it was based. In our table, the footnote makes clear that the data are abstracted from several different sources.

3. Read the *headings* along the top and left-hand side of the table. (Sometimes tables are arranged with "headings" at the foot rather than the top.) These tell you what type of information is contained in each row and column. In reading the table, each set of headings has to be kept in mind as you scan the figures. In the present table, the headings on the left give the countries involved, while the headings at the top refer to selected years in which levels of car ownership are compared.

4. Identify the *units* used—the figures in the body of the table may represent a number of cases, percentages, averages, or other measures. Sometimes it may be useful to convert the figures given in a table to a form more relevant for the purposes to which you wish to put it. If percentages are not provided, for example, it may be worthwhile calculating them. In the case given here, no percentages are provided, but it would be easy to work them out.

5. Consider the conclusions that might be reached from the information in the table. Most tables are discussed by the author presenting them, and what he or she has to say should of course be borne in mind when you assess the tabulated material yourself. However, you should also think about what further issues or questions may be suggested by the data given.

Several interesting trends can be seen in the figures in our table. First, the level of car ownership varies considerably between different countries. The number of cars per thousand people is nearly ten times greater in the United States than in Chile. Second, there are clear connections revealed in the table between car ownership and the level of affluence of a country. In fact, we could probably use car ownership ratios as rough indicators of differential prosperity. Third, in all countries represented, the level of car ownership increased from 1971 to 1984. But in some, the rate of increase is higher than in others—probably indicating differences in the degree to which countries have successfully generated economic growth.

CHAPTER TWENTY-TWO

THE DEVELOPMENT OF SOCIOLOGICAL THEORY

WHEN THEY FIRST START STUDYING SOCIOLOGY, MANY PEOple are puzzled by the diversity of approaches they encounter. Sociology is not a discipline in which there has ever been a body of theoretical ideas that everyone accepts as valid. Sociologists quite often quarrel among themselves about how to go about studying human behavior and how research results might best be interpreted. Why should this be so? Why can't sociologists agree with one another more consistently, as natural scientists seem able to do?

The answer to these questions is bound up with the very nature of sociology itself. Sociology is about our own lives and our own behavior. Studying ourselves is the most complex and difficult endeavor we can undertake. In all academic disciplines—including the natural sciences—there is far more disagreement over theoretical approaches than over empirical research, because empirical work can be directly checked, and often repeated if there are differing views about its factual findings. Theoretical disputes are always more dependent upon interpretation, and can rarely be decisively settled in the same way. In sociology, the difficulties inherent in subjecting our own behavior to study further complicate this problem.

Challenging though it may be, theoretical thinking is a central part of sociology. Factual materials do not "speak for themselves." Without a theoretical orientation, we would not know what to look for in beginning a study, or in interpreting the results. Theoretical thinking and empirical research are necessarily closely connected. However, the illumination of empirical analysis is not the only reason for the prime position of theoretical work in sociology. Theoretical thinking has to respond to general problems posed by the study of human social life, including issues that are to some extent philosophical in nature. Deciding to what extent sociology can and should be modeled upon the natural sciences, how we should best conceptualize human consciousness, action, and institutions—these are questions that do not admit of easy solutions. They have been handled in different ways in the various theoretical traditions that have sprung up in the discipline.

In this chapter, we shall analyze the development of the major **theoretical approaches** in sociology and identify the dilemmas to which they point. We shall start out by looking at the views of some of the founders of modern sociology—for many of the ideas they pioneered are still influential. We shall then analyze the theoretical perspectives that dominate the discipline in the present day and then go on to discuss some of the problems they raise.

EARLY ORIGINS

HUMAN BEINGS HAVE NO DOUBT ALWAYS BEEN CURIOUS about the sources of their own behavior. Yet our attempts to understand ourselves relied for thousands of years on ways of thinking, usually expressed in religious terms, passed down from generation to generation. The systematic study of human behavior and human society is a relatively recent enterprise, whose beginnings are found in the late eighteenth century. The background to this novel enterprise was the series of sweeping changes (referred to many times in this book) associated with industrialization and urbanism. The shattering of traditional ways of life prompted the endeavor to develop new understandings of both the social and the natural worlds.

AUGUSTE COMTE

No single individual, of course, can found a whole discipline, and there were many contributors to the early formation of sociological thinking. Pride of place is usually given to the French author, Auguste Comte (1789–1857), if only because he actually coined the word "sociology." Comte originally used the term "social physics" to refer to the new field of study. Since other writers were also beginning to use that term, and he wanted to separate his views from theirs, Comte invented a new word of his own to refer to the new subject he wished to establish. Comte regarded sociology as the last science to fully develop, but as the most significant and complex of all of them. Sociology, he believed, should contribute to the welfare of humanity; in the latter part of his career, he drew up ambitious plans for the reconstruction of French society in particular and future human societies in general.

August Comte

ÉMILE DURKHEIM

The work of Comte had a direct influence on another French writer, Émile Durkheim (1858–1917). Although he drew upon aspects of Comte's writing, Durkheim thought much of Comte's work too speculative and vague. He believed that Comte had not successfully carried out his program—to establish sociology on a scientific basis. To become scientific, according to Durkheim, sociology must study "social facts." That is to say, it must pursue the analysis of social institutions with the same objectivity as scientists achieve when studying nature. Durkheim's famous first principle of sociology was "Study social facts as *things*." By this he meant that social life can be analyzed as rigorously as objects or events in nature.

Like all the major founders of sociology, Durkheim was preoccupied with the changes transforming society in the nineteenth century. He tried to understand these changes by focusing on the development of the **division of labor** as part of the process of industrialization. The division of labor refers to the growth of ever more complex distinctions between different occupations in modern societies. Durkheim argued that the division of labor would gradually replace religion as the main basis of social cohesion. As the division of labor expands, people become more and more dependent on one another, because each person needs goods and services that those in other occupations supply. According to Durkheim, processes of change in the modern world are so rapid and intense they give rise to

Émile Durkheim

major social tensions, which he linked to **anomie.** Anomie is the feeling of aimlessness or purposelessness provoked by certain social conditions. Traditional moral controls and standards, which used to be supplied by religion, have been largely broken down by modern social development. As a consequence, many individuals in modern societies experience the feeling that their day-to-day lives lack meaning.

One of Durkheim's most famous studies was his sociological analysis of suicide (Durkheim, 1966; original edition, 1897). While suicide seems to be a purely personal act, the outcome of extreme personal unhappiness, Durkheim showed that social factors have a fundamental influence on suicidal behavior—anomie being one of these influences. Suicide rates show regular patterns from year to year, and these patterns can be explained sociologically. There are many objections that can be made against Durkheim's study, but it remains a classic work whose relevance to sociology today is by no means exhausted.

Karl Marx

KARL MARX

The ideas of Karl Marx contrast quite sharply with those of Comte and Durkheim. Marx was born in Germany in 1818, and died in England in 1883. Although originally trained in German traditions of thought, he spent much of his life in Britain and produced his major works there. Marx was not able to pursue a university career, since as a young man his political activities brought him into conflict with the German authorities. After a brief stay in France, he settled permanently in exile in Britain. Marx's writings cover a diversity of areas. Even his sternest critics regard his work a major contribution to the development of sociology, though Marx did not see himself as a "sociologist." Much of his writing concentrates on economic issues, but since he was always concerned with connecting economic problems to social institutions, his work is rich in sociological insights.

Marx's viewpoint was founded upon what came to be known as **historical materialism** (see Chapter 20: "Understanding Social Change"). It is not the ideas or values which human beings hold that are the main sources of social change, according to Marx; rather, social change is prompted primarily by economic influences. Such influences are clearly linked to the conflicts between classes, which provides the motive power of historical development. In Marx's words: "All human history thus far is the history of class struggles" (Marx and Engels, 1965; orig. pub., 1848).

Though he wrote about various phases of history, Marx concentrated on change in modern times. For him, the most important changes involved in the modern period were bound up with the development of **capitalism.** Capitalism is a system of production that contrasts radically with previous economic orders in history, involving as it does the production of goods and services sold to a wide range of consumers. Those who own capital—factories, machines, and large sums of money—form a ruling class. The mass of the population make up a class of wage workers, or a working class, who do not own the means of their livelihood, but have to find employment provided by the owners of capital. Capitalism is thus a class system, in which conflict between classes is a commonplace occurrence.

According to Marx, capitalism in the future would be supplanted by socialism or communism (he used these words interchangeably). In a socialist society, there would be no classes. Marx did not mean by this that all inequalities between individuals would disappear. Rather, societies would no longer be split into a small class who monopolized economic and political power and the large mass of people who benefited little from the wealth their labor created. The economic system would come under communal ownership, and a more egalitarian and participatory social order would be established.

For Marx, the study of the development and likely future of capitalism would provide the means of actively transforming it through political action. Marx's sociological observations were thus closely related to a political program—one that has had a far-reaching effect upon the twentieth-century world. Even following the changes in Eastern Europe, one-half of the world's population live in societies whose governments claim to derive their inspiration from Marx's ideas.

It is important to try to approach the study of Marx's work without prejudice. This is not easy, because the widespread influence of Marx's writings has produced major differences of opinion about their value—even among those who call themselves "Marxists" there are large differences. Many Marxists living in the West today, for example, are extremely critical of the Soviet Union and other communist countries, where Marx's ideas supposedly form the basis of the social system.

MAX WEBER

Like Marx, Max Weber (1864–1920) cannot simply be labeled a "sociologist"—his interests and concerns ranged across many disciplines.

Max Weber

Weber was born in Germany and spent the whole of his academic career there. He was somewhat depressive in character and for much of his life was unable to sustain a full-time teaching post in a university. A private income allowed him to devote himself to scholarship. Weber was an individual of extraordinarily wide learning: his writings covered the fields of economics, law, philosophy, and comparative history as well as sociology. Much of his work was concerned with the development of modern capitalism. He was influenced by Marx, but was also strongly critical of some of Marx's major views. He rejected the materialist conception of history and saw class conflict as being less significant than Marx did. In Weber's view, ideas and values have as much impact as economic conditions upon social change.

Some of Weber's most important writings were concerned with analyzing the distinctiveness of Western society and culture, as compared to those of other major civilizations. He produced extensive studies of the traditional Chinese empire, India, and the Near East (Weber, 1951; 1958; 1952). In the course of these researches, he made major contributions to the sociology of religion. Comparing the leading religious systems in China and India with those of the West, Weber concluded that certain aspects of Christian beliefs strongly influenced the rise of capitalism (see Chapter 14: "Religion").

One of the most persistent concerns of Weber's work was the study of **bureaucracy.** A bureaucracy is a large organization that is divided into offices based on specific functions and staffed by officials ranked according to a hierarchy. Industrial firms, government organizations, hospitals, and schools are all examples of bureaucracies. Weber believed the advance of bureaucracy to be an inevitable feature of our era. Bureaucracy makes it possible for these large organizations to run efficiently, but poses problems for effective democratic participation in modern societies. Bureaucracy involves the rule of experts, whose decisions are made without much consultation with those whose lives are affected by them.

Weber's contributions range over many other areas, including the study of the development of cities, systems of law, types of economy, and the nature of classes. He also produced a range of writings concerned with the overall character of sociology itself. Weber was more cautious than either Durkheim or Marx in proclaiming sociology to be a science. According to Weber, it is misleading to imagine that we can study people using the same procedures that are applied to investigate the physical world. Humans are thinking, reasoning beings; we attach meaning and significance to most of what we do, and any discipline that deals with human behavior must acknowledge this.

MODERN THEORETICAL APPROACHES

WHILE THE ORIGINS OF SOCIOLOGY WERE MAINLY EUROpean, in the present century the subject has become firmly established worldwide, and some of the most important developments have taken place in the United States. The work of George Herbert Mead (1863–1931), a philosopher teaching at the University of Chicago, has had an important influence on the development of sociological theory. Mead emphasized the centrality of language, and of symbols as a whole, in human social life. The perspective he developed later came to be called *symbolic interactionism.*

Talcott Parsons (1902–1979) was the most prominent American sociological theorist of the postwar period. Parsons was a very productive author, who wrote on many empirical areas of sociology in addition to producing theoretical writings. He made contributions to the study of the family, bureaucracy, the professions, and the study of politics among other areas. He was one of the main contributors to the development of *functionalism,* a theoretical approach originally pioneered by Durkheim and Comte. According to the functionalist viewpoint, in studying any given society we should look at how its various "parts," or institutions, combine to give that society continuity over time.

However, European thinkers continue to be prominent in the development of sociological theory in this century. An approach that has achieved particular prominence is *structuralism.* Structuralist thought was originally pioneered in linguistics, and imported into the social sciences by the anthropologist, Claude Lévi-Strauss (b. 1908). But its origins can also be traced back to Durkheim and Marx.

FUNCTIONALISM

Functionalism as was pointed out, was originally developed by Comte and was closely bound up with his overall view of sociology. Durkheim also regarded functional analysis as a key part of his formulation of the tasks of sociological theorizing and research. The development of functionalism in its modern form, however, was strongly influenced by the work of anthropologists. Until the early years of the present century, anthropology was based mainly upon reports and documents produced by colonial administrators, missionaries, and travelers. Nineteenth-century anthropology therefore was rather speculative in character and inadequately documented. Writers produced books collecting examples from all over the world without bothering too much about how authentic their material was, or about the particular cultural context from which they came. For instance, religion was analyzed by comparing examples of belief and practice drawn from very diverse cultures.

Modern anthropology dates from the time at which researchers became dissatisfied with this procedure, and started to spend long periods of field-study in different cultures around the world. Two of the originators of anthropological fieldwork were a British author strongly influenced by Durkheim, A. R. Radcliffe-Brown (1881–1955), and Bronislaw Malinowski (1884–1942), a Pole who spent much of his career in Britain. Malinowski produced some of the most celebrated anthropological studies ever written, as a result of spending a lengthy period in the Trobriand Islands, in the Pacific. Radcliffe-Brown studied the Andaman Islanders, who lived on an archipelago just off the coast of Burma.

Radcliffe-Brown and Malinowski both believed that a society or a culture must be studied as a whole to understand its major institutions and why its members behave as they do. For example, the religious beliefs and customs of a society could only be analyzed by showing how they relate to other institutions within it, for the different parts of a society develop in close relation to one another.

To study the *function* of a social practice or institution is to analyze the contribution which that practice or institution makes to the continuation of the society as a whole. The best way to understand this is by analogy to the human body, a comparison which Comte, Durkheim, and many subsequent functionalist authors have made. To study a bodily organ, like the heart, we need to show how it relates to other parts of the body. By pumping blood around the body, the heart plays a vital role in the continuation of the life of the organism. Similarly, analyzing the function of a social item means showing the part it plays in the continuing existence of a society. According to Durkheim, for instance, religion reaffirms people's adherence to core social values, thereby contributing to the maintenance of social cohesion. (For more detail on Durkheim's theory of religion, see Chapter 14: "Religion.")

Merton's Version of Functionalism

Functionalism "moved back" into sociology through the writings of Talcott Parsons (1902–1979) and Robert K. Merton (b. 1910). Each of these authors saw functionalist analysis as key to the development of sociological theory and research. Merton's version of functionalism has been particularly influential, serving particularly to focus the work of a whole generation of American sociologists, but it also has been used by many other authors elsewhere. Merton produced a more sophisticated account of functionalist analysis than was offered by either Radcliffe-Brown or Malinowski. At the same time, he readapted it to the study of industrialized societies, which differ in certain basic ways from the simpler cultures studied by anthropologists.

Merton distinguished between **manifest** and **latent functions.** Manifest functions are those known to, and intended by, the participants in a specific type of social activity. Latent functions are consequences of that activity of which participants are unaware (Merton, 1957). To illustrate this distinction, Merton used the example of a rain dance performed by the Hopi Indians of New Mexico. The Hopi believed that the ceremony would bring the rain they needed for their crops (manifest function), which was why they organized and participated in it. But the rain dance, Merton argued, using Durkheim's theory of religion, also had the effect of promoting the cohesion of the society (latent function). A major part of sociological explanation, according to Merton, consists of uncovering the latent functions of social activities and institutions.

Merton also distinguished between functions and *dysfunctions*. The small cultures anthropologists study, he pointed out, tend to be more integrated and solitary than the large, industrialized societies that are the main concern of sociology. Radcliffe-Brown and Malinowski could concentrate solely upon identifying functions, because the cultures which they analyzed were stable and integrated. In studying the modern world, however, we must be aware of disintegrative tendencies. Dysfunction refers to aspects of social activity that tend to produce change, because they *threaten* social cohesion.

To look for the dysfunctional aspects of social behavior means focusing upon features of social life that challenge the existing order of things. For example, it is mistaken to suppose that religion is always functional—that it contributes only to social cohesion. When two groups support different religions, or even different versions of the same religion, the result can be major social conflicts, causing widespread social disruption. Thus wars have often been fought between religious communities—as in the case of the struggles between Protestants and Catholics in European history.

Limitations of Functionalism

For a long while functionalist thought was probably the leading theoretical tradition in sociology, particularly in the United States. In recent years its popularity has begun to wane, as its limitations have become apparent—although it still has articulate defenders (Alexander, 1985). While this was not true of Merton, many functionalist thinkers—Talcott Parsons among them—have been criticized for unduly stressing factors leading to social cohesion at the expense of those producing division and conflict. In addition, it has seemed to many critics that functional analysis attributes societies with qualities they do not have. Functionalists often write as though societies have "needs" and "purposes," even though these concepts only make sense when applied to individual human beings. Take, for instance, Merton's analysis of the Hopi rain dance. Merton argues that, if we can show that the ceremonial rain dance helps integrate Hopi culture, we have explained why it "really" exists—because, after all, the dance does not actually bring rain. But we would have to imagine that somehow Hopi *society* propels its members to act in ways that it needs to hold together. But this cannot be the case, critics claim, for societies are not endowed with willpower or purposes; only human individuals have these qualities.

STRUCTURALISM

Like functionalism, **structuralism** has been influenced by Durkheim's writings, although it largely developed in linguistics, particularly as a result of the work of the Swiss linguist Ferdinand de Saussure (1857–1913). Although Saussure only wrote about language, the views he developed were subsequently incorporated into numerous disciplines in the social sciences as well as in the humanities.

Before Saussure's work, the study of language was concerned mainly with tracing detailed changes in the way words were used. According to Saussure, this procedure omits the central features of language. We can never identify the basic characteristics—or "structures"—of language if we look only at the words people use when they speak (Saussure, 1986). Language consists of rules of grammar and meaning which "lie behind" the words, but are not stated in them. To take a simple example: in English we usually add "-ed" to a verb when we want to signal that we are referring to an event in the past. This is one grammatical rule among thousands of others that we use to *construct* what we say. According to Saussure, analyzing the structures of language means looking for the rules that underlie our speech. Most of these rules are known to us only implicitly: we could not easily state what they are. The task of linguistics, in fact, is to uncover what we implicitly know, but only on the level of being able to use language in practice.

Language and Meaning

Saussure argued that the meaning of words derive from the structure of language, not from the objects to which the words refer. We might naively imagine that the meaning of the word "tree" is the leafy object to which the term refers. According to Saussure, however, this is not so. We can see this by the fact that there are plenty of words in language that do not refer to anything—like "and," "but," or "nevertheless." Moreover, there are perfectly meaningful words that refer to mythical objects and have no existence in reality at all—like "unicorn." If the meaning of a word does not derive from the object to which it refers, where does it come from? Saussure's answer is that meaning is created by the *differences* between related concepts which the rules of a language recognize. The meaning of the word "tree" comes from the fact that we distinguish "tree" from "bush," "shrub," "forest," and a host of words that have similar—but distinct —meanings. The meaning of a word is created internally within a language, not by the object in the world that we refer to by means of it.

Structuralism and Semiotics

To this analysis, Saussure added the important observation that it is not only sounds (speaking) or marks on paper (writing) that can create meaning. Any objects, which we can systematically distinguish, can be used to *make meanings.* An example is a traffic light. We use the contrast between green and red to mean "stop" and "go." (Yellow, in the United States, means "get ready to stop," but in England it means "get ready to start.") Notice that it is the *difference* that creates the meaning, not the actual colors themselves. It would not matter if we used green to mean "stop" and red to mean "go"—so long as we were consistent in recognizing the difference. Saussure called the study of nonlinguistic meanings *semiology,* but the term most often used today is **semiotics.**

Semiotic studies can be made of many different aspects of human culture. One example is clothing and fashion: what makes a certain style of clothing fashionable at a given time? It is not the actual clothes that are worn. For short skirts might be fashionable one year and unfashionable the next. What makes something fashionable is again the *difference* between what is worn by those who are "in the know," and those who lag behind. Another example from the sphere of clothing is the wearing of mourning dress. In our culture, we show we are in mourning by wearing black. In other cultures, on the other hand, people who are in mourning wear white. What matters once more is not the color itself, but the fact that people in mourning dress differently from their normal style.

The structuralist approach has been used more widely in anthropology than sociology. Following the lead of Claude Lévi-Strauss—who popularized the term *structuralism*—structuralist analysis has been employed in the study of kinship, myth, religion, and other areas. However, many writers on sociological theory have been influenced by notions drawn from structuralism. Structuralist concepts have been applied to the study of the media (newspapers, magazines, television), ideology, and culture in general.

Structuralist thought has weaknesses that limit its appeal as a general theoretical framework in sociology. Structuralism originated in the study of language and has proved more relevant to analyzing certain aspects of human behavior than others. It is useful for exploring communication and culture, but has less application to more practical concerns of social life, such as economic or political activity.

SYMBOLIC INTERACTIONISM

Symbolic interactionism gives more weight to the active, creative individual than either of the other theoretical approaches. Since Mead's time it has been further developed by many other writers, and in the United States has been the principal rival to the functionalist standpoint. As in the case of structuralism, symbolic interactionism springs from a concern with language; but Mead developed this in a different direction from structuralist thought.

Symbols

Mead claimed that language allows us to become self-conscious beings—aware of our own individuality. The key to this view is the **symbol.** A symbol is something which *stands for* something else. Pursuing the example used by Saussure, the word "tree" is a symbol by means of which we represent the object, tree. Once we have mastered such a concept, Mead argued, we can think of a tree even if none is visible: we have learned to think of the object *symbolically.* Symbolic thought frees us from being limited in our experience to what we actually see, hear, or feel.

Unlike the lower animals, human beings live in a richly symbolic universe. This applies to our very sense of self. Animals do not have a sense of self as human beings do. Each of us is a self-conscious being, because we learn to "look at" ourselves as if from the outside—seeing ourselves as others see us. When a child begins to use "I" to refer to that object (himself or herself) which others call "you," he or she is exhibiting the beginnings of self-consciousness. (Further discussion of Mead's theory of the development of self can be found in Chapter 3: "Socialization and the Life Cycle.")

Virtually all interaction between human individuals, symbolic interactionists point out, involves an exchange of symbols. When we interact with others, we constantly look for "clues" about what type of behavior is appropriate in the context, and about how to interpret what others intend. Symbolic interactionism directs our attention to the details of interpersonal interaction, and how those details are used to make sense of what others say and do. For instance, suppose a man and a woman are out on a date for the first time. Each is likely to spend a good part of the evening sizing the other up and assessing how the relationship is likely to develop—if it will at all. Neither wishes to be seen doing this too openly, although each recognizes that it is going on. Each one is careful about his or her own behavior, and is anxious to appear in a favorable light. But, knowing this, each is likely to be looking for aspects of the other's behavior that would reveal that person's true opinions. A complex and subtle process of symbolic interpretation shapes the interaction between the two.

Sociologists influenced by symbolic interactionism usually focus on face-to-face interaction in the contexts of everyday life. Erving Goffman, whose work is discussed in Chapter 4 ("Social Interaction and Everyday Life"), has made particularly illuminating contributions to this type of study, introducing wit and verve into what in the hands of Mead was a drier, abstract theoretical approach. In the hands of Goffman and others, symbolic interactionism has yielded many insights into the nature of our actions in the course of day-to-day social life. But symbolic interactionism is open to the criticism that it concentrates too much on the small-scale. Symbolic interactionists have usually found difficulty in dealing with more large-scale social structures and processes—the very phenomena that the other two traditions most strongly emphasize.

A White House press conference is abundant material for symbolic interactionists as they seek to explain a politician's face-to-face interaction with the press, and his "impression management."

MARXISM

Functionalism, structuralism, and symbolic interactionism are not the only theoretical traditions of any importance in sociology. A fur-

FIGURE 22.1   **THEORETICAL APPROACHES IN SOCIOLOGY**

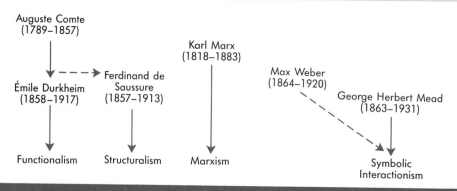

The unbroken lines indicate direct influence, the dotted lines an indirect connection. It is not certain that Saussure owed many of his ideas directly to Durkheim, but there are several major areas of overlap. Mead is not indebted to Weber, but Weber's views—stressing the meaningful, purposive nature of human action—have affinities with the themes of symbolic interactionism.

ther influential approach is **Marxism.** Marxists, of course, all trace their views back in some way to the writings of Marx. But numerous interpretations of Marx's major ideas are possible, and there are today schools of Marxist thought that take very different theoretical positions.

Broadly speaking, Marxism can be subdivided along lines that correspond to the boundaries between the three theoretical traditions previously described. Many Marxists have implicitly or openly adopted a functionalist approach to historical materialism (Cohen, 1980). Their version of Marxism is quite different from that of Marxists influenced by structuralism, the most well-known writer developing this standpoint being the French author Louis Althusser (Althusser, 1969). Both these types of Marxist thought differ from that of Marxists who have laid stress upon the active, creative character of human behavior. Few of these writers have been directly influenced by symbolic interactionism, but some, like Erich Fromm (1967) and Herbert Marcuse (1986), have adopted a perspective quite close to it.

In all of its versions, Marxism differs from non-Marxist traditions of sociology in that its authors see it as a combination of sociological analysis and political reform. Marxism is supposed to generate a program of radical political change. Moreover, Marxists lay more emphasis on class divisions, conflict, power, and ideology than many non-Marxist sociologists, especially most of those influenced by functionalism. It is best to see Marxism not as an approach within sociology, but as a body of writing existing alongside sociology; each overlaps and is quite frequently influenced by the other. Non-Marxist sociology and Marxism have always existed in a relationship of mutual influence and opposition.

THEORETICAL DILEMMAS

HOW SHOULD WE ASSESS THE RELATIVE VALUE OF THESE four differing theoretical approaches? Although each has its committed advocates, there are obvious respects in which they are complementary to one another. Functionalism and most versions of Marxism concentrate upon the more large-scale properties of social groups or societies. These approaches are principally concerned with the "grand questions" like "How do societies hold together?" or "What are the main conditions producing social change?" Symbolic interaction is, by contrast, more concentrated upon face-to-face contexts of social life. Structuralism differs from the other approaches by being focused mainly upon cultural features of social activity.

To some extent, therefore, we can draw selectively upon each of these various standpoints in discussing specific sociological problems. But in certain respects they clearly do clash, and there are a number of basic **theoretical dilemmas**—matters of continuing controversy or dispute—which these clashes of viewpoint bring to our attention. Some of these concern very general matters about how we should interpret human activities and social institutions. We shall discuss four such dilemmas here.

1. HUMAN ACTION AND SOCIAL STRUCTURE. One dilemma concerns human action and social structure: To what degree are we creative human actors, actively controlling the conditions of our own lives? Or, alternatively, is most of what we do the result of general social forces outside our control? This issue has always divided, and continues to divide, sociologists. Symbolic interactionism stresses the active, creative aspects of human behavior. The other three approaches (with the exception of some variants of Marxism) emphasize the constraining nature of social influences upon our actions.

2. CONSENSUS AND CONFLICT. A second theoretical dilemma concerns consensus and conflict in society. Some standpoints in sociology—including many linked to functionalism—place a marked emphasis on the inherent order and harmony of human societies. Those taking this position—such as Talcott Parsons—regard continuity and **consensus** as the most evident

characteristics of societies, however much they may change over time. Other sociologists, on the other hand—particularly those strongly influenced by Marx or Weber—accentuate the pervasiveness of social **conflict** (Collins, 1974). They see societies as plagued with divisions, tensions, and struggles. To them, it is illusory to claim that people tend to live amicably with one another most of the time; even when there are no open confrontations, they say, there remain deep divisions of interest which at some point are liable to break out into active conflicts.

3.   MODERN SOCIAL DEVELOPMENT. A third dilemma concerns not so much the general characteristics of human behavior or of societies as a whole, but rather as features of modern social development. This dilemma has to do with the determining influences affecting the origins and nature of modern societies. It derives from the differences between non-Marxist and Marxist approaches, and centers on the following issue: How much has the modern world been shaped by the economic factors that Marx singled out—in particular, the mechanisms of capitalist enterprise? How much, alternatively, have other influences (such as social, political, or cultural factors) shaped social development in the modern era?

4.   GENDER AND SOCIAL DEVELOPMENT. There is a fourth basic problem of theory which hardly figures at all in orthodox traditions of sociology, but which can no longer be ignored. This is the problem of how we are to incorporate a satisfactory understanding of *gender* within sociological analysis. All the major figures in the early development of sociological theory were men, and their writings gave virtually no attention to the fact that human beings are gendered (Sydie, 1987). In their works, humans appear as if they were "neuter"—they are abstract "actors," rather than differentiated women and men. Since we have very little to build upon in relating issues of gender to the more established forms of theoretical thinking in sociology, this is now perhaps the most acutely difficult problem of the four to grapple with.

One of the main theoretical dilemmas associated with gender is the following: Shall we build "gender" as a general category into our sociological thinking. Or, alternatively, do we need to analyze gender issues by breaking them down into more specific influences affecting the behavior of women and men in different contexts? Put in another way: Are there characteristics that separate men and women in terms of their identities and social behavior in all cultures? Or are gender differences always to be explained mainly in terms of other differences that divide societies (such as class divisions)?

We shall look at each of these dilemmas in turn.

HUMAN ACTION AND SOCIAL STRUCTURE

A major theme pursued by Durkheim, and by many others since, is that the societies of which we are members exert **social constraint** over our actions. Durkheim argued that society has primacy over the individual person. Society is far more than the sum of individual acts; when we analyze social structures, we are studying characteristics that have a "firmness" or "solidity" comparable to those of structures in the material environment. Think of a person standing in a room with several doors. The structure of the room constrains the range of her or his possible activities. The position of the walls and the doors, for example, defines the routes of exit and entry. Social structure, according to Durkheim, constrains our activities in a parallel way, setting limits to what we can do as individuals. It is "external" to us, just as the walls of the room are.

This point of view was expressed by Durkheim in a famous statement:

When I perform my duties as a brother, a husband or a citizen and carry out the commitments I have entered into, I fulfil obligations which are defined in law and custom and which are external to myself and my actions. . . . Similarly, the believer has discovered from birth, ready fashioned, the beliefs and practices of his religious life; if they existed before he did, it follows that they exist outside him. The system of signs that I employ to express my thoughts, the monetary system I use to pay my debts, the credit instru-

ments I utilize in my commercial relationships, the practices
I follow in my profession, etc.—all function independently
of the use I make of them. (Durkheim, 1982)

Although the viewpoint that Durkheim expressed has many adherents, it has also met with sharp criticism. What is "society," the
critics have asked, if it is not the composite of many individual actions? If we study a group, we do not see a collective entity, only individuals interacting with one another in various ways. Society is only
many individuals behaving in habitual ways in relation to each other.
According to the critics (which include most sociologists influenced
by symbolic interactionism), as human beings we have reasons for
what we do, and we inhabit a social world permeated by cultural
meanings. Social phenomena, according to them, are precisely *not*
like "things," but depend upon the symbolic meanings we invest in
what we do. We are not the *creatures* of society, but its *creators.*

Assessment

It is unlikely that the controversy between social structure and
human action will ever be fully resolved, since it has been continuing
ever since modern thinkers first started systematically trying to explain human behavior. Moreover, it is a debate that is not just confined to sociology but preoccupies scholars in all fields of the social
sciences. You must decide, in the light of your reading the chapters of
this book, which position you think more nearly correct.

Yet the differences between the two views can be exaggerated, and
we can fairly easily see connections between them. Durkheim's view
is clearly in some respects valid. Social institutions do precede the existence of any given individual; it is also evident that they exert constraint over us. Thus, for example, I did not invent the monetary
system that exists in the United States. Nor do I have a choice about
whether I want to use it or not, if I wish to have the goods and services that money can buy. The system of money, like all other established institutions, exists independently of any individual member of
society and constrains that individual's activities.

On the other hand, it is obviously mistaken to suppose that society
is external to us in the same way the physical world is. For the physical world would go on existing whether or not any human being
were alive, whereas it would plainly be nonsensical to say this of society. While society is external to each individual taken singly, by definition it cannot be external to *all* individuals taken together.

Moreover, although what Durkheim called "social facts" might constrain what we do, they do not *determine* what we do. I could choose to live without using money, should I be firmly resolved to do so, even if it might prove difficult to eke out an existence from day to day. As human beings, we do make choices, and we do not simply respond passively to events around us. The way forward in bridging the gap between "structural" and "action" approaches is to recognize that we *actively make and remake* social institutions during the course of our everyday activities. For example, the fact that I use the monetary system contributes in a minor, yet necessary, way to the very existence of that system. If everyone, or even a majority of people, at some point decided to stop using money, the monetary system would dissolve.

How much influence does work and economic life have on an individual's behavior, and free choice?

CONSENSUS AND CONFLICT

It is also useful to begin with Durkheim when contrasting the consensus and conflict viewpoints. Durkheim saw society as a set of interdependent parts. For most functionalist thinkers, in fact, society is treated as an *integrated whole,* composed of structures that mesh closely with one another. This is very much in accord with Durkheim's emphasis on the constraining, "external" character of "social facts." However, the analogy here is not that of the walls of a building, but the physiology of the body.

A body consists of various specialized parts (such as the brain, heart, lungs, liver, etc.), each of which contributes to sustaining the continuing life of the organism. These necessarily work in harmony with one another; if they do not, the life of the organism is under threat. So it is, according to Durkheim (and Parsons), with society. For a society to have a continuing existence over time, its specialized institutions (such as the political system, religion, the family, and the educational system) must work in harmony with one another. The continuation of a society thus depends upon cooperation, which in turn presumes a general consensus, or agreement, among its members over basic values.

Those who focus mainly on conflict have a very different outlook. Their guiding assumptions can easily be outlined using Marx's account of class conflict as an example. According to Marx, societies are divided into classes having unequal resources. Since such marked inequalities exist, there are divisions of interest that are built into the social system. These interest conflicts at some point break out into active struggle between classes—which can generate processes of radi-

Some conflict-oriented theorists will examine life in terms of class tensions—here, between this South American government and its urban guerrillas.

cal change. Not all of those influenced by this viewpoint concentrate upon class conflict to the degree that Marx did. Other divisions are regarded as important in promoting conflict—for example, divisions between racial groups or political factions. Whichever division is emphasized, society is seen as essentially *tensionful*—even the most stable social system represents an uneasy balance of antagonistic groupings.

Assessment

As with the case of structure and action, it is not likely that this theoretical debate can be completely brought to a close. Yet once more the difference between the consensus and conflict standpoints seem wider than is in fact the case. The two positions are by no means wholly incompatible. All societies probably involve some kind of general agreement over values, and all certainly involve conflict.

Moreover, as a general rule of sociological analysis we have always to examine the connections *between* consensus and conflict within social systems. The values different groups hold, and the goals their members pursue, often reflect a mixture of common and opposed interests. For instance, even in Marx's portrayal of class conflict different classes share common interests in addition to being pitted against one another. Thus capitalists depend upon a labor force to work in their enterprises, just as workers depend upon the capitalists to provide their wages. Open conflict is not continuous in such circumstances. Rather, in some circumstances what both sides share in common tends to override their differences, while in other situations the reverse is the case.

One way to analyze the interrelations of conflict and consensus in a society is to look at the influence of *ideology*. An ideology is made up of values and beliefs that help secure the position of more-powerful groups at the expense of less-powerful ones. Power, ideology, and conflict are always closely connected. Many conflicts are *about* power, because of the rewards it can bring. Those who hold the most power may depend mainly on the influence of ideology to retain their situation of dominance, but are usually able also to use force if necessary. For instance, in feudal times aristocratic rule was supported by values emphasizing that a minority of people were "born to govern." The aristocratic rulers also resorted to the use of violence against those who dared to question their power.

UNDERSTANDING THE MODERN WORLD

From Marx's time to the present day many sociological debates have centered upon the ideas that Marx set out about the influence of economics on the development of modern societies. According to Marx, as was mentioned earlier, modern societies are *capitalistic*—the driving impulse behind social change in the modern era is to be found in the pressure towards constant economic transformation produced by the spread of capitalist production. Capitalism is a vastly more dynamic economic system than any other that preceded it in history. Capitalists compete with one another to sell their goods to consumers, and to survive in a competitive market, firms have to produce their wares as cheaply and efficiently as possible. This leads to constant technological innovation, because increasing the effectiveness of the technology used in a particular production process is one way in which companies can secure an edge over their rivals.

There are also strong incentives to seek out new markets in which to sell goods, acquire cheap raw materials, and make use of cheap labor power. Capitalism, therefore, according to Marx, is a restlessly expanding system, pushing outwards across the world. This is how Marx explains the spread of Western industry globally.

Marx's interpretation of the influence of capitalism has found many supporters. Subsequent Marxist authors have considerably refined Marx's own portrayal. On the other hand, numerous critics have set out to rebut Marx's view, offering alternative analyses of the influences shaping the modern world. Virtually everyone accepts that capitalism *has* played a major part in creating the world in which we live today. But other sociologists have argued both that Marx exaggerated the impact of purely *economic* factors in producing change, and that capitalism is *less central* to modern social development than he claimed. Most of these writers have also been sceptical of Marx's belief that a socialist system would eventually replace capitalism.

One of Marx's earliest, and most acute, critics was Max Weber. Weber's writings, in fact, have been described as involving a lifelong struggle with "the ghost of Marx"—with the intellectual legacy that Marx left. The alternative position that Weber worked out remains important today. According to Weber, noneconomic factors have played the key role in modern social development. Weber's celebrated and much discussed work, *The Protestant Ethic and the Spirit of Capitalism,* proposes that religious values—especially those associated with Puritanism—were of fundamental importance in creating a capitalistic outlook. This outlook did not emerge, as Marx supposed, only from economic changes.

Weber's understanding of the nature of modern societies, and the reasons for the spread of Western ways of life across the world, also contrasts substantially with that of Marx. According to Weber, capitalism—a distinct way of organizing economic enterprise—is one among other major factors shaping social development in the modern period. Underlying capitalistic mechanisms, and in some ways more fundamental than them, is the impact of *science* and *bureaucracy.* Science has shaped modern technology and will presumably continue to do so in any future socialist society. Bureaucracy is the only way of organizing large numbers of people effectively, and therefore inevitably expands with economic and political growth. The development of science, modern technology, and bureaucracy, Weber refers to collectively as **rationalization.** Rationalization means the organization of social and economic life according to principles of efficiency, on the basis of technical knowledge.

Which interpretation of modern societies, that deriving from Marx, or that coming from Weber, is correct? Again, scholars are divided on the issue. Table 22.1 lists some of these differences. It must be remembered that within each camp there are variations, so not every theorist will agree with all the points.

The contrasts between these two standpoints inform many areas of sociology. They influence not only how we analyze the nature of the industrialized societies, but our view of Third World societies also. In addition, the two perspectives are also linked to differing political po-

TABLE 22.1	INTERPRETING THE MODERN WORLD
Broadly Marxist ideas	**Broadly Weberian ideas**
1. The main dynamic of modern development is the expansion of capitalistic economic mechanisms.	1. The main dynamic of modern development is the rationalization of production.
2. Modern societies are riven with class inequalities, which are basic to their very nature.	2. Class is one type of inequality among others—such as inequalities between men and women—in modern societies.
3. Major divisions of power, like those affecting the differential position of men and women, derive ultimately from economic inequalities.	3. Power in the economic system is separable from power derived from other sources. For instance, male-female inequalities cannot be explained only in economic terms.
4. Modern societies (capitalist societies) are transitional; we may expect them to become radically reorganized in the future. Socialism or communism, of one type or another, will eventually replace capitalism.	4. Rationalization is bound to progress further in the future, in all spheres of social life. All modern societies are dependent on the same basic modes of social and economic organization. There is no chance of setting up a radically different system than that of the industrialized societies at present.
5. The spread of Western influence across the world is mainly a result of the expansionist tendencies of capitalist economic enterprise.	5. The global impact of the West comes from its command over industrial resources, together with superior military power.

sitions: Leftist authors on the whole adopt the views influenced by a broadly Marxist standpoint; Liberals and Conservatives are more in accord with a Weberian view.

THE QUESTION OF GENDER

Issues of gender are scarcely central in the writings of the major figures who established modern sociology. The few passages in which they did touch upon gender questions, however, allow us at least to specify the outlines of a basic theoretical dilemma—even if there is little in their works to help us try to resolve it. We can best describe this dilemma by contrasting a theme that occasionally occurs in Durkheim's writings with one that appears in those of Marx. Durkheim notes at one point, in the course of his discussion of suicide, that man is "almost entirely the product of society," while woman is "to a far greater extent the product of nature." Expanding upon these observations, he says of man: "his tastes, aspirations and humor have in large part a collective origin, while his companion's are more directly influenced by [her body]. His needs, therefore, are quite different from hers . . ." (Durkheim, 1966). In other words, women and men have different identities, tastes, and inclinations because women are less socialized, and are "closer to nature" than men.

No one today would accept a view stated in quite this manner. Female identity is as much shaped by socialization as that of males. Yet, when modified somewhat, Durkheim's claim does represent one possible view of the formation and nature of gender differences—that they rest fundamentally upon biologically-given variations between men and women. Such a view does not necessarily mean believing that gender differences are mostly inborn. Rather, it presumes that women's social position and identity are mainly shaped by their involvement in reproduction and child rearing (see Chapter 6: "Gender and Sexuality"). If this view is correct, differences of gender are deeply embedded in all societies. The discrepancies in power between women and men reflect the fact that women bear children, and are their primary caretakers, whereas men are active in the "public" spheres of politics, work, and war.

Marx's view is substantially at odds with this. For Marx, gender differences in power and status between men and women mainly reflect other divisions—in his eyes, especially class divisions. According to him, neither gender nor class divisions were present in the earliest forms of human society. The power of men over women developed as class divisions appeared; women came to be a form of "private property" owned by men through the institution of marriage. Women will become freed from their situation of bondage when class divisions are overcome. Again, few if any would accept this analysis today. But we can make it a much more plausible view by generalizing it further. Class is not the only factor shaping social divisions that affect the behavior of men and women. Other factors include ethnicity and cultural background. For instance, it might be argued that women in a minority group (say, blacks in the United States) have more in common with men in that minority group than they do with women in the majority (that is, white women). Or it may be the case that women from a particular culture (like a small hunting and gathering culture) share more common characteristics with the males of that culture than they do with women from an industrial society.

Evaluation

The issues involved in this fourth dilemma are highly important and bear directly upon the challenge that feminist authors have thrown down to sociology. No one can seriously dispute that a great deal of sociological analysis in the past has either ignored women or has operated with interpretations of female identity and behavior that are drastically inadequate. In spite of all the new research on women that has been carried out in sociology over the past twenty years, there still are many areas in which the distinctive activities and concerns of women have been insufficiently studied. But "bringing the study of women into sociology" is not in and of itself the same as coping with problems of gender, because gender concerns the relations between the identities and behavior of women *and* men. For the moment it is an open question how much gender differences can be illuminated by means of other sociological concepts (class, ethnicity, cultural background, and so forth) or, on the contrary, how much other social divisions need to be explained in terms of gender. Certainly some of the major explanatory tasks of sociology in the future will depend upon tackling this dilemma effectively.

THEORIES

SO FAR IN THIS CHAPTER WE HAVE BEEN CONCERNED WITH theoretical approaches, which refer to broad, overall orientations to the subject matter of sociology. However, we can draw a distinction between theoretical approaches and **theories.** Theories are more narrowly focused and represent attempts to explain particular social conditions or types of event. They are usually formed as part of the process of research, and in turn suggest problems to which research investigations should be devoted. An example would be Durkheim's theory of suicide, referred to earlier in this chapter (p. 848).

Innumerable theories have been developed in the many different areas of research in which sociologists work. Sometimes theories are very precisely set out, and are even occasionally expressed in mathematical form—although this is more common in other social sciences (especially economics) than in sociology.

Some theories are also much more encompassing than others. Opinions vary about whether it is desirable or useful for sociologists to concern themselves with very wide-ranging theoretical endeavors. Robert Merton (1957), for example, argues forcefully that sociologists should concentrate their attention upon what he calls *theories of the middle range.* Rather than attempting to create grand theoretical schemes (in the manner of Marx, for instance), we should be concerned with developing more modest theories.

Middle-range theories are specific enough to be directly tested by empirical research, yet sufficiently general to cover a range of different phenomena. A case in point is the theory of relative deprivation. This theory holds that how people evaluate their circumstances depends upon who they compare themselves to. Thus, feelings of deprivation do not conform directly to the level of material poverty individuals experience. A family living in a small home in a poor area, where everyone is in more or less similar circumstances, is likely to feel less deprived that one living in a similar house in a neighborhood where the majority of homes are much larger and more affluent.

It is indeed true that the more wide-ranging and ambitious a theory is, the more difficult it is to test empirically. Yet there seems no obvious reason why theoretical thinking in sociology should be confined to the "middle range." To see why this is so, let us return, as an example, to the theory that Weber advanced in *The Protestant Ethic and the Spirit of Capitalism.*

AN EXAMPLE OF A THEORY: THE PROTESTANT ETHIC

In *The Protestant Ethic,* (1977; first ed. 1904–5) Weber set out to tackle a major problem: why capitalism developed in the Western world and nowhere else. For some fifteen centuries following the fall of ancient Rome, other civilizations were much more prominent in world history than the West. Europe in fact was a rather insignificant area of the globe compared to China, India, and the Ottoman Empire in the Near East. The Chinese in particular were a long way ahead of the West in terms of their level of technological and economic development. What happened to bring about a surge in economic development in Europe from the seventeenth century onward?

To answer this question, Weber reasoned, we must show what separates modern industry from earlier types of economic activity. We find the desire to accumulate wealth in many different civilizations, and this is not difficult to explain: people have valued wealth for the security, power, and enjoyment it can bring. They wish to be free of want, and having accumulated wealth, they use it to make themselves comfortable.

If we look at the early economic development of the West, Weber argued, we find something quite different. There developed in Western Europe a unique attitude towards the accumulation of wealth found nowhere else in history. This attitude is what Weber called the *spirit of capitalism*—a set of beliefs and values held by the first capitalist merchants and industrialists. These individuals had a strong drive to accumulate personal wealth, yet quite unlike the wealthy elsewhere, they did not seek to use their accumulated riches to follow a luxurious lifestyle. Their way of life was in fact self-denying and frugal. They lived soberly and quietly, shunning the ordinary manifestations of affluence. This very unusual combination of characteristics, Weber tried to show, was vital to early Western economic development. For unlike the wealthy in previous ages, and in other cultures, these groups did not dissipate their wealth. Instead, they reinvested it to promote the further expansion of the enterprises they headed.

The core of Weber's theory is that the attitudes involved in the spirit of capitalism derived from the impact of religion. Christianity in general played a part in fostering this outlook. But the essential motive force was provided by the impact of Protestantism, and especially one variety of Protestantism, Puritanism. The early capitalists were mostly Puritans, but a substantial proportion were Calvinists. Weber argued that certain Calvinist doctrines were the direct source of the spirit of capitalism. One was the idea that human beings are God's instruments on earth, required by the Almighty to work in a vocation—a "calling"—for the greater glory of God.

A second important aspect of Calvinism was the notion of *predestination*. According to this idea, only a certain number of those born upon earth are destined to be among the "elect"—to enter heaven in the afterlife. In John Calvin's original doctrine, nothing a person does on this earth can alter whether he or she happens to be one of the elect. This is predetermined by God. However, this belief set up such anxiety among Calvin's followers that the doctrine was modified to allow believers to recognize certain signs of election. Success in a vocation, indicated by material prosperity, became *the main sign that a person was truly one of the elect*. A tremendous dynamic impulse towards economic success was created among groups influenced by these ideas. At the same time, the believer was compelled to live a sober and frugal life. The Puritans believed luxury to be an evil, so the drive to accumulate wealth became joined to a severe and unadorned lifestyle.

The early entrepreneurs were not aware that they were helping to produce momentous changes in society. They were impelled above all by religious motives. The ascetic—that is, self-denying—lifestyle of the Puritans has subsequently become an intrinsic part of the modern civilization in which we now live. As Weber wrote:

> The Puritan wanted to work in a calling; we are forced to do so. For when asceticism was carried out of the monastic cells into everyday life, and began to dominate worldly morality, it did its part in building the tremendous cosmos of the modern economic order. . . . Since asceticism undertook to remodel the world and to work out its ideals in the world, material goods have gained an increasingly and finally an inexorable power over the lives of men as at no previous period in history. . . . The idea of duty in one's calling prowls about in our lives like the ghost of dead religious beliefs. Where the fulfilment of the calling cannot directly be related to the highest spiritual and cultural values, or when, on the other hand, it need not be felt simply as economic compulsion, the individual generally abandons the attempt to justify it at all. In the field of its highest development, in the United States, the pursuit of wealth, stripped of its religious and ethical meaning, tends to become associated with purely mundane passions. (Weber, 1976)

Weber's theory has been criticized from many angles. Some have argued, for example, that the outlook he called the spirit of capitalism can be discerned in the early Italian merchant cities—long before Calvinism was ever heard of. Others have claimed that the key notion of "working in a vocation," which Weber associated with Protestantism, already existed previously in Catholic beliefs. Yet the essentials of Weber's account are still accepted by many, and the ideas he advanced remain as bold and illuminating as when he first formulated them. If Weber's view is valid, modern economic and social development was decisively influenced by something that seems at first sight utterly distant from it—a set of religious ideals.

Weber's theory meets several criteria important in theoretical thinking in sociology:

1. The theory develops a *fresh perspective* on sociological issues. Further, it is counterintuitive, that is, it suggests an interpretation that breaks with what "common sense" would suggest. Most authors prior to Weber gave little thought to the

possibility that religious ideals could have played a fundamental role in the origins of the capitalistic outlook.

2. The theory is *neither a purely "structural" nor purely "individual" account.* The early development of capitalism, an economic structure that dominates the West, was an unintended consequence of what individual Puritan business leaders aspired to—to live virtuously according to God's will.

3. The theory *makes sense of something that is otherwise puzzling,* why individuals would want to live in a frugal manner while making great efforts to accumulate wealth.

4. The theory is capable of *illuminating circumstances beyond those it was originally developed to understand.* Weber emphasized that he was trying only to understand the early origins of modern capitalism. Nonetheless, it seems reasonable to suppose that parallel values to those instilled by Puritanism might be involved in other more recent situations of successful capitalist development.

5. A good theory is not just one that happens to be valid. It is also one that is *fruitful* in terms of generating new ideas and stimulating further research work. Weber's theory has certainly been highly successful in these respects, providing the springboard for a vast amount of subsequent research and theory.

THEORETICAL THINKING IN SOCIOLOGY

ASSESSING THEORIES, AND ESPECIALLY THEORETICAL APproaches, in sociology is a challenging and formidable task. Theoretical debates are by definition more abstract than controversies of a more empirical kind. The fact that there is not a single theoretical approach that dominates the whole of sociology might seem to be a sign of weakness in the subject. But this is not the case at all: the jostling of rival theoretical approaches and theories is an expression of the vitality of the sociological enterprise. In studying human beings—ourselves—theoretical variety rescues us from dogma. Human behavior is complicated and many-sided, and it is very unlikely that a single theoretical perspective could cover all of its aspects. Diversity in theoretical thinking provides a rich source of ideas that can be drawn upon in research, and stimulates the imaginative capacities so essential to progress in sociological work.

SUMMARY

1. A diversity of theoretical approaches is found in sociology (and also in the other social sciences). The reason for this is not particularly puzzling. Theoretical disputes are difficult to resolve even in the natural sciences, and in sociology we face special difficulties because of the complex problems involved in subjecting our own behavior to study.

2. Important figures in the early development of sociological theory include Auguste Comte (1789–1857), Émile Durkheim (1858–1917), Karl Marx (1818–1883), and Max Weber (1864–1920). Many of their ideas remain important in sociology today.

3. The main theoretical approaches in sociology are *functionalism, structuralism, symbolic interactionism,* and *Marxism.* To some extent, these approaches are complementary to one another. However, there are also major contrasts between them, which influence the ways in which theoretical issues are handled by authors following different approaches.

4. One main theoretical dilemma in sociology concerns how we should relate human action to social structure. Are we the creators of society, or created by it? The gap between these two views is not as wide as may initially appear, as we actually make and remake social structures constantly in our everyday activities.

5. A second dilemma concerns whether societies should be pictured as harmonious and orderly, or whether they should be seen as marked by persistent conflict. Again, these two views are not completely opposed, and we need to show how *consensus* and *conflict* interrelate. The concepts of *ideology* and *power* are useful in undertaking this task.

6. A third focus of continuing debate in sociology has to do with the analysis of modern social development. Are processes of change in the modern world mainly shaped by capitalist economic development, or by other factors, including noneco-

nomic ones? Positions taken in this debate to some extent are influenced by the political beliefs and attitudes different sociologists hold.

7. A fourth dilemma concerns how we should cope with gender issues in sociological analysis. Feminists have thrown down a challenge to sociology that is slowly being met on the level of empirical research: far more studies of the concerns and outlooks of women are being carried out today than previously was the case. But these do not in and of themselves resolve the question of how we should best analyze gender in relation to the existing approaches and concepts of sociological theory.

8. Weber's thesis about the influence of Puritanism upon modern economic development provides a useful example in thinking about what makes a theory valuable. Weber's ideas remain controversial, but in several respects his theory broke new ground, stimulating a great deal of subsequent research.

BASIC CONCEPTS

THEORETICAL APPROACH
CONSENSUS
CONFLICT
THEORY

IMPORTANT TERMS

DIVISION OF LABOR
ANOMIE
HISTORICAL MATERIALISM
CAPITALISM
BUREAUCRACY
FUNCTIONALISM
MANIFEST FUNCTIONS
LATENT FUNCTIONS

STRUCTURALISM
SEMIOTICS
SYMBOLIC INTERACTIONISM
SYMBOL
MARXISM
THEORETICAL DILEMMA
SOCIAL CONSTRAINT
RATIONALIZATION

APPENDIX:
HOW TO
USE LIBRARIES

Libraries, especially large ones, can seem like daunting places. Many people feel somewhat lost when confronted with the apparently innumerable sources of information that libraries contain. They may therefore end up using only a small proportion of what a library has to offer, perhaps with damaging effects on their academic work. It is a good idea to get to know—at the beginning of your course—the range of resources libraries have. If you do this early on, the "lost" feeling won't last long!

All the information available in the library is stored and cataloged systematically, in order to make finding things easy. Most smaller libraries operate with *open stacks*—the books can be visibly inspected on the shelves, and the user can select whichever volume he or she wants directly. Most larger collections keep only a proportion of their books on open shelves, and store others in vaults where less space is required to keep them. In these libraries, anyone who wishes to use or borrow a book must ask for it, or fill in a request slip. Some libraries have some books in each system.

If you are looking for a particular book, you'll be able to look it up under author or title in the index or catalog. This may be a computerized list, drawerfuls of index cards, or a microfiche—or all three! Once you find its catalog number, you can then either order it from library staff quoting that number, or find it on the open shelves, which are always arranged by catalog numbers. All—or most—sociology books will be in one area. Any librarian will be able to explain how the cataloging system works.

Finding books on a particular topic when you don't know any names or titles involves using a subject index (again, this may be computerized or on cards). A subject index lists books by topics—such as "class," "bureaucracy," etc.

Many of the larger libraries today have computer-trace systems, which are very easy to operate, and are normally available to all library users. You simply key in the area or areas about which you require bibliographical information, and the computer will display a list of titles relevant to them.

Most libraries provide very similar services, but different libraries do have their own ways of doing things, and there are variations in cataloging systems. Never be afraid to ask the librarian or assistants for their help, if there is any aspect of library procedure that puzzles you, or about which you need guidance. You should not be worried about bothering them; librarians are trained professionals, committed to making sure that the library resources are available to everyone who wants to make use of them. They are usually highly knowledgeable about the range of material the library contains, and only too willing to provide guidance if asked.

SOURCES OF GENERAL INFORMATION IN SOCIOLOGY

If you are beginning the study of a particular topic in sociology, and want to find some general information about it, there are a number of useful sources. Several dictionaries of sociology are available. These provide brief discussions of the major concepts in the subject, and also accounts of the ideas of some of the leading contributors to the discipline. The major encyclopedias—like the *World Book Encyclopedia*—contain many entries relevant to sociological topics. The entries in dictionaries and encyclopedias virtually always provide short lists of books or articles as a guide to further reading.

There are various other ways in which books and articles relevant to a given problem or issue can be traced. The *International Bibliography of the Social Sciences,* published annually by UNESCO, offers a comprehensive listing of works that have appeared in different social science subjects over the course of any year. Thus, for example, you can look up the heading "sociology of education," and find a range of up-to-date materials in that field. An equally useful source is *Sociological Abstracts,* which not only lists books and articles in the different areas of sociology, but gives a short description of the contents of each of them.

SOCIOLOGICAL JOURNALS

It is worth familiarizing yourself with the main journals in sociology. Journals usually appear three or four times a year. The information and debates they contain are often more up-to-date than those in books, which take longer to write and publish. Journal articles are sometimes quite technical, and a person fairly new to sociology may well not find them readily understandable. But all the leading journals regularly publish articles of general interest, accessible to those with only limited knowledge of the subject.

The most important journals include the *Sociological Review* and the *American Journal of Sociology*, as well as *Sociology* (the official journal of the British Sociological Association) and the *British Journal of Sociology*.

RESEARCH FOR DISSERTATIONS OR LONGER PROJECTS

On some occasions you may wish to use the library to pursue a particular research project, perhaps in the course of writing a dissertation. Such a task might involve carrying out a more "in-depth" search of relevant sources than is required for normal study.

If you require statistical information concerning the United States, a good place to start is *Statistical Abstract of the United States,* which is available from the U.S. Government Printing Office. This volume contains selected statistical information on many aspects of American social life.

Newspaper articles provide a mine of valuable information for the sociological researcher. A few newspapers are what are sometimes called "journals of record." That is to say, they not only carry news stories, but also record sections from parliamentary speeches, government reports, and other official sources. The *New York Times, Washington Post,* and *Los Angeles Times* are the most important examples, and each produces an index of topics and names that have appeared in its pages.

Once you start using a library regularly, you are likely to find that it is more common to feel overwhelmed by the number of works available in a particular area than to experience difficulty in tracing relevant literature. One way of dealing with this problem, of course, is to base your selection of books or articles on reading lists provided by lecturers and professors. Where such lists are not available, or are inadequate, the best procedure to follow is to define the information you require as precisely as possible. This will allow you to narrow the range of choice to feasible limits. If your library is an open-stack one, it is worth looking through a number of potentially relevant books or articles before selecting those you decide to work with. In making the decision, apart obviously from considerations of the subject matter, keep in mind *when* the book was written. New developments are constantly taking place in sociology, and in the other social sciences, and obviously older books won't cover these.

GLOSSARY OF
BASIC CONCEPTS

Words in bold type within entries refer to concepts or terms found elsewhere in the glossaries.

ALIENATION. The sense that our own abilities, as human beings, are taken over by other entities. The term as originally used by Marx to refer to the projection of human powers onto gods. Subsequently he employed the term to refer to the loss of control on the part of workers over the nature of the labor task, and over the products of their labor.

CAUSATION. The causal influence of one factor or **variable** upon another. A "cause and effect" relationship exists wherever a particular event or state of affairs (the effect) is produced by the existence of another (the cause). Causal factors in sociology include the reasons individuals have for what they do, as well as many external influences on their behavior.

CLASS. Although it is one of the most frequently used concepts in sociology, there is no clear agreement about how the notion should best be defined. However, most sociologists use the term to refer to socioeconomic differences between groups of individuals that create differences in their material prosperity and power.

COLLECTIVE ACTION. Action undertaken in a relatively spontaneous way by a large number of people assembled together in a particular place or area. One of the most important forms of collective action is crowd behavior. In crowds, individuals can seek to achieve objectives that in ordinary circumstances are denied to them.

COMMUNICATION. The transmission of information from one individual or group to another. Communication is the necessary basis of all social interaction. In face-to-face contexts, communication is carried on by the use of language, but also by many bodily cues that individuals interpret in understanding what others say and do. With the development of writing, and electronic media, like radio, television, or computer transmission systems, communication becomes in some part detached from immediate contexts of face-to-face social relationships.

CONFLICT. Antagonism between individuals or groups in society. Conflict may take two forms. One occurs where there is a clash of interests between two or more individuals or groups; the other happens where people or collectivities engage in active struggle with one another. Interest conflict does not always lead to open struggle, while active conflicts may sometimes occur between parties who mistakenly believe their interests are opposed.

CONFORMITY. Behavior that follows the established norms of a group or society. People do not always conform to social norms because they accept the **values** that underlie them. They may behave in the approved ways simply because it is expedient to do so, or because of **sanctions.**

CONSENSUS. Agreement over basic social values by the members of a group, community, or society. Some thinkers in sociology strongly emphasize the importance of consensus as a basis for social stability. These writers believe that all societies that endure over any substantial period of time involve a "common value system" of consensual beliefs held by the majority of the population.

CORRELATION. The regular relationship between two dimensions or **variables,** often expressed in statistical terms. Correlations may be positive or negative. A positive correlation between two variables exists where a high rank on one variable is associated with a high rank on the other. A negative correlation is where a high rank on one variable is associated with a low rank on the other.

THE CREATED ENVIRONMENT. Those aspects of the physical world that derive from the use of humanly created **technology.** The created environment refers to constructions established by human beings to serve their needs—including, for example, roads, railways, factories, offices, private homes, and other buildings.

CRIME. Any action that contravenes the laws established by a political authority. Although we may tend to think of "criminals" as a distinct subsection of the population, there are few people who have not broken the law in one way or another during the course of their lives. While laws are formulated by state authorities, it is by no means unknown for those authorities to engage in criminal behavior in certain contexts.

CRUDE BIRTH RATE. A statistical measure representing the number of births within a given population per year. Crude birth rates are normally calculated in terms of the number of births per thousand members of a population. Although the crude birth rate is a useful index for many purposes, it is only a general measure, because it does not specify numbers of births in relation to the age distribution of society in question.

CRUDE DEATH RATE. A statistical measure representing the number of deaths that occur annually in a given population. Crude death rates are normally calculated as the ratio of deaths to every thousand members of a population in a particular year. Crude death rates give a general indication of the mortality levels of a community or society, but are limited in their usefulness because they do not take into account the age distribution of the population in question.

CULTURAL REPRODUCTION. The transmission of cultural **values** and **norms** from generation to generation. Cultural reproduction refers to the mechanisms by which continuity of cultural experience is sustained across time. The processes of schooling in modern societies are among the main mechanisms of cultural reproduction, and do not operate solely through what is taught in courses of formal instruction. Cultural reproduction occurs in a more profound way through the **hidden curriculum**—aspects of behavior that individuals learn informally while at school.

CULTURE. The **values, norms,** and material goods characteristic of a given group. Like the concept of **society,** the notion of culture is very widely used in sociology, as well as in the other social sciences (particularly anthropology). Culture is one of the most distinctive properties of human social association.

DEMOGRAPHIC TRANSITION. An interpretation of population change which holds that a stable ratio of births to deaths is achieved once a certain level of economic prosperity has been reached. According to this notion, in preindustrial societies there is a rough balance between births and deaths, because population increase is kept in check by a lack of available food, and by disease or war. In modern societies, by contrast, population equilibrium is achieved because families are moved by economic incentives to limit numbers of children.

DEVIANCE. Modes of action that do not conform to the **norms** or **values** held by most of the members of a group or society. What is regarded as "deviant" is as widely variable as the norms and values that distinguish different cultures and subcultures from one another. Many forms of behavior that are highly esteemed in one context, or by one group, are regarded negatively by others.

DISCRIMINATION. Activities that deny to the members of a particular group resources or rewards that can be obtained by others. Discrimination has to be distinguished from prejudice, although the two are usually quite closely associated. It can be the case that individuals who are prejudiced against others do not engage in discriminatory practices against them; conversely, people may act in a discriminatory fashion even though they are not prejudiced against those subject to such discrimination.

DIVISION OF LABOR. The specialization of work tasks, by means of which different occupations are combined within a production system. All societies have at least some rudimentary form of division of labor, especially between the tasks allocated to men and those performed by women. With the development of industrialism, however, the division of labor becomes vastly more complex than in any prior type of production system. In the modern world, the division of labor is international in scope.

THE ECONOMY. The system of production and exchange that provides for the material needs of individuals living in a given society. Economic institutions are of key importance in all social orders. What goes on in the economy usually influences many other aspects of social life. Modern economies differ very substantially from traditional ones, because the majority of the population is no longer engaged in agricultural production.

EDUCATION. The transmission of knowledge from one generation to another by means of direct instruction. Although educational processes exist in all societies, it is only in the modern period that mass education takes the form of schooling—that is, instruction in specialized educational environments in which individuals spend several years of their lives.

ENCOUNTER. A meeting between two or more individuals in a situation of face-to-face interaction. Our day-to-day lives can be seen as a series of different encounters strung out across the course of the day. In modern societies, many of the encounters we have with others involve strangers rather than people we know well.

ETHNICITY. Culture **values** and **norms** which distinguish the members of a given group from others. An ethnic group is one whose members share a distinct awareness of a common cultural identity, separating them from other groups around them. In virtually all societies ethnic differences are associated with variations in power and material wealth. Where ethnic differences are also racial, such divisions are sometimes especially pronounced.

FAMILY. A group of individuals related to one another by blood ties, **marriage,** or adoption, who form an economic unit, the adult members of which are responsible for the upbringing of children. All known societies involve some form of family system, although the nature of family relationships varies widely. While in modern societies the main family form is the **nuclear family,** a variety of **extended family** relationships are also often found.

FEMINISM. Advocacy of the rights of women to equality with men in all spheres of life. Feminism dates from the late eighteenth century in Europe, and feminist movements exist in most countries of the world today.

FERTILITY. The average number of liveborn children produced by women of childbearing age in a particular society. Fertility has to be distinguished from **fecundity,** which refers to the potential numbers of births of which women in a given population are capable. Fertility always falls well short of fecundity.

FORMAL RELATIONS. Relations that exist in groups and organizations laid down by the **norms** or rules of the "official" system of authority.

GENDER. Social expectations about behavior regarded as appropriate for the members of each sex. Gender does not refer to the physical attributes in terms of which men and women differ, but to socially formed traits of masculinity and femininity. The study of gender relations has become one of the most important areas of sociology in recent years, although for a long time it received little attention.

GENDER SOCIALIZATION. The learning of gender roles through social factors such as schooling, the media, and family.

GLOBALIZATION. The development of social and economic relationships stretching worldwide. In current times, many aspects of people's lives are influenced by organizations and social networks located thousands of miles away from the societies in which they live. A key aspect of the study of globalization is the emergence of a **world system**—that is to say, for some purposes we have to regard the world as forming a single social order.

GOVERNMENT. The process of the enacting of policies and decisions on the part of **officials** within a political apparatus. We can speak of "government" as a process, or *the* government to refer to the officialdom responsible for the taking of binding political decisions. While in the past virtually all governments were headed by monarchs or emperors, in most modern societies governments are run by officials, who do not inherit their positions of power, but are elected or appointed on the basis of expertise and qualifications.

IDEOLOGY. Shared ideas or beliefs that serve to justify the interests of dominant groups. Ideologies are found in all societies in which there are systematic and engrained inequalities between groups. The concept of ideology connects closely with that of **power,** since ideological systems serve to legitimize the differential power that groups hold.

IMPERIALISM. The establishing of empires during the period of colonialism.

INDUSTRIALIZATION OF WAR. The application of modes of industrial production to weaponry, coupled with the organization of fighting forces as "military machines." The industrialization of war is as fundamental an aspect of the development of modern societies as is industry evolved for peaceful purposes. It is closely associated with the emergence of **total war** in the twentieth century

—warfare involving hundreds of thousands or millions of soldiers, plus the overall mobilizing of the **economy** for war-related needs.

INFORMAL RELATIONS. Relations that exist in groups and organizations developed on the basis of personal connections; ways of doing things that depart from formally recognized modes of procedure.

INNER CITY. The areas composing the central neighborhoods of a city, which normally have distinct characteristics from the **suburbs.** In many modern urban settings in the First World, inner-city areas are subject to dilapidation and decay, the more affluent residents having moved to outlying areas.

KINSHIP. A relation that links individuals through blood ties, **marriage,** or adoption. Kinship relations are by definition involved in marriage and the **family,** but extend much more broadly than these institutions. While in most modern societies few social obligations are involved in kinship relations extending beyond the immediate family, in many other cultures kinship is of vital importance for most aspects of social life.

MAGIC. Rites that attempt to influence spirits or supernatural beings in order to achieve human aims. In most societies, magic exists in a relation of some tension with religion. In contrast to religion, magic tends to be more of an "individual" activity, practiced by a sorcerer or **shaman.**

MARRIAGE. A socially approved sexual relationship between two individuals. Marriage almost always involves two persons of opposite sexes, but in some cultures types of homosexual marriage are tolerated. Marriage normally forms the basis of a **family procreation**—that is, it is expected that the married couple will produce and bring up children. Many societies permit **polygamous** marriage, in which an individual may have several spouses at the same time.

MENTAL ILLNESS. Disorder of the personality or mental processes. In the past, psychiatrists recognized two general types of mental disorder, neuroses (milder forms of illness, such as anxiety states) and psychoses (more serious forms of disturbance, in which individuals lose touch with reality as defined by the majority of the population). Today, however, psychiatrists follow *The Diagnostic and Statistical Manual*, Third Edition, Revised (DSM-III-R), a classification of disorders organized around specific categories instead of the broad neuroses and psychoses dichotomy.

MILITARY RULE. Government by military leaders, rather than by elected officials. Military governments have existed in many parts of the world in the current century. There are several types of military rule; in some instances the military tends to govern directly, while in others, government is conducted by officials appointed by, and directly responsible to, military leaders.

NATION-STATE. A particular type of **state,** characteristic of the modern world, in which a government has sovereign power within a defined territorial area, and the mass of the population are **citizens** who know themselves to be part of a single nation. Nation-states are closely associated with the rise of **nationalism,** although nationalist loyalties do not always conform to the boundaries of specific states that exist today. Nation-states developed as part of an emerging nation-state system, originating in Europe, but in current times spanning the whole globe.

NORMS. Rules of conduct that specify appropriate behavior in a given range of social contexts. A norm either prescribes a given type of behavior, or forbids it.

All human groups follow definite types of norms, which are always backed by sanctions of one kind or another—varying from informal disapproval to physical punishment or execution.

OBJECTIVITY. In common with those working in the natural sciences, sociologists seek to be objective in assessing the result of studies of the social world. Objectivity means giving rival interpretations a "fair hearing"—that is, striving as far as possible to reduce or eliminate bias in the interpretation of findings. A crucial dimension of objectivity, however, is that the conclusions drawn by any particular author are open to critical assessment by other members of the social scientific community.

ORGANIZATION. A large group of individuals, involving a definite set of authority relations. Many types of organization exist in industrial societies, influencing most aspects of our lives. While not all organizations are bureaucratic, there are quite close links between the development of organizations and bureaucratic tendencies.

PATRIARCHY. The dominance of men over women. All known societies are patriarchal, although there are many variations in the degree and nature of the power men exercise, as compared to women. One of the prime objectives of women's movements in modern societies is to combat existing patriarchal institutions.

POLITICS. The means by which power is employed to influence the nature and content of governmental activities. The sphere of the "political" includes the activities of those in **government,** but also the actions of many other groups and individuals. There are many ways in which people outside the governmental apparatus seek to influence it.

POSTINDUSTRIAL SOCIETY. A notion advocated by those who believe that processes of social change are taking us beyond the industrialized order. A postindustrial society is one based on the production of information, rather than on the production of material goods. According to those who favor this concept, we are currently experiencing a series of social changes as profound as those which initiated the industrial era some two hundred years ago.

POWER. The ability of individuals, or the members of a group, to achieve aims or further the interests they hold. Power is a pervasive aspect of all human relationships. Many **conflicts** in society are struggles over power, because how much power an individual or group is able to achieve governs how far they are able to put their wishes into practice at the expense of those of others.

PREJUDICE. The holding of preconceived ideas about an individual or group, ideas that are resistant to change even in the face of new information. Prejudice may be either positive or negative.

RACISM. The attribution of characteristics of superiority or inferiority to a population sharing certain physically inherited characteristics. Racism is one specific form of prejudice, focusing on physical variations between people. Racist attitudes became entrenched during the period of Western colonial expansion, but seem also to rest on mechanisms of prejudice and discrimination found in very many contexts of human societies.

REBELLION. A revolt against the political authorities, involving the use, or threat, of force. Rebellions, unlike revolutions, are mainly aimed at removing particular rulers or regimes, rather than bringing about structural change in a society.

RELIGION. A set of beliefs adhered to by the members of a community, involving **symbols** regarded with a sense of awe or wonder, together with **ritual** practices in which members of the community engage. Religions do not universally involve a belief in supernatural entities. Although distinctions between religion and **magic** are difficult to draw, it is often held that magic is primarily practiced by individuals rather than being the focus of community ritual.

RESEARCH METHODS. The diverse methods of investigation used to gather empirical (factual) material. Numerous different research methods exist in sociology, but perhaps the most commonly used are fieldwork (or **participant observation**) and **survey** methods. For many purposes it is useful to combine two or more methods within a single research project.

REVOLUTION. A process of political change, involving the mobilizing of a mass **social movement,** which by the use of violence successfully overthrows an existing regime and forms a new government. A revolution is distinguished from a *coup d'état* because it involves a mass movement and the occurrence of major change in the political system as a whole. A *coup d'état* refers to the seizure of power through the use of arms by individuals who then replace the existing political leaders, but without otherwise radically transforming the governmental system. Revolutions can also be distinguished from **rebellions,** which involve challenges to the existing political authorities, but again aim at the replacement of personnel rather than the transformation of the political structure as such.

RITUAL. Formalized modes of behavior in which the members of a group or community regularly engage. **Religion** represents one of the main contexts in which rituals are practiced, but the scope of ritual behavior extends well beyond this particular sphere. Most groups have ritual practices of some kind or another.

ROLE. The expected behavior of an individual occupying a particular **social position.** The idea of social role originally comes from the theater, referring to the parts that actors play in a stage production. In every society individuals play a number of different social roles, according to the varying contexts of their activities.

SCIENCE. Science, in the sense of physical science, is the systematic study of the physical world. Science involves the disciplined marshalling of empirical data, combined with the construction of **theoretical approaches** and **theories** that illuminate or explain those data. Scientific activity combines the creation of boldly new modes of thought with the careful testing of **hypotheses** and ideas. One major feature that helps distinguish science from other types of idea system (such as that involved in religion) is the assumption that *all* scientific ideas are open to mutual criticism and revision on the part of the members of the scientific community.

SECULARIZATION. A process of decline in the influence of religion. Although modern societies have become increasingly secularized, tracing the extent of secularization is a complex matter. Secularization can refer to levels of involvement with religious organizations (such as rates of church attendance), the social and material influence wielded by religious organizations, and the degree to which people hold religious beliefs.

SELF-CONSCIOUSNESS. Awareness of one's distinct social identity, as a person separate from others. Human beings are not born with self-consciousness, but acquire an awareness of self as a result of early **socialization.** The learning of language is of vital importance to the processes by which the child learns to become a self-conscious being.

SOCIAL CHANGE. Alteration in basic structures of a social group or society. Social change is an ever-present phenomenon in social life, but has become especially intense in the modern era. The origins of modern **sociology** can be traced to attempts to understand the dramatic changes shattering the traditional world and promoting new forms of **social order.**

SOCIAL EVOLUTIONISM. An approach to social change that draws upon concepts and ideas from evolutionary theory in biology. Although evolutionary thought was particularly influential in sociology in the nineteenth century, evolutionary ideas have continued to exert some influence in contemporary sociology. There are many versions of sociological evolutionism, but most such theories hold that human societies move progressively from simple to more complex forms of association.

SOCIAL GROUP. A collection of individuals who interact in systematic ways with one another. Groups may range from very small associations to large-scale **organizations** or **societies.** Whatever their size, it is a defining feature of a group that its members have an awareness of a common identity. Most of our lives are spent in group contact; in modern societies, most people belong to numerous different types of group.

SOCIAL INSTITUTION. Basic modes of social activity followed by the majority of the members of a given society. Institutions involve **norms** and **values** to which large numbers of individuals conform, and all institutionalized modes of behavior are protected by strong sanctions. Institutions form the "bedrock" of a society, because they represent relatively fixed modes of behavior that endure over time.

SOCIAL MOBILITY. Movement of individuals or groups between different social positions. **Vertical mobility** refers to movement up or down a hierarchy in a stratification system. **Lateral mobility** is physical movement of individuals or groups from one region to another. When analyzing vertical mobility, sociologists distinguish between how far an individual is mobile in the course of his or her own career, and to what degree the position that the person reaches differs from that of his or her parents.

SOCIAL MOVEMENT. A large grouping of people who have become involved in seeking to accomplish, or to block, a process of **social change.** Social movements normally exist in relations of **conflict** with **organizations,** whose objectives and outlook they frequently oppose. However, movements that successfully challenge for power, once they become institutionalized, can develop into organizations.

SOCIAL POSITION. The social identity an individual has in a given group or society. Social positions may be very general in nature (such as those associated with **gender** roles) or may be much more specific (as in the case of occupational positions).

SOCIAL REPRODUCTION. The processes that sustain or perpetuate characteristics of social structure over periods of time.

SOCIAL STRATIFICATION. The existence of structured inequalities between groups in society, in terms of their access to material or symbolic rewards.

While all societies involve some forms of stratification, only with the development of state-based systems do wide differences in wealth and power arise. The most distinctive form of stratification in modern societies involves **class** divisions.

SOCIAL STRUCTURE. The underlying regularities or patterns in how people behave and in their relationships with one another.

SOCIALIZATION. The social processes through which children develop an awareness of social **norms** and **values,** and achieve a distinct sense of self. Although socialization processes are particularly significant in infancy and childhood, they continue to some degree throughout life. No human individuals are immune from the reactions of others around them, which influence and modify their behavior at all phases of the **life cycle.**

SOCIETY. The concept of society is one of the most important of all sociological notions. A society is a group of people who live in a particular territory, are subject to a common system of political authority, and are aware of having a distinct identity from other groups around them. Some societies, like those of hunters and gatherers, are very small, numbering no more than a few dozen people. Others are very large, involving many millions—modern Chinese society, for instance, has a population of more than a billion individuals.

SOCIOLOGY. The study of human groups and societies, giving particular emphasis to the analysis of the industrialized world. Sociology is one of a group of social sciences, which include also anthropology, economics, political science, and human geography. The divisions between the various social sciences are not clear-cut, and all share a certain range of common interests, concepts, and methods.

THE STATE. A **political apparatus** (**government** institutions, plus civil-service **officials**) ruling over a given territorial order, whose authority is backed by **law** and the ability to use **force.** Not all societies are characterized by the existence of a state. Hunting and gathering cultures, and smaller agrarian societies, lack state institutions. The emergence of the state marks a distinctive transition in human history, because the centralization of political power involved in state formation introduces new dynamics into processes of **social change.**

STATUS. The social honor or prestige that a particular group is accorded by other members of a society. Status groups normally involve distinct styles of life —patterns of behavior that the members of a group follow. Status privilege may be positive or negative. **"Pariah"** status groups are regarded with disdain, or treated as outcasts, by the majority of the population.

THEORETICAL APPROACH. A perspective on social life derived from a particular theoretical tradition. Some of the major theoretical traditions in sociology include **functionalism, structuralism, symbolic interactionism,** and **Marxism.** Theoretical approaches supply overall "perspectives" within which sociologists work, and influence the areas of their research as well as the modes in which research problems are identified and tackled.

THEORY. An attempt to identify general properties that explain regularly observed events. The construction of theories forms an essential element of all sociological works. While theories tend to be linked to broader **theoretical approaches,** they are also strongly influenced by the research results they help generate.

THE UNCONSCIOUS. Motives and ideas unavailable to the conscious mind of the individual. A key psychological mechanism involved in the unconscious is repression—parts of the mind are "blocked off" from an individual's direct awareness. According to Freud's theory, unconscious wishes and impulses established in childhood continue to play a major part in the life of the adult.

URBAN ECOLOGY. An approach to the study of urban life based on an analogy with the adjustment of plants and organisms to the physical environment. According to ecological theorists, the various neighborhoods and zones within cities are formed as a result of natural processes of adjustment on the part of urban populations as they compete for resources.

VALUES. Ideas held by human individuals or groups about what is desirable, proper, good, or bad. Differing values represent key aspects of variations in human **culture.** What individuals value is strongly influenced by the specific culture in which they happen to live.

WORK. The activity by which human beings produce from the natural world and so ensure their survival. Work should not be thought of exclusively as paid employment. In traditional cultures, there was only a rudimentary monetary system, and very few people worked for money payments. In modern societies, there remain many types of work that do not involve direct payment of wages or salary (such as housework).

WORLD SYSTEM. A social system of global dimensions, linking all societies within a world social order. The world system may most easily be thought of as a "single global society." The world system has only come into being since the period of the expansion of the West from about the seventeenth century onwards. Today, however, the existence of an increasingly integrated world system is one of the most important features affecting the lives of most individuals.

WORLD-SYSTEM THEORY. Pioneered by Immanuel Wallerstein, this theory emphasizes the interconnections among countries based on the expansion of a capitalist world economy. This economy is made up of **core countries,** the **semi-periphery,** the **periphery,** and the **external arena.**

GLOSSARY OF IMPORTANT TERMS

Words in bold type within entries refer to concepts or terms found elsewhere in the glossaries.

ABSOLUTE POVERTY. Poverty as defined in terms of the minimal requirements necessary to sustain a healthy existence.

ACTION-REACTION. An aspect of the arms race, in which each side develops its defense strategy and spending in relation to the anticipated response of the others.

ADAPTATION. Refers to the ability of a biological organism to survive within a given environment.

AFFECTIVE INDIVIDUALISM. The belief in romantic attachment as a basis for contracting **marriage** ties.

AFFIRMATIVE ACTION. Reforms designed to reduce inequalities by the taking of positive steps to ensure the representation of minorities in educational and other organizations.

AGE-GRADES. The system found in many small, traditional cultures, according to which individuals belonging to a similar age-group are categorized together, and hold similar rights and obligations.

AGEISM. **Discrimination** or prejudice against a person on the grounds of age.

AGENCIES OF SOCIALIZATION. Groups or social contexts within which significant processes of **socialization** take place.

AGGREGATE. A collection of people present in a public setting, all going their separate ways rather than composing a solidary group.

AGRARIAN SOCIETIES. Societies whose means of subsistence is based on agricultural production (crop growing).

AGRIBUSINESS. The mass production of agricultural goods on the basis of mechanized agriculture.

AIDS. A disease that attacks the immune system of the body.

ALIENATION. The sense that our own abilities, as human beings, are taken over by other entities. The term was originally used by Marx to refer to the projection of human powers onto gods. Subsequently he employed the term to refer to the loss of control on the part of workers over the nature of the labor task, and over the products of their labor.

ALTERATIVE MOVEMENT. A movement concerned with altering individuals' behavior or consciousness.

ANDROGENITAL SYNDROME. An endocrinal abnormality that produces male-like genitals in individuals who have female hormonal makeup.

ANGLO-CONFORMITY. The process of **assimilation** by which immigrants abandon their own cultures and values and take on the culture and values of the English-speaking majority.

ANIMISM. A belief that events in the world are mobilized by the activities of spirits.

ANOMIE. A concept first brought into wide usage in sociology by Durkheim, referring to a situation in which social **norms** lose their hold over individual behavior.

ANTHROPOLOGY. A social science, closely linked to sociology, which concentrates on the study of traditional cultures and on the **evolution** of the human species.

APARTHEID. The system of racial segregation established in South Africa.

ARMS RACE. A competition between two or more nations to achieve military superiority over the other or others.

ARMS TRADE. The selling of armaments for profit, whether carried on by **governments** or by private contractors.

ASSIMILATION. The acceptance of a minority group by a majority population, in which the new group takes on the values and norms of the dominant **culture.**

AUTHORITARIAN PERSONALITY. A set of specific personality characteristics, involving a rigid and intolerant outlook and an inability to accept ambiguity.

AUTOMATION. Production processes monitored and controlled by machines with only minimal supervision from human beings.

BACK REGION. An area away from "front region" performances, as specified by Erving Goffman, in which individuals are able to relax and behave informally.

BUREAUCRACY. A type of **organization** marked by a clear hierarchy of authority, the existence of written rules of procedure, and staffed by full-time, salaried **officials.**

CAPITALISM. An economic system based on the private ownership of wealth, which is invested and reinvested in order to produce profit.

CAPITALISTS. Those who own companies, land, or stocks and shares, using these to generate economic returns.

CARCERAL ORGANIZATION. An **organization** in which individuals are shut away for long periods of time from the outside world—such as a prison, mental hospital, army barrack, or boarding school.

CASH-CROP PRODUCTION. Production of crops sold on world markets, rather than being consumed by the local population.

CASTE. A form of stratification in which an individual's social position is fixed at birth and cannot be changed. There is virtually no intermarriage between the members of different caste groups.

CAUSAL RELATIONSHIP. A relationship whereby one state of affairs (the effect) is brought about by another (the cause).

CHURCH. A large body of people belonging to an established religious organization. The term is also used to refer to the place in which religious ceremonials are carried on.

CITIZEN. A member of a political community, having both rights and duties associated with that membership.

CIVIL INATTENTION. The process whereby individuals who are in the same physical setting of interaction demonstrate to one another that they are aware of each other's presence.

CIVIL RELIGION. Forms of ritual and belief similar to those involved in **religion,** but concerning secular activities—such as political parades or ceremonials.

CIVIL RIGHTS. Legal rights held by all **citizens** in a given national community.

CLAN. A kin group stretching more broadly than the family, found in many preindustrial societies.

CLASS CONSCIOUSNESS. Awareness of the class system, including the class an individual believes him- or herself to be in, together with the imagery of the class system he or she possesses.

CLIENTSHIP. A system of patronage, in which services are available to specific individuals in positions of influence or power. Those "patrons" tie others to them by means of the rewards they control.

CLOCK TIME. Time as measured by the clock—that is, assessed in terms of hours, minutes, or seconds. Before the invention of clocks, time-reckoning was based on events in the natural world, such as the rising and setting of the sun.

CLOSED DOMESTICATED NUCLEAR FAMILY. The **nuclear family** system characteristic of the modern West, in which the domestic unit is largely separate from the surrounding community.

COGNITION. Human thought processes involving perception, reasoning, and remembering.

COHABITATION. Two people living together in a sexual relationship of some permanence, without being married to one another.

COLLECTIVE CONSUMPTION. A concept used by Manuel Castells to refer to processes of urban consumption—such as the buying and selling of property.

COLONIALISM. The process whereby Western nations established their rule in parts of the world away from their home territories.

COMMON-SENSE BELIEFS. Widely shared beliefs about the social or natural worlds held by lay members of society.

COMMUNISM. A set of political ideas associated with Marx, as developed particularly by Lenin, and institutionalized in the Soviet Union, Eastern Europe, and in some Third World countries.

COMPARATIVE QUESTIONS. Questions concerned with the drawing of comparisons between different human societies for the purposes of sociological **theory** or research.

COMPETITION. A concept used in ecology to refer to the struggle of different species to occupy the most advantageous locations in a given territory.

CONCESSION COMPANIES. European companies that established themselves in colonial areas on the basis of exclusive rights of production in a given area or industry.

CONCRETE OPERATIONAL STAGE. A stage of cognitive development, as formulated by Piaget, in which the child's thinking is based primarily on physical perception of the world. In this phase, the child is not yet capable of dealing with abstract concepts or hypothetical situations.

CONGLOMERATES. Corporations made up of companies producing or trading in a variety of different products and services.

CONSTITUTIONAL MONARCH. A king or queen who is largely a "figurehead," real power rests in the hands of other political leaders.

CONTRADICTION. A term used by Marx to refer to mutually antagonistic tendencies in a society.

CONTRADICTORY CLASS LOCATIONS. Positions in the class structure, particularly involving routine white-collar and lower managerial jobs, which share characteristics of the class positions both above and below them.

CONTROL. A statistical or experimental means of holding some **variables** constant in order to examine the causal influence of others.

CONURBATION. An agglomeration of towns or cities into an unbroken urban environment.

CONVERGENCE THEORY. The thesis that the more economically developed a society becomes, the more it resembles other industrialized countries.

CONVERSATION. Verbal communication between two or more individuals.

CONVERSATION ANALYSIS. The empirical study of conversations, employing techniques drawn from **ethnomethodology.**

CORE COUNTRIES. The core countries in the world economy are those that occupy a central position as a result of being most fully industrialized (they include primarily the United States, Western Europe, and Japan).

CORPORATENESS. A sense of belonging to a body of people having a similar outlook to one's own.

CORPORATIONS. Business firms or companies.

CORRELATION COEFFICIENT. A measure of the degree of correlation between variables.

COUNTER-INTUITIVE THINKING. Thinking that suggests ideas contrary to common-sense assumptions.

COUP D'ÉTAT. An armed takeover of **government.** Unlike in the case of **revolutions,** no mass **social movement** is involved.

CRIMES OF THE POWERFUL. Criminal activity carried out by those in positions of power.

CRIMINAL NETWORK. A network of social relations between individuals engaging in criminal activities.

CRITICAL SITUATIONS. Social circumstances in which individuals are compelled to cope with radically new demands, which put a strain upon their existing behavior and attitudes.

CROWD ACTIVITY. Actions carried on by individuals when associated together as a crowd.

CULT. A fragmentary religious grouping, to which individuals are loosely affiliated, but which lacks any permanent structure.

CULTURAL PLURALISM. The coexistence of several subcultures within a given society on equal terms.

CULTURAL UNIVERSALS. Values or modes of behavior shared by all human cultures.

DECARCERATION. The release of large numbers of individuals from mental hospitals and prisons to live in the outside world.

DEMOCRACY. A political system that allows the citizens to participate in political decision making, or to elect representatives to government bodies.

DEMOCRATIC CENTRALISM. A mode of political organization characteristic of Eastern Europe and the Soviet Union, which takes the form of a pyramid of electoral bodies. Those in groups at each level elect representatives to groups at higher levels, who in turn elect representatives to yet higher-level organizations.

DEMOCRATIC ELITISM. A theory of the limits of **democracy,** which holds that democratic participation in large-scale societies is necessarily limited to the regular election of political leaders.

DEMOGRAPHY. The study of populations.

DENOMINATION. A religious **sect** that has lost its revivalist dynamism, and has become an institutionalized body, commanding the adherence of significant numbers of people.

DEPENDENCY THEORY. The term for the thesis that a range of countries, particularly in the **Third World,** lack the ability to control major aspects of their economic life, because of the dominance of the industrialized societies in the world economy.

DEPENDENT VARIABLE. A **variable** or factor causally influenced by another (the **independent variable**).

DETERRENCE. The prevention of military conflict on the basis of ensuring that an aggressor would suffer too many losses to make the initiation of hostilities worthwhile.

DEVIANT SUBCULTURE. A subculture whose members have values that differ substantially from those of the majority in a society.

DEVELOPMENTAL QUESTIONS. Questions that sociologists pose when looking at the origins and path of development of **social institutions** from the past to the present.

DIALECTICAL INTERPRETATION OF CHANGE. An interpretation of change emphasizing the clash of opposing influences or groups as the impulse for social transformation.

DIFFERENTIAL ASSOCIATION. An interpretation of the development of criminal behavior proposed by Edwin H. Sutherland. According to him, criminal behavior is learned through association with others who regularly engage in crime.

DIFFERENTIATION. The development of increasing complexity within organic systems or societies.

DISEQUILIBRIUM. The breakdown of social equilibrium or **consensus.**

DISPLACEMENT. The transferring of ideas or emotions from their true source to another object.

DIVISION OF LABOR. The specialization of work tasks, by means of which different occupations are combined within a production system. All societies have at least some rudimentary form of division of labor, especially between the tasks allocated to men and those performed by women. With the development of industrialism, however, the division of labor becomes vastly more complex than in any prior type of production system. In the modern world, the division of labor is international in scope.

DOCUMENTARY RESEARCH. Research based on evidence drawn from the study of documents, such as archives or official statistics.

DOMESTIC VIOLENCE. Violent behavior directed by one member of a household against another. Most serious domestic violence is carried out by males against females.

DOUBLING TIME. The time it takes for a particular level of population to double.

DRAMATURGICAL MODEL. An approach to the study of social interaction based on the use of metaphors derived from the theater.

ECOLOGICAL APPROACH. A perspective on urban analysis emphasizing the "natural" distribution of city neighborhoods into areas having contrasting characteristics.

ECONOMIC INTERDEPENDENCE. Refers to the fact that, in the **division of labor,** individuals depend on others to produce many or most of the goods they need to sustain their lives.

EDUCATIONAL SYSTEM. The system of educational provision operating within a given society.

EGOCENTRISM. The characteristic outlook of a child, according to Piaget, during the early years of its life. Egocentric thinking involves understanding objects and events in the environment solely in terms of the child's own position.

ELABORATED CODE. A form of speech involving the deliberate and constructed use of words to designate precise meanings.

EMPIRICAL INVESTIGATION. Factual enquiry carried out in any given area of sociological study.

ENDOGAMY. A system in which an individual may only marry another person from within the same kin group as herself or himself.

ENTREPRENEUR. The owner of a business firm.

ENVIRONMENTAL ECOLOGY. The term refers to a concern with preserving the integrity of the physical environment in the face of the impact of modern industry and technology.

EPISODES OF CHANGE. Sequences of **social change** occurring in a similar way in several societies.

ESTATE. A form of stratification involving inequalities between groups of individuals established by law.

ETHICAL RELIGIONS. Religions that depend on the ethical appeal of a "great teacher" (like Buddha or Confucius), rather than on a belief in supernatural beings.

ETHNOCENTRIC TRANSNATIONALS. Transnational companies largely run directly from the headquarters of the parent company.

ETHNOCENTRISM. The tendency to look at other cultures through the eyes of one's own culture, and thereby misrepresent them.

ETHNOMETHODOLOGY. The study of how people make sense of what others say and do in the course of day-to-day social interaction. Ethnomethodology is concerned with the "ethno-methods" by means of which human beings sustain meaningful interchanges with one another.

EVOLUTION. The development of biological organisms by means of the adaptation of species to the demands of the physical environment.

EXOGAMY. A system in which individuals may only marry a spouse from a kinship group different from their own.

EXPERIMENT. A research method in which **variables** can be analyzed in a controlled and systematic way, either in an artificial situation constructed by the researcher, or in naturally occurring settings.

EXPONENTIAL GROWTH. A geometric, rather than linear, rate of progression, producing a very fast rise in the numbers of a population experiencing such growth.

EXTENDED FAMILY. A family group consisting of more than two generations of relatives living either within the same household or very close to one another.

EXTERNAL ARENA. Countries that remain outside the world economy at any particular period of time.

FACTUAL QUESTIONS. Questions that raise issues concerning matters of fact (rather than theoretical or moral issues).

FAMILY. A group of individuals related to one another by blood ties, **marriage,** or adoption, who form an economic unit, the adult members of which are responsible for the upbringing of children. All known societies involve some form of family system, although the nature of family relationships varies widely.

While in modern societies the main family form is the **nuclear family,** a variety of **extended family** relationships are also often found.

FAMILY CAPITALISM. Capitalistic enterprise owned and administered by entrepreneurial families.

FAMILY OF ORIENTATION. The family into which an individual is born.

FAMILY OF PROCREATION. The family an individual initiates through marriage or by having children.

FASCISM. A set of political ideas, or an actual political system, based on notions of the superiority of some races over others.

FECUNDITY. A measure of the number of children that is biologically possible for a woman to produce.

FEMININITY. The characteristic forms of behavior expected of women in any given culture.

FIELD OF ACTION. The arena within which **social movements** interact with established **organizations,** the ideas and outlook of the members of both thereby often becoming modified.

FIRST WORLD. The group of nation-states that possesses mature industrialized economies, based upon capitalistic production.

FOCUSED CROWD. A crowd of people acting in pursuit of common objectives.

FOCUSED INTERACTION. Interaction between individuals engaged in a common activity or in direct conversation with one another.

FORCE. Compulsion, based on the threat or actual use of violence.

FORCES OF PRODUCTION. A term used by Marx to refer to the factors promoting economic growth in a society.

FORDISM. The system of production pioneered by Henry Ford, involving the introduction of the assembly line.

FORMAL-OPERATIONAL STAGE. A stage of cognitive development, according to Piaget's theory, at which the growing child becomes capable of handling abstract concepts and hypothetical situations.

FRONT REGION. A setting of social activity in which individuals seek to put on a definite "performance" for others.

FUNCTIONALISM. A theoretical perspective based on the notion that social events can best be explained in terms of the functions they perform—that is, the contributions they make to the continuity of a society.

FUNDAMENTALISM. A belief in returning to the literal meanings of scriptural texts.

GANG. An informal group of individuals meeting regularly to engage in common activities, which may be outside the framework of the law.

GENERALIZED OTHER. A concept in the theory of G. H. Mead, according to which the individual takes over the general **values** of a given group or society during the **socialization** process.

GENTRIFICATION. A process of urban renewal in which older, deteriorated housing is refurbished by affluent people moving into the area.

GEOCENTRIC TRANSNATIONALS. Transnational companies whose administrative structure is global, rather than organized from any particular country.

GROSS NATIONAL PRODUCT (GNP). The amount of wealth produced in a country per year, usually measured as the average per head of population.

GROUP PRODUCTION. Production organized by means of small groups rather than individuals.

GUERRILLA MOVEMENT. A nongovernmental military **organization.**

HEADQUARTERS CITY. A city that has a coordinating role in the international **division of labor**—a headquarters of world finance or commerce.

HEALTH-CARE SYSTEM. The organization of medical services in a given country.

HETEROSEXUALITY. An orientation in sexual activity or feelings towards people of the opposite sex.

HIDDEN CURRICULUM. Traits of behavior or attitudes that are learned at school, but which are not included within the formal curriculum. The hidden curriculum is the "unstated agenda" involved in schooling—teaching, for example, aspects of gender differences.

HIGH-TRUST SYSTEMS. Organizations, or work settings, in which individuals are permitted a great deal of autonomy and control over the work task.

HIGHER EDUCATION. Education beyond school level, in colleges or universities.

HISTORICAL MATERIALISM. Marx's interpretation of **social change** in history, according to which processes of change are determined primarily by economic factors.

HISTORICITY. The use of an understanding of history as a basis for trying to change history—that is, producing informed processes of **social change.**

HOMOSEXUALITY. An orientation of sexual activities or feelings towards others of the same sex.

HOUSEWORK (domestic labor). Unpaid work carried on, usually by women, in the home, concerned with day-to-day domestic chores such as cooking, cleaning, and shopping.

HUNTING AND GATHERING SOCIETIES. Societies whose mode of subsistence is gained from hunting animals, fishing, and gathering edible plants.

HYPOTHESIS. An idea, or a guess, about a given state of affairs, put forward as a basis for empirical testing.

IDEAL TYPE. A "pure type," constructed by emphasizing certain traits of a given social item that do not necessarily exist anywhere in reality. An example is Max Weber's ideal type of bureaucratic **organization.**

INCOME. Payment, usually derived from wages, salaries, or investments.

INDEPENDENT VARIABLE. A **variable** or factor that causally affects another (the **dependent variable**).

INDUSTRIAL DEMOCRACY. Types of democratic participation or representation in the workplace.

INDUSTRIALIZED SOCIETIES. The main characteristics are that the majority of the population works in factories or offices rather than in agriculture, most people live in urban areas, and **nation-states** are more strongly developed.

INFANT MORTALITY RATE. The number of infants who die during the first year of life, per thousand live births.

THE INFORMAL ECONOMY. Economic transactions carried on outside the sphere of orthodox paid employment.

INFORMATION TECHNOLOGY. Forms of technology based on information processing and involving micro-electronic circuitry.

INNOVATION CENTER. A city or town whose prosperity depends on being a center of technological innovation or creativity.

INSTINCT. A fixed pattern of behavior that has genetic origins and which appears in all normal animals within a given species.

INSTITUTIONAL CAPITALISM. Capitalistic enterprise organized on the basis of institutional shareholding.

INSTITUTIONAL RACISM. Patterns of discrimination based on ethnicity that have become structured into existing social institutions.

INTELLIGENCE. Level of intellectual ability, particularly as measured by **IQ (Intelligence Quotient)** tests.

INTEREST GROUP. A group organized to pursue specific interests in the political arena, operating primarily by lobbying the members of legislative bodies.

INTERGENERATIONAL MOBILITY. Movement up or down a social stratification hierarchy from one generation to another.

INTERNATIONAL DIVISION OF LABOR. The phrase refers to the interdependence of countries or regions that trade on global markets.

INTRAGENERATIONAL MOBILITY. Movement up or down a social stratification hierarchy within the course of a personal career.

INVASION. A notion used in ecology to refer to the intrusion of a new species into an area previously dominated by others.

IQ (Intelligence Quotient). A score attained on tests of symbolic or reasoning abilities.

KIBBUTZIM. Communities established in Israel in which production is carried on cooperatively and inequalities of wealth and income are kept to a minimum.

LABELING THEORY. An approach to the study of **deviance** that suggests that people become "deviant" because certain labels are attached to their behavior by political authorities and others.

LATENT FUNCTIONS. Functional consequences that are not intended or recognized by the members of a social system in which they occur.

LATERAL MOBILITY. Movement of individuals from one region of a country to another, or across countries.

LAW. A rule of behavior established by a political authority and backed by state power.

LEGITIMACY. The belief that a particular political order is just and valid.

LEGITIMATION CRISIS. The failure of a political order to generate a sufficient level of commitment and involvement on the part of its **citizens** to be able properly to govern.

LESBIANISM. Homosexual activities or attachment between women.

LIBERAL DEMOCRACY. A system of **democracy** based on parliamentary institutions, coupled to the free-market system in the area of economic production.

LIFE EXPECTANCY. The number of years that people at any given age can on average expect to live.

LIFE HISTORIES. Studies of the overall lives of individuals, often based both on self-reporting and documents such as letters.

LIFE SPAN. The maximum length of life that is biologically possible for a member of a given species.

LIMITED WAR. Warfare involving relatively small numbers of the population, and fought principally by soldiers.

LITERACY. The ability of individuals to read and write.

LOCAL KNOWLEDGE. Knowledge of a local community, or context of action, possessed by individuals who spend long periods of their lives in them.

LOW-TRUST SYSTEMS. An **organizational** or work setting in which individuals are allowed little responsibility for, or control over, the work task.

MACHINE PRODUCTION. Economic production carried on through the use of machinery driven by inanimate sources of power.

MACROSEGREGATION. Segregation between very large numbers of the members of different racial groups, separated territorially.

MACROSOCIOLOGY. The study of large-scale groups, **organizations,** or social systems.

MALE INEXPRESSIVENESS. The difficulties men have in expressing, or talking about, their feelings to others.

MALTHUSIANISM. A doctrine about population dynamics developed by Thomas Malthus, according to which population increase comes up against "natural limits," represented by famine and war.

MANAGEMENT OF VIOLENCE. The way in which the military, together with armaments, are organized within a given society, in respect of their relation to the civil authorities.

MANAGERIAL CAPITALISM. Capitalistic enterprises administered by managerial executives, rather than by owners.

MANIFEST FUNCTIONS. The functions of an aspect or type of social activity that are known to, and intended by, the individuals involved in a given situation of social life.

MARXISM. A body of thought deriving its main elements from Marx's ideas.

MASCULINITY. The characteristic forms of behavior expected of men in any given culture.

MASS CIRCULATION. The larege-scale audiences reached by modern media of communication, such as newspapers or television.

MASS MEDIA. Forms of communication, such as newspapers, magazines, radio, or television, designed to reach mass audiences.

MATERIALIST CONCEPTION OF HISTORY. The view developed by Marx, according to which "material" or economic factors have a prime role in determining historical change.

MATERNAL DEPRIVATION. The situation in which infants or very young children are deprived of close contact with the mother for a period of several weeks or longer.

MATRILINEAL INHERITANCE. The inheritance of property or titles through the female line.

MATRILOCAL FAMILY. A family system in which the husband is expected to live near to the wife's parents.

MEAN. A statistical measure of "central tendency" or average based on dividing a total by the number of individual cases involved.

MEANINGFUL ACTIVITIES. Human action that is carried out for definite reasons, and with specific purposes in mind. The vast bulk of human behavior is composed of meaningful activities, this being one of the main characteristics that separates human conduct from the movement of objects and events in the natural world.

MEANS OF PRODUCTION. The means whereby the production of material goods is carried on in a society, including not just technology but the social relations between producers.

MEDIAN. The number that falls halfway in a range of numbers—a way of calculating "central tendency" that is sometimes more useful than calculating a **mean.**

MEGALOPOLIS. The "city of all cities" in ancient Greece—used in modern times to refer to very large **conurbations.**

MELTING POT. The idea that ethnic differences can be combined to create new patterns of behavior drawing on diverse cultural sources.

MEZZOSEGREGATION. Segregation between racial groups in terms of areas of neighborhood residence.

MICROSEGREGATION. Segregation between racial groups enforced in the details of daily life—for example separate waiting rooms in bus or railway stations.

MICROSOCIOLOGY. The study of human behavior in contexts of face-to-face interaction.

MIDDLE CLASS. A social class composed broadly of those working in white-collar and lower managerial occupations.

MILITARY-INDUSTRIAL COMPLEX. A set of institutional connections between business firms and the armed forces, based upon common interests in weapons production.

MILITARY MIND. A concept used by Samuel Huntington to refer to the typical outlook that the soldier has towards the world.

MILLENARIAN MOVEMENT. Beliefs held by the members of certain types of religious movements, according to which cataclysmic changes will occur in the near future, heralding the arrival of a new epoch.

MINORITY GROUP (OR ETHNIC MINORITY). A group of people, in a minority in a given society who, because of their distinct physical or cultural characteristics, find themselves in situations of inequality within that society.

MOBILIZATION. The "gearing up" of groups for collective action.

MODE. The number that appears most often in a given set of data. This can sometimes be a helpful way of portraying central tendency.

MODULE PRODUCTION PLACE. An urban area in which parts are made for products whose final assembly are carried out elsewhere.

MONOGAMY. A form of marriage in which each married partner is allowed only one spouse at any given time.

MONOPOLY. A situation in which a single firm dominates in a given industry.

MONOTHEISM. Belief in a single god.

MORTALITY. The number of deaths in a population.

MULTILINEAR EVOLUTION. An interpretation of social evolution which holds that there are varying "paths" of evolutionary development followed by different societies.

MULTIPLE SOVEREIGNTY. A situation in which there is no single sovereign power in a society.

MUTATION. A process of random genetic change introducing an alteration in the physical characteristics of an animal or plant. The vast majority of mutations lead "nowhere" in the course of **evolution**—that is the mutant organisms fail to survive. In a tiny proportion of cases, however, mutation produces characteristics that allow new species to flourish.

NATIONALISM. A set of beliefs and **symbols** expressing identification with a given national community.

NATION-STATE. A particular type of **state,** characteristic of the modern world, in which a government has sovereign power within a defined territorial area, and the mass of the population are **citizens** who know themselves to be part of a single nation. Nation-states are closely associated with the rise of **nationalism,** although nationalist loyalties do not always conform to the boundaries of specific states that exist today. Nation-states developed as part of an emerging nation-state system, originating in Europe, but in current times spanning the whole globe.

NEO-IMPERIALISM. The dominance of some nations over others by means of unequal conditions of economic exchange. Neo-imperialism, unlike older empires, is not founded upon the direct imposition of political power by one society upon another. The most important global context in which relations of neo-imperialism are established are between industrialized societies and the **Third World** countries.

NEOLOCAL RESIDENCE. A family pattern in which the married couple sets up home away from the place of residence of either the wife's or the husband's parents.

NEUROSES. Less-severe mental disorders according to the traditional method of diagnosing mental disorders. Those afflicted suffered from anxiety but retained a sense of reality.

NEWLY INDUSTRIALIZING COUNTRIES (NIC). **Third World** countries that over the past two or three decades have begun to develop a strong industrial base, such as Singapore or Hong Kong.

NONCONFORMITY. The failure or refusal to conform to established social norms.

NONSTATE ACTORS. International agencies, other than states, which play a part in the world system.

NONVERBAL COMMUNICATION. Communication between individuals based on facial expression or bodily gesture, rather than on the use of language.

NUCLEAR FAMILY. A family group consisting of wife, husband (or one of these), and dependent children.

OCCUPATION. Any form of paid employment in which an individual regularly works.

OEDIPUS COMPLEX. A phase of early human psychological development, according to Freud, in which a boy experiences intense feeling of love for the mother, together with hatred for the father. The overcoming of the Oedipus complex marks a key transition, in Freud's view, in the development of the boy as an autonomous being.

OFFICIALS. Individuals who occupy formal positions in large-scale **organizations.**

OLIGARCHY. Rule by a small minority within an organization or society.

OLIGOPOLY A situation in which a small number of firms dominates in a given industry.

OPEN-LINEAGE FAMILY. A family system found in traditional Europe, in which domestic relationships are closely intertwined with the local community.

ORGANIZATION. A large group of individuals, involving a definite set of authority relations. Many types of organization exist in industrial societies, influencing most aspects of our lives. While not all organizations are bureaucratic, there are quite close links between the development of organizations and bureaucratic tendencies.

ORGANIZED CRIME. Criminal activities carried out by organizations established as businesses.

PACIFISM. The belief that war is morally wrong.

PARIAH GROUPS. Groups who suffer from negative **status discrimination** —in other words, they are "looked down on" by most other members of society. The Jews have been a pariah group throughout much of European history.

PARTICIPANT OBSERVATION (field-work). A method of research widely used in sociology and anthropology, in which the researcher takes part in the activities of a group or community being studied.

PARTICIPATORY DEMOCRACY. A system of democracy in which all members of a group or community participate collectively in making major decisions.

PASTORAL SOCIETIES. Societies whose subsistence derives from the rearing of domesticated animals.

PATRILINEAL INHERITANCE. The inheritance of property or titles through the male line.

PATRILOCAL FAMILY. A family system in which the wife is expected to live near to the husband's parents.

PEASANTS. People who produce food from the land, using traditional farming methods.

PEER GROUP. A friendship group composed of individuals of similar age and social status.

PERIPHERY. The term refers to countries that have a marginal role in the world economy, and are thus dependent on the "core" producing societies for their trading relationships.

PERSONAL SPACE. The physical space individuals maintain between themselves and others when they know them on a personal basis.

PLURAL SOCIETY. A society in which several ethnic groupings coexist, each living in communities or regions largely separate from the others.

PLURALISM. A model for ethnic relations by which all ethnic groups in the United States retain their independent and separate identities, yet share equally in the rights and powers of citizenship.

PLURALIST THEORIES OF DEMOCRACY. Theories that emphasize the role of diverse and competing interest groups in preventing too much power being accumulated in the hands of political leaders.

POLITICAL APPARATUS. A set of governmental **organizations** making possible the regular political administration of a given territorial area.

POLITICAL PARTY. An organization established with the aim of achieving governmental power and using that power to pursue a specific program.

POLITICAL RIGHTS. Rights of political participation, such as the right to vote in local and national elections, held by **citizens** of a given national community.

POLYANDRY. A form of **marriage** in which a woman may simultaneously have two or more husbands.

POLYCENTRIC TRANSNATIONALS. Transnational corporations run from two or several main administrative centers in different countries.

POLYGAMY. A form of **marriage** in which a person may have two or more spouses simultaneously.

POLYGYNY. A form of **marriage** in which a man may have more than one wife at the same time.

POLYTHEISM. Belief in two or more gods.

POSITIVISM. A philosophical position according to which there are close ties between the social and natural sciences, which share a common logical framework.

POWER ELITE. Small networks of individuals who, according to the interpretation of C. Wright Mills, hold concentrated power in modern societies.

PREOPERATIONAL STAGE. A stage of cognitive development, in Piaget's theory, in which the child has advanced sufficiently to master basic modes of logical thought.

PRESTIGE. The respect accorded to an individual or group in virtue of their **status.**

PRIMARY GROUP. A group of individuals standing in a personal relationship to one another.

PRIMARY LABOR MARKET. The term refers to the economic position of groups of individuals who have secure jobs and good conditions of work.

PRIMARY SECTOR. That part of a modern economy based on the gathering or extraction of natural resources (including agricultural production).

PRIVATE HEALTH CARE. Health-care services available only to those who pay the full cost of them.

PROFANE. That which belongs to the mundane, everyday world.

PROFESSIONALS. Occupants of jobs requiring high-level educational qualifications, whose behavior is subject to codes of conduct laid down by central bodies (or professional associations).

PROJECTION. Attributing to others feelings that one actually has oneself.

PROPHETS. Religious leaders who mobilize followers through their interpretation of sacred texts.

PROSTITUTION. The sale of sexual favors.

PSYCHOANALYSIS. The technique of psychotherapy invented by Sigmund Freud. The word "psychoanalysis" has also come to be used for the intellectual system of psychological theory that Freud constructed.

PSYCHOPATH. A specific personality type; such individuals lack the moral sense and concern for others held by most normal people.

PSYCHOSES. The most severe type of mental disorders according to the traditional method of diagnosis. Those afflicted had a severely disturbed sense of reality and could not deal with everyday life.

PUBLIC DISTANCE. The physical space individuals maintain between themselves and others when engaged in a public performance, such as giving a lecture.

PUBLIC HEALTH CARE. Health-care services available to all members of the population, supported by government funding.

RACE. Differences in human physical stock regarded as categorizing large numbers of individuals together.

RAPE. The threat, or use, of force to compel one individual to engage in a sexual act with another.

RATIONALIZATION. A concept used by Max Weber to refer to the process by which modes of precise calculation and organization, involving abstract rules and procedures, increasingly come to dominate the social world.

REDEMPTIVE MOVEMENT. A **social movement** aiming to produce a return to a past state of affairs believed to be superior to the current one.

REFORMATIVE MOVEMENT. A **social movement** concerned to implement a practical, but limited program of **social change.**

REGIONALIZATION. The division of social life into different regional settings or zones.

RELATIVE DEPRIVATION. Feelings of deprivation relative to a group with which an individual compares him- or herself.

RELATIVE POVERTY. Poverty defined by reference to the living standards of the majority in any given society.

RELIGIOUS MOVEMENT. An association of people who join together to seek to spread a new religion or to promote a new interpretation of an existing religion.

REPRESENTATIVE MULTIPARTY DEMOCRACY. A democratic system based on the existence of two or more political parties, in which voters elect political leaders to represent them.

REPRESENTATIVE ONE-PARTY DEMOCRACY. A democratic system involving a single party, in which voters elect candidates from the party to represent them in government.

REPRODUCTIVE TECHNOLOGIES. Techniques of influencing the human reproductive process.

RESIDUAL RULE-BREAKING. The transgressing of **norms** that control basic aspects of day-to-day **social interaction.**

RESOCIALIZATION. A pattern of personality change whereby a mature individual adopts modes of behavior distinct from those he or she previously accepted.

RESPONSE CRIES. Seemingly involuntary exclamations individuals make when, for example, being taken by surprise, dropping something inadvertently, or expressing pleasure.

RESTRICTED CODE. A mode of speech that rests on strongly developed cultural understandings, such that many ideas do not need to be put into words.

RESTRICTED PATRIARCHAL FAMILY. A transitional **family** type found in Europe from the late seventeenth to the mid-nineteenth centuries, in which the domestic unit becomes largely separated from the external community and where the power of the father within the family circle is stressed.

RETIREMENT CENTER. A city or town, normally having a favorable climate, to which many people move when they retire.

REVOLUTIONARY TERROR. The use of violence, or threat of its use, by revolutionary leaders to induce a compliant attitude towards their policies.

RIOT. An outbreak of illegal violence, directed against persons, property, or both.

SACRED. Something that inspires attitudes of awe or reverence among believers in a given set of religious ideas.

SAMPLING. Taking a proportion of individuals or cases from a larger population, studied as representative of that population as a whole.

SANCTION. A mode of reward or punishment that reinforces socially expected forms of behavior.

SCAPEGOATING. Blaming an individual or group for wrongs that were not of their doing.

SCHIZOPHRENIA. A serious form of **mental illness** in which an individual's sense of reality is distorted.

SCIENCE. The application of systematic methods of research, and careful logical analysis, to the study of objects, events or people; and the body of knowledge produced by such means.

SECOND WORLD. Before the 1989–1990 democracy movements, this included the industrialized, communist societies of Eastern Europe and the Soviet Union; now, primarily the Soviet Union.

SECONDARY GROUP. A group of individuals who do not know one another intimately on a personal level.

SECONDARY LABOR MARKET. Refers to the economic position of individuals who have insecure jobs and poor conditions of work.

SECONDARY SECTOR. That part of an economy devoted to the manufacture of goods.

SECT. A religious movement that breaks away from orthodoxy.

SELF-ENLIGHTENMENT. The increased understanding that sociology can provide for people to understand the circumstances of their own actions.

SEMI-PERIPHERY. Countries that supply sources of labor and raw materials to the core industrial countries and the world economy, but are not themselves fully industrialized.

SEMIOTICS. The study of the ways in which nonlinguistic phenomena can generate meaning—as in the example of a traffic light.

SENSORIMOTOR STAGE. A stage of human cognitive development, according to Piaget, in which the child's awareness of its environment is dominated by perception and touch.

SERIAL MONOGAMY. The practice of a person contracting several marriages in succession, but not having more than one spouse at any one time.

SERVICE INDUSTRIES. Industries concerned with the production of services rather than manufactured goods, such as the travel industry.

SEX. The biological and anatomical differences distinguishing females from males.

SEXISM. Attitudes or beliefs that falsely attribute, or deny, certain capacities to the members of one of the sexes, thereby justifying sexual inequalities.

SEXUAL ABUSE. The carrying out of sexual acts by adults with children below the age of consent (usually sixteen years old).

SEXUAL ACTIVITY. Activity engaged in for the purpose of sexual gratification.

SEXUAL HARASSMENT. The making of unwanted sexual advances by one individual towards another, in which the first individual persists even though it is made clear that the other party is resistant.

SHAMAN. An individual believed to have special magical powers; a sorcerer or witch doctor.

SLAVERY. A form of social stratification in which some individuals are literally owned by others as their property.

SOCIAL CATEGORY. A statistical grouping of individuals who share a common trait—such as all the individuals in a given society earning a certain level of income.

SOCIAL CLOSURE. Practices by which groups separate themselves off from other groups.

SOCIAL CONSTRAINT. The term refers to the fact that the groups and societies of which we are a part exert a conditioning influence on our behavior. Social constraint was regarded by Émile Durkheim as one of the distinctive properties of "social facts."

SOCIAL DARWINISM. A view of social evolution emphasizing the importance of struggle or warfare between groups or societies as the motor of development.

SOCIAL DISTANCE. The level of spatial separation maintained when individuals interact with others whom they do not know well.

SOCIAL RIGHTS. Rights of social and welfare provision held by all **citizens** in a given national community involving, for example, the right to claim unemployment benefits or sickness payments provided by the state.

SOCIAL SELF. The basis of self-consciousness in human individuals, according to the theory of G. H. Mead. The social self is the identity conferred upon an individual by the reactions of others. A person achieves self-consciousness by becoming aware of this social identity.

SOCIAL TRANSFORMATION. Processes of change in "societies" or social systems.

SOCIALISM. A set of political ideas emphasizing the cooperative nature of modern industrial production and stressing the need to achieve an egalitarian social community.

SOCIOBIOLOGY. An approach that attempts to explain the behavior of both animals and human beings in terms of biological principles.

THE SOCIOLOGICAL IMAGINATION. The application of imaginative thought to the asking and answering of sociological questions. The sociological imagination involves the individual in "thinking herself or himself away" from the familiar routines of day-to-day life.

SOVEREIGNTY. The undisputed political rule of a **state** over a given territorial area.

STANDARD DEVIATION. A way of calculating the spread of a group of figures.

STANDING ARMY. A full-time, professional army having a relatively permanent existence.

STATE OVERLOAD. A **theory** that holds that modern states face major difficulties as a result of being overburdened with complex administrative decisions.

STATE SOCIETY. A **society** that possesses a formal apparatus of **government.**

STATELESS SOCIETY. A **society** that lacks formal institutions of **government.**

STEPFAMILY. A family in which at least one partner has children from a previous marriage, either living in the home or nearby.

STEREOTYPICAL THINKING. Thought processes involving rigid and inflexible categories.

STRIKE. A temporary stoppage of work by a group of employees in order to express a grievance or enforce a demand.

STRUCTURALISM. A **theoretical approach,** derived originally from the study of language, concerned with the identification of structures in social or cultural systems.

SUBCULTURE. **Values** and **norms** distinct from those of the majority, held by a group within a wider society.

SUBURBANIZATION. The development of suburbia, areas of housing outside inner cities.

SUCCESSION. An ecological term referring to the replacement of one dominant type of species in a particular environment by another.

SUFFRAGISTS. Members of early women's movements who pressed for equal voting rights for women and men.

SURPLUS VALUE. The value of an individual's labor-power, in Marxist theory, which is "left over" when an employer has repaid the cost involved in hiring a worker.

SURROGATE PARENTHOOD. A situation in which a woman bears a child on behalf of a couple because the female partner is unable to do so.

SURVEILLANCE. The supervising of the activities of some individuals or groups by others in order to ensure compliant behavior.

SURVEY. A method of sociological research involving the administration of questionnaires to a population being studied.

SYMBOL. One item used to stand for or represent another—as in the case of a flag which symbolizes a nation.

SYMBOLIC INTERACTIONISM. A **theoretical approach** in sociology developed by G. H. Mead, which places strong emphasis on the role of symbols and language as core elements of all human interaction.

TALK. The carrying on of conversations or verbal exchanges in the course of day-to-day social life.

TAYLORISM. A set of ideas, also referred to as "scientific management," developed by Frederick Winslow Taylor, involving simple, coordinated operations in industry.

TECHNOLOGY. The application of knowledge to production from the material world. Technology involves the creation of material instruments (such as machines) used in human interaction with nature.

TERRORISM. The use of violence on the part of nongovernmental groups to achieve political ends.

TERTIARY SECTOR. That part of an economy concerned with the provision of services.

TESTICULAR FEMINIZATION SYNDROME. An endrocrinal abnormality that produces physically female genitals in individuals who are male in terms of their chromosomal makeup.

THEORETICAL DILEMMA. A basic theoretical problem that forms the focus of long-standing debates in sociology.

THEORETICAL QUESTIONS. Questions posed by the sociologist when seeking to explain a particular range of observed events. The asking of theoretical questions is crucial to allowing us to generalize about the nature of social life.

THIRD WORLD. The less-developed societies, in which industrial production is either virtually nonexistent or only developed to a limited degree. The majority of the world's population live in Third World countries.

THIRD WORLD ENTREPÔT. A city serving as an entry point for migration from less-developed countries to a more developed one.

TIME GEOGRAPHY. An approach to the study of human behavior, pioneered by the Swedish geographer Torsten Hägerstrand, which emphasizes the movement of individuals simultaneously across time and space.

TIME-SPACE CONVERGENCE. The process whereby distances become "shortened in time," as the speed of methods of transportation increases.

TOTAL WAR. Warfare involving several nations, large numbers of their populations, directly or indirectly, the mobilization of their overall economies, and which deploys hundreds of thousands or millions of soldiers.

TOTALITARIANISM. A form of political administration in which power is concentrated in the hands of a dictator, who operates through a mixture of cultivating a devoted following and terrorizing those who do not agree with his policies.

TOTEMISM. A system of religious belief that attributes divine properties to a particular type of animal or plant.

TRADING NETWORKS. Networks of economic exchange linking companies or countries.

TRADITIONAL STATES. State-based societies in which the main basis of production is agriculture or pastoralism. Traditional states are also often referred to as "early civilizations."

TRANSFORMATIVE MOVEMENT. A **social movement** aiming to produce major processes of **social change.**

TRANSITIONAL CLASSES. A term used by Marx to refer to classes belonging to a declining type of society that linger on in a new one—such as peasants or large landowners in a system that has become capitalist.

TRANSNATIONAL COMPANIES. Business corporations located in two or more countries.

TRIANGULATION. The use of multiple research methods as a way of producing more reliable empirical data than is available from any single method used in isolation.

UNDERCLASS. A class of individuals situated right at the bottom of the class system, normally composed of people from ethnic minority backgrounds.

UNFOCUSED INTERACTION. Interaction occurring among people present in a particular setting, but where they are not engaged in direct face-to-face communication.

UNILINEAR EVOLUTION. An account of social evolution according to which all societies must pass through the same sequence of stages in order to develop.

UNINTENDED CONSEQUENCES. Consequences that result from behavior initiated for other purposes. Many of the major features of social activity are unintended by those who participate in it.

UNION. A body of people set up to represent workers' interests in an industrial setting.

UNIVERSAL CONSCRIPTION. A system of national service, under which every individual of a certain age (or, more commonly, all males of a certain age) have to undergo a period of military training.

UPPER CLASS. A social class broadly composed of the more affluent members of society, especially those who have inherited wealth, own businesses, or hold large numbers of stocks and shares.

URBAN RENEWAL. The process of renovating deteriorating neighborhoods by encouraging the renewal of old buildings and the construction of new ones.

URBANISM. A term used by Louis Wirth to denote distinctive characteristics of urban social life, such as its impersonality.

URBANIZATION. The development of towns and cities.

VARIABLE. A dimension along which an object, individual, or group may be categorized, such as income or height.

VERTICAL INTEGRATION. The centralized coordination of the world-wide activities of **transnational companies.**

VERTICAL MOBILITY. Movement up or down a hierarchy of positions in a social stratification system.

VICTIMLESS CRIME. An activity in which an individual engages, which is defined as criminal, but where no other person is directly involved, such as drug taking or illegal gambling.

WEALTH. Money and material possessions held by an individual or group.

WELFARE STATE. A political system that provides a wide range of welfare benefits for its citizens.

WHITE-COLLAR CRIME. Criminal activities carried out by those in white-collar or professional jobs.

WORKING CLASS. A social class broadly composed of people involved in blue-collar or manual occupations.

WORLD INFORMATION ORDER. A global system of communications, operating through satellite links, radio and TV transmission, telephone and computer links.

CREDITS

■

PHOTO ILLUSTRATIONS

Page vi, Anthrophoto File ▪ p. vii, Leonard Freed/Magnum Photos, Inc. ▪ p. viii, Wayne Miller/1964 Magnum Photos, Inc. ▪ p. ix, Alex Webb/Magnum Photos, Inc. ▪ p. x, Alex Webb/Magnum Photos, Inc. ▪ p. xi, Philip Jones Griffiths/Magnum Photos, Inc. ▪ p. xii, Reuters/Bettmann Newsphotos ▪ p. xiv, Anthrophoto File ▪ p. xv, Peter Marlow/Magnum Photos, Inc. ▪ p. xvi, Sepp Seitz 1984/Woodfin Camp Associates, Inc. ▪ p. xvii, Rene Burri/Magnum Photos, Inc. ▪ p. xviii, Bruno Barbey/Magnum Photos, Inc. ▪ p. xix, Wide World Photos, Inc.

Chapter 1
Page 3, Erich Hartmann/Magnum Photos, Inc. ▪ p. 4, Susanne Anderson ▪ p.6, Bibliotheque Royale Albert ▪ p. 7, UPI/Bettmann Newsphotos ▪ p. 10, Franco Zeichin/Magnum Photos, Inc. ▪ p. 11, Bettmann Archives ▪ p. 11, Tom Stoddart/Katz Pictures, Woodfin Camp and Associates, Inc. ▪ p. 16, Ian Berry/Magnum Photos, Inc. ▪ p. 17, Alex Webb/Magnum Photos, Inc. ▪ p. 23, Gary Larson, United Press International

Chapter 2
Page 28, AT&T Bell Laboratories and Kim Hill ▪ p. 33, Scala Art Resource ▪ p. 34, Peabody Museum, Salem ▪ p. 35, Robert Osborn ▪ p. 36, American Museum of Natural History ▪ p. 37, *The Far Side Cartoons* by Gary Larson on pages 37, 97, 448, 681, 782, 823 are reprinted by permission of Chronicle Features, San Francisco, CA ▪ p. 39, Michael K. Nichols/Magnum Photos, Inc. ▪ p. 45, Marjorie Shostak/Anthrophoto File ▪ p. 45, Gamma-Liaison Agency, Inc. ▪ p. 47, Anthrophoto File ▪ p. 48, Art Resource, Inc. ▪ p. 49, Staatliche Museen zu Berlin ▪ p. 53, N. R. Farbman/*Life* magazine ▪ p. 53, Marjorie Shostak/Anthrophoto File ▪ p. 58, Warder Collection ▪ p. 64, Rene Millon

Chapter 3
Page 72, Scott Eklund ▪ p. 73, British Museum ▪ p. 76, Suzanne Szasz ▪ p. 78, Marjorie Shostak/Anthrophoto File ▪ p. 79, Bettmann Archive ▪ p. 87, Warder Collection ▪ p. 89, Suzanne Szasz ▪ p. 90, Yurs de Braine/Blackstar, Inc. ▪ p. 91, Suzanne Szasz ▪ p.95, Suzanne Szasz ▪ p. 99, Margaret Bourke-White/*Life* magazine ▪ p. 101, National Archives

Chapter 4
Page 102, National Archives ▪ p. 113, Paul Ekman ▪ p. 114, Warder Collection ▪ p.123, Rene Burri/Magnum Photos, Inc. ▪ p. 124, Gary Larson/Universal Press Syndicate ▪ p. 126, AP/Wide World Photos, Inc. ▪ p. 130, Wallace Litwin ▪ p. 130, Animals, Animals, Inc. ▪ p. 137, Anthrophoto, Inc.

Chapter 5
Page 143, Wide World Photos, Inc. ▪ p. 144, NYT Pictures ▪ p. 147, Brown Brothers ▪ p. 154, NYT Pictures ▪ p. 154, Magnum Photos, Inc. ▪ p. 164, Cornell Capa/Magnum Photos, Inc. ▪ p. 173, Sidney Harris ▪ p. 178, Ed Gamble/*Florida Times-Union* ▪ p. 178,

Chapter 15
Page 594, Denver Institute of Art ▪ p. 596, Metropolitan Museum of Art ▪ p. 596, Bildarchiv Preussischer Kulturbesitz ▪ p. 599, Henry Ford Museum ▪ p. 603, Chrysler Corporation ▪ p. 612, *Star Tribune,* Minneapolis ▪ p. 617, Wide World Photos, Inc. ▪ p. 627, Warder Collection

Chapter 16
Page 647, Sebastian Selgado, Jr./Magnum Photos, Inc. ▪ p. 658, Adam J. Stoultman/ Doumo ▪ p. 661, CBS News ▪ p. 663, (left) Philip Jones Griffiths/Magnum Photos Inc.; (right) James R. Holland, Stock, Boston ▪ p. 667 Bettmann Archive ▪ p. 669, Richard Kalver/Magnum Photos, Inc.

Chapter 17
Page 674, Michael K. Nichols/Magnum Photos, Inc. ▪ p. 675, (top) Eli Reed/Magnum Photos Inc.; (bottom) Philip Jones Griffiths/Magnum Photos Inc. ▪ p. 677, (left) Warder Collection; (right) UPI/Bettmann ▪ p. 680, Wayne Miller/Magnum Photos, Inc. ▪ p. 682, Eli Reed/Magnum Photos, Inc. ▪ p. 683, Leo Heizel/Photo Reporters ▪ p. 685, *Punch* Publications ▪ p. 689, Bruno Barby/Magnum Photos, Inc. ▪ p. 695, (left) Library of Congress; (right) Philip Jones Griffiths/Magnum Photos, Inc. ▪ p. 703, Ernest Haas

Chapter 18
Page 735, UPI/Bettmann

Chapter 19
Page 742, Bettmann Archive ▪ p. 744, Warder Collection ▪ p. 747, Warder Collection ▪ p. 748, Eastfoto ▪ p. 749, (left) UPI/Bettmann; (right) Blackstar ▪ p. 757, AP/Wide World Photos, Inc. ▪ p. 768, (left) Bettmann Archive; (right) H. Roger Violett

Chapter 20
Page 779, (left) Bettmann Archive; (right) Bettmann Archive ▪ p. 785, *Punch* Publications ▪ p. 792, Consulate General of Japan ▪ p. 801, NYT Pictures ▪ p. 804, Bettmann Archive ▪ p. 805, Museum of Modern Art

Chapter 21
Page 813, AP/Wide World Photos ▪ p. 818, Tom Beckett/Women Against Pornography ▪ p. 819, Magnum Photos, Inc. ▪ p. 820, Anthrophoto File

Chapter 22
Page 847, Warder Collection ▪ p. 848, Warder Collection ▪ p. 850, Bettmann Archive ▪ p. 856, Terry Arthur/White House ▪ p. 862, Bettmann Archive ▪ p.864, Alan Keiler/Sygma

EXCERPTS

Chapter 1
Page 5, Michel Foucault, *Discipline and Punish.* New York: Penguin, 1979. ▪ p. 6, John Loftland, "The dramaturgy of state executions," in Horace Bleackley and John Loftland, *State Execution Viewed Historically and Sociologically.* Montclair, NJ: Patterson Smith, 1977.

Chapter 2
Page 43, Horace Miner, "Body ritual among the Nacirema," *American Anthropologist,* 58 (1956). ▪ p. 51, Marvin Harris, *Cannibals and Kings: The Origins of Cultures.* New York: Random House, 1978.

Chapter 3

Page 78, Selma Fraiberg, *The Magic Years: Understanding and Handling the Problems of Early Childhood*. New York: Scribners, 1949. ▪ p. 92, Laurie Lee, *Cider with Rosie*. London: Hogarth Press, 1965. ▪ p. 100, Bruno Bettelheim, *The Informed Heart*. New York: Free Press, 1986.

Chapter 4

Page 117, Harold Garfinkel, *Studies in Ethnomethodology*. Englewood Cliffs: Prentice-Hall, 1967. ▪ p. 118, John Heritage, *Garfinkel and Ethnomethodology*. New York: Basil Blackwell, 1984. ▪ p. 117, Harold Garfinkel, "A conception of, and experiments with, 'trust' as a condition of stable concerted actions," in O. J. Harvey (ed.), *Motivation and Social Interaction*. New York: Roland Press, 1963. ▪ p. 132, Erving Goffmann, *Frame Analysis*. New York: Harper and Row, 1974. ▪ p. 135 Murray Melbin, "Night as Frontier." *American Sociological Review,* 43.

Chapter 5

Page 143, Donald L. Bartlett and James B. Steele, *Empire: The Life, Legend and Madness of Howard Hughes*. New York: Norton, 1981. ▪ p. 152, Cathy Spatz Widom and Joseph P. Newman, "Characteristics of non-institutionalized psychopaths," in David P. Farraington and John Gunn, *Aggression and Dangerousness*. New York: John Wiley, 1985. ▪ p. 164, Marvin Wolfgang, *Patterns of Homicide*. Philadelphia: University of Pennsylvania Press, 1958; Anne Campbell and John T. Gibbs (eds.), *Violent Transactions*. New York: Basil Blackwell, 1986. ▪ p. 171, Pat Carlen, et al., *Criminal Women: Autobiographical Accounts*. Boston: Allen and Unwin, 1985.

Chapter 6

Page 189–90, Laurel Richardson Walum, *The Dynamics of Sex and Gender: A Sociological Perspective*. Chicago: Rand McNally, 1977. ▪ p. 191–92, Jan Morris, *Condondrum*. New York: Harcourt, Brace Jovanovich, 1974. ▪ p. 198, Richard Lewontin, *Human Diversity*. New York: W. H. Freeman, 1984 ▪ p. 202, Judith Viorst, "And the prince knelt down and tried to put the glass slipper on Cinderella's foot," in Jack Zipes, *Don't Bet on the Prince: Contemporary Feminist Fairy Tales in North America and England*. New York: Metheun, 1977. ▪ p. 204, June Statham, *Daughters and Sons: Experiences of Non-Sexist Childraising*. New York: Oxford University Press, 1986. ▪ p. 209, Carol Gilligan, *In a Different Voice: Psychological Theory and Women's Development*. Cambridge, MA: Harvard University Press, 1982. ▪ p. 213, Graham S. Lowe, *Women in the Administrative Revolution: The Feminisation of Clerical Work*. Cambridge: Polity Press, 1987. ▪ p. 215, Hilary Homans, "Man-made myth: The reality of being a woman scientist in the NHS," in Anne Spencer and David Podmore (eds.), *In a Man's World: Essays on Women in Male-Dominated Professions*. London: Tavistock, 1987. ▪ p. 229, Sedelle Katz and Mary Ann Mazur, *Understanding the Rape Victim: A Synthesis of Research Findings*. London: Wiley, 1979.

Chapter 7

Page 254, Ellen Israel Rosen, *Bitter Choices: Blue-Collar Women In and Out of Work*. Chicago: University of Chicago Press, 1987. ▪ p. 269, David Halle, *America's Working Man: Work, Home and Politics Among Blue Collar Property Owners*. Chicago: University of Chicago Press, 1984. ▪ p. 270, Frank Parkin, *Class Inequality and Political Order*. London: McGibbon and Kee, 1971. ▪ p. 273, Roslyn Feldberg and Evelyn Nakano Glenn, "Male and female: Job versus gender models in the sociology of work," in Janet Siltaman and Michelle Stanworth, *Women and the Public Sphere: A Critique of Sociology and Politics*. New York: St. Martin's Press, 1984 ▪ p. 283, John Kenneth Galbraith, *The Affluent Society*. New York: New American Library, 1985.

Chapter 8
Page 314, Martin Murray, *South Africa: Time of Agony, Time of Destiny: The Upsurge of Popular Protest in South Africa.* New York: Schocken Books, 1987. ▪ p. 318, Eva Morawska, *For Bread with Butter: Life-Worlds of the East Central Europeans in Johnstown, Pennsylvania, 1890–1940.* New York: Cambridge University Press, 1985. ▪ p. 324, Vincent Harding, *The Other American Revolution.* University of California, Los Angeles: Center for Afro-American Studies, Culture and Society Monograph Series, 4, 1980. ▪ p. 325, Stokely Carmichael and Charles Hamilton, *Black Power: The Politics of Liberation in America.* New York: Random House, 1968.

Chapter 9
Page 359, Satoshi Kamata, *Japan in the Passing Lane.* Boston: Allen and Unwin, 1982. ▪ p. 368, Katherine Archibald, *Wartime Shipyard.* Berkeley: University of California Press, 1947.

Chapter 10
Page 408, Peter Hall, "The presidency and impression management," *Studies in Symbolic Interactionism,* 2, 1982. ▪ p. 419, Frederick Barghoorn and Thomas Remington, *Politics in the U.S.S.R,* Third Edition. Boston: Little, Brown, 1986.

Chapter 11
Page 434, Samuel P. Huntington, *The Solider and the State: The Theory and Politics of Civil-Military Relations.* Cambridge, MA: Harvard University Press, 1981. ▪ p. 442, Jonathan Schell, *The Fate of the Earth.* New York: Alfred A. Knopf, 1982. ▪ p. 450, Sean O'Casey, *Shadow of a Gunman,* quoted in Paul Wilkinson, *Political Terrorism.* London: Macmillan, 1974. ▪ p. 456, Elizabeth Cady Stanton and Susan B. Anthony (eds.), *History of Woman's Suffrage.* Rochester, NY: Charles Mann, 1889. ▪ p. 457, Shelley Saywell, *Women in War.* New York: Viking, 1982. ▪ p. 460, Gwynne Dyer, *War.* London: Bodley Head, 1985.

Chapter 12
Page 496, Emily B. Vischer and John S. Vischer, *Step Families: A Guide to Working with Step-Parents and Step-Children.* Secaucus, NJ: Citadel Press, 1979. ▪ p. 500, David Finkelhor, *Child Sexual Abuse: New Theory and Research.* New York: Free Press, 1984.

Chapter 13
Page 522, Eleanor Orr, *Twice As Less: Black English and the Performance of Black Students in Mathematics.* New York: Norton, 1987. ▪ p. 527, Paul Willis, *Learning to Labor: How Working Class Kids Get Working Class Jobs.* New York: Columbia University Press, 1981.

Chapter 14
Page 575, Elizabeth Cady Stanton, *The Woman's Bible: The Original Feminist Attack on the Bible.* Edinburgh: Polygon Books, 1985.

Chapter 15
Page 600, R. Linhart, *The Assembly Line.* Amherst, MA: University of Massachusetts Press, 1981. ▪ p. 602, Karl Marx, "Economic and philosophical manuscripts," in T. B. Bottomore (ed.), *Karl Marx: Early Writings.* New York: Penguin, 1963. ▪ p. 604, Steven Miller and Robert Ayres, "Industrial robots on the line," in Tom Forrester (ed.), *The Information Technology Revolution.* Cambridge, MA: MIT Press, 1985. ▪ p. 606, Paul Blumberg, *Industrial Democracy: The Sociology of Participation.* London: Constable, 1968.

Chapter 16
Page 642, Agostino Neto, quoted in Jon Bennett and Susan George, *The Hunger Machine.* New York: Basil Blackwell, 1987. ▪ p. 665, Anthony Smith, *How Western Culture Dominates the World.* New York: Oxford University Press, 1980b.

Chapter 17

Page 678, Andrew Lees, *Cities Perceived: Urban Society in European and American Thought, 1820–1940.* New York: Columbia University Press, 1985. ▪ p. 690, Ajit Singh, "Urbanization, Poverty and Employment: The Large Metropolis in the Third World." Unpublished monograph, Cambridge University, 1988. ▪ p. 696, Louis Wirth, "Urbanism as a way of life," *American Journal of Sociology,* 44, July 1938, pp. 1–24. ▪ p. 699, Edward Krupat, *People in Cities: The Urban Environment and its Effects.* New York: Cambridge University Press, 1985.

Chapter 18

Page 706, Paul Erlich, *The Population Bomb.* New York: Ballantine Books, 1976.

Chapter 20

Page 776, David Landes, *The Unbound Prometheus.* New York: Cambridge University Press, 1969. ▪ p. 791, Karl Marx and Freidrich Engels, *The Communist Manifesto* New York: Amereon Ltd, 1968.

Chapter 21

Page 819, Erving Goffman, *Essays on the Social Situation of Mental Patients and Other Inmates.* New York: Doubleday/Anchor, 1961.

Chapter 22

Page 861, Emile Durkheim, *The Rules of Sociological Method.* New York: Free Press, 1982. ▪ p. 872, Max Weber, *The Protestant Ethic and the Spirit of Capitalism.* New York: Macmillan, 1977.

FIGURES AND TABLES

Figure 2.2, N. Tinbergen, *The Study of Instinct.* Oxford: Oxford University Press, 1951. ▪ Figures 6.1, 6.2, 6.4, Women on Words and Images, 1972. ▪ Table 6.3, Lisa Tuttle, *Encyclopedia on Feminism.* New York: Facts on File, 1986. ▪ Table 6.5, Kinsey, 1948, 1953. ▪ Table 7.2, "Homeless in Chicago." 1988 study by the School of Social Service Administration of the University of Chicago. ▪ Table 11.1, Ruth Leger Sivard, *World Military and Social Expenditures.* Washington, D.C.: World Priorities, 1983. ▪ Table 11.2, Ruth Leger Sivard, *World Military and Social Expenditures.* Washington, D.C.: World Priorities, 1983. ▪ Table 13.3, Statistical Office of the United Nations, *Statistical Yearbook.* New York, NY ▪ Table 15.1, David G. Blanchflower and Andrew J. Oswald, "International Patterns of Work," in Roger Jowell, et al., eds., *British Social Attitudes.* Brookfield, VT: Gower, 1989. ▪ Table 15.2, *Fortune Magazine,* August 3, 1987, p. 18. ▪ Figure 16.1, Burns, *World Civilizations,* Seventh Edition. New York: W. W. Norton and Company, Inc., 1986. ▪ Figure 16.4, Peter Dicken, *Global Shift.* New York: 1986. ▪ Figure 18.1, World Bank Atlas, 1988. ▪ Table 18.1, World Bank Atlas, 1988. ▪ Table 18.3, Leslie Watkins, Robert M. Worcester, *Private Opinion, Public Polls.* London: Thames and Hudson, 1986. ▪ Table 18.4, World Bank Atlas, 1988.

BIBLIOGRAPHY

ABERLE, DAVID. 1966. *The Peyote Religion among the Navaho*. Chicago: Aldine Press.

ABRAMS, PHILIP. 1968, 1982. *Historical Sociology*. Ithaca, NY: Cornell University Press.

———. 1978. *Work, Urbanism, and Inequality: U.K. Society Today*. London: Weidenfeld and Nicolson.

ACHESON, E. D., ET AL. 1981. *The Impending Crisis of Old Age: A Challenge to Ingenuity*. New York: Oxford University Press.

ACQUAVIVA, S. S. 1979. *The Decline of the Sacred in Industrial Society*. Oxford: Basil Blackwell.

ADORNO, THEODORE W., ET AL. 1950. *The Authoritarian Personality*. New York: Harper and Row.

———. 1974. "The stars down to earth: The *Los Angeles Times* astrology column." *Telos*, no. 19.

AGELL, ANDERS. 1980. "Co-habitation without marriage in Swedish law," in John M. Eekelaar, Sanford, and Katz (eds.), *Marriage and Co-Habitation in Contemporary Societies*. Toronto: Butterworths.

AINSWORTH, MARY D. S. 1977. *Infancy in Uganda*. Baltimore, MD: Johns Hopkins University Press.

ALAVI, H. 1983. "Colonial and post-colonial societies," in Tom B. Bottomore, (ed.), *A Dictionary of Marxist Thought*. Cambridge, MA: Harvard University Press.

ALBA, R. 1985. *Italian Americans: Into the Twilight of Ethnicity*. Englewood Cliffs, NJ: Prentice-Hall.

ALBROW, MARTIN. 1970. *Bureaucracy*. London: Pall Mall Press.

ALDRIDGE, ALAN. 1987. "In the absence of the minister: Structures of subordination in the role of deaconess in the Church of England." *Sociology*, 21.

ALEXANDER, JEFFREY C. 1985. *Neofunctionalism*. Beverly Hills, CA: Sage.

ALLAND, ALEXANDER. 1967. *Evolution and Human Behavior*. Garden City, NY: Natural History Press.

———. 1970. *Adaptation in Cultural Evolution*. New York: Columbia University Press.

ALLEN, MICHAEL P. 1981. "Managerial power and tenure in the large corporation." *Social Forces*, 60.

ALLEN, ROBERT L. 1970. *A Guide to Black Power in America: A Historical Analysis*. London: Gollancz.

ALLMÄN/MÅNAD STATISTIK 1987. 1987. *Sveriges Officiella Statistik*. Stockholm: Statistika Centralbyrån.

ALTHUSSER, LOUIS. 1969. *For Marx*. London: Allen Lane.

ALTMAN, DENNIS. 1986. *AIDS in the Mind of America*. Garden City, NY: Doubleday.

AMIR, MENACHIM. 1971. *Patterns in Forcible Rape*. Chicago: University of Chicago Press.

ANDERSON, F. S. 1977. "TV violence and viewer aggression: Accumulation of study results 1956–1976." *Public Opinion Quarterly*, 41.

ANDERSON, MICHAEL. 1980. *Approaches to the History of the Western Family.* Atlantic Highlands, NJ: Humanities Press.

———. 1981. *Family Structure in Nineteenth-Century Lancashire.* Cambridge: Cambridge University Press.

ANNETT, T. S. 1976. *The Many Ways of Being: A Guide to Spiritual Groups and Growth Centres in Britain.* London: Abacus.

ANYON, JEAN. 1987. "Intersections of gender and class: Accommodation and resistance by working class and affluent females to contradictory sex-role ideologies," in Stephen Walker and Len Barton (eds.), *Gender, Class, and Education.* New York: International Publications Service.

ARCHIBALD, KATHERINE. 1947. *Wartime Shipyard.* Berkeley, CA: University of California Press.

ARENDT, HANNAH. 1963. *Eichmann in Jerusalem.* Rev. Ed. New York: Viking.

———. 1977. *On Revolution.* New York: Penguin.

ARIÈS, PHILIPPE. 1965. *Centuries of Childhood.* New York: Random House.

ARON, RAYMON. 1981. *The Century of Total War.* Westport, CT: Greenwood Press.

ASCHENBRENNER, JOYCE. 1983. *Lifelines: Black families in Chicago.* Prospect Heights, IL: Waveland Press.

ASHFORD, DOUGLAS E. 1988. *The Emergence of Welfare States.* New York: Basil Blackwell.

ASHWORTH, ANTHONY E. 1980. *Trench Warfare: 1914–1918.* London: Macmillan.

ATCHLEY, ROBERT C. 1985. *Social Forces and Aging.* 4th ed. Belmont, CA: Wadsworth.

ATHOLL, JUSTIN. 1954. *Shadow of the Gallows.* London: Hutchinson.

ATKINSON, J. MAXWELL, and **JOHN HERITAGE (EDS.).** 1985. *Structures of Social Action: Studies in Conversation Analysis.* New York: Cambridge University Press.

ATTWOOD, LYNNE, and **MAGGIE MCANDREW.** 1984. "Women at work in the U.S.S.R.," in Marilyn J. Davidson and Cary L . Cooper (eds.), *Working Women: An International Survey.* Chichester, England: Wiley.

AYRES, ROBERT, and **STEVEN MILLER.** 1983. *Robotics: Applications and Social Implications.* Cambridge, MA: Ballinger Press.

———. 1985. "Industrial robots on the line," in Tom Forester (ed.), *The Information Technology Revolution.* Cambridge, MA: MIT Press.

BABBAGE, CHARLES. 1986. *On the Economy of Machinery and Manufactures.* 4th ed. New York: Kelley.

BACH, R. 1980. "The new Cuban immigrants: Their background and prospects." *Monthly Labour Review,* no. 103.

BAILYN, BERNARD. 1960. *Education in the Forming of American Society.* New York: Random House.

BAKAL, DONALD A. 1974. *Psychology and Medicine: Psychobiological Dimensions of Health and Illness.* New York: Springer.

BALSWICK, J. O. 1983. "Male inexpressiveness," in Kenneth Soloman and Norman B. Levy (eds.), *Men in Transition: Theory and Therapy.* New York: Plenum Press.

BARGHOORN, FREDERICK C., and **THOMAS REMINGTON.** 1986. *Politics in the U.S.S.R.* 3rd ed. Boston: Little, Brown.

BARKER, EILEEN. 1984. *The Making of a Moonie: Choice or Blackmail.* New York: Basil Blackwell.

BARKER, SHEILA, and **DIANA ALLEN (EDS.)** 1976. *Dependence and Exploitation in Work and Marriage.* New York: Longman.

BARLETT, DONALD L., and **JAMES B. STEELE.** 1981. *Empire: The Life, Legend, and Madness of Howard Hughes.* New York: Norton.

BARNES, JOHN A. 1979. *Who Should Know What? Social Science, Privacy, and Ethics.* Harmondsworth: Penguin.

BARNOUW, ERIC. 1982. *Tube of Plenty: The Evolution of American Television.* New York: Oxford University Press.

BARTH, FREDERICK. 1969. *Ethnic Groups and Boundaries.* London: Allen and Unwin.

BARTOLLE, K., ET AL. 1980. *Integrated Cooperatives in the Industrial Society: The Example of the Kibbutz.* Amsterdam: Van Gorum.

BARTON, S. E., ET AL. 1985. "HTLV–III antibody in prostitutes." *Lancet,* no. 1424.

BASTIDE, ROGER. 1967. "Color, Racism, and Christianity." *Daedalus,* Spring.

———. 1978. *The African Religions of Brazil.* Baltimore, MD: Johns Hopkins University Press.

BATE, J. ST. JOHN. 1985. *The Automated Office: Information Technology and Its Effect on Management and Office Staff.* London: Collins.

BATER, JAMES H. 1977. "Soviet town planning: Theory and practice in the 1970s." *Progress in Human Geography,* 1, pp. 177–207.

BAUMRIND, D. 1964. "Some thoughts on ethics of research: After reading Milgram's 'Behavioural study of obedience.'" *American Psychologist,* 19.

BAXTER, SANDRA, and **MARJORIE LANSING.** 1983. *Women and Politics: The Visible Majority.* Ann Arbor: University of Michigan Press.

BEATTIE, JOHN. 1968. *Other Cultures.* New York: Free Press.

BEAUVOIR, SIMONE DE. 1974. *The Second Sex.* New York: Random House.

BECKER, HOWARD S. 1950. *Through Values to Social Interpretation.* Durham, NC: Duke University Press.

———. 1967. "Whose side are we on?" *Social Problems,* 14.

———. 1974. "Labelling theory reconsidered," in P. Rock and M. McIntosh (eds.), *Deviance and Social Control.* London: Tavistock.

———. 1976. "Problems in the publication of field studies," in *Sociological Work: Methods and Substance.* New Brunswick, NJ: Transaction Books.

BELL, COLIN, and **HOWARD NEWBY.** 1977. *Doing Sociological Research.* London: Allen and Unwin.

BELL, DANIEL. 1953. "Crime as an American way of life." *Antioch Review,* 13.

———. 1976. *The Coming of Post-Industrial Society: A Venture in Social Forecasting.* New York: Basic Books.

BELLAH, ROBERT N. 1970. *Beyond Belief.* New York: Harper and Row.

———, and **PHILLIP E. HAMMOND.** 1980. *Varieties of Civil Religion.* San Francisco: Harper & Row.

BENNETT, JON, and **SUSAN GEORGE.** 1987. *The Hunger Machine.* New York: Basil Blackwell.

BENNETT, LERONE. 1967. *Black Power U.S.A.: The Human Side of Reconstruction.* Chicago: Johnson Publishing.

BENSON, IAN, and **JOHN LLOYD.** 1983. *New Technology and Industrial Change.* New York: Nichols Publishing.

BENTHAM, JEREMY L. 1791. *Panopticon: Or, the Inspection House.*

BEQUAI, A. 1980. *Organized Crime: The Fifth Estate.* Lexington, MA: D.C. Heath.

BERGER, JOHN. 1977. *Ways of Seeing.* New York: Penguin.

BERGMANN, THEODOR. 1977. *The Development Models of India, the Soviet Union, and China.* Amsterdam: Van Gorrum.

BERK, RICHARD A. 1974. "A gaming approach to crowd behavior." *American Sociological Review,* 37.

BERLE, ADOLF, and **GARDINER C. MEANS.** 1982. *The Modern Corporation and Private Property.* Buffalo, NY: William S. Heim.

BERMAN, L. V. 1982. "The United States of America: A cooperative model for worker management," in F. H. Stephen (ed.), *The Performance of Labor-Managed Firms.* New York: St. Martin's Press.

BERNSTEIN, BASIL. 1977. *Class, Codes, and Control.* 3 vols. New York: Methuen.

BERRY, BREWTON, and HENRY L. TISCHLER. 1978. *Race and Ethnic Relations.* Boston: Houghton Mifflin.

BERTAUX, DANIEL. 1981. *Biography and Society: The Life History Approach in the Social Sciences.* Beverly Hills, CA: Sage.

BERTELSON, DAVID. 1986. *Snowflakes and Snowdrifts: Individualism and Sexuality in America.* Lanham, MD: University Press of America.

BETTELHEIM, BRUNO. 1971. *The Informed Heart.* New York: Avon.

BEYNON, HUGH. 1975. *Working for Ford.* England: EP Publishing.

BICCHIERI, M. G. (ED.). 1972. *Hunters and Gatherers Today.* New York: Holt, Rinehart and Winston.

BINDER, A., and P. SCHARF. 1982. "Deadly force in law enforcement." *Crime and Delinquency,* 28.

BINGHAM, RICHARD D., ROY E. GREEN, and SAMMIS WHITE (EDS.). 1987. *The Homeless in Contemporary Society.* Beverly Hills, CA: Sage.

BIRDWHISTELL, RAY L. 1970. *Kinesics and Context.* Philadelphia: University of Pennsylvania Press

BLACKSTONE, TESSA, and O. FULTON. 1975. "Sex discrimination among university teachers: A British-American comparison." *British Journal of Sociology,* 26.

BLANCHFLOWER, DAVID G., and ANDREW J. OSWALD. 1989. "International Patterns of Work," in Roger Jowell, Sharon Witherspoon, and Lindsay Brook (eds.), *British Social Attitudes.* Brookfield, VT: Gower. ©Social and Community Planning Research.

BLAU, PETER. 1963. *The Dynamics of Bureaucracy.* Chicago: University of Chicago Press.

———, and OTIS DUDLEY DUNCAN. 1967. *The American Occupational Structure.* New York: Wiley.

BLAUNER, ROBERT. 1964. *Alienation and Freedom.* Chicago: University of Chicago Press.

———. 1972. *Racial Oppression in America.* New York: Harper & Row.

BLAUSTEIN, ALBERT P. and L. ZANGRANDO (EDS.). 1968. *Civil Rights and the Black American.* New York: Simon and Schuster.

BLOCH, S., and P. REDDAWAY. 1977. *Russia's Political Hospitals.* London: Victor Gollancz.

BLOCK, FRED, ET AL. 1987. *The Mean Season: The Attack on the Welfare State.* New York: Pantheon.

BLOMSTROM, MAGNUS, and BJORN HETTNE. 1984. *Development Theory in Transition. The Dependency Debate and Beyond: Third World Responses.* London: Zed Books.

BLUMBERG, PAUL. 1968. *Industrial Democracy: The Sociology of Participation.* London: Constable.

———. 1987. *Inequality in an Age of Decline.* New York: Oxford University Press.

BLYTON, PAUL. 1986. *Changes in Working Time: An International Review.* New York: St. Martin's Press.

BOBBIO, NORBERTO. 1987. *The Future of Democracy.* Minneapolis: University of Minnesota Press.

BODEN, DEIRDRE. 1987. "Temporal frames: Time, talk, and organizations." Department of Sociology, Washington University, St. Louis. Mimeo.

BOGART, LEO. 1975. "The future of the metropolitan daily." *Journal of Communication,* 25.

BOHANNAN, PAUL (ED.). 1960. *African Homicide and Suicide.* Princeton, NJ: Princeton University Press.

———. 1970. "The six stations of divorce," in *Divorce and After.* New York: Doubleday.

BOORSTEIN, EDWARD. 1969. *The Economic Transformation of Cuba.* New York: Monthly Review Press.

BOOTH, ALAN. 1977. "Food riots in the North-West of England, 1770–1801." *Past and Present,* no. 77.

BOOTH, CHARLES. 1904. *Labour and Life of the People.* Vol. I of *Life and Labour of the People in London, 1890–1900.* Reprint of 1904 ed. New York: AMS Press.

BOOTH, WILLIAM. 1984. *In Darkest England and the Way Out.* Reprint of 1890 ed. Montclair, NJ: Smith, Patterson Pub.

BOTTOMLEY, ALLEN, and **KEN PEASE.** 1986. *Crime and Punishment: Interpreting the Data.* Philadelphia: Taylor and Francis.

BOURDIEU, PIERRE. 1984. *Distinction: A Social Critique of Judgements of Taste.* Cambridge, MA: Harvard University Press.

————. 1988. *Language and Symbolic Power.* Cambridge: Polity Press.

————, and **JEAN-CLAUDE PASSERON.** 1977. *Reproduction: In Education, Society, and Culture.* Beverly Hills, CA: Sage.

BOWLBY, JOHN. 1951. *Maternal Care and Mental Health.* Geneva, Switzerland: World Health Organization.

————. 1958. "The nature of the child's tie to its mother." *International Journal of Psychoanalysis,* 39.

BOWLES, SAMUEL, and **HERBERT GINTIS.** 1976. *Schooling in Capitalist America.* New York: Basic Books.

BOX, STEVEN. 1984. *Power, Crime, and Mystification.* New York: Routledge, Chapman and Hall.

BRANDT COMMISSION. 1983. *Common Crisis North-South: Co-operation for World Recovery.* Cambridge, MA: MIT Press.

BRAUN, ERNEST. 1984. *Wayward Technology.* Westport, CT: Greenwood Press.

BRAVERMAN, HARRY. 1976. *Labor and Monopoly Capital: The Degradation of Work in the Twentieth Century.* New York: Monthly Review Press.

BREESE, GERALD. 1966. *Urbanization in Newly Developing Countries.* Englewood Cliffs, NJ: Prentice-Hall.

BREKKE, TORIL, ET AL. 1985. *Women: A World Report.* New York: Methuen.

BRENNAN, TERESA. 1988. "Controversial discussions and feminist debate," in Naomi Segal and Edward Timms, *The Origins and Evolution of Psychoanalysis.* New Haven, CT: Yale University Press.

BRENNER, MICHAEL. 1978. "Interviewing: The social phenomenology of a research instrument," in Michael Brenner, Peter Marsh, and Marilyn Brenner, *The Social Contexts of Method.* London: Croom Helm.

BRENNER, ROBERT. 1977. "The origins of capitalist development: A critique of neo-Smithian Marxism." *New Left Review,* no. 105.

BREUILLY, JOHN. 1982. *Nationalism and the State.* New York: St. Martin's Press.

BRINTON, CRANE. 1965. *The Anatomy of Revolution.* New York: Knopf.

BRITTAN, SAMUEL. 1975. "The economic contradictions of democracy." *British Journal of Political Science,* 15.

BROCH, T., ET AL. 1966. "Belligerence among the primitives." *Journal of Peace Research,* 3.

BROTHERS, JOAN. 1971. *Religious Institutions.* Atlantic Highlands, NJ: Humanities International Press.

BROWN, JUDITH K. 1977. "A note on the division of labor by sex," in Nona Glazer, and Helen Y. Waehrer, *Woman in a Man-Made World.* 2nd ed. Chicago: Rand McNally.

BROWN, LESTER R., ET AL. 1974. *By Bread Alone.* Washington, D.C.: Overseas Development Council.

BROWN, ROGER. 1973. *A First Language: The Early Stages.* Cambridge, MA: Harvard University Press.

BROWNMILLER, SUSAN. 1986. *Against Our Will: Men, Women, and Rape.* rev. ed. New York: Bantam.

BRUMMER, ALEX. 1987. "San Francisco gives the pope a rough ride." *The Guardian,* September 19.

BRUNER, JEROME S. 1975. "From communication to language—a psychological perspective." *Cognition,* 3.

BRYAN, BEVERLEY, STELLA DADZIE, and **SUZANNE SCAFE.** 1987. "Learning to resist: Black women and education," in Gaby Weiner and Madeleine Arnot, *Gender under Scrutiny: New Inquiries in Education.* London: Hutchinson.

BRZEZINSKI, ZBIGNIEW, and **SAMUEL P. HUNTINGTON.** 1982. *Political Power: USA, USSR.* Westport, CT: Greenwood Press.

BUCKLE, ABIGAIL, and **DAVID P. FARRINGTON.** 1984. "An observational study of shoplifting." *British Journal of Criminology,* 24.

BUCKLEY, P. J., and **M. CASSON.** 1976. *The Future of Multinational Enterprise.* New York: Holmes and Meier.

BULKELEY, RIP, and **GRAHAM SPINARDI.** 1986. *Space Weapons: Deterrence or Delusion?* Savage, MD: Barnes and Noble.

BULL, PETER. 1983. *Body Movement and Interpersonal Communication.* New York: Wiley.

BULLOCK, CHARLES, III. 1983. "Equal education opportunity," in Charles S. Bullock, III and Charles M. Lamb (eds.), *Implementation of Civil Rights Policy.* Monterey, CA: Brooks and Cole.

BULMER, MARTIN (ED.). 1975. *Working-Class Images of Society.* New York: Routledge and Kegan Paul.

———. 1984. *Sociological Research Methods.* 2nd ed. New Brunswick, NJ: Transaction Books.

BURAWOY, MICHAEL. 1979. *Manufacturing Consent.* Chicago: University of Chicago Press.

BURGOYNE, JACQUELINE, ROGER ORMROD, and **MARTIN RICHARDS.** 1987. *Divorce Matters.* Harmondsworth, England: Pelican.

BURNS, EDWARD MCNALL, ET AL. 1986. *World Civilizations.* 7th ed. New York: Norton.

BURRIDGE, KENELM. 1969. *New Haven, New Earth: A Study of Millenarian Activities.* New York: Basil Blackwell.

BURT, CYRIL. 1977. *The Subnormal Mind.* 3rd ed. Oxford: Oxford University Press.

BUTLER, MATILDA, and **WILLIAM PAISLEY.** 1980. *Women and the Mass Media: Sourcebook for Research Action.* New York: Human Sciences Press.

BYNUM, CAROLINE WALKER, STEVEN HARRELL, and **PAULA RICHMAN (EDS.).** 1986. *Gender and Religion: On the Complexity of Symbols.* Boston: Beacon Press.

BYRD, MAX. 1978. *London Transformed: Images of the City in the Eighteenth Century.* New Haven, CT: Yale University Press.

CALIFANO, JOSEPH A. 1986. *America's Health Care Revolution: Who Lives? Who Dies? Who Pays?* New York: Random House.

CAMPAGNA, DAVID. 1985. "The economics of juvenile prostitution in the USA." *International Children's Rights Monitor,* 2.

CAMPBELL, ANNE. 1984. *The Girls in the Gang.* New York: Basil Blackwell.

———. 1986. "Self-reporting of fighting by females." *British Journal of Criminology,* 26.

———, and **JOHN T. GIBBS (EDS.).** 1986. *Violent Transactions.* New York: Basil Blackwell.

CAMPBELL, DUNCAN. 1982. *War Plan U.K.: The Truth about Civil Defense in Britain.* London: Burnett Books.

CAMPBELL-JONES, SUZANNE. 1979. *In Habit: An Anthropoligical Study of Working Nuns.* London: Faber and Faber.

CAMPORESI, PIERO. 1988. *Bread of Dreams.* Cambridge: Polity Press.

CANCIAN, FRANCESCA M. 1987. *Love in America: Gender and Self-Development.* New York: Cambridge University Press.

CANNON, GEOFFREY. 1987. *The Politics of Food.* London: Century.

CANTRIL, HADLEY. 1963. *The Psychology of Social Movements.* New York: Wiley.

CAPLAN, ARTHUR L. (ED.). 1978. *The Sociobiology Debate: Readings on Ethical and Scientific Issues.* New York: Harper and Row.

CAPLAN, PAT (ED.). 1987. *The Cultural Construction of Sexuality.* New York: Routledge, Chapman and Hall.

CAPLIN, L., and **D. KESSLER.** 1976. *An Economic Analysis of Crime.* Springfield, IL: Charles Thomas.

CARDOSO, F. H. 1972. "Dependency and under-development in Latin America." *New Left Review,* no. 74.

CARDOSO, G. 1983. *Negro Slavery in the Sugar Plantations of Veracruz and Pernambuco, 1550–1680.* Washington, D.C.: University Press of America.

CARLEN, PAT, ET AL. (EDS.). 1985. *Criminal Women: Some Autobiographical Accounts.* New York: Basil Blackwell.

CARLEY, MICHAEL. 1981. *Social Measurement and Social Indicators.* Winchester, MA: Allen and Unwin.

CARLSTEIN, TOMMY. 1982. *Time Resources, Society, and Ecology.* Preindustrial Society Series, Vol. 1. Winchester, MA: Allen and Unwin.

————, **DON PARKES,** and **NIGEL THRIFT (EDS.).** 1978. *Making Sense of Time.* 3 vols. New York: Wiley.

CARMICHAEL, STOKELY, and **CHARLES HAMILTON.** 1987. *Black Power: The Politics of Liberation in America.* New York: Random House.

CARNEIRO, ROBERT L. 1970. "A theory of the origin of the state." *Science,* no. 169.

CARR, EDWARD HALLETT. 1970. *The October Revoution: Before and After.* London: Macmillan.

CARRIER, FRED J. 1976. *The Third World Revolution.* Amsterdam: B. R. Gruner.

CARRINGTON GOODRICH, L. 1946. "The early development of firearms in China." *Isis,* 36.

CARSWELL, JOHN. 1986. *Government and the Universities in Britain: Program and Performance, 1960–1980.* New York: Cambridge University Press.

CASTEL, ROBERT. 1988. *The Regulation of Madness: The Origins of Incarceration in France.* Berkeley, CA: University of California Press.

CASTELLS, MANUEL. 1977. *The Urban Question: A Marxist Approach.* Cambridge, MA: MIT Press.

————. 1983. *The City and the Grass Roots: A Cross-Cultural Theory of Urban Social Movements.* Berkeley, CA: University of California Press.

CASTLES, STEPHEN, with **HEATHER BOOTH** and **TINA WALLACE.** 1984. *Here for Good: Western Europe's New Ethnic Minorities.* Wolfeboro, NH: Longwood Publishing Group.

CENTERS, RICHARD. 1949. *The Psychology of Social Classes.* Princeton, NJ: Princeton University Press.

CHAFE, WILLIAM H. 1974. *The American Woman: Her Changing Social, Economic, and Political Roles, 1920–1970.* New York: Oxford University Press.

————. 1977. *Women and Equality: Changing Patterns in American Culture.* New York: Oxford University Press.

CHALFANT, PAUL H., ROBERT E. BECKLEY, and C. EDDIE PALMER. 1986. *Religion in Contemporary Society.* 2nd ed. Palo Alto, CA: Mayfield.

CHALLENER, R. D. 1965. *The French Theory of the Nation in Arms: 1866–1939.* New York: Russell and Russell.

CHAMBLISS, WILLIAM J., and ROBERT SEIDMAN. 1982. *Law, Order, and Power.* 2nd ed. Reading, MA: Addison-Wesley.

CHAPMAN, KAREN. 1986. *The Sociology of Schools.* London: Tavistock.

CHERLIN, ANDREW J. 1981. *Marriage, Divorce, Re-Marriage.* Cambridge, MA: Harvard University Press.

CHILDE, V. GORDON. 1979. "Prehistory and Marxism." *Antiquity,* 53.

———. 1983. *Man Makes Himself.* New York: New American Library.

CHODOROW, NANCY. 1978. *The Reproduction of Mothering.* Berkeley, CA: University of California Press.

———. 1988. *Psychoanalytic Theory and Feminism.* Cambridge: Polity Press.

CHOMSKY, NOAM. 1976. *Reflections on Language.* New York: Pantheon.

CHRISTIE, BRUCE (ED.). 1985. *Human Factors of Information Technology in the Office.* New York: Wiley.

CHURCH OF ENGLAND. 1985. *Faith in the City: The Report of the Archbishop of Canterbury's Commission on Urban Priority Areas.* London: Christian Action.

CIBA FOUNDATION. 1985. *Child Sexual Abuse within the Family.* New York: Routledge, Chapman and Hall.

CIPOLLA, CARLO M. 1965. *Guns and Sails in the Early Phase of European Expansion 1400–1700.* London: Collins.

CLAESSEN, HENRI J. M., and PETER SKALNIK (EDS.). 1976. *The Early State.* Hawthorne, NY: Mouton.

CLARK, BURTON R. 1985. *The School and the University: An International Perspective.* Berkeley, CA: University of California Press.

CLARK, K., and M. CLARK. 1963. *Prejudice and Your Child.* 2nd ed. Boston: Beacon Press.

CLARK, LORENNE M. G., and DEBRA J. LEWIS. 1977. *Rape: The Price of Coercive Sexuality.* Toronto: The Women's Press.

CLAYTON, RICHARD R., and HARWIN L. VOSS. 1977. "Shacking up: Co-habitation in the 1970s." *Journal of Marriage and the Family,* 39.

CLEMENS, JOHN. 1983. *Polls, Politics, and Populism.* Brookfield, VT: Gower.

CLINARD, MARSHALL. 1978. *Cities with Little Crime: The Case of Switzerland.* New York: Cambridge University Press.

CLOWARD, RICHARD A. and L. OHLIN. 1960. *Delinquency and Opportunity.* New York: Free Press.

CLYNE, P. 1973. *Guilty But Insane.* London: Thomas Nelson and Sons.

COBB, JONATHAN, and RICHARD SENNETT. 1973. *The Hidden Injuries of Class.* New York: Random House.

COCKERHAM, WILLIAM C. 1986. *Medical Sociology.* 3rd ed. Englewood Cliffs, NJ: Prentice-Hall.

COHEN, ALBERT. 1955. *Delinquent Boys.* New York: Free Press.

COHEN, BERNARD. 1980. *Deviant Street Networks: Prostitution in New York City.* Lexington, MA: D. C. Heath.

COHEN, G. A. 1980. *Karl Marx's Theory of History: A Defense.* Princeton, NJ: Princeton University Press.

COHEN, STANLEY. 1985. *Visions of Social Control: Crime, Punishment, and Classification.* New York: Basil Blackwell.

COHN, NORMAN. 1970a. *The Pursuit of the Millennium.* New York: Oxford University Press.

_____. 1970b. "Medieval Millenarianism," in Sylvia L. Thrupp, *Millennial Dreams in Action: Studies in Revolutionary Religious Movements*. New York: Shocken Books.

COLEMAN, JAMES S., ET AL. 1966. *Equality of Educational Opportunity*. Washington, D.C.: U.S. Government Printing Office.

_____, THOMAS HOFFER, and SALLY KILGORE. 1981. *Public and Private Schools*. Chicago: National Opinion Research Center.

COLLINS, RANDALL. 1974. *Conflict Sociology: Toward an Explanatory Science*. New York: Academic Press.

_____. 1979. *The Credential Society: An Historical Sociology of Education*. New York: Academic Press.

_____. 1981. "On the micro-foundations of macro-sociology." *American Journal of Sociology*, 86.

CONE, JAMES H. 1984. *For My People: Black Theology and the Black Church*. Mary Knoll, NY: Orbis Books.

CONGRESSIONAL BUDGET OFFICE. 1988. *Trends in Family Income: 1970–1986*. Washington, D.C.: U.S. Government Printing Office.

CONNELLY, MARK THOMAS. 1980. *The Response to Prostitution in the Progressive Era*. Chapel Hill, NC: University of North Carolina Press.

CONVERSE, JEAN M., and HOWARD SCHUMAN. 1974. *Conversations at Random: Survey Research as Interviewers See It*. New York: Wiley.

COOK, ALICE, and GWYN KIRK. 1983. *Greenham Women Everywhere: Dreams, Ideas, and Actions from the Women's Peace Movement*. Boston: South End Press.

COOK, P. J. 1982. "The role of firearms in violent crime," in Marvin E. Wolfgang and Neil Alan Wiener, *Criminal Violence*. London: Sage.

COOK, THOMAS D. ET AL. 1975. *Sesame Street Revisited*. New York: Russell Sage.

_____, and DONALD T. CAMPBELL. 1979. *Quasi-Experimentation: Design and Analysis Issues for Field Settings*. Chicago: Rand McNally.

COOLEY, CHARLES HORTON. 1969. *Sociological Theory and Social Research*. New York: Wiley.

COOMBS, PHILIP H. 1985. *The World Crisis in Education*. New York: Oxford University Press.

COOPER, R. 1986. *The Economics of Interdepenence*. New York: McGraw-Hill.

CORCORAN, P. E. 1983. "The limits of democratic theory," in Graeme Duncan (ed.), *Democratic Theory and Practice*. New York: Cambridge University Press.

CORNISH, DEREK B., and RONALD V. CLARKE. 1986. *The Reasoning Criminal: Rational Choice Perspectives on Offending*. New York: Springer-Verlag.

COTTAM, JEAN. 1980. "Soviet women in combat in World War 2: The ground forces and the navy." *International Journal of Women's Studies*, 3.

COWAN, RUTH SCHWARTZ. 1985. "The industrial revolution in the home," in Donald MacKenzie and Judy Wajcman, *The Social Shaping of Technology*. Philadelphia: Open University Press.

COWARD, ROSALIND. 1984. *Female Desire: Women's Sexuality Today*. London: Paladin.

DOWEN, P. 1979. "An XYY Man." *British Journal of Psychiatry*, 135, pp. 255–58.

COX, OLIVER C. 1948. *Caste, Class, and Race*. New York: Doubleday.

_____. 1964. "The Pre-industrial city reconsidered." *Sociological Quarterly*, 5.

COX, PETER R. 1976. *Demography*. 5th ed. New York: Cambridge University Press.

CRAFT, M. and A. 1985. "The participation of ethnic minority pupils in further and higher education." *Education Research*, 25.

CRENSHAW, MARTHA, (ED.). 1983. *Terrorism, Legitimacy, and Power: The consequences of Political Violence*. Middletown, CT: Wesleyan University Press.

CREWE, IVOR. 1987. "The campaign of confusion." *New Society*, May 8.

CROZIER, MICHAEL. 1967. *The Bureaucratic Phenomenon.* Chicago: University of Chicago Press.

CRUIKSHANK, MARGARET, (ED.). 1982. *Lesbian Studies, Present and Future.* Old Westbury, NY: The Feminist Press.

CURRELL, MELVILLE E. 1974. *Political Woman.* Totowa, NJ: Rowman and Littlefield.

CURTISS, SUSAN. 1977. *Genie: A Linguistic Study of a Modern Day "Wild Child."* New York: Academic Press.

CUSHING, FRANK H. 1967. *My Adventures in Zuni.* Orig. pub. 1882–83. Palmer Lake, CO: Filter Press.

CYBRINSKY, ROMAN A., ET AL. 1986. "The political and social construction of revitalized neighborhoods: Society Hill, Philadelphia, and False Creek, Vancouver," in Neil Smith and Peter Williams (ed.), *Gentrification of the City.* Winchester, MA: Allen and Unwin.

DAHL, ROBERT. 1971. *Polyarchy: Participation and Opposition.* New Haven, CT: Yale University Press.

———. 1985. *A Preface to Economic Democracy.* Berkeley, CA: University of California Press.

DAVENPORT, W. 1965. "Sexual patterns and their regulations in a society of the southwest Pacific," in F. Beech (ed.), *Sex and Behavior.* New York: Wiley.

DAVIDSON, BASIL. 1974. *Africa in History: Themes and Outlines.* New York: Macmillan.

DAVIES, D. 1986. *Information Technology at Work.* London: Heinemann.

DAVIES, JAMES C. 1962. "Towards a theory of revolution." *American Sociological Review,* 27.

DAVIES, R. 1979. *Capital, State, and White Labour in Soth Africa, 1900–1960.* East Sussex, England: Harvester Press.

DAVIS, ANGELA. 1971. "Reflections on black woman's role in the community of slaves." *The Black Scholar,* 3.

DAVIS, JAMES A., and **ROGER JOWELL.** 1989. "Measuring national differences," in Roger Jowell, Sharon Witherspoon, and Lindsay Brook (eds.), *British Social Attitudes.* Brookfield, VT: Gower. ©Social and Community Planning Research.

DAVIS, KINGSLEY. 1940. "Extreme social isolation of a child." *American Journal of Sociology,* 45.

———. 1976. "The world's population crisis," in Robert K. Merton and Robert Nisbet (eds.), *Contemporary Social Problems.* 4th ed. New York: Harcourt Brace Jovanovich.

DAVIS, MIKE, ET AL. (EDS.). 1987. *The Year Left 2: Toward a Rainbow Socialism. Essays on Race, Ethnicity, Class and Gender.* London: Verso.

DEAR, MICHAEL, and **JENNIFER WOLCH.** 1987. *Landscapes of Despair.* Princeton, NJ: Princeton University Press.

DEFLEUR, MELVIN, and **EVERETTE E. DENNIS.** 1985. *Understanding Mass Communication.* Boston: Houghton Mifflin.

DELAMONT, SARAH. 1983. *Interaction in the Classroom.* New York: Routledge, Chapman and Hall.

DELGARD, P., and **E. KRINGLEN.** 1976. "A Norwegian twin study of criminality." *British Journal of Criminology,* 29, pp. 71–74.

DEMARS, O. 1974. *Dirty Business.* New York: Harper and Row.

DE YOUNG, MARY. 1982. *The Sexual Victimization of Children.* Jefferson, NC: McFarland.

DIAMOND, STANLEY. 1974. *In Search of the Primitive.* New Brunswick, NJ: Transaction Books.

DICKEN, PETER. 1986. *Global Shift: Industrial Change in a Turbulent World.* New York: Harper and Row.

DILLOWAY, JAMES. 1986. *Is World Order Evolving? An Adventure into Human Potential.* New York: Pergamon Press.

DINGWALL, ROBERT. 1980. "Ethics and ethnography." *Sociological Review,* 28.

DINHAM, BARBARA, and **COLIN HINES.** 1983. *Agribusiness in Africa.* San Francisco: Institute for Food Development Policy).

DITTON, JASON. 1977. *Part-Time Crime: An Ethnography of Fiddling and Pilferage.* London: MacMillan.

DIZARD, WILSON P. 1982. *The Coming Information Age: An Overview of Technology, Economics, and Politics.* New York: Longman.

DJILAS, MILOVAN. 1967. *The New Class: An Analysis of the Communist System.* New York: Praeger.

DOBASH, RUSSELL, R. EMERSON DOBASH, and **SUE GUTTERIDGE.** 1986. *The Imprisonment of Women.* New York: Basil Blackwell.

DOERNER, KLAUS. 1984. *Madmen and the Bourgeoisie: A Social History of Insanity and Psychiatry.* New York: Basil Blackwell.

DOLBEARE, KENNETH M., and **MURRAY J. EDLEMAN.** 1974. *American Politics, Policies, Power, and Change.* Lexington, MA: D. C. Heath.

DOMHOFF, G. WILLIAM. 1967. *Who Rules America?* Englewood Cliffs, N.J.: Prentice-Hall.

————. 1971. *The Higher Circles: The Governing Class in America.* New York: Random House.

————. 1979. *The Powers That Be: Process of Ruling Class Domination in America.* New York: Random House.

————. 1983. *Who Rules America Now? A View from the Eighties.* Englewood Cliffs, NJ: Prentice-Hall.

DONALDSON, MARGARET. 1979. *Children's Minds.* New York: Norton.

DORE, RONALD. 1980. *British Factory, Japanese Factory: The Origins of National Diversity in Industrial Relations.* Berkeley, CA: University of California Press.

————, and **K. AOYAGI.** 1965. "The Burakumin minority in urban Japan," in A. Rose and C. Rose (eds.), *Minority Problems.* New York: Harper and Row.

DOWLING, COLETTE. 1982. *The Cinderella Complex: Women's Hidden Fear of Independence.* New York: Pocket Books.

DOYAL, LESLEY, and **IMOGEN PENNELL.** 1981. *The Political Economy of Health.* Boston: South End Press.

DREW, PAUL and **TONY WOOTTON.** 1988. *Erving Goffman and the Interaction Order.* Cambridge: Polity Press.

DUBOS, RENÉ. 1959. *Mirage of Health.* New York: Doubleday/Anchor.

DUCHEN, CLAIRE. 1986. *Feminism in France.* New York: Routledge, Chapman and Hall.

DUGDALE, RICHARD L. 1970. *The Dukes: A Study in Crime, Pauperism, Disease, and Heredity.* Reprint of 1877 ed. New York: AMS Press.

DUMONT, LOUIS. 1981. *Homo Hierarchicus: The Caste System and its Implications.* Chicago: University of Chicago Press.

DUNCAN, OTIS DUDLEY. 1971. "Observations on population." *The New Physician,* April 20.

DUNN, JOHN. 1972. *Modern Revolutions: An Introduction to the Analysis of a Political Phenomenon.* New York: Cambridge University Press.

————. 1985. "Understanding revolutions," in *Rethinking Modern Political Theory.* New York: Cambridge University Press.

DURIE, SHEILA, and **ROB EDWARDS.** 1982. *Fueling the Nuclear Arms Race: The Links between Nuclear Power and Nuclear Weapons.* Wolfeboro, NH: Longwood Publishing Group.

DURKHEIM, ÉMILE. 1965. *The Elementary Forms of the Religious Life.* Orig. pub. 1912. New York: Free Press.

———. 1966. *Suicide.* Orig. pub. 1897. New York: Free Press.

———. 1982. *The Rules of Sociological Method.* Orig. pub. 1895. New York: Free Press.

DUVERGER, MAURICE. 1954. *Political Parties.* New York: Wiley.

DWYER, D. J. 1975. *People and Housing in Third World Cities.* London: Longman.

DYE, THOMAS R. 1986. *Who's Running America?* 4th ed. Englewood Cliffs, NJ: Prentice-Hall.

DYER, GWYNNE. 1985. *War.* London: Bodley Head.

EBERHARD, WOLFRAM. 1970. *Conquerors and Rulers: Social Forces in Medieval China.* New York: W.S. Heinman.

ECKSTEIN, HARRY. 1958. *The English Health Service.* Cambridge, MA: Harvard University Press.

EDGELL, STEPHEN R. 1980. *Middle-Class Couples.* London: Allen and Unwin.

EDWARDS, RICHARD, and MICHAEL PODGURSKY. 1986. "The unravelling accord: American unions in crisis," in Richard Edwards, Paolo Garonna, and Franz Todtling, *Unions in Crisis and Beyond: Perspectives from Six Countries.* Dover, MA: Auburn House.

EHRLICH, PAUL R. 1976. *The Population Bomb.* New York: Ballantine.

———, and ANNE H. EHRLICH. 1979. "What happened to the population bomb?" *Human Nature,* 2.

EHRENREICH, BARBARA. 1983. *The Hearts of Men: The American Dream and the Flight from Commitment.* Garden City, NY: Doubleday.

EIBL-EIBESFELDT, I. 1972. "Similarities and differences between cultures in expressive movements," in Robert A. Hinde (ed.), *Nonverbal Communication.* New York: Cambridge University Press.

———. 1973. "The expressive behavior of the deaf-and-blind born," in M. von Cranach and I. Vine (eds.), *Social Communication and Movement.* New York: Academic Press.

EISENSTADT, S. N. 1963. *The Political System of Empires.* New York: Free Press.

EKMAN, PAUL, and W. V. FRIESEN. 1971. "Constants across culture in the face and emotion," *Journal of Personality and Social Psychology,* 17.

———. 1978. *Facial Action Coding System.* New York: Consulting Psychologists Press.

ELKIND, DAVID. 1984. *All Grown Up and No Place to Go: Teenagers in Crisis.* Reading, MA: Addison-Wesley.

ELLMAN, MICHAEL. 1980. "Against convergence." *Cambridge Journal of Economics,* 4.

ELLWOOD, ROBERT S. 1979. *Alternative Altars: Unconventional and Eastern Spirituality in America.* Chicago: University of Chicago Press.

ELSHTAIN, JEAN BETHKE 1981. *Public Man: Private Woman.* Princeton, NJ: Princeton University Press.

———. 1987. *Women and War.* New York: Basic Books.

ELSTON, M. 1980. "Medicine: Half our future doctors?" in R. Silverstone and A. Ward (eds.), *Careers of Professional Women.* New York: Routledge, Chapman and Hall.

ENGERMAN, STANLEY L. 1977. "Black fertility and family structure in the United States, 1880–1940." *Journal of Family History,* 2.

ENGLAND, PAULA, and GEORGE FARKAS. 1986. *Households, Employment, and Gender: A Social, Economic, and Democratic View.* New York: Aldine.

ENNEW, JUDITH. 1986. *The Sexual Exploitation of Children.* New York: St. Martin's Press.

EPSTEIN, CYNTHIA FUCHS. 1988. *Deceptive Distinctions: Sex, Gender, and the Social Order.* New Have, CT: Yale University Press.

———, and ROSE LAUB COSER (EDS.). 1981. *Access to Power: Cross-National Studies of Women and Elites.* Boston: Allen and Unwin.

ERICKSON, JOHN. 1974. "Some military and political aspects of the 'Militia Army' controversy, 1919–1920." in C. Abramsky et al. (eds.), *Essay in Honor of E. H. Carr.* Hamden, CT: Shoe String Press.

ERIKSON, ERIK H. 1986. *Childhood and Society.* Orig. pub. 1950. New York: Norton.

ERIKSON, ROBERT, and JOHN J. GOLDTHORPE. 1986. "National variation in social fluidity," CASMIN Project Working Paper, no. 9.

ERMANN, DAVID, and RICHARD LUNDMAN. 1982. *Corporate and Governmental Deviance.* New York: Oxford University Press.

ESTABROOK, A. 1916. *The Dukes in 1915.* Washington, D.C.: Carnegie Institution.

ESTRICH, SUSAN. 1987. *Real Rape.* Cambridge, MA: Harvard University Press.

ETZIONI-HALÉVY, EVA. 1985. *Bureaucracy and Democracy: A Political Dilemma.* New York: Routledge, Chapman and Hall.

EVANS, RICHARD J. 1977. *The Feminists: Women's Emancipation Movements in Europe, America, and Australasia,, 1840–1920.* New York: Barnes and Noble Imports.

EVANS, ROBIN. 1982. *The Fabrication of Virtue: English Prison Architecture: 1750–1840.* New York: Cambridge University Press.

EVANS-PRITCHARD, E. E. 1940. *The Nuer: A Description of the Modes of Livelihood and Political Institutions of a Nilotic People.* New York: Oxford University Press.

———. 1950. *Witchcraft, Oracles, and Magic among the Azande.* Oxford: Oxford University Press.

———. 1956. *Nuer Religion.* New York: Oxford University Press.

EYSENCK, HANS. 1977. *Crime and Personality.* St. Albans, England: Paladin.

FAGAN, JEFFREY A., DOUGLAS A. STEWART, and KAREN V. HANSEN. 1983. "Violent men or violent husbands? Background factors and situational correlates," in David Finkelhor and Richard J. Galles (eds.), *The Dark Side of Families: Current Family Violence Research.* Beverly Hills, CA: Sage.

FANCHER, RAYMOND E. 1987. *The Intelligence Men: Makers of the IQ Controversy.* New York: Norton.

FARLEY, R. 1985. "Three steps forward and two back? Recent changes in the social and economic status of blacks," in Richard D. Alba (ed.), *Ethnicity and Race in the U.S.A.: Toward the Twenty-First Century.* New York: Methuen.

FARLEY, REYNOLDS, and WALTER ALLEN. 1987. *The Color Line and the Quality of Life: The Problem of the Twentieth Century.* New York: Russel Sage.

FARRINGTON, DAVID, and R. KIDD. 1980. "Stealing from a 'lost' letter: Effects of victim characteristics." *Criminal Justice and Behavior,* 7.

———, and J. GUNN (EDS.). 1985. *Aggression and Dangerousness.* New York: Wiley.

———, LLOYD E. OHLIN, and JAMES Q. WILSON. 1986. *Understanding and Controlling Crime: Toward a New Research Strategy.* New York: Springer-Verlag.

FAUSTO-STERLING, ANNE. 1985. *Myths of Gender: Biological Theories about Men and Women.* New York: Basic Books.

FEENEY, FLOYD. 1986. "Robbers as decision-makers," in Derek Cornish and Ronald Clarke (eds.), *The Reasoning Criminal: Rational Choice Perspectives on Offending.* New York: Springer-Verlag.

FEIGE, L. 1981. *The Theory and Measurement of the Unobserved Sector of the U. S. Economy.* Lieden, Netherlands: Reidel.

FEIN, RASHI. 1986. *Medical Care, Medical Costs.* Cambridge, MA: Harvard University Press.

FELD, MAURY D. 1977. *The Structure of Violence: Armed Forces as Social Systems.* Washington, D.C.: Seven Locks Press.

FELDBERG, ROSLYN, and EVELYN NAKANO GLENN. 1984. "Male and female: Job versus gender models in the sociology of work," in Janet Siltanen and Michelle Stanworth (eds.), *Women and the Public Sphere: A Critique of Sociology and Politics.* New York: St. Martin's Press.

FELDMAN, PHILIP, and **MALCOLM MACCULLOCH.** 1980. *Human Sexual Behavior.* New York: Wiley.

FENSTERMAKER BERK, SARAH. 1985. *The Gender Factory: The Apportionment of Work in American Households.* New York: Plenum Press.

FETTNER, ANN G., and **WILLIAM A. CHECK.** 1984. *The Trush About AIDS: Evolution of an Epidemic.* New York: Holt, Rinehart and Winston.

FEUERBACH, LUDWIG. 1957. *The Essence of Christianity.* New York: Harper & Row.

FINCH, MINNIE. 1981. *The NAACP: Its Fight for Justice.* Metuchen, NJ: Scarecrow Press.

FINE, BEN. 1977. "Labelling theory." *Economy and Society,* 4. pp. 166–93.

FINEMAN, STEPHEN, ET AL. 1987. *Unemployment: Personal and Social Consequences.* London: Tavistock.

FINER, SAMUEL E. 1962. *The Man on Horseback: The Role of the Military in Politics.* London: Pall Mall Press.

———. 1975. "State and nation building in Europe: The role of the military," in Charles Tilley (ed.), *The Formation of National States in Europe.* Princeton, NJ: Princeton University Press.

FINKELHOR, DAVID. 1984. *Child Sexual Abuse: New Theory and Research.* New York: Free Press.

———, and **K. YLLO.** 1982. "Forced sex in marriage: A Preliminary report." *Crime and Delinquency,* 28.

FINLEY, MOSES I. (ED.). 1968. *Slavery in Classical Antiquity.* Cambridge: Heffer.

———. 1980. *Ancient Slavery and Modern Ideology.* London: Chatto and Windus.

FIRESTONE, SHULAMITH. 1971. *The Dialectic of Sex.* London: Paladin.

FISCHER, CLAUDE S. 1975. "Toward a subcultural theory of urbanism." *American Journal of Sociology,* 80.

———. 1984. *The Urban Experience.* 2nd ed. New York: Harcourt Brace Jovanovich.

FISHER, B. 1972. *The Gay Mystique: The Myth and Reality of Male Homosexuality.* New York: Stein and Day.

FITZGERALD, R., and **L. FULLER.** 1982. " 'I hear you knocking but you can't come in': The effects of reluctant respondents and refusers on sample survey estimates." *Sociological Methods and Research,* 2.

FITZPATRICK, J. 1971. *Puerto Rican Americans: The Meaning of Migration to the Mainland.* Englewood Cliffs, NJ: Prentice-Hall.

FLAKE, CAROL. 1984. *Redemptorama: Culture, Politics, and the New Evangelicalism.* Garden City, NY: Anchor.

FLANZ, GISBERT H. 1983. *Comparative Women's Rights and Political Participation in Europe.* Ardsley on Hudson, NY: Transnational Publishers.

FLOWERS, RONALD BARRI. 1987. *Women and Criminality: The Women as Victim, Offender, and Practitioner.* Westport, CT: Greenwood Press.

FLYNN, JAMES R. 1985. "The mean IQ of Americans: Massive gains 1932 to 1978." *Psychological Bulletin,* 95.

FOGEL, ROBERT W., and **STANLEY L. ENGERMAN.** 1974. *Time on the Cross.* 2 vols. Lanham, MD: University Press of America.

FORD, CLELLAN S., and **FRANK A. BEACH.** 1951. *Patterns of Sexual Behavior.* New York: Harper and Row.

FORM, WILLIAM. 1985. *Divided We Stand: Working Class Stratification in America.* Urbana, IL: University of Illinois Press.

FORRESTER, TOM, (ED.). 1985. *The Information Technology Revolution.* Oxford: Basil Blackwell.

FOUCAULT, MICHEL. 1973. *Madness and Civilization: A History of Insanity in the Age of Reason.* New York: Random House.

———. 1979. *Discipline and Punish: The Birth of the Prison.* New York: Random House.

FOX, ALAN. 1974. *Beyond Contract: Work, Power, and Trust Relations.* London: Faber and Faber.

FOX, D. J. 1972. "Patterns of morbidity and morality in Mexico City." *Geographical Review*, 62.

FOX, OLIVER C. 1964. "The Pre-industrial city reconsidered." *Sociological Quarterly*, 5.

FRAIBERG. SELMA H. 1984. *The Magic Years: Understanding and Handling the Problems of Early Childhood.* New York: Scribners.

FRANCIS, ARTHUR. 1980. "Company objectives, managerial motivation and the behaviour of large firms: An empirical test of the theory of 'managerial' capitalism." *Cambridge Journal of Economics*, 4.

FRANK, ANDRÉ GUNDER. 1969. *Capitalism and Under-development in Latin America.* New York: Monthly Review Press.

————. 1981. *Crisis: In the Third World.* New York: Holmes and Meier.

FRAZIER, FRANKLIN. 1939. *The Negro Family in the United States.* Chicago: University of Chicago Press.

FRAZIER, NANCY, and **MYRA SADKER.** 1973. *Sexes in School and Society.* New York: Harper and Row.

FREEMAN, R. B., and **D. A. WISE.** 1982. *The Youth Labor Market Problem: Its Nature, Causes, and Consequences.* Chicago: University of Chicago Press.

FREIDSON, ELIOT. 1980. *Doctoring Together: A Study of Professional Social Control.* Chicago: University of Chicago Press.

————. 1986. *Professional Powers: A Study of the Institutionalization of Formal Knowledge.* Chicago: University of Chicago Press.

FREMLIN, J. H. 1964. "How many people can the world support?" *New Scientist*, October 19.

FRENCH, R. A. 1979. "The individuality of the Soviety city," in R. A. French and F. E. I. Hamilton (eds.), *The Socialist City: Spatial Structure and Urban Policy.* New York: Wiley.

FREUD, SIGMUND. 1971. *The Psychopathology of Everyday Life.* New York: Norton.

————. 1982. *Three Essays on the Theory of Sexuality.* New York: Basic Books.

FRIEDEN, BETTY. 1981. *The Second Stage.* New York: Summit.

FRIEDL, JOHN. 1981. *The Human Portrait: Introduction to Cultural Anthropology.* Englewood Cliffs, NJ: Prentice-Hall.

FRIEDMAN, L. 1977. *Sex-Role Stereotyping in the Mass Media: An Annotated Bibliography.* New York: Garland Publishing.

FRIEDRICH, CARL. 1954. *Totalitarianism.* Cambridge, MA: Harvard University Press.

————. 1969. *Totalitarianism in Perspective: Three Views.* London: Pall Mall Press.

FRÖBEL, FOLKER, ET AL. 1980. *The New International Division of Labor.* New York: Cambridge University Press.

FROMM, ERICH, (ED.). 1967. *Socialist Humanism.* London: Allen Lane.

FRYER, DAVID, and **STEPHEN MCKENNA.** 1987. "The laying off of hands—unemployment and the experience of time," in Stephen Fineman, (ed.), *Unemployment: Personal and Social Consequences.* London: Tavistock.

FRYER, PETER. 1984. *Staying Power.* Atlantic Highlands, NJ: Humanities Press International.

FURNIVALL, J. 1956. *Colonial Policy and Practice: A Comparative Study of Burma and Netherlands India.* New York: New York University Press.

FURSTENBERG, FRANK F., JR., THEODORE HERSHBERG, and **JOHN MODELL.** 1975. "The origins of the female-headed black family: The impact of the urban experience." *Journal of Interdisciplinary History*, 6.

FURTADO, C. 1984. *The Economic Growth of Brazil: A Survey from Colonial to Modern Times.* Westport, CT: Greenwood Press.

GAERTNER, W., and **A. WENIG (EDS.).** 1985. *The Economics of the Shadow Economy.* Berlin: Springer-Verlag.

GAGE, MATILDA JOSLYN. 1972. *Women, Church, and State.* Orig. pub. 1893. Salem, NH: Ayer.

GAILEY, H. A. 1970–72. *A History of Africa: 1800 to the Present.* 2 vols. Boston: Houghton Mifflin.

GALBRAITH, JOHN KENNETH. 1980. *Economics and the Public Purpose.* New York: New American Library.

————. 1984. *The Affluent Society.* 4th ed. Boston: Houghton Mifflin.

————. 1985. *The New Industrial State.* 4th ed. Boston: Houghton Mifflin.

GALLIE, DUNCAN. 1978. *In Search of the New Working Class: Automation and Social Integration within the Capitalist Enterprise.* New York: Cambridge University Press.

GALLUP OPINION INDEX., 1976. "Religion in America," Report no. 130.

GANS, HERBERT J. 1968. *People and Plans: Essays on Urban Problems and Solutions.* New York: Basic Books.

————. 1982. *The Urban Villagers: Group and Class in the Life of Italian-Americans.* Rev. expanded ed. New York: Free Press.

GANSLER, JACQUES. 1980. *The Defense Industry.* Cambridge, MA: MIT Press.

GARDNER, BEATRICE, and **ALLEN GARDNER.** 1969. "Teaching sign language to a chimpanzee." *Science,* no. 165.

————. 1975. "Evidence for sentence constituents in the early utterances of child and chimpanzee." *Journal of Experimental Psychology,* 104.

GARFINKEL, HAROLD. 1963. "A conception of, and experiments with, 'trust' as a condition of stable concerted actions," in O. J. Harvey (ed.), *Motivation and Social Interaction.* New York: Ronald Press.

————. 1985. *Studies in Ethnomethodology.* New York: Basil Blackwell.

GEARY, DICK. 1981. *European Labor Protest, 1848–1939.* New York: St. Martin's Press.

GEERTZ, CLIFFORD. 1983. *Local Knowledge: Further Essays in Interpretative Anthropology.* New York: Basic Books.

GEIS, GILBERT. 1979. *Not the Law's Business: An Examination of Homosexuality, Abortion, Prostitution and Gambling in the United States.* New York: Schocken Books.

————, and **EZRA STOTLAND (EDS.).** 1980. *White Collar Crime: Theory and Research.* Beverly Hills: Sage.

GELB, I. J. 1952. *A Study of Writing.* Chicago: University of Chicago Press.

GELLNER, ERNEST. 1964. *Thought and Change.* London: Weidenfeld and Nicolson.

————. 1983. *Nations and Nationalism.* Ithaca, NY: Cornell University Press.

GEORGES, ROBERT A., and **MICHAEL O. JONES.** 1980. *People Studying People: The Human Element in Fieldwork.* Berkeley, CA: University of California Press.

GERBNER, GEORGE, ET AL. 1979. "The demonstration of power: Violence profile no. 10." *Journal of Communication,* 29.

————. 1980. "The 'mainstreaming' of America: Violence profile no. 11." *Journal of Communication,* 30.

GERSHUNY, J. I. 1978. *After Industrial Society?* London: Macmillan.

————, and **I. D. MILES.** 1983. *The New Service Economy: The Transformation of Employment in Industrial Societies.* London: Francis Pinter.

GERSON, KATHLEEN. 1985. *Hard Choices: How Women Decide About Work, Career, and Motherhood.* Berkeley: University of California Press.

GIBBONS, DON. 1979. *The Criminological Enterprise: Theories and Perspectives.* Englewood Cliffs, NJ: Prentice-Hall.

GIDDENS, ANTHONY. 1977. *New Rules of Sociological Method.* New York: Basic Books.

————. 1985a. *The Constitution of Society.* Berkeley, CA: University of California.

————. 1985b. *The Nation-State and Violence.* Berkeley, CA: University of California Press.

GILIOMEE, HERMANN, and **LAWRENCE SCHLEMMER (EDS.).** 1985. *Up Against the Fences: Poverty, Passes and Privilege in South Africa.* New York: St. Martin's Press.

GILL, COLIN. 1985. *Work, Unemployment, and the New Technology.* New York: Basil Blackwell.

GILLEN, R. 1978. "A study of women shoplifters." *Excerpta Medica Psychiatrica,* 123.

GILLIGAN, CAROL. 1982. *In a Different Voice: Psychological Theory and Women's Development.* Cambridge, MA: Harvard University Press.

GILROY, PAUL. 1987. *"There Ain't No Black in the Union Jack."* London: Hutchinson.

GINZBURG, CARLO. 1982. *The Cheese and the Worms.* Tr. by John Tedeschi and Anne Tedeschi. New York: Penguin.

GISSING, GEORGE. 1983. *Demos: A Story of English Socialism.* Orig. pub. 1892. New York: Roultedge, Chapmann and Hall.

GLASS, DAVID (ED.). 1954. *Social Mobility in Britain.* London: Routledge and Kegan Paul.

GLEITMAN, HENRY. 1986. *Psychology.* 2nd ed. New York: Norton.

GLENN, NORVAL D., and **CHARLES N. WEAVER.** 1956. "The marital happiness of remarried divorced persons." *Journal of Marriage and The Family.* 39.

GLUECK, SHELDON W., ET AL. 1949. *Varieties of Delinquent Youth.* New York: Harper and Row.

———, and **ELEANOR GLUECK.** 1956. *Physique and Delinquency.* New York: Harper and Row.

GOFFMAN, ERVING. 1961. *Asylums: Essays on the Social Situation of Mental Patients and Other Inmates.* New York: Doubleday/Anchor.

———. 1963. *Behavior in Public Places.* New York: Free Press.

———. 1967. *Interaction Ritual.* New York: Doubleday/Anchor.

———. 1970. *Stigma: Notes on the Management of a Spoiled Identity.* Harmondsworth, England: Penguin.

———. 1972. *Relations in Public: Microstudies of the Public Order.* New York: Harper and Row.

———. 1973. *The Presentation of Self in Everyday Life.* New York: Overlook Press.

———. 1974. *Frame Analysis.* New York: Harper and Row.

———. 1979. *Gender Advertisements.* Cambridge, MA: Harvard University Press.

———. 1981. *Forms of Talk.* Philadelphia; University of Pennsylvania Press.

GOLDFIELD, MICHAEL. 1987. *The Decline of Organized Labor in the United States.* Chicago: University of Chicago Press.

GOLDING, PETER and **SUE MIDDLETON.** 1982. *Images of Welfare: Press and Public Attitudes to Poverty.* Oxford: Martin Robertson.

GOLDING, P. (ED.). 1982. *Alcoholism: A Modern Perspective.* Ridgewood, NJ: Bogden and Son.

GOLDSTEIN, PAUL J. 1979. *Prostitution and Drugs.* Lexington, MA: D. C. Heath.

GOLDTHORPE, J. E. 1984. *The Sociology of the Third World: Disparity and Development.* 2nd ed. Cambridge: Cambridge University Press.

GOLDTHORPE, JOHN H. 1971. "Theories of industrial society." *Archives Européennes de Sociologie,* 12.

———. 1983. "Women and class analysis: In defence of the conventional view." *Sociology,* 17.

———, **ET AL.** 1969. *The Affluent Worker in the Class Structure.* 3 vols. New York: Cambridge University Press.

———, **C. LLEWELLYN, AND C. PAYNE.** 1982. *Social Mobility and Class Structure in Modern Britain.* New York: Oxford University Press.

———, and **C. PAYNE.** 1986. "Trends in intergenerational class mobility in England and Wales 1972–1983." *Sociology,* 20.

GOLEMAN, DANIEL. 1987. "An emerging theory on blacks' IQ scores." *New York Times*. April 9.

GOODE, E. 1972. *Drugs in American Society*. New York: Alfred Knopf.

GOODE, WILLIAM J. 1963. *World Revolution in Family Patterns*. New York: Free Press.

GOODHARDT, G. J., A. S. C. EHRENBERG, and M. A. COLLINS. 1987. *The Television Audience: Patterns of Voting*. 2nd ed. London: Gower.

GOODWIN, CHARLES. 1981. *Conversational Organization: Interaction between Speakers and Hearers*. New York: Academic Press.

GOODWIN, JEAN. 1982. *Sexual Abuse: Incest Victims and Their Families*. Littleton, MA: PSG Publishing.

GOODY, JACK. 1977. *The Domestication of the Savage Mind*. New York: Cambridge University Press.

GORDON, MILTON. 1964. *Assimilation in American Life: The Role of Race, Religion, and National Origins*. New York: Oxford University Press.

———. 1978. *Human Nature, Class, and Ethnicity*. New York: Oxford University Press.

GORZ, ANDRÉ. 1982. *Farewell to the Working Class*. London: Pluto.

GOSSETT, THOMAS F. 1963. *Race: The History of an Idea in America*. Dallas, TX: Southern Methodist University Press.

GOTTMAN, JEAN. 1961. *Megalopolis: The Urbanized Northeastern Seaboard of the United States*. New York: Twentieth Century Fund.

GOULDNER, ALVIN. 1982. *The Future of Intellectuals and the Rise of the New Class*. New York: Oxford University Press.

GOYDER, JOHN. 1988. *The Silent Minority: Nonrespondents on Sample Surveys*. Boulder, CO: Westview.

GREELEY, ANDREW. 1977. *The American Catholic: A Social Portrait*. New York: Basic Books.

GREENBAUM, JOAN. 1979. *In the Name of Efficiency: Management Theory and Shopfloor Practice in Data-Processing Work*. Philadelphia: Temple University Press.

GREENBERG, DAVID F., and MARCIA H. BYSTRYN. 1984. "Capitalism bureaucracy and male homosexuality." *Contemporary Crises*, 8.

GREENBERG, MARTIN S., CHAUNCEY E. WILSON, and MICHAEL K. MILLS. 1978. "Victim decision-making: An experimental approach," in D. Walsh, *Shoplifting: Controlling a Major Crime*. London: Macmillan Press.

GREENBLAT, CATHY STEIN. 1983. "A hit is a hit is a hit . . . or is it? Approval and tolerance of the use of physical force by spouses," in David Finkelhor and Richard J. Gelles (eds.), *The Dark Side of Families: Current Family Violence Research*. Beverly Hills, CA: Sage.

GREENFIELD, P. M., and J. H. SMITH. 1976. *The Structure of Communication in Early Language Development*. New York: Academic Press.

GREGORY, DEREK, and JOHN URRY. 1985. *Social Relations and Spatial Structures*. New York: St. Martin's Press.

GRIFFIN, CHRISTINE. 1980. In Edwin M. Schur (ed.), *The Politics of Deviance: Stigma Contests and the Uses of Power*. Englewood Cliffs, NJ: Prentice-Hall.

GRINKER, ROY, and P. SPIEGEL. 1945. *Men under Stress*. Philadelphia: Balkiston.

GRUSKY, DAVID B., and ROBERT M. HAUSER. 1984. "Comparative social mobility revisited: Models of convergence and divergence in 16 countries." *American Sociological Review*, 49.

GUNTER, BARRIE. 1985. *Dimensions of Television Violence*. New York: St. Martin's Press.

GUPTE, PRANAY. 1984. *The Crowded Earth: People and the Politics of Population*. New York: Norton.

GUTMAN, HEBERT. 1975. "Extended review of 'Time on the Cross.' " *Journal of Negro History*, 60.

———. 1976. *The Black Family in Slavery and Freedom: 1750–1925.* New York: Pantheon.

HABERMAS, JÜRGEN. 1975. *Legitimation Crisis.* Tr. by Thomas McCarthy. Boston: Beacon Press.

———. 1979. *Communication and the Evolution of Society.* Tr. by Thomas McCarthy. Boston: Beacon Press.

———. 1985. *Theory of Communicative Action,* vol. 1. Tr. by Thomas McCarthy. Boston: Beacon Press.

HAGEN, JOHN. 1988. *Structural Criminology.* Cambridge: Polity Press.

HÄGERSTRAND, TORSTEN. 1973. "The domain of human geography," in R. J. Chorley (ed.), *Directions in Geography.* London: Methuen.

HAKIM, CATHERINE C. 1982. *Secondary Analysis in Social Research: A Guide to Data Services and Methods with Examples.* Winchester, MA: Allen and Unwin.

HALE, ROBERT B. 1971. *The Strengths of Black Families.* New York: Emerson Hall.

HALL, EDWARD T. 1969. *The Hidden Dimension.* New York: Doubleday.

———. 1973. *The Silent Language.* New York: Doubleday.

HALL, PETER. 1979. "The presidency and impression management." *Studies in Symbolic Interaction,* 2.

HALL, RUTH E. 1986. *Ask Any Woman: A London Enquiry into Rape and Sexual Assault.* New York: Falling Wall Press.

———, SELMA JAMES, and JUDITH KERTESZ. 1982. *The Rapist Who Pays the Rent.* New York: Falling Wall Press.

HALL, STUART, and MARTIN JACQUES (EDS.). 1983. *The Politics of Thatcherism.* London: Lawrence and Wishart.

HALLE, DAVID. 1984. *America's Working Man: Work, Home, and Politics among Blue Collar Property Owners.* Chicago: University of Chicago Press.

HALSEY, A. H., A. F. HEATH, and J. M. RIDGE. 1980. *Origins and Destinations.* Oxford: Oxford University Press.

HAMILTON, RICHARD. 1967. *Affluence and the French Worker in the Fourth Republic.* Princeton, NJ: Princeton University Press.

HAMMOND, PHILLIP E. (ED.). 1985. *The Sacred in a Secular Age: Toward Revision in the Scientific Study of Religion.* Berkeley, CA: University of California Press.

HANDY, CHARLES. 1984. *The Future of Work: A Guide to a Changing Society.* New York: Basil Blackwell.

HANSCOMBE, GILLIAN E., and MARTIN HUMPHREYS. (EDS.). 1987. *Heterosexuality.* Boston: Alyson Publications.

HANSEN, I. 1980. "Sex education for young children," quoted in J. Scanzoni and G. L. Fox "Sex role, family and society." *Journal of Marriage and the Family,* 42.

HARDER, MARY WHITE, ET AL. 1972. "Jesus people." *Psychology Today,* 6.

HARDING, VINCENT. 1980. *The Other American Revolution.* University of California, Los Angeles: Center for Afro-American Studies, Culture and Society Monograph Series, 4.

HARDYMENT, CHRISTINA. 1987. *Labour Saved?* Cambridge: Polity Press.

HARLOW, HARRY F., and MARGARET K. HARLOW. 1962. "Social deprivation in monkeys." *Scientific American,* no. 207.

———, and R. R. ZIMMERMAN. 1959. "Affectional response in the infant monkey." *Science,* no. 130.

HARRINGTON, MICHAEL. 1963. *The Other America.* New York: Firethorn.

———. 1984. *The New American Poverty.* New York: Firethorn.

HARRIS, CHRISTOPHER. 1983. *The Family and Industrial Society.* Winchester, MA: Allen and Unwin.

HARRIS, MARVIN. 1978. *Cannibals and Kings: The Origins of Cultures.* New York: Random House.

HARRIS, NIGEL. 1987. *The End of the Third World: Newly Industrializing Countries and the Decline of an Ideology.* New York: Penguin.

HARTLEY, EUGENE. 1946. *Problems in Prejudice.* New York: Kings Crown Press.

HARTMAN, MARY, and LOIS BANNER (EDS.). 1974. *Clio's Consciousness Raised: New Perspectives on the History of Women.* New York: Norton.

HARTMANN, HEIDI. 1981. "The family as the locus of class, gender, and political struggle: The example of housework." *Signs,* 6.

HARVEY, DAVID. 1973. *Social Justice and the City.* Baltimore, MD: Johns Hopkins University Press.

———. 1984. *The Limits to Capital.* Chicago: University of Chicago Press.

———. 1985. *Consciousness and the Urban Experience: Studies in the History and Theory of Capitalist Urbanization.* Baltimore, MD: Johns Hopkins University Press.

HATCH, S., and R. KICKBUSCH 1983. *Self-Help and Health in Europe.* Genova, Switzerland: World Health Organization.

HAUSSON, CAROLA, and KARIN LINDIN. 1984. *Moscow Women.* London: Allison and Busby.

HAWKES, TERENCE. 1977. *Structuralism and Semiotics.* Berkeley, CA: University of California Press.

HAWLEY, AMOS H. 1950. *Human Ecology: A theory of Community Structure.* New York: Ronald Press Company.

———. 1968. "Human ecology." *International Encyclopedia of Social Science,* vol 4. New York: Free Press.

HEARNSHAW, LESLIE. 1979. *Cyril Burt: Psychologist.* Ithaca, NY: Cornell University Press.

HEATH, ANTHONY. 1981. *Social Mobility.* London: Fontana.

———, ET AL. 1986. *How Britain Votes.* London: Pergamon Press.

HEITLINGER, ALENA. 1979. *Women and State Socialism: Sex Inequality in the Soviety Union and Czechoslovakia.* Buffalo, NY: McGill-Queens University Press.

HELD, DAVID. 1987. *Models of Democracy.* Stanford, CA: Stanford University Press.

HEMMING, JOHN. 1987. *Amazon Frontier: The Defeat of the Brazilian Indians.* Cambridge, MA: Harvard University Press.

HENNIG, MARGARET, and ANNE JARDIN. 1977. *The Managerial Woman.* Garden City, NY: Doubleday/Anchor.

HENRIQUES, FERNANDO. 1963. *Prostitution and Society,* vol. 2. London: MacGibbon and Kee.

HENRY, S. 1978. *The Hidden Economy.* London: Martin Robertson.

HENSLIN, JAMES M., and MAE A. BRIGGS. 1971. "Dramaturgical desexualization: The sociology of the vaginal examination," in James M. Henslin (ed.), *Studies in the Sociology of Sex.* New York: Appleton-Century-Crofts.

HERITAGE, JOHN. 1985. *Garfinkel and Ethnomethodology.* New York: Basil Blackwell.

HIEBERT, PAUL G. 1983. *Cultural Anthropology,* 2nd ed. Grand Rapids, MI: Baker Book.

HILL, RICHARD C. 1984. "Transnational capitalism and urban crisis: A case of the auto industry and Detroit," in Ivan Szelenyi (ed.), *Cities in Recession: Critical Responses to the Urban Policies of the New Right.* Beverly Hills, CA: Sage.

———. 1984. "Economic crisis and political response in the motor city," in Larry Sawer and William K. Tabb (eds.), *Sunbelt-Snowbelt: Urban Development and Regional Restructuring.* Oxford: Oxford University press.

HILL, RONALD J. 1985. *The Soviet Union: Politics, Economy, and Society.* Boulder, CO: Lynne Riener.

———, and PETER FRANK. 1986. *The Soviet Communist Party.* Winchester, MA: Allen and Unwin.

HIMMELSTRAND, ULF, ET AL. 1981. *Beyond Welfare Capitalism.* New York: Gower Publishing.

HINDELANG, MICHAEL J. 1979. "Sex differences in criminal activity," in *Social Problems,* 27.

HIRSH-PASEK, K., and **R. TREIMAN.** 1982. "Doggerel: Motherese in a new context." *Journal of Child Language,* 9.

HIRST, PAUL, and **PENNY WOOLLEY.** 1982. *Social Relations and Human Attributes.* New York: Routledge, Chapman and Hall.

HOBSON, JOHN A. 1965. *Imperialism: A Study.* Ann Arbor, MI: University of Michigan Press.

HODGE, ROBERT, and **DAVID TRIPP.** 1986. *Children and Television: A Semiotic Approach.* Cambridge: Polity Press.

HOLLOWAY, DAVID. 1984. *The Soviet Union and the Arms Race.* 2nd ed. New Haven, CT: Yale University Press.

HOLMAN, ROBERT. 1978. *Poverty: Explanations of Social Deprivation.* New York: St. Martin's Press.

HOLMES, LESLIE. 1987. *Politics in the Communist World.* New York: Oxford University Press.

HOLTON, ROBERT J. 1978. "The crowds in history: Some problems of theory and method." *Social History,* 3.

HOMANS, HILARY. 1987. "Man-made myth: The reality of being a woman scientist in the NHS," in Anne Spencer and david Podmore (eds.), *In a Man's World: Essays on Women in Male-Dominated Professions.* London: Tavistock.

HOOKS, BELL. 1981. *Ain't I a Woman: Black Women and Feminism.* Boston: South End Press.

HOOPER, JUDITH O., and **FRANK H. HOOPER.** 1985. "Family and individual development theories: Conceptual analysis and speculations," in J. A. Meacham, *Family and Individual Development.* New York: S. Karger.

HOPKINS, A. 1980. "Controlling corporate deviance." *Criminology,* 18: pp. 198–214.

HOPKINS, MARK W. 1970. *Mass Media in the Soviet Union.* New York: Pegasus.

HOPPER, EARL. 1981. *Social Mobility: A Study of Control and Instability.* Oxford: Basil Blackwell.

HOUGH, JERRY W. F., and **MERLE FAINSOD.** 1979. *How the Soviet Union Is Governed.* Cambridge, MA: Harvard University Press.

HOUNSHELL, DAVID A. 1984. *From the American System to Mass Production, 1800–1932: The Development of Manufacturing Technology in the United States.* Baltimore, MD: Johns Hopkins University Press.

HOWARD, MICHAEL. 1976. *War in European History.* New York: Oxford University Press.

HOY STEELE, C. 1975. "Urban Indian identity in Kansas: Some implications for research," in J. Bennett (ed.), *The New Ethnicity: Perspectives from Ethnology.* St. Paul, MN: West Publishing.

HUGHES, BARRY. 1985. *World Futures: A Critical Analysis of Alternatives.* Baltimore, MD: Johns Hopkins University Press.

HUGHES, C. C., and **J. M. HUNTER.** 1971. "Disease and 'development' in Africa," in H. P. Dreitzel (ed.), *The Social Organization of Health.* New York: Macmillan/Collier.

HUMPHRIES, JUDITH. 1983. *Part-Time Work.* London: Kogan Page.

HUNDLEY, N. (ED.). 1975. *The Chicano.* Santa Barbara, CA: Clio Press.

HUNTINGTON, SAMUEL P. 1981. *The Soldier and the State: The Theory and Politics of Civil-Military Relations.* Cambridge, MA: Harvard University press.

HURN, CHRISTOPHER J. 1985. *The Limits and Possibilities of Schooling: An Introduction to the Sociology of Education.* Boston: Allyn and Bacon.

HUTCHINSON, E. 1981. *Legislative History of American Immigration Policy, 1785–1965.* Philadelphia: University of Pennsylvania Press.

HUTTENBACK, ROBERT A. 1976. *Racism and Empire: White Settlers v. Colored Immigrants in British Self-Governing Colonies, 1830–1910.* Ithaca, NY: Cornell University Press.

HYDE, H. M. 1970. *The Other Love: An Historical and Contemporary Survey of Homosexuality in Britain.* London: Heinemann.

HYDE, JANET SHIBLEY. 1986. *Understanding Human Sexuality.* New York: McGraw-Hill.

HYMAN, RICHARD. 1984. *Strikes.* 2nd ed. London: Fontana.

IANNI, FRANCIS A. J. 1974. *Black Mafia.* New York: Simon and Schuster.

———, and **ELIZABETH REUSS-IANNI.** 1973. *A Family Business: Kinship and Social Control in Organized Crime.* New York: Mentor.

IDELL, ALBERT. 1956. *The Bernal Diaz Chronicles.* New York: Doubleday.

IGNATIEFF, MICHAEL. 1978. *A Just Measure of Pain: The Penitentiary in the Industrial Revolution, 1750–1850.* New York: Random House.

ILLICH, IVAN D. 1983. *Deschooling Society.* New York: Harper and Row.

INSTITUTE FOR SOCIAL SESEARCH. 1987. "The U.S. economy: Who owns the wealth, who needs welfare, who saves, and why." Newsletter. Ann Arbor, MI: University of Michigan, Winter.

INTERNATIONAL INSTITUTE FOR STRATEGIC STUDIES. 1987. *Strategic Survey, 1986–1987.* London.

ISSEL, WILLIAM. 1985. *Social Change in the United States 1945–1983.* New York: Schocken Books.

JACKMAN, MARY R., and **ROBERT W. JACKMAN.** 1983. *Class Awareness in the United States.* Berkeley, CA: University of California Press.

JACKSON, K. 1967. *The Klu Klux Klan in the City, 1915–1930.* New York: Oxford University Press.

JACKSON, KENNETH T. 1981. "The spatial dimensions of social control: Race, ethnicity and government housing policy in the United States, 1918–1968," in Bruce N. Stave (ed.), *Modern Industrial Cities: History, Policy, and Survival.* Beverly Hills, CA: Sage Publications.

———. 1985. *Crabgrass Frontier: The Suburbanization of the United States.* New York: Oxford University Press.

JACKSON, MICHAEL P. 1985. *Industrial Relations.* 3rd ed. New York: Routledge, Chapman and Hall.

JACOBS, JANE. 1961. *The Death and Life of Great American Cities.* New York: Random House.

JAHER, FREDERIC COPLE (ED.). 1973. *The Rich, the Well Born, and the Powerful.* Urbana, IL: University of Illinois Press.

———. 1980. "The gilded elite: American multimillionaires, 1865 to the present," in William D. Rubinstein (ed.), *Wealth and the Wealthy in the Modern World.* London: Croom Helm.

JAMES, JENNIFER, ET AL. 1975. *The Politics of Prostitution.* Seattle, WA: Social Research.

JAMES, WILLIAM. 1981. *Principles of Psychology.* Orig. pub. 1890. Cambridge, MA: Harvard University Press.

JANELLE, D. G. 1968. "Central place development in a time-space framework." *Professional Geographer,* 20.

JANOWITZ, MORRIS. 1977. *Military Institutions and Coercion in the Developing Nations: An Essay in Comparative Analysis.* Chicago: University of Chicago Press.

JANUS, S. S., and D. H. HEID BRACEY. 1980. "Runaways: Pornography and prostitution." New York: Mimeo.

JAYNES, GERALD D., ET AL. 1987. "Contributions to 'American dilemmas and black responses.' " *Society*, 24.

JENCKS, CHRISTOPHER, ET AL. 1972. *Inequality: A Reassessment of the Effects of Family and School in America*. New York: Basic Books.

JENKINS, SIMON. 1986. *The Market for Glory: Fleet Street Ownership in the Twentieth Century*. Boston: Faber and Faber.

_____. 1987. "Eve versus the Adams of the Church." *Sunday Times* (London). September, 6.

JENSEN, ARTHUR. 1967. "How much can we boost IQ and scholastic achievement?" *Harvard Educational Review*, 29.

_____. 1979. *Bias in Mental Testing*. New York: Free Press.

JOHNSON, CHALMERS. 1964. *Revolution and the Social System*. Stanford, CA: Stanford University Press.

_____. 1966. *Revolutionary Change*. Boston: Little Brown.

JONES, BARRY. 1985. *Sleepers Awake! Technology and the Future of Work*. New York: Oxford University Press.

JONES, R., and P. SCHNEIDER. 1984. "Self-Help production cooperatives: Government-administered cooperatives during the Depression," in R. Jackall and H. Levin (eds.), *Worker Cooperatives in America*. Berkeley, CA: University of California Press.

JORDAN, WINTHROP. 1968. *White over Black*. Chapter Hill, NC: University of North Carolina Press.

JORGENSEN, JAMES. 1980. *The Graying of America*. New York: Dial Press.

JOWELL, ROGER ET AL. (EDS.). 1986. *British Social Attitudes: The Nineteen Eighty-Six Report*. Brookfield, VT: Gower.

KAHN, R. N. 1986. "Multinational companies and the world economy: Economic and technological impact." *Impact of Science on Society*, 36.

KALDOR, MARY. 1982. *The Baroque Arsenal*. New York: Hill and Wang.

KAMATA, SATOSHI. 1982. *Japan in the Passing Lane*. London: Allen and Unwin.

KAMIN, LEON J. 1974. *The Science and Politics of IQ*. Hillsdale, NJ: L. Erlbaum Assoc.

KANTER, ROSABETH MOSS. 1977. *Work and Family in the United States*. New York: Russell Sage Foundation.

KARABEL, JEROME, and A. H. HALSEY (EDS.). 1977. *Power and Ideology in Education*. New York: Oxford University Press.

KART, GARY S. 1985. *The Social Realities of Aging*. Boston: Allyn and Bacon.

KASARDA, JOHN, and MORRIS JANOWITZ. 1974. "Community attachment in mass society." *American Sociological Review*, 39.

KATZ, ELIHU, ET AL. 1978. *Broadcasting in the Third World: Promise and Performance*. London: Macmillan.

KATZ, G. (ED.). 1976. *Gay American History: Lesbians and Gay Men in the U.S.A.* New York: Thomas Y. Crowell.

KATZ, SEDELLE, and MARY ANN MAZUR. 1979. *Understanding the Rape Victim: A Synthesis of Research Findings*. New York: Wiley.

KAUTSKY, JOHN J. 1982. *The Politics of Aristocratic Empires*. Chapel Hill, NC: University of North Carolina Press.

KAVANAGH, DENNIS A. 1987. *Thatcherism and British Politics*. New York: Oxford University Press.

KEIN, RUDOLPH. 1974. "Accountability in the National Health Service." *Political Quarterly*, 41.

KELLY, J. E. 1982. *Scientific Management: Job Re-Design and Work Performance*. New York: Academic Press.

KELSO, WILLIAM. 1984. *Kingsmill Plantations, 1620–1800: An Archaeology of Rural Colonial Virginia.* Orlando, FL: Academic Press.

KENNEDY, GAVIN. 1983. *Defense Economics.* New York: St. Martin's Press.

KEOHANE, ROBERT. 1984. *After Hegemony.* Princeton, NJ: Princeton University Press.

KERN, STEVEN. 1983. *The Culture of Time and Space: 1880–1918.* Cambridge, MA: Harvard University Press.

KERNER COMMISSION. 1968. *Report of the National Advisory Commission on Civil Disorders.* New York: Bantam.

KERR, CLARK. 1983. *The Future of Industralized Societies.* Cambridge, MA: Harvard University Press.

———, **ET AL.** 1960. *Industrialism and Industrial Man: The Problems of Labor and Management in Economic Growth.* Cambridge, MA: Harvard University Press.

KESSELMAN, MARK, ET AL. 1987. *European Politics in Transition.* Lexington, MA: D. C. Heath.

KING, D. (ED.). 1979. *The Cherokee Indian Nation.* Knoxville, TN: University of Tennessee Press.

KINSEY, ALFRED C., ET AL. 1948. *Sexual Behavior in the Human Male.* Philadelphia: W. B. Saunders.

———, **ET AL.** 1953. *Sexual Behavior in the Human Female.* Philadelphia: W. B. Saunders.

KITCHER, PHILIP. 1985. *Vaulting Ambition: Sociobiology and the Quest for Human Nature.* Cambridge, MA: MIT Press.

KJEKSHUS, H. 1977. *Ecology, Control, and Economic Development in East African History.* Berkeley, CA: University of California Press.

KLEIN, RUDOLF. 1983. *The Politics of the National Health Service.* London: Longman.

KLUCKHOHN, CLYDE. 1985. *Mirror for Man.* Tucson, AZ: University of Arizona Press.

KNORR-CETINA, KAREN, and **AARON V. CICOUREL (EDS.).** 1981. *Advances in Social Theory and Methodology: Towards an Integration of Micro and Macro-Sociologies.* Boston: Routledge and Kegan Paul.

KOESTLER, ARTHUR. 1976. *The Act of Creation.* London: Hutchinson.

KOGAN, MAURICE, with **DAVID KOGAN.** 1983. *The Attack on High Education.* London: Kogan Page.

KOHN, MELVIN. 1969. *Class and Conformity.* Homewood, IL: Dorsey Press.

KOMAROVSKY, MIRRA. 1976. *Dilemmas of Masculinity.* New York: Norton.

KOSA, JOHN, and **IRVING KENNETH ZOLA (EDS.).** 1975. *Poverty and Health: A Sociological Analysis.* Cambridge, MA: Harvard University Press.

KOVEL, JOEL. 1970. *White Racism: A Psychohistory.* New York: Random House.

KRAMER, SAMUEL N. 1981. *History Begins at Sumer.* Philadelphia: University of Pennsylvania Press.

KRAUSE, ELLIOT A. 1977. *Power and Illness: The Political Sociology of Health and Health Care.* New York: Elsevier.

KRIEGER, JOEL. 1986. *Reagan, Thatcher, and the Politics of Decline.* New York: Oxford University Press.

KRUPAT, EDWARD. 1985. *People in Cities: The Urban Environment and Its Effects.* New York: Cambridge University Press.

KUBALKOVA, V. and **A. A. CRUIKSHANK.** 1981. *International Inequality.* New York: St. Martin's Press.

KÜBLER-ROSS, ELISABETH. 1981. *Living with Death and Dying.* New York: Macmillan.

———. 1986. *Death: The Final Stage of Growth.* New York: Simon and Schuster.

KUMAR, KRISHAN. 1978. *Prophecy and Progress: The Sociology of Industrial and Post-Industrial Society.* London: Penguin.

LABOV, WILLIAM. 1973. *Sociolinguistic Patterns.* Philadelphia: University of Pennsylvania Press.

LADD, EVERETT CARLL. 1989. *The American Polity: The People and Their Government.* 3rd ed. New York: Norton.

LAKE, R. 1981. *The New Suburbanites: Race and Housing in the Suburbs.* New Brunswick, NJ: Center for Urban Policy Research, Rutgers University Press.

LANCET. 1974. "World Health Losing Ground." May, 18.

LANDES, DAVID S. 1969. *The Unbound Prometheus.* New York: Cambridge University Press.

LANDRY, BART. 1988. *The New Black Middle Class.* Berkeley, Ca: University of California Press.

LANE, HARLAN. 1976. *The Wild Boy of Aveyron.* Cambridge, MA: Harvard University Press.

LANE, JAMES B. 1974. *Jacob A. Riis: The American City.* New York: Kennikat Press.

LANGONE, JOHN. 1987. *AIDS: The Facts.* Boston: Little Brown.

LANTENARI, VITTORIO. 1963. *The Religions of the Oppressed: A Study of Modern Messianic Cults.* New York: Knopf.

LANTZ, HERMAN, MARTIN SCHULTZ, and **MARY O'HARA.** 1977. "The changing American family from the preindustrial to the industrial period: A final report." *American Sociological Review,* 42.

LAPPÉ, FRANCES MOORE, and **JOSEPH COLLINS.** 1979. *Food First.* New York: Ballantine.

_____. 1980. *Aid as an Obstacle.* San Francisco: Institute for Food and Development Policy.

LAPPING, BRIAN. 1987. *Apartheid: A History.* New York: Braziller.

LAQUEUR, WALTER. 1976. *Guerrilla: A Historical and Critical Study.* Boston: Little Brown.

LARGE, PETER. 1984. *The Micro Revolution Revisited.* Totowa, NJ: Rowman and Littlefield.

LASLETT, PETER. 1977. *Family Life and Illicit Love in Earlier Generations.* New York: Cambridge University Press.

_____. 1984. *The World We Have Lost: England Before the Industrial Age.* 3rd ed. New York: Macmillan.

LATANE, B., and **J. DARLEY.** 1970. *The Unresponsive Bystander: Why Doesn't He Help?* New York: Appleton-Century-Crofts.

LAZARSFELD, PAUL F., BERNARD BERELSON, and **HAZEL GAUDET.** 1948. *The People's Choice.* New York: Columbia University Press.

LEACH, EDMUND. 1976. *Culture and Communication: The Logic by which Symbols Are Connected.* New York: Cambridge University Press.

LE BON, GUSTAVE. 1960. *The Crowd.* Orig. pub. 1895. New York: Viking.

LEE, LAURIE. 1965. *Cider with Rosie.* London: Hogarth Press.

LEE, R. 1960. *The Chinese in the United States of America.* Oxford: Oxford University Press.

LEE, RICHARD B. 1968. "What hunters do for a living or, how to make out on scarce resources," in Richard B. Lee and Irven DeVore (eds.), *Man the Hunter.* Chicago: Aldine.

_____. 1969. "!Kung Bushman subsistence: An input-output analysis," in A. P. Vayda (ed.), *Environment and Cultural Behavior.* New York: Natural History Press.

LEES, ANDREW. 1985. *Cities Perceived: Urban Society in European and American Thought, 1820–1940.* New York: Columbia University Press.

LEIUFFSRUD, HAKON, and **ALISON WOODWARD.** 1987. "Women at class crossroads: Repudiating conventional theories of family class." *Sociology,* 21.

LEMERT, EDWIN. 1972. *Human Deviance, Social Problems, and Social Control.* Englewood Cliffs, NJ: Prentice-Hall.

LENSKI, GERHARD. 1966. *Power and Privilege.* New York: McGraw-Hill.

——, and **JEAN LENSKI.** 1982. *Human Societies.* 4th ed. New York: McGraw-Hill.

LERNER, BARBARA. 1982. "American education: How are we doing?" *The Public Interest, 69.*

LESLIE, GERALD R. 1982. *The Family in Social Context.* 5th ed. New York: Oxford University Press.

LEVISON, ANDREW. 1974. *The Working Class Majority.* New York: Coward, McGann and Geoghegan.

LEWONTIN, RICHARD. 1984. *Human Diversity.* New York: W. H. Freeman.

LIAZOS, A. 1972. "The poverty of the sociology of deviance: Nuts, sluts and perverts." *Social Problems, 20.*

LIEBERMAN, M. 1978. *Power for the Poor—The Family Center Project: An Experiment in Self-Help.* London: Allen and Unwin.

LIEBERSON, STANLEY. 1962. *Ethnic Patterns in American Cities.* New York: Free Press.

——. 1972. "An empirical study of military-industrial linkages," in Sam C. Sarkesian (ed.). *The Military-Industrial Complex: A Reassessment.* Washington, D.C.: Seven Locks Press.

LIEBERT, ROBERT M., JOYCE N. SPRAFKIN, and **M. A. S. DAVIDSON.** 1985. *The Early Window: Effects of Television on Children and Youth.* New York: Pergamon Press.

LIEDERMAN, P. HERBERT, STEPHEN R. TULKIN, and **ANN ROSENFELD.** 1977. *Culture and Infancy: Variations in the Human Experience.* New York: Academic Press.

LIFTON, ROBERT J., ET AL. 1982. *Indefensible Weapons: The Political and Psychological Case against Nuclearism.* New York: Basic Books.

LIGHT, DONALD W. 1986. "Corporate medicine for profit." *Scientific American, 255.*

——. 1987. "Social control and the American health-care system," in Howard E. Freeman and Sol Levine (eds.), *Handbook of Medical Sociology.* 4th ed. Englewood Cliffs, NJ: Prentice-Hall.

LIGHT, PAUL C. 1988. *Baby Boomers.* New York: Norton.

LINDBLOM, CHARLES E. 1977. *Politics and Markets.* New York: Basic Books.

LINDEN, E. 1976. *Apes, Men, and Language.* New York: Penguin.

LINHART, R. 1981. *The Assembly Line.* Amherst, MA: University of Massachusetts Press.

LINTON, RALPH. 1937. "One hundred percent American." *The American Mercury,* no. 40, April.

LIPSET, SEYMOUR MARTIN (ED.). 1981. *Party Coalitions in the 1980s.* San Francisco: Institute for Contemporary Affairs.

——, and **REINHARD BENDIX.** 1959. *Social Mobility in Industrial Society.* Berkeley, CA: University of California Press.

LIPTON, M. 1986. *Capitalism and Apartheid.* Aldershot, England: Wildwood House.

LITTLEJOHN, JAMES. 1972. *Social Stratification.* London: Allen and Unwin.

LITTLER, CRAIG, and **GRAEME SALAMAN.** 1984. *Class at Work: The Design, Allocation, and Control of Jobs.* London: Batsford.

LOCKWOOD, DAVID. 1966. *The Blackcoated Worker: A Study in Class Consciousness.* London: Allen and Unwin.

LODGE, JULIET (ED.). 1981. *Terrorism: A Challenge to the State.* New York: St. Martin's Press.

LOFLAND, JOHN. 1977. "The dramaturgy of state executions," in Horace bleackley and John Lofland, *State Executions, Viewed Historically and Sociologically.* Montclair, NJ: Patterson Smith.

LOGAN, JOHN R., and **HARVEY L. MOLOTCH.** 1987. *Urban Fortunes: The Political Economy of Place.* Berkeley, CA: University of California Press.

LOMBROSO, CESARE. 1911. *Crime: Its Causes and Remedies.* Boston: Little Brown.

LOPATA, HELENA. 1977. "Widows and widowers." *The Humanist, 37.*

LOWE, GRAHAM S. 1987. *Women in the Administrative Revolution: The Feminization of Clerical Work.* Toronto: University of Toronto Press.

LOWE, J. R. 1967. *Cities in a Race with Time: Progress and Poverty in America's Renewing Cities.* New York: Random House.

LOWE, STUART. 1986. *Urban Social Movements: The City after Castells.* New York: St. Martin's Press.

LUARD, EVAN. 1977. *International Agencies: The Emerging Framework of Interdependence.* Dobbs Ferry, NY: Oceana.

LUEPTOW, L. B. 1975. "Parental status and influence on the achievement orientations of high school seniors." *Sociology of Education,* 48.

LUFT, HAROLD S. 1978. *Poverty and Health: Economic Causes and Consequences of Health Problems.* Cambridge, MA: Ballinger.

LUIA, A. 1974. "Recent women college graduates: A study of rising expectations." *American Journal of Ortho Psychiatry,* 44, pp. 14–15.

LYNCH, K. 1976. *Making Sense of a Region.* Cambridge, MA: MIT Press.

LYON, DAVID. 1989. *The Information Society: Issues and Illusions.* New York: Basil Blackwell.

LYSTAD, MARY (ED.). 1986. *Violence in the Home: Interdisciplinary Perspectives.* New York: Brunner and Mazel.

MCCONVILLE, SEAN. 1981. *A History of English Prison Administration,* vol. 1. London: Routledge and Kegan Paul.

MCGILL, PETER. 1987. "Sunset in the East." *The Observer,* August 2.

MCGOLDRICK, ANN. 1973. "Early retirement: A new leisure opportunity?" Leisure Studies Association Conference Paper No. 15. London: Continued Education Center, Polytechnic of Central London.

MCHALE, MAGDA CORDELL, ET AL. 1979. *Children in the World.* Washington, D.C.: Population Reference Bureau.

MCKAY, DAVID. 1985. *American Politics and Society.* 2nd ed. New York: Basil Blackwell.

MCKEE, D. 1977. *Chinese Exclusion versus the Open Door Policy.* Detroit, MI: Wayne State University Press.

MACKENZIE, DONALD, and **JUDY WAJCMAN.** 1985. *The Social Shaping of Technology.* New York: Taylor and Francis.

MACKENZIE, GAVIN. 1973. *The Aristocracy of Labor: The Position of Skilled Craftsmen in the American Class Structure.* New York: Cambridge University Press.

MCKENZIE, R. R. 1933. *The Metropolitan Community.* New York: Russell and Russell.

MACKINNON, CATHERINE A. 1979. *Sexual Harassment of Working Women: A Case of Sex Discrimination.* New Haven, CT: Yale University Press.

MACKLIN, ELEANORE D. 1978. "Non-marital heterosexual co-habitation." *Marriage and Family Review,* 1.

MCLEAN, CHARLES. 1978. *The Wolf Children.* New York: Hill and Wang.

MCNEILL, WILLIAM H. 1982. *The Pursuit of Power: Technology, Armed Force, and Society Since AD 1000.* Chicago: University of Chicago Press.

MCPHAIL, THOMAS L. 1987. *Electronic Communication: The Future of International Broadcasting and Communication.* 2nd ed. Beverly Hills, CA: Sage.

MADDOX, BRENDA. 1975. *The Half Parent.* New York: Evans.

MAIR, LUCY. 1974. *African Societies.* Cambridge: Cambridge University Press.

MALINOWSKI, BRONISLAW. 1982. *"Magic: Science and Religion," and Other Essays.* London: Sourvenir Press.

MALLIER, A. T., and **M. J. ROSSER.** 1986. *Women and the Economy: A Comparative Study of Britain and the U.S.A.* New York: St. Martin's Press.

MALTHUS, THOMAS. 1976. *Essay on the Principle of Population.* Edited by Philip Appleman. Orig. pub. 1798. New York: Norton.

MACQUET, JACQUES JEROME. 1961. *The Premise of Inequality in Ruanda.* London: Greenwood.

MALVEAUX, JULIANNE. 1985. "Similarities and differences in the economic interests of black and white women." *Review of Black Political Economy.* Summer.

MANN, MICHAEL. 1986. *The Sources of Social Power: Vol. I: A History of Power from the Beginning to 1760.* New York: Cambridge University Press.

MANN, PETER H. 1970. *An Approach to Urban Sociology.* New York: Humanities Press.

———. 1985. *Methods of Social Investigation.* New York: Basil Blackwell.

MANSBRIDGE, J. J. 1983. *Beyond Adversary Democracy.* Chicago: University of Chicago Press.

MANWARING, T., and **S. SIGLER (EDS.).** 1985. *Breaking the Nation.* London: Pluto Press.

MARCUSE, HERBERT. 1983. *Reason and Revolution: Hegel and the Rise of Social Theory.* 2nd ed. Atlantic Highlands, NJ: Humanities.

MARSH, CATHERINE. 1982. *The Survey Method: The Contribution of Surveys to Sociological Explanat***MARSTRAND, PAULINE K., ET AL.** 1978. "Food and agriculture: When enough is not enough—the world food paradox," in Christopher Freeman and Marie Jahoda (eds.), *World Futures: The Great Debate.* London: Martin Robertson.

MARTY, MARTIN E. 1970. *The Righteous Empire.* New York: Dial Press.

MARWICK, ARTHUR. 1974. *War and Social Change in the Twentieth Century.* London: Macmillan.

MARX, KARL. 1963. "Alienated labour," in T. B. Bottomore (ed.), *Karl Marx: Early Writings.* New York: McGraw Hill.

———. 1963. "Economic and philosophical manuscripts," in T. B. Bottomore (ed.), *Karl Marx: Early Writings.* New York: McGraw Hill.

———. 1977. *Capital: A Critique of Political Economy, Vol. I.* Orig. pub. 1864. New York: Random House.

———, and **FREIDRICH ENGELS.** 1965. *Manifesto of the Communist Party.* San Francisco: China Bks.

MASON, P. 1971. *Patterns of Dominance.* New York: Oxford University Press.

MASSEY, DOREEN. 1984. *Spatial Divisions of Labor: Social Structures and the Geography of Production.* New York: Methuen.

MASTERS, WILLIAM H., VIRGINIA E. JOHNSON, and **ROBERT C. KOLODNY.** 1987. *Crisis: Heterosexual Behavior in the Age of AIDS.* New York: Grove Press.

MATTEIS, R. 1979. "The new bank office on customer service." *Harvard Business Review,* March/April.

MATTELART, A. 1979. *Multinational Corporations and the Control of Culture: The Ideological Apparatuses of Imperialism.* Atlantic Highlands, NJ: Humanities Press.

MATTHEWS, MERVYN. 1972. *Class and Society in Soviet Russia.* London: Allen and Unwin.

MATTHEWS, SARAH H. 1979. *The Social World of Old Women: Management of Self-Identity.* Beverly Hills, CA: Sage.

MAYO, ELTON. 1977. *The Human Problems of an Industrial Civilization.* New York: Arno Press.

———. 1977. *The Social Problems of an Industrial Civilization.* New York: Arno Press.

MEAD, GEORGE HERBERT. 1967. *Mind, Self, and Society.* Chicago: University of Chicago Press.

MEADOWS, DONNELLA H., ET AL. 1972. *The Limits to Growth.* New York: Universe Books.

MEDNICK, S. 1982. "Biology and violence," in Marvin E. Wolfgang and N. A. Wiener (eds.), *Criminal Violence.* Beverly Hills, CA: Sage.

———, and **T. MOFFITT (EDS.).** 1984. *The New Biocriminology.* New York: Cambridge University Press.

MEIER, AUGUST, and **ELLIOT RUDWICK.** 1973. *CORE: A Study in the Civil Rights Movement, 1945–1968.* New York: Oxford University Press.

MELBIN, MURRAY. 1978. "The colonisation of time," in Tommy Carlstein, Don Parkes, and Nigel J. Thrift, *Human Activity and Time Geography.* London: Arnold.

———. 1978. "Night as frontier." *American Sociological Review, 43.*

———. 1987. *Night as Frontier: Colonizing the World after Dark.* New York: Free Press.

MELTON, J. GORDON. 1978. *Encyclopedia of American Religions.* 2 vols. Wilmington, NC: McGrath.

MERRITT, GILES. 1982. *World Out of Work.* London: Collins.

MERTON, ROBERT K. 1949. "Discrimination and the American creed," in R. M. McIver, *Discrimination and National Welfare.* New York: Harper and Row.

———. 1957.*Social Theory and Social Structure.* Rev. ed. New York: Free Press.

MEYER, ALFRED G. 1970. "Theories of convergence," in Chalmers Johnson (ed.), *Change in Communist Systems.* Stanford, CA: Stanford University Press.

MEYER, JOHN W., and **BRIAN ROWAN.** 1977. "Institutionalized organizations: Formal structure as myth and ceremony." *American Journal of Sociology, 83.*

MEYER, STEPHEN III. 1981. *The Five Dollar Day: Labor Management and Social Control in the Ford Motor Company, 1908–1921.* Albany, NY: State University of New York Press.

MICHELS, ROBERT. 1967. *Political Parties.* Orig. pub. 1911. New York: Free Press.

MICKLIN, MICHAEL, and **HARVEY M. CHOLDIN.** 1984. *Sociological Human Ecology: Contemporary Issues and Applications.* Boulder, CO: Westview.

MILES, AGNES. 1981. *The Mentally Ill in Contemporary Society.* New York: St. Martin's Press.

MILGRAM, STANLEY. 1973. *Obedience to Authority: An Experimental View.* New York: Harper and Row.

———. 1977. *The Individual in a Social World: Essays and Experiments.* Reading, MA: Addison-Wesley.

MILLER, ELEANOR M. 1986. *The Street Woman.* Philadelphia: Temple University Press.

MILLER, GALE. 1978. *Odd Jobs: The World of Deviant Work.* Englewood Cliffs, NJ: Prentice-Hall.

MILLER, S. M. 1960. "Comparative social mobility." *Journal of Current Sociology, 9.*

———. 1971. "A comment: The future of social mobility studies." *American Journal of Sociology, 77.*

MILLER, WILLIAM L. 1983. *The Survey Method in Social and Political Sciences: Achievements, Failures, Prospects.* New York: St. Martin's Press.

MILLS, C. WRIGHT. 1956. *The Power Elite.* New York: Oxford University Press.

———. 1967. *The Sociological Imagination.* New York: Oxford University Press.

MILLS, D. QUINN, and **JANICE MCCORMICK.** 1985. *Industrial Relations in Transition: Cases and Text.* New York: Wiley.

MILWARD, ALAN S. 1984. *The Economic Effects of the World Wars on Britain.* New York: Humanities Press.

MINER, HORACE. 1956. "Body ritual among the Nacirema." *American Anthropologist, 58.*

MINTZ, F., and **MICHAEL SCHWARTZ.** 1985. *The Power Structure of American Business.* Chicago: University of Chicago Press.

MIRSKY, JONATHAN. 1982. "China and the one child family." *New Society,* no. 59, February 18.

MITCHELL, JULIET. 1975. *Psychoanalysis and Feminism.* New York: Random House.

MITTERAUER, MICHAEL. and REINHARD SIDER. 1984. *The European Family, Patriarchy to Partnership from the Middle Ages to the Present.* Chicago: University of Chicago Press.

MOLOTCH, HARVEY, and DEIRDRE BODEN. 1985. "Talking social structure: Discourse, dominance, and the Watergate hearings." *American Sociological Review*, 50.

MOMMSEN, WOLFGANG J. 1982. "Violence and terrorism in Western industrial societies," in W. J. Mommsen, et al, *Social Protest. Violence and Terror in Nineteenth and Twentieth-Century Europe.* New York: St. Martin's Press.

MONEY, JOHN, and ANKE A. EHRHARDT. 1973. *Man and Woman, Boy and Girl.* Baltimore, MD: Johns Hopkins Press.

MONTAGU, ASHLEY. 1980. *Sociobiology Examined.* New York: Oxford University Press.

MONTER, E. WILLIAM. 1977. "The pedestal and the stake: Courtly love and witchcraft," in Renate Bridenthal and Claudia Koouz, *Becoming Visible: Women in European History.* Boston: Houghton Mifflin.

MOORE, BARRINGTON. 1965. *Political Power and Social Theory.* New York: Harper and Row.

MOQUIN, W. (ED.). 1974. *A Documentary History of the Italian-American.* New York: Praeger.

MORAWSKA, EVA. 1986. *For Bread with Butter: Life-Worlds of East-Central Europeans in Johnstown, Pennsylvania, 1890–1940.* New York: Cambridge University Press.

MORGAN, KEVIN, and ANDREW SAYER. 1988. *Microcircuits of Capital: Sunrise Industry and Uneven Development.* Boulder, CO: Westview.

MORRIS, ALLISON. 1987. *Women, Crime, and Justice.* New York: Basil Blackwell.

MORRIS, DESMOND. 1977. *Manwatching: A Field Guide to Human Behavior.* New York: Abrams.

MORRIS, JAN. 1974. *Conundrum.* New York: Harcourt Brace Jovanovich.

MORTIMER, EDWARD. 1982. *Faith and Power: The Politics of Islam.* New York, Random House.

MOYNIHAN, DANIEL P. 1965. *The Negro Family: A Case for National Action.* Washington D.C.: U.S. Government Printing Office.

MULLER, PETER O. 1981. *Contemporary Suburban American.* Englewood Cliffs, NJ: Prentice-Hall.

MUMFORD, LEWIS. 1973. *Interpretations and Forecasts.* New York: Harcourt Brace Jovanovich.

MUNCK, RONALDO. 1984. *Politics and Dependency in the Third World: The Case of Latin America.* Atlantic Highlands, NJ: Humanities Press.

MURDOCK, GEORGE PETER. 1945. "The common denominator of cultures," in Ralph Linton (ed.), *The Science of Man in a World of Crisis.* New York: Columbia University Press.

———. 1949. *Social Structure.* New York: McMillan.

MURRAY, MARTIN. 1987. *Time of Agony: Time of Destiny: The Upsurge of Popular Protest in South Africa.* New York: Schocken Books.

NAIPAUL, V. S. 1978. *India: A Wounded Civilization.* New York: Random House.

NAIRN. TOM. 1977. *The Break-up of Britain.* London: New Left Books.

NAKSASE, T. 1981. "Some characteristics of Japanese-type multinational enterprises." *Capital and Class*, 13.

NAPES, G. 1970. "Unequal justice: A growing disparity in criminal sentences troubles legal experts." *The Wall Street Journal*, Sept. 9.

NEARY, IAN J. 1986. "Socialist and communist party attitudes towards discrimination against Japan's Burakumin." *Political Studies*, 34.

NEEDHAM, JOSEPH. 1975. *The Development of Iron and Steel Technology in China.* New York: Cambridge University Press.

NELSON, Q. 1975. *Americanization of the Common Law: The Impact of Legal Change on Massachusett's Society, 1760–1830.* Cambridge, MA: Harvard University Press.

NEWMAN, PHILIP L. 1965. *Knowing the Gururumba.* New York: Holt, Rinehart and Winston.

NEWSPAPER ADVERTISING BUREAU. 1978. *Seven Days in March: Major News Stories in the Press and on TV.* New York.

NICHOLS, EVE K. 1986. *Mobilizing against AIDS.* Cambridge, MA: Harvard University Press.

NICHOLS, THEO, and **HUGH BEYNON.** 1977. *Living with Capitalism: Class Relations and the Modern Factory.* New York: Routledge, Chapman and Hall.

NIE, NORMAN H., SIDNEY VERBA, and **JOHN R. PETROCIK.** 1976. *The Changing American Voter.* Cambridge, MA: Harvard University Press.

NORC. 1981. *Social Survey.* Princeton, NJ: National Opinion Research Center.

NOEL, GERARD. 1980. *The Anatomy of the Catholic Church.* London: Hodder and Stoughton.

NORDHAUS, W. D. 1975. "The political business cycle." *Review of Economic Studies,* 42.

NOTTINGHAM, ELIZABETH K. 1971. *Religion: A Sociological View.* New York: Random House.

NOVAK, M. A. 1979. "Social recovery of monkeys isolated for the first year of life: II. Long-term assessment." *Developmental Psychology,* 2.

NYILAS, JOZSEF. 1982. *The World Economy and Its Main Development Tendencies.* Norwell, MA: Kluwer Press.

OAKES, JEANNIE. 1985. *Keeping Track: How Schools Structure Inequality.* New Haven, CT: Yale University Press.

OAKLEY, ANN. 1975. *The Sociology of Housework.* New York: Pantheon.

———. 1976. *Woman's Work: The Housewife, Past and Present.* New York: Random House.

———. 1981. *Subject Woman.* New York: Pantheon.

OBERG, JAN. 1980. "The new international military order: A threat to human security," in Eide Asbjorn et al. (eds.), *Problems of Contemporary Militarism.* New York: St. Martin's Press.

OFFE, CLAUS. 1984. *Contradictions of the Welfare State.* Cambridge, MA: MIT Press.

———. 1985. *Disorganized Capitalism.* Cambridge, MA: MIT Press.

OLTMAN, RUTH. 1970. "Campus 1970—Where do women stand?" *American Association of University Women Journal.* 64.

ORENSTEIN, ALAN, and **WILLIAM R. F. PHILLIPS.** 1984. *Understanding Social Research: An Introduction.* Boston: Allyn and Bacon.

ORR, ELEANOR WILSON. 1987 *Twice As Less: Black English and the Performance of Black Students in Mathematics.* New York: Norton.

OSWALT, WENDELL HILLMAN. 1972. *Other Peoples, Other Customs: World Ethnography and its History.* New York: Doubleday.

OTTERBEIN, KEITH F. 1985. *The Evolution of War: A Cross-Cultural Study.* New Haven, CT: Human Relations Area Files Press.

OUCHI, WILLIAM G. 1979. "A conceptual framework for the design of organizational control mechanisms." *Management Science,* 25.

———. 1982. *Theory Z: How American Business Can Meet the Japanese Challenge.* New York: Avon Books.

PAGDEN, ANTHONY. 1982. *The Fall of Natural Man: The American Indian and the origins of Comparative Ethnology.* New York: Cambridge University Press.

PAHL, JAN. 1978. *A Refuge for Battered Women.* London: HMSO.

PAHL, RAY. E. 1977. "Collective consumption and the state in capitalist and state socialist societies." in Richard Scase (ed.), *Industrial Society, Class, Cleavage, and Control.* New York: St. Martin's Press.

———. 1984. *Divisions of Labor.* New York: Basil Blackwell.

———. 1987. "A comparative approach to the study of the informal economy." Paper Presented at the 1987 Meeting of the American Sociological Association, August.

———, and **P. A. WILSON.** 1987. "The family as a hologram: First you see it then you don't." *Sociological Review,* 35.

———, and **J. WINKLER.** 1974. "The economic elite: Theory and practice," in Philip Stanworth and Anthony Giddens, *Elites and Power in British Society.* New York: Cambridge University Press.

PALLEY, MARIAN LIEF. 1987. "The women's movement in recent American politics," in Sara E. Rix, *The American Women, 1987–1988.* New York: Norton.

PAN AMERICAN HEALTH ORGANIZATION. 1982. *Health Conditions in the Americas.* Washington, D.C.

PANDEY, TRIKOLI NATH. 1972. "Anthropologists at Zuñi." *Proceedings of the American Philosophical Society,* 166.

———. 1975. " 'India man' among American Indians," in André Beteille and T. N. Madan (eds.), *Encounter and Experience: Personal Accounts of Fieldwork.* Honolulu: University Press of Hawaii.

PAPALIA, DIANE E., and **SALLY WENDKOS OLDS.** 1987. *A Child's World: Infancy through Adolescence.* 4th ed. New York: McGraw-Hill.

PARK, ROBERT E. 1952. *Human Communities: The City and Human Ecology.* New York: Free Press.

PARKES, DON, and **NIGEL THRIFT.** 1980. *Times, Spaces and Places: A Chronogeographic Perspective.* New York: Wiley.

PARKIN, FRANK. 1971. *Class Inequality and Political Order.* London: McGibbon and Kee.

———. 1979. *Marxism and Class Theory: A Bourgeois Critique.* New York: Columbia University Press.

PARKINSON, C. NORTHCOTE. 1957. *Parkinson's Law.* Boston: Houghton Mifflin.

PARKS, E. 1976. "From constabulary to police society," in Williams Chambliss and Milton Mankoff, *Whose Law? What Order?* New York: Wiley.

PARNES, HERBERT S., ET AL. 1985. *Retirement among American Men.* Lexington, MA: Lexington Books.

PARSONS, TALCOTT. 1964. *The Social System.* New York: Free Press.

———. 1964. "Evolutionary universals in society." *American Sociological Review,* 29.

———. 1966. *Societies: Evolutionary and Comparative Perspectives.* Englewood Cliffs, NJ: Prentice-Hall.

PARTEN, MILDRED. 1932. "Social play among preschool children." *Journal of Abnormal and Social Psychology,* 27.

PASCALE, RICHARD, and **ANTHONY ATHOS.** 1982. *The Art of Japanese Management.* New York: Warner Books.

PATRICK, DONALD L., and **GRAHAM SCAMBLER (EDS.).** 1982. *Sociology as Applied to Medicine.* New York: Macmillan.

PAUL, DIANA Y. 1985. *Women in Buddhism: Images of the Feminine in the Mahayana Tradition.* Berkeley, CA: University of California Press.

PAYNE, E. J. 1899. *History of the New World Called America.* 2 vols. London: Oxford University Press.

PEARSON, GEOFFREY. 1980. *The Deviant Imagination: Psychiatry, Social Work, and Social Change.* New York: Holmes and Meier.

PEARTON, MAURICE. 1984. *Diplomacy: War, and Technology Since 1830.* Lawrence, KS: University Press of Kansas.

PERLMUTTER, AMOS. 1977. *The Military and Politics in Modern Times: On Professionals, Praetorians, and Revolutionary Soldiers.* New Haven, CT: Yale University Press.

PERLMUTTER, HOWARD V. 1972. "Towards research on and development of nations, unions, and firms as worldwide institutions," in H. Gunter (ed.), *Transnational Industrial Relations.* New York: St. Martin's Press.

PICKVANCE, CHRIS. 1985. "The rise and fall of urban movements and the role of comparative analysis." *Society and Space,* 3.

PINKNEY, A. 1984. *The Myth of Black Progress.* New York: Cambridge University Press.

PIVEN, FRANCES FOX, and RICHARD A. CLOWARD. 1977. *Poor People's Movements: Why They Succeed, How They Fail.* New York: Pantheon.

PLATT, ANTHONY. 1969. *The Child Savers.* Chicago: University of Chicago Press.

PLUMMER, KENNETH. 1975. *Sexual Stigma: An Interactive Account.* Boston: Routledge and Kegan Paul.

POLLACK, O. 1950. *The Criminality of Women.* Westport, CT: Greenwood Press.

PORTER, J. 1971. *Black Child, White Child: The Development of Racial Attitudes.* Cambridge, MA: Harvard University Press.

PORTER, ROY. 1986. *Patients and Practitioners: Lay Perceptions of Medicine in Pre-Industrial Society.* New York: Cambridge University Press.

———. 1988. *A Social History of Madness: The World Throughout the Eyes of the Insane.* New York: Weidenfeld & Nicolson.

PRAGNALL, A. 1985. *Television in Europe.* Manchester, England: European Institute for the Media.

PRED, ALLAN. 1986. *Place, Practice and Structure: Social and Spatial Transformation in Southern Sweden, 1750–1850.* New York: Barnes and Noble Imports.

PRESIDENT'S COMMISSION ON ORGANIZED CRIME. 1985 and 1986. *Records of Hearings, March 14, 1984 and June 24–26, 1985.* Washington, D.C.: Government Printing Office.

PRINS, HERSCHEL. 1980. *Offenders, Deviants or Patients?* New York: Routledge, Chapman and Hall.

RAMIREZ, FRANCISCO O., and JOHN BOLI. 1987. "The political construction of mass schooling: European origins and worldwide institutionalism." *Sociology of Education,* 60.

RANDALL, VICKY. 1984. *Women and Politics.* New York: St. Martin's Press.

RAPOPORT, ROBERT AND RHONA. 1982. "British families in transition," in R. N. Rapaport et al, *Families in Britain.* London: Routledge and Kegan Paul.

RAY, AAKLEY S. 1978. *Drugs, Society, and Human Behavior.* 2nd ed. St. Louis, MO: C. V. Mosby.

RAYNER, ERIC. 1986. *Human Development: An Introduction to the Psychodynamics of Growth, Maturity, and Ageing.* 3rd ed. Winchester, MA: Unwin Hyman.

REED, ANDREW. 1987. *The Developing World.* London: Bell and Hyman.

REISS, IRA L. 1960. *Premarital Sexual Standards in America.* New York: Free Press.

———. 1972. "Premarital sexuality: Past, Present and future," in *Readings on the Family System.* New York: Holt, Rinehard and Winston.

REITLINGER, GERALD. 1957. *The SS: Alibi of a Nation, 1922–1945.* New York: Viking Press.

RENNINGER, C., and J. WILLIAMS. 1966. "Black-White color-connotations and race awareness in pre-school children." *Journal of Perceptual and Motor Skills,* 22.

REX, JOHN. 1986. *Race and Ethnicity.* New York: Taylor and Francis.

RICHARDS, M. P. M. (ED.). 1974. *The Integration of a Child into a Social World.* New York: Cambridge University Press.

RICHARDS, MARTIN, and PAUL LIGHT. 1986. *Children of Social Worlds.* Cambridge, MA: Harvard University Press.

RICHARDSON, JAMES T., MARY WHITE STEWART, and ROBERT B. SIMMONDS. 1979. *Organized Miracles.* New Brunswick, NJ: Transaction Books.

RICHARDSON, KEN, and DAVID SPEARS. 1972. *Race, Culture and Intelligence.* Harmondsworth, England: Penguin.

RICHMAN, JOEL. 1987. *Medicine and Health.* New York: Longman.

RIDDELL, PETER. 1986. *The Thatcher Government.* 2nd ed. New York: Basil Blackwell.

RIGHTS OF WOMEN LESBIAN CUSTODY GROUP. 1986. *Lesbian Mothers' Legal Handbook.* London: Women's Press.

RIIS, JACOB A. 1957. *How the Other Half Lives: Studies Among the Tenements of New York.* Orig. pub. 1890. New York: Dover.

RILEY, MATILDA WHITE. 1987. "On the significance of age in sociology." *American Sociological Review,* 52.

———, and JOAN WARING. 1976. "Age and ageing," in Robert K. Merton and Robert Nisbet (eds.), *Contemporary Social Problems.* 4th ed. New York: Harcourt Brace Jovanovich.

RINGER, BENJAMIN B. 1985. *"We the People" and Others: Duality and America's Treatment of its Racial Minorities.* New York: Tavistock.

ROBINSON, D. 1977. *Self-Help and Health: Mutual Aid for Modern Problems.* London: Martin Robertson.

———. 1979. *Talking Out of Alcoholism: The Self-Help Process of AA.* London: Croom Helm.

———. 1980. "Self-help groups," in P. Smith, *Small Groups and Personal Change.* London: Methuen.

ROCKFORD, E. BURKE. 1985. *Hare Krishna in America.* New Brunswick, NJ: Rutgers University Press.

RODGERS, HARRELL R., JR. 1986. *Poor Women, Poor Families: The Economic Plight of America's Female-Headed Households.* Armonk, NY: M. E. Sharpe.

ROLLE, A. 1980. *The Italian-Americans: Troubled Roots.* New York: Free Press.

ROPER ORGANIZATION. 1977. *Changing Public Attitudes Toward Television and Other Mass Media, 1959–1976.* Washington, D.C.: Television Information Office.

ROPP, T. 1959. *War in the Modern World.* Durham, N.C.: Duke University Press.

ROSECRANCE, RICHARD. 1986. *The Rise of the Trading State: Commerce and Conquest in the Modern World.* New York: Basic Books.

ROSEN, ELLEN ISRAEL. 1987. *Bitter Choices: Blue-Collar Women In and Out of Work.* Chicago: University of Chicago Press.

ROSEN, RUTH. 1982. *The Lost Sisterhood: Prostitution in America: 1900–1918.* Baltimore, MD: Johns Hopkins University Press.

ROSENHAN, DAVID. 1973. "On being sane in an insane place." *Science.* 179.

ROSENTHAU, J. N. 1980. *The Study of Global Interdependence.* London: Frances Pinter.

ROSNER, MENACHEM, and ARNOLD S. TANENBAUM. 1987. "Organisational efficiency and egalitarian democracy in an intentional communal society: The Kibbutz." *British Journal of Sociology,* 38.

ROSS, ARTHUR M. 1954. "The natural history of the strike," in Arthur Kornhauser, Robert Dubin, and Arthur M. Ross, *Industrial Conflict.* New York: McGraw-Hill.

———, and P. T. HARTMAN. 1960. *Changing Patterns of Industrial Conflict.* New York: Wiley.

ROSS, GEORGE, STANLEY HOFFMANN, and SYLVIA MALZACHER. 1987. *The Mitterand Experiment: Continuity and Change in Modern France.* New York: Oxford University Press.

ROSSI, ALICE S., and ANN CALDERWOOD. 1973. *Academic Women on the Move.* New York: Russell Sage.

ROTH, MARTIN, and **JEROME KROLL.** 1986. *The Reality of Mental Illness.* Cambridge: Cambridge University Press.

ROTHMAN, D. 1971. *The Discovery of the Asylum.* Boston: Little, Brown.

ROWBOTHAM, SHEILA. 1974. *Women's Consciousness, Man's World.* New York: Penguin.

ROYAL COMMISSION ON THE NATIONAL HEALTH SERVICE. 1979. *Report.* London: HMSO.

RUBENSTEIN, E. A., ET AL (EDS.). 1972a. *Television and Social Behavior.* Washington D.C.: U.S. Government Printing Office.

————. 1972b. *Television in Day to Day Life: Patterns of Use.* Washington, D.C.: U.S. Government Printing Office.

RUBINSTEIN, W. D. 1986. *Wealth and Inequality in Britain.* Winchester, MA: Faber and Faber.

RUDÉ, GEORGE. 1959. *The Crowd in the French Revolution.* Oxford: Oxford University Press.

————. 1985. *The Crowd in History.* London: Lawrence and Wishart.

RUMBLE, GREVILLE. 1986. *The Politics of Nuclear Defense: A Comprehensive Introduction.* New York: Basil Blackwell.

RUSSELL, D. 1984. *Sexual Exploitation: Rape, Child Abuse, and Sexual Harassment.* Beverly Hills, CA: Sage.

RUTHERFORD, A. 1984. *Prisons and the Process of Justice.* London: Heinemann.

RUTTER, M., and **H. GILLER.** 1984. *Juvenile Delinquency: Trends and Perspectives.* New York: Guilford Press.

RYAN, TOM. 1985. "The roots of masculinity," in Andy Metcalf and Martin Humphries (eds.), *Sexuality of Men.* London: Pluto.

SABEL, CHARLES F. 1982. *Work and Politics: The Division of Labor in Industry.* New York: Cambridge University Press.

SACK, ROBERT DAVID. 1986. *Human Territoriality: Its Theory and History.* New York: Cambridge University Press.

SAHLINS, MARSHALL D. 1972. *Stone Age Economics.* Chicago: Aldine.

————. 1976. *The Use of Abuse and Biology.* Ann Arbor, MI: University of Michigan Press.

————, and **ELMAN R. SERVICE.** 1960. *Evolution and Culture.* Ann Arbor, MI: University of Michigan Press.

SAID, EDWARD. 1979. *Orientalism.* New York: Random House.

SAKHAROV, ANDREI D. 1974. *Sakharov Speaks.* Ed. Harrison E. Salisbury. New York: Vintage.

SALAMAN, GRAEME. 1981. *Class and the Corporation.* London: Fontana.

————. 1986. *Working.* New York: Routledge, Chapman, and Hall.

SAMPSON, ANTHONY. 1983. *The Changing Anatomy of Britain.* New York: Random House.

SANDERS, WILLIAM B. 1974. *The Sociologist as Detective: An Introduction to Research Methods.* New York: Praeger.

SARGANT, WILLIAM. 1959. *Battle for the Mind.* London: Pan.

SARSBY, H. 1983. *Romantic Love and Society: Its Place in the Modern World.* Harmondsworth, England: Penguin.

SAUL, JOHN, and **STEPHEN GELB.** 1986. *The Crisis in South Africa.* New York: Monthly Review Press.

SAUNDERS, CHRISTOPHER. 1981. *The Political Economy of the New and Old Industrial Countries.* London: Butterworths.

SAUNDERS, PETER. 1987. *Social Theory and the Urban Question.* 2nd ed. New York: Holmes and Meier.

SAUSSURE, FERDINAND DE 1986. *Course in General Linguistics*. Peru, IL: Open Court.

SAYERS, JANET. 1986. *Sexual Contradiction: Psychology, Psychoanalysis, and Feminism*. New York: Methuen.

SAYWELL, SHELLEY. 1985. *Women in War*. New York: Viking.

SCARMAN, LESLIE GEORGE. 1982. *The Scarman Report*. Harmondsworth, England: Penguin.

SCHAFER, KERMIT. 1965. *Prize Bloopers*. Greenwich, CT: Fawcett.

SCHAFFER, H. R. 1976. *The Growth of Sociability*. Harmondsworth, England: Penguin.

SCHAPIRO, LEONARD. 1972. *Totalitarianism*. London: Pall Mall.

SCHEFF, THOMAS. 1966. *Being Mentally Ill*. Chicago: Aldine.

SCHELL, JONATHAN. 1982. *The Fate of the Earth*. New York: Knopf.

SCHILLER, HERBERT I. 1969. *Mass Communications and American Empire*. New York: Augustus M. Kelley.

———. 1978. "Computer Systems: Power for whom and for what?" *Journal of Communication, 28*.

SCHMID, ALEX P., and JANNY DEGRAAF. 1982. *Violence as Communication: Insurgent Terrorism and the Western News Media*. Beverly Hills, CA: Sage.

SCHORSKE, CARL. 1963. "The idea of the city in European thought: Voltaire to Spengler," in Oscar Handlin and John Burchard (eds.), *The Historian and the City*. Cambridge, MA: Harvard University Press.

SCHRIRE, CARMEL (ED.). 1984. *Past and Present in Hunter Gatherer Studies*. New York: Academic Press.

SCHUMAN, HOWARD, CHARLOTTE STEEL, and LAWRENCE BOBO. 1985. *Racial Attitudes in America: Trends and Interpretations*. Cambridge, MA: Harvard University Press.

SCHUMPETER, JOSEPH. 1983. *Capitalism, Socialism and Democracy*. Orig. pub. 1942. Magnolia, MA: Peter Smith.

SCHUR, EDWIN. 1965. *Crimes without Victims*. Englewood Cliffs, NJ: Prentice-Hall.

SCHWARTZ, GARY. 1970. *Sect Ideologies and Social Status*. Chicago: University of Chicago Press.

SCOTT, J. 1969. *The White Poppy*. New York: Harper and Row.

SCOTT, JAMES BROWN. 1918. *President Wilson's Foreign Policy: Messages, Addresses, Papers*. New York: Oxford University Press.

SCOTT, JAMES C. 1986. *Weapons of the Weak: Everyday Forms of Peasant Resistance*. New Haven, CT: Yale University Press.

SCOTT, JOHN. 1980. *Corporations, Classes, and Capitalism*. New York: St. Martin's Press.

SCRIVEN, JEANNIE. 1984. "Women at work in Sweden," in Marily J. Davidson and Cory L. Cooper (eds.), *Working Women: An International Survey*. New York: Wiley.

SCULL, ANDREW T. 1979. *Museums of Madness: The Social Organization of Insanity in Nineteenth-Century England*. New York: St. Martin's Press.

———. 1984. *Decarceration: Community Treatment and the Deviant—A Radical View*. New Brunswick, NJ: Rutgers University Press.

SEGAL, ALEXANDER. 1976. "The sick role concept: Understanding illness behavior." *Journal of Health and Social Behavior, 17*.

SEIDENBERG, M. S., ET AL. 1979. "Signing behavior in apes: A critical review." *Cognition, 7*.

SERENY, GITTA. 1985. *The Invisible Children: Child Prostitution in America, West Germany, and Great Britain*. New York: Knopf.

SEWELL, WILLIAM H. 1971. "Inequality of opportunity for higher education." *American Sociological Review, 36*.

SHARP, SUE. 1976. *Just Like a Girl*. Harmondsworth, England: Penguin.

SHATTUCK, ROGER. 1980. *The Forbidden Experiment: The Story of the Wild Boy of Aveyron.* New York: Farrar, Straus and Giroux.

SHAWCROSS, TIM, and **KIM FLETCHER.** 1987. "How crime is organized in London." *Illustrated London News,* October.

SHEEHAN, MICHAEL. 1983. *The Arms Race.* New York: St. Martin's Press.

SHEEHY, GAIL. 1973. *Hustling: Prostitution in our Wide Open Society.* New York: Delacorte.

SHELDON, WILLIAM A., ET AL. 1949. *Varieties of Delinquent Youth.* New York: Harper and Row.

————, and **E. GLUECK.** 1956. *Physique and Delinquency.* New York: Harper and Row.

SHEPHERD, GILL. 1987. "Rank, gender, and homosexuality: Mombasa as a key to understanding sexual options," in Pat Caplan, *The Social Construction of Sexuality.* New York: Tavistock.

SHILTS, RANDY. 1977. *And the Band Played On: Politics, People, and the AIDS Epidemic.* New York: St. Martin's Press.

SEIBER, SAM. 1981. *Fatal Remedies: The Ironies of Social Intervention.* New York: Plenum Press.

SILVERMAN, DAVID. 1982. *Secondary Analysis in Social Research: A Guide to Data Sources and Methods with Examples.* Boston: Allen and Unwin.

SILVERMAN, IRWIN. 1985. *Qualitative Methodology and Sociology.* Aldershot, England: Gower.

SIMON, JULIAN L. 1981. *The Ultimate Resource.* Princeton, NJ: Princeton University Press.

SIMPSON, GEORGE EATON, and **J. MILTON YINGER.** 1986. *Racial and Cultural Minorities: An Analysis of Prejudice and Discrimination.* New York: Plenum Press.

SINCLAIR, PETER. 1987. *Unemployment: Economic Theory and Evidence.* New York: Basil Blackwell.

SINGH, AJIT. 1988. "Urbanisation, poverty and employment: The large metropolis in the Third World." Unpublished monograph. Cambridge University.

SINGH, J. A. L., and **ROBERT M. ZINGG.** 1942. *Wolf Children and Feral Man.* New York: Harper and Row.

SIPRI (STOCKHOLM INTERNATIONAL PEACE RESEARCH INSTITUTE). 1986. *World Armament and Disarmament: Yearbook 1986.* Philadelphia: Taylor and Francis.

SITKOFF, HARVARD. 1981. *The Struggle for Black Equality, 1954–1980.* New York: Hill and Wang.

SIVARD, RUTH LEGER. 1983. *World Military and Social Expenditures, 1983.* Washington, D.C.: World Priorities.

SJOBERG, GIDEON. 1960. *The Pre-Industrial City: Past and Present.* New York: The Free Press.

————. 1963. "The rise and fall of cities: A theoretical perspective." *International Journal of Comparative Sociology,* 4.

SKIDMORE, THOMAS E. 1974. *Black into White: Race and Nationality in Brazilian Thought.* New York: Oxford University Press.

SKILLING, H. GORDON, and **FRANKLYN GRIFFITH (EDS.).** 1971. *Interest Groups in Soviet Politics.* Princeton, NJ: Princeton University Press.

SKOCPOL, THEDA. 1977. "Wallerstein's world capitalist system: A theoretical and historical critique." *American Journal of Sociology,* 82.

————. 1979. *States and Social Resolutions: A Comparative Analysis of France, Russia and China.* New York: Cambridge University Press.

SMART, CAROL. 1978. *Women, Crime and Criminology: A Feminist Critique.* New York: Routledge, Chapman and Hall.

SMELSER, NEIL J. 1963. *Theory of Collective Behavior.* New York: Free Press.

SMITH, ADAM. 1982. *The Wealth of Nations.* New York: Penguin.

SMITH, ANTHONY D. 1973. *The Concept of Social Change: A Critique of the Functionalist Theory of Social Change.* Boston: Routledge Kegan Paul.

————. 1979. *Nationalism in the Twentieth Century.* New York: New York University.

SMITH, ANTHONY. 1980. *Goodbye Gutenberg: The Newspaper Revolution of the 1980s.* New York: Oxford University Press.

————. 1981. *The Geopolitics of Information: How Western Culture Dominates the World.* New York: Oxford University Press.

SMITH, DAVID M. (ED.). 1982. *Living under Apartheid.* Winchester, MA: Allen and Unwin.

SMITH, DOROTHY E. 1978. "K is mentally ill: The anatomy of a factual account." *Sociology,* 12.

SMITH, H. W. 1975. *Strategies of Social Research: The Methodological Imagination.* Englewood Cliffs, NJ: Prentice-Hall.

SMITH, R. 1981. *Moon of Popping Trees.* Lincoln, NE: University of Nebraska Press.

SMITH, TOM W. 1989. "Inequality and Welfare," in Roger Jowell, Sharon Witherspoon, and Lindsay Brook (eds.), *British Social Attitudes.* Brookfield, VT: Gower. ©Social and Community Planning Research.

SOMMERVILLE, I. 1983. *Information Unlimited: The Applications of Information Technology.* London: Addison-Wesley.

SORENSON, THEODORE. 1966. *Kennedy.* New York: Bantam.

SOROKIN, PITIRIM A. 1927. *Social Mobility.* New York: Harper.

SOUSTELLE, J. 1970. *Daily Life of the Aztecs on the Eve of the Spanish Conquest.* Stanford, CA: Stanford University Press.

SPADA, J. 1979. *The Spada Report: The Newest Survey of Gay Male Sexuality.* New York: New American Library.

SPITZ, RENÉ A. 1945. "Hospitalism: An enquiry into the genesis of psychiatric conditions in early childhood," in Anna Freud, et al. (eds.), *The Psychoanalytic Study of the Child.* New York: International Universities Press.

SPRAFKIN, JOYCE N., and **ROBERT M. LIEBERT.** 1978. "Sex typing and children's television preferences," in Gaye Tuchman, Arlene Kaplan Daniels, and James Benet (eds.), *Hearth and Home: Images of Women in the Mass Media.* New York: Oxford University Press.

STACK, CAROL B. 1974. *All Our Kin.* New York: Harper and Row.

STAMPP, KENNETH. 1956. *The Peculiar Institution.* New York: Knopf.

STANTON, ELIZABETH CADY. 1972. *The Woman's Bible.* Orig. pub. 1895. Salem, NH: Ayer Co. Publishers.

————, **SUSAN B. ANTHONY,** and **MATILDA JOSLYN GAGE (EDS.).** 1969. *History of Woman Suffrage,* Vol. I. Reprint of 1922 ed. Orig. pub. in 1889. Salem, NH: Ayer Co. Pub.

STANWORTH, MICHELLE. 1984. "Women and class analysis: A reply to John Goldthorpe." *Sociology,* 18.

————, **(ED.).** 1988. *Reproductive Technologies.* Minneapolis, MN: University of Minnesota Press.

STANWORTH, PHILIP, and **ANTHONY GIDDENS (EDS.).** 1974. *Elites and Power in British Society.* New York: Cambridge University Press.

STAPLES, ROBERT. 1973. *The Black Woman in America.* Chicago: Nelson Hill.

STARK, RODNEY, and **WILLIAM SIMS BAINBRIDGE.** 1985. *The Future of Religion, Secularization, Revival, and Cult Formation.* Berkeley, CA: University of California Press.

STARR, PAUL. 1982. "Medicine and the waning of professional sovereignty." *Daedalus,* no. 107.

STATHAM, JUNE. 1986. *Daughters and Sons: Experiences of Non-Sexist Childraising.* New York: Basil Blackwell.

STAVRIANOS, L. S. 1981. *Global Rift: The Third World Comes of Age.* New York: Morrow.

STEIN, PETER J. 1980. *Single Life: Unmarried Adults in Social Context.* New York: St. Martin's Press.

STEINBERG, C. S. 1980. *TV Facts.* New York: Facts on File.

STEINSON, BARBARA J. 1980. " 'The mother half of humanity': American women in peace and preparedness movements in World War I," in Carol R. Berkin and Clara M. Lovett, *Women, War, and Revolution.* New York: Holmes and Meier.

STERN, DANIEL N. 1985. *The Interpersonal World of the Infant: A View from Psychoanalysis and Development Psychology.* New York: Basic Books.

STINCHCOMBE, ARTHUR. 1982. "The growth of the world system." *American Journal of Sociology,* 8.

STRINNER, WILLIAM F. 1979. "Modernization and the family extension in the Philippines: A social-demographic analysis." *Journal of Marriage and the Family,* 41.

STOLLMAN, FRANS N., ROLF ZIEGLER, and **JOHN SCOTT.** 1985. *Networks of Corporate Power: A Comparative Analysis of Ten Countries.* New York: Basil Blackwell.

STONE, JOHN. 1986. *Racial Conflict in Contemporary Society.* Cambridge, MA: Harvard University Press.

STONE, LAWRENCE. 1980. *The Family, Sex, and Marriage in England, 1500–1800.* New York: Harper and Row.

STRAUS, MURRAY A. 1978. "Wife-beating: How common and why?" *Victimology,* 2.

————, **RICHARD J. GELLES,** and **SUZANNE K. STEINMETZ.** 1980. *Behind Closed Doors: Violence in the American Family.* Garden City, NY: Anchor.

STROMBERG, A. H., and **S. HARKNESS (EDS.).** 1977. *Women Working, Theories and Facts in Perspective.* Palo Alto, CA: Mayfield.

SURANSKY, VALERIE P. 1982. *The Erosion of Childhood.* Chicago: University of Chicago Press.

SURGEON GENERAL'S SCIENTIFIC ADVISORY COMMITTEE. 1972. *Television and Social Behavior.* Washington, D.C.: Government Printing Office.

SUSSMAN, MARVIN B. 1953. "The help pattern in the middle-class family." *American Sociological Review,* 18.

SUTHERLAND, EDWIN H. 1949. *Principles of Criminology.* Chicago: Lippincott.

————, and **CHIC CONWELL.** 1937. *The Professional Thief.* Chicago: University of Chicago Press.

SUTTLES, GERALD. 1968. *The Social Order of the Slum.* Chicago: University of Chicago Press.

SWANN REPORT. 1985. *Education for All.* London: HMSO.

SWARTZ, S. 1985. *Sugar Plantations in the Formation of Brazilian Society: Bahia, 1550–1835.* Cambridge: Cambridge University Press.

SYDIE, R. A. 1987. *Natural Women, Cultured Men: A Feminist Perspective on Sociological Theory.* New York: Methuen.

SZASZ, THOMAS. 1970. *The Manufacture of Madness.* New York: Harper and Row.

SZELENYI, IVAN. 1983. *Urban Inequalities Under State Socialism.* New York: Oxford University Press.

SZRETER, R. 1983. "Opportunities for women as university teachers in England since the Robbins Report of 1963." *Studies in Higher Education,* 8.

TABB, WILLIAM K. 1982. *The Long Default: New York City and the Urban Fiscal Crisis.* New York: Monthly Review Press.

TANNENBAUM, A., ET AL. 1974. *Hierarchy in Organizations.* San Francisco, CA: Josey-Bass.

TANNENBAUM, FRANK. 1964. *The Fine Society: A Philosophy of Labour.* London: Cape.

TASK FORCE ON ASSESSMENT. 1967. "Crime rates: Impact and assessment." *Report to*

The President's Commission on Law Enforcement and the Administration of Justice. Washington, D.C.: Government Printing Office.

TATARIAN, ROGER. 1978. "News Flow in the Third World—An Overview," in C. Horton (ed.), *The Third World and Press Freedom.* New York: Praeger.

TAYLOR, P. 1982. "Schizophrenia and Violence," in John Gunn and David P. Farrington (eds.), *Abnormal Offenders; Delinquency and the Criminal Justice System.* New York: Wiley.

TERKEL, STUDS. 1984. *The Good War.* New York: Ballantine.

———. 1985. *Working: People Talk about What They Do All Day and How They Feel about What They Do.* New York: Ballantine.

THOMAS, KEITH. 1986. *Religion and the Decline of Magic.* New York: Scribners.

THOMAS, W. I., and FLORIAN ZNANIECKI. 1966. *The Polish Peasant in Europe and America: Monograph of Our Immigrant Group.* 5 Vols. Orig. pub. 1918–20. New York: Dover.

THOMPSON, E. P. 1967. "Time, work-discipline and industrial capitalism." *Past and Present,* 38.

———. 1971. "The moral economy of the English crowd in the eighteenth century." *Past and Present,* 50.

THOMPSON, PAUL. 1983. *The Nature of Work.* Atlantic Highlands, NJ: Humanities Press.

THOMPSON, WARREN S. 1929. "Population." *American Journal of Sociology,* 34.

THORNLEY, JENNY. 1981. *Workers' Co-operatives, Jobs and Dreams.* New York: Portsmouth, NH: Heinemann Educational Books.

THRALL, CHARLES. 1970. "Household Technology and the Division of Labor in Families." Unpublished Ph.D. dissertation, Harvard University.

TILLY, CHARLES. 1975. "Reflections on the History of European State Making," in *The Formation of National States in Europe.* Princeton, NJ: Princeton University Press.

———. 1978. *From Mobilization to Revolution.* Reading, MA: Addison-Wesley.

TILLY, LOUISE A., and JOAN W. SCOTT. 1978. *Women, Work, and Family.* New York: Holt, Rinehart and Winston.

TINBERGEN, NIKO. 1974. *The Study of Instinct.* Oxford: Oxford University Press.

TIZARD, BARBARA, and MARTIN HUGHES. 1985. *Young Children Learning, Talking, and Thinking at Home and at School.* Cambridge, MA: Harvard University Press.

TOBIAS, J. 1967. *Crime and Industrial Society in the Nineteenth Century.* London: Batsford.

TOCQUEVILLE, ALEXIS DE. 1969. *Democracy in America.* Orig. pub. 1835. New York: Doubleday.

———. 1955. *The Ancien Regime and the French Revolution.* Orig. pub. 1856. New York: Doubleday.

TOFFLER, ALVIN. 1970. *Future Shock.* New York: Random House.

———. 1984. *The Third Wave.* New York: Bantam.

TOLLIDAY, STEVEN, and JONATHAN ZEITLIN (EDS.). 1987. *The Automobile Industry and Its Workers: Between Fordism and Flexibility.* Cambridge, MA: Harvard University Press.

TOUGH, JOAN. 1983. *Listening to Children Talking.* Portsmouth, NH: Heinemann Educational Books.

TOURAINE, ALAIN. 1974. *The Post-Industrial Society.* London: Wildwood.

———. 1977. *The Self-Production of Society.* Chicago: University of Chicago Press.

———. 1981. *The Voice and the Eye: An Analysis of Social Movements.* New York: Cambridge University Press.

TOWNSEND, PETER. 1979. *Poverty in the United Kingdom: A Survey of Household Resources and Standards of Living.* Berkeley, CA: University of California Press.

TROELTSCH, ERNST. 1981. *The Social Teaching of the Christian Churches.* 2 vols. New York: Macmillan.

TROW, MARTIN. 1961. "The second transformation of American secondary education." *Comparative Sociology,* 2.

TRUMAN, DAVID B. 1981. *The Governmental Process.* Westport, CT: Greenwood Press.

TUNSTALL, JEREMY. 1977. *The Media are American: Anglo-American Media in the World.* New York: Columbia University Press.

TURNBULL, COLIN. 1983. *The Mbuti Pygmies: Change and Adaptation.* New York: Holt, Rinehart and Winston.

———. 1983. *The Human Cycle.* New York: Simon and Schuster.

TURNER, A. 1981. "The San José Recall Study," in R. Lehlen and W. Skogan (eds.), *The National Crime Survey Working Papers. Vol. 1: Current and Historical Perspectives.* Washington, D.C.: Bureau of Justice Statistics.

TURNER, BRYAN S. 1983. *Religion and Social Theory: A Methodist Perspective.* London: Heinemann.

TURNER, JOHN. 1985. *Arms in the Eighties: New Developments in the Global Arms Race.* Philadelphia: Taylor and Francis.

TURNER, RALPH H., and LEWIS M. KILLIAN. 1972. *Collective Behavior.* Englewood Cliffs, NJ: Prentice-Hall.

TUROWSKI, JAN. 1977. "Inadequacy of the theory of the nuclear family: The Polish experience," in Luis Lenero-Otero, *Beyond the Nuclear Family Model: Cross-Cultural Perspectives.* Beverly Hills, CA: Sage.

TUTTLE, LISA. 1986. *Encyclopedia of Feminism.* New York: Facts on File.

TYREE, ANDREA, MOSHE SEMYONOV, and ROBERT W. HODGE. 1979. "Gaps and glissandas: Inequality, economic development, and social mobility in 24 countries." *American Sociological Review,* 44.

UNICEF. 1983. *The State of the World's Children.* New York: Oxford University Press.

UNITED NATIONS CENTRE ON TRANSNATIONAL CORPORATIONS (UNCTC). 1983. *Transnational Corporations in the International Auto Industry.* New York: United Nations.

U.S. BUREAU OF THE CENSUS. 1986. *Current Population Reports,* ser. P-60, No. 159.

U.S. BUREAU OF THE CENSUS. 1987. *Current Population Reports,* ser. P-60, No. 161.

U.S. BUREAU OF THE CENSUS. 1989. *Statistical Abstract of the United States: 1990.* Washington, D.C.: U.S. Government Printing Office.

U.S. BUREAU OF STATISTICS. April 1961; 1988; and unpublished BLS data. *Statistical Abstract of the United States.* Washington, D.C.: U.S. Government Printing Office.

U.S. BUREAU OF STATISTICS. 1987. *Statistical Abstract of the United States.* Washington, D.C.: U.S. Government Printing Office.

U.S. DEPARTMENT OF HEALTH, EDUCATION AND WELFARE. 1973. *Work in America: Report of a Special Task Force to the Secretary of Health, Education and Welfare.* Washington, D.C.: U.S. Government Printing Office.

U.S. NATIONAL CENTER FOR HEALTH STATISTICS. 1985. *Vital and Health Statistics,* ser. 10. Washington, D.C.: U.S. Government Printing Office.

U.S. RIOT COMMISSION. 1968. *Report of the National Advisory Commission on Civil Disorder.* New York: Bantam.

USEEM, MICHAEL. 1986. *The Inner Circle: Large Corporations and the Rise of Business Political Activity in the U.S. and the U.K.* New York: Oxford University Press.

VAILLANT, G. 1983. *The Natural History of Alcoholism.* Cambridge, MA: Harvard University Press.

VAN DEN BERGHE, PIERRE L. 1970. *Race and Ethnicity: Essays in Comparative Sociology.* New York: Basic Books.

VAN GENNEP, ARNOLD. 1977. *The Rites of Passage.* Orig. pub. 1908. London: Routledge and Kegan Paul.

VANCE, CAROLE S. (ED.). 1984. *Pleasure and Danger: Exploring Female Sexuality.* New York: Routledge, Chapman and Hall.

VANEK, JOANNE. 1974. "Time spent on housework." *Scientific American,* no. 231.

VANVELEY, T., ET AL. 1977. "Trends in racial segregation 1960–70." *American Journal of Sociology,* 82.

VASS, ANTHONY A. 1986. *Aids: A Plague in Us. A Social Perspective on the Condition and Its Social Consequences.* St. Ives, England: Venus Academicus.

VAUGHAN, DIANE. 1986. *Uncoupling: Turning Points in Intimate Relationships.* New York: Oxford University Press.

VIORST, JUDITH. 1986. "And the prince knelt down and tried to put the glass slipper on Cinderella's foot," in Jack Zipes, *Don't Bet On The Prince: Contemporary Feminist Fairy Tales in North America and England.* New York: Methuen.

VISCHER, EMILY B., and **JOHN S. VISCHER.** 1979. *Step Families: A Guide to Working With Step-Parents and Step-Children.* Secaucus, NJ: Citadel Press.

VITERITTI, JOSEPH P. 1979. *Bureaucracy and Social Justice: The Allocation of Jobs and Services to Minority Groups.* Port Washington, NY: Kennikat Press.

VOGEL, EZRA F. 1979. *Japan as Number One: Lessons for America.* New York: Harper Colophon.

WADE, WYN CRAIG. 1987. *The Fiery Cross: The Ku Klux Klan in America.* New York: Simon & Schuster.

WAGENHEIM, K. 1975. *A Survey of Puerto Ricans on the U.S. Mainland in the 1970s.* New York: Praeger.

WAITZKIN, HOWARD. 1986. *The Second Sickness: Contradictions of Capitalist Health Care.* Chicago: University of Chicago Press.

WALBY, SYLVIA A. 1986. "Gender, class and stratification: Toward a new approach," in Rosemary Crompton and Michael Mann (eds.), *Gender and Stratification.* New York: Basil Blackwell.

WALKER, MARTIN. 1987. *The Walking Giant.* New York: Pantheon.

WALKER, STEPHEN, and **LEN BARTON.** 1983. *Gender, Class and Education.* London: Falmer Press.

WALL, RICHARD, JEAN ROBIN, and **PETER LASLETT.** 1983. *Family Forms in Historic Europe.* New York: Cambridge University Press.

WALLACE, M. 1987. "A Caring Community?" *Sunday Times,* May 3.

WALLACE, MICHELLE. 1982. "A black feminist's search for sisterhood," in Gloria T. Hull, Patricia Bell Scott and Barbara Smith: *All the Women Are White, All the Blacks Are Men, But Some of Us Are Brave: Black Women's Studies.* Old Westbury, NY: Feminist Press.

WALLERSTEIN, IMMANUEL. 1974. *The Modern World System.* New York: Academic Press.

———. 1979. *The Capitalist World Economy.* New York: Cambridge University Press.

WALLERSTEIN, JUDITH S., and **JOAN BERLIN KELLY.** 1980. *Surviving the Break-Up: How Children and Parents Cope with Divorce.* New York: Basic Books.

WALLIS, ROY. 1977. *The Road to Total Freedom.* New York: Columbia University Press.

———. 1987. "My secret life: Dilemmas of integrity in the conduct of field research," in Ragnhild Kristensen and Ole Riis, *Religiose Minoriteter.* Aarhus: Aarhus Universitetsfarlag.

WALSH, DERMOT. 1986. *Heavy Business: Commercial Burglary and Robbery.* New York: Routledge, Chapman and Hall.

WALUM, LAUREL RICHARDSON. 1977. *The Dynamics of Sex and Gender: A Sociological Perspective.* Chicago: Rand McNally.

WALVIN, JAMES. 1984. *Passage to Britain: Immigration in British History and Politics.* Harmondsworth: Penguin.

WARD, PETER M. 1981. "Mexico City," in Michael Pacione, *Problems and Planning in Third World Cities.* New York: St. Martin's Press.

WARDLAW, GRANT. 1983. *Political Terrorism: Theory, Tactics and Counter-Measures.* New York: Cambridge University Press.

WARREN, BILL. 1981. *Imperialism: Pioneer of Capitalism.* New York: Shocken.

WARREN, ROBERT PENN. 1965. *Who Speaks for the Negro?* New York: Macmillan.

WARNER, W. LLOYD, ET AL. 1949. *Social Class in America.* New York: Harper.

————, and **PAUL S. LUNT.** 1941. *The Social Life of a Modern Community.* New Haven, CT: Yale University Press.

————, and **PAUL S. LUNT.** 1947. *The Status System of a Modern Community.* New Haven, CT: Yale University Press.

WATSON, K. 1982. *Education in the Third World.* New York: Routledge, Chapman, and Hall.

WATKINS, LESLIE AND ROBERT M. WORCESTER. 1986. *Private Opinions, Public Polls.* London: Thames and Hudson.

WAXMAN, C. I. 1983. *The Stigma of Poverty: A Critique of Poverty Theories and Policies.* 2nd ed. Elmsford, NY: Pergamon Press.

WEATHERBY, JOSEPH, ET AL. 1987. *The Other World: Issues and Politics in the Third World.* New York: Macmillan.

WEBER, MAX. 1946. *From Max Weber: Essays in Sociology.* Tr. and ed. by H. Gerth and C. Wright-Mills. New York: Oxford University Press.

————. 1951. *The Religion of China.* New York: Free Press.

————. 1952. *Ancient Judaism.* New York: Free Press.

————. 1958. *The Religion of India.* New York: Free Press.

————. 1963. *The Sociology of Religion.* Boston: Beacon Press.

————. 1977. *The Protestant Ethic and the Spirit of Capitalism.* New York: Macmillan.

————. 1979. *Economy and Society: An Outline of Interpretive Sociology.* 2 Vols. Berkeley, CA: University of California Press.

WEEKS, JEFFREY. 1986. *Sexuality.* New York: Routledge, Chapman and Hall.

WEINSTEIN, FRED. 1980. *The Dynamics of Nazism: Leadership, Ideology, and the Holocaust.* New York: Academic Press.

WEISS, ROBERT. 1976. *Going it Alone.* New York: Basic Books.

————. 1975. *Marital Separation.* New York: Basic Books.

WEITZMAN, LENORE. 1985. *Divorce Revolution: The Unexpected Social and Economic Consequences for Women and Children in America.* New York: Free Press.

————. **ET AL.** 1972. "Sexual socialization in picture books for preschool children." *American Journal of Sociology,* 77.

WELLFORD, C. 1975. "Labelling Theory and Criminology: An assessment." *Social Problems,* 22.

WELLMAN, DAVID T. (ED.). 1977. *Portraits of White Racism.* New York: Cambridge University Press.

WELLS, ALAN. 1972. *Picture Tube Imperialism? The Impact of U.S. Television on Latin America.* Maryknoll, NY: Orbis Books.

WESTERN, JOHN. 1981. *Outcast Cape Town.* Minneapolis, MN: University of Minnesota Press.

WESTON, R. G. 1967. *The Imperial Order.* Berkeley, CA: University of California Press.

WHEATLEY, PAUL. 1971. *The Pivot of the Four Quarters.* Edinburgh, Scotland: Edinburgh University Press.

WHITE, MICHAEL, and **MALCOLM TREVOR.** 1983. *Under Japanese Management: The Experience of British Workers.* New York: Gower Publishing.

WIDOM, CATHY SPATZ, and **JOSEPH P. NEWMAN.** 1985. "Characteristics of non-institutionalized psychopaths," in David P. Farrington and John Gunn, *Aggression and Dangerousness.* Chichester, England: Wiley.

WIEGELE, THOMAS C. (ED.). 1982. *Biology and the Social Sciences: An Emerging Revolution.* Boulder, CO: Westview.

WILKINSON, PAUL. 1974. *Political Terrorism.* London: Macmillan.

————. 1986. *Terrorism and the Liberal State.* 2nd ed. New York: New York University Press.

WILL, J., P. SELF, and **N. DATAN.** 1976. "Maternal behavior and perceived sex of infant." *American Journal of Orthopsychiatry,* 46.

WILLIAMS, JUANITA H. 1987. *Psychology of Women.* Third Edition. New York: Norton.

WILLIAMS, PHILIP M., ET AL. 1979. *De Gaulle's Republic.* Westport, CT: Greenwood Press.

WILLIAMS, RAYMOND., 1984. *Towards 2000.* Harmondsworth: Penguin.

WILLIAMS, ROBIN. 1983. "Sociological tropes: A tribute to Erving Goffman." *Theory, Culture and Society,* 2.

WILLIAMS, W. M. 1956. *Gosforth: The Sociology of an English Village.* London: Routledge.

WILLIS, PAUL. 1981. *Learning to Labor: How Working Class Kids Get Working Class Jobs.* New York: Columbia University Press.

WILSON, BRYAN. 1982. *Religion in Sociological Perspective.* New York: Oxford University Press.

WILSON, EDWARD O. 1975. *Sociobiology: The New Synthesis.* Cambridge, MA: Harvard University Press.

————. 1978. *On Human Nature.* Cambridge, MA: Harvard University Press.

WILSON, J. 1946. "Egypt," in H. Frankfort et al., *The Intellectual Adventure of Ancient Man.* Chicago: University of Chicago Press.

WILSON, JOHN. 1972. *Religion.* London: Heinemann.

WILSON, MONICA. 1987. *Good Company: A Study of Nyakyusa Age Villages.* Prospect Heights, IL: Waveland Press.

WILSON, TREVOR. 1986. *The Myriad Faces of War: Britain and the Great War, 1914–1918.* New York: Basil Blackwell.

WILSON, WILLIAM JULIUS. 1980. *The Declining Significance of Race: Blacks and Changing American Institutions.* Chicago: University of Chicago Press.

————. 1987. *The Truly Disadvantaged: The Inner City, the Underclass, and Public Policy.* Chicago: University of Chicago Press.

————, **ET AL.** 1987. "The changing structure of urban poverty." Paper presented at the annual meeting of the American Sociological Association.

WILTSHER, ANNE. 1985. *Most Dangerous Women: Feminist Peace Campaigners of the Great War.* New York: Routledge, Chapman and Hall.

WINCH, G. (ED.). 1983. *Information technology in Manufacturing Processes: Case Studies in Technological Change.* London: Rossendale.

WINICK, CHARLES, and **PAUL M. KINSIE.** 1971. *The Lively Commerce.* Chicago: Quadrangle.

WINN, MARIE. 1983. *Children Without Childhood.* New York: Pantheon.

WIRTH, LOUIS. 1938. "Urbanism as a way of life." *American Journal of Sociology,* 44: 1–24, July.

WISTRAND, BIRGITTA. 1981. *Swedish Women on the Move.* Ed. and trans. by Jeanne Rosen. Stockholm: Swedish Institute.

WITTKE, CARL. 1956. *The Irish in America.* Baton Rouge: Louisiana State University Press.

WOLF, ERIC R. 1983. *Europe and the People Without History.* Berkeley, CA: University of California Press.

WOLFGANG, MARVIN. 1958. *Patterns of Homicide.* Philadelphia: University of Pennsylvania Press.

WOLLSTONECRAFT, MARY. 1982. *A Vindication of the Rights of Women.* Orig. pub. 1792. New York: Penguin.

WOMEN ON WORDS AND IMAGES. 1972. *Dick and Jane as Victims: Sex Stereotyping in Children's Readers.* Princeton, NJ: Women on Words and Images.

WOOD, STEPHEN (ED.). 1984. *The Degradation of Work.* Wolfeboro, NH: Longwood Publishing Group.

WORLD BANK. 1985. *World Development Report, 1985.* New York: Oxford University Press.

WORLD COUNCIL OF CHURCHES. 1979. *Programme to Combat Racism.* London: Institute for the Study of Conflict.

WORSLEY, PETER. 1968. *The Trumpet Shall Sound: A Study of Cargo Cults in Melanesia.* New York: Schocken Books.

———. 1973. *The Third World.* Chicago: University of Chicago Press.

———. 1984. *The Three Worlds of Culture and World Development.* Chicago: University of Chicago Press.

WRIGHT, ERIK OLIN. 1978. *Class, Crisis, and the State.* London: New Left Books.

———. 1985. *Classes.* New York: Shocken Books.

WRIGHT, HARRISON M. 1977. *The Burden of the Present.* Cape Town, South Africa: David Philip.

WRIGHT, LAWRENCE. 1968. *Clockwork Man.* London: Elek.

WRIGLEY, E. A. 1968. *Population and History.* New York: McGraw-Hill.

WUTHNOW, ROBERT. 1986. "Religious movements in North America." in James A. Beckford (ed.), *New Religious Movements and Rapid Social Change.* Beverly Hills, CA: Sage.

YOFFIE, D. B. 1983. *Power and Protectionism: Strategies of the Newly Industrializing Countries.* New York: Columbia University Press.

YOUNG, ALLEN. 1972. "Out of the closets into the streets," in Karla Jay and Allen Young (eds.), *Out of the Closets: Voices of Gay Liberation.* New York: Douglas.

ZAGORIN, PEREZ. 1982. *Rebels and Rulers, 1550–1660.* Vol. I: *Society, States, and Early Modern Revolution: Agrarian and Urban Rebellions.* New York: Cambridge University Press.

ZAMMUNER, VANDA LUCIA. 1986. "Children's sex-role stereotypes: A cross-cultural analysis," in Phillip Shaver and Clyde Hendrick, *Sex and Gender.* Beverly Hills, CA: Sage.

ZANGRANDO, ROBERT L. 1980. *The NAACP Crusade against Lynching, 1909–1950.* Philadelphia: Temple University Press.

ZEITLIN, IRVING. 1985. *Ancient Judaism: Biblical Criticism from Max Weber to the Present.* New York: Basil Blackwell.

———. 1988. *The Historical Jesus.* Cambridge: Polity Press.

ZERUBAVEL, EVIATAR. 1979. *Patterns of Time in Hospital Life.* Chicago: University of Chicago Press.

———. 1982. "The standardization of time: A sociohistorical perspective." *American Journal of Sociology,* 88.

ZIMBARDO, PHILIP. 1972. "Pathology of imprisonment." *Society,* 9.

ZIMBLAST, A. (ED.). 1979. *Case Studies in the Labor Process.* New York: Monthly Review Press.

ZIMMERMAN, DON, and **CANDACE WEST.** 1975. "Sex roles, interruptions and silences in conversation," in B. Thorne and N. Henley (eds.), *Language and Sex: Difference and Dominance.* Rowley, MA: Newbury House.

ZOLA, IRVING KENNETH, and **J. KOSA (EDS.).** 1975. *Poverty and Health: A Sociological Analysis.* Rev. ed. Cambridge, MA: Commonwealth Fund.

ZOPF, PAUL E. 1986. *America's Older Population.* Houston, TX: Cap and Gown Press.

INDEX

Page numbers in *italics* refer to illustrations, tables, and figures.